2001

INTERNET AND COMPUTER LAW

Cases — Comments — Questions

By

Peter B. Maggs
Peer and Sarah Pedersen Professor of Law
University of Illinois at Urbana-Champaign

John T. Soma
Professor of Law
University of Denver

James A. Sprowl
Of Counsel
Foley & Lardner

AMERICAN CASEBOOK SERIES®

**WEST
GROUP**

ST. PAUL, MINN., 2001

 *TEXT IS PRINTED ON 10% POST CONSUMER RECYCLED PAPER*

Introduction

Is there such a subject as "Internet and Computer Law"? If so, what should an "Internet and Computer Law" casebook include? The answers to these questions are not obvious. Certainly there are many cases involving computers. A recent WESTLAW search for the word "INTERNET" found 1262 cases in the "allfeds" data base and 391 cases in "allstates". A similar search for "SHOE" found 28,269 Federal and 37,0373 state cases! No one is suggesting that law students should study "shoe law" as a separate course. Students will read *Brown Shoe Co. v. United States*, 370 U.S. 294 (1962), a leading vertical merger case, in their antitrust course and may read a few more cases involving shoes in other courses. Little or nothing in these cases turns on anything peculiar about shoes. Cases involving shoes do not cite other cases involving shoes. Internet and computer cases, in contrast, often turn on the special nature of the Internet and of computer software and hardware, and regularly cite other cases involving the Internet or computers.

Why are computers "special" when shoes are not? First, computer software and hardware are the most complex and rapidly developing intellectual creations of modem man. Second, computers provide unprecedented power in accessing and manipulating data. Third, computers work in complex systems that require standardization and compatibility to function. Each of these special features has engendered one or more bodies of law. Complex intellectual creation demands comprehensive intellectual property protection. Computer technology, however, differs fundamentally from previous objects of intellectual property protection, and thus does not fit easily into traditional copyright and patent law. Courts and legislatures, consequently, have had to exert great efforts to adapt old legal forms and create new ones. The power of the computer to access and manipulate data requires new types of government regulation. Antisocial individuals may steal or destroy information in ways that involve no physical trespass on property and thus may fall outside traditional regulatory and criminal prohibitions.

Potential enemies seek access to our computers and data banks to catch up with our high technology military power. Litigators seek access to opposing parties' computer data. Tax assessors try to tax this valuable asset. Standardization is essential, but provides opportunities for companies that can set standards to exploit the public by monopolizing software and hardware markets.

These special qualities of computers have determined the scope of this casebook. The book opens with chapters on copyright and patent issues. These chapters serve a dual purpose. They have the utilitarian purpose of introducing an area of law that is of considerable importance in practice. But they also attempt to build an understanding of the unique features of computer technology as an intellectual creation. Then the book continues with other intellectual property issues, with particular focus on attempts by businesses to use intellectual property to seize or maintain ownership of industry standards. This theme also appears in the antitrust chapter A chapter on electronic commerce explores the issue of definition further-just what is the seller of computer hardware and software selling—pieces of metal and plastic or solutions to problems? The book ends with chapters dealing with public law issues, particularly the right to privacy and freedom of speech.

This casebook deals with one of the fastest-moving areas of the law. Important new cases will arise soon after the book is published. Many of the cases in this book have been discussed in law review articles; many more articles will be published mentioning these cases. Therefore any reader interested in following up these cases in depth is urged to use West Group's KeyCite system to find current information supplementing the cases reproduced or mentioned herein.

Preface

Ten years ago we created a casebook on the then uncharted territory of computer law. We began work on a new edition of that book, but soon realized that the development of the Internet and the rapid change of legal institutions required us to create an almost entirely new casebook. We have tried to choose cases that are both important and teachable. We have edited them, trying to preserve the key ideas intact, but removing irrelevant issues, lengthy string citations, and minor footnotes. We have retained the original numbering of those footnotes that we have kept.

We owe thanks to those who have helped us with the volume. University of Illinois Law student Sandra Gallini provided an invaluable service in carefully proofreading, cite-checking, and correcting the entire manuscript. University of Illinois Law student Kevin Baird performed an essential final cite-check. University of Denver law students Renée Albersheim, Lori Lucas Barbara, Kevin Brad Davis, Patrick J. Kelly, Lisa J. Loerzel, Sumaya Vanderhorst, and Steve L. Webb provided valuable research assistance. Ms. Ma Antionieta Murphy of the University of Denver helped greatly in preparation of the manuscript. The technology aspects of various chapters were much improved by comments from Computer Consultant Robert T. Voorhees of Littleton, Colorado. Co-author Jim Sprowl is particularly indebted to his wife Susan for her editorial contributions to this and previous West casebooks.

P.B.M.
J.T.S.
J.A.S.

August 2000

*

v

Summary of Contents

		Page
INTRODUCTION		iii
PREFACE		v
TABLE OF CASES		xix

Chapter I. Internet and Software Copyright 1
A. Introduction 1
B. Copyrightability 4
C. Ownership of Copyright 65
D. Exclusive Rights of the Copyright Owner 66
E. Limitations on the Exclusive Rights 93
F. Infringement 146
G. Preemption of State Law 200
H. Copyright–Like Protection 208

Chapter II. Patentability of Computer Software, Programmed Computers, and Internet Business Systems 217
A. Introduction 217
B. A Networked Computer Methods Patent 219
C. Eligibility for Patent Protection 229
D. Patentable Subject Matter—§ 101 232
E. Novelty and Anticipation—§ 102 283
F. Non–Obviousness—§ 103 287
G. Enablement—§ 112 304
H. Claim Interpretation and Infringement: "means for," The Doctrine of Equivalents, and File Wrapper Estoppel 319

Chapter III. Trade Secrecy 342
A. Introduction 342
B. Protecting Trade Secrets Against Taking by "improper Means" 342
C. Protecting Trade Secrets Against Disclosure by Government Agencies 355
D. Protecting Trade Secrets by Negotiated Contracts 366
E. Protecting Trade Secrets by "Shrinkwrap" Licenses 370

Chapter IV. Trademarks, Unfair Competition, and Unfair Business Practices 387
A. Trademark Rights in Internet Domain Names 387
B. Domain Name Arbitration 399
C. Misappropriation, Product Standards, and Trademarks ... 408
D. Interfering With Internet Communications 461

Page

Chapter V. Internet Jurisdiction _____ 472
A. Reach of "Long–Arm" Statutes _____ 472
B. Constitutional Limits on the Reach of Long–Arm Statutes _____ 476
C. In Rem Jurisdiction Over Domain Names _____ 484
D. Jurisdiction Over Persons Not Doing Business on the Internet _____ 489

CHAPTER VI. E–Commerce and Software Contracts _____ 495
A. Old Law and New Situations _____ 495
B. Paperfree Transactions _____ 498
C. Authentication of Signatures _____ 510
D. Applicable Law _____ 513
E. Tort as an Alternative to Contract Claims _____ 518
F. Bankruptcy–Protecting Software Users _____ 530
G. Self–Help _____ 531
H. Consumer Protection By The Federal Trade Commission _____ 535
I. Taxation _____ 541
J. Restricting E–Competition _____ 542

Chapter VII. Telecommunications and the Internet _____ 570
A. Introduction _____ 570
B. Line Sharing _____ 570
C. Internet Access Over Cable Television Facilities _____ 572

Chapter VIII. Antitrust _____ 582
A. Introduction _____ 582
B. Tie–In Sales _____ 583
C. Agreements in Violation of the Antitrust Laws _____ 621
D. Horizontal Restraints _____ 632

Chapter IX. Privacy _____ 634
A. Introduction _____ 634
B. Restricting the Power of Government to Use Compulsion to Force Disclosure of Personal Information _____ 635
C. Restricting Non–Governmental Collection of Information _____ 649
D. Restricting Use by the Government of Information in Government Records _____ 657
E. Restricting Use by Private Parties of Information in Private Records _____ 668
F. Restricting Disclosure by the Government of Information in Government Records _____ 671
G. Restriction of Disclosure by Private Parties of Information in Their Records _____ 676
H. The Effect of European Union Privacy Law _____ 684

Chapter X. Right to Accuracy of Information _____ 692
A. Defamation _____ 692
B. Immunity of Internet Service Providers _____ 706
C. Duty to Provide Accurate Information to Those Affected _____ 715
D. Duty of Government Agencies to Operate on the Basis of Accurate Information _____ 717

Page

E.   Computerized Business Records as Evidence ----------------------- 724
F.   Computer–Generated Evidence ------------------------------------- 728

Chapter XI.   Access to Information in Computerized Form -- **734**
A.   Access to Government Databanks ------------------------------------ 734
B.   Access to Computerized Data in Litigation --------------------------- 742

Chapter XII.   First Amendment Rights ----------------------------- **759**
A.   Introduction --- 759
B.   Is There a Right to Have E–Mail Delivered? ------------------------ 759
C.   Pornography and Indecency --- 770
D.   Intellectual Property Rights Versus Free Speech ------------------- 808
E.   Anonymous and Pseudonymous Communications ------------------- 812
F.   Encryption Software and the First Amendment --------------------- 819

INDEX -- 825

*

Table of Contents

	Page
INTRODUCTION	iii
PREFACE	v
TABLE OF CASES	xix

Chapter I.   Internet and Software Copyright — 1

A. Introduction — 1
  Copyright Act of 1976—§§ 101–102 — 2
  Notes and Questions — 3
B. Copyrightability — 4
  1. Fixation — 4
    Williams Electronics, Inc. v. Arctic International, Inc. — 4
    Note — 9
  2. Creativity — 10
    Feist Publications, Inc. v. Rural Telephone Service Company, Inc. — 10
    Notes and Questions — 19
    Oasis Publishing Company, Inc. v. West Publishing Co. — 20
    Notes — 21
    Matthew Bender & Co., Inc. v. West Publishing Co. — 22
    Notes — 29
  3. Methods of Operation — 30
    Apple Computer, Inc. v. Franklin Computer Corp. — 31
    Notes — 37
    Lotus Development Corp. v. Borland International, Inc. — 38
    Note — 47
    Compaq Computer Corp. v. Procom Technology, Inc. — 47
    Question — 54
  4. Merger of Idea and Expression — 54
    NEC Corp. v. Intel Corp. — 55
    Compaq Computer Corp. v. Procom Technology, Inc. — 59
    Question — 60
  5. Scenes a Faire — 60
    Data East USA, Inc. v. Epyx, Inc. — 60
    Note — 65
C. Ownership of Copyright — 65
D. Exclusive Rights of the Copyright Owner — 66
  1. Introduction — 66
    Copyright Act of 1976—§ 106 — 66
  2. Copies—§ 106(1) — 66
    MAI Systems Corp. v. Peak Computer, Inc. — 66
    Note — 71
  3. Derivative Works—§ 102(2) — 71
    Lewis Galoob Toys, Inc. v. Nintendo of America, Inc. — 71
    Notes — 75

                                                                    Page
D. Exclusive Rights of the Copyright Owner—Continued
   4. Rental—§ 106(3) -- 75
     Copyright Act of 1976—§ 106(3) ------------------------------- 75
   5. Performance And Display—§ 106(4) § 106(5) ------------------ 75
   6. Digital Audio Works—§ 106(6) and Copyright Management
      Rights—§ 1001 -- 75
     Recording Industry Association of America, v. Diamond Multime-
      dia Systems Inc. --- 75
     Notes -- 85
   7. Circumvention of Technological Measures—§§ 1201—1205 -- 85
     Universal City Studios, Inc. v. Reimerdes ------------------------- 85
     Notes -- 92
E. Limitations on the Exclusive Rights --------------------------------- 93
   1. Fair Use -- 93
     Copyright Act of 1976—§ 107 ----------------------------------- 93
     Sega Enterprises Ltd. v. Accolade, Inc. --------------------------- 94
     Note --- 106
     UMG Recordings, Inc. v. MP3.Com, Inc. ------------------------ 107
     A & M Records, Inc. v. Napster, Inc. ---------------------------- 110
   2. Backup Copies -- 120
     Copyright Act of 1976—§ 117 ----------------------------------- 120
     Atari, Inc. v. JS & A Group, Inc. ------------------------------- 121
   3. Privileges of Internet Service Providers—§ 512 ---------------- 126
     A & M Records, Inc. v. Napster, Inc. ---------------------------- 126
     Notes -- 136
   4. First Sale --- 136
     Copyright Act of 1976—§ 109 ----------------------------------- 136
     Note --- 137
     DSC Communications Corp. v. Pulse Communications, Inc. --------- 137
F. Infringement --- 146
   1. Direct Infringement -- 146
     NEC Corp. and NEC Electronics, Inc. v. Intel Corp. ------------- 146
     Note --- 151
     Whelan Associates, Inc. v. Jaslow Dental Laboratory, Inc. ------- 151
     Note --- 164
     Computer Associates International, Inc., v. Altai, Inc. ------------ 165
     Notes -- 182
   2. Contributory Infringement -------------------------------------- 182
     Vault Corp. v. Quaid Software Ltd. ------------------------------ 182
     In Re Certain Personal Computers and Components Thereof --------- 190
     Note --- 193
     Intellectual Reserve, Inc. v. Utah Lighthouse Ministry, Inc. ------- 193
   3. Vicarious Infringement --- 197
     Microsoft Corp. v. Grey Computer ------------------------------- 197
     Note --- 200
G. Preemption of State Law --- 200
   Ohio v. Perry --- 202
   Vault Corp. v. Quaid Software Ltd. ------------------------------- 206
   Question -- 207
H. Copyright–Like Protection -- 208
   Brooktree Corp. v. Advanced Micro Devices, Inc. ----------------- 208
   Note -- 216

Chapter II. Patentability of Computer Software, Programmed Computers, and Internet Business Systems   **217**

A. Introduction 217
B. A Networked Computer Methods Patent 219
C. Eligibility for Patent Protection 229
    Patent Act, ... 229
    35 U.S.C. §§ 101–103,112 229
D. Patentable Subject Matter—§ 101 232
    Gottschalk v. Benson 232
    Notes 237
    Diamond v. Diehr 238
    Notes 244
    In Re Alappat 244
    Notes 255
    State Street Bank & Trust Co. v. Signature Financial Group, Inc. 256
    Notes 264
    International Business Machines Corporation 265
    Note 272
    AT&T Corp. v. Excel Communications, Inc. 272
    Notes 281
E. Novelty and Anticipation—§ 102 283
    Notes on § 102 283
    Application of Bergy 285
    Note 287
F. Non–Obviousness—§ 103 287
    Amazon.com, Inc. v. Barnesandnoble.com, Inc. 289
    Notes and Questions 302
G. Enablement—§ 112 304
    In re Buchner 305
    Notes 307
    Notes 310
    Mossman v. Broderbund Software 311
    Notes 317
H. Claim Interpretation and Infringement: "Means for," The Doctrine of Equivalents, and File Wrapper Estoppel 319
    CIVIX–DDI, LLC v. Microsoft Corporation 320
    Notes 332
    Hilgraeve Corporation v. McAfee Associates, Inc. 333
    Notes 337
    Notes on the "Doctrine of Equivalents" 338
    Question 339

Chapter III. Trade Secrecy **342**

A. Introduction 342
B. Protecting Trade Secrets Against Taking by "Improper Means"   342
    Uniform Trade Secrets Act 343
    Economic Espionage Act of 1996 345
    Note 346
    Religious Technology Center v. Lerma 346
    Notes 349
    Vermont Microsystems, Inc. v. Autodesk, Inc. 350
    Note 355

Page

C. Protecting Trade Secrets Against Disclosure by Government Agencies --- 355
    Gilmore v. U.S. Department of Energy ------------------------ 355
    Note -- 366
D. Protecting Trade Secrets by Negotiated Contracts ------------- 366
    Hogan Systems, Inc. v. Cybresource Int'l., Inc. ----------- 366
    Notes --- 370
E. Protecting Trade Secrets by "Shrinkwrap" Licenses ------------ 370
    Vault Corp. v. Quaid Software Ltd. ------------------------- 370
    ProCD, Inc. v. Zeidenberg --------------------------------- 373
    Notes --- 382
    Uniform Computer Information Transactions Act --------- 383

Chapter IV. Trademarks, Unfair Competition, and Unfair Business Practices --- 387
A. Trademark Rights in Internet Domain Names ------------------- 387
    Sporty's Farm L.L.C. v. Sportsman's Market, Inc. --------- 387
    Note -- 399
B. Domain Name Arbitration -- 399
    Olly's B.V. v. CPS Korea ----------------------------------- 399
    Weber–Stephen Products Co. v. Armitage Hardware and Building Supply, Inc. --- 405
C. Misappropriation, Product Standards, and Trademarks --------- 408
    United States Golf Association v. St. Andrews Systems, Data–Max, Inc. 408
    Note And Question -- 419
    Compaq Computer Corp. v. Procom Technology, Inc. ----- 419
    Notes --- 426
    Playboy Enterprises, Inc. v. Terri Welles, Inc. ----------- 426
    Note -- 456
    Playboy Enterprises, Inc. v. Netscape Communications Corp. ---- 456
    Playboy Enterprises, Inc. v. Excite, Inc. ------------------ 456
D. Interfering With Internet Communications ----------------------- 461
    America Online, Inc. v. LCGM, Inc. ------------------------ 461
    Note -- 469
    Hartford House, LTD v. Microsoft Corp. ------------------- 469
    Note -- 471

Chapter V. Internet Jurisdiction ------------------------------- 472
A. Reach of "Long–Arm" Statutes ---------------------------------- 472
    Bensusan Restaurant Corp. v. King ------------------------ 472
    Note -- 475
B. Constitutional Limits on the Reach of Long–Arm Statutes ------- 476
    Cybersell, Inc. v. Cybersell, Inc. -------------------------- 476
    Note -- 483
C. In Rem Jurisdiction Over Domain Names ------------------------- 484
    Lucent Technologies, Inc. v. Lucentsucks.Com ----------- 484
    Note -- 488
D. Jurisdiction Over Persons Not Doing Business on the Internet -- 489
    Bochan v. La Fontaine ------------------------------------- 489
    Notes --- 494

CHAPTER VI. E–Commerce and Software Contracts --------- 495
A. Old Law and New Situations ------------------------------------- 495
    Walgreen v. Wisconsin Pharmacy Examining Board ------- 495

Page

B. Paperfree Transactions --------------------------------------- 498
   Prefatory Note to the Uniform Electronic Transactions Act ---------------- 499
   Electronic Signatures in Global and National Commerce Act ------------- 501
   Note --- 502
   The Uniform Computer Information Transactions Act ------------------ 502
   Summary of the Uniform Computer Information Transactions Act -------- 503
   Letter From the Federal Trade Commission Bureau of Consumer
      Protection, Bureau of Competition, and Policy Planning Office ning
      Office --- 507

C. Authentication of Signatures ---------------------------------- 510
   Question -- 511
   Electronic Signatures in Global and National Commerce Act ------------- 511
   Uniform Electronic Transactions Act ---------------------------------- 513

D. Applicable Law --- 513
   Uniform Computer Information Transactions Act ---------------------- 513
   Notes And Question -- 516

E. Tort as an Alternative to Contract Claims --------------------- 518
   A.T. Kearney, Inc. v. International Business Machines Corp. -------------- 518
   Note --- 524
   Glovatorium, Inc. v. NCR Corp. ------------------------------------- 524
   Notes and Questions -- 529

F. Bankruptcy–Protecting Software Users ------------------------- 530
   Bankruptcy Code --- 530

G. Self–Help --- 531
   Clayton X–Ray Co. v. Professional Systems Corp. ----------------------- 531
   Uniform Computer Information Transactions Act § 816 ----------------- 534

H. Consumer Protection By The Federal Trade Commission ---------- 535
   In Re Beylen Telecom, LTD. --- 536
   Note --- 540

I. Taxation --- 541
   Quill Corporation v. North Dakota --------------------------------- 541
   Notes -- 542

J. Restricting E–Competition ----------------------------------- 542
   State v. Amoroso --- 543
   Arizona Revised Statutes § 28–4460 -------------------------------- 548
   Note --- 550
   People v. World Interactive Gaming Corporation ----------------------- 550
   Questions --- 557
   Unauthorized Practice of Law Committee v. Parsons Technology, Inc. --- 557
   Unauthorized Practice of Law Committee v. Parsons Technology, Inc. --- 569
   Note And Questions --- 569

Chapter VII.   Telecommunications and the Internet ------------ **570**
A. Introduction -- 570
B. Line Sharing -- 570
   Before the Federal Communications Commission in the Matters of
      Deployment Of Wireline Services Offering Advanced Telecommunica-
      tions Capability and Implementation of the Local Competition Provi-
      sions of the Telecommunications Act of 1996 --------------------- 570
   Note --- 572

C. Internet Access Over Cable Television Facilities --------------- 572
   AT&T Corp. v. City of Portland ------------------------------------ 573
   Note --- 581

Page

Chapter VIII. Antitrust--- **582**
A. Introduction --- 582
B. Tie–In Sales --- 583
   Caldera, Inc. v. Microsoft Corp. ---------------------------- 584
   Note -- 601
   United States v. Microsoft Corporation ---------------------- 601
   Note -- 619
   United States v. Microsoft Corp. ---------------------------- 619
   New York v. Microsoft Corp. -------------------------------- 619
   Note -- 620
C. Agreements in Violation of the Antitrust Laws ---------------------- 621
   In re Intel Corp. -- 621
   Note -- 625
   Business Electronics Corporation v. Sharp Electronics Corporation ------- 625
   Note -- 632
D. Horizontal Restraints --- 632

Chapter IX. Privacy--- **634**
A. Introduction --- 634
B. Restricting the Power of Government to Use Compulsion to Force Disclosure of Personal Information ------------------------- 635
   Whalen v. Roe -- 635
   Note -- 640
   Electronic Communications Privacy Act § 2703 ---------------- 640
   Note -- 642
   United States v. Charbonneau ------------------------------- 642
C. Restricting Non–Governmental Collection of Information -------- 649
   Children's Online Privacy Protection Act --------------------- 649
   In re Liberty Financial Companies, Inc. ----------------------- 652
   Notes and Questions --- 654
   Electronic Communications Privacy Act § 2701 ---------------- 657
D. Restricting Use by the Government of Information in Government Records--- 657
   Pippinger v. Rubin -- 657
   Note -- 663
   Bohach v. City of Reno --- 663
E. Restricting Use by Private Parties of Information in Private Records--- 668
   Smyth v. Pillsbury -- 668
   Notes and Questions --- 671
F. Restricting Disclosure by the Government of Information in Government Records --- 671
   Reno v. Condon -- 671
   Note -- 676
G. Restriction of Disclosure by Private Parties of Information in Their Records --- 676
   In re Trans Union Corp. -- 676
   Electronic Communications Privacy Act § 2702 ---------------- 682
H. The Effect of European Union Privacy Law ---------------------- 684
   Directive On The Protection Of Individuals With Regard To The Processing Of Personal Data And On The Free Movement Of Such Data --- 684
   Note -- 688
   Safe Harbor Principles -- 688

Page

Chapter X.   Right to Accuracy of Information 692

A. Defamation 692
  Andrews v. TRW, Inc. 692
  Note 698
  Rogan v. City of Los Angeles 698
  Notes and Questions 705
B. Immunity of Internet Service Providers 706
  Zeran v. America Online, Inc. 706
  Note 714
C. Duty to Provide Accurate Information to Those Affected 715
  Hermes v. Pfizer, Inc. 715
  Questions 716
D. Duty of Government Agencies to Operate on the Basis of
    Accurate Information 717
  Mesiar v. Heckman 717
E. Computerized Business Records as Evidence 724
  United States v. Whitaker 724
F. Computer–Generated Evidence 728
  Commercial Union Insurance Co. v. Boston Edison Co. 728
  Questions 733

Chapter XI.   Access to Information in Computerized Form ... 734

A. Access to Government Databanks 734
  *DeLorme Publishing Company, Inc. v. National Oceanic and Atmo-
    spheric Administration of the United States Department of Commerce* 734
  Notes 741
B. Access to Computerized Data in Litigation 742
  *National Union Electric Corporation v. Matsushita Electric Industrial
    Co., Ltd.* 742
  In re Japanese Electrical Products Antitrust Litigation 742
  Discovery of Computerized Data 747
  Notes And Questions 749
  Anti–Monopoly, Inc. v. Hasbro, Inc. 749
  In re Potash Antitrust Litigation 751

Chapter XII.   First Amendment Rights 759

A. Introduction 759
B. Is There a Right to Have E–Mail Delivered? 759
  Cyber Promotions, Inc. v. America Online, Inc. 759
  America Online, Inc. v. Cyber Promotions, Inc. 759
  Note And Question 769
C. Pornography and Indecency 770
  Reno v. American Civil Liberties Union 770
  Notes and Comments 789
  American Civil Liberties Union v. Reno 790
  Note 797
  *Mainstream Loudoun v. Board of Trustees of the Loudoun County
    Library* 797
D. Intellectual Property Rights Versus Free Speech 808
  CPC International, Inc. v. Skippy Inc. 808
  Note 812

                                                                        Page
E. Anonymous and Pseudonymous Communications 812
    American Civil Liberties Union of Georgia v. Miller 812
    Notes 819
F. Encryption Software and the First Amendment 819
    Junger v. Daley 819
    Note 823

INDEX 825

Table of Cases

The principal cases are in bold type. Cases cited or discussed in the text
are roman type. References are to pages. Cases cited in principal
cases and within other quoted materials are not included.

Abele, In re, 684 F.2d 902 (Cust. & Pat. App.1982), 244

Advanced Display Systems, Inc. v. Kent State University, 212 F.3d 1272 (Fed. Cir.2000), 303

Alappat, In re, 33 F.3d 1526 (Fed.Cir. 1994), 218, **244**

Amazon.com, Inc. v. Barnesandnoble.com, Inc., 73 F.Supp.2d 1228 (W.D.Wash.1999), **289**

American Civil Liberties Union v. Reno, 217 F.3d 162 (3rd Cir.2000), **790**

American Civil Liberties Union of Georgia v. Miller, 977 F.Supp. 1228 (N.D.Ga.1997), **812**

America Online, Inc. v. Cyber Promotions, Inc., 948 F.Supp. 436 (1996), **759**

America Online, Inc. v. LCGM, Inc., 46 F.Supp.2d 444 (E.D.Va.1998), **461**

Amoroso, State v., 975 P.2d 505 (Utah App.1999), **543**

A & M Records, Inc. v. Napster, Inc., 114 F.Supp.2d 896 (N.D.Cal.2000), **110**

A & M Records, Inc. v. Napster, Inc., 54 U.S.P.Q.2d 1746, 2000 WL 573136 (N.D.Cal.2000), **126**

Andrews v. TRW, Inc., 225 F.3d 1063 (9th Cir.2000), **692**

Anti–Monopoly, Inc. v. Hasbro, Inc., 1996 WL 22976 (S.D.N.Y.1996), **749**

Apollo Group, Inc. v. Avnet, Inc., 58 F.3d 477 (9th Cir.1995), 524

Apple Computer, Inc. v. Franklin Computer Corp., 714 F.2d 1240 (3rd Cir. 1983), **31**

Application of (see name of party)

Arizona v. Evans, 514 U.S. 1, 115 S.Ct. 1185, 131 L.Ed.2d 34 (1995), 705

Atari, Inc. v. JS & A Group, Inc., 597 F.Supp. 5 (N.D.Ill.1983), **121**

A.T. Kearney, Inc. v. International Business Machines Corp., 73 F.3d 238 (9th Cir.1995), **518**

AT & T Corp. v. City of Portland, 216 F.3d 871 (9th Cir.2000), **573**

AT & T Corp. v. Excel Communications, Inc., 172 F.3d 1352 (Fed.Cir. 1999), 219, **272**

Autoskill Inc. v. National Educational Support Systems, Inc., 994 F.2d 1476 (10th Cir.1993), 47, 182

Baker v. Selden, 101 U.S. 99, 11 Otto 99, 25 L.Ed. 841 (1879), 30

Bally Total Fitness Holding Corp. v. Faber, 29 F.Supp.2d 1161 (C.D.Cal.1998), 399, 812

Barrows, People v., 177 Misc.2d 712, 677 N.Y.S.2d 672 (N.Y.Sup.1998), 789

Bateman v. Mnemonics, Inc., 79 F.3d 1532 (11th Cir.1996), 182

Bechhoefer v. United States Dept. of Justice D.E.A., 209 F.3d 57 (2nd Cir.2000), 705

Bensusan Restaurant Corp. v. King, 126 F.3d 25 (2nd Cir.1997), **472**

Bergy, Application of, 596 F.2d 952 (Cust. & Pat.App.1979), 238, **285**

Bernstein v. United States Dept. of Justice, 176 F.3d 1132 (9th Cir.1999), 823

Beylen Telecom, Ltd., In re, No. 972–3128 (1997), **536**

Blumenthal v. Drudge, 992 F.Supp. 44 (D.D.C.1998), 714

Bochan v. La Fontaine, 68 F.Supp.2d 692 (E.D.Va.1999), **489**

Bohach v. City of Reno, 932 F.Supp. 1232 (D.Nev.1996), **663**

Brooktree Corp. v. Advanced Micro Devices, Inc., 977 F.2d 1555 (Fed.Cir. 1992), **208**

Brower v. Gateway 2000, Inc., 246 A.D.2d 246, 676 N.Y.S.2d 569 (N.Y.A.D. 1 Dept. 1998), 382

Buchner, In re, 929 F.2d 660 (Fed.Cir. 1991), **305**

Burrow–Giles Lithographic Co. v. Sarony, 111 U.S. 53, 4 S.Ct. 279, 28 L.Ed. 349 (1884), 31

Business Electronics Corp. v. Sharp Electronics Corp., 485 U.S. 717, 108 S.Ct. 1515, 99 L.Ed.2d 808 (1988), **625**

Caldera, Inc. v. Microsoft Corp., 72 F.Supp.2d 1295 (D.Utah 1999), **584**
Certain Personal Computers and Components Thereof, In re, 224 U.S.P.Q. 270, 1984 WL 64146 (U.S.Intern.Trade Com'n 1984), **190**
Charbonneau, United States v., 979 F.Supp. 1177 (S.D.Ohio 1997), **642**
Chevron, U.S.A., Inc. v. Natural Resources Defense Council, Inc., 467 U.S. 837, 104 S.Ct. 2778, 81 L.Ed.2d 694 (1984), **282**
CIVIX–DDI, LLC v. Microsoft Corp., 84 F.Supp.2d 1132 (D.Colo.2000), **320**
Clayton X–Ray Co. v. Professional Systems Corp., 812 S.W.2d 565 (Mo.App. W.D.1991), **531**
Commercial Union Ins. Co. v. Boston Edison Co., 412 Mass. 545, 591 N.E.2d 165 (Mass.1992), **728**
Compaq Computer Corp. v. Procom Technology, Inc., 908 F.Supp. 1409 (S.D.Tex.1995), **47, 59, 419**
Computer Associates Intern., Inc. v. Altai, Inc., 982 F.2d 693 (2nd Cir.1992), **165**
CPC Intern., Inc. v. Skippy Inc., 214 F.3d 456 (4th Cir.2000), **808**
Cyber Promotions, Inc. v. American Online, Inc., 948 F.Supp. 436 (E.D.Pa. 1996), **759**
Cybersell, Inc. v. Cybersell, Inc., 130 F.3d 414 (9th Cir.1997), **476**
Cyberspace, Communications, Inc. v. Engler, 55 F.Supp.2d 737 (E.D.Mich.1999), 789

Dahlmann v. Sulcus Hospitality Technologies, Corp., 63 F.Supp.2d 772 (E.D.Mich. 1999), 517
Dann v. Johnston, 425 U.S. 219, 96 S.Ct. 1393, 47 L.Ed.2d 692 (1976), 237, 283
Data East USA, Inc. v. Epyx, Inc., 862 F.2d 204 (9th Cir.1988), **60**
Delorise Brown, M.D., Inc. v. Allio, 86 Ohio App.3d 359, 620 N.E.2d 1020 (Ohio App. 8 Dist.1993), 517
DeLorme Pub. Co., Inc. v. National Oceanic and Atmospheric Admin. of United States Dept. of Commerce, 917 F.Supp. 867 (D.Me.1996), **734**
Destination Ventures, Ltd. v. F.C.C., 46 F.3d 54 (9th Cir.1995), 769
Diamond v. Chakrabarty, 447 U.S. 303, 100 S.Ct. 2204, 65 L.Ed.2d 144 (1980), 238, 287
Diamond v. Diehr, 450 U.S. 175, 101 S.Ct. 1048, 67 L.Ed.2d 155 (1981), 218, **238**
Dickinson v. Zurko, 527 U.S. 150, 119 S.Ct. 1816, 144 L.Ed.2d 143 (1999), 282

D.M.I., Inc. v. Deere & Co., 755 F.2d 1570 (Fed.Cir.1985), 332
Donaldson Co., Inc., In re, 16 F.3d 1189 (Fed.Cir.1994), 319
DSC Communications Corp. v. Pulse Communications, Inc., 170 F.3d 1354 (Fed.Cir.1999), **137**

Eastman Kodak Co. v. Image Technical Services, Inc., 504 U.S. 451, 112 S.Ct. 2072, 119 L.Ed.2d 265 (1992), 583
Ed Nowogroski Ins., Inc. v. Rucker, 137 Wash.2d 427, 971 P.2d 936 (Wash.1999), 343
Egbert v. Lippmann, 104 U.S. 333, 14 Otto 333, 26 L.Ed. 755 (1881), 283
Engineering Dynamics, Inc. v. Structural Software, Inc., 46 F.3d 408 (5th Cir. 1995), 47
Engineering Dynamics, Inc. v. Structural Software, Inc., 26 F.3d 1335 (5th Cir. 1994), 182

Feist Publications, Inc. v. Rural Telephone Service Co., Inc., 499 U.S. 340, 111 S.Ct. 1282, 113 L.Ed.2d 358 (1991), **10**
Fisher v. National Institutes of Health, 934 F.Supp. 464 (D.D.C.1996), 705
Flotec, Inc. v. Southern Research, Inc., 16 F.Supp.2d 992 (S.D.Ind.1998), 343
Foley, People v., 257 A.D.2d 243, 692 N.Y.S.2d 248 (N.Y.A.D. 4 Dept.1999), 789
Ford Motor Co. v. Lane, 67 F.Supp.2d 745 (E.D.Mich.1999), 350
Foster, Application of, 52 C.C.P.A. 1808, 343 F.2d 980 (Cust. & Pat.App.1965), 288

Gartside, In re, 203 F.3d 1305 (Fed.Cir. 2000), 282
Gates Rubber Co. v. Bando Chemical Industries, Ltd., 9 F.3d 823 (10th Cir.1993), 182
Gilmore v. United States Dept. of Energy, 4 F.Supp.2d 912 (N.D.Cal.1998), **355**
Glovatorium, Inc. v. NCR Corp., 684 F.2d 658 (9th Cir.1982), **524**
Gottschalk v. Benson, 409 U.S. 63, 93 S.Ct. 253, 34 L.Ed.2d 273 (1972), 217, **232**
Graham v. John Deere Co. of Kansas City, 383 U.S. 1, 86 S.Ct. 684, 15 L.Ed.2d 545 (1966), 288, 303
Graver Tank & Mfg. Co. v. Linde Air Products Co., 339 U.S. 605, 70 S.Ct. 854, 94 L.Ed. 1097 (1950), 338, 339

Haggar Apparel Co., United States v., 526 U.S. 380, 119 S.Ct. 1392, 143 L.Ed.2d 480 (1999), 282
Hartford House, Ltd. v. Microsoft Corp., Case No. CV778550 (1988), **469**

Hermes v. Pfizer, Inc., 848 F.2d 66 (5th Cir.1988), **715**

Hilgraeve Corp. v. McAfee Associates, Inc., 224 F.3d 1349 (Fed.Cir.2000), **333**

Hill v. Gateway 2000, Inc., 105 F.3d 1147 (7th Cir.1997), 382

Hoehling v. Universal City Studios, Inc., 618 F.2d 972 (2nd Cir.1980), 60

Hogan Systems, Inc. v. Cybresource Intern., Inc., 158 F.3d 319 (5th Cir.1998), **366**

IBM Peripheral EDP Devices Antitrust Litigation, In re, 5 Computer L.Serv. 878 (N.D.Calif.1975), 749

In re (see name of party)

Intel Corp., In re, Docket No. 9288 (1999), **621**

Intellectual Reserve, Inc. v. Utah Lighthouse Ministry, Inc., 75 F.Supp.2d 1290 (D.Utah 1999), **193**

International Business Machines Corporation, Case Number T 0935/97–3.5.1 (1999), **265**

In the Matters of Deployment of Wireline Services Offering Advanced Telecommunications Capability and Implementation of the Local Competition Provisions of the Telecommunications Act of 1996, 14 F.C.C.R. 20,912, 1999 WL 1124073 (F.C.C.1999), **570**

Japanese Electrical Products Antitrust Litigation, In re, 494 F.Supp. 1257 (1980), **742**

Junger v. Daley, 209 F.3d 481 (6th Cir. 2000), **819**

Lee v. A.R.T. Co., 125 F.3d 580 (7th Cir. 1997), 75

Lewis Galoob Toys, Inc. v. Nintendo of America, Inc., 964 F.2d 965 (9th Cir. 1992), **71**

Liberty Financial Companies, Inc., In re, File No. 982 3522 (1999), **652**

Lotus Development Corp. v. Borland Intern., Inc., 49 F.3d 807 (1st Cir. 1995), 3, **38**

Lowry, In re, 32 F.3d 1579 (Fed.Cir.1994), 255

Lucent Technologies, Inc. v. Lucentsucks.Com, 95 F.Supp.2d 528 (E.D.Va. 2000), **484**

Mainstream Loudoun v. Board of Trustees of Loudoun County Library, 2 F.Supp.2d 783 (E.D.Va.1998), **797**

MAI Systems Corp. v. Peak Computer, Inc., 991 F.2d 511 (9th Cir.1993), **66**

M.A. Mortenson Co., Inc. v. Timberline Software Corp., 140 Wash.2d 568, 998 P.2d 305 (Wash.2000), 382

Markman v. Westview Instruments, Inc., 517 U.S. 370, 116 S.Ct. 1384, 134 L.Ed.2d 577 (1996), 303

Markman v. Westview Instruments, Inc., 52 F.3d 967 (Fed.Cir.1995), 319

Matthew Bender & Co., Inc. v. West Pub. Co., 158 F.3d 693 (2nd Cir.1998), **22**

McLaren v. Microsoft Corp., 1999 WL 339015 (Tex.App.-Dallas 1999), 671

Mesiar v. Heckman, 964 P.2d 445 (Alaska 1998), **717**

Metallizing Engineering Co. v. Kenyon Bearing & Auto Parts Co., 153 F.2d 516 (2nd Cir.1946), 283

Micro–Managers, Inc. v. Gregory, 147 Wis.2d 500, 434 N.W.2d 97 (Wis.App. 1988), 517

Microsoft Corp. v. Grey Computer, 910 F.Supp. 1077 (D.Md.1995), **197**

Microsoft Corp., United States v., 84 F.Supp.2d 9 (D.D.C.1999), **619**

Microsoft Corp., United States v., 147 F.3d 935, 331 U.S.App.D.C. 121 (D.C.Cir.1998), **601**

Mirage Editions, Inc. v. Albuquerque A.R.T. Co., 856 F.2d 1341 (9th Cir.1988), 75

MiTek Holdings, Inc. v. Arce Engineering Co., Inc., 89 F.3d 1548 (11th Cir.1996), 182

Morrissey v. Procter & Gamble Co., 379 F.2d 675 (1st Cir.1967), 54

Mossman v. Broderbund Software Inc., 51 U.S.P.Q.2d 1752, 1999 WL 696007 (E.D.Mich.1999), **311**

National Basketball Ass'n v. Motorola, Inc., 105 F.3d 841 (2nd Cir.1997), 29

National Union Elec. Corp. v. Matsushita Elec. Indus. Co., Ltd., 494 F.Supp. 1257 (E.D.Pa.1980), **742**

NEC Corp. v. Intel Corp., 1989 WL 67434, 10 U.S.P.Q.2d 1177 (N.D.Cal. 1989), **55, 146**

New York v. Microsoft Corp., 82 F.Supp.2d 9 (1999), **619**

Nichols v. Universal Pictures Corporation, 45 F.2d 119 (2nd Cir.1930), 151

Novamedix, Ltd. v. NDM Acquisition Corp., 166 F.3d 1177 (Fed.Cir.1999), 517

Oasis Pub. Co., Inc. v. West Pub. Co., 924 F.Supp. 918 (D.Minn.1996), **20**

Olly's B.V. v. CPS Korea, Case No. D2000–0203 (2000), **399**

Pardo, In re, 684 F.2d 912 (Cust. & Pat. App.1982), 244

Parker v. Flook, 437 U.S. 584, 98 S.Ct. 2522, 57 L.Ed.2d 451 (1978), 237

Pennwalt Corp. v. Durand–Wayland, Inc., 833 F.2d 931 (Fed.Cir.1987), 332

People v. _____ (see opposing party)

People ex rel. v. _____ (see opposing party and relator)

Perry, Ohio v., 83 Ohio St.3d 41, 697 N.E.2d 624 (Ohio 1998), **202**

Pfaff v. Wells Electronics, Inc., 525 U.S. 55, 119 S.Ct. 304, 142 L.Ed.2d 261 (1998), 284

Pippinger v. Rubin, 129 F.3d 519 (10th Cir.1997), **657**, 705

Playboy Enterprises, Inc. v. Excite, Inc., 55 F.Supp.2d 1070 (1999), **456**

Playboy Enterprises, Inc. v. Netscape Communications Corp., 55 F.Supp.2d 1070 (C.D.Cal.1999), **456**

Playboy Enterprises, Inc. v. Terri Welles, Inc., 78 F.Supp.2d 1066 (S.D.Cal.1999), **426**

Potash Antitrust Litigation, In re, 1996 WL 757185 (D.Minn.1996), **751**

Prater, Application of, 56 C.C.P.A. 1381, 415 F.2d 1393 (Cust. & Pat.App.1969), 232

ProCD, Inc. v. Zeidenberg, 86 F.3d 1447 (7th Cir.1996), **373**

Quill Corp. v. North Dakota By and Through Heitkamp, 504 U.S. 298, 112 S.Ct. 1904, 119 L.Ed.2d 91 (1992), **541**

RealNetworks, Inc. v. Streambox, Inc., 2000 WL 127311 (W.D.Wash.2000), 93

Recording Industry Ass'n of America v. Diamond Multimedia Systems, Inc., 180 F.3d 1072 (9th Cir.1999), **75**

Red Baron–Franklin Park, Inc. v. Taito Corp., 883 F.2d 275 (4th Cir.1989), 75

Reiss v. National Quotation Bureau, 276 F. 717 (S.D.N.Y.1921), 30

Religious Technology Center v. Lerma, 908 F.Supp. 1362 (E.D.Va.1995), **346**

Reno v. American Civil Liberties Union, 521 U.S. 844, 117 S.Ct. 2329, 138 L.Ed.2d 874 (1997), **770**

Reno v. Condon, 528 U.S. 141, 120 S.Ct. 666, 145 L.Ed.2d 587 (2000), **671**

Rogan v. City of Los Angeles, 668 F.Supp. 1384 (C.D.Cal.1987), **698**

Sega Enterprises Ltd. v. Accolade, Inc., 977 F.2d 1510 (9th Cir.1992), **94**

Smyth v. Pillsbury Co., 914 F.Supp. 97 (E.D.Pa.1996), **668**

Softel, Inc. v. Dragon Medical and Scientific Communications, Inc., 118 F.3d 955 (2nd Cir.1997), 182

Sony Computer Entertainment, Inc. v. Connectix Corp., 203 F.3d 596 (9th Cir. 2000), 106

Sony Corp. of America v. Universal City Studios, Inc., 464 U.S. 417, 104 S.Ct. 774, 78 L.Ed.2d 574 (1984), 92

Sporty's Farm L.L.C. v. Sportsman's Market, Inc., 202 F.3d 489 (2nd Cir. 2000), **387**

SRI Intern. v. Matsushita Elec. Corp. of America, 775 F.2d 1107 (Fed.Cir.1985), 338

State v. _____ (see opposing party)

State Street Bank & Trust Co. v. Signature Financial Group, Inc, 149 F.3d 1368 (Fed.Cir.1998), 3, 219, **256**

Telectronics, Inc., United States v., 857 F.2d 778 (Fed.Cir.1988), 226

Trans Union Corp., In re, Docket No. 9255 (2000), **676**

UMG Recordings, Inc. v. MP3.Com, Inc., 92 F.Supp.2d 349 (S.D.N.Y.2000), **107**

Unauthorized Practice of Law Committee v. Parsons Technology, Inc., 179 F.3d 956 (5th Cir.1999), **569**

Unauthorized Practice of Law Committee v. Parsons Technology, Inc., 1999 WL 47235 (N.D.Tex.1999), **557**

United States v. _____ (see opposing party)

United States Golf Ass'n v. St. Andrews Systems, Data–Max, Inc., 749 F.2d 1028 (3rd Cir.1984), **408**

Universal Camera Corp. v. N.L.R.B., 340 U.S. 474, 71 S.Ct. 456, 95 L.Ed. 456 (1951), 282

Universal City Studios, Inc. v. Reimerdes, 111 F.Supp.2d 294 (S.D.N.Y. 2000), **85**

Vacco, People ex rel. v. World Interactive Gaming Corp., 1999 WL 591995 (N.Y.Sup.1999), **550**

Vault Corp. v. Quaid Software Ltd., 847 F.2d 255 (5th Cir.1988), **182, 206, 370**

Vermont Microsystems, Inc. v. Autodesk, Inc., 88 F.3d 142 (2nd Cir.1996), **350**

Walgreen Co. v. Wisconsin Pharmacy Examining Bd., 217 Wis.2d 290, 577 N.W.2d 387 (Wis.App.1998), **495**

Warmerdam, In re, 33 F.3d 1354 (Fed.Cir. 1994), 255

Warner–Jenkinson Co., Inc. v. Hilton Davis Chemical Co., 520 U.S. 17, 117 S.Ct. 1040, 137 L.Ed.2d 146 (1997), 338

Weber–Stephen Products Co. v. Armitage Hardware and Bldg. Supply, Inc., 54 U.S.P.Q.2d 1766, 2000 WL 562470 (N.D.Ill.2000), **405**

Western Marine Electronics, Inc. v. Furuno Elec. Co., Ltd., 764 F.2d 840 (Fed.Cir. 1985), 283

West Pub. Co. v. Mead Data Cent., Inc., 799 F.2d 1219 (8th Cir.1986), 19

Whalen v. Roe, 429 U.S. 589, 97 S.Ct. 869, 51 L.Ed.2d 64 (1977), **635**

Whelan Associates, Inc. v. Jaslow Dental Laboratory, Inc., 797 F.2d 1222 (3rd Cir.1986), **151**

Whitaker, United States v., 127 F.3d 595 (7th Cir.1997), **724**

Williams Electronics, Inc. v. Artic Intern., Inc., 685 F.2d 870 (3rd Cir.1982), **4**

Wilson Sporting Goods Co. v. David Geoffrey & Associates, 904 F.2d 677 (Fed.Cir. 1990), 338

WMS Gaming, Inc. v. International Game Technology, 184 F.3d 1339 (Fed.Cir. 1999), 338

World Interactive Gaming Corp., People ex rel. Vacco v., 1999 WL 591995 (N.Y.Sup.1999), **550**

Zeran v. America Online, Inc., 129 F.3d 327 (4th Cir.1997), **706**

*

INTERNET AND COMPUTER LAW

Cases — Comments — Questions

*

Chapter I

INTERNET AND SOFTWARE COPYRIGHT

A. INTRODUCTION

Article I, sec. 8, of the United States Constitution grants Congress the power: "To promote the Progress of Science and useful Arts, by securing for limited Times to Authors and Inventors the exclusive Right to their respective Writings and Discoveries." The drafters of the Constitution thereby interwove the patent and copyright powers. Translated into modern English, this clause might read as follows: "To promote the progress of knowledge by securing for limited times to authors the exclusive right to their writings; and to promote the progress of technology by securing for limited times to inventors the exclusive right to their inventions."

While explicitly recognizing the power of Congress to promote progress by granting copyright and patent protection, this same clause put important restrictions on the power, with the requirements that the exclusive rights be granted only for "limited times" and only for "writings and discoveries." The economics of copyright protection are very different from the economics of the protection of physical property, such as a single-family house. Providing strong and perpetual ownership rights for houses ensure that homeowners will spend an optimum amount on upkeep and that the market will allocate the house to the one who values it most. On the other hand, once sufficient incentive has been provided to ensure creation of a literary work, it can require little or no upkeep and can be shared at little or no cost by anyone in the world. So continuing strong ownership rights may lead to suboptimal access to the work. The theoretical aspects are discussed in detail in William M. Landes & Richard A. Posner, *An Economic Analysis of Copyright Law*, 18 J. LEGAL STUD. 325 (1989). Clearly the draftsmen of the Constitution were worried about some of the abuses of monopolies granted in England over everyday necessities such as matches and playing cards. Much of the work of the courts and Congress in interpreting this clause in the last two centuries has been in drawing the line this clause says must be drawn between the legitimate rewards of the innovator and the granting of monopoly power to the undeserving. Congress most recently exercised its Constitutional power of "securing" to "authors" the "exclusive rights" to "their writings" in the Copyright

Act of 1976, now codified in Title 17 of the U.S. Code. A 1978 Report of the National Commission on New Technological Uses of Copyrighted Works (CONTU) led Congress to amend the Act in 1980, adding provisions specifically dealing with computer programs. These provisions made it clear that computer programs were eligible for copyright protection. Because computer software and computer data are very different from traditional "writings," the courts have had an uneasy time applying copyright law to the computer area.

The Copyright Act has a relatively straightforward structure. Section 101 contains definitions; § 102 defines copyrightable subject matter. Section 106 lists the exclusive rights of the copyright owner. Sections 107–121 provided limitations upon (and exceptions to) the exclusive rights granted by § 106.

COPYRIGHT ACT OF 1976—§§ 101–102

§ 101 Definitions

* * *

A "computer program" is a set of statements or instructions to be used directly or indirectly in a computer in order to bring about a certain result.

* * *

§ 102 Subject matter of copyright: In general

(a) Copyright protection subsists, in accordance with this title, in original works of authorship fixed in any tangible medium of expression, now known or later developed, from which they can be perceived, reproduced, or otherwise communicated, either directly or with the aid of a machine or device. Works of authorship include the following categories:

(1) literary works;

(2) musical works, including any accompanying words;

(3) dramatic works, including any accompanying music;

(4) pantomimes and choreographic works;

(5) pictorial, graphic, and sculptural works;

(6) motion pictures and other audiovisual works; and

(7) sound recordings.

(b) In no case does copyright protection for an original work of authorship extend to any idea, procedure, process, system, method of operation, concept, principle, or discovery regardless of the form in which it is described, explained, illustrated, or embodied in such work.

Notes and Questions

1.   The list of categories in § 102 is not exhaustive, merely illustrative. It is now well established that computer programs are "works of authorship" protected under § 102. However, not everything fixed on a computer disk is a work of authorship. Suppose a scientist buys a data recording program and uses it to record temperatures from a thermometer connected to a computer. Is the record of temperatures the "writing of an author"? Probably it lacks the creative element that the Supreme Court has held is necessary to constitute authorship. But if somehow it is the "writing of an author," who is the author—the scientist or the company that prepared the computer program or the company that made the thermometer—or are they coauthors?

2.   Section 102(b) excludes from copyright protection ideas, procedures, processes, systems, methods of operation, concepts, principles, and discoveries because protection for such things is available in the form of a patent. Many computer programs have highly utilitarian purposes, such as controlling the rate at which fuel is fed to an automobile engine. Accused infringers may argue § 102(b) precludes protection for such programs. The matter remains in doubt because the Supreme Court divided 4 to 4 in the leading case on the subject, *Lotus Development Corp. v. Borland International, Inc.* 49 F.3d 807 (1st Cir.1995), *aff'd by an equally divided Court*, 516 U.S. 233. A recent decision *State Street Bank & Trust Co. v. Signature Financial Group, Inc.*, 149 F.3d 1368 (Fed.Cir.1998), has clarified and expanded the scope of possible patent protection for ways of doing business implemented in software. Nevertheless, copyright, rather than patent, remains the primary intellectual property right used by the computer industry. Since the 1976 Copyright Act was passed, computer technology has progressed at lightning speed, and industry lobbying for and against expanded intellectual property protection has moved even faster. Congress amended the Copyright Act in 1980, 1990, 1995, 1998, and 1999 to deal with issues related to computers and the Internet, mainly in the direction of strengthening and expanding intellectual property rights. These amendments to the Copyright Act and court decisions interpreting them will be discussed in more detail throughout this text.

3.   To understand the development of copyright principles relating to software, one must understand the basic structure of a modern personal computer. A computer runs by the positioning of a series of gates. The hardware is the basis of this system of gates. The hard-wired logic chips determine everything the computer can ultimately do. On top of that is the microcode level. Microcode sequences define the operations which the computer can perform by sequencing the use of the hard-wired logic chips. On top of this is the machine language level. At this level, the computer receives specific instructions for carrying out an operation in its native tongue. On top of machine language lies the operating system and the high-level programming language. These are the programs and syntax that can be controlled by the person operating the computer through use of the screen displays, input formats and keyboard and mouse input.

4. Above this last level, we are no longer dealing in terms of computer expertise, but rather in the domain of the discipline for which the computer is being put to use, i.e. business man, engineer, social scientist, librarian, attorney, doctor, and "video game freak" just to name a few. Thus, the complexity of the technology industries is apparent. There is no such thing as an all around "computer expert." There can be expertise at any given level or the expertise can be specific to a discipline in which computers are used for very specific purposes. Copyrightable material may be created at any of these levels or in any of the disciplines for which a new and unique computer usage can be found.

5. As computer law developed, it was necessary for the courts to consider whether each component merited copyright protection. There were decisions that recognized the copyrightability of microcode, source code and of eventually operating systems. There are also cases that recognize the copyrightability of screen displays and graphical user interfaces (also known as GUIs). Today, it is recognized that any form of computer software is protected by copyright, provided that it meets the requirements of § 102 that it be fixed in a tangible medium, be an original and somewhat creative work of authorship, and not be an idea, procedure, process, system, method of operation, concept, principle, or discovery.

B. COPYRIGHTABILITY

1. FIXATION

WILLIAMS ELECTRONICS, INC. v. ARCTIC INTERNATIONAL, INC.

United States Court of Appeals, Third Circuit, 1982.
685 F.2d 870.

SLOVITER, CIRCUIT JUDGE.

Defendant Arctic International, Inc. appeals from the district court's entry of a final injunction order permanently restraining and enjoining it from infringing plaintiff's copyrights on audiovisual works and a computer program relating to the electronic video game DEFENDER. The district court severed plaintiff's demand for injunctive relief from its demand for monetary damages, and further severed plaintiff's claims of copyright infringement from its claims of trademark infringement and unfair competition. These latter claims have not yet been adjudicated. However, because the injunction granted by the district court goes to the merits of the dispute and has "serious, perhaps irreparable, consequences", the order can be considered a "routine interlocutory injunctive order" and appealable under 28 U.S.C. § 1292(a)(1).

Plaintiff-appellee Williams Electronics, Inc. manufactures and sells coin-operated electronic video games. A video game machine consists of a cabinet containing, inter alia, a cathode ray tube (CRT), a sound system, hand controls for the player, and electronic circuit boards. The electronic circuitry includes a microprocessor and memory devices, called ROMs (*R*ead *O* nly *M* emory), which are tiny computer "chips" containing thousands of data locations which store the instructions and data of a computer program. The microprocessor executes the computer program to cause the game to operate. Judge Newman of the Second Circuit described a similar type of memory device as follows: "The (ROM) stores the instructions and data from a computer program in such a way that when electric current passes through the circuitry, the interaction of the program stored in the (ROM) with the other components of the game produces the sights and sounds of the audiovisual display that the player sees and hears. The memory devices determine not only the appearance and movement of the (game) images but also the variations in movement in response to the player's operation of the hand controls." *Stern Electronics, Inc. v. Kaufman*, 669 F.2d 852, 854 (2d Cir.1982).

In approximately October 1979 Williams began to design a new video game, ultimately called DEFENDER, which incorporated various original and unique audiovisual features. The DEFENDER game was introduced to the industry at a trade show in 1980 and has since achieved great success in the marketplace. One of the attractions of video games contributing to their phenomenal popularity is apparently their use of unrealistic fantasy creatures, a fad also observed in the popularity of certain current films. In the DEFENDER game, there are symbols of a spaceship and aliens who do battle with symbols of human figures. The player operates the flight of and weapons on the spaceship, and has the mission of preventing invading aliens from kidnaping the humans from a ground plane.

Williams obtained three copyright registrations relating to its DEFENDER game: one covering the computer program, Registration No. TX 654–755, effective date December 11, 1980; the second covering the audiovisual effects displayed during the game's "attract mode", Registration No. PA 97–373, effective date March 3, 1981; and the third covering the audiovisual effects displayed during the game's "play mode", Registration No. PA 94–718, effective date March 11, 1981. Readily visible copyright notices for the DEFENDER game were placed on the game cabinet, appeared on the CRT screen during the attract mode and at the beginning of the play mode, and were placed on labels which were attached to the outer case of each memory device (ROM). In addition, the Williams program provided that the words "Copyright 1980–Williams Electronics" in code were to be stored in the memory devices, but were not to be displayed on the CRT at any time.

Defendant-appellant Arctic International, Inc. is a seller of electronic components for video games in competition with Williams. The district court made the following relevant findings which are not disputed on this appeal. Arctic has sold circuit boards, manufactured by others, which contain electronic circuits including a microprocessor and memory devices (ROMs). These memory devices incorporate a computer program which is virtually identical to Williams' program for its DEFENDER game. The result is a circuit board "kit" which is sold by Arctic to others and which, when connected to a cathode ray tube, produces audiovisual effects and a game almost identical to the Williams DEFENDER game including both the attract mode and the play mode. The play mode and actual play of Arctic's game, entitled "DEFENSE COMMAND", is virtually identical to that of the Williams game, *i.e.*, the characters displayed on the cathode ray tube including the player's spaceship are identical in shape, size, color, manner of movement and interaction with other symbols. Also, the attract mode of the Arctic game is substantially identical to that of Williams' game, with minor exceptions such as the absence of the Williams name and the substitution of the terms "DEFENSE" and/or "DEFENSE COMMAND" for the term "DEFENDER" in its display. Based on the evidence before it, the district court found that the defendant Arctic had infringed the plaintiff's computer program copyright for the DEFENDER game by selling kits which contain a computer program which is a copy of plaintiff's computer program, and that the defendant had infringed both of the plaintiff's audiovisual copyrights for the DEFENDER game by selling copies of those audiovisual works.

In the appeal before us, defendant does not dispute the findings with respect to copying but instead challenges the conclusions of the district court with respect to copyright infringement and the validity and scope of plaintiff's copyrights. The recent market interest in electronic audiovisual games has created an active market for original work, and as frequently happens, has also spawned copies, many of which have been the subject of a flurry of recent opinions.

In the case before us, the parties agreed at the district court level that the only issues to be decided on the injunction were legal ones. Essentially, defendant Arctic attacks the validity and the scope of the copyrights which it has been found by the district court to have infringed. Plaintiff possesses certificates of registration issued by the Copyright Office. Under the Copyright Act, these certificates constitute *prima facie* evidence of the validity of plaintiff's copyright. 17 U.S.C. § 410(c). Defendant, therefore, has the burden of overcoming this presumption of validity.

With respect to the plaintiff's two audiovisual copyrights, defendant contends that there can be no copyright protection for the DEFENDER game's attract mode and play mode because these works fail to meet the statutory requirement of "fixation." Section 101 of the 1976 Copyright Act, 17 U.S.C. § 102, provides in part:

(a) Copyright protection subsists . . . in original works of authorship *fixed in any tangible medium of expression,* now known or later developed, from which they can be perceived, reproduced, or otherwise communicated, either directly or with the aid of a machine or device. Works of authorship include the following categories:

(1) literary works;

. . . .

(6) motion pictures and other audiovisual works;

. . . .

(emphasis added). The fixation requirement is defined in section 101 in relevant part as follows:

> A work is "fixed" in a tangible medium of expression when its embodiment in a copy or phonorecord, by or under the authority of the author, is sufficiently permanent or stable to permit it to be perceived, reproduced, or otherwise communicated for a period of more than transitory duration.

Defendant claims that the images in the plaintiff's audiovisual game are transient, and cannot be "fixed." Specifically, it contends that there is a lack of "fixation" because the video game generates or creates "new" images each time the attract mode or play mode is displayed, notwithstanding the fact that the new images are identical or substantially identical to the earlier ones.

We reject this contention. The fixation requirement is met whenever the work is "sufficiently permanent or stable to permit it to be ... reproduced, or otherwise communicated" for more than a transitory period. Here the original audiovisual features of the DEFENDER game repeat themselves over and over. The identical contention was previously made by this defendant and rejected by the court in *Midway Manufacturing Co. v. Arctic International, Inc., supra,* slip op. at 16–18. Moreover, the rejection of a similar contention by the Second Circuit is also applicable here. The court stated:

> The (video game's) display satisfies the statutory definition of an original "audiovisual work," and the *memory devices of the game satisfy the statutory requirement of a "copy" in which the work is "fixed."* The Act defines "copies" as "material objects ... in which a work is fixed by any method now known or later developed, and from which the work can be perceived, reproduced, or otherwise communicated, either directly or with the aid of a machine or device" and specifies that a work is "fixed" when "its embodiment in a copy ... is sufficiently permanent or stable to permit it to be perceived, reproduced, or otherwise communicated for a period of more than transitory duration." 17 U.S.C.App. § 101 (1976). *The audiovisual work is permanently embodied in a material object, the memory devices,* from which it can be perceived with the aid of the other components of the game.

Stern Electronics, Inc. v. Kaufman, 669 F.2d at 855–56 (footnote omitted; emphasis added). *See also Midway Manufacturing Co. v. Drikschneider, supra,* at 479–80; *Atari, Inc. v. Amusement World, Inc., supra.*

Defendant also apparently contends that the player's participation withdraws the game's audiovisual work from copyright eligibility because there is no set or fixed performance and the player becomes a co-author of what appears on the screen. Although there is player interaction with the machine during the play mode which causes the audiovisual presentation to change in some respects from one game to the next in response to the player's varying participation, there is always a repetitive sequence of a substantial portion of the sights and sounds of the game, and many aspects of the display remain constant from game to game regardless of how the player operates the controls. *See Stern Electronics, Inc. v. Kaufman*, 669 F.2d at 855–56. Furthermore, there is no player participation in the attract mode which is displayed repetitively without change.

* * *

Defendant argues that the basic question presented is whether the ROMs, which it views as part of a machine, can be considered a "copy" of a copyrighted work within the meaning of the Copyright Act. Defendant argues that a copyright for a computer program is not infringed when the program is loaded into electronic memory devices (ROMs) and used to control the activity of machines. That use, it claims, is a utilitarian one not within the scope of the Copyright Act. We have already rejected defendant's similar argument in the context of the copyrights for the audiovisual works. Defendant makes the further point that when the issue is the copyright on a computer program, a distinction must be drawn between the "source code" version of a computer program, which it would hold can be afforded copyright protection, and the "object code" stage, which it contends cannot be so protected.[7] Its theory is that a "copy" must be intelligible to human beings and must be intended as a medium of communication to human beings.

The answer to defendant's contention is in the words of the statute itself. A "copy" is defined to include a material object in which a work is fixed "by *any* method now known or later developed, and *from which the work can be perceived*, reproduced, or otherwise communicated, either directly or *with the aid of a machine or device*." 17 U.S.C. § 101 (emphasis added). By this broad language, Congress opted for an expansive interpretation of the terms "fixation" and "copy" which encompass technological advances such as those represented by the electronic devices in this case.[8] We reject any contention that this broad language

---

7. According to the *Final Report of the National Commission on New Technological Uses of Copyrighted Works*,

A source code is a computer program written in any of several programming languages employed by computer programmers. An object code is the version of a program in which the source code language is converted or translated into the machine language of the computer with which it is to be used.

Id. at 21 n.109 (majority report). A somewhat different explanation of these terms is provided in Commissioner Hersey's dissent to the CONTU Report:

All computer programs go through various stages of development....

. . . .

The stages of development of a program usually are: a definition, in eye-legible form, of the program's task or function; a description; a listing of the program's steps and/or their expression in flow charts; the translation of these steps into a "source code," often written in a high-level programming language, such as FORTRAN or COBOL; the transformation of this source code within the computer, through intervention of a so-called compiler or assembler program, into an "object code." This last is most often physically embodied, in the present state of technology, in punched cards, magnetic disks, magnetic tape, or silicon chips-its mechanical phase.

Id. at 28.

8. The legislative history of the 1976 Copyright Act supports this interpretation. It emphasizes the expanded scope of the fixation requirement:

should nonetheless be interpreted in a manner which would severely limit the copyrightability of computer programs which Congress clearly intended to protect. We cannot accept defendant's suggestion that would afford an unlimited loophole by which infringement of a computer program is limited to copying of the computer program text but not to duplication of a computer program fixed on a silicon chip. This was also the conclusion reached in *Tandy Corp. v. Personal Micro Computers, Inc.*, 524 F.Supp. 171, 175 (N.D.Cal.1981) (Peckham, C. J.), albeit in the context of computers rather than video games.

The only authority upon which defendant relies for its claim that plaintiff is entitled to no copyright protection is the district court's opinion in *Data Cash Systems, Inc. v. JS&A Group, Inc.*, 480 F.Supp. 1063 (N.D.Ill.1979), *aff'd on other grounds*, 628 F.2d 1038 (7th Cir.1980). Significantly, the statements of the district court in that case that the copying of ROMs was not actionable under the copyright laws was not the basis of the affirmance by the Court of Appeals which expressly stated that it did not reach the merits of this issue. 628 F.2d at 1041. It has been suggested that the Court of Appeals implicitly reversed the district court on that issue. *See* 2 *Nimmer on Copyright*, § 8.08 at 8–106.3 n.18 (1981); *Tandy Corp. v. Personal Micro Computers, Inc.*, 524 F.Supp. at 175. The district court's analysis in Data Cash has been expressly rejected in both the video game audiovisual copyright context, *Midway Manufacturing Co. v. Arctic International, Inc.*, *supra*, slip op. at 27–29, and the computer program copyright context, *Tandy Corp. v. Personal Micro Computers, Inc.*, 524 F.Supp. at 175. Accordingly, we find that defendant has failed to provide any persuasive reason which would overcome the statutory presumption of validity of the copyright registration and we will affirm the district court's grant of an injunction.

* * *

For the above reasons, the district court's order granting the injunction will be affirmed except for Conclusion of Law No. 8 finding that the infringement was willful and deliberate. The case will be remanded for further proceedings consistent with this opinion.

Note

The case above is the leading case establishing the principle that software is copyrightable. The important Supreme Court decision below,

This broad language is intended to avoid the artificial and largely unjustifiable distinctions, derived from cases such as White–Smith Publishing Co. v. Apollo Co., 209 U.S. 1, 28 S.Ct. 319, 52 L.Ed. 655 (1908), under which statutory copyrightability in certain cases has been made to depend upon the form or medium in which the work is fixed. Under the bill it makes no difference what the form, manner, or medium of fixation may be—whether it is in words, numbers, notes, sounds, pictures, or any other graphic or symbolic indicia, whether embodied in a physical object in written, printed, photographic, sculptural, punched, magnetic, or any other stable form, and whether it is capable of perception directly or by means of any machine or device "now known or later developed."

H.R.Rep.No. 94–1476, at 52; S.Rep.No. 94–473, at 51, U.S.Code Cong. & Admin.News 1976, at 5665.

however, restricts the copyrightability of a computer-created compilation of factual data.

2. CREATIVITY

FEIST PUBLICATIONS, INC. v. RURAL TELEPHONE SERVICE COMPANY, INC.

Supreme Court of the United States, 1991.
499 U.S. 340, 111 S.Ct. 1282, 113 L.Ed.2d 358.

JUSTICE O'CONNOR delivered the opinion of the Court.

This case requires us to clarify the extent of copyright protection available to telephone directory white pages.

I

Rural Telephone Service Company, Inc., is a certified public utility that provides telephone service to several communities in northwest Kansas. It is subject to a state regulation that requires all telephone companies operating in Kansas to issue annually an updated telephone directory. Accordingly, as a condition of its monopoly franchise, Rural publishes a typical telephone directory, consisting of white pages and yellow pages. The white pages list in alphabetical order the names of Rural's subscribers, together with their towns and telephone numbers. The yellow pages list Rural's business subscribers alphabetically by category and feature classified advertisements of various sizes. Rural distributes its directory free of charge to its subscribers, but earns revenue by selling yellow pages advertisements.

Feist Publications, Inc., is a publishing company that specializes in area-wide telephone directories. Unlike a typical directory, which covers only a particular calling area, Feist's area-wide directories cover a much larger geographical range, reducing the need to call directory assistance or consult multiple directories. The Feist directory that is the subject of this litigation covers 11 different telephone service areas in 15 counties and contains 46,878 white pages listings—compared to Rural's approximately 7,700 listings. Like Rural's directory, Feist's is distributed free of charge and includes both white pages and yellow pages. Feist and Rural compete vigorously for yellow pages advertising.

As the sole provider of telephone service in its service area, Rural obtains subscriber information quite easily. Persons desiring telephone service must apply to Rural and provide their names and addresses; Rural then assigns them a telephone number. Feist is not a telephone company, let alone one with monopoly status, and therefore lacks independent access to any subscriber information. To obtain white pages listings for its area-wide directory, Feist approached each of the 11 telephone companies operating in northwest Kansas and offered to pay for the right to use its white pages listings.

Of the 11 telephone companies, only Rural refused to license its listings to Feist. Rural's refusal created a problem for Feist, as omitting these listings would have left a gaping hole in its area-wide directory, rendering it less attractive to potential yellow pages advertisers. In a decision subsequent to that which we review here, the District Court determined that this was precisely the reason Rural refused to license its listings. The refusal was motivated by an unlawful purpose "to extend its monopoly in telephone service to a monopoly in yellow pages advertising." *Rural Telephone Service Co. v. Feist Publications, Inc.*, 737 F.Supp. 610, 622 (D.Kan.1990).

Unable to license Rural's white pages listings, Feist used them without Rural's consent. Feist began by removing several thousand listings that fell outside the geographic range of its area-wide directory, then hired personnel to investigate the 4,935 that remained. These employees verified the data reported by Rural and sought to obtain additional information. As a result, a typical Feist listing includes the individual's street address; most of Rural's listings do not. Notwithstanding these additions, however, 1,309 of the 46,878 listings in Feist's 1983 directory were identical to listings in Rural's 1982–1983 white pages. Four of these were fictitious listings that Rural had inserted into its directory to detect copying.

Rural sued for copyright infringement in the District Court for the District of Kansas taking the position that Feist, in compiling its own directory, could not use the information contained in Rural's white pages. Rural asserted that Feist's employees were obliged to travel door-to-door or conduct a telephone survey to discover the same information for themselves. Feist responded that such efforts were economically impractical and, in any event, unnecessary because the information copied was beyond the scope of copyright protection. The District Court granted summary judgment to Rural, explaining that "[c]ourts have consistently held that telephone directories are copyrightable" and citing a string of lower court decisions. 663 F.Supp. 214, 218 (1987). In an unpublished opinion, the Court of Appeals for the Tenth Circuit affirmed "for substantially the reasons given by the district court." We granted certiorari to determine whether the copyright in Rural's directory protects the names, towns, and telephone numbers copied by Feist.

II

A

This case concerns the interaction of two well-established propositions. The first is that facts are not copyrightable; the other, that compilations of facts generally are. Each of these propositions possesses an impeccable pedigree. That there can be no valid copyright in facts is universally understood. The most fundamental axiom of copyright law is that "[n]o author may copyright his ideas or the facts he narrates." *Harper & Row, Publishers, Inc. v. Nation Enterprises*, 471 U.S. 539, 556, 105 S.Ct. 2218, 2228, 85 L.Ed.2d 588 (1985). Rural wisely concedes this point, noting in its brief that "[f]acts and discoveries, of course, are not themselves subject to copyright protection." Brief for Respondent 24. At the same time, however, it is beyond dispute that compilations of facts are within the subject matter of copyright. Compilations were expressly mentioned in the Copyright Act of 1909, and again in the Copyright Act of 1976.

There is an undeniable tension between these two propositions. Many compilations consist of nothing but raw data—*i.e.*, wholly factual information not accompanied by any original written expression. On what basis may one claim a copyright in such a work? Common sense tells us that 100 uncopyrightable facts do not magically change their status when gathered together in one place. Yet copyright law seems to contemplate that compilations that consist exclusively of facts are potentially within its scope.

The key to resolving the tension lies in understanding why facts are not copyrightable. The *sine qua non* of copyright is originality. To qualify for copyright protection, a work must be original to the author. See *Harper & Row, supra*, at 547–549. Original, as the term is used in copyright, means only that the work was independently created by the author (as opposed to copied from other works), and that it possesses at least some minimal degree of creativity. 1 M. Nimmer & D. Nimmer, Copyright §§ 2.01[A], [B] (1990) (hereinafter Nimmer). To be sure, the requisite level of creativity is extremely low; even a slight amount will suffice. The vast majority of works make the grade quite easily, as they possess some creative spark, "no matter how crude, humble or obvious" it might be. *Id.*, § 1.08[C] [1]. Originality does not signify novelty; a work may be original even though it closely resembles other works so long as the similarity is fortuitous, not the result of copying. To illustrate, assume that two poets, each ignorant of the other, compose identical poems. Neither work is novel, yet both are original and, hence, copyrightable. See *Sheldon v. Metro–Goldwyn Pictures Corp.*, 81 F.2d 49, 54 (C.A.2 1936).

Originality is a constitutional requirement. The source of Congress' power to enact copyright laws is Article I, § 8, cl. 8, of the Constitution, which authorizes Congress to "secur[e] for limited Times to Authors . . . the exclusive Right to their respective Writings." In two decisions from the late 19th century—*The Trade–Mark Cases*, 100 U.S. 82, 25 L.Ed. 550 (1879); and *Burrow-Giles Lithographic Co. v. Sarony*, 111 U.S. 53, 4 S.Ct. 279, 28 L.Ed. 349 (1884)—this Court defined the crucial terms "authors" and "writings." In so doing, the Court made it unmistakably clear that these terms presuppose a degree of originality.

In *The Trade–Mark Cases*, the Court addressed the constitutional scope of "writings." For a particular work to be classified "under the head of writings of authors," the Court determined, "originality is required." 100 U.S., at 94. The Court explained that originality requires independent creation plus a modicum of creativity: "[W]hile the word *writings* may be liberally construed, as it has been, to include original designs for engraving, prints, & c., it is only such as are *original*, and are founded in the creative powers of the mind. The writings which are to be protected are *the fruits of intellectual labor*, embodied in the form of books, prints, engravings, and the like." *Ibid.* (emphasis in original).

In *Burrow-Giles*, the Court distilled the same requirement from the Constitution's use of the word "authors." The Court defined "author," in a constitutional sense, to mean "he to whom anything owes its origin; originator; maker." 111 U.S., at 58, 4 S.Ct., at 281 (internal quotation marks omitted). As in *The Trade–Mark Cases*, the Court emphasized the creative component of originality. It described copyright as being limited to "original intellectual conceptions of the author," 111 U.S., at 58, 4 S.Ct., at 281, and stressed the importance of requiring an author who accuses another of infringement to prove "the existence of those facts of originality, of intellectual production, of thought, and conception." *Id.* at 59–60.

The originality requirement articulated in *The Trade–Mark Cases* and *Burrow-Giles* remains the touchstone of copyright protection today. See *Goldstein v. California*, 412 U.S. 546, 561–562, 93 S.Ct. 2303, 2312, 37 L.Ed.2d 163 (1973). It is the very "premise of copyright law." *Miller v. Universal City Studios, Inc.*, 650 F.2d 1365, 1368 (C.A.5 1981). Leading scholars agree on this point. As one pair of commentators succinctly puts it: "The originality requirement is *constitutionally mandated* for all works." Patterson & Joyce, Monopolizing the Law: The Scope of Copyright Protection for Law Reports and Statutory Compilations, 36 UCLA L.Rev. 719, 763, n. 155 (1989) (emphasis in original) (hereinafter Patterson & Joyce). Accord *id.*, at 759–760, and n. 140; Nimmer § 106[A] ("originality is a statutory as well as a constitutional requirement"); *id.*, § 108[C][1] ("a modicum of intellectual labor ... clearly constitutes an essential constitutional element").

It is this bedrock principle of copyright that mandates the law's seemingly disparate treatment of facts and factual compilations. "No one may claim originality as to facts." *Id.*, § 2.11[A], p. 2–157. This is because facts do not owe their origin to an act of authorship. The distinction is one between creation and discovery: The first person to find and report a particular fact has not created the fact; he or she has merely discovered its existence. To borrow from *Burrow-Giles*, one who discovers a fact is not its "maker" or "originator." 111 U.S., at 58, 4 S.Ct., at 281. "The discoverer merely finds and records." Nimmer § 2.03[E]. Census takers, for example, do not "create" the population figures that emerge from their efforts; in a sense, they copy these figures from the world around them. Denicola, Copyright in Collections of Facts: A Theory for the Protection of Nonfiction Literary Works, 81 Colum.L.Rev. 516, 525 (1981) (hereinafter Denicola). Census data therefore do not trigger copyright because these data are not "original" in the constitutional sense. Nimmer § 2.03[E]. The same is true of all facts—scientific, historical, biographical, and news of the day. "[T]hey may not be copyrighted and are part of the public domain available to every person." *Miller, supra,* at 1369.

Factual compilations, on the other hand, may possess the requisite originality. The compilation author typically chooses which facts to include, in what order to place them, and how to arrange the collected data so that they may be used effectively by readers. These choices as to selection and arrangement, so long as they are made independently by the compiler and entail a minimal degree of creativity, are sufficiently original that Congress may protect such compilations through the copyright laws. Nimmer §§ 2.11[D], 3.03; Denicola 523, n. 38. Thus, even a directory that contains absolutely no protectible written expression, only facts, meets the constitutional minimum for copyright protection if it features an original selection or arrangement. See *Harper & Row*, 471 U.S., at 547, 105 S.Ct., at 2223. Accord, Nimmer § 3.03.

This protection is subject to an important limitation. The mere fact that a work is copyrighted does not mean that every element of the work may be protected. Originality remains the *sine qua non* of copyright; accordingly, copyright protection may extend only to those components of a work that are original to the author. Patterson & Joyce 800–802. Thus, if the compilation author clothes facts with an original collocation of words, he or she may be able to claim a copyright in this written expression. Others may copy the underlying facts from the publication, but not the precise words used to present them. In *Harper & Row*, for example, we explained that President Ford could not prevent others from copying bare historical facts from his autobiography, see 471 U.S., at 556–557, 105 S.Ct., at 2228–2229, but that he could prevent others from copying his "subjective descriptions and portraits of public figures." *Id.*, at 563, 105 S.Ct., at 2232. Where the compilation author adds no written expression but rather lets the facts speak for themselves, the expressive element is more elusive. The only conceivable expression is the manner in which the compiler has selected and arranged the facts. Thus, if the selection and arrangement are original, these elements of the work are eligible for copyright protection. See Patry, Copyright in Compilations of Facts (or Why the "White Pages" Are Not Copyrightable), 12 Com. & Law 37, 64 (Dec. 1990) (hereinafter Patry). No matter how original the format, however, the facts themselves do not become original through association. See Patterson & Joyce 776.

This inevitably means that the copyright in a factual compilation is thin. Notwithstanding a valid copyright, a subsequent compiler remains free to use the facts contained in another's publication to aid in preparing a competing work, so long as the competing work does not feature the same selection and arrangement. As one commentator explains it: "[N]o matter how much original authorship the work displays, the facts and ideas it exposes are free for the taking. . . . [T]he very same facts and ideas may be divorced from the context imposed by the author, and restated or reshuffled by second comers, even if the author was the first to discover the facts or to propose the ideas." Ginsburg 1868.

It may seem unfair that much of the fruit of the compiler's labor may be used by others without compensation. As Justice Brennan has correctly observed, however, this is not "some unforeseen byproduct of a statutory scheme." *Harper & Row*, 471 U.S., at 589, 105 S.Ct., at 2245 (dissenting opinion). It is, rather, "the essence of copyright," *ibid.*, and a constitutional requirement. The primary objective of copyright is not to reward the labor of authors, but "[t]o promote the Progress of Science and useful Arts." Art. I, § 8, cl. 8. Accord, *Twentieth Century Music Corp. v. Aiken*, 422 U.S. 151, 156, 95 S.Ct. 2040, 2044, 45 L.Ed.2d 84 (1975). To this end, copyright assures authors the right to their original expression, but encourages others to build freely upon the ideas and information conveyed by a work. *Harper & Row, supra*, 471 U.S., at 556–557, 105 S.Ct., at 2228–2229. This principle, known as the idea/expression or fact/expression dichotomy, applies to all works of authorship. As applied to a factual compilation, assuming the absence of original written expression, only the compiler's selection and arrangement may be protected; the raw facts may be copied at will. This result is neither unfair nor unfortunate. It is the means by which copyright advances the progress of science and art.

This Court has long recognized that the fact/expression dichotomy limits severely the scope of protection in fact-based works. More than a century ago, the Court observed: "The very object of publishing a book on science or the useful arts is to communicate to the world the useful knowledge which it contains. But this object would be frustrated if the knowledge could not be used without incurring the guilt of piracy of the book." *Baker v. Selden*, 101 U.S. 99, 103, 25 L.Ed. 841 (1880). We reiterated this point in *Harper & Row*:

> "[N]o author may copyright facts or ideas. The copyright is limited to those aspects of the work—termed 'expression'—that display the stamp of the author's originality.

> "[C]opyright does not prevent subsequent users from copying from a prior author's work those constituent elements that are not original—for example ... facts, or materials in the public domain— as long as such use does not unfairly appropriate the author's original contributions." 471 U.S., at 547–548, 105 S.Ct., at 2223– 2224 (citation omitted).

This, then, resolves the doctrinal tension: Copyright treats facts and factual compilations in a wholly consistent manner. Facts, whether alone or as part of a compilation, are not original and therefore may not be copyrighted. A factual compilation is eligible for copyright if it features an original selection or arrangement of facts, but the copyright is limited to the particular selection or arrangement. In no event may copyright extend to the facts themselves.

B

As we have explained, originality is a constitutionally mandated prerequisite for copyright protection. The Court's decisions announcing this rule predate the Copyright Act of 1909, but ambiguous language in the 1909 Act caused some lower courts temporarily to lose sight of this requirement.

* * *

Making matters worse, these courts developed a new theory to justify the protection of factual compilations. Known alternatively as "sweat of the brow" or "industrious collection," the underlying notion was that copyright was a reward for the hard work that went into compiling facts. * * *

The "sweat of the brow" doctrine had numerous flaws, the most glaring being that it extended copyright protection in a compilation beyond selection and arrangement—the compiler's original contributions—to the facts themselves. * * *

Decisions of this Court applying the 1909 Act make clear that the statute did not permit the "sweat of the brow" approach. The best example is *International News Service v. Associated Press*, 248 U.S. 215, 39 S.Ct. 68, 63 L.Ed. 211 (1918). In that decision, the Court stated unambiguously that the 1909 Act conferred copyright protection only on those elements of a work that were original to the author.

* * *

[T]he originality requirement is not particularly stringent. A compiler may settle upon a selection or arrangement that others have used; novelty is not required. Originality requires only that the author make the selection or arrangement independently (i.e., without copying that selection or arrangement from another work), and that it display some minimal level of creativity. Presumably, the vast majority of compilations will pass this test, but not all will. There remains a narrow category of works in which the creative spark is utterly lacking or so trivial as to be virtually nonexistent. See generally *Bleistein v. Donaldson Lithographing Co.*, 188 U.S. 239, 251, 23 S.Ct. 298, 300, 47 L.Ed. 460 (1903) (referring to "the narrowest and most obvious limits"). Such works are incapable of sustaining a valid copyright. Nimmer § 2.01[B].

Even if a work qualifies as a copyrightable compilation, it receives only limited protection. This is the point of § 103 of the Act. Section 103 explains that "[t]he subject matter of copyright . . . includes compilations," § 103(a), but that copyright protects only the author's original contributions—not the facts or information conveyed:

> "The copyright in a compilation . . . extends only to the material contributed by the author of such work, as distinguished from the preexisting material employed in the work, and does not imply any exclusive right in the preexisting material." § 103(b).

As § 103 makes clear, copyright is not a tool by which a compilation author may keep others from using the facts or data he or she has collected. "The most important point here is one that is commonly misunderstood today: copyright . . . has no effect one way or the other on the copyright or public domain status of the preexisting material." H.R.Rep., at 57; S.Rep., at 55. * * *

In summary, the 1976 revisions to the Copyright Act leave no doubt that originality, not "sweat of the brow," is the touchstone of copyright protection in directories and other fact-based works. Nor is there any doubt that the same was true under the 1909 Act. The 1976 revisions were a direct response to the Copyright Office's concern that many lower courts had misconstrued this basic principle, and Congress emphasized repeatedly that the purpose of the revisions was to clarify, not change, existing law. The revisions explain with painstaking clarity that copyright requires originality, § 102(a); that facts are never original, § 102(b); that the copyright in a compilation does not extend to the facts it contains, § 103(b); and that a compilation is copyrightable only to the extent that it features an original selection, coordination, or arrangement, § 101.

* * *

III

There is no doubt that Feist took from the white pages of Rural's directory a substantial amount of factual information. At a minimum, Feist copied the names, towns, and telephone numbers of 1,309 of Rural's subscribers. Not all copying, however, is copyright infringement. To establish infringement, two elements must be proven: (1) ownership of a valid copyright, and (2) copying of constituent elements of the work that are original. See *Harper & Row*, 471 U.S., at 548, 105 S.Ct., at 2224. The first element is not at issue here; Feist appears to concede that Rural's directory, considered as a whole, is subject to a valid copyright because it contains some foreword text, as well as original material in its yellow pages advertisements. See Brief for Petitioner 18; Pet. for Cert. 9.

The question is whether Rural has proved the second element. In other words, did Feist, by taking 1,309 names, towns, and telephone numbers from Rural's white pages, copy anything that was "original" to Rural? Certainly, the raw data does not satisfy the originality requirement. Rural may have been the first to discover and report the names, towns, and telephone numbers of its subscribers, but this data does not " 'ow[e] its origin' " to Rural. *Burrow-Giles*, 111 U.S., at 58, 4 S.Ct., at 281. Rather, these bits of information are uncopyrightable facts; they existed before Rural reported them and would have continued to exist if Rural had never published a telephone directory. The originality requirement "rule[s] out protecting . . . names, addresses, and telephone numbers of which the plaintiff by no stretch of the imagination could be called the author." Patterson & Joyce 776.

Rural essentially concedes the point by referring to the names, towns, and telephone numbers as "preexisting material." Brief for Respondent 17. Section 103(b) states explicitly that the copyright in a compilation does not extend to "the preexisting material employed in the work."

The question that remains is whether Rural selected, coordinated, or arranged these uncopyrightable facts in an original way. As mentioned, originality is not a stringent standard; it does not require that facts be presented in an innovative or surprising way. It is equally true, however, that the selection and arrangement of facts cannot be so mechanical or routine as to require no creativity whatsoever. The standard of originality is low, but it does exist. * * *

The selection, coordination, and arrangement of Rural's white pages do not satisfy the minimum constitutional standards for copyright protection. As mentioned at the outset, Rural's white pages are entirely typical. Persons desiring telephone service in Rural's service area fill out an application and Rural issues them a telephone number. In preparing its white pages, Rural simply takes the data provided by its subscribers and lists it alphabetically by surname. The end product is a garden-variety white pages directory, devoid of even the slightest trace of creativity.

Rural's selection of listings could not be more obvious: It publishes the most basic information—name, town, and telephone number—about each person who applies to it for telephone service. This is "selection" of a sort, but it lacks the modicum of creativity necessary to transform mere selection into copyrightable expression. Rural expended sufficient effort to make the white pages directory useful, but insufficient creativity to make it original.

We note in passing that the selection featured in Rural's white pages may also fail the originality requirement for another reason. Feist points out that Rural did not truly "select" to publish the names and telephone numbers of its subscribers; rather, it was required to do so by the Kansas Corporation Commission as part of its monopoly franchise. See 737 F.Supp., at 612. Accordingly, one could plausibly conclude that this selection was dictated by state law, not by Rural.

Nor can Rural claim originality in its coordination and arrangement of facts. The white pages do nothing more than list Rural's subscribers in alphabetical order. This arrangement may, technically speaking, owe its origin to Rural; no one disputes that Rural undertook the task of alphabetizing the names itself. But there is nothing remotely creative about arranging names alphabetically in a white pages directory. It is an age-old practice, firmly rooted in tradition and so commonplace that it has come to be expected as a matter of course. See Brief for Information Industry Association et al. as *Amici Curiae* 10 (alphabetical arrangement "is universally observed in directories published by local exchange telephone companies"). It is not only unoriginal, it is practically inevitable. This time-honored tradition does not possess the minimal creative spark required by the Copyright Act and the Constitution.

We conclude that the names, towns, and telephone numbers copied by Feist were not original to Rural and therefore were not protected by the copyright in Rural's combined white and yellow pages directory. As a constitutional matter, copyright protects only those constituent elements of a work that possess more than a *de minimis* quantum of creativity. Rural's white pages, limited to basic subscriber information and arranged alphabetically, fall short of the mark. As a statutory matter, 17 U.S.C. § 101 does not afford protection from copying to a collection of facts that are selected, coordinated, and arranged in a way that utterly lacks originality. Given that some works must fail, we cannot imagine a more likely candidate. Indeed, were we to hold that Rural's white pages pass muster, it is hard to believe that any collection of facts could fail.

Because Rural's white pages lack the requisite originality, Feist's use of the listings cannot constitute infringement. This decision should not be construed as demeaning Rural's efforts in compiling its directory, but rather as making clear that copyright rewards originality, not effort. As this Court noted more than a century ago, " 'great praise may be due to the plaintiffs for their industry and enterprise in publishing this paper, yet the law does not contemplate their being rewarded in this way.' " *Baker v. Selden*, 101 U.S., at 105.

The judgment of the Court of Appeals is

Reversed.

JUSTICE BLACKMUN concurs in the judgment.

Notes and Questions

1. The record and briefs in *Feist* indicate that plaintiff's telephone directories were generated by computers, which retrieved the names and numbers in plaintiff telephone company's files, alphabetized them, and typeset them to create plaintiff's directories.

2. In *Feist*, the Supreme Court held that neither the unselective collection of all the telephone numbers for a given city nor the alphabetization of the names of the subscribers meets the requirements of creativity necessary to support a valid copyright. Suppose a telephone company hires artists to design the Yellow Pages to maximize the eye-appeal of the placement of different sizes of advertisements. Is the resulting arrangement copyrightable?

3. Numerous bills have been introduced in Congress to provide database protection, so as to fill what the proponents of these bills see as the gap created by *Feist*. Should non-copyrightable databases be protected and, if so, what types of databases should be protected and what form should the protection take?

4. *West Publishing Co. v. Mead Data Central, Inc.*, 799 F.2d 1219 (8th Cir.1986) held that the arrangement of cases in West's National Reporter System was copyrightable and that Mead's inclusion of "star page" references to this arrangement in the LEXIS system (which was owned by Mead at that time) would infringe. The *Oasis* decision below considered the effect of *Feist* upon *West v. Mead*.

OASIS PUBLISHING COMPANY, INC.
v. WEST PUBLISHING CO.

United States District Court, D. Minn., 1996.
924 F.Supp. 918.

MAGNUSON, CHIEF JUDGE.

This matter is before the Court upon West Publishing Company's (West's) Motion for Partial Summary Judgment and on Oasis Publishing Company, Inc.'s (Oasis') Cross–Motion for Partial Summary Judgment. For the following reasons the Court grants West's motion and denies Oasis' motion.

BACKGROUND

Oasis Publishing Company, Inc., (Oasis) publishes the statutes and cases of several states in Compact Disc Read Only Memory (CD–ROM) format. Among other works, West Publishing Company (West) publishes case reports of both state and federal courts in print in the National Reporter System, in its on-line computer database service (WESTLAW) and also in CD–ROM format. Both parties are private, for-profit corporations.

West publishes the *Southern Reporter*, a regional reporter that includes state court appellate decisions from Alabama, Florida, Louisiana and Mississippi. The *Southern Reporter* is a part of West's National Reporter System.

* * *

Oasis has announced its intent to publish reports of Florida court decisions on CD–ROM, having both parallel citation and star pagination to *Florida Cases*. Pagination to *Florida Cases*, of course, is pagination to the *Southern Reporter*, since pagination in the *Florida Cases* intentionally mirrors the pagination of the *Southern Reporter*. Oasis intends to obtain a set of *Florida Cases* in bound form and send the volumes to a service in order to translate the Florida decisions into computer data, ultimately to convert the decisions into CD–ROM format and market the CD–ROM product. Oasis does not intend to include the digest material (case synopsis, syllabi, etc.) authored by West. While West concedes that use of parallel citation is a fair use under the Copyright Act, it objects to Oasis' planned use of star pagination to *Florida Cases/Southern Reporter*.

* * *

* * * Oasis cross-moves for partial summary judgment, seeking a declaratory judgment that West has no copyright in the arrangement of the decisions in the *Florida Cases* * * *.

DISCUSSION

* * *

I. Copyright in Arrangement of Cases

* * *

The mainstay of Oasis' primary argument is that *Feist* has implicitly overruled *Mead*. In *Mead*, the Eighth Circuit affirmed this Court's (Rosenbaum, J.) decision to grant West a temporary injunction prohibiting Mead from using West's internal citations in Mead's proposed LEXIS star pagination computer research product. The *Mead* court found internal pagination part of West's arrangement, and found West's arrangement copyrightable. 799 F.2d at 1226–29. Finally, the court held that on the facts before it, LEXIS' proposed use would violate West's copyrightable arrangement. In *Feist*, the Supreme Court considered whether a publisher could duplicate selected listings from white pages that had been published by the local telephone company. It held that neither the information copied from the original white pages nor their selection and arrangement were copyrightable, and therefore the Court found no infringement by the duplication. 499 U.S. at 362–64, 111 S.Ct. at 1296–97.

Oasis insists that *Mead* applied a "sweat-of-the-brow" standard, which *Feist* rejected. In *Feist*, Justice O'Conner clarified that "[t]he sine qua non of copyright is originality." 499 U.S. at 345, 111 S.Ct. at 1287. The opinion reiterates that while choices concerning selection and arrangement are eligible for copyright protection if they are sufficiently original, the underlying compiled facts themselves do not become original or copyrightable merely through association with the selection or arrangement. *Id.* at 348–49, 111 S.Ct. at 1289–90.

In *Mead*, the Eighth Circuit applied essentially the same creativity standard discussed and applied in *Feist*. Instead of a mere "sweat-of-the-brow" analysis of West's arrangement of cases in the National Reporter System, the court considered the "originality and intellectual-creation requirements" of the arrangement. *Mead*, 799 F.2d at 1225–26. *Feist* did not overrule *Mead*. * * *

* * *

Notes

1. Oasis originally brought this suit in Florida. West successfully persuaded the Federal District Court in Florida to transfer the case to Minnesota, where West is located. Why might West's lawyers have wanted to do this?

2. The issue of the effect of *Feist* upon *Mead v. West* also arose in the Second Circuit case below.

MATTHEW BENDER & CO., INC.
v. WEST PUBLISHING CO.

United States Court of Appeals, Second Circuit, 1998.
158 F.3d 693, *cert. denied*, 526 U.S. 1124, 199
S.Ct. 2039, 143 L.Ed.2d 1048 (1999).

JACOBS, CIRCUIT JUDGE.

Defendants-appellants West Publishing Co. and West Publishing Corp. (collectively "West") create and publish printed compilations of federal and state judicial opinions. Plaintiff-appellee Matthew Bender & Company, Inc. and intervenor-plaintiff-appellee HyperLaw, Inc. (collectively "plaintiffs") manufacture and market compilations of judicial opinions stored on compact disc-read only memory ("CD–ROM") discs, in which opinions they embed (or intend to embed) citations that show the page location of the particular text in West's printed version of the opinions (so-called "star pagination"). Bender and HyperLaw seek judgment declaring that star pagination will not infringe West's copyrights in its compilations of judicial opinions. West now appeals from a judgment of the United States District Court for the Southern District of New York (Martin, J.), granting summary judgment of noninfringement to Bender and partial summary judgment of noninfringement to HyperLaw.

West's primary contention on appeal is that star pagination to West's case reporters allows a user of plaintiffs' CD–ROM discs (by inputting a series of commands) to "perceive" West's copyright-protected arrangement of cases, and that plaintiffs' products (when star pagination is added) are unlawful copies of West's arrangement. We reject West's argument for two reasons:

A.   Even if plaintiffs' CD–ROM discs (when equipped with star pagination) amounted to unlawful copies of West's arrangement of cases under the Copyright Act, (i) West has conceded that specification of the *initial* page of a West case reporter in plaintiffs' products ("parallel citation") is permissible under the fair use doctrine, (ii) West's arrangement may be perceived through parallel citation and thus the plaintiffs may lawfully create a copy of West's arrangement of cases, (iii) the incremental benefit of star pagination is that it allows the reader to perceive West's page breaks within each opinion, which are not protected by its copyright, and (iv) therefore star pagination does not create a "copy" of any protected elements of West's compilations or infringe West's copyrights.

B.   In any event, under a proper reading of the Copyright Act, the insertion of star pagination does not amount to infringement of West's arrangement of cases.

BACKGROUND

* * * West then publishes these case reports (first in paperbacked advance sheets, and then in hardbound volumes) in various series of

"case reporters." These case reporters are collectively known as West's "National Reporter System," and include (as relevant to this case): the *Supreme Court Reporter*, which contains all Supreme Court opinions and memorandum decisions; the *Federal Reporter*, which contains all federal court of appeals opinions designated for publication, as well as tables documenting the disposition of cases that are unpublished; the *Federal Rules Decisions* and *Federal Supplement*, which contain selected federal district court opinions; and the *New York Supplement*, which contains selected New York State case reports. Cases appearing in West's case reporters are universally cited by the volume and page number of the case reporter series in which they appear. One citation guide recommends—and some courts require—citation to the West version of federal appellate and trial court decisions and New York State court decisions.

Bender markets a series of CD–ROM discs called *Authority from Matthew Bender*. One product in this series—the "New York product"— consists of three elements: (i) "New York Law and Practice" (one disc), which contains New York statutory and treatise materials; (ii) "New York Federal Cases" (three discs), which contains cases from the Second Circuit and New York's federal district courts from 1789 to the present; and (iii) "New York State Cases" (four discs), which contains New York State judicial opinions from 1912 to the present (the New York State Court of Appeals cases begin in 1884). These CD–ROM discs contain published opinions and unpublished opinions and orders from these courts.

Bender obtains the text of the judicial opinions through a license from LEXIS (an on-line database containing legal and non-legal data), and stores the opinions and orders on the discs arranged by court and date, which is also the order in which they would be seen by a user who for some reason browses through the discs without sorting the case reports in a search. For each case that appears in West's case reporters, Bender intends to insert (and in some cases already has inserted) a parallel citation (*e.g.*, 100 F.3d 101) to the West case reporter at the beginning of the opinion and a citation to the successive West page numbers at the points in the opinion where page breaks occur in the West volume (*e.g.*, *104 or 100 F.3d 104).

Bender uses the FOLIO file-retrieval program, which allows a user to access opinions in several ways, including in the order in which they are stored on the disc, or through term searches, or through a West or LEXIS parallel or page citation. In addition, citations appearing within judicial opinions are "hot linked," so that a user may retrieve the cited case by clicking the mouse on the case citation.

West claims (and for the purposes of this summary judgment motion, we accept as true) that the FOLIO retrieval system permits a user of Bender's product to view (and print) judicial opinions in the same order in which they are printed in a West volume by repeating the following steps: (i) a user activates the jump feature in the program to go to the first page in a West case reporter volume, (ii) pages through to the bottom of the case, (iii) finds the last star pagination reference, and (iv) activates the jump cite feature to retrieve the case beginning on the same or next West page number.

HyperLaw markets *Supreme Court on Disc*, an annual CD–ROM disc containing opinions of the United States Supreme Court since 1991, and *Federal Appeals on Disc*, a quarterly CD–ROM disc containing nearly all opinions (published and unpublished) of the federal courts of appeals since January 1993. HyperLaw currently obtains the text of its opinions directly from the courts and includes in its *Federal Appeals* CD–ROM disc many more cases than published by West. The opinions are organized on the CD–ROM disc in an order that is "approximately chronological." HyperLaw includes parallel citations to West's case reporters for all cases appearing in the *Supreme Court Reporter* and the *Federal Reporter*, and intends to add star pagination as well.

Bender's complaint sought a judgment declaring that star pagination to West's case reporters will not copy West's arrangement or infringe West's copyright. HyperLaw intervened seeking the same relief. All parties then moved for summary judgment. The district court granted summary judgment to plaintiffs on the star pagination issue, concluding that the insertion of star pagination to West's volumes on the CD–ROM version of the cases would not reproduce any protectable element of West's compilation. The court noted that "the protection extends only to those aspects of the compilation that embody the original creation of the compiler" and that "where and on what particular pages the text of a court opinion appears does not embody any original creation of the compiler, and therefore ... is not entitled to protection." The court further ruled that star pagination would be permitted under the fair use doctrine even if West's pagination were copyrightable.

DISCUSSION

West's case reporters are compilations of judicial opinions. The Copyright Act defines a "compilation" as "a work formed by the collection and assembling of preexisting materials or of data that are selected, coordinated, or arranged in such a way that the resulting work as a whole constitutes an original work of authorship." 17 U.S.C. § 101 (1994). Compilations are copyrightable, but the copyright "extends only to the material contributed by the author of such work, as distinguished from the preexisting material employed in the work." 17 U.S.C. § 103 (1994). Works of the federal government are not subject to copyright protection, 17 U.S.C. § 105 (1994), although they may be included in a compilation.

* * *

Under *Feist*, two elements must be proven to establish infringement: "(1) ownership of a valid copyright, and (2) copying of constituent elements of the work that are original." *Id.* at 361, 111 S.Ct. at 1296. Bender and HyperLaw concede that West has proven the first element of infringement, *i.e.*, that West owns a valid copyright in each of its case reporters.

However, as is clear from the second Feist element, copyright protection in compilations "may extend only to those components of a work that are original to the author." *Id.* at 348, 111 S.Ct. at 1289. The "originality" requirement encompasses requirements both "that the work was independently created . . ., *and* that it possesses at least some minimal degree of creativity." *Id.* at 345, 111 S.Ct. at 1287 (emphasis added). At issue here are references to West's volume and page numbers distributed through the text of plaintiffs' versions of judicial opinions. West concedes that the pagination of its volumes—*i.e.*, the insertion of page breaks and the assignment of page numbers—is determined by an automatic computer program, and West does not seriously claim that there is anything original or creative in that process. As Judge Martin noted, "where and on what particular pages the text of a court opinion appears does not embody any original creation of the compiler." Because the internal pagination of West's case reporters does not entail even a modicum of creativity, the volume and page numbers are not original components of West's compilations and are not themselves protected by West's compilation copyright.

Because the volume and page numbers are unprotected features of West's compilation process, they may be copied without infringing West's copyright. However, West proffers an alternative argument based on the fact (which West has plausibly demonstrated) that plaintiffs have inserted or will insert all of West's volume and page numbers for certain case reporters. West's alternative argument is that even though the page numbering is not (by itself) a protectable element of West's compilation, (i) plaintiffs' star pagination to West's case reporters embeds West's arrangement of cases in plaintiffs' CD–ROM discs, thereby allowing a user to perceive West's protected arrangement through the plaintiffs' file-retrieval programs, and (ii) that under the Copyright Act's definition of "copies," 17 U.S.C. § 101, a work that allows the perception of a protectable element of a compilation through the aid of a machine amounts to a copy of the compilation. We reject this argument for two separate reasons.

A

West asserts an indirect infringement theory: (i) the embedding of unprotectable volume and page numbers in a CD–ROM disc (so-called "compilation markers" or "tags"), (ii) permits a user to perceive West's arrangement of cases through the aid of a machine, and (iii) this amounts to a copy of the compilation's arrangement under § 101's definition of "copies." Assuming for the moment that West has properly read the Act, i.e., that a copy of the arrangement is created when the arrangement can be perceived with the aid of a user *and* a machine, we think it is clear that the copy is not created by insertion of star pagination.

West concedes that insertion of parallel citations (identifying the volume and first page numbers on which a particular case appears) to West's case reporters in plaintiffs' products (as well as any other compilations of judicial opinions) is permissible under the fair use doctrine. * * *

Once the copy has thus been created through parallel citation—assuming that anyone would wish to avail themselves of the capability of perceiving this copy—the only incremental data made perceivable (through the aid of a machine) by star pagination is the location of page breaks within each judicial opinion. But since page breaks do not result from any original creation by West, their location may be lawfully copied. We therefore conclude that star pagination's volume and page numbers merely convey unprotected information, and that their duplication does not infringe West's copyright.

* * *

B

But our rejection of West's position is even more fundamental. If one browses through plaintiffs' CD–ROM discs from beginning to end, using the computer software that reads and sorts it, the sequence of cases owes nothing to West's arrangement. West's argument is that the CD–ROM discs are infringing copies because a user who manipulates the data on the CD–ROM discs could at will re-sequence the cases (discarding many of them) into the West arrangement. To state West's theory in the statutory words on which West (mistakenly) relies, each of the plaintiffs' CD–ROM discs is a "copy" because West's copyrighted arrangement is "fixed" on the disc in a way that can be "perceived ... with the aid of a machine or device." 17 U.S.C. § 101 (1994).

For reasons set forth below, we conclude that a CD–ROM disc infringes a copyrighted arrangement when a machine or device that reads it perceives the embedded material in the copyrighted arrangement or in a substantially similar arrangement. At least absent some invitation, incentive, or facilitation not in the record here, a copyrighted arrangement is not infringed by a CD–ROM disc if a machine can perceive the arrangement only after another person uses the machine to re-arrange the material into the copyrightholder's arrangement.

1. Section 101's Definition of "Copies"

* * *

To recapitulate a bit, West relies on the definition of "copies" to argue that plaintiffs' CD–ROM discs duplicate its copyrighted arrangement of cases because star pagination permits a user to "perceive" the copyrighted element "with the aid of" a computer and the FOLIO retrieval system, *i.e.*, by manipulating the data embedded on a CD–ROM disc to retrieve the cases in the order in which they appear in the West case reporters. West's definition of a copy, as applied to a CD–ROM disc, would expand the embedded work to include all arrangements and re arrangements that could be made by a third-party user who manipulates the data on his or her own initiative. But the relevant statutory wording refers to material objects in which "a work" readable by technology "is fixed," not to another work or works that can be created, unbidden, by using technology to alter the fixed embedding of the work, by rearrangement or otherwise. The natural reading of the statute is that the arrangement of the work is the one that can be perceived by a machine without an uninvited manipulation of the data.

West cites no case which supports its interpretation of § 101's definition of "copies," and every case we have found has relied upon the definition solely to ascertain whether a work has met the fixation requirement, not to determine the arrangements and rearrangements of the work fixed on the material object.

2. *Substantial Similarity*

The question presented—whether an element of West's copyrighted work has been reproduced in a "copy"—is answered by comparing the original and the allegedly infringing works, and inquiring whether the copyrightable elements are substantially similar. Under the facts of this case, the arrangement of the "work" on plaintiffs' CD–ROM discs is the arrangement of cases that is displayed by a CD player reading the information in the order in which it is physically embedded or "fixed" in the discs and not all possible arrangements that can be perceived through the manipulation and rearrangement of the embedded data by a third party user with a machine.

The Supreme Court in *Feist* emphasized that copyright protection for a factual compilation is "thin," and that a compilation containing the same facts or non-copyrightable elements will not infringe unless it "*feature[s]* the same selection and arrangement" as the original compilation. *Feist*, 499 U.S. at 349, 111 S.Ct. at 1289 (emphasis added). To determine whether two works contain a substantially similar arrangement, courts compare the ordering of material in the two works, finding infringement only when both compilations have featured a very similar literal ordering or format. "If the similarity concerns only noncopyrightable elements of [a copyright holder's] work, or no reasonable trier of fact could find the works substantially similar, summary judgment is appropriate." *Williams v. Crichton*, 84 F.3d 581, 587 (2d Cir.1996) (internal quotation marks and citations omitted). We agree with plaintiffs and *amicus* United States that West fails to demonstrate the requisite substantial similarity. West's case reporters contain many fewer cases than plaintiffs' CD–ROM discs, and are arranged according to classification such as court, date, and genre (opinions, per curiam opinions, orders, etc.), subject to certain exceptions characterized by West as features of originality, whereas plaintiffs organize their cases simply by court and date. Comparison of the works reveals that cases that appear adjacent in the West case reporters are separated on plaintiffs' products by many other cases; and even if these other cases are disregarded, the West cases included on plaintiffs' products are not in an order at all resembling West's arrangement.

Star pagination (in addition to revealing the page location of the text of judicial opinions) may incidentally reveal to *the reader* how the reader could create a copy of West's arrangement by various computer key operations; but by the same token, if the CD–ROM discs were published on paper in the same order as the cases are embedded in the CD–ROM disc, a reader so minded could assemble a "copy" of the West arrangement by use of scissors.

True, CD–ROM technology is different from paper, for as West points out, the arrangement of judicial opinions in a CD–ROM disc does not correspond necessarily to how the information will be displayed or printed by the user, because the file-retrieval system allows users to retrieve cases in a variety of ways. But having rejected West's argument under § 101, we can conclude that the arrangement of plaintiffs' work is the sequence of cases as embedded on the plaintiffs' CD–ROM discs and as displayed to the user browsing through plaintiffs' products. That sequence is not substantially similar to West's case reporters. There is no evidence that Bender and HyperLaw's case-retrieval systems allow a user to browse the cases in the West arrangement without first taking steps to create that arrangement. Thus, an actionable copy of West's sequence of cases, *i.e.*, a work with a substantially similar arrangement fixed in a tangible medium (probably a print-out of the cases), could be created by a user of the CD–ROM discs, but only by using the file-retrieval program as electronic scissors. We cannot find that plaintiffs' products directly infringe West's copyright by inserting star pagination to West's case reporters.

* * *

C

We differ with the Eighth Circuit's opinion in *West Publishing Co. v. Mead Data Central, Inc.*, 799 F.2d 1219 (8th Cir.1986). In that case, LEXIS (an on-line database provider) announced plans to star paginate its on-line version of cases to West case reporters. West claimed that the star pagination would allow users to page through cases as if they were reading West volumes, and in that way copied West's arrangement of cases. *Id.* at 1222. The court held that "West's arrangement is a copyrightable aspect of its compilation of cases, that the pagination of West's volumes reflects and expresses West's arrangement, and that MDC's intended use of West's page numbers infringes West's copyright in the arrangement." *Id.* at 1223. Even if it was not "possible to use LEXIS to page through cases as they are arranged in West volumes," the court said that insertion of comprehensive star pagination amounted to infringement: * * *.

The Eighth Circuit in *West Publishing Co.* adduces no authority for protecting pagination as a "reflection" of arrangement, and does not explain how the insertion of star pagination creates a "copy" featuring an arrangement of cases substantially similar to West's—rather than a dissimilar arrangement that simply references the location of text in West's case reporters and incidentally simplifies the task of someone who wants to reproduce West's arrangement of cases. It is true that star pagination enables users to locate (as closely as is useful) a piece of text within the West volume. But this location does not result in any proximate way from West's original arrangement of cases (or any other exercise of original creation) and may be lawfully copied So any damage to the marketability of West's reporters resulting from such copying is not cognizable under the Copyright Act. It is interesting that the Eighth Circuit's quotation from the Senate Report on supplanting use is drawn from the Report's discussion of the fair use doctrine, which applies only when the copyright holder has first demonstrated infringement of a protectable element of its work.

At bottom, *West Publishing Co.* rests upon the now defunct "sweat of the brow" doctrine. That court found that LEXIS had infringed West's copyright simply because it supplanted much of the need for West's case reporters through wholesale appropriation of West's page numbers. In reaching this conclusion, the court (i) noted that LEXIS's appropriation would deprive West of a large part of what it "[had] spent so much labor and industry in compiling," *West Publ'g Co.*, 799 F.2d at 1227, and (ii) cited *Hutchinson Telephone v. Fronteer Directory Co.*, 770 F.2d 128 (8th Cir.1985), *see West Publ'g Co.*, 799 F.2d at 1228, which in turn relied on *Leon v. Pacific Telephone & Telegraph Co.*, 91 F.2d 484 (9th Cir.1937), and *Jeweler's Circular Pub. Co. v. Keystone Pub. Co*, 281 F. 83 (C.C.A.2, 1922)—classic "sweat of the brow" cases that were overruled in *Feist*. Thus, the Eighth Circuit in *West Publishing Co.* erroneously protected West's industrious collection rather than its original creation. Because *Feist* undermines the reasoning of *West Publishing Co.*, we decline to follow it.

Conclusion

We hold that Bender and HyperLaw will not infringe West's copyright by inserting star pagination to West's case reporters in their CD–ROM disc version of judicial opinions. The judgement of the district court is affirmed.

Notes

1. After *Oasis* and *Matthew Bender*, would a competitor be safe in copying West's case reporters (without West's headnotes) into the competitor's commercial databank?

2. *National Basketball Association v. Motorola, Inc.*, 105 F.3d 841 (2d Cir.1997), was a recent case concerning the creative element. Motorola was distributing play-by-play sports information over a website and a pager network. The NBA argued that the information fell under the copyright protection afforded their broadcasts of professional basketball games. The Court found that the information was purely factual and, therefore, not protectable.

3. METHODS OF OPERATION

Competing software and hardware—computer operating systems, spreadsheet software, modems, etc., are subject to what economists call "network effects" and "switching costs." A "network effect" occurs when it is advantageous to have a product that functions to the same standard as the product that most other people have. It was important to each of the coauthors of this book to use a word processor that created files compatible with the word processors of the other coauthors. Often a widely used core product will attract the development of additional products developed to enhance the use and enjoyment of the core product. For instance, when Microsoft Windows became the most widely used operating system, more and more software was written that was designed for Microsoft Windows and would not work on competing operating systems. In some cases of network effects there can be a "tipping effect." Once VHS VCRs were in the majority, producers of videotapes concentrated on VHS production and the competing Betamax format disappeared. "Switching costs" are the costs associated with changing to a new system. For instance, when a company or an independent computer user wishes to change word processors, there are labor requirements for loading the new word processor onto computers, costs for retraining, effect on productivity during the learning cycle, etc. With traditional subjects of copyright, network effects and switching costs are largely absent. A glance at lists of motion picture box office hits will show different movies at the top every few weeks. Unless you are in a film discussion club, you don't really care what films other people are watching, so there is no network effect. Indeed if your friends have already seen the movie you want to watch, they will not want to go with you to see it again. With motion pictures there is a switching benefit rather than a cost. It is more fun to watch a new movie than to watch the same movie over and over again. The economic differences between traditional media and software publishing have led to arguments over whether software copyright owners should get the extra benefits of the "lock-in" nature of network effects and switching costs.

Copyright Act § 102(b) expressly forbids copyright protection for a "method of operation." This section codifies the holding of *Baker v. Selden*, 101 U.S. 99 (1879), which involved an accounting system developed by Selden. Selden had filed registered copyright in various blank accounting forms. The Court found that he had no protection against a competitor who "uses a similar plan so far as results are concerned; but makes a different arrangement of the columns, and uses different headings." In the 1921 decision of *Reiss v. National Quotation Bureau, Inc.* 276 F. 717, (S.D.N.Y.1921), Judge Learned Hand upheld copyright protection in a code book that used sequences of letters succinctly and efficiently express meaning when sending cables. The letter sequences were designed in a clever manner so that common errors in telegraphy would not distort messages. Defendant had copied the letter sequences exactly. Judge Hand wrote:

Not all words communicate ideas; some are mere spontaneous ejaculations. Some are used for their sound alone, like nursery jingles, or the rhymes of children in their play. Might not some one, with a gift for catching syllables, devise others? . . . .

Works of plastic art need not be pictorial. They may be merely patterns, or designs, and yet they are within the statute. A pattern or an ornamental design depicts nothing; it merely pleases the eye. If such models or paintings are "writings," I can see no reason why words should not be such because they communicate nothing. They may have their uses for all that aesthetic or practical, and they may be productions of high ingenuity, or even genius . . .

. . . grants of power to Congress comprise, not only what was then known, but what the ingenuity of men should devise thereafter. Of course, the new subject-matter must have some relation to the grant; but we interpret it by general practices of civilized people in similar fields, for it is not a strait-jacket, but a charter for living people.

Obviously the authors of the Constitution did not have computer programs in mind when they drafted the patent and copyright clause. The courts, however, have always interpreted the clause broadly to incorporate new technology. For instance a famous nineteenth century case, *Burrow-Giles Lithographic Co. v. Sarony*, 111 U.S. 53 (1884), held that photographs were copyrightable. Thus, the stage was set for the courts to find computer operating systems eligible for copyright, as we see in the following case.

APPLE COMPUTER, INC. v. FRANKLIN COMPUTER CORP.

United States Court of Appeals, Third Circuit, 1983.
714 F.2d 1240.

SLOVITER, CIRCUIT JUDGE.

I.

INTRODUCTION

Apple Computer, Inc. appeals from the district court's denial of a motion to preliminarily enjoin Franklin Computer Corp. from infringing the copyrights Apple holds on fourteen computer programs.

* * *

In this case the district court denied the preliminary injunction, *inter alia*, because it had "some doubt as to the copyrightability of the programs." *Apple Computer, Inc. v. Franklin Computer Corp.*, 545 F.Supp. 812, 812 (E.D.Pa.1982). This legal ruling is fundamental to all future proceedings in this action and, as the parties and amici curiae seem to agree, has considerable significance to the computer services industry. Because we conclude that the district court proceeded under an erroneous view of the applicable law, we reverse the denial of the preliminary injunction and remand.

II.

FACTS AND PROCEDURAL HISTORY

Apple, one of the computer industry leaders, manufactures and markets personal computers (microcomputers), related peripheral equipment such as disk drives (peripherals), and computer programs (software). It presently manufactures Apple II computers and distributes over 150 programs. Apple has sold over 400,000 Apple II computers, employs approximately 3,000 people, and had annual sales of $335,000,000 for fiscal year 1981. One of the byproducts of Apple's success is the independent development by third parties of numerous computer programs which are designed to run on the Apple II computer.

Franklin, the defendant below, manufactures and sells the ACE 100 personal computer and at the time of the hearing employed about 75 people and had sold fewer than 1,000 computers. The ACE 100 was designed to be "Apple compatible," so that peripheral equipment and software developed for use with the Apple II computer could be used in conjunction with the ACE 100. Franklin's copying of Apple's operating system computer programs in an effort to achieve such compatibility precipitated this suit.

* * *

Computer programs can be categorized by function as either application programs or operating system programs. Application programs usually perform a specific task for the computer user, such as word processing, checkbook balancing, or playing a game. In contrast, operating system programs generally manage the internal functions of the computer or facilitate use of application programs. The parties agree that the fourteen computer programs at issue in this suit are operating system programs.

Apple filed suit in the United States District Court for the Eastern District of Pennsylvania pursuant to 28 U.S.C. § 1338 on May 12, 1982, alleging that Franklin was liable for copyright infringement of the fourteen computer programs, patent infringement, unfair competition, and misappropriation. Franklin's answer in respect to the copyright counts included the affirmative defense that the programs contained no copyrightable subject matter. Franklin counterclaimed for declaratory judgment that the copyright registrations were invalid and unenforceable, and sought affirmative relief on the basis of Apple's alleged misuse. * * *

* * *

Franklin did not dispute that it copied the Apple programs. * * *

Franklin's principal defense at the preliminary injunction hearing and before us is primarily a legal one, directed to its contention that the

Apple operating system programs are not capable of copyright protection.

The district court denied the motion for preliminary injunction by order and opinion dated July 30, 1982. * * * We have jurisdiction of Apple's appeal pursuant to 28 U.S.C. § 1292(a)(1).

III.

THE DISTRICT COURT OPINION

* * *

We read the district court opinion as presenting the following legal issues: * * * (3) whether copyright can exist in an operating system program, * * *.

IV.

DISCUSSION

* * *

C.

Copyrightability of Computer Operating System Programs

We turn to the heart of Franklin's position on appeal which is that computer operating system programs, as distinguished from application programs, are not the proper subject of copyright "regardless of the language or medium in which they are fixed." Brief of Appellee at 15 (emphasis deleted). Apple suggests that this issue too is foreclosed by our *Williams* decision because some portion of the program at issue there was in effect an operating system program. Franklin is correct that this was not an issue raised by the parties in *Williams* and it was not considered by the court. Thus we consider it as a matter of first impression.

Franklin contends that operating system programs are *per se* excluded from copyright protection under the express terms of section 102(b) of the Copyright Act, and under the precedent and underlying principles of *Baker v. Selden*, 101 U.S. 99, 25 L.Ed. 841 (1879). These separate grounds have substantial analytic overlap.

In *Baker v. Selden*, plaintiff's testator held a copyright on a book explaining a bookkeeping system which included blank forms with ruled lines and headings designed for use with that system. Plaintiff sued for copyright infringement on the basis of defendant's publication of a book containing a different arrangement of the columns and different headings, but which used a similar plan so far as results were concerned. The Court, in reversing the decree for the plaintiff, concluded that blank account-books were not the subject of copyright and that "the mere copyright of Selden's book did not confer upon him the exclusive right to make and use account-books, ruled and arranged as designated by him and described and illustrated in said book." *Id.* at 107. The Court stated that copyright of the books did not give the plaintiff the exclusive right to use the system explained in the books, noting, for example, that "copyright of a work on mathematical science cannot give to the author an exclusive right to the methods of operation which he propounds." *Id.* at 103.

Franklin reads *Baker v. Selden* as "stand[ing] for several fundamental principles, each presenting ... an insuperable obstacle to the copyrightability of Apple's operating systems." It states:

> *First*, Baker teaches that use of a system itself does not infringe a copyright on the description of the system. *Second*, Baker enunciates the rule that copyright does not extend to purely utilitarian works. *Finally*, Baker emphasizes that the copyright laws may not be used to obtain and hold a monopoly over an idea. In so doing, Baker highlights the principal difference between the copyright and patent laws—a difference that is highly pertinent in this case.

Brief of Appellee at 22.

Section 102(b) of the Copyright Act, the other ground on which Franklin relies, appeared first in the 1976 version, long after the decision in *Baker v. Selden*. It provides:

> In no case does copyright protection for an original work of authorship extend to any idea, procedure, process, system, method of operation, concept, principle, or discovery, regardless of the form in which it is described, explained, illustrated, or embodied in such work.

It is apparent that section 102(b) codifies a substantial part of the holding and dictum of *Baker v. Selden*. *See* 1 *Nimmer on Copyright* § 2.18[D], at 2–207.

We turn to consider the two principal points of Franklin's argument.

1. "Process", "System" or "Method of Operation"

Franklin argues that an operating system program is either a "process", "system", or "method of operation" and hence uncopyrightable. Franklin correctly notes that underlying section 102(b) and many of the statements for which *Baker v. Selden* is cited is the distinction which must be made between property subject to the patent law, which protects discoveries, and that subject to copyright law, which protects the writings describing such discoveries. However, Franklin's argument misapplies that distinction in this case. Apple does not seek to copyright the method which instructs the computer to perform its operating functions but only the instructions themselves. * * *

Franklin's attack on operating system programs as "methods" or "processes" seems inconsistent with its concession that application programs are an appropriate subject of copyright. Both types of programs instruct the computer to do something. Therefore, it should make no difference for purposes of section 102(b) whether these instructions tell the computer to help prepare an income tax return (the task of an application program) or to translate a high level language program from source code into its binary language object code form (the task of an operating system program such as "Applesoft", see note 4 *supra*). Since it is only the instructions which are protected, a "process" is no more involved because the instructions in an operating system program may be used to activate the operation of the computer than it would be if instructions were written in ordinary English in a manual which described the necessary steps to activate an intricate complicated machine. There is, therefore, no reason to afford any less copyright protection to the instructions in an operating system program than to the instructions in an application program.

Franklin's argument, receptively treated by the district court, that an operating system program is part of a machine mistakenly focuses on the physical characteristics of the instructions. But the medium is not the message. We have already considered and rejected aspects of this contention in the discussion of object code and ROM. The mere fact that the operating system program may be etched on a ROM does not make the program either a machine, part of a machine or its equivalent. Furthermore, as one of Franklin's witnesses testified, an operating system does not have to permanently in the machine in ROM, but it may be on some other medium, such as a diskette or magnetic tape, where it could be readily transferred into the temporary memory space of the computer. In fact, some of the operating systems at issue were on diskette. * * *

Franklin also argues that the operating systems cannot be copyrighted because they are "purely utilitarian works" and that Apple is seeking to block the use of the art embodied in its operating systems. This argument stems from the following dictum in *Baker v. Selden*:

> The very object of publishing a book on science or the useful arts is to communicate to the world the useful knowledge which it contains. But this object would be frustrated if the knowledge could not be used without incurring the guilt of piracy of the book. And where the art it teaches cannot be used without employing the methods and diagrams used to illustrate the book, or such as are similar to them, such methods and diagrams are to be considered as necessary incidents to the art, and given therewith to the public; not given for the purpose of publication in other works explanatory of the art, but for the purpose of practical application.

101 U.S. at 103. * * *

Although a literal construction of this language could support Franklin's reading that precludes copyrightability if the copyright work is put to a utilitarian use, that interpretation has been rejected by a later Supreme Court decision. In *Mazer v. Stein*, 347 U.S. 201, 218, 74 S.Ct. 460, 471, 98 L.Ed. 630 (1954), the Court stated: "We find nothing in the copyright statute to support the argument that the intended use or use in industry of an article eligible for copyright bars or invalidates its registration. We do not read such a limitation into the copyright law." *Id.* at 218, 74 S.Ct. at 471. * * *

Perhaps the most convincing item leading us to reject Franklin's argument is that the statutory definition of a computer program as a set of instructions to be used in a computer in order to bring about a certain result, 17 U.S.C. § 101, makes no distinction between application programs and operating programs. Franklin can point to no decision which adopts the distinction it seeks to make. In the one other reported case to have considered it, *Apple Computer, Inc. v. Formula International, Inc.*, 562 F.Supp. 775 (C.D.Cal.1983), the court reached the same conclusion which we do, *i.e.* that an operating system program is not per se precluded from copyright. It stated, "There is nothing in any of the statutory terms which suggest a different result for different types of computer programs based upon the function they serve within the machine." *Id.* at 780. * * *

2. Idea/Expression Dichotomy

Franklin's other challenge to copyright of operating system programs relies on the line which is drawn between ideas and their expression. *Baker v. Selden* remains a benchmark in the law of copyright for the reading given it in *Mazer v. Stein, supra*, where the Court stated, "Unlike a patent, a copyright gives no exclusive right to the art disclosed; protection is given only to the expression of the idea—not the idea itself." 347 U.S. at 217, 74 S.Ct. at 470 (footnote omitted).

The expression/idea dichotomy is now expressly recognized in section 102(b) which precludes copyright for "any idea." This provision was not intended to enlarge or contract the scope of copyright protection but "to restate . . . that the basic dichotomy between expression and idea remains unchanged." H.R.Rep. No. 1476, *supra*, at 57, *reprinted in* 1976 U.S.Code Cong. & Ad.News at 5670. The legislative history indicates that section 102(b) was intended "to make clear that the expression adopted by the programmer is the copyrightable element in a computer program, and that the actual processes or methods embodied in the program are not within the scope of the copyright law." *Id.*

Many of the courts which have sought to draw the line between an idea and expression have found difficulty in articulating where it falls. See, *e.g., Nichols v. Universal Pictures Corp.*, 45 F.2d 119, 121 (2d Cir.1930) (L. Hand, J). We believe that in the context before us, a program for an operating system, the line must be a pragmatic one, which also keeps in consideration "the preservation of the balance between competition and protection reflected in the patent and copyright laws". *Herbert Rosenthal Jewelry Corp. v. Kalpakian*, 446 F.2d 738, 742 (9th Cir.1971). * * *

* * * If other programs can be written or created which perform the same function as an Apple's operating system program, then that program is an expression of the idea and hence copyrightable. In essence, this inquiry is no different than that made to determine whether the

expression and idea have merged, which has been stated to occur where there are no or few other ways of expressing a particular idea.

The district court made no findings as to whether some or all of Apple's operating programs represent the only means of expression of the idea underlying them. Although there seems to be a concession by Franklin that at least some of the programs can be rewritten, we do not believe that the record on that issue is so clear that it can be decided at the appellate level. Therefore, if the issue is pressed on remand, the necessary finding can be made at that time.

Franklin claims that whether or not the programs can be rewritten, there are a limited "number of ways to arrange operating systems to enable a computer to run the vast body of Apple-compatible software", Brief of Appellee at 20. This claim has no pertinence to either the idea/expression dichotomy or merger. The idea which may merge with the expression, thus making the copyright unavailable, is the idea which is the subject of the expression. The idea of one of the operating system programs is, for example, how to translate source code into object code. If other methods of expressing that idea are not foreclosed as a practical matter, then there is no merger. Franklin may wish to achieve total compatibility with independently developed application programs written for the Apple II, but that is a commercial and competitive objective which does not enter into the somewhat metaphysical issue of whether particular ideas and expressions have merged.

In summary, Franklin's contentions that operating system programs are *per se* not copyrightable is unpersuasive. The other courts before whom this issue has been raised have rejected the distinction. Neither the CONTU majority nor Congress made a distinction between operating and application programs. We believe that the 1980 amendments reflect Congress' receptivity to new technology and its desire to encourage, through the copyright laws, continued imagination and creativity in computer programming. Since we believe that the district court's decision on the preliminary injunction was, to a large part, influenced by an erroneous view of the availability of copyright for operating system programs and unnecessary concerns about object code and ROMs, we must reverse the denial of the preliminary injunction and remand for reconsideration.

* * *

V.

For the reasons set forth in this opinion, we will reverse the denial of the preliminary injunction and remand to the district court for further proceedings in accordance herewith.

Notes

1. Analyze *Apple v. Franklin* in terms of the "network effects" and "switching costs" discussed above.

2. Was Franklin's argument against copyrightability of "operating system programs" as weak as the court seems to indicate? Increasingly, computer software performs functions previously performed by machine parts. One of the reasons for Apple's success was that its brilliant developers found ways to use software instead of hardware to control disk drives, allowing them to reduce dramatically the number of hardware components needed, so as to produce a lighter-weight, cheaper, and more reliable personal computer. Competitors' disk drive controller hardware certainly was ineligible for copyright protection. Why should Apple's software, which performed exactly the same function, receive protection? Why should an automobile manufacturer who makes a computer-controlled fuel injection system receive protection against copying when a manufacturer of a mechanical fuel injection system receives no protection even against exact copying?

3. The United States Supreme Court has not provided guidance involving the eligibility of "operating system programs" for copyright protection. *Apple v. Franklin* (above) and *Lotus v. Borland* (below) are the leading cases on these issues.

LOTUS DEVELOPMENT CORP. v. BORLAND INTERNATIONAL, INC.

United States Court of Appeals, First Circuit, 1995.
49 F.3d 807, *aff'd by an equally divided Court*, 516 U.S.
233, 116 S.Ct. 804, 133 L.Ed.2d 610 (1996).

STAHL, CIRCUIT JUDGE.

This appeal requires us to decide whether a computer menu command hierarchy is copyrightable subject matter. In particular, we must decide whether, as the district court held, plaintiff-appellee Lotus Development Corporation's copyright in Lotus 1–2–3, a computer spreadsheet program, was infringed by defendant-appellant Borland International, Inc., when Borland copied the Lotus 1–2–3 menu command hierarchy into its Quattro and Quattro Pro computer spreadsheet programs.

I.

Background

Lotus 1–2–3 is a spreadsheet program that enables users to perform accounting functions electronically on a computer. Users manipulate and control the program via a series of menu commands, such as "Copy," "Print," and "Quit." Users choose commands either by highlighting them on the screen or by typing their first letter. In all, Lotus 1–2–3 has 469 commands arranged into more than 50 menus and submenus.

Lotus 1–2–3, like many computer programs, allows users to write what are called "macros." By writing a macro, a user can designate a series of command choices with a single macro keystroke. Then, to execute that series of commands in multiple parts of the spreadsheet, rather than typing the whole series each time, the user only needs to type the single pre-programmed macro keystroke, causing the program to recall and perform the designated series of commands automatically.

Thus, Lotus 1–2–3 macros shorten the time needed to set up and operate the program.

Borland released its first Quattro program to the public in 1987, after Borland's engineers had labored over its development for nearly three years. Borland's objective was to develop a spreadsheet program far superior to existing programs, including Lotus 1–2–3. In Borland's words, "[f]rom the time of its initial release ... Quattro included enormous innovations over competing spreadsheet products."

The district court found, and Borland does not now contest, that Borland included in its Quattro and Quattro Pro version 1.0 programs "a *virtually identical* copy of the entire 1–2–3 menu tree." *Borland III*, 831 F.Supp. at 212 (emphasis in original). In so doing, Borland did not copy any of Lotus's underlying computer code; it copied only the words and structure of Lotus's menu command hierarchy. Borland included the Lotus menu command hierarchy in its programs to make them compatible with Lotus 1–2–3 so that spreadsheet users who were already familiar with Lotus 1–2–3 would be able to switch to the Borland programs without having to learn new commands or rewrite their Lotus macros.

In its Quattro and Quattro Pro version 1.0 programs, Borland achieved compatibility with Lotus 1–2–3 by offering its users an alternate user interface, the "Lotus Emulation Interface." By activating the Emulation Interface, Borland users would see the Lotus menu commands on their screens and could interact with Quattro or Quattro Pro as if using Lotus 1–2–3, albeit with a slightly different looking screen and with many Borland options not available on Lotus 1–2–3. In effect, Borland allowed users to choose how they wanted to communicate with Borland's spreadsheet programs: either by using menu commands designed by Borland, or by using the commands and command structure used in Lotus 1–2–3 augmented by Borland-added commands.

* * *

Immediately following the district court's summary judgment decision, Borland removed the Lotus Emulation Interface from its products. Thereafter, Borland's spreadsheet programs no longer displayed the Lotus 1–2–3 menus to Borland users, and as a result Borland users could no longer communicate with Borland's programs as if they were using a more sophisticated version of Lotus 1–2–3. Nonetheless, Borland's programs continued to be partially compatible with Lotus 1–2–3, for Borland retained what it called the "Key Reader" in its Quattro Pro programs. Once turned on, the Key Reader allowed Borland's programs to understand and perform some Lotus 1–2–3 macros. With the Key Reader on, the Borland programs used Quattro Pro menus for display, interaction, and macro execution, except when they encountered a slash ("/") key in a macro (the starting key for any Lotus 1–2–3 macro), in which case they interpreted the macro as having been written for Lotus 1–2–3. Accordingly, people who wrote or purchased macros to shorten the time needed to perform an operation in Lotus 1–2–3 could still use those macros in Borland's programs. The district court permitted Lotus to file a supplemental complaint alleging that the Key Reader infringed its copyright.

The parties agreed to try the remaining liability issues without a jury. The district court held two trials, the Phase I trial covering all remaining issues raised in the original complaint (relating to the Emulation Interface) and the Phase II trial covering all issues raised in the supplemental complaint (relating to the Key Reader). * * *

* * *

This appeal concerns only Borland's copying of the Lotus menu command hierarchy into its Quattro programs and Borland's affirmative defenses to such copying. Lotus has not cross-appealed; in other words, Lotus does not contend on appeal that the district court erred in finding that Borland had not copied other elements of Lotus 1–2–3, such as its screen displays.

II.

Discussion

On appeal, Borland does not dispute that it factually copied the words and arrangement of the Lotus menu command hierarchy. Rather, Borland argues that it "lawfully copied the unprotectable menus of Lotus 1–2–3." Borland contends that the Lotus menu command hierarchy is not copyrightable because it is a system, method of operation, process, or procedure foreclosed from protection by 17 U.S.C. § 102(b). Borland also raises a number of affirmative defenses.

A. *Copyright Infringement Generally*

To establish copyright infringement, a plaintiff must prove "(1) ownership of a valid copyright, and (2) copying of constituent elements of the work that are original." *Feist Publications, Inc. v. Rural Tel. Serv. Co.*, 499 U.S. 340, 361, 111 S.Ct. 1282, 1296, 113 L.Ed.2d 358 (1991). To show ownership of a valid copyright and therefore satisfy *Feist's* first prong, a plaintiff must prove that the work as a whole is original and that the plaintiff complied with applicable statutory formalities. *See Engineering Dynamics, Inc. v. Structural Software, Inc.*, 26 F.3d 1335, 1340 (5th Cir.1994). "In judicial proceedings, a certificate of copyright registration constitutes *prima facie* evidence of copyrightability and shifts the burden to the defendant to demonstrate why the copyright is not valid." *Bibbero Sys., Inc. v. Colwell Sys., Inc.*, 893 F.2d 1104, 1106 (9th Cir.1990)

To show actionable copying and therefore satisfy *Feist's* second prong, a plaintiff must first prove that the alleged infringer copied plaintiff's copyrighted work as a factual matter; to do this, he or she may either present direct evidence of factual copying or, if that is unavailable, evidence that the alleged infringer had access to the copyrighted work and that the offending and copyrighted works are so similar that the court may infer that there was factual copying (i.e., probative similarity).

Engineering Dynamics, 26 F.3d at 1340. The plaintiff must then prove that the copying of copyrighted material was so extensive that it rendered the offending and copyrighted works substantially similar. *See Engineering Dynamics*, 26 F.3d at 1341.

In this appeal, we are faced only with whether the Lotus menu command hierarchy is copyrightable subject matter in the first instance, for Borland concedes that Lotus has a valid copyright in Lotus 1–2–3 as a whole and admits to factually copying the Lotus menu command hierarchy. As a result, this appeal is in a very different posture from most copyright-infringement cases, for copyright infringement generally turns on whether the defendant has copied protected expression as a factual matter. Because of this different posture, most copyright-infringement cases provide only limited help to us in deciding this appeal. This is true even with respect to those copyright-infringement cases that deal with computers and computer software.

B.　*Matter of First Impression*

Whether a computer menu command hierarchy constitutes copyrightable subject matter is a matter of first impression in this court. While some other courts appear to have touched on it briefly in dicta, we know of no cases that deal with the copyrightability of a menu command hierarchy standing on its own (i.e., without other elements of the user interface, such as screen displays, in issue). Thus we are navigating in uncharted waters.

Borland vigorously argues, however, that the Supreme Court charted our course more than 100 years ago when it decided *Baker v. Selden*, 101 U.S. 99 (1879). In *Baker v. Selden*, the Court held that Selden's copyright over the textbook in which he explained his new way to do accounting did not grant him a monopoly on the use of his accounting system. * * *

We do not think that *Baker v. Selden* is nearly as analogous to this appeal as Borland claims. Of course, Lotus 1–2–3 is a computer spreadsheet, and as such its grid of horizontal rows and vertical columns certainly resembles an accounting ledger or any other paper spreadsheet. Those grids, however, are not at issue in this appeal for, unlike Selden, Lotus does not claim to have a monopoly over its accounting system. Rather, this appeal involves Lotus's monopoly over the commands it uses to operate the computer. Accordingly, this appeal is not, as Borland contends, "identical" to *Baker v. Selden*.

C.　*Altai*

Before we analyze whether the Lotus menu command hierarchy is a system, method of operation, process, or procedure, we first consider the applicability of the test the Second Circuit set forth in *Computer Assoc. Int'l, Inc. v. Altai, Inc.*, 982 F.2d 693 (2d Cir.1992). The Second Circuit designed its *Altai* test to deal with the fact that computer programs, copyrighted as "literary works," can be infringed by what is known as "nonliteral" copying, which is copying that is paraphrased or loosely paraphrased rather than word for word. When faced with nonliteral-copying cases, courts must determine whether similarities are due mere-ly to the fact that the two works share the same underlying idea or whether they instead indicate that the second author copied the first author's expression. The Second Circuit designed its *Altai* test to deal with this situation in the computer context, specifically with whether one computer program copied nonliteral expression from another pro-gram's code.

*　*　*

While the *Altai* test may provide a useful framework for assessing the alleged nonliteral copying of computer code, we find it to be of little help in assessing whether the literal copying of a menu command hierarchy constitutes copyright infringement. In fact, we think that the *Altai* test in this context may actually be misleading because, in instruct-ing courts to abstract the various levels, it seems to encourage them to find a base level that includes copyrightable subject matter that, if literally copied, would make the copier liable for copyright infringement. While that base (or literal) level would not be at issue in a nonliteral-copying case like *Altai*, it is precisely what is at issue in this appeal. We think that abstracting menu command hierarchies down to their individ-ual word and menu levels and then filtering idea from expression at that stage, as both the *Altai* and the district court tests require, obscures the more fundamental question of whether a menu command hierarchy can be copyrighted at all. The initial inquiry should not be whether individu-al components of a menu command hierarchy are expressive, but rather whether the menu command hierarchy as a whole can be copyrighted. *But see Gates Rubber Co. v. Bando Chem. Indus., Ltd.*, 9 F.3d 823 (10th Cir.1993) (endorsing *Altai's* abstraction-filtration-comparison test as a way of determining whether "menus and sorting criteria" are copyright-able).

D.　The Lotus Menu Command Hierarchy: A "Method of Operation"

Borland argues that the Lotus menu command hierarchy is uncopy-rightable because it is a system, method of operation, process, or proce-dure foreclosed from copyright protection by 17 U.S.C. § 102(b). *　*　* Because we conclude that the Lotus menu command hierarchy is a method of operation, we do not consider whether it could also be a system, process, or procedure.

We think that "method of operation," as that term is used in § 102(b), refers to the means by which a person operates something, whether it be a car, a food processor, or a computer. Thus a text describing how to operate something would not extend copyright protec-tion to the method of operation itself; other people would be free to employ that method and to describe it in their own words. Similarly, if a new method of operation is used rather than described, other people would still be free to employ or describe that method.

We hold that the Lotus menu command hierarchy is an uncopyright-able "method of operation." The Lotus menu command hierarchy provides the means by which users control and operate Lotus 1–2–3. If users wish to copy material, for example, they use the "Copy" command. If users wish to print material, they use the "Print" command. Users must use the command terms to tell the computer what to do. Without the menu command hierarchy, users would not be able to access and control, or indeed make use of, Lotus 1–2–3's functional capabilities.

The Lotus menu command hierarchy does not merely explain and present Lotus 1–2–3's functional capabilities to the user; it also serves as the method by which the program is operated and controlled. The Lotus menu command hierarchy is different from the Lotus long prompts, for the long prompts are not necessary to the operation of the program; users could operate Lotus 1–2–3 even if there were no long prompts. The Lotus menu command hierarchy is also different from the Lotus screen displays, for users need not "use" any expressive aspects of the screen displays in order to operate Lotus 1–2–3; because the way the screens look has little bearing on how users control the program, the screen displays are not part of Lotus 1–2–3's "method of operation." The Lotus menu command hierarchy is also different from the underlying computer code, because while code is necessary for the program to work, its precise formulation is not. In other words, to offer the same capabilities as Lotus 1–2–3, Borland did not have to copy Lotus's underlying code (and indeed it did not); to allow users to operate its programs in substantially the same way, however, Borland had to copy the Lotus menu command hierarchy. Thus the Lotus 1–2–3 code is not a uncopyrightable "method of operation."

* * *

The fact that Lotus developers could have designed the Lotus menu command hierarchy differently is immaterial to the question of whether it is a "method of operation." In other words, our initial inquiry is not whether the Lotus menu command hierarchy incorporates any expression. Rather, our initial inquiry is whether the Lotus menu command hierarchy is a "method of operation." Concluding, as we do, that users operate Lotus 1–2–3 by using the Lotus menu command hierarchy, and that the entire Lotus menu command hierarchy is essential to operating Lotus 1–2–3, we do not inquire further whether that method of operation could have been designed differently. The "expressive" choices of what to name the command terms and how to arrange them do not magically change the uncopyrightable menu command hierarchy into copyrightable subject matter.

* * *

In many ways, the Lotus menu command hierarchy is like the buttons used to control, say, a video cassette recorder ("VCR"). A VCR is a machine that enables one to watch and record video tapes. Users operate VCRs by pressing a series of buttons that are typically labeled

"Record, Play, Reverse, Fast Forward, Pause, Stop/Eject." That the buttons are arranged and labeled does not make them a "literary work," nor does it make them an "expression" of the abstract "method of operating" a VCR via a set of labeled buttons. Instead, the buttons are themselves the "method of operating" the VCR.

When a Lotus 1–2–3 user chooses a command, either by highlighting it on the screen or by typing its first letter, he or she effectively pushes a button. Highlighting the "Print" command on the screen, or typing the letter "P," is analogous to pressing a VCR button labeled "Play."

Just as one could not operate a buttonless VCR, it would be impossible to operate Lotus 1–2–3 without employing its menu command hierarchy. Thus the Lotus command terms are not equivalent to the labels on the VCR's buttons, but are instead equivalent to the buttons themselves. Unlike the labels on a VCR's buttons, which merely make operating a VCR easier by indicating the buttons' functions, the Lotus menu commands are essential to operating Lotus 1–2–3. Without the menu commands, there would be no way to "push" the Lotus buttons, as one could push unlabeled VCR buttons. While Lotus could probably have designed a user interface for which the command terms were mere labels, it did not do so here. Lotus 1–2–3 depends for its operation on use of the precise command terms that make up the Lotus menu command hierarchy.

One might argue that the buttons for operating a VCR are not analogous to the commands for operating a computer program because VCRs are not copyrightable, whereas computer programs are. VCRs may not be copyrighted because they do not fit within any of the § 102(a) categories of copyrightable works; the closest they come is "sculptural work." Sculptural works, however, are subject to a "useful-article" exception whereby "the design of a useful article . . . shall be considered a pictorial, graphic, or sculptural work only if, and only to the extent that, such design incorporates pictorial, graphic, or sculptural features that can be identified separately from, and are capable of existing independently of, the utilitarian aspects of the article." 17 U.S.C. § 101. A "useful article" is "an article having an intrinsic utilitarian function that is not merely to portray the appearance of the article or to convey information." *Id*. Whatever expression there may be in the arrangement of the parts of a VCR is not capable of existing separately from the VCR itself, so an ordinary VCR would not be copyrightable.

Computer programs, unlike VCRs, are copyrightable as "literary works." 17 U.S.C. § 102(a). Accordingly, one might argue, the "buttons" used to operate a computer program are not like the buttons used to operate a VCR, for they are not subject to a useful-article exception. The response, of course, is that the arrangement of buttons on a VCR would not be copyrightable even without a useful-article exception, because the buttons are an uncopyrightable "method of operation." Similarly, the "buttons" of a computer program are also an uncopyrightable "method of operation."

That the Lotus menu command hierarchy is a "method of operation" becomes clearer when one considers program compatibility. Under Lotus's theory, if a user uses several different programs, he or she must learn how to perform the same operation in a different way for each program used. For example, if the user wanted the computer to print material, then the user would have to learn not just one method of operating the computer such that it prints, but many different methods. We find this absurd. The fact that there may be many different ways to operate a computer program, or even many different ways to operate a computer program using a set of hierarchically arranged command terms, does not make the actual method of operation chosen copyrightable; it still functions as a method for operating the computer and as such is uncopyrightable.

Consider also that users employ the Lotus menu command hierarchy in writing macros. Under the district court's holding, if the user wrote a macro to shorten the time needed to perform a certain operation in Lotus 1–2–3, the user would be unable to use that macro to shorten the time needed to perform that same operation in another program. Rather, the user would have to rewrite his or her macro using that other program's menu command hierarchy. This is despite the fact that the macro is clearly the user's own work product. We think that forcing the user to cause the computer to perform the same operation in a different way ignores Congress's direction in § 102(b) that "methods of operation" are not copyrightable. That programs can offer users the ability to write macros in many different ways does not change the fact that, once written, the macro allows the user to perform an operation automatically. As the Lotus menu command hierarchy serves as the basis for Lotus 1–2–3 macros, the Lotus menu command hierarchy is a "method of operation."

* * *

III.

Conclusion

Because we hold that the Lotus menu command hierarchy is uncopyrightable subject matter, we further hold that Borland did not infringe Lotus's copyright by copying it. Accordingly, we need not consider any of Borland's affirmative defenses. The judgment of the district court is

Reversed.

BOUDIN, CIRCUIT JUDGE, concurring.

* * *

I.

* * *

[T]he argument for protection is undiminished, perhaps even enhanced, by utility: if we want more of an intellectual product, a temporary monopoly for the creator provides incentives for others to create other, different items in this class. But the "cost" side of the equation may be different where one places a very high value on public access to a useful innovation that may be the most efficient means of performing a given task. Thus, the argument for extending protection may be the same; but the stakes on the other side are much higher.

Requests for the protection of computer menus present the concern with fencing off access to the commons in an acute form. A new menu may be a creative work, but over time its importance may come to reside more in the investment that has been made by *users* in learning the menu and in building their own mini-programs—macros—in reliance upon the menu. Better typewriter keyboard layouts may exist, but the familiar QWERTY keyboard dominates the market because that is what everyone has learned to use. *See* P. David, *CLIO and the Economics of QWERTY*, 75 *Am.Econ.Rev.* 332 (1985). The QWERTY keyboard is nothing other than a menu of letters.

* * *

II.

In this case, the raw facts are mostly, if not entirely, undisputed. Although the inferences to be drawn may be more debatable, it is very hard to see that Borland has shown any interest in the Lotus menu except as a fall-back option for those users already committed to it by prior experience or in order to run their own macros using 1–2–3 commands. At least for the amateur, accessing the Lotus menu in the Borland Quattro or Quattro Pro program takes some effort.

Put differently, it is unlikely that users who value the Lotus menu for its own sake—independent of any investment they have made themselves in learning Lotus' commands or creating macros dependent upon them—would choose the Borland program in order to secure access to the Lotus menu. Borland's success is due primarily to other features. Its rationale for deploying the Lotus menu bears the ring of truth.

Now, any use of the Lotus menu by Borland is a commercial use and deprives Lotus of a portion of its "reward," in the sense that an infringement claim if allowed would increase Lotus' profits. But this is circular reasoning: broadly speaking, every limitation on copyright or privileged use diminishes the reward of the original creator. Yet not every writing is copyrightable or every use an infringement. The provision of reward is one concern of copyright law, but it is not the only one. If it were, copyrights would be perpetual and there would be no exceptions.

The present case is an unattractive one for copyright protection of the menu. The menu commands (*e.g.*, "print," "quit") are largely for standard procedures that Lotus did not invent and are common words that Lotus cannot monopolize. What is left is the particular combination and sub-grouping of commands in a pattern devised by Lotus. This arrangement may have a more appealing logic and ease of use than some other configurations; but there is a certain arbitrariness to many of the choices.

If Lotus is granted a monopoly on this pattern, users who have learned the command structure of Lotus 1–2–3 or devised their own macros are locked into Lotus, just as a typist who has learned the QWERTY keyboard would be the captive of anyone who had a monopoly on the production of such a keyboard. Apparently, for a period Lotus 1–2–3 has had such sway in the market that it has represented the *de facto* standard for electronic spreadsheet commands. So long as Lotus is the superior spreadsheet—either in quality or in price—there may be nothing wrong with this advantage.

But if a better spreadsheet comes along, it is hard to see why customers who have learned the Lotus menu and devised macros for it should remain captives of Lotus because of an investment in learning made by the users and not by Lotus. Lotus has already reaped a substantial reward for being first; assuming that the Borland program is now better, good reasons exist for freeing it to attract old Lotus customers: to enable the old customers to take advantage of a new advance, and to reward Borland in turn for making a better product. If Borland has not made a better product, then customers will remain with Lotus anyway.

* * *

Note

This case was one of the few computer-related cases to reach the Supreme Court. However, the Court upheld the decision by a vote of 4 to 4 (Justice Stevens not participating). A decision by an equally divided Supreme Court is of no precedential value and thus does not resolve existing conflicts among the circuits. The First Circuit's decision in *Lotus v. Borland* conflicts directly with the Tenth Circuit's decision in *Autoskill, Inc. v. National Educational Support Systems, Inc.*, 994 F.2d 1476 (10th Cir.1993), *cert. denied*, 510 U.S. 916 (1993), and is flatly inconsistent with *Engineering Dynamics v. Structural Software, Inc.*, 46 F.3d 408 (5th Cir.1995) as well. Is it also inconsistent with *Apple v. Franklin*?

COMPAQ COMPUTER CORP. v. PROCOM TECHNOLOGY, INC.

United States District Court, S.D. Texas, Houston Division, 1995.
908 F.Supp. 1409.

HITTNER, DISTRICT JUDGE.

In May, 1995, Compaq Computer Corporation ("Compaq") filed suit against Procom Technology, Inc. ("Procom"). Compaq's suit alleges that Procom has infringed its trademark, trade dress, copyright and patent rights, engaged in unfair competition, and in false advertising. Procom asserts several affirmative defenses to Compaq's claims and also maintains that Compaq's claims are barred by unclean hands and that Compaq has engaged in unfair competition. Procom also seeks declaratory judgment that Compaq's patents are invalid.

The case was tried to the Court on August 21, 1995 through August 23, 1995 on all except the patent claims. After reviewing the evidence, the submissions of the parties, and the applicable law, the Court enters the following findings of fact and conclusions of law.

FACTUAL FINDINGS

A. The Parties

Compaq is a large computer company whose product line includes both hardware and software. Compaq advertises and sells all its products under its COMPAQ trademark. The name Compaq is well known throughout the United States and the world. The COMPAQ trademark is registered with the United States Patent and Trademark Office under registration number 1,467,066.

Procom is also a computer company whose relevant business is the sale and distribution of hard drives and hard drive trays for use with specific Compaq products.

B. Compaq Servers & Hard Drives

One of Compaq's products is the ProLiant line of network servers. The ProLiant server, like other servers, requires the use of hard disk drives for data storage purposes. One of the attractive features of the ProLiant server is that the hard drives may be added or removed while the server is in operation. This feature is called "hot-pluggability."

Compaq markets hot-pluggable hard drives specifically for use with its ProLiant servers. At issue in this lawsuit are three models of hot-pluggable drives: the 2 gigabyte ("GB") drives which come in a "high-profile" and a "low-profile model," and the 4 GB drive which has only one profile. All three of these drives are manufactured for Compaq by a third party, Seagate Technology, Inc. ("Seagate"). In addition to the Compaq drives, ProLiant servers are also compatible with hard drives sold by third parties.

C. Hard Drive Trays

Hard drives used with the ProLiant server are mounted on a tray specially designed to enable hot-pluggability. The tray consists of a plastic base containing a circuit board that plugs into the server to make the necessary connections.

Compaq sells trays designed for this purpose. Compaq trays may be used with both Compaq drives and third party drives. Compaq sells these trays separately as well as premounted with hard drives.

Compaq trays feature a light gray and medium gray color scheme. The trays have lights and icons which indicate the light's function. The placement of the lights is in part dictated by the design of the server. The server houses the drives in individual bays, covered by a protective hinged panel. The panel contains slots through which the indicator lights may be viewed.

Compaq trays comply with Underwriters Laboratories' safety requirements for electronic devices. The bottom of the tray contains no large openings through which a user might inadvertently touch the drive when removing the drive and tray from the server. This is important because the drives operate at high temperatures and can become quite hot.

During the development of the drives, Compaq discovered that there is a risk of data loss to surrounding drives when another hot-pluggable drive was inserted into the server. The cause of this potential problem is electrostatic discharge ("ESD"). To solve this problem, Compaq developed a special metal shield to dissipate the effects of ESD and protect data. A different shield was developed for each drive model.

D. Compaq Insight Manager

Customers purchasing a ProLiant server have the option of purchasing two additional items, the SMART controller and Compaq's Insight Manager program ("CIM"). CIM was developed by Compaq in order to allow the network administrator to monitor the performance of the hard drives running in the server. CIM works in conjunction with the SMART Controller to track numerous elements in the ProLiant server and provide the network administrator warnings of potential problems. Based on this information, the network administrator can dispatch service technicians, call for warranty service, or take other action to remedy the problem.

Some of the components monitored by CIM are the hard drives used by the server. CIM reports certain data for all drives; however, the amount of data reported depends on the type of drive being used and whether the customer has received upgrade software from Compaq. For example, for all drives, including third party drives, CIM will report whether the drive is working, drive capacity, service hours, and firmware version. In addition, Compaq will provide a software upgrade to customers using third party drives which enable CIM to report supplementary information regarding the drive's operating history. Finally, customers who use Compaq drives receive the full range of data the CIM is capable of reporting, including a feature known as prefailure warnings.

E. Prefailure Warnings & Threshold Values

One of the more desirable attributes of CIM is its ability to generate "prefailure warnings." A prefailure warning is an indication to the network administrator that a drive has reached a point in its life where failure may be imminent. This allows the administrator to replace the drive prior to failure and avoid the risk of having the drive fail while in operation.

The prefailure warning program was developed as part of a warranty package provided by Compaq to those customers who buy Compaq drives. When a hard drive has degraded below a predetermined "threshold value," a prefailure warning is triggered. Once this happens, Compaq will replace the drive that triggered the warning even though it has not actually failed. Although the prefailure warning system was developed as part of a warranty program, CIM will continue to issue the warning even if the drive is no longer under warranty.

In designing the prefailure warning component of CIM, Compaq made several choices. Compaq had to determine both the number and the particular parameters which it would monitor through CIM. In addition, Compaq had to decide upon the appropriate threshold value for each of the five parameters selected. In selecting the threshold value, Compaq had to consider the point at which the drive would actually fail and then select a threshold that would be reached before actual failure. However, Compaq did not want to set the prefailure point too early in the life of the drive, otherwise Compaq would incur unnecessary expenses. Thus, the point at which the warning is triggered is based on both engineering and business related judgments.

The threshold values are contained in a portion of the hard drive known as the Monitor and Performance Partition ("M & P Partition"). The M & P Partition contains data in addition to the threshold values, however, only the latter are necessary for Compaq's prefailure warning program. Compaq registered the threshold values for each of its three drives with the United States Copyright Office under registration numbers TX–3–926–599, TX–3–924–600, and TX–3–924–601. The threshold values are but a small percentage of the total amount of information registered by Compaq. The registrations were issued under the "Rule of Doubt." The Rule of Doubt is used by the Copyright Office for registrations submitted in formats that are not understandable to humans.

Compaq provides warranty service for Compaq hard drives only. Thus, the prefailure component of CIM was designed solely to work with Compaq drives. All Compaq drives are intended to be sold complete with a copy of the threshold values. In contrast, third party drives do not contain the same data in the M & P Partition. In particular, third party drives do not contain the Compaq copyright notice and the threshold values. Without the threshold values, the prefailure warning system will not work.

In the event that Compaq drives are sold without the necessary threshold values, Compaq has designed a method by which the correct values are written onto the drive. In a portion of the drive known as the firmware, all hard drives contain a vendor identification string ("vendor ID"). The vendor ID allows computers to identify themselves electronically to each other. The placement of the vendor ID in the firmware is dictated by an industry standard called the Small Computer System Interface. Compaq drives contain the word Compaq in the vendor ID portion of the drive firmware.

When a new drive is added to a ProLiant server, the network administrator runs a Compaq program called EISA Config. EISA Config determines whether the drive is a Compaq drive by checking the vendor ID. If the drive is a Compaq drive, but does not contain the threshold values, EISA Config writes those values to the drive. Once the values are added, CIM will report prefailure warnings for the drive.

F. Procom's Products

Procom distributes two products which are at issue in this lawsuit. The first product at issue is Procom's line of hard drives designed for use with the ProLiant server. Like Compaq, Procom purchases its drives from Seagate. Like Compaq, Procom offers a warranty program in which it agrees to replace its drives prior to failure. However, Procom did not develop its own prefailure notification system. Instead, after receiving drives from Seagate, Procom modifies the drives so that they access all features of CIM, including the prefailure warnings.

Procom understood that its customers valued the features offered by CIM. Therefore, it set out to discover how it could modify its product to work in the same manner that Compaq drives work. In the early stages of developing drives that were compatible with CIM, Procom learned that it could access all features of CIM by modifying the firmware of the drives. When received from Seagate, the drives identified Seagate as the vendor in the vendor ID portion of the firmware. However, Procom discovered that by changing the vendor ID to Compaq, the requisite threshold values would be written to the drive, as described above. However, Procom decided not to market this drive because it was uncomfortable with the idea of shipping a product that incorrectly identified the vendor as Compaq.

Next, Procom determined that the M & P Partition contained data which enabled the prefailure warnings. The data are the threshold values, described above. Although Procom did not understand what the data represented, it was able to copy the necessary data to its drives and thereby enable the warnings. Procom began selling these drives to ProLiant server owners. However, a percentage of these drives contained incorrect copies of the threshold data. Procom corrected this mistake and continued selling these drives until it was sued by Compaq for copyright infringement.

After being sued, Procom reverted to the method of manufacture in which it changed the vendor ID in the firmware to specify Compaq as the vendor. This way, Procom did not actually copy any of the necessary data. The copying was done when the customer installed the drive and ran the EISA Config program. However, this alteration of the vendor ID has an unavoidable and unintentional consequence. When the network administrator runs CIM, a portion of the screen display identifies the vendor of the drive as Compaq. Had the drive been properly labeled as a Procom or a Seagate drive, those identifiers would appear on the screen. This result is of particular significance because the specific hard drive may not be located where it is easily accessible. Consequently, greater reliance may be placed on the screen display than would otherwise be the case if the user could simply reach over and pull the hard drive out of the server.

The second Procom product at issue in this suit is the drive tray sold by Procom for use with its hard drives. Initially, when Procom began selling drives for use in the ProLiant, it purchased genuine Compaq trays for use with the drives. However, in March or April 1995, Procom switched from Compaq trays to trays manufactured by a third party, CI Designs. These trays were virtually identical to the Compaq trays. However, the Procom trays did not display the Compaq logo and instead featured the Procom logo "P" and the word "Procom" marked on the tray faceplate. In addition, the Procom trays lacked front panel slits which were part of the Compaq tray.

In August, 1995, Procom began selling a new design of the tray that differs significantly from the tray it replaced. Differences include redesigned locking mechanisms and the use of words rather than icons above the indicator lights on the trays. Procom no longer sells the trays complained of by Compaq.

G. Compaq's Service Advisories

After becoming aware of Procom's sale of hard drives for use with ProLiant servers, Compaq notified its customer service personnel and resellers about potential problems that Compaq perceived with third party drives.

Compaq prepared a product problem report ("PPR 1203") which identified several potential problems with Procom drives. PPR 1203 discussed three issues: the risk of improper contact with drives because of large openings on the bottom of the tray, the inaccurate copy of the threshold values, and the risk of data loss from electrostatic discharge. PPR 1203 states "Compaq Confidential—Compaq only." Although PPRs are prepared for Compaq internal use only, PPR 1203 was distributed to at least one non-Compaq employee.

Compaq also issued a document entitled Service Advisory 877 which describes risks in using third party drives. Service Advisory 877 does not mention Procom by name but does address third party drives "advertised as 100% Compaq compatible." The advisory warns that third party drives may be at risk for data loss, false prefailure notification, and safety hazards.

Any finding of fact that should be construed as a conclusion of law is adopted as such.

Legal Conclusions

I. Procom's First Drives

Compaq contends that Procom's first line of hard drives contained an unauthorized copy of Compaq's copyrighted threshold values in violation of the Copyright Act, 17 U.S.C. § 101 *et seq.* Procom counters that the threshold values are not protectable expression, or alternatively, that its use of those numbers is permissible according to the doctrines of merger, fair use, and the scènes à faire doctrine. For Compaq to prevail on its claim, it must show that the threshold values, either individually or as a compilation, are copyrightable expression and that Procom copied the protected material.

A. *Copyrightability*

Compaq registered the threshold values with the United States Copyright Office. However, the registrations were issued under the Rule of Doubt. This means that the Copyright Office was unable to verify that the data was copyrightable because it is not in a format that is understandable to humans. The legal effect of such a registration is that it is not entitled to the usual presumption of validity. Accordingly, the burden is on Compaq to establish that the threshold values, or the compilation of the threshold values, are copyrightable.

It is fundamental in copyright law that facts cannot be copyrighted. However, in certain situations, compilations of facts are protectable. The key consideration in determining whether a compilation is copyrightable is the degree of originality embodied in the work. If the compilation reflects choices by the author such as "which facts to include, in what order to place them, and how to arrange the collected data so that they may be used effectively by readers," then the work probably reflects sufficient originality to merit protection.

Compaq's compilation of the five threshold values meets the standard announced in *Feist*. In deciding which parameters to monitor through CIM, Compaq had numerous choices. Compaq exercised its discretion in choosing both the number of parameters to monitor—five, and which five particular parameters those would be. Presumably Compaq could have chosen to track a higher or lower number of parameters. Compaq could also have chosen a different combination of parameters. Accordingly, the choices made by Compaq reflect the requisite degree of creativity and judgment necessary to protect its compilation.

Not only does Compaq's compilation reflect originality, but perhaps more importantly, the underlying elements of the compilation are not facts. Unlike a telephone number, or the date a bond is redeemed, the threshold value is not empirically verifiable. Instead, the particular threshold value is the result of a decision making process by Compaq based on at least two variables. First, Compaq must estimate when the drive will actually fail. This conclusion is factual in nature although ultimately it is more a prediction than a fact. In addition to making this prediction, Compaq must make a business decision as to the point in the life of the drive that Compaq is willing to replace it under its warranty program. In making this decision, Compaq must weigh several considerations such as the cost of replacing drives too early in their life versus the risk of waiting too long to replace and drive and having it fail while in use. It seems unlikely that other drive manufacturers, facing different economic considerations and different customer expectations, would choose the exact same point in time to replace a drive that Compaq chose.

* * *

Based on the foregoing, the Court

ORDERS that Procom, its officers, agents, servants, employees and attorneys, and all persons in active concert or participation with any of them, be permanently enjoined from:

(a) reproducing, selling, distributing, or using unauthorized copies of Compaq's copyrighted data compilations, threshold values, or any portion thereof;

(b) manufacturing, advertising, offering for sale, selling, or distributing hard disk drives which cause the reproduction of unauthorized copies of Compaq's copyrighted data compilations, threshold values, or any portion thereof.

All other relief not specifically granted herein is DENIED.

Question

How would the First Circuit have decided this case in view of its opinion in *Lotus*?

4. MERGER OF IDEA AND EXPRESSION

The doctrine of merger relating to copyright can operate to deny copyright protection to material which otherwise on its face appears to qualify for such protection. When the basic nature of an idea limits the number of forms in which it can be expressed, the expression and idea are said to "merge." Since, under § 102(b), ideas may not be protected, expressions merged with ideas are unprotectable, since to protect such expressions would protect ideas. The leading case is *Morrissey v. Procter & Gamble Co.*, 379 F.2d 675 (1st Cir.1967). Morrissey alleged that Proctor & Gamble had "copied" the first rule of a set of copyrighted rules for a promotional contest. The Court found that the rule (contestant should give name, address, etc.) was so fundamental to such contests that the idea of the contest dictated the formulation and expression of the rule. Thus, the idea and expression were merged, so there was no protection available for the rule, since to protect plaintiff's rule would give plaintiff a monopoly on the idea. Morrissey suggested that in cases of merger, the subject matter was not copyrightable. The case below takes a different approach.

NEC CORP. v. INTEL CORP.

United States District Court, N.D. California, 1989.
10 U.S.P.Q.2d 1177, 1989 WL 67434.

Gray, Senior District Judge.

In this action, NEC seeks a declaration that Intel's copyrights on its 8086 and 8088 microcodes are invalid and/or are not infringed by NEC. Intel has filed a counterclaim for infringement of its copyrights on those microcodes. This case was tried without a jury for eighteen days between April 25 and July 18, 1988. Post-trial briefs were filed, final arguments were heard on July 29, 1988, and the case then was submitted for decision. The issues to be determined and the decision that the court now renders on each are as follows:

1. Are Intel's microcodes for its 8086 and 8088 microprocessors proper subject matter for protection under United States copyright laws (17 U.S.C. § 101 et seq.)? This question is answered in the affirmative.

* * *

The reasons for the foregoing decision are contained in the following discussion:

I. The Copyrightability of Intel's Microcode

A microcode consists of a series of instructions that tell a microprocessor which of its thousands of transistors to actuate in order to perform the tasks directed by the macroinstruction set. As such, it comes squarely within the definition of a "computer program," which Congress added to the Copyright Act in 1980, namely, "a set of statements or instructions to be used directly or indirectly in a computer in order to bring about a certain result." 17 U.S.C. § 101.

A computer program, even though articulated in object code, is afforded copyright protection as a "literary work" under Section 101, which includes works "expressed in words, numbers, or other verbal or numerical symbols or indicia, regardless of the nature of the material objects . . . in which they are embodied." *See Apple Computer, Inc. v. Franklin Computer Corp.*, 714 F.2d 1240, 1249 (3d Cir.1983); 17 U.S.C. § 101. For a particular literary work to be copyrightable, two requirements must be satisfied: the work must be "fixed in any tangible medium of expression," and it must be "original." *See* 17 U.S.C. § 102(a). It is undisputed that Intel's microcode is fixed in a tangible medium of expression. However, NEC challenges the originality of Intel's microcode, and urges two other bases for denying copyright protection.

* * *

C. *Idea v. Expression.*

It is an axiom of copyright law that only the expression of an idea is copyrightable, not the idea, itself. This doctrine was announced in *Baker* *v. Selden*, 101 U.S. 99, 103 (1879), and a substantial portion has been codified in 17 U.S.C. § 102(b). * * *

NEC contends that if substantial similarities do exist between its accused microroutines and those of Intel, they are because of constraints that severely limit the ways in which the "ideas" therein contained can be expressed. NEC therefore urges that such merger of idea and expression forestalls copyrightability, and relies basically upon *Morrissey v. Procter & Gamble Co.*, 379 F.2d 675 (1st Cir.1967), which so held.

However, Mr. Nimmer suggests the appropriate rule to be that the "merger" of idea and expression "will preclude a finding of substantial similarity", thus forestalling a finding of infringement, and he criticized Morrissey as "a questionable extension of this principle." 3 M. Nimmer, *Nimmer on Copyright*, § 13.03[A] at 13–33 to 13–34.

Although Ninth Circuit cases have not specifically discussed this issue raised by NEC, they appear uniformly to treat the "merger" issue as a question of whether or not there is infringement rather than copyrightability.

It also seems to me that, as a matter of practicality, the issue of a limited number of ways to express an idea is relevant to infringement, but should not be the basis for denying the initial copyright. The Register of Copyrights will not know about the presence or absence of constraints that limit ways to express an idea. The burden of showing such constraints should be left to the alleged infringer. Accordingly, in the absence of Ninth Circuit authority to the contrary, it is concluded that the relationship between "idea" and "expression" will not be considered on the issue of copyrightability, but will be deferred to the discussion of infringement.

It is the view of this court that NEC's above mentioned objections to the copyrightability of Intel's microcode are not persuasive. On the contrary, the statutory references discussed at the outset of this section on copyrightability, and particularly the specific definition of "computer program" that Congress enacted in 1980, "reflect Congress' receptivity to new technology and its desire to encourage, through the copyright laws, continued imagination and creativity in computer programming." *Apple Computer, Inc. v. Franklin Computer Corp.*, 714 F.2d 1240, 1254 (3d Cir.1983). In light of the foregoing, it is concluded that Intel's microcode was a proper subject for copyright protection and that the copyright registrations contained thereon were initially valid.

* * *

C. *The Constraints.*

1. *The Hardware, Architecture And Specifications.*

In seeking to show that there were many alternate ways in which Mr. Kaneko's various microprograms could have been written, and therefore that the substantial similarities to Intel's microcode that did exist stemmed from copying, Intel declined to take into consideration the constraints that limited Mr. Kaneko's choices. Intel contends that NEC could have created a microprocessor compatible with Intel's 8086/88 by using "different hardware, different architecture, different specifications and a different microinstruction format." Intel's Memorandum for the Trial Court, dated June 7, 1988, page 18. However, NEC had a license from Intel to duplicate the 8086/88 microprocessor hardware to the extent comprehended by the Intel patents. Both Dr. Patterson and Dr. Frieder acknowledged that the use of such hardware limited substantially the choices available to Mr. Kaneko in creating the microcode for the V-series. Having granted to NEC a license to duplicate the hardware of its 8086/88 to the extent comprehended by the Intel patents, and having conceded at trial that NEC had a right to duplicate the hardware of the 8086/88 because it was not otherwise protected by Intel, Intel is in no position to challenge NEC's right to use the aspects of Intel's microcode that are mandated by such hardware.

2. The Storage Space.

Intel also asserts that if NEC had utilized all of the storage area (ROM) available to it on its microprocessor, which would have been double the storage space that was available to Intel, any constraint imposed by size would have been removed and a different and better microcode would have resulted. Intel's Memorandum for the Trial Court, dated June 7, 1988, page 18. NEC elected to use part of the ROM space existing on the V-series, in order to accommodate microcode for additional macroinstructions on the same ROM. This also was a legitimate constraint; NEC was not obliged to avoid the similarity that other constraints imposed by creating a larger microcode.

3. The Clean Room.

The Clean Room microcode constitutes compelling evidence that the similarities between the NEC microcode and the Intel microcode resulted from constraints. The Clean Room microcode was governed by the same constraints of hardware, architecture and specifications as applied to the NEC microcode, and copying clearly was not involved. Mr. McKevitt, who created the 8086 microcode for Intel, readily acknowledged that the microarchitecture of the 8086 microprocessor affected the manner in which he created his microcode, and that he would expect that another independently created microcode for the 8086 would have some similarities to his. (See Tr. Vol. 8 1358:10–24). Accordingly, the similarities between the Clean Room microcode and the Intel microcode must be attributable largely to the above mentioned constraints. But the similarities between the Clean Room microcode and Rev. 2 are at least as great as are the similarities between the latter and the Intel microcode. This is made evident by an examination of Exhibit 705. The strong likelihood follows that these similarities, also resulted from the same constraints.

Mr. McKevitt also acknowledged that he would expect that independently created microcode for the 8086 would have fewer similarities in the longer sequences than in the shorter sequences because "there is more opportunity for the longer sequences to be expressed differently."

(Tr. Vol. 8 1359:5–10). This is exactly what occurred here; the longer sequences in Rev. 2 and Intel's microcode are not nearly so much alike as are the shorter sequences.

In light of the foregoing, it is reasonable to conclude that the same constraints, rather than copying, were responsible for the principal similarities between Rev. 2 and the Intel microcode.

D. Idea v. Expression

As concluded above, overall, and particularly with respect to the longer microroutines, NEC's microcode is not substantially similar to Intel's; but some of the shorter, simpler microroutines resemble Intel's. None, however, are identical. As to these shorter, simpler microroutines, if their underlying ideas are capable of only a limited range of expression, they "may be protected only against virtually identical copying." *Frybarger v. International Business Machines Corp.*, 812 F.2d 525, 530 (9th Cir.1987). *See also Worth v. Selchow & Righter Co.*, 827 F.2d 569 (9th Cir.1987).

In determining an idea's range of expression, constraints are relevant factors to consider. *See Data East USA v. Epyx, Inc.*, No. 87–2294 (9th Cir. Nov.30, 1988). In this case, the expression of NEC's microcode was constrained by the use of the macroinstruction set and hardware of the 8086/88. Mr. McKevitt so testified, Dr. Patterson initially expressed the same opinion, and the close similarities of the Clean Room microcode to Intel's and NEC's microcodes emphatically concur.

Mr. Davidian and Dr. Frieder testified that, in light of these constraints, the shorter, simpler microroutines can be expressed only in a few limited ways, and I agree. Frieder as cited in (NEC's Supplemented and Annotated Findings of Fact and Conclusions of Law & 75). These include those microroutines identified as similar in Section A, pages 20–21 above. A good illustration is "ESCAPE". The Clean Room and NEC's version are identical, which is evidence of its constrained nature. Further, Dr. Frieder testified that "ESCAPE" was highly constrained given the existing hardware.

Accordingly, it is the conclusion of this court that the expression of the ideas underlying the shorter, simpler microroutines (including those identified earlier as substantially similar) may be protected only against virtually identical copying, and that NEC properly used the underlying ideas, without virtually identically copying their limited expression.

* * *

CONCLUSION

For reasons hereinabove set forth, judgment will be entered holding that:

1. The Intel microcode for its 8086 and 8088 microprocessors were proper subjects for protection under United States copyright laws.

COMPAQ COMPUTER CORP. v. PROCOM TECHNOLOGY, INC.

United States District Court, S.D. Texas, Houston Division, 1995.
908 F.Supp. 1409.

[The factual background of this case is reproduced above, p. 47.]

LEGAL CONCLUSIONS

I. *Procom's First Drives*

Compaq contends that Procom's first line of hard drives contained an unauthorized copy of Compaq's copyrighted threshold values in violation of the Copyright Act, 17 U.S.C. § 101 *et seq.* Procom counters that the threshold values are not protectable expression, or alternatively, that its use of those numbers is permissible according to the doctrines of merger, fair use, and the *scènes à faire* doctrine. For Compaq to prevail on its claim, it must show that the threshold values, either individually or as a compilation, are copyrightable expression and that Procom copied the protected material.

* * *

B. *Merger*

The doctrine of merger denies copyright protection to a work if that work is the only way to express a particular idea. In this situation, the expression is viewed as having merged with the idea itself. To allow copyright of the expression would result in a grant of a monopoly over the underlying idea. "In the computer context, this means that when specific instructions, even though previously copyrighted, are the only and essential means of accomplishing a given task, their later use by another will not amount to infringement." National Commission on New Technological Uses of Copyrighted Works, Final Report at 20 (1979).

The specific question presented here is whether the copying of the threshold data is permissible because those data are the only way to express the idea of predictive drive failure. It has already been determined that to obtain prefailure warnings through CIM, the drive must have the five numbers representing the five parameters monitored by the program. A third party attempting to gain access to CIM has no choice but to also select those five parameters for observation. If a third party selected other parameters, then any warnings that CIM issued would be meaningless.

However, the third party is not limited to the selection of the five precise numbers chosen by Compaq as its "as-new values." As described above, these numbers do not simply represent the point at which the drive will fail. They represent the point that *Compaq* deems most optimal to replace the drives. There are numerous ways that a drive supplier may express its opinion as to when it should replace its drives.

Therefore, the Court finds that the doctrine of merger does not strip Compaq's threshold values of copyright protection.

* * *

Question

Compaq tested its hard drives and arrived at a mathematical formulation for determining when the drive was likely to fail and when would be the most cost-efficient time to replace a drive nearing the period when failure was most likely to occur. Would a formula used as the basis of a computer program for flight scheduling based on wind speed and distance be copyrightable? What if the airplane's engine power and loaded weight were included in the calculation? What if the airline kept records for average times for passenger loading and maintenance? Obviously, under the theory of the preceding cases, the more variables used in a calculation, the more likely the formula used in the program will be copyrightable because the possible combinations and weighting of factors increase tremendously with each variable. But aren't we thus giving a copyright for the clever selection of the best method of operation—something that should be the province of patents, not copyrights?

5. SCENES A FAIRE

The doctrine of scènes à faire is another way which seemingly copyrightable expression can be denied protection. The doctrine falls somewhere between the denial of copyright under § 102(a) for lack of originality and denial under § 102(b) for merger. The doctrine prevents an author from receiving protection for a work that is too dependent on basic, common ways of treating particular subject matter. Only blatant identical copying of such expression can support a claim of infringement.

A leading case applying this doctrine is *Hoehling v. Universal City Studios, Inc.,* 618 F.2d 972 (2d Cir.1980). The dispute arose among three authors recounting the final voyage of the Hindenburg, the German airship which crashed in Lakehurst, New Jersey on May 6, 1937. Both plaintiff's and defendant's works depicted German soldiers drinking in a beer hall, "Heil Hitler" greetings, and the singing of the German national anthem. The court held that these were standard literary devices ("scènes à faire") for works dealing with Germany in the 1930s and therefore they could not be protected by copyright. The following case applies the scènes à faire doctrine to computer games.

DATA EAST USA, INC. v. EPYX, INC.
United States Court of Appeals, Ninth Circuit, 1988.
862 F.2d 204.

TROTT, CIRCUIT JUDGE.

Plaintiff-appellee Data East USA, Inc., brought this action against defendant-appellant Epyx, Inc. for copyright, trademark, and trade dress infringement. The district court found a copyright infringement and issued a permanent injunction and impoundment. Epyx appeals the grant of the permanent injunction.

Epyx contends * * * (2) the district court erred in finding substantial similarity * * * . We reverse.

I. FACTS

Data East is a California corporation engaged in the design, manufacture, and sale of audio-visual works embodied in video games for coin-operated and home computer use. In July 1984, Data East commenced distribution in Japan of an arcade game entitled "Karate Champ" ("Arcade #1"). In September 1984, Data East commenced distribution in Japan and later in the United States and Europe of an updated version of "Karate Champ" ("Arcade #2" or more generally as "arcade game"). Finally, on October 12, 1985, Data East commenced distribution in the United States of a home computer game version of "Karate Champ" ("home game"). Data East applied for and received audio-visual copyright certificates for each game.

In November of 1985, System III Software, Ltd., an English company, commenced distribution in England of a home computer game entitled "International Karate." Epyx, a California corporation engaged in the development and distribution of audio-visual works for use on home computers, obtained a license agreement with System III and commenced distribution in the United States on April 30, 1986 of a Commodore-compatible version of "International Karate" under the name "World Karate Championship."

Each competing product, "Karate Champ" and "World Karate Championship," consists of the audio-visual depiction of a karate match or matches conducted by two combatants, one clad in a typical white outfit and the other in red. Successive phases of combat are conducted against varying stationary background images depicting localities or geographic scenes. The match is supervised by a referee who directs the beginning and end of each phase of combat and announces the winning combatant of each phase by means of a cartoon-style speech balloon. Each game has a bonus round where the karate combatant breaks bricks and dodges objects. Similarities also exist in the moves used by the combatants and the scoring method.

Data East alleged that the overall appearance, compilation, and sequence of the audio-visual display of the video game "World Karate Championship" infringed its copyright for "Karate Champ" as embodied in the arcade and home versions of the video game. Data East also charged Epyx with trademark and trade dress infringement.

The district court found that except for the graphic quality of Epyx's expressions, part of the scoreboard, the referee's physical appearance, and minor particulars in the "bonus phases," Data East's and Epyx's games are qualitatively identical. The district court then held that Epyx's game infringes the copyright Data East has in "Karate Champ."

The district court, however, found no trademark or trade dress infringement. Based upon its decision, the district court permanently restrained and enjoined Epyx from copying, preparing derivative works, distributing, performing, or displaying the copyrighted work in the "Karate Champ" video game, the "World Karate Championship" game, or the "International Karate" game. A recall of all Commodore computer games of "World Karate Championship" and "International Karate" was ordered. This appeal followed.

II.   DISCUSSION

A district court's determination of findings of fact is subject to the clearly erroneous standard of review. The issues of access and substantial similarity are findings of fact reviewable for clear error. Under the clearly erroneously standard of review, an appellate court must accept the lower court's findings of fact unless upon review the appellate court is left with the definite and firm conviction that a mistake has been committed.

To establish copyright infringement, Data East must prove both ownership of a valid copyright and "copying" by Epyx of the copyrighted work. It is undisputed that Data East is the registered copyright owner of the audio-visual work for each version of "Karate Champ." Thus we need only determine whether Epyx copied "Karate Champ." This sounds simple and straightforward. It is not.

As in most infringement cases of this kind, no direct evidence was developed that System III Software or anybody else copied any version of Data East's product. There seldom is any direct evidence of copying in these matters. Therefore, copying may be established instead by circumstantial evidence of (1) the defendant's access to the copyrighted work prior to defendant's creation of its work, and (2) the substantial similarity of both the general ideas and expression between the copyrighted work and defendant's work. In essence, the question of copying becomes a matter of reasonable inferences. Because we find no substantial similarity, we decline to address the issue of access.

* * *

B.   *Substantial Similarity*

"To show that two works are substantially similar, plaintiff must demonstrate that the works are substantially similar in both *ideas* and *expression*." Although plaintiff must first show that the ideas are substantially similar, the ideas themselves are not protected by copyright and therefore, cannot be infringed. It is an axiom of copyright law that copyright protects only an author's expression of an idea, not the idea itself. There is a strong public policy corollary to this axiom permitting all to use freely ideas contained in a copyrightable work, so long as the protected expression itself is not appropriated. Thus, to the extent the similarities between plaintiff's and defendant's works are confined to ideas and general concepts, these similarities are noninfringing.

The Ninth Circuit has developed a two-step test for the purposes of determining substantial similarity. First, an "extrinsic" test is used to determine whether two ideas are substantially similar. This is an objective test which rests upon specific criteria that can be listed and analyzed. Second, an "intrinsic" test is used to compare forms of expression. This is a subjective test which depends on the response of the ordinary reasonable person.

In applying the extrinsic test, the district court found that the idea expressed in plaintiff's game and in defendant's game is identical. The *idea* of the games was described by the court as follows:

" . . . a martial arts karate combat game conducted between two combatants, and presided over by a referee, all of which are represented by visual images, and providing a method of scoring accomplished by full and half point scores for each player, and utilizing dots to depict full point scores and half point scores."

The district court further found that:

"In each of the games, the phases of martial arts combat are conducted against still background images purporting to depict geographic or locality situses and located at the top of the screen as the game is viewed. The action of the combatants in each of the games takes place in the lower portion of the screen as the game is viewed, and is against a one color background in that portion of the screen as the game is viewed."

Once an idea is found to be similar or identical, as in this case, the second or intrinsic step is applied to determine whether similarity of the expression of the idea occurs. This exists when the "total concept and feel of the works" is substantially similar. Analytic dissection of the dissimilarities as opposed to the similarities is not appropriate under this test because it distracts a reasonable observer from a comparison of the total concept and feel of the works.

* * *

Nor can copyright protection be afforded to elements of expression that necessarily follow from an idea, or to "scenes à faire," i.e., expressions that are "as a practical matter, indispensable or at least standard in the treatment of a given [idea]."

To determine whether similarities result from unprotectable expression, analytic dissection of similarities may be performed. If this demonstrates that all similarities in expression arise from use of common ideas, then no substantial similarity can be found.

The district court performed what can be described as an analytic dissection of similarities in its findings of fact and stated:

Plaintiff's and defendant's games each encompass the idea of depicting the performance of karate martial arts combat in each of the following respects:

A. Each game has fourteen moves.

B.   Each game has a two-player option.

C.   Each game has a one-player option.

D.   Each game has forward and backward somersault moves and about-face moves.

E.   Each game has a squatting reverse punch wherein the heel is not on the ground.

F.   Each game has an upper-lunge punch.

G.   Each game has a back-foot sweep.

H.   Each game has a jumping sidekick.

I.   Each game has low kick.

J.   Each game has a walk-backwards position.

K.   Each game has changing background scenes.

L.   Each game has 30–second countdown rounds.

M.   Each game uses one referee.

N.   In each game the referee says "begin," "stop," "white," "red," which is depicted by a cartoon-style speech balloon.

O.   Each game has a provision for 100 bonus points per remaining second.

The district court found that the visual depiction of karate matches is subject to the constraints inherent in the sport of karate itself. The number of combatants, the stance employed by the combatants, established and recognized moves and motions regularly employed in the sport of karate, the regulation of the match by at least one referee or judge, and the manner of scoring by points and half points are among the constraints inherent in the sport of karate. Because of these constraints, karate is not susceptible of a wholly fanciful presentation. Furthermore, the use of the Commodore computer for a karate game intended for home consumption is subject to various constraints inherent in the use of that computer. Among the constraints are the use of sprites, and a somewhat limited access to color, together with limitations upon the use of multiple colors in one visual image.

The fifteen features listed by the court "encompass the idea of karate." These features, which consist of the game procedure, common karate moves, the idea of background scenes, a time element, a referee, computer graphics, and bonus points, result from either constraints inherent in the sport of karate or computer restraints. After careful consideration and viewing of these features, we find that they necessarily follow from the idea of a martial arts karate combat game, or are inseparable from, indispensable to, or even standard treatment of the idea of the karate sport. As such, they are not protectable. "When idea and expression coincide, there will be protection against nothing other than identical copying." A comparison of the works in this case demonstrates that identical copying is not an issue.

Accordingly, we hold that the court did not give the appropriate weight and import to its findings which support Epyx's argument that the similarities result from unprotectable expression. Consequently, it was clear error for the district court to determine that protectable substantial similarity existed based upon these facts.

The lower court erred by not limiting the scope of Data East's copyright protection to the author's contribution—the scoreboard and background scenes. In actuality, however, the backgrounds are quite dissimilar and the method of scorekeeping, though similar, is inconsequential. Based upon these two features, a discerning 17.5 year-old boy could not regard the works as substantially similar. Accordingly, Data East's copyright was not infringed on this basis either.

Because we reverse in its entirety the district court's finding of copyright infringement, it follows that the injunction was improvidently granted. Accordingly, we remand to the district court to lift the injunction.

Each party is to bear its own costs.

REVERSED and REMANDED.

Note

Copyright protection for many computer programs today may be limited by the "scènes à faire" doctrine, given the Microsoft Windows environment in which they were written.

C. OWNERSHIP OF COPYRIGHT

As the word copyright implies, there is a right involved. Intellectual property rights, like all property rights tend to give rise to the disputes over ownership. It is easy to determine who is the author of a novel, because novelists work alone. Determining the ownership of copyright to a computer program or a website is much more complex, because these are typically created by commercial enterprises, typically using numerous staff employees and outside consultants.

United States copyright law in some cases considers the employer or other person for whom a work was prepared to be the author. (In the rest of the world, the "author" is the human being who actually created the work, though an employer may have some rights in an employee's work product.) Many disputes could be avoided by carefully negotiated contracts. But in practice, smaller businesses often fail to have a clear written agreement covering rights in commissioned works. The position of a consultant commissioned to write software is often on the borderline between employee and independent contractor, thus inviting litigation in the absence of a clear contract.

D. EXCLUSIVE RIGHTS OF THE COPYRIGHT OWNER

1. INTRODUCTION

Section 106 of the Copyright Act lists the exclusive rights of the copyright owner. The cases below involve the application of the various Section 106 rights to computer data and software. Further exclusive rights are provided by § 1001 and §§ 1201–1205. A later section of the casebook will deal with the exceptions to exclusive rights found in §§ 107–121 and § 512 of the Copyright Act.

COPYRIGHT ACT OF 1976—§ 106

§ 106. Exclusive rights in copyrighted works

Subject to sections 107 through 121, the owner of copyright under this title has the exclusive rights to do and to authorize any of the following:

(1) to reproduce the copyrighted work in copies or phonorecords;

(2) to prepare derivative works based upon the copyrighted work;

(3) to distribute copies or phonorecords of the copyrighted work to the public by sale or other transfer of ownership, or by rental, lease, or lending;

(4) in the case of literary, musical, dramatic, and choreographic works, pantomimes, and motion pictures and other audiovisual works, to perform the copyrighted work publicly;

(5) in the case of literary, musical, dramatic, and choreographic works, pantomimes, and pictorial, graphic, or sculptural works, including the individual images of a motion picture or other audiovisual work, to display the copyrighted work publicly; and

(6) in the case of sound recordings, to perform the copyrighted work publicly by means of a digital audio transmission.

2. COPIES—§ 106(1)

MAI SYSTEMS CORP. v. PEAK COMPUTER, INC.

United States Court of Appeals, Ninth Circuit, 1993.
991 F.2d 511.

BRUNETTI, CIRCUIT JUDGE.

Peak Computer, Inc. and two of its employees appeal the district court's order issuing a preliminary injunction pending trial as well as the district court's order issuing a permanent injunction following the grant of partial summary judgment.

I. FACTS

MAI Systems Corp., until recently, manufactured computers and designed software to run those computers. The company continues to service its computers and the software necessary to operate the computers. MAI software includes operating system software, which is necessary to run any other program on the computer.

Peak Computer, Inc. is a company organized in 1990 that maintains computer systems for its clients. Peak maintains MAI computers for more than one hundred clients in Southern California. This accounts for between fifty and seventy percent of Peak's business.

Peak's service of MAI computers includes routine maintenance and emergency repairs. Malfunctions often are related to the failure of circuit boards inside the computers, and it may be necessary for a Peak technician to operate the computer and its operating system software in order to service the machine.

In August, 1991, Eric Francis left his job as customer service manager at MAI and joined Peak. Three other MAI employees joined Peak a short time later. Some businesses that had been using MAI to service their computers switched to Peak after learning of Francis's move.

II.   PROCEDURAL HISTORY

On March 17, 1992, MAI filed suit in the district court against Peak, Peak's president Vincent Chiechi, and Francis. The complaint includes counts alleging copyright infringement, misappropriation of trade secrets, trademark infringement, false advertising, and unfair competition.

MAI asked the district court for a temporary restraining order and preliminary injunction pending the outcome of the suit. The district court issued a temporary restraining order on March 18, 1992 and converted it to a preliminary injunction on March 26, 1992. On April 15, 1992, the district court issued a written version of the preliminary injunction along with findings of fact and conclusions of law.

* * *

Since the permanent injunction covers some of the same issues appealed in the preliminary injunction, the appeal of those issues in the context of the preliminary injunction has become moot. *See Burbank–Glendale–Pasadena Airport Authority v. Los Angeles*, 979 F.2d 1338, 1340 n. 1 (9th Cir.1992). Therefore, we grant MAI's motion to dismiss the appeal of the preliminary injunction relative to the issues of copyright infringement and trade secret misappropriation. Since other issues covered in the preliminary injunction are not covered in the permanent injunction, the appeals have been consolidated and both the permanent injunction and parts of the preliminary injunction are reviewed here.

III.   JURISDICTION AND STANDARD OF REVIEW

* * *

IV. COPYRIGHT INFRINGEMENT

The district court granted summary judgment in favor of MAI on its claims of copyright infringement and issued a permanent injunction against Peak on these claims. The alleged copyright violations include: (1) Peak's running of MAI software licenced to Peak customers; (2) Peak's use of unlicensed software at its headquarters; and, (3) Peak's loaning of MAI computers and software to its customers. Each of these alleged violations must be considered separately.

A. *Peak's running of MAI software licenced to Peak customers*

To prevail on a claim of copyright infringement, a plaintiff must prove ownership of a copyright and a " 'copying' of protectable expression" beyond the scope of a license. *S.O.S., Inc. v. Payday, Inc.*, 886 F.2d 1081, 1085 (9th Cir.1989).

MAI software licenses allow MAI customers to use the software for their own internal information processing. This allowed use necessarily includes the loading of the software into the computer's random access memory ("RAM") by a MAI customer. However, MAI software licenses do not allow for the use or copying of MAI software by third parties such as Peak. Therefore, any "copying" done by Peak is "beyond the scope" of the license.

It is not disputed that MAI owns the copyright to the software at issue here, however, Peak vigorously disputes the district court's conclusion that a "copying" occurred under the Copyright Act.

The Copyright Act defines "copies" as:

material objects, other than phonorecords, in which a work is fixed by any method now known or later developed, and from which the work can be perceived, reproduced, or otherwise communicated, either directly or with the aid of a machine or device.

17 U.S.C. § 101.

The Copyright Act then explains:

A work is "fixed" in a tangible medium of expression when its embodiment in a copy or phonorecord, by or under the authority of the author, is sufficiently permanent or stable to permit it to be perceived, reproduced, or otherwise communicated for a period of more than transitory duration.

17 U.S.C. § 101.

The district court's grant of summary judgment on MAI's claims of copyright infringement reflects its conclusion that a "copying" for purposes of copyright law occurs when a computer program is transferred from a permanent storage device to a computer's RAM. This conclusion is consistent with its finding, in granting the preliminary injunction, that: "the loading of copyrighted computer software from a storage medium (hard disk, floppy disk, or read only memory) into the memory of a central processing unit ('CPU') causes a copy to be made." In the absence of ownership of the copyright or express permission by license, such acts constitute copyright infringement." We find that this conclusion is supported by the record and by the law.

Peak concedes that in maintaining its customer's computers, it uses MAI operating software "to the extent that the repair and maintenance process necessarily involves turning on the computer to make sure it is functional and thereby running the operating system." It is also uncontroverted that when the computer is turned on the operating system is loaded into the computer's RAM. As part of diagnosing a computer problem at the customer site, the Peak technician runs the computer's operating system software, allowing the technician to view the systems error log, which is part of the operating system, thereby enabling the technician to diagnose the problem.

Peak argues that this loading of copyrighted software does not constitute a copyright violation because the "copy" created in RAM is not "fixed." However, by showing that Peak loads the software into the RAM and is then able to view the system error log and diagnose the problem with the computer, MAI has adequately shown that the representation created in the RAM is "sufficiently permanent or stable to permit it to be perceived, reproduced, or otherwise communicated for a period of more than transitory duration."

After reviewing the record, we find no specific facts (and Peak points to none) which indicate that the copy created in the RAM is not fixed.
* * *

The law also supports the conclusion that Peak's loading of copyrighted software into RAM creates a "copy" of that software in violation of the Copyright Act. In *Apple Computer, Inc. v. Formula Int'l, Inc.*, 594 F.Supp. 617, 621 (C.D.Cal.1984), the district court held that the copying of copyrighted software onto silicon chips and subsequent sale of those chips is not protected by § 117 of the Copyright Act. Section 117 allows "the 'owner'[5] of a copy of a computer program to make or authorize the making of another copy" without infringing copyright law, if it "is an essential step in the utilization of the computer program" or if the new copy is "for archival purposes only." 17 U.S.C. § 117 (Supp.1988).[6] One of the grounds for finding that § 117 did not apply was the court's conclusion that the permanent copying of the software onto the silicon chips was not an "essential step" in the utilization of the software

---

5. Since MAI licensed its software, the Peak customers do not qualify as "owners" of the software and are not eligible for protection under § 117.

6. The current § 117 was enacted by Congress in 1980, as part of the Computer Software Copyright Act. This Act adopted the recommendations contained in the *Final Report of the National Commission on New Technological Uses of Copyrighted Works* ("CONTU") (1978). H.R.Rep. No. 1307, 96th Cong., 2d Sess., pt. 1, at 23. The CONTU was established by Congress in 1974 to perform research and make recommendations concerning copyright protection for computer programs. The new § 117 reflects the CONTU's conclusion that: "Because the placement of a work into a computer is the preparation of a copy, the law should provide that persons in rightful possession of copies of programs be able to use them freely without fear of exposure to copyright liability." *Final Report* at 13.

because the software could be used through RAM without making a permanent copy. The court stated:

> RAM can be simply defined as a computer component in which data and computer programs can be temporarily recorded. Thus, the purchaser of [software] desiring to utilize all of the programs on the diskette could arrange to copy [the software] into RAM. This would only be a temporary fixation. It is a property of RAM that when the computer is turned off, the copy of the program recorded in RAM is lost.

Apple Computer at 622.

While we recognize that this language is not dispositive, it supports the view that the copy made in RAM is "fixed" and qualifies as a copy under the Copyright Act.

We have found no case which specifically holds that the copying of software into RAM creates a "copy" under the Copyright Act. However, it is generally accepted that the loading of software into a computer constitutes the creation of a copy under the Copyright Act. *See e.g. Vault Corp. v. Quaid Software Ltd.*, 847 F.2d 255, 260 (5th Cir.1988) ("the act of loading a program from a medium of storage into a computer's memory creates a copy of the program"); 2 *Nimmer on Copyright*, § 8.08 at 8–105 (1983) ("Inputting a computer program entails the preparation of a copy."); *Final Report of the National Commission on the New Technological Uses of Copyrighted Works*, at 13 (1978) ("the placement of a work into a computer is the preparation of a copy"). We recognize that these authorities are somewhat troubling since they do not specify that a copy is created regardless of whether the software is loaded into the RAM, the hard disk or the read only memory ("ROM"). However, since we find that the copy created in the RAM can be "perceived, reproduced, or otherwise communicated," we hold that the loading of software into the RAM creates a copy under the Copyright Act. 17 U.S.C. § 101. We affirm the district court's grant of summary judgment as well as the permanent injunction as it relates to this issue.

B. *Use of unlicensed software at headquarters*

It is not disputed that Peak has several MAI computers with MAI operating software "up and running" at its headquarters. It is also not disputed that Peak only has a license to use MAI software to operate one system. As discussed above, we find that the loading of MAI's operating software into RAM, which occurs when an MAI system is turned on, constitutes a copyright violation. We affirm the district court's grant of summary judgment in favor of MAI on its claim that Peak violated its copyright through the unlicensed use of MAI software at Peak headquarters, and also affirm the permanent injunction as it relates to this issue.

* * *

Note

This decision gave software providers the opportunity to establish monopolies on the provision of maintenance. Book publishers cannot require homeowners to use their services to rebind books or repair bookcases. Why should software publishers be able to require what book publishers cannot? Congress decided that *MAI v. Peak* threatened competition in repair services. It did not touch the basic ruling in the case, that reading a program into RAM constituted making a copy of the program and hence was a violation of the exclusive § 106 right of the copyright holder to make copies. But Congress did deal with the problem of monopolization of repair services, by adding the following subsections to § 117 of the Copyright Act:

(c) Machine Maintenance or Repair. Notwithstanding the provisions of section 106, it is not an infringement for the owner or lessee of a machine to make or authorize the making of a copy of a computer program if such copy is made solely by virtue of the activation of a machine that lawfully contains an authorized copy of the computer program, for purposes only of maintenance or repair of that machine, if:

(1) such new copy is used in no other manner and is destroyed immediately after the maintenance or repair is completed; and

(2) with respect to any computer program or part thereof that is not necessary for that machine to be activated, such program or part thereof is not accessed or used other than to make such new copy by virtue of the activation of the machine.

(d) Definitions. For purposes of this section

(1) the "maintenance" of a machine is the servicing of the machine in order to make it work in accordance with its original specifications and any changes to those specifications authorized for that machine; and

(2) the "repair" of a machine is the restoring of the machine to the state of working in accordance with its original specifications and any changes to those specifications authorized for that machine.

3. DERIVATIVE WORKS—§ 102(2)

LEWIS GALOOB TOYS, INC. v. NINTENDO OF AMERICA, INC.

United States Court of Appeals, Ninth Circuit, 1992.
964 F.2d 965.

FARRIS, CIRCUIT JUDGE.

Nintendo of America appeals the district court's judgment following a bench trial (1) declaring that Lewis Galoob Toys' Game Genie does not violate any Nintendo copyrights and dissolving a temporary injunction and (2) denying Nintendo's request for a permanent injunction enjoining Galoob from marketing the Game Genie. *Lewis Galoob Toys, Inc. v. Nintendo of America, Inc.*, 780 F.Supp. 1283 (N.D.Cal.1991). We have appellate jurisdiction pursuant to 15 U.S.C. § 1121 and 28 U.S.C. §§ 1291 and 1292(a)(1). We affirm.

The Nintendo Entertainment System is a home video game system marketed by Nintendo. To use the system, the player inserts a cartridge containing a video game that Nintendo produces or licenses others to produce. By pressing buttons and manipulating a control pad, the player controls one of the game's characters and progresses through the game. The games are protected as audiovisual works under 17 U.S.C. § 102(a)(6).

The Game Genie is a device manufactured by Galoob that allows the player to alter up to three features of a Nintendo game. For example, the Game Genie can increase the number of lives of the player's character, increase the speed at which the character moves, and allow the character to float above obstacles. The player controls the changes made by the Game Genie by entering codes provided by the Game Genie Programming Manual and Code Book. The player also can experiment with variations of these codes.

The Game Genie functions by blocking the value for a single data byte sent by the game cartridge to the central processing unit in the Nintendo Entertainment System and replacing it with a new value. If that value controls the character's strength, for example, then the character can be made invincible by increasing the value sufficiently. The Game Genie is inserted between a game cartridge and the Nintendo Entertainment System. The Game Genie does not alter the data that is stored in the game cartridge. Its effects are temporary.

DISCUSSION

1. Derivative work

The Copyright Act of 1976 confers upon copyright holders the exclusive right to prepare and authorize others to prepare derivative works based on their copyrighted works. Nintendo argues that the district court erred in concluding that the audiovisual displays created by the Game Genie are not derivative works. The court's conclusions of law are reviewed *de novo*. Its findings of fact are reviewed for clear error.

A derivative work must incorporate a protected work in some concrete or permanent "form." * * * The examples of derivative works provided by the Act all physically incorporate the underlying work or works. The Act's legislative history similarly indicates that "the infringing work must incorporate a portion of the copyrighted work in some form."

Our analysis is not controlled by the Copyright Act's definition of "fixed." The Act defines copies as "material objects, other than phonorecords, in which a work is *fixed* by any method." 17 U.S.C. § 101 (emphasis added). The Act's definition of "derivative work," in contrast, lacks any such reference to fixation. Further, we have held in a copyright infringement action that "[i]t makes no difference that the derivation may not satisfy certain requirements for statutory copyright registration itself." *Lone Ranger Television v. Program Radio Corp.*, 740 F.2d 718,

722 (9th Cir.1984). A derivative work must be fixed to be *protected* under the Act, *see* 17 U.S.C. § 102(a), but not to *infringe*.

The argument that a derivative work must be fixed because "[a] 'derivative work' is a work," 17 U.S.C. § 101, and "[a] work is 'created' when it is fixed in a copy or phonorecord for the first time," *id.*, relies on a misapplication of the Copyright Act's definition of "created":

> A work is "created" when it is fixed in a copy or phonorecord for the first time; where a work is prepared over a period of time, the portion of it that has been fixed at any particular time constitutes the work as of that time, and where the work has been prepared in different versions, each version constitutes a separate work.

Id. The definition clarifies the *time* at which a work is *created*. If the provision were a definition of "work," it would not use that term in such a casual manner. The Act does not contain a definition of "work." Rather, it contains specific definitions: "audiovisual works," "literary works," and "pictorial, graphic and sculptural works," for example. The definition of "derivative work" does not require fixation.

The district court's finding that no independent work is created, is supported by the record. The Game Genie merely enhances the audiovisual displays (or underlying data bytes) that originate in Nintendo game cartridges. The altered displays do not incorporate a portion of a copyrighted work in some concrete or permanent *form*. Nintendo argues that the Game Genie's displays are as fixed in the hardware and software used to create them as Nintendo's original displays. Nintendo's argument ignores the fact that the Game Genie cannot produce an audiovisual display; the underlying display must be produced by a Nintendo Entertainment System and game cartridge. Even if we were to rely on the Copyright Act's definition of "fixed," we would similarly conclude that the resulting display is not "embodied" in the Game Genie. It cannot be a derivative work.

* * *

Nintendo asserted at oral argument that the existence of a $150 million market for the Game Genie indicates that its audiovisual display must be fixed. We understand Nintendo's argument; consumers clearly would not purchase the Game Genie if its display was not "sufficiently permanent or stable to permit it to be perceived . . . for a period of more than transitory duration." But, Nintendo's reliance on the Act's definition of "fixed" is misplaced. Nintendo's argument also proves too much; the existence of a market does not, and cannot, determine conclusively whether a work is an infringing derivative work. For example, although there is a market for kaleidoscopes, it does not necessarily follow that kaleidoscopes create unlawful derivative works when pointed at protected artwork. The same can be said of countless other products that enhance, but do not replace, copyrighted works.

Nintendo also argues that our analysis should focus exclusively on the audiovisual displays created by the Game Genie, *i.e.*, that we should compare the altered displays to Nintendo's original displays. Nintendo emphasizes that " '[a]udiovisual works' are works that consist of a series of related images . . . *regardless of the nature of the material objects . . . in which the works are embodied.*" 17 U.S.C. § 101 (emphasis added). The Copyright Act's definition of "audiovisual works" is inapposite; the only question before us is whether the audiovisual displays created by the Game Genie are "derivative works." The Act does not similarly provide that a work can be a derivative work regardless of the nature of the material objects in which the work is embodied. A derivative work must incorporate a protected work in some concrete or permanent form. We cannot ignore the actual source of the Game Genie's display.

Nintendo relies heavily on *Midway Mfg. Co. v. Artic Int'l, Inc.*, 704 F.2d 1009 (7th Cir.), *cert. denied*, 464 U.S. 823 (1983). *Midway* can be distinguished. The defendant in *Midway*, Artic International, marketed a computer chip that could be inserted in Galaxian video games to speed up the rate of play. The Seventh Circuit held that the speeded-up version of Galaxian was a derivative work. Artic's chip substantially copied and *replaced* the chip that was originally distributed by Midway. Purchasers of Artic's chip also benefited economically by offering the altered game for use by the general public. The Game Genie does not physically incorporate a portion of a copyrighted work, nor does it supplant demand for a component of that work. The court in *Midway* acknowledged that the Copyright Act's definition of "derivative work" "must be stretched to accommodate speeded-up video games." *Id.* at 104. Stretching that definition further would chill innovation and fail to protect "society's competing interest in the free flow of ideas, information, and commerce."

In holding that the audiovisual displays created by the Game Genie are not derivative works, we recognize that technology often advances by improvement rather than replacement. Some time ago, for example, computer companies began marketing spell-checkers that operate within existing word processors by signaling the writer when a word is misspelled. These applications, as well as countless others, could not be produced and marketed if courts were to conclude that the word processor and spell-checker combination is a derivative work based on the word processor alone. The Game Genie is useless by itself, it can only enhance, and cannot duplicate or recaste, a Nintendo game's output. It does not contain or produce a Nintendo game's output in some concrete or permanent form, nor does it supplant demand for Nintendo game cartridges. Such innovations rarely will constitute infringing derivative works under the Copyright Act.

* * *

3. *Temporary and permanent injunction*

Galoob has not violated the Copyright Act. Nintendo therefore is not entitled to a temporary or permanent injunction.

AFFIRMED.

Notes

1. For a discussion of Internet-related derivative works issues, see Lydia Pallas Loren, *"The Changing Nature of Derivative Works in the Face of New Technologies,"* 4 J. SMALL & EMERGING BUSINESS L. 57 (2000).

2. In *Mirage Editions, Inc. v. Albuquerque A.R.T. Co.*, 856 F.2d 1341 (9th Cir.1988), the Ninth Circuit held that defendant created an infringing derivative work when it bought genuine copies of an original work and glued them to tiles. On essentially identical facts in *Lee v. A.R.T. Co.*, 125 F.3d 580 (7th Cir.1997), the Seventh Circuit held that there was no infringement. Commentators unanimously agree that the Seventh Circuit decision is the better interpretation. What implications do these decisions have for the practice using a "frame" from one's own Internet site to "frame" content from other Internet sites?

4. RENTAL—§ 106(3)

COPYRIGHT ACT OF 1976—§ 106(3)

§ 106(3) Exclusive Rights in Copyrighted Works—Rental

(3) to distribute copies or phonorecords of the copyrighted work to the public by sale or other transfer of ownership, or by rental, lease, or lending;

5. PERFORMANCE AND DISPLAY—§ 106(4) § 106(5)

In *Red Baron—Franklin Park, Inc. v. Taito Corporation*, 883 F.2d 275 (4th Cir.1989), the court decided that a video arcade owner infringed the copyright of a video game manufacturer, when the arcade purchased the circuit boards of the manufacturer and used them in coin-operated video game machines. Congress promptly overturned *Red Baron* by an amendment to § 109 of the Copyright Act.

6. DIGITAL AUDIO WORKS—§ 106(6) AND COPYRIGHT MANAGEMENT RIGHTS—§ 1001

RECORDING INDUSTRY ASSOCIATION OF AMERICA, v. DIAMOND MULTIMEDIA SYSTEMS INC.

United States Court of Appeals, Ninth Circuit. 1999.
180 F.3d 1072.

O'SCANNLAIN, CIRCUIT JUDGE.

In this case involving the intersection of computer technology, the Internet, and music listening, we must decide whether the Rio portable music player is a digital audio recording device subject to the restrictions of the Audio Home Recording Act of 1992.

I

This appeal arises from the efforts of the Recording Industry Association of America and the Alliance of Artists and Recording Companies (collectively, "RIAA") to enjoin the manufacture and distribution by Diamond Multimedia Systems ("Diamond") of the Rio portable music player. The Rio is a small device (roughly the size of an audio cassette) with headphones that allows a user to download MP3 audio files from a computer and to listen to them elsewhere. The dispute over the Rio's design and function is difficult to comprehend without an understanding of the revolutionary new method of music distribution made possible by digital recording and the Internet; thus, we will explain in some detail the brave new world of Internet music distribution.

A

The introduction of digital audio recording to the consumer electronics market in the 1980's is at the root of this litigation. Before then, a person wishing to copy an original music recording—e.g., wishing to make a cassette tape of a record or compact disc—was limited to analog, rather than digital, recording technology. With analog recording, each successive generation of copies suffers from an increasingly pronounced degradation in sound quality. For example, when an analog cassette copy of a record or compact disc is itself copied by analog technology, the resulting "second-generation" copy of the original will most likely suffer from the hiss and lack of clarity characteristic of older recordings. With digital recording, by contrast, there is almost no degradation in sound quality, no matter how many generations of copies are made. Digital copying thus allows thousands of perfect or near perfect copies (and copies of copies) to be made from a single original recording. Music "pirates" use digital recording technology to make and to distribute near perfect copies of commercially prepared recordings for which they have not licensed the copyrights.

Until recently, the Internet was of little use for the distribution of music because the average music computer file was simply too big: the digital information on a single compact disc of music required hundreds of computer floppy discs to store, and downloading even a single song from the Internet took hours. However, various compression algorithms (which make an audio file "smaller" by limiting the audio bandwidth) now allow digital audio files to be transferred more quickly and stored more efficiently. MPEG–1 Audio Layer 3 (commonly known as "MP3") is the most popular digital audio compression algorithm in use on the Internet, and the compression it provides makes an audio file "smaller" by a factor of twelve to one without significantly reducing sound quality. MP3's popularity is due in large part to the fact that it is a standard, non-proprietary compression algorithm freely available for use by anyone, unlike various proprietary (and copyright-secure) competitor algorithms. Coupled with the use of cable modems, compression algorithms like MP3 may soon allow an hour of music to be downloaded from the Internet to a personal computer in just a few minutes.

These technological advances have occurred, at least in part, to the traditional music industry's disadvantage. By most accounts, the predominant use of MP3 is the trafficking in illicit audio recordings, presumably because MP3 files do not contain codes identifying whether the compressed audio material is copyright protected. Various pirate websites offer free downloads of copyrighted material, and a single pirate site on the Internet may contain thousands of pirated audio computer files.

RIAA represents the roughly half-dozen major record companies (and the artists on their labels) that control approximately ninety percent of the distribution of recorded music in the United States. RIAA asserts that Internet distribution of serial digital copies of pirated copyrighted material will discourage the purchase of legitimate recordings, and predicts that losses to digital Internet piracy will soon surpass the $300 million that is allegedly lost annually to other more traditional forms of piracy. RIAA fights a well-nigh constant battle against Internet piracy, monitoring the Internet daily, and routinely shutting down pirate websites by sending cease-and-desist letters and bringing lawsuits. There are conflicting views on RIAA's success—RIAA asserts that it can barely keep up with the pirate traffic, while others assert that few, if any, pirate sites remain in operation in the United States and illicit files are difficult to find and download from anywhere online.

In contrast to piracy, the Internet also supports a burgeoning traffic in legitimate audio computer files. Independent and wholly Internet record labels routinely sell and provide free samples of their artists' work online, while many unsigned artists distribute their own material from their own websites. Some free samples are provided for marketing purposes or for simple exposure, while others are teasers intended to entice listeners to purchase either mail order recordings or recordings available for direct download (along with album cover art, lyrics, and artist biographies). Diamond cites a 1998 "Music Industry and the Internet" report by Jupiter Communications which predicts that online sales for pre-recorded music will exceed $1.4 billion by 2002 in the United States alone.

Prior to the invention of devices like the Rio, MP3 users had little option other than to listen to their downloaded digital audio files through headphones or speakers at their computers, playing them from their hard drives. The Rio renders these files portable. More precisely, once an audio file has been downloaded onto a computer hard drive from the Internet or some other source (such as a compact disc player or digital audio tape machine), separate computer software provided with the Rio (called "Rio Manager") allows the user further to download the file to the Rio itself via a parallel port cable that plugs the Rio into the computer. The Rio device is incapable of effecting such a transfer, and is incapable of receiving audio files from anything other than a personal computer equipped with Rio Manager.

Generally, the Rio can store approximately one hour of music, or sixteen hours of spoken material (e.g., downloaded newscasts or books on tape). With the addition of flash memory cards, the Rio can store an additional half-hour or hour of music. The Rio's sole output is an analog audio signal sent to the user via headphones. The Rio cannot make duplicates of any digital audio file it stores, nor can it transfer or upload such a file to a computer, to another device, or to the Internet. However, a flash memory card to which a digital audio file has been downloaded can be removed from one Rio and played back in another.

B

RIAA brought suit to enjoin the manufacture and distribution of the Rio, alleging that the Rio does not meet the requirements for digital audio recording devices under the Audio Home Recording Act of 1992, 17 U.S.C. § 1001 *et seq.* (the "Act"), because it does not employ a Serial Copyright Management System ("SCMS") that sends, receives, and acts upon information about the generation and copyright status of the files that it plays. *See id.* § 1002(a)(2). RIAA also sought payment of the royalties owed by Diamond as the manufacturer and distributor of a digital audio recording device. *See id.* § 1003.

The district court denied RIAA's motion for a preliminary injunction, holding that RIAA's likelihood of success on the merits was mixed and the balance of hardships did not tip in RIAA's favor. *See generally Recording Indus. Ass'n of America, Inc. v. Diamond Multimedia Sys., Inc.,* 29 F.Supp.2d 624 (C.D.Cal.1998) ("RIAA I"). RIAA brought this appeal.

II

The initial question presented is whether the Rio falls within the ambit of the Act. The Act does not broadly prohibit digital serial copying of copyright protected audio recordings. Instead, the Act places restrictions only upon a specific type of recording device. Most relevant here, the Act provides that "[n]o person shall import, manufacture, or distribute any *digital audio recording device* ... that does not conform to the Serial Copy Management System ['SCMS'] [or] a system that has the same functional characteristics." 17 U.S.C. § 1002(a)(1), (2) (emphasis added). The Act further provides that "[n]o person shall import into and distribute, or manufacture and distribute, any *digital audio recording device* ... unless such person records the notice specified by this section and subsequently deposits the statements of account and applicable royalty payments." *Id.* § 1003(a) (emphasis added). Thus, to fall within the SCMS and royalty requirements in question, the Rio must be a "digital audio recording device," which the Act defines through a set of nested definitions.

The Act defines a "digital audio recording device" as:

> any machine or device of a type commonly distributed to individuals for use by individuals, whether or not included with or as part of some other machine or device, the digital recording function of which is designed or marketed for the primary purpose of, and that is capable of, making a *digital audio copied recording* for private use....

Id. § 1001(3) (emphasis added).

A "digital audio copied recording" is defined as:

a reproduction in a digital recording format of a *digital musical recording*, whether that reproduction is made directly from another digital musical recording or indirectly from a transmission.

Id. § 1001(1) (emphasis added).

A "digital musical recording" is defined as:

a material object—

(i) in which are fixed, in a digital recording format, *only sounds, and material, statements, or instructions incidental to those fixed sounds*, if any, and

(ii) from which the sounds and material can be perceived, reproduced, or otherwise communicated, either directly or with the aid of a machine or device.

Id. § 1001(5)(A) (emphasis added).

In sum, to be a digital audio recording device, the Rio must be able to reproduce, either "directly" or "from a transmission," a "digital music recording."

III

We first consider whether the Rio is able directly to reproduce a digital music recording—which is a specific type of material object in which only sounds are fixed (or material and instructions incidental to those sounds). *See id.*

A

The typical computer hard drive from which a Rio directly records is, of course, a material object. However, hard drives ordinarily contain much more than "only sounds, and material, statements, or instructions incidental to those fixed sounds." *Id.* Indeed, almost all hard drives contain numerous programs (e.g., for word processing, scheduling appointments, etc.) and databases that are not incidental to any sound files that may be stored on the hard drive. Thus, the Rio appears not to make copies from digital music recordings, and thus would not be a digital audio recording device under the Act's basic definition unless it makes copies from transmissions.

Moreover, the Act expressly provides that the term "digital musical recording" does not include:

a material object—

(i) in which the fixed sounds consist entirely of spoken word recordings, or

(ii) *in which one or more computer programs are fixed*, except that a digital recording may contain statements or instructions constituting the fixed sounds and incidental material, and statements or instructions to be used directly or indirectly in order to bring about the perception, reproduction, or communication of the fixed sounds and incidental material.

Id. § 1001(5)(B) (emphasis added). As noted previously, a hard drive is a material object in which one or more programs are fixed; thus, a hard drive is excluded from the definition of digital music recordings. This provides confirmation that the Rio does not record "directly" from "digital music recordings," and therefore could not be a digital audio recording device unless it makes copies "from transmissions."

B

The district court rejected the exclusion of computer hard drives from the definition of digital music recordings under the statute's plain language (after noting its "superficial appeal") because it concluded that such exclusion "is ultimately unsupported by the legislative history, and contrary to the spirit and purpose of the [Act]." *RIAA I*, 29 F.Supp.2d at 629. We need not resort to the legislative history because the statutory language is clear. *See City of Auburn v. United States*, 154 F.3d 1025, 1030 (9th Cir.1998) ("[W]here statutory command is straightforward, 'there is no reason to resort to legislative history.'" (quoting *United States v. Gonzales*, 520 U.S. 1, 6, 117 S.Ct. 1032, 137 L.Ed.2d 132 (1997))). Nevertheless, we will address the legislative history here, because it is consistent with the statute's plain meaning and because the parties have briefed it so extensively.

1

The Senate Report states that "if the material object contains computer programs or data bases that are not incidental to the fixed sounds, then the material object would not qualify" under the basic definition of a digital musical recording. S. Rep. 102–294 (1992), *reprinted at* 1992 WL 133198, at *118–19. The Senate Report further states that the definition "is intended to cover those objects commonly understood to embody sound recordings and their underlying works." *Id.* at *97. A footnote makes explicit that this definition only extends to the material objects in which songs are normally fixed: "[t]hat is recorded compact discs, digital audio tapes, audio cassettes, long-playing albums, digital compact cassettes, and mini-discs." *Id.* at n. 36. There are simply no grounds in either the plain language of the definition or in the legislative history for interpreting the term "digital musical recording" to include songs fixed on computer hard drives.

RIAA contends that the legislative history reveals that the Rio does not fall within the specific exemption from the digital musical recording definition of "a material object in which one or more computer programs are fixed." 17 U.S.C. § 1001(5)(B)(ii). The House Report describes the exemption as "revisions reflecting exemptions for talking books and *computer programs*." H.R. Rep. 102–873(I) (1992), reprinted at 1992 WL 232935, at *35 (emphasis added); *see also id.* at *44 ("In addition to containing an *express exclusion of computer programs* in the definition of

'digital musical recording'. . . . '') (emphasis added). We first note that
limiting the exemption to computer programs is contrary to the plain
meaning of the exemption. As Diamond points out, a computer program
is not a material object, but rather, a literary work, *see, e.g., Apple
Computer, Inc. v. Franklin Computer Corp.*, 714 F.2d 1240, 1249 (3d
Cir.1983) ("[A] computer program . . . is a 'literary work.' ''), that can be
fixed in a variety of material objects, *see* 17 U.S.C. § 101 (" 'Literary
works' are works . . . expressed in words, numbers, or other verbal or
numerical symbols or indicia, *regardless of the nature of the material
objects, such as books . . . tapes, disks, or cards, in which they are
embodied*.'') (emphasis added). Thus, the plain language of the exemption at issue does not exclude the copying of programs from coverage by
the Act, but instead, excludes copying from various types of material
objects. Those objects include hard drives, which indirectly achieve the
desired result of excluding copying of programs. But by its plain language, the exemption is not limited to the copying of programs, and
instead extends to any copying from a computer hard drive.

Moreover, RIAA's assertion that computer hard drives do not fall
within the exemption is irrelevant because, regardless of that portion of
the legislative history which addresses the *exemption* from the definition
of digital music recording, *see id.* § 1001(5)(B)(ii), the Rio does not
reproduce files from something that falls within the plain language of
the basic *definition* of a digital music recording, *see id.* § 1001(5)(A).

2

The district court concluded that the exemption of hard drives from
the definition of digital music recording, and the exemption of computers
generally from the Act's ambit, "would effectively eviscerate the [Act]"
because "[a]ny recording device could evade [ ] regulation simply by
passing the music through a computer and ensuring that the MP3 file
resided momentarily on the hard drive." *RIAA I*, 29 F.Supp.2d at 630.
While this may be true, the Act seems to have been expressly designed to
create this loophole.

A

Under the plain meaning of the Act's definition of digital audio
recording devices, computers (and their hard drives) are not digital audio
recording devices because their "primary purpose" is not to make digital
audio copied recordings. *See* 17 U.S.C. § 1001(3). Unlike digital audio
tape machines, for example, whose primary purpose is to make digital
audio copied recordings, the primary purpose of a computer is to run
various programs and to record the data necessary to run those programs and perform various tasks. The legislative history is consistent
with this interpretation of the Act's provisions, stating that "the typical
personal computer would not fall within the definition of 'digital audio
recording device,' " S. Rep. 102–294, at *122, because a personal computer's "recording function is designed and marketed primarily for the
recording of data and computer programs," *id.* at *121. Another portion

of the Senate Report states that "[i]f the 'primary purpose' of the recording function is to make objects other than digital audio copied recordings, then the machine or device is not a 'digital audio recording device,' *even if the machine or device is technically capable of making such recordings.*" *Id.* (emphasis added). The legislative history thus expressly recognizes that computers (and other devices) have recording functions capable of recording digital musical recordings, and thus implicate the home taping and piracy concerns to which the Act is responsive. Nonetheless, the legislative history is consistent with the Act's plain language—computers are *not* digital audio recording devices.

B

In turn, because computers are not digital audio recording devices, they are not required to comply with the SCMS requirement and thus need not send, receive, or act upon information regarding copyright and generation status. *See* 17 U.S.C. § 1002(a)(2). And, as the district court found, MP3 files generally do not even carry the codes providing information regarding copyright and generation status. *See RIAA I*, 29 F.Supp.2d. at 632. Thus, the Act seems designed to allow files to be "laundered" by passage through a computer, because even a device with SCMS would be able to download MP3 files lacking SCMS codes from a computer hard drive, for the simple reason that there would be no codes to prevent the copying.

Again, the legislative history is consistent with the Act's plain meaning. As the Technical Reference Document that describes the SCMS system explains, "[d]igital audio signals ... that have no information concerning copyright and/or generation status *shall be recorded* by the [digital audio recording] device so that the digital copy is copyright asserted and original generation status." *Technical Reference Document for the Audio Home Recording Act of 1992*, II–A, § 10, *reprinted in* H.R. Rep. 102–780(I), 32, 43 (1992) (emphasis added). Thus, the incorporation of SCMS into the Rio would allow the Rio to copy MP3 files lacking SCMS codes so long as it marked the copied files as "original generation status." And such a marking would allow another SCMS device to make unlimited further copies of such "original generation status" files, *see, e.g.*, H.R. Rep. 102–873(I), at *47 ("Under SCMS ... consumers will be able to make an unlimited number of copies from a digital musical recording."), despite the fact that the Rio does not permit such further copies to be made because it simply cannot download or transmit the files that it stores to any other device. Thus, the Rio without SCMS inherently allows *less* copying than SCMS permits.

C

In fact, the Rio's operation is entirely consistent with the Act's main purpose—the facilitation of personal use. As the Senate Report explains, "[t]he purpose of [the Act] is to ensure the right of consumers to make analog or digital audio recordings of copyrighted music for their *private, noncommercial use.*" S. Rep. 102–294, at *86 (emphasis added). The Act does so through its home taping exemption, see 17 U.S.C. § 1008, which "protects all noncommercial copying by consumers of digital and analog musical recordings," H.R. Rep. 102–873(I), at *59. The Rio merely makes copies in order to render portable, or "space-shift," those files that already reside on a user's hard drive. *Cf. Sony Corp. of America v. Universal City Studios*, 464 U.S. 417, 455, 104 S.Ct. 774, 78 L.Ed.2d 574 (1984) (holding that "time-shifting" of copyrighted television shows with VCR's constitutes fair use under the Copyright Act, and thus is not an infringement). Such copying is paradigmatic noncommercial personal use entirely consistent with the purposes of the Act.

IV

Even though it cannot directly reproduce a digital music recording, the Rio would nevertheless be a digital audio recording device if it could reproduce a digital music recording "from a transmission." 17 U.S.C. § 1001(1).

A

The term "transmission" is not defined in Act, although the use of the term in the Act implies that a transmission is a communication to the public. *See id.* § 1002(e) (placing restrictions upon "[a]ny person who transmits or *otherwise communicates to the public* any sound recording in digital format") (emphasis added). In the context of copyright law (from which the term appears to have been taken), "[t]o 'transmit' a performance or display is to communicate it by any device or process whereby images or sounds are received beyond the place from which they are sent." 17 U.S.C. § 101. The legislative history confirms that the copyright definition of "transmission" is sufficient for our purposes here. The Act originally (and circularly) provided that "[a] 'transmission' is any audio or audiovisual transmission, now known or later developed, whether by a broadcast station, cable system, multipoint distribution service, subscription service, direct broadcast satellite, or other form of analog or digital communication." S. Rep. 102–294, at *10. The Senate Report provides a radio broadcast as an example of a transmission. *See id.*, at *119 (referring to "a transmission (e.g., a radio broadcast of a commercially released audio cassette)."). The parties do not really dispute the definition of transmission, but rather, whether *indirect* reproduction of a transmission of a digital music recording is covered by the Act.

B

RIAA asserts that indirect reproduction of a transmission is sufficient for the Rio to fall within the Act's ambit as a digital audio recording device. *See* 17 U.S.C. § 1001(1) (digital audio recording devices are those devices that are capable of making "a reproduction in a digital recording format of a digital musical recording, whether that reproduction is made directly from another digital musical recording or *indirectly* from a transmission") (emphasis added). Diamond asserts that the adverb "indirectly" modifies the recording of the underlying "digital music recording," rather than the recording "from the transmission." Diamond effectively asserts that the statute should be read as covering devices that are capable of making a reproduction of a digital musical recording, "whether that reproduction is made directly[,] from another digital musical recording[,] or indirectly[,] from a transmission."

While the Rio can only directly reproduce files from a computer hard drive via a cable linking the two devices (which is obviously not a transmission), the Rio can indirectly reproduce a transmission. For example, if a radio broadcast of a digital audio recording were recorded on a digital audio tape machine or compact disc recorder and then uploaded to a computer hard drive, the Rio could indirectly reproduce the transmission by downloading a copy from the hard drive. Thus, if indirect reproduction of a transmission falls within the statutory definition, the Rio would be a digital audio recording device.

1

RIAA's interpretation of the statutory language initially seems plausible, but closer analysis reveals that it is contrary to the statutory language and common sense. The focus of the statutory language seems to be on the two means of reproducing the underlying digital music recording—either directly from that recording, or indirectly, by reproducing the recording from a transmission. RIAA's interpretation of the Act's language (in which "indirectly" modifies copying "from a transmission," rather than the copying of the underlying digital music recording) would only cover the indirect recording of transmissions, and would omit restrictions on the direct recording of transmissions (e.g., recording songs from the radio) from the Act's ambit. This interpretation would significantly reduce the protection afforded by the Act to transmissions, and neither the statutory language nor structure provides any reason that the Act's protections should be so limited. Moreover, it makes little sense for the Act to restrict the indirect recording of transmissions, but to allow unrestricted direct recording of transmissions (e.g., to regulate second-hand recording of songs from the radio, but to allow unlimited direct recording of songs from the radio). Thus, the most logical reading of the Act extends protection to direct copying of digital music recordings, and to indirect copying of digital music recordings from transmissions of those recordings.

2

Because of the arguable ambiguity of this passage of the statute, recourse to the legislative history is necessary on this point. *Cf. Moyle v. Director, Office of Workers' Compensation Programs*, 147 F.3d 1116, 1120 (9th Cir.1998) ("[I]f the statute is ambiguous, [this court] consult[s] the legislative history, to the extent that it is of value, to aid in [its] interpretation."), *cert. denied*, ___ U.S. ___, 119 S.Ct. 1454, 143 L.Ed.2d 541 (1999). The Senate Report states that "a digital audio recording made from a commercially released compact disc or audio cassette, or *from a radio broadcast* of a commercially released compact disc or audio cassette, would be a 'digital audio copied recording.' " S. Rep. 102–294, at * 119 (emphasis added). This statement indicates that the recording of a transmission need not be indirect to fall within the scope of the Act's restrictions, and thus refutes RIAA's proposed interpretation of the relevant language. Moreover, the statement tracks the statutory definition by providing an example of direct copying of a digital music recording from that recording, and an example of indirect copying of a digital music recording from a transmission of that recording. Thus the legislative history confirms the most logical reading of the statute, which we adopt: "indirectly" modifies the verb "is made"—in other words, modifies the making of the reproduction of the underlying digital music recording. Thus, a device falls within the Act's provisions if it can indirectly copy a digital music recording by making a copy from a transmission of that recording. Because the Rio cannot make copies from transmissions, but instead, can only make copies from a computer hard drive, it is not a digital audio recording device.[7]

V

For the foregoing reasons, the Rio is not a digital audio recording device subject to the restrictions of the Audio Home Recording Act of 1992. The district court properly denied the motion for a preliminary injunction against the Rio's manufacture and distribution. Having so determined, we need not consider whether the balance of hardships or the possibility of irreparable harm supports injunctive relief.

AFFIRMED.

Notes

1.   At the time of the *RIAA* case, a memory card that could contain an hour's worth of music cost over $50. Thus it appears that the Recording Industry Association of America ("RIAA") was more interested in establishing a legal principle that in stopping current copying. Of course all concerned knew that computer memory costs drop rapidly.

7.   CIRCUMVENTION OF TECHNOLOGICAL MEASURES— §§ 1201—1205

UNIVERSAL CITY STUDIOS, INC. v. REIMERDES

United States District Court, S.D. New York, 2000.
111 F.Supp.2d 294, 2000 WL 1160678.

KAPLAN, DISTRICT JUDGE.

Plaintiffs, eight major United States motion picture studios, distribute many of their copyrighted motion pictures for home use on digital

---

7. We further note that any transmission reproduced indirectly must pass through a computer, as an MP3 file, to reach the Rio. As we explained in part III.B.2, *supra*, computers are exempted from the requirement of reading and transmitting SCMS codes, and MP3 files do not incorporate such codes. Thus, requiring the Rio to implement SCMS because it can indirectly reproduce a transmission of a digital music recording would be, as the district court concluded, "an exercise in futility." *RIAA I*, 29 F.Supp.2d at 632. SCMS would not alter the Rio's ability to reproduce such transmissions, just as it would not alter the Rio's ability to reproduce digital music recordings uploaded to a computer hard drive.

versatile disks ("DVDs"), which contain copies of the motion pictures in digital form. They protect those motion pictures from copying by using an encryption system called CSS. CSS-protected motion pictures on DVDs may be viewed only on players and computer drives equipped with licensed technology that permits the devices to decrypt and play—but not to copy—the films.

Late last year, computer hackers devised a computer program called DeCSS that circumvents the CSS protection system and allows CSS-protected motion pictures to be copied and played on devices that lack the licensed decryption technology. Defendants quickly posted DeCSS on their Internet web site, thus making it readily available to much of the world. Plaintiffs promptly brought this action under the Digital Millennium Copyright Act (the "DMCA") to enjoin defendants from posting DeCSS and to prevent them from electronically "linking" their site to others that post DeCSS. Defendants responded with what they termed "electronic civil disobedience"—increasing their efforts to link their web site to a large number of others that continue to make DeCSS available.

Defendants contend that their actions do not violate the DMCA * * *and, in any case, that the DMCA, as applied to computer programs, or code, violates the First Amendment.This is the Court's decision after trial, and the decision may be summarized in a nutshell.

Defendants argue first that the DMCA should not be construed to reach their conduct, principally because the DMCA, so applied, could prevent those who wish to gain access to technologically protected copyrighted works in order to make fair—that is, non-infringing—use of

them from doing so. They argue that those who would make fair use of technologically protected copyrighted works need means, such as DeCSS, of circumventing access control measures not for piracy, but to make lawful use of those works.

Technological access control measures have the capacity to prevent fair uses of copyrighted works as well as foul. Hence, there is a potential tension between the use of such access control measures and fair use. Defendants are not the first to recognize that possibility. As the DMCA made its way through the legislative process, Congress was preoccupied with precisely this issue. Proponents of strong restrictions on circumvention of access control measures argued that they were essential if copyright holders were to make their works available in digital form because digital works otherwise could be pirated too easily. Opponents contended that strong anti-circumvention measures would extend the copyright monopoly inappropriately and prevent many fair uses of copyrighted material.

Congress struck a balance. The compromise it reached, depending upon future technological and commercial developments, may or may not prove ideal. But the solution it enacted is clear. The potential tension to which defendants point does not absolve them of liability under the statute. There is no serious question that defendants' posting of DeCSS violates the DMCA. * * *

5.   THE TECHNOLOGY HERE AT ISSUE

CSS, or Content Scramble System, is an access control and copy prevention system for DVDs developed by the motion picture companies, including plaintiffs. It is an encryption-based system that requires the use of appropriately configured hardware such as a DVD player or a computer DVD drive to decrypt, unscramble and play back, but not copy, motion pictures on DVDs. The technology necessary to configure DVD players and drives to play CSS-protected DVDs has been licensed to hundreds of manufacturers in the United States and around the world.

DeCSS is a software utility, or computer program, that enables users to break the CSS copy protection system and hence to view DVDs on unlicenced players and make digital copies of DVD movies. The quality of motion pictures decrypted by DeCSS is virtually identical to that of encrypted movies on DVD.

* * *

CSS involves encrypting, according to an encryption algorithm, the digital sound and graphics files on a DVD that together constitute a motion picture. A CSS-protected DVD can be decrypted by an appropriate decryption algorithm that employs a series of keys stored on the DVD and the DVD player. In consequence, only players and drives containing the appropriate keys are able to decrypt DVD files and thereby play movies stored on DVDs.

* * *

In late September 1999, Jon Johansen, a Norwegian subject then fifteen years of age, and two individuals he "met" under pseudonyms over the Internet, reverse engineered a licensed DVD player and discovered the CSS encryption algorithm and keys. They used this information to create DeCSS, a program capable of decrypting or "ripping" encrypted DVDs, thereby allowing playback on non-compliant computers as well as the copying of decrypted files to computer hard drives. Mr. Johansen then posted the executable code on his personal Internet web site and informed members of an Internet mailing list that he had done so. Neither Mr. Johansen nor his collaborators obtained a license from the DVD CCA.

Although Mr. Johansen testified at trial that he created DeCSS in order to make a DVD player that would operate on a computer running the Linux operating system, DeCSS is a Windows executable file; that is, it can be executed only on computers running the Windows operating system. Mr. Johansen explained the fact that he created a Windows rather than a Linux program by asserting that Linux, at the time he created DeCSS, did not support the file system used on DVDs. Hence, it was necessary, he said, to decrypt the DVD on a Windows computer in order subsequently to play the decrypted files on a Linux machine. Assuming that to be true, however, the fact remains that Mr. Johansen created DeCSS in the full knowledge that it could be used on computers running Windows rather than Linux. Moreover, he was well aware that the files, once decrypted, could be copied like any other computer files.

* * *

In the months following its initial appearance on Mr. Johansen's web site, DeCSS has become widely available on the Internet, where hundreds of sites now purport to offer the software for download. A few other applications said to decrypt CSS-encrypted DVDs also have appeared on the Internet.

In November 1999, defendants' web site began to offer DeCSS for download.

* * *

II.   The Digital Millennium Copyright Act

A.   Background and Structure of the Statute

In December 1996, the World Intellectual Property Organization ("WIPO"), held a diplomatic conference in Geneva that led to the adoption of two treaties. Article 11 of the relevant treaty, the WIPO Copyright Treaty, provides in relevant part that contracting states "shall provide adequate legal protection and effective legal remedies against the circumvention of effective technological measures that are used by authors in connection with the exercise of their rights under this Treaty or the Berne Convention and that restrict acts, in respect of their works, which are not authorized by the authors concerned or permitted by law."

The adoption of the WIPO Copyright Treaty spurred continued Congressional attention to the adaptation of the law of copyright to the digital age. Lengthy hearings involving a broad range of interested parties both preceded and succeeded the Copyright Treaty. As noted above, a critical focus of Congressional consideration of the legislation was the conflict between those who opposed anti-circumvention measures as inappropriate extensions of copyright and impediments to fair use and those who supported them as essential to proper protection of copyrighted materials in the digital age. The DMCA was enacted in October 1998 as the culmination of this process.

The DMCA contains two principal anticircumvention provisions. The first, Section 1201(a)(1), governs "[t]he act of circumventing a technological protection measure put in place by a copyright owner to control access to a copyrighted work," an act described by Congress as "the electronic equivalent of breaking into a locked room in order to obtain a copy of a book." The second, Section 1201(a)(2), which is the focus of this case, "supplements the prohibition against the act of circumvention in paragraph (a)(1) with prohibitions on creating and making available certain technologies ... developed or advertised to defeat technological protections against unauthorized access to a work." As defendants are accused here only of posting and linking to other sites posting DeCSS, and not of using it themselves to bypass plaintiffs' access controls, it is principally the second of the anticircumvention provisions that is at issue in this case.

B. Posting of DeCSS

1. Violation of Anti–Trafficking Provision

Section 1201(a)(2) of the Copyright Act, part of the DMCA, provides that:

> "No person shall . . . offer to the public, provide or otherwise traffic in any technology . . . that—
>
> > "(A) is primarily designed or produced for the purpose of circumventing a technological measure that effectively controls access to a work protected under [the Copyright Act];
> >
> > "(B) has only limited commercially significant purpose or use other than to circumvent a technological measure that effectively controls access to a work protected under [the Copyright Act]; or
> >
> > "(C) is marketed by that person or another acting in concert with that person with that person's knowledge for use in circumventing a technological measure that effectively controls access to a work protected under [the Copyright Act]."

In this case, defendants concededly offered and provided and, absent a court order, would continue to offer and provide DeCSS to the public by making it available for download on the 2600.com web site. DeCSS, a computer program, unquestionably is "technology" within the meaning of the statute. "[C]ircumvent a technological measure" is defined to mean descrambling a scrambled work, decrypting an encrypted work, or "otherwise to avoid, bypass, remove, deactivate, or impair a technological measure, without the authority of the copyright owner," so DeCSS clearly is a means of circumventing a technological access control measure. In consequence, if CSS otherwise falls within paragraphs (A), (B) or (C) of Section 1201(a)(2), and if none of the statutory exceptions applies to their actions, defendants have violated and, unless enjoined, will continue to violate the DMCA by posting DeCSS.

a. Section 1201(a)(2)(A)

(1) CSS Effectively Controls Access to Copyrighted Works

* * *

(2) DeCSS Was Designed Primarily to Circumvent CSS

* * *

d. Fair use

Finally, defendants rely on the doctrine of fair use. Stated in its most general terms, the doctrine, now codified in Section 107 of the

Copyright Act, limits the exclusive rights of a copyright holder by permitting others to make limited use of portions of the copyrighted work, for appropriate purposes, free of liability for copyright infringement. For example, it is permissible for one other than the copyright owner to reprint or quote a suitable part of a copyrighted book or article in certain circumstances. The doctrine traditionally has facilitated literary and artistic criticism, teaching and scholarship, and other socially useful forms of expression. It has been viewed by courts as a safety valve that accommodates the exclusive rights conferred by copyright with the freedom of expression guaranteed by the First Amendment.

The use of technological means of controlling access to a copyrighted work may affect the ability to make fair uses of the work. Focusing specifically on the facts of this case, the application of CSS to encrypt a copyrighted motion picture requires the use of a compliant DVD player to view or listen to the movie. Perhaps more significantly, it prevents exact copying of either the video or the audio portion of all or any part of the film. This latter point means that certain uses that might qualify as "fair" for purposes of copyright infringement—for example, the preparation by a film studies professor of a single CD–ROM or tape containing two scenes from different movies in order to illustrate a point in a lecture on cinematography, as opposed to showing relevant parts of two different DVDs—would be difficult or impossible absent circumvention of the CSS encryption. Defendants therefore argue that the DMCA cannot properly be construed to make it difficult or impossible to make any fair use of plaintiffs' copyrighted works and that the statute therefore does not reach their activities, which are simply a means to enable users of DeCSS to make such fair uses.

Defendants have focused on a significant point. Access control measures such as CSS do involve some risk of preventing lawful as well as unlawful uses of copyrighted material. Congress, however, clearly faced up to and dealt with this question in enacting the DMCA.

The Court begins its statutory analysis, as it must, with the language of the statute. Section 107 of the Copyright Act provides in critical part that certain uses of copyrighted works that otherwise would be wrongful are "not ... infringement[s] of copyright." Defendants, however, are not here sued for copyright infringement. They are sued for offering and providing technology designed to circumvent technological measures that control access to copyrighted works and otherwise violating Section 1201(a)(2) of the Act. If Congress had meant the fair use defense to apply to such actions, it would have said so. Indeed, as the legislative history demonstrates, the decision not to make fair use a defense to a claim under Section 1201(a) was quite deliberate.

Congress was well aware during the consideration of the DMCA of the traditional role of the fair use defense in accommodating the exclusive rights of copyright owners with the legitimate interests of noninfringing users of portions of copyrighted works. It recognized the contention, voiced by a range of constituencies concerned with the legislation, that technological controls on access to copyrighted works might erode fair use by preventing access even for uses that would be deemed "fair" if only access might be gained. And it struck a balance among the competing interests.

The first element of the balance was the careful limitation of Section 1201(a)(1)'s prohibition of the act of circumvention to the act itself so as not to "apply to subsequent actions of a person once he or she has obtained authorized access to a copy of a [copyrighted] work.... " [FN163] By doing so, it left "the traditional defenses to copyright infringement, including fair use, ... fully applicable" provided "the access is authorized."

Second, Congress delayed the effective date of Section 1201(a)(1)'s prohibition of the act of circumvention for two years pending further investigation about how best to reconcile Section 1201(a)(1) with fair use concerns. Following that investigation, which is being carried out in the form of a rule-making by the Register of Copyright, the prohibition will not apply to users of particular classes of copyrighted works who demonstrate that their ability to make noninfringing uses of those classes of works would be affected adversely by Section 1201(a)(1).

Third, it created a series of exceptions to aspects of Section 1201(a) for certain uses that Congress thought "fair," including reverse engineering, security testing, good faith encryption research, and certain uses by nonprofit libraries, archives and educational institutions.

Defendants claim also that the possibility that DeCSS might be used for the purpose of gaining access to copyrighted works in order to make fair use of those works saves them under *Sony Corp. v. Universal City Studios, Inc.* But they are mistaken. Sony does not apply to the activities with which defendants here are charged. Even if it did, it would not govern here. *Sony* involved a construction of the Copyright Act that has been overruled by the later enactment of the DMCA to the extent of any inconsistency between *Sony* and the new statute.

Sony was a suit for contributory infringement brought against manufacturers of video cassette recorders on the theory that the manufacturers were contributing to infringing home taping of copyrighted television broadcasts. The Supreme Court held that the manufacturers were not liable in view of the substantial numbers of copyright holders who either had authorized or did not object to such taping by viewers. But *Sony* has no application here.

When *Sony* was decided, the only question was whether the manufacturers could be held liable for infringement by those who purchased equipment from them in circumstances in which there were many noninfringing uses for their equipment. But that is not the question now before this Court. The question here is whether the possibility of noninfringing fair use by someone who gains access to a protected copyrighted work through a circumvention technology distributed by the defendants saves the defendants from liability under Section 1201. But nothing in Section 1201 so suggests. By prohibiting the provision of circumvention technology, the DMCA fundamentally altered the landscape. A given device or piece of technology might have "a substantial noninfringing use, and hence be immune from attack under Sony's construction of the Copyright Act—but nonetheless still be subject to suppression under Section 1201." Indeed, Congress explicitly noted that Section 1201 does not incorporate *Sony*.

The policy concerns raised by defendants were considered by Congress. Having considered them, Congress crafted a statute that, so far as the applicability of the fair use defense to Section 1201(a) claims is concerned, is crystal clear. In such circumstances, courts may not undo what Congress so plainly has done by "construing" the words of a statute to accomplish a result that Congress rejected. The fact that Congress elected to leave technologically unsophisticated persons who wish to make fair use of encrypted copyrighted works without the technical means of doing so is a matter for Congress unless Congress' decision contravenes the Constitution, a matter to which the Court turns below. Defendants' statutory fair use argument therefore is entirely without merit.

* * *

Each side is entitled to its views. In our society, however, clashes of competing interests like this are resolved by Congress. For now, at least, Congress has resolved this clash in the DMCA and in plaintiffs' favor. Given the peculiar characteristics of computer programs for circumventing encryption and other access control measures, the DMCA as applied to posting and linking here does not contravene the First Amendment. Accordingly, plaintiffs are entitled to appropriate injunctive and declaratory relief.

SO ORDERED.

Notes

1. In *Sony Corp. of America v. Universal City Studios, Inc.*, 464 U.S. 417, 104 S.Ct. 774, 78 L.Ed.2d 574 (1984), the Supreme Court held that consumers had a fair use right to record copyrighted television broadcasts to view at a later time ("time-shifting") and that manufacturers of VCR's were not contributory infringers since there was a substantial non-infringing use for the VCR's, namely "time-shifting." In view of the foregoing, was the court in the DeCSS case too quick to dismiss the fair use defense? Or has Universal City Studios, which was the loser in the *Sony* case really won in Congress what it lost in the Supreme Court?

2. In the *Sony* case cited in the previous note, Universal City Studios sought to restrict sales of VCR's in order to protect Universal's movie business. After Universal lost the Sony case and VCR's became common household items, the major movie studios found that sales of motion pictures on videocassettes at affordable prices created a huge and very profitable new market. Given the ever-present willingness of someone in cyberspace to break and publish the techniques of commercial encryption systems, would

the entertainment industry be better off it it responded by mass-marketing its products at very low prices over the Internet? This lower price would make copying substantially less attractive, and could lead to increased profits given the elasticity of demand for entertainment products, just as was the case with videocassettes.

3. Libraries holding printed books can allow an unlimited number of readers (one at a time, of course) to read these publications. Publishers would like to charge libraries higher prices than individual book buyers, the way airlines charge higher prices to business travelers who buy tickets on short notice and do not stay over Saturday nights. With printed books this is impossible. However, if publications were sold not on paper, but on CD–ROM's or DVD's, they could be encased in encrypted software that would limit the number of times the publications could be read. This would not inconvenience ordinary buyers, who rarely read a book more than once or twice. But libraries would have to pay a renewal fee for a reactivation code or buy a new copy when the number of permitted readings were exhausted.

4. On October 27, 2000, the Copyright Office issued a very restricted list of classes of copyrighted works exempted from Section 1201(a)(1): "(1) Compilations consisting of lists of websites blocked by filtering software applications; and (2) Literary works, including computer programs and databases, protected by access control mechanisms that fail to permit access because of malfunction, damage or obsoleteness." 65 Fed. Reg. 64555.

5. A preliminary injunction based on § 1201 was granted in the case *RealNetworks, Inc. v. Streambox, Inc.*, 2000 WL 127311 (W.D.Wash.2000). RealNetworks, with permission of copyright owners, delivered "streaming" audio and video over the Internet. At the insistence of the copyright owners, RealNetworks used cryptographic techniques to ensure that Internet users could not record the audio and video streams. Streambox broke the codes and distributed software that allowed ordinary Internet users to record the audio and video transmitted by Real Networks.

E.   LIMITATIONS ON THE EXCLUSIVE RIGHTS

1. FAIR USE

COPYRIGHT ACT OF 1976—§ 107

§ 107. Fair Use

Notwithstanding the provisions of sections 106 and 106A, the fair use of a copyrighted work, including such use by reproduction in copies or phonorecords or by any other means specified by that section, for purposes such as criticism, comment, news reporting, teaching (including multiple copies for classroom use), scholarship, or research, is not an infringement of copyright. In determining whether the use made of a work in any particular case is a fair use the factors to be considered shall include—

    (1) the purpose and character of the use, including whether such use is of a commercial nature or is for nonprofit educational purposes;

(2) the nature of the copyrighted work;

(3) the amount and substantiality of the portion used in relation to the copyrighted work as a whole; and

(4) the effect of the use upon the potential market for or value of the copyrighted work.

The fact that a work is unpublished shall not itself bar a finding of fair use if such finding is made upon consideration of all the above factors.

SEGA ENTERPRISES LTD. v. ACCOLADE, INC.

United States Court of Appeals, Ninth Circuit, 1992.
977 F.2d 1510.

REINHARDT, CIRCUIT JUDGE.

This case presents several difficult questions of first impression involving our copyright and trademark laws. We are asked to determine, first, whether the Copyright Act permits persons who are neither copyright holders nor licensees to disassemble a copyrighted computer program in order to gain an understanding of the unprotected functional elements of the program. In light of the public policies underlying the Act, we conclude that, when the person seeking the understanding has a legitimate reason for doing so and when no other means of access to the unprotected elements exists, such disassembly is as a matter of law a fair use of the copyrighted work. * * * Accordingly, we reverse the district court's grant of a preliminary injunction in favor of plaintiff-appellee Sega Enterprises, Ltd. on its claims of copyright and trademark infringement. We decline, however, to order that an injunction *pendente lite* issue precluding Sega from continuing to use its security system, even though such use may result in a certain amount of false labeling. We prefer to leave the decision on that question to the district court initially.

I. BACKGROUND

Plaintiff-appellee Sega Enterprises, Ltd. ("Sega"), a Japanese corporation, and its subsidiary, Sega of America, develop and market video entertainment systems, including the "Genesis" console (distributed in Asia under the name "Mega–Drive") and video game cartridges. Defendant-appellant Accolade, Inc., is an independent developer, manufacturer, and marketer of computer entertainment software, including game cartridges that are compatible with the Genesis console, as well as game cartridges that are compatible with other computer systems.

Sega licenses its copyrighted computer code and its "SEGA" trademark to a number of independent developers of computer game software. Those licensees develop and sell Genesis-compatible video games in competition with Sega. Accolade is not and never has been a licensee of Sega. Prior to rendering its own games compatible with the Genesis console, Accolade explored the possibility of entering into a licensing agreement with Sega, but abandoned the effort because the agreement would have required that Sega be the exclusive manufacturer of all games produced by Accolade.

Accolade used a two-step process to render its video games compatible with the Genesis console. First, it "reverse engineered" Sega's video game programs in order to discover the requirements for compatibility with the Genesis console. As part of the reverse engineering process, Accolade transformed the machine-readable object code contained in commercially available copies of Sega's game cartridges into human-readable source code using a process called "disassembly" or "decompilation".[2] Accolade purchased a Genesis console and three Sega game cartridges, wired a decompiler into the console circuitry, and generated printouts of the resulting source code. Accolade engineers studied and annotated the printouts in order to identify areas of commonality among the three game programs. They then loaded the disassembled code back into a computer, and experimented to discover the interface specifications for the Genesis console by modifying the programs and studying the results. At the end of the reverse engineering process, Accolade created a development manual that incorporated the information it had discovered about the requirements for a Genesis-compatible game. According to the Accolade employees who created the manual, the manual contained only functional descriptions of the interface requirements and did not include any of Sega's code.

In the second stage, Accolade created its own games for the Genesis. According to Accolade, at this stage it did not copy Sega's programs, but relied only on the information concerning interface specifications for the Genesis that was contained in its development manual. Accolade maintains that with the exception of the interface specifications, none of the code in its own games is derived in any way from its examination of Sega's code. In 1990, Accolade released "Ishido", a game which it had originally developed and released for use with the Macintosh and IBM personal computer systems, for use with the Genesis console.

Even before Accolade began to reverse engineer Sega's games, Sega had grown concerned about the rise of software and hardware piracy in Taiwan and other Southeast Asian countries to which it exported its products. Taiwan is not a signatory to the Berne Convention and does not recognize foreign copyrights. Taiwan does allow prosecution of trademark counterfeiters. However, the counterfeiters had discovered how to modify Sega's game programs to blank out the screen display of

---

2. Computer programs are written in specialized alphanumeric languages, or "source code". In order to operate a computer, source code must be translated into computer readable form, or "object code". Object code uses only two symbols, 0 and 1, in combinations which represent the alphanumeric characters of the source code. A program written in source code is translated into object code using a computer program called an "assembler" or "compiler", and then imprinted onto a silicon chip for commercial distribution. Devices called "dissassemblers" or "decompilers" can reverse this process by "reading" the electronic signals for "0" and "1" that are produced while the program is being run, storing the resulting object code in computer memory, and translating the object code into source code. Both assembly and disassembly devices are commercially available, and both types of devices are widely used within the software industry.

Sega's trademark before repackaging and reselling the games as their own. Accordingly, Sega began to explore methods of protecting its trademark rights in the Genesis and Genesis-compatible games. While the development of its own trademark security system (TMSS) was pending, Sega licensed a patented TMSS for use with the Genesis home entertainment system.

The most recent version of the Genesis console, the "Genesis III", incorporates the licensed TMSS. When a game cartridge is inserted, the microprocessor contained in the Genesis III searches the game program for four bytes of data consisting of the letters "S–E–G–A" (the "TMSS initialization code"). If the Genesis III finds the TMSS initialization code in the right location, the game is rendered compatible and will operate on the console. In such case, the TMSS initialization code then prompts a visual display for approximately three seconds which reads "PRODUCED BY OR UNDER LICENSE FROM SEGA ENTERPRISES LTD" (the "Sega Message"). All of Sega's game cartridges, including those disassembled by Accolade, contain the TMSS initialization code.

Accolade learned of the impending release of the Genesis III in the United States in January, 1991, when the Genesis III was displayed at a consumer electronics show. When a demonstration at the consumer electronics show revealed that Accolade's "Ishido" game cartridges would not operate on the Genesis III, Accolade returned to the drawing board. During the reverse engineering process, Accolade engineers had discovered a small segment of code—the TMSS initialization code—that was included in the "power-up" sequence of every Sega game, but that had no identifiable function. The games would operate on the original Genesis console even if the code segment was removed. Mike Lorenzen, the Accolade engineer with primary responsibility for reverse engineering the interface procedures for the Genesis console, sent a memo regarding the code segment to Alan Miller, his supervisor and the current president of Accolade, in which he noted that "it is possible that some future Sega peripheral device might require it for proper initialization."

In the second round of reverse engineering, Accolade engineers focused on the code segment identified by Lorenzen. After further study, Accolade added the code to its development manual in the form of a standard header file to be used in all games. The file contains approximately twenty to twenty-five bytes of data. Each of Accolade's games contains a total of 500,000 to 1,500,000 bytes. According to Accolade employees, the header file is the only portion of Sega's code that Accolade copied into its own game programs.

In 1991, Accolade released five more games for use with the Genesis III, "Star Control", "Hardball!", "Onslaught", "Turrican", and "Mike Ditka Power Football." With the exception of "Mike Ditka Power Football", all of those games, like "Ishido", had originally been developed and marketed for use with other hardware systems. All contained the standard header file that included the TMSS initialization code.

According to Accolade, it did not learn until after the Genesis III was released on the market in September, 1991, that in addition to enabling its software to operate on the Genesis III, the header file caused the display of the Sega Message. All of the games except "Onslaught" operate on the Genesis III console; apparently, the programmer who translated "Onslaught" for use with the Genesis system did not place the TMSS initialization code at the correct location in the program.

All of Accolade's Genesis-compatible games are packaged in a similar fashion. The front of the box displays Accolade's "Ballistic" trademark and states "for use with Sega Genesis and Mega Drive Systems." The back of the box contains the following statement: "Sega and Genesis are registered trademarks of Sega Enterprises, Ltd. Game 1991 Accolade, Inc. All rights reserved. Ballistic is a trademark of Accolade, Inc. Accolade, Inc. is not associated with Sega Enterprises, Ltd. All product and corporate names are trademarks and registered trademarks of their respective owners."

* * *

III. Copyright Issues

Accolade raises four arguments in support of its position that disassembly of the object code in a copyrighted computer program does not constitute copyright infringement. First, it maintains that intermediate copying does not infringe the exclusive rights granted to copyright owners in section 106 of the Copyright Act unless the end product of the copying is substantially similar to the copyrighted work. Second, it argues that disassembly of object code in order to gain an understanding of the ideas and functional concepts embodied in the code is lawful under section 102(b) of the Act, which exempts ideas and functional concepts from copyright protection. Third, it suggests that disassembly is authorized by section 117 of the Act, which entitles the lawful owner of a copy of a computer program to load the program into a computer. Finally, Accolade contends that disassembly of object code in order to gain an understanding of the ideas and functional concepts embodied in the code is a fair use that is privileged by section 107 of the Act.

Neither the language of the Act nor the law of this circuit supports Accolade's first three arguments. Accolade's fourth argument, however, has merit. Although the question is fairly debatable, we conclude based on the policies underlying the Copyright Act that disassembly of copyrighted object code is, as a matter of law, a fair use of the copyrighted work if such disassembly provides the only means of access to those elements of the code that are not protected by copyright and the copier has a legitimate reason for seeking such access. Accordingly, we hold that Sega has failed to demonstrate a likelihood of success on the merits of its copyright claim. Because on the record before us the hardships do not tip sharply (or at all) in Sega's favor, the preliminary injunction issued in its favor must be dissolved, at least with respect to that claim.

* * *

D.   Fair Use

Accolade contends, finally, that its disassembly of copyrighted object code as a necessary step in its examination of the unprotected ideas and functional concepts embodied in the code is a fair use that is privileged by section 107 of the Act. Because, in the case before us, disassembly is the only means of gaining access to those unprotected aspects of the program, and because Accolade has a legitimate interest in gaining such access (in order to determine how to make its cartridges compatible with the Genesis console), we agree with Accolade. Where there is good reason for studying or examining the unprotected aspects of a copyrighted computer program, disassembly for purposes of such study or examination constitutes a fair use.

1.

As a preliminary matter, we reject Sega's contention that the assertion of a fair use defense in connection with the disassembly of object code is precluded by statute. First, Sega argues that not only does section 117 of the Act *not* authorize disassembly of object code, but it also constitutes a legislative determination that any copying of a computer program *other* than that authorized by section 117 cannot be considered a fair use of that program under section 107. That argument verges on the frivolous. Each of the exclusive rights created by section 106 of the Copyright Act is expressly made subject to all of the limitations contained in sections 107 through 120. Nothing in the language or the legislative history of section 117, or in the CONTU Report, suggests that section 117 was intended to preclude the assertion of a fair use defense with respect to uses of computer programs that are not covered by section 117, nor has section 107 been amended to exclude computer programs from its ambit.

Moreover, sections 107 and 117 serve entirely different functions. Section 117 defines a narrow category of copying that is lawful *per se.* Section 107, by contrast, establishes a *defense* to an otherwise valid claim of copyright infringement. It provides that particular instances of copying that otherwise would be actionable are lawful, and sets forth the factors to be considered in determining whether the defense applies. The fact that Congress has not chosen to provide a *per se* exemption to section 106 for disassembly does not mean that particular instances of disassembly may not constitute fair use.

Second, Sega maintains that the language and legislative history of section 906 of the Semiconductor Chip Protection Act of 1984 (SCPA) establish that Congress did not intend that disassembly of object code be considered a fair use. Section 906 of the SCPA authorizes the copying of the "mask work" on a silicon chip in the course of reverse engineering the chip. The mask work in a standard ROM chip, such as those used in the Genesis console and in Genesis-compatible cartridges, is a physical representation of the computer program that is embedded in the chip. The zeros and ones of binary object code are represented in the circuitry of the mask work by open and closed switches. Sega contends that

Congress's express authorization of copying in the particular circumstances set forth in section 906 constitutes a determination that other forms of copying of computer programs are prohibited.

The legislative history of the SCPA reveals, however, that Congress passed a separate statute to protect semiconductor chip products because it believed that semiconductor chips were intrinsically utilitarian articles that were not protected under the Copyright Act. Accordingly, rather than amend the Copyright Act to extend traditional copyright protection to chips, it enacted "a sui generis form of protection, apart from and independent of the copyright laws." H.R.Rep. No. 781, 98th Cong., 2d sess. 10, *reprinted in*1984 U.S.C.C.A.N. at 5759. Because Congress did not believe that semiconductor chips were eligible for copyright protection in the first instance, the fact that it included an exception for reverse engineering of mask work in the SCPA says nothing about its intent with respect to the lawfulness of disassembly of computer programs under the Copyright Act. Nor is the fact that Congress did not contemporaneously amend the Copyright Act to permit disassembly significant, since it was focusing on the protection to be afforded to semiconductor chips. Here we are dealing not with an alleged violation of the SCPA, but with the copying of a computer program, which is governed by the Copyright Act. Moreover, Congress expressly stated that it did not intend to "limit, enlarge or otherwise affect the scope, duration, ownership or subsistence of copyright protection ... in computer programs, data bases, or any other copyrightable works embodied in semiconductor chip products." *Id.* at 28, 1984 U.S.C.C.A.N. at 5777. Accordingly, Sega's second statutory argument also fails. We proceed to consider Accolade's fair use defense.

2.

Section 107 lists the factors to be considered in determining whether a particular use is a fair one. Those factors include:

(1) the purpose and character of the use, including whether such use is of a commercial nature or is for nonprofit educational purposes;

(2) the nature of the copyrighted work;

(3) the amount and substantiality of the portion used in relation to the copyrighted work as a whole; and

(4) the effect of the use upon the potential market for or value of the copyrighted work.

The statutory factors are not exclusive. Rather, the doctrine of fair use is in essence "an equitable rule of reason." *Harper & Row, Publishers, Inc. v. Nation Enterprises*, 471U.S. 539, 560, 105 S.Ct. 2218, 2230, 85 L.Ed.2d 588 (1985). Fair use is a mixed question of law and fact. "Where the district court has found facts sufficient to evaluate each of the statutory factors," an appellate court may resolve the fair use question as a matter of law.

In determining that Accolade's disassembly of Sega's object code did not constitute a fair use, the district court treated the first and fourth statutory factors as dispositive, and ignored the second factor entirely. Given the nature and characteristics of Accolade's direct use of the copied works, the ultimate use to which Accolade put the functional information it obtained, and the nature of the market for home video entertainment systems, we conclude that neither the first nor the fourth factor weighs in Sega's favor. In fact, we conclude that both factors support Accolade's fair use defense, as does the second factor, a factor which is important to the resolution of cases such as the one before us.

(A)

With respect to the first statutory factor, we observe initially that the fact that copying is for a commercial purpose weighs against a finding of fair use. However, the presumption of unfairness that arises in such cases can be rebutted by the characteristics of a particular commercial use. Further "[t]he commercial nature of a use is a matter of degree, not an absolute...." *Maxtone-Graham v. Burtchaell*, 803 F.2d 1253, 1262 (2d Cir.1986), *cert. denied* 481 U.S. 1059, 107 S.Ct. 2201, 95 L.Ed.2d 856 (1987).

Sega argues that because Accolade copied its object code in order to produce a competing product, the *Harper & Row* presumption applies and precludes a finding of fair use. That analysis is far too simple and ignores a number of important considerations. We must consider other aspects of "the purpose and character of the use" as well. As we have noted, the use at issue was an intermediate one only and thus any commercial "exploitation" was indirect or derivative.

The declarations of Accolade's employees indicate, and the district court found, that Accolade copied Sega's software solely in order to discover the functional requirements for compatibility with the Genesis console—aspects of Sega's programs that are not protected by copyright. With respect to the video game programs contained in Accolade's game cartridges, there is no evidence in the record that Accolade sought to avoid performing its own creative work. Indeed, most of the games that Accolade released for use with the Genesis console were originally developed for other hardware systems. Moreover, with respect to the interface procedures for the Genesis console, Accolade did not seek to avoid paying a customarily charged fee for use of those procedures, nor did it simply copy Sega's code; rather, it wrote its own procedures based on what it had learned through disassembly. Taken together, these facts indicate that although Accolade's ultimate purpose was the release of Genesis-compatible games for sale, its direct purpose in copying Sega's code, and thus its direct use of the copyrighted material, was simply to study the functional requirements for Genesis compatibility so that it could modify existing games and make them usable with the Genesis console. Moreover, as we discuss below, no other method of studying those requirements was available to Accolade. On these facts, we conclude that Accolade copied Sega's code for a legitimate, essentially nonexploitative purpose, and that the commercial aspect of its use can best be described as of minimal significance.

We further note that we are free to consider the public benefit resulting from a particular use notwithstanding the fact that the alleged infringer may gain commercially. Public benefit need not be direct or tangible, but may arise because the challenged use serves a public interest. In the case before us, Accolade's identification of the functional requirements for Genesis compatibility has led to an increase in the number of independently designed video game programs offered for use with the Genesis console. It is precisely this growth in creative expression, based on the dissemination of other creative works and the unprotected ideas contained in those works, that the Copyright Act was intended to promote. The fact that Genesis-compatible video games are not scholarly works, but works offered for sale on the market, does not alter our judgment in this regard. We conclude that given the purpose and character of Accolade's use of Sega's video game programs, the presumption of unfairness has been overcome and the first statutory factor weighs in favor of Accolade.

(B)

As applied, the fourth statutory factor, effect on the potential market for the copyrighted work, bears a close relationship to the "purpose and character" inquiry in that it, too, accommodates the distinction between the copying of works in order to make independent creative expression possible and the simple exploitation of another's creative efforts. We must, of course, inquire whether, "if [the challenged use] should become widespread, it would adversely affect the potential market for the copyrighted work," *Sony Corp. v. Universal City Studios*, 464 U.S. 417, 451, 104 S.Ct. 774, 793, 78 L.Ed.2d 574 (1984), by diminishing potential sales, interfering with marketability, or usurping the market. If the copying resulted in the latter effect, all other considerations might be irrelevant. The *Harper & Row* Court found a use that effectively usurped the market for the copyrighted work by supplanting that work to be dispositive. However, the same consequences do not and could not attach to a use which simply enables the copier to enter the market for works of the same type as the copied work.

Unlike the defendant in *Harper & Row*, which printed excerpts from President Ford's memoirs verbatim with the stated purpose of "scooping" a *Time* magazine review of the book, Accolade did not attempt to "scoop" Sega's release of any particular game or games, but sought only to become a legitimate competitor in the field of Genesis-compatible video games. Within that market, it is the characteristics of the game program as experienced by the user that determine the program's commercial success. As we have noted, there is nothing in the record that suggests that Accolade copied any of those elements.

By facilitating the entry of a new competitor, the first lawful one that is not a Sega licensee, Accolade's disassembly of Sega's software undoubtedly "affected" the market for Genesis-compatible games in an indirect fashion. We note, however, that while no consumer except the most avid devotee of President Ford's regime might be expected to buy more than one version of the President's memoirs, video game users typically purchase more than one game. There is no basis for assuming that Accolade's "Ishido" has significantly affected the market for Sega's "Altered Beast", since a consumer might easily purchase both; nor does it seem unlikely that a consumer particularly interested in sports might purchase both Accolade's "Mike Ditka Power Football" and Sega's "Joe Montana Football", particularly if the games are, as Accolade contends, not substantially similar. In any event, an attempt to monopolize the market by making it impossible for others to compete runs counter to the statutory purpose of promoting creative expression and cannot constitute a strong equitable basis for resisting the invocation of the fair use doctrine. Thus, we conclude that the fourth statutory factor weighs in Accolade's, not Sega's, favor, notwithstanding the minor economic loss Sega may suffer.

(c)

The second statutory factor, the nature of the copyrighted work, reflects the fact that not all copyrighted works are entitled to the same level of protection. The protection established by the Copyright Act for original works of authorship does not extend to the ideas underlying a work or to the functional or factual aspects of the work. To the extent that a work is functional or factual, it may be copied, *Baker v. Selden*, 101 U.S. 99 (1879), as may those expressive elements of the work that "must necessarily be used as incident to" expression of the underlying ideas, functional concepts, or facts, *id.* at 104. Works of fiction receive greater protection than works that have strong factual elements, such as historical or biographical works, *Maxtone-Graham*, 803 F.2d at 1263, or works that have strong functional elements, such as accounting textbooks, *Baker*, 101 U.S. at 104. Works that are merely compilations of fact are copyrightable, but the copyright in such a work is "thin."

Computer programs pose unique problems for the application of the "idea/expression distinction" that determines the extent of copyright protection. To the extent that there are many possible ways of accomplishing a given task or fulfilling a particular market demand, the programmer's choice of program structure and design may be highly creative and idiosyncratic. However, computer programs are, in essence, utilitarian articles—articles that accomplish tasks. As such, they contain many logical, structural, and visual display elements that are dictated by the function to be performed, by considerations of efficiency, or by external factors such as compatibility requirements and industry demands. In some circumstances, even the exact set of commands used by the programmer is deemed functional rather than creative for purposes of copyright. "[W]hen specific instructions, even though previously copyrighted, are the only and essential means of accomplishing a given task, their later use by another will not amount to infringement." CONTU

Report at 20; see *Computer Assoc. Int'l, Inc. v. Altai, Inc.*, 23 U.S.P.Q.2d 1241, 1254 (2d Cir.1992) ("*CAI*").

Because of the hybrid nature of computer programs, there is no settled standard for identifying what is protected expression and what is unprotected idea in a case involving the alleged infringement of a copyright in computer software. We are in wholehearted agreement with the Second Circuit's recent observation that "[t]hus far, many of the decisions in this area reflect the courts' attempt to fit the proverbial square peg in a round hole." *CAI*, 23 U.S.P.Q.2d at 1257. In 1986, the Third Circuit attempted to resolve the dilemma by suggesting that the idea or function of a computer program is the idea of the program as a whole, and "everything that is not necessary to that purpose or function [is] part of the expression of that idea." *Whelan Assoc., Inc. v. Jaslow Dental Laboratory, Inc.*, 797 F.2d 1222, 1236 (3d Cir.1986) (emphasis omitted). The *Whelan* rule, however, has been widely—and soundly— criticized as simplistic and overbroad. *See CAI*, 23 U.S.P.Q.2d at 1252 (citing cases, treatises, and articles). In reality, "a computer program's ultimate function or purpose is the composite result of interacting subroutines. Since each subroutine is itself a program, and thus, may be said to have its own 'idea,' *Whelan's* general formulation ... is descriptively inadequate." *Id.* For example, the computer program at issue in the case before us, a video game program, contains at least two such subroutines—the subroutine that allows the user to interact with the video game and the subroutine that allows the game cartridge to interact with the console. Under a test that breaks down a computer program into its component subroutines and sub-subroutines and then identifies the idea or core functional element of each, such as the test recently adopted by the Second Circuit in *CAI*, many aspects of the program are not protected by copyright. In our view, in light of the essentially utilitarian nature of computer programs, the Second Circuit's approach is an appropriate one.

Sega argues that even if many elements of its video game programs are properly characterized as functional and therefore not protected by copyright, Accolade copied protected expression. Sega is correct. The record makes clear that disassembly is wholesale copying. Because computer programs are also unique among copyrighted works in the form in which they are distributed for public use, however, Sega's observation does not bring us much closer to a resolution of the dispute.

> The unprotected aspects of most functional works are readily accessible to the human eye. The systems described in accounting textbooks or the basic structural concepts embodied in architectural plans, to give two examples, can be easily copied without also copying any of the protected, expressive aspects of the original works. Computer programs, however, are typically distributed for public use in object code form, embedded in a silicon chip or on a floppy disk. For that reason, humans often cannot gain access to the unprotected ideas and functional concepts contained in object code without disassembling that code—i.e., making copies.

Sega argues that the record does not establish that disassembly of its object code is the only available method for gaining access to the interface specifications for the Genesis console, and the district court agreed. An independent examination of the record reveals that Sega misstates its contents, and demonstrates that the district court committed clear error in this respect.

First, the record clearly establishes that humans cannot *read* object code. Sega makes much of Mike Lorenzen's statement that a reverse engineer can work directly from the zeros and ones of object code but "[i]t's not as fun." In full, Lorenzen's statements establish only that the use of an *electronic* decompiler is not absolutely necessary. Trained programmers can disassemble object code by hand. Because even a trained programmer cannot possibly remember the millions of zeros and ones that make up a program, however, he must make a written or computerized copy of the disassembled code in order to keep track of his work. The relevant fact for purposes of Sega's copyright infringement claim and Accolade's fair use defense is that *translation* of a program from object code into source code cannot be accomplished without making copies of the code.

Second, the record provides no support for a conclusion that a viable alternative to disassembly exists. The district court found that Accolade could have avoided a copyright infringement claim by "peeling" the chips contained in Sega's games or in the Genesis console, as authorized by section 906 of the SCPA. Even Sega's amici agree that this finding was clear error. The declaration of Dr. Harry Tredennick, an expert witness for Accolade, establishes that chip peeling yields only a physical diagram of the *object code* embedded in a ROM chip. It does not obviate the need to translate object code into source code.

The district court also suggested that Accolade could have avoided a copyright infringement suit by programming in a "clean room". That finding too is clearly erroneous. A "clean room" is a procedure used in the computer industry in order to prevent direct copying of a competitor's code during the development of a competing product. Programmers in clean rooms are provided only with the functional specifications for the desired program. As Dr. Tredennick explained, the use of a clean room would not have avoided the need for disassembly because disassembly was necessary in order to discover the functional specifications for a Genesis-compatible game.

In summary, the record clearly establishes that disassembly of the object code in Sega's video game cartridges was necessary in order to understand the functional requirements for Genesis compatibility. The interface procedures for the Genesis console are distributed for public use only in object code form, and are not visible to the user during operation of the video game program. Because object code cannot be read by humans, it must be disassembled, either by hand or by machine. Disassembly of object code necessarily entails copying. Those facts dictate our analysis of the second statutory fair use factor. If disassembly of copyrighted object code is *per se* an unfair use, the owner of the copyright gains a *de facto* monopoly over the functional aspects of his work—aspects that were expressly denied copyright protection by Congress. In order to enjoy a lawful monopoly over the idea or functional principle underlying a work, the creator of the work must satisfy the more stringent standards imposed by the patent laws. Sega does not hold a patent on the Genesis console.

Because Sega's video game programs contain unprotected aspects that cannot be examined without copying, we afford them a lower degree of protection than more traditional literary works. In light of all the considerations discussed above, we conclude that the second statutory factor also weighs in favor of Accolade.

(D)

As to the third statutory factor, Accolade disassembled entire programs written by Sega. Accordingly, the third factor weighs against Accolade. The fact that an entire work was copied does not, however, preclude a finding a fair use. In fact, where the ultimate (as opposed to direct) use is as limited as it was here, the factor is of very little weight.

(E)

In summary, careful analysis of the purpose and characteristics of Accolade's use of Sega's video game programs, the nature of the computer programs involved, and the nature of the market for video game cartridges yields the conclusion that the first, second, and fourth statutory fair use factors weigh in favor of Accolade, while only the third weighs in favor of Sega, and even then only slightly. Accordingly, Accolade clearly has by far the better case on the fair use issue.

We are not unaware of the fact that to those used to considering copyright issues in more traditional contexts, our result may seem incongruous at first blush. To oversimplify, the record establishes that Accolade, a commercial competitor of Sega, engaged in wholesale copying of Sega's copyrighted code as a preliminary step in the development of a competing product. However, the key to this case is that we are dealing with computer software, a relatively unexplored area in the world of copyright law. We must avoid the temptation of trying to force "the proverbial square peg in[to] a round hole." *CAI*, 23 U.S.P.Q.2d at 1257.

In determining whether a challenged use of copyrighted material is fair, a court must keep in mind the public policy underlying the Copyright Act. " 'The immediate effect of our copyright law is to secure a fair return for an "author's" creative labor. But the ultimate aim is, by this incentive, to stimulate artistic creativity for the general public good.' " *Sony Corp.*, 464 U.S. at 432, 104 S.Ct. at 783 (quoting *Twentieth Century Music Corp. v. Aiken*, 422 U.S. 151, 156, 95 S.Ct. 2040, 2044, 45 L.Ed.2d 84 (197)). When technological change has rendered an aspect or application of the Copyright Act ambiguous, " 'the Copyright Act must be construed in light of this basic purpose.' " *Id.* As discussed above, the fact that computer programs are distributed for public use in object code form often precludes public access to the ideas and functional concepts contained in those programs, and thus confers on the copyright owner a *de facto* monopoly over those ideas and functional concepts. That result defeats the fundamental purpose of the Copyright Act—to encourage the production of original works by protecting the expressive elements of those works while leaving the ideas, facts, and functional concepts in the public domain for others to build on.

Sega argues that the considerable time, effort, and money that went into development of the Genesis and Genesis-compatible video games militate against a finding of fair use. Borrowing from antitrust principles, Sega attempts to label Accolade a "free rider" on its product development efforts. In *Feist Publications, Inc.* v. *Rural Tel. Serv. Co.*, 499 U.S. 340, 349–359, 111 S.Ct. 1282, 1290–95, 113 L.Ed.2d 358 (1991), however, the Court unequivocally rejected the "sweat of the brow" rationale for copyright protection. Under the Copyright Act, if a work is largely functional, it receives only weak protection. "This result is neither unfair nor unfortunate. It is the means by which copyright advances the progress of science and art." *Id.* at 499 U.S. at 350, 111 S.Ct. at 1290. Here, while the work may not be largely functional, it incorporates functional elements which do not merit protection. The equitable considerations involved weigh on the side of public access. Accordingly, we reject Sega's argument.

(F)

We conclude that where disassembly is the only way to gain access to the ideas and functional elements embodied in a copyrighted computer program and where there is a legitimate reason for seeking such access, disassembly is a fair use of the copyrighted work, as a matter of law. Our conclusion does not, of course, insulate Accolade from a claim of copyright infringement with respect to its finished products. Sega has reserved the right to raise such a claim, and it may do so on remand.

* * *

AFFIRMED IN PART; REVERSED IN PART; AND REMANDED.

Note

Sony Computer Entertainment, Inc. v. *Connectix Corp.*, 203 F.3d 596 (9th Cir.2000), extended the holding of *Sega*. Defendant Connectix, seeking to learn how to inter-operate with Sony's video game software, repeatedly disassembled the software and also adapted the software to operate in a different environment where its features could be more closely observed. In ruling for the defendant, the Ninth Circuit took a broad reading *Sega*: "The 'necessity' we addressed in *Sega* was the necessity of the method, i.e., disassembly, not the necessity of the number of times that method was applied." The effect of *Sega* and later cases that have followed its holding has been to cause software owners to redouble their efforts to find contractual protection against reverse engineering and to obtain legislative blessing for such protection through the Uniform Computer Information Transactions Act ("UCITA"). *See* <http://www.law.upenn.edu/bll/ulc/ulc_frame.htm>.

UMG RECORDINGS, INC. v. MP3.COM, INC.

United States District Court, S.D. New York, 2000.
92 F.Supp.2d 349.

RAKOFF, DISTRICT JUDGE.

The complex marvels of cyberspatial communication may create difficult legal issues; but not in this case. Defendant's infringement of plaintiffs' copyrights is clear. Accordingly, on April 28, 2000, the Court granted defendant's motion for partial summary judgment holding defendant liable for copyright infringement. This opinion will state the reasons why.

The pertinent facts, either undisputed or, where disputed, taken most favorably to defendant, are as follows:

The technology known as "MP3" permits rapid and efficient conversion of compact disc recordings ("CDs") to computer files easily accessed over the Internet. See generally Recording Industry Ass'n of America v. Diamond Multimedia Systems Inc., 180 F.3d 1072, 1073–74 (9th Cir. 1999). Utilizing this technology, defendant MP3.com, on or around January 12, 2000, launched its "My.MP3.com" service, which is advertised as permitting subscribers to store, customize and listen to the recordings contained on their CDs from any place where they have an Internet connection. To make good on this offer, defendant purchased tens of thousands of popular CDs in which plaintiffs held the copyrights, and, without authorization, copied their recordings onto its computer servers so as to be able to replay the recordings for its subscribers.

Specifically, in order to first access such a recording, a subscriber to MP3.com must either "prove" that he already owns the CD version of the recording by inserting his copy of the commercial CD into his computer CD–Rom drive for a few seconds (the "Beam-it Service") or must purchase the CD from one of defendant's cooperating online retailers (the "instant Listening Service"). Thereafter, however, the subscriber can access via the Internet from a computer anywhere in the world the copy of plaintiffs' recording made by defendant. Thus, although defendant seeks to portray its service as the "functional equivalent" of storing its subscribers' CDs, in actuality defendant is re-playing for the subscribers converted versions of the recordings it copied, without authorization, from plaintiffs' copyrighted CDs. On its face, this makes out a presumptive case of infringement under the Copyright Act of 1976 ("Copyright Act"), 17 U.S.C. § 101 *et seq. See, e.g., Castle Rock Entertainment, Inc. v. Carol Publishing Group, Inc.*, 150 F.3d 132, 137 (2d Cir.1998); *Hasbro Bradley, Inc. v. Sparkle Toys, Inc.*, 780 F.2d 189, 192 (2d Cir.1985).

Defendant argues, however, that such copying is protected by the affirmative defense of "fair use." See 17 U.S.C. § 107. In analyzing such a defense, the Copyright Act specifies four factors that must be considered: "(1) the purpose and character of the use, including whether such use is of a commercial nature or is for nonprofit educational purposes; (2) the nature of the copyrighted work; (3) the amount and substantiality of the portion used in relation to the copyrighted work as a whole; and (4) the effect of the use upon the potential market for or value of the copyrighted work." Id. Other relevant factors may also be considered, since fair use is an "equitable rule of reason" to be applied in light of the overall purposes of the Copyright Act. *Sony Corporation of America v. Universal City Studios, Inc.*, 464 U.S. 417, 448, 454, 104 S.Ct. 774, 78 L.Ed.2d 574 (1984); see *Harper & Row, Publishers, Inc. v. Nation Enterprises*, 471 U.S. 539, 549, 105 S.Ct. 2218, 85 L.Ed.2d 588 (1985).

Regarding the first factor—"the purpose and character of the use"— defendant does not dispute that its purpose is commercial, for while subscribers to My.MP3.com are not currently charged a fee, defendant seeks to attract a sufficiently large subscription base to draw advertising and otherwise make a profit. Consideration of the first factor, however, also involves inquiring into whether the new use essentially repeats the old or whether, instead, it "transforms" it by infusing it with new meaning, new understandings, or the like. *See, e.g., Campbell v. Acuff– Rose Music, Inc.*, 510 U.S. 569, 579, 114 S.Ct. 1164, 127 L.Ed.2d 500 (1994); *Castle Rock*, 150 F.3d at 142; See also Pierre N. Leval, "Toward a Fair Use Standard," 103 Harv.L.Rev. 1105, 111 (1990). Here, although defendant recites that My.MP3.com provides a transformative "space shift" by which subscribers can enjoy the sound recordings contained on their CDs without lugging around the physical discs themselves, this is simply another way of saying that the unauthorized copies are being retransmitted in another medium—an insufficient basis for any legitimate claim of transformation, *See, e.g., Infinity Broadcast Corp. v. Kirkwood*, 150 F.3d 104, 108 (2d Cir.1998) (rejecting the fair use defense by operator of a service that retransmitted copyrighted radio broadcasts over telephone lines); *Los Angeles News Serv. v. Reuters Television Int'l Ltd.*, 149 F.3d 987 (9th Cir.1998) (rejecting the fair use defense where television news agencies copied copyrighted news footage and retransmitted it to news organizations), *cert. denied*, 525 U.S. 1141, 119 S.Ct. 1032, 143 L.Ed.2d 41 (1999); *see also American Geophysical Union v. Texaco Inc.*, 60 F.3d 913, 923 (2d Cir.), *cert. dismissed*, 516 U.S. 1005, 116 S.Ct. 592, 133 L.Ed.2d 486 (1995); *Basic Books, Inc. v. Kinko's Graphics Corp.*, 758 F.Supp. 1522, 1530–31 (S.D.N.Y.1991); see generally Leval, supra, at 1111 (repetition of copyrighted material that "merely repackages or republishes the original" is unlikely to be deemed a fair use).

Here, defendant adds no new "new aesthetics, new insights and understandings" to the original music recordings it copies, see *Castle Rock*, 150 F.3d at 142 (internal quotation marks omitted), but simply repackages those recordings to facilitate their transmission through another medium. While such services may be innovative, they are not transformative.

Regarding the second factor—"the nature of the copyrighted work"—the creative recordings here being copied are "close[ ] to the core of intended copyright protection," *Campbell*, 510 U.S. at 586, 114 S.Ct. 1164, and, conversely, far removed from the more factual or descriptive work more amenable to "fair use," *see Nihon Keizai Shimbun, Inc. v. Comline Business Data, Inc.*, 166 F.3d 65, 72–73 (2d Cir.1999); *see also Castle Rock*, 150 F.3d at 143–44.

Regarding the third factor—"the amount and substantiality of the portion [of the copyrighted work] used [by the copier] in relation to the copyrighted work as a whole"—it is undisputed that defendant copies, and replays, the entirety of the copyrighted works here in issue, thus again negating any claim of fair use. *See Infinity Broadcast*, 150 F.3d at 109 ("[T]he more of a copyrighted work that is taken, the less likely the use is to be fair. . . ."); *see generally* Leval, *supra*, at 1122 ("[T]he larger the volume . . . of what is taken, the greater the affront to the interests of the copyright owner, and the less likely that a taking will qualify as a fair use").

Regarding the fourth factor—"the effect of the use upon the potential market for or value of the copyrighted work"—defendant's activities on their face invade plaintiffs' statutory right to license their copyrighted sound recordings to others for reproduction. See 17 U.S.C. § 106. Defendant, however, argues that, so far as the derivative market here involves is concerned, plaintiffs have not shown that such licensing is "traditional, reasonable, or likely to be developed." *American Geophysical*, 60 F.3d at 930 & n. 17. Moreover, defendant argues, its activities can only enhance plaintiffs' sales, since subscribers cannot gain access to particular recordings made available by MP3.com unless they have already "purchased" (actually or purportedly), or agreed to purchase, their own CD copies of those recordings.

Such arguments—though dressed in the garb of an expert's "opinion" (that, on inspection, consists almost entirely of speculative and conclusory statements)—are unpersuasive. Any allegedly positive impact of defendant's activities on plaintiffs' prior market in no way frees defendant to usurp a further market that directly derives from reproduction of the plaintiffs' copyrighted works. *See Infinity Broadcast*, 150 F.3d at 111. This would be so even if the copyrightholder had not yet entered the new market in issue, for a copyrighterholder's "exclusive" rights, derived from the Constitution and the Copyright Act, include the right, within broad limits, to curb the development of such a derivative market by refusing to license a copyrighted work or by doing so only on terms the copyright owner finds acceptable. *See Castle Rock*, 150 F.3d at 145–46; *Salinger v. Random House, Inc.*, 811 F.2d 90, 99 (2d Cir.), *cert. denied*, 484 U.S. 890, 108 S.Ct. 213, 98 L.Ed.2d 177 (1987). Here, moreover, plaintiffs have adduced substantial evidence that they have in fact taken steps to enter that market by entering into various licensing agreements.

Finally, regarding defendant's purported reliance on other factors, *see Campbell*, 510 U.S. at 577, 114 S.Ct. 1164, this essentially reduces to the claim that My.MP3.com provides a useful service to consumers that, in its absence, will be served by "pirates." Copyright, however, is not designed to afford consumer protection or convenience but, rather, to protect the copyrightholders' property interests. Moreover, as a practical matter, plaintiffs have indicated no objection in principle to licensing their recordings to companies like MP3.com; they simply want to make sure they get the remuneration the law reserves for them as holders of copyrights on creative works. Stripped to its essence, defendant's "consumer protection" argument amounts to nothing more than a bald claim that defendant should be able to misappropriate plaintiffs' property simply because there is a consumer demand for it. This hardly appeals to the conscience of equity.

In sum, on any view, defendant's "fair use" defense is indefensible and must be denied as a matter of law. * * *

Accordingly, the Court, for the foregoing reasons, has determined that plaintiffs are entitled to partial summary judgment holding defendant to have infringed plaintiffs' copyrights.

A & M RECORDS, INC. v. NAPSTER, INC.

United States District Court, N.D. California, 2000.
114 F.Supp.2d 896, 55 U.S.P.Q.2d 1780.

PATEL, CHIEF J.

The matter before the court concerns the boundary between sharing and theft, personal use and the unauthorized worldwide distribution of copyrighted music and sound recordings. On December 6, 1999, A & M Records and seventeen other record companies ("record company plaintiffs") filed a complaint for contributory and vicarious copyright infringement, violations of the California Civil Code section 980(a)(2), and unfair competition against Napster, Inc., an Internet start-up that enables users to download MP3 music files without payment. On January 7, 2000, plaintiffs Jerry Leiber, Mike Stoller, and Frank Music Corporation filed a complaint for vicarious and contributory copyright infringement on behalf of a putative class of similarly-situated music publishers ("music publisher plaintiffs") against Napster, Inc. and former CEO Eileen Richardson. The music publisher plaintiffs filed a first amended complaint on April 6, 2000, and on May 24, 2000, the court entered a stipulation of dismissal of all claims against Richardson. Now before this court is the record company and music publisher plaintiffs' joint motion to preliminarily enjoin Napster, Inc. from engaging in or assisting others in copying, downloading, uploading, transmitting, or distributing copyrighted music without the express permission of the rights owner.

In opposition to this motion, defendant seeks to expand the "fair use" doctrine articulated in *Sony Corp. of America v. Universal City Studios, Inc.*, 464 U.S. 417, 104 S.Ct. 774, 78 L.Ed.2d 574 (1984), to encompass the massive downloading of MP3 files by Napster users. Alternatively, defendant contends that, even if this third-party activity constitutes direct copyright infringement, plaintiffs have not shown probable success on the merits of their contributory and vicarious infringement claims. Defendant also asks the court to find that copyright holders are not injured by a service created and promoted to facilitate the free downloading of music files, the vast majority of which are copyrighted.

Having considered the parties' arguments, the court grants plaintiffs' motion for a preliminary injunction against Napster, Inc. The court makes the following Findings of Fact and Conclusions of Law to support the preliminary injunction under Federal Rules of Civil Procedure 65(d).

I. FINDINGS OF FACT

A. *MP3 Technology*

1. Digital compression technology makes it possible to store audio recordings in a digital format that uses less memory and may be uploaded and downloaded over the Internet. MP3 is a popular, standard format used to store such compressed audio files. Compressing data into MP3 format results in some loss of sound quality. However, because MP3 files are smaller, they require less time to transfer and are therefore better suited to transmission over the Internet.

2. Consumers typically acquire MP3 files in two ways. First, users may download audio recordings that have already been converted into MP3 format by using an Internet service such as Napster. Second, "ripping" software makes it possible to copy an audio compact disc ("CD") directly onto a computer hard-drive; ripping software compresses the millions of bytes of information on a typical CD into a smaller MP3 file that requires a fraction of the storage space.

B. *Defendant's Business*

1. Napster, Inc. is a start-up company based in San Mateo, California. It distributes its proprietary file-sharing software free of charge via its Internet website. People who have downloaded this software can log-on to the Napster system and share MP3 music files with other users who are also logged-on to the system. It is uncontradicted that Napster users currently upload or download MP3 files without payment to each other, defendant, or copyright owners.

* * *

10. Defendant employs the term "space-shifting" to refer to the process of converting a CD the consumer already owns into MP3 format and using Napster to transfer the music to a different computer—from home to office, for example. The court finds that space-shifting accounts

for a de minimis portion of Napster use and is not a significant aspect of defendant's business.

* * *

C.   The Napster Technology

* * *

3.   The software features a browser interface, search engine, and chat functions that operate in conjunction with defendant's online network of servers. The software also contains a "hotlist" tool that allows users to compile and store lists of other account holders' user names. In addition, the Napster software may be used to play and categorize audio files, which users can store in specific file directories on their hard drives. Those directories, which allow account holders to share files on Napster, constitute the "user library." Id. Some users store their MP3 files in such directories; others do not. See id.

4.   Defendant maintains clusters of servers that compose its network or system. Account holders who access the Napster network may communicate, share files, and learn of designated hotlist names only within the cluster to which they are assigned. See id. Users can access the network of servers free of charge.

5.   Once an account holder signs on to the Napster network, the Napster browser interacts with its proprietary server-side software. If a user sets the "allowable uploads" function of the MusicShare software above zero, all of the MP3 file names she stores in her user library automatically become available to other online Napster users.

However, before the client software uploads MP3 file names to defendant's master servers, it "validates" the files stored in the user library directories. The client software reads those files to ensure they are indeed MP3 files, checking to see whether they contain the proper syntax specification and content. If the files are not properly formatted, their file names will not be not uploaded to the Napster servers.

Once the file names are successfully uploaded to the servers, each user library, identified by a user name, becomes a "location" on the servers. Napster locations are short-lived; they are respectively added or purged every time a user signs on or off of the network. Thus, a user's MP3 files are only accessible to other users while she is online.

6.   A user who is logged-on to the Napster servers via the client software may access the content of other users' uploaded "locations" in one of two ways: (a) by utilizing defendant's proprietary search engine, or (b) by employing the hotlist tool featured in the client software.

7.   An account holder may use the search tools included in the Napster client software to find MP3 files. The server-side application software maintains a search index that is updated in real time as users log-on and-off of the system. The file-name index contains the names of MP3 files that on-line users save in their designated user library directo-

ries. Users who wish to search for a song or artist may do so by entering the name of the song or artist in the search fields of the client software and then clicking the "Find It" button. When the search form is transmitted to the Napster network, the Napster servers send the requesting user a list of files that include the same term(s) she entered on the search form.

After the application software returns a list of specific MP3 file names to the requesting user, the user then must peruse the list to determine whether she desires any of those files. She must read through the list because the Napster application software does not search for a particular song or recording artist per se. Napster does not organize MP3 files based on content because, currently, they are not designed for such indexing. Instead, Napster performs a text search of the file names indexed in a particular cluster. Those file names may contain typographical errors or otherwise inaccurate descriptions of the content of the files since they are designated by other users.

In addition to listed text results from an executed search, Napster's servers provide other information about particular MP3 files. For instance, the client software can sort the results of "echo packets" or "ping requests" that it sends out to host users; these requests help gauge the "responsiveness value" of a transmission between two users by calculating the amount of time it takes for ping responses to be returned to the client software. Users can also search for files that meet certain technical criteria, such as the host user's bandwidth. Finally, the file name or "data object description" includes the size and bytes stored and "attributes of quality," such as bit rate. These Napster options contribute to the ease with which the user can locate and obtain the music she wants.

8. Alternatively, users may access MP3 files via the hotlist function. This function enables a Napster user to archive other user names and learn whether account holders who access the network under those names are online. A requesting user can access or browse all files listed in the user libraries of hotlisted users. Then she can request a particular file in a host user's user library by selecting, or clicking on, that file name. The hotlist function is a feature that helps make Napster users a virtual community—they are not only able to download the music they desire, but also to obtain files from particular individuals whom they know by user name.

9. The Napster network facilitates the same mode of file-transfer, whether a requesting user accesses a specific MP3 file with the search engine or the hotlist. Once a requesting user locates and selects the file she wishes to download, the server-side software engages in a dialogue with her browser and that of the "host user" (that is, the user who makes the MP3 available for downloading). Napster servers obtain the necessary IP addsress information from the host user. The servers then communicate the host user's address or routing information to the requesting user; the requesting user's computer employs this informa-

tion to establish a connection with the host user's browser software and download the MP3 file from the host user's library. The content of the actual MP3 file is transferred over the Internet between users, not through the Napster servers. However, users would not be able to access the uploaded file names and corresponding routing data without signing on to the Napster system.

* * *

II. CONCLUSIONS OF LAW

* * *

B. Proof of Direct Infringement

To prevail on a contributory or vicarious copyright infringement claim, a plaintiff must show direct infringement by a third party. *See Sony Corp. of Am. v. Universal City Studios, Inc.*, 464 U.S. 417, 434, 104 S.Ct. 774, 78 L.Ed.2d 574 (1984). As a threshold matter, plaintiffs in this action must demonstrate that Napster users are engaged in direct infringement.

Plaintiffs have established a prima facie case of direct copyright infringement. As discussed above, virtually all Napster users engage in the unauthorized downloading or uploading of copyrighted music; as much as eighty-seven percent of the files available on Napster may be copyrighted, and more than seventy percent may be owned or administered by plaintiffs.

C. Affirmative Defense of Fair Use and Substantial Non–Infringing Use

1. Defendant asserts the affirmative defenses of fair use and substantial non-infringing use. The latter defense is also known as the staple article of commerce doctrine. *See Sony*, 464 U.S. at 442. *Sony* stands for the rule that a manufacturer is not liable for selling a "staple article of commerce" that is "capable of commercially significant noninfringing uses." *Id.* The Supreme Court also declared in Sony, "Any individual may reproduce a copyrighted work for a 'fair use'; the copyright holder does not possess the exclusive right to such a use." *Id.* at 433. Defendant bears the burden of proving these affirmative defenses. *See Bateman v. Mnemonics, Inc.*, 79 F.3d 1532, 1542 n. 22 (11th Cir.1996) ("[I]t is clear the burden of proving fair use is always on the putative infringer.").

2. For the reasons set forth below, the court finds that any potential non-infringing use of the Napster service is minimal or connected to the infringing activity, or both. The substantial or commercially significant use of the service was, and continues to be, the unauthorized downloading and uploading of popular music, most of which is copyrighted.

3. Section 107 of the Copyright Act provides a non-exhaustive list of fair use factors. These factors include:

(1) the purpose and character of the use, including whether such use is of a commercial nature or is for nonprofit educational purposes;

(2) the nature of the copyrighted work;

(3) the amount and substantiality of the portion used in relation to the copyrighted work as a whole; and

(4) the effect of the use upon the potential market for or value of the copyrighted work.

17 U.S.C. § 107.

4. In the instant action, the purpose and character of the use militates against a finding of fair use. Ascertaining whether the new work transforms the copyrighted material satisfies the main goal of the first factor. *See Campbell v. Acuff–Rose Music, Inc.*, 510 U.S. 569, 579, 114 S.Ct. 1164, 127 L.Ed.2d 500 (1994). Plaintiff persuasively argues that downloading MP3 files does not transform the copyrighted music. *See UMG Recordings, Inc. v. MP3.com, Inc.*, 92 F.Supp.2d 349, 351 (S.D.N.Y.2000) (concluding that repackaging copyrighted recordings in MP3 format suitable for downloading "adds no 'new aesthetics, new insights and understandings' to the original").

5. Under the first factor, the court must also determine whether the use is commercial. In *Acuff-Rose*, the Supreme Court clarified that a finding of commercial use weighs against, but does not preclude, a determination of fairness. *See Acuff–Rose*, 510 U .S. at 584.

6. If a use is non-commercial, the plaintiff bears the burden of showing a meaningful likelihood that it would adversely affect the potential market for the copyrighted work if it became widespread. *See Sony*, 464 U.S. at 451.

7. Although downloading and uploading MP3 music files is not paradigmatic commercial activity, it is also not personal use in the traditional sense. Plaintiffs have not shown that the majority of Napster users download music to sell—that is, for profit. However, given the vast scale of Napster use among anonymous individuals, the court finds that downloading and uploading MP3 music files with the assistance of Napster are not private uses. At the very least, a host user sending a file cannot be said to engage in a personal use when distributing that file to an anonymous requester. Moreover, the fact that Napster users get for free something they would ordinarily have to buy suggests that they reap economic advantages from Napster use. *See Sega Enters. Ltd. v. MAP-HIA*, 857 F.Supp. 679, 687 (N.D.Cal.1994) ("*Sega I*") (holding that copying to save users expense of purchasing authorized copies has commercial character and thus weighs against finding of fair use); cf. American Geophysical Union v. Texaco, Inc., 60 F.3d 913, 922 (2d Cir.1994) (holding that for-profit enterprise which made unauthorized copies of scholarly articles to facilitate scientific research reaped indirect

economic advantage from copying and, hence, that copying constituted commercial use).

8.   The court finds that the copyrighted musical compositions and sound recordings are creative in nature; they constitute entertainment, which cuts against a finding of fair use under the second factor. *See Harper & Row Publishers, Inc. v. Nation Enters.*, 471 U.S. 539, 563, 105 S.Ct. 2218, 85 L.Ed.2d 588 (1985); Sega I, 857 F.Supp. at 687; *Playboy Enters., Inc. v. Frena*, 839 F.Supp. 1552, 1558 (M.D.Fla.1993) *(citing In re New Era Publications Int'l v. Carol Publ'g*, 904 F.2d 152, 157–58 (2d Cir.), *cert. denied*, 498 U.S. 921, 111 S.Ct. 297, 112 L.Ed.2d 251 (1990)).

9.   With regard to the third factor, it is undisputed that downloading or uploading MP3 music files involves copying the entirety of the copyrighted work. The Ninth Circuit held prior to *Sony* that "wholesale copying of copyrighted material precludes application of the fair use doctrine." *Marcus v. Rowley*, 695 F.2d 1171, 1176 (9th Cir.1983). Even after *Sony*, wholesale copying for private home use tips the fair use analysis in plaintiffs' favor if such copying is likely to adversely affect the market for the copyrighted material. See *Sony*, 464 U.S. at 449–50, 456.

10.   The fourth factor, the effect on the potential market for the copyrighted work, also weighs against a finding of fair use. Plaintiffs have produced evidence that Napster use harms the market for their copyrighted musical compositions and sound recordings in at least two ways. First, it reduces CD sales among college students. Second, it raises barriers to plaintiffs' entry into the market for the digital downloading of music.

11.   Defendant asserts several potential fair uses of the Napster service—including sampling, space-shifting, and the authorized distribution of new artists' work. Sampling on Napster is not a personal use in the traditional sense that courts have recognized—copying which occurs within the household and does not confer any financial benefit on the user. *See, e.g, Sony*, 464 U.S. at 423, 449–50. Instead, sampling on Napster amounts to obtaining permanent copies of songs that users would otherwise have to purchase; it also carries the potential for viral distribution to millions of people. Defendant ignores critical differences between sampling songs on Napster and VCR usage in *Sony*. First, while "time-shifting [TV broadcasts] merely enables a viewer to see . . . a work which he ha[s] been invited to witness in its entirety free of charge," plaintiffs in this action almost always charge for their music—even if it is downloaded song-by-song. *Sony*, 464 U.S. at 449–50. They only make promotional downloads available on a highly restricted basis. Copyright owners also earn royalties from streamed song samples on retail websites like Amazon.com. Second, the majority of VCR purchasers in Sony did not distribute taped television broadcasts, but merely enjoyed them at home. In contrast, a Napster user who downloads a copy of a song to her hard drive may make that song available to millions of other individuals, even if she eventually chooses to purchase the CD. So-called sampling on

Napster may quickly facilitate unauthorized distribution at an exponential rate.

* * *

The court concludes that, even assuming the sampling alleged in this case is a non-commercial use, the record company plaintiffs have demonstrated a meaningful likelihood that it would adversely affect their entry into the online market if it became widespread. See Sony, 464 U.S. at 451. Moreover, it deprives the music publisher plaintiffs of royalties for individual songs. The unauthorized downloading of plaintiffs' music to sample songs would not constitute a fair use, even if it enhanced CD sales.

* * *

15. Defendant argues that, if space-shifting is deemed a fair use, the staple article of commerce doctrine precludes liability for contributory or vicarious infringement. Under *Sony*, the copyright holder cannot extend his monopoly to products "capable of substantial noninfringing uses." *Sony*, 464 U.S. at 442. Defendant fails to show that space-shifting constitutes a commercially significant use of Napster. Indeed, the most credible explanation for the exponential growth of traffic to the website is the vast array of free MP3 files offered by other users—not the ability of each individual to space-shift music she already owns. Thus, even if space-shifting is a fair use, it is not substantial enough to preclude liability under the staple article of commerce doctrine. *See Cable/Home Communication Corp. v. Network Prods., Inc.*, 902 F.2d 829, 846 (11th Cir.1990) (affirming finding of contributory infringement where defendant primarily promoted pirate computer chips and other devices capable of descrambling pay-TV broadcasts as infringement aids); *A & M Records v. General Audio Video Cassettes, Inc.*, 948 F.Supp. 1449, 1456 (C.D.Cal.1996) (rejecting *Sony* defense because counterfeiting was chief purpose of time-loaded cassettes that defendant sold).

16. This court also declines to apply the staple article of commerce doctrine because, as paragraphs (D)(6) and (E)(2) of the legal conclusions explain, Napster exercises ongoing control over its service. In Sony, the defendant's participation did not extend past manufacturing and selling the VCRs: "[t]he only contact between Sony and the users of the Betamax ... occurred at the moment of sale." *Sony*, 464 U.S. at 438. Here, in contrast, Napster, Inc. maintains and supervises an integrated system that users must access to upload or download files. Courts have distinguished the protection *Sony* offers to the manufacture and sale of a device from scenarios in which the defendant continues to exercise control over the device's use. See General Audio Video, 948 F.Supp. at 1456–57 (finding Sony doctrine inapplicable to seller of blank tapes who "acted as a contact between his customers and suppliers of other material necessary for counterfeiting"); *RCA Records v. All–Fast Sys., Inc.*, 594 F.Supp. 335, 339 (S.D.N.Y.1984) (holding that defendant in position to control cassette-copying machine could not invoke Sony); *see*

also Columbia Pictures Indus., Inc. v. Aveco, Inc., 800 F.2d 59, 62 & n. 3 (3d Cir.1986) (holding that business which rented rooms where public viewed copyrighted video cassettes engaged in contributory infringement, even when it was not source of cassettes). Napster, Inc.'s facilitation of unauthorized file-sharing smacks of the contributory infringement in these cases, rather than the legitimate conduct of the VCR manufacturers. Given defendant's control over the service, as opposed to mere manufacturing or selling, the existence of a potentially unobjectionable use like space-shifting does not defeat plaintiffs' claims.

17.   Nor do other potential non-infringing uses of Napster preclude contributory or vicarious liability. Defendant claims that it engages in the authorized promotion of independent artists, ninety-eight percent of whom are not represented by the record company plaintiffs. However, the New Artist Program may not represent a substantial or commercially significant aspect of Napster. The evidence suggests that defendant initially promoted the availability of songs by major stars, as opposed to "page after page of unknown artists." Its purported mission of distributing music by artists unable to obtain record-label representation appears to have been developed later.

Other facts point to the conclusion that the New Artists Program was an afterthought, not a major aspect of the Napster business plan. Former CEO Eileen Richardson claimed in her deposition that she told the press Napster is not about known artists like Madonna. But, tellingly, discovery related to downloads by Napster executives reveals that Richardson's own computer contained about five Madonna files obtained using Napster. Defendant did not launch the website aspect of its New Artist Program until after plaintiffs filed suit, and as recently as July 2000, bona fide new artists constituted a very small percentage of music available on Napster.

In any event, Napster's primary role of facilitating the unauthorized copying and distribution established artists' songs renders Sony inapplicable.

18.   Plaintiffs do not object to all of the supposedly non-infringing uses of Napster. They do not seek an injunction covering chat rooms or message boards, the New Artist Program or any distribution authorized by rights holders. Nor do they seek to enjoin applications unrelated to the music recording industry. Because plaintiffs do not ask the court to shut down such satellite activities, the fact that these activities may be non-infringing does not lessen plaintiffs' likelihood of success. The court therefore finds that plaintiffs have established a reasonable probability of proving third-party infringement.

* * *

D.   Contributory Copyright Infringement

1.   Once they have shown direct infringement by Napster users, plaintiffs must demonstrate a likelihood of success on their contributory infringement claim. A contributory infringer is "one who, with knowl-

edge of the infringing activity, induces, causes or materially contributes to the infringing conduct of another." *Gershwin Publ'g Corp. v. Columbia Artists Management, Inc.*, 443 F.2d 1159, 1162 (2d Cir.1971); *see Fonovisa, Inc. v. Cherry Auction, Inc.*, 76 F.3d 259, 264 (9th Cir.1996). Courts do not require actual knowledge; rather, a defendant incurs contributory copyright liability if he has reason to know of the third party's direct infringement. *See Cable/Home Communication Corp.*, 902 F.2d at 846; *Sega Enter. Ltd. v. MAPHIA*, 948 F.Supp. 923, 933 (N.D.Cal.1996) ("*Sega II*").

* * *

7. Because they have made a convincing showing with regard to both the knowledge and material contribution elements, plaintiffs have established a reasonable likelihood of success on their contributory infringement claims.

E.   *Vicarious Copyright Infringement*

1. Even in the absence of an employment relationship, a defendant incurs liability for vicarious copyright infringement if he "has the right and ability to supervise the infringing activity and also has a direct financial interest in such activities." *Fonovisa*, 76 F.3d at 262 (quoting *Gershwin*, 443 F.2d at 1162).

* * *

4. Plaintiffs has shown a reasonable likelihood of success on their vicarious infringement claims.

F.   *Defendant's First Amendment Challenge*

1. According to Napster, Inc., the requested injunction would impose a prior restraint on its free speech, as well as that of its users and the unsigned artists that depend upon its service. This First Amendment argument centers on the fact that defendant offers an electronic directory, which does not itself contain copyrighted material. Directories have been accorded First Amendment protection. *See Princeton Community Phone Book, Inc. v. Bate*, 582 F.2d 706, 710–11 (3d Cir.) (holding that First Amendment affords as much protection to listing in directory as it does to newspaper advertisement), cert. denied, 439 U.S. 966, 99 S.Ct. 454, 58 L.Ed.2d 424 (1978).

2. Although an overbroad injunction might implicate the First Amendment, free speech concerns "are protected by and coextensive with the fair use doctrine." *Nihon Keizai Shimbun, Inc. v. Comline Bus. Data, Inc.*, 166 F.3d 65, 74 (2d Cir.1999); *Religious Tech. Ctr.*, 907 F.Supp. at 1377 (stating that, where otherwise appropriate, imposing liability for copyright infringement does not necessarily create First Amendment concerns because the fair use defense encompasses this issue). This court has already determined that plaintiffs do not seek to

enjoin any fair uses of the Napster service that are not completely contrived or peripheral to its existence.

* * *

III. CONCLUSION

For the foregoing reasons, the court GRANTS plaintiffs' motion for a preliminary injunction against Napster, Inc. Defendant is hereby preliminarily ENJOINED from engaging in, or facilitating others in copying, downloading, uploading, transmitting, or distributing plaintiffs' copyrighted musical compositions and sound recordings, protected by either federal or state law, without express permission of the rights owner. This injunction applies to all such works that plaintiffs own; it is not limited to those listed in Schedules A and B of the complaint.

Plaintiffs have shown persuasively that they own the copyrights to more than seventy percent of the music available on the Napster system. Because defendant has contributed to illegal copying on a scale that is without precedent, it bears the burden of developing a means to comply with the injunction. Defendant must insure that no work owned by plaintiffs which neither defendant nor Napster users have permission to use or distribute is uploaded or downloaded on Napster. The court ORDERS plaintiffs to cooperate with defendant in identifying the works to which they own copyrights. To this end, plaintiffs must file a written plan no later than September, 5, 2000, describing the most expedient method by which their rights can be ascertained. The court also ORDERS plaintiffs to post a bond for the sum of $5,000,000.00 to compensate defendant for its losses in the event that this injunction is reversed or vacated.[32]

IT IS SO ORDERED.

2. BACKUP COPIES

COPYRIGHT ACT OF 1976—§ 117

§ 117—Limitations on exclusive rights: Computer programs

(a) Making of additional copy or adaptation by owner of copy.— Notwithstanding the provisions of section 106, it is not an infringement for the owner of a copy of a computer program to make or authorize the making of another copy or adaptation of that computer program provided:

(1) that such a new copy or adaptation is created as an essential step in the utilization of the computer program in conjunction with a machine and that it is used in no other manner, or

(2) that such new copy or adaptation is for archival purposes only and that all archival copies are destroyed in the event that continued possession of the computer program should cease to be rightful.

---

32. On July 26, 2000, the court ordered defendant to comply with the preliminary injunction by midnight on July 28, 2000; however, on July 28, a Ninth Circuit panel stayed the injunction. That same day, plaintiffs posted their bond.

(b) Lease, sale, or other transfer of additional copy or adaptation.—Any exact copies prepared in accordance with the provisions of this section may be leased, sold, or otherwise transferred, along with the copy from which such copies were prepared, only as part of the lease, sale, or other transfer of all rights in the program. Adaptations so prepared may be transferred only with the authorization of the copyright owner.

(c) Machine maintenance or repair.—Notwithstanding the provisions of section 106, it is not an infringement for the owner or lessee of a machine to make or authorize the making of a copy of a computer program if such copy is made solely by virtue of the activation of a machine that lawfully contains an authorized copy of the computer program, for purposes only of maintenance or repair of that machine, if—

(1) such new copy is used in no other manner and is destroyed immediately after the maintenance or repair is completed; and

(2) with respect to any computer program or part thereof that is not necessary for that machine to be activated, such program or part thereof is not accessed or used other than to make such new copy by virtue of the activation of the machine.

(d) Definitions.—For purposes of this section—

(1) the "maintenance" of a machine is the servicing of the machine in order to make it work in accordance with its original specifications and any changes to those specifications authorized for that machine; and

(2) the "repair" of a machine is the restoring of the machine to the state of working in accordance with its original specifications and any changes to those specifications authorized for that machine.

ATARI, INC. v. JS & A GROUP, INC.

United States District Court, N.D. Illinois, 1983.
597 F.Supp. 5.

DECKER, DISTRICT JUDGE.

This is a suit for declaratory and injunctive relief and for damages for contributory copyright infringement, patent infringement, unfair competition, and various state law torts. The plaintiff, Atari, Inc. ("Atari"), brought this suit because the defendant, JS & A, Inc., ("JS & A") sells and advertises a device called the "PROM BLASTER". The case is before the court on plaintiff's motion for a preliminary injunction on the copyright infringement claim.

FACTUAL BACKGROUND

Atari manufactures and sells a home computer video game system, the "2600", and game cartridges such as "CENTIPEDE" and "PAC–MAN" for use in the 2600. In order to play the games at home, the consumer connects the Atari computer to a television set and plugs his controls, or "joysticks", into the computer. A game cartridge, which is usually purchased separately, is then inserted into the computer. The computer program in the cartridge causes the audiovisual aspects of the game to emanate from the television. The 2600 has been a resounding commercial success.

The various game cartridges consist of a heavy plastic housing which contains an electronic circuit, or "chip", which in turn contains the game's computer program. The chips in Atari 2600 game cartridges are "Ready Only Memory", or "ROM", chips. The parties have stipulated that a ROM can neither be reprogrammed nor erased. The game cartridges sell for as much as $40 apiece.

Atari has copyrighted its video games as audiovisual works. In addition, it is seeking to register a copyright of the computer program for the CENTIPEDE game. Plaintiff's Exhibit D.

JS & A is a retailer of electronic products. It began this fall an effort to market its PROM BLASTER, a device for the duplication of those video games which are compatible with the Atari 2600 home computer. The machine has two slots, one for a 2600–compatible cartridge and one for a blank cartridge sold by JS & A for $10. In the words of JS & A's advertisements, "[y]ou simply plug in your Atari© or Activision© cartridge in one slot and a blank cartridge in another, press a button and three minutes later you've created an exact duplicate." Plaintiff's Exhibit A. The PROM BLASTER sells for $119, and JS & A currently has $12,000 in inventory on hand. The defendant agreed not to fill any orders for the product pending the disposition of this motion.

JS & A markets the PROM BLASTER primarily as a means of making "back-up" copies of 2600–compatible games. The advertisements urge the consumer to protect his investment in video game cartridges which "can easily be ruined." Plaintiff's Exhibit A. The advertisements assure the public that this copying does not violate the copyright laws because "[i]n 1980, Congress passed an amendment to the copyright act that clearly permitted consumers to duplicate their cartridges" but warn that "[y]ou can't sell, lease or give away a duplicate cartridge produced from a copyrighted original that you own." *Id.* A related selling point for the PROM BLASTER is that the buyer "can make copies for [his] friends who wish to own archival copies of their favorite games and charge them for the service." *Id.*

JS & A also sells nine 2600–compatible video games of its own. JS & A grants the purchaser of a PROM BLASTER the right to copy the games, and even to sell the copies, without any limitation.

Atari alleges that any copying of its video games infringes its copyrights, even if the consumer does it for "archival purposes." Atari also contends that "[t]he purpose and effect of JS & A's acts are actively to induce, cause, and materially contribute to the making of infringing copies of ATARI's copyrighted home video games." Atari seeks a preliminary injunction against JS & A to prevent the use, advertising, offering for sale, and the sale of the PROM BLASTER and the blank cartridges.

DISCUSSION

To establish its right to a preliminary injunction, Atari must show that it is likely to prevail on the merits, that it will suffer irreparable harm if the injunction does not issue, that the balance of hardships is in its favor, and that granting the injunction is in the public interest.

1. Likelihood of Success on the Merits

Atari's copyright claim against JS & A is for contributory infringement. "[O]ne who, with knowledge of the infringing activity, induces, causes or materially contributes to the infringing conduct of another, may be held liable as a 'contributory' infringer." *Gershwin Publishing Corp. v. Columbia Artists Management, Inc.*, 443 F.2d 1159, 1162 (2d Cir.1971) (footnote omitted). JS & A raises no issue as to its knowledge or encouragement of the use of the PROM BLASTER to copy copyrighted Atari and other 2600–compatible video games. The defendant argues instead that the copying of those games is legal and, even if it is not, the court may not enjoin the sale of the PROM BLASTER because it has other, legal uses.

Whether the copying of others' video games is an infringing activity is an issue the court discusses in detail below. Here, it must be noted that if JS & A is wrong, and such copying does infringe, its misinterpretation of the Copyright Act is no defense to a charge of contributory infringement. Furthermore, it is not enough for JS & A to establish that the PROM BLASTER has *a* legal use. The machine must have a *substantial* noninfringing use to preclude an injunction against its sale. The PROM BLASTER can perform only two functions: copy others' video games or duplicate JS & A's own games. JS & A argues that the later use, which is of course noninfringing, is enough. This argument fails because that use is not substantial. JS & A markets only nine games. Since they evidently went on the market with the PROM BLASTER, quite recently, no one knows if consumers want to play these games, much less copy them. Furthermore, PROM BLASTERS sell for $119. It strains credulity to assert that consumers would spend that much for a machine that could only copy JS & A's games. This capability of the PROM BLASTER is by itself insufficient to make its sale legal.

JS & A's liability as a infringer thus turns ultimately on the legality of the primary use of the machine, that which JS & A encourages with its advertisements, the duplication of others' video games. This is the machine's only substantial use, and if it is an infringing use the PROM BLASTER is fatally limited.

Section 106 of the Copyright Act details the exclusive rights of copyright owners, and it states in relevant part:

"Subject to sections 107 through 118, the owner of copyright under this title has the exclusive right to do and to authorize any of the following:

(1) To reproduce the copyrighted work in copies...."

17 U.S.C. § 106. Absent an exception, therefore, the duplication of Atari's copyrighted games is an infringement of its rights. Atari is likely to prevail unless JS & A can establish that an exception applies. JS & A has the burden because it "claims the benefits of an exception to the prohibition of a statute."

The exception on which JS & A seeks to rely is the new § 117 of the Copyright Act, which was enacted in 1980 to replace the original § 117. That provision states in relevant part:

> "Notwithstanding the provisions of section 106, it is not an infringement for the owner of a copy of a computer program to make or authorize the making of another copy or adaptation of that computer program provided:

> * * *

> "(2) that any such new copy or adaptation is for archival purposes only and that all archival copies are destroyed in the event that the continued possession of the computer program should cease to be rightful."

17 U.S.C. § 117. This "archival exception," according to JS & A, legalizes the PROM BLASTER and its use in making back-up copies.

Apparently, no other court has interpreted § 117, and the legislative history is scant. Congress' only statement is that the section "embodies the recommendations of the Commission on New Technological Works ['the Commission'] with respect to clarifying the law of copyright of computer software." H.R.Rep. No. 96–1307 (Part I), *reprinted in* 1980 U.S.Code Congressional and Administrative News 6460, 6492.

Congress created the Commission in 1974 to study copyright problems with respect to computers and photocopying and to make recommendations for statutory changes. The Final Report of the Commission ("CONTU Report") sets forth and explains those recommendations, which Congress in 1980 adopted. "Although the Congressional action in 1980 does not appear to be supported by a legislative history, it is fair to conclude, since Congress adopted its recommendations without alteration, that the CONTU Report reflects the Congressional intent." *Midway Mfg. Co. v. Strohon*, 564 F.Supp. 741, 750 n. 6 (N.D.Ill.1983) (Will, J.).

The CONTU Report does provide some guidance in that it explains the limited purpose of the archival exception:

> "One who rightfully possesses a copy of a program, therefore, should be provided with a legal right to copy it to that extent which will permit its use by that possessor. This would include the right to load it into a computer and *to prepare archival copies of it to guard against destruction or damage by mechanical or electrical failure.* But this permission would not extend to other copies of the program."

CONTU Report at 31 (emphasis added). The purpose of the exception is to protect the use of a copy against a particular type of risk: "destruction or damage by mechanical or electrical failure." The parties accept that this is the purpose of the exception. They disagree, however, as to the applicability of the exception to computer programs embodied in ROMs.

Computer programs are stored in a wide variety of media. Not all of these are subject to the same risks, and not all are subject to mechanical or electrical failure. For example, the instructions of the program can be printed on paper in a human-readable form. That piece of paper could be burned or shredded, yet it could not be destroyed by mechanical or electrical failure. The medium of storage must, therefore, determine whether the archival exception applies. Where, and only where, a medium may be destroyed by mechanical or electrical failure, the archival exception protects the owners of programs stored in that medium by granting them the right to make back-up copies.

The parties stipulated at the December 1 hearing in this case that the programs in ROMs can be neither reprogrammed nor erased. Atari concludes from this that the programs are not susceptible to destruction or damage through mechanical or electrical failure. JS & A disagrees, and argues that ROMs can be destroyed "as a result of a wire becoming disconnected, liquid spillage, crushing, etc." In support of its argument, JS & A offered Exhibit 1, a letter from a customer who wrote that four of his cartridges "died." The customer did not, however, specify the cause of death. This is the only evidence JS & A presented as to the nature of the danger to the ROMs, despite the court's invitation on December 1 to present expert or other testimony on this point.

The court concludes that JS & A has not met its burden of bringing itself within the § 117 exception. The dangers to ROMs presented by JS & A are *physical* dangers not unlike the risk that a handwritten computer program will be shredded accidentally. Virtually every copy of a copyrighted work, be it a book, a phonograph record, or a videotape, faces that kind of risk. Yet Congress did not enact a general rule that making back-up copies of copyrighted works would not infringe. Rather, according to the CONTU report, it limited its exception to computer programs which are subject to "destruction or damage by mechanical or electrical failure." Some media must be especially susceptible to this danger. JS & A has simply offered no evidence that a ROM in a 2600–compatible video game cartridge is such a medium.

In sum, the PROM BLASTER would have a substantial noninfringing use only if it could legally be used to make archival copies of copyrighted 2600–compatible video games. That use is legal only if the § 117 exception applies, and JS & A has the burden of showing that it does. JS & A has not done so. The court must conclude, therefore, that Atari is likely to prevail on its arguments that the exception does not apply, that the PROM BLASTER has no substantial noninfringing use, and that its sale should be enjoined.

* * *

CONCLUSION

For the reasons stated above, the court grants plaintiff's motion for a preliminary injunction. Defendant JS & A and its agents and servants will be preliminarily enjoined from selling, marketing, distributing or otherwise disposing of PROM BLASTERS. Plaintiff will prepare an appropriate order to submit to the court, and at that time bond will be fixed.

3. PRIVILEGES OF INTERNET SERVICE PROVIDERS—§ 512

A & M RECORDS, INC. v. NAPSTER, INC.

United States District Court, N.D. California, 2000.
54 U.S.P.Q.2d 1746, 2000 WL 573136.

PATEL, CHIEF J.

On December 6, 1999, plaintiff record companies filed suit alleging contributory and vicarious federal copyright infringement and related state law violations by defendant Napster, Inc. ("Napster"). Now before this court is defendant's motion for summary adjudication of the applicability of a safe harbor provision of the Digital Millennium Copyright Act ("DMCA"), 17 U.S.C. section 512(a), to its business activities. Defendant argues that the entire Napster system falls within the safe harbor and, hence, that plaintiffs may not obtain monetary damages or injunctive relief, except as narrowly specified by subparagraph 512(j)(1)(B). In the alternative, Napster asks the court to find subsection 512(a) applicable to its role in downloading MP3 music files,[1] as opposed to searching for or indexing such files. Having considered the parties' arguments and for the reasons set forth below, the court enters the following memorandum and order.

BACKGROUND

Napster—a small Internet start-up based in San Mateo, California-makes its proprietary MusicShare software freely available for Internet users to download. Users who obtain Napster's software can then share MP3 music file s with others logged-on to the Napster system. MP3 files, which reproduce nearly CD-quality sound in a compressed format, are available on a variety of websites either for a fee or free-of-charge. Napster allows users to exchange MP3 files stored on their own computer hard-drives directly, without payment, and boasts that it "takes the frustration out of locating servers with MP3 files." Def. Br. at 4.

Although the parties dispute the precise nature of the service Napster provides, they agree that using Napster typically involves the

---

1. The Motion Picture Experts Group first created MP3 in the early 1980s as the audio layer 3 of the MPEG–1 audiovisual format. MP3 technology allows for the fast and efficient conversion of compact disc recordings into computer files that may be downloaded over the Internet. *See generally Recording Industry Ass'n of America v. Diamond Multimedia Systems Inc.*, 180 F.3d 1072, 1073–74 (9th Cir.1999) (discussing MP3 technology).

following basic steps: After downloading MusicShare software from the Napster website, a user can access the Napster system from her computer. The MusicShare software interacts with Napster's server-side software when the user logs on, automatically connecting her to one of some 150 servers that Napster operates. The MusicShare software reads a list of names of MP3 files that the user has elected to make available. This list is then added to a directory and index, on the Napster server, of MP3 files that users who are logged-on wish to share. If the user wants to locate a song, she enters its name or the name of the recording artist on the search page of the MusicShare program and clicks the "Find It" button. The Napster software then searches the current directory and generates a list of files responsive to the search request. To download a desired file, the user highlights it on the list and clicks the "Get Selected Song(s)" button. The user may also view a list of files that exist on another user's hard drive and select a file from that list. When the requesting user clicks on the name of a file, the Napster server communicates with the requesting user's and host user's[2] MusicShare browser software to facilitate a connection between the two users and initiate the downloading of the file without any further action on either user's part.

According to Napster, when the requesting user clicks on the name of the desired MP3 file, the Napster server routes this request to the host user's browser. The host user's browser responds that it either can or cannot supply the file. If the host user can supply the file, the Napster server communicates the host's address and routing information to the requesting user's browser, allowing the requesting user to make a connection with the host and receive the desired MP3 file. The parties disagree about whether this process involves a hypertext link that the Napster server-side software provides. However, plaintiffs admit that the Napster server gets the necessary IP address information from the host user, enabling the requesting user to connect to the host. The MP3 file is actually transmitted over the Internet, but the steps necessary to make that connection could not take place without the Napster server.

The Napster system has other functions besides allowing users to search for, request, and download MP3 files. For example, a requesting user can play a downloaded song using the MusicShare software. Napster also hosts a chat room.

Napster has developed a policy that makes compliance with all copyright laws one of the "terms of use" of its service and warns users that:

> Napster will terminate the accounts of users who are repeat infringers of the copyrights, or other intellectual property rights, of others. In addition, Napster reserves the right to terminate the account of a user upon any single infringement of the rights of others in conjunction with use of the Napster service.

2. Napster uses the term "host user" to refer to the user who makes the desired   MP3 file available for downloading.

Kessler Dec. ¶ 19. However, the parties disagree over when this policy was instituted and how effectively it bars infringers from using the Napster service. Napster claims that it had a copyright compliance policy as early as October 1999, but admits that it did not document or notify users of the existence of this policy until February 7, 2000.

* * *

DISCUSSION

Section 512 of the DMCA addresses the liability of online service and Internet access providers for copyright infringements occurring online. Subsection 512(a) exempts qualifying service providers from monetary liability for direct, vicarious, and contributory infringement and limits injunctive relief to the degree specified in subparagraph 512(j)(1)(B). Interpretation of subsection 512(a), or indeed any of the section 512 safe harbors, appears to be an issue of first impression.

Napster claims that its business activities fall within the safe harbor provided by subsection 512(a). This subsection limits liability "for infringement of copyright by reason of the [service] provider's transmitting, routing, or providing connections for, material through a system or network controlled or operated by or for the service provider, or by reason of the intermediate and transient storage of that material in the course of such transmitting, routing, or providing connections," if five conditions are satisfied:

(1) the transmission of the material was initiated by or at the direction of a person other than the service provider;

(2) the transmission, routing, provision of connections, or storage is carried out through an automatic technical process without selection of the material by the service provider;

(3) the service provider does not select the recipients of the material except as an automatic response to the request of another person;

(4) no copy of the material made by the service provider in the course of such intermediate or transient storage is maintained on the system or network in a manner ordinarily accessible to anyone other than the anticipated recipients, and no such copy is maintained on the system or network in a manner ordinarily accessible to such anticipated recipients for a longer period than is reasonably necessary for the transmission, routing, or provision of connections; and

(5) the material is transmitted through the system or network without modification of its content.

17 U.S.C. § 512(a).

Citing the "definitions" subsection of the statute, Napster argues that it is a "service provider" for the purposes of the 512(a) safe harbor. *See* 17 U.S.C. § 512(k)(1)(A).[4] First, it claims to offer the "transmission,

---

4. Subparagraph 512(k)(1)(A) provides: As used in subsection (a), the term "ser-

vice provider" means an entity offering the transmission, routing, or providing of con-

routing, or providing of connections for digital online communications" by enabling the connection of users' hard-drives and the transmission of MP3 files "directly from the Host hard drive and Napster browser through the Internet to the user's Napster browser and hard drive." Def. Reply Br. at 3. Second, Napster states that users choose the online communication points and the MP3 files to be transmitted with no direction from Napster. Finally, the Napster system does not modify the content of the transferred files. Defendant contends that, because it meets the definition of "service provider,"[5] it need only satisfy the five remaining requirements of the safe harbor to prevail in its motion for summary adjudication.

Defendant then seeks to show compliance with these requirements by arguing: (1) a Napster user, and never Napster itself, initiates the transmission of MP3 files; (2) the transmission occurs through an automatic, technical process without any editorial input from Napster; (3) Napster does not choose the recipients of the MP3 files; (4) Napster does not make a copy of the material during transmission; and (5) the content of the material is not modified during transmission. Napster maintains that the 512(a) safe harbor thus protects its core function— "transmitting, routing and providing connections for sharing of the files its users choose." Def. Reply Br. at 2.

Plaintiffs disagree. They first argue that subsection 512(n) requires the court to analyze each of Napster's functions independently and that not all of these functions fall under the 512(a) safe harbor. In their view, Napster provides information location tools-such as a search engine, directory, index, and links-that are covered by the more stringent eligibility requirements of subsection 512(d), rather than subsection 512(a).

Plaintiffs also contend that Napster does not perform the function which the 512(a) safe harbor protects because the infringing material is not transmitted or routed *through* the Napster system, as required by subsection 512(a). They correctly note that the definition of "service provider" under subparagraph 512(k)(1)(A) is not identical to the prefatory language of subsection 512(a). The latter imposes the additional requirement that transmitting, routing, or providing connections must occur "through the system or network." Plaintiffs argue in the alterna-

---

nections for digital online communications, between or among points specified by a user, of material of the user's choosing, without modification to the content of the material sent or received.

Subparagraph 512(k)(1)(B) states:

As used in this section, other than subsection (a), the term "service provider" means a provider of online services or network access, or the operator of facilities therefor, and includes an entity described in subparagraph (A).

5. It is not entirely clear to the court that Napster qualifies under the narrower subparagraph 512(k)(1)(A). However, plaintiffs appear to concede that Napster is a "service provider" within the meaning of subparagraph 512(k)(1)(A), arguing instead that Napster does not satisfy the additional limitations that the prefatory language of subsection 512(a) imposes. The court assumes, but does not hold, that Napster is a "service provider" under subparagraph 512(k)(1)(A).

tive that, if users' computers are part of the Napster system, copies of MP3 files are stored on the system longer than reasonably necessary for transmission, and thus subparagraph 512(a)(4) is not satisfied.

Finally, plaintiffs note that, under the general eligibility requirements established in subsection 512(i), a service provider must have adopted, reasonably implemented, and informed its users of a policy for terminating repeat infringers. Plaintiffs contend that Napster only adopted its copyright compliance policy after the onset of this litigation and even now does not discipline infringers in any meaningful way. Therefore, in plaintiffs' view, Napster fails to satisfy the DMCA's threshold eligibility requirements or show that the 512(a) safe harbor covers any of its functions.

I. Independent Analysis of Functions

Subsection 512(n) of the DMCA states:

Subsections (a), (b), (c), and (d) describe separate and distinct functions for purposes of applying this section. Whether a service provider qualifies for the limitation on liability in any one of those subsections shall be based solely on the criteria in that subsection and shall not affect a determination of whether that service provider qualifies for the limitations on liability under any other such subsections.

Citing subsection 512(n), plaintiffs argue that the 512(a) safe harbor does not offer blanket protection to Napster's entire system. Plaintiffs consider the focus of the litigation to be Napster's function as an information location tool—eligible for protection, if at all, under the more rigorous subsection 512(d). They contend that the system does not operate as a passive conduit within the meaning subsection 512(a). In this view, Napster's only possible safe harbor is subsection 512(d), which applies to service providers "referring or linking users to an online location containing infringing material or infringing activity, by using information location tools, including a directory, index, reference, pointer, or hypertext link...." Subsection 512(d) imposes more demanding eligibility requirements because it covers active assistance to users.

Defendant responds in two ways. First, it argues that subsection 512(a), rather than 512(d), applies because the information location tools it provides are incidental to its core function of automatically transmitting, routing, or providing connections for the MP3 files users select. In the alternative, defendant maintains that, even if the court decides to analyze the information location functions under 512(d), it should hold that the 512(a) safe harbor protects other aspects of the Napster service.

Napster undisputedly performs some information location functions. The Napster server stores a transient list of the files that each user currently logged-on to that server wants to share. This data is maintained until the user logs off, but the structure of the index itself continues to exist. If a user wants to find a particular song or recording artist, she enters a search, and Napster looks for the search terms in the index. Edward Kessler, Napster's Vice President of Engineering, admitted in his deposition that, at least in this context, Napster functions as a free information location tool. *See* [Kessler's deposition] at 21:12–19; *cf.* Farmer Dec. ¶ 16 (stating that "Napster operates exactly like a search engine or information location tool to the user"). Napster software also has a "hot list" function that allows users to search for other users' login names and receive notification when users with whom they might want to communicate have connected to the service. In short, the parties agree on the existence of a searchable directory and index, and Napster representatives have used the phrase "information location tool," which appears in the heading for subsection 512(d), to characterize some Napster functions.

There the agreement ends. According to Napster, the information location tools upon which plaintiffs base their argument are incidental to the system's core function of transmitting MP3 music files, and for this reason, the court should apply subsection 512(a). Napster also disputes the contention that it organizes files or provides links to other Internet sites in the same manner as a search engine like Yahoo!. *See* Kessler Reply Dec. ¶ ¶ 16–20 (discussing differences between Napster and other search engines). Consequently, it deems subsection 512(d) inapplicable to its activities. *Cf.* H.R.Rep. No. 105–551(II), 105th Cong., 2d Sess. (1998), 1998 WL 414916, at (using Yahoo! as an example of an information location tool covered by 512(d)). Napster contrasts its operations, which proceed automatically after initial stimuli from users, with search engines like Yahoo! that depend upon the "human judgment and editorial discretion" of the service provider's staff. *Id.*

Napster's final and most compelling argument regarding subsection 512(d) is that the DMCA safe harbors are not mutually exclusive. According to subsection 512(n), a service provider could enjoy the 512(a) safe harbor even if its information location tools were also protected by (or failed to satisfy) subsection 512(d). *See* 17 U.S.C. § 512(n) ("Whether a service provider qualifies for the limitation on liability in any one of those subsections . . . shall not affect a determination of whether that service provider qualifies for the limitations on liability under any other such subsections.") Similarly, finding *some* aspects of the system outside the scope of subsection 512(a) would not preclude a ruling that *other* aspects *do* meet 512(a) criteria.

Because the parties dispute material issues regarding the operation of Napster's index, directory, and search engine, the court declines to hold that these functions are peripheral to the alleged infringement, or that they should not be analyzed separately under subsection 512(d).[6] Indeed, despite its contention that its search engine and indexing functions are incidental to the provision of connections and transmission of MP3 files, Napster has advertised the ease with which its users can locate "millions of songs" online without "wading through page after

---

6. The court need not rule on the applicability of subsection 512(d) to the functions plaintiffs characterize as information location tools because defendant does not rely on subsection 512(d) as grounds for its motion for summary adjudication.

page of unknown artists." Frackman Dec., Exh. 5, 4. Such statements by Napster to promote its service are tantamount to an admission that its search and indexing functions are essential to its marketability. Some of these essential functions-including but not limited to the search engine and index-should be analyzed under subsection 512(d).

However, the potential applicability of subsection 512(d) does not completely foreclose use of the 512(a) safe harbor as an affirmative defense. *See* 17 U.S.C. § 512(n). The court will now turn to Napster's eligibility for protection under subsection 512(a). It notes at the outset, though, that a ruling that subsection 512(a) applies to a given function would not mean that the DMCA affords the service provider blanket protection.

II. Subsection 512(a)

Plaintiffs' principal argument against application of the 512(a) safe harbor is that Napster does not perform the passive conduit function eligible for protection under this subsection. As defendant correctly notes, the words "conduit" or "passive conduit" appear nowhere in 512(a), but are found only in the legislative history and summaries of the DMCA. The court must look first to the plain language of the statute, "construing the provisions of the entire law, including its object and policy, to ascertain the intent of Congress." *United States v. Hockings*, 129 F.3d 1069, 1071 (9th Cir.1997) (quoting *Northwest Forest Resource Council v. Glickman*, 82 F.3d 825, 830 (9th Cir.1996)) (internal quotation marks omitted). If the statute is unclear, however, the court may rely on the legislative history. *See Hockings*, 129 F.3d at 1071. The language of subsection 512(a) makes the safe harbor applicable, as a threshold matter, to service providers "transmitting, routing or providing connections for, material *through a system or network* controlled or operated by or for the service provider...." 17 U.S.C. § 512(a) (emphasis added). According to plaintiffs, the use of the word "conduit" in the legislative history explains the meaning of "through a system."

Napster has expressly denied that the transmission of MP3 files ever passes through its servers. *See* Kessler Dec. ¶ 14. Indeed, Kessler declared that "files reside on the computers of Napster users, and are transmitted directly between those computers." *Id.* MP3 files are transmitted "from the Host user's hard drive and Napster browser, *through the Internet* to the recipient's Napster browser and hard drive." Def. Reply Br. at 3 (citing Kessler Dec. ¶ 12–13). The Internet cannot be considered "a system or network controlled or operated by or for the service provider," however. 17 U.S.C. § 512(a). To get around this problem, Napster avers (and plaintiffs seem willing to concede) that "Napster's servers and Napster's MusicShare browsers on its users' computers are all part of Napster's overall system." Defendant narrowly defines its system to include the browsers on users' computers. In contrast, plaintiffs argue that either (1) the system does not include the browsers, or (2) it includes not only the browsers, but also the users' computers themselves.

Even assuming that the system includes the browser on each user's computer, the MP3 files are not transmitted "through" the system within the meaning of subsection 512(a). Napster emphasizes the passivity of its role-stating that "[a]ll files transfer directly from the computer of one Napster user *through the Internet* to the computer of the requesting user." Def. Br. at 5 (emphasis added). It admits that the transmission bypasses the Napster server. This means that, even if each user's Napster browser is part of the system, the transmission goes *from* one part of the system *to* another, or *between* parts of the system, but not "through" the system. The court finds that subsection 512(a) does not protect the transmission of MP3 files.

The prefatory language of subsection 512(a) is disjunctive, however. The subsection applies to "infringement of copyright by reason of the provider's transmitting, routing, *or* providing connections through a system or network controlled or operated by or for the service provider." 17 U.S.C. § 512(a) (emphasis added). The court's finding that transmission does not occur "through" the system or network does not foreclose the possibility that subsection 512(a) applies to "routing" or "providing connections." Rather, each of these functions must be analyzed independently.

Napster contends that providing connections between users' addresses "constitutes the value of the system to the users and the public." Def. Br. at 15. This connection cannot be established without the provision of the host's address to the Napster browser software installed on the requesting user's computer. *See* Kessler Dec. ¶ 10–13. The central Napster server delivers the host's address. *See id.* While plaintiffs contend that the infringing material is not *transmitted* through the Napster system, they provide no evidence to rebut the assertion that Napster supplies the requesting user's computer with information necessary to facilitate a connection with the host.

Nevertheless, the court finds that Napster does not provide connections "through" its system. Although the Napster server conveys address information to establish a connection between the requesting and host users, the connection itself occurs through the Internet. The legislative history of section 512 demonstrates that Congress intended the 512(a) safe harbor to apply only to activities "in which a service provider plays the role of a 'conduit' for the communications of others." H.R.Rep. No. 105–551(II), 105th Cong., 2d Sess. (1998), 1998 WL 414916, at *130. Drawing inferences in the light most favorable to the non-moving party, this court cannot say that Napster serves as a conduit for the connection itself, as opposed to the address information that makes the connection possible. Napster enables or facilitates the initiation of connections, but these connections do not pass through the system within the meaning of subsection 512(a).

Neither party has adequately briefed the meaning of "routing" in subsection 512(a), nor does the legislative history shed light on this issue. Defendant tries to make "routing" and "providing connections" appear synonymous-stating, for example, that "the central Napster server *routes* the transmission by providing the Host's address to the Napster browser that is installed on and in use by User's computer." Def. Br. at 16. However, the court doubts that Congress would have used the terms "routing" and "providing connections" disjunctively if they had the same meaning. It is clear from both parties' submissions that the route of the allegedly infringing material goes through the Internet from the host to the requesting user, not through the Napster server. *See, e.g.*, Def. Br. at 13 ("Indeed, the content of the MP3 files are routed without even passing through Napster's Servers."). The court holds that routing does not occur through the Napster system.

Because Napster does not transmit, route, or provide connections through its system, it has failed to demonstrate that it qualifies for the 512(a) safe harbor. The court thus declines to grant summary adjudication in its favor.

III. Copyright Compliance Policy

Even if the court had determined that Napster meets the criteria outlined in subsection 512(a), subsection 512(i) imposes additional requirements on eligibility for any DMCA safe harbor. This provision states:

The limitations established by this section shall apply to a service provider only if the service provider-

(A) has adopted and reasonably implemented, and informs subscribers and account holders of the service provider's system or network of, a policy that provides for the termination in appropriate circumstances of subscribers and account holders of the service provider's system or network who are repeat infringers; and

(B) accommodates and does not interfere with standard technical measures.

17 U.S.C. § 512(i).

Plaintiffs challenge Napster's compliance with these threshold eligibility requirements on two grounds. First, they point to evidence from Kessler's deposition that Napster did not adopt a written policy of which its users had notice until on or around February 7, 2000–two months after the filing of this lawsuit. Kessler testified that, although Napster had a copyright compliance policy as early as October 1999, he is not aware that this policy was reflected in any document or communicated to any user. Congress did not intend to require a service provider to "investigate possible infringements, monitor its service or make difficult judgments as to whether conduct is or is not infringing," but the notice requirement is designed to insure that flagrant or repeat infringers "know that there is a realistic threat of losing [their] access." H.R. Rep. 105–551(II), 1998 WL 414916, at *154.

Napster attempts to refute plaintiffs' argument by noting that subsection 512(i) does not specify when the copyright compliance policy must be in place. Although this characterization of subsection 512(i) is facially accurate, it defies the logic of making formal notification to users or subscribers a prerequisite to exemption from monetary liability. The fact that Napster developed and notified its users of a formal policy *after* the onset of this action should not moot plaintiffs' claim to monetary relief for past harms. Without further documentation, defendant's argument that it has satisfied subsection 512(i) is merely conclusory and does not support summary adjudication in its favor.

Summary adjudication is also inappropriate because Napster has not shown that it *reasonably* implemented a policy for terminating repeat infringers. *See* 17 U.S.C. § 512(i)(A) (requiring "reasonable" implementation of such a policy). If Napster is formally notified of infringing activity, it blocks the infringer's password so she cannot log on to the Napster service using that password. Napster does not block the IP addresses of infringing users, however, and the parties dispute whether it would be feasible or effective to do so.

Plaintiffs aver that Napster wilfully turns a blind eye to the identity of its users—that is, their real names and physical addresses—because their anonymity allows Napster to disclaim responsibility for copyright infringement. Hence, plaintiffs contend, "infringers may readily reapply to the Napster system to recommence their infringing downloading and uploading of MP3 music files." Pl. Br. at 24. Plaintiffs' expert, computer security researcher Daniel Farmer, declared that he conducted tests in which he easily deleted all traces of his former Napster identity, convincing Napster that "it had never seen me or my computer before ." Farmer also cast doubt on Napster's contention that blocking IP addresses is not a reasonable means of terminating infringers. He noted that Napster bans the IP addresses of users who runs "bots"[8] on the service.

Hence, plaintiffs raise genuine issues of material fact about whether Napster has reasonably implemented a policy of terminating repeat infringers. They have produced evidence that Napster's copyright compliance policy is neither timely nor reasonable within the meaning of subparagraph 512(i)(A).

Conclusion

This court has determined above that Napster does not meet the requirements of subsection 512(a) because it does not transmit, route, or provide connections for allegedly infringing material through its system. The court also finds summary adjudication inappropriate due to the existence of genuine issues of material fact about Napster's compliance with subparagraph 512(i)(A), which a service provider must satisfy to enjoy the protection of any section 512 safe harbor. Defendant's motion for summary adjudication is DENIED.

IT IS SO ORDERED.

---

8. Farmer informed that court that "A 'bot' is a robot, or program, that performs actions continuously, in a sort of manic or robotic fashion." Farmer Dec. ¶ 27.

Notes

1. In a related decision, ___ F.Supp.2d ___, 55 U.S.P.Q.2d 1780, the District Court held that Napster's users were not engaged in "fair use," since the only significant use of Napster replaced the purchase of copyrighted materials. The District Court granted the record companies a preliminary injunction against Napster, 2000 WL 1009483, but the Ninth Circuit had granted a stay of the injunction as this casebook was going to press. 2000 WL 1055915.

2. If Napster loses this case on appeal, how would you advise it to revise its system so as to fall under the safe harbor provisions of § 512? Would routing all files through a huge Napster server be enough? Would Napster's intent matter?

4. FIRST SALE

COPYRIGHT ACT OF 1976—§ 109

§ 109. Limitations on Exclusive Rights: Effect of transfer of particular copy or phonorecord

(a) Notwithstanding the provisions of section 106(3), the owner of a particular copy or phonorecord lawfully made under this title, or any person authorized by such owner, is entitled, without the authority of the copyright owner, to sell or otherwise dispose of the possession of that copy or phonorecord. Notwithstanding the preceding sentence, copies or phonorecords of works subject to restored copyright under section 104A that are manufactured before the date of restoration of copyright or, with respect to reliance parties, before publication or service of notice under section 104A(e), may be sold or otherwise disposed of without the authorization of the owner of the restored copyright for purposes of direct or indirect commercial advantage only during the 12–month period beginning on—

(1) the date of the publication in the Federal Register of the notice of intent filed with the Copyright Office under section 104A(d)(2)(A), or

(2) the date of the receipt of actual notice served under section 104A(d)(2)(B), whichever occurs first.

(b)(1)(A) Notwithstanding the provisions of subsection (a), unless authorized by the owners of copyright in the sound recording or the owner of copyright in a computer program (including any tape, disk, or other medium embodying such program), and in the case of a sound recording in the musical works embodied therein, neither the owner of a particular phonorecord nor any person in possession of a particular copy of a computer program (including any tape, disk, or other medium embodying such program), may, for the purposes of direct or indirect commercial advantage, dispose of, or authorize the disposal of, the possession of that phonorecord or computer program (including any tape, disk, or other medium embodying such program) by rental, lease, or lending, or by any other act or practice in the nature of rental, lease, or lending. Nothing in the preceding sentence shall apply to the rental, lease, or lending of a phonorecord for nonprofit purposes by a nonprofit library or nonprofit educational institution. The transfer of possession of a lawfully made copy of a computer program by a nonprofit educational institution to another nonprofit educational institution or to faculty, staff, and students does not constitute rental, lease, or lending for direct or indirect commercial purposes under this subsection.

(B) This subsection does not apply to—

(i) a computer program which is embodied in a machine or product and which cannot be copied during the ordinary operation or use of the machine or product; or

(ii) a computer program embodied in or used in conjunction with a limited purpose computer that is designed for playing video games and may be designed for other purposes.

(C) Nothing in this subsection affects any provision of chapter 9 of this title.

Note

The Uniform Computer Information Transactions Act ("UCITA") contains provisions which will allow software licensors to eliminate the restrictions of 17 U.S.C. § 109 within the language of "shrinkwrap licenses." UCITA § 503(2). UCITA § 509 and § 510 validate standard form contract provisions that would choose UCITA as the applicable law and a state that has enacted UCITA as the forum for deciding a case. UCITA § 102(a)(20) and § 307(b) validate provisions in "shrinkwrap licenses" that prohibit reverse engineering. What are the implications of these UCITA provisions? Do they give too much power to the copyright owners? Or does this give those who invested in the development of software more appropriate protection for their investment? Are they preempted by the United States Copyright Act—see the discussion at p. 200.

DSC COMMUNICATIONS CORP. v. PULSE COMMUNICATIONS, INC.

United States Court of Appeals, Federal Circuit, 1999.
170 F.3d 1354, *cert. denied* ___ U.S. ___, 120 S.Ct. 286, 145 L.Ed.2d 240.

BRYSON, CIRCUIT JUDGE.

DSC Communications Corporation (DSC) and Pulse Communications, Inc., (Pulsecom) make products for the telephone industry and compete for the business of the Regional Bell Operating Companies, more commonly known as the "RBOCs." Competition between the two parties led to this litigation over certain products that the two produce for use in commercial telephone systems.

DSC struck first, filing an action in the United States District Court for the Eastern District of Virginia in which it alleged that Pulsecom had committed various federal and state law violations, including (1) contributory infringement of DSC's copyright in certain software used with one of DSC's products; (2) direct infringement of DSC's copyright in that software; (3) misappropriation of DSC's trade secrets; and (4) tortious interference with DSC's business expectancy. Pulsecom then counterclaimed, charging that DSC had infringed Pulsecom's U.S. Patent No. 5,263,081 (the '081 patent).

The parties went to trial on DSC's claims, and at the close of DSC's case-in-chief, Pulsecom moved for judgment as a matter of law. The court granted the motion and dismissed all four of DSC's claims. With respect to Pulsecom's counterclaim of patent infringement, the court held a hearing to construe the claims, and the parties subsequently filed cross-motions for summary judgment. The court granted DSC's motion and entered a summary judgment of noninfringement.

I

This case involves certain components of digital loop carrier systems (DLCs), electronic devices that allow telephone companies to serve large numbers of subscribers efficiently. Before the advent of DLCs, telephone companies had to run copper wire from their central offices to the telephones of each of their subscribers. DLCs allow the individual copper lines to be run over much shorter distances, resulting in large savings for telephone companies. Typically, a DLC is placed in a location central to a number of subscribers, and copper lines are run over the relatively short distances from the DLC to the subscribers.

The DLC acts as an analog-to-digital converter and as a signal modulator-demodulator. The electrical signals that travel over the copper lines between the DLC and the subscribers are voice-frequency analog signals, but the signals that travel between the DLC and the central telephone office are digital signals that travel over a high-bandwidth (e.g., fiber optic) digital channel. The DLC converts the various analog signals it receives from individual subscribers to a digital format and modulates those digital signals into a high-bandwidth composite signal that is sent to the central office through the digital channel. The DLC performs the reverse process on signals traveling from the central office to individual subscribers.

The devices at the heart of the dispute in this case are the "Litespan 2000" DLC, which is manufactured by DSC, and the interface cards, which DSC and Pulsecom designed to work with the Litespan. The Litespan has a backplane connecting 500 interface card slots, through interface circuitry, to a microprocessor. The backplane is controlled by an application-specific integrated circuit that uses a particular signaling protocol. The purpose of the interface cards is to comport with the backplane protocol while providing a particular type of service to subscribers. For example, a single Litespan might have some interface cards providing POTS (plain old telephone service) service and other interface cards providing PBX (private branch exchange) service. The analog signals traveling between the subscribers and the two types of interface cards may be quite different, but the interface cards process the signals so that they are compatible with the Litespan's backplane protocol.

Litespans and individual interface cards each have their own microprocessors and interface circuitry, which require software to operate. Two software packages are at issue here. The first is the Litespan System software, which includes both the Litespan operating system software and various Litespan utility programs. The second is the POTS–DI (download image) software, which DSC developed to operate its POTS interface cards. Both the Litespan System software and the POTS–DI software normally reside in nonvolatile storage within Litespan systems. When a DSC POTS card is inserted into a Litespan and powered up, a copy of the POTS–DI software is downloaded into volatile memory on the POTS card. When the POTS card is powered down, its copy of the POTS–DI software ceases to exist. This design allows changes to be made to the POTS–DI software in a central location (*i.e.,* in the Litespan system) with no need to update software in the individual POTS cards.

DSC designed the Litespan to be used in the telephone networks of the RBOCs, and it transferred the Litespan technology to the RBOCs through a series of comprehensive agreements. The seven agreements at issue here—DSC–Ameritech, DSC–NYNEX, DSC–Bell Atlantic (1993–96 and 1996–99), DSC–U.S. West, DSC–Pacific Bell, and DSC–BellSouth—have generally similar provisions. The agreements all contain provisions that license, under a variety of restrictions, the Litespan System software and POTS–DI software to the RBOCs.

Pulsecom has developed a Litespan-compatible POTS card to compete with DSC's POTS card. Pulsecom decided not to develop the software necessary to operate its POTS card, but rather to design the card so that—like DSC's POTS card—it downloads the POTS–DI software from the host Litespan into its resident memory upon power-up. Pulsecom's design has the obvious advantage of allowing Pulsecom's POTS cards to remain compatible with the Litespan system if DSC modifies its Litespan System software and POTS–DI software.

II

A

Although DSC's complaint alleged only copyright and state law claims, we have jurisdiction over this appeal under 28 U.S.C. § 1295(a)(1) because Pulsecom filed a counterclaim that raised a non-frivolous claim of patent infringement. Section 1295(a)(1) gives this court exclusive jurisdiction over an appeal from a final judgment of a district court "if the jurisdiction of that court was based, in whole or in part, on [28 U.S.C. § 1338]." The congressional policy underlying section 1295(a)(1) was to ensure uniform resolution of patent law disputes. In light of that policy and the plain language of section 1295(a)(1), we have held that our appellate jurisdiction extends to cases in which nonfrivolous claims of patent infringement have been raised in compulsory counterclaims. While the court in Aerojet–General did not need to decide whether to apply that principle to permissive counterclaims, we see no sufficient basis in the language or purpose of section 1295(a)(1) to distinguish between compulsory and permissive counterclaims. We therefore hold that any counterclaim raising a nonfrivolous claim of patent infringement is sufficient to support this court's appellate jurisdiction.

DSC's principal contention on appeal is that the district court improperly granted judgment to Pulsecom on DSC's contributory copyright infringement claim at the close of DSC's case. On that issue, as on the other copyright and state law issues before us, we follow the law of the circuit from which this appeal is taken. With respect to the issues raised in DSC's appeal, our task is therefore to determine how the Fourth Circuit would decide those issues.

DSC's theory of contributory infringement is that each time an RBOC powers up a Pulsecom POTS card in one of its Litespan systems, it directly infringes DSC's POTS–DI software copyright by copying the POTS–DI software from the Litespan into the resident memory of a Pulsecom POTS card. An act of direct infringement is a necessary predicate for any derivative liability on the part of Pulsecom; absent direct infringement, there can be no contributory infringement. The district court disposed of DSC's claim on the ground that DSC had not made a prima facie showing of direct infringement.

Pivotal to the proper resolution of DSC's copyright infringement claim is the interpretation and application of section 117 of the Copyright Act, 17 U.S.C. § 117. Because the Fourth Circuit has not had occasion to construe section 117, we have no direct guidance as to how that court would approach the problem in this case. We therefore look to general principles of copyright law in addressing the copyright infringement issue.

Section 117 provides a limitation on the exclusive rights of the owner of the copyright in a piece of software. It provides, in pertinent part:

> [I]t is not an infringement for the owner of a copy of a computer program to make or authorize the making of another copy or adaptation of that computer program provided: (1) that such a new copy or adaptation is created as an essential step in the utilization of the computer program in conjunction with a machine and that it is used in no other manner. . . .

17 U.S.C. § 117. The district court concluded that making copies of the POTS–DI software (in the resident memory of POTS cards) was an "essential step in the utilization" of the POTS–DI software and that there was no evidence that the RBOCs used the software in any other manner that would constitute infringement. Accordingly, under the district court's theory of the case there was no direct infringement (and thus no contributory infringement) if the RBOCs were section 117 "owners" of copies of the POTS–DI software.

The district court then held that the RBOCs were "owners" of copies of the POTS–DI software because they obtained the software by making a single payment and obtaining a right to possession of the software for an unlimited period. Those attributes of the transaction, the court concluded, made the transaction a "sale."

DSC challenges the district court's conclusion that, based on the terms of the purchase transactions between DSC and the RBOCs, the RBOCs were "owners" of copies of the POTS–DI software. In order to resolve that issue, we must determine what attributes are necessary to constitute ownership of copies of software in this context.

Unfortunately, ownership is an imprecise concept, and the Copyright Act does not define the term. Nor is there much useful guidance to be obtained from either the legislative history of the statute or the cases that have construed it. The National Commission on New Technological Uses of Copyrighted Works ("CONTU") was created by Congress to recommend changes in the Copyright Act to accommodate advances in computer technology. In its final report, CONTU proposed a version of section 117 that is identical to the one that was ultimately enacted, except for a single change. The proposed CONTU version provided that "it is not an infringement for the *rightful possessor of a copy* of a computer program to make or authorize the making of another copy or adaptation of that program...." Congress, however, substituted the words "owner of a copy" in place of the words "rightful possessor of a copy." The legislative history does not explain the reason for the change, but it is clear from the fact of the substitution of the term "owner" for "rightful possessor" that Congress must have meant to require more than "rightful possession" to trigger the section 117 defense.

In the leading case on section 117 ownership, the Ninth Circuit considered an agreement in which MAI, the owner of a software copyright, transferred copies of the copyrighted software to Peak under an agreement that imposed severe restrictions on Peak's rights with respect to those copies. *See MAI Sys. Corp. v. Peak Computer, Inc.*, 991 F.2d 511, 26 USPQ 2d 1458, 1462 (9th Cir.1993). The court held that Peak was not an "owner" of the copies of the software for purposes of section 117 and thus did not enjoy the right to copy conferred on owners by that statute. The Ninth Circuit stated that it reached the conclusion that Peak was not an owner because Peak had licensed the software from MAI. That explanation of the court's decision has been criticized for failing to recognize the distinction between ownership of a copyright, which can be licensed, and ownership of copies of the copyrighted software. Plainly, a party who purchases copies of software from the copyright owner can hold a license under a copyright while still being an "owner" of a copy of the copyrighted software for purposes of section 117. We therefore do not adopt the Ninth Circuit's characterization of all licensees as non-owners. Nonetheless, the *MAI* case is instructive, because the agreement between MAI and Peak, like the agreements at issue in this case, imposed more severe restrictions on Peak's rights with respect to the software than would be imposed on a party who owned copies of software subject only to the rights of the copyright holder under the Copyright Act. And for that reason, it was proper to hold that Peak was not an "owner" of copies of the copyrighted software for purposes of section 117. We therefore turn to the agreements between DSC and the RBOCs to determine whether those agreements establish that the RBOCs are section 117 "owners" of copies of the copyrighted POTS–DI software.

Each of the DSC–RBOC agreements contains a provision that is similar in effect to the following, taken from the DSC–BellSouth agreement: "All rights, title and interest in the Software are and shall remain with seller, subject, however, to a license to Buyer to use the Software solely in conjunction with the Material [*i.e.*, the Litespan–2000 and related equipment] during the useful life of the Material." Two of the agreements also contain clauses that provide for the passage of title to all the material transferred from DSC to the RBOCs, except for the software. The language and the context of those clauses makes it clear that the clauses refer to DSC's rights to the copies of the software in the RBOCs' possession, not DSC's copyright interest in the software. There was no need for a contract clause making clear that DSC was not selling its copyrights in its software to its customers, as it was obvious that DSC did not intend to convey any ownership rights in its copyright as part of the licensing agreements with the RBOCs. The question of ownership of the copies of the software, by contrast, was a matter that needed to be addressed in the contracts.

Not only do the agreements characterize the RBOCs as non-owners of copies of the software, but the restrictions imposed on the RBOCs' rights with respect to the software are consistent with that characterization. In particular, the licensing agreements severely limit the rights of the RBOCs with respect to the POTS–DI software in ways that are inconsistent with the rights normally enjoyed by owners of copies of software.

Section 106 of the Copyright Act, 17 U.S.C. § 106, reserves for a copyright owner the following exclusive rights in the copyrighted work: the right to reproduce the work; the right to prepare derivative works; the right to distribute copies of the work; the right to perform the work publicly; and the right to display the work publicly. Those rights are expressly limited, however, by sections 107 through 120 of the Act. Of particular importance are the limitations of sections 109 and 117. As we have seen, section 117 limits the copyright owner's exclusive rights by allowing an owner of a copy of a computer program to reproduce or adapt the program if reproduction or adaptation is necessary for the program to be used in conjunction with a machine. Section 109, which embodies the "first sale" doctrine, limits the copyright owner's otherwise exclusive right of distribution by providing, in relevant part, that

> the owner of a particular copy ... is entitled, without the authority of the copyright owner, to sell or otherwise dispose of the possession of that copy....

* * *

Notwithstanding [the above], unless authorized by . . . the owner of copyright in a computer program . . . [no] person in possession of a particular copy of a computer program . . . may, for the purposes of direct or indirect commercial advantage, dispose of, or authorize the disposal of, the possession of that . . . computer program . . . by rental, lease, or lending. . . .

17 U.S.C. § 109. Each of the DSC–RBOC agreements limits the contracting RBOC's right to transfer copies of the POTS–DI software or to disclose the details of the software to third parties. For example, the DSC–Ameritech agreement provides that Ameritech shall "not provide, disclose or make the Software or any portions or aspects thereof available to any person except its employees on a 'need to know' basis without the prior written consent of [DSC]. . . ." Such a restriction is plainly at odds with the section 109 right to transfer owned copies of software to third parties. The agreements also prohibit the RBOCs from using the software on hardware other than that provided by DSC. If the RBOCs were "owners of copies" of the software, section 117 would allow them to use the software on any hardware, regardless of origin. Because the DSC-RBOC agreements substantially limit the rights of the RBOCs compared to the rights they would enjoy as "owners of copies" of the POTS–DI software under the Copyright Act, the contents of the agreements support the characterization of the RBOCs as non-owners of the copies of the POTS-DI software.

In finding that the RBOCs were owners of copies of the POTS–DI software, the district court relied heavily on its finding that the RBOCs obtained their interests in the copies of the software through a single payment and for an unlimited period of time. It is true that the transfer of rights to the POTS-DI software in each of the agreements did not take the form of a lease, and that the transfer in each case was in exchange for a single payment and was for a term that was either unlimited or nearly so. One commentator has argued that when a copy of a software program is transferred for a single payment and for an unlimited term, the transferee should be considered an "owner" of the copy of the software program regardless of other restrictions on his use of the software. That view has not been accepted by other courts, however, and we think it overly simplistic. The concept of ownership of a copy entails a variety of rights and interests. The fact that the right of possession is perpetual, or that the possessor's rights were obtained through a single payment, is certainly relevant to whether the possessor is an owner, but those factors are not necessarily dispositive if the possessor's right to use the software is heavily encumbered by other restrictions that are inconsistent with the status of owner.

In passing, the district court found added support for its ruling on the contributory infringement issue in the "non-exclusive market rights" clause in DSC's contracts with the RBOCs. The court concluded that the market rights clause supported its view that the RBOCs were entitled to use the POTS–DI software in connection with Pulsecom's POTS cards, because otherwise there would be no point in permitting the RBOCs to buy equipment such as POTS cards from another source.

We conclude that the district court read the market rights clause too broadly. The market rights clause gave the RBOCs the right to obtain competing products and software from other sources, but it did not give the RBOCs the right to copy DSC's copyrighted software in the course of using other companies' products. In fact, the contracts specifically prohibited the RBOCs from copying DSC's software except for use with DSC equipment.

In light of the restrictions on the RBOCs' rights in the copies of the POTS–DI software, we hold that it was improper for the court to conclude, as a matter of law, that the RBOCs were "owners" under section 117 of the copies of DSC's software that were in their possession. The court was therefore incorrect to rule, at the close of DSC's case, that section 117 of the Copyright Act gave the RBOCs the right to copy the POTS–DI software when using Pulsecom's POTS cards without violating DSC's copyright in the software. Accordingly, we reverse the district court's order granting judgment for Pulsecom on DSC's contributory infringement claim.

B

DSC next challenges the district court's ruling—again at the close of DSC's case-in-chief—dismissing DSC's claim of direct copyright infringement.

In its amended complaint, DSC charged that Pulsecom committed direct copyright infringement by creating copies of the POTS–DI software, both in two Litespan systems that Pulsecom obtained on the open market, and in the RBOCs' own Litespan systems. The district court found no infringement on the ground that the RBOCs' rights under 17 U.S.C. § 117 allowed them to authorize the making of copies of the POTS–DI software and thus shielded Pulsecom from liability for making copies of the software on the RBOCs' Litespan systems. Our rejection of the district court's ruling that the RBOCs were entitled under section 117 to make such copies requires that we also reject the court's conclusion that Pulsecom was legally entitled to make copies of the POTS–DI software by using the RBOCs' Litespan systems. Accordingly, that aspect of DSC's direct infringement claim must be remanded to the district court for further proceedings.

With respect to Pulsecom's activities in creating copies of the POTS–DI software with its own Litespan systems, we reach a different conclusion. Pulsecom obtained its Litespan systems on the open market. It was thus an owner of those systems and the associated software, and it was not subject to any restriction on its ownership interest through a licensing agreement or otherwise. As such, it was entitled, under 17

U.S.C. § 117, to make such copies of the POTS–DI software as were necessary to operate the systems. To the extent that DSC's direct infringement claim is directed at Pulsecom's conduct in making copies of the POTS–DI software during the operation of its own Litespan systems, DSC has no valid claim, and the district court's ruling is correct. Although DSC characterizes Pulsecom's activities in obtaining the Litespan systems as devious because Pulsecom did not purchase the systems in its own name, we attach no legal significance to the fact that Pulsecom used a third party to purchase the Litespan systems. Pulsecom's agent obtained the Litespan systems without restriction on their use, and there is no evidence that the copies were obtained through any misrepresentations that would affect the use that Pulsecom could lawfully make of the systems.

The district court dismissed DSC's direct copyright infringement claim on the ground that Pulsecom's conduct was excused by the affirmative defense of fair use for reverse engineering, as discussed in *Sega Enterprises, Ltd. v. Accolade, Inc.* The *Sega* case, however, does not stand for the proposition that any form of copyright infringement is privileged as long as it is done as part of an effort to explore the operation of a product that uses the copyrighted software. On the basis of DSC's evidence at trial, Pulsecom's activities in creating copies of the POTS–DI software on its POTS cards by using the RBOCs' Litespan systems does not qualify as "fair use" under the *Sega* analysis. DSC's evidence showed that Pulsecom representatives made copies of the POTS–DI software on Pulsecom POTS cards as part of the ordinary operation of those cards, not as part of an effort to determine how the Litespan system worked. Rather than being part of an attempt at reverse engineering, the copying appears to have been done after Pulsecom had determined how the system functioned and merely to demonstrate the interchangeability of the Pulsecom POTS cards with those made and sold by DSC.

Of course, Pulsecom has not put in its evidence on direct infringement, since the court granted judgment for Pulsecom at the close of the DSC's case. It is possible that Pulsecom may be able to make out a case of fair use under the *Sega* case or that there was no prohibited copying of the DSC software by Pulsecom, but in light of the state of the evidence at the close of DSC's case-in-chief, it was error for the district court to take the direct infringement case away from the jury with respect to the claims relating to the copies Pulsecom allegedly made of the POTS–DI software.

* * *

AFFIRMED IN PART, REVERSED IN PART, VACATED IN PART, and REMANDED.

F. INFRINGEMENT

1. DIRECT INFRINGEMENT

NEC CORP. AND NEC ELECTRONICS, INC. v. INTEL CORP.

United States District Court, N.D. California, 1989.
1989 WL 67434, 10 U.S.P.Q.2d 1177.

Gray, J.

In this action, NEC seeks a declaration that Intel's copyrights on its 8086 and 8088 microcodes are invalid and/or are not infringed by NEC. Intel has filed a counterclaim for infringement of its copyrights on those microcodes. This case was tried without a jury for eighteen days between April 25 and July 18, 1988, Post-trial briefs were filed, final arguments were heard on July 29, 1988, and the case then was submitted for decision. The issues to be determined and the decision that the court now renders on each are as follows:

* * *

3.   Do the microcodes that NEC produced for its V20, V30, V40 and V50 microprocessors infringe the Intel copyrights for its 8086 and 8088 microcodes? NEC's microcodes do not so infringe.

4.   Are NEC's V20 and V30 microprocessors no more than "improvements" upon its uPD 8086 and uPD 8088 microprocessors, which were licensed by Intel under its copyrights? NEC's V20 and V30 microprocessors are not simply "improvements" upon its uPD 8086 and uPD 8088 microprocessors.

The reasons for the foregoing decision are contained in the following discussion:

* * *

III.   THE NONINFRINGEMENT BY NEC'S MICROCODE

A.   The Issue Of Substantial Similarity.

In order to make a prima facie case of infringement, Intel must have a valid copyright, which it did obtain as noted above, establish access by NEC to the copyrighted microcode, which is admitted, and show substantial similarity between the latter and the accused microcode of NEC. In seeking to resolve the issue of substantial similarity, I have given careful consideration to the testimony and the conflicting conclusions of the two eminent experts, Dr. Patterson and Dr. Frieder, and I have also taken into account my own impressions upon comparing the respective microcodes in light of the other testimony and the exhibits in the case. In pursuing this study, I have sought to adhere to the admonition that

[i]n deciding whether there is substantial similarity between the copyrighted work and the accused work, courts do not allow the

accused work to be dissected into pieces, and the pieces isolated, as if each stood alone. Where the accused work reflects an accumulation of similarities, the totality of the taking is to be considered: "When analyzing two works to determine whether they are substantially similar, courts should be careful not to lose sight of the forest for the trees." In programming infringement cases involving comprehensive nonliteral similarity, the "trees" are the individual lines of code, and the "forest" is the detailed design.

Clapes, Lynch & Steinberg, *Silicon Epics And Binary Bards: Determining The Proper Scope of Copyright Protection For Computer Programs*, 34 UCLA L.Rev. 1493, 1570 (1987). Having pondered all of these matters, it is my conclusion that the NEC microcode (Rev. 2), when considered as a whole, is not substantially similar to the Intel microcode within the meaning of the copyright laws.

In the first place, none of the approximately ninety microroutines in the accused microcode are identical to Intel's copyrighted microcode. Some of the shorter ones are, indeed, substantially similar. But most of these involve simple, straightforward operations in which close similarity in approach is not surprising. On the other hand, others of the shorter microroutines of the NEC microcode are substantially different from the comparable Intel items.

Most of the approximately forty NEC microroutines that Intel acknowledges not to be substantially similar are much longer than the accused NEC items and are quite different from the comparable Intel items in the manner in which the instructions are expressed.

As I have pondered upon the testimony of the experts and studied the exhibits, I have developed a sympathetic understanding of what Judge Learned Hand meant when he observed in a relevant situation that "the more the court is led into the intricacies of dramatic craftsmanship, the less likely it is to stand upon the firmer, if more naive, ground of its considered impressions upon its own perusal." *Nichols v. Universal Pictures Corp.*, 45 F.2d 119, 123 [7 USPQ 84, 88] (2d Cir. 1930). Also, Intel has proposed a finding and has cited valid authority to the effect that "[t]he test for infringement or substantial similarity is whether the work is recognized by an ordinary observer as having been taken from the copyrighted source." Intel's Proposed Conclusions Of Law, ¶ 5. For the reasons set forth above, this court concludes, based upon its own perusal, as well as upon the conflicting testimony of the experts, that the ordinary observer, considering the accused microcode as a whole, would not recognize it as having been taken from the copyrighted source.

I believe that the foregoing conclusion comes close to resolving the issue of infringement. However, as pointed out, several of the shorter accused microroutines are substantially similar to Intel's corresponding items, and it is my obligation to "make a qualitative, not quantitative, judgment about the character of the work as a whole and the importance of the substantially similar portions of the work." *Whelan Assoc. v.*

Jaslow Dental Laboratory, 797 F.2d 1222, 1245 [230 USPQ 481, 498] (3d Cir.1986). Some of these similar microroutines may be very important, and if they result from copying of protected expressions their use by NEC may be enjoined, irrespective of the general lack of similarity between the two microcodes. Accordingly, we shall discuss what the evidence indicates as to whether or not actionable copying is responsible for the similarities that do exist in some of the microroutines.

B.   The Evidence Regarding Copying.

In preparing this portion of this memorandum, I am assuming that it will be of particular interest only to Intel and NEC and their respective counsel, and therefore that anyone who reads it will be familiar with the facts. Accordingly, I shall refrain from the extremely arduous and lengthy task of describing or explaining the background circumstances involving the specific issues.

Intel urges several bases for its contention that Mr. Kaneko created NEC's microcode for its V20/V30 microprocessors by copying substantial portions of Intel's 8086/88 microcode. These arguments are found not to be compelling.

1.   Assessment Of Mr. Kaneko's Expertise.

Intel contends that the indications are that Mr. Kaneko must have copied because of his relative inexperience with microprograms, the arduous schedule imposed upon him within which to write the microprograms and the specifications for the hardware, and the fact that he made relatively few notes as compared to his work on other microprograms. The record shows Mr. Kaneko to have been a very talented young man with an outstanding academic record that is highly relevant to microprocessors, and he previously had completed a substantial assembly language compiler program. Mr. Kaneko testified very creditably that he did not feel himself to have been under great pressure to complete his assignment and that he easily was able to accomplish it in two months, well within the time requested of him. The court also accepts Mr. Kaneko's testimony that the lack of notes stemmed from his conclusion that the task was relatively simple and that he was working alone, as compared with other assignments in which the participation of others made greater note taking more appropriate.

Mr. Kaneko testified in a straightforward manner and displayed considerable technical knowledge in explaining the decisions that he made in the creation of the V20/V30 microcode. He did not contend that he had not been influenced by his experience in previously having disassembled the 8086/88 microcode. Such experience inevitably became part of his expertise, and the acquired knowledge of how Mr. McKevitt created instructions to be executed by the 8086/88 microcode very well may have been a source of ideas that Mr. Kaneko utilized in preparing a microcode for the V20/V30. However, he testified creditably that he did not undertake to copy the 8086/88 microcode, and, as is noted herein, the other evidence received in the trial of this action by no means impels a contrary conclusion.

* * *

C. The Constraints.

1. The Hardware, Architecture And Specifications.

In seeking to show that there were many alternate ways in which Mr. Kaneko's various microprograms could have been written, and therefore that the substantial similarities to Intel's microcode that did exist stemmed from copying, Intel declined to take into consideration the constraints that limited Mr. Kaneko's choices. Intel contends that NEC could have created a microprocessor compatible with Intel's 8086/88 by using "different hardware, different architecture, different specifications and a different microinstruction format." Intel's Memorandum for the Trial Court, dated June 7, 1988, page 18. However, NEC had a license from Intel to duplicate the 8086/88 microprocessor hardware to the extent comprehended by the Intel patents. Both Dr. Patterson and Dr. Frieder acknowledged that the use of such hardware limited substantially the choices available to Mr. Kaneko in creating the microcode for the V-series. Having granted to NEC a license to duplicate the hardware of its 8086/88 to the extent comprehended by the Intel patents, and having conceded at trial that NEC had a right to duplicate the hardware of the 8086/88 because it was not otherwise protected by Intel, Intel is in no position to challenge NEC's right to use the aspects of Intel's microcode that are mandated by such hardware.

2. The Storage Space.

Intel also asserts that if NEC had utilized all of the storage area (ROM) available to it on its microprocessor, which would have been double the storage space that was available to Intel, any constraint imposed by size would have been removed and a different and better microcode would have resulted. Intel's Memorandum for the Trial Court, dated June 7, 1988, page 18. NEC elected to use part of the ROM space existing on the V-series, in order to accommodate microcode for additional macroinstructions on the same ROM. This also was a legitimate constraint; NEC was not obliged to avoid the similarity that other constraints imposed by creating a larger microcode.

3. The Clean Room.

The Clean Room microcode constitutes compelling evidence that the similarities between the NEC microcode and the Intel microcode resulted from constraints. The Clean Room microcode was governed by the same constraints of hardware, architecture and specifications as applied to the NEC microcode, and copying clearly was not involved. Mr. McKevitt, who created the 8086 microcode for Intel, readily acknowledged that the microarchitecture of the 8086 microprocessor affected the manner in which he created his microcode, and that he would expect that another independently created microcode for the 8086 would have some similarities to his. (See Tr. Vol. 8 1358: 10–24). Accordingly, the similarities between the Clean Room microcode and the Intel microcode must be attributable largely to the above mentioned constraints. But the similarities between the Clean Room microcode and Rev. 2 are at least as great as are the similarities between the latter and the Intel microcode. This is made evident by an examination of Exhibit 705. The strong likelihood follows that these similarities, also resulted from the same constraints.

Mr. McKevitt also acknowledged that he would expect that independently created microcode for the 8086 would have fewer similarities in the longer sequences than in the shorter sequences because "there is more opportunity for the longer sequences to be expressed differently." (Tr. Vol. 8 1359: 5–10). This is exactly what occurred here; the longer sequences in Rev. 2 and Intel's microcode are not nearly so much alike as are the shorter sequences.

In light of the foregoing, it is reasonable to conclude that the same constraints, rather than copying, were responsible for the principal similarities between Rev. 2 and the Intel microcode.

D. Idea v. Expression.

As concluded above, overall, and particularly with respect to the longer microroutines, NEC's microcode is not substantially similar to Intel's; but some of the shorter, simpler microroutines resemble Intel's. None, however, are identical. As to these shorter, simpler microroutines, if their underlying ideas are capable of only a limited range of expression, they "may be protected only against virtually identical copying." *Frybarger v. International Business Machines Corp.*, 812 F.2d 525, 530 [2 USPQ2d 1135, 1138–39] (9th Cir.1987). *See also Worth v. Selchow & Righter Co.*, 827 F.2d 569, 572 [4 USPQ2d 1144] (9th Cir.1987).

In determining an idea's range of expression, constraints are relevant factors to consider. *See Data East USA v. Epyx, Inc.*, No. 87–2294 [9 USPQ2d 1322, 1325] (9th Cir. Nov.30, 1988). In this case, the expression of NEC's microcode was constrained by the use of the macroinstruction set and hardware of the 8086/88. Mr. McKevitt so testified (Tr. Vol. 8 1358: 10–24), Dr. Patterson initially expressed the same opinion (Exhibit R, pages 7598 and 7601), and the close similarities of the Clean Room microcode to Intel's and NEC's microcodes emphatically concur.

Mr. Davidian and Dr. Frieder testified that, in light of these constraints, the shorter, simpler microroutines can be expressed only in a few limited ways, and I agree. (Davidian Tr. Vol. 18 3092: 18—3093: 13; Frieder as cited in NEC's Supplemented and Annotated Findings of Fact and Conclusions of Law P75). These include those microroutines identified as similar in Section A, pages 20–21 above. A good illustration is "ESCAPE". The Clean Room and NEC's version are identical, which is evidence of its constrained nature. Further, Dr. Frieder testified that "ESCAPE" was highly constrained given the existing hardware. (Tr. Vol. 14 2479: 10—2480: 1).

Accordingly, it is the conclusion of this court that the expression of the ideas underlying the shorter, simpler microroutines (including those identified earlier as substantially similar) may be protected only against virtually identical copying, that NEC properly used the underlying ideas, without virtually identically copying their limited expression.

* * *

CONCLUSION

For reasons hereinabove set forth, judgment will be entered holding that:

* * *

3. The microcodes that NEC produced for its V20, V30, V40 and V50 microprocessors do not infringe the Intel copyrights for its 8086 and 8088 microcodes.

4. NEC's V20 and V30 microprocessors are not simply "improvements" upon its uPD 8086 and uPD 8088 microprocessors, which were licensed by Intel under its copyrights.

This memorandum shall constitute findings of fact and conclusion of law, pursuant to Federal Rule of Civil Procedure 52(a).

* * *

Note

Copyright protects expression but not ideas. In a seminal copyright case, *Nichols v. Universal Pictures Corp.*, 45 F.2d 119 (2d Cir.1930), Judge Learned Hand found a taking of ideas that did not involve infringing protectible expression. The case involved the scripts of two plays with a number of similarities in their plots. In this leading case, Judge Learned Hand ruled that the defendant, if he copied anything, took no more than the law allowed from the plaintiff's play. In dealing with software copyright, courts have had to try to draw the line between copying protected expression and copying unprotected ideas.

WHELAN ASSOCIATES, INC. v. JASLOW DENTAL LABORATORY, INC.

United States Court of Appeals, Third Circuit, 1986.
797 F.2d 1222.

BECKER, CIRCUIT JUDGE.

This appeal involves a computer program for the operation of a dental laboratory, and calls upon us to apply the principles underlying our venerable copyright laws to the relatively new field of computer technology to determine the scope of copyright protection of a computer program. More particularly, in this case of first impression in the courts of appeals, we must determine whether the structure (or sequence and organization) of a computer program is protectible by copyright, or whether the protection of the copyright law extends only as far as the literal computer code. The district court found that the copyright law covered these non-literal elements of the program, and we agree. This conclusion in turn requires us to consider whether there was sufficient evidence of substantial similarity between the structures of the two programs at issue in this case to uphold the district court's finding of copyright infringement. Because we find that there was enough evidence, we affirm.

I. FACTUAL BACKGROUND

Appellant Jaslow Dental Laboratory, Inc. ("Jaslow Lab") is a Pennsylvania corporation in the business of manufacturing dental prosthetics and devices. Appellant Dentcom, Inc. ("Dentcom") is a Pennsylvania corporation in the business of developing and marketing computer programs for use by dental laboratories. Dentcom was formed out of the events that gave rise to this suit, and its history will be recounted below. Individual appellants Edward Jaslow and his son Rand Jaslow are officers and shareholders in both Jaslow Lab and Dentcom. Appellants were defendants in the district court. Plaintiff-appellee Whelan Associates, Inc. ("Whelan Associates") is also a Pennsylvania corporation, engaged in the business of developing and marketing custom computer programs.

Jaslow Lab, like any other small-or medium-sized business of moderate complexity, has significant bookkeeping and administrative tasks. Each order for equipment must be registered and processed; inventory must be maintained; customer lists must be continually updated; invoicing, billing, and accounts receivable, must be dealt with. While many of these functions are common to all businesses, the nature of the dental prosthetics business apparently requires some variations on the basic theme.

Although Rand Jaslow had not had extensive experience with computers, he believed that the business operations of Jaslow Lab could be made more efficient if they were computerized. In early 1978, he therefore bought a small personal computer and tried to teach himself how to program it so that it would be of use to Jaslow Lab. Although he wrote a program for the computer, he was ultimately not successful, limited by both his lack of expertise and the relatively small capacity of his particular computer.

A few months later, stymied by his own lack of success but still confident that Jaslow Lab would profit from computerization, Rand Jaslow hired the Strohl Systems Group, Inc. ("Strohl"), a small corporation that developed custom-made software to develop a program that would run on Jaslow Lab's new IBM Series One computer and take care of the Lab's business needs. Jaslow Lab and Strohl entered into an agreement providing that Strohl would design a system for Jaslow Lab's needs and that after Strohl had installed the system Strohl could market it to other dental laboratories. Jaslow Lab would receive a 10% royalty on all such sales. The person at Strohl responsible for the Jaslow Lab account was Elaine Whelan, an experienced programmer who was an officer and half-owner of Strohl.

Ms. Whelan's first step was to visit Jaslow Lab and interview Rand Jaslow and others to learn how the laboratory worked and what its needs were. She also visited other dental laboratories and interviewed people there, so that she would better understand the layout, workflow, and administration of dental laboratories generally. After this education into the ways of dental laboratories, and Jaslow Lab, in particular, Ms. Whelan wrote a program called Dentalab for Jaslow Lab. Dentalab was written in a computer language known as EDL (Event Driven Language), so that it would work with IBM Series One machines. The program was completed and was operative at Jaslow Lab around March 1979.

Presumably with an eye towards exploiting the economic potential of the Dentalab program, Ms. Whelan left Strohl in November, 1979, to form her own business, Whelan Associates, Inc., which acquired Strohl's interest in the Dentalab program. Shortly thereafter, Whelan Associates entered into negotiations with Jaslow Lab for Jaslow Lab to be Whelan Associates' sales representative for the Dentalab program. Whelan Associates and Jaslow Lab entered into an agreement on July 30, 1980, according to which Jaslow Lab agreed to use its "best efforts and to act diligently in the marketing of the Dentalab package," and Whelan Associates agreed to "use its best efforts and to act diligently to improve and augment the previously successfully designed Dentalab package." App. at 1779. The agreement stated that Jaslow Lab would receive 35% of the gross price of any programs sold and 5% of the price of any modifications to the programs. The agreement was for one year and was then terminable by either party on thirty days' notice.

The parties' business relationship worked successfully for two years. During this time, as Rand Jaslow became more familiar with computer programming, he realized that because Dentalab was written in EDL it could not be used on computers that many of the smaller dental prosthetics firms were using, for which EDL had not been implemented. Sensing that there might be a market for a program that served essentially the same function as Dentalab but that could be used more widely, Rand Jaslow began in May or June of 1982 to develop in his spare time a program in the BASIC language for such computers. That program, when completed, became the alleged copyright infringer in this suit; it was called the Dentcom PC program ("Dentcom program").

It appears that Rand Jaslow was sanguine about the prospects of his program for smaller computers. After approximately a year of work, on May 31, 1983, his attorney sent a letter to Whelan Associates giving one month notice of termination of the agreement between Whelan Associates and Jaslow Lab. The letter stated that Jaslow Lab considered itself to be the exclusive marketer of the Dentalab program which, the letter stated, "contains valuable trade secrets of Jaslow Dental Laboratory."

The letter concluded with a thinly veiled threat to Whelan Associates: "I . . . look for your immediate response confirming that you will respect the rights of Jaslow and not use or disclose to others the trade secrets of Jaslow." App. at 1221.

Approximately two months later, on about August 1, Edward and Rand Jaslow, Paul Mohr, and Joseph Cerra formed defendant-appellant Dentcom to sell the Dentcom program. At about the same time, Rand Jaslow and Jaslow Lab employed a professional computer programmer, Jonathan Novak, to complete the Dentcom program. The program was soon finished, and Dentcom proceeded to sell it to dental prosthetics companies that had personal computers. Dentcom sold both the Dentalab and Dentcom programs, and advertised the Dentcom program as "a new version of the Dentalab computer system." App. at 178; 1567–73; 1766–69.

Despite Jaslow Lab's May 31 letter warning Whelan Associates not to sell the Dentalab program, Whelan Associates continued to market Dentalab. This precipitated the present litigation.

* * *

III. TECHNOLOGICAL BACKGROUND

* * *

As this brief summary demonstrates, the coding process is a comparatively small part of programming. By far the larger portion of the expense and difficulty in creating computer programs is attributable to the development of the structure and logic of the program, and to debugging, documentation and maintenance, rather than to the coding. The evidence in this case shows that Ms. Whelan spent a tremendous amount of time studying Jaslow Labs, organizing the modules and subroutines for the Dentalab program, and working out the data arrangements, and a comparatively small amount of time actually coding the Dentalab program.

IV. LEGAL BACKGROUND

A. *The elements of a copyright infringement action*—To prove that its copyright has been infringed, Whelan Associates must show two things: that it owned the copyright on Dentalab, and that Rand Jaslow copied Dentalab in making the Dentacom program. Although it was disputed below, *see supra* 1228, the district court determined, and it is not challenged here, that Whelan Associates owned the copyright to the Dentalab program. We are thus concerned only with whether it has been shown that Rand Jaslow copied the Dentalab program.

As it is rarely possible to prove copying through direct evidence, *Roth Greeting Cards v. United Card Co.*, 429 F.2d 1106, 1110 (9th Cir.1970), copying may be proved inferentially by showing that the defendant had access to the allegedly infringed copyrighted work and that the allegedly infringing work is substantially similar to the copyrighted work. The district court found, and here it is uncontested, that Rand Jaslow had access to the Dentalab program, both because Dentalab was the program used in Jaslow Labs and because Rand Jaslow acted as a sales representative for Whelan Associates. *See Whelan Associates v. Jaslow Dental Laboratory*, 609 F.Supp. at 1314. Thus, the sole question is whether there was substantial similarity between the Dentcom and Dentalab programs.

B. *The appropriate test for substantial similarity in computer program cases*—The leading case of *Arnstein v. Porter*, 154 F.2d 464, 468–69 (2d Cir.1946), suggested a bifurcated substantial similarity test whereby a finder of fact makes two findings of substantial similarity to support a copyright violation. First, the fact-finder must decide whether there is sufficient similarity between the two works in question to conclude that the alleged infringer used the copyrighted work in making his own. On this issue, expert testimony may be received to aid the trier of fact. (This has been referred to as the "extrinsic" test of substantial similarity. *Sid & Marty Krofft Television Prods., Inc. v. McDonald's Corp.*, 562 F.2d at 1164–65.) Second, if the answer to the first question is in the affirmative, the fact-finder must decide without the aid of expert testimony, but with the perspective of the "lay observer," whether the copying was "illicit," or "an unlawful appropriation" of the copyrighted work. (This has been termed an "intrinsic" test of substantial similarity. *Id.*) The *Arnstein* test has been adopted in this circuit. *See Universal Athletic Sales Co.*, 511 F.2d at 907.

The district court heard expert testimony. It did not bifurcate its analysis, however, but made only a single finding of substantial similarity. *See Whelan Associates v. Jaslow Dental Laboratory*, 609 F.Supp. at 1321–22. It would thus appear to have contravened the law of this circuit. Nevertheless, for the reasons that follow, we believe that the district court applied an appropriate standard.

The ordinary observer test, which was developed in cases involving novels, plays, and paintings, and which does not permit expert testimony, is of doubtful value in cases involving computer programs on account of the programs' complexity and unfamiliarity to most members of the public. Moreover, the distinction between the two parts of the *Arnstein* test may be of doubtful value when the finder of fact is the same person for each step: that person has been exposed to expert evidence in the first step, yet she or he is supposed to ignore or "forget" that evidence in analyzing the problem under the second step. Especially in complex cases, we doubt that the "forgetting" can be effective when the expert testimony is essential to even the most fundamental understanding of the objects in question.

On account of these problems with the standard, we believe that the ordinary observer test is not useful and is potentially misleading when the subjects of the copyright are particularly complex, such as computer programs. We therefore join the growing number of courts which do not apply the ordinary observer test in copyright cases involving exceptionally difficult materials, like computer programs, but instead adopt a single substantial similarity inquiry according to which both lay and expert testimony would be admissible. That was the test applied by the district court in this case.

C. *The arguments on appeal*—On appeal, the defendants attack on two grounds the district court's holding that there was sufficient evidence of substantial similarity. First, the defendants argue that because the district court did not find any similarity between the "literal" elements (source and object code) of the programs, but only similarity in their overall structures, its finding of substantial similarity was incorrect, for the copyright covers only the literal elements of computer programs, not their overall structures. Defendants' second argument is that even if the protection of copyright law extends to "non-literal" elements such as the structure of computer programs, there was not sufficient evidence of substantial similarity to sustain the district court's holding in this case. We consider these arguments in turn.

V.   THE SCOPE OF COPYRIGHT PROTECTION OF COMPUTER PROGRAMS

It is well, though recently, established that copyright protection extends to a program's source and object codes. In this case, however, the district court did not find any copying of the source or object codes, nor did the plaintiff allege such copying. Rather, the district court held that the Dentalab copyright was infringed because the *overall structure* of Dentcom was substantially similar to the overall structure of Dentalab. *Whelan Associates v. Jaslow Dental Laboratory*, 609 F.Supp. at 1321–22. The question therefore arises whether mere similarity in the overall structure of programs can be the basis for a copyright infringement, or, put differently, whether a program's copyright protection covers the structure of the program or only the program's literal elements, *i.e.*, its source and object codes.

Title 17 U.S.C. § 102(a)(1) extends copyright protection to "literary works," and computer programs are classified as literary works for the purposes of copyright. *See* H.R.Rep. No. 1476, 94th Cong., 2d Sess. 54, reprinted in 1976 U.S.Code Cong. & Ad.News 5659, 5667. The copyrights of other literary works can be infringed even when there is no substantial similarity between the works' literal elements. One can violate the copyright of a play or book by copying its plot or plot devices. By analogy to other literary works, it would thus appear that the copyrights of computer programs can be infringed even absent copying of the literal elements of the program. Defendants contend, however, that what is true of other literary works is not true of computer programs. They assert two principal reasons, which we consider in turn.

A.   *Section 102(b) and the dichotomy between idea and expression*— It is axiomatic that copyright does not protect ideas, but only expressions of ideas. This rule, first enunciated in *Baker v. Selden*, 101 U.S. (11 Otto) 99, 25 L.Ed. 841 (1879), has been repeated in numerous cases. The rule has also been embodied in statute. Title 17 U.S.C. § 102(b) (1982) states:

In no case does copyright protection for an original work of authorship extend to any idea, procedure, process, system, method of operation, concept, principle, or discovery, regardless of the form in which it is described, explained, illustrated, or embodied in such work.

The legislative history of this section, adopted in 1976, makes clear that § 102(b) was intended to express the idea-expression dichotomy.

Defendants argue that the structure of a computer program is, by definition, the idea and not the expression of the idea, and therefore that the structure cannot be protected by the program copyright. Under the defendants' approach, any other decision would be contrary to § 102(b). We divide our consideration of this argument into two parts. First, we examine the caselaw concerning the distinction between idea and expression, and derive from it a rule for distinguishing idea from expression in the context of computer programs. We then apply that rule to the facts of this case.

* * *

We begin our analysis with the case of *Baker v. Selden*, which, in addition to being a seminal case in the law of copyright generally, is particularly relevant here because, like the instant case, it involved a utilitarian work, rather than an artistic or fictional one. In *Baker v. Selden*, the plaintiff Selden obtained a copyright on his book, "Selden's Condensed Ledger, or Bookkeeping Simplified," which described a new, simplified system of accounting. Included in the book were certain "blank forms," pages with ruled lines and headings, for use in Selden's accounting system. Selden alleged that Baker had infringed Selden's copyright by making and selling accounting books that used substantially the same system as Selden's and that reproduced Selden's blank forms. No one disputed that Baker had the right to use and promulgate Selden's system of accounting, for all parties agreed that the system could not be copyrighted, although the Court opined that it might be patentable. *Id.*, 101 U.S. at 102. Nor did the parties dispute that the text of Baker's book on accounting did not infringe Selden's copyright. The dispute centered on whether Selden's blank forms were part of the method (idea) of Selden's book, and hence non-copyrightable, or part of the copyrightable text (expression). *Id.* at 101.

In deciding this point, the Court distinguished what was protectible from what was not protectible as follows:

> [W]here the art [*i.e.*, the method of accounting] it teaches cannot be used without employing the methods and diagrams used to illustrate the book, or such as are similar to them, such methods and diagrams are to be considered as necessary incidents to the art, and given to the public.

Id. at 103. Applying this test, the Court held that the blank forms were necessary incidents to Selden's method of accounting, and hence were not entitled to any copyright protection. *Id.* at 104.

The Court's test in *Baker v. Selden* suggests a way to distinguish idea from expression. Just as *Baker v. Selden* focused on the end sought to be achieved by Selden's book, the line between idea and expression may be drawn with reference to the end sought to be achieved by the work in question. In other words, *the purpose or function of a utilitarian work would be the work's idea, and everything that is not necessary to that purpose or function would be part of the expression of the idea.* Where there are various means of achieving the desired purpose, then the particular means chosen is not necessary to the purpose; hence, there is expression, not idea.[28]

Consideration of copyright doctrines related to *scènes à faire* and fact-intensive works supports our formulation, for they reflect the same underlying principle. *Scènes à faire* are "incidents, characters or settings which are as a practical matter indispensable ... in the treatment of a given topic." *Atari, Inc. v. North American Philips Consumer Elecs. Corp.*, 672 F.2d 607, 616 (7th Cir.), *cert. denied*, 459 U.S. 880, 103 S.Ct. 176, 74 L.Ed.2d 145 (1982). It is well-settled doctrine that *scènes à faire* are afforded no copyright protection.

Scènes à faire are afforded no protection because the subject matter represented can be expressed in no other way than through the particular *scène à faire*. Therefore, granting a copyright "would give the first author a monopoly on the commonplace ideas behind the *scènes à faire*." *Landsberg v. Scrabble Crossword Game Players, Inc.*, 736 F.2d at 489. This is merely a restatement of the hypothesis advanced above, that the purpose or function of a work or literary device is part of that device's "idea" (unprotectable portion). It follows that anything necessary to effecting that function is also, necessarily, part of the idea, too.

* * *

* * * As we stated above, *see supra* at 1231, among the more significant costs in computer programming are those attributable to developing the structure and logic of the program. The rule proposed here, which allows copyright protection beyond the literal computer code, would provide the proper incentive for programmers by protecting their most valuable efforts, while not giving them a stranglehold over the development of new computer devices that accomplish the same end.

The principal economic argument used against this position—used, that is, in support of the position that programs' literal elements are the only parts of the programs protected by the copyright law—is that computer programs are so intricate, each step so dependent on all of the

---

28. This test is necessarily difficult to state, and it may be difficult to understand in the abstract. It will become more clear as we discuss and explain it in the textual discussion that follows this footnote. *See also infra* at 1242–44 (discussion of the copyrightability of file structures that raise many of the issues considered here). As will be seen, *see infra* at 1238–39, the idea of the Dentalab program was the efficient management of a dental laboratory (which presumably has significantly different requirements from those of other businesses). Because that idea could be accomplished in a number of different structures, the structure of the Dentalab program is part of the program's expression, not its idea.

other steps, that they are almost impossible to copy except literally, and that anyone who attempts to copy the structure of a program without copying its literal elements must expend a tremendous amount of effort and creativity. In the words of one commentator: "One cannot simply 'approximate' the entire copyrighted computer program and create a similar operative program without the expenditure of almost the same amount of time as the original programmer expended." Note, 68 Minn. L.Rev. at 1290 (footnote omitted). According to this argument, such work should not be discouraged or penalized. A further argument against our position is not economic but jurisprudential; another commentator argues that the concept of structure in computer programs is too vague to be useful in copyright cases. Radcliffe, *Recent Developments in Copyright Law Related to Computer Software*, 4 Computer L.Rep. 189, 194–97 (1985). He too would therefore appear to advocate limiting copyright protection to programs' literal codes.

Neither of the two arguments just described is persuasive. The first argument fails for two reasons. In the first place, it is simply not true that "approximation" of a program short of perfect reproduction is valueless. To the contrary, one can approximate a program and thereby gain a significant advantage over competitors even though additional work is needed to complete the program. Second, the fact that it will take a great deal of effort to copy a copyrighted work does not mean that the copier is not a copyright infringer. The issue in a copyrighted case is simply whether the copyright holder's expression has been copied, not how difficult it was to do the copying. Whether an alleged infringer spent significant time and effort to copy an original work is therefore irrelevant to whether he has pirated the expression of an original work.

As to the second argument, it is surely true that limiting copyright protection to computers' literal codes would be simpler and would yield more definite answers than does our answer here. Ease of application is not, however, a sufficient counterweight to the considerations we have adduced on behalf of our position.

Finally, one commentator argues that the process of development and progress in the field of computer programming is significantly different from that in other fields, and therefore requires a particularly restricted application of the copyright law. According to this argument, progress in the area of computer technology is achieved by means of "stepping-stones," a process that "requires plagiarizing in some manner the underlying copyrighted work." Note, 68 Minn.L.Rev. at 1292 (footnote omitted). As a consequence, this commentator argues, giving computer programs too much copyright protection will retard progress in the field.

We are not convinced that progress in computer technology or technique is qualitatively different from progress in other areas of science or the arts. In balancing protection and dissemination, *see supra* at 1235, the copyright law has always recognized and tried to accommodate the fact that all intellectual pioneers build on the work of their predecessors. Thus, copyright principles derived from other areas are applicable in the field of computer programs.

2. *Application of the general rule to this case*—The rule proposed here is certainly not problem-free. The rule has its greatest force in the analysis of utilitarian or "functional" works, for the purpose of such works is easily stated and identified. By contrast, in cases involving works of literature or "non-functional" visual representations, defining the purpose of the work may be difficult. Since it may be impossible to discuss the purpose or function of a novel, poem, sculpture or painting, the rule may have little or no application to cases involving such works. The present case presents no such difficulties, for it is clear that the purpose of the utilitarian Dentalab program was to aid in the business operations of a dental laboratory.[34] *See supra* 1225. It is equally clear that the structure of the program was not essential to that task: there are other programs on the market, competitors of Dentalab and Dentcom, that perform the same functions but have different structures and designs.

* * * The conclusion is thus inescapable that the detailed structure of the Dentalab program is part of the expression, not the idea, of that program.

Our conclusion is supported by *SAS Institute, Inc. v. S & H Computer Systems, Inc.*, 605 F.Supp. 816 (M.D.Tenn.1985), the only other case that has addressed this issue specifically, in which the court found that a program's copyright could extend beyond its literal elements to its structure and organization. * * * After a brief discussion of the programs' literal similarities, the court said:

> In addition, the copying proven at trial does not affect only the specific lines of code cited by Dr. Peterson in his testimony. Rather, to the extent that it represents copying of the organization and structural details of SAS, such copying pervades the entire S & H product.

Id. at 830. Although the *SAS* court did not analyze the point in great depth, we are encouraged by its conclusion.

Our solution may put us at odds with Judge Patrick Higginbotham's scholarly opinion in *Synercom Technology, Inc. v. University Computing Co.*, 462 F.Supp. 1003 (N.D.Tex.1978), which dealt with the question whether the "input formats" of a computer program—the configurations and collations of the information entered into the program—were idea or expression. The court held

34. We do not mean to imply that the idea or purpose behind *every* utilitarian or functional work will be precisely what it accomplishes, and that structure and organization will therefore always be part of the expression of such works. The idea or purpose behind a utilitarian work may be to accomplish a certain function *in a certain way, see, e.g., Baker v. Selden*, 101 U.S. at 100 (referring to Selden's book as explaining "a peculiar system of book-keeping"), and the structure or function of a program might be essential to that task. There is no suggestion in the record, however, that the purpose of the Dentalab program was anything so refined; it was simply to run a dental laboratory in an efficient way.

that the input formats were ideas, not expressions, and thus not protectible. *Synercom* did not deal with precisely the materials at issue here—input formats are structurally simple as compared to full programs—and it may therefore be distinguishable. However, insofar as the input formats are devices for the organization of data into forms useful for computers, they are *similar* to programs; thus, *Synercom* is relevant and we must come to grips with it.

Central to Judge Higginbotham's analysis was his conviction that the organization and structure of the input formats was inseparable from the idea underlying the formats. Although the court acknowledged that in some cases structure and sequence might be part of expression, not idea, *see id.* at 1014, it stated that in the case of input formats, structure and organization were inherently part of the idea. The court put its position in the form of a powerful rhetorical question: "if sequencing and ordering [are] expression, what separable idea is being expressed?" *Id.* at 1013.

To the extent that *Synercom* rested on the premise that there was a difference between the copyrightability of sequence and form in the computer context and in any other context, we think that it is incorrect. As just noted, the Copyright Act of 1976 demonstrates that Congress intended sequencing and ordering to be protectible in the appropriate circumstances, *see supra* p. 1237–1238, and the computer field is not an exception to this general rule. Although Congress was aware that computer programs posed a novel set of issues and problems for the copyright law, Congress did not then make, and has not since made, any special provision for ordering and sequencing in the context of computer programs. There is thus no statutory basis for treating computer programs differently from other literary works in this regard.

Despite the fact that copyright protection extends to sequence and form in the computer context, unless we are able to answer Judge Higginbotham's powerful rhetorical question—"if sequencing and ordering [are] expression, what separable idea is being expressed?"—in our own case, we would have to hold that the structure of the Dentalab program is part of its idea and is thus not protectible by copyright. Our answer has already been given, however: the idea is the efficient organization of a dental laboratory (presumably, this poses different problems from the efficient organization of some other kinds of laboratories or businesses). Because there are a variety of program structures through which that idea can be expressed, the structure is not a necessary incident to that idea.

* * *

VI.   EVIDENCE OF SUBSTANTIAL SIMILARITY

Defendants' second argument is that even if copyright protection is not limited to computer programs' literal elements as a matter of law, there is insufficient evidence of substantial similarity presented in this case to support a finding of copyright infringement. The defendants claim that all three parts of Dr. Moore's expert testimony as to the similarity of the programs, see supra at 1228, were flawed, and also that the district court erred in evaluating the relative weight of Dr. Moore's and Mr. Ness' testimony. We consider these arguments in turn.

A. *File structures*—Defendants claim that Dr. Moore's examination and conclusions with respect to file structures are irrelevant to the question whether there was a copyright violation. Defendants analogize files to blank forms, which contain no information but merely collect and organize information that is entered from another source. They argue, relying on *Baker v. Selden*, that, as a matter of law, blank forms cannot be copyrighted. Thus, they conclude, neither can file structures be part of the copyright of a program.

Defendants' description of the file structures is indeed correct. Dr. Moore himself described a computer's file as "a storage place for data, and it's really no different in a computer than it is in a file drawer, it's like a manila folder that contains all the data on a particular subject category in a computer." App. at 682. (Another analogy, particularly accessible to lawyers, is to a very complex cataloguing structure like the structure of Lexis or Westlaw without any entries yet made.) Defendants' legal conclusion is not correct, however. Although some courts have stated that the meaning of *Baker v. Selden* is that blank forms cannot be copyrighted, this circuit, like the majority of courts that have considered the issue, has rejected this position and instead have held that blank forms may be copyrighted if they are sufficiently innovative that their arrangement of information is itself informative.

This is not to say that *all* blank forms or computer files are copyrightable. Only those that by their arrangement and organization convey some information can be copyrighted. *Cf.* 1 Nimmer at 2–201: "Thus books intended to record the events of baby's first year, or a record of a European trip, or any one of a number of other subjects, may evince considerable originality in suggestions of specific items of information which are to be recorded, and in the arrangement of such items." (footnote omitted). Defendants do not contend, however, that the file structures convey no information, and it appears to us that the structures are sufficiently complex and detailed that such an argument would not succeed. As we have noted, *supra* at 1239, there are many ways in which the same goal—the organization of the business aspects of a dental laboratory—might be accomplished, and several of these approaches might use significantly different file structures. The file structures in the Dentalab and Dentcom systems require certain information and order that information in a particular fashion. Other programs might require different information or might use the same information differently. When we compare the comprehensiveness and complexity of the file structures at issue here with the "blank forms" at issue in the cases mentioned above, we have no doubt that these file structures are sufficiently informative to deserve copyright protection.

B. *Screen outputs*—Defendants' second line of argument is slightly confusing. Defendants appear to argue that to the extent that the district court relied upon the similarity of the screen outputs of Dentalab and Dentcom its finding of substantial similarity was erroneous because (1) the screen outputs are covered by a different copyright from the program's, and/or (2) the screen outputs bear no relation to the programs that produce them. Although these arguments are not always clearly distinguished, Appellants' Br. at 38–41; Reply Br. at 8–10, the distinction is important because whereas the first argument is weak, we feel that the second is more persuasive.

It is true that screen outputs are considered audio-visual works under the copyright code, and are thus covered by a different copyright than are programs, which are literary works, *see supra* at 1233. It is also true that Whelan Associates asserts no claim of copyright infringement with respect to the screen outputs. But the conclusion to be drawn from this is not, as defendants would have it, that screen outputs are completely irrelevant to the question whether the copyright in the program has been infringed. Rather, the only conclusion to be drawn from the fact of the different copyrights is that the screen output cannot be *direct* evidence of copyright infringement. There is no reason, however, why material falling under one copyright category could not be indirect, inferential evidence of the nature of material covered by another copyright.

Thus, the question is whether the screen outputs have probative value concerning the nature of the programs that render them sufficient to clear the hurdles of Fed.R.Evid. 401 and 403. The defendants argue that the screen outputs have *no* probative value with respect to the programs because many different programs can create the same screen output. * * *

Insofar as everything that a computer does, including its screen outputs, is related to the program that operates it, there is necessarily a causal relationship between the program and the screen outputs. The screen outputs must bear *some* relation to the underlying programs, and therefore they have some probative value. The evidence about the screen outputs therefore passes the low admissibility threshold of Fed.R.Evid. 401.

* * *

C. *The five subroutines*—With respect to the final piece of evidence, Dr. Moore's testimony about the five subroutines found in Dentalab and Dentcom, defendants state that they "fail to understand how a substantial similarity in *structure* can be established by a comparison of only a small fraction of the two works." Appellants' Brief at 43, *see also* Reply Br. at 12. The premise underlying this declaration is that one cannot prove substantial similarity of two works without comparing the entirety, or at least the greater part, of the works. We take this premise to be the defendants' argument.

The premise does not apply in other areas of copyright infringement. There is no general requirement that most of each of two works be compared before a court can conclude that they are substantially similar. In the cases of literary works—novels, movies, or plays, for example—it is often impossible to speak of "most" of the work. The substantial similarity inquiry cannot be simply quantified in such instances. Instead, the court must make a qualitative, not quantitative, judgment about the character of the work as a whole and the importance of the substantially similar portions of the work.

Computer programs are no different. Because all steps of a computer program are not of equal importance, the relevant inquiry cannot therefore be the purely mechanical one of whether most of the programs' steps are similar. Rather, because we are concerned with the overall similarities between the programs, we must ask whether the most significant steps of the programs are similar. This is precisely what Dr. Moore did. He testified as follows:

> What I decided to do was to look at the programs that had the primary, or let's say most important, tasks of the system, and also ones which manipulate files, because there are a lot of programs that simply print lists, or answer a question when you ask him it, but I thought that the programs which actually showed the flow of information, through the system, would be the ones that would illustrate the system back.

App. at 704. Dr. Moore's testimony was thus in accord with general principles of copyright law. As we hold today that these principles apply as well to computer programs, we therefore reject the defendants' argument on this point.

* * *

VII. Conclusion

We hold that (1) copyright protection of computer programs may extend beyond the programs' literal code to their structure, sequence, and organization, and (2) the district court's finding of substantial similarity between the Dentalab and Dentcom programs was not clearly erroneous. The judgment of the district court will therefore be affirmed.

Note

Whelan has not fared well in other Circuits. Numerous decisions have criticized or rejected its holding as leaning too far toward the protection of ideas rather than expression, and as improperly providing protection for standard operating procedures for dental labs that were part of the public domain. Two decisions subsequent to *Whelan* show how tricky it can be to determine what constitutes infringement of the "look and feel" of another computer program. It may seem fairly obvious when a video game appears on the market that closely resembles the play of another video game. When the program's function is utilitarian, however, the substantial similarity may result, as in the *Intel* case above, from the necessary utilitarian aspects of the program. Granting copyright on such aspects of a program would give something close to patent rights to a the program author without compliance with the requirements of the patent law. For this reason, courts have been reluctant to extend copyright protection to necessary utilitarian functions of a program.

COMPUTER ASSOCIATES INTERNATIONAL, INC., v. ALTAI, INC.

United States Court of Appeals, Second Circuit,1992.
982 F.2d 693.

WALKER, CIRCUIT JUDGE.

* * *

II. FACTS

CA [Computer Associates] is a Delaware corporation, with its principal place of business in Garden City, New York. Altai is a Texas corporation, doing business primarily in Arlington, Texas. Both companies are in the computer software industry—designing, developing and marketing various types of computer programs.

The subject of this litigation originates with one of CA's marketed programs entitled CA–SCHEDULER. CA–SCHEDULER is a job scheduling program designed for IBM mainframe computers. Its primary functions are straightforward: to create a schedule specifying when the computer should run various tasks, and then to control the computer as it executes the schedule. CA–SCHEDULER contains a sub-program entitled ADAPTER, also developed by CA. ADAPTER is not an independently marketed product of CA; it is a wholly integrated component of CA–SCHEDULER and has no capacity for independent use.

Nevertheless, ADAPTER plays an extremely important role. It is an "operating system compatibility component," which means, roughly speaking, it serves as a translator. An "operating system" is itself a program that manages the resources of the computer, allocating those resources to other programs as needed. The IBM System 370 family of computers, for which CA–SCHEDULER was created, is, depending upon the computer's size, designed to contain one of three operating systems: DOS/VSE, MVS, or CMS. As the district court noted, the general rule is that "a program written for one operating system, e.g., DOS/VSE, will not, without modification, run under another operating system such as MVS." *Computer Assocs. Int'l, Inc. v. Altai, Inc.*, 775 F.Supp. 544, 550 (E.D.N.Y.1991). ADAPTER's function is to translate the language of a given program into the particular language that the computer's own operating system can understand.

The district court succinctly outlined the manner in which ADAPTER works within the context of the larger program. In order to enable

CA–SCHEDULER to function on different operating systems, CA divided the CA–SCHEDULER into two components:

> —a first component that contains only the task-specific portions of the program, independent of all operating system issues, and

> —a second component that contains all the interconnections between the first component and the operating system.

In a program constructed in this way, whenever the first, task-specific, component needs to ask the operating system for some resource through a "system call", it calls the second component instead of calling the operating system directly.

The second component serves as an "interface" or "compatibility component" between the task-specific portion of the program and the operating system. It receives the request from the first component and translates it into the appropriate system call that will be recognized by whatever operating system is installed on the computer, *e.g.*, DOS/VSE, MVS, or CMS. Since the first, task-specific component calls the adapter component rather than the operating system, the first component need not be customized to use any specific operating system. The second, interface, component insures that all the system calls are performed properly for the particular operating system in use.

Id. at 551. ADAPTER serves as the second, "common system interface" component referred to above.

A program like ADAPTER, which allows a computer user to change or use multiple operating systems while maintaining the same software, is highly desirable. It saves the user the costs, both in time and money, that otherwise would be expended in purchasing new programs, modifying existing systems to run them, and gaining familiarity with their operation. The benefits run both ways. The increased compatibility afforded by an ADAPTER-like component, and its resulting popularity among consumers, makes whatever software in which it is incorporated significantly more marketable.

Starting in 1982, Altai began marketing its own job scheduling program entitled ZEKE. The original version of ZEKE was designed for use in conjunction with a VSE operating system. By late 1983, in response to customer demand, Altai decided to rewrite ZEKE so that it could be run in conjunction with an MVS operating system.

At that time, James P. Williams ("Williams"), then an employee of Altai and now its President, approached Claude F. Arney, III ("Arney"), a computer programmer who worked for CA. Williams and Arney were longstanding friends, and had in fact been co-workers at CA for some time before Williams left CA to work for Altai's predecessor. Williams wanted to recruit Arney to assist Altai in designing an MVS version of ZEKE.

At the time he first spoke with Arney, Williams was aware of both the CA-SCHEDULER and ADAPTER programs. However, Williams was not involved in their development and had never seen the codes of either program. When he asked Arney to come work for Altai, Williams did not know that ADAPTER was a component of CA–SCHEDULER.

Arney, on the other hand, was intimately familiar with various aspects of ADAPTER. While working for CA, he helped improve the VSE version of ADAPTER, and was permitted to take home a copy of ADAPTER'S source code. This apparently developed into an irresistible habit, for when Arney left CA to work for Altai in January, 1984, he took with him copies of the source code for both the VSE and MVS versions of ADAPTER. He did this in knowing violation of the CA employee agreements that he had signed.

Once at Altai, Arney and Williams discussed design possibilities for adapting ZEKE to run on MVS operating systems. Williams, who had created the VSE version of ZEKE, thought that approximately 30% of his original program would have to be modified in order to accommodate MVS. Arney persuaded Williams that the best way to make the needed modifications was to introduce a "common system interface" component into ZEKE. He did not tell Williams that his idea stemmed from his familiarity with ADAPTER. They decided to name this new component-program OSCAR.

Arney went to work creating OSCAR at Altai's offices using the ADAPTER source code. The district court accepted Williams' testimony that no one at Altai, with the exception of Arney, affirmatively knew that Arney had the ADAPTER code, or that he was using it to create OSCAR/VSE. However, during this time period, Williams' office was adjacent to Arney's. Williams testified that he and Arney "conversed quite frequently" while Arney was "investigating the source code of ZEKE" and that Arney was in his office "a number of times daily, asking questions." In three months, Arney successfully completed the OSCAR/VSE project. In an additional month he developed an OSCAR/MVS version. When the dust finally settled, Arney had copied approximately 30% of OSCAR's code from CA's ADAPTER program.

The first generation of OSCAR programs was known as OSCAR 3.4. From 1985 to August 1988, Altai used OSCAR 3.4 in its ZEKE product, as well as in programs entitled ZACK and ZEBB. In late July 1988, CA first learned that Altai may have appropriated parts of ADAPTER. After confirming its suspicions, CA secured copyrights on its 2.1 and 7.0 versions of CA–SCHEDULER. CA then brought this copyright and trade secret misappropriation action against Altai.

Apparently, it was upon receipt of the summons and complaint that Altai first learned that Arney had copied much of the OSCAR code from ADAPTER. After Arney confirmed to Williams that CA's accusations of copying were true, Williams immediately set out to survey the damage. Without ever looking at the ADAPTER code himself, Williams learned from Arney exactly which sections of code Arney had taken from ADAPTER.

Upon advice of counsel, Williams initiated OSCAR's rewrite. The project's goal was to save as much of OSCAR 3.4 as legitimately could be used, and to excise those portions which had been copied from ADAPT-ER. Arney was entirely excluded from the process, and his copy of the ADAPTER code was locked away. Williams put eight other programmers on the project, none of whom had been involved in any way in the development of OSCAR 3.4. Williams provided the programmers with a description of the ZEKE operating system services so that they could rewrite the appropriate code. The rewrite project took about six months to complete and was finished in mid-November 1989. The resulting program was entitled OSCAR 3.5.

From that point on, Altai shipped only OSCAR 3.5 to its new customers. Altai also shipped OSCAR 3.5 as a "free upgrade" to all customers that had previously purchased OSCAR 3.4. While Altai and Williams acted responsibly to correct Arney's literal copying of the ADAPTER program, copyright infringement had occurred.

After CA originally instituted this action in the United States District Court for the District of New Jersey, the parties stipulated its transfer in March, 1989, to the Eastern District of New York where it was assigned to Judge Jacob Mishler. On October 26, 1989, Judge Mishler transferred the case to Judge Pratt who was sitting in the district court by designation. Judge Pratt conducted a six day trial from March 28 through April 6, 1990. He entered judgment on August 12, 1991, and this appeal followed.

DISCUSSION

While both parties originally appealed from different aspects of the district court's judgment, Altai has now abandoned its appellate claims. In particular, Altai has conceded liability for the copying of ADAPTER into OSCAR 3.4 and raises no challenge to the award of $364,444 in damages on that score. Thus, we address only CA's appeal from the district court's rulings that: (1) Altai was not liable for copyright infringement in developing OSCAR 3.5 * * *.

* * * CA contends that the district court applied an erroneous method for determining whether there exists substantial similarity between computer programs, and thus, erred in determining that OSCAR 3.5 did not infringe the copyrights held on the different versions of its CA-SCHEDULER program. * * *

I. COPYRIGHT INFRINGEMENT

In any suit for copyright infringement, the plaintiff must establish its ownership of a valid copyright, and that the defendant copied the copyrighted work. *See Novelty Textile Mills, Inc. v. Joan Fabrics Corp.*, 558 F.2d 1090, 1092 (2d Cir.1977); *see also* 3 Melville B. Nimmer & David Nimmer, *Nimmer on Copyright* § 13.01, at 13–4 (1991) (hereinafter "Nimmer"). The plaintiff may prove defendant's copying either by direct evidence or, as is most often the case, by showing that (1) the defendant had access to the plaintiff's copyrighted work and (2) that defendant's work is substantially similar to the plaintiff's copyrightable material. *See Walker v. Time Life Films, Inc.*, 784 F.2d 44, 48 (2d Cir.), *cert. denied*, 476 U.S. 1159 (1986).

For the purpose of analysis, the district court assumed that Altai had access to the ADAPTER code when creating OSCAR 3.5. *See Computer Assocs.*, 775 F.Supp. at 558. Thus, in determining whether Altai had unlawfully copied protected aspects of CA's ADAPTER, the district court narrowed its focus of inquiry to ascertaining whether Altai's OSCAR 3.5 was substantially similar to ADAPTER. Because we approve Judge Pratt's conclusions regarding substantial similarity, our analysis will proceed along the same assumption.

As a general matter, and to varying degrees, copyright protection extends beyond a literary work's strictly textual form to its non-literal components. As we have said, "[i]t is of course essential to any protection of literary property ... that the right cannot be limited literally to the text, else a plagiarist would escape by immaterial variations." *Nichols v. Universal Pictures Corp.*, 45 F.2d 119, 121 (2d Cir.1930) (L. Hand, J.), *cert. denied*, 282 U.S. 902 (1931). Thus, where "the fundamental essence or structure of one work is duplicated in another," 3 Nimmer, § 13.03[A][1], at 13–24, courts have found copyright infringement. This black letter proposition is the springboard for our discussion.

A. Copyright Protection for the Non-literal Elements of Computer Programs

* * *

In this case, the hotly contested issues surround OSCAR 3.5. As recounted above, OSCAR 3.5 is the product of Altai's carefully orchestrated rewrite of OSCAR 3.4. After the purge, none of the ADAPTER source code remained in the 3.5 version; thus, Altai made sure that the literal elements of its revamped OSCAR program were no longer substantially similar to the literal elements of CA's ADAPTER.

According to CA, the district court erroneously concluded that Altai's OSCAR 3.5 was not substantially similar to its own ADAPTER program. CA argues that this occurred because the district court "committed legal error in analyzing [its] claims of copyright infringement by failing to find that copyright protects expression contained in the non-literal elements of computer software." We disagree.

CA argues that, despite Altai's rewrite of the OSCAR code, the resulting program remained substantially similar to the *structure* of its ADAPTER program. As discussed above, a program's structure includes its non-literal components such as general flow charts as well as the more specific organization of inter-modular relationships, parameter lists, and macros. In addition to these aspects, CA contends that OSCAR 3.5 is also substantially similar to ADAPTER with respect to the list of services that both ADAPTER and OSCAR obtain from their respective operating systems. We must decide whether and to what extent these elements of computer programs are protected by copyright law.

The statutory terrain in this area has been well explored. *See Lotus Dev. Corp. v. Paperback Software Int'l*, 740 F.Supp. 37, 47–51 (D.Mass. 1990); *see also Whelan*, 797 F.2d at 1240–42; Englund, at 885–90; Spivack, at 731–37. The Copyright Act affords protection to "original works of authorship fixed in any tangible medium of expression...." 17 U.S.C. § 102(a). This broad category of protected "works" includes "literary works," *id.* at § 102(a)(1), which are defined by the Act as

> works, other than audiovisual works, expressed in words, numbers, or other verbal or numerical symbols or indicia, regardless of the nature of the material objects, such as books, periodicals, manuscripts, phonorecords, film tapes, disks, or cards, in which they are embodied.

17 U.S.C. § 101. While computer programs are not specifically listed as part of the above statutory definition, the legislative history leaves no doubt that Congress intended them to be considered literary works. *See* H.R.Rep. No. 1476, 94th Cong., 2d Sess. 54, *reprinted in* 1976 U.S.C.C.A.N. 5659, 5667 (hereinafter "House Report"); *Whelan*, 797 F.2d at 1234; *Apple Computer*, 714 F.2d at 1247.

The syllogism that follows from the foregoing premises is a powerful one: if the non-literal structures of literary works are protected by copyright; and if computer programs are literary works, as we are told by the legislature; then the non-literal structures of computer programs are protected by copyright. *See Whelan*, 797 F.2d at 1234 ("By analogy to other literary works, it would thus appear that the copyrights of computer programs can be infringed even absent copying of the literal elements of the program."). We have no reservation in joining the company of those courts that have already ascribed to this logic. *See, e.g., Johnson Controls, Inc. v. Phoenix Control Sys., Inc.*, 886 F.2d 1173, 1175 (9th Cir.1989); *Lotus Dev. Corp.*, 740 F.Supp. at 54; *Digital Communications Assocs., Inc. v. Softklone Distrib. Corp.*, 659 F.Supp. 449, 455–56 (N.D.Ga.1987); *Q-Co Industries, Inc. v. Hoffman*, 625 F.Supp. 608, 615 (S.D.N.Y.1985); *SAS Inst., Inc. v. S & H Computer Sys., Inc.*, 605 F.Supp. 816, 829–30 (M.D.Tenn.1985). However, that conclusion does not end our analysis. We must determine the scope of copyright protection that extends to a computer program's non-literal structure.

* * *

1) Idea vs. Expression Dichotomy

It is a fundamental principle of copyright law that a copyright does not protect an idea, but only the expression of the idea. *See Baker v. Selden* (1879); *Mazer v. Stein*, 347 U.S. 201, 217 (1954). This axiom of common law has been incorporated into the governing statute. Section 102(b) of the Act provides:

> In no case does copyright protection for an original work of authorship extend to any idea, procedure, process, system, method of

operation, concept, principle, or discovery, regardless of the form in which it is described, explained, illustrated, or embodied in such work.

17 U.S.C. § 102(b). *See also House Report*, at 5670 ("Copyright does not preclude others from using ideas or information revealed by the author's work.").

Congress made no special exception for computer programs. To the contrary, the legislative history explicitly states that copyright protects computer programs only "to the extent that they incorporate authorship in programmer's expression of original ideas, as distinguished from the ideas themselves." *Id.* at 5667.

Similarly, the National Commission on New Technological Uses of Copyrighted Works ("CONTU") established by Congress to survey the issues generated by the interrelationship of advancing technology and copyright law, *see* Pub.L. No. 93–573, § 201, 88 Stat. 1873 (1974), recommended, *inter alia*, that the 1976 Copyright Act "be amended ... to make it explicit that computer programs, to the extent that they embody the author's original creation, are proper subject matter for copyright." *See* National Commission on New Technological Uses of Copyrighted Works, *Final Report* 1 (1979) (hereinafter "*CONTU Report*"). To that end, Congress adopted CONTU's suggestions and amended the Copyright Act by adding, among other things, a provision to 17 U.S.C. § 101 which defined the term "computer program." *See* Pub.L. No. 96–517, § 10(a), 94 Stat. 3028 (1980). CONTU also "concluded that the idea-expression distinction should be used to determine which aspects of computer programs are copyrightable." *Lotus Dev. Corp.*, 740 F.Supp. at 54 (citing *CONTU Report*, at 44).

Drawing the line between idea and expression is a tricky business. Judge Learned Hand noted that "[n]obody has ever been able to fix that boundary, and nobody ever can." *Nichols*, 45 F.2d at 121. Thirty years later his convictions remained firm. "Obviously, no principle can be stated as to when an imitator has gone beyond copying the 'idea,' and has borrowed its 'expression,' " Judge Hand concluded. "Decisions must therefore inevitably be *ad hoc*." *Peter Pan Fabrics, Inc. v. Martin Weiner Corp.*, 274 F.2d 487, 489 (2d Cir.1960).

The essentially utilitarian nature of a computer program further complicates the task of distilling its idea from its expression. *See SAS Inst.*, 605 F.Supp. at 829; *cf.* Englund, at 893. In order to describe both computational processes and abstract ideas, its content "combines creative and technical expression." *See* Spivack, at 755. The variations of expression found in purely creative compositions, as opposed to those contained in utilitarian works, are not directed towards practical application. For example, a narration of Humpty Dumpty's demise, which would clearly be a creative composition, does not serve the same ends as, say, a recipe for scrambled eggs—which is a more process oriented text. Thus, compared to aesthetic works, computer programs hover even more closely to the elusive boundary line described in § 102(b).

The doctrinal starting point in analyses of utilitarian works, is the seminal case of *Baker v. Selden*, 101 U.S. 99 (1879). In *Baker*, the Supreme Court faced the question of "whether the exclusive property in a system of bookkeeping can be claimed, under the law of copyright, by means of a book in which that system is explained?" *Id.* at 101. Selden had copyrighted a book that expounded a particular method of bookkeeping. The book contained lined pages with headings intended to illustrate the manner in which the system operated. Baker's accounting publication included ledger sheets that employed "substantially the same ruled lines and headings...." *Id.* Selden's testator sued Baker for copyright infringement on the theory that the ledger sheets were protected by Selden's copyright.

The Supreme Court found nothing copyrightable in Selden's bookkeeping system, and rejected his infringement claim regarding the ledger sheets. The Court held that:

> The fact that the art described in the book by illustrations of lines and figures which are reproduced in practice in the application of the art, makes no difference. Those illustrations are the mere language employed by the author to convey his ideas more clearly. Had he used words of description instead of diagrams (which merely stand in the place of words), there could not be the slightest doubt that others, applying the art to practical use, might lawfully draw the lines and diagrams which were in the author's mind, and which he thus described by words in his book.

> The copyright of a work on mathematical science cannot give to the author an exclusive right to the methods of operation which he propounds, or to the diagrams which he employs to explain them, so as to prevent an engineer from using them whenever occasion requires.

Id. at 103.

To the extent that an accounting text and a computer program are both "a set of statements or instructions ... to bring about a certain result," 17 U.S.C. § 101, they are roughly analogous. In the former case, the processes are ultimately conducted by human agency; in the latter, by electronic means. In either case, as already stated, the processes themselves are not protectable. But the holding in *Baker* goes farther. The Court concluded that those aspects of a work, which "must necessarily be used as incident to" the idea, system or process that the work describes, are also not copyrightable. 101 U.S. at 104. Selden's ledger sheets, therefore, enjoyed no copyright protection because they were "necessary incidents to" the system of accounting that he described. *Id.* at 103. From this reasoning, we conclude that those elements of a computer program that are necessarily incidental to its function are similarly unprotectable.

While *Baker v. Selden* provides a sound analytical foundation, it offers scant guidance on how to separate idea or process from expression, and moreover, on how to further distinguish protectable expression from that expression which "must necessarily be used as incident to" the work's underlying concept. In the context of computer programs, the Third Circuit's noted decision in *Whelan* has, thus far, been the most thoughtful attempt to accomplish these ends.

The court in *Whelan* faced substantially the same problem as is presented by this case. There, the defendant was accused of making off with the non-literal structure of the plaintiff's copyrighted dental lab management program, and employing it to create its own competitive version. In assessing whether there had been an infringement, the court had to determine which aspects of the programs involved were ideas, and which were expression. In separating the two, the court settled upon the following conceptual approach:

> [T]he line between idea and expression may be drawn with reference to the end sought to be achieved by the work in question. In other words, the *purpose or function of a utilitarian work would be the work's idea, and everything that is not necessary to that purpose or function would be part of the expression of the idea* . . . . Where there are various means of achieving the desired purpose, then the particular means chosen is not necessary to the purpose; hence, there is expression, not idea.

797 F.2d at 1236 (citations omitted). The "idea" of the program at issue in *Whelan* was identified by the court as simply "the efficient management of a dental laboratory." *Id.* at n. 28.

So far, in the courts, the *Whelan* rule has received a mixed reception. * * *

Whelan has fared even more poorly in the academic community, where its standard for distinguishing idea from expression has been widely criticized for being conceptually overbroad. See, e.g., Englund, at 881; Menell, at 1074, 1082; Kretschmer, at 837–39; Spivack, at 747–55; Thomas M. Gage, Note, Whelan Associates v. Jaslow Dental Laboratories: *Copyright Protection for Computer Software Structure—What's the Purpose?*, 1987 Wis.L.Rev. 859, 860–61 (1987). The leading commentator in the field has stated that "[t]he crucial flaw in [*Whelan*'s] reasoning is that it assumes that only one 'idea,' in copyright law terms, underlies any computer program, and that once a separable idea can be identified, everything else must be expression." 3 Nimmer § 13.03(F), at 13–62.34. This criticism focuses not upon the program's ultimate purpose but upon the reality of its structural design. As we have already noted, a computer program's ultimate function or purpose is the composite result of interacting subroutines. Since each subroutine is itself a program, and thus, may be said to have its own "idea," *Whelan*'s general formulation that a program's overall purpose equates with the program's idea is descriptively inadequate.

Accordingly, we think that Judge Pratt wisely declined to follow *Whelan. See Computer Assocs.*, 775 F.Supp. at 558–60. In addition to noting the weakness in the *Whelan* definition of "program-idea," mentioned above, Judge Pratt found that *Whelan*'s synonymous use of the terms "structure, sequence, and organization," *see Whelan*, 797 F.2d at 1224 n. 1, demonstrated a flawed understanding of a computer program's method of operation. *See Computer Assocs.*, 775 F.Supp. at 559–60 (discussing the distinction between a program's "static structure" and "dynamic structure"). Rightly, the district court found *Whelan's* rationale suspect because it is so closely tied to what can now be seen—with the passage of time—as the opinion's somewhat outdated appreciation of computer science.

2) Substantial Similarity Test for Computer Program Structure: Abstraction–Filtration–Comparison

We think that *Whelan's* approach to separating idea from expression in computer programs relies too heavily on metaphysical distinctions and does not place enough emphasis on practical considerations. *Cf. Apple Computer*, 714 F.2d at 1253 (rejecting certain commercial constraints on programming as a helpful means of distinguishing idea from expression because they did "not enter into the somewhat metaphysical issue of whether particular ideas and expressions have merged"). As the cases that we shall discuss demonstrate, a satisfactory answer to this problem cannot be reached by resorting, *a priori*, to philosophical first principals.

As discussed herein, we think that district courts would be well-advised to undertake a three-step procedure, based on the abstractions test utilized by the district court, in order to determine whether the non-literal elements of two or more computer programs are substantially similar. This approach breaks no new ground; rather, it draws on such familiar copyright doctrines as merger, *scènes à faire*, and public domain. In taking this approach, however, we are cognizant that computer technology is a dynamic field which can quickly outpace judicial decision-making. Thus, in cases where the technology in question does not allow for a literal application of the procedure we outline below, our opinion should not be read to foreclose the district courts of our circuit from utilizing a modified version.

In ascertaining substantial similarity under this approach, a court would first break down the allegedly infringed program into its constituent structural parts. Then, by examining each of these parts for such things as incorporated ideas, expression that is necessarily incidental to those ideas, and elements that are taken from the public domain, a court would then be able to sift out all non-protectable material. Left with a kernel, or possible kernels, of creative expression after following this process of elimination, the court's last step would be to compare this material with the structure of an allegedly infringing program. The result of this comparison will determine whether the protectable elements of the programs at issue are substantially similar so as to warrant a finding of infringement. It will be helpful to elaborate a bit further.

Step One: Abstraction

As the district court appreciated, *see Computer Assocs.*, 775 F.Supp. at 560, the theoretic framework for analyzing substantial similarity expounded by Learned Hand in the *Nichols* case is helpful in the present context. In *Nichols*, we enunciated what has now become known as the "abstractions" test for separating idea from expression:

> Upon any work ... a great number of patterns of increasing generality will fit equally well, as more and more of the incident is left out. The last may perhaps be no more than the most general statement of what the [work] is about, and at times might consist only of its title; but there is a point in this series of abstractions where they are no longer protected, since otherwise the [author] could prevent the use of his "ideas," to which, apart from their expression, his property is never extended.

Nichols, 45 F.2d at 121.

While the abstractions test was originally applied in relation to literary works such as novels and plays, it is adaptable to computer programs. * * *

As applied to computer programs, the abstractions test will comprise the first step in the examination for substantial similarity. Initially, in a manner that resembles reverse engineering on a theoretical plane, a court should dissect the allegedly copied program's structure and isolate each level of abstraction contained within it. This process begins with the code and ends with an articulation of the program's ultimate function. * * *

As an anatomical guide to this procedure, the following description is helpful:

> At the lowest level of abstraction, a computer program may be thought of in its entirety as a set of individual instructions organized into a hierarchy of modules. At a higher level of abstraction, the instructions in the lowest-level modules may be replaced conceptually by the functions of those modules. At progressively higher levels of abstraction, the functions of higher-level modules conceptually replace the implementations of those modules in terms of lower-level modules and instructions, until finally, one is left with nothing but the ultimate function of the program.... A program has structure at every level of abstraction at which it is viewed. At low levels of abstraction, a program's structure may be quite complex; at the highest level it is trivial.

Englund, at 897–98; *cf.* Spivack, at 774.

Step Two: Filtration

Once the program's abstraction levels have been discovered, the substantial similarity inquiry moves from the conceptual to the concrete. Professor Nimmer suggests, and we endorse, a "successive filtering method" for separating protectable expression from non-protectable material. *See generally* 3 Nimmer § 13.03[F]. This process entails examining the structural components at each level of abstraction to determine whether their particular inclusion at that level was "idea" or was dictated by considerations of efficiency, so as to be necessarily incidental to that idea; required by factors external to the program itself; or taken from the public domain and hence is nonprotectable expression. *See also* Kretschmer, at 844–45 (arguing that program features dictated by market externalities or efficiency concerns are unprotectable). The structure of any given program may reflect some, all, or none of these considerations. Each case requires its own fact specific investigation.

Strictly speaking, this filtration serves "the purpose of defining the scope of plaintiff's copyright." *Brown Bag Software v. Symantec Corp.*, 960 F.2d 1465, 1475 (9th Cir.) (endorsing "analytic dissection" of computer programs in order to isolate protectable expression), *cert. denied*, 506 U.S. 869 (1992). By applying well developed doctrines of copyright law, it may ultimately leave behind a "core of protectable material." 3 Nimmer § 13.03[F][5], at 13–72. Further explication of this second step may be helpful.

(a) Elements Dictated by Efficiency

The portion of *Baker v. Selden*, discussed earlier, which denies copyright protection to expression necessarily incidental to the idea being expressed, appears to be the cornerstone for what has developed into the doctrine of merger. The doctrine's underlying principle is that "[w]hen there is essentially only one way to express an idea, the idea and its expression are inseparable and copyright is no bar to copying that expression." *Concrete Machinery Co. v. Classic Lawn Ornaments, Inc.*, 843 F.2d 600, 606 (1st Cir.1988). Under these circumstances, the expression is said to have "merged" with the idea itself. In order not to confer a monopoly of the idea upon the copyright owner, such expression should not be protected. *See Herbert Rosenthal Jewelry Corp. v. Kalpakian*, 446 F.2d 738, 742 (9th Cir.1971).

CONTU recognized the applicability of the merger doctrine to computer programs. In its report to Congress it stated that:

> [C]opyrighted language may be copied without infringing when there is but a limited number of ways to express a given idea.... In the computer context, this means that when specific instructions, even though previously copyrighted, are the only and essential means of accomplishing a given task, their later use by another will not amount to infringement.

CONTU Report, at 20. While this statement directly concerns only the application of merger to program code, that is, the textual aspect of the program, it reasonably suggests that the doctrine fits comfortably within the general context of computer programs.

Furthermore, when one considers the fact that programmers generally strive to create programs "that meet the user's needs in the most efficient manner," Menell, at 1052, the applicability of the merger doctrine to computer programs becomes compelling. In the context of computer program design, the concept of efficiency is akin to deriving the most concise logical proof or formulating the most succinct mathematical computation. Thus, the more efficient a set of modules are, the more closely they approximate the idea or process embodied in that particular aspect of the program's structure.

While, hypothetically, there might be a myriad of ways in which a programmer may effectuate certain functions within a program,—i.e., express the idea embodied in a given subroutine—efficiency concerns may so narrow the practical range of choice as to make only one or two forms of expression workable options. *See* 3 Nimmer § 13.03. Of course, not all program structure is informed by efficiency concerns. *See* Menell, at 1052 (besides efficiency, simplicity related to user accommodation has become a programming priority). It follows that in order to determine whether the merger doctrine precludes copyright protection to an aspect of a program's structure that is so oriented, a court must inquire "whether the use of *this particular set* of modules is necessary efficiently to implement that part of the program's process" being implemented. Englund, at 902. If the answer is yes, then the expression represented by the programmer's choice of a specific module or group of modules has merged with their underlying idea and is unprotected. *Id.* at 902–03.

* * *

Efficiency is an industry-wide goal. Since, as we have already noted, there may be only a limited number of efficient implementations for any given program task, it is quite possible that multiple programmers, working independently, will design the identical method employed in the allegedly infringed work. Of course, if this is the case, there is no copyright infringement. *See Roth Greeting Cards v. United Card Co.*, 429 F.2d 1106, 1110 (9th Cir.1970); *Sheldon*, 81 F.2d at 54.

Under these circumstances, the fact that two programs contain the same efficient structure may as likely lead to an inference of independent creation as it does to one of copying. *See* 3 Nimmer § 13.03[F][2], at 13–65; *cf. Herbert Rosenthal Jewelry Corp.*, 446 F.2d at 741 (evidence of independent creation may stem from defendant's standing as a designer of previous similar works). Thus, since evidence of similarly efficient structure is not particularly probative of copying, it should be disregarded in the overall substantial similarity analysis. *See* 3 Nimmer § 13.03[F][2], at 13–65.

We find support for applying the merger doctrine in cases that have already addressed the question of substantial similarity in the context of computer program structure. Most recently, in *Lotus Dev. Corp.*, 740 F.Supp. at 66, the district court had before it a claim of copyright infringement relating to the structure of a computer spreadsheet program. The court observed that "the basic spreadsheet screen display that resembles a rotated 'L' . . . , if not present in every expression of such a program, is present in most expressions." *Id.* Similarly, the court found that "an essential detail present in most if not all expressions of an electronic spreadsheet—is the designation of a particular key that, when pressed, will invoke the menu command system." *Id.* Applying the merger doctrine, the court denied copyright protection to both program elements.

* * *

We agree with the approach taken in these decisions, and conclude that application of the merger doctrine in this setting is an effective way to eliminate non-protectable expression contained in computer programs.

(b) Elements Dictated By External Factors

We have stated that where "it is virtually impossible to write about a particular historical era or fictional theme without employing certain 'stock' or standard literary devices," such expression is not copyrightable. *Hoehling v. Universal City Studios, Inc.*, 618 F.2d 972, 979 (2d Cir.), *cert. denied*, 449 U.S. 841 (1980). * * * This is known as the *scènes à faire* doctrine, and like "merger," it has its analogous application to computer programs. *Cf. Data East USA*, 862 F.2d at 208 (applying *scènes à faire* to a home computer video game).

Professor Nimmer points out that "in many instances it is virtually impossible to write a program to perform particular functions in a specific computing environment without employing standard techniques." 3 Nimmer § 13.03[F][3], at 13–65. This is a result of the fact that a programmer's freedom of design choice is often circumscribed by extrinsic considerations such as (1) the mechanical specifications of the computer on which a particular program is intended to run; (2) compatibility requirements of other programs with which a program is designed to operate in conjunction; (3) computer manufacturers' design standards; (4) demands of the industry being serviced; and (5) widely accepted programming practices within the computer industry. *Id.* at 13–66–71.

Courts have already considered some of these factors in denying copyright protection to various elements of computer programs. * * *

* * *

Building upon this existing case law, we conclude that a court must also examine the structural content of an allegedly infringed program for elements that might have been dictated by external factors.

(c) Elements taken From the Public Domain

Closely related to the non-protectability of *scènes à faire*, is material found in the public domain. Such material is free for the taking and cannot be appropriated by a single author even though it is included in a copyrighted work. *See E.F. Johnson Co. v. Uniden Corp. of America*, 623 F.Supp. 1485, 1499 (D.Minn.1985); *see also Sheldon*, 81 F.2d at 54. We see no reason to make an exception to this rule for elements of a computer program that have entered the public domain by virtue of freely accessible program exchanges and the like. *See* 3 Nimmer § 13.03[F][4]. Thus, a court must also filter out this material from the allegedly infringed program before it makes the final inquiry in its substantial similarity analysis.

Step Three: Comparison

The third and final step of the test for substantial similarity that we believe appropriate for non-literal program components entails a comparison. Once a court has sifted out all elements of the allegedly infringed program which are "ideas" or are dictated by efficiency or external factors, or taken from the public domain, there may remain a core of protectable expression. In terms of a work's copyright value, this is the golden nugget. *See Brown Bag Software*, 960 F.2d at 1475. At this point, the court's substantial similarity inquiry focuses on whether the defendant copied any aspect of this protected expression, as well as an assessment of the copied portion's relative importance with respect to the plaintiff's overall program.

3) Policy Considerations

We are satisfied that the three step approach we have just outlined not only comports with, but advances the constitutional policies underlying the Copyright Act. Since any method that tries to distinguish idea from expression ultimately impacts on the scope of copyright protection afforded to a particular type of work, "the line [it draws] must be a pragmatic one, which also keeps in consideration 'the preservation of the balance between competition and protection. . . . ' " *Apple Computer,* 714 F.2d at 1253 (citation omitted).

* * *

B.   The District Court Decision

1) Use of Expert Evidence in Determining Substantial Similarity Between Computer Programs

* * *

2) Evidentiary Analysis

The district court had to determine whether Altai's OSCAR 3.5 program was substantially similar to CA's ADAPTER. We note that Judge Pratt's method of analysis effectively served as a road map for our own, with one exception—Judge Pratt filtered out the non-copyrightable aspects of OSCAR 3.5 rather than those found in ADAPTER, the allegedly infringed program. We think that our approach—i.e., filtering out the unprotected aspects of an allegedly infringed program and then comparing the end product to the structure of the suspect program—is preferable, and therefore believe that district courts should proceed in this manner in future cases.

We opt for this strategy because, in some cases, the defendant's program structure might contain protectable expression and/or other elements that are not found in the plaintiff's program. Since it is extraneous to the allegedly copied work, this material would have no bearing on any potential substantial similarity between the two programs. Thus, its filtration would be wasteful and unnecessarily time consuming. Furthermore, by focusing the analysis on the infringing rather than on the infringed material, a court may mistakenly place too little emphasis on a quantitatively small misappropriation which is, in reality, a qualitatively vital aspect of the plaintiff's protectable expression.

The fact that the district court's analysis proceeded in the reverse order, however, had no material impact on the outcome of this case. Since Judge Pratt determined that OSCAR effectively contained no protectable expression whatsoever, the most serious charge that can be leveled against him is that he was overly thorough in his examination.

The district court took the first step in the analysis set forth in this opinion when it separated the program by levels of abstraction. The district court stated:

> As applied to computer software programs, this abstractions test would progress in order of "increasing generality" from object code, to source code, to parameter lists, to services required, to general outline. In discussing the particular similarities, therefore, we shall focus on these levels.

Computer Assocs., 775 F.Supp. at 560. While the facts of a different case might require that a district court draw a more particularized blueprint of a program's overall structure, this description is a workable one for the case at hand.

Moving to the district court's evaluation of OSCAR 3.5's structural components, we agree with Judge Pratt's systematic exclusion of non-protectable expression. With respect to code, the district court observed that after the rewrite of OSCAR 3.4 to OSCAR 3.5, "there remained virtually no lines of code that were identical to ADAPTER." *Id.* at 561. Accordingly, the court found that the code "present[ed] no similarity at all." *Id.* at 562.

Next, Judge Pratt addressed the issue of similarity between the two programs' parameter lists and macros. He concluded that, viewing the conflicting evidence most favorably to CA, it demonstrated that "only a few of the lists and macros were similar to protected elements in ADAPTER; the others were either in the public domain or dictated by the functional demands of the program." *Id.* As discussed above, functional elements and elements taken from the public domain do not qualify for copyright protection. With respect to the few remaining parameter lists and macros, the district court could reasonably conclude that they did not warrant a finding of infringement given their relative contribution to the overall program. *See Warner Bros., Inc. v. American Broadcasting Cos., Inc.*, 720 F.2d 231, 242 (2d Cir.1983) (discussing *de minimis* exception which allows for literal copying of a small and usually insignificant portion of the plaintiff's work); 3 Nimmer § 13.03[F][5], at 13–74. In any event, the district court reasonably found that, for lack of persuasive evidence, CA failed to meet its burden of proof on whether the macros and parameter lists at issue were substantially similar. *See Computer Assocs.*, 775 F.Supp. at 562.

The district court also found that the overlap exhibited between the list of services required for both ADAPTER and OSCAR 3.5 was "determined by the demands of the operating system and of the applications program to which it [was] to be linked through ADAPTER or OSCAR. . . ." *Id.* In other words, this aspect of the program's structure was dictated by the nature of other programs with which it was designed to interact and, thus, is not protected by copyright.

Finally, in his infringement analysis, Judge Pratt accorded no weight to the similarities between the two programs' organizational charts, "because [the charts were] so simple and obvious to anyone exposed to the operation of the program[s]." *Id.* CA argues that the district court's action in this regard "is not consistent with copyright law"—that "obvious" expression is protected, and that the district court erroneously failed to realize this. However, to say that elements of a work are "obvious," in the manner in which the district court used the word, is to say that they "follow naturally from the work's theme rather than from the author's creativity." 3 Nimmer § 13.03 [F][3], at 13–65. This is but one formulation of the *scènes à faire* doctrine, which we have already endorsed as a means of weeding out unprotectable expression.

CA argues, at some length, that many of the district court's factual conclusions regarding the creative nature of its program's components are simply wrong. Of course, we are limited in our review of factual findings to setting aside only those that we determine are clearly erroneous. *See* Fed.R.Civ.P. 52. Upon a thorough review of the voluminous record in this case, which is comprised of conflicting testimony and other highly technical evidence, we discern no error on the part of Judge Pratt, let alone clear error.

Since we accept Judge Pratt's factual conclusions and the results of his legal analysis, we affirm his denial of CA's copyright infringement claim based upon OSCAR 3.5. We emphasize that, like all copyright infringement cases, those that involve computer programs are highly fact specific. The amount of protection due structural elements, in any given case, will vary according to the protectable expression found to exist within the program at issue.

* * *

CONCLUSION

In adopting the above three step analysis for substantial similarity between the non-literal elements of computer programs, we seek to insure two things: (1) that programmers may receive appropriate copyright protection for innovative utilitarian works containing expression; and (2) that non-protectable technical expression remains in the public domain for others to use freely as building blocks in their own work.
* * *

* * *

Accordingly, we affirm the judgment of the district court in part; vacate in part; and remand for further proceedings. The parties shall bear their own costs of appeal, including the petition for rehearing.

Notes

1. Unlike *Whelan*, *Computer Associates* has been widely followed as a judicial "test" for separating protectable expression from unprotected ideas in the context of computer software. See for example, *Softel, Inc. v. Dragon Medical and Scientific Communications, Inc.*, 118 F.3d 955 (2d Cir.1997), *Engineering Dynamics, Inc. v. Structural Software, Inc.*, 26 F.3d 1335 (5th Cir.1994); *Gates Rubber Co. v. Bando Chemical Industries, Ltd.*, 9 F.3d 823 (10th Cir.1993); *Autoskill Inc. v. National Educational Support Systems, Inc.*, 994 F.2d 1476 (10th Cir.1993); *MiTek Holdings, Inc. v. Arce Engineering Co., Inc.*, 89 F.3d 1548 (11th Cir.1996); and *Bateman v. Mnemonics, Inc.*, 79 F.3d 1532 (11th Cir.1996).

2. *Computer Associates* provides an approach, but not an answer. Inevitably, judges are faced with making ad hoc determinations of what constitutes protectable expression vs. unprotectable "idea, procedure, process, system, method of operation, concept, principle, or discovery". 17 U.S.C. § 102(b). This has led to unpredictable and conflicting outcomes.

2. CONTRIBUTORY INFRINGEMENT

VAULT CORP. v. QUAID SOFTWARE LTD.

United States Court of Appeals, Fifth Circuit, 1988.
847 F.2d 255.

REAVLEY, CIRCUIT JUDGE.

Vault brought this copyright infringement action against Quaid seeking damages and preliminary and permanent injunctions. The district court denied Vault's motion for a preliminary injunction, holding that Vault did not have a reasonable probability of success on the merits. *Vault Corp. v. Quaid Software Ltd.*, 655 F.Supp. 750 (E.D.La.1987). By stipulation of the parties, this ruling was made final and judgment was entered accordingly. We affirm.

I

Vault produces computer diskettes under the registered trademark "PROLOK" which are designed to prevent the unauthorized duplication of programs placed on them by software computer companies, Vault's customers. Floppy diskettes serve as a medium upon which computer companies place their software programs. To use a program, a purchaser loads the diskette into the disk drive of a computer, thereby allowing the computer to read the program into its memory. The purchaser can then remove the diskette from the disk drive and operate the program from the computer's memory. This process is repeated each time a program is used.

The protective device placed on a PROLOK diskette by Vault is comprised of two parts: a "fingerprint" and a software program ("Vault's program"). The "fingerprint" is a small mark physically placed on the magnetic surface of each PROLOK diskette which contains certain information that cannot be altered or erased. Vault's program is a set of instructions to the computer which interact with the "fingerprint" to prevent the computer from operating the program recorded on a PROLOK diskette (by one of Vault's customers) unless the computer verifies that the original PROLOK diskette, as identified by the "fingerprint," is in the computer's disk drive. While a purchaser can copy a PROLOK protected program onto another diskette, the computer will not read the program into its memory from the copy unless the original PROLOK diskette is also in one of the computer's disk drives. The fact that a fully functional copy of a program cannot be made from a PROLOK diskette prevents purchasers from buying a single program and making unauthorized copies for distribution to others.

Vault produced PROLOK in three stages. The original commercial versions, designated as versions 1.01, 1.02, 1.03, 1.04 and 1.06 ("version 1.0") were produced in 1983. Vault then incorporated improvements into the system and produced version 1.07 in 1984. The third major revision occurred in August and September of 1985 and was designated as versions 2.0 and 2.01 ("version 2.0"). Each version of PROLOK has been copyrighted and Vault includes a license agreement with every PROLOK package that specifically prohibits the copying, modification, translation, decompilation or disassembly of Vault's program. Beginning with version 2.0 in September 1985, Vault's license agreement contained a choice of law clause adopting Louisiana law.

Quaid's product, a diskette called "CopyWrite," contains a feature called "RAMKEY" which unlocks the PROLOK protective device and facilitates the creation of a fully functional copy of a program placed on a PROLOK diskette. The process is performed simply by copying the contents of the PROLOK diskette onto the CopyWrite diskette which can then be used to run the software program without the original PROLOK diskette in a computer disk drive. RAMKEY interacts with Vault's program to make it appear to the computer that the CopyWrite diskette contains the "fingerprint," thereby making the computer function as if the original PROLOK diskette is in its disk drive. A copy of a program placed on a CopyWrite diskette can be used without the original, and an unlimited number of fully functional copies can be made in this manner from the program originally placed on the PROLOK diskette.

Quaid first developed RAMKEY in September 1983 in response to PROLOK version 1.0. In order to develop this version of RAMKEY, Quaid copied Vault's program into the memory of its computer and analyzed the manner in which the program operated. When Vault developed version 1.07, Quaid adapted RAMKEY in 1984 to defeat this new version. The adapted version of RAMKEY contained a sequence of approximately 30 characters found in Vault's program and was discontinued in July 1984. Quaid then developed the current version of

RAMKEY which also operates to defeat PROLOK version 1.07, but does not contain the sequence of characters used in the discontinued version. Quaid has not yet modified RAMKEY to defeat PROLOK version 2.0, and has agreed not to modify RAMKEY pending the outcome of this suit. Robert McQuaid, the sole owner of Quaid, testified in his deposition that while a CopyWrite diskette can be used to duplicate programs placed on all diskettes, whether copy-protected or not, the only purpose served by RAMKEY is to facilitate the duplication of programs placed on copy-protected diskettes. He also stated that without the RAMKEY feature, CopyWrite would have no commercial value. * * *

* * *

III. VAULT'S FEDERAL CLAIMS

An owner of a copyrighted work has the exclusive right to reproduce the work in copies, to prepare derivative works based on the copyrighted work, to distribute copies of the work to the public, and, in the case of certain types of works, to perform and display the work publicly. 17 U.S.C. § 106. Sections 107 through 118 of the Copyright Act limit an owner's exclusive rights, and section 501(a) provides that "[a]nyone who violates any of the exclusive rights of the copyright owner as provided by sections 106 through 118 . . . is an infringer of the copyright."

It is not disputed that Vault owns the copyright to the program it places on PROLOK diskettes and is thus an "owner of copyright" under § 106. Therefore, Vault has, subject to the exceptions contained in sections 107 through 118, the exclusive right to reproduce its program in copies and to prepare derivative works based on its program. Vault claims that Quaid infringed its copyright under § 501(a) by: (1) directly copying Vault's program into the memory of Quaid's computer; (2) contributing to the unauthorized copying of Vault's program and the programs Vault's customers place on PROLOK diskettes; and (3) preparing derivative works of Vault's program.

Section 117 of the Copyright Act limits a copyright owner's exclusive rights under § 106 by permitting an owner of a computer program to make certain copies of that program without obtaining permission from the program's copyright owner. With respect to Vault's first two claims of copyright infringement, Quaid contends that its activities fall within the § 117 exceptions and that it has, therefore, not infringed Vault's exclusive rights under § 501(a).

* * *

C. Contributory Infringement

Vault contends that, because purchasers of programs placed on PROLOK diskettes use the RAMKEY feature of CopyWrite to make unauthorized copies, Quaid's advertisement and sale of CopyWrite diskettes with the RAMKEY feature violate the Copyright Act by contributing to the infringement of Vault's copyright and the copyrights owned by Vault's customers. Vault asserts that it lost customers and substantial revenue as a result of Quaid's contributory infringement because software companies which previously relied on PROLOK diskettes to protect their programs from unauthorized copying have discontinued their use. While a purchaser of a program on a PROLOK diskette violates sections 106(1) and 501(a) by making and distributing unauthorized copies of the program, the Copyright Act "does not expressly render anyone liable for the infringement committed by another." *Sony Corp. of Am. v. Universal City Studios*, 464 U.S. 417, 434, 104 S.Ct. 774, 785, 78 L.Ed.2d 574 (1984). The Supreme Court in Sony, after examining the express provision in the Patent Act which imposes liability on an individual who "actively induces infringement of a patent," 35 U.S.C. § 271(b) & (c), and noting the similarity between the Patent and Copyright Acts, recognized the availability, under the Copyright Act, of vicarious liability against one who sells a product that is used to make unauthorized copies of copyrighted material. *Id.* at 434–42, 104 S.Ct. at 785–89. The Court held that liability based on contributory infringement could be imposed only where the seller had constructive knowledge of the fact that its product was used to make unauthorized copies of copyrighted material, *id.* at 339, 104 S.Ct. at 787, and that the sale of a product "does not constitute contributory infringement if the product is widely used for legitimate, unobjectionable purposes. Indeed, it need merely be capable of substantial noninfringing uses." *Id.* at 442, 104 S.Ct. at 789.

While Quaid concedes that it has actual knowledge that its product is used to make unauthorized copies of copyrighted material, it contends that the RAMKEY portion of its CopyWrite diskettes serves a substantial noninfringing use by allowing purchasers of programs on PROLOK diskettes to make archival copies as permitted under 17 U.S.C. § 117(2), and thus that it is not liable for contributory infringement. The district court held that Vault lacked standing to raise a contributory infringement claim because "it is not Vault, but the customers of Vault who place their programs on PROLOK disks, who may assert such claims. Clearly the copyright rights to these underlying programs belong to their publishers, not Vault." *Vault*, 655 F.Supp. at 759. Alternatively the court held that CopyWrite is capable of "commercially significant noninfringing uses" because the RAMKEY feature permits the making of archival copies of copy-protected software, and CopyWrite diskettes (without the RAMKEY feature) are used to make copies of unprotected software and as a diagnostic tool to analyze the quality of new computer programs. *Id.* Therefore, the court held that the sale of CopyWrite did not constitute contributory infringement.

While we hold that Vault has standing to assert its contributory infringement claim, we find that RAMKEY is capable of substantial noninfringing uses and thus reject Vault's contention that the advertisement and sale of CopyWrite diskettes with RAMKEY constitute contributory infringement.

1. *Standing*

The Copyright Act provides that the "legal or beneficial owner of an exclusive right under a copyright is entitled, subject to the requirements of sections 205(d) and 411 [concerning the recordation and registration of copyrights], to institute an action for any infringement of that particular right committed while he or she is the owner of it." 17 U.S.C. § 501(b). The Supreme Court in *Sony* noted that it was the taping of plaintiff's "own copyrighted programs that provides them with standing to charge Sony with contributory infringement." 464 U.S. at 434, 104 S.Ct. at 785.

The focus of Vault's allegation of contributory infringement in its amended complaint is that CopyWrite, through RAMKEY, enables purchasers of PROLOK protected programs to infringe the copyrights of Vault's customers and that, as a result, Vault has suffered damages due to its loss of customers. While Vault does not own the copyrights to its customer's programs, it does own the copyright to the program it places on each PROLOK diskette. This program operates in conjunction with the "fingerprint" to prevent the duplication of Vault's customer's programs. Uncontroverted testimony established that both Vault's protective program and its customer's program are copied onto a CopyWrite diskette when an individual executes a computer's "copy" function in order to duplicate the customer's program from a PROLOK diskette onto a CopyWrite diskette, and that RAMKEY then interacts with Vault's program to defeat its protective function and to make the computer operate as if the original PROLOK diskette was in one of its disk drives. Therefore, CopyWrite diskettes, through RAMKEY, facilitate not only the copying of Vault's customer's software programs but also the copying of Vault's protective program, and, in addition, RAMKEY interacts with Vault's program to destroy its purpose.

Quaid does not take issue with the validity of Vault's copyright under § 501(b) but instead contends that Vault lacks standing because it failed to allege contributory infringement based on the copying of its program, as opposed to the programs of its customers. Vault responds that its pleadings should be broadly construed to include its contributory infringement claim based on the copying of its program, and that even if its pleadings are narrowly construed, they were amended, pursuant to Fed.R.Civ.P. 15(b), to include this claim by trial testimony which established that Quaid's product contributes to the unauthorized copying of Vault's program.

Rule 15(b) provides that "[w]hen issues not raised by the pleadings are tried by express or implied consent of the parties, they shall be treated in all respects as if they had been raised in the pleadings." While Vault's pleadings do not allege contributory infringement based on the copying of its copyrighted program, Quaid's consent to this claim is evidenced by a pretrial memorandum, signed by counsel for both Vault and Quaid, which listed as a contested issue of law "[w]hether Quaid has contributorily infringed *Vault's* and Vault's customer copyrights" (emphasis added). Quaid does not contend that it has been unfairly prejudiced by Vault's contention of contributory infringement based on the copying of its own program, *see Mason v. Hunter*, 534 F.2d 822, 825 (8th Cir.1976), nor does Quaid contend that it had inadequate notice of the nature of Vault's claim or an inadequate opportunity to fully and fairly respond, *see Henry v. Coahoma County Bd. of Educ.*, 246 F.Supp. 517, 519 (N.D.Miss.1963), *aff'd*, 353 F.2d 648 (5th Cir.1965), *cert. denied*, 384 U.S. 962, 86 S.Ct. 1586, 16 L.Ed.2d 674 (1966). Vault's proposed interpretation or amendment of its pleadings in no way changes the character of the case. *See id.* at 518. It is beyond dispute that RAMKEY destroys the commercial value of PROLOK diskettes, and while the extent of Vault's damages were not fully developed at trial, the evidence indicated that Vault sustained substantial injuries as a result of RAMKEY and thus has a significant personal stake in the outcome of this litigation. Under these circumstances, we hold that, pursuant to Fed.R.Civ.P. 15(b), Vault has fairly alleged contributory infringement of its copyrighted program and has standing to pursue this claim.

2. *Substantial Noninfringing Uses of RAMKEY*

Vault's allegation of contributory infringement focuses on the RAMKEY feature of CopyWrite diskettes, not on the non-RAMKEY portions of these diskettes. Vault has no objection to the advertising and marketing of CopyWrite diskettes without the RAMKEY feature, and this feature is separable from the underlying diskette upon which it is placed. Therefore, in determining whether Quaid engaged in contributory infringement, we do not focus on the substantial noninfringing uses of CopyWrite, as opposed to the RAMKEY feature itself. *See Vault*, 655 F.Supp. at 759. The issue properly presented is whether the RAMKEY feature has substantial noninfringing uses.

The starting point for our analysis is with *Sony*. The plaintiffs in *Sony*, owners of copyrighted television programs, sought to enjoin the manufacture and marketing of Betamax video tape recorders ("VTR's"), contending that VTR's contributed to the infringement of their copyrights by permitting the unauthorized copying of their programs. 464 U.S. at 419–20, 104 S.Ct. at 777. After noting that plaintiffs' market share of television programming was less than 10%, and that copyright holders of a significant quantity of television broadcasting authorized the copying of their programs, the Court held that VTR's serve the legitimate and substantially noninfringing purpose of recording these programs, as well as plaintiffs' programs, for future viewing (authorized and unauthorized time-shifting respectively), and therefore rejected plaintiffs' contributory infringement claim. *Id.* at 442–55, 104 S.Ct. at 789–95.

Quaid asserts that RAMKEY serves the legitimate purpose of permitting purchasers of programs recorded on PROLOK diskettes to make archival copies under § 117(2) and that this purpose constitutes a substantial noninfringing use. At trial, witnesses for Quaid testified that software programs placed on floppy diskettes are subject to damage by *physical and human mishap* and that RAMKEY protects a purchaser's investment by providing a fully functional archival copy that can be used if the original program on the PROLOK protected diskette, or the diskette itself, is destroyed. Quaid contends that an archival copy of a PROLOK protected program, made without RAMKEY, does not serve to protect against these forms of damage because a computer will not read the program into its memory from the copy unless the PROLOK diskette containing the original undamaged program is also in one of its disk drives, which is impossible if the PROLOK diskette, or the program placed thereon, has been destroyed due to physical or human mishap.

Computer programs can be stored on a variety of mediums, including floppy diskettes, hard disks, non-erasable read only memory ("ROM") chips, and a computer's random access memory, and may appear only as printed instructions on a sheet of paper. Vault contends that the archival exception was designed to permit *only* the copying of programs which are subject to "destruction or damage by *mechanical or electrical failure.*" CONTU Report at 31 (emphasis added). While programs stored on all mediums may be subject to damage due to physical abuse or human error, programs stored on certain mediums are not subject to damage by mechanical or electrical failure. Therefore, Vault argues, the medium of storage determines whether the archival exception applies, thus providing only owners of programs, placed on mediums of storage which subject them to damage by mechanical or electrical failure, the right to make back-up copies. To support its construction of § 117(2), Vault notes that one court has held that the archival exception does not apply to the copying of programs stored on ROM chips where there was no evidence that programs stored on this medium were subject to damage by mechanical or electrical failure, *Atari*, 597 F.Supp. at 9–10, and another court has likewise held that the archival exception does not apply to the copying of programs which appear only in the form of printed instructions in a magazine, *Micro-Sparc*, 592 F.Supp. at 35–36.

Vault contends that the district court's finding that programs stored on floppy diskettes are subject to damage by mechanical or electrical failure is erroneous because there was insufficient evidence presented at trial to support it, and, based on this contention, Vault asserts that the archival exception does not apply to permit the unauthorized copying of these programs. Vault performed a trial demonstration to prove that even if a program on an original PROLOK diskette, and Vault's protective program, were completely erased from this diskette, these programs could be restored on the original diskette using a copy made *without* RAMKEY. Therefore, Vault argues that even if a program recorded on a PROLOK diskette is subject to damage by mechanical or electrical failure, the non-operational copy of a PROLOK protected program made without RAMKEY is sufficient to protect against this type of damage. Vault concludes that, in light of the fact that RAMKEY facilitates the making of unauthorized copies and owners of PROLOK protected programs can make copies to protect against damage by mechanical and electrical failure without RAMKEY, the RAMKEY feature is not capable of substantial noninfringing uses.

The narrow construction of the archival exception, advanced by Vault and accepted in the *Atari* and *Micro-Sparc* decisions, has undeniable appeal. This construction would leave the owner of a protected software program free to make back-up copies of the software to guard against erasures, which is probably the primary concern of owners as well as the drafters of the CONTU Report. Software producers should perhaps be entitled to protect their product from improper duplication, and Vault's PROLOK may satisfy producers and most purchasers on this score—*if* PROLOK cannot be copied by the purchaser onto a CopyWrite diskette without infringing the PROLOK copyright. That result does have appeal, but we believe it is an appeal that must be made to Congress. "[I]t is not our job to apply laws that have not yet been written." *Sony*, 464 U.S. at 456, 104 S.Ct. at 796. We read the statute as it is now written to authorize the owner of the PROLOK diskette to copy both the PROLOK program and the software program for any reason so long as the owner uses the copy for archival purposes only and not for an unauthorized transfer.

The CONTU Report's words of "mechanical or electrical failure" are contained in a paragraph quoted in the footnote. We read the stated causes of damage to be illustrative only, and not exclusive. Similarly, the statement follows with the prohibited use of the archival copies which does not include a prohibition against copying for purposes other than to protect against "mechanical or electrical failure." The Report, or Congress, could have easily limited the scope of § 117(2) to authorize the making of archival copies of programs subject to damage, and to guard against, only mechanical or electrical failure. CONTU did not recommend that language, nor did Congress enact it. Congress, following CONTU's advice, provided that an owner of a computer program may make a copy of that program provided that "such new copy . . . is for archival purposes only." 17 U.S.C. § 117(2). Congress did not choose to spell out detailed restrictions on the copying as was done in sections 108 and 112. Congress imposed no restriction upon the purpose or reason of the owner in making the archival copy; only the use made of that copy is restricted. *See* CONTU Report at 31 ("one could not, for example, make archival copies of a program and later sell some to another while retaining some for use"). An owner of a program is entitled, under § 117(2), to make an archival copy of that program in order to guard against *all* types of risks, including physical and human mishap as well as mechanical and electrical failure.

A copy of a PROLOK protected program made with RAMKEY protects an owner from all types of damage to the original program, while a copy made without RAMKEY only serves the limited function of protecting against damage to the original program by mechanical and electrical failure. Because § 117(2) permits the making of fully functional archival copies, it follows that RAMKEY is capable of substantial noninfringing uses. Quaid's advertisement and sale of CopyWrite diskettes with the RAMKEY feature does not constitute contributory infringement.

* * *

V. CONCLUSION

We hold that: (1) Quaid did not infringe Vault's exclusive right to reproduce its program in copies under § 106(1); (2) Quaid's advertisement and sale of RAMKEY does not constitute contributory infringement; (3) RAMKEY does not constitute a derivative work of Vault's program under § 106(2); and (4) the provision in Vault's license agreement, which prohibits the decompilation or disassembly of its program, is unenforceable.

The judgment of the district court is AFFIRMED.

IN RE CERTAIN PERSONAL COMPUTERS AND COMPONENTS THEREOF

U.S. International Trade Commission, 1984.
224 U.S.P.Q. 270, 1984 WL ___, 1984 WL 64146.

On January 20, 1984, the Commission determined to review the initial determination (ID) of the administrative law judge (ALJ) in Certain Personal Computers and Components Thereof, Inv. No. 337–TA–140. n2 The ALJ issued the ID on December 9, 1983, and determined that there was a violation of section 337 of the Tariff Act of 1930 on the basis that: (1) the patents and copyrights involved are valid, enforceable and infringed; (2) there is an "industry, efficiently and economically operated, in the United States," within the meaning of section 337; and (3) the importation of the subject articles has the tendency to substantially injure that industry.

We concur in the finding of a violation of section 337 on the basis that (1) the patents and copyrights involved are valid, enforceable, and infringed; (2) there is an "industry, efficiently and economically operated, in the United States;" and (3) the importation of the subject articles has the tendency to substantially injure that industry. However, we have modified the ID in accordance with the standards adopted for review in our rules. We have found some conclusions of material fact clearly erroneous and some legal conclusions erroneous. Additionally, we have provided more complete reasoning in some instances where we have concurred in the finding of the ALJ.

* * *

COPYRIGHTS INVOLVED

1. Registration No. TX 873–203

The copyright which is the subject of this registration is for a work entitled "Autostart ROM," a computer program. The deposit copy, which was introduced into evidence, is a hard copy printout in hexadecimal-coded machine language, i.e., each byte is represented as two hexadecimal numbers. The program is 2048 bytes long, filling the hexadecimal-coded memory addresses F800 to FFFF.

The Autostart ROM program is an operating system program, as opposed to a translator or applications program. It is a relatively short program and, indeed, is actually a collection of about 70 shorter programs which are referred to as "subroutines." These subroutines or groups of these subroutines instruct the microprocessor to perform certain housekeeping functions. Like all operating system programs, the Autostart ROM program is used every time the computer is used, no matter what applications program is being run. For this reason, like many other operating system programs, it is permanently stored in "read-only memory," referred to as ROM. The machine language in which the Autostart ROM program is written is that used by the 6502 microprocessor; it cannot be used on any other type of microprocessor. ROM is incorporated in a ROM chip, of which there may be several in a given computer. The Autostart ROM program is stored on such a ROM chip, known as an F8 ROM, since for the 6502 microprocessor, it must be located in that area of memory, i.e., beginning at memory address F8, i.e., F800. In the Apple II+ the F8 ROM chip is located at approximately location F3 on the printed circuit board (PCB) or motherboard.

PRODUCTS INVOLVED

Complainant Apple

Apple's products subject to this investigation are all complete personal computers: the Apple II, Apple II+, Apple IIe and Apple III. The Apple II and Apple II+ are no longer being manufactured, however. The Apple II, Apple II+, and Apple IIe incorporate the patented inventions and have ROM chips incorporating the Applesoft and Autostart ROM programs. The Apple III incorporates the patented inventions, but does not incorporate the Applesoft and Autostart ROM programs.

* * *

COPYRIGHT VALIDITY

The copyrights, including the Apple II System Monitor copyright, were registered within five years of publication of the copyrighted works and are thus presumed valid. Their validity is not disputed here.

* * *

CONTRIBUTORY COPYRIGHT INFRINGEMENT

The ALJ found contributory copyright infringement with regard to ROMless computers and motherboards which Apple had established were associated with parallel importations of infringing ROM chips. However, the ALJ found that for all other ROMless computers and motherboards, contributory copyright infringement could not be found because of the availability of non-infringing copies of the Applesoft or Autostart ROM programs from Apple or other suppliers. We agree with the ALJ's former finding, but find the latter clearly erroneous, for the reasons discussed below.

In *Sony Corporation of America v. Universal City Studios, Inc.,* ___ U.S. ___ (1984), slip opinion at 17, the Supreme Court stated that contributory copyright infringement "is merely a species of the broader problem of identifying the circumstances in which it is just to hold one individual accountable for the actions of another." As a general rule, a contributory infringer is one who with knowledge of the infringing activity, induces, causes or materially contributes to the infringing conduct of another. Knowledge includes reason to have knowledge. However, where the contributory infringement is alleged to lie in the sale or distribution of an article, it will not be found if that article is capable of commercially significant non-infringing uses. Of course, there must first be a finding that direct copyright infringement is occurring.

Dr. Hulina testified with regard to several ROMless computers and motherboards. Among these were the ROMless Guan Haur Golden II computer and the ROMless NAR MIND II computer. Dr. Hulina testified that the motherboards for these computers, which apparently are identical to Apple II series motherboards, had room for sockets for six ordinary ROM chips, but had sockets for 3 large 2732 EPROM chips. Dr. Hulina testified that these EPROM chips contain twice as much information as ordinary ROM chips, and their use as a substitute is a well-known expedient. He also testified that other than the Apple programs, he knew of no presently available programs which could be placed in those ROM chips to make these computers, or computers like them, useful. Dr. Hulina testified similarly with regard to the Formula/Leader motherboard. The foregoing evidence is sufficient to imply the existence of direct copyright infringement by at least third parties, i.e., copying of the copyrighted programs onto ROM chips and their insertion into the ROMless computers and motherboards. Persons who import or sell ROMless computers or components with identical motherboards have reason to know that activity which results in such direct infringement is occurring or will occur.

Finally, such ROMless computers and components are not capable of a commercially significant non-infringing use. The Commission investigative attorney argues that the availability of the Applesoft program on disk from Apple or others indicates that at least with regard to the Applesoft program, ROMless computers and components in general have a substantial non-infringing use. Guan Haur would go even further and include the Autostart ROM program as well, which is still available as part of one or more card inserts formerly manufactured by Apple and still available from inventory of some distributors and retailers. The mere availability of these programs, however, does not avoid contributory copyright infringement; it does not provide sufficient probative evidence of any commercially significant use of these Apple program cards or disks in conjunction with an imported unstuffed motherboard or ROMless computer to make a fully operational computer.

Apple argues that in addition to finding that ROMless computers and components having identical motherboards contributorily infringe the copyrights, the Commission should also find that ROMless computers and components having motherboards which are not identical to the Apple motherboard contributorily infringe the copyrights. We have found no expert testimony in the record with regard to this and no such ROMless computers or motherboards have been placed in the record. We therefore decline to make such a finding.

* * *

Note

If infringing or contributorily infringing products are all foreign-made, the use of procedures for stopping imports may be more cost-effective for the copyright owner than an attempt to track down and sue the distributors within the United States.

INTELLECTUAL RESERVE, INC. v. UTAH LIGHTHOUSE MINISTRY, INC.

United States District Court, D. Utah, Central Division, 1999.
75 F.Supp.2d 1290.

CAMPBELL, DISTRICT JUDGE.

This matter is before the court on plaintiff's motion for preliminary injunction. Plaintiff claims that unless a preliminary injunction issues, defendants will directly infringe and contribute to the infringement of its copyright in the *Church Handbook of Instructions* ("Handbook"). Defendants do not oppose a preliminary injunction, but argue that the scope of the injunction should be restricted to only prohibit direct infringement of plaintiff's copyright.

Having fully considered the arguments of counsel, the submissions of the parties and applicable legal authorities, the court grants plaintiff's motion for a preliminary injunction. However, the scope of the preliminary injunction is limited. * * *

* * *

B. *Contributory Infringement*

According to plaintiff, after the defendants were ordered to remove the Handbook from their website, the defendants began infringing plaintiff's copyright by inducing, causing, or materially contributing to the infringing conduct of others. It is undisputed that defendants placed a notice on their website that the Handbook was online, and gave three website addresses of websites containing the material defendants were ordered to remove from their website. Defendants also posted e-mails on their website that encouraged browsing those websites, printing copies of the Handbook and sending the Handbook to others.

Although the copyright statute does not expressly impose liability for contributory infringement,

[t]he absence of such express language in the copyright statute does not preclude the imposition of liability for copyright infringements on certain parties who have not themselves engaged in the infringing activity. For vicarious liability is imposed in virtually all areas of the law, and the concept of contributory infringement is merely a species of the broader problem of identifying the circumstances in which it is just to hold one accountable for the actions of another.

Sony Corp. v. Universal City Studios, Inc., 464 U.S. 417, 435, 104 S.Ct. 774, 78 L.Ed.2d 574 (1984) (footnote omitted). Even though " 'the lines between direct infringement, contributory infringement and vicarious liability are not clearly drawn' " distinctions can be made between them. *Id.* at n. 17 (quoting *Universal City Studios, Inc. v. Sony Corp.,* 480 F.Supp. 429, 457–58 (C.D.Cal.1979)). Vicarious liability is grounded in the tort concept of respondeat superior, and contributory infringement is founded in the tort concept of enterprise liability. * * *

Liability for contributory infringement is imposed when "one who, with knowledge of the infringing activity, induces, causes or materially contributes to the infringing conduct of another." *Gershwin Publ'g Corp. v. Columbia Artists Mgt., Inc.,* 443 F.2d 1159, 1162 (2d Cir.1971). Thus, to prevail on its claim of contributory infringement, plaintiff must first be able to establish that the conduct defendants allegedly aided or encouraged could amount to infringement. Defendants argue that they have not contributed to copyright infringement by those who posted the Handbook on websites nor by those who browsed the websites on their computers.

     1. *Can the Defendants Be Liable Under a Theory of Contributory Infringement for the Actions of Those Who Posted the Handbook on the Three Websites?*

     a. *Did those who posted the Handbook on the websites infringe plaintiff's copyright?*

During a hearing on the motion to vacate the temporary restraining order, defendants accepted plaintiff's proffer that the three websites contain the material which plaintiff alleges is copyrighted. Therefore, plaintiff at trial is likely to establish that those who have posted the material on the three websites are directly infringing plaintiff's copyright.

     b. *Did the defendants induce, cause or materially contribute to the infringement?*

The evidence now before the court indicates that there is no direct relationship between the defendants and the people who operate the three websites. The defendants did not provide the website operators with the plaintiff's copyrighted material, nor are the defendants receiving any kind of compensation from them. The only connection between the defendants and those who operate the three websites appears to be the information defendants have posted on their website concerning the infringing sites. Based on this scant evidence, the court concludes that plaintiff has not shown that defendants contributed to the infringing action of those who operate the infringing websites.

2. *Can the Defendants Be Liable Under a Theory of Contributory Infringement for the Actions of Those Who Browse the Three Infringing Websites?*

Defendants make two arguments in support of their position that the activities of those who browse the three websites do not make them liable under a theory of contributory infringement. First, defendants contend that those who browse the infringing websites are not themselves infringing plaintiff's copyright; and second, even if those who browse the websites are infringers, defendants have not materially contributed to the infringing conduct.

a. *Do those who browse the websites infringe plaintiff's copyright?*

The first question, then, is whether those who browse any of the three infringing websites are infringing plaintiff's copyright. Central to this inquiry is whether the persons browsing are merely viewing the Handbook (which is not a copyright infringement), or whether they are making a copy of the Handbook (which is a copyright infringement). *See* 17 U.S.C. § 106.

"Copy" is defined in the Copyright Act as: "material objects ... in which a work is fixed by any method now known or later developed, and from which the work can be perceived, reproduced, or otherwise communicated, either directly or with the aid of a machine or device." 17 U.S.C. § 101. "A work is 'fixed' ... when its ... sufficiently permanent or stable to permit it to be perceived, reproduced, or otherwise communicated for a period of more than transitory duration." *Id.*

When a person browses a website, and by so doing displays the Handbook, a copy of the Handbook is made in the computer's random access memory (RAM), to permit viewing of the material. And in making a copy, even a temporary one, the person who browsed infringes the copyright. * * *

b. *Did the defendants induce, cause or materially contribute to the infringement?*

The court now considers whether the defendants' actions contributed to the infringement of plaintiff's copyright by those who browse the three websites.

The following evidence establishes that defendants have actively encouraged the infringement of plaintiff's copyright After being ordered to remove the Handbook from their website, defendants posted on their website: "Church Handbook of Instructions is back online!" and listed the three website addresses. (*See* Pl.'s Reply Supp.Mot.Prelim.Inj., Ex. 1; Memo. Re: Contributory Infringement, at 9 n. 6.) Defendants also posted e-mail suggesting that the lawsuit against defendants would be affected by people logging onto one of the websites and downloading the complete handbook. (*See id.*, Ex. 2.) One of the e-mails posted by the defendants mentioned sending a copy of the copyrighted material to the media. (*See id.*) In response to an e-mail stating that the sender had unsuccessfully tried to browse a website that contained the Handbook, defendants gave further instruction on how to browse the material. * * *

Based on the above, the court finds that the first element necessary for injunctive relief is satisfied.

II. *Irreparable Injury*

Because this is a copyright infringement case and plaintiff has demonstrated a likelihood of success on the merits, there is a presumption of injury. *See Country Kids 'N City Slicks, Inc. v. Sheen*, 77 F.3d 1280, 1288–89 (10th Cir.1996). In addition, plaintiff will suffer additional immediate and real irreparable harm if defendants are permitted to post the copyrighted material or to knowingly induce, cause or materially contribute to the infringement of plaintiff's copyright by others.

III. *Harm to Defendants*

Defendants argue that their First Amendment rights will be infringed by a preliminary injunction. However, the First Amendment does not give defendants the right to infringe on legally recognized rights under the copyright law. *See Cable/Home Comm. Corp. v. Network Productions, Inc.*, 902 F.2d 829, 849 (11th Cir.1990). "[C]opyright interests [ ] must be guarded under the Constitution, and injunctive relief is a common judicial response to infringement of a valid copyright." *Id.* The court, in fashioning the scope of injunctive relief, is aware of and will protect the defendants' First Amendment rights.

IV. *The Public Interest*

Finally, it is in the public's interest to protect the copyright laws and the interests of copyright holders.

Order

Therefore, for the reasons stated, the court orders the following preliminary injunction:

1. Defendants, their agents and those under their control, shall remove from and not post on defendants' website the material alleged to infringe plaintiff's copyright;

2. Defendants, their agents and those under their control, shall not reproduce or distribute verbatim, in a tangible medium, material alleged to infringe plaintiff's copyright;

3. Defendants, their agents and those under their control, shall remove from and not post on defendants' website, addresses to websites that defendants know, or have reason to know, contain the material alleged to infringe plaintiff's copyright;

Defendants have not requested that a security be obtained from plaintiff. If defendants consider a security to be appropriate in this case, defendants shall file a motion and memorandum within twenty days from this date. Plaintiff shall then have fifteen days after service to respond. A reply memorandum may be filed by defendants within seven days after service.

3. VICARIOUS INFRINGEMENT

MICROSOFT CORP. v. GREY COMPUTER

United States District Court, D. Maryland, Southern Division, 1995.
910 F.Supp. 1077.

WILLIAMS, DISTRICT JUDGE.

Microsoft Corporation ("Microsoft") instituted this civil action against Grey Computer, Inc. ("Grey"), Integrated Computer Electronic, Inc. ("ICE"), Intelligent Data Systems ("IDS") and their respective principals. Microsoft claims that Defendants infringed upon their copyrights and trademarks by selling or distributing counterfeit copies of Microsoft's software products.

* * *

I.

Microsoft is the worldwide leader in computer software. It offers a wide range of products and services for businesses and personal use, each designed with the mission of making it easier and more enjoyable for people to take advantage of the full power of personal computing every day. Microsoft is the owner of valid and incontestible registered trademarks in and to "Microsoft" and "MS–DOS" for use in connection with computer software. It is the owner of registered copyrights in and to all MS–DOS 5.0, 6.0 and 6.2 software products, including User's Reference Manuals and User's Guides and Screen Displays ("Windows Software Products"). Microsoft has caused it trademarks to be registered in the United States Patent and Trademark Office on the Principal Register.

Direct Wholesale opened for business in February 1993. Mazoch and Williams are equal and sole shareholders. Ninety to ninety-five percent of Direct Wholesale's business was in distributing software products. While almost all of the software products Direct Wholesale distributed were Microsoft products, Microsoft has never licensed Direct Wholesale, Timothy Mazoch or Dewitt Williams to manufacture, replicate, distribute, market or advertise any MS–DOS or Windows Software Product, manuals, or packaging.

During it operations, Direct Wholesale received at least two news releases regarding Microsoft software. The releases provided:

Microsoft has alleged that Micro Innovation, Inc. of Houston, also known as MIC, was producing unlicensed MS–DOS 5 and Windows 3.1 under its own tradename, and distributing its product throughout the PC Innovations stores and other resellers nationally. Simultaneously seizures at seven Houston-area locations netted 35,000 units of MS–DOS and Windows, with a street value of approximately $2 million.

Microsoft legally licenses MS–DOS and Windows to computer manufacturers to include with their PCs for sale. However, Microsoft's license agreements prohibit the sale and/or distribution of Microsoft's products by themselves, without an accompanying PC.... Any consumers or resellers having questions about the legitimacy of Microsoft products should contact the Microsoft piracy hotline at (800) NO–COPYN.

Despite having received notice of Microsoft's prohibition of selling its software without an accompanying PC, Direct Wholesale continued to buy purported Microsoft software products from its California suppliers without accompanying PCs.

Direct Wholesale then sold the software to companies like ICE. From 23 July 1993 through 27 December 1993, ICE paid Direct Wholesale $195,773.63 for the purported Microsoft software to use in its PC sales. Direct Wholesale represented to ICE that it had good and merchantable title. Direct Wholesale also represented that it was an authorized distributor of Microsoft products.

On 31 January 1994, Microsoft commenced this action by filing its Complaint against Grey Computer, ICE and their respective principals, among others. In its original complaint Microsoft alleged copyright infringement, trademark infringement, false designation of origin and unfair competition arising out of the Defendants' purported sale of counterfeit copies of Microsoft's software products. * * *

* * *

III.

Microsoft urges that this is a clear cut case of copyright and trademark infringement. Microsoft alleges Defendants distributed counterfeit goods, bearing Microsoft's marks. Microsoft asserts that Defendants distributed poor quality copies of its copyrighted works and deceived consumers.

Defendants urge that they were innocent infringers. Williams and Mazoch posit that they conducted Direct Wholesale's business according to the practices and procedures they learned while working as salesmen/brokers in the computer software field.

* * *

F. Individual Liability

Microsoft asserts that Williams and Mazoch are contributorily and vicariously liable for Direct Wholesale's infringement of Microsoft's registered copyrights and trademarks. It claims that both Williams and Mazoch were each personally involved in acquiring and distributing the infringing software products. Microsoft urges that Williams and Mazoch not only had the right and ability to supervise the acquisition and distribution of counterfeit Microsoft software products, but they, themselves, conducted the infringing activities.

Defendants do not deny that they were not licensed to distribute Microsoft's products. They do not deny that they knew that the products were to be sold only with a new personal computer. Rather than providing the Court genuine issues of material fact, Williams and Mazoch simply argue theories and suppositions regarding Microsoft's claims. The Court, however, will not deny an otherwise valid motion for summary judgment because of Defendants' supposition and theory.

Williams and Mazoch knew about and participated in the infringing activities of Direct Wholesale because, for all intents and purposes, they were Direct Wholesale. A party who, with knowledge of the infringing activity, induces, causes, or materially contributes to the infringing conduct of another, will be held liable as a contributory infringer and is jointly and severally liable for the infringement. *See Polymer Technology Corp. v. Mimran*, 975 F.2d at 64. This general rule is applicable to trademark infringement and unfair trade practices cases. *See Polo Fashions, 816 F.2d at 149.* Even assuming, arguendo, Mazoch and Williams acted primarily for the benefit of Direct Wholesale, they may still be held personally liable. *See id.* ("A corporate official may be held personally liable for tortious conduct committed by him, though committed primarily for the benefit of the corporation.").

Moreover, a party will be held vicariously liable for another's infringement if that party had (1) the right and ability to supervise the activity and (2) an obvious and direct financial interest in the exploitation of the copyrighted materials. *Southern Bell Telephone & Telegraph Co. v. Associated Telephone Directory Publishers*, 756 F.2d 801, 811 (11th Cir.1985); *Major League Baseball Promotion Corp. v. Colour–Tex, Inc.*, 729 F.Supp. 1035, 1043 (D.N.J.1990); *Boz Scaggs Music v. KND Corp.*, 491 F.Supp. 908, 913–914 (D.C.Conn.1980). As Direct Wholesale's sole shareholders and directors, Williams and Mazoch had the ability to supervise the activity. They shared a financial interest so direct and obvious that they willfully turned a blind eye to their acquisition of counterfeit Microsoft software from suppliers.

Even assuming, *arguendo*, that they initially lacked experience for conducting Direct Wholesale's affairs, Williams and Mazoch learned shortly after initiating business with their California suppliers that something was awry. They knew about Microsoft's licensing requirements. They knew that the California suppliers and Williams and Mazoch personally violated those requirements because they were not authorized licensees and because they sold the purported Microsoft software without personal computers. Their actions amounted to infringement and ignorance of the law, if there was ignorance, is no excuse. *See Lambert v. California*, 355 U.S. 225, 228, 78 S.Ct. 240, 242, 2 L.Ed.2d 228 (1957). Thus, Williams and Mazoch are contributorily and vicariously liable. They are jointly, and, thus, jointly and severally liable. Since the Court concludes that Williams and Mazoch willfully participated in the infringement, they are also personally liable. *See Gershwin Publishing Corp. v. Columbia Artists Management, Inc.*, 443 F.2d 1159, 1162 (2d Cir.1971).

* * *

CONCLUSION

For the foregoing reasons, the Court will issue an order granting Microsoft's motion for summary judgment. The Court will award Microsoft all profits earned by Direct Wholesale from its sell of the counterfeit Microsoft software products from February 1993 through January 1994. Because this is an exceptional case of infringement, the Court will also treble damages consistent with the Lanham Act and award Microsoft reasonable attorneys' fees and costs. Moreover, because of the deliberateness of Defendants' infringing activities, the Court will enter a permanent injunction against Defendants. The Court will so order.

Note

If the defendants were selling outright counterfeit software, of course the court was right to be extremely harsh with them. But if the were selling software packages that Microsoft had provided to computer manufacturers who had promised not to resell them, the situation is much less clear. As will be discussed in other chapters, it is far from obvious that Microsoft, by calling a transaction with one party a "license" rather than a "sale" can avoid the provisions of the Copyright Act that provide that the buyer of a copy of a copyrighted work can transfer title to the copy to third parties. Even if the party to whom Microsoft originally provided the software was breaking a contract in selling it to the defendants in this case, these defendants might have obtained the right to resell the software without violating copyright, though they might be liable to Microsoft for inducing breach of contract.

G. PREEMPTION OF STATE LAW

Prior to the Copyright Act of 1976, all states provided common law or statutory copyright protection for unpublished works of authorship. Under the 1976 Act, all works, published and unpublished gained Federal protection. To avoid the existence of overlapping and possibly contradictory protection schemes, § 301 of the Copyright Act preempted state law copyright protection of unpublished works. However, § 301 was broadly worded, so that it did more than this. How much more continues to be a matter of debate.

17 U.S.C. § 301. Preemption with respect to other laws

(a) On and after January 1, 1978, all legal or equitable rights that are equivalent to any of the exclusive rights within the general scope of copyright as specified by section 106 in works of authorship that are fixed in a tangible medium of expression and come within the subject matter of copyright as specified by sections 102 and 103, whether created before or after that date and whether published or unpublished, are governed exclusively by this title. Thereafter, no person is entitled to any such right or equivalent right in any such work under the common law or statutes of any State.

(b) Nothing in this title annuls or limits any rights or remedies under the common law or statutes of any State with respect to—

(1) subject matter that does not come within the subject matter of copyright as specified by sections 102 and 103, including works of authorship not fixed in any tangible medium of expression; or

(2) any cause of action arising from undertakings commenced before January 1, 1978;

(3) activities violating legal or equitable rights that are not equivalent to any of the exclusive rights within the general scope of copyright as specified by section 106; or

(4) State and local landmarks, historic preservation, zoning, or building codes, relating to architectural works protected under section 102(a)(8).

(c) With respect to sound recordings fixed before February 15, 1972, any rights or remedies under the common law or statutes of any State shall not be annulled or limited by this title until February 15, 2067. The preemptive provisions of subsection (a) shall apply to any such rights and remedies pertaining to any cause of action arising from undertakings commenced on and after February 15, 2067. Notwithstanding the provisions of section 303, no sound recording fixed before February 15, 1972, shall be subject to copyright under this title before, on, or after February 15, 2067.

(d) Nothing in this title annuls or limits any rights or remedies under any other Federal statute.

(e) The scope of Federal preemption under this section is not affected by the adherence of the United States to the Berne Convention or the satisfaction of obligations of the United States thereunder.

(f)(1) On or after the effective date set forth in section 610(a) of the Visual Artists Rights Act of 1990, all legal or equitable rights that are equivalent to any of the rights conferred by section 106A with respect to works of visual art to which the rights conferred by section 106A apply are governed exclusively by section 106A and section 113(d) and the provisions of this title relating to such sections. Thereafter, no person is entitled to any such right or equivalent right in any work of visual art under the common law or statutes of any State.

(2) Nothing in paragraph (1) annuls or limits any rights or remedies under the common law or statutes of any State with respect to—

(A) any cause of action from undertakings commenced before the effective date set forth in section 610(a) of the Visual Artists Rights Act of 1990;

(B) activities violating legal or equitable rights that are not equivalent to any of the rights conferred by section 106A with respect to works of visual art; or

(C) activities violating legal or equitable rights which extend beyond the life of the author.

OHIO v. PERRY

Supreme Court of Ohio, 1998.
83 Ohio St.3d 41, 697 N.E.2d 624.

MOYER, CHIEF JUSTICE.

We hold that prosecution of state charges of unauthorized use that are based solely upon the unauthorized uploading, downloading, and posting of computer software on a computer bulletin board is preempted by the federal copyright laws.

I

The federal copyright laws expressly preempt any state law actions which govern "legal or equitable rights that are equivalent to any of the exclusive rights within the general scope of copyright as specified by section 106 in works of authorship that are fixed in a tangible medium of expression and come within the subject matter of copyright as specified by sections 102 and 103 * * *." Section 301(a), Title 17, U.S.Code. The statute thus creates a two-part inquiry: (1) whether a work fixed in a tangible medium of expression is within the subject matter of copyright and (2) whether the rights addressed are equivalent to the exclusive copyright rights set out in Section 106, Title 17, U.S.Code.

Section 106 of the copyright statute gives owners of a copyrighted work exclusive rights to reproduce, prepare derivatives, perform, distribute, and display their work. Thus, "a right is equivalent to one of the rights comprised by a copyright if it 'is infringed by the mere act of reproduction, performance, distribution or display.'" *Baltimore Orioles, Inc. v. Major League Baseball Players Assn.* (C.A.7, 1986), 805 F.2d 663, 677 (quoting Nimmer, Nimmer on Copyright [1985], Section 1.01[B][I]).

The preemption provisions of Section 301 of the Copyright Act are broad and absolute and are "stated in the most unequivocal language possible, so as to foreclose any conceivable misinterpretation of its unqualified intention that Congress shall act preemptively, and to avoid the development of any vague borderline areas between State and Federal protection." Notes of the Committee on the Judiciary, H.R.Rep. No. 94–1476, U.S.Code Cong. & Adm. News (1976) 5659, 5746. Federal courts have repeatedly recognized that allowing state claims where the core of the complaint centers on wrongful copying would render the preemption provisions of the Copyright Act useless .. The same effect would arise where issues of wrongful distribution or display are the core of the state law claim, as these rights are also exclusively governed by federal copyright laws and are expressly preempted under Section 301 of the Copyright Act.

In order to survive a preemption challenge based on equivalency of protected rights, the state law claim must contain an extra element. *Del Madera Properties v. Rhodes & Gardner, Inc.* (C.A.9, 1987), 820 F.2d 973, 977. The extra element must not only distinguish the claim from a claim in copyright but also must change the state law so that it is "*qualitatively* different from a copyright infringement claim." (Emphasis in the original.) *Berge* at 1463 (citing *Rosciszewski v. Arete Assocs., Inc.* [C.A. 4, 1993], 1 F.3d 225, 229–230).

II

* * *

The indictment alleged that on or about June 16, 1995, Perry knowingly used or operated computer software belonging to Microsoft Corporation and knowingly used or operated computer software belonging to Clark Development Corporation, without the consent of the owner or person authorized to give consent. The state's explanation added the following relevant facts to those alleged in the indictment:

In reference to count two of the indictment, alleging unauthorized use of Microsoft software, the state explained that Perry had been running a bulletin board for people to share computer software. The prosecutor informed the court that Perry was "exchanging and moving" computer software, including the Microsoft software referred to in the indictment.

In reference to count four, alleging unauthorized use of Clark Development Corp. software, the state said, "The software or the fourth count of the indictment was the software that actually let his [Perry's] bulletin board work, so he was not only *distributing* that, but he was also using it to facilitate the distribution of other items * * *." (Emphasis added.)

None of the uses or attendant circumstances argued by the state is sufficient to satisfy the "extra element" requirement that would except the charge of unauthorized use in this case from the express preemption clause in the copyright statute. Section 301, Title 17, U.S.Code. The facts established in the record simply do not support a finding that Perry engaged in any unauthorized use other than that which is preempted by federal copyright laws.

The state has struggled to pinpoint which of Perry's activities are not preempted by federal copyright laws and has cited very little from the record to support its contentions. The state admits that charges based on unauthorized copying and unauthorized distribution are preempted by federal copyright laws and then argues without explanation that "copying" is something entirely different from "use."

Significantly, the state even concedes at the end of its brief that the record in this case does not reveal whether the nature of Perry's use of the software was that of copying or of some other use. Though conceding that it failed to establish any non-copying use on the record at the time the no contest plea was accepted, the state, on appeal to this court, now contends "that the offense consisted of use beyond the scope of [a license agreement that also was not established on the record], not the act of copying." Based on the current case law and the explicit language of the copyright preemption clause, we cannot agree that the activities proved by the state constitute uses that are qualitatively different from the exclusive copyright rights.

* * * [U]nauthorized uploading and unauthorized downloading are unauthorized uses governed by the copyright laws and prosecution of state charges of unauthorized use for uploading and downloading is preempted.

Posting software on a bulletin board where others can access and download it is distribution. See, *e.g., Playboy.* Unauthorized distribution is a use which is governed by the copyright laws. See, *e.g., Dowling* at 217, 105 S.Ct. at 3133, 87 L.Ed.2d at 160. Unauthorized posting may also be viewed as facilitating unauthorized downloading or copying by a third party and as such is also a violation of the exclusive right of reproduction under the copyright laws. See, *e.g., Sega*; *Playboy*; *Central Point Software, Inc. v. Nugent* (E.D.Tex.1995), 903 F.Supp. 1057. Posting also implicates the display rights of copyright owners. *Playboy* at 1556. It follows that unauthorized posting is an unauthorized use governed by the copyright laws and prosecution of state charges of unauthorized use for posting is preempted.

As these are the only uses addressed by the state on appeal and because these are uses regulated exclusively by the copyright laws, we hold that Perry cannot be prosecuted for unauthorized use under the state statute.

III

In an attempt to circumvent preemption, the state argues that the violation of a licensing agreement is an "extra element" rendering the charge of unauthorized use in this case qualitatively different from a charge of infringement under federal copyright laws. However, we find no reference to any license or licensing agreement in the record. As indicated above, neither the indictment nor the prosecutor's explanation establishes the existence of any license or licensing agreement, let alone any agreement to which Perry was a party. An unauthorized use charge obviously cannot be based on the terms of a licensing agreement that, so far as the record reveals, does not exist.

* * *

Further, a consumer software licensing agreement is generally treated as a contract between the copyright owner or "seller" of the software and the licensee or "buyer" and is therefore governed by general contract law and the U.C.C. There can be legal differences between licenses and sales contracts that affect the parties' rights under the copyright doctrine of first sale, but these differences are not implicated in this case. Accordingly, in the context of this case, licenses are treated as general contracts. What is important to this discussion is the fact that third-party users, whether authorized or unauthorized, are not parties to the licensing agreement and generally cannot be bound by its terms. Copyrights are rights "against the world," but a licensing agreement affects only its parties and, as such, any licensing agreement involving the software would be between the copyright owner and the purchaser. Therefore, any licensing terms that did exist would not apply to Perry.

* * *

V

We do not find the state's arguments on appeal to be persuasive. Neither do we find any indication in the hearing transcripts that an unauthorized use, other than copyright infringement, has been alleged. The hearing transcripts indicate, in reference to Perry's use of Microsoft software in count two, that the state did not allege an unauthorized use other than one that is equivalent to the exclusive usage rights governed in the copyright statute. Its only allegation was that Perry was "exchanging and moving" the software through the running of a bulletin board. This amounts to no more than reproduction and distribution by means of uploading and posting. Thus, we hold that Perry's prosecution on count two is clearly preempted.

* * *

VI

We acknowledge that there are factual situations where prosecution of "unauthorized use" under the state statute would not be preempted, but this case does not present those facts. It is also important to recognize that preemption of Perry's criminal prosecution under the state statute does not leave Microsoft or Clark without a remedy. They may pursue their rights under civil copyright law. Nor does preemption necessarily relieve Perry of criminal culpability. The federal copyright law includes a criminal cause of action, and charges could have been brought under that federal law. Section 506, Title 17, U.S.Code; Section 2319, Title 18, U.S.Code; No Electronic Theft (NET) Act, Section 2311 note, Title 18, U.S.Code, as amended by P.L. 105–147 (H.R. 2265) (Dec. 16, 1997), 111 Stat. 2678.

For the foregoing reasons, we hold that prosecution of the state charge of "unauthorized use" in this case is preempted by federal copyright laws. The judgment of the court of appeals is affirmed.

Judgment affirmed.

VAULT CORP. v. QUAID SOFTWARE LTD.

United States Court of Appeals, Fifth Circuit, 1988.
847 F.2d 255.

REAVLEY, CIRCUIT JUDGE,

[The factual background of this case appears on p. 182.]

* * *

IV. VAULT'S LOUISIANA CLAIMS

Seeking preliminary and permanent injunctions and damages, Vault's original complaint alleged that Quaid breached its license agreement by decompiling or disassembling Vault's program in violation of the Louisiana Software License Enforcement Act (the "License Act"), La.Rev.Stat.Ann. § 51:1961 *et seq.* (West 1987) * * * and, with respect to its breach of license claim, Vault only seeks an injunction to prevent Quaid from decompiling or disassembling PROLOK version 2.0.[27]

Louisiana's License Act permits a software producer to impose a number of contractual terms upon software purchasers provided that the terms are set forth in a license agreement which comports with La.Rev. Stat.Ann. "51:1963 & 1965, and that this license agreement accompanies the producer's software." Enforceable terms include the prohibition of: (1) any copying of the program for any purpose; and (2) modifying and/or adapting the program in any way, including adaptation by reverse engineering, decompilation or disassembly. La.Rev.Stat.Ann. § 51:1964. The terms "reverse engineering, decompiling or disassembling" are defined as "any process by which computer software is converted from one form to another form which is more readily understandable to human beings, including without limitation any decoding or decrypting of any computer program which has been encoded or encrypted in any manner." La.Rev.Stat.Ann. § 51:1962(3).

Vault's license agreement, which accompanies PROLOK version 2.0 and comports with the requirements of La.Rev.Stat.Ann. '51:1963 & 1965, provides that "[y]ou may not ... copy, modify, translate, convert to another programming language, decompile or disassemble" Vault's program. Vault asserts that these prohibitions are enforceable under Louisiana's License Act, and specifically seeks an injunction to prevent Quaid from decompiling or disassembling Vault's program.

The district court held that Vault's license agreement was "a contract of adhesion which could only be enforceable if the [Louisiana License Act] is a valid and enforceable statute." *Vault*, 655 F.Supp. at 761. The court noted numerous conflicts between Louisiana's License Act and the Copyright Act, including: (1) while the License Act authorizes a total prohibition on copying, the Copyright Act allows archival copies and copies made as an essential step in the utilization of a

---

27. Beginning with PROLOK version 2.0, Vault's license agreement contained a   choice of law clause adopting Louisiana law. *See supra* note 3.

computer program, 17 U.S.C. § 117; (2) while the License Act authorizes a perpetual bar against copying, the Copyright Act grants protection against unauthorized copying only for the life of the author plus fifty years, 17 U.S.C. § 302(a); and (3) while the License Act places no restrictions on programs which may be protected, under the Copyright Act, only "original works of authorship" can be protected, 17 U.S.C. § 102. *Vault*, 655 F.Supp. at 762–63. The court concluded that, because Louisiana's License Act "touched upon the area" of federal copyright law, its provisions were preempted and Vault's license agreement was unenforceable. *Id.* at 763.

In *Sears, Roebuck & Co. v. Stiffel Co.*, 376 U.S. 225, 84 S.Ct. 784, 11 L.Ed.2d 661 (1964), the Supreme Court held that "[w]hen state law touches upon the area of [patent or copyright statutes], it is 'familiar doctrine' that the federal policy 'may not be set at naught, or its benefits denied' by the state law." *Id.* at 229, 84 S.Ct. at 787 (quoting *Sola Elec. Co. v. Jefferson Elec. Co.*, 317 U.S. 173, 176, 63 S.Ct. 172, 173, 87 L.Ed. 165 (1942)). Section 117 of the Copyright Act permits an owner of a computer program to make an adaptation of that program provided that the adaptation is either "created as an essential step in the utilization of the computer program in conjunction with a machine," § 117(1), or "is for archival purpose only," § 117(2). The provision in Louisiana's License Act, which permits a software producer to prohibit the adaptation of its licensed computer program by decompilation or disassembly, conflicts with the rights of computer program owners under § 117 and clearly "touches upon an area" of federal copyright law. For this reason, and the reasons set forth by the district court, we hold that at least this provision of Louisiana's License Act is preempted by federal law, and thus that the restriction in Vault's license agreement against decompilation or disassembly is unenforceable.

* * *

The judgment of the district court is AFFIRMED

Question

If a state law has additional elements beyond Federal copyright law, then the state law will generally be upheld. In *Pro-CD,* a "shrinkwrap" license was upheld by the Seventh Circuit. As previously discussed, UCITA purports to validate "shrinkwrap" licenses not only against the parties thereto but also against third parties. As states adopt UCITA and some form of the "shrinkwrap" provision, will these provisions be preempted?

H.   COPYRIGHT–LIKE PROTECTION

BROOKTREE CORP. v. ADVANCED MICRO DEVICES, INC.

United States Court of Appeals, Federal Circuit, 1992.
977 F.2d 1555.

PAULINE NEWMAN, CIRCUIT JUDGE.

Brooktree Corporation brought suit against Advanced Micro Devices, Inc. (herein AMD) for patent infringement, 35 U.S.C. § 271, and infringement of mask work registrations, 17 U.S.C. § 910, in connection with certain semiconductor chips used in color video displays. The United States District Court for the Southern District of California entered judgment that the patents were valid and infringed and that the registered mask works were infringed, assessing damages.

The principal issues on appeal arise under the Patent Act, of which the Federal Circuit has exclusive appellate jurisdiction, 28 U.S.C. § 1295(a)(1), and the Semiconductor Chip Protection Act, of which this court's appellate jurisdiction is pendent. Thus for issues of fact and law under the Semiconductor Chip Protection Act we apply the discernable law of the Ninth Circuit, in accordance with the principles set forth in *Atari, Inc. v. JS & A Group, Inc.*, 747 F.2d 1422, 1438–40, 223 USPQ 1074, 1086–87 (Fed.Cir.1984) (en banc) (applying copyright law of the circuit in which the case was tried, thus avoiding creating new opportunities for forum shopping). Judicial consideration of the Semiconductor Chip Protection Act has thus far been sparse, and we have given particular attention to the statute and its history, for the parties dispute significant aspects of statutory interpretation.

This case occasioned a lengthy trial over the course of seven weeks before the jury, in consecutive determinations of liability and damages. The jury verdicts were the subject of duly filed motions for judgment notwithstanding the verdict and for a new trial, which motions were denied by the district court. AMD charges error on issues of mask work infringement and damages, and also on issues of patent validity, infringement, and willfulness. Brooktree cross-appeals certain damages rulings, and the denial of attorney fees under both the Patent Act and the Semiconductor Chip Protection Act.

I

MASK WORKS

The Semiconductor Chip Protection Act

The Semiconductor Chip Protection Act of 1984, Pub.L. 98–620, Title III, 98 Stat. 3347, codified at 17 U.S.C. §§ 901–914, arose from concerns that existing intellectual property laws did not provide adequate protection of proprietary rights in semiconductor chips that had been designed to perform a particular function. The Act, enacted after extensive congressional consideration and hearings over several years, adopted relevant aspects of existing intellectual property law, but for the most part created a new law, specifically adapted to the protection of design layouts of semiconductor chips.

Chip design layouts embody the selection and configuration of electrical components and connections in order to achieve the desired electronic functions. The electrical elements are configured in three dimensions, and are built up in layers by means of a series of "masks" whereby, using photographic depositing and etching techniques, layers of metallic, insulating, and semiconductor material are deposited in the desired pattern on a wafer of silicon. This set of masks is called a "mask work", and is part of the semiconductor chip product. The statute defines a mask work as:

a series of related images, however fixed or encoded

(A) having or representing the predetermined, three dimensional pattern of metallic, insulating, or semiconductor material present or removed from the layers of a semiconductor chip product; and

(B) in which series the relation of the images to one another is that each image has the pattern of the surface of one form of a semiconductor chip product.

17 U.S.C. § 901(a)(2). The semiconductor chip product in turn is defined as:

the final or intermediate form of any product—

(A) having two or more layers of metallic, insulating, or semiconductor material, deposited or otherwise placed on, or etched away or otherwise removed from, a piece of semiconductor material in accordance with a predetermined pattern; and

(B) intended to perform electronic circuitry functions.

17 U.S.C. § 901(a)(1).

The design of a satisfactory chip layout may require extensive effort and be extremely time consuming, particularly as new and improved electronic capabilities are sought to be created. A new semiconductor chip may incur large research and development costs, yet after the layout is imprinted in the mask work and the chip is available in commerce, it can be copied at a fraction of the cost to the originator. Thus there was concern that widespread copying of new chip layouts would have adverse effects on innovative advances in semiconductor technology, as stated in the Senate Report:

In the semiconductor industry, innovation is indispensable; research breakthroughs are essential to the life and health of the industry. But research and innovation in the design of semiconductor chips are threatened by the inadequacies of existing legal protection against piracy and unauthorized copying. This problem, which is so critical to this essential sector of the American economy, is addressed by the Semiconductor Chip Protection Act of 1984.

* * *

The Semiconductor Chip Protection Act of 1984, ... would prohibit "chip piracy"—the unauthorized copying and distribution of semiconductor chip products copied from the original creators of such works.

S.Rep. No. 425, 98th Cong., 2d Sess., 1 (1984) (hereinafter *Senate Report*).

* * *

The Semiconductor Chip Protection Act provides for the grant of certain exclusive rights to owners of registered mask works, including the exclusive right "to reproduce the mask work by optical, electronic, or any other means", and the exclusive right "to import or distribute a semiconductor chip product in which the mask work is embodied". 17 U.S.C. § 905. Mask works that are not "original", or that consist of "designs that are staple, commonplace, or familiar in the semiconductor industry, or variations of such designs, combined in a way that, considered as a whole, is not original", are excluded from protection. 17 U.S.C. § 902(b). Protection is also not extended to any "idea, procedure, process, system, method of operation, concept, principle, or discovery, regardless of the form in which it is described, explained, illustrated or embodied" in the mask work. 17 U.S.C. § 902(c).

Brooktree's Mask Work Registrations

Brooktree was granted mask work registration MW 2873 on August 6, 1987, and registration MW 3838 on July 6, 1988, for its chips identified as Bt451 and Bt458. These Brooktree chips embody a circuit design that combines the functions of a static random access memory (SRAM) and a digital to analog converter (DAC). This circuitry, sometimes referred to as RAMDAC, acts as a "color palette", producing the colors in color video displays having high speed and enhanced picture resolution. A Brooktree witness described these chips as a technological breakthrough, exceeding limits in speed and performance that had been believed impossible to exceed. Brooktree stated that a single Bt458 chip replaced a previously used set of 36 chips (an AMD product) and offered many advantages. A Brooktree witness testified that these chips were extremely successful commercially, and were soon incorporated into new designs for video display systems made by several large manufacturers.

A critical component of the Brooktree chips is the core cell, a ten-transistor SRAM cell which is repeated over six thousand times in an array covering about eighty percent of the chip area. Each core cell consists of ten transistors and metal conductors electrically connecting the transistors throughout the three dimensions of the multilayered cell. Brooktree charged that this core cell was copied by AMD, thus infringing Brooktree's mask work registrations.

AMD does not challenge the validity of these mask work registrations, or dispute Brooktree's position that its chips are protected under the Semiconductor Chip Protection Act. AMD does, however, assert that its accused chips are not infringements, for reasons we shall discuss.

Infringement

The Semiconductor Chip Protection Act defines an "infringing semiconductor chip product" as one which is "made, imported, or distributed in violation of the exclusive rights" of the mask work owner. 17 U.S.C. § 901(a)(9). The text of the Semiconductor Chip Protection Act sets forth the subject matter of protection in terms of certain exclusive rights, including, *inter alia*, the exclusive right to "reproduce the mask work", 17 U.S.C. § 905. This usage mirrors the words of the Copyright Act, which states the exclusive rights of copyright owners "to reproduce the copyrighted work". 17 U.S.C. § 106. Although the Semiconductor Chip Protection Act does not use the word "copy" to describe infringement, the parallel language reflects the incorporation of the well-explicated copyright principle of substantial similarity into the Semiconductor Chip Protection Act, as discussed *infra*.

The jury instruction on the criteria for establishing infringement included the instruction that infringement requires substantial similarity to a material portion of the registered mask work:

> To establish infringement, Brooktree must show that A.M.D.'s mask works are substantially similar to a material portion of the mask works in Brooktree's chips covered by Brooktree's mask work registration. No hard and fast rule or percentage governs what constitutes a, quote, "substantial similarity." Substantial similarity may exist where an important part of the mask work is copied, even though the percentage of the entire chip which is copied may be relatively small. It is not required that A.M.D. make a copy of the entire mask work embodied in the Brooktree chip.

AMD states that it does not on appeal challenge this jury instruction. Instead, AMD argues that because the non-SRAM portion of its accused chip was not copied, the chips are not "substantially similar", whatever the materiality of the SRAM cell to the total mask work. It was undisputed that there was not duplication of the entire chip. AMD states that the Semiconductor Chip Protection Act requires copying of the entire chip, and therefore that it was entitled to judgment in its favor as a matter of law, or at least to a new trial on the issue.

The principle of substantial similarity recognizes that the existence of differences between an accused and copyrighted work may not negate infringement if a material portion of the copyrighted work is appropriated. If the copied portion is qualitatively important, the finder of fact may properly find substantial similarity under copyright law, and under the Semiconductor Chip Protection Act.

Brooktree agrees that the SRAM portion of the accused chips covers only eighty percent of the chip area, and that the remaining circuitry was not copied by AMD. Infringement under the statute does not require that all parts of the accused chip be copied. The district court's explanation to the jury was in full accord with the statutory grant of exclusive rights to reproduce the mask work. The statutory interpretation now pressed by AMD, *viz.*, that the entire chip must have been copied, is unsupported. Indeed, the House Report states that it was contemplated that the cell layout alone could be misappropriated:

> Mask works sometimes contain substantial areas of (so-called "cells") whose layouts involve creativity and are commercially valuable. In appropriate fact settings, the misappropriation of such a cell—assuming it meets the original standards of this chapter—could be the basis for an infringement action under this chapter.

* * *

Whether an appropriation of a cell layout constitutes infringement in a particular case is for the trier of fact, and can not be decided as a matter of law.

The Reverse Engineering Defense

AMD's position at trial, and on appeal, was that its core cell was the product of reverse engineering of the Brooktree chip, and therefore does not constitute infringement under the Semiconductor Chip Protection Act. Reverse engineering is a statutory defense, included in the Act upon extensive congressional attention to the workings of the semiconductor chip industry.

The statute provides that it is not an infringement of a registered mask work for

> (1) a person to reproduce the mask work solely for the purpose of teaching, analyzing, or evaluating the concepts or techniques embodied in the mask work or the circuitry, logic flow, or organization of components used in the mask work; or

> (2) a person who performs the analysis or evaluation described in paragraph (1) to incorporate the results of such conduct in an original mask work which is made to be distributed.

17 U.S.C. § 906(a). The statute thus provides that one engaged in reverse engineering shall not be liable for infringement when the end product is itself original. In performing reverse engineering a person may disassemble, study, and analyze an existing chip in order to understand it. This knowledge may be used to create an original chip having a different design layout, but which performs the same or equivalent function as the existing chip, without penalty or prohibition. Congress was told by industry representatives that reverse engineering was an accepted and fair practice, and leads to improved chips having "form, fit, and function" compatibility with the existing chip, thereby serving competition while advancing the state of technology.

Much attention was given by Congress and by witnesses to the question of how to determine whether a chip layout was born of legitimate reverse engineering or of copying. It was foreseen that there would be a "gray area" wherein the rights of the parties, on the facts of a particular chip design, would require resolution on a fact-dependent, case-by-case basis. The following colloquy illustrates concerns raised at the hearings:

> Rep. EDWARDS: ... Is the chief reservation here the idea that reverse engineering, which all the witnesses agree is appropriate, might be confused with pirating and that any kind of reverse engineering might be interpreted under this law as pirating?

> Mr. MacPHERSON (of Fairchild Camera & Instrument Corp.): I think that's one of the very strong concerns that we have, yes. There is a very gray area here in the very nature of reverse engineering, which would leave an individual engaged in that practice uncertain what his ultimate rights would be should he use that particular result in another product.

Copyright Protection for Imprinted Design Patterns on Semiconductor Chips: Hearings Before the Subcomm. on Courts, Civil Liberties, and the Administration of Justice of the House Comm. on the Judiciary, 96th Cong., 1st Sess., 66 (1979).

This aspect was explored over the several years of legislative gestation. The reverse engineering procedure was described by witnesses, and distinguished in purpose and mechanism from the copying against which the Semiconductor Chip Protection Act was intended to guard. It was explained that a person engaged in reverse engineering seeks to understand the design of the original chip with the object of improving the circuitry, the chip layout, or both. The presence of innovation and improvement was stressed as the hallmark of an original layout. A witness explained the difference as determining "was anything innovative done in the process or was it simply a reproduction of what was already there?" Another witness explained that reverse engineering generally produces a "paper trail" recording the engineer's efforts to understand the original chip and to design a different version after reverse engineering:

> "Whenever there is a true case of reverse engineering, the second firm will have prepared a great deal of paper—logic and circuit diagrams, trial layouts, computer simulations of the chip, and the like; it will also have invested thousands of hours of work. All of these can be documented by reference to the firm's ordinary business records. A pirate has no such papers, for the pirate does none of this work. Therefore, whether there has been a true reverse engineering job or just a job of copying can be shown by looking at the defendant's records. The paper trail of a chip tells a discerning observer whether the chip is a copy or embodies the effort of reverse engineering."

The Committee reports and the statements of the Semiconductor Chip Protection Act's supporters show the belief that evidence of the presence or absence of such a paper trail would significantly reduce the gray area between legitimate and illegitimate behavior. *See Mathias–Leahy Memorandum* at S12,917; *House Report* at 21.

Senators Mathias and Leahy explained that § 906(a) includes a provision

> to clarify the intent of both chambers that competitors are permitted not only to study the protected mask works, but also to use the results of that study to design, distribute and import semiconductor chip products embodying their own original mask works.

*   *   *

> The end product of the reverse engineering process is not an infringement, and itself qualifies for protection under the Act, if it is an original mask work as contrasted with a substantial copy. If the resulting semiconductor chip product is not substantially identical to the original, and its design involved significant toil and investment, so that it is not mere plagiarism, it does not infringe the original chip, even if the layout of the two chips is, in substantial part, similar.

Mathias-Leahy Memorandum at S12,917.

In illuminating the meaning of "original" in the context of reverse engineering, Senators Mathias and Leahy distinguished between a substantial copy, on one hand, and the product of reverse engineering which might be similar to the original, but if not a substantial copy would not be an infringement. For the latter, the "paper trail" was expected to document efforts in "analyzing, or evaluating the concepts or techniques embodied in the mask work or the circuitry, logic flow, or organization of components used in the mask work", as the effort required would be reflected in the documents. *Id.*

AMD's defense was that its chips were independently designed after the Brooktree chips were subjected to reverse engineering to learn the Brooktree design. The question of whether AMD's activities were acceptable reverse engineering, or unacceptable copying, was explained to the jury as follows:

> Reverse engineering is permitted and is authorized by the Chip Protection Act. It is not infringement of an owner's exclusive right and protected mask work for another person, through reverse-engineering, to photograph and to study the mask work for the purpose of analyzing its circuitry—correction—the circuitry, logic flow and organization of the components used in the mask work and to incorporate such analysis into an original mask work.

> The end product of the reverse-engineering process may be an original mask work, and therefore not an infringing mask work, if the resulting semiconductor chip product is not substantially identical to the protected mask work and its design involved significant toil and investment so that it is not mere plagiarism.

You should place great weight on the existence of reverse paperwork trail in determining whether the defendant's mask work is an original mask work from reverse-engineering.

A.M.D. mask work constitutes an original mask work if A.M.D.'s mask work incorporates its own new design elements which offered improvements over or an alternative to Brooktree's mask work.

These instructions focus the jury on whether AMD produced an original mask work, as the statute requires. The instructions were not challenged by AMD on its motion for new trial or on appeal, and were adapted from AMD's proposed instructions. Brooktree calls the instructions "too lenient". Whether or not too lenient, they were not objected to by AMD at trial, and are not now criticized by AMD as incorrect. They are the law applied in this case. *See* Fed.R.Civ.P. 51; *Herrington v. County of Sonoma*, 834 F.2d 1488, 1500 n. 12 (9th Cir.1987), *cert. denied*, 489 U.S. 1090, 109 S.Ct. 1557, 103 L.Ed.2d 860 (1989) (failure to object to a jury instruction precludes appellate review).

* * *

These fact-dependent areas were thoroughly aired at trial. The grant of judgment as a matter of law, by the trial judge or by the appellate court, is appropriate only when the evidence, with inferences drawn favorably to the party with the verdict, could not reasonably support the verdict.

We conclude that there was a legally sufficient evidentiary basis whereby a reasonable jury could have found infringement of the mask work registrations. The judgment is affirmed.

III

Damages and Attorney Fees

* * *

Costs and Attorney Fees Under the Semiconductor Chip Protection Act

The Semiconductor Chip Protection Act provides that in

> any civil action arising under this chapter, the court in its discretion may allow the recovery of full costs, including reasonable attorneys' fees, to the prevailing party.

17 U.S.C. § 911(f). This provision is commensurate with 17 U.S.C. § 505 of the copyright statute. Both parties argued to the district court that copyright precedent applies to § 911(f), and the district court relied on Ninth Circuit copyright precedent in its decision. On this appeal both sides rely on Federal Circuit precedent in patent cases.

Many aspects of the Semiconductor Chip Protection Act are based on copyright concepts. The House Report states that this section "provides for counsel fees, similar to 17 U.S.C. § 505." In contrast with the attorney fee provision of the patent law, 35 U.S.C. § 285, there is no requirement for a threshold finding of "exceptional case". However, the award under the Semiconductor Chip Protection Act continues to be consigned to the court's discretion. We conclude that copyright law principles are more aptly applied to the application of 17 U.S.C. § 911(f).

The Ninth Circuit has held that attorney fees are generally awarded to a prevailing plaintiff under § 505 of the Copyright Act, explaining that the fee-shifting provision is intended to encourage assertion of "colorable" copyright claims, to deter infringement, and to make the plaintiff whole. *McCulloch v. Albert E. Price, Inc.*, 823 F.2d 316, 323 (9th Cir.1987). However, attorney fees are not awarded in every case, *id.*, and fees may be denied in various situations, including:

> (1) the presence of a complex or novel issue of law that the defendant litigates vigorously and in good faith, (2) the defendant's status as innocent, rather than willful or knowing, infringer, (3) the plaintiff's prosecution of the case in bad faith, and (4) the defendant's good faith attempt to avoid infringement.

Id. (citations omitted). The district court relied on *McCulloch*, and in particular the first factor, remarking that this was a case of first impression under the Semiconductor Chip Protection Act, and that it involved complex technology as well as novel issues of law.

Attorney fee decisions under the Copyright Act are reviewed under the abuse of discretion standard. The denial of attorney fees under 17 U.S.C. § 911(f) was not, in these circumstances, an abuse of the court's discretionary authority, and is sustained.

Conclusion

The judgment entered on the jury verdicts, and the district court's rulings, are

AFFIRMED.

Note

The Semiconductor Chip Protection Act has led to remarkably little litigation. The above case is the only case listed in West Group's United States Code Annotated as having applied the Act.

Chapter II

PATENTABILITY OF COMPUTER SOFTWARE, PROGRAMMED COMPUTERS, AND INTERNET BUSINESS SYSTEMS

A. INTRODUCTION

In the nineteenth century, computers did not exist. Mathematical calculations and business systems were implemented by humans, not machines. The U.S. Patent and Trademark Office ("PTO") and the courts denied patent protection for such human activity. Gradually, during the last decades of the twentieth century, first mathematical calculations and later business systems came to be implemented by programmed computers. In the early days of computers, the programs did little more than solve mathematical equations. Since mathematical equations were traditionally not patentable, initially the PTO and the courts refused to grant patents on computer programs or on programmed computers. Starting in 1969, the Court of Customs and Patent Appeals [C.C.P.A.], a Federal appellate tribunal which had supervisory jurisdiction over the PTO, began to reverse the patent examiners and the PTO's Board of Patent Appeals and to compel the issuance of software patents. Accordingly, the PTO was forced to issue computer program patents from 1969 until 1972. In 1972, the United States Supreme Court, at the request of the PTO, reversed the C.C.P.A. and blocked the issuance of a patent directed to a method of converting one form of number into another. *Gottschalk v. Benson,* 409 U.S. 63 (1972).

The C.C.P.A. reacted to this Supreme Court decision with hostility, construing *Benson* as narrowly as possible. But even so, the PTO issued very few computer program or programmed computer patents between 1972 and 1981 (when the Supreme Court again ruled on programmed computer patents). Between 1972 and 1981 most attorneys advised their clients not to file patents directed to software. Many fundamental software inventions (for example, the spreadsheet program) were not patented. Attorneys advised their clients to utilize copyright and trade secret protection as substitutes for software patent protection. The World Intellectual Property Organization (WIPO) even proposed a new form of intellectual property protection designed especially for computer

217

programs. Europe, taking its lead from the United States Supreme Court, enacted statutes prohibiting the patenting of computer programs. The United Kingdom Patents Act of 1977, for example, contains the following language "(2) It is hereby declared that the following (among other things) are not inventions for the purposes of this Act, that is to say, anything which consists of—* * * a program for a computer * * *." In both Europe and the United States, however, attorneys for proprietors of software inventions tried to circumvent the restrictions on patenting programs by seeking patents for programmed computers.

In *Diamond v. Diehr, 450 U.S.* 175 (1981), the Supreme Court authorized the grant of a software-hardware patent. This decision opened the door to the patentability of programmed computers but did not overrule the earlier Supreme Court precedents holding some computer programs unpatentable. Most programmed computer inventions are now patentable. However, a "black hole" of unpatentability, centered about *Benson,* remains.

The C.C.P.A.'s appellate jurisdiction was limited to appeals from the PTO and several other federal agencies, so it could not establish uniform nationwide patent precedents. Patent holders had to file patent infringement suits in the Federal district courts. Prior to 1980, appeals from the district courts went to the respective circuit courts of appeals. Perceived nonuniformity in the appellate decisions in patent cases produced considerable "forum shopping," since some circuits were considered more "pro-patent" than others. The 8th Circuit, for example, was reputed to be extremely "anti-patent." Conflicting circuit court decisions created considerable uncertainty. In 1980 the C.C.P.A. was expanded, renamed the "United States Court of Appeals For The Federal Circuit" (commonly called the "Federal Circuit") and given exclusive appellate jurisdiction over all patent-related appeals, even in cases where there are other non-patent issues.

The creation of this new appellate court eliminated conflicts between Circuits in patent law and has thereby reduced the need for Supreme Court certiorari supervision. Because lawyers perceive the Federal Circuit as "pro-patent," they now more readily advise clients to obtain patents and sue infringers. This court has also increased the importance of prior C.C.P.A. decisions, particularly since several of the former C.C.P.A. judges were appointed to this new court and wrote many of its patent decisions. Judge Rich, in particular, came to be regarded as highly by many patent attorneys as the late Judge Learned Hand is by copyright attorneys.

In re Alappat, 33 F.3d 1526 (Fed.Cir.1994), was a key decision. The Federal Circuit, sitting en banc, characterized the Supreme Court decisions on software patents very narrowly, interpreting them as holding only "that certain types of mathematical subject matter, standing alone, represent nothing more than abstract ideas until reduced to some type of practical application, and thus that subject matter is not, in and of itself, entitled to patent protection." The Federal Circuit went on to hold that a general-purpose computer, when performing particular functions pursuant to instructions from program software, becomes a special purpose computer. This special purpose computer may be patentable, provided that the claimed subject matter meets all of the other requirements for patentability.

In *State Street Bank v. Signature Financial Group,* 149 F.3d 1368 (Fed.Cir.1998), *cert. denied* 525 U.S. 1093 (1999), Judge Rich reaffirmed the Federal Circuit's position that a programmed computer using a mathematical algorithm that produces useful, concrete and tangible results is statutory subject matter under § 101. *State Street* also eliminated the business method exception to patentable subject matter, thus opening the door for patents on Internet business systems.

The European Patent Office has also moved to allow at least some software to be patented. An important European case, the decision in *International Business Machines,* is included in this Chapter.

The Federal Circuit clarified its position in *AT&T v. Excel,* 172 F.3d 1352 (Fed.Cir.1999), *cert. denied,* ___ U.S. ___, 120 S.Ct. 368 (1999), which held that the mathematical algorithm need not involve physical transformation or conversion to be deemed patentable subject matter. With this decision it is clear that today a general-purpose computer, when operating according to software instructions that transform or convert data from one form into another new and useful form, is patentable subject matter.

The last few cases in this Chapter, also from the Federal Circuit, provide additional details on patent law, particularly with regard to the use of "means for" terminology which is frequently included in claims to define the metes and bounds of software inventions, as well as the "doctrine of equivalents," an equitable doctrine that permits a court to find infringement even when a patent is not literally infringed.

B. A NETWORKED COMPUTER METHODS PATENT

This patent is a typical networked computer business methods patent. All the claims are method claims, and the figure is a flow chart. We have reproduced the entire patent to give an idea of what a patent is like. We have omitted, however, two certificates of correction filed after the patent was granted.

US005963921A

United States Patent [19]
Longfield

[11] **Patent Number:**   **5,963,921**

[45] **Date of Patent:**   **Oct. 5, 1999**

[54] **ELECTRONIC INCOME TAX REFUND EARLY PAYMENT SYSTEM WITH MEANS FOR CREATING OF A NEW DEPOSIT ACCOUNT FOR RECEIPT OF AN ELECTRONICALLY TRANSFERRED REFUND FROM THE IRS**

[75] Inventor: **Ross N. Longfield**, Far Hills, N.J.

[73] Assignee: **Beneficial Financial Corporation**, Wilmington, Del.

[21] Appl. No.: **08/982,807**

[22] Filed: **Oct. 15, 1997**

Related U.S. Application Data

[63] Continuation of application No. 08/000,270, Jan. 4, 1993, abandoned, which is a continuation of application No. 07/615,903, Nov. 20, 1990, Pat. No. 5,193,057, which is a continuation of application No. 07/384,654, Jul. 25, 1989, abandoned, which is a continuation of application No. 07/146,324, Jan. 21, 1988, Pat. No. 4,890,228.

[51] **Int. Cl.⁶** **G06F 17/60**
[52] **U.S. Cl.** **705/31**; 705/30
[58] **Field of Search** 705/1, 30, 31

[56] **References Cited**

U.S. PATENT DOCUMENTS

4,890,228   12/1989   Longfield 705/31

5,193,057   3/1993   Longfield 705/31
5,694,322   12/1997   Westerlage et al. 705/417

Primary Examiner—Edward R. Cosimano
Attorney, Agent, or Firm—Connolly & Hutz

[57]   **ABSTRACT**

Electronic data processing system for preparation of electronically filed tax returns and authorization and payment of refunds based on the data supplied in those returns. Electronic data processing programs are provided for creating an electronic tax return that is filed with a tax collecting authority. At the same time as the electronic tax return is created, a loan application is processed to create an electronic deposit/loan account for the tax filer at an authorized credit institution. As early as the day after completion of the tax return and loan application, the tax filer receives initial refund payment from the loan account. The authorized credit institution electronically files the electronic tax return with the tax collecting authority which processes the return and transfers by electronic fund transfer the refund amount to the deposit/loan account at the authorized credit institution. Any refund in excess of the initial refund payment is then forwarded to the tax filer. Provision is also made for checking the credit worthiness of the tax filer.

15 Claims, 1 Drawing Sheet

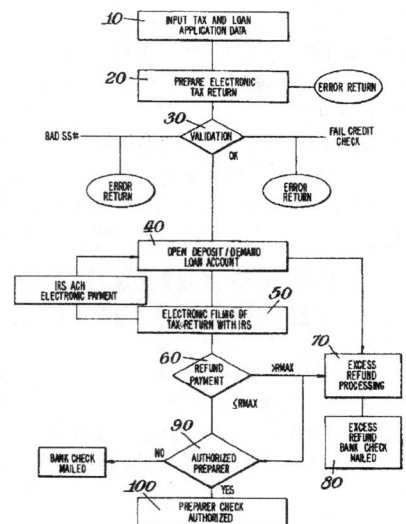

U.S. Patent   Oct. 5, 1999   **5,963,921**

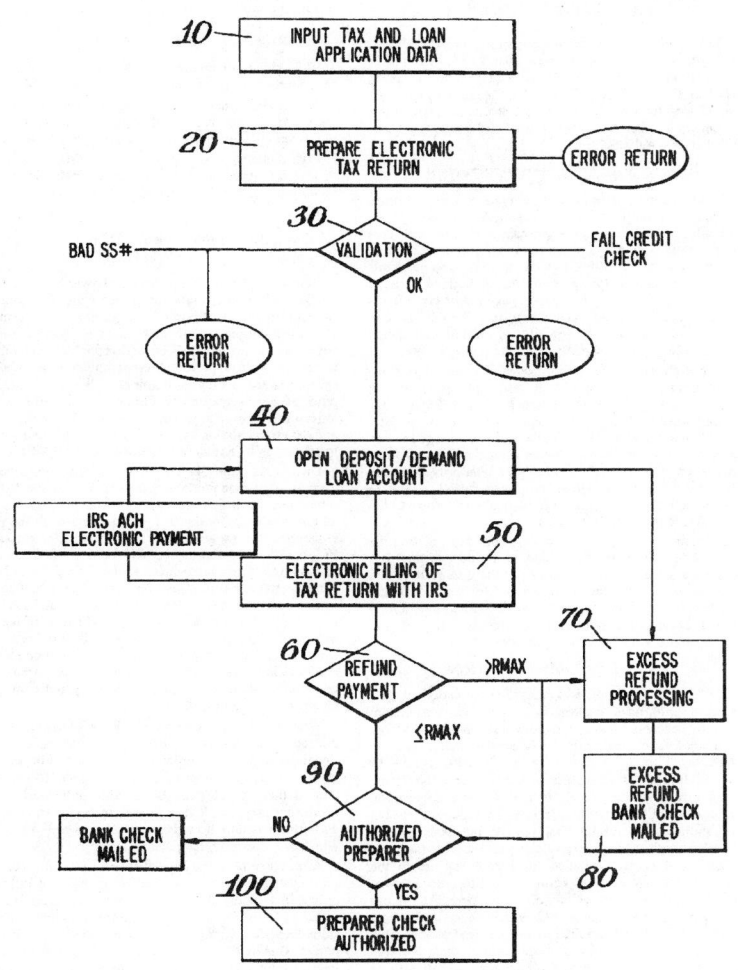

5,963,921

1

ELECTRONIC INCOME TAX REFUND EARLY PAYMENT SYSTEM WITH MEANS FOR CREATING OF A NEW DEPOSIT ACCOUNT FOR RECEIPT OF AN ELECTRONICALLY TRANSFERRED REFUND FROM THE IRS

This application is a continuation of Ser. No. 08/000,270 filed Jan. 4, 1993, which is now abandoned. Which is a continuation of Ser. No. 07/615,903 filed Nov. 20, 1990, now U.S. Pat. No. 5,193,057, which is a continuation of Ser. No. 384,654 filed Jul. 25, 1989, now abandoned, which is a continuation of Ser. No. 146,324, filed on Jan. 21, 1988 now U.S. Pat. No. 4,890,228.

BACKGROUND OF THE INVENTION

This invention relates to a data processing system for use on programmable data processing machines. More particularly, the invention comprises a data processing program for the preparation of tax returns, for electronic filing thereof with a taxing authority and data processing programs for creating a deposit/loan account at an authorized financial institution for providing immediate payment of tax refunds based on such prepared and filed returns. The deposit/loan account is created with the capability of receiving electronic fund transfer deposits directly from the taxing authority.

In recent years, taxing authorities have increasingly automated the tax collecting and tax return filing process. In particular, the United States Internal Revenue Service has instituted a system for the electronic filing of tax return data. In conjunction with that system, the IRS has arranged to pay refunds by electronic funds transfer using the Treasury ACH origination system. While this has greatly improved the tax filing and refund process it still requires a period of three to six weeks from the filing of an individual's tax return to the time of receipt of a refund check.

In contrast, the system of the invention shortens the time from filing to receipt of a refund to as little as one day. Additional advantages and features of the instant invention will become more readily apparent from the following detailed description of a specific illustrative embodiment thereof presented hereinbelow in conjunction with the accompanying drawing and appendices.

BRIEF SUMMARY INVENTION

The present invention is a unique combination of data processing programs resulting in a data processing system that provides a tax refund payment within 24–48 hours from the time of filing a tax return. In the present embodiment an Electronic Filing Program prepares a 1040, 1040A or 1040EZ federal tax return acceptable for electronic transmission to the United States Internal Revenue Service, on the basis of tax filer provided data. At the same time, the tax filer applies for a refund loan and, on the basis of filer provided credit data, a deposit/loan account is opened at a authorized financial institution. In a preferred use of the system of the invention, the entire transaction takes place at the offices of an authorized tax return preparer. Such a use of the system provides the tax filer with the benefit of having a tax return prepared and filed on one day and picking up a check at the same office for any refund due, less tax preparation fees and filing fees, on the next day; all without any out of pocket payment by the tax filer.

The specific embodiment of the data processing system of the invention is disclosed in the form of program flow charts enabling a skilled programmer to write programs in any of

2

a variety of computer programming languages (e.g., COBOL) which can be executed on any of a number of data processing machines. It is also anticipated that programs equivalent to the disclosed programs can be written by those skilled in the art to achieve the unique benefits of the data processing system of the invention.

BRIEF DESCRIPTION OF THE DRAWINGS

FIG. 1 is a schematic flow diagram of data processing functions of the invention.

Microfiche Appendix I is a program flow diagram for the Electronic Filing Program of the disclosed embodiment of the invention. Appendix I is one page with 9 sheets.

Microfiche Appendix II is a program flow diagram of the deposit/loan program of the disclosed embodiment of the invention. microfiche Appendix II is one page with 22 sheets.

DETAILED DESCRIPTION OF THE INVENTION

Referring now to FIG. 1, there is shown in schematic flow diagram form an overall depiction of the data processing functions for implementing the invention. Input means **10** is used for inputting tax preparer, taxpayer identification, taxpayer tax return information and refund anticipation loan information. In a preferred embodiment input means **10** comprises and intelligent terminal such as a personal computer having programmable data processing arithmetic and logical functions, a keyboard, a visual monitor, data storage and data transmission capabilities. Data input using such an input means is hereinafter described in more detail.

Once data input is complete, a program process is executed by a data processing means to create electronic tax return files **20** which are in a form accepted by the taxing authority processing the taxpayer tax return. In the present embodiment, a program flow chart of an Electronic Filing Program for preparing 1040, 1040A and 1040EZ tax returns in electronic format acceptable to the United States Internal Revenue Service comprises Microfiche Appendix I hereto. It is also necessary to validate tax return data and loan application data as is shown in block **30**. Validation of tax return data including mathematical checking is performed by the Electronic Filing Program of Microfiche Appendix I. In addition, individual identification data is compared to a file containing credit information to identify individuals with unacceptable credit histories.

When validation is complete, a deposit/loan account **40** is created at a authorized financial institution, e.g., bank, financial union, Savings and Loan Association, etc., that issues advance payments of taxpayer refunds. To accomplish this in the present embodiment the authorized financial institution programs a data processor means in accordance with the program flow chart of Microfiche Appendix II which is more fully described hereinafter.

After creation of the deposit/loan account file **40**, the tax return data is electronically filed with the taxing authority as indicated in block **50**. In the present embodiment, the taxing authority is the IRS and the tax preparer and return data is supplied via electronic transmission to designated IRS computers. This data also includes identification of the deposit/loan account which is designated to receive electronic fund transfer refunds directly from the IRS through the Treasury Department's ACH system.

As soon as the validated tax return data and loan application data have been processed and a refund amount is

5,963,921

3

determined, the refund loan payment procedure **60** is initiated. The payor authorized financial institution may have set a maximum amount (Rmax), for example $2,500, which it will immediately pay out as a refund loan. Therefore a determination is made as to whether or not the claimed refund exceeds this amount. If that is the case, excess refund processing is entered and an excess refund payment **80** is generated when the electronic funds payment is received. Simultaneously, the maximum authorized amount of refund anticipation loan is processed by determining whether or not payment is to be made through an authorized preparer **90** or directly by the authorized financial institution **100**. In the case of an authorized preparer a financial institution check is issued by the preparer for delivery the next day. In the case of direct payment by the authorized financial institution, a check is mailed to the tax filer the next day. The foregoing constitutes an overall description of the data processing system of the invention.

Returning now to the Electronic Filing Program **20** of the present embodiment which is set forth in the program flow charts of Microfiche Appendix I. The Electronic Filing Program (EFP) is designed to be used by tax preparers having an intelligent terminal input means **10**. The program enables preparers **20** to electronically enter tax returns and transmit them to a remote processing center. The remote processing center gathers tax returns from many tax preparers and collectively transmits them to the IRS. The System Specifications of the EFP are divided into four main sections these sections describe the tax preparers duties and systems operations as they pertain to 1. SYSTEM INITIALIZATION, 2. DATA ENTRY, 3. TRANSMIT, and 4. FOLLOW-UP.

The system initialization process is designed to make it as easy as possible for the tax preparer. It sets up all the files required by the EFP software, and guides him through the terminal screen provided for the entry of the tax preparer information (Microfiche Appendix I). The system is designed for the entry of the tax preparer information separately so that it needs only be entered once, but provides the tax preparer the opportunity to change this information if needed. In the present embodiment, such tax preparer data is in the form required by the IRS for preparers eligible to file tax return data electronically.

The tax preparer gathers all the necessary information from a client to file a tax return. The EFP can handle the three basic tax returns, 1040, 1040A, and 1040EZ and certain supported schedules and forms. The tax preparer then goes to his intelligent terminal and enables the EFP program.

After the preparer has completed the 1040, 1040A or 1040EZ form by following the input procedures, the EFP software performs two major functions. First, it determines the presence of errors in the entry of most of the major fields. Second, it determines from the information entered on the 1040 if any of the supported forms or schedules are required. If any of the supported forms or schedules are required it automatically brings to the screen the required data entry format for completion by the preparer.

After the preparer has entered all of the information for the 1040, 1040A, or 1040EZ, and all related forms and schedules, the software automatically displays a summary screen.

The preparer then enters his code on the summary screen and the system automatically displays all of the information from the preparer file. The information on the preparer file is entered only once and can be updated as needed by using option seven from the main menu. It is attached to each tax

4

return through the summary screen. The summary screen also provides for the input of authorized financial institution route information and displays a list of the required documents.

When the summary screen is completed the system displays the screen for the entry of W-2 information.

When all of the required W-2's have been completed the software automatically returns to the main screen. At this time the preparer can either enter another 1040, 1040A, or 1040EZ, or select which returns are to be transmitted to the remote processing center.

After all required tax returns have been entered the preparer can transmit the returns to the remote processing center. This is accomplished by selecting the 'NEW TRANSMISSION FILE' entry from the main screen. When this item is selected the transmit screen is displayed, the preparer indicates the returns to be transmitted by changing the status code on the transmit screen to 'T'. The system then adds these tax returns to the transmit file, dials the remote processor center number, and transmits the data over either dedicated or ordinary telecommunication lines.

The week after a tax return has been accepted by the IRS, the preparer must ship a form 8453 and supporting documents such as W2's to the IRS. IRS rejected returns are corrected by the central processing center unless the tax meaning of the return would be altered, in which case the preparer is informed and asked to re-process the return.

In the present embodiment the validation **30**, account file creation **40** electronic filing **50**, and refund payment processing **60**, **70**, **80**, **90** and **100** are all performed at the remote processing center. These functions are performed by data processing programs created in accordance with microfiche appendix II hereto. In overview this embodiment of the system of the invention permits a taxpayer to obtain a refund loan within one or two days of filing his tax return through an authorized preparer directly or by mail from the participating authorized financial institution. This is in contrast to the typical 6 to 8 weeks required to receive a refund directly from the IRS.

Rapid refund payment is accomplished by the authorized financial institution issuing to the tax filer a demand loan for an amount of the tax filer's calculated IRS refund. This loan is in the form of a check issued by the authorized financial institution and has the loan terms on the check document. A deposit account is opened for the customer at the authorized financial institution to which the tax filer's IRS tax refund is sent via the IRS electronic funds transfer ACH system. This IRS refund payment, when received is automatically applied as payment of the tax filer's loan, paying it off, assuming that none of the refund was withheld by the IRS. In the event that a cap has been set by the lender, any refund in excess of the amount of the loan is subsequently issued in an additional check for that excess amount and mailed to the tax filer.

To accomplish this in the Refund Anticipated Loan (RAL) system of the embodiment of Microfiche Appendix II,, an issue file will be transmitted from the remote processing center. Multiple files are allowed on a daily basis. This file will be posted to a masterfile on the authorized financial institution data processing means, in this instance an NCR 8250. Validation will be performed on the file received from the remote processing center. Fields validated include the Social Security Number field for numerics and non duplicate Social Security Number, the amount file for numerics and the Name and Address filed for Alpha/Numerics. The individual items and amounts are summed up and compared against the trailer record for control. The loan application is

5,963,921

5

also compared to a master credit data file to validate the credit worthiness of the applicant tax filer. A failure of this test will result in an error return to the originating tax preparer the next day. The RAL refund checks are generated from the file transmission and update. The checks are mailed within 24 hours from receipt of file from the authorized financial institution or in the case of authorized preparers will be issued the next day by the preparer. Four reports are generated by this program. They are the Input Validation, Update Report, RAL Checks, and Check Register.

Each day three reconciliations are performed against the RAL Masterfile. One is for the clearing of the cashed RAL checks. The information from all captured bank checks is searched and RAL refund check information extracted. This is posted against the RAL Masterfile. The checks are matched by serial number to the RAL Masterfiles Serial Number to insure that the amount cleared equals the amount issued. All exceptions are noted as an exception for manual exception item handling. All validated checks are posted against the RAL Masterfile, and the date cleared is stored.

A second reconciliation is performed daily. This is a reconciliation against all incoming IRS ACH items. The IRS ACH Incoming file is searched for RAL IRS Tax Refunds. This is keyed off of the account number field in the IRS ACH record. A unique constant eight digit number followed by the tax filer's Social Security number is used in the Account Number field for the IRS ACH Refund. Based upon this unique number, the IRS ACH items are searched and information pulled for validation and update to the RAL Masterfiles. Four reports are generated. They are the IRS ACH RAL Validation Report, the Update Report, Excess Refund Checks, and Excess Refund Check Register. These Excess Refund Check Issues are posted to another reconciliation masterfile.

A third reconciliation is made for the Excess Refund Checks. This is a basic reconciliation system. Each day all data from the captured checks is searched and Excess Refund check information is extracted to post against the Excess Refund reconciliation Masterfile. Again two reports are generated, one is a Validation Report and the second an Update Report.

On a periodic basis, a program is run to strip off from the RAL Masterfile and Excess RAL Refund Masterfile, all completely cleared items to a history file.

Having described the unique properties of the system of the invention and without limitation illustrated the invention in a specific embodiment;

What is claimed is:

1. A method of operating at least one programmable electronic data processing machine comprising the programmed steps of:

  a) receiving inputted tax preparer data, tax return data and refund payment data from a tax preparer site prepared by a tax preparer and not the tax payer;

  b) creating electronic tax return data files from said tax return data;

  c) immediately after creating said electronic tax return data files, creating a new, previously unopened electronic deposit account files for said tax return data and said refund payment data to an authorized financial institution and the sole purpose of the account files if for receiving IRS funds to offset against the loan debit;

  d) designating said electronic deposit account file at said authorized financial institution as the recipient of electronic funds;

  e) electronically transmitting said electronic tax return data files to at least one tax collecting authority;

6

  f) authorizing receipt by said authorized financial institution of tax refund electronic fund transfers, based on said tax return data, from said tax collecting authority;

  g) processing said tax return data files and said electronic deposit account files and authorizing payment, at said tax preparer site, by said authorized financial institution from said deposit account files of a tax refund amount based on said tax return data upon completion of tax return processing and electronic fund transfer refund payment by said tax collecting authority;

  h) electronically closing said electronic deposit account file after payment of the tax refund amount from the IRS is received by said financial institution to the taxpayer.

2. The method of claim 1 further comprising the steps of deducting processing fees from said refund amount and transmitting at least part of said fees by electronic funds transfer.

3. The method as claimed in claim 1, wherein said electronic tax return data is inputted by an input means into a computer system.

4. The method as claimed in claim 3, wherein said input means includes keyboard input means, visual monitor means, data storage means, data transmission means and programmable data process means for executing said program means for processing said tax preparer data and said tax return data and transmitting said electronic tax return data files and said payment data, to a remote processing center.

5. The method as claimed in claim 4, wherein said remote processing center includes at least one programmable data processing means for executing said program means for processing payment data and creating electronic deposit account files, for transmitting electronic tax return data to and for authorizing receipt of by said authorized financial institution electronic funds transfer data from, at least one electronic data processing means controlled by at least one tax collecting authority and for executing said program means for processing said tax return data files and said electronic deposit account files and program means for transmitting said files to said authorized financial institution for authorizing payment of a tax refund amount from said electronic deposit account whereby said payment made be made at a tax preparer site upon tax return processing and electronic funds transfer refund payment by said tax collecting authority.

6. The method as claimed in claim 4, further including program means for deducting processing fees from said refund amount and program means for transmitting at least a part of said fees by electronic funds transfer.

7. The method as claimed in claim 1, wherein a check for the loan amount is mailed within twenty-four hours of receipt of the file from the authorized financial institution or in the case of an authorized preparer, will be issued the next day by the preparer.

8. The method as claimed in claim 7, which further comprises generating an input validation report, an update report, refund anticipation loan check and check register.

9. The method as claimed in claim 8, which further comprises performing a reconciliation for clearing of the cashed refund anticipation loan check whereby the information from the captured check is searched and the refund anticipation loan check information extracted.

10. The method as claimed in claim 9, which further comprises removing, from the refund anticipation loan master file and excess refund anticipation loan refund master file, all of the completely cleared items to a history file.

5,963,921

7

11. A method of operating at least one programmable electronic data processing machine comprising the programmed steps of:

    a) receiving tax return data from a taxpayer prepared by a tax preparer and not the taxpayer at said tax preparer's site;

    b) calculating tax refund data based on the tax return data;

    c) inputting said tax refund data and taxpayer identification data into a database on a computer;

    d) electronically transmitting taxpayer identification data and the tax refund data to an authorized financial institution;

    e) immediately after transmitting said tax refund data to the financial institution, electronically requesting the creation of a single transaction deposit account file at the financial institution and said single transaction deposit account file's sole purpose is of receiving IRS funds to offset against the loan debit in the account and electronically receiving information identifying the account file from the financial institution;

    f) electronically communicating the taxpayer identification data, tax refund data and the single transaction account file data to at least one tax collecting authority;

    g) transmitting authorization to the tax collecting authority to perform tax refund electronic fund transfers based on the tax return data to the single transaction account file;

    h) disbursing funds to the taxpayer from the single transaction account file based on the tax refund data; and

    i) electronically closing said electronic deposit account file after payment of the tax refund amount to the taxpayer is sent from the IRS by said financial institution.

8

12. The method as claimed in claim 11, further including program means for deducting processing fees from said refund amount and program means for transmitting at least a part of said fees by electronic funds transfer.

13. The method of claimed in claim 11, further comprising the steps of deducting processing fees from said refund amount and transmitting at least part of said fees by electronic funds transfer.

14. The method as claimed in claim 11 wherein said computer includes an input means which includes keyboard input means, visual monitor means, data storage means, data transmission means and programmable data processing means for executing said program means for processing said tax preparer data and said tax return data and transmitting said electronic tax return data files and said payment data, to a remote processing center.

15. The method as claimed in claim 14, wherein said remote processing center includes at least one programmable data processing means for executing said program means for processing payment data and creating electronic deposit account files, for transmitting electronic tax return data to and for authorizing receipt of by said authorized financial institution electronic funds transfer data from, at least one electronic data processing means controlled by at least one tax collecting authority and for executing said program means for processing said tax return data files and said electronic deposit account files and program means for transmitting said files to said authorized financial institution for authorizing payment of a tax refund amount from said electronic deposit account whereby said payment made be made at a tax preparer site upon tax return processing and electronic funds transfer refund payment by said tax collecting authority.

* * * * *

1.   A patent begins with a "Title," an "Abstract," and an illustrative drawing on a cover page that together summarize the teachings of the patent. One or more drawings of the invention come next, and these are required. (See 35 U.S.C. § 113 and 37 C.F.R. § 1.83(a)). The specification begins by summarizing what the inventor knows about the "prior art"—the prior work of others that relates to the invention. The specification then continues with a brief summary of the invention that defines generally what the inventor believes is new and unobvious and worthy of patent protection. A completely detailed description of the "preferred embodiments" of the invention comes next. This is the inventor's statement of what is the best way to practice the invention, together with a listing of alternative ways to practice the invention, and it may go on for many pages. The detailed description contains frequent references to the drawings and to reference numbers that the rules require to be affixed to the individual elements shown in the drawings.

At the very end of the patent specification, the most important part of the patent appears in a series of numbered paragraphs that are called "claims." Each claim precisely defines an invention itself—what the inventor believes is new and patentable and what the inventor desires to exclude others from making, using, selling, offering for sale, and importing. (The claims are not to be confused with the detailed description of the "preferred embodiment," which may define the invention much more narrowly than the claims do.) *See* 35 U.S.C. §§ 111, 112. During "prosecution" of the patent application before the patent examiner, it is the precise wording of the claims that is the subject of most of the discussions and negotiations between the examiner and the patent attorney representing the inventor/applicant for a patent. Before a patent finally issues, the claims may be amended many times.

2.   The inventions defined by the Longfield patent's claims are "pure software" in the sense that the inventions can be implemented on a general-purpose computer having no new or novel elements other than the software converting one type of data into a new and useful second type of data. Note that only a very simple "flow diagram" of the program is defined by one or more of these claims. In cases where hardware or software elements are novel, they must be disclosed. Sometimes complete or partial program listings are essential, and they may be submitted in appropriate format. Section 112 of the Patent Act requires "a written description of the invention, and of the manner and process of making and using it, in such full, clear, concise, and exact terms as to enable any person skilled in the art to which it pertains, or with which it is most nearly connected, to make and use the same ..." This description must enable one skilled in the art to make the invention "without undue experimentation." *U.S. v. Telectronics*, 857 F.2d 778, 785 (Fed. Cir.1988).

3.   Note that the date when the patent application was filed appears in the patent along with an application serial number. Once approved by the patent examiner, a patent is assigned a unique patent number and a date of issuance. Once issued, a patent grants the inventors, or their assignee, a monopoly on making, using, offering to sell, selling, and importing the invention (35 U.S.C. § 271(a)) that lasts twenty years from the date of filing (35 U.S.C. § 154(a)(2)). If the application claims the priority of an earlier (non-provisional) U.S. application, the twenty-year term commences with the filing date of that earlier application. Patents issued from an application filed prior to June 8, 1995 expire 20 years from the date of filing or 17 years from the date of issue, whichever is longer (35 U.S.C.§ 154(c)(1)).

4.   Note the list of "prior art" references on the cover page of the patent. These patents and articles were examined by the patent examiner, and the inventions defined by the claims in the patent are presumed by the courts to be "valid"—to define inventions that are new (35 U.S.C. § 102) and unobvious (35 U.S.C. § 103)—over these "prior art" references (this presumption is set forth at 35 U.S.C. § 282). Accordingly, to successfully attack the "validity" of a patent in court, an alleged infringer must usually find and present to the court new and different "prior art" that the patent examiner did not see during the prosecution of the patent application. The inventor/applicant for a patent and his or her attorney both have an ethical duty to send copies of any relevant prior art references that they know of to the examiner, and failure to do so may constitute fraud and may also invalidate the patent (37 C.F.R. § 1.56), with the defendant possibly recovering its attorney's fees (35 U.S.C. § 285).

5. The process of applying for and obtaining a patent is called the "prosecution" of a patent. Individual inventors may "prosecute" their own patents (usually a very unwise approach), or they may be represented by a "registered" patent attorney or patent agent. To register one must meet educational requirements in science and engineering (or have equivalent experience) and also pass a rigorous examination on patent procedure. 37 C.F.R. § 10.7. The examination covers Title 35, the Rules of Practice set forth in 37 C.F.R. Chapter 1, and the Manual of Patent Examining Procedure, or M.P.E.P. (a set of two bulky three-ring binders containing numerous additional rules of practice). Non-registered attorneys may not practice before the patent section of the PTO. They may practice before the Trademark section, however. See 37 C.F.R. § 10.14.

6. Large corporations usually require employees to sign contracts agreeing to assign their inventions to the corporation. If the corporation decides that the benefits of a potential patent outweigh the costs of the application procedure, it will pay patent attorneys to prosecute the patent application. The inventor here, Ross N. Longfield, assigned his patent to Beneficial Financial, Corp., which then hired the firm of Connolly & Hutz to represent it. Assignments of patents must be recorded in the PTO. 35 U.S.C. § 261. An assignment is void as against a subsequent purchaser for value if not recorded within three months or prior to the subsequent assignment. If there is more than one owner of a patent, each owns the whole in the sense that each joint owner may grant licenses and collect royalties, and there is no obligation to account to the other joint owners (35 U.S.C. § 262) unlike the case with joint owners of a copyright (see NIMMER ON COPYRIGHT, 6.12[A]). Accordingly, an agreement on ownership, licensing and distribution of royalties is essential. Liens against patents must be recorded at the state level under Article 9 of the U.C.C. A lien on "general intangibles" is sufficient to cover patents. Recording of patent liens in the PTO is also desirable. (Copyright liens, however, must be recorded with the Register of Copyright, not at the state level.)

7. Each claim appended to the end of a patent, for instance each of the 15 claims of the "Longfield" patent, defines a unique invention. The patent examiner studies the "prior art" and then negotiates with the inventor's patent attorney or agent over the precise wording of the patent claims. Initially, the examiner typically rejects all of the claims, sends the "prior art" to the applicant's attorney or agent, and awaits a response. The applicant's attorney or agent responds with an "amendment" to the claims, typically narrowing the inventions defined by the claims. The patent may then issue, or negotiations may continue for years, with the patent applicant paying fees periodically to continue the examination process (35 U.S.C. § 132(b)), or the applicant may re-file an application several times as a "continuation" or "division" of the original application, claiming the benefit of the original application's filing date under 35 U.S.C. § 120. However, the patent will still expire twenty years from the date of the original filing. Another option is to re-file a

patent application with additional inventive material added (a "continuation-in-part" patent application).

8. An adverse decision of the Examiner may be appealed first to the Board of Patent Appeals and Interferences within the PTO (35 U.S.C. § 134) and then to the Court of Appeals for the Federal Circuit (35 U.S.C. § 141). Alternatively, the Commissioner of Patents may be sued in the United States District Court for the District of Columbia (35 U.S.C. § 145), but that is not a particularly favorable forum for inventors.

9. A patent application, unless withdrawn, is normally published eighteen months after it is filed. 35 U.S.C. § 122. Publication destroys any trade secrets contained in the application. Publication can also give rise to "provisional rights" to recover a reasonable royalty from infringers commencing on the date of publication, providing the patent ultimately issues with claims "substantially identical" to the claims as published (35 U.S.C. § 154(d)).

10. While not reproduced here, the original patent application, plus all correspondence between the applicant and the Examiner, is open to public inspection once the patent issues, with copies available at nominal cost. It is stored in a large manila folder called a "file wrapper." Statements made by the applicant during "prosecution" of the patent before the examiner are frequently used later by the courts in construing the meaning of the "claim" language and thus the scope of the invention. These statements can give rise to "prosecution history estoppel" (also called "file wrapper estoppel"). If an applicant has interpreted a claim narrowly to get the examiner to issue a patent, the patent-holder is "estopped" to argue later for a broader interpretation of the same claim. Accordingly, it is essential to review the file wrapper of a patent before rendering an opinion on patent validity or patent infringement.

11. The process of suing a patent infringer before a United States district court is called "litigation". Any attorney admitted to practice may "litigate" a patent. The trend in recent years is toward more jury trials in patent cases. Patent infringement is for the trier of fact to determine, as are damages. The patent claims, such as claims 1–15 in the "Longfield" patent, define the scope of the patent for the purpose of determining infringement. The Judge determines the meaning of the claim language in what is called a "Markman" hearing preceding the trial. In some instances, the claims may be interpreted to cover "equivalents" outside the scope of their literal language. The successful litigant may receive actual damages or, if greater, a "reasonable royalty," typically 3 to 5 percent of the sale price of the invention as claimed in the patent claims. 35 U.S.C. § 284. Compare this to copyright damages, which include actual damages plus defendant's profits not included in actual damages, 17 U.S.C. § 504(b) or, in the alternative, "statutory damages" set by the judge, 17 U.S.C. § 504(c). Injunction against further infringement is also available under 35 U.S.C. § 283 (patent) and 17 U.S.C. § 502 (copyright).

12.   A patent owner may normally seek up to six year's of damages for infringement arising before the date when litigation commences. 35 U.S.C. § 286. However, if the patent owner or its licensees have been selling the invention and not marking the patent number of the invention, then past damages can only go back to the date when the infringer was notified of the infringement. 35 U.S.C. § 287(a). If the jury finds the infringement to be willful, the court may treble the damages (35 U.S.C. § 284), and the court may award attorney fees to the prevailing party in "exceptional cases." (35 U.S.C.§ 285) In an effort to protect against such punitive damages, many companies routinely ask their attorneys to provide them with an opinion of invalidity/noninfringement if they plan to continue engaging in the allegedly infringing activity following formal notification of infringement.

C. ELIGIBILITY FOR PATENT PROTECTION

In general, an invention must be "useful" and patentable subject matter under 35 U.S.C. § 101, "novel" under § 102, "nonobvious" under § 103, and meet "procedural requirements" set forth in § 102(b), § 112, and other sections for the PTO to issue a valid patent. The issue of whether or not a patent application meets the requirements of the patent act (title 35 U.S.C.) may arise before the PTO. This happens when the patent examiner rejects the application and the applicant contests the rejection. The issue of validity may also be raised by the defendant in patent infringement litigation, who may (and usually does) argue that the PTO erred in issuing a patent because the applicant had failed to meet the statutory standards. (The defendant usually will also argue in the alternative, that if the patent is valid, the defendant has not infringed it because the defendant's process or product does not fall within the claims of the patent.)

PATENT ACT,

35 U.S.C. §§ 101–103,112

§ 101. Inventions patentable

Whoever invents or discovers any new and useful process, machine, manufacture, or composition of matter, or any new and useful improvement thereof, may obtain a patent therefor, subject to the conditions and requirements of this title.

§ 102. Conditions for patentability; novelty and loss of right to patent

A person shall be entitled to a patent unless—

(a) the invention was known or used by others in this country, or patented or described in a printed publication in this or a foreign country, before the invention thereof by the applicant for patent, or

(b) the invention was patented or described in a printed publication in this or a foreign country or in public use or on sale in this country, more than one year prior to the date of the application for patent in the United States, or

(c) he has abandoned the invention, or

(d) the invention was first patented or caused to be patented, or was the subject of an inventor's certificate, by the applicant or his legal representatives or assigns in a foreign country prior to the date of the application for patent in this country on an application for patent or inventor's certificate filed more than twelve months before the filing of the application in the United States, or

(e) the invention was described in–

(1) an application for a patent, published under section 122(b), by another filed in the United States before the invention by the applicant for patent, except that an international application filed under the treaty defined in section 351(a) shall have the effect under this subsection of a national application published under section 122(b) only if the international application designating the United States was published under Article 21(2)(a) of such treaty in the English language; or

(2) a patent granted on an application for a patent by another filed in the United States before the invention by the applicant for patent, except that a patent shall not be deemed filed in the United States for the purposes of this subsection based on the filing of an international application defined under the treaty defined in section 351(a); or

(f) he did not himself invent the subject matter sought to be patented, or

(g)(1) during the course of an interference conducted under section 135 or section 291, another inventor involved therein establishes, to the extent permitted in section 104, that before such person's invention thereof the invention was made by such other inventor and not abandoned, suppressed, or concealed, or

(2) before such person's invention thereof, the invention was made in this country by another inventor who had not abandoned, suppressed, or concealed it. In determining priority of invention under this subsection, there shall be considered not only the respective dates of conception and reduction to practice of the invention, but also the reasonable diligence of one who was first to conceive and last to reduce to practice, from a time prior to conception by the other.

§ 103. Conditions for patentability; non-obvious subject matter

(a) A patent may not be obtained though the invention is not identically disclosed or described as set forth in section 102 of this title, if the differences between the subject matter sought to be patented and the prior art are such that the subject matter as a whole would have been obvious at the time the invention was made to a person having ordinary skill in the art to which said subject matter pertains. Patentability shall not be negatived by the manner in which the invention was made.

(b) * * * [§ 103 (b) is directed to special problems relating to "biotechnological" process and composition of matter patents, and is not relevant to the subject matter of this casebook.—Eds.]

(c) Subject matter developed by another person, which qualifies as prior art only under subsection (e), (f), and (g) of section 102 of this title, shall not preclude patentability under this section where the subject matter and the claimed invention were, at the time the invention was made, owned by the same person or subject to an obligation of assignment to the same person.

§ 112. Specification

The specification shall contain a written description of the invention, and of the manner and process of making and using it, in such full, clear, concise, and exact terms as to enable any person skilled in the art to which it pertains, or with which it is most nearly connected, to make and use the same, and shall set forth the best mode contemplated by the inventor of carrying out his invention.

The specification shall conclude with one or more claims particularly pointing out and distinctly claiming the subject matter which the applicant regards as his invention.

A claim may be written in independent or, if the nature of the case admits, in dependent or multiple dependent form.

Subject to the following paragraph, a claim in dependent form shall contain a reference to a claim previously set forth and then specify a further limitation of the subject matter claimed. A claim in dependent form shall be construed to incorporate by reference all the limitations of the claim to which it refers.

A claim in multiple dependent form shall contain a reference, in the alternative only, to more than one claim previously set forth and then specify a further limitation of the subject matter claimed. A multiple dependent claim shall not serve as a basis for any other multiple dependent claim. A multiple dependent claim shall be construed to incorporate by reference all the limitations of the particular claim in relation to which it is being considered.

An element in a claim for a combination may be expressed as a means or step for performing a specified function without the recital of structure, material, or acts in support thereof, and such claim shall be construed to cover the corresponding structure, material, or acts described in the specification and equivalents thereof.

D. PATENTABLE SUBJECT MATTER—§ 101

In general, § 101 patentable subject matter issues arise rather rarely in non-computer cases. The typical invention, for instance the proverbial "better mousetrap," clearly falls into the category of a "process, machine, manufacture, or composition of matter." Computer programs, however, have had to overcome precedents to the effect that mental steps, mathematical equations, and ways of doing business are not patentable subject matter under § 101.

The President's Commission on the Patent System issued a report in 1966 opposing the patentability of software. In the *Benson* case (set forth below), the Supreme Court relies heavily upon this report as part of its basis for its holding that mathematical algorithms are unpatentable. The PTO was opposed to software patents at the time the President's Commission met, having been overwhelmed with voluminous hardware logic patents that defied classification. (In patent libraries, patents are or should be arranged for searching by Class and Subclass.) The real problem was that integrated circuit designers were highly prolific inventors, and software designers were and are ever so much more prolific at invention. The PTO was simply overwhelmed by the number and complexity of the hardware and software inventions that occurred during the 1960s.

As is noted in the *Benson* case, below, this inability of the PTO to process software inventions was a major reason why the Commission Report opposed software patent protection.

The original Court of Customs and Patent Appeals decision holding software to be patentable, *In re Prater*, 415 F.2d 1393 (C.C.P.A. 1969) involved an "analog computer," not a "digital computer." An analog computer is a mechanical device whose action mimics action in the real world. Therefore, there was no computer program in the usual sense.

GOTTSCHALK v. BENSON

Supreme Court of the United States, 1972.
409 U.S. 63, 93 S.Ct. 253, 34 L.Ed.2d 273.

MR. JUSTICE DOUGLAS delivered the opinion of the Court.

Respondents filed in the Patent Office an application for an invention which was described as being related "to the processing of data by program and more particularly to the programmed conversion of numerical information" in general-purpose digital computers. They claimed a method for converting binary-coded decimal (BCD) numerals into pure binary numerals. The claims were not limited to any particular art or technology, to any particular apparatus or machinery, or to any particular end use. They purported to cover any use of the claimed method in a general-purpose digital computer of any type. Claims 8 and 13[1] were rejected by the Patent Office but sustained by the Court of Customs and

---

1. They are set forth in the Appendix to this opinion.

Patent Appeals, 441 F.2d 682. The case is here on a petition for a writ of certiorari.

The question is whether the method described and claimed is a "process" within the meaning of the Patent Act.

* * *

A digital computer, as distinguished from an analog computer, operates on data expressed in digits, solving a problem by doing arithmetic as a person would do it by head and hand. Some of the digits are stored as components of the computer. Others are introduced into the computer in a form which it is designed to recognize. The computer operates then upon both new and previously stored data. The general-purpose computer is designed to perform operations under many different programs.

* * *

The patent sought is on a method of programming a general-purpose digital computer to convert signals from binary-coded decimal form into pure binary form. A procedure for solving a given type of mathematical problem is known as an "algorithm." The procedures set forth in the present claims are of that kind; that is to say, they are a generalized formulation for programs to solve mathematical problems of converting one form of numerical representation to another. From the generic formulation, programs may be developed as specific applications.

The decimal system uses as digits the 10 symbols 0, 1, 2, 3, 4, 5, 6, 7, 8, and 9. The value represented by any digit depends, as it does in any positional system of notation, both on its individual value and on its relative position in the numeral. Decimal numerals are written by placing digits in the appropriate positions or columns of the numerical sequence, i.e., "unit" (10^0), "tens" (10^1), "hundreds" (10^2), "thousands" (10^3) , etc. Accordingly, the numeral 1492 signifies $(1 \times 10^3) + (4 \times 10^2) + (9 \times 10^1) + (2 \times 10^0)$.

The pure binary system of positional notation uses two symbols as digits—0 and 1, placed in a numerical sequence with values based on consecutively ascending powers of 2. In pure binary notation, what would be the tens position is the twos position; what would be hundreds position is the fours position; what would be the thousands position is the eights. Any decimal number from 0 to 10 can be represented in the binary system with four digits or positions as indicated in the following table.

Shown as the sum of powers of 2

		2^3		2^2		2^1		2^0		
Decimal		(8)		(4)		(2)		(1)		Pure Binary
0	=	0	+	0	+	0	+	0	=	0000
1	=	0	+	0	+	0	+	2^0	=	0001
2	=	0	+	0	+	2^1	+	0	=	0010
3	=	0	+	0	+	2^1	+	2^0	=	0011
4	=	0	+	2^2	+	0	+	0	=	0100
5	=	0	+	2^2	+	0	+	2^0	=	0101
6	=	0	+	2^2	+	2^1	+	0	=	0110
7	=	0	+	2^2	+	2^1	+	2^0	=	0111
8	=	2^3	+	0	+	0	+	0	=	1000
9	=	2^3	+	0	+	0	+	2^0	=	1001
10	=	2^3	+	0	+	2^1	+	0	=	1010

The BCD system using decimal numerals replaces the character for each component decimal digit in the decimal numeral with the corresponding four-digit binary numeral, shown in the right-hand column of the table. Thus decimal 53 is represented as 0101 0011 in BCD, because decimal 5 is equal to binary 0101 and decimal 3 is equivalent to binary 0011. In pure binary notation, however, decimal 53 equals binary 110101. The conversion of BCD numerals to pure binary numerals can be done mentally through use of the foregoing table. The method sought to be patented varies the ordinary arithmetic steps a human would use by changing the order of the steps, changing the symbolism for writing the multiplier used in some steps, and by taking subtotals after each successive operation. The mathematical procedures can be carried out in existing computers long in use, no new machinery being necessary. And, as noted, they can also be performed without a computer.

The Court stated in *MacKay Co. v. Radio Corp.*, 306 U.S. 86, 94, that "[w]hile a scientific truth, or the mathematical expression of it, is not patentable invention, a novel and useful structure created with the aid of knowledge of scientific truth may be." That statement followed the longstanding rule that "[a]n idea of itself is not patentable." *Rubber-Tip Pencil Co. v. Howard*, 20 Wall. (87 U.S.) 498, 507. "A principle, in the abstract, is a fundamental truth; an original cause; a motive; these cannot be patented, as no one can claim in either of them an exclusive right." *Le Roy v. Tatham*, 14 How. (55 U.S.) 156, 175. Phenomena of nature, though just discovered, mental processes, and abstract intellectual concepts are not patentable, as they are the basic tools of scientific and technological work. As we stated in *Funk Bros. Seed Co. v. Kalo Co.*, 333 U.S. 127, 130, "He who discovers a hitherto unknown phenomenon of nature has no claim to a monopoly of it which the law recognizes. If there is to be invention from such a discovery, it must come from the application of the law of nature to a new and useful end." We dealt there with a "product" claim, while the present case deals with a "process" claim. But we think the same principle applies.

Here the "process" claim is so abstract and sweeping as to cover both known and unknown uses of the BCD to pure binary conversion. The end use may (1) vary from the operation of a train to verification of drivers' licenses to researching the law books for precedents and (2) be performed through any existing machinery or future-devised machinery or without any apparatus.

In *O'Reilly v. Morse*, 15 How. (56 U.S.) 62, Morse was allowed a patent for a process of using electromagnetism to produce distinguishable signs for telegraphy. *Id.*, at 111. But the Court denied the eighth claim in which Morse claimed the use of "electromagnetism, however developed for marking or printing intelligible characters, signs, or letters, at any distances." *Id.*, at 112. The Court in disallowing that claim said, "If this claim can be maintained, it matters not by what process or machinery the result is accomplished. For aught that we now know, some future inventor, in the onward march of science, may discover a mode of writing or printing at a distance by means of the electric or galvanic current, without using any part of the process or combination set forth in the plaintiffs specification. His invention may be less complicated-less liable to get out of order-less expensive in construction, and in its operation. But yet, if it is covered by this patent, the inventor could not use it, nor the public have the benefit of it, without the permission of this patentee." *Id.*, at 113.

* * *

It is argued that a process patent must either be tied to a particular machine or apparatus or must operate to change articles or materials to a "different state or thing." We do not hold that no process patent could ever qualify if it did not meet the requirements of our prior precedents. It is said that the decision precludes a patent for any program servicing a computer. We do not so hold. It is said that we have before us a program for a digital computer but extend our holding to programs for analog computers. We have, however, made clear from the start that we deal with a program only for digital computers. It is said we freeze process patents to old technologies, leaving no room for the revelations of the new, onrushing technology. Such is not our purpose. What we come down to in a nutshell is the following.

It is conceded that one may not patent an idea. But in practical effect that would be the result if the formula for converting BCD numerals to pure binary numerals were patented in this case. The mathematical formula involved here has no substantial practical application except in connection with a digital computer, which means that if the judgment below is affirmed, the patent would wholly pre-empt the mathematical formula and in practical effect would be a patent on the algorithm itself

It may be that the patent laws should be extended to cover these programs, a policy matter to which we are not competent to speak.

* * *

If these programs are to be patentable, considerable problems are raised which only committees of Congress can manage, for broad powers of investigation are needed, including hearings which canvass the wide variety of views which those operating in this field entertain. The technological problems tendered in the many briefs before us indicate to us that considered action by the Congress is needed.

Reversed.

MR. JUSTICE STEWART, MR. JUSTICE BLACKMUN, and MR. JUSTICE POWELL took no part in the consideration or decision of this case.

APPENDIX TO OPINION OF THE COURT

Claim 8 reads:

"The method of converting signals from binary coded decimal form into binary which comprises the steps of

"(1) storing the binary coded decimal signals in a reentrant shift register,

"(2) shifting the signals to the right by at least three places, until there is a binary '1' in the second position of said register,

"(3) masking out said binary '1' in said second position of said register,

"(4) adding a binary '1' to the first position of said register,

"(5) shifting the signals to the left by two positions,

"(6) adding a '1' to said first position, and

"(7) shifting the signals to the right by at least three positions in preparation for a succeeding binary '1' in the second position of said register."

Claim 13 reads:

"A data processing method for converting binary coded decimal number representations into binary number representations comprising the steps of

"(1) testing each binary digit position '1,' beginning with the least significant binary digit position, of the most significant decimal digit representation for a binary 0 or a binary '1';

"(2) if a binary 0 is detected, repeating step (1) for the next least significant binary digit position of said most significant decimal digit representation;

"(3) if a binary '1' is detected, adding a binary '1' at the $(i + 1)$th and $(i + 3)$th least significant binary digit positions of the next lesser significant decimal digit representation, and repeating step (1) for the next least significant binary digit position of said most significant decimal digit representation;

"(4) upon exhausting the binary digit positions of said most significant decimal digit representation, repeating steps (1) through (3) for the next lesser significant decimal digit representation as modified by the previous execution of steps (1) through (3); and

"(5) repeating steps (1) through (4) until the second least significant decimal digit representation has been so processed."

Notes

1.   Computers use true binary numbers internally, since this simplifies the design of a computer's arithmetic logic unit. But when one types on a computer's keyboard, each keystroke produces a binary code representing the number or letter key that is struck. Every time one strikes a number key, a binary code representing the decimal number printed on the key cap flows into the computer. Accordingly, all numeric computer input from keyboards is inherently "binary-coded decimal" input and must be converted into true binary numbers. Likewise, true binary numbers flowing from a computer must be converted back into binary coded decimal numbers which can then be sent to a printer or written upon a display. Thus, all personal computers must contain the *Benson* algorithm, or a slower "prior art" algorithm. The *Benson* algorithm works something like long division, proceeding into a BCD number from the left and computing partial results. "Prior art" algorithms would simply multiply each BCD number by binary representations of 1000 (for the fourth digit), 100 (for the third digit), 10 (for the second digit), and 1 (for the first digit) using binary multiplication, and then add these results using binary arithmetic. Had the Benson patent issued, then all computer companies not having an AT&T (now Lucent) license would have "designed around" this patent by using this older, slower way of converting.

2.   In response to the *Benson* decision, the PTO suspended all pending computer program patent applications, and the legal community in the U.S. and in Europe took the *Benson* decision as a signal that computer programs were not patentable. Copyright and trade secret law were used to protect software inventions during the decade following *Benson*.

3.   *Dann v. Johnston,* 425 U.S. 219, 96 S.Ct. 1393, 47 L.Ed.2d 692 (1976) was the second Supreme Court decision involving software patentability. The invention was a bank computer system that permitted one to indicate on a bank check whether the payment was "medical," "charitable," etc. At the end of the year, the checking account statement would include a breakdown of payments into "medical," "charitable," etc. categories that would assist one in preparing tax returns. The Supreme Court ruled that the invention was "obvious" and therefore unpatentable under 35 U.S.C. § 103 and never addressed the "patentability" issue under § 101. Today, with the popularity of "business methods" patents on ways of doing business on the Internet, the *Johnson* decision may be used by defendants faced with patents on automated ways of conducting business transactions previously done in a semimanual or manual manner.

4.   In *Parker v. Flook,* 437 U.S. 584, 98 S.Ct. 2522, 57 L.Ed.2d 451 (1978), the Supreme Court rejected an application for a patent covering a petrochemical process, where the novelty was in a computerized alarm limit updating process, and where the remainder of the petrochemical process was

disclosed only in very general terms. Justice Stevens, in holding this invention to be unpatentable, proposed the rule that the unpatentable computer program should be deemed "obvious," and then the invention should be examined to see if the combination of the "obvious" program with other (non-computer program) elements of the invention contained any novelty at all. If not, the invention is unpatentable under § 101. This analysis was strongly rejected by Judge Rich (*Application of Bergy,* 596 F.2d 952 (C.C.P.A. 1979)) who objected to this combining of the tests under § 103 (obviousness) and § 101 (patentable subject matter). According to Judge Rich, there are "three doors" to achieving a patent—§ 101 ("statutory subject matter"), § 102 ("novelty"), and § 103 ("unobviousness").

5. In *Diamond v. Chakrabarty,* 447 U.S. 303, 100 S.Ct. 2204, 65 L. Ed.2d 144 (1980), the Supreme Court, in a split decision, upheld the patentability of living organisms. The rationale underlying this decision seems to be totally contra to that in the *Benson* decision, with the Court emphasizing that the patent system, by its very nature, was intended to cover new innovations. "The Committee Reports accompanying the 1952 Act inform us that Congress intended statutory subject matter to 'include anything under the sun that is made by man.' ...." Query: can this decision be reconciled with that in *Benson?*

6. In *Diamond v. Diehr,* below, the Supreme Court opened the door to a way around *Benson.*

DIAMOND v. DIEHR

Supreme Court of the United States, 1981.
450 U.S. 175, 101 S.Ct. 1048, 67 L.Ed.2d 155.

JUSTICE REHNQUIST delivered the opinion of the Court.

We granted certiorari to determine whether a process for curing synthetic rubber which includes in several of its steps the use of a mathematical formula and a programmed digital computer is patentable subject matter under 35 U.S.C. § 101.

I

The patent application at issue was filed by the respondents on August 6, 1975. The claimed invention is a process for molding raw, uncured synthetic rubber into cured precision products. The process uses a mold for precisely shaping the uncured material under heat and pressure and then curing the synthetic rubber in the mold so that the product will retain its shape and be functionally operative after the molding is completed.[1]

Respondents claim that their process ensures the production of molded articles which are properly cured. Achieving the perfect cure depends upon several factors including the thickness of the article to be

---

1. A "cure" is obtained by mixing curing agents into the uncured polymer in advance of molding and then applying heat over a period of time. If the synthetic rubber is cured for the right length of time at the right temperature, it becomes a usable product.

molded, the temperature of the molding process, and the amount of time that the article is allowed to remain in the press. It is possible using well-known time, temperature, and cure relationships to calculate by means of the Arrhenius equation[2] when to open the press and remove the cured product. Nonetheless, according to the respondents, the industry has not been able to obtain uniformly accurate cures because the temperature of the molding press could not be precisely measured, thus making it difficult to do the necessary computations to determine cure time.[3] Because the temperature *inside* the press has heretofore been viewed as an uncontrollable variable, the conventional industry practice has been to calculate the cure time as the shortest time in which all parts of the product will definitely be cured, assuming a reasonable amount of mold-opening time during loading and unloading. But the shortcoming of this practice is that operating with an uncontrollable variable inevitably led in some instances to overestimating the mold-opening time and overcuring the rubber, and in other instances to underestimating that time and undercuring the product.

Respondents characterize their contribution to the art to reside in the process of constantly measuring the actual temperature inside the mold. These temperature measurements are then automatically fed into a computer which repeatedly recalculates the cure time by use of the Arrhenius equation. When the recalculated time equals the actual time that has elapsed since the press was closed, the computer signals a device to open the press. According to the respondents, the continuous measuring of the temperature inside the mold cavity, the feeding of this information to a digital computer which constantly recalculates the cure time, and the signaling by the computer to open the press, are all new in the art.

The patent examiner rejected the respondents' claims on the sole ground that they were drawn to nonstatutory subject matter under 35 U.S.C. § 101.[5] He determined that those steps in respondents' claims

2. The equation is named after its discoverer Svante Arrhenius and has long been used to calculate the cure time in rubber-molding presses. The equation can be expressed as follows:

$$\ln v = CZ + x$$

wherein ln v is the natural logarithm of v, the total required cure time; C is the activation constant, a unique figure for each batch of each compound being molded, determined in accordance with rheometer measurements of each batch; Z is the temperature in the mold; and x is a constant dependent on the geometry of the particular mold in the press. A rheometer is an instrument to measure flow of viscous substances.

3. During the time a press is open for loading, it will cool. The longer it is open, the cooler it becomes and the longer it takes to reheat the press to the desired temperature range. Thus, the time necessary to raise the mold temperature to curing temperature is an unpredictable variable. The respondents claim to have overcome this problem by continuously measuring the actual temperature in the closed press through the use of a thermocouple.

5. Respondents' application contained 11 different claims. Three examples are claims 1, 2, and 11 which provide:

"1. A method of operating a rubbermolding press for precision molded compounds with the aid of a digital computer, comprising:

"providing said computer with a data base for said press including at least,

"natural logarithm conversion data (ln),

that are carried out by a computer under control of a stored program constituted nonstatutory subject matter under this Court's decision in *Gottschalk v. Benson,* 409 U.S. 63, 93 S.Ct. 253, 34 L.Ed.2d 273 (1972). The remaining steps-installing rubber in the press and the subsequent closing of the press-were "conventional and necessary to the process and cannot be the basis of patentability." The examiner concluded that respondents' claims defined and sought protection of a computer program for operating a rubber-molding press.

The Patent and Trademark Office Board of Appeals agreed with the examiner, but the Court of Customs and Patent Appeals reversed. *In re Diehr,* 602 F.2d 982 (1979). The court noted that a claim drawn to subject matter otherwise statutory does not become nonstatutory because a computer is involved. The respondents' claims were not directed to a mathematical algorithm or an improved method of calculation but rather recited an improved process for molding rubber articles by solving a practical problem which had risen in the molding of rubber products.

The Commission of Patents and Trademarks sought certiorari arguing that the decision of the Court of Customs and Patent Appeals was inconsistent with prior decisions of this Court. Because of the importance of the question presented, we granted the writ. 445 U.S. 926 (1980).

II

Last Term in *Diamond v. Chakrabarty,* 447 U.S. 303, 100 S.Ct. 2204, 65 L.Ed.2d 144 (1980), this Court discussed the historical purposes of the patent laws and in particular 35 U.S.C. § 101. * * *

In cases of statutory construction, we begin with the language of the statute. Unless otherwise defined, "words will be interpreted as taking their ordinary, contemporary, common meaning," *Perrin v. United States,* 444 U.S. 37, 42 (1979), and, in dealing with the patent laws, we have more than once cautioned that "courts 'should not read into the patent laws limitations and conditions which the legislature has not

"the activation energy constant (C) unique to each batch of said compound being molded, and

"a constant (x) dependent upon the geometry of the particular mold of the press,

"initiating an interval timer in said computer upon the closure of the press for monitoring the elapsed time of said closure,

"constantly determining the temperature (Z) of the mold at a location closely adjacent to the mold cavity in the press during molding,

"constantly providing the computer with the temperature (Z),

"repetitively calculating in the computer, at frequent intervals during each cure, the Arrhenius equation for reaction time during the cure, which is

"$\ln v = CZ + x$

"where v is the total required cure time,

"repetitively comparing in the computer at said frequent intervals during the cure each said calculation of the total required cure time calculated with the Arrhenius equation and said elapsed time, and

"opening the press automatically when a said comparison indicates equivalence.

"2. The method of claim 1 including measuring the activation energy constant for the compound being molded in the press with a rheometer and automatically updating said data base within the computer in the event of changes in the compound being molded in said press as measured by said rheometer. * * * "

expressed.' " *Diamond v. Chakrabarty, supra,* at 308, 100 S.Ct., at 2207 quoting *United States v. Dubilier Condenser Corp.,* 289 U.S. 178, 199, 53 S.Ct. 554, 561, 77 L.Ed. 1114 (1933).

* * *

Analyzing respondents' claims according to the above statements from our cases, we think that a physical and chemical process for molding precision synthetic rubber products falls within the § 101 categories of possibly patentable subject matter. That respondents' claims involve the transformation of an article, in this case raw, uncured synthetic rubber, into a different state or thing cannot be disputed. The respondents' claims describe in detail a step-by-step method for accomplishing such, beginning with the loading of a mold with raw, uncured rubber and ending with the eventual opening of the press at the conclusion of the cure. Industrial processes such as this are the types which have historically been eligible to receive the protection of our patent laws.

III

Our conclusion regarding respondents' claims is not altered by the fact that in several steps of the process a mathematical equation and a programmed digital computer are used. This Court has undoubtedly recognized limits to § 101 and every discovery is not embraced within the statutory terms. Excluded from such patent protection are laws of nature, natural phenomena, and abstract ideas."An idea of itself is not patentable," *Rubber-Tip Pencil Co. v. Howard,* 20 Wall. 498 (1874). "A principle, in the abstract, is a fundamental truth; an original cause; a motive; these cannot be patented, as no one can claim in either of them an exclusive right." * * *

In *Benson,* we held unpatentable claims for an algorithm used to convert binary code decimal numbers to equivalent pure binary numbers. The sole practical application of the algorithm was in connection with the programming of a general purpose digital computer. We defined "algorithm" as a "procedure for solving a given type of mathematical problem," and we concluded that such an algorithm, or mathematical formula, is like a law of nature, which cannot be the subject of a patent.[9] *Parker v. Flook, supra,* presented a similar situation. The claims were

---

9. The term "algorithm" is subject to a variety of definitions. The petitioner defines the term to mean:

" '1. A fixed step-by-step procedure for accomplishing a given result; usually a simplified procedure for solving a complex problem, also a full statement of a finite number of steps. 2. A defined process or set of rules that leads [sic] and assures development of a desired output from a given input. A sequence of formulas and/or algebraic/logical steps to calculate or determine a given task; processing rules.' " Brief for Petitioner in *Diamond v. Bradley,* O.T.1980,

No. 79–855, p. 6, n. 12, quoting C. Sippl & R. Sippl, Computer Dictionary and Handbook 23 (2d ed 1972).

This definition is significantly broader than the definition this Court employed in *Benson* or *Flook.* Our previous decisions regarding the patentability of "algorithms" are necessarily limited to the more narrow definition employed by the Court, and we do not pass judgment on whether processes falling outside the definition previously used by this Court, but within the definition offered by the petitioner, would be patentable subject matter.

drawn to a method for computing an "alarm limit." An "alarm limit" is simply a number and the Court concluded that the application sought to protect a formula for computing this number. Using this formula, the updated alarm limit could be calculated if several other variables were known. The application, however, did not purport to explain how these other variables were to be determined, nor did it purport "to contain any disclosure relating to the chemical processes at work, the monitoring of process variables, or the means of setting off an alarm or adjusting an alarm system. All that it provides is a formula for computing an updated alarm limit." 437 U.S., at 586.

In contrast, the respondents here do not seek to patent a mathematical formula. Instead, they seek patent protection for a process of curing synthetic rubber. Their process admittedly employs a well-known mathematical equation, but they do not seek to pre-empt the use of that equation. Rather, they seek only to foreclose from others the use of that equation in conjunction with all of the other steps in their claimed process. These include installing rubber in a press, closing the mold, constantly determining the temperature of the mold, constantly recalculating the appropriate cure time through the use of the formula and a digital computer, and automatically opening the press at the proper time. Obviously, one does not need a "computer" to cure natural or synthetic rubber, but if the computer use incorporated in the process patent significantly lessens the possibility of "overcuring" or "undercuring," the process as a whole does not thereby become unpatentable subject matter.

Our earlier opinions lend support to our present conclusion that a claim drawn to subject matter otherwise statutory does not become nonstatutory simply because it uses a mathematical formula, computer program, or digital computer. In *Gottschalk v. Benson,* we noted: "It is said that the decision precludes a patent for any program servicing a computer. We do not so hold." 409 U.S., at 71. Similarly, in *Parker v. Flook,* we stated that "a process is not unpatentable simply because it contains a law of nature or a mathematical algorithm." 437 U.S., at 590. It is now commonplace that an *application* of a law of nature or mathematical formula to a known structure or process may well be deserving of patent protection. As Justice Stone explained four decades ago:

> "While a scientific truth, or the mathematical expression of it, is not a patentable invention, a novel and useful structure created with the aid of knowledge of scientific truth may be." *Mackay Radio & Telegraph Co. v. Radio of America,* 306 U.S. 86, 94 (1939).[11]

---

11. We noted in *Funk Bros. Seed Co. v. Kalo Inoculant Co.,* 333 U.S. 127, 130 (1948):

"He who discovers a hitherto unknown phenomenon of nature has no claim to a monopoly of it which the law recognizes. If there is to be invention from such a discovery, it must come from the application of the law of nature to a new and useful end."

Although we were dealing with a "product" claim in *Funk Bros.,* the same principle applies to a process claim. *Gottschalk v. Benson,* 409 U.S. 63, 68 (1972).

We think this statement in *Mackay* takes us a long way toward the correct answer in this case. Arrhenius' equation is not patentable in isolation, but when a process for curing rubber is devised which incorporates in it a more efficient solution of the equation, that process is at the very least not barred at the threshold by § 101.

In determining the eligibility of respondents' claimed process for patent protection under § 101, their claims must be considered as a whole. It is inappropriate to dissect the claims into old and new elements and then to ignore the presence of the old elements in the analysis. This is particularly true in a process claim because a new combination of steps in a process may be patentable even though all the constituents of the combination were well known and in common use before the combination was made. The "novelty" of any element or steps in a process, or even of the process itself, is of no relevance in determining whether the subject matter of a claim falls within the § 101 categories of possibly patentable subject matter.

It has been urged that novelty is an appropriate consideration under § 101. Presumably, this argument results from the language in § 101 referring to any "new and useful" process, machine, etc. Section 101, however, is a general statement of the type of subject matter that is eligible for patent protection "subject to the conditions and requirements of this title." Specific conditions for patentability follow and § 102 covers in detail the conditions relating to novelty. The question therefore of whether a particular invention is novel is "wholly apart from whether the invention falls into a category of statutory subject matter." *In re Bergy,* 596 F.2d 952, 961 (C.C.P.A., 1979) (emphasis deleted). See also *Nickola v. Peterson,* 580 F.2d 898 (C.A.6 1978). The legislative history of the 1952 Patent Act is in accord with this reasoning. * * *

* * *

In this case, it may later be determined that the respondents' process is not deserving of patent protection because it fails to satisfy the statutory conditions of novelty under § 102 or nonobviousness under § 103. A rejection on either of these grounds does not affect the determination that respondents' claims recited subject matter which was eligible for patent protection under § 101.

IV

We have before us today only the question of whether respondents' claims fall within the § 101 categories of possibly patentable subject matter. We view respondents' claims as nothing more than a process for molding rubber products and not as an attempt to patent a mathematical formula. We recognize, of course, that when a claim recites a mathematical formula (or scientific principle or phenomenon of nature), an inquiry must be made into whether the claim is seeking patent protection for that formula in the abstract. A mathematical formula as such is not accorded the protection of our patent laws, *Gottschalk v. Benson,* 409 U.S. 63, 93 S.Ct. 253, 34 L.Ed.2d 273 (1972), and this principle cannot be circumvented by attempting to limit the use of the formula to a particular technological environment. *Parker v. Flook,* 437 U.S. 584, 98 S.Ct. 2522, 57 L.Ed.2d 451 (1978). Similarly, insignificant post-solution activity will not transform an unpatentable principle into a patentable process. *Ibid. To* hold otherwise would allow a competent draftsman to evade the recognized limitations on the type of subject matter eligible for patent protection. On the other hand, when a claim containing a mathematical formula implements or applies that formula in a structure or process which, when considered as a whole, is performing a function which the patent laws were designed to protect (*e.g.,* transforming or reducing an article to a different state or thing), then the claim satisfies the requirements of § 101. Because we do not view respondents' claims as an attempt to patent a mathematical formula, but rather to be drawn to an industrial process for the molding of rubber products, we affirm the judgment of the Court of Customs and Patent Appeals.

It is so ordered.

JUSTICE STEVENS, with whom JUSTICE BRENNAN, JUSTICE MARSHALL, and JUSTICE BLACKMUN join, dissenting.

* * *

Notes

1.   Following the *Diehr* decision, the PTO began to accept and to issue patents on computer programs again. But the PTO construed *Diehr* narrowly. The Court of Customs and Patent Appeals produced what was later called the "Freeman–Walter–Abele" test of the patentability of a computer program: "First, the claim is analyzed to determine whether a mathematical algorithm is directly or indirectly recited. Next, if a mathematical algorithm is found, the claim as a whole is further analyzed to determine whether the algorithm is 'applied in any manner to physical elements or process steps,' and, if it is, it 'passes muster under § 101.' " *In re Pardo,* 684 F.2d 912, 915 (C.C.P.A. 1982). A claim is patentable if the mathematical algorithm is applied to physical elements or process steps, "provided that its application is circumscribed by more than a field of use limitation or non-essential post-solution activity." *In re Abele,* 684 F.2d 902, 907 (C.C.P.A. 1982). Recent decisions of the Court of Appeals for the Federal Circuit (set forth below) have found this test to be too restrictive, and have departed from it.

Clearly *Diamond v. Diehr* involved some unacknowledged backtracking by the Supreme Court from the anti-software patent positions in *Benson* and *Flook.* But how far had it backtracked? This was left for the Federal Circuit to decide 13 years later.

IN RE ALAPPAT

United States Court of Appeals, Federal Circuit, 1994.
33 F.3d 1526.

RICH, CIRCUIT JUDGE, with whom:

as to Part I (Jurisdiction): PAULINE NEWMAN, LOURIE and RADER, CIRCUIT JUDGES, join; ARCHER, CHIEF JUDGE, NIES and PLAGER, CIRCUIT JUDGES, concur in conclusion; and MAYER, MICHEL, CLEVENGER and SCHALL, CIRCUIT JUDGES, dissent; and

as to Part II (Merits): PAULINE NEWMAN, LOURIE, MICHEL, PLAGER, and RADER, CIRCUIT JUDGES, join; ARCHER, CHIEF JUDGE, and NIES, CIRCUIT JUDGE, dissent; and MAYER, CLEVENGER and SCHALL, CIRCUIT JUDGES, take no position.

Kuriappan P. Alapatt, Edward E. Averill, and James G. Larsen (collectively Alappat) appeal the April 22, 1992, reconsideration decision of the Board of Patent Appeals and Interferences (Board) of the United States Patent and Trademark Office (PTO), *Ex Parte Alappat*, 23 USPQ2d 1340, 1992 WL 176684 (BPAI, 1992), which sustained the Examiner's rejection of claims 15–19 of application Serial No. 07/149,792 ('792 application) as being unpatentable under 35 U.S.C. § 101 (1988).

I. JURISDICTION

* * * [The Court found that it had jurisdiction.—Eds.]

II. THE MERITS

Our conclusion is that the appealed decision should be reversed because the appealed claims are directed to a "machine" which is one of the categories named in 35 U.S.C. § 101, as the first panel of the Board held.

A. *Alappat's Invention*

Alappat's invention relates generally to a means for creating a smooth waveform display in a digital oscilloscope. The screen of an oscilloscope is the front of a cathode-ray tube (CRT), which is like a TV picture tube, whose screen, when in operation, presents an array (or raster) of pixels arranged at intersections of vertical columns and horizontal rows, a pixel being a spot on the screen which may be illuminated by directing an electron beam to that spot, as in TV. Each column in the array represents a different time period, and each row represents a different magnitude. An input signal to the oscilloscope is sampled and digitized to provide a waveform data sequence (vector list), wherein each successive element of the sequence represents the magnitude of the waveform at a successively later time. The waveform data sequence is then processed to provide a bit map, which is a stored data array indicating which pixels are to be illuminated. The waveform ultimately displayed is formed by a group of vectors, wherein each vector has a straight line trajectory between two points on the screen at elevations representing the magnitudes of two successive input signal samples and at horizontal positions representing the timing of the two samples.

Because a CRT screen contains a finite number of pixels, rapidly rising and falling portions of a waveform can appear discontinuous or jagged due to differences in the elevation of horizontally contiguous pixels included in the waveform. In addition, the presence of "noise" in an input signal can cause portions of the waveform to oscillate between contiguous pixel rows when the magnitude of the input signal lies between values represented by the elevations of the two rows. Moreover, the vertical resolution of the display may be limited by the number of rows of pixels on the screen. The noticeability and appearance of these effects is known as *aliasing*.

To overcome these effects, *Alappat's invention employs an anti-aliasing system* wherein each vector making up the waveform is represented by modulating the illumination intensity of pixels having center points bounding the trajectory of the vector. The intensity at which each of the pixels is illuminated depends upon the distance of the center point of each pixel from the trajectory of the vector. Pixels lying squarely on the waveform trace receive maximum illumination, whereas pixels lying along an edge of the trace receive illumination decreasing in intensity proportional to the increase in the distance of the center point of the pixel from the vector trajectory. Employing this *anti-aliasing* technique eliminates any apparent discontinuity, jaggedness, or oscillation in the waveform, *thus giving the visual appearance of a smooth continuous waveform*. In short, and in lay terms, the invention is an improvement in an oscilloscope comparable to a TV having a clearer picture.

* * *

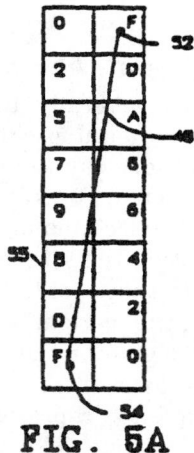

FIG. 5A

[The numbers "52," "54", and "55" referred to below are reference numbers used to label "pixels," or "picture elements," in Figure 5A (above) of the Alappat patent drawings. In this Figure, the "trace" drawn upon the oscilloscope's screen slopes steeply and crosses seven horizontal rows of pixels for every vertical column of pixels that it crosses. The trace passes through the precise centers of the two pixels 52 and 54 which occupy adjacent columns but which occupy rows that are separated by six rows. These two pixels are called "observation points," and since they fall right on the trace, they are illuminated to the full brightness value of "F" (hexadecimal), which is "15" (decimal). The trace does not pass through the precise centers of the twelve pixels that occupy the same two columns as the pixels 52 and 54 and that occupy the six rows which separate the two pixels 52 and 54. These twelve pixels must be dimmed. The pixel 55, one of these twelve intervening pixels, lies in the same column with pixel 54 and is spaced vertically two pixels away from pixel 54. Alappat teaches that the brightness of the pixel 55 must be reduced in proportion to the pixel's distance from the trace. Alappat's equation, set forth below, achieves this result by dimming each pixel's brightness in proportion to how far away (vertically) the pixel is from the "observation point" pixel in the same column, and by forcing the pixel's brightness to go to zero as the pixel's (vertical) position nears the (vertical) position of the "observation point" pixel in an adjoining column. Since the pixel 55 is spaced (vertically) 2/7ths of the way from the "same column" pixel 54 to the "adjacent column" pixel 52, it is dimmed to 2/7ths of the brightness "F" of the pixels 52 and 54.—Eds.]

* * *

The intensity at which each pixel is to be illuminated is determined as follows, using pixel 55 as an example First, the vertical distance between the y coordinates of observation points 54 and 52 (Δy_i) is determined. In this example, this difference equals 7 units, with one unit representing the center-to-center distance of adjacent pixels. Then, the elevation of pixel 55 above pixel 54 ($\Delta y_{i,j}$) is determined, which in this case is 2 units. The Δy_i and $\Delta y_{i,j}$ values are then "normalized," which Alappat describes as converting these values to larger values which are easier to use in mathematical calculations. In Alappat's example, a barrel shifter is used to shift the binary input to the left by the number of bits required to set the most significant (leftmost) bit of its output signal to "1." The Δy_i and $\Delta y_{i,j}$ values are then plugged into a mathematical equation for determining the intensity at which the particular pixel is to be illuminated. In this particular example, the equation $I'(i, j) = [1-(\Delta y_{i,j}/\Delta y_i)]$ F, wherein F is 15 in hexadecimal notation, suffices. The intensity of pixel 55 in this example would thus be calculated as follows:

$$[1 - (\tfrac{2}{7})]15 = (\tfrac{5}{7})15 = 10.71 \sim 11 \text{ (or B)}.$$

Accordingly, pixel 55 is illuminated at $^{11}/_{15}$ of the intensity of the pixels in which observation points 54 and 52 lie. Alappat discloses that the particular formula used will vary depending on the shape of the waveform.

B.   The Rejected Claims

Claim 15, the only independent claim in issue, reads:

A rasterizer for converting vector list data representing sample magnitudes of an input waveform into anti-aliased pixel illumination intensity data to be displayed on a display means comprising:

(a) means for determining the vertical distance between the endpoints of each of the vectors in the data list;

(b) means for determining the elevation of a row of pixels that is spanned by the vector;

(c) means for normalizing the vertical distance and elevation; and

(d) means for outputting illumination intensity data as a predetermined function of the normalized vertical distance and elevation.

Each of claims 16–19 depends directly from claim 15 and more specifically defines an element of the rasterizer claimed therein. Claim 16 recites that means (a) for determining the vertical distance between the endpoints of each of the vectors in the data list, Δy_i, comprises *an arithmetic logic circuit* configured to perform an absolute value function. Claim 17 recites that means (b) for determining the elevation of a row of pixels that is spanned by the vector, $\Delta y_{i,j}$ described above, comprises *an arithmetic logic circuit* configured to perform an absolute value function. Claim 18 recites that means (c) for normalizing the vertical distance and elevation comprises *a pair of barrel shifters*. Finally, claim 19 recites that means (d) for outputting comprises *a read only memory (ROM)* containing illumination intensity data. As the first Board panel found, each of (a)-(d) was a *device* known in the electronics arts before Alappat made his invention.

C.   The Examiner's Rejection and Board Reviews

The Examiner's final rejection of claims 15–19 was under 35 U.S.C. § 101 "because the claimed invention is non statutory subject matter," and the original three-member Board panel reversed this rejection. That Board panel held that, although claim 15 *recites* a mathematical algorithm, *the claim as a whole is directed to a machine* and thus to statutory subject matter named in § 101. In reaching this decision, the original panel construed the means clauses in claim 15 pursuant to 35 U.S.C. § 112, paragraph six (§ 112 ¶ 6), as corresponding to the respective structures disclosed in the specification of Alappat's application, and equivalents thereof.

In its reconsideration decision, the five-member majority of the expanded, eight-member Board panel "modified" the decision of the original panel and affirmed the Examiner's § 101 rejection. [*Ex Parte Alappat*, 23 USPQ2d 1340, 1992 WL 176684 (BPAI, 1992)] The majority *held that the PTO need not apply § 112 ¶ 6 in rendering patentability determinations*, characterizing this court's statements to the contrary in *In re Iwahashi*, 888 F.2d 1370, 1375(Fed.Cir.1989), "as dicta," and dismissing this court's discussion of § 112 ¶ 6 in *Arrhythmia Research Technology, Inc. v. Corazonix Corp.*, 958 F.2d 1053, 1060 (Fed.Cir.1992) on the basis that the rules of claim construction in infringement actions differ from the rules for claim interpretation during prosecution in the PTO. The majority stated that, during examination, the PTO gives means-plus-function clauses in claims their broadest interpretation and does not impute limitations from the specification into the claims. *See Applicability of the Last Paragraph of 35 USC § 112 to Patentability Determinations Before the Patent and Trademark Office*, 1134 TMOG 633 (1992); *Notice Interpreting In Re Iwahashi* (Fed.Cir.1989), 1112 OG 16 (1990). Accordingly, the majority held that each of the means recited in claim 15 reads on any and every means for performing the particular function recited.

The majority further held that, because claim 15 is written completely in "means for" language and because these means clauses are read broadly in the PTO to encompass each and every means for performing the recited functions, claim 15 amounts to nothing more than a process claim wherein each means clause represents only a step in that process. The majority stated that each of the steps in this postulated process claim recites a mathematical operation, which steps combine to form a "mathematical algorithm for computing pixel information," *Alappat*, 23 USPQ2d at 1345, and that, "when the claim is viewed without the steps of this mathematical algorithm, no other elements or steps are found." *Alappat*, 23 USPQ2d at 1346. The majority thus concluded that the claim was directed to nonstatutory subject matter.

In its analysis, the majority further stated:

> It is further significant that claim 15, as drafted, reads on a digital computer "means" to perform the various steps under program control. In such a case, it is proper to treat the claim as if drawn to a method. We will not presume that a stored program digital computer is not within the § 112 ¶ 6 range of equivalents of the structure disclosed in the specification. The disclosed ALU, ROM and shift registers are all common elements of stored program digital computers. Even if appellants were willing to admit that a stored program digital computer were not within the range of equivalents, § 112 ¶ 2 requires that this be clearly apparent from the claims based upon limitations recited in the claims.

Alappat, 23 USPQ2d at 1345. The Board majority also stated that dependent claims 16–19 were not before them for consideration because they had not been argued by Alappat and thus not addressed by the Examiner or the original three-member Board panel. *Alappat*, 23 USPQ2d at 1341 n. 1.

D. Analysis

(1) *Section 112, Paragraph Six*

As recently explained in *In re Donaldson*, 16 F.3d 1189, 1193 (Fed.Cir.1994), *the PTO is not exempt* from following the statutory mandate of § 112 ¶ 6, which reads:

> An element in a claim for a combination may be expressed as *a means* or step for performing a specified function without the recital of structure, material, or acts in support thereof, and such claim *shall be construed* to cover the corresponding structure, material, or acts described in the specification and equivalents thereof.

35 U.S.C. § 112, paragraph 6 (1988) (emphasis added). The Board majority therefore erred as a matter of law in refusing to apply § 112 ¶ 6 in rendering its § 101 patentable subject matter determination.

Given Alappat's disclosure, it was error for the Board majority to interpret each of the means clauses in claim 15 so broadly as to "read on any and every means for performing the functions" recited, as it said it was doing, and then to conclude that claim 15 is nothing more than a process claim wherein each means clause represents a step in that process. Contrary to suggestions by the Commissioner, this court's precedents do not support the Board's view that the particular apparatus claims at issue in this case may be viewed as nothing more than process claims. The cases relied upon by the Commissioner, namely, *In re Abele*, 684 F.2d 902 (C.C.P.A. 1982), *In re Pardo*, 684 F.2d 912, 214 USPQ 673 (C.C.P.A. 1982), *In re Meyer*, 688 F.2d 789, 215 USPQ 193 (C.C.P.A. 1982), *In re Walter*, 618 F.2d 758, 205 USPQ 397 (C.C.P.A. 1980), and *In re Maucorps*, 609 F.2d 481, 203 USPQ 812 (C.C.P.A. 1979), differ from the instant case. In *Abele*, *Pardo*, and *Walter*, given the apparent lack of any supporting structure in the specification corresponding to the claimed "means" elements, the court reasonably concluded that the claims at issue were in effect nothing more than process claims in the guise of apparatus claims. This is clearly not the case now before us. As to *Maucorps* and *Meyer*, despite suggestions therein to the contrary, the claimed means-plus-function elements at issue in those cases were not construed as limited to those means disclosed in the specification and equivalents thereof. As reaffirmed in *Donaldson*, such claim construction is improper, and therefore, those cases are of limited value in dealing with the issue presently before us. We further note that *Maucorps* dealt with a business methodology for deciding how salesmen should best handle respective customers and *Meyer* involved a "system" for aiding a neurologist in diagnosing patients. Clearly, neither of the alleged "inventions" in those cases falls within any § 101 category.

When independent claim 15 is construed in accordance with § 112 ¶ 6, claim 15 reads as follows, the subject matter in brackets representing the structure which Alappat discloses in his specification as corresponding to the respective means language recited in the claims:

A rasterizer [a "machine"] for converting vector list data representing sample magnitudes of an input waveform into anti-aliased pixel illumination intensity data to be displayed on a display means comprising:

(a) [an arithmetic logic *circuit* configured to perform an absolute value function, or an equivalent thereof] for determining the vertical distance between the endpoints of each of the vectors in the data list;

(b) [an arithmetic logic *circuit* configured to perform an absolute value function, or an equivalent thereof] for determining the elevation of a row of pixels that is spanned by the vector;

(c) [a pair of *barrel shifters*, or equivalents thereof] for normalizing the vertical distance and elevation; and

(d) [a *read only memory (ROM)* containing illumination intensity data, or an equivalent thereof] for outputting illumination intensity data as a predetermined function of the normalized vertical distance and elevation.

As is evident, claim 15 unquestionably recites a machine, or apparatus, made up of a combination of known electronic circuitry elements.

Despite suggestions by the Commissioner to the contrary, each of dependent claims 16–19 serves to *further limit* claim 15. Section 112 ¶ 6 requires that each of the means recited in independent claim 15 be construed to cover at least the structure disclosed in the specification corresponding to the "means." Each of dependent claims 16–19 is in fact limited to one of the structures disclosed in the specification.

(2) *Section 101*

The reconsideration Board majority affirmed the Examiner's rejection of claims 15–19 on the basis that these claims are not directed to statutory subject matter as defined in § 101, which reads:

Whoever invents or discovers any new and useful process, *machine*, manufacture, or composition of matter, or any new and useful improvement thereof, may obtain a patent therefor, subject to the conditions and requirements of this title. [Emphasis ours.]

As discussed in section II.D.(1), supra, claim 15, properly construed, claims a machine, namely, a rasterizer "for converting vector list data representing sample magnitudes of an input waveform into anti-aliased pixel illumination intensity data to be displayed on a display means," which machine is made up of, at the very least, the specific structures disclosed in Alappat's specification corresponding to the means-plus-function elements (a)-(d) recited in the claim. According to Alappat, the claimed rasterizer performs the same overall function as prior art rasterizers, but does so in a different way, which is represented by the combination of four elements claimed in means-plus-function terminology. Because claim 15 is directed to a "machine," which is one of the four categories of patentable subject matter enumerated in § 101, claim 15 appears on its face to be directed to § 101 subject matter.

This does not quite end the analysis, however, because the Board majority argues that the claimed subject matter falls within a judicially created exception to § 101 which the majority refers to as the "mathematical algorithm" exception. Although the PTO has failed to support the premise that the "mathematical algorithm" exception applies to true apparatus claims, we recognize that our own precedent suggests that this may be the case. *See In re Johnson*, 589 F.2d 1070, 1077, 200 USPQ 199, 206 (C.C.P.A. 1978) ("*Benson* [referring to *Gottschalk v. Benson*, 409 U.S. 63, 93 S.Ct. 253, 34 L.Ed.2d 273 (1972)] applies equally whether an invention is claimed as an apparatus or process, because the form of the claim is often an exercise in drafting."). Even if the mathematical subject matter exception to § 101 does apply to true apparatus claims, the claimed subject matter in this case does not fall within that exception.

(a)

The plain and unambiguous meaning of § 101 is that any new and useful process, machine, manufacture, or composition of matter, or any new and useful improvement thereof, may be patented if it meets the requirements for patentability set forth in Title 35, such as those found in §§ 102, 103, and 112. The use of the expansive term "any" in § 101 represents Congress's intent not to place any restrictions on the subject matter for which a patent may be obtained beyond those specifically recited in § 101 and the other parts of Title 35. Indeed, the Supreme Court has acknowledged that Congress intended § 101 to extend to "anything under the sun that is made by man." *Diamond v. Chakrabarty*, 447 U.S. 303, 309, 100 S.Ct. 2204, 2208, 65 L.Ed.2d 144 (1980), *quoting* S.Rep. No. 1979, 82nd Cong., 2nd Sess., 5 (1952); H.R.Rep. No. 1923, 82nd Cong., 2nd Sess., 6 (1952). Thus, it is improper to read into § 101 limitations as to the subject matter that may be patented where the legislative history does not indicate that Congress clearly intended such limitations. *See Chakrabarty*, 447 U.S. at 308, 100 S.Ct. at 2207 ("We have also cautioned that courts 'should not read into the patent laws limitations and conditions which the legislature has not expressed.' "), *quoting United States v. Dubilier Condenser Corp.*, 289 U.S. 178, 199, 53 S.Ct. 554, 561, 77 L.Ed. 1114 (1933).

Despite the apparent sweep of § 101, the Supreme Court has held that certain categories of subject matter are not entitled to patent protection. In *Diamond v. Diehr*, 450 U.S. 175, 101 S.Ct. 1048, 67 L.Ed.2d 155 (1981), its most recent case addressing § 101, the Supreme Court explained that there are three categories of subject matter for which one may not obtain patent protection, namely "laws of nature, natural phenomena, and abstract ideas." *Diehr*, 450 U.S. at 185, 101 S.Ct. at 1056. Of relevance to this case, the Supreme Court also has held that certain mathematical subject matter is not, standing alone, entitled to patent protection. *See Diehr*, 450 U.S. 175, 101 S.Ct. 1048; *Parker v. Flook*, 437 U.S. 584, 98 S.Ct. 2522, 57 L.Ed.2d 451; *Gottschalk v. Benson*, 409 U.S. 63, 93 S.Ct. 253, 34 L.Ed.2d 273. A close analysis of *Diehr*, *Flook*, and *Benson* reveals that the Supreme Court never intended to create an overly broad, fourth category of subject matter excluded from § 101. Rather, at the core of the Court's analysis in each of these cases lies an attempt by the Court to explain a rather straightforward concept, namely, that certain types of mathematical subject matter, standing alone, represent nothing more than *abstract ideas* until reduced to some type of practical application, and thus that subject matter is not, in and of itself, entitled to patent protection.

Diehr also demands that the focus in any statutory subject matter analysis be on *the claim as a whole*. Indeed, the Supreme Court stated in *Diehr*:

[W]hen a claim containing a mathematical formula [, mathematical equation, mathematical algorithm, or the like,] implements or applies that formula [, equation, algorithm, or the like,] in a structure or process which, when considered as a whole, is performing a function which the patent laws were designed to protect (e.g., transforming or reducing an article to a different state or thing), then the claim satisfies the requirements of § 101.

Diehr, 450 U.S. at 192, 101 S.Ct. at 1059–60 (emphasis added). *In re Iwahashi*, 888 F.2d at 1375, 12 USPQ2d at 1911; *In re Taner*, 681 F.2d 787, 789, 214 USPQ 678, 680 (C.C.P.A. 1982). It is thus not necessary to determine whether a claim contains, as merely a part of the whole, any mathematical subject matter which standing alone would not be entitled to patent protection. Indeed, because the dispositive inquiry is whether the claim *as a whole* is directed to statutory subject matter, it is irrelevant that a claim may contain, as part of the whole, subject matter which would not be patentable by itself. "A claim drawn to subject matter otherwise statutory does not become nonstatutory simply because it uses a mathematical formula, [mathematical equation, mathematical algorithm,] computer program or digital computer." *Diehr*, 450 U.S. at 187, 101 S.Ct. at 1057.

(b)

Given the foregoing, the proper inquiry in dealing with the so called mathematical subject matter exception to § 101 alleged herein is to see whether the claimed subject matter *as a whole* is a disembodied mathematical concept, whether categorized as a mathematical formula, mathematical equation, mathematical algorithm, or the like, which in essence represents nothing more than a "law of nature," "natural phenomenon," or "abstract idea." If so, *Diehr* precludes the patenting of that subject matter. That is not the case here.

Although many, or arguably even all, of the means elements recited in claim 15 represent circuitry elements that perform mathematical calculations, which is essentially true of all digital electrical circuits, the claimed invention as a whole is directed to a combination of interrelated elements which combine to form a machine for converting discrete waveform data samples into anti-aliased pixel illumination intensity data to be displayed on a display means. This is not a disembodied mathematical concept which may be characterized as an "abstract idea," but rather a specific machine to produce a useful, concrete, and tangible result.

The fact that the four claimed means elements function to transform one set of data to another through what may be viewed as a series of mathematical calculations does not alone justify a holding that the claim as a whole is directed to nonstatutory subject matter. *See In re Iwahashi*, 888 F.2d at 1375, 12 USPQ2d at 1911. Indeed, claim 15 as written is not "so abstract and sweeping" that it would "wholly preempt" the use of any apparatus employing the combination of mathematical calculations recited therein. *See Benson*, 409 U.S. at 68–72, 93

S.Ct. at 255–58 (1972). Rather, claim 15 is limited to the use of a particularly claimed combination of elements performing the particularly claimed combination of calculations to transform, i.e., rasterize, digitized waveforms (data) into anti-aliased, pixel illumination data to produce a smooth waveform.

Furthermore, the claim preamble's recitation that the subject matter for which Alappat seeks patent protection is a rasterizer for creating a smooth waveform is not a mere field-of-use label having no significance. Indeed, the preamble specifically recites that the claimed rasterizer converts waveform data into output illumination data for a display, and the means elements recited in the body of the claim make reference not only to the inputted waveform data recited in the preamble but also to the output illumination data also recited in the preamble. Claim 15 thus defines a combination of elements constituting a machine for producing an anti-aliased waveform.

The reconsideration Board majority also erred in its reasoning that claim 15 is unpatentable merely because it "reads on a general purpose digital computer 'means' to perform the various steps under program control." *Alappat*, 23 USPQ2d at 1345. The Board majority stated that it would "not presume that a stored program digital computer is not within the § 112 ¶ 6 range of equivalents of the structure disclosed in the specification." *Alappat*, 23 USPQ2d at 1345. Alappat admits that claim 15 would read on a general purpose computer programmed to carry out the claimed invention, but argues that this alone also does not justify holding claim 15 unpatentable as directed to nonstatutory subject matter. We agree. We have held that such programming creates a new machine, because a general purpose computer in effect becomes a special purpose computer once it is programmed to perform particular functions pursuant to instructions from program software. *In re Freeman*, 573 F.2d 1237, 1247 n. 11, 197 USPQ 464, 472 n. 11 (C.C.P.A. 1978); *In re Noll*, 545 F.2d 141, 148, 191 USPQ 721, 726 (C.C.P.A. 1976); *In re Prater*, 415 F.2d at 1403 n. 29, 162 USPQ at 549–50 n. 29.

Under the Board majority's reasoning, a programmed general purpose computer could never be viewed as patentable subject matter under § 101. This reasoning is without basis in the law. The Supreme Court has never held that a programmed computer may never be entitled to patent protection. Indeed, the *Benson* court specifically stated that its decision therein did not preclude "a patent for any program servicing a computer." *Benson*, 409 U.S. at 71, 93 S.Ct. at 257. Consequently, a computer operating pursuant to software *may* represent patentable subject matter, provided, of course, that the claimed subject matter meets all of the other requirements of Title 35. In any case, a computer, like a rasterizer, is apparatus not mathematics.

CONCLUSION

For the foregoing reasons, the appealed decision of the Board affirming the examiner's rejection is

REVERSED.

Notes

1.   Does Judge Rich successfully deal with the prior Supreme Court decisions on computer program patents? Does he successfully tie together the Supreme Court decisions of *Benson*, *Flook*, and *Diehr*?

2.   What is the importance of the "means for" claim language being tied to a specific structure in the specification? (See 35 U.S.C. § 112, 6th paragraph.)

3.   *Alappat* rules that a general purpose computer becomes a special purpose computer once it is programmed to perform particular functions pursuant to instructions from software. *Alappat* goes on to say that a special purpose computer fits into the machine category of statutory subject matter under § 101. Would the outcome of *Benson* be the same under this test?

4.   At about the same time that *Alappat* held an equation-based claim to be patentable, another Federal Circuit decision held some claims to be unpatentable. *See In re Warmerdam*, 33 F.3d 1354 (Fed.Cir.1994). But some data structures have been held to be patentable, since they do not fall into the unpatentable category of "printed matter." *In re Lowry*, 32 F.3d 1579 (Fed.Cir.1994).

5.   Prior to *Alappat*, the PTO had refused to follow the Federal Circuit's holdings in *Iwahashi* and in *ART* (cited in Alappat). Following *Alappat*, the PTO published *Guidelines for the Examination of Computer–Related Inventions*, 61 Fed. Reg. 7478 (1996) that recognized the patentability of a wide range of software-related inventions. The following chart on patentability under 35 U.S.C. § 101 is reproduced from those guidelines:

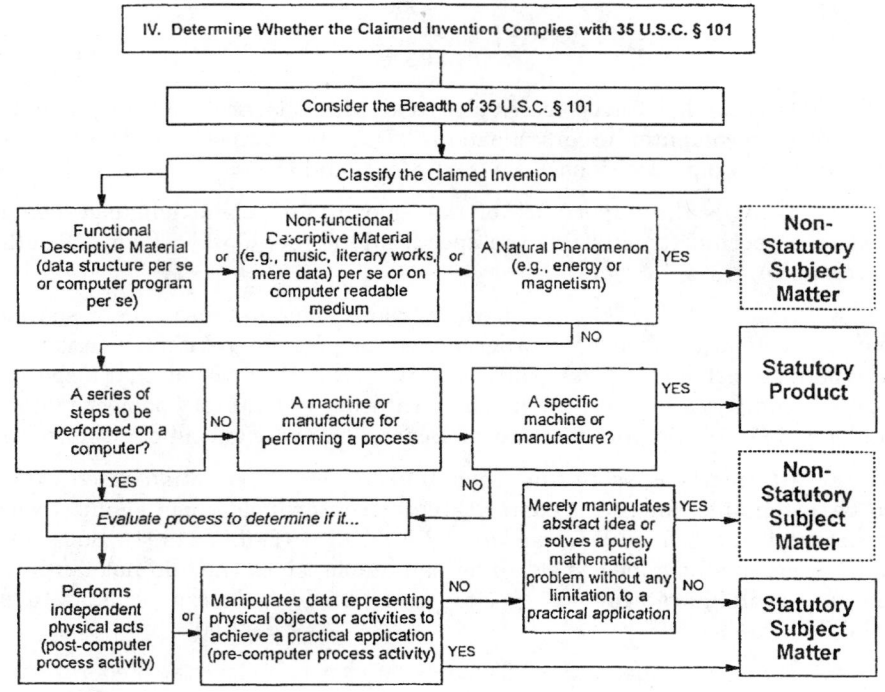

STATE STREET BANK & TRUST CO. v. SIGNATURE FINANCIAL GROUP, INC.

United States Court of Appeals, Federal Circuit, 1998.
149 F.3d 1368, *cert. denied*, 525 U.S. 1093, 119 S.Ct. 851, 142 L.Ed.2d 704 (1999).

RICH, CIRCUIT JUDGE.

Signature Financial Group, Inc. (Signature) appeals from the decision of the United States District Court for the District of Massachusetts granting a motion for summary judgment in favor of State Street Bank & Trust Co. (State Street), finding U.S. Patent No. 5,193,056 (the '056 patent) invalid on the ground that the claimed subject matter is not encompassed by 35 U.S.C. § 101 (1994). *See State Street Bank & Trust Co. v. Signature Financial Group, Inc.*, 927 F.Supp. 502, 38 USPQ2d 1530 (D.Mass.1996). We reverse and remand because we conclude that the patent claims are directed to statutory subject matter.

BACKGROUND

Signature is the assignee of the '056 patent which is entitled "Data Processing System for Hub and Spoke Financial Services Configuration." The '056 patent issued to Signature on 9 March 1993, naming R. Todd Boes as the inventor. The '056 patent is generally directed to a data processing system (the system) for implementing an investment structure which was developed for use in Signature's business as an administrator and accounting agent for mutual funds. In essence, the system, identified by the proprietary name Hub and Spoke®, facilitates a structure whereby mutual funds (Spokes) pool their assets in an investment portfolio (Hub) organized as a partnership. This investment configuration provides the administrator of a mutual fund with the advantageous combination of economies of scale in administering investments coupled with the tax advantages of a partnership.

State Street and Signature are both in the business of acting as custodians and accounting agents for multi-tiered partnership fund financial services. State Street negotiated with Signature for a license to use its patented data processing system described and claimed in the '056 patent. When negotiations broke down, State Street brought a declaratory judgment action asserting invalidity, unenforceability, and noninfringement in Massachusetts district court, and then filed a motion for partial summary judgment of patent invalidity for failure to claim statutory subject matter under § 101. The motion was granted and this appeal followed.

DISCUSSION

* * *

The following facts pertinent to the statutory subject matter issue are either undisputed or represent the version alleged by the nonmovant. The patented invention relates generally to a system that allows an administrator to monitor and record the financial information flow and make all calculations necessary for maintaining a partner fund financial services configuration. As previously mentioned, a partner fund financial services configuration essentially allows several mutual funds, or "Spokes," to pool their investment funds into a single portfolio, or "Hub," allowing for consolidation of, inter alia, the costs of administering the fund combined with the tax advantages of a partnership. In particular, this system provides means for a daily allocation of assets for two or more Spokes that are invested in the same Hub. The system determines the percentage share that each Spoke maintains in the Hub, while taking into consideration daily changes both in the value of the Hub's investment securities and in the concomitant amount of each Spoke's assets.

In determining daily changes, the system also allows for the allocation among the Spokes of the Hub's daily income, expenses, and net realized and unrealized gain or loss, calculating each day's total investments based on the concept of a book capital account. This enables the determination of a true asset value of each Spoke and accurate calculation of allocation ratios between or among the Spokes. The system additionally tracks all the relevant data determined on a daily basis for the Hub and each Spoke, so that aggregate year end income, expenses, and capital gain or loss can be determined for accounting and for tax purposes for the Hub and, as a result, for each publicly traded Spoke.

It is essential that these calculations are quickly and accurately performed. In large part this is required because each Spoke sells shares to the public and the price of those shares is substantially based on the Spoke's percentage interest in the portfolio. In some instances, a mutual fund administrator is required to calculate the value of the shares to the nearest penny within as little as an hour and a half after the market closes. Given the complexity of the calculations, a computer or equivalent device is a virtual necessity to perform the task.

The '056 patent application was filed 11 March 1991. It initially contained six "machine" claims, which incorporated means-plus-function clauses, and six method claims. According to Signature, during prosecution the examiner contemplated a § 101 rejection for failure to claim statutory subject matter. However, upon cancellation of the six method claims, the examiner issued a notice of allowance for the remaining present six claims on appeal. Only claim 1 is an independent claim.

The district court began its analysis by construing the claims to be directed to a process, with each "means" clause merely representing a step in that process. However, "machine" claims having "means" clauses may only be reasonably viewed as process claims if there is no supporting structure in the written description that corresponds to the claimed "means" elements. *See In re Alappat*, 33 F.3d 1526, 1540–41, 31 USPQ2d 1545, 1554 (Fed.Cir.1994) (*in banc*). This is not the case now before us.

When independent claim 1 is properly construed in accordance with § 112, ¶ 6, it is directed to a machine, as demonstrated below, where representative claim 1 is set forth, the subject matter in brackets stating the structure the written description discloses as corresponding to the respective "means" recited in the claims.

1. A data processing system for managing a financial services configuration of a portfolio established as a partnership, each partner being one of a plurality of funds, comprising:

(a) computer processor means [a personal computer including a CPU] for processing data;

(b) storage means [a data disk] for storing data on a storage medium;

(c) first means [an arithmetic logic circuit configured to prepare the data disk to magnetically store selected data] for initializing the storage medium;

(d) second means [an arithmetic logic circuit configured to retrieve information from a specific file, calculate incremental increases or decreases based on specific input, allocate the results on a percentage basis, and store the output in a separate file] for processing data regarding assets in the portfolio and each of the funds from a previous day and data regarding increases or decreases in each of the funds, [sic, funds'] assets and for allocating the percentage share that each fund holds in the portfolio;

(e) third means [an arithmetic logic circuit configured to retrieve information from a specific file, calculate incremental increases and decreases based on specific input, allocate the results on a percentage basis and store the output in a separate file] for processing data regarding daily incremental income, expenses, and net realized gain or loss for the portfolio and for allocating such data among each fund;

(f) fourth means [an arithmetic logic circuit configured to retrieve information from a specific file, calculate incremental increases and decreases based on specific input, allocate the results on a percentage basis and store the output in a separate file] for processing data regarding daily net unrealized gain or loss for the portfolio and for allocating such data among each fund; and

(g) fifth means [an arithmetic logic circuit configured to retrieve information from specific files, calculate that information on an aggregate basis and store the output in a separate file] for processing data regarding aggregate year-end income, expenses, and capital gain or loss for the portfolio and each of the funds.

Each claim component, recited as a "means" plus its function, is to be read, of course, pursuant to § 112, ¶ 6, as inclusive of the "equivalents" of the structures disclosed in the written description portion of the specification. Thus, claim 1, properly construed, claims a machine, namely, a data processing system for managing a financial services configuration of a portfolio established as a partnership, which machine is made up of, at the very least, the specific structures disclosed in the written description and corresponding to the means-plus-function elements (a)-(g) recited in the claim. A "machine" is proper statutory subject matter under § 101. We note that, for the purposes of a § 101 analysis, it is of little relevance whether claim 1 is directed to a "machine" or a "process," as long as it falls within at least one of the four enumerated categories of patentable subject matter, "machine" and "process" being such categories.

This does not end our analysis, however, because the court concluded that the claimed subject matter fell into one of two alternative judicially-created exceptions to statutory subject matter. The court refers to the first exception as the "mathematical algorithm" exception and the second exception as the "business method" exception. Section 101 reads:

Whoever invents or discovers any new and useful process, machine, manufacture, or composition of matter, or any new and useful improvement thereof, may obtain a patent therefor, subject to the conditions and requirements of this title.

The plain and unambiguous meaning of § 101 is that any invention falling within one of the four stated categories of statutory subject matter may be patented, provided it meets the other requirements for patentability set forth in Title 35, i.e., those found in §§ 102, 103, and 112, ¶ 2.

The repetitive use of the expansive term "any" in § 101 shows Congress's intent not to place any restrictions on the subject matter for which a patent may be obtained beyond those specifically recited in § 101. Indeed, the Supreme Court has acknowledged that Congress intended § 101 to extend to "anything under the sun that is made by man." *Diamond v. Chakrabarty*, 447 U.S. 303, 309, 100 S.Ct. 2204, 65 L.Ed.2d 144 (1980); *see also Diamond v. Diehr*, 450 U.S. 175, 182, 101 S.Ct. 1048, 67 L.Ed.2d 155 (1981). Thus, it is improper to read limitations into § 101 on the subject matter that may be patented where the legislative history indicates that Congress clearly did not intend such limitations. *See Chakrabarty*, 447 U.S. at 308, 100 S.Ct. 2204 ("We have also cautioned that courts 'should not read into the patent laws limitations and conditions which the legislature has not expressed.' "(citations omitted)).

The "Mathematical Algorithm" Exception

The Supreme Court has identified three categories of subject matter that are unpatentable, namely "laws of nature, natural phenomena, and abstract ideas." *Diehr*, 450 U.S. at 185, 101 S.Ct. 1048. Of particular relevance to this case, the Court has held that mathematical algorithms are not patentable subject matter to the extent that they are merely abstract ideas. *See Diehr*, 450 U.S. 175, 101 S.Ct. 1048, *passim*; *Parker v. Flook*, 437 U.S. 584, 98 S.Ct. 2522, 57 L.Ed.2d 451 (1978); *Gottschalk v. Benson*, 409 U.S. 63, 93 S.Ct. 253, 34 L.Ed.2d 273 (1972). In *Diehr*, the Court explained that certain types of mathematical subject matter, standing alone, represent nothing more than abstract ideas until reduced to some type of practical application, i.e., "a useful, concrete and tangible result." *Alappat*, 33 F.3d at 1544, 31 USPQ2d at 1557.

Unpatentable mathematical algorithms are identifiable by showing they are merely abstract ideas constituting disembodied concepts or truths that are not "useful." From a practical standpoint, this means that to be patentable an algorithm must be applied in a "useful" way. In *Alappat*, we held that data, transformed by a machine through a series of mathematical calculations to produce a smooth waveform display on a rasterizer monitor, constituted a practical application of an abstract idea (a mathematical algorithm, formula, or calculation), because it produced "a useful, concrete and tangible result"—the smooth waveform.

Similarly, in *Arrhythmia Research Technology Inc. v. Corazonix Corp.*, 958 F.2d 1053, 22 USPQ2d 1033 (Fed.Cir.1992), we held that the transformation of electrocardiograph signals from a patient's heartbeat by a machine through a series of mathematical calculations constituted a practical application of an abstract idea (a mathematical algorithm, formula, or calculation), because it corresponded to a useful, concrete or tangible thing—the condition of a patient's heart.

Today, we hold that the transformation of data, representing discrete dollar amounts, by a machine through a series of mathematical calculations into a final share price, constitutes a practical application of a mathematical algorithm, formula, or calculation, because it produces "a useful, concrete and tangible result"—a final share price momentarily fixed for recording and reporting purposes and even accepted and relied upon by regulatory authorities and in subsequent trades.

The district court erred by applying the Freeman–Walter–Abele test to determine whether the claimed subject matter was an unpatentable abstract idea. The Freeman–Walter–Abele test was designed by the Court of Customs and Patent Appeals, and subsequently adopted by this court, to extract and identify unpatentable mathematical algorithms in the aftermath of *Benson* and *Flook*. *See In re Freeman*, 573 F.2d 1237, 197 USPQ 464 (C.C.P.A. 1978) as modified by *In re Walter*, 618 F.2d 758, 205 USPQ 397 (C.C.P.A. 1980). The test has been thus articulated:

> First, the claim is analyzed to determine whether a mathematical algorithm is directly or indirectly recited. Next, if a mathematical algorithm is found, the claim as a whole is further analyzed to determine whether the algorithm is "applied in any manner to physical elements or process steps," and, if it is, it "passes muster under § 101."

In re Pardo, 684 F.2d 912, 915, 214 USPQ 673, 675–76 (C.C.P.A. 1982) (citing *In re Abele*, 684 F.2d 902, 214 USPQ 682 (C.C.P.A. 1982)).

After *Diehr* and *Chakrabarty*, the Freeman–Walter–Abele test has little, if any, applicability to determining the presence of statutory subject matter. As we pointed out in *Alappat*, 33 F.3d at 1543, 31 USPQ2d at 1557, application of the test could be misleading, because a process, machine, manufacture, or composition of matter employing a law of nature, natural phenomenon, or abstract idea is patentable subject matter even though a law of nature, natural phenomenon, or abstract idea would not, by itself, be entitled to such protection. The test determines the presence of, for example, an algorithm. Under *Benson*, this may have been a sufficient indicium of nonstatutory subject matter. However, after *Diehr* and *Alappat*, the mere fact that a claimed invention involves inputting numbers, calculating numbers, outputting numbers, and storing numbers, in and of itself, would not render it nonstatutory subject matter, unless, of course, its operation does not produce a "useful, concrete and tangible result." *Alappat*, 33 F.3d at 1544, 31 USPQ2d at 1557. After all, as we have repeatedly stated,

> every step-by-step process, be it electronic or chemical or mechanical, involves an algorithm in the broad sense of the term. Since § 101 expressly includes processes as a category of inventions which may be patented and § 100(b) further defines the word "process" as meaning "process, art or method, and includes a new use of a known process, machine, manufacture, composition of matter, or material," it follows that it is no ground for holding a claim is directed to nonstatutory subject matter to say it includes or is directed to an

algorithm. This is why the proscription against patenting has been limited to *mathematical* algorithms. . . .

In re Iwahashi, 888 F.2d 1370, 1374, 12 USPQ2d 1908, 1911 (Fed.Cir. 1989) (emphasis in the original).

The question of whether a claim encompasses statutory subject matter should not focus on *which* of the four categories of subject matter a claim is directed to—process, machine, manufacture, or composition of matter—but rather on the essential characteristics of the subject matter, in particular, its practical utility. Section 101 specifies that statutory subject matter must also satisfy the other "conditions and requirements" of Title 35, including novelty, nonobviousness, and adequacy of disclosure and notice. *See In re Warmerdam*, 33 F.3d 1354, 1359, 31 USPQ2d 1754, 1757–58 (Fed.Cir.1994). For purpose of our analysis, as noted above, claim 1 is directed to a machine programmed with the Hub and Spoke software and admittedly produces a "useful, concrete, and tangible result." *Alappat*, 33 F.3d at 1544, 31 USPQ2d at 1557. This renders it statutory subject matter, even if the useful result is expressed in numbers, such as price, profit, percentage, cost, or loss.

The Business Method Exception

As an alternative ground for invalidating the '056 patent under § 101, the court relied on the judicially-created, so-called "business method" exception to statutory subject matter. We take this opportunity to lay this ill-conceived exception to rest. Since its inception, the "business method" exception has merely represented the application of some general, but no longer applicable legal principle, perhaps arising out of the "requirement for invention"—which was eliminated by § 103. Since the 1952 Patent Act, business methods have been, and should have been, subject to the same legal requirements for patentability as applied to any other process or method.

The business method exception has never been invoked by this court, or the C.C.P.A., to deem an invention unpatentable. Application of this particular exception has always been preceded by a ruling based on some clearer concept of Title 35 or, more commonly, application of the abstract idea exception based on finding a mathematical algorithm. Illustrative is the C.C.P.A.'s analysis in *In re Howard*, 55 C.C.P.A. 1121, 394 F.2d 869, 157 USPQ 615 (C.C.P.A. 1968), wherein the court affirmed the Board of Appeals' rejection of the claims for lack of novelty and found it unnecessary to reach the Board's section 101 ground that a method of doing business is "inherently unpatentable." *Id.* at 872, 55 C.C.P.A. 1121, 394 F.2d 869, 157 USPQ at 617.

Similarly, *In re Schrader*, 22 F.3d 290, 30 USPQ2d 1455 (Fed.Cir. 1994), while making reference to the business method exception, turned on the fact that the claims implicitly recited an abstract idea in the form of a mathematical algorithm and there was no "transformation or conversion of subject matter representative of or constituting physical activity or objects." 22 F.3d at 294, 30 USPQ2d at 1459 (emphasis omitted).

State Street argues that we acknowledged the validity of the business method exception in *Alappat* when we discussed *Maucorps* and *Meyer*:

> *Maucorps* dealt with a business methodology for deciding how salesmen should best handle respective customers and *Meyer* involved a "system" for aiding a neurologist in diagnosing patients. Clearly, neither of the alleged "inventions" in those cases falls within any § 101 category.

Alappat, 33 F.3d at 1541, 31 USPQ2d at 1555. However, closer scrutiny of these cases reveals that the claimed inventions in both *Maucorps* and *Meyer* were rejected as abstract ideas under the mathematical algorithm exception, not the business method exception. *See In re Maucorps*, 609 F.2d 481, 484, 203 USPQ 812, 816 (C.C.P.A. 1979); *In re Meyer*, 688 F.2d 789, 796, 215 USPQ 193, 199 (C.C.P.A. 1982).

Even the case frequently cited as establishing the business method exception to statutory subject matter, *Hotel Security Checking Co. v. Lorraine Co.*, 160 F. 467 (2d Cir.1908), did not rely on the exception to strike the patent. In that case, the patent was found invalid for lack of novelty and "invention," not because it was improper subject matter for a patent. The court stated "the fundamental principle of the system is as old as the art of bookkeeping, i.e., charging the goods of the employer to the agent who takes them." *Id.* at 469. "If at the time of [the patent] application, there had been no system of bookkeeping of any kind in restaurants, we would be confronted with the question whether a new and useful system of cash registering and account checking is such an art as is patentable under the statute." *Id.* at 472.

This case is no exception. The district court announced the precepts of the business method exception as set forth in several treatises, but noted as its primary reason for finding the patent invalid under the business method exception as follows:

> If Signature's invention were patentable, any financial institution desirous of implementing a multi-tiered funding complex modelled (sic) on a Hub and Spoke configuration would be required to seek Signature's permission before embarking on such a project. *This is so because the '056 Patent is claimed [sic] sufficiently broadly to foreclose virtually any computer-implemented accounting method necessary to manage this type of financial structure.*

927 F.Supp. 502, 516, 38 USPQ2d 1530, 1542 (emphasis added). Whether the patent's claims are too broad to be patentable is not to be judged under § 101, but rather under §§ 102, 103 and 112. Assuming the above statement to be correct, it has nothing to do with whether what is claimed is statutory subject matter.

In view of this background, it comes as no surprise that in the most recent edition of the Manual of Patent Examining Procedures (MPEP) (1996), a paragraph of § 706.03(a) was deleted. In past editions it read:

> Though seemingly within the category of process or method, a method of doing business can be rejected as not being within the statutory classes. *See Hotel Security Checking Co. v. Lorraine Co.*, 160 F. 467 (2d Cir.1908) and *In re Wait*, 24 USPQ 88, 22 C.C.P.A. 822, 73 F.2d 982 (1934).

MPEP § 706.03(a) (1994). This acknowledgment is buttressed by the U.S. Patent and Trademark 1996 Examination Guidelines for Computer Related Inventions which now read:

> Office personnel have had difficulty in properly treating claims directed to methods of doing business. Claims should not be categorized as methods of doing business. Instead such claims should be treated like any other process claims.

Examination Guidelines, 61 Fed.Reg. 7478, 7479 (1996). We agree that this is precisely the manner in which this type of claim should be treated. Whether the claims are directed to subject matter within § 101 should not turn on whether the claimed subject matter does "business" instead of something else.

CONCLUSION

The appealed decision is reversed and the case is remanded to the district court for further proceedings consistent with this opinion.

REVERSED and *REMANDED*.

Notes

1. State Street uses the same "useful, concrete and tangible result" test as *Alappat* for avoiding the "mathematical algorithm" exception to patentability.

2. The Supreme Court denied certiorari in both *Alappat* and *State Street*. Now that huge numbers of patents are being granted on "programmed computers" including computers implementing business methods, what would be the economic effect of a Supreme Court decision rejecting *Alappat* and *State Street*?

3. The business exception to § 101 statutory subject matter is eliminated in *State Street*. Did this open the door completely to software business methodology patents? Is a very clever scheme for selling time-shared resort accommodations, involving the use of special props, special scripts, and a special sequence of events now patentable? How about the same very clever scheme implemented entirely as an interactive web site on the Internet? Can a business method's patentability be altered depending upon whether it is implemented manually or by computers? Can one patent an Internet-based, computerized version of a business method that has been practiced manually in the past?

4. In view of the above cases, would it be possible now to get a pure software patent?

5. The European Patent Office has also moved far toward allowing computer program patents, as the next case shows.

INTERNATIONAL BUSINESS MACHINES CORPORATION

Technical Board of Appeal of the European Patent Office, 1999.
Case Number T 0935/97–3.5.1.

SUMMARY OF FACTS AND SUBMISSIONS

I. The appeal was lodged against a decision of the examining division, dated 18 June 1997, refusing the European patent application No. 96 305 851.6 (publication number 0 767 419). The decision was based on claims 1 to 9 filed with letter of 1 January 1997 and claim 10 filed with letter of 19 February 1997. The reason for the refusal was that claims 7 to 10, defining a computer program product and element, respectively, were directed to a computer program as such and, therefore, concerned subject-matter excluded from patentability under Article 52(2)(c) and (3) EPC. * * *

* * *

Claim 7 * * * read as follows: * * * "7. A computer program product comprising a computer readable medium, having thereon: computer program code means, when said program is loaded, to make the computer execute procedure to display information within a first window in a display; and responsive to the obstruction of a portion of said first window information by a second window, to display in said first window said portion of said information that had been obscured by said second window, including moving said portion of said information that had been obscured by said second window to a location within said first window that is not obscured by said second window."

* * *

REASONS FOR THE DECISION

* * *

The only question to be decided by the Board in this case, therefore, is whether the subject-matter of present claims 7 to 10 is excluded from patentability under Article 52(2) and (3) EPC.

2. *TRIPS*

[Agreement on Trade–Related Aspects of Intellectual Property Rights (TRIPS Agreement January 1, 1995)—*see* Agreement on Trade–Related Aspects of Intellectual Property Rights, April 15, 1994, Marrakesh Agreement Establishing the World Trade Organization, Annex 1C, 33 I.L.M. 1125, 1197 (1994), also on the Internet at *<http://www.wto.org>* under the trade related topics tab—Eds.]

2.1   To a large extent the Board shares the appellant's opinion about the significance of TRIPS with regard to the case under consideration.

However, for the time being it is not convinced that TRIPS may be applied directly to the EPC. [European Patent Convention—*see* Convention on the Grant of European Patents (European Patent Convention), Oct. 5, 1973, 12 I.L.M. 271 (1974), also on the Internet at <http://www.european-patent-office.org>—Eds.] Apart from any other considerations TRIPS is binding only on its member states. The European Patent Organisation itself is not a member of the WTO [World Trade Organisation–*see* Agreement Establishing the World Trade Organization, April 15, 1994, 33 I.L.M. 1125, 1144 (1994), also on the Internet at <http://www.wto.org>—Eds.] and did not sign the TRIPS Agreement.

2.2   Nor has the Board been able to find any justification under the Vienna Convention on the Law of Treaties for the direct application of TRIPS to the EPC.

Although, according to Article 4, the Vienna Convention, which was signed on 23 May 1969, but did not enter into force until 27 January 1980, is not applicable to the EPC, it has considerable authority and has frequently been cited by the boards of appeal when applying principles laid down in it. However, in the Board's opinion Article 30, which deals with the "application of successive treaties relating to the same subject-matter", does not provide any justification for applying TRIPS to the EPC. For instance, there is not even full correspondence between the contracting states to the EPC and the member states of TRIPS, i.e. not all the contracting states to the EPC are simultaneously members of TRIPS.

2.3   But although TRIPS may not be applied directly to the EPC, the Board thinks it appropriate to take it into consideration, since it is aimed at setting common standards and principles concerning the availability, scope and use of trade-related intellectual property rights, and therefore of patent rights. Thus TRIPS gives a clear indication of current trends.

Article 27(1) TRIPS states that "patents shall be available for any inventions, whether products or processes, in all fields of technology, provided they are new, involve an inventive step and are capable of industrial application". This general principle, when considered together with the provisions pursuant to paragraphs 2 and 3 of Article 27 concerning exclusion from patentability (which, however, do not comprise any of the subject-matter mentioned in Article 52(2) EPC), can be correctly interpreted, in the Board's opinion, as meaning that it is the clear intention of TRIPS not to exclude from patentability any inventions, whatever field of technology they belong to, and therefore, in particular, not to exclude programs for computers as mentioned in and excluded under Article 52(2)(c) EPC.

European Patent Convention—Article 52—Patentable inventions

(1) European patents shall be granted for any inventions which are susceptible of industrial application, which are new and which involve an inventive step.

(2) The following in particular shall not be regarded as inventions within the meaning of paragraph 1:

  (a) discoveries, scientific theories and mathematical methods;

  (b) aesthetic creations;

  (c) schemes, rules and methods for performing mental acts, playing games or doing business, and programs for computers;

  (d) presentations of information.

(3) The provisions of paragraph 2 shall exclude patentability of the subject-matter or activities referred to in that provision only to the extent to which a European patent application or European patent relates to such subject-matter or activities as such.

—Casebook editors' note.]

2.4   The Board is fully aware that, according to Article 10(1) TRIPS, "computer programs, whether in source or object code, shall be protected as literary works under the Berne Convention (1971)". This provision does not, however, weaken the above conclusion that computer programs are patentable under TRIPS, as based on its Article 27. The fact that Article 10 is the only provision in TRIPS which expressly mentions programs for computers and that copyright is the means of protection provided for by said provision does not give rise to any conflict between Articles 10 and 27 TRIPS. Copyright and protection by patents constitute two different means of legal protection, which may, however, also cover the same subject-matter (e.g. programs for computers), since each of them serves its own purpose.

2.5   The appellant also referred to current practice in the US and Japanese patent offices. The Board has taken due notice of these developments, but wishes to emphasise, that the situation under these two legal systems (US, JP) differs greatly from that under the EPC in that it is only the EPC which contains an exclusion such as the one in Article 52(2) and (3). 2.6 Nevertheless these developments represent a useful indication of modern trends. In the Board's opinion they may contribute to the further highly desirable (world-wide) harmonisation of patent law.

3.   *The relevant source of substantive patent law*

The outcome of the above considerations is that the only source of substantive patent law for examining European patent applications at this moment is the European Patent Convention. The examining division's conclusion in the decision under appeal that the EPC is the only relevant system of substantive patent law to be taken into account is therefore correct. In applying the EPC the examining division relied on the Guidelines for Examination in the European Patent Office and thus only applied the interpretation of the EPC as given therein.

However, the Guidelines are not binding upon the boards of appeal. In particular, according to Article 23(3) EPC, "in their decisions the members of the Boards shall not be bound by any instructions and shall comply only with the provisions of this Convention".

The Board will therefore now investigate what in its view would be the proper interpretation of the exclusion from patentability of programs for computers under Article 52(2) and (3) EPC.

4. *Exclusion under Article 52(2) and (3) EPC*

4.1 Turning to the exclusion clause itself, the Board notes the following:

Article 52(2)(c) EPC states that programs for computers shall not be regarded as inventions within the meaning of Article 52(1) EPC and are therefore excluded from patentability.

Article 52(3) EPC establishes an important limitation to the scope of this exclusion. According to this provision, the exclusion applies only to the extent to which a European patent application or a European patent relates to programs for computers "as such". The combination of the two provisions (Article 52(2) and (3) EPC) demonstrates that the legislators did not want to exclude from patentability all programs for computers. In other words the fact that only patent applications relating to programs for computers as such are excluded from patentability means that patentability may be allowed for patent applications relating to programs for computers where the latter are not considered to be programs for computers as such.

4.2 In order to establish the scope of the exclusion from patentability of programs for computers, it is necessary to determine the exact meaning of the expression "as such". This may result in the identification of those programs for computers which, as a result of not being considered programs for computers as such, are open to patentability.

5. *Interpretation of "as such"*

5.1 Within the context of the application of the EPC the technical character of an invention is generally accepted as an essential requirement for its patentability. This is illustrated, for instance, by Rules 27 and 29 EPC.

5.2 The exclusion from patentability of programs for computers as such (Article 52(2) and (3) EPC) may be construed to mean that such programs are considered to be mere abstract creations, lacking in technical character. The use of the expression "shall not be regarded as inventions" seems to confirm this interpretation.

5.3   This means that programs for computers must be considered as patentable inventions when they have a technical character.

5.4   This conclusion seems to be consistent with the three different provisions concerned:

(a) the exclusion from patentability provided for in Article 52(2) EPC;

(b) the general provision of Article 52(1) EPC, according to which European patents shall be granted for any inventions (therefore having technical features) which are susceptible of industrial application, which are new and which involve an inventive step;

(c) the provision of Article 52(3) EPC, which does not allow a broad interpretation of the scope of the exclusion.

5.5   The main problem for the interpretation of said exclusion is therefore to define the meaning of the feature "technical character", in the present case with specific reference to programs for computers.

6.   *Technical character of programs for computers*

6.1   For the purpose of interpreting the exclusion from patentability of programs for computers under Article 52(2) and (3) EPC, it is assumed that programs for computers cannot be considered as having a technical character for the very reason that they are programs for computers.

6.2   This means that physical modifications of the hardware (causing, for instance, electrical currents) deriving from the execution of the instructions given by programs for computers cannot *per se* constitute the technical character required for avoiding the exclusion of those programs.

6.3   Although such modifications may be considered to be technical, they are a common feature of all those programs for computers which have been made suitable for being run on a computer, and therefore cannot be used to distinguish programs for computers with a technical character from programs for computers as such.

6.4   It is thus necessary to look elsewhere for technical character in the above sense: It could be found in the further effects deriving from the execution (by the hardware) of the instructions given by the computer program. Where said further effects have a technical character or where they cause the software to solve a technical problem, an invention which brings about such an effect may be considered an invention, which can, in principle, be the subject-matter of a patent.

6.5   Consequently a patent may be granted not only in the case of an invention where a piece of software manages, by means of a computer, an industrial process or the working of a piece of machinery, but in every case where a program for a computer is the only means, or one of the necessary means, of obtaining a technical effect within the meaning specified above, where, for instance, a technical effect of that kind is achieved by the internal functioning of a computer itself under the influence of said program.

In other words, on condition that they are able to produce a technical effect in the above sense, all computer programs must be considered as inventions within the meaning of Article 52(1) EPC, and may be the subject-matter of a patent if the other requirements provided for by the EPC are satisfied.

6.6 As already indicated in the previous paragraph, said technical effect may also be caused by the functioning of the computer itself on which the program is being run, i.e. by the functioning of the hardware of that computer. It is clear that also in this situation the physical modifications of the hardware deriving from the execution of the instructions given by the program within the meaning indicated under points 6.2 and 6.3 above cannot *per se* constitute the technical character required for avoiding exclusion.

In this case it is only said further technical effect which matters when considering the patentability requirements, and no importance should be attached to the specific further use of the system as a whole. The expression "the system as a whole" means the hardware plus the software, that is the system consisting of the hardware as programmed in accordance with the program concerned (hardware + software).

* * *

9. *Claim for a computer program product*

9.1 As already pointed out under reason 1, the only question to be decided in this appeal is whether the subject-matter of claims 7 to 10 is excluded from patentability under Article 52(2) and (3) EPC. These claims are directed to a computer program product and have to be examined from the point of view of what may be called "the further technical effect", which, if present, may lead to the subject-matter not being excluded under Article 52(2) and (3) EPC.

9.2 Such products normally comprise a set of instructions which, when the program is loaded, makes the hardware execute a specific procedure producing a particular result.

9.3 It is self-evident that in this instance the basic idea underlying the invention resides in the computer program. It is also clear that, in such a case, the hardware on which the program is intended to run is outside the invention, i.e. the hardware is not part of the invention. It is the material object on which the physical changes carried out by running the program take place.

Furthermore it is clear that if, for instance, the computer program product comprises a computer-readable medium on which the program is stored, this medium only constitutes the physical support on which the program is saved, and thus constitutes hardware.

9.4 Every computer program product produces an effect when the program concerned is made to run on a computer. The effect only shows in physical reality when the program is being run. Thus the computer program product itself does not directly disclose the said effect in physical reality. It only discloses the effect when being run and consequently only possesses the "potential" to produce said effect.

This effect may also be technical in the sense as explained under reason 6, in which case it constitutes the "further technical effect" mentioned there. This means that a computer program product may possess the potential to produce a "further" technical effect. Once it has been clearly established that a specific computer program product, when run on a computer, brings about a technical effect in the above sense, the Board sees no good reason for distinguishing between a direct technical effect on the one hand and the potential to produce a technical effect, which may be considered as an indirect technical effect, on the other hand.

A computer program product may therefore possess a technical character because it has the potential to cause a predetermined further technical effect in the above sense. According to the above, having technical character means not being excluded from patentability under the "as such" provision pursuant to Article 52(3) EPC.

This means that a computer program product having the potential to cause a predetermined further technical effect is, in principle, not excluded from patentability under Article 52(2) and (3). Consequently, computer program products are not excluded from patentability under all circumstances.

* * *

Order

For these reasons it is decided that:

1. The decision under appeal is set aside.

2. The case is remitted to the first instance for further prosecution on the basis of the appellant's request, and in particular for examination of whether the wording of the present claims 7 to 10 avoids exclusion from patentability under Article 52(2)and (3) EPC, taking into account the fact that a computer program product is not so excluded under all circumstances.

THE REGISTRAR: M. KIEL
THE CHAIRMAN: P. K. J. VAN DEN BERG

Note

When the *Benson* decision came down in the United States, the world responded by deciding that computer programs were not patentable. In Europe, the countries individually amended their patent laws to rule software unpatentable. Then the United States Supreme Court, in *Diehr* and later decisions, in effect reversed itself. The courts all over Europe have more-or-less followed suit, on the fiction that a "programmed computer" is not a computer program but is a machine. This is the first decision, coming from the European Patent Office, to go beyond this fiction and simply hold a computer program to be patentable, in actual effect reversing the clear meaning of the treaty language.

AT&T CORP. v. EXCEL COMMUNICATIONS, INC.

United States Court of Appeals, Federal Circuit, 1999.
172 F.3d 1352.

PLAGER, CIRCUIT JUDGE.

This case asks us once again to examine the scope of section 1 of the Patent Act, 35 U.S.C. § 101 (1994). The United States District Court for the District of Delaware granted summary judgment to Excel Communications, Inc., Excel Communications Marketing, Inc., and Excel Telecommunications, Inc. (collectively "Excel"), holding U.S. Patent No. 5,333,-184 (the '184 patent) invalid under § 101 for failure to claim statutory subject matter. *See AT & T Corp. v. Excel Communications, Inc.*, No. CIV.A.96–434–SLR, 1998 WL 175878, at *7 (D.Del. Mar.27, 1998). AT&T Corp. ("AT&T"), owner of the '184 patent, appeals. Because we find that the claimed subject matter is properly within the statutory scope of § 101, we reverse the district court's judgment of invalidity on this ground and remand the case for further proceedings.

BACKGROUND

A.

The '184 patent, entitled "Call Message Recording for Telephone Systems," issued on July 26, 1994. It describes a message record for long-distance telephone calls that is enhanced by adding a primary interexchange carrier ("PIC") indicator. The addition of the indicator aids long-distance carriers in providing differential billing treatment for subscribers, depending upon whether a subscriber calls someone with the same or a different long-distance carrier.

The invention claimed in the '184 patent is designed to operate in a telecommunications system with multiple long-distance service providers. The system contains local exchange carriers ("LECs") and long-distance service (interexchange) carriers ("IXCs"). The LECs provide local telephone service and access to IXCs. Each customer has an LEC for local service and selects an IXC, such as AT&T or Excel, to be its primary long-distance service (interexchange) carrier or PIC. IXCs may own their own facilities, as does AT & T. Others, like Excel, called "resellers" or "resale carriers," contract with facility-owners to route their subscribers' calls through the facility-owners' switches and transmission lines. Some IXCs, including MCI and U.S. Sprint, have a mix of their own lines and leased lines.

The system thus involves a three-step process when a caller makes a direct-dialed (1+) long-distance telephone call: (1) after the call is transmitted over the LEC's network to a switch, and the LEC identifies the caller's PIC, the LEC automatically routes the call to the facilities used by the caller's PIC; (2) the PIC's facilities carry the call to the LEC serving the call recipient; and (3) the call recipient's LEC delivers the call over its local network to the recipient's telephone.

When a caller makes a direct-dialed long-distance telephone call, a switch (which may be a switch in the interexchange network) monitors and records data related to the call, generating an "automatic message account" ("AMA") message record. This contemporaneous message record contains fields of information such as the originating and terminating telephone numbers, and the length of time of the call. These message records are then transmitted from the switch to a message accumulation system for processing and billing.

Because the message records are stored in electronic format, they can be transmitted from one computer system to another and reformatted to ease processing of the information. Thus the carrier's AMA message subsequently is translated into the industry-standard "exchange message interface," forwarded to a rating system, and ultimately forwarded to a billing system in which the data resides until processed to generate, typically, "hard copy" bills which are mailed to subscribers.

B.

The invention of the '184 patent calls for the addition of a data field into a standard message record to indicate whether a call involves a particular PIC (the "PIC indicator"). This PIC indicator can exist in several forms, such as a code which identifies the call recipient's PIC, a flag which shows that the recipient's PIC is or is not a particular IXC, or a flag that identifies the recipient's and the caller's PICs as the same IXC. The PIC indicator therefore enables IXCs to provide differential billing for calls on the basis of the identified PIC.

The application that issued as the '184 patent was filed in 1992. The U.S. Patent and Trademark Office ("PTO") initially rejected, for reasons unrelated to § 101, all forty-one of the originally filed claims. Following amendment, the claims were issued in 1994 in their present form. The '184 patent contains six independent claims, five method claims and one apparatus claim, and additional dependent claims. The PTO granted the '184 patent without questioning whether the claims were directed to statutory subject matter under § 101.

AT&T in 1996 asserted ten of the method claims against Excel in this infringement suit. The independent claims at issue (claims 1, 12, 18, and 40) include the step of "generating a message record for an interexchange call between an originating subscriber and a terminating subscriber," and the step of adding a PIC indicator to the message record. Independent claim 1, for example, adds a PIC indicator whose value depends upon the call recipient's PIC:

> A method for use in a telecommunications system in which interexchange calls initiated by each subscriber are automatically routed over the facilities of a particular one of a plurality of interexchange carriers associated with that subscriber, said method comprising the steps of:
>
> *generating a message record for an interexchange* call between an originating subscriber and a terminating subscriber, and
>
> *including, in said message record, a primary interexchange carrier (PIC) indicator* having a value which is *a function of whether or not the interexchange carrier associated with said terminating subscriber is a predetermined one* of said interexchange carriers.

(Emphasis added.) Independent claims 12 and 40 add a PIC indicator that shows if a recipient's PIC is the same as the IXC over which that particular call is being made. Independent claim 18 adds a PIC indicator designed to show if the caller and the recipient subscribe to the same IXC. The dependent claims at issue add the steps of accessing an IXC's subscriber database (claims 4, 13, and 19) and billing individual calls as a function of the value of the PIC indicator (claims 6, 15, and 21).

The district court concluded that the method claims of the '184 patent implicitly recite a mathematical algorithm. *See AT&T*, 1998 WL 175878, at * 6. The court was of the view that the only physical step in the claims involves data-gathering for the algorithm. *See id.* Though the court recognized that the claims require the use of switches and computers, it nevertheless concluded that use of such facilities to perform a non-substantive change in the data's format could not serve to convert non-patentable subject matter into patentable subject matter. *See id.* at *6–7. Thus the trial court, on summary judgment, held all of the method claims at issue invalid for failure to qualify as statutory subject matter. *See id.* at *7.

DISCUSSION

A.

* * *

The issue on appeal, whether the asserted claims of the '184 patent are invalid for failure to claim statutory subject matter under 35 U.S.C. § 101, is a question of law which we review without deference. *See Arrhythmia Research Technology v. Corazonix Corp.*, 958 F.2d 1053, 1055–56, 22 USPQ2d 1033, 1035 (Fed.Cir.1992). In matters of statutory interpretation, it is this court's responsibility independently to determine what the law is. *See Hodges v. Secretary of the Dep't of Health & Human Servs.*, 9 F.3d 958, 960 (Fed.Cir.1993).

B.

Our analysis of whether a claim is directed to statutory subject matter begins with the language of 35 U.S.C. § 101, which reads:

> Whoever invents or discovers any new and useful process, machine, manufacture, or composition of matter, or any new and useful improvement thereof, may obtain a patent therefor, subject to the conditions and requirements of this title.

The Supreme Court has construed § 101 broadly, noting that Congress intended statutory subject matter to "include anything under the sun that is made by man." *See Diamond v. Chakrabarty*, 447 U.S. 303, 309, 100 S.Ct. 2204, 65 L.Ed.2d 144 (1980) (quoting S.Rep. No. 82–1979, at 5 (1952); H.R.Rep. No. 82–1923, at 6 (1952)); *see also Diamond v. Diehr*, 450 U.S. 175, 182, 101 S.Ct. 1048, 67 L.Ed.2d 155 (1981). Despite this seemingly limitless expanse, the Court has specifically identified three categories of unpatentable subject matter: "laws of nature, natural phenomena, and abstract ideas." *See Diehr*, 450 U.S. at 185, 101 S.Ct. 1048.

In this case, the method claims at issue fall within the "process" category of the four enumerated categories of patentable subject matter in § 101. The district court held that the claims at issue, though otherwise within the terms of § 101, implicitly recite a mathematical algorithm, *see AT&T*, 1998 WL 175878, at *6, and thus fall within the judicially created "mathematical algorithm" exception to statutory subject matter.

A mathematical formula alone, sometimes referred to as a mathematical algorithm, viewed in the abstract, is considered unpatentable subject matter. *See Diamond v. Diehr*, 450 U.S. 175, 101 S.Ct. 1048, 67 L.Ed.2d 155 (1981); *Parker v. Flook*, 437 U.S. 584, 98 S.Ct. 2522, 57 L.Ed.2d 451 (1978); *Gottschalk v. Benson*, 409 U.S. 63, 93 S.Ct. 253, 34 L.Ed.2d 273 (1972). Courts have used the terms "mathematical algorithm," "mathematical formula," and "mathematical equation," to describe types of nonstatutory mathematical subject matter without explaining whether the terms are interchangeable or different. Even assuming the words connote the same concept, there is considerable question as to exactly what the concept encompasses. *See, e.g., Diehr*, 450 U.S. at 186 n. 9, 101 S.Ct. 1048 ("The term 'algorithm' is subject to a variety of definitions ... [Petitioner's] definition is significantly broader than the definition this Court employed in *Benson* and *Flook*."); *accord In re Schrader*, 22 F.3d 290, 293 n. 5, 30 USPQ2d 1455, 1457 n. 5 (Fed.Cir.1994).

This court recently pointed out that any step-by-step process, be it electronic, chemical, or mechanical, involves an "algorithm" in the broad sense of the term. *See State Street Bank & Trust Co. v. Signature Fin. Group, Inc.*, 149 F.3d 1368, 1374–75, 47 USPQ2d 1596, 1602 (Fed.Cir.

1998), *cert. denied*, ___ U.S. ___, 119 S.Ct. 851, 142 L.Ed.2d 704 (1999). Because § 101 includes processes as a category of patentable subject matter, the judicially-defined proscription against patenting of a "mathematical algorithm," to the extent such a proscription still exists, is narrowly limited to mathematical algorithms in the abstract. *See id.*; *see also Benson*, 409 U.S. at 65, 93 S.Ct. 253 (describing a mathematical algorithm as a "procedure for solving a given type of mathematical problem").

Since the process of manipulation of numbers is a fundamental part of computer technology, we have had to reexamine the rules that govern the patentability of such technology. The sea-changes in both law and technology stand as a testament to the ability of law to adapt to new and innovative concepts, while remaining true to basic principles. In an earlier era, the PTO published guidelines essentially rejecting the notion that computer programs were patentable. As the technology progressed, our predecessor court disagreed, and, overturning some of the earlier limiting principles regarding § 101, announced more expansive principles formulated with computer technology in mind. In our recent decision in *State Street*, this court discarded the so-called "business method" exception and reassessed the "mathematical algorithm" exception, *see* 149 F.3d at 1373–77, 47 USPQ2d at 1600–04, both judicially-created "exceptions" to the statutory categories of § 101. As this brief review suggests, this court (and its predecessor) has struggled to make our understanding of the scope of § 101 responsive to the needs of the modern world.

The Supreme Court has supported and enhanced this effort. In *Diehr*, the Court expressly limited its two earlier decisions in *Flook* and *Benson* by emphasizing that these cases did no more than confirm the "long-established principle" that laws of nature, natural phenomena, and abstract ideas are excluded from patent protection. 450 U.S. at 185, 101 S.Ct. 1048. The *Diehr* Court explicitly distinguished *Diehr's* process by pointing out that "the respondents here do not seek to patent a mathematical formula. Instead, they seek patent protection for a process of curing synthetic rubber." *Id.* at 187, 101 S.Ct. 1048. The Court then explained that although the process used a well-known mathematical equation, the applicants did not "pre-empt the use of that equation." *Id.* Thus, even though a mathematical algorithm is not patentable in isolation, a process that applies an equation to a new and useful end "is at the very least not barred at the threshold by § 101." *Id.* at 188, 101 S.Ct. 1048. In this regard, it is particularly worthy of note that the argument for the opposite result, that "the term 'algorithm' ... is synonymous with the term 'computer program,' " *id.* at 219, 101 S.Ct. 1048 (Stevens, J., dissenting), and thus computer-based programs as a general proposition should not be patentable, was made forcefully in dissent by Justice Stevens; his view, however, was rejected by the *Diehr* majority.

As previously noted, we most recently addressed the "mathematical algorithm" exception in *State Street. See* 149 F.3d at 1373–75, 47

USPQ2d at 1600–02. In *State Street*, this court, following the Supreme Court's guidance in *Diehr*, concluded that "[u]npatentable mathematical algorithms are identifiable by showing they are merely abstract ideas constituting disembodied concepts or truths that are not 'useful.' . . . [T]o be patentable an algorithm must be applied in a 'useful' way." *Id.* at 1373, 47 USPQ2d at 1601. In that case, the claimed data processing system for implementing a financial management structure satisfied the § 101 inquiry because it constituted a "practical application of a mathematical algorithm, . . . [by] produc[ing] 'a useful, concrete and tangible result.'"*Id.* at 1373, 47 USPQ2d at 1601.

The State Street formulation, that a mathematical algorithm may be an integral part of patentable subject matter such as a machine or process if the claimed invention as a whole is applied in a "useful" manner, follows the approach taken by this court en banc in *In re Alappat*, 33 F.3d 1526, 31 USPQ2d 1545 (Fed.Cir.1994). In *Alappat*, we set out our understanding of the Supreme Court's limitations on the patentability of mathematical subject matter and concluded that:

> [The Court] never intended to create an overly broad, fourth category of [mathematical] subject matter excluded from § 101. Rather, at the core of the Court's analysis . . . lies an attempt by the Court to explain a rather straightforward concept, namely, that certain types of mathematical subject matter, *standing alone*, represent nothing more than *abstract ideas until reduced to some type of practical application*, and thus that subject matter is not, in and of itself, entitled to patent protection.

Id. at 1543, 31 USPQ2d at 1556–57 (emphasis added). Thus, the *Alappat* inquiry simply requires an examination of the contested claims to see if the claimed subject matter as a whole is a disembodied mathematical concept representing nothing more than a "law of nature" or an "abstract idea," or if the mathematical concept has been reduced to some practical application rendering it "useful." *Id.* at 1544, 31 USPQ2d at 1557. In *Alappat*, we held that more than an abstract idea was claimed because the claimed invention as a whole was directed toward forming a specific machine that produced the useful, concrete, and tangible result of a smooth waveform display. *See id.* at 1544, 31 USPQ2d at 1557.

In both *Alappat* and *State Street*, the claim was for a machine that achieved certain results. In the case before us, because Excel does not own or operate the facilities over which its calls are placed, AT&T did not charge Excel with infringement of its apparatus claims, but limited its infringement charge to the specified method or process claims. Whether stated implicitly or explicitly, we consider the scope of § 101 to be the same regardless of the form—machine or process—in which a particular claim is drafted. *See, e.g., In re Alappat*, 33 F.3d at 1581, 31 USPQ2d at 1589 (Rader, J., concurring) ("Judge Rich, with whom I fully concur, reads *Alappat's* application as claiming a machine. In fact, whether the invention is a process or a machine is irrelevant. The language of the Patent Act itself, as well as Supreme Court rulings, clarifies that *Alappat's* invention fits comfortably within 35 U.S.C. § 101 whether viewed as a process or a machine."); *State Street*, 149 F.3d at 1372, 47 USPQ2d at 1600 ("[F]or the purposes of a § 101 analysis, it is of little relevance whether claim 1 is directed to a 'machine' or a 'process,'.... "). Furthermore, the Supreme Court's decisions in *Diehr*, *Benson*, and *Flook*, all of which involved method (i.e., process) claims, have provided and supported the principles which we apply to both machine—and process-type claims. Thus, we are comfortable in applying our reasoning in *Alappat* and *State Street* to the method claims at issue in this case.

C.

In light of this review of the current understanding of the "mathematical algorithm" exception, we turn now to the arguments of the parties in support of and in opposition to the trial court's judgment. We note that, at the time the trial court made its decision, that court did not have the benefit of this court's explication in *State Street* of the mathematical algorithm issue.

As previously explained, AT&T's claimed process employs subscribers' and call recipients' PICs as data, applies Boolean algebra to those data to determine the value of the PIC indicator, and applies that value through switching and recording mechanisms to create a signal useful for billing purposes. In *State Street*, we held that the processing system there was patentable subject matter because the system takes data representing discrete dollar amounts through a series of mathematical calculations to determine a final share price—a useful, concrete, and tangible result. *See* 149 F.3d at 1373, 47 USPQ2d at 1601.

In this case, Excel argues, correctly, that the PIC indicator value is derived using a simple mathematical principle (p and q). But that is not determinative because AT&T does not claim the Boolean principle as such or attempt to forestall its use in any other application. It is clear from the written description of the '184 patent that AT&T is only claiming a process that uses the Boolean principle in order to determine the value of the PIC indicator. The PIC indicator represents information about the call recipient's PIC, a useful, non-abstract result that facilitates differential billing of long-distance calls made by an IXC's subscriber. Because the claimed process applies the Boolean principle to produce a useful, concrete, tangible result without pre-empting other uses of the mathematical principle, on its face the claimed process comfortably falls within the scope of § 101. *See Arrhythmia Research Technology, Inc. v. Corazonix Corp.*, 958 F.2d 1053, 1060, 22 USPQ2d 1033, 1039 (Fed.Cir. 1992) ("That the product is numerical is not a criterion of whether the claim is directed to statutory subject matter.").

Excel argues that method claims containing mathematical algorithms are patentable subject matter only if there is a "physical transformation" or conversion of subject matter from one state into another. The physical transformation language appears in *Diehr*, *see* 450 U.S. at 184, 101 S.Ct. 1048 ("That respondents' claims involve the transformation of an article, in this case raw, uncured synthetic rubber, into a different state or thing cannot be disputed."), and has been echoed by this court in *Schrader*, 22 F.3d at 294, 30 USPQ2d at 1458 ("Therefore, we do not find in the claim any kind of data transformation.").

The notion of "physical transformation" can be misunderstood. In the first place, it is not an invariable requirement, but merely one example of how a mathematical algorithm may bring about a useful application. As the Supreme Court itself noted, when [a claimed invention] is performing a function which the patent laws were designed to protect (*e.g.*, transforming or reducing an article to a different state or thing), then the claim satisfies the requirements of § 101. *Diehr*, 450 U.S. at 192, 101 S.Ct. 1048 (emphasis added). The "e.g." signal denotes an example, not an exclusive requirement.

This understanding of transformation is consistent with our earlier decision in *Arrhythmia*, 958 F.2d 1053, 22 USPQ2d 1033 (Fed.Cir.1992). Arrhythmia's process claims included various mathematical formulae to analyze electrocardiograph signals to determine a specified heart activity. *See id.* at 1059, 22 USPQ2d at 1037–38. The *Arrhythmia* court reasoned that the method claims qualified as statutory subject matter by noting that the steps transformed physical, electrical signals from one form into another form—a number representing a signal related to the patient's heart activity, a non-abstract output. *See id.*, 958 F.2d at 1059, 22 USPQ2d at 1038. The finding that the claimed process "transformed" data from one "form" to another simply confirmed that Arrhythmia's method claims satisfied § 101 because the mathematical algorithm included within the process was applied to produce a number which had specific meaning—a useful, concrete, tangible result—not a mathematical abstraction. *See id.* at 1060, 22 USPQ2d at 1039.

Excel also contends that because the process claims at issue lack physical limitations set forth in the patent, the claims are not patentable subject matter. This argument reflects a misunderstanding of our case law. The cases cited by Excel for this proposition involved machine claims written in means-plus-function language. *See, e.g., State Street*, 149 F.3d at 1371, 47 USPQ2d at 1599; *Alappat*, 33 F.3d at 1541, 31 USPQ2d at 1554–55. Apparatus claims written in this manner require supporting structure in the written description that corresponds to the claimed "means" elements. *See* 35 U.S.C. § 112, para. 6 (1994). Since the claims at issue in this case are directed to a process in the first instance, a structural inquiry is unnecessary.

The argument that physical limitations are necessary may also stem from the second part of the *Freeman–Walter–Abele* test, an earlier test which has been used to identify claims thought to involve unpatentable mathematical algorithms. That second part was said to inquire "whether the claim is directed to a mathematical algorithm that is not applied to or limited by physical elements." *Arrhythmia*, 958 F.2d at 1058, 22 USPQ2d at 1037. Although our en banc *Alappat* decision called this test "not an improper analysis," we then pointed out that "the ultimate issue always has been whether the claim as a whole is drawn to statutory subject matter." 33 F.3d at 1543 n. 21, 31 USPQ2d at 1557 n. 21. Furthermore, our recent *State Street* decision questioned the continuing viability of the *Freeman–Walter–Abele* test, noting that, "[a]fter *Diehr* and *Chakrabarty*, the *Freeman–Walter–Abele* test has little, if any, applicability to determining the presence of statutory subject matter." 149 F.3d at 1374, 47 USPQ2d at 1601. Whatever may be left of the earlier test, if anything, this type of physical limitations analysis seems of little value because "after *Diehr* and *Alappat*, the mere fact that a claimed invention involves inputting numbers, calculating numbers, outputting numbers, and storing numbers, in and of itself, would not render it nonstatutory subject matter, unless, of course, its operation does not produce a 'useful, concrete and tangible result.'" *Id.* at 1374, 47 USPQ2d at 1602 (quoting *Alappat*, 33 F.3d at 1544, 31 USPQ2d at 1557).

Because we focus on the inquiry deemed "the ultimate issue" by *Alappat*, rather than on the physical limitations inquiry of the *Freeman–Walter–Abele* test, we find the cases cited by Excel in support of its position to be inapposite. For example, in *In re Grams*, the court applied the *Freeman–Walter–Abele* test and concluded that the only physical step in the claimed process involved data-gathering for the algorithm; thus, the claims were held to be directed to unpatentable subject matter. *See* 888 F.2d 835, 839, 12 USPQ2d 1824, 1829 (Fed.Cir.1989). In contrast, our inquiry here focuses on whether the mathematical algorithm is applied in a practical manner to produce a useful result. *In re Grams* is unhelpful because the panel in that case did not ascertain if the end result of the claimed process was useful, concrete, and tangible.

* * *

D.

In his dissent in *Diehr*, Justice Stevens noted two concerns regarding the § 101 issue, and to which, in his view, federal judges have a duty to respond:

> First, the cases considering the patentability of program-related inventions do not establish rules that enable a conscientious patent lawyer to determine with a fair degree of accuracy which, if any, program-related inventions will be patentable. Second, the inclusion of the ambiguous concept of an "algorithm" within the "law of nature" category of unpatentable subject matter has given rise to the concern that almost any process might be so described and therefore held unpatentable.

Diehr, 450 U.S. at 219, 101 S.Ct. 1048 (Stevens, J., dissenting).

Despite the almost twenty years since Justice Stevens wrote, these concerns remain important. His solution was to declare all computer-based programming unpatentable. That has not been the course the law has taken. Rather, it is now clear that computer-based programming constitutes patentable subject matter so long as the basic requirements of § 101 are met. Justice Stevens's concerns can be addressed within that framework.

His first concern, that the rules are not sufficiently clear to enable reasonable prediction of outcomes, should be less of a concern today in light of the refocusing of the § 101 issue that *Alappat* and *State Street* have provided. His second concern, that the ambiguous concept of "algorithm" could be used to make any process unpatentable, can be laid to rest once the focus is understood to be not on whether there is a mathematical algorithm at work, but on whether the algorithm-containing invention, as a whole, produces a tangible, useful, result.

In light of the above, and consistent with the clearer understanding that our more recent cases have provided, we conclude that the district court did not apply the proper analysis to the method claims at issue. Furthermore, had the court applied the proper analysis to the stated claims, the court would have concluded that all the claims asserted fall comfortably within the broad scope of patentable subject matter under § 101. Accordingly, we hold as a matter of law that Excel was not entitled to the grant of summary judgment of invalidity of the '184 patent under § 101.

Since the case must be returned to the trial court for further proceedings, and to avoid any possible misunderstandings as to the scope of our decision, we note that the ultimate validity of these claims depends upon their satisfying the other requirements for patentability such as those set forth in 35 U.S.C. §§ 102, 103, and 112. Thus, on remand, those questions, as well as any others the parties may properly raise, remain for disposition.

Conclusion

The district court's summary judgment of invalidity is reversed, and the case is remanded for further proceedings consistent with this opinion.

REVERSED & REMANDED.

Notes

1.   By ruling that the transformation need not be physical has the Federal Circuit opened the door to pure software patents? Is the court here refusing to follow the Supreme Court's decision in *Benson*? Now that there is only one court of appeals for all patent cases, will the Supreme Court no longer involve itself in issues of substantive patent law?

2.   In this decision, the Federal Circuit says that "patentability" under 35 U.S.C. § 101 is a "question of law which we review without deference." Contrary to the practice of the Federal Circuit in this case, most reviewing courts today review agency rulemaking, whether done by "notice-comment" rulemaking or by decisions in individual cases, under a highly deferential "arbitrary and capricious" standard of review. § 706(2)(a) of the Administrative Procedure Act (APA), 5 U.S.C. § 706(2)(a). The logic underlying this

deference is that the administrative agencies have considerably more expertise than do the courts, and accordingly the agencies should be permitted to "flesh out" their enabling statutes with substantive rules. *U.S. v. Haggar*, 526 U.S. 380, 119 S.Ct. 1392, 143 L.Ed.2d 480 (1999); *Chevron v. Natural Resources Defense Council*, 467 U.S. 837, 104 S.Ct. 2778, 81 L.Ed.2d 694 (1984). Why should a different standard of review be applied to patent law decisions of the PTO than is applied, for example, to labor law and environmental law decisions of the NLRB and EPA? Does the *Zurko* case (see next paragraph), which directs the Federal Circuit to apply the APA standards of review when reviewing findings of fact, also direct the Federal Circuit to grant much more deference towards the PTO's decisions and rules on substantive patent law?

3. When reviewing a factual decision made by a trial court, Federal appellate courts are mildly deferential and reverse only if the decision is "clearly erroneous." (Federal Rules of Civil Procedure 52(a)) This "clearly erroneous" standard would apply when the Federal Circuit is reviewing a decision of a Federal District Court in patent litigation. When reviewing the factual basis for a refusal of the PTO to issue a patent, the Federal Circuit must apply an even more deferential standard of review that is defined in § 706 of the APA (5 U.S.C. § 706). *Dickinson v. Zurko*, 527 U.S. 150, 119 S.Ct. 1816, 144 L.Ed.2d 143 (1999). A factual finding of the PTO is reversed by the Federal Circuit only if it is not supported by "substantial evidence." *In re Gartside*, 203 F.3d 1305 (Fed.Cir.2000). The "substantiality" of the "evidence" must be weighed against the "entire record or those portions cited" to the reviewing court. *Universal Camera v. NLRB*, 340 U.S. 474, 71 S.Ct. 456, 95 L.Ed. 456 (1951) Accordingly, this agency "substantial evidence" standard of review is not as deferential as the similarly-named jury "substantial evidence" standard applied when testing whether a jury finding of fact can be overturned. (Courts and law students frequently confuse these two standards.)

4. In this decision, the Federal Circuit does not address "obviousness" under 35 U.S.C. § 103, since it is reviewing a "summary judgment" dismissal based upon § 101. Is this invention, which enables a long distance service to grant a special discount when two of its subscribers talk to each other, "obvious" in view of the prior-art "friends and family discount" promotional and pricing scheme that is briefly described in the patent itself? (*see* U.S. Patent No. 5,333,184, Column 2, lines 5 to 16). Once a patent issues, the patent is "presumed" to be valid, 35 U.S.C. § 282, and this presumption normally applies to prior art reviewed by the patent Examiner and identified on the cover page of the patent in the listing of "References Cited." Does brief mention of the "Friends and Family" long distance discount plan prior art in the "Summary of The Invention" portion of the '184 patent also give rise to this presumption of validity? If so, how can this presumption that the patent is valid over the "Friends and Family" prior art be overcome at trial? (Under the "Friends and Family" plan, the long distance company offered a discount for all calls to numbers on a list submitted by the subscriber.)

5. Since the Court says questions of patentability are questions of law, are questions of "novelty" under § 102 and "obviousness" under § 103 also questions of law? Does the Federal Circuit review "not novel" and "obvious" holdings "without deference" to the trial court and to the PTO? Think about

this issue as you read the cases which follow. Contrast the Federal Circuit's handling of the § 101 and § 103 issues in this case with the very different approach taken by the Supreme Court in *Dann v. Johnston,* 425 U.S. 219 (1976), where the Court did not address the § 101 issue at all but ruled instead that a modification to a bank accounting system was "obvious" under § 103.

E. NOVELTY AND ANTICIPATION—§ 102

Notes on § 102

1. Section 102 of Title 35 defines what is meant by "novelty"—the requirement that an invention be new. It is written as a set of seven rules any one of which can prevent one from obtaining a patent.

2. Under § 102(a), the applicant for a patent must be the true first inventor: the applicant must have invented the invention prior to its use in this country by others and also prior to the appearance of its description in a printed publication anywhere in the world published by others.

Use of the invention in another country, without any publication of the invention, does not prevent the patenting of the invention by someone else in this country, but one cannot borrow an invention from overseas and patent it here, since one must be a true inventor and not a plagarist (§ 102(f)).

The filing in the United States of a patent application is not a "publication" under § 102(a). However, if the patent application is later published, or if it matures into a patent which is published, this publication is statutorily construed by § 102(e) to have occurred when the application was first filed. This publication thus prevents one who invents after the application filing date from obtaining a patent.

If there are two inventors each claiming to be the first, § 102(g) says that the first to conceive the invention who was also diligent in reducing the invention to practice (by building a working model or by filing a patent application) is the true first inventor. Contests between two such inventors are resolved by interference proceedings in the PTO (§ 135) or in the courts (§ 291). And, of course, if one abandons one's invention, one cannot go back later and claim the original date of invention (§ 102(c)). Unlike the United States, other countries generally award the patent to the first inventor to file an application.

3. Under § 102(b), the applicant must file a patent application promptly: no later than 12 months after the first "sale" or "public use" of the invention in the United States or "publication" of a description of the invention anywhere in the world.

The "public use" of an invention can be completely private and secret so long as the use is not an experimental use. Private use of a corset for ten years was held to be "public use". *Egbert v. Lippmann,* 104 U.S. 333, 26 L.Ed. 755 (1881). Likewise secret use of a process was held to be "public use", *Metallizing Engineering Co. v. Kenyon Bearing & Auto Parts Co.,* 153 F.2d 516 (2d Cir.1946), and market testing has been held to be "public use," not experimental use. *Western Marine Electronics, Inc. v. Furuno Electric*

Co., Ltd., 764 F.2d 840 (Fed.Cir.1985). When developing software, it is important to document "bug" reports and fixes to establish proof of experimental use that is product testing and not market testing. "Beta testing," the testing of new software by friendly users, is essential in software development. It is important to monitor Beta testing to avoid unintended "public use." A "printed publication" can be ten to twenty handouts at a show, a microfilm in a public library, or a newspaper article printed in Mongolian in a provincial newspaper in Mongolia.

An invention normally cannot be "on sale" before it is built, but it can be "on sale" if it is offered to buyers when the specifications have been worked out in such full detail that implementation will be straightforward. *Pfaff v. Wells*, 525 U.S. 55, 119 S.Ct. 304, 142 L.Ed.2d 261 (1998).

Another way that one can delay too long is by waiting for more than a year after filing a foreign patent application and then failing to file in the U.S. before the foreign patent issues (§ 102(d)).

4. In virtually all countries other than the United States, the application for a patent must file *before* the invention is disclosed publicly in any way. If foreign patents are desired, the initial U.S. filing must precede public disclosure of the invention, and foreign filing must occur within 12 months thereafter, to obtain the priority date of the United States invention in accordance with Article 4 of the Paris Convention for the Protection of Intellectual Property. To protect foreign rights, it is important to have employees and outside organizations that test the programs sign and obey confidentiality agreements.

5. Foreign inventors may claim the priority of their foreign filing dates if they file in the United States within twelve months. 35 U.S.C. § 119. Likewise, U.S. citizens, by treaty, may claim the priority of their U.S. filing date before a foreign Patent Office, if they file in the foreign country within twelve months.

6. The Patent Act, 35 U.S.C. § 351 *et seq.*, also provides for the filing of an "International Application" under the Patent Cooperation Treaty which may be effective in many countries, including the U.S.A. A "national" phase of patent prosecution in each designated country follows an initial search of the "prior art" and optional examination conducted by the United States Patent and Trademark Office acting as an "international searching authority" under the treaty.

7. It is important to distinguish the concept of novelty (§ 102) from that of "non-obviousness" (§ 103). In § 102, the term "invention" has a very precise meaning. You will recall that every patent, and every patent application, contains numbered paragraphs called "claims." Each of these "claims" precisely defines and lists the elements that comprise an "invention." Accordingly, a patent or patent application that contains 23 claims also contains 23 precisely-defined inventions.

When § 102(a) and § 102(b) say an "invention was ... described in a printed publication," this means that the publication contains every element of the claim which defines that particular invention. If the claim lists six separate elements, and if the publication contains all six elements, then the publication "anticipates" the claimed invention, and the invention "lacks novelty." Such a claim is invalid if the publication date precedes the date of the invention (under § 102(a)) or if the publication date precedes the application filing date by more than one year (under § 102(b)). Likewise, to "anticipate" a claimed invention, the thing that was "known or used" or "patented" or "in public use" or "on sale" must contain each and every element of the claim.

If the publication, or the thing placed on sale or into public use, lacks even one element of the claim, even if it contains all of the other elements of the claim, then the claim is "novel," and the § 102 test has been passed. The invention is then "new." One then moves on to the § 103 "obviousness" test to see if the invention, while new, is so obvious to one skilled in the art that it does not merit patent protection. If two separately published articles must be combined to reveal all the elements of an invention as claimed, then the invention is "novel", since it is not fully revealed in a single published article. The invention may still be obvious if there is some suggestion in one of the articles to combine the teachings of the two articles.

APPLICATION OF BERGY

United States Court of Customs and Patent Appeals, 1979.
596 F.2d 952.

RICH, JUDGE

* * *

ANATOMY OF THE PATENT STATUTE

* * *

All of the statutory law relevant to the present case is found in four of the five sections in Chapter 10, the first chapter of Part II:

Sec. 100 Definitions

Sec. 101 Inventions patentable [if they qualify]

Sec. 102 Conditions for patentability; novelty and loss of right to patent

Sec. 103 Conditions for patentability; non-obvious subject matter

More strictly speaking, these cases involve only § 101, as did *Flook*. Achieving the ultimate goal of a patent under those statutory provisions involves, to use an analogy, having the separate keys to open in succession the three doors of sections 101, 102, and 103, the last two guarding the public interest by assuring that patents are not granted which would take from the public that which it already enjoys (matters already within its knowledge whether in actual use or not) or *potentially* enjoys by reason of obviousness from knowledge which it already has.

Inventors of patentable inventions, as a class, are those who bridge the chasm between the known and the obvious on the one side and that which promotes progress in useful arts or technology on the other.

The first door which must be opened on the difficult path to patentability is § 101 (augmented by the § 100 definitions), * * *. The person approaching that door is *an inventor*, whether his invention is patentable or not. There is always an inventor; being an inventor might be regarded as a preliminary legal requirement, for if he has not invented something, if he comes with something he knows was invented by someone else, he has no right even to approach the door. Thus, section 101 begins with the words "Whoever invents or discovers," and since 1790 the patent statutes have always said substantially that. Being an inventor or having an invention, however, is no guarantee of opening even the first door. What *kind* of an invention or discovery is it? In dealing with the question of kind, as distinguished from the qualitative conditions which make the invention patentable, § 101 is broad and general; its language is: "any * * * process, machine, manufacture, or composition of matter, or any * * * improvement thereof." Section 100(b) further expands "process" to include "art or method and * * * a new use of a known process, machine, manufacture, composition of matter, or material." If the invention, as the inventor defines it in his claims (pursuant to § 112, second paragraph), falls into any one of the named categories, he is allowed to pass through to the second door, which is § 102; "novelty and loss of right to patent" is the sign on it. Notwithstanding the words "new and useful" in § 101, the invention is not examined under that statute for novelty because that is not the statutory scheme of things or the long-established administrative practice.

Section 101 *states* three requirements: novelty, utility, and statutory subject matter. The understanding that these three requirements are *separate and distinct* is long-standing and has been universally accepted. The text writers are all in accord and treat these requirements under separate chapters and headings. Thus, the questions of whether a particular invention is *novel* or *useful* are questions wholly apart from whether the invention falls into a category of *statutory subject matter*. Of the three requirements *stated* in § 101, only two, utility and statutory subject matter, are *applied* under § 101. As we shall show, in 1952 Congress voiced its intent to consider the novelty of an invention under § 102 where it is first made clear what the statute means by "new", notwithstanding the fact that this requirement is first *named* in § 101.

The PTO, in administering the patent laws, has, for the most part, consistently applied § 102 in making rejections for lack of novelty. * * *

* * *

The second door then, as we have already seen, is § 102 pursuant to which the inventor's claims are examined for novelty, requiring, for the first time in the examination process, comparison with the prior art which, up to this point, has therefore been irrelevant.

Section 102 also contains other conditions under the heading "loss of right" which need not be considered here. An *invention* may be in a statutory category and not be patentable for want of *novelty*, or it may be novel and still not be patentable because it must meet yet another condition existing in the law since 1850 when *Hotchkiss v. Greenwood*, 11 How. 248, 13 L.Ed. 683, was decided. This condition developed in the ensuing century into the *"requirement for invention."*

The third door, under the 1952 Act, is § 103 which was enacted *to take the place of the requirement for "invention."* We need not examine this requirement in detail for it is not involved in the present appeals, and was not involved in *Flook*. It will suffice to quote what the House and Senate reports, cited *supra*—"signals" from Congress—say about the third requirement, from which it will be seen that, again, the claimed invention for which a patent is sought must be compared with the prior art.

* * *

If the inventor holds the three different keys to the three doors, his *invention* (here assumed to be "useful") qualifies for a patent, otherwise not; but he, as *inventor*, must meet still other statutory requirements in the preparation and prosecution of his patent application. We need not here consider the latter because appellants have not been faulted by the PTO in their paperwork or behavior. * * *

Note

Judge Rich then went on to find that both Bergy's and Chakrabarty's claims, directed to living products of genetic engineering, defined subject matter that falls within the categories named in § 101. Judge Baldwin concurred, disagreeing with Rich on some points. Judge Miller dissented. A badly divided Supreme Court later affirmed the *Chakrabarty* portion of this decision in *Diamond v. Chakrabarty*, 447 U.S. 303 (1980), the pioneering decision under § 101 holding genetically-modified life forms to be patentable.

F. NON–OBVIOUSNESS—§ 103

The *novelty* test, administered under § 102, is a fairly objective test: a publication either contains all the elements of a patent claim, or it does not. Contrariwise, the *obviousness* test under § 103 is a subjective test upon which reasonable minds can and do differ. Granted, the invention is new, because all of its elements do not appear together in one publication. But there are two publications which, when laid side by side, disclose all the elements of the invention. Would it be obvious to an engineer skilled in the technology to which the invention relates to combine the teachings of the two publications? Here we have the makings of many grand arguments presented to patent examiners and juries and judges alike.

Although § 103 speaks of "nonobviousness" "at the time the invention was made," any public use or sale in this country or any publication anywhere occurring after the invention was made but more than one year prior to the application filing date may be included in the "prior art" that one "skilled in the art" is presumed to know about. *Application of Foster*, 343 F.2d 980 (C.C.P.A. 1965). (Note the characterization of the holding in Judge Smith's strong dissent: "... [F]rom this day forward obviousness under § 103 will be tested, not as of the time the invention was made, but as of one year prior to the filing date of the application.") For example, if the invention was "made" four years before the application filing date, and if two publications, published just over a year before the filing date, disclose all the elements of the invention, then *Foster* holds that these two publications are part of the "prior art" that one skilled in the art four years before the filing date is presumed to know about, even though this is obviously not true. This fiction means, in practical effect, that the "prior art" includes all public uses (in this country), all sales (in this country) and all publications (anywhere) occurring: (1) more than a year before a patent's filing date; or (2) prior to the date of invention. This "prior art" is used both to test the invention for novelty under § 102 and also to test it for nonobviousness under § 103.

To test an invention for patentability, you first assemble the "prior art." If all the elements of a patent claim (which defines an invention) can be found in a single item of "prior art" (a single article, for example), then the invention is not "novel," and § 102 blocks patentability. If the novelty test is passed, the invention is "new," and one moves on to the § 103 test. If all the elements of a patent claim (which defines an invention) can be found in two or more items of "prior art" (two or more articles or patents, for example), and if a hypothetical individual "skilled in the art" and familiar with these items of "prior art" would find the invention to be "obvious," then § 103 blocks patentability.

The cryptic language of § 103 provides little guidance to the application of the "nonobviousness" test in practice. The Supreme Court has offered some suggestions in the leading case of *Graham v. John Deere Co.*, 383 U.S. 1, 17–18, 86 S.Ct. 684, 694, 15 L.Ed.2d 545 (1966):

> While the ultimate question of patent validity is one of law, *Great A. & P. Tea Co. v. Supermarket Equipment Corp.*, *supra*, 340 U.S. [147] at 155 [71 S.Ct. 127 at 132, 95 L.Ed. 162 at 545], the § 103 condition, which is but one of three conditions, each of which must be satisfied, lends itself to several basic factual inquiries. Under § 103, the scope and content of the prior art are to be determined; differences between the prior art and the claims at issue are to be ascertained; and the level of ordinary skill in the pertinent art resolved. Against this background, the obviousness or nonobviousness of the subject matter is determined. Such secondary considerations as commercial success, long felt but unsolved needs, failure of others, etc., might be utilized to give light to the circumstances surrounding the origin of the subject matter sought to be patented. As indicia of obviousness or nonobviousness, these inquiries may have relevancy. *See* Note, Subtests of "Nonobviousness": A Nontechnical Approach to Patent Validity, 112 U.Pa.L.Rev. 1169 (1964).

This is not to say, however, that there will not be difficulties in applying the nonobviousness test. What is obvious is not a question upon which there is likely to be uniformity of thought in every given factual context. The difficulties, however, are comparable to those encountered daily by the courts in such frames of reference as negligence and scienter, and should be amenable to a case-by-case development. We believe that strict observance of the requirements laid down here will result in that uniformity and definiteness which Congress called for in the 1952 Act.

The following case illustrates the application of § 103 in an Internet context.

AMAZON.COM, INC.
v. BARNESANDNOBLE.COM, INC.

United States District Court, W.D. Washington, 1999.
73 F.Supp.2d 1228.

PECHMAN, DISTRICT JUDGE.

I. INTRODUCTION

On October 21, 1999, Plaintiff Amazon.com filed a complaint in this Court alleging patent infringement by Defendants Barnesandnoble.com Inc. and Barnesandnoble.com LLC (hereinafter referred to collectively as "Barnesandnoble.com"). The patent in question is United States Patent No. 5,960,411 (the '411 patent), which was issued on September 28, 1999. The '411 patent describes a Method and System for Placing a Purchase Order Via a Communications Network and includes 26 claims.

The '411 patent, in essence, describes a method and system in which a consumer can complete a purchase order for an item via the Internet using only a single action (such as a single click of a computer mouse button) once information identifying the item is displayed to the consumer. This method and system is only applicable in situations where a retailer already has in its files various information about the purchaser (such as the purchaser's address and credit card number) and where the purchaser's client system (e.g., a personal computer) has been provided with an identifier that enables the retailer's server system to identify the purchaser.

Amazon.com alleges that Defendants' "Express Lane" ordering feature infringes various claims of the '411 patent. Concurrently with its complaint, Amazon.com filed a motion for a preliminary injunction to enjoin Barnesandnoble.com from infringing the '411 patent. * * *

* * *

Defendants raised a number of defenses in their pleadings and during the hearing. In support of their position that Amazon.com is not likely to succeed at a trial on the merits, Defendants placed particular emphasis on arguments that the '411 patent is invalid on obviousness and anticipation grounds and that the Express Lane feature does not infringe any claims in the '411 patent. To a lesser extent, Defendants also suggested that the '411 patent is unenforceable. In addition, Defendants argued that Amazon.com could not demonstrate irreparable harm, that the balance of hardships did not tip in Amazon.com's favor, and that the public interest would not be served by issuance of a preliminary injunction.

On November 22, 1999, following the testimony of all witnesses and the submission of evidence, the parties presented proposed findings of fact and conclusions of law to the Court. The Court heard closing arguments on November 23, 1999. Based on the papers, pleadings, testimony, evidence, and arguments presented by the parties, the Court finds that Plaintiff has demonstrated: (1) a reasonable likelihood of success on the merits at trial; (2) it will suffer irreparable harm if the preliminary injunction is not granted; (3) the balance of hardships tips in its favor; and (4) the preliminary injunction sought is in the public interest. Although Defendants have raised a number of defenses concerning the validity of the patent and infringement of the patent, Plaintiff has shown that the defenses asserted by Defendant lack substantial merit. Therefore, the Court hereby GRANTS Plaintiff's motion for a preliminary injunction.

The Preliminary Injunction is effective at 12:01 a.m. P.S.T. on Saturday, December 4, 1999, and upon Amazon.com's filing an undertaking in the sum of $10,000,000, and shall remain in effect during the pendency of this action. Defendants may, however, continue to offer an Express Lane feature if the feature is modified in a manner that is consistent with this Order to avoid infringement of the '411 patent.

Pursuant to Fed.R.Civ.P. 52(a), the Court's findings of facts and conclusions of law are set forth below.

II. FINDINGS OF FACT

Background

1. Plaintiff Amazon.com, Inc. ("Amazon.com") is a Delaware corporation with its principal place of business at Seattle, Washington. Through its website, www.amazon.com, the company enables customers to find and purchase books, music, videos, consumer electronics, games, toys, gifts, electronic greeting cards, and other items over the World Wide Web. Amazon.com is the leading online retailer of books.

2. Defendant Barnesandnoble.com LLC is a Delaware limited liability company with its principal place of business at New York, New York. Barnesandnoble.com LLC operates a website through which it distributes books, software, music, and other items.

* * *

4. Sometime before May 1997, Amazon.com CEO Jeffrey Bezos conceived of an idea to enable Amazon.com customers to purchase items

with a single-click of a computer mouse button. This idea was commercially implemented by Amazon.com in September of 1997.

5.   On September 28, 1999, United States Patent No. 5,960,411 (the " '411 patent"), entitled "Method and System for Placing a Purchase Order Via a Communications Network," was issued. The filing date for the '411 patent is September 21, 1997. The patent was assigned to and is owned by Amazon.com.

* * *

Prior Art

7.   Plaintiff's expert Geoffrey Mulligan testified that except for single-action ordering and the implementation of single-action ordering without a shopping cart model, everything in the independent claims of the '411 patent (claims 1, 6, 9, and 11) is in prior art.

8.   In support of their arguments that the single-action ordering element of the '411 patent is invalid on obviousness and anticipation grounds, Defendants offered evidence concerning several prior art references. This evidence of prior art falls into two general categories: systems for ordering tangible items online (such as groceries or computer equipment) and electronic document delivery systems. In the former category were Dr. John Lockwood's Web Basket system, the Netscape Merchant System described in the "Creating a Virtual Store" reference, and the "Oliver's Market" web pages. In the latter category were the CompuServe financial information service represented by Mr. Alexander Trevor's testimony regarding the "Trend" feature, and U.S. Patent No. 5,708,780 (the '780 patent). It is undisputed that these prior art references were not before the PTO when the '411 patent was examined.

[The Court then goes on to describe the prior art in considerable detail. None of the prior art enabled one to purchase something with one click of a mouse button.—Eds.]

* * *

Netscape Merchant System

13.   Defendants also presented as a prior art reference an excerpt from a book entitled "Creating the Virtual Store" that was copyrighted in 1996. Defendants focused on the following language from this reference: "Merchants also can provide shoppers with an instant buy button for some or all items, enabling them to skip check out review. This provides added appeal for customers who already know the single item they want to purchase during their shopping excursion." Defendants argue that the Netscape Marchant System reference anticipates each of the independent claims of the '411 patent and that this reference, either alone or in combination with other prior art references, renders the claims of the '411 patent obvious.

* * *

15. Read in context, the few lines relied on by Defendants appear to describe only the elimination of the checkout review step, leaving at least two other required steps to complete a purchase. Thus, apart from the words "instant buy," there is no indication that the Netscape system implements a single-action ordering component as required by claims 6 and 9 of the '411 patent or a single action as required by claims 1 and 11 of the '411 patent. Moreover, Defendants' expert acknowledged that he did not know how the Netscape instant buy feature worked.

* * *

Summary of Prior Art

27. There are key differences between each of the prior art references cited by Defendants and the method and system described in the claims of the '411 patent. The Court finds that none of the prior art references offered by Defendants anticipate the claims of the '411 patent. On the question of obviousness, the Court finds that the differences between the prior art references submitted by Defendants and the '411 patent claims are significant. Moreover, there is insufficient evidence in the record regarding a teaching, suggestion, or motivation in the prior art that would lead one of ordinary skill in the art of e-commerce to combine the references. The Court finds particularly telling Dr. Lockwood's admission that it never occurred to him to modify his Web Basket program to enable single-action ordering, despite his testimony that such a modification would be easy to implement. This admission serves to negate Dr. Lockwood's conclusory statements that prior art references teach to one of ordinary skill in the art the invention of the '411 patent.

Barnesandnoble.com's Shopping Cart and Express Lane

28. Barnesandnoble.com offers customers two purchasing options. One is called Shopping Cart and the other is called Express Lane. The two methods are separate and cannot be combined. (Ex. 9, Mulligan Decl. at Ex. I (noting "Express Lane and the Shopping Cart are two different ways to place your order. You can't combine them")). The Barnesandnoble.com Shopping Cart option includes the steps of a standard shopping cart model, including adding items to a virtual shopping cart and "checking out" to complete the purchase.

29. Barnesandnoble.com's Express Lane allows customers who have registered for the feature to purchase items by simply clicking on the Express Lane button shown on the detail or product page that describes and identifies the book or other item to be purchased. The text beneath the Express Lane button invites the user to "Buy it now with just 1 click!"

30. Throughout its web site, Barnesandnoble.com consistently describes Express Lane as a one-click ordering method. In its May 1999 prospectus, Barnesandnoble.com consistently described Express Lane as making one-click ordering possible. In its November 1999 10–Q Report to shareholders, Barnesandnoble.com describes Express Lane as a one-

click ordering system. It does not appear that Barnesandnoble.com has ever described the Express Lane ordering process as requiring more than one action, other than in the course of this litigation.

31.   Barnesandnoble.com began using the Express Lane feature in May of 1998, describing the feature in a press release as "Express Lane (SM) One Click Ordering" and noting that "[n]ow, visitors can click one button to order books, software and magazines."

32.   Clicking on the shopping cart icon on the top of every Barnesandnoble.com page will not show the items that the user has purchased using the Express Lane.

33.   The strong similarities between the Amazon.com 1–click feature and the Express Lane feature subsequently adopted by Barnesandnoble.com suggest that Barnesandnoble.com copied Amazon.com's feature.

Direct Evidence of Nonobviousness

34.   Amazon.com has provided direct evidence of nonobviousness. Jeff Bezos, Amazon.com's founder and an inventor on the '411 patent, testified that because "many customers were tentative and somewhat fearful of on-line purchasing, conventional wisdom was that they had to be slowly and incrementally led to the point of purchase. In addition, consumers were not acclimated to rely without confirmation on stored personal information for correct shipping and billing."

35.   Professor Eric Johnson of Columbia Business School testified in his declaration that "Amazon.com's 1–Click (R) purchasing was a major innovation in on-line retailing that allows for purchasing without disrupting the consumer's shopping experience; and by eliminating additional confirmation requirements, recasts the default in a way that both maximizes the likelihood that consumers will complete their purchases and minimizes consumer anxiety over real or perceived issues of internet security."

36.   Moreover, despite their experience with prior art shopping cart models of on-line purchasing, both sides' technical experts acknowledged that they had never conceived of the invention. Mr. Mulligan testified that ordering with one click was "a huge leap from what was done in the past." Mr. Mulligan testified further that: "I've been working in electronic commerce for years now. And I've never thought of the idea of being able to turn a shopping cart or take the idea of clicking on an item and suddenly having the item ship—having the complete process done." Mr. Mulligan also testified that he believed it was "a huge leap of faith for the website and the consumer to implement something like this." Additionally, as noted above, Dr. Lockwood testified that he never thought of modifying Web Basket to provide single-action ordering.

Objective Factors

37.   Plaintiff's single-action ordering method addressed an unsolved need that had been long-felt (at least in the relatively short period of

time that e-commerce has existed), namely streamlining the on-line ordering process to reduce the high percentage of orders that are begun but never completed, *i.e.*, abandoned shopping carts. The problem of on-line consumers starting but abandoning shopping carts was acknowledged by both parties and their experts.

* * *

40.   Amazon.com's single-action ordering is used by millions of customers, indicating the commercial success of the feature. Barnesandnoble.com's Express Lane also accounts for a significant portion of its sales. Further evidence of commercial success of single-action ordering is suggested by the fact that Barnesandnoble.com promoted its Express Lane feature in a press release after it was announced and in its prospectus Indeed, Barnesandnoble.com described Express Lane as one of its "major enhancements" to its on-line business.

* * *

Irreparable Harm

42.   The harm that would be suffered by Amazon.com due to Barnesandnoble.com's infringement during the pendency of this case would be irreparable. The invention described in the '411 patent is of significant commercial value, as evidenced, among other things, by the large number of customers who make use of single-action ordering available on the websites of both Amazon.com and Barnesandnoble.com, and by the large number of other e-commerce retailers whom Barnesandnoble.com claims have adopted single-action ordering.

43.   The harm Amazon.com would suffer if denied the benefit of using its invention to distinguish itself from its competitor Barnesandnoble.com could not easily be measured in dollars.

* * *

III.   Conclusions of Law

* * *

Preliminary Injunction Standard

4.   "[T]o obtain a preliminary injunction, pursuant to 35 U.S.C. § 283, a party must establish a right thereto in light of four factors: (1) reasonable likelihood of success on the merits; (2) irreparable harm; (3) the balance of hardships tipping in its favor; and (4) the impact of the injunction on the public interest." *Hybritech, Inc. v. Abbott Labs.*, 849 F.2d 1446, 1451 (Fed.Cir.1988).

A.   Likelihood of Success on the Merits

Validity

5.   The statutory presumption of validity, 35 U.S.C. § 282, applies to all patents and is meant "to contribute stability to the grant of patent

rights." *Magnivision, Inc. v. Bonneau Co.*, 115 F.3d 956, 958 (Fed.Cir. 1997). This presumption operates at every stage of the litigation, including in a motion for preliminary injunction against an alleged infringer. *See Canon Computer Systems, Inc. v. Nu–Kote Int'l, Inc.*, 134 F.3d 1085, 1088 (Fed.Cir.1998). * * *

Anticipation

6. Anticipation is a question of fact, *see Atlas Powder Co. v. Ireco Inc.*, 190 F.3d 1342, 1346 (Fed.Cir.1999), and is a defense only if "all of the same elements are found in exactly the same situation and united in the same way . . . in a single prior art reference." *Perkin-Elmer Corp. v. Computervision Corp.*, 732 F.2d 888, 894 (Fed.Cir.1984). Although anticipation is a factual inquiry, the Court reiterates its findings and the applicable law here for ease of reference.

7. The Court finds that Web Basket does not anticipate any claim of the '411 patent. Each claim of the '411 patent requires either "a single-action ordering component" [claims 1–10] or "a single action that is to be performed to order the identified item" [claims 11–26]. The Web Basket ordering process requires that the user perform at least five actions to complete the order. Web Basket, therefore, does not include "a single-action ordering component" or "a single action that is to be performed to order the identified item."

8. In addition, claims 1–5 and 11–26 require that "the item is ordered without using a shopping cart ordering model" [claims 1–5] or "the item is ordered independently of a shopping cart model" [claims 11–26]. Because Web Basket is itself a shopping cart model, it lacks these required elements as well.

9. The description of the Netscape Instant Buy option presented by Defendants consisted of a total of four lines. Defendants' expert Dr. Lockwood was unable to supply any additional information regarding the feature described by this reference and ultimately admitted that he did not know how the feature worked. The Netscape reference therefore does not teach the invention to one of ordinary skill in the art (e.g., Dr. Lockwood) as is required for an anticipatory reference.

* * *

Obviousness

19. "Included within the presumption of validity mandated by 35 U.S.C. § 282 is a presumption of nonobviousness which the patent challenger must overcome by proving facts with clear and convincing evidence. The presumption remains intact even upon proof of prior art not cited by the Patent and Trademark Office (PTO), though such art, if more relevant than that cited, may enable the challenger to sustain its burden." *Perkin-Elmer Corp. v. Computervision Corp.*, 732 F.2d 888, 894 (Fed.Cir.1984) (citations omitted).

20. The issue of obviousness is a mixed question of fact and law. The ultimate question is one of law, but it is based on several factual

inquiries, including: (1) the scope and content of the prior art; (2) the differences between the prior art and the claims; (3) the level of ordinary skill in the pertinent art; and (4) applicable secondary considerations. *See Weatherchem Corp. v. J.L. Clark, Inc.*, 163 F.3d 1326, 1332 (Fed.Cir. 1998).

21. Defendants' evidence relating to invalidity of claims of the '411 patent on the ground of obviousness consists largely of Dr. Lockwood's statements that he could modify his Web Basket system to actually be a single-action ordering system, and that doing so would be an "obvious" or "trivial" modification of the Web Basket system. Dr. Lockwood, however, testified (as did Mr. Mulligan), that it had never occurred to him to do this. Mr. Mulligan further produced credible testimony why one skilled in the art would not, at the time the invention was made, have considered this modification.

22. In any event, whether it would be, at the present time, an "obvious" or "trivial" modification of the Web Basket system to include the "single action" feature of the '411 patent is legally irrelevant. The law is clear that the time period for any obviousness determination is "at the time the invention was made." 35 U.S.C. § 103(a). *See also, In re Dembiczak*, 175 F.3d 994, 998–99 (Fed.Cir.1999).

* * *

26. The adoption of single-action ordering by other e-commerce retailers following Amazon.com's introduction of the feature, coupled with the need to solve the problem of abandoned shopping carts by e-commerce customers, is additional evidence of nonobviousness. *See In re Hayes Microcomputer Products, Inc. Patent Litigation*, 982 F.2d 1527, 1540 (Fed.Cir.1992) ("[T]he commercial success of the invention, the failure of others to solve the problem addressed by the patented invention, and the fact that the [invention] has become the industry standard is compelling objective evidence of the nonobviousness of the claimed invention").

27. In light of its consideration of the factors and evidence related to the question of obviousness, the Court finds Barnesandnoble.com is unlikely to succeed in showing by clear and convincing evidence that the claims of the '411 patent were obvious. Barnesandnoble.com's reliance on the simplicity of the invention is unavailing. "Defining the problem in terms of its solution reveals improper hindsight in the selection of the prior art relevant to obviousness." *Monarch Knitting Machinery Corp. v. Sulzer Morat Gmbh*, 139 F.3d 877, 881 (Fed.Cir.1998).

* * *

Infringement Analysis

30. Defendants have also argued that Plaintiff has not demonstrated that the "Express Lane" feature infringes any claims of the '411 patent. "[A]nalysis of patent infringement involves two steps: (1) claim construction to determine what the claims cover, i.e., their scope, fol-

lowed by (2) determination of whether the properly construed claims encompass the accused structure." *Cole v. Kimberly–Clark Corp.*, 102 F.3d 524, 528 (Fed.Cir.1996). The former is a question of law; the latter is a question of fact. *See Voice Technologies Group v. VMC Systems, Inc.*, 164 F.3d 605, 612 (Fed.Cir.1999). For ease of reference, the Court includes its entire infringement analysis in the Conclusions of Law section, even though it presents mixed questions of law and fact.

Claim Construction

31. The parties do not dispute the meaning of most of the terms in the patent claims including: "client system"; "server system"; and "method for ordering." The parties disagree, however, as to the meaning of the terms "shopping cart model," "fulfillment," "single action," and "single-action ordering component."

* * *

34. The definition of shopping cart model in the background section of the '411 patent is consistent with that provided by Amazon.com's e-commerce experts Dr. Johnson and Mr. Mulligan.

35. Dr. Lockwood defined a shopping cart model more broadly in a manner that could potentially include any method for buying on-line. In general, the Court found Dr. Lockwood's description of the term "shopping cart model" to be confusing and inconsistent. Barnesandnoble.com's Chief Information Officer, Mr. King, gave a similarly broad definition of shopping cart model. According to its own expert Dr. Lockwood, under Defendants' definition of shopping cart model, claims 1 and 11 would appear to be internally inconsistent. Similarly, Mr. King testified that with Barnesandnoble.com's definition of shopping cart model, claims 1 and 11 would not cover the single-action purchasing method described in the '411 patent.

36. A claim interpretation that excludes the preferred embodiment is "rarely, if ever, correct." *Vitronics Corp. v. Conceptronic, Inc.*, 90 F.3d 1576, 1583 (Fed.Cir.1996). "When claims are amenable to more than one construction, they should when reasonably possible be interpreted so as to preserve their validity." *Modine Mfg. Co. v. U.S. Int'l Trade Comm'n*, 75 F.3d 1545, 1557 (Fed.Cir.1996). The Court, therefore, rejects the definition of "shopping cart model" propounded by Defendants.

37. The Court adopts instead a definition which is consistent with the patent specification, preserves the validity of the claims, and allows the claims to be read on the preferred embodiment described in the patent specification. In construing the claims, the Court, therefore, takes the term "shopping cart model" to mean a method for on-line ordering in which a user selects and accumulates items to be purchased while browsing a merchant's site and then must proceed to one or more checkout or confirmation steps in order to complete the purchase.

38. The second point of disagreement is the meaning of the terms "fulfill" and "order fulfillment component" in claims 6 and 9, and in particular whether "fulfill" or "fulfillment" refer to computer or physi-

cal process. Though the patent specification does not explicitly define the phrase, order "filling" and "fulfillment" is discussed at length at column 8 and figure 7 in the context of Amazon.com's order consolidation algorithm. That discussion and the entire specification describe only computer processes and an order is defined to be filled "when all its items are currently in inventory (i.e. available) and can be shipped." In addition, Amazon.com's expert Mr. Mulligan testified that an "order fulfillment component" of a "server system" as required by claim 9 is "the software that takes the information provided by the database of the user information and the inventory database and combines those into a shipment order ... and then notifies that the order is ready for shipment."

* * *

41. The third point of disagreement concerns the terms "single action" and "single-action ordering component" as used in claims 1, 6, 9, and 11.

42. The term "single action" is not defined by patent specification. However, the patent specification provides that "once the description of an item is displayed, the purchaser need only take a single action to place the order to purchase that item." The specification also provides that "a single action may be preceded by multiple physical movements of the purchaser (*e.g.*, moving a mouse so that a mouse pointer is over a button)." In addition, the specification indicates "[i]n general, the purchaser need only be aware of the item or items to be ordered by the single action *and* of the single action needed to place the order." As a result, the term "single action" as used in the '411 patent appears to refer to one action (such as clicking a mouse button) that a user takes to purchase an item once the following information is displayed to the user: (1) a description of the item; and (2) a description of the single action the user must take to complete a purchase order for that item.

43. The parties dispute what mouse clicks "count" in determining whether the single-action requirement of the '411 patent claims is satisfied. The Court finds that clicks "count" after both information identifying the item and a description of the single action the user must take to complete a purchase order for that item are displayed to the user.

Comparison of the '411 Patent Claims to Defendants' Express Lane Feature

44. In its opening papers, Amazon.com provided a declaration from its expert Mr. Mulligan explaining in detail where every element of claims 1, 2, 3, 5, 6, 7, 8, 9, 10, 11, 12, 14, 15, 16, 17, 21, 22, 23, 24 is presented in Barnesandnoble.com's Express Lane ordering system. Mr. Mulligan described his analysis with respect to independent claims 9 and 11 in his testimony before the Court.

45. In their pre-hearing briefing, Defendants only disputed Mr. Mulligan's analysis with respect to the meaning of fulfillment in claims 6 and 9 and the meaning of "shopping cart model" in claims 1 and 11. Mr.

King acknowledged that Barnesandnoble.com's Express Lane included every element of claims 11 except the last, which requires that the item is ordered independently of a shopping cart model.

46. Because the Court adopts the patent specification's description of the term "shopping cart model," which is consistent with Mr. Mulligan's testimony, the Court finds that Barnesandnoble.com infringes claims, 1, 2, 3, 5, 11, 12, 14, 15, 16, 17, 21, 22, 23, 24.

47. The Court has also found that the terms "fulfill" and "order fulfillment component" in claims 6 and 9 do not include the retailer's acts of physically locating, packaging, and shipping a tangible item after a purchase order is completed. The Court, therefore finds that Barnesandnoble.com also infringes claims 6–10 of the '411 patent.

* * *

Summary

50. Based on the foregoing, the Court finds that Plaintiff has demonstrated a reasonable likelihood of success on the merits at trial.

B. *Irreparable Harm*

51. The Court finds that Plaintiff has made a strong showing that the '411 patent is valid and that Defendants' Express Lane feature infringes the patent. Plaintiff is therefore entitled to a presumption of irreparable harm. *See, e.g., Smith Int'l, Inc. v. Hughes Tool Co.*, 718 F.2d 1573, 1581 (Fed.Cir.1983) (holding "where validity and continuing infringement have been clearly established ... immediate irreparable harm is presumed"). While Defendants have raised a number of defenses regarding validity, noninfringement, and enforceability, the Court finds that Plaintiff has established that these defenses lack substantial merit.

* * *

55. Beyond the presumption of irreparable harm, there is additional evidence of irreparable harm in the record. Irreparable harm can also be shown by demonstrating that damages are an inadequate remedy. The Federal Circuit uses a variety of factors to determine whether irreparable harm exists. *See* Mills, "The Developing Standard for Irreparable Harm in Preliminary Injunctions to Prevent Patent Infringement," 81 J. Pat. & Trademark Off. Soc'y 51, 65–66 (Jan.1999) (listing factors); *see also Jacobson v. Cox Paving Co.*, 19 U.S.P.Q.2d 1641, 1653 (D.Ariz. 1991) (listing factors and noting that courts have issued injunctions after finding only a few), *aff'd*, 949 F.2d 404 (Fed.Cir.1991).

56. All of the following factors here weigh in favor of a finding of irreparable harm: the parties are direct competitors trying to influence the same group of customers; Amazon.com spent significant time and effort on market development; Defendants' continuing infringement is likely to undermine Amazon.com's market position; and Defendants' unchecked infringement will encourage others to infringe. *See* Mills, *supra*; *see also Atlas Powder Co.*, 773 F.2d at 1233 ("If monetary relief

were the sole relief afforded by the patent statute then … infringers could become compulsory licensees for as long as the litigation lasts"). These sorts of indirect effects are the reason the statute includes injunctive remedies. *See Hybritech*, 849 F.2d at 1457 ("The patent statute provides injunctive relief to preserve the legal interests of the parties against future infringement which may have market effects never fully compensable in money").

* * *

59. Defendants argue that Amazon.com is not entitled to an injunction because its injuries can be compensated in money damages. The cases they cite all hinge on a finding, not applicable here, that the patentee was not entitled to a presumption of irreparable harm because it had not made a clear showing of validity and infringement. *See Nutrition 21 v. Thorne Research, Inc.*, 930 F.2d 867, 871 (Fed.Cir.1991); *Eli Lilly & Co. v. American Cyanamid Co.*, 896 F.Supp. 851, 860 (S.D.Ind.1995). Where the presumption of irreparable harm applies, that plaintiff's injuries are fully compensable cannot alone justify a finding that defendants rebutted the presumption of irreparable harm. *Polymer Technologies*, 103 F.3d at 975–76.

60. Here, Amazon.com has presented ample evidence that the harm it asks the Court to prevent—losing the opportunity to distinguish itself and build customer loyalty at a critical time—cannot be reduced to a simple formula. *See Hybritech*, 849 F.2d at 1456–57 ("It is well-settled that … the nature of the patent grant weighs against holding that monetary damages will always suffice to make the patentee whole"). There is no easy way to determine the value of the relationships and loyalties that millions of customers establish with Internet retailers over the next several months.

61. Neither side is able to offer any formula that is readily available for determining what damages might be.

62. Amazon.com's patent entitles it to the exclusive right to offer its single-action ordering invention, and to reap the value that feature adds to its site. Defendants' use of the Express Lane feature, as currently configured, would deny Amazon.com of the benefit of its patent. Barnesandnoble.com has failed to demonstrate that the value of the use of the patent can be calculated in dollars.

63. Amazon.com is presumptively and actually suffering irreparable injury because of Defendants' infringement. The Court concludes that only a preliminary injunction will prevent that harm.

C. *Balance Of Hardships*

64. The balance of hardships between the parties also favors granting Amazon.com's motion for preliminary injunction. The Court must weigh the threatened injury to the patent holder if injunctive relief is not granted against the injury to the accused infringer if the preliminary injunction is granted. *See Hybritech Inc.*, 849 F.2d at 1457. Here, the

balance of hardships tips in Amazon.com's favor. Any harm suffered by Barnesandnoble.com would result directly from its misappropriation of Amazon.com's patented purchasing method. The balance of hardships does not favor a defendant where the defendant "took a calculated risk that it might infringe [plaintiff's] patents." *Smith Int'l, Inc. v. Hughes Tool Co.*, 718 F.2d 1573, 1581 (Fed.Cir.1983).

65. Moreover, the evidence indicates that Barnesandnoble.com can modify its "Express Lane" feature with relative ease to avoid infringement of the '411 patent. For instance, infringement can be avoided by simply requiring users to take an additional action to confirm orders placed by using Express Lane. (Tr. at 530:8–13).

66. The harm to Amazon.com is more extensive. Without this injunction, Amazon.com will lose the primary value of the 1–Click (R) option: its role in distinguishing the Amazon.com site from the site of a key competitor. (See Ex. 10, Johnson Dec. ¶ ¶ 8–12).

* * *

D. Public Interest

71. The public is served by innovation on the Internet and in electronic commerce, particularly now while it is still developing rapidly. Competition to provide unique, effective and enjoyable consumer experiences will lead to innovation and diversity in on-line commerce. (Ex. 11, Bezos Decl. ¶ 22). On the other hand, innovation will be discouraged if competitors are permitted a free ride on each other's patented inventions. Protection of intellectual property rights in innovations will foster greater competition and innovation. (Ex. 11, Bezos Decl. ¶ 22; Ex. 10, Johnson Decl. ¶ 15).

72. Granting Amazon.com's preliminary injunction will serve the public interest.* * *

* * *

IV. CONCLUSION

Therefore, the Court hereby ORDERS that Defendants Barnesandnoble.com LLC and Barnesandnoble.com Inc., their offers, agents, servants, employees and attorneys and those in active concert or participation with them or Defendants ARE HEREBY RESTRAINED AND ENJOINED from continuing to infringe United States Patent No. 5,960,-411, including by continuing to make or use within the United States Defendants' Express Lane feature as currently configured or any other single-action ordering system that employs the methods or systems of the '411 patent, or by inducing others to make or use within the United States Defendants' Express Lane feature as currently configured or any other single-action ordering system that employs the methods of systems of the '411 patent. Defendants may continue to offer an Express Lane feature if the feature is modified to avoid infringement of the '411 patent in a manner that is consistent with the findings of fact and conclusions of law set forth above.

The above Preliminary Injunction is effective at 12:01 a.m. P.S.T. on Saturday, December 4, 1999, and upon Amazon.com's filing an undertaking in the sum of $10,000,000 and shall remain in effect during the pendency of this action.

Notes and Questions

1. A patent case normally does not go to trial until several years after the complaint is filed. The preliminary injunction in this case went into effect on December 4th, less than two months after the case was filed on October 21, 1999. In many instances, particularly if the invention is essential to the defendant continuing in business, such a preliminary injunction forces the defendant to take a license to stay in business, and thus ends the dispute. Note that the plaintiff had to post a $10 million bond in case the plaintiff loses in the actual trial. Following a trial, it is customary for the Court to enjoin the defendant from further infringement when the plaintiff prevails. The grant of an injunction does not necessarily mean that the defendant will have to stop what it was doing—the winning plaintiff can decide to grant a license to the losing defendant. Of course after winning an injunction, the plaintiff is in a much better bargaining position over licensing terms.

2. Anyone can set up a brokerage account that is backed up by cash or by a line of credit. Once having done so, the customer may telephone the broker. After the broker presents a stock purchase proposal, the customer may simply say "buy" and hang up the telephone. Thus, a single word consummates the purchase of shares of stock. Isn't Amazon.com's "single-action" purchasing invention identical to that just described? Does the decades-old brokerage arrangement just described, as a "public use" more than a year prior to the filing of the patent, "anticipate" the patent under § 102(b)? Isn't the automation of something previously done manually "obvious" under § 103? Why was such "prior art" not discussed during the trial? Is it always patentable to do something with a computer that was previously done manually? If not, what does it take to lend patentability to an automated version of a manual process? Why is the Court so careful to conclude that the term "fulfill" used in claim 6 "does not include the physical steps of handling or packing tangible items"? Why is this important?

3. Computer system designers are trained to try and prevent erroneous data from ever entering a computer. One way to do this is to request confirmation of a command already given, particularly when that command may be irreversible. For example, when one commands a computer to erase an entire set of files, the computer, before erasing the files, asks "Are you sure?" and then requires one to click the mouse button a second time. In the design of Internet purchasing systems, this same technique is frequently used to gain verification of the command to purchase, to make sure that such commands are not mistakes and do not reflect misunderstandings. Thus, from the point of view of many Internet system designers, the

Amazon.com one-click purchase system is defective, in that it does not give the purchaser a chance to recover from a mistaken mouse click. But the difference between a "bug" and a "feature" in a software system is frequently highly subjective. Can an argument be made that this leaving off of a safeguard to gain speed is not patentable but is simply a "reasonable mind" tradeoff of speed versus security? Could one patent a boiler that omits the safety overpressure relief valve because it is simpler and less costly to manufacture? Could one patent a multiple file delete program that did not ask: "Are you sure?"

4. The Judge appears to have been influenced by his conclusion that Barnesandnoble.com copied Amazon.com's feature. This conclusion followed from the "strong similarities" between the two systems. If there was no copying, can there still be patent infringement? If so, then why is "copying" important to the "nonobviousness" determination? (Read once again the quotation taken from *Graham v. John Deere Co.*, 383 U.S. 1, 17–18, 86 S.Ct. 684, 694, 15 L.Ed.2d 545 (1966)).

5. Could the "one click" feature be protected by the copyright on the program? Why not? When reading the following chapters on trade secrets and trademarks consider: (1) could the "one click" feature be protected as a trade secret and (2) could "one click shopping" or "one stop shopping" be registered as a trademark?

6. The Court concluded that "Anticipation is a question of fact ...." Later, it concluded that "... obviousness is a mixed question of fact and law." Why are these two treated differently by the trial court? By a reviewing court? What would be the role of a jury in determining novelty or anticipation under § 102? In determining obviousness under § 103? Note that the Court reserved to itself the task of defining what the terms in the claim mean. *See Markman v. Westview Instruments,* 517 U.S. 370, 134 L.Ed.2d 577 (1996).

7. The Court rejects the "Netacape Instant Buy" prior art because it "consisted of a total of four lines." The court further noted that "Defendants' expert ... was unable to supply any additional information ... and ultimately admitted that he did not know how the feature worked." The Court concluded, "The Netscape reference therefore does not teach the invention to one of ordinary skill in the art ... as is required of an anticipatory reference." Recall that "anticipation" is governed by § 102, while the phrase "obvious ... to a person having ordinary skill in the art" appears in § 103. Is it proper to apply, when determining the "anticipation" value of "prior art," a test that the statute says applies to determinations of "obviousness?" Section 112 requires a patent application to teach the invention in such a manner "as to enable any person skilled in the art to which it pertains ... to make and use the same ...." Does "prior art" submitted to prove the invention is not novel under § 102 also have to comply with this same high standard? What about a public use or an offer to sell? If a public use or sale occurred, would it matter whether defendants' expert understood how the thing sold or used worked? *See Advanced Display Systems, Inc. v. Kent State University*, 212 F.3d 1272, 54 U.S.P.Q.2d 1673 (Fed.Cir.2000):

Accordingly, invalidity by anticipation requires that the four corners of a single, prior art document describe every element of the claimed invention, either expressly or inherently, such that a person of ordinary skill in the art could practice the invention without undue experimentation.

G. ENABLEMENT—§ 112

A patent application includes a specification (or textual part), one or more drawings, and an oath and must be accompanied by a fee. The oath and fee may be submitted after the specification and drawings are filed. (35 U.S.C. § 111) The filing date of a patent application is the date upon which the specification and drawing are filed.

Section 112 specifies what must be included in the "specification" of a patent application. Briefly summarized, paragraph 1 of § 112 requires the specification to "contain a written description of the invention, and of the manner and process of making and using it …." Paragraph 2 requires the specification to "conclude with one or more claims particularly pointing out and distinctly claiming the subject matter which the applicant regards as his invention." The remaining paragraphs talk more specifically about what type of claims may be used.

1. § 112, paragraph 1–Enablement, and Best Mode Requirements

Under the first paragraph of § 112, the written description must "enable any person skilled in the art … to make and use" the invention. The invention, of course, is defined by the claims. Normally, patent examiners do not question the whether the description of the invention in the patent is sufficiently detailed and complete to enable one skilled in the art to make and use it. But when they do, the result can be devastating for the applicant. The problem is this: After a patent application is filed and assigned a filing date, no "new matter" may be added to the patent application without the application losing its priority date, which date may be crucial to avoiding the adverse impact under § 102(b) of publications, public uses, or offers to sell that may occur after the priority date. And since the examiner typically does not get around to examining the application for a year or two, it may then be too late to add to the description in the patent without losing the patentability of one or more inventions due to such later-occurring publications, uses, or offers.

Enablement arises most often in the PTO, when it is raised by the examiner. It commonly arises in interference proceedings, where two parties are contending to obtain the same patent claim by proving up their respective dates of conception, diligence and reduction to practice under § 102(g). It sometimes arises during patent litigation, but if the examiner has approved the application in this regard, it is difficult to gain the court's interest in this issue.

Accordingly, some thought should always be given to the need for providing an adequate disclosure. The rules of practice permit a program appendix to be submitted with a patent application. So if a program implementation of the invention exists, it may be submitted to the PTO. The problem with this approach is that once the patent is published, the program is also published, thereby dedicating any trade secrets that it contains to the public. Another approach is to disclose some of the program subroutines in such an appendix, selecting only those at the heart of the invention as claimed or only those whose implementation would not be obvious to one skilled in the art. But flow chart and block diagram representations of hardware elements, signal paths, program algorithms, data structures, and program signaling paths are routinely accepted by the examiners as adequate in most cases. Thus, the filing of program appendices is the exception, rather than the rule. But if a program is truly unconventional and difficult to design, it may be best to submit it to the PTO.

In addition to being enabling, the written description must "set forth the best mode contemplated by the inventor of carrying out his invention." This means one should not submit a description of the invention that is six months old if the program has been rewritten and radically changed in the meanwhile. Just before a patent application is filed, a check should be made for recent changes and improvements, and these should be described in what may be a simple addition to the very end of the description to insure compliance with this rule. The examiner, of course, will not know if the "best mode" has been described. Failure to describe the best mode typically comes up during litigation and enforcement of the patent and can give the infringer grounds to seek punitive damages if it was done willfully.

IN RE BUCHNER

U.S. Court of Appeals Federal Circuit, 1991.
929 F.2d 660.

J. LOURIE, CIRCUIT JUDGE

Johannes B. Buchner appeals from the July 17, 1990, decision of the Board of Patent Appeals and Interferences (Board), Appeal No. 89–2590, affirming the examiner's rejection of all of his claims for failure to provide an enabling disclosure under the first paragraph of 35 U.S.C. § 112. We affirm.

BACKGROUND

The claimed invention relates to a higher order digital transmission system which communicates a plurality of separate digital streams over a common channel. It includes a transmitter portion (block encoding arrangements and multiplexer) and receiver portion (a demultiplexer and block decoding arrangements). The receiver portion of the system further includes a phase comparator having four inputs and one output and a divider having two inputs and one output.

Buchner's application was rejected by the Patent and Trademark Office (PTO) on the ground that it failed to describe how to make and use the phase comparator and divider without undue experimentation. Although the functions of the phase comparator and divider were adequately disclosed, the examiner rejected the application because the design structures of the two elements were not disclosed. The examiner asserted that the comparator was not a typical two input phase comparator and the divider was not a typical one input divider.

Buchner offered a declaration of Professor Jan Louis de Kroes which stated that "the elements referred to in the application as divider 19 and phase comparator 16 were well-known to those of ordinary skill in the art as of June 17, 1985," the filing date of a foreign priority application. The declaration also stated that these elements were "routinely built"; it provided details concerning the structure and function of the elements.

The PTO did not accept the declaration as overcoming the rejection, stating that it was mere conclusion unsupported by factual documentation and that it provided inadequate indication that the technology concerning the comparator and divider was well-known.

The Board, on all the evidence before it, found that there was a reasonable basis for the examiner to question the sufficiency of the disclosure with respect to the structure of the comparator and divider and that the declarant's assertions that these elements were "well-known" and "routinely built" were conclusory statements unsupported by any other evidence.

DISCUSSION

Buchner claims that the Board erred in affirming the examiner's rejection, arguing that the declaration of de Kroes, an expert, unequivocally establishes a fact that cannot be dismissed "in the absence of a . . . contrary inference from other evidence." We affirm the Board's decision.

In order to be enabling under 35 U.S.C. § 112, a patent application must sufficiently disclose an invention to enable those skilled in the art to make and use it. The specification need not disclose what is well known in the art. *Lindemann Maschinenfabrik GMBH v. American Hoist & Derrick Co.*, 730 F.2d 1452, 1463, 221 USPQ 481, 489 (Fed.Cir. 1984). However, an examiner may reject a claim if it is reasonable to conclude that one skilled in the art would be unable to carry out the claimed invention. *See In re Eynde*, 480 F.2d 1364, 1370, 178 USPQ 470, 474 (C.C.P.A. 1973).

We conclude that it was reasonable in this case for the examiner to doubt that the claimed invention could have been carried out based on the disclosure since the elements at issue are integral to the practice of the invention and neither the application nor the prior art described their structure. The applicant thus had the burden of overcoming this rejection. *Id*.

The declaration of de Kroes did provide significant detail concerning the structure and function of the elements in question. However, § 112 requires that, unless the information is well known in the art, the application itself must contain this information; it is not sufficient to provide it only through an expert's declaration. *In re Smyth*, 189 F.2d 982, 990, 90 USPQ 106, 112 (C.C.P.A. 1951).

Moreover, an expert's opinion on the ultimate legal issue must be supported by something more than a conclusory statement. *See In re Brandstadter*, 484 F.2d 1395, 1405, 179 USPQ 286, 294 (C.C.P.A. 1973). De Kroes only stated that "the elements referred to in the application as divider 19 and phase comparator 16 were well known to those of ordinary skill in the art as of June 17, 1985" and that they were "routinely built." He did not provide adequate support for his conclusion. What he did describe was how *he* would construct the divider and phase comparator, but he did not demonstrate that such construction was well-known to those of ordinary skill in the art.

As stated by the Board, "[i]f the relatively complex phase comparator and divider arrangement described in the declaration were so "well-known" and "routinely built" as of the effective filing date, the declarant should have [had] no trouble documenting the same...."

We conclude that the Board did not err in affirming the examiner's rejection of all the claims in Buchner's application for failure to comply with 35 U.S.C. § 112, paragraph 1.

AFFIRMED

Notes

1. Note that this is a foreign application, filed initially in another country, and then filed less than 12 months thereafter in the United States. A copy of the foreign patent application, certified by the foreign patent office, must be supplied and accompanied by a translation. 35 U.S.C. § 119(a) and (b). (If these formalities are met, in accordance with international patent treaties the United States application is treated as having been filed as of its original foreign filing date.) "Enablement" problems arise most frequently with such foreign applications, since the disclosure requirements are more lenient in other countries than in the U.S.

2. The Court objects to the wording of the declaration of de Kroes. How would you have worded this declaration to satisfy the Federal Circuit and the examiner that the divider and phase comparator were "well-known to those of ordinary skill in the art"? Is it too late to approach the examiner one more time with another declaration? This could possibly be done in a continuation application.

3. The lesson to be learned from this and similar cases is: Any time you place a labeled block into a patent drawing, with little or no description of its contents, you should be prepared to demonstrate that the contents of the block can be found in the "prior art."

2. § 112, paragraphs 2 to 4: Patent Claims

The second paragraph of § 112 requires the specification to conclude with "one or more claims" that define the invention. The claims are numbered sequentially, and each claim defines a unique invention. If a claim stands by itself, and doesn't incorporate some other claim by reference, it is called an "independent" claim. Normally, as is explained in the third and fourth paragraphs of § 112, an applicant files, perhaps, three or four broad "independent" claims, each claim defining the invention as containing only a limited number of elements. Each such "independent" claim is typically followed by a series of "dependant" claims each of which incorporates by reference either the preceding independent claim or else a preceding dependant claim. Sometimes an independent claim is followed by five or six claims each of which incorporates by reference the immediately preceding claim, so that the last claim incorporates all of the limitations of the preceding claims. The filing fee for a patent application depends in part on how many "independent" claims there are, and on the total number of claims. And if an amendment is filed that increases the number of "independent" claims or the total number of claims, an extra fee must be paid.

Paragraph 5 of § 112 explains that a claim may incorporate two or more preceding claims by reference, but this practice is not followed much in the United States and must be done quite carefully to comply with the rules set out in this paragraph. Such a "multiple dependant" claim is not treated as one claim but, rather, as a multiple set of claims each differing in what it incorporates into itself. An extra fee is charged when a patent application contains this type of claim.

In computer software related patent applications, three types of claims are most commonly used: method claims, apparatus claims, and program claims. Here is an exemplary claim of each type taken from a recent IBM patent, U.S. Patent No. 6,064,990:

Title: **System for electronic notification of account activity**

Abstract:

Disclosed is a system for notifying a user of account activity, such as a withdrawal from a savings or checking account. A computer system maintains information on financial accounts and electronic user contact information for at least one of the financial accounts, such as a telephone number, e-mail address or pager number. Information on a transaction with respect to one of the financial accounts is received and processed. The computer system then processes the information on the transaction and generates an electronic message providing information on the transaction. The user contact information for the financial account involved in the transaction is processed. The message is then electronically transmitted to the location identified by the user contact information for the financial account.

Claims:

1. A method implemented within a financial institution computer system for notifying a user of account activity, wherein the account is maintained within the financial institution computer system, comprising:

(a) maintaining electronic information in the financial institution computer system on financial accounts;

(b) maintaining electronic user contact information for at least one of the financial accounts;

(c) processing information on a completed financial transaction with respect to one of the financial accounts in the financial institution computer system, wherein all completed financial transactions regardless of amount are processed;

(d) generating a message providing information on the completed transaction;

(e) processing the user contact information for the financial account involved in the completed transaction; and

(f) electronically transmitting the message immediately from the financial institution computer system to the location identified by the user contact information for the financial account.

* * *

11. A system for notifying a user of account activity, comprising:

(a) a computer system including a database including information on financial accounts and user contact information for at least one of the financial accounts, wherein the financial accounts are maintained in the financial institution computer system;

(b) program logic implemented in the financial institution computer system, comprising:

(i) means for processing information on a completed transaction with respect to one of the financial accounts in the computer system, wherein all completed financial transactions regardless of amount are processed;

(ii) means for generating an electronic message providing information on the completed transaction; and

(iii) means for processing the user contact information for the account involved in the completed transaction; and

(c) a communication port including means for electronically transmitting the electronic message immediately from the financial institution computer system to the location identified by the user contact information for the account.

* * *

19. An article of manufacture for use in programming a financial institution computer system maintaining a database including information on a plurality of user accounts, the article of manufacture comprising a computer usable storage medium having at least one computer program stored therein that causes the financial institution computer system to perform the steps of:

(a) maintaining electronic information on financial accounts in the financial institution computer system;

(b) maintaining electronic user contact information for at least one of the financial accounts;

(c) processing information on a completed transaction with respect to one of the financial accounts, wherein all completed financial transactions regardless of amount are processed;

(d) generating a message providing information on the completed transaction;

(e) processing the user contact information for the financial account involved in the completed transaction; and

(f) electronically transmitting the message immediately from the computer system to the location identified by the user contact information for the financial account.

* * *

Notes

1. When drafting claims, one must think about whom one may wish to sue, and draft claims accordingly. In the case of this IBM system, one could sue: the bank; the developer of the bank's software; the developer of the software that runs on the user's home computer and that gives off an indication of each transaction; the individual home user; the manufacturer of the user's PC which comes with the user software built-in; and the network manager. Can you think of anyone else that you might wish to sue? Who has the most money? Who would be the most inconvenienced by a preliminary injunction? Who is easiest to find? Does the manufacturer of the software ever infringe a "method" claim directly? If "direct" infringement (35 U.S.C.§ 271(a)) cannot be proved, what about "contributory" infringement (35 U.S.C. § 271(c)) or inducement to infringe (35 U.S.C.§ 271(b))? How good a job has IBM done of targeting its claims at easy-to-find, wealthy potential infringers?

Section 271 reads as follows

§ 271. Infringement of patent

(a) Except as otherwise provided in this title, whoever without authority makes, uses, offers to sell, or sells any patented invention, within the United States, or imports into the United States any patented invention during the term of the patent therefor, infringes the patent.

(b) Whoever actively induces infringement of a patent shall be liable as an infringer.

(c) Whoever offers to sell or sells within the United States or imports into the United States a component of a patented machine, manufacture, combination, or composition, or a material or apparatus for use in practicing a patented process, constituting a material part of the invention, knowing the same to be especially made or especially adapted for use in an infringement of such patent, and not a staple article or commodity of commerce suitable for substantial noninfringing use, shall be liable as a contributory infringer.

* * *

2.   Another good test of a claim is: How hard is it to determine if one is infringing the claim? Ideally, one can walk through a trade show and spot the infringers by simply looking into each display booth, without extensive reverse engineering. How well do IBM's claims stand up under this test of claim quality?

3.   There are various reasons for obtaining patents. Sometimes they are obtained simply for the good of the morale of the engineering staff, and to increase the size of the company's patent portfolio. Other times they are obtained to prevent others from copying a company's new product and to protect the investment in new product design. Other patents, with broader claims, are intended for aggressive use against a wide range of infringers. Since one doesn't know in advance what prior art is out there, one tries to provide a range of different claims in each patent to satisfy all of these potential needs. If one knows in advance that one patent is being obtained simply to please the engineers, another to give investors minimal assurance that a new product is "patented," and yet another to strike at the heart of the competition and to earn big royalties, how much money should be budgeted for the prosecution of each patent? Does it make sense to spend hundreds of thousands of dollars asserting a patent after having only paid $3,000 to have the least competent attorney spend minimal time writing and prosecuting the patent application?

MOSSMAN v. BRODERBUND SOFTWARE

District Court, Eastern District of Michigan, 1999.
51 USPQ2d 1752, 1999 WL 696007.

J. Zatkoff, District Court Judge

I. Introduction

This matter is before the Court on the following motions: (1) Defendants' Motion for Summary Judgment For Invalidity; * * *. All of the motions have been fully briefed. The facts and legal arguments are adequately presented in the briefs submitted, and the decisional process will not be aided by oral arguments. Therefore, pursuant to E.D. Mich. Local R. 7.1(e)(2), it is hereby ORDERED that the motion be resolved on the briefs submitted. For the reasons that follow, defendants' Motion for Summary Judgment for Invalidity is GRANTED.

II. Background

This patent infringement case arises from a dispute over a method of teaching children how to read using video presentations. Plaintiff Robert Mossman (hereinafter "Mossman" or "plaintiff") is the named inventor and owner of U.S. Patent 4,636,173 (hereinafter "the '173 patent"). In particular, the '173 patent involves a method of teaching children in which words or syllables are displayed on a video screen. Along with the pronunciation of the displayed syllable or work, the corresponding letters are temporarily highlighted by a change in appearance. Mossman filed suit against defendants, claiming that series of CD–ROM interactive animated stories called Living Books, produced by defendant Broderbund and formerly produced by a joint venture between Broderbund and Random House, infringes his patent. Defendants deny that the Living Books infringe plaintiff's patent and claim that plaintiff's patent is invalid.

III. SUMMARY JUDGMENT STANDARDS

* * *

IV. OPINION

A. Claim Construction

Before this Court determines if any or all of the claims of patent '173 are anticipated by the prior art references cited by the Defendants, this Court must first analyze each claim of the patent to determine what the claims cover. Claim construction is a question of law and strictly for this Court to determine. *See Markman v. Westview Instruments, Inc.*, 517 U.S. 370 (1996).

In analyzing the patent claim, this Court must first analyze the claims themselves, the patent's specification, and the prosecution history. *Vitronics Corp. v. Conceptronics, Inc.*, 90 F.3d 1576, 1582 (Fed.Cir. 1996). The words of the patent are generally given their ordinary and customary meaning. *Vitronics*, 90 F.3d at 1582. However, the patentee may choose to be his own lexicographer and use terms in a manner other than their ordinary meaning, as long as the special definition of the term is clearly stated in the patent specification or file history. *Hoechst Celanese Corp. v. BP Chems. Ltd.*, 78 F.3d 1575, 1578 (Fed.Cir.1996).

Next, the Court must review the specification to ensure that the terms used in the patent claim are used consistently with the patent specification. "Claims must be read in light of the specification, of which they are a part." *Markman,* 52 F.3d at 979. However, "while it is true that claims are to be interpreted in light of the specification ... it does not follow that limitations from the specification may be read into the claims." *Sjolund v. Musland,* 847 F.2d 1573, 1581 (Fed.Cir.1988).

Third, the Court must examine the prosecution history of the patent in the event that the first two steps are not dispositive of the claim construction. In this case, there is no reason to discuss the prosecution history as there was none.

Admissions by the party inventor may also be relevant. *See Moll v. Northern Telecom, Inc.* 1996 WL 11355, *3 (E.D.Pa.1996) (construing patent based on plaintiff inventor's testimony). In some situations, for example a highly technical field, a court may rely upon extrinsic evidence to give proper meaning to the words contained in the patent claim. However, the Federal Circuit made it clear in *Vitronics* that, with few exceptions, it is improper to rely upon extrinsic evidence. In most situations, an analysis of the intrinsic evidence alone will resolve any ambiguity in a disputed claim term. *Vitronics*, 90 F.3d at 1582.

Claim 1 of the '173 patent states:

1. In a method for teaching reading of the type characterized by a combined video and oral recording which comprises (1) a visual display of information in the form of alphabetic characters arranged either individually or in groups which are combined to represent words and (2) an audible soundtrack which records spoken pronunciation of such displayed information, the improvement which comprises the steps of:

synchronizing the recorded audible pronunciation of each syllable or work with a temporary recorded visible highlighting of such syllable or word as it is pronounced, the highlighting being in the form of a temporary change in the visual characteristics of the pronounced syllable or word,

whereby the viewer can readily follow the reading of the visual display and correlate the sound of the displayed syllable or word with its written representation merely by following the visible highlighting as such highlighting progresses through the visual display.

Therefore, by clear language of claim 1 of the '173 patent, in order for the claim to be anticipated, the prior art must be both 1) a method for teaching reading, and 2) a combined video and oral recording. This Court will address additional requirements and specifications below.

1. JEPSON FORM

The '173 patent has four claims. Claim 1 is the only independent claim and claims 2–4 depend on claim 1. Therefore, both parties agree that claims 2–4 incorporate all of the requirements of claim 1, as well as the particular elements set forth in each claim. Claim 1 is in the Jepson form. A Jepson claim is one that begins with a preamble that recites a public domain method, apparatus or combination, and continues with a transition that states "wherein the improvement comprises ..." See Ex Parte Jepson, 243 O.G. 525 (Ass't Comm'r of Pat. 1917); 37 C.F.R. § 1.75. The terms in both the preamble describing the prior art and those elements constituting the improvement are substantive claim limitations. 37 C.F.R. § 1.75(e).

In this case, the claimed method for teaching reading that was previously known consisted of a "combined video and oral recording" including the video display of letters, alone or grouped to form words, and a soundtrack with the spoken pronunciation of the letters and words. Stated differently, words are displayed on the screen, and those words are read on the recorded audible soundtrack.

2. SYNCHRONIZING

Mossman's improvement consists of synchronizing a temporary visual highlighting of the displayed words or syllables with the recorded soundtrack. Synchronizing is not defined in the claim or in the specifications. Therefore, the word synchronizing should be given its ordinary and customary meaning. *Vitronics*, 90 F.3d at 1582. Synchronizing is defined in the field of motion pictures and television as "to arrange (sound) so as to coincide with the action of a scene . . ." Random House College Dictionary (Rev. ed. 1975). Therefore, as to claim 1, synchronizing is defined as the temporary visual highlighting of the displayed words or syllables so as to coincide with the audible soundtrack.

3. *EACH SYLLABLE OR WORD*

According to the '173 patent, each syllable or word is highlighted and the highlighting is to be synchronized with the pronunciation of the displayed word or syllable. Therefore, each of the syllables or words displayed must be highlighted individually as that word or syllable is spoken.

4. *TEMPORARY HIGHLIGHTING*

Moreover, the synchronized highlighting must be temporary, meaning that after the word or syllable is spoken (and therefore highlighted), it must return to the original state. The temporary highlighting is discussed in the column 2, lines 17–23 of the '173 patent.

As the pronounced syllable or word is passed, the temporary highlighting disappears so that the intensity or boldness or color thereof returns to the normal state. In this manner, even after a momentary lapse of attention by the student, the student will instantly be redirected to the portion of the visual display which is being pronounced on the soundtrack.

The '173 patent clarifies that the temporary highlighting of the words as they are pronounced distinguished the patent from the prior art "bouncing ball" videos discussed in the specification at column 1, lines 15–21.

5. *VISUAL DISPLAY*

The patent also specifies that the temporary visual highlighting must progress through the visual display. The '173 patent claim defines "visual display" as the "alphabetic characters arranged either individually or in groups which are combined to represent words." The patent specification further elaborates on the definition as "a format similar to the pages of a book. That is, the format preferably should have a conventional number of printed words per line and lines per page, giving due consideration to the age and attention span of the students." The description also permits the use of "interspersed pictures that are related to the subject of the printed text." (Defendant's Ex. 1). Therefore, the visual display should, but need not resemble the pages of a book. *Sjolund*, 847 F.2d at 1581 (while it is true that claims are to be interpreted in light of the specification, it does not follow that limitations from the specification may be read into the claims).

6. *"READILY FOLLOW" AS SUCH HIGHLIGHTING "PROGRESSES"*

The highlighting on the visual display must allow the viewer to readily follow the synchronized highlighting and audible pronunciation of the word or syllable "merely by following the visible highlighting as such highlighting progresses through the visual display." The '173 patent describes a highlighting method in which "the eye of the student is encouraged to progress across the printed message." The '173 patent describes the term "progression" in the specification. "In this manner, even after a momentary lapse of attention by the student, the student will be redirected to the portion of the visual display which is being pronounced on the soundtrack." As defined, the term "progression" does not adequately specify how the words are to "progress" through the visual display. Therefore, extrinsic evidence and party admissions may be admitted to clarify an ambiguity. Mossman testified in depositions that the term "progress through the visual display" means "to move from left to right." (Mossman Dep. at 203:13–15).

B. Defendants' Motion for Summary Judgment for Invalidity

Plaintiff filed this lawsuit claiming that two reading aids produced by the defendants infringe on his patent. Plaintiff therefore filed suit against Defendants, Broderbund Software, Inc. and Random House, Inc., for patent infringement.

Defendants filed a motion for summary judgment in which they claimed that the '173 patent is invalid on two separate grounds. First, the patent at issue is invalid under 35 U.S.C. § 102(a) because prior art existed that met each element of the claims asserted in the patent. Second, Defendants argue that the '173 patent is invalid for indefiniteness.

* * *

[The Court next compares the claim elements to the prior art, and concludes that the prior art, and in particular a children's television program segment named "Dear Louisa, will you marry me?" (written by "The Electric Company") does contain the first four of five claim elements identified by the court. The court now proceeds to discuss the fifth and last significant claim element.—Eds]

5. "READILY FOLLOW"

The final element is that the segment must allow the reader to "readily follow" as the highlighting progresses. The final claim reads, "whereby the viewer can readily follow the reading of the visual display and correlate the sound of the displayed syllable or word with its written representation merely by following the visible highlighting as such highlighting progresses through the visual display." Plaintiff maintains that the animation or movement on the screen during the "Dear Louisa" segment distracts the eyes of the viewer, thereby preventing the viewer from being able to "readily follow" as the highlighting of words progresses. Plaintiff therefore, argues that the "Dear Louisa" segment fails to meet the final element of being able to "readily follow" as the highlighting progresses. The defendants claim that the final claim [element] is invalid for indefiniteness.

Patent law requires each patent specification to conclude with one or more claims "particularly pointing out and distinctly claiming the subject matter which the applicant regards as his invention." 35 U.S.C. § 112 ¶ 2. Despite Plaintiff's claim to the contrary, the issue of indefiniteness is a question of law and is properly resolved at the summary judgment stage. *See Miles Lab., Inc. v. Shandon Inc.,* 997 F.2d 870, 874 (Fed.Cir.1993) *citing Orthokinetics, Inc. v. Safety Travel Chairs, Inc.,* 806 F.2d 1565, 1576, 1 USPQ2d 1081, 1088 (Fed.Cir.1986). The "definiteness" requirement means that a claim must have a clear and definite meaning when construed in light of the complete patent document. *Standard Oil Co. v. American Cyanamid Co.,* 774 F.2d 448, 452 (Fed.Cir. 1985). A claim complies with § 112 ¶ 2 if one of ordinary skill in the art would understand what is being claimed when the claim is read in light of the patent specification. *Seattle Box Co. v. Industrial Crating & Packing, Inc.,* 731 F.2d 818, 826 (Fed.Cir.1984), *appeal after remand,* 756 F.2d 1574 (Fed.Cir.1985). If the claims read in light of the specification reasonably apprize those skilled in the art of the scope of the invention, section 112 demands no more. *Hybritech,* 802 F.2d at 1385. The degree of precision necessary for adequate claims is a function of the nature of the subject matter. *Id.* Indefiniteness is construed in light of the prior art. *Standard Oil,* 774 F.2d at 453 (patent is invalid for indefiniteness if it does not distinguish claimed invention from close prior art); *Amgen, Inc. v. Chugai Pharmaceutical Co., Ltd.,* 927 F.2d 1200, 1218 (Fed.Cir.1991), *cert. denied,* 502 U.S. 856 (1991). Further, "[w]hen the meaning of the claim is in doubt, especially when, as in the case here, there is close prior art, they are properly declared invalid." *Amgen,* 927 F.2d at 1218 (invalidating as indefinite a claim using the term "at least about 160,-000'").

According to Patent '173, paragraph 2 of claim 1 requires that the synchronized highlighting and recorded pronunciation allow the viewers to "readily follow" the reading of the visual display and and related audio. (Defendants' Ex. 1). Patent '173 does not mention or even attempt to establish a criteria for determining whether a display can be "readily followed." Moreover, the term "readily follow" is not defined and has no particular meaning in the '173 patent claims.

In this case, as discussed above, the prior art is substantially identical to the claims in Patent '173. Further, Plaintiff's patent provides no insight as to how one of ordinary skill in the art would identify a segment in which the viewer could "readily follow" the correlation of the display and the pronunciation of the word, let alone distinguish it from the prior art.

Plaintiff claims that the animation in the "Dear Louisa" segment distinguishes his patent claim from the prior art. This Court disagrees. Patent '173 uses the word "comprises" to describe both the prior art portion of his method and his improvement. The prior art comprises a visual display of letters and an audible soundtrack of the pronunciation of the displayed letters. Mossman's improvement comprises the steps of synchronizing the recorded pronunciation of each word or syllable with a temporary visual highlighting of each syllable or word as it is pronounced. (Greenberg Decl. Ex. 1 at 2:39–51.

It is well settled in patent law that the word "compromises" means that the recited elements are only a part of the device. *See Genentech, Inc. v. Chiron Corp.*, 112 F.3d 495, 501 [42 USPQ2d 1608] (Fed.Cir. 1997). Therefore, to be covered by the '173 patent claims, the prior art reference must simply include all the elements listed above. *Id.* If these elements are included, it does not matter if the method includes other additional elements. In fact, plaintiff made videos incorporating all of the elements outlined in the patent claim, but also included the additional elements of music and animation. Although these videos used elements not included in the patent claim, plaintiff did mark these videos with his patent number. Therefore, if all of the elements discussed above are included in the prior art reference, the claim is anticipated even if additional elements are used in the reference.

In *The Electric Company* example discussed extensively above, the displayed syllables or words are highlighted and the highlighting is synchronized with the recorded pronunciation on the soundtrack as the highlighting progresses through the screen. The reader can just as readily follow the reading in *The Electric Company* as one could by following the teaching of the patent. Plaintiff's argument that the animation or movement on the screen during *The Electric Company* segment distracts the eyes of the viewer, thereby preventing the viewer from being able to "readily follow" as the highlighting of words progresses is unpersuasive. The patent does not mention the lack of animation or movement, nor does it require that the product be without animation. In fact, the preferred embodiment encourages the use of interspersed pictures to enhance the student's reading experience. Because the term "readily follow" does not distinguish the highlighting technique in the prior art from that described in the '173 patent, one skilled in the art could not know what highlighting technique would be infringing. *Morton International, Inc. v. Cardinal Chemical Co.*, 5 F.3d 1464, 1470 (Fed.Cir.1993). Claim 1 of the '173 patent is therefore fatally indefinite. Because claim 1 fails, so do claims 2–4 which depend on claim 1.

Therefore, defendant's "Motion For Summary Judgment For Invalidity" is GRANTED.

* * *

Notes

1. U.S. Patent No. 4,636,173 is only two pages long–a cover page, and one page of description. There is no drawing. The entire specification, including four claims, fits into two columns on a single page.

2. In general, claims begin with a preamble phrase that ends with the word "comprising," and that is followed by a list of the claim's elements. Every element must be present in an infringing device. The preamble itself

may contain claim elements essential to infringement, or it may simply state background information, in which case the claim can be infringed even when there is non-infringement of the preamble. As the Court explains, use of the word "comprising" means that the claimed invention includes the listed elements plus, possibly, additional elements that are not listed. If the phrase "consisting of" is used instead of "comprising," then no additional elements are permitted–but "consisting of" is not commonly used in computer-related inventions. It is used frequently in chemical inventions, where extra ingredients beyond those listed are not permitted. Watch out: these are special patent law definitions of the words "comprising" and "consisting of." Dictionary definitions, and usage around the world, frequently assign just the opposite meaning to these two words, and patent offices (outside of the U.S.) may use different conventions.

3. Jepson claims are customarily used by many foreign patent offices, particularly Germany. A long preamble lists the elements of the claim that can be found in the "prior art," and these elements are separated from the new elements by the phrase: ". . . . wherein the improvement comprises . . . ." Jepson claims are not required by the U.S. PTO.

4. Note that the Court held a Markman hearing before he ruled upon the motions. At the Markman hearing, the parties presented arguments as to the meaning of the claim terms that were in dispute: "synchronizing," "each syllable or word," "temporary highlighting," "visual display," "readily follow," and "progresses." Note the rules of construction used by the Court. Do they resemble those used for construing contracts? In what ways do these rules differ from those used when construing language in a contract?

5. Having decided the meaning of the claim terminology, the Court next went through to see if the claims were "anticipated" by the prior art. "Anticipation" is a matter of fact, but since there is no dispute as to what the prior art shows, the Court is comfortable deciding anticipation on summary judgment. Query: if no single piece of prior art contained all the elements of each claim, so that two or more pieces of prior art had to be combined to invalidate the claims, then "obviousness" under § 103 would have to be addressed. Who would make the "obviousness" determination? Would it be possible to gain a summary judgment decision that the claims were obvious and therefore invalid? Would it be likely? Would it make any difference if this was a jury trial?

6. The patent examiner examines the claim language for clarity, and rejects any claim under paragraph two of § 112 that is not clear, requiring amendment of the claim. Why isn't there a presumption (arising under 35 U.S.C.§ 282) that the claims in all issued patents are clear and unambiguous? Does the Court's decision that "Despite Plaintiff's claim to the contrary, the issue of indefiniteness is a question of law" have anything to do with the answer to this question?

3. § 112, Last Paragraph: "Means For" Claim Terminology

All through this chapter, you have encountered claims containing elements written in the form: "means for . . ." followed by language defining the function of the claim element, rather than its structure. The last paragraph of § 112 specifically permits this type of claim drafting to be used, and it says that when the language "means for ..." or "step for ..." appears "without the recital of structure, material, or acts in support thereof," the claim is to be "construed to cover the corresponding structure, material, or acts described in the specification and equivalents thereof."

Up until the 1990s, many patent practitioners assumed that a claim containing a "means for ..." element would be infringed if the allegedly infringing device or method performed the recited function, regardless of how it performed that function. In other words, practitioners assumed great breadth for such claim language. But the Federal Circuit has made it clear that "means for ..." terminology is not as broad as this. To infringe, the infringing structure must be equivalent to what is disclosed in the specification. And to anticipate or render obvious, the "prior art" must match or be equivalent to what is disclosed in the specification, rather than simply performing the function recited in the "means for" claim element language. *See In re Donaldson,* 16 F.3d 1189 (Fed.Cir. 1994). Accordingly, when drafting a patent, if "means for ..." language is used in a claim, the claim draftsman must read over the specification and see whether the description of the apparatus that performs the function lists a sufficient range of equivalent alternative embodiments. If not, then the specification should be revised (before the patent application is filed) to list other ways of carrying out the specified function and to give the claim more breadth of coverage. Many practitioners who used to use "means for ..." language routinely now use it sparingly, preferring to describe the structure in the claim elements and then rely upon the "doctrine of equivalents" to give the claims more breadth.

H. CLAIM INTERPRETATION AND INFRINGEMENT: "MEANS FOR," THE DOCTRINE OF EQUIVALENTS, AND FILE WRAPPER ESTOPPEL

A patent is infringed by one who makes, without authorization, an invention described in one of the claims of a valid patent. The decision as to infringement is a two step process. *Markman v. Westview Instruments, Inc.,* 52 F.3d 967 (Fed.Cir.1995), *aff'd,* 517 U.S. 370, 116 S.Ct. 1384, 134 L.Ed.2d 577 (1996). First, the court determines the meaning of the claims. In making this determination, the court usually holds a "Markman hearing" in which it has the benefit of expert testimony and other evidence. Second, the meaning as determined by the court is applied to the alleged infringement. If there is a jury, only the second step involves the jury and then only if there is enough doubt to create a "jury question." Prior to the *Markman* decision in 1995, many courts permitted the jury to perform both steps.

The decisions studied so far make it clear that a programmed computer or computer program invention can be claimed either as an apparatus or as a method. Under 35 U.S.C. § 112, "An element in a claim for a combination may be expressed as a means or step for performing a specified function without the recital of structure, material, or acts in support thereof, and such claims shall be construed to cover the corresponding structure, material, or acts described in the specification and equivalents thereof." Accordingly, patent claims directed to apparatus frequently contain a series of "means for" steps. Since the "means for" language utilized in a claim is "construed to cover the corresponding structure ... described ... and equivalents thereof" under § 112, the question arises as to how widely a court should read a claim as covering substituted equivalents for the structure disclosed in the patent. The patent holder will argue for a broad interpretation of the claims; the alleged infringer will argue that what it has substituted in some way is not "equivalent" to the "structure ... described" in the claims. The infringer will also argue the doctrine of prosecution history estoppel, under which a claim's scope cannot be enlarged by the § 112 "equivalents" doctrine (or by the similar "doctrine of equivalents" which is discussed below) to cover a process or apparatus that was specifically disclaimed by the applicant during the prosecution of the patent.

Because of the great commercial importance of the Internet, holders of pre-Internet patents have tried to use broad claim interpretation and the doctrine of equivalents to expand them to cover basic Internet processes.

CIVIX–DDI, LLC v. MICROSOFT CORPORATION

United States District Court, D. Colorado, 2000.
84 F.Supp.2d 1132.

BABCOCK, DISTRICT JUDGE.

Plaintiff, CIVIX–DDI, LLC ("CIVIX"), asserts claims for infringement of United States Patents Nos. 4,974,170 (" '170 patent") and/or 5,682,525 (" '525 patent") against seven remaining Defendants, Microsoft Corporation ("Microsoft"), DeLorme Publishing Company, Inc., d/b/a DeLorme Mapping Company ("DeLorme"), InfoUSA, Inc. ("InfoUSA"), Zip2 Corporation ("Zip2"), Infoseek Corporation ("Infoseek"), Lycos, Inc. ("Lycos"), and Excite, Inc. ("Excite") (collectively "Defendants"). CIVIX moves for summary judgment against each Defendant. Defendants plead the affirmative defenses of non-infringement and invalidity. All Defendants, except Microsoft and Infoseek, cross-move for summary judgment on grounds of non-infringement. Pursuant to *Markman v. Westview Instruments, Inc.*, 517 U.S. 370, 116 S.Ct. 1384, 134 L.Ed.2d 577 (1996), I held a hearing on December 10, 1999, and permitted the parties to brief the interpretation of the claims in question. I have reserved the question of invalidity pending determination on the cross-motions for summary judgment on infringement/non-infringement grounds. Having the benefit of the *Markman* hearing to construe the claims in question, and for the following reasons, I deny CIVIX' motions for summary judgment and grant the moving Defendants' motions for summary judgment. Therefore, the issue of invalidity is moot as to these Defendants. Jurisdiction is proper in this Court pursuant to 28 U.S.C. § 1338.

I. BACKGROUND

The following facts are undisputed. The '170 patent, entitled "Electronic Directory for Identifying a Selected Group of Subscribers," was issued November 27, 1990 to Lincoln Bouve and Edward Holmes. The '170 patent matured from an application filed on January 25, 1990, Application No. 470,221 (" '221 application"). The '221 application is a continuation from a parent application, Application No. 07/146,692, filed January 21, 1988, now abandoned. The '170 patent contains seven claims, three of which are at issue in this Order.

As explained in the '170 patent's specification:

Travelers are typically unaware of the locations of businesses or historical sites and must use directories to find such. Commonly, a tourist bureau provides a list of historical sites, or a Chamber of Commerce may provide a directory of businesses. Generally, one must first find a visitor's center or other location which distributes this kind of directory. This is quite time consuming, their having to know where the directories are distributed before they can have access to the information.

('170 Patent, Col. 1 lines 15–24). The '170 patent sought to address this problem by providing publicly accessible "user stations" with electronic directories and methods for locating businesses within the directories. ('170 Patent, Col. 1 lines 25–32). Figures 1 and 2 of the '170 patent illustrate a preferred embodiment of a base or user station. The invention can be used to identify and locate selected "subscribers" within a fixed geographical region surrounding the user station. ('170 Patent, Col. 1 lines 35–42). The user can query the database for the identification and location of subscribers with desired characteristics. ('170 Patent, Col. 1 lines 45–55). For example, a person can query the database for the names and locations of drugstores within a one mile radius of the user station. A map showing the locations of these subscribers is then provided to the user. Figure 6 of the '170 patent is an illustration of a map produced by the user station.

The '525 patent, entitled "System and Methods for Remotely Accessing a Selected Group of Items of Interest from a Database," was issued October 28, 1997 to Lincoln Bouve, William Semple, and Steven Oxman. The '525 patent matured from an application filed on January 11, 1995, Application No. 371,425 (" '425 application"). The '525 patent contains thirty-seven claims, eight of which are specifically at issue in this Order.

As explained in the "Background of the Invention" section of the '525 patent, this newer invention was created, in part, to overcome limitations inherent in the '170 patent:

Electronic directories for identifying selected subscribers within a city are known in the prior art. For example, U.S. Pat. No. 4,974,170 [the '170 patent] describes one system which includes a fixed kiosk with an internal memory for storing locations such as businesses and historical sites within a predetermined distance from the kiosk. . . .

However, such a system is inflexible. The map generated by the system is predefined; and thus the user cannot access or select information about businesses and historical sites outside of the predefined map. A user of the system must also know the exact location of the kiosk in order to use the system. Tourists and business travelers to the city are unlikely to know of the kiosk; and thus the kiosk system is of little use to such users. Further, a user must be physically present at the kiosk in order to access the information about the businesses and/or sites in the surrounding area.

('525 Patent, Col. 1 lines 19–38). The '525 patent addresses these insufficiencies by allowing remote access to select items of interest from a database, and for displaying the location of items of interests to the user at the remote location. ('525 Patent, Col. 1 lines 48–52). A user can access a common data base from a remote location to generate a map which locates selected items of interest. For example, a user in Denver, from a personal computer with a modem, can select a display of drugstores in the area surrounding the Chicago O'Hare International Airport. ('525 Patent, Abstract). A user can also display locations of items of interest relative to the user's own position.

The Defendants manufacture and sell various types of mapping technology and services. Each Defendant's product and/or service will be discussed, as relevant, in the respective summary judgment sections. CIVIX commenced this action on January 26, 1999, alleging that Defendants' individual products and/or services infringe either the '525 or the '170 patents.

II.   Summary Judgment Standards

* * *

III.   Claim Construction

CIVIX and most of the Defendants cross-move for summary judgment, on grounds of infringement and non-infringement respectively. However, prior to determining issues of summary judgment, I construe the claims and decide the meaning and scope of any disputed terms in the claims as a matter of law. *See, e.g., Blumenthal v. Barber–Colman Holdings Corp.,* 62 F.3d 1433, 1995 WL 453120 (Fed.Cir.1995). Determining infringement is a two-step process: "First, the claims of the patent must be construed to determine their scope. Second, a determination must be made as to whether the properly construed claims read on the accused device." *Pitney Bowes, Inc.,* 182 F.3d at 1304 (citing *Carroll*

Touch, Inc. v. Electro Mechanical Sys., Inc., 15 F.3d 1573, 1576 (Fed.Cir. 1993)). Thus, only after construing the disputed claims do I apply these claims to summary judgment infringement analysis.

A. Standards of Claim Construction

Claim construction is a matter of law exclusively for the court's determination. *See Markman*, 517 U.S. at 379, 116 S.Ct. 1384. In interpreting a patent's claims, I first look to the intrinsic evidence of record, including the claims of the patent, the written description, and the prosecution history. *See Phillips Petroleum Co. v. Huntsman Polymers Corp.*, 157 F.3d 866, 870 (Fed.Cir.1998). Such evidence is "the most significant source of the legally operative meaning of disputed claim language." *Vitronics Corp. v. Conceptronic, Inc.*, 90 F.3d 1576, 1582 (Fed.Cir.1996). Only if the intrinsic evidence is ambiguous in delineating the scope of the patent should I resort to extrinsic evidence. *See Phillips Petroleum*, 157 F.3d at 870.

I must read the claims in the context provided by the patent specification. Two canons of claim construction assist in this reading:

> (a) one may not read a limitation into a claim from the written description, but (b) one may look to the written description to define a term already in a claim limitation, for a claim must be read in view of the specification of which it is a part. These two rules lay out the general relationship between the claims and the written description.

Renishaw PLC v. Marposs Societa' per Azioni, 158 F.3d 1243, 1248 (Fed.Cir.1998); *see also Burke, Inc. v. Bruno Independent Living Aids, Inc.*, 183 F.3d 1334, 1341 (Fed.Cir.1999) ("an attribute of the preferred embodiment cannot be read into the claim as a limitation."). The specification contains a written description of the invention which may also act as a dictionary explaining the invention and defining terms in the claims. *See Markman*, 52 F.3d at 979; *Process Control Corp. v. Hydreclaim Corp.*, 190 F.3d 1350, 1357 (Fed.Cir.1999) ("a patentee can act as his own lexicographer to specifically define terms of a claim contrary to their ordinary meaning").

Additionally, I consider the prosecution history in construing the claims. *See Biodex Corp. v. Loredan Biomedical, Inc.*, 946 F.2d 850, 862 (Fed.Cir.1991). Although the doctrine of prosecution estoppel applies only to the doctrine of equivalents and not claim construction, reference to prosecution history may be instructive of the meaning of disputed claim language. *See id.* For example, during prosecution a patentee may disclaim a particular interpretation of claim language to avoid replicating prior art. *See id.* at 863; *see also Alpex Computer Corp. v. Nintendo Co.*, 102 F.3d 1214, 1220 (Fed.Cir.1996) ("Prosecution history is relevant not only for purposes of prosecution history estoppel but also for construing the meaning and scope of the claims.").

Furthermore, I may receive extrinsic evidence to correctly interpret the true meaning of the patent's language. *See Markman*, 52 F.3d at 980. Nevertheless, the type of extrinsic evidence considered and the extent of its use are circumscribed. In *Vitronics*, the Federal Circuit criticized a district court for relying on expert testimony in interpreting the claim language:

> Had the district court relied on the expert testimony and other extrinsic evidence solely to help it understand the underlying technology, we could not say the district court was in error. But testimony on the technology is far different from other expert testimony, whether it be of an attorney, a technical expert, or the inventor, on the proper construction of a disputed claim term, relied on by the district court in this case. The latter kind of testimony may only be relied upon if the patent documents, taken as a whole, are insufficient to enable the court to construe disputed claim terms. Such instances will rarely, if ever, occur.... Even in those rare instances, prior art documents and dictionaries, although to a lesser extent, are more objective and reliable guides. Unlike expert testimony, these sources are accessible to the public in advance of litigation. They are to be preferred over opinion testimony, whether by an attorney or artisan in the field of technology to which the patent is directed. Indeed, opinion testimony on claim construction should be treated with the utmost caution, for it is no better than opinion testimony on the meaning of statutory terms.

Vitronics, 90 F.3d at 1585.

Ultimately, "the interpretation to be given a term can only be determined and confirmed with a full understanding of what the inventors actually invented and intended to envelop with the claim." *See Renishaw*, 158 F.3d at 1251. I begin with the language of the claims, specification, and prosecution history and will only resort to extrinsic evidence if the disputed claim terms are not clear in that context.

B. Claim Construction of the '170 Patent

The '170 patent contains the following disputed claims with disputed terms underlined:

[Claim 1] Apparatus for identifying locations within a **predetermined region of a selected group** of a **set of a plurality of subscribers** relative to the location of a **user station comprising**,

a user station within said predetermined region for interrogating said apparatus,

means for generating a map of said predetermined region,

data base means having data regarding each **subscriber** of said **set of subscribers**, said data including coordinates of said map identifying the location for each **subscriber** in said **predetermined region** of said **set of subscribers** and a characteristic for each **subscriber**, wherein said characteristic is common to a group of said **subscribers**,

input means at said user station for identifying at least one characteristic of said group,

means responsive to the identification at said user station of said at least one characteristic for searching said data base means with reference to said at least one characteristic to determine the members of said **selected group** as at least those **subscribers** having locations in said **predetermined region** and said at least one characteristic,

and **means for displaying said map** at said **user station** with the locations thereon of said members of said **selected group** relative to the location of said **user station**.

[Claim 2] Apparatus according to claim 1 wherein said **means for generating said map** comprises an electronic memory element.

[Claim 5] A method for identifying the location within a **predetermined region** of a **selected group** of a **set of a plurality of subscribers** relative to the location of a **user station** comprising,

providing to said user station map electronic information representing a map of said **predetermined region** around said **user station**,

providing to said user station subscriber electronic information representing the location and at least one characteristic for each **subscriber** of said **set of subscribers**,

said at least one characteristic being common to the members of a group,

selecting at said user station at least one of said characteristics as a group characterization identifying a **group of said subscribers**,

searching said subscriber electronic information with respect to said group characterization,

and **providing said map at said user location displaying the locations of members of said selected group** identified by said group characterization relative to the location of said **user station**.

1. Claims 1 & 5—"User Station"

The term "user station" appears throughout the '170 patent and is a term crucial to the invention. Defendants argue that "user station" is a fixed, public structure and not a non-fixed, non-public structure, such as a personal computer. CIVIX, on the other hand, contends that "user station" should not be so narrowly defined and instead is any computer or other electronic device, available to a user for interrogating a database.

CIVIX bases its interpretation of "user station" on the view that "*work* station," a common computer term, is defined as "a computer terminal or microcomputer connected to a mainframe, minicomputer, or data-processing network.'' Random House Webster's Unabridged Dictionary, Second Edition 1997. Additionally, CIVIX stresses that the '170 patent itself explains that the ''user station'' is designed to interrogate a database containing a map and subscriber electronic information. ('170 Patent, Col. 1 lines 46–55). Furthermore, CIVIX looks to the prosecution history where the applicants added the phrase ''user station, such as'' before the word ''kiosks'' to emphasize the fact that a kiosk is merely a type of user station. ('170 Patent, Col. 1 line 31) ('170 Prosecution History File, CIV000015, CIV 000058). Finally, CIVIX argues that the terms ''kiosk'' and/or ''fixed'' never appear in the claims themselves and, therefore, I should not read this limitation into them. Instead, a fixed kiosk is merely one embodiment of a user station.

I first address Defendants' means-plus-function argument surrounding the term ''user station.'' Defendants urge that the term ''user station'' appears as part of a functional term and is thus limited to the kiosk specification. Claim 1 of the '170 patent teaches, ''a user station within said predetermined region for interrogating said apparatus.'' Defendants argue that this phrase denotes only a place for interrogating the apparatus, recites no structure and, accordingly, must be construed as limited to the corresponding structure disclosed in the patent specification. 35 U.S.C. § 112 ¶ 6. I disagree that this phrase implies a means-plus-function limitation.

Paragraph 6 of 35 U.S.C. § 112 provides that limitations ''expressed as a means ... for performing a specified function without the recital of structure ... in support thereof, ... shall be construed to cover the corresponding structure ... described in the specification and equivalents thereof.'' Paragraph 6 ''operates to cut back on the type of means which could literally satisfy the claim language.'' *Johnston v. IVAC Corp.*, 885 F.2d 1574, 1580 (Fed.Cir.1989). More specifically, ''where a claim sets forth a means for performing a specific function, without reciting any specific structure for performing that function, the structure disclosed in the specification must be considered, and the patent claim construed to cover both the disclosed structure and equivalents thereof.'' *Data Line Corp. v. Micro Technologies, Inc.*, 813 F.2d 1196, 1201 (Fed.Cir.1987).

The phrase at issue here does not use the word ''means,'' and although a claim element might still meet the requirements of § 112, ¶ 6, this does not. In *Personalized Media Communications, LLC v. International Trade Com'n*, 161 F.3d 696, 703 (Fed.Cir.1998), the Federal Circuit stated:

> We also made clear that use of the term ''means'' is central to the analysis: ''the use of the term 'means' has come to be so closely associated with 'means-plus function' claiming that it is fair to say that the use of the term 'means' ... generally invokes [§ 112, ¶ 6] and that the use of a different formulation generally does not.'' ... [F]ailure to use the word ''means'' creates a presumption that § 112, ¶ 6 does not apply.... In deciding whether either presump-

tion has been rebutted, the focus remains on whether the claim as properly construed recites sufficiently definite structure to avoid the ambit of § 112, ¶ 6.

Id. at 703–704 (internal citations omitted); *see also Cole v. Kimberly–Clark Corp.*, 102 F.3d 524, 531 (Fed.Cir.1996) ("To invoke [35 U.S.C. § 112 ¶ 6], the alleged means-plus-function claim element must not recite a definite structure which performs the described function.").

In *Cole*, the claim recited a "perforation means . . . for tearing." The court held that the statute did not apply because the claim "describes the structure supporting the tearing function (i.e., perforations)." *Id.* In addition, the claim "describes not only the structure that supports the tearing function, but also its location (extending from the leg band to the waist band) and extent (extending through the outer impermeable layer)." *Id.* The court concluded that "an element with such a detailed recitation of its structure, as opposed to its function, cannot meet the requirements of the statute." *Id.*

The same rationale applies here. The phrase at issue provides for a "a user station within said predetermined region for interrogating said apparatus." ('525 patent, Claim 1). Although the latter part of the quoted phrase describes a function, the claim includes a specific recitation of the structure to support that function—a "user station." In addition, as in *Cole*, this phrase includes a limitation on the user station—it must be "within said predetermined region." Furthermore, the phrase "user station" is expressed throughout Claims 1 & 5 as a specific structural element, such as a kiosk. Accordingly, the phrase at issue does not meet the requirements of 35 U.S.C. § 112 ¶ 6, and I will not analyze it as a means-plus-function element. Although I do not find that 35 U.S.C. § 112 ¶ 6 limits the scope of the term "user station," the overwhelming weight of relevant evidence supports a more limited construction than that proposed by CIVIX.

This invention was intended to provide travelers a convenient substitute for visitor's centers and Chambers of Commerce. ('170 Patent, Col. 1 lines 25–27). For example, the '170 patent states that a kiosk is to be "placed on the sidewalk of the downtown area of a city. Preferably, user station, such as kiosks are placed on the sidewalks at a plurality of locations throughout the city." ('170 Patent, Col. 1 lines 29–32). The preferred embodiment in figure 1 shows a "base station 2 in the form of a kiosk. The kiosk is preferably placed on a sidewalk, and receives power from cables (not shown) buried beneath the sidewalk." ('170 Patent, Col. 2 lines 40–43). The patent explains that a user station "may be located on a sidewalk at a street intersection for easy access by pedestrians." ('170 Patent, Col. 2 lines 53–54). Further, the patent proudly states that,

> It will be appreciated that a unique method and apparatus has been described wherein *anyone in the city may obtain a map* of the area immediately surrounding where they are, the map having information regarding the locations of businesses, historical sites, or the like by simply activating an input key on a kiosk.

('170 Patent, Col. 3 lines 62–67) (emphasis added). The patent specification does not detail or teach any mobile, private, or non-fixed user station. In fact, the patent's stated purpose to provide travelers with information about local businesses could not be furthered without an accessible public structure.

I look to the ordinary meaning of these terms because there is no specialized meaning asserted. *See, e.g., Karlin Technology, Inc. v. Surgical Dynamics, Inc.,* 177 F.3d 968 (Fed.Cir.1999). A "station" merely denotes "a place established to provide a public service," such as a fire station, police station, or gas station. Webster's Third New Int'l Dictionary 2229 (3d ed.1986). The modifying word "user," in this context, not surprisingly, means that the station is one for users. I conclude that in early 1990, the time of the filing of the '170 patent application, one of ordinary skill in the art would not have understood the term "user station" to mean a personal computer or "work station," *see Markman,* 52 F.3d at 986 ("the focus is on the objective test of what one of ordinary skill in the art at the time of the invention would have understood the term to mean."), especially in light of the other language and specifications of the '170 patent. (Waite Declaration, ¶ 17). Therefore, I am not persuaded by CIVIX' citation of the term "work station" in the 1997 Random House Webster's Unabridged Dictionary, as this definition was created subsequent to the patent application.

Finally, if any ambiguity remains in the meaning of the term "user station," the '525 patent is illuminating. The '525 patent notes the insufficiencies of the '170 patent: "such a system is inflexible.... *A user of the system must also know the exact location of the kiosk in order to use the system.* Tourists and business travelers to the city are unlikely to know of the kiosk; and thus the kiosk system is of little use to such users. Further, a user must be *physically present at the kiosk in order to access the information* about the businesses and/or sites in the surrounding area." ('525 Patent, Col. 1 lines 29–37) (emphasis added). This characterization by the '525 patentees are also those of Mr. Bouve, a named inventor on both the '170 and '525 patents. Therefore, these comments are relevant to the construction of the terms and corroborate my interpretation. Although I do not limit the term "user station" to include only "kiosks," I conclude that "user station," as used in the '170 patent, is limited to a fixed public structure.

* * *

4. Claim 1—"Input Means"

Defendants' argue, and I agree, that "input means" is a means-plus-function term. The entire phrase reads, "input means at said user station for identifying at least one characteristic of said group." Defendants urge that "input means" are thus limited to the only means of input disclosed in the '170 patent (an input panel with input keys each labeled with a corresponding characteristic) and its equivalents. 35 U.S.C. § 112 ¶ 6. CIVIX, on the other hand, argues that the "input means" limitation is not the "means" of a means-plus-function limitation. Instead, CIVIX argues that the term "input" provides sufficient structure for performing the function of identifying characteristics.

As stated above, 35 U.S.C. § 112 ¶ 6, provides that limitations "expressed as a means ... for performing a specified function without the recital of structure ... in support thereof, ... shall be construed to cover the corresponding structure ... described in the specification and equivalents thereof." Paragraph 6 "operates to cut back on the type of means which could literally satisfy the claim language." *Johnston*, 885 F.2d at 1580. More specifically, "where a claim sets forth a means for performing a specific function, without reciting any specific structure for performing that function, the structure disclosed in the specification must be considered, and the patent claim construed to cover both the disclosed structure and equivalents thereof." *Data Line*, 813 F.2d at 1201.

The phrase at issue here uses the word "means," and although this does not dictate that a claim falls under § 112, ¶ 6, I conclude that this claim does. *See Personalized Media*, 161 F.3d at 703 ("use of the word 'means' has come to be so closely associated with 'means-plus-function' claiming that it is fair to say that the use of the term 'means' ... generally invokes [§ 112, ¶ 6].... [U]se of the word 'means' creates a presumption that § 112, ¶ 6 applies") (internal citations omitted).

There is no definite structure recited in this phrase that is used to perform the described function. "Input" is not structural. Thus, I construe the patent to cover both the disclosed structure and equivalents thereof. The structure disclosed by the '170 patent is "an input panel having a plurality of input keys." ('170 Patent, Abstract). Further, Figure 2 depicts an "input panel includ[ing] a plurality of input keys." ('170 Patent, Col. 2 lines 55–56). In operation, "a user selects one of the input keys 12 corresponding to the characteristic of the organization desired. For example, if a key labeled 'Drugstores' is activated, internal electronic means ... searches ... for the group of subscribers which are drugstores." ('170 Patent, Col. 2 lines 60–65). Thus, I conclude that "input means" is limited to an input panel with input keys each labeled with a corresponding subscriber characteristic, and equivalent structures.

* * *

7. Claim 1—"Means for Displaying Said Map"

Again, the parties agree that "means for displaying said map at said user station" is a means-plus-function limitation controlled by 35 U.S.C. § 112 ¶ 6. CIVIX contends that the means is not limited to a printer as described in the specification. Instead, CIVIX argues that a skilled artisan would have recognized that a monitor or similar device for presenting the map in visual form could perform the claimed function. Defendants, on the other hand, argue that this term is to be narrowly construed as a printer and the structural equivalents of a printer.

The only "means for displaying" a map indicated in the '170 patent is through a printer providing a hard copy of the map. For example,

> In operation, a user selects one of the input keys 12 corresponding to the characteristic of the organization.... Then, the apparatus prints a map having the locations of the drugstores indicated thereon, and that map is dispensed into a hopper 16. The user then withdraws the map and ascertains which drugstore to use.

('170 Patent, Col. 2 line 60 through Col. 3 line 4). Nowhere in the '170 patent does the inventor indicate that a monitor or similar device for presenting a map in visual form could be used. In construing a means-plus-function claim controlled by 35 U.S.C. § 112 ¶ 6, I am limited to the specifications of the patent and their equivalents. I cannot find that a monitor or similar device is a structural equivalent of a printer. Therefore, the means are thus limited.

* * *

C. Claim Construction of the '525 Patent

* * *

IV. CROSS MOTIONS FOR SUMMARY JUDGMENT

* * * Having completed claim construction of both the '170 and '525 patents, I move to the second stage * * *

B. The '170 Patent

CIVIX asserts infringement of the '170 patent against only two of the seven Defendants, DeLorme and Microsoft. CIVIX moves for summary judgment on grounds of infringement of Claims 1, 2, and 5 of the '170 patent against both Defendants DeLorme and Microsoft. De-Lorme cross-moves for summary judgment on non-infringement of the '170 patent. Microsoft, on the other hand, has not yet moved for summary judgment on the basis of non-infringement.

1. The Accused Products

DeLorme: Only two DeLorme products are accused of infringement, Street Atlas USA Versions 5.0 and 7.0 Street Atlas USA Version 5.0 ("Atlas 5.0") and Street Atlas USA Version 7.0 ("Atlas 7.0") are both sold in the form of CD ROM disks. Atlas 5.0 includes a "Setup" disk for installing on a computer the programs necessary to use the product, and a "Runtime" disk which actually runs the product. Similarly, Atlas 7.0 includes an "Install" disk and a "Program Data" disk which serve the same respective functions. DeLorme customers receive a license to install and use the software on a personal computer. This same license would prohibit a customer from installing the software in a structure accessible by the general public. (Gray Declaration, ¶ 3). The Introductory Guide to Atlas 5.0 describes the product as,

> the original and best mapping software available! Street Atlas USA 5.0 combines DeLorme's extraordinary map detail with address-to-

address routing. High-quality maps and easy-to-use tools help you plan your trips quickly. Street Atlas USA 5.0 not only helps you map the route of your choice, but also lets you explore and select from over two million points of interest along the way.

Plan your route based upon your travel preferences and driving habits. Make your trip more enjoyable by avoiding expensive toll roads or heavily congested traffic areas. Street Atlas USA 5.0 lets you choose the route that best fits your needs and then automatically calculates the distance and driving time for you. Take the Scenic route to see the country, save gas by taking the Shortest route or save time by taking the Quickest route.

Best of all, when you've finished planning your trip, you can print a Travel Plan of strip maps, complete with your customized list of places to see along the way. You can also print out a separate list of detailed directions for your journey. Street Atlas USA 5.0 is the complete street-level travel planner.

(Street Atlas USA 5.0 Introductory Guide, D 0028). The introductory language to the Atlas 7.0 product describes a very similar system. (Street Atlas USA 7.0 Introductory Guide, p. 4).

Microsoft: Only one Microsoft software product is accused of infringing the '170 patent, Microsoft Expedia Streets 98 Version 6.0 ("Streets 98"). It is sold in the form of a CD ROM disk. Microsoft's Streets 98 product allows users to find street addresses anywhere in the Country and to display or print them on custom maps. (Microsoft's Motion, p. 5).

2. The '170 Patent Summary Judgment Conclusions

As judges and commentators have noted, to decide what the claims mean will almost always decide the case. See *Markman*, 52 F.3d at 989 (Mayer, J., concurring in the judgment), *aff'd.* 517 U.S. 370, 116 S.Ct. 1384, 134 L.Ed.2d 577 (1996); *Baxa*, 981 F.Supp. at 1360; Gregory D. Leibold, *In Juries We Do Not Trust: Appellate Review of Patent–Infringement Litigation*, 67 U. Colo. L.Rev. 623, 635 (1996). To establish literal infringement, CIVIX has the burden of showing that "every limitation set forth in a claim [is] found in an accused product, exactly." *Southwall*, 54 F.3d at 1575. If any physical component recited in an apparatus claim is not present in an accused product, the product cannot literally infringe that claim. *See Mannesmann Demag Corp. v. Engineered Metal Prods. Co.*, 793 F.2d 1279, 1282 (Fed.Cir.1986). Where, as here, "the parties do not dispute any relevant facts regarding the accused product but disagree over which of two possible meanings of [the claim] is the proper one, the question of literal infringement collapses to one of claim construction and is thus amenable to summary judgment." *Athletic Alternatives, Inc. v. Prince Mfg., Inc.*, 73 F.3d 1573, 1578 (Fed.Cir.1996). Now that I have construed properly the claims as a matter of law, there is no genuine issue of fact whether DeLorme or Microsoft's products infringe the claims. I hold that they do not.

As contained in the only independent claims at issue in the '170 patent, Claims 1 and 5, per my construction, "user station" is limited to a fixed public structure, and is not broad enough to include a non-fixed personal computer. DeLorme's Atlas 5.0 and 7.0 products and Microsoft's Streets 98 do not employ a fixed, public structure, but are rather in the form of CD ROM disks to be installed on a personal computer. My construction of this term alone warrants a grant of summary judgment in favor of Defendants. * * *

* * *

For the above reasons, I deny CIVIX' motions for summary judgment against DeLorme and Microsoft on grounds of infringement. Accordingly, I grant DeLorme's motion for summary judgment on non-infringement of the '170 patent. Microsoft has not yet filed a motion for summary judgment on grounds of non-infringement.

* * *

Notes

1.   Prior to Markman, the Court would probably have delegated the claim language construction task to the jury, possibly through the use of a special verdict. Would a jury have reached the same result as did the Court? Do you think that Markman takes some of the uncertainty out of patent litigation?

2.   Do you agree with the Court that a monitor is not the equivalent of a printer as "means for displaying" under § 112, last paragraph? The Court reaches this conclusion because the patent specification never mentions a monitor as an alternative for a printer. Is this a proper reading of the statute? When we consider the "doctrine of equivalents" in the next case, you may wish to think about whether the "doctrine of equivalents" is applicable to "means for" claim elements or only to other types of claim elements; and whether the test for "equivalents" under § 112, last paragraph, is the same or different than the "doctrine of equivalents" doctrine described in the next case. See *D.M.I. v. Deere*, 755 F.2d 1570, 1575 (Fed.Cir.1985) and *Pennwalt v. Durand–Wayland*, 833 F.2d 931, 933–34 (Fed.Cir.1987).

3.   In determining the meaning of the phrase "user station," the Court quotes language from a later patent having one inventor in common with the earlier patent that contains the phrase "user station" in its claims. The later patent notes as a deficiency that the "kiosk" of the earlier patent resides at a fixed location. But this defines the term "kiosk," not the phrase "user station" in the claim. By assigning the meaning of the term "kiosk" to the phrase "user station" in the claim, isn't the Court construing this claim language to cover the corresponding structure "described in the specification" and thus applying the last paragraph of § 112 after having specifically decided that this statutory provision was inapplicable to this claim element?

HILGRAEVE CORPORATION v. McAFEE ASSOCIATES, INC.

United States Court of Appeals, Federal Circuit, 2000.
___ F.3d ___, 2000 WL 1059659.

RADER, CIRCUIT JUDGE.

On summary judgment, the United States District Court for the Eastern District of Michigan determined that the VirusScan product of McAfee Associates, Inc. (MC) does not literally infringe Hilgraeve Corporation's U.S. Patent No. 5,319,776 (the '776 patent). *See Hilgraeve Corp. v. McAfee Assocs., Inc.*, 70 F.Supp.2d 738 (E.D.Mich.1999). The district court also estopped Hilgraeve from arguing that VirusScan infringes any claim of the '776 patent under the doctrine of equivalents. This court affirms the district court's finding that prosecution history estoppel bars application of the doctrine of equivalents. This court vacates, however, the grant of summary judgment of no literal infringement and remands for appropriate further proceedings.

I.

Hilgraeve's '776 patent, entitled "In Transit Detection of Computer Virus with Safeguard," describes a program that scans for computer viruses. The claimed invention scans a body of data during its transfer, i.e., before storage of the data with potential viruses on the destination storage medium. If the program detects signs of a virus during the scan, the program automatically blocks storage.

Claims 1 and 18 of the '776 patent are at issue. Claim 1 reads as follows, with language in dispute underlined:

1. In a system for transferring digital data for storage in a computer storage medium, a method of screening the data as it is being transferred and automatically inhibiting the storage of screened data containing at least one predefined sequence, comprising the steps of:

   causing a quantity of digital data resident on a source storage medium to be transferred to a computer system having a destination storage medium;

   receiving and screening the transferred digital data prior to storage on the destination storage medium to determine if at least one of a plurality of predefined sequences are present in the digital data received; and in response to said screening step:

   (a) automatically causing the screened digital data to be stored on said destination storage medium if none of the plurality of predefined sequences are present and

   (b) automatically inhibiting the screened digital data from being stored on said destination storage medium if at least one predefined sequence is present.

'776 patent, col. 17, ll. 9–29 (emphasis added). Claim 18 reads as follows:

18.   A method of preventing the spread of computer viruses to a computer having a storage medium, comprising the steps of:

> simultaneously searching for a plurality of virus signatures, each of which comprising an identifiable digital sequence, while said computer is receiving a stream of digital data for storage on said storage medium;

> providing an indication of the detection of a virus from said searching step; and

> automatically inhibiting the storage of said digital stream on said storage medium if any of said virus signatures have been detected.

Id. at col. 28, ll. 45–57 (emphasis added). Because these claims require inhibition of storage, the district court construed the meaning of the word "storage" in the temporal context of the patent. The district court construed "storage" as occurring "when the incoming digital data is sufficiently present on the destination storage medium, and accessible by the operating system or other programs, so that any viruses contained in the data can spread and infect the computer system." *Hilgraeve*, 70 F.Supp.2d at 745. This definition is consistent with the district court's interpretation of the patent claims as requiring scanning prior to storage. See id. at 748. Neither party disputes the court's claim construction.

Hilgraeve contended that McAfee's accused product, VirusScan, infringes independent claims 1 and 18 and dependent claims 2 and 6 of the '776 patent. In other words, Hilgraeve alleged that VirusScan screens incoming digital data for viruses during transfer and before "storage" on the destination storage medium. McAfee, on the other hand, asserted that VirusScan does not infringe because it screens the incoming digital data only after it has been transferred and "stored" on the destination storage medium. Thus, the critical issue in the infringement analysis is whether VirusScan screens before, or after, the time at which incoming data is present on the destination storage medium and accessible by the operating system and other programs.

To resolve this issue on summary judgment, the district court relied solely upon expert testimony about the operation of VirusScan. The district court declined to entertain a declaration and accompanying exhibits offered by one of the co-inventors of the '776 patent, terming this evidence "a thinly veiled effort to introduce expert testimony in an improper manner." *Id.* at 754. The district court also declined to consider McAfee promotional materials describing VirusScan. Hilgraeve asserted that these promotional materials showed that a user of Virus-Scan would perceive that the program operates as outlined in the claims of the '776 patent. The district court pointed out that infringement is not a question of user perception of operation, but of actual operation. Therefore it declined to consider the promotional literature. *See Id.* at 156. * * *

III.

The district court based its summary judgment on the testimony of experts who had tested VirusScan and interpreted the VirusScan code. In examining the appellate record for genuine issues of material fact, this court notes disagreements between the experts. McAfee's expert, Mr. Belgard, opined on the basis of his studies that VirusScan first stores digital data and then screens for viruses, and so does not infringe the '776 patent. Hilgraeve's expert, Dr. Geske, on the basis of his own technical studies and consideration of deposition testimony of McAfee's designated witness on infringement, Mr. Kuo, reached a different conclusion. Dr. Geske characterized Mr. Belgard's description of VirusScan's operation as over-simplified and opined that his tests were not probative on the question of infringement. Thus, Dr. Geske concluded that Virus-Scan infringes the '776 patent. While disagreements do not always create genuine issues of material fact, on this record the conflicting allegations of experts leaves material factual questions unanswered. * * *

These differences in the experts' descriptions of VirusScan's operation raise a genuine issue of material fact. The record shows a genuine and material conflict over the interaction of VirusScan with the computer's operating system arising from the differing explanations of the operation of VirusScan. Moreover the record does not conclusively describe VirusScan's interaction with the computer's operating system. McAfee's expert does not describe VirusScan's inhibition or manipulation of the operating system. Instead, this expert states that VirusScan makes the infected program available to the computer in general (an operation which defeats infringement) by a normal call from the application program to the operating system to close the file. Hilgraeve's expert, however, understands VirusScan to interact with the operating system itself to make an infected program inaccessible. The determination of whether either description (or neither) is correct requires a factual determination of the actual operation of the VirusScan program, particularly its interaction with the operating system. The testimony of neither party's expert reveals enough of such a determination to resolve the issues on this record. * * *

IV.

Although the parties nominally agree on the district court's claim interpretation, Hilgraeve also argued before that court that the phrase "prior to storage" must be construed from the ordinary user's perspective, i.e., that whether or not VirusScan screens before or after storage, it will infringe if the user perceives that screening occurs before storage. As support for this argument, Hilgraeve refers to comments the applicant made to the Patent and Trademark Office (PTO) during prosecution, in support of the amendments to its application which resulted in allowance. The amendments added, inter alia, the phrase "prior to storage on the destination storage medium" to claim 1. *See Hilgraeve*, 70 F.Supp.2d at 750. In its comments to the PTO, Hilgraeve asserted that "the Applicants' invention requires only one step. The user simply initiates the data transfer. The program automatically screens the data, as it is being transferred...." Hilgraeve asserts that this comment means that the patented invention requires only that the user perceive screening before storage, regardless of how the program actually operates.

The district court correctly found nothing in the intrinsic evidence to support Hilgraeve's argument based on the perception of the program's operation. *See Hilgraeve*, 70 F.Supp.2d. at 756. Neither the claims nor the rest of the specification of the '776 patent show that the invention involves the user's perception of the program's operation. The written description supplies some suggestions for user interaction with the program to direct inspection for certain specific error protocols. The claims of the '776 patent, however, do not claim a method of screening data "so that the user perceives that screening occurs before storage," but instead claims a method of actually screening before storage. The patentee claimed a technical method, not a method for projecting a perception.

V.

The district court found Hilgraeve estopped from claiming infringement under the doctrine of equivalents by any product that screens for viruses after "storage." As originally submitted, the application that led to the '776 patent did not contain claim 18. Claim 18 was added in the applicant's first response to rejection of all its claims. In this response, the applicant stated to the examiner that "[t]he present invention also has the capability to respond to the detection of a virus by not only preventing the copying of the complete file, but also...." (Emphasis added.) In other words, the applicant was stating that when the scanning program detected a virus, it prevented the copying of the complete file (among other things). Because an incomplete file would not be "sufficiently present on the destination storage medium, and accessible by the operating system or other programs" (except perhaps for erasure), the patentee may not now assert equivalents to claim 18 that allow screening after storage. *See Hilgraeve*, 70 F.Supp. at 748–50. Claim 1 acquired the phrase "prior to storage on the destination storage medium" in a later amendment, after which the patent was granted. Hilgraeve admits that it amended its claims to specify screening "prior to storage" to procure its patent. A surrender of subject matter during patent prosecution may preclude recapturing any part of that subject matter, even if it is equivalent to the matter expressly claimed. *See Warner–Jenkinson Co. v. Hilton Davis Chem. Co.*, 117 S.Ct. 1040, 1044 (1997). In other words, prosecution history estoppel bars recapture of subject matter surrendered during prosecution. By limiting the added claim 18 to screening before storage, and specifically adding "screening ... prior to storage" to claim 1, Hilgraeve surrendered the possibility of infringement by equivalence of any process that does not contain this modification, i.e., that screens after storage.

VI.

Because neither McAfee's three tests nor either expert's analysis of the VirusScan code definitively answers the fundamental factual question of whether "storage," as defined by the district court, occurs before or after scanning in VirusScan, this court vacates the district court's grant of summary judgment of non-infringement and remands for further proceedings consistent with this opinion. Because Hilgraeve surrendered, during prosecution, the option of accusing a product of infringing its patent by equivalents if it does not screen before storage, this court affirms the district court's holding that a product that screens for viruses after "storage" cannot infringe any claim of the '776 patent under the doctrine of equivalents. * * *

VACATED–IN–PART, AFFIRMED–IN–PART, and REMANDED.

Notes

1.   This patent had a fairly typical prosecution history, where the application is filed, and then rejected, amended, finally rejected, a further amendment is not entered, and then a "continuation" application is filed, and then the second amendment is entered and the patent is granted. Examiners get credit for "dispositions." In this case, the Examiner received credit for two "dispositions." Experienced patent practitioners know that at the end of a quarter, when an examiner may be up for promotion depending upon the number of dispositions, the examiner may be more inclined to bargain than at other times. Would it have been smarter in this case for the applicant to go up on appeal after the final rejection, rather than compromising and introducing narrower language into the claims? Appeals can take several years and are relatively expensive. Today, instead of filing new "continuation" applications to keep patent prosecution going, the applicant pays an additional fee and thereby continues the examination of the original application.

2.   In finding prosecution history estoppel in this case, did the Court rely more upon what the applicant said, or upon what new limitations were added to the claim language by amendment? Personal and telephone interviews with the examiner are not normally recorded on the record in any detail, and so what is said orally may have less of an impact on later litigation than what is said in the "remarks" portion of a written amendment to the claims.

3.   Compare the final form of claim 1 to its form just before the final amendment. Notice how the changes emphasize that the screening precedes storage, and the determination to store or not to store is done automatically after screening for viruses is complete. This is a fairly major revision of the wording of the claim, done to distinguish the claim language from the prior art before the examiner.

Notes on the "Doctrine of Equivalents"

1. Routinely today, patent litigation first looks for literal infringement of the patent claims, and then looks for "doctrine of equivalents" infringement of the patent claims. The court determines the meaning of the claim language. The jury, or judge acting as trier of fact, then determines whether there is literal infringement, or "doctrine of equivalents" infringement, or no infringement of each claim.

2. The "doctrine of equivalents" is applied to the claim language element by element, rather than to the claim as a whole. If an element of a claim is not infringed literally, the question is asked whether the element in the infringing device is "equivalent" to the element of the claim.

3. There are two tests for "doctrine of equivalents" infringement. The first test is the function, way, result test, referred to by the Court as the "triple identity" test: If the non-literally-infringing element of the allegedly infringing device is, in fact, substantially the same thing, used in substantially the same way, to achieve substantially the same result as the claim element, then "doctrine of equivalents" infringement is established. *Graver Tank v. Linde Air*, 339 U.S. 605, 609, 70 S.Ct. 854, 856–57, 94 L.Ed. 1097 (1950). The second test is referred to by the Court as the "insubstantial differences" test. *WMS Gaming v. International Game Technology*, 184 F.3d 1339, 1359 (1999). The Supreme Court summarizes the "doctrine of equivalents" as follows: "Does the accused product or process contain elements identical or equivalent to each claimed element of the patented invention?" *Warner–Jenkinson v. Hilton Davis*, 520 U.S. 17, 19, 117 S.Ct. 1040, 1044, 137 L.Ed.2d 146 (1997).

4. There are two outer limits on this doctrine: first, "prosecution history estoppel" (also called "file wrapper estoppel") still applies and can prevent finding a claim element equivalent. Secondly, any given claim can only be expanded in scope until it runs into the "prior art." Any claim construed so broadly that it reads upon and encompasses the prior art is, of course, invalid when so construed. Accordingly, the doctrine of equivalents may be applied differently (and more narrowly) when applied to elements of a broader independent claim, which is closer to the prior art, than when applied to elements of a narrower, dependent claim, which is farther away from the prior art. For example, the very same element may be found to be not equivalent in the case of independent claim 1 and to be equivalent in the case of narrower dependent claim 2 which incorporates claim 1 by reference. *See Wilson Sporting Goods v. David Geoffrey*, 904 F.2d 677 (Fed.Cir.1990). Practically speaking, these outer limits define areas of noninfringement where a potential infringer can feel safe and secure, not subject to the whims of a jury's decision on the doctrine of equivalents.

5. There is also a "reverse doctrine of equivalents," which permits the court or jury to find non-infringement even when there is literal infringement. This doctrine is not often applied. *See SRI International v. Matsushita Electric*, 775 F.2d 1107 (Fed.Cir.1985). "Thus, where a device is so far changed in principle from a patented article that it performs the same or a similar function in a substantially different way, but nevertheless falls

within the literal words of the claim, the doctrine of equivalents may be used to restrict the claim and defeat the patentee's action for infringement." *Graver Tank v. Linde Air*, 339 U.S. 605, 608–09, 70 S.Ct. 854, 856, 94 L.Ed.1097 (1950).

Question

1.   An Internet computer expert and a young musician and music lover come to you and describe a business that they are going to set up on the Internet that will permit anyone to buy and sell music CDs over the Internet. They plan to set up a central server to coordinate the sales and the purchases. Anyone will be permitted to place an order to purchase any CD, and each order must be backed up by a valid credit card guarantee. An order to buy may take the form of a bid to purchase a specific CD at no more than a stated price, or it can take the form of a bid to purchase the CD at whatever the market price may be. Sellers, likewise, will be permitted to place an order to sell either at a stated minimum price or at the market price.

The system is to be implemented on the Internet by means of a computer that will accept orders to buy and to sell during successive 15 minute "order acceptance" periods. At the end of each "order acceptance" period, the system matches up all compatibly-priced orders to buy and orders to sell, and it then computes a market price that is applied to all of the trades.

The computer proceeds in the following manner: It matches the highest-priced offer to buy with the lowest-priced offer to sell; next, it matches the next-highest offer to buy against the next-lowest offer to sell; and so it proceeds until all the orders with compatible prices have been matched up. The average of the final two prices of the last two "priced" orders is then taken as the "market price" for all of the sales consummated. The "at market" orders are then also matched up, to the extent possible, at this same price. In this manner, as many sales are accomplished as is theoretically possible, at the best possible price for all concerned.

Your new clients ask you about patent protection for their proposed system.

As a first step, you conduct a search using the PTO's searchable data base of patents looking for any patent that might be relevant to the patentability of this invention. You come across U.S. Patent No. 5,794,207, issued on August 11, 1998 to Walker Asset Management Limited Partnership. This patent discloses an internet-based marketing system for such things as new cars, airline tickets, and hotel reservations, where the purchasers bid at named prices, guaranteeing their bids with credit card information, and the sellers then respond. The "Abstract" and claim 1 of this patent read as follows (you may obtain a full copy of this 40–page patent from the PTO's web site, <http://www.uspto.gov>):

Abstract

The present invention is a method and apparatus for effectuating bilateral buyer-driven commerce. The present invention allows prospective buyers of goods and services to communicate a binding purchase offer globally to potential sellers, for sellers conveniently to search for relevant buyer purchase offers, and for sellers potentially to bind a buyer to a contract based on the buyer's purchase offer. In a preferred embodiment, the apparatus of the present invention includes a controller which receives binding purchase offers from prospective buyers. The controller makes purchase offers available globally to potential sellers. Potential sellers then have the option to accept a purchase offer and thus bind the corresponding buyer to a contract. The method and apparatus of the present invention have applications on the Internet as well as conventional communications systems such as voice telephony.

Claim 1

1. A method for using a computer to facilitate a transaction between a buyer and at least one of sellers, comprising:

inputting into the computer a conditional purchase offer which includes an offer price;

inputting into the computer a payment identifier specifying a credit card account, the payment identifier being associated with the conditional purchase offer;

outputting the conditional purchase offer to the plurality of sellers after receiving the payment identifier;

inputting into the computer an acceptance from a seller, the acceptance being responsive to the conditional purchase offer; and

providing a payment to the seller by using the payment identifier.

You run a computer check to see if this patent has ever been asserted, and you learn that on October 13, 1999, the web site Priceline.com asserted this patent against Microsoft's Expedia.com travel agency web site.

This patent was filed on September 4, 1996, and it issued on August 11, 1998. Assuming that it is relevant prior art, what specific information from your clients will negate this patent as possibly anticipatory "prior art" under § 102(a)? Under § 102(b)? Under § 102(e)? Under § 102(g)? What information will negate it as prior art that possibly could be used to prove your client's invention is obvious under § 103?

Assuming that this patent does fall within the category of relevant prior art as to your clients' invention under §§ 102 and 103, try drafting a claim for your client that will define invention over this prior art.

What advice should you give your clients to avoid the risk of infringing this patent, assuming that it is valid? In particular, should you suggest changes or restrictions in the design of the system? And when you communicate with your clients on this subject, should you do so in writing when discussing design modifications?

Assuming that your clients are going to reveal their new system to the public in two weeks, what precautions must you take to preserve their rights to seek a foreign patent? Are confidential agreements needed?

What three actions by your clients will trigger the start of the one year clock defined by § 102(b) that requires a U.S. patent application to be filed less than one year later?

What steps must you take to insure that the Internet music company that you plan set up for your clients owns all the patent rights? Must inventor-employees sign some form of agreement?

Chapter III

TRADE SECRECY
A. INTRODUCTION

In the early days of software, trade secrets were the primary means of protection. Three major changes affecting the use of trade protection occurred in the 1980s. As demonstrated in the previous chapters, copyright and patent law developed into significant forms of protection for computer technology. Personal computer manufacturers discovered that hardware sales depended upon software availability for their computers, and that software developers needed extensive access to technical data about the computers and operating systems for which they were developing software. The incredible growth of personal computer ownership made it impossible to negotiate traditional, signed trade secret contracts with every purchaser of hardware and software. These three factors resulted in a major, but not complete shift, from trade secrecy to copyright and patents in the software and computer industries. Currently the software industry is lobbying for passage of the Uniform Computer Information Transactions Act (UCITA), which would allow it to impose "contractual" trade secrecy requirements without obtaining traditional signed contracts.

Mainframe manufacturers and custom software houses continue to use trade secrecy as they have since the 1960s. Software developers nearly always keep the "source code" secret when they sell "object code" to the general public or license "object code" to individual users. Developers often keep new products secret until they are released, to delay market entry by competitors. Because of the need to test new products and adapt software for them, developers do, however, distribute advance versions to trusted organizations, but require those organizations to sign trade secrecy agreements. Due to the high demand for and resulting job-hopping by technology professionals, and the resulting high turnover rate in the late 1990's, non-compete and non-disclosure agreements in employment contracts are widely used. However, in some states, particularly California, there are serious legal restrictions upon the enforceability of non-compete contracts.

B. PROTECTING TRADE SECRETS AGAINST TAKING BY "IMPROPER MEANS"

Over 40 states have enacted trade secrecy legislation, generally patterned on the Uniform Trade Secrets Act. The trade secret provisions of Restatement (Third) of Unfair Competition (which superseded the trade secret provisions of Restatement (Second) of Torts) largely track the provisions of the Uniform Trade Secrets Act. The Act and the Restatement provide protection against outright theft of trade secrets but they do not govern contracts safeguarding of trade secrets. Courts have been using Restatement (Third) of Unfair Competition to complement and supplement decisions involving existing trade secrets statutes. *See Ed Nowogroski Insurance, Inc. v. Rucker,* 137 Wash. 2d 427, 971 P.2d 936 (1999); *Flotec Inc. v. Southern Research Inc.,* 16 F.Supp.2d. 992 (S.D.Ind., 1998). In 1996 Congress passed the Economic Espionage Act, 18 U.S.C. 90, which provides severe criminal penalties for trade secret theft.

UNIFORM TRADE SECRETS ACT

14 U.L.A. 433 (1990).
© 1990 National Council of Commissioners on
State Laws; reprinted with permission.

§ 1. Definitions

As used in this [Act], unless the context requires otherwise:

(1) "Improper means" includes theft, bribery, misrepresentation, breach or inducement of a breach of a duty to maintain secrecy, or espionage through electronic or other means;

(2) "Misappropriation" means:

(i) acquisition of a trade secret of another by a person who knows or has reason to know that the trade secret was acquired by improper means; or

(ii) disclosure or use of a trade secret of another without express or implied consent by a person who

(A) used improper means to acquire knowledge of the trade secret; or

(B) at the time of disclosure or use, knew or had reason to know that his knowledge of the trade secret was

(I) derived from or through a person who had utilized improper means to acquire it;

(II) acquired under circumstances giving rise to a duty to maintain its secrecy or limit its use; or

(III) derived from or through a person who owed a duty to the person seeking relief to maintain its ()secrecy or limit its use; or

(C) before a material change of his [or her] position, knew or had reason to know that it was a trade secret and that knowledge of it had been acquired by accident or mistake.

(3) "Person" means a natural person, corporation, business trust, estate, trust, partnership, association, joint venture, government, governmental subdivision or agency, or any other legal or commercial entity.

(4) "Trade secret" means information, including a formula, pattern, compilation, program, device, method, technique, or process, that:

 (i) derives independent economic value, actual or potential, from not being generally known to, and not being readily ascertainable by proper means by, other persons who can obtain economic value from its disclosure or use, and

 (ii) is the subject of efforts that are reasonable under the circumstances to maintain its secrecy.

§ 2. Injunctive Relief

(a) Actual or threatened misappropriation may be enjoined. Upon application to the court, an injunction shall be terminated when the trade secret has ceased to exist, but the injunction may be continued for an additional reasonable period of time in order to eliminate commercial advantage that otherwise would be derived from the misappropriation.

(b) In exceptional circumstances, an injunction may condition future use upon payment of a reasonable royalty for no longer than the period of time for which use could have been prohibited. Exceptional circumstances include, but are not limited to, a material and prejudicial change of position prior to acquiring knowledge or reason to know of misappropriation that renders a prohibitive injunction inequitable.

(c) In appropriate circumstances, affirmative acts to protect a trade secret may be compelled by court order.

§ 3. Damages

(a) Except to the extent that a material and prejudicial change of position prior to acquiring knowledge or reason to know of misappropriation renders a monetary recovery inequitable, a complainant is entitled to recover damages for misappropriation. Damages can include both the actual loss caused by misappropriation and the unjust enrichment caused by misappropriation that is not taken into account in computing actual loss. In lieu of damages measured by any other methods, the damages caused by misappropriation may be measured by the imposition of liability for a reasonable royalty for a misappropriator's unauthorized disclosure or use of a trade secret.

(b) If willful and malicious misappropriation exists, the court may award exemplary damages in an amount not exceeding twice any award made under subsection (a).

§ 4. Attorney's Fees

If (i) a claim of misappropriation is made in bad faith, (ii) a motion to terminate an injunction is made or resisted in bad faith, or (iii) willful and malicious misappropriation exists, the court may award reasonable attorney's fees to the prevailing party.

§ 5. Preservation of Secrecy

In an action under this [Act], a court shall preserve the secrecy of an alleged trade secret by reasonable means, which may include granting protective orders in connection with discovery proceedings, holding in-camera hearings, sealing the records of the action, and ordering any person involved in the litigation not to disclose an alleged trade secret without prior court approval.

§ 6. Statute of Limitations

An action for misappropriation must be brought within 3 years after the misappropriation is discovered or by the exercise of reasonable diligence should have been discovered. For the purposes of this section, a continuing misappropriation constitutes a single claim.

§ 7. Effect on Other Law

(a) Except as provided in subsection (b), this [Act] displaces conflicting tort, restitutionary, and other law of this State providing civil remedies for misappropriation of trade secret.

(b) This [Act] does not affect:

(1) Contractual remedies, whether or not based upon misappropriation of a trade secret;

(2) other civil remedies that are not based upon misappropriation of a trade secret; or

(3) criminal remedies, whether or not based upon misappropriation of a trade secret.

§ 8. Uniformity of Application and Construction

This [Act] shall be applied and construed to effectuate its general purpose to make uniform the law with respect to the subject of this [Act] among states enacting it. * * *

ECONOMIC ESPIONAGE ACT OF 1996
18 U.S.C. § 1831.

§ 1839—Definitions

(3) the term "trade secret" means all forms and types of financial, business, scientific, technical, economic, or engineering information, including patterns, plans, compilations, program devices, formulas, designs, prototypes, methods, techniques, processes, procedures, programs, or codes, whether tangible or intangible, and whether or how stored, compiled, or memorialized physically, electronically, graphically, photographically, or in writing if–

(A) the owner thereof has taken reasonable measures to keep such information secret; and

(B) the information derives independent economic value, actual or potential, from not being generally known to, and not being readily ascertainable through proper means by, the public; and

(4) the term owner, with respect to a trade secret, means the person or entity in whom or in which rightful legal or equitable title to, or license in, the trade secret is reposed.

Note

Note that the trade secret definition in the Economic Espionage Act is broader than the definition in the Uniform Trade Secrets Act. It is wise to include a broad definition of trade secrets in an employment contract to minimize eventual disputes over whether or not particular information was a trade secret.

RELIGIOUS TECHNOLOGY CENTER v. LERMA

United States District Court, E.D. Virginia, 1995.
908 F.Supp. 1362.

BRINKEMA, DISTRICT JUDGE.

Before the Court is the Motion for Summary Judgment filed by defendants, The Washington Post, and two of its reporters, Marc Fisher and Richard Leiby (hereinafter referred to collectively as "The Post"). * * * [T]he Court finds that summary judgment should be entered in favor of the defendants.

I. UNDISPUTED FACTS

The essential facts are not in dispute. In 1991, the Church of Scientology sued Steven Fishman, a disgruntled former member of the Church of Scientology, in the United States District Court for the Central District of California. *Church of Scientology Int'l v. Fishman*, No. CV 91–6426. On April 14, 1993, Fishman filed in the open court file what has come to be known as the Fishman affidavit, to which were attached 69 pages of what the Religious Technology Center ("RTC") describes as various Advanced Technology works, specifically levels OT–I through OT–VII documents. Plaintiff claims that these documents are protected from both unauthorized use and unauthorized disclosure under the copyright laws of the United States and under trade secret laws, respectively.

In California, the RTC moved to seal the Fishman affidavit, arguing that the attached AT documents were trade secrets. That motion was denied and the Ninth Circuit upheld the district court's decision not to seal the file. *Church of Scientology Int'l v. Fishman*, 35 F.3d 570 (9th Cir.1994). The case was remanded for further proceedings and the district court again declined to seal the file, which remained unsealed until August 15, 1995.

Defendant Arnaldo Lerma, another former Scientologist, obtained a copy of the Fishman affidavit and the attached AT documents. Lerma admits that on July 31 and August 1, 1995, he published the AT documents on the Internet through defendant Digital Gateway Systems ("DGS"), an Internet access provider. RTC, which regularly scans the Internet, discovered the publication of documents and on August 11, 1995, warned Lerma to return the AT documents and not publish them any further. After Lerma refused to cooperate, RTC obtained a Temporary Restraining Order prohibiting Lerma from any further publication of the documents and a seizure warrant which authorized the United States Marshal to seize Lerma's personal computer, floppy disks and any copies of the copyrighted works of L. Ron Hubbard, the author of the AT documents.

During the same time period, on or about August 5 or 6, 1995, Lerma sent a hard copy of the Fishman affidavit and AT attachments to Richard Leiby, an investigative reporter for The Washington Post. On August 12, 1995, counsel for RTC discovered this disclosure and approached The Post, which was told that the Fishman affidavit might be stolen. In response to the RTC's representations, The Post returned the actual copy which Lerma had given it. However, The Post had by then learned that a copy of the same Fishman affidavit was available in the open court file in the United States District Court for the Central District of California. On August 14, 1995, The Post sent Kathryn Wexler, a news aide stationed in California, to that court to obtain a copy of the Fishman affidavit. The Clerk's office made a copy for Wexler, who then mailed it to Washington. Although it is undisputed that RTC staff members had been checking that file out and holding it all day to prevent anyone from seeing it, the file was not sealed and obviously was available, upon request, to any member of the public who wished to see it.

The day after The Post obtained its copy of the Fishman affidavit, the RTC applied for a sealing order and the trial judge ordered the file sealed. However, there is no evidence in the record that the judge ordered The Post to return the copy made by the Clerk's office or that any kind of a restraining order was issued by that court against The Post.

Five days later, on August 19, 1995, The Post published a news article, entitled "Church in Cyberspace: Its Sacred Writ is on the Net. Its Lawyers are on the Case," written by defendant Marc Fisher. In that article, RTC's lawsuit against Lerma and the seizure of his computer equipment were discussed, as was the history of Scientology litigation against its critics and the growing use of the Internet by Scientology dissidents. The article included three brief quotes (totaling 46 words) from three of the AT documents. On August 22, 1995, the RTC filed its First Amended Verified Complaint for Injunctive Relief and Damages in which it added The Washington Post and its two reporters, Fisher and Leiby, as additional defendants. A Second Amended Verified was later filed and is now the subject of this summary judgment motion.

II. THE COPYRIGHT CLAIM

* * *

IV. MISAPPROPRIATION CLAIM

To prove misappropriation of a trade secret, the RTC must show (1) that it possessed a valid trade secret, (2) that the defendant acquired its trade secret, and (3) that the defendant knew or should have known that the trade secret was acquired by improper means. *Trandes Corporation v. Guy F. Atkinson*, 996 F.2d 655, 660 (4th Cir.1993), cert. denied, 510 U.S. 965, 114 S.Ct. 443, 126 L.Ed.2d 377 (1993).

The Post argues persuasively that the AT documents were no longer trade secrets by the time The Post acquired them. They point to the following undisputed facts. First, the Fishman affidavit had been in a public court file from April 14, 1993 until August 15, 1995, for a total of 28 months. Although RTC has shown that it went to extraordinary efforts to control access to that file by having church members sign out the file and keep it in their custody at the courthouse, the file nevertheless was an open file, available to the public. The Post was able to obtain a copy of the Fishman affidavit without any difficulty, by merely asking the Clerk of the court to copy it. Thus, having been in the public domain for an extensive period of time, these AT documents cannot be deemed "trade secrets." *Kewanee Oil Co. v. Bicron Corp.*, 416 U.S. 470, 484, 94 S.Ct. 1879, 1887, 40 L.Ed.2d 315 (1974).

Of even more significance is the undisputed fact that these documents were posted on the Internet on July 31 and August 1, 1995. (Lerma Affidavit). On August 11, 1995, this Court entered a Temporary Restraining Order among other orders which directed Lerma to stop disseminating the AT documents. However, that was more than ten days after the documents were posted on the Internet, where they remained potentially available to the millions of Internet users around the world.

As other courts who have dealt with similar issues have observed, "posting works to the Internet makes them 'generally known' "at least to the relevant people interested in the news group. *Religious Technology Center v. Netcom On–Line Communications Services, Inc.*, No. C. 95–20091 RMW (N.D.Cal.) Slip Opinion entered 9/22/95 at 30. Once a trade secret is posted on the Internet, it is effectively part of the public domain, impossible to retrieve. Although the person who originally posted a trade secret on the Internet may be liable for trade secret misappropriation, the party who merely down loads Internet information cannot be liable for misappropriation because there is no misconduct involved in interacting with the Internet.

Even if one were to assume that the AT documents are still trade secrets, under Virginia law, the tort of misappropriation of trade secrets is not committed by a person who uses or publishes a trade secret unless that person has used unlawful means, or breached some duty created by contract or implied by law resulting from some employment or similar relationship.

> It is the *employment of improper means to procure the trade secret, rather than the mere copying or use*, which is the basis of [liability] . . . Apart from breach of contract, abuse of confidence or impropriety in the means of procurement, trade secrets may be copied freely as devices or processes which are not secret.

Trandes Corporation v. Guy F. Atkinson Company, 996 F.2d at 660 (quoting the Restatement (First of Torts)) (emphasis in original). The *Trandes* court notes that abuse of confidence or impropriety in the means of procurement represented the "essential element" and the "core" of a misappropriation claim. *Id.*

The RTC claims that because The Post was on notice of the RTC's allegations that the AT documents were stolen and were both trade secrets and unpublished copyrighted works, The Post was under a legal obligation not to copy or use the documents. This Court knows of no law which required The Post to sit on its hands and do no further investigation into what was obviously becoming a newsworthy event and newsworthy documents. The RTC's allegations are still just allegations. The very court from which the Fishman affidavit was obtained still has under advisement the issue of whether the AT documents are trade secrets. Although The Post was on notice that the RTC made certain proprietary claims about these documents, there was nothing illegal or unethical about The Post going to the Clerk's office for a copy of the documents or downloading them from the Internet.

Because there is no evidence that The Post abused any confidence, committed an impropriety, violated any court order or committed any other improper act in gathering information from the court file or down loading information from the Internet, there is no possible liability for The Post in its acquisition of the information. This is true regardless of the documents status as trade secrets. As for the disclosure of the information, The Post did nothing more than briefly quote from publicly available materials. These acts simply do not approach a trade secret misappropriation, and, therefore, summary judgment must be entered for the defendants.

The Clerk is directed to forward copies of this Memorandum Opinion to counsel of record.

Notes

1. The information about the Church of Scientology that was the subject of this and other intellectual property litigation has reappeared at various foreign sites on the Internet.

2. Older cases held that limited distribution of a trade secret by someone who had taken it improperly did not destroy the secret. But now a trade secret thief can instantly and utterly destroy the secret merely by posting on the Internet. And likewise, of course, a company foolish enough to post its trade secrets on the Internet will lose them instantly.

3. Note the decision in *Ford Motor Co. v. Lane*, 67 F.Supp.2d 745 (E.D.Mich.1999). Although the defendant in that case was found likely to have violated the Michigan Uniform Trade Secrets Act, the court held that the issuance of an injunction against posting the trade secrets on a website would violate the prior restraint doctrine and the First Amendment as applied under these circumstances. Existing precedent required Ford to demonstrate that publication of the trade secrets on a website threatened an interest more fundamental than the First Amendment itself before an injunction would issue. In the absence of a confidentiality agreement or fiduciary duty between the parties, Ford's commercial interest in its trade secrets and Lane's alleged improper conduct in obtaining the trade secrets were not grounds for issuing an injunction.

VERMONT MICROSYSTEMS, INC. v. AUTODESK, INC.

United States Court of Appeals, Second Circuit, 1996.
88 F.3d 142.

VAN GRAAFEILAND, CIRCUIT JUDGE.

This litigation involves the alleged misappropriation of trade secrets. In a judgment of the United States District Court for the District of Vermont (Niedermeier, Magistrate J.) Autodesk, Inc. and Otto G. Berkes were held liable to Vermont Microsystems, Inc. ("VMI") for trade secret misappropriation, and Autodesk was assessed $25.5 million in damages.

At issue is certain computer aided design ("CAD") software. CAD is highly sophisticated software used primarily by engineers and architects to render computer drawings. Autodesk is the largest provider of CAD software in the world. Its premier product, AutoCAD, has nearly 80 percent of the CAD market. VMI, a small company based in Winooski, Vermont, is one of many "third party developers" that create AutoCAD accessories to increase the program's functionality. VMI initially concentrated on hardware accessories such as graphics boards, which could be added to a computer to improve the graphics resolution. In 1989, VMI realized that the hardware accessory market was limited and decided to concentrate on software accessories that could be used directly with the AutoCAD program.

Berkes began working for VMI while it was making this shift, first as a summer intern in 1988 and then as a full-time employee in 1989. As a full-time employee, Berkes signed an Invention and Nondisclosure Agreement in which he acknowledged that all trade secrets developed on VMI's time were company property and promised not to disclose such trade secrets for the benefit of himself or others. Berkes worked as a software programmer and was assigned a variety of projects by VMI. He was a gifted programmer who made valuable contributions to VMI's library of software.

When Berkes left VMI in the fall of 1991 and joined Autodesk, Peter Reed, the President and Chief Executive Officer of VMI, sent a letter to Autodesk advising that because Berkes was privy to VMI's trade secrets,

Autodesk should exercise caution in assigning him projects. Berkes also was given a copy of this letter. Although Berkes initially was assigned to noncompeting projects, by the fall of 1992, VMI learned that his assignments had changed and that his new work implicated VMI trade secrets. After some unproductive discourse between the two companies, VMI sued Autodesk and Berkes alleging copyright infringement and misappropriation of trade secrets. Berkes, against whom VMI sought only injunctive relief, counterclaimed against VMI and Reed for libel and sought a declaratory judgment that he had a non-exclusive right to use the Berkes–Pilcher Shading ("BPS") algorithm, which bears his name and that of VMI employee Steven Pilcher.

In the course of a seventeen day bench trial, VMI abandoned its copyright infringement claim. However, it was successful on its claim for trade secret misappropriation. Both of Berkes' counterclaims were rejected. The primary trade secrets at issue are the architecture of VMI's display list driver, and its triangle shading algorithm, which are described hereafter in the language of the untutored layman.

* * *

LIABILITY

Display List Driver

With the parties in agreement, the district court applied California law of trade secret misappropriation. Cal. Civ.Code §§ 3426.1–3426.11. To assert a cause of action for trade secret misappropriation under California law, VMI was required to "identify the trade secret with reasonable particularity." Cal.Civ.Proc.Code § 2019(d). VMI complied with this directive by submitting to the court a list of eleven trade secrets that Autodesk allegedly misappropriated. The first of these trade secrets was the "architecture" of the display list driver. The next eight trade secrets listed were component trade secrets which contributed to VMI's display list driver. Since they were largely subsumed by the scope of the first secret, the district court directed its attention primarily to the latter. Secrets ten and eleven were the triangle shading and BPS algorithms which are discussed separately *infra*. With reference to the first trade secret, VMI claimed that it "has been able to attain higher performance AutoCAD graphics and create AutoMate 'tools' via its unique display list architecture, which comprises its data format and organization, its collection of associated display list data processing algorithms, and its software code implementation."

The parties agree that this "combination" trade secret qualifies as a trade secret under California law. " '[A] trade secret can exist in a combination of characteristics and components, each of which, by itself, is in the public domain, but the unified process, design and operation of which, in unique combination, affords a competitive advantage and is a protectable secret.' "*Integrated Cash Management Servs., Inc. v. Digital Transactions, Inc.*, 920 F.2d 171, 174 (2d Cir.1990) (quoting *Imperial Chem. Indus. Ltd. v. National Distillers & Chem. Corp.*, 342 F.2d 737,

742 (2d Cir.1965)); *see Cybertek Computer Prods., Inc. v. Whitfield*, 203 U.S.P.Q. 1020, 1024 (Cal.Super.Ct.1977).

The parties disagree, however, on whether VMI has carried its burden of demonstrating misappropriation. Under California law, the onus was on VMI to show that the display list driver incorporated in R12 Windows was substantially derived from the architecture of its AutoMate display list driver. *See Forro Precision, Inc. v. International Business Machs. Corp.*, 673 F.2d 1045, 1056–57 (9th Cir.1982), *opinion following remand*, 745 F.2d 1283 (9th Cir.1984), *cert. denied*, 471 U.S. 1130, 105 S.Ct. 2664, 86 L.Ed.2d 280 (1985). VMI did not, however, have to prove that the display list drivers were identical. Our review of the record satisfies us that the district court's findings of fact concerning substantial derivation are fully supported by the evidence. * * *

* * *

TRIANGLE SHADING ALGORITHM

Autodesk also was held to have misappropriated the triangle shading algorithm developed by VMI. On appeal, Autodesk does not deny the similarity between the two algorithms. That argument was foreclosed by the overwhelming evidence of the algorithms' correspondence. Indeed, one expert witness reported that "[t]he resemblance goes right down to the names of variables, names of macros, and even many of the comments." Another pronounced the algorithms "identical."

Instead, Autodesk takes issue with the district court's implicit finding that the triangle shading algorithm qualifies as a trade secret under California law. California law affords protection only to those trade secrets which meet a two-part definition. In addition to being subject to reasonable measures to insure their secrecy, trade secrets also must "[d]erive [ ] independent economic value, actual or potential, from not being generally known to the public or to other persons who can obtain economic value from [their] disclosure or use." Cal.Civ.Code § 3426.1(d)(1); *see also Religious Technology Ctr. v. Wollersheim*, 796 F.2d 1076, 1090 (9th Cir.1986), *cert. denied*, 479 U.S. 1103 (1987). Autodesk concedes that VMI diligently protected its trade secrets. Its argument on appeal is that, since VMI's triangle shading technique is simply a variation of the well-known Gouraud Shading technique, the algorithm had no "independent economic value." *See id.* at 1091; *Scott v. Snelling & Snelling, Inc.*, 732 F.Supp. 1034, 1045 (N.D.Cal.1990).

This argument is unavailing here. The economic value of VMI's triangle shading algorithm is readily apparent. The inclusion of this algorithm in AutoMate contributed, if only in small part, to its commercial attractiveness. One witness indicated that acquisition of this algorithm "would save any developer a great deal of time and would provide them with an efficient, polished, and proven fill algorithm." That is exactly what occurred here when, within weeks of signing on with Autodesk, Berkes created a nearly identical triangle shading algorithm for inclusion in AutoCAD Release 12 for MS–DOS. While alternative triangle shading algorithms might have been acceptable to Autodesk, it nonetheless received value from Berkes' infringement of VMI's version. Simply because other developers might independently create their own version of a triangle shading routine does not deprive VMI's version of its trade secret status. *See Gates Rubber Co. v. Bando Chem. Indus., Ltd.*, 9 F.3d 823, 848 (10th Cir.1993) ("Although there is some evidence that some of the constants might be 'reverse engineered' through mathematical trial and error, that fact alone does not deprive the constants of their status as trade secrets."). In sum, the district court did not err in concluding that VMI's triangle shading algorithm constituted a trade secret.

THE LEGALITY OF THE AGREEMENT

Berkes makes a separate argument against the district court's findings of liability. He contends that, by failing to specify which trade secrets it considered proprietary under the Invention and Nondisclosure Agreement, VMI was seeking to transform the agreement into a de facto noncompetition agreement that would unfairly foreclose his future employment options. According to Berkes, the broad language of the Invention and Nondisclosure Agreement, which prohibited disclosure of "any and all inventions, discoveries, trade secrets and improvements," gave VMI greater protection than it could have received under a noncompetition agreement. Noncompetition agreements generally are construed narrowly by courts, and must contain time, geographic and/or industry limitations. *See, e.g., Deringer v. Strough*, 918 F.Supp. 129, 132–33 (D.Vt.1996); *Fine Foods, Inc. v. Dahlin*, 147 Vt. 599, 523 A.2d 1228 (1986). Berkes argues that, if VMI was concerned about his future competitive threat, the company should have sought a noncompetition agreement, not an Invention and Nondisclosure Agreement.

Trade secret cases often balance an employer's right to proprietary information against an employee's right to use his or her knowledge, training, and experience to gain a livelihood. Milgrim, 1 MILGRIM ON TRADE SECRETS § 5.01 (1994). Courts must weigh "the policy which strives to extend some protection to an employer from the breach of confidence of a former employee in taking away and utilizing trade secrets with the policy of the law which protects an employee in his right to carry on his trade or profession after he leaves his employer." *Cybertek*, 203 U.S.P.Q. at 1024. Where that balance is struck in individual cases depends largely upon the facts and circumstances surrounding the employer-employee relationship. *See Integrated Cash Management Servs., Inc. v. Digital Transactions, Inc.*, 732 F.Supp. 370, 377 (S.D.N.Y. 1989), *aff'd*, 920 F.2d 171 (2d Cir.1990). Here, we perceive no injustice to Berkes in upholding VMI's proprietary rights under the Invention and Nondisclosure Agreement.

As VMI's key software programmer, Berkes was well aware of the value of the main trade secret at issue—the architecture of the display list driver. He was proud of his many contributions to the product and even referred to himself in his resume as the "chief architect of Auto-

Mate." In two separate exit interviews with VMI, Berkes was reminded of his confidentiality obligations under the Invention and Nondisclosure Agreement. He also was given a copy of the letter that Reed sent Autodesk warning against an inadvertent technology transfer. In view of these oral and written warnings, the district court did not err in finding that "Berkes understood the concept of intellectual property ownership rights when he left VMI and had every reason to know what VMI considered its proprietary technology."

The Invention and Nondisclosure Agreement included within its scope the component trade secrets contained in AutoMate. Contrary to Berkes' assertions, VMI was under no obligation to provide him with an itemized list of AutoMate's component trade secrets upon his departure from the company. To enforce its rights under the Invention and Nondisclosure Agreement, VMI must demonstrate that it took reasonable steps to guard its trade secrets. *See Balboa Ins. Co. v. Trans Global Equities*, 218 Cal.App.3d 1327, 267 Cal.Rptr. 787, 798 n. 22, *cert. denied*, 498 U.S. 940, 111 S.Ct. 347, 112 L.Ed.2d 311 (1990). There was ample testimony at trial describing the security precautions that VMI had in place during Berkes' employment. In addition to having employees sign an Invention and Nondisclosure Agreement, VMI management periodically issued reminders about the need to keep developments confidential. On those occasions when VMI provided proprietary information to outsiders, as it did with Autodesk in the early stages of this case, appropriate confidentiality assurances were sought and obtained. VMI also maintained a secure workplace as a precaution against burglary. Berkes' contention that VMI should have provided him with a list of the specific component trade secrets it considered proprietary upon his resignation from VMI is unpersuasive inasmuch as such a practice could have jeopardized VMI's security. We conclude that VMI took reasonable steps to protect its trade secrets. Moreover, in so doing, VMI did not unfairly preclude Berkes from pursuing his profession. Berkes himself acknowledged that he could have created a display list driver for Autodesk without using any VMI trade secrets.

* * *

DAMAGES

* * *

CONCLUSION

The amended judgment of the district court is affirmed in all respects except as to the $25.5 million damage award. That portion of the judgment is vacated and the matter is remanded to the district court with instructions to recalculate the damage award.

Note

As this case makes clear, it can be very difficult to distinguish the general skill in programming techniques that an employee learns on the job, skills that the employee is free to take to the next job, from specific secret programming techniques that the employee may not use with a new employer.

C. PROTECTING TRADE SECRETS AGAINST DISCLOSURE BY GOVERNMENT AGENCIES

GILMORE v. U.S. DEPARTMENT OF ENERGY

United States District Court, N.D. California, 1998.
4 F.Supp.2d 912.

ORRICK, DISTRICT JUDGE.

In this action brought by John Gilmore ("Gilmore") against the United States Department of Energy ("DOE") under the Freedom of Information Act ("FOIA"), 5 U.S.C. § 552, both parties now move for summary judgment. For the reasons set forth below, DOE's motion for summary judgment is granted in part, and denied in part. Gilmore's motion for summary judgment is denied in its entirety.

I.

On December 8, 1993, Gilmore filed a FOIA request with DOE, seeking access to all agency records pertaining to the CLERVER conferencing technology. CLERVER was created by Sandia National Laboratories/New Mexico ("SNL"), is owned by Sandia Corporation ("Sandia"), and has been licensed to several private parties, including SunSolutions, Inc. ("Sun"). CLERVER is video conferencing software that allows people in different geographical locations to simultaneously collaborate on complex technical drawings and schematics using their desktop computers. Gilmore requested a copy of CLERVER, as well as all documentation relating to CLERVER, including the source code. He also requested all records that pertain to the rationale for making CLERVER available to Sun, but not to the general public. Gilmore intends to disseminate all of these records on the Internet.

By letter dated May 2, 1994, DOE denied Gilmore's request in its entirety on the ground that (1) the software was not an agency record; (2) the other information about the software was not in DOE's possession; and (3) the information was exempt from disclosure because it was commercially valuable. On May 27, 1994, Gilmore appealed DOE's denial of his request. On June 29, 1994, DOE denied his appeal.

This action was filed on January 24, 1995, and an amended complaint was filed on March 2, 1995. Gilmore seeks:

1. disclosure of CLERVER and related documents;

2.　to enjoin DOE from denying FOIA requests for computer software on the ground that software is not an agency record;

3.　a declaration that DOE's failure to publicly define the terms "contractor" or "contractor records" renders its "contractor records" regulations null and void as applied to Gilmore and any other person without actual notice of their terms, and requiring DOE to publish definitions of these terms in the Federal Register;

4.　a declaration that federal laboratories such as SNL are agencies of DOE subject to the FOIA, and that records of federal laboratories produced under their management and operations contracts with DOE are agency records subject to the FOIA that cannot be withheld under FOIA Exemption 4;

5.　a declaration that DOE's pattern and practice of failing to issue a determination of FOIA requests within the ten-day statutory period is unlawful;

6.　a declaration that DOE's failure to provide adequate information during the administrative process about the withholding of records is unlawful; and

7.　an award of costs and fees.

Gilmore brings these claims under the FOIA, the Administrative Procedures Act, and the Fifth Amendment of the United States Constitution. The parties have now filed cross-motions for summary judgment.

II.

A.

"The basic purpose of the [FOIA] is to ensure an informed citizenry, vital to the functioning of a democratic society, needed to check against corruption and to hold the governors accountable to the governed." *NLRB v. Robbins Tire & Rubber Co.*, 437 U.S. 214, 242, 98 S.Ct. 2311, 57 L.Ed.2d 159 (1978) (citations omitted). The FOIA was intended to establish a general philosophy of full agency disclosure and to close the loopholes that allowed agencies to deny legitimate information to the public. *GTE Sylvania, Inc. v. Consumers Union of the United States*, 445 U.S. 375, 385, 100 S.Ct. 1194, 63 L.Ed.2d 467 (1980). In accordance with those goals, the FOIA provides that "each agency, upon any request for records which (i) reasonably describes such records and (ii) is made in accordance with published rules stating the time, place, fees (if any), and procedures to be followed, shall make the records promptly available to any person." 5 U.S.C. § 552(a)(3). Nine specific categories of records are not required to be disclosed. 5 U.S.C. § 552(b). "But unless the requested material falls within one of these nine statutory exemptions, the FOIA requires that records and material in the possession of federal agencies be made available on demand to any member of the general public." *Robbins Tire*, 437 U.S. at 221, 98 S.Ct. 2311. The only exemption claimed to be relevant here is Exemption 4, the exemption for "trade secrets and commercial or financial information obtained from a person and privileged or confidential." 5 U.S.C. 552(b)(4).

The FOIA vests jurisdiction in federal district courts to enjoin an agency from withholding agency records and to order the production of any agency records improperly withheld from the complainant. 5 U.S.C. § 552(a)(4)(B). Federal jurisdiction is thus dependent upon a showing that an agency has (1) improperly (2) withheld (3) agency records. *Kissinger v. Reporters Comm. for Freedom of the Press*, 445 U.S. 136, 150, 100 S.Ct. 960, 63 L.Ed.2d 267 (1980). The threshold question in this case is whether the requested documents relating to CLERVER are agency records within the meaning of the FOIA.

Under the FOIA, the term "agency" includes "any executive department, military department, Government corporation, Government controlled corporation, or other establishment in the executive branch of the Government (including the Executive Office of the President), or any independent regulatory agency." 5 U.S.C. § 552(f). Private organizations receiving federal financial assistance grants are not within the FOIA definition of "agency," absent extensive, detailed, and virtually day-to-day supervision. *Forsham v. Harris*, 445 U.S. 169, 179, 100 S.Ct. 977, 63 L.Ed.2d 293 (1980).

"Records" include "all books, papers, maps, photographs, machine readable materials, or other documentary materials, regardless of physical form or characteristics made or received by an agency of the United States Government under Federal law or in connection with the transaction of public business." *Id.* at 183, 100 S.Ct. 977 (applying the definition of a "record" from the Records Disposal Act, 44 U.S.C. § 3301, to the FOIA).

Two requirements must be satisfied for materials to qualify as "agency records." *United States Dep't of Justice v. Tax Analysts*, 492 U.S. 136, 144, 109 S.Ct. 2841, 106 L.Ed.2d 112 (1989) ("*Tax Analysts I*"). First, an agency must either create or obtain the materials. *Id.* Second, the agency must be in control of the requested materials at the time the FOIA request is made. *Id.* at 145, 109 S.Ct. 2841. "By control we mean that the materials must have come into the agency's possession in the legitimate conduct of its official duties." *Id.* The FOIA applies only to records that have in fact been obtained, and not to records that merely could have been obtained, by the agency. *Id.* at 144, 109 S.Ct. 2841. The relevant issue is whether a FOIA agency has created or obtained the material sought, not whether the organization from which the documents originated is itself covered by the FOIA. *Id.* at 146, 109 S.Ct. 2841.

Records of a nonagency can become agency records by contract. *Forsham*, 445 U.S. at 181, 100 S.Ct. 977. For instance, "Congress could have provided that the records generated by a federally funded grantee were federal property even though the grantee has not been adopted as a federal entity." *Id.* at 180, 100 S.Ct. 977. Under this test, it appears that records that are contractually owned by the government are agency records regardless of whether they are physically in the government's possession, because they have been obtained by the government and are within the government's control.

The burden is on the agency to demonstrate that the materials sought are not agency records or have not been improperly withheld. *Tax Analysts I*, 492 U.S. at 142 n. 3, 109 S.Ct. 2841. Placing the burden of proof upon the agency puts the task of justifying the withholding on the only party able to explain it. *Id.*

B.

1.

The Court begins by examining who was in control of CLERVER and the related CLERVER records on December 8, 1993, the date of Gilmore's FOIA request. The contracts between DOE and Sandia for the operation of SNL provide that, subject to exceptions not relevant here, all records acquired or generated by Sandia in its performance of the contract are the property of the government. (Index to Exs. ("Index"), Vol. II, Ex. C, app. B, art. B–XXXI at B65; id. Vol. I, Ex. B, ¶ H–18(a) at 16.) The contracts also provide that the government will control the rights to all intellectual property created pursuant to the contracts, but that Sandia can request that it be permitted to retain title if it intends to take reasonable steps to commercialize the intellectual property that it has created. If permission to retain title is granted, the government receives a nonexclusive license to use the intellectual property on behalf of the United States. On July 2, 1993, DOE granted permission for Sandia to assert copyright in the CLERVER software. Previously, in 1992, the government also had assigned to Sandia the title to a patented invention that is incorporated into CLERVER.

Accordingly, on December 8, 1993, the date of Gilmore's FOIA request, the government owned all records relating to the development of CLERVER, and owned a nonexclusive license to use CLERVER itself. Sandia owned the copyright in CLERVER, which gave it the exclusive right, subject to the license retained by the government, to make copies of CLERVER and to distribute it to the public. 17 U.S.C. § 106. Sandia also owned exclusive rights in a patented invention that is incorporated into CLERVER, subject to a license to the government. *Id.*

The government does not, however, own CLERVER itself, but merely possesses a license to use it for government purposes. At least one recent case has found that the government does not control a record for FOIA purposes if it does not have unrestricted use of it. *See Tax Analysts v. United States Dep't of Justice*, 913 F.Supp. 599 (D.D.C.1996), *aff'd without opinion*, 107 F.3d 923 (D.C.Cir.1997), *cert. denied*, ___ U.S. ___, 118 S.Ct. 336, 139 L.Ed.2d 260 (1997) ("*Tax Analysts II*").[1]

---

1. To distinguish this case from the Supreme Court's 1989 *Tax Analysts* decision, the Court will refer to this case as *Tax* *Analysts II*, and to the Supreme Court case as *Tax Analysts I*. Other than the similarity in names, the two cases are not related.

In Tax Analysts II, the plaintiff had submitted a FOIA request seeking to compel the United States Department of Justice ("DOJ") to disclose its JURIS electronic legal research database. *Id.* at 600. The DOJ refused to disclose the portion of JURIS that was provided to it by West Publishing Company on the ground that it either was not an agency record or was confidential commercial information excluded from disclosure by FOIA Exemption 4. *Id.* West had granted the DOJ a nonexclusive license for limited use of the JURIS materials, which specifically provided that West remained the exclusive owner of the materials. *Id.* at 604. The court focused on the definition of "control" under the FOIA. The court found that although the Supreme Court had stated that "[b]y control, we mean that the materials have come into the agency's possession in the legitimate conduct of its official duties," it did not suggest that mere possession was synonymous with control. *Id.* at 602 (quoting *Tax Analysts I*, 492 U.S. at 144, 109 S.Ct. 2841.) Indeed, the Court had cited approvingly an earlier case in which it had declined to hold that the mere physical location of the records in a government agency rendered them agency records. *Id.* (citing *Kissinger*, 445 U.S. at 157, 100 S.Ct. 960). In the district court's view, the key element of "control" was whether the records at issue were subject to the free disposition of the agency. *Id.* at 603 (citing *Goland v. CIA*, 607 F.2d 339, 347 (D.C.Cir.1978)). The court found that "although DOJ certainly possessed the West-provided data, its right to use, transfer and/or dispose it was greatly restricted, and thus DOJ did not 'control' the data in any common sense reading of that word." *Id.* at 607. Thus, the West-provided database materials were not agency records within the meaning of the FOIA. As DOE's right to use CLERVER is similarly restricted, the Court finds that DOE lacks sufficient control over CLERVER to make it an agency record of DOE.

2.

It is undisputed that CLERVER and its related documentation were in the physical possession of Sandia on the date of Gilmore's FOIA request. The Court turns to whether Sandia can be considered a government agency. Under the FOIA, the term "agency" includes "any executive department, military department, Government corporation, Government controlled corporation, or other establishment in the executive branch of the Government (including the Executive Office of the President), or any independent regulatory agency." 5 U.S.C. § 552(f). At the time CLERVER was developed, Sandia was owned in its entirety by American Telephone and Telegraph Company. It is currently 100 percent owned by Lockheed Martin. Accordingly, the only definition of "agency" that might conceivably apply to Sandia is that of a government controlled corporation.

Whether an entity should be considered a government controlled corporation is determined on a case-by-case basis. *Irwin Mem'l Blood Bank of San Francisco Med. Society v. American Nat'l Red Cross*, 640 F.2d 1051, 1053 (9th Cir.1981). The definition of "government controlled corporation" excludes corporations that receive appropriated federal funds, but are neither chartered nor controlled by the federal government. *Id.* at 1054. A substantial degree of federal control or supervision must be demonstrated before an entity can be charactered [*sic*] as federally controlled. *Id.* at 1054–55.

In *Irwin*, the Ninth Circuit found that the American National Red Cross ("Red Cross") was not a government controlled corporation because its employees were not considered employees of the United States, the United States does not appropriate funds for the Red Cross, although the Red Cross receives money from government contracts and specific purpose grants, and government officials do not direct its everyday affairs. The court found not to be determinative the Red Cross's use of government buildings, the requirement that it submit financial reports to the Secretary of Defense, and the government's power to appoint eight of the fifty members of the Red Cross' Board of Governors. The court concluded that although the Red Cross is "undoubtedly a close ally" of the United States, "its operations are not subject to substantial federal control or supervision." *Id.* at 1057–58. *See also Public Citizen Health Research Group v. Department of HEW*, 668 F.2d 537 (D.C.Cir. 1981) (Professional Standards Review Organization that provides oversight for Medicare and Medicaid programs found not to be a government controlled corporation); *Dong v. Smithsonian Inst.*, 125 F.3d 877 (D.C.Cir.1997) (Smithsonian not a government controlled corporation); *Ehm v. National R.R. Passenger Corp.*, 732 F.2d 1250 (5th Cir.1984) (Amtrak not a government controlled corporation).

The Federal Home Loan Mortgage Corporation ("FHLMC") was found to be a government controlled corporation in *Rocap v. Indiek*, 539 F.2d 174 (D.C.Cir.1976). The court found that the FHLMC was subject to substantial federal control over its day-to-day operations, and noted that the FHLMC is federally chartered, its Board of Directors is presidentially appointed, it is subject to federal supervision and control over its business transactions, it is subject to federal auditing and reporting requirements, it is expressly designated as an agency, and its employees are officers and employees of the United States. *Id.* at 180. Like other agencies, it is empowered to make and enforce bylaws, rules and regulations necessary to carry out the purposes of its enabling act. *Id.*

It is undisputed that none of Sandia's employees receive any federal salaries or federal benefits. The contract between DOE and Sandia that was in effect at the time of Gilmore's FOIA request specifically provides that "[p]ersons employed by the Contractor shall be and remain employees of the Contractor, and shall not be deemed employees of DOE or the Government [.]" (Index, Vol. I, Ex. B, attachment 1, pt. III, § J, app. A at A–1.) Although Sandia uses SNL, a government-owned facility, to conduct research, the management who run the day-to-day operations of SNL are Sandia employees, not employees of the federal government.

Sandia is incorporated in Delaware, New Mexico, Nevada, Virginia, and Texas under state law, and was not established pursuant to federal law. Although the members of the board of directors and other key personnel must be acceptable to DOE, it does not select people for those positions. No member of the current board of directors of Sandia, which consists of prominent scientists and researchers, was recommended or chosen by DOE, nor does any DOE employee sit on the board. Sandia retains complete autonomy in implementing policies for the company, as long as they are within the terms and conditions of the contract between it and DOE. DOE does not participate at all in the formulation of policies to guide Sandia in conducting its business, other than its participation in establishing the directives set forth in the parties' negotiated contract.

On the other hand, there have been complaints that DOE micromanages the SNL laboratories. (Index, Vol. I, Ex. B at 78.) In addition, Lockheed Martin cannot transfer control of Sandia to another party without DOE's permission. At the end of the contract period, DOE retains the right to buy all shares of Sandia, require the resignation of the board of directors, and transfer the shares to a new contractor. (*Id.* attachment 1 at 13.) This demonstrates only that DOE retains the ultimate authority to change the private contractors who oversee operation of the SNL; it does not show that DOE retains day-to-day supervision over the contractor's operation of SNL. Similarly, DOE's regular reviews of Sandia's performance to ensure that contractual requirements are being complied with does not constitute day-to-day supervision. There is a great deal of difference between DOE's prudent system of checks and balances, and actual control of Sandia.

The Court finds that there is no dispute of material fact and that the facts demonstrate that Sandia is not a government-controlled corporation, as a matter of law. Unlike the Red Cross and the Smithsonian, both of which are run by a certain percentage of federal appointees or officials but were found not to be government controlled, no employee of Sandia is a federal employee, and DOE has no control over Sandia's employees. Like the Red Cross and the Smithsonian, Sandia receives federal funding, but is not subject to day-to-day federal supervision. DOE's detailed contractual objectives for the operation of SNL by Sandia do not translate into the day-to-day supervision and control required for Sandia to be deemed a government-controlled corporation. Accordingly, the Court finds that Sandia is not a government agency for FOIA purposes.

3.

Even if DOE actually owned and controlled CLERVER at the time of Gilmore's FOIA request, CLERVER still would not be an agency record subject to the FOIA because CLERVER does not illuminate the structure, operation, or decision-making structure of DOE. In *Tax Analysts II*, the court found, as an alternate basis for its holding that the West database materials were not agency records, that the data was not the type of information that Congress intended to make available to the public under the FOIA, because it provided no information about the structure, operation or decision-making procedures of the DOJ.

Ninth Circuit authority is in accord. In *Baizer v. United States Department of the Air Force*, 887 F.Supp. 225 (N.D.Cal.1995) (Smith, J.), the plaintiff requested that the Air Force provide the decisions of the United States Supreme Court in electronic form, from the JURIS database, but specifically excluded from his request any privately owned information. *Id.* at 226. The court found that because the material did not provide any insight into agency decision making, it did not constitute an agency record. *Id.* at 228. The court distinguished the Supreme Court's opinion in *Tax Analysts I*, and relied on an earlier Ninth Circuit opinion, *SDC Development Corp. v. Mathews*, 542 F.2d 1116 (9th Cir. 1976).

In *Tax Analysts I*, the Supreme Court held that the Tax Division of the DOJ was required under the FOIA to produce copies of opinions in district court tax cases that it received in the course of litigating tax cases on behalf of the federal government. *Tax Analysts I*, 492 U.S. at 138, 109 S.Ct. 2841. In *Baizer*, Judge Smith noted that the tax opinions at issue in *Tax Analysts I* were integrated into the Tax Division's active case files, and were utilized by the Tax Division in making decisions whether to appeal or file post-trial motions in those very cases when the government lost, and to collect judgments when the government won. 887 F.Supp. at 228 (citing *Tax Analysts I*, 492 U.S. at 138–39, 109 S.Ct. 2841, and *Tax Analysts v. United States Department of Justice*, 845 F.2d 1060, 1068 (D.C.Cir.1988), *aff'd* 492 U.S. 136, 109 S.Ct. 2841, 106 L.Ed.2d 112 (1989)). The Ninth Circuit had previously found that a research database was not an agency record because it did not reflect the structure, operation, or decisionmaking functions of the agency. *SDC Development*, 542 F.2d at 1120; *see also Tax Analysts I*, 492 U.S. at 141, 109 S.Ct. 2841 (affirming the Court of Appeals' decision that the tax decisions were agency records because "the Department has the discretion to use the decisions as it sees fit, because the Department routinely uses the decisions in performing its official duties, and because the decisions are integrated into the Department's official case files"). Thus, the court in Baizer found that "[i]f an agency integrates material into its files and relies on it in decision making, then the agency controls the material." 887 F.Supp. at 228.

> The Air Force simply does not control the decisions of the Supreme Court in the same manner that the Tax Division controlled the decisions it received as a party litigant, integrated into its case files, and used to prosecute appeals. As a result, the database of Supreme Court decisions is not an agency record.

Id. at 228–29.

Similarly, here, CLERVER illuminates nothing about DOE's decision-making process and thus is not an agency record subject to disclosure under the FOIA. Cases in which computer software has been found to be an agency record subject to FOIA disclosure are distinguishable on their facts. In *Cleary, Gottlieb, Steen & Hamilton v. Department of Health & Human Services.*, 844 F.Supp. 770 (D.D.C.1993), the court found that a software program was an agency record where it was necessary to understand and manipulate the data in a government study. *Id.* at 781–782. In *Windels, Marx, Davies & Ives v. Department of Commerce*, 576 F.Supp. 405 (D.D.C.1983), the software program at issue was used by the government agency to determine how to perform audits. Here, the parties have stipulated that CLERVER was not designed to be unique or responsive to any particular database, not does CLERVER contain any database of information about DOE's operations. (Joint Statement of Undisputed Facts No. 24.) CLERVER does not illuminate anything about DOE's structure or decision-making process.

Gilmore cites a number of cases predating *Tax Analysts I* for the proposition that a record does not have to expose the government decision-making process to be an agency record under the FOIA. All of these cases did, in fact, involve records that were used in government decision making. In *Stephenson v. Internal Revenue Service*, 629 F.2d 1140 (5th Cir.1980), the plaintiff sought tax records from the IRS that were being used in civil and criminal investigations of the plaintiff. In *Irons & Sears v. Dann*, 606 F.2d 1215 (D.C.Cir.1979), the documents at issue were decisions of the United States Patent and Trademark Office. In *Weisberg*, the court expressly found that photographs of the scene of the Martin Luther King assassination permitted evaluation of the FBI's performance in investigating the King assassination and thus reflected the operation and decision-making functions of the agency. 631 F.2d at 828.

Following *Tax Analysts I* and *Tax Analysts II*, *SDC Development*, and *Baizer*, the Court finds that CLERVER would not be an agency record even if DOE owned or controlled it, because it does not provide information about the government's operation, structure, or decision-making processes.

4.

Even if the CLERVER software could be considered an agency record, it would still be exempt from disclosure under FOIA Exemption 4. Exemption 4 provides that "trade secrets and commercial or financial information obtained from a person and privileged or confidential" need not be disclosed pursuant to a FOIA request. 5 U.S.C. § 552(b)(4). In evaluating whether a request for information falls within the scope of a FOIA exemption, the Court must balance the public interest in disclosure against the interest Congress intended the exemption to protect. *United States Dep't of Defense v. Federal Labor Relations Auth.*, 510 U.S. 487, 495, 114 S.Ct. 1006, 127 L.Ed.2d 325 (1994). The only relevant public interest in disclosure to be weighed in this balancing test is the extent to which disclosure would serve the core purpose of the FOIA of contributing significantly to public understanding of the operations or activities of the government. *Id.*; *Bibles v. Oregon Natural Desert Ass'n*, 519 U.S. 335, 117 S.Ct. 795, 795, 136 L.Ed.2d 825 (1997).

A record is confidential for purposes of Exemption 4 "if disclosure is likely to have either of the following effects: (1) to impair the Government's ability to obtain necessary information in the future; or (2) to cause substantial harm to the competitive position of the person from whom the information was obtained." *GC Micro Corp. v. Defense Logistics Agency*, 33 F.3d 1109, 1112 (9th Cir.1994) (quoting *National Parks & Conservation Ass'n v. Morton*, 498 F.2d 765 (D.C.Cir.1974)). The term "person" as used in Exemption 4 refers to a wide range of entities including corporations, associations and public or private organizations other than agencies. *Allnet Communication Servs. v. FCC*, 800 F.Supp. 984, 988 (D.D.C.1992) (citing *Critical Mass Energy Project v. NRC*, 830 F.2d 278, 281 n. 15 (D.C.Cir.1987)). The test for confidentiality is an objective one. *GC Micro*, 33 F.3d at 1113. The party seeking to withhold information under a FOIA exemption bears the burden of proving that the information falls within the claimed exemption. *Id.* "[E]vidence revealing (1) actual competition and (2) a likelihood of substantial competitive injury is sufficient to bring commercial information under Exemption 4." *Id.*

Here, both prongs of the test for confidentiality are satisfied. At the time CLERVER was developed, Sandia was owned in its entirety by American Telephone and Telegraph Company. It is now 100 percent owned by Lockheed Martin. The contract between DOE and Sandia for the operation of SNL, which was in effect at the time CLERVER was created, provided that one of the objectives of the contract was to expeditiously and efficiently transfer technology developed at SNL to domestic industry, in order to contribute to national well-being by aiding United States industrial competitiveness. Sandia was required to "undertake a vigorous licensing program whereby Sandia Corporation technology is moved expeditiously into the commercial marketplace." Pursuant to this mandate, Sandia has licensed CLERVER to SunSolutions, Inc., the University of New Mexico, the University of Delaware, and Sterling Winthrop, Inc. It has received inquiries from other companies, and is engaged in ongoing efforts to market CLERVER to other commercial entities. Under the license granted to Sun Solutions, Sandia has received approximately $164,000 in royalties, and a portable computer valued at $62,000. Sandia owns the copyright on CLERVER, but gave the government a limited license to use CLERVER for government purposes only.

There can be no doubt that disclosure of CLERVER to Gilmore so that he can distribute CLERVER on the Internet will cause substantial commercial harm to Sandia and its current owner Lockheed Martin. If the technology is freely available on the Internet, there is no reason for anyone to license CLERVER from Sandia, and the value of Sandia's copyright effectively will have been reduced to zero. There also can be no doubt that corporations will be less likely to enter into joint ventures with the government to develop technology if that technology can be distributed freely through the FOIA, irrespective of any intellectual property rights retained by the corporations. Accordingly, the government's access to such information is likely to be impaired. Moreover, there is no countervailing public interest in disclosure because CLER-

VER sheds no light whatsoever on DOE's performance of its duties. As both of the prongs of the test for confidentiality under FOIA Exemption 4 are met, the FOIA would not require that CLERVER be disclosed, even if CLERVER were an agency record.

For all of these reasons, Gilmore's FOIA request for CLERVER was properly denied.

5.

Because the government, by contract, owns the records relating to the development of CLERVER, those records are agency records under the FOIA, whether or not Sandia or SNL are themselves government agencies. *Forsham*, 445 U.S. at 180, 100 S.Ct. 977. The parties have stipulated, however, that the only materials that are currently at issue in this litigation are the CLERVER software and its technical documentation and associated materials in the possession of Sandia Corporation. It appears that Gilmore has abandoned his request for documents related to CLERVER that do not include CLERVER's technical documentation. In any event, because DOE owns the technical documentation, those records must be disclosed under the FOIA unless they fall within the scope of one of the enumerated FOIA exemptions. *Robbins Tire & Rubber Co.*, 437 U.S. at 221, 98 S.Ct. 2311.

For the same reasons Gilmore's FOIA request for CLERVER was properly denied, his request for the CLERVER technical documentation owned by DOE was also properly denied under FOIA Exemption 4. The information in those documents reflects confidential information, the disclosure of which would cause commercial damage to Sandia and Lockheed Martin, and would likely impair the government's access to such information in the future.

Gilmore attempts to rely on an unpublished DOE internal order to force the government to disclose the CLERVER documentation. DOE Order 1700.1 provides that "[w]here a contract with DOE stipulated that any documents relating to work under the contract shall be the property of the Government, such records shall be considered to be agency records and subject to disclosure under the FOIA." (Tien Decl. Ex. R.) This order adds nothing to the Supreme Court's *Forsham* opinion, in which the Court noted that records of a nonagency could become records of the agency by contract, 445 U.S. at 180, 100 S.Ct. 977, nor does it add anything to the contractual language providing that all records created pursuant to the contract between DOE and Sandia are the property of DOE. Although these records were owned by DOE at creation, however, DOE later transferred copyright in CLERVER to Sandia, before the date of Gilmore's FOIA request. Sandia thus has the exclusive right, subject to the license retained by the government, to make copies of CLERVER and to distribute it to the public. 17 U.S.C. § 106.

At that point, DOE no longer had control over the technical documentation of CLERVER because it could not distribute the documents to the public without violating Sandia's copyright and the terms of DOE's own license to use CLERVER. Accordingly, on the date of Gilmore's FOIA request, the CLERVER technical documentation was no longer an agency record under the FOIA because the government no longer controlled its dissemination. *See Tax Analysts II*, 913 F.Supp. at 607.

Alternately, the documentation contains confidential information of Sandia that could not be disclosed without causing commercial harm to Sandia and Lockheed Martin, or without impairing the government's access to such information in the future. As a result, even if the technical documentation was an agency record, it would be exempt from disclosure under FOIA Exemption 4.

For all of these reasons, Gilmore's FOIA request for the CLERVER technical documentation was properly denied by DOE.

* * *

III.

For the reasons set forth above,

IT IS HEREBY ORDERED that:

1. Summary judgment is GRANTED for DOE, and DENIED for Gilmore, on Gilmore's claim that CLERVER and its related documentation was improperly withheld from disclosure under the FOIA; * * *

Note

The Internet itself and a great deal of computer hardware, software, and data have been developed under government contract. There is a tension between the private companies that do development under government contract and third parties that seek, through the Freedom of Information Act, to obtain the results of government-sponsored work. In this and other cases, the courts have had to struggle with applying definitions meant for traditional government recordkeeping to the new, computer-related technologies.

D. PROTECTING TRADE SECRETS BY NEGOTIATED CONTRACTS

HOGAN SYSTEMS, INC. v. CYBRESOURCE INT'L., INC.

United States Court of Appeals, Fifth Circuit, 1998.
158 F.3d 319.

STEWART, CIRCUIT JUDGE.

Plaintiff–Appellant appeals the district court's grant of summary judgment in favor of defendants-appellees on its claims of copyright infringement, misappropriation of trade secrets and breach of contract. Additionally, Plaintiff–Appellant appeals the district court's award of costs and attorney's fees to defendants-appellees. For the reasons set forth below, we AFFIRM both of these decisions by the district court.

FACTUAL & PROCEDURAL BACKGROUND

Plaintiff–Appellant Hogan Systems, Inc. ("Hogan") is the developer and owner of copyrighted data processing software used by major banks worldwide. Such software—including the source code, object code and related documentation for Hogan's Umbrella System and the other programs at issue in this case (the "Software")—is stipulated to be a trade secret. Hogan owns the copyright in the Software. Hogan maintains that since the early 1980's, it has required its employees to sign a confidentiality agreement—agreeing not to disclose or use the Software and related secrets without Hogan's express written consent. Hogan requires its licensees to maintain the confidentiality of the Software and related trade secrets as well. Hogan does not sell the Software to third parties, but instead licenses it to its customers. Norwest is one of the many major banks that is one of Hogan's licensees.

Hogan entered into an initial license (the "Initial License") with Norwest in 1980, permitting Norwest's use of the Software. Hogan suggests that in the Initial License Agreement, Norwest stipulated to the trade secret status of the Software, and agreed not to distribute or disclose the Software to third parties. The Initial License was non-assignable.

In 1987, Hogan entered into a marketing agreement with IBM whereby IBM assumed responsibility for marketing the Software in North America. As part of that arrangement, Hogan, Norwest, and IBM signed an agreement effective in 1988 (the "1988 Agreement"). The 1988 Agreement applied the terms of a pre-existing 1983 IBM–Norwest license agreement (the "IBM–Norwest License") to the Software. The 1988 Agreement provides that the IBM–Norwest License terms prevail over the Initial License to the extent of any conflict. After the conclusion of the IBM–Norwest marketing arrangement in 1993, IBM and Hogan entered into another agreement, in which Hogan reaffirmed the validity of IBM's various sublicense agreements, including those with Norwest. Together, these license agreements shall be referred to as the "License Agreements."

The four individual defendants/appellees, David Boehr, Douglas Paradowski, James Helms, and Michael Greene (together the "Individual Defendants"), are former employees of Hogan who terminated their employment on various dates between September 29, 1995 and July 15, 1996. During their employment at Hogan each of the four signed substantially similar confidentiality agreements (the "Confidentiality Agreements") with Hogan, containing identical commitments concerning the restricted use and non-disclosure of Hogan's trade secrets and confidential materials. Each of the Confidentiality Agreements indicates that the employee's general skill, knowledge, and experience is not encompassed by the confidentiality obligation.

Following his departure from Hogan, Greene formed Cybresource International, Inc. ("Cybresource") an independent service organization ("ISO") at which Boehr, Paradowski, and Helms later became employees. In anticipation of a symbiotic relationship with Hogan, Greene signed a Professional Services Agreement (the "Cybresource–Hogan Agreement") with Hogan dated October 18, 1995. In that Agreement, Hogan alleges that Cybresource stipulates to the trade secret status of the Software and related processes, technical mastery, and ideas of Hogan. Hogan insists that Cybresource pledged that its representatives would keep Hogan's proprietary information secret, and that they would not copy or otherwise use the information except as expressly authorized by Hogan in the performance of the Cybresource–Hogan Agreement. These promises and stipulations expressly survive any termination of the Cybresource–Hogan Agreement.

Several months after the execution of the Cybresource–Hogan Agreement, Greene entered into a contract with Norwest (for Cybresource to provide software support services to Norwest), without the consent required by the Cybresource-Hogan Agreement. That agreement (the "Cybresource–Norwest Agreement"), dated March 18, 1996 is the focus of the litigation. Hogan suggests that the Cybresource–Norwest Agreement (1) characterizes Cybresource and its employees as independent contractors; (2) contemplates possible access by Cybresource to Software owned by Hogan and other third parties; and (3) mandates that for Cybresource to perform services on third-party software as the Agreement outlines, consents, and licenses from that third party (in this case, Hogan) must be obtained. Hogan maintains, however, that such consents and licenses were never obtained from it.

Cybresource insists that the applicable Norwest License Agreements provide that the licensee (Norwest) does not violate its confidentiality obligations if it provides or otherwise makes the Software available to non-employees (here, the Individual Defendants) of the licensee during the periods such persons are on the premises of the licensee for purposes related to authorized use of the Software. Cybresource further suggests that Norwest is authorized under its license agreements to tailor Hogan products through modifications, customizations, and enhancements to meet Norwest's specific business needs. Further, Cybresource contends that Paradowski and Boehr first acquired experience with Hogan Software not while employed by Hogan, but by two of its other licensees. Cybresource notes that familiarity with Hogan's Software is gained through other methods than by employment at Hogan. Finally, Cybresource indicates that many other ISO and individuals in the computer marketplace are performing substantially similar work to that being performed by the Individual Defendants at Norwest.

Hogan filed this action on July 25, 1996, seeking injunctive and monetary relief for copyright infringement, contract breach, trade secret misappropriation, unfair competition, tortious interference, and misappropriation. Hogan contends that Cybresource and the Individual Defendants are infringing upon its copyrights and misappropriating its trade secrets by utilizing its copyrighted Software and related trade secrets to perform support services for the benefit of Norwest. Hogan also alleges that the Individual Defendants violated the provisions of their Confidentiality Agreements with Hogan by conducting these same activities. Hogan also asserts claims against Greene individually, based on his apparent wrongful solicitation of Hogan's former employees.

On December 12, 1996, after conducting an evidentiary hearing, the district court denied Hogan's application for preliminary injunction. On June 2, 1997, the district court granted Cybresource's motion for summary judgment and entered the final judgment which Hogan challenges in this appeal. On July 15, 1997, the district court granted Cybresource's request for an award of costs and attorney's fees under 17 U.S.C. § 505.

DISCUSSION

I. Summary Judgment

The district court granted summary judgement against all of Hogan's claims. Hogan appeals the lower court's action on two sets of these claims, the first being copyright infringement, and the second being misappropriation of trade secrets and a breach of contract. We review a district court's grant of summary judgment *de novo. See, e.g., Hirras v. National Railroad Passenger Corp.*, 95 F.3d 396, 399 (5th Cir.1996). The party seeking summary judgment, who in this case is Cybresource, bears the burden of demonstrating that there is an absence of evidence to support the non-movant's case, who in this case is Hogan. *Id.* The summary judgment evidence must be viewed in the light most favorable to Hogan, with all permissible inferences drawn in favor of Hogan as non-movant. *Id.*

A. Copyright Infringement

* * *

B. Trade Secrets

Hogan also appeals the district court's decision to grant summary judgment upon Hogan's misappropriation of trade secrets claim and its breach of contract claim. The district court's decision was based upon its finding that the information Hogan complained about was not a trade secret, but rather was "general knowledge, skill, and experience" that the Individual Defendants garnered as a result of their former employment with Hogan, and which their Confidentiality Agreements with Hogan recognized as not being a trade secret. On appeal, Hogan submits that the summary judgment evidence proves that the Individual Defendants have acquired specialized knowledge about the process and structure of the Software that they are now exploiting to their own commercial advantage.

In order for information to be a trade secret, it must not be generally known or readily ascertainable by independent investigation. *See, e.g., Rugen v. Interactive Business Systems, Inc.*, 864 S.W.2d 548, 552 (Tex.App.—Dallas 1993, no writ). Here, Hogan stipulated to the fact that many individuals in the field obtain comparable abilities and expertise without ever being employed by Hogan. We thus disagree with Hogan's argument and affirm the district court's decision.

II. Costs and Attorneys' Fees

* * *

CONCLUSION

For the foregoing reasons, we AFFIRM the district court's grants of summary judgement against Hogan and its award of costs and attorney's fees to Cybresource.

Notes

Drafting contracts for the protection of computer-related trade secrets requires a detailed knowledge of the operation of the computer systems in question. How could Hogan have drafted its contracts so as to have secured more effective trade secret protection?

E.   PROTECTING TRADE SECRETS BY "SHRINKWRAP" LICENSES

VAULT CORP. v. QUAID SOFTWARE LTD.

United States Court of Appeals, Fifth Circuit, 1988.
847 F.2d 255.

REAVLEY, CIRCUIT JUDGE:

I.

[For a full statement of the facts, see pp. 182–184 of this casebook]

* * * Vault includes a license agreement with every PROLOK package that specifically prohibits the copying, modification, translation, decompilation or disassembly of Vault's program.[2] Beginning with version 2.0

---

2. The license agreement refers to the program placed on the diskette by Vault, not the software program placed on the diskette by Vault's customers. * * * The companies that place their software programs on PROLOK diskettes, not Vault, own the copyright to their programs and may include a license agreement covering their programs in the package for sale to the public.

Vault's license agreement reads:

IMPORTANT! VAULT IS PROVIDING THE ENCLOSED MATERIALS TO YOU ON THE EXPRESS CONDITION THAT YOU ASSENT TO THIS SOFTWARE LICENSE. BY USING ANY OF THE ENCLOSED DISKETTE(S), YOU AGREE TO THE FOLLOWING PROVISIONS. IF YOU DO NOT AGREE WITH THESE LICENSE PROVISIONS, RETURN THESE MATERIALS TO YOUR DEALER, IN ORIGINAL PACKAGING WITHIN 3 DAYS FROM RECEIPT, FOR A REFUND.

1. This copy of the PROLOK Software Protection System and this PROLOK Software Protection Diskette (the "Licensed Software") are licensed to you, the end-user, for your own internal use. Title to the Licensed Software and all copyrights and proprietary rights in the Licensed Software shall remain with VAULT. You may not transfer, sublicense, rent, lease, convey, copy, modify, translate, convert to another programming language, decompile or disassemble the Licensed Software for any purpose without VAULT's prior written consent.

2. THE LICENSED SOFTWARE IS PROVIDED "AS–IS". VAULT DISCLAIMS ALL WARRANTIES AND REPRESENTATIONS OF ANY KIND WITH REGARD TO THE LICENSED SOFTWARE, INCLUDING THE IMPLIED WARRANTIES OF MERCHANTABILITY AND FITNESS FOR A PARTICULAR PURPOSE. UNDER NO CIRCUMSTANCES WILL VAULT BE LIA-

in September 1985, Vault's license agreement contained a choice of law clause adopting Louisiana law.[3]

* * *

III. Vault's Federal Claims

[See p. 184 of this casebook]

* * *

IV. Vault's Louisiana Claims

Seeking preliminary and permanent injunctions and damages, Vault's original complaint alleged that Quaid breached its license agreement by decompiling or disassembling Vault's program in violation of the Louisiana Software License Enforcement Act (the "License Act"), La.Rev.Stat.Ann. § 51:1961 *et seq.* (West 1987), and that Quaid misappropriated Vault's program in violation of the Louisiana Uniform Trade Secrets Act, La.Rev.Stat.Ann. § 51:1431 *et seq.* (West 1987). On appeal, Vault abandons its misappropriation claim,[26] and, with respect to its breach of license claim, Vault only seeks an injunction to prevent Quaid from decompiling or disassembling PROLOK version 2.0.[27]

Louisiana's License Act permits a software producer to impose a number of contractual terms upon software purchasers provided that the terms are set forth in a license agreement which comports with La.Rev. Stat.Ann. §§ 51:1963 & 1965, and that this license agreement accompanies the producer's software. Enforceable terms include the prohibition of: (1) any copying of the program for any purpose; and (2) modifying and/or adapting the program in any way, including adaptation by reverse engineering, decompilation or disassembly. La.Rev.Stat.Ann. § 51:1964.[28]

BLE FOR ANY CONSEQUENTIAL, INCIDENTAL, SPECIAL OR EXEMPLARY DAMAGES EVEN IF VAULT IS APPRISED OF THE LIKELIHOOD OF SUCH DAMAGES OCCURRING. SOME STATES DO NOT ALLOW THE LIMITATION OR EXCLUSION OF LIABILITY FOR INCIDENTAL OR CONSEQUENTIAL DAMAGES, SO THE ABOVE LIMITATION OR EXCLUSION MAY NOT APPLY TO YOU.

3. The license agreement included the following language beginning with version 2.0:

To the extent the laws of the United States of America are not applicable, this license agreement shall be governed by the laws of the State of Louisiana.

26. While the district court held that the Louisiana Uniform Trade Secrets Act, La.Rev.Stat.Ann. § 51:1431 et seq., was not preempted by the Copyright Act, the court held that the process of ascertaining information by "reverse engineering," used by Quaid to analyze the operation of Vault's

program, did not constitute a violation of the Louisiana Trade Secrets Act. *Vault*, 655 F.Supp. at 761. This holding is not challenged on appeal.

27. Beginning with PROLOK version 2.0, Vault's license agreement contained a choice of law clause adopting Louisiana law. *See supra* note 3.

28. Section 51:1964 reads, in full:

Terms of which shall be deemed to have been accepted under R.S. 51:1963, if included in an accompanying license agreement which conforms to the provisions of R.S. 51:1965, may include any or all of the following:

(1) Provisions for the retention by the licensor of title to the copy of the computer software.

(2) If title to the copy of computer software has been retained by the licensor, provisions for the prohibition of any copying of the copy of computer software for any purpose and/or limitations on the purposes

The terms "reverse engineering, decompiling or disassembling" are defined as "any process by which computer software is converted from one form to another form which is more readily understandable to human beings, including without limitation any decoding or decrypting of any computer program which has been encoded or encrypted in any manner." La.Rev.Stat.Ann. § 51:1962(3).

Vault's license agreement, which accompanies PROLOK version 2.0 and comports with the requirements of La.Rev.Stat.Ann. §§ 51:1963 & 1965, provides that "[y]ou may not ... copy, modify, translate, convert to another programming language, decompile or disassemble" Vault's program. Vault asserts that these prohibitions are enforceable under Louisiana's License Act, and specifically seeks an injunction to prevent Quaid from decompiling or disassembling Vault's program.

The district court held that Vault's license agreement was "a contract of adhesion which could only be enforceable if the [Louisiana License Act] is a valid and enforceable statute." *Vault*, 655 F.Supp. at 761. The court noted numerous conflicts between Louisiana's License Act and the Copyright Act, including: (1) while the License Act authorizes a total prohibition on copying, the Copyright Act allows archival copies and copies made as an essential step in the utilization of a computer program, 17 U.S.C. § 117; (2) while the License Act authorizes a perpetual bar against copying, the Copyright Act grants protection against unauthorized copying only for the life of the author plus fifty years, 17 U.S.C. § 302(a); and (3) while the License Act places no restrictions on programs which may be protected, under the Copyright Act, only "original works of authorship" can be protected, 17 U.S.C. § 102. *Vault*, 655 F.Supp. at 762–63. The court concluded that, because Louisiana's License Act "touched upon the area" of federal copyright law, its provisions were preempted and Vault's license agreement was unenforceable. *Id.* at 763.

In *Sears, Roebuck & Co. v. Stiffel Co.*, 376 U.S. 225, 84 S.Ct. 784, 11 L.Ed.2d 661 (1964), the Supreme Court held that "[w]hen state law touches upon the area of [patent or copyright statutes], it is 'familiar doctrine' that the federal policy 'may not be set at naught, or its benefits denied' by the state law." * * * Section 117 of the Copyright Act permits

for which copies of the computer software can be made and/or limitations on the number of copies of the computer software which can be made.

(3) If title to the copy of computer software has been retained by the licensor, provisions for the prohibition or limitation of rights to modify and/or adapt the copy of the computer software in any way, including without limitation prohibitions on translating, reverse engineering, decompiling, disassembling, and/or creating derivative works based on the computer software.

(4) If title to the copy of computer software has been retained by the licensor,

provisions for prohibitions on further transfer, assignment, rental, sale, or other disposition of that copy or any other copies made from that copy of the computer software, provided that terms which prohibit the transfer of a copy of computer software in connection with the sale or transfer by operation of law of all or substantially all of the operating assets of a licensee's business shall to that extent only not be deemed to have been accepted under R.S. 51:1963.

(5) Provisions for the automatic termination without notice of the license agreement if any provisions of the license agreement are breached by the licensee.

an owner of a computer program to make an adaptation of that program provided that the adaptation is either "created as an essential step in the utilization of the computer program in conjunction with a machine," § 117(1), or "is for archival purpose only," § 117(2). The provision in Louisiana's License Act, which permits a software producer to prohibit the adaptation of its licensed computer program by decompilation or disassembly, conflicts with the rights of computer program owners under § 117 and clearly "touches upon an area" of federal copyright law. For this reason, and the reasons set forth by the district court, we hold that at least this provision of Louisiana's License Act is preempted by federal law, and thus that the restriction in Vault's license agreement against decompilation or disassembly is unenforceable.

V. Conclusion

We hold that: * * * (4) the provision in Vault's license agreement, which prohibits the decompilation or disassembly of its program, is unenforceable.

The judgment of the district court is AFFIRMED.

PROCD, INC. v. ZEIDENBERG

United States Court of Appeals, Seventh Circuit, 1996.
86 F.3d 1447.

EASTERBROOK, CIRCUIT JUDGE.

Must buyers of computer software obey the terms of shrinkwrap licenses? The district court held not, for two reasons: first, they are not contracts because the licenses are inside the box rather than printed on the outside; second, federal law forbids enforcement even if the licenses are contracts. 908 F.Supp. 640 (W.D.Wis.1996). The parties and numerous amici curiae have briefed many other issues, but these are the only two that matter—and we disagree with the district judge's conclusion on each. Shrinkwrap licenses are enforceable unless their terms are objectionable on grounds applicable to contracts in general (for example, if they violate a rule of positive law, or if they are unconscionable). Because no one argues that the terms of the license at issue here are troublesome, we remand with instructions to enter judgment for the plaintiff.

I

ProCD, the plaintiff, has compiled information from more than 3,000 telephone directories into a computer database. We may assume that this database cannot be copyrighted, although it is more complex, contains more information (nine-digit zip codes and census industrial codes), is organized differently, and therefore is more original than the single alphabetical directory at issue in *Feist Publications, Inc. v. Rural Telephone Service Co.*, 499 U.S. 340 (1991). See Paul J. Heald, The Vices of Originality, 1991 Sup.Ct. Rev. 143, 160–68. ProCD sells a version of the database, called SelectPhone (trademark), on CD–ROM discs. (CD–ROM means "compact disc—read only memory." The "shrinkwrap license" gets its name from the fact that retail software packages are covered in plastic or cellophane "shrinkwrap," and some vendors, though not ProCD, have written licenses that become effective as soon as the customer tears the wrapping from the package. Vendors prefer "end user license," but we use the more common term.) A proprietary method of compressing the data serves as effective encryption too. Customers decrypt and use the data with the aid of an application program that ProCD has written. This program, which is copyrighted, searches the database in response to users' criteria (such as "find all people named Tatum in Tennessee, plus all firms with 'Door Systems' in the corporate name"). The resulting lists (or, as ProCD prefers, "listings") can be read and manipulated by other software, such as word processing programs.

The database in SelectPhone (trademark) cost more than $10 million to compile and is expensive to keep current. It is much more valuable to some users than to others. The combination of names, addresses, and SIC codes enables manufacturers to compile lists of potential customers. Manufacturers and retailers pay high prices to specialized information intermediaries for such mailing lists; ProCD offers a potentially cheaper alternative. People with nothing to sell could use the database as a substitute for calling long distance information, or as a way to look up old friends who have moved to unknown towns, or just as an electronic substitute for the local phone book. ProCD decided to engage in price discrimination, selling its database to the general public for personal use at a low price (approximately $150 for the set of five discs) while selling information to the trade for a higher price. It has adopted some intermediate strategies too: access to the SelectPhone (trademark) database is available via the America Online service for the price America Online charges to its clients (approximately $3 per hour), but this service has been tailored to be useful only to the general public.

If ProCD had to recover all of its costs and make a profit by charging a single price—that is, if it could not charge more to commercial users than to the general public—it would have to raise the price substantially over $150. The ensuing reduction in sales would harm consumers who value the information at, say, $200. They get consumer surplus of $50 under the current arrangement but would cease to buy if the price rose substantially. If because of high elasticity of demand in the consumer segment of the market the only way to make a profit turned out to be a price attractive to commercial users alone, then all consumers would lose out—and so would the commercial clients, who would have to pay more for the listings because ProCD could not obtain any contribution toward costs from the consumer market.

To make price discrimination work, however, the seller must be able to control arbitrage. An air carrier sells tickets for less to vacationers than to business travelers, using advance purchase and Saturday-night-stay requirements to distinguish the categories. A producer of movies segments the market by time, releasing first to theaters, then to pay-per-view services, next to the videotape and laserdisc market, and finally to cable and commercial tv. Vendors of computer software have a harder task. Anyone can walk into a retail store and buy a box. Customers do not wear tags saying "commercial user" or "consumer user." Anyway, even a commercial-user-detector at the door would not work, because a consumer could buy the software and resell to a commercial user. That arbitrage would break down the price discrimination and drive up the minimum price at which ProCD would sell to anyone.

Instead of tinkering with the product and letting users sort themselves—for example, furnishing current data at a high price that would be attractive only to commercial customers, and two-year-old data at a low price—ProCD turned to the institution of contract. Every box containing its consumer product declares that the software comes with restrictions stated in an enclosed license. This license, which is encoded on the CD–ROM disks as well as printed in the manual, and which appears on a user's screen every time the software runs, limits use of the application program and listings to non-commercial purposes.

Matthew Zeidenberg bought a consumer package of SelectPhone (trademark) in 1994 from a retail outlet in Madison, Wisconsin, but decided to ignore the license. He formed Silken Mountain Web Services, Inc., to resell the information in the SelectPhone (trademark) database. The corporation makes the database available on the Internet to anyone willing to pay its price—which, needless to say, is less than ProCD charges its commercial customers. Zeidenberg has purchased two additional SelectPhone (trademark) packages, each with an updated version of the database, and made the latest information available over the World Wide Web, for a price, through his corporation. ProCD filed this suit seeking an injunction against further dissemination that exceeds the rights specified in the licenses (identical in each of the three packages Zeidenberg purchased). The district court held the licenses ineffectual because their terms do not appear on the outside of the packages. The court added that the second and third licenses stand no different from the first, even though they are identical, because they might have been different, and a purchaser does not agree to—and cannot be bound by— terms that were secret at the time of purchase. 908 F.Supp. at 654.

II

Following the district court, we treat the licenses as ordinary contracts accompanying the sale of products, and therefore as governed by the common law of contracts and the Uniform Commercial Code. Whether there are legal differences between "contracts" and "licenses" (which may matter under the copyright doctrine of first sale) is a subject for another day. See *Microsoft Corp. v. Harmony Computers & Electronics, Inc.,* 846 F.Supp. 208 (E.D.N.Y.1994). Zeidenberg does not argue that Silken Mountain Web Services is free of any restrictions that apply to Zeidenberg himself, because any effort to treat the two parties as distinct would put Silken Mountain behind the eight ball on ProCD's argument that copying the application program onto its hard disk violates the copyright laws. Zeidenberg does argue, and the district court held, that placing the package of software on the shelf is an "offer," which the customer "accepts" by paying the asking price and leaving the store with the goods. *Peeters v. State*, 154 Wis. 111, 142 N.W. 181 (1913). In Wisconsin, as elsewhere, a contract includes only the terms on which the parties have agreed. One cannot agree to hidden terms, the judge concluded. So far, so good—but one of the terms to which Zeidenberg agreed by purchasing the software is that the transaction was subject to a license. Zeidenberg's position therefore must be that the printed terms on the outside of a box are the parties' contract—except for printed terms that refer to or incorporate other terms. But why would Wisconsin fetter the parties' choice in this way? Vendors can put the entire terms of a contract on the outside of a box only by using microscopic type, removing other information that buyers might find more useful (such as what the software does, and on which computers it works), or both. The "Read Me" file included with most software, describing system requirements and potential incompatibilities, may be equivalent to ten pages of type; warranties and license restrictions take still more space. Notice on the outside, terms on the inside, and a right to return the software for a refund if the terms are unacceptable (a right that the license expressly extends), may be a means of doing business valuable to buyers and sellers alike. See E. Allan Farnsworth, 1 *Farnsworth on Contracts* § 4.26 (1990); *Restatement (2d) of Contracts* § 211 comment a (1981) ("Standardization of agreements serves many of the same functions as standardization of goods and services; both are essential to a system of mass production and distribution. Scarce and costly time and skill can be devoted to a class of transactions rather than the details of individual transactions."). Doubtless a state could forbid the use of standard contracts in the software business, but we do not think that Wisconsin has done so.

Transactions in which the exchange of money precedes the communication of detailed terms are common. Consider the purchase of insurance. The buyer goes to an agent, who explains the essentials (amount of coverage, number of years) and remits the premium to the home office, which sends back a policy. On the district judge's understanding, the terms of the policy are irrelevant because the insured paid before receiving them. Yet the device of payment, often with a "binder" (so that the insurance takes effect immediately even though the home office reserves the right to withdraw coverage later), in advance of the policy, serves buyers' interests by accelerating effectiveness and reducing transactions costs. Or consider the purchase of an airline ticket. The traveler calls the carrier or an agent, is quoted a price, reserves a seat, pays, and gets a ticket, in that order. The ticket contains elaborate terms, which the traveler can reject by canceling the reservation. To use the ticket is to accept the terms, even terms that in retrospect are disadvantageous. See *Carnival Cruise Lines, Inc. v. Shute*, 499 U.S. 585, 111 S.Ct. 1522, 113 L.Ed.2d 622 (1991); see also *Vimar Seguros y Reaseguros, S.A. v. M/V Sky Reefer*, ___ U.S. ___, 115 S.Ct. 2322, 132 L.Ed.2d 462 (1995) (bills of lading). Just so with a ticket to a concert. The back of the ticket states that the patron promises not to record the concert; to attend is to agree. A theater that detects a violation will confiscate the tape and escort the violator to the exit. One *could* arrange things so that every concertgoer signs this promise before forking over the money, but that cumbersome way of doing things not only would lengthen queues and raise prices but also would scotch the sale of tickets by phone or electronic data service.

Consumer goods work the same way. Someone who wants to buy a radio set visits a store, pays, and walks out with a box. Inside the box is a leaflet containing some terms, the most important of which usually is the warranty, read for the first time in the comfort of home. By Zeidenberg's lights, the warranty in the box is irrelevant; every consumer gets the standard warranty implied by the UCC in the event the contract is silent; yet so far as we are aware no state disregards warranties furnished with consumer products. Drugs come with a list of ingredients on the outside and an elaborate package insert on the inside. The package insert describes drug interactions, contraindications, and other vital information—but, if Zeidenberg is right, the purchaser need not read the package insert, because it is not part of the contract.

Next consider the software industry itself. Only a minority of sales take place over the counter, where there are boxes to peruse. A customer may place an order by phone in response to a line item in a catalog or a review in a magazine. Much software is ordered over the Internet by purchasers who have never seen a box. Increasingly software arrives by wire. There is no box; there is only a stream of electrons, a collection of information that includes data, an application program, instructions, many limitations ("MegaPixel 3.14159 cannot be used with BytePusher 2.718"), and the terms of sale. The user purchases a serial number, which activates the software's features. On Zeidenberg's arguments, these unboxed sales are unfettered by terms—so the seller has made a broad warranty and must pay consequential damages for any shortfalls in performance, two "promises" that if taken seriously would drive prices through the ceiling or return transactions to the horse-and-buggy age.

According to the district court, the UCC does not countenance the sequence of money now, terms later. (Wisconsin's version of the UCC does not differ from the Official Version in any material respect, so we use the regular numbering system. Wis. Stat. § 402.201 corresponds to UCC § 2–201, and other citations are easy to derive.) One of the court's reasons—that by proposing as part of the draft Article 2B a new UCC § 2–2203 that would explicitly validate standard-form user licenses, the American Law Institute and the National Conference of Commissioners on Uniform Laws have conceded the invalidity of shrinkwrap licenses under current law, see 908 F.Supp. at 655–56—depends on a faulty inference. To propose a change in a law's *text* is not necessarily to propose a change in the law's *effect*. New words may be designed to fortify the current rule with a more precise text that curtails uncertainty. To judge by the flux of law review articles discussing shrinkwrap licenses, uncertainty is much in need of reduction—although businesses seem to feel less uncertainty than do scholars, for only three cases (other than ours) touch on the subject, and none directly addresses it. See *Step-Saver Data Systems, Inc. v. Wyse Technology*, 939 F.2d 91 (3d Cir.1991); *Vault Corp. v. Quaid Software Ltd.*, 847 F.2d 255, 268–70 (5th Cir.1988); *Arizona Retail Systems, Inc. v. Software Link, Inc.*, 831 F.Supp. 759 (D.Ariz.1993). As their titles suggest, these are not consumer transactions. Step–Saver is a battle-of-the-forms case, in which the parties exchange incompatible forms and a court must decide which prevails. See *Northrop Corp. v. Litronic Industries*, 29 F.3d 1173 (7th Cir.1994) (Illinois law); Douglas G. Baird & Robert Weisberg, *Rules, Standards, and the Battle of the Forms: A Reassessment of § 2–207*, 68 Va. L.Rev. 1217, 1227–31 (1982). Our case has only one form; UCC § 2–207 is irrelevant. Vault holds that Louisiana's special shrinkwrap-license statute is preempted by federal law, a question to which we return. And *Arizona Retail Systems* did not reach the question, because the court found that the buyer knew the terms of the license before purchasing the software.

What then does the current version of the UCC have to say? We think that the place to start is § 2–204(1): "A contract for sale of goods may be made in any manner sufficient to show agreement, including conduct by both parties which recognizes the existence of such a contract." A vendor, as master of the offer, may invite acceptance by conduct, and may propose limitations on the kind of conduct that constitutes acceptance. A buyer may accept by performing the acts the vendor proposes to treat as acceptance. And that is what happened. ProCD proposed a contract that a buyer would accept by *using* the software after having an opportunity to read the license at leisure. This Zeidenberg did. He had no choice, because the software splashed the license on the screen and would not let him proceed without indicating acceptance. So although the district judge was right to say that a contract can be, and often is, formed simply by paying the price and walking out of the store, the UCC permits contracts to be formed in other ways. ProCD proposed such a different way, and without protest Zeidenberg agreed. Ours is not a case in which a consumer opens a package to find an insert saying "you owe us an extra $10,000" and the seller files suit to collect. Any buyer finding such a demand can prevent formation of the contract by returning the package, as can any consumer who concludes that the terms of the license make the software worth less than the purchase price. Nothing in the UCC requires a seller to maximize the buyer's net gains.

Section 2–606, which defines "acceptance of goods", reinforces this understanding. A buyer accepts goods under § 2–606(1)(b) when, after an opportunity to inspect, he fails to make an effective rejection under § 2–602(1). ProCD extended an opportunity to reject if a buyer should find the license terms unsatisfactory; Zeidenberg inspected the package, tried out the software, learned of the license, and did not reject the goods. We refer to § 2–606 only to show that the opportunity to return goods can be important; acceptance of an offer differs from acceptance of goods after delivery, *see Gillen v. Atalanta Systems, Inc.*, 997 F.2d 280, 284 n. 1 (7th Cir.1993); but the UCC consistently permits the parties to structure their relations so that the buyer has a chance to make a final decision after a detailed review.

Some portions of the UCC impose additional requirements on the way parties agree on terms. A disclaimer of the implied warranty of merchantability must be "conspicuous." UCC § 2–316(2), incorporating UCC § 1–201(10). Promises to make firm offers, or to negate oral modifications, must be "separately signed." UCC §§ 2–205, 2–209(2). These special provisos reinforce the impression that, so far as the UCC is concerned, other terms may be as inconspicuous as the forum-selection clause on the back of the cruise ship ticket in Carnival Lines. Zeidenberg has not located any Wisconsin case—for that matter, any case in any state—holding that under the UCC the ordinary terms found in shrink-wrap licenses require any special prominence, or otherwise are to be undercut rather than enforced. In the end, the terms of the license are conceptually identical to the contents of the package. Just as no court would dream of saying that SelectPhone (trademark) must contain 3,100 phone books rather than 3,000, or must have data no more than 30 days old, or must sell for $100 rather than $150—although any of these changes would be welcomed by the customer, if all other things were held constant—so, we believe, Wisconsin would not let the buyer pick and choose among terms. Terms of use are no less a part of "the product" than are the size of the database and the speed with which the software compiles listings. Competition among vendors, not judicial revision of a package's contents, is how consumers are protected in a market economy. *Digital Equipment Corp. v. Uniq Digital Technologies, Inc.*, 73 F.3d 756 (7th Cir.1996). ProCD has rivals, which may elect to compete by offering superior software, monthly updates, improved terms of use, lower price, or a better compromise among these elements. As we stressed above, adjusting terms in buyers' favor might help Matthew Zeidenberg today (he already has the software) but would lead to a response, such as a higher price, that might make consumers as a whole worse off.

III

The district court held that, even if Wisconsin treats shrinkwrap licenses as contracts, § 301(a) of the Copyright Act, 17 U.S.C. § 301(a), prevents their enforcement. 908 F.Supp. at 656–59. The relevant part of § 301(a) preempts any "legal or equitable rights [under state law] that are equivalent to any of the exclusive rights within the general scope of copyright as specified by section 106 in works of authorship that are fixed in a tangible medium of expression and come within the subject matter of copyright as specified by sections 102 and 103". ProCD's software and data are "fixed in a tangible medium of expression", and the district judge held that they are "within the subject matter of copyright". The latter conclusion is plainly right for the copyrighted application program, and the judge thought that the data likewise are "within the subject matter of copyright" even if, after Feist, they are not sufficiently original to be copyrighted. 908 F.Supp. at 656–57. *Baltimore Orioles, Inc. v. Major League Baseball Players Ass'n*, 805 F.2d 663, 676 (7th Cir.1986), supports that conclusion, with which commentators agree. E.g., Paul Goldstein, III *Copyright* § 15.2.3 (2d ed.1996); Melville B. Nimmer & David Nimmer, *Nimmer on Copyright* § 101[B] (1995); William F. Patry, II *Copyright Law and Practice* 1108–09 (1994). One function of § 301(a) is to prevent states from giving special protection to works of authorship that Congress has decided should be in the public domain, which it can accomplish only if "subject matter of copyright" includes all works of a *type* covered by sections 102 and 103, even if federal law does not afford protection to them. Cf. *Bonito Boats, Inc. v. Thunder Craft Boats, Inc.*, 489 U.S. 141, 109 S.Ct. 971, 103 L.Ed.2d 118 (1989) (same principle under patent laws).

But are rights created by contract "equivalent to any of the exclusive rights within the general scope of copyright"? Three courts of appeals have answered "no." *National Car Rental System, Inc. v. Computer Associates International, Inc.*, 991 F.2d 426, 433 (8th Cir.1993); *Taquino v. Teledyne Monarch Rubber*, 893 F.2d 1488, 1501 (5th Cir. 1990); *Acorn Structures, Inc. v. Swantz*, 846 F.2d 923, 926 (4th Cir.1988). The district court disagreed with these decisions, 908 F.Supp. at 658, but we think them sound. Rights "equivalent to any of the exclusive rights within the general scope of copyright" are rights established *by law*— rights that restrict the options of persons who are strangers to the author. Copyright law forbids duplication, public performance, and so on, unless the person wishing to copy or perform the work gets permission; silence means a ban on copying. A copyright is a right against the world. Contracts, by contrast, generally affect only their parties; strangers may do as they please, so contracts do not create "exclusive rights." Someone who found a copy of SelectPhone (trademark) on the street would not be affected by the shrinkwrap license—though the federal copyright laws of their own force would limit the finder's ability to copy or transmit the application program.

Think for a moment about trade secrets. One common trade secret is a customer list. After *Feist*, a simple alphabetical list of a firm's customers, with address and telephone numbers, could not be protected by copyright. Yet *Kewanee Oil Co. v. Bicron Corp.*, 416 U.S. 470 (1974), holds that contracts about trade secrets may be enforced—precisely because they do not affect strangers' ability to discover and use the information independently. If the amendment of § 301(a) in 1976 overruled *Kewanee* and abolished consensual protection of those trade secrets that cannot be copyrighted, no one has noticed—though abolition is a logical consequence of the district court's approach. Think, too, about everyday transactions in intellectual property. A customer visits a video store and rents a copy of *Night of the Lepus*. The customer's contract with the store limits use of the tape to home viewing and requires its return in two days. May the customer keep the tape, on the ground that § 301(a) makes the promise unenforceable?

A law student uses the LEXIS database, containing public-domain documents, under a contract limiting the results to educational endeavors; may the student resell his access to this database to a law firm from which LEXIS seeks to collect a much higher hourly rate? Suppose ProCD hires a firm to scour the nation for telephone directories, promising to pay $100 for each that ProCD does not already have. The firm locates 100 new directories, which it sends to ProCD with an invoice for $10,000. ProCD incorporates the directories into its database; does it have to pay the bill? Surely yes; *Aronson v. Quick Point Pencil Co.*, 440 U.S. 257 (1979), holds that promises to pay for intellectual property may be enforced even though federal law (in *Aronson*, the patent law) offers no protection against third-party uses of that property. See also *Kennedy v. Wright*, 851 F.2d 963 (7th Cir.1988). But these illustrations are what our case is about. ProCD offers software and data for two prices: one for personal use, a higher price for commercial use. Zeidenberg wants to use the data without paying the seller's price; if the law student and Quick Point Pencil Co. could not do that, neither can Zeidenberg.

Although Congress possesses power to preempt even the enforcement of contracts about intellectual property—or railroads, on which see *Norfolk & Western Ry. v. Train Dispatchers*, 499 U.S. 117 (1991)—courts usually read preemption clauses to leave private contracts unaffected. *American Airlines, Inc. v. Wolens*, 513 U.S. 219 (1995), provides a nice illustration. A federal statute preempts any state "law, rule, regulation, standard, or other provision ... relating to rates, routes, or services of any air carrier." 49 U.S.C.App. § 1305(a)(1). Does such a law preempt the law of contracts—so that, for example, an air carrier need not honor a quoted price (or a contract to reduce the price by the value of frequent flyer miles)? The Court allowed that it is possible to read the statute that broadly but thought such an interpretation would make little sense. Terms and conditions offered by contract reflect private ordering, essential to the efficient functioning of markets. 513 U.S. at ___–___ 115 S.Ct. at 824–25. Although some principles that carry the name of contract law are designed to defeat rather than implement consensual transactions, *id.* at ___ n. 8, 115 S.Ct. at 826 n. 8, the rules that respect private choice are not preempted by a clause such as § 1305(a)(1). Section 301(a) plays a role similar to § 1301(a)(1): it prevents states from substituting their own regulatory systems for those of the national government. Just as § 301(a) does not itself interfere with private transactions in intellectual property, so it does not prevent states from respecting those transactions. Like the Supreme Court in *Wolens*, we think it prudent to refrain from adopting a rule that anything with the label "contract" is necessarily outside the preemption clause: the variations and possibilities are too numerous to foresee. *National Car Rental* likewise recognizes the possibility that some applications of the law of contract could interfere with the attainment of national objectives and therefore come within the domain of § 301(a). But general enforcement of shrinkwrap licenses of the kind before us does not create such interference.

Aronson emphasized that enforcement of the contract between Aronson and Quick Point Pencil Company would not withdraw any information from the public domain. That is equally true of the contract between ProCD and Zeidenberg. Everyone remains free to copy and disseminate all 3,000 telephone books that have been incorporated into ProCD's database. Anyone can add SIC codes and zip codes. ProCD's rivals have done so. Enforcement of the shrinkwrap license may even make information more readily available, by reducing the price ProCD charges to consumer buyers. To the extent licenses facilitate distribution of object code while concealing the source code (the point of a clause forbidding disassembly), they serve the same procompetitive functions as does the law of trade secrets. *Rockwell Graphic Systems, Inc. v. DEV Industries, Inc.*, 925 F.2d 174, 180 (7th Cir.1991). Licenses may have other benefits for consumers: many licenses permit users to make extra copies, to use the software on multiple computers, even to incorporate the software into the user's products. But whether a particular license is generous or restrictive, a simple two-party contract is not "equivalent to any of the exclusive rights within the general scope of copyright" and therefore may be enforced.

Reversed and Remanded.

Notes

1. The Seventh Circuit reaffirmed its *ProCD* holding in *Hill v. Gateway 2000, Inc.*, 105 F.3d 1147 (7th Cir.1997). Hill had ordered a computer from Gateway by telephone. He was held to be bound by contract terms that Gateway shipped in the box with the computer. The particular terms called for arbitration of all disputes. Computer hardware and software manufacturers sell huge quantities of very complex products. Because of the complexities, almost all software and much hardware contains "bugs." This situation opens the manufacturers to expensive class action litigation. Gateway's arbitration clause kept it out of the courts and ensured that it would not be open to class action litigation. *Hill v. Gateway* was followed in *Brower v. Gateway 2000, Inc.*, 676 N.Y.S.2d 569, 571 (N.Y.A.D. 1 Dept.1998) and *M.A. Mortenson Company, Inc. v. Timberline Software Corporation*, 140 Wash.2d 568, 998 P.2d 305 (2000).

2. To one of the coauthors of this casebook, *Vault and ProCD* appear to be inconsistent with each other, and ProCD appears to be inconsistent with § 301 of the Copyright Act and with *Feist*. Another coauthor, however, thinks that if one looks at what is being protected, at the actions of the defendants, and at the interface between § 301 of the Copyright Act and copyright, trade secret, patent, and other intellectual property principles, the two cases may be views as consistent. In *Vault*, the plaintiff was attempting to obtain patent-type protection under Louisiana state unfair competition law, while defendant was simply attempting to discover the unpatented ideas by reverse engineering–an action clearly permitted under traditional copyright and trade secret law. In *ProCD*, the plaintiff was simply using traditional state trade secret law to protect its product, while the defendant was

clearly breaching a contract valid under the applicable state law. Which coauthor is right and why?

3. The Uniform Computer Information Transactions Act ("UCITA") is designed to allow software and database companies to retain rights comparable to trade secret rights in software and databases, even when the software and databases is mass-marketed and no formal contracts are negotiated. One aspect of UCITA operates by changing the traditional contract concepts of offer, acceptance, and consideration, to create what it calls a "contract" even in situations when traditional contract doctrine might not find that any contract exists. It has been supported as providing important incentives to the software industry. It has been attacked as special interest legislation. Some have argued, along the lines of *Vault v. Quaid, supra,* that these provisions of UCITA are preempted by the Copyright Act. UCITA will be discussed further below, in the chapter on "E–Commerce."

UNIFORM COMPUTER INFORMATION TRANSACTIONS ACT

http://www.law.upenn.edu/bll/ulc/ulc_frame.htm
© 1999 National Council of Commissioners on
State Laws; reprinted with permission.

§ 112. MANIFESTING ASSENT; OPPORTUNITY TO REVIEW.

(a) A person manifests assent to a record or term if the person, acting with knowledge of, or after having an opportunity to review the record or term or a copy of it:

    (1) authenticates the record or term with intent to adopt or accept it; or

    (2) intentionally engages in conduct or makes statements with reason to know that the other party or its electronic agent may infer from the conduct or statement that the person assents to the record or term.

(b) An electronic agent manifests assent to a record or term if, after having an opportunity to review it, the electronic agent:

    (1) authenticates the record or term; or

    (2) engages in operations that in the circumstances indicate acceptance of the record or term.

(c) If this [Act] or other law requires assent to a specific term, a manifestation of assent must relate specifically to the term.

(d) Conduct or operations manifesting assent may be proved in any manner, including a showing that a person or an electronic agent obtained or used the information or informational rights and that a procedure existed by which a person or an electronic agent must have engaged in the conduct or operations in order to do so. Proof of compliance with subsection (a)(2) is sufficient if there is conduct that assents and subsequent conduct that reaffirms assent by electronic means.

(e) With respect to an opportunity to review, the following rules apply:

(1) A person has an opportunity to review a record or term only if it is made available in a manner that ought to call it to the attention of a reasonable person and permit review.

(2) An electronic agent has an opportunity to review a record or term only if it is made available in manner that would enable a reasonably configured electronic agent to react to the record or term.

(3) If a record or term is available for review only after a person becomes obligated to pay or begins its performance, the person has an opportunity to review only if it has a right to a return if it rejects the record. However, a right to a return is not required if:

(A) the record proposes a modification of contract or provides particulars of performance under Section 305; or

(B) the primary performance is other than delivery or acceptance of a copy, the agreement is not a mass-market transaction, and the parties at the time of contracting had reason to know that a record or term would be presented after performance, use, or access to the information began.

(4) The right to a return under paragraph (3) may arise by law or by agreement.

(f) The effect of provisions of this section may be modified by an agreement setting out standards applicable to future transactions between the parties.

§ 207. FORMATION: RELEASES OF INFORMATIONAL RIGHTS.

(a) A release is effective without consideration if it is:

(1) in a record to which the releasing party agrees, such as by manifesting assent, and which identifies the informational rights released; or

(2) enforceable under estoppel, implied license, or other law.

(b) A release continues for the duration of the informational rights released if the release does not specify its duration and does not require affirmative performance after the grant of the release by:

(1) the party granting the release; or

(2) the party receiving the release, except for relatively insignificant acts.

(c) In cases not governed by subsection (b), the duration of a release is governed by Section 308.

§ 208.   ADOPTING TERMS OF RECORDS.

Except as otherwise provided in Section 209, the following rules apply:

(1) A party adopts the terms of a record, including a standard form, as the terms of the contract if the party agrees to the record, such as by manifesting assent.

(2) The terms of a record may be adopted pursuant to paragraph (1) after beginning performance or use if the parties had reason to know that their agreement would be represented in whole or part by a later record to be agreed on and there would not be an opportunity to review the record or a copy of it before performance or use begins. If the parties fail to agree to the later terms and did not intend to form a contract unless they so agreed, Section 202(e) applies.

(3) If a party adopts the terms of a record, the terms become part of the contract without regard to the party's knowledge or understanding of individual terms in the record, except for a term that is unenforceable because it fails to satisfy another requirement of this [Act].

§ 209.   MASS–MARKET LICENSE.

(a) A party adopts the terms of a mass-market license for purposes of Section 208 only if the party agrees to the license, such as by manifesting assent, before or during the party's initial performance or use of or access to the information. A term is not part of the license if:

(1) the term is unconscionable or is unenforceable under Section 105(a) or (b); or

(2) subject to Section 301, the term conflicts with a term to which the parties to the license have expressly agreed.

(b) If a mass-market license or a copy of the license is not available in a manner permitting an opportunity to review by the licensee before the licensee becomes obligated to pay and the licensee does not agree, such as by manifesting assent, to the license after having an opportunity to review, the licensee is entitled to a return under Section 112 and, in addition, to:

(1) reimbursement of any reasonable expenses incurred in complying with the licensor's instructions for returning or destroying the computer information or, in the absence of instructions, expenses incurred for return postage or similar reasonable expense in returning the computer information; and

(2) compensation for any reasonable and foreseeable costs of restoring the licensee's information processing system to reverse changes in the system caused by the installation, if:

(A) the installation occurs because information must be installed to enable review of the license; and

(B) the installation alters the system or information in it but does not restore the system or information after removal of the installed information because the licensee rejected the license.

(c) In a mass-market transaction, if the licensor does not have an opportunity to review a record containing proposed terms from the licensee before the licensor delivers or becomes obligated to deliver the information, and if the licensor does not agree, such as by manifesting assent, to those terms after having that opportunity, the licensor is entitled to a return.

Chapter IV

TRADEMARKS, UNFAIR COMPETITION, AND UNFAIR BUSINESS PRACTICES

A. TRADEMARK RIGHTS IN INTERNET DOMAIN NAMES

SPORTY'S FARM L.L.C. v. SPORTSMAN'S MARKET, INC.

United States Court of Appeals, Second Circuit, 2000.
202 F.3d 489, *cert. denied*, U.S. ___, 120 S.Ct. 2719, 147 L.Ed.2d 984.

CALABRESI, CIRCUIT JUDGE.

This case originally involved the application of the Federal Trademark Dilution Act ("FTDA") to the Internet. *See* Federal Trademark Dilution Act of 1995, Pub.L. No. 104–98, 109 Stat. 985 (codified at 15 U.S.C. §§ 1125, 1127 (Supp.1996)). While the case was pending on appeal, however, the Anticybersquatting Consumer Protection Act ("ACPA"), Pub.L. No. 106–113 (1999), *see* H.R.Rep. No. 106–479 (Nov. 18, 1999), was passed and signed into law. That new law applies to this case.

Plaintiff–Counter–Defendant–Appellant–Cross–Appellee Sporty's Farm L.L.C. ("Sporty's Farm") appeals from a judgment, following a bench trial, of the United States District Court for the District of Connecticut (Alfred V. Covello, *Chief Judge*) dated March 13, 1998. Defendant–Third-Party–Plaintiff–Counter–Claimant–Appellee–Cross–Appellant Sportsman's Market, Inc. ("Sportsman's") cross-appeals from the same judgment.

The district court held: (1) that the Sportsman's trademark ("*sporty's* ") was a *famous* mark entitled to protection under the FTDA; (2) that Sporty's Farm and its parent company, Third–Party–Defendant–Appellee Omega Engineering, Inc. ("Omega"), diluted the *sporty's* mark by using the Internet domain name "sportys.com" to sell Christmas trees and by preventing Sportsman's from using its trademark as a domain name; (3) that applying the FTDA to Sporty's Farm through an injunction requiring it to relinquish sportys.com was both equitable and not a retroactive application of the statute; (4) that Sportsman's was

387

limited to injunctive relief since the conduct of Sporty's Farm and Omega did not constitute a willful intent to dilute under the FTDA; and (5) that Sporty's Farm and Omega did not violate the Connecticut Unfair Trade Practices Act ("CUTPA"), Conn. Gen.Stat. Ann. §§ 42–110a to 42–110q (West 1992 & Supp.1999). We apply the new anticybersquatting law and affirm the judgment in all respects, but, given the new law, on different grounds from those relied upon by the district court.

BACKGROUND

I

Although the Internet is on its way to becoming a familiar aspect in our daily lives, it is well to begin with a brief explanation of how it works. The Internet is a network of computers that allows a user to gain access to information stored on any other computer on the network. Information on the Internet is lodged on files called web pages, which can include printed matter, sound, pictures, and links to other web pages. An Internet user can move from one page to another with just the click of a mouse.

Web pages are designated by an address called a domain name. A domain name consists of two parts: a top level domain and a secondary level domain. The top level domain is the domain name's suffix. Currently, the Internet is divided primarily into six top level domains: (1) .edu for educational institutions; (2) .org for non-governmental and non-commercial organizations; (3) .gov for governmental entities; (4) .net for networks; (5) .com for commercial users, and (6) a nation-specific domain, which is .us in the United States. The secondary level domain is the remainder of the address, and can consist of combinations of letters, numbers, and some typographical symbols.[2] To take a simple example, in the domain name "cnn.com," cnn ("Cable News Network") represents the secondary level domain and .com represents the top level domain. Each domain name is unique.

Over the last few years, the commercial side of the Internet has grown rapidly. Web pages are now used by companies to provide information about their products in a much more detailed fashion than can be done through a standard advertisement. Moreover, many consumers and businesses now order goods and services directly from company web pages. Given that Internet sales are paperless and have lower transaction costs than other types of retail sales, the commercial potential of this technology is vast.

For consumers to buy things or gather information on the Internet, they need an easy way to find particular companies or brand names. The most common method of locating an unknown domain name is simply to type in the company name or logo with the suffix .com. If this proves unsuccessful, then Internet users turn to a device called a search engine. A search engine will find all web pages on the Internet with a particular word or phrase. Given the current state of search engine technology,

---

2. Certain symbols, such as apostrophes ('), cannot be used in a domain name.

that search will often produce a list of hundreds of web sites through which the user must sort in order to find what he or she is looking for. As a result, companies strongly prefer that their domain name be comprised of the company or brand trademark and the suffix .com. *See* H.R.Rep. No. 106–412, at 5 (1999).

Until recently, domain names with the .com top level domain could only be obtained from Network Solutions, Inc. ("NSI"). Now other registrars may also assign them. But all these registrars grant such names primarily on a first-come, first-served basis upon payment of a small registration fee. They do not generally inquire into whether a given domain name request matches a trademark held by someone other than the person requesting the name. *See id.*

Due to the lack of any regulatory control over domain name registration, an Internet phenomenon known as "cybersquatting" has become increasingly common in recent years. *See, e.g., Panavision Int'l, L.P. v. Toeppen*, 141 F.3d 1316 (9th Cir.1998). Cybersquatting involves the registration as domain names of well-known trademarks by non-trademark holders who then try to sell the names back to the trademark owners. Since domain name registrars do not check to see whether a domain name request is related to existing trademarks, it has been simple and inexpensive for any person to register as domain names the marks of established companies. This prevents use of the domain name by the mark owners, who not infrequently have been willing to pay "ransom" in order to get "their names" back. *See* H.R.Rep. No. 106–412, at 5–7; S.Rep. No. 106–140, at 4–7 (1999).

II

Sportsman's is a mail order catalog company that is quite well-known among pilots and aviation enthusiasts for selling products tailored to their needs. In recent years, Sportsman's has expanded its catalog business well beyond the aviation market into that for tools and home accessories. The company annually distributes approximately 18 million catalogs nationwide, and has yearly revenues of about $50 million. Aviation sales account for about 60% of Sportsman's revenue, while non-aviation sales comprise the remaining 40%.

In the 1960s, Sportsman's began using the logo "*sporty*" to identify its catalogs and products. In 1985, Sportsman's registered the trademark *sporty's* with the United States Patent and Trademark Office. Since then, Sportsman's has complied with all statutory requirements to preserve its interest in the *sporty's* mark. *Sporty's* appears on the cover of all Sportsman's catalogs; Sportsman's international toll free number is 1–800–4*sportys*; and one of Sportsman's domestic toll free phone numbers is 1–800–*Sportys*. Sportsman's spends about $10 million per year advertising its *sporty's* logo.

Omega is a mail order catalog company that sells mainly scientific process measurement and control instruments. In late 1994 or early 1995, the owners of Omega, Arthur and Betty Hollander, decided to enter the aviation catalog business and, for that purpose, formed a wholly-owned subsidiary called Pilot's Depot, LLC ("Pilot's Depot"). Shortly thereafter, Omega registered the domain name sportys.com with NSI. Arthur Hollander was a pilot who received Sportsman's catalogs and thus was aware of the *sporty's* trademark.

In January 1996, nine months after registering sportys.com, Omega formed another wholly-owned subsidiary called Sporty's Farm and sold it the rights to sportys.com for $16,200. Sporty's Farm grows and sells Christmas trees, and soon began advertising its Christmas trees on a sportys.com web page. When asked how the name Sporty's Farm was selected for Omega's Christmas tree subsidiary, Ralph S. Michael, the CEO of Omega and manager of Sporty's Farm, explained, as summarized by the district court, that

> in his own mind and among his family, he always thought of and referred to the Pennsylvania land where Sporty's Farm now operates as *Spotty's farm*. The origin of the name . . . derived from a childhood memory he had of his uncle's farm in upstate New York. As a youngster, Michael owned a dog named Spotty. Because the dog strayed, his uncle took him to his upstate farm. Michael thereafter referred to the farm as Spotty's farm. The name Sporty's Farm was . . . a subsequent derivation.

Joint Appendix ("JA") at 277 (emphasis added). There is, however, no evidence in the record that Hollander was considering starting a Christmas tree business when he registered sportys.com or that Hollander was ever acquainted with Michael's dog Spotty.

In March 1996, Sportsman's discovered that Omega had registered sportys.com as a domain name. Thereafter, and before Sportsman's could take any action, Sporty's Farm brought this declaratory action seeking the right to continue its use of sportys.com. Sportsman's counterclaimed and also sued Omega as a third-party defendant for, *inter alia*, (1) trademark infringement, (2) trademark dilution pursuant to the FTDA, and (3) unfair competition under state law. Both sides sought injunctive relief to force the other to relinquish its claims to sportys.com. While this litigation was ongoing, Sportsman's used "sportys-catalogs.com" as its primary domain name.

After a bench trial, the court rejected Sportsman's trademark infringement claim and all related claims that are based on a "likelihood of [consumer] confusion" since "the parties operate wholly unrelated businesses [and t]herefore, confusion in the marketplace is not likely to develop." *Id.* at 282–83. But on Sportsman's trademark dilution action, where a likelihood of confusion was not necessary, the district court found for Sportsman's. The court concluded (1) that *sporty's* was a *famous* mark entitled to protection under the FTDA since "the 'Sporty's'mark enjoys general name recognition in the consuming public,"*id.* at 288, and (2) that Sporty's Farm and Omega had diluted *sporty's* because "registration of the 'sportys.com' domain name effectively compromises Sportsman's Market's ability to identify and distinguish its goods on the Internet.... [by] preclud[ing] Sportsman's Market from using its 'unique identifier,' "*id.* at 289. The court also held, however, that Sportsman's could only get injunctive relief and was not entitled to "punitive damages ... profits, and attorney's fees and costs" pursuant to the FTDA since Sporty Farm and Omega's conduct did not constitute willful dilution under the FTDA. *Id.* at 292–93.

Finally, the district court ruled that, although Sporty's Farm had violated the FTDA, its conduct did not constitute a violation of CUTPA. This conclusion was based on the district court's finding that Sportsman's had failed to show by a preponderance of the evidence (1) that Sporty's Farm and Omega's "conduct was immoral, unethical, oppressive, or unscrupulous," and (2) that Sportsman's "suffered a substantial injury sufficient to establish a CUTPA claim." *Id.* at 291–92.

The district court then issued an injunction forcing Sporty's Farm to relinquish all rights to sportys.com. And Sportsman's subsequently acquired the domain name. Both Sporty's Farm and Sportsman's appeal. Specifically, Sporty's Farm appeals the judgment insofar as the district court granted an injunction in favor of Sportsman's for the use of the domain name. Sportsman's, on the other hand, in addition to urging this court to affirm the district court's injunction, cross-appeals, quite correctly as a procedural matter, the district court's denial of damages under both the FTDA and CUPTA. *See* 16A Charles Alan Wright, Arthur R. Miller, Edward H. Cooper, *Federal Practice and Procedure* § 3974.4 (3d ed.1999) ("[A] cross-appeal is required to support modification of the judgment.... ").

III

As we noted above, while this appeal was pending, Congress passed the ACPA. That law was passed "to protect consumers and American businesses, to promote the growth of online commerce, and to provide clarity in the law for trademark owners by prohibiting the bad-faith and abusive registration of distinctive marks as Internet domain names with the intent to profit from the goodwill associated with such marks—a practice commonly referred to as 'cybersquatting'." S.Rep. No. 106–140, at 4. In particular, Congress viewed the legal remedies available for victims of cybersquatting before the passage of the ACPA as "expensive and uncertain." H.R.Rep. No. 106–412, at 6. The Senate made clear its view on this point:

> While the [FTDA] has been useful in pursuing cybersquatters, cybersquatters have become increasingly sophisticated as the case law has developed and now take the necessary precautions to insulate themselves from liability. For example, many cybersquatters are now careful to no longer offer the domain name for sale in any manner that could implicate liability under existing trademark dilution case law. And, in cases of warehousing and trafficking in domain names, courts have sometimes declined to provide assistance to trademark holders, leaving them without adequate and effective judicial remedies. This uncertainty as to the trademark law's appli-

cation to the Internet has produced inconsistent judicial decisions and created extensive monitoring obligations, unnecessary legal costs, and uncertainty for consumers and trademark owners alike. S.Rep. No. 106–140, at 7. In short, the ACPA was passed to remedy the perceived shortcomings of applying the FTDA in cybersquatting cases such as this one.

The new act accordingly amends the Trademark Act of 1946, creating a specific federal remedy for cybersquatting. New 15 U.S.C. § 1125(d)(1)(A) reads:

A person shall be liable in a civil action by the owner of a mark, including a personal name which is protected as a mark under this section, if, without regard to the goods or services of the parties, that person—

(i) has a bad faith intent to profit from that mark, including a personal name which is protected as a mark under this section; and

(ii) registers, traffics in, or uses a domain name that—

(I) in the case of a mark that is distinctive at the time of registration of the domain name, is identical or confusingly similar to that mark;

(II) in the case of a famous mark that is famous at the time of registration of the domain name, is identical or confusingly similar to or dilutive of that mark; . . .

The Act further provides that "a court may order the forfeiture or cancellation of the domain name or the transfer of the domain name to the owner of the mark," 15 U.S.C. § 1125(d)(1)(C), if the domain name was "registered before, on, or after the date of the enactment of this Act," Pub.L. No. 106–113, § 3010. It also provides that damages can be awarded for violations of the Act,[9] but that they are not "available with respect to the registration, trafficking, or use of a domain name that occurs before the date of the enactment of this Act." *Id.*

DISCUSSION

This case has three distinct features that are worth noting before we proceed further. First, our opinion appears to be the first interpretation of the ACPA at the appellate level. Second, we are asked to undertake the interpretation of this new statute even though the district court made its ruling based on the FTDA. Third, the case before us presents a factual situation that, as far as we can tell, is rare if not unique: A Competitor X of Company Y has registered Y's trademark as a domain name and then transferred that name to Subsidiary Z, which operates a

---

9. The new Act permits a plaintiff to "elect, at any time before final judgment is rendered by the trial court, to recover, instead of actual damages and profits, an award of statutory damages in the amount of not less than $1,000 and not more than $100,000 per domain name, as the court considers just." Pub.L. No. 106–113, § 3003. If the plaintiff does not so elect, the court may award damages under 15 U.S.C. § 1117(a) and (b), based on damages, profits, and the cost of the action. *See id.*

business wholly unrelated to Y. These unusual features counsel that we decide no more than is absolutely necessary to resolve the case before us.

A. *Application of the ACPA to this Case*

The first issue before us is whether the ACPA governs this case. The district court based its holding on the FTDA since the ACPA had not been passed when it made its decision. Because the ACPA became law while this case was pending before us, we must decide how its passage affects this case. As a general rule, we apply the law that exists at the time of the appeal. *See, e.g., Hamm v. City of Rock Hill*, 379 U.S. 306, 312–13, 85 S.Ct. 384, 13 L.Ed.2d 300 (1964) (" '[I]f subsequent to the judgment and before the decision of the appellate court, a law intervenes and positively changes the rule which governs, the law must be obeyed, or its obligation denied.' " (quoting *United States v. Schooner Peggy*, 5 U.S. (1 Cranch) 103, 110, 2 L.Ed. 49 (1801))).

But even if a new law controls, the question remains whether in such circumstances it is more appropriate for the appellate court to apply it directly or, instead, to remand to the district court to enable that court to consider the effect of the new law. We therefore asked for additional briefing from the parties regarding the applicability of the ACPA to the case before us. After receiving those briefs and fully considering the arguments there made, we think it is clear that the new law was adopted specifically to provide courts with a preferable alternative to stretching federal dilution law when dealing with cybersquatting cases. Indeed, the new law constitutes a particularly good fit with this case. Moreover, the findings of the district court, together with the rest of the record, enable us to apply the new law to the case before us without difficulty. Accordingly, we will do so and forego a remand.

B. *"Distinctive" or "Famous"*

Under the new Act, we must first determine whether *sporty's* is a distinctive or famous mark and thus entitled to the ACPA's protection. *See* 15 U.S.C. § 1125(d)(1)(A)(ii)(I), (II). The district court concluded that *sporty's* is both distinctive and famous. We agree that *sporty's* is a "distinctive" mark. As a result, and without casting any doubt on the district court's holding in this respect, we need not, and hence do not, decide whether *sporty's* is also a "famous" mark.[10]

More vexing is the question posed by the criterion that focuses on "the degree of recognition of the mark in the trading areas and channels of trade used by the marks' owner and the person against whom the

---

10. In most respects, *sporty's* meets the rigorous criteria laid out in § 1125(c)(1), requiring both fame and distinctiveness for protection under the FTDA. *See Nabisco Brands Co. v. PF Brands, Inc.*, 191 F.3d 208, 216 (2d Cir.1999). The mark (1) is sufficiently distinctive (as we discuss in the text), (2) has been used by Sportsman's for an extended period of time, (3) has had millions of dollars in advertising spent on it, (4) is used nationwide, and (5) is traded in a wide variety of retail channels. *See* 15 U.S.C. § 1125(c)(1)(A)-(E). Moreover, the record does not indicate that anyone else besides Sportsman's uses sporty's, and the mark is, of course, registered with federal authorities. *See id.* at § 1125(c)(1)(G)-(H). * * *

injunction is sought." *Id.* at § 1125(c)(1)(F). Sporty's Farm contends that, although sporty's is a very well-known mark in the pilot and aviation niche market, Sportsman's did not (and could not) prove that the mark was well-known to Sporty's Farm's customers. We need not reach this question, as we would have had to do under the FTDA, since the ACPA provides protection not only to famous marks but also to distinctive marks regardless of fame.

Distinctiveness refers to inherent qualities of a mark and is a completely different concept from fame. A mark may be distinctive before it has been used—when its fame is nonexistent. By the same token, even a famous mark may be so ordinary, or descriptive as to be notable for its lack of distinctiveness. *See Nabisco, Inc. v. PF Brands, Inc.*, 191 F.3d 208, 215–26 (2d Cir.1999). We have no doubt that *sporty's*, as used in connection with Sportsman's catalogue of merchandise and advertising, is inherently distinctive. Furthermore, Sportsman's filed an affidavit under 15 U.S.C. § 1065 that rendered its registration of the *sporty's* mark incontestable, which entitles Sportsman's "to a presumption that its registered trademark is inherently distinctive." *Equine Technologies, Inc. v. Equitechnology, Inc.*, 68 F.3d 542, 545 (1st Cir. 1995). We therefore conclude that, for the purposes of § 1125(d)(1)(A)(ii)(I), the *sporty's* mark is distinctive.

C.   "Identical and Confusingly Similar"

The next question is whether domain name sportys.com is "identical or confusingly similar to" the *sporty's* mark. 15 U.S.C. § 1125(d)(1)(A)(ii)(I). As we noted above, apostrophes cannot be used in domain names. *See supra* note 2. As a result, the secondary domain name in this case (sportys) is indistinguishable from the Sportsman's trademark (*sporty's*). *Cf. Brookfield Communications, Inc. v. West Coast Entertainment Corp.*, 174 F.3d 1036, 1055 (9th Cir.1999) (observing that the differences between the mark "MovieBuff" and the domain name "moviebuff.com" are "inconsequential in light of the fact that Web addresses are not caps-sensitive and that the '.com' top-level domain signifies the site's commercial nature"). We therefore conclude that, although the domain name sportys.com is not precisely identical to the *sporty's* mark, it is certainly "confusingly similar" to the protected mark under § 1125(d)(1)(A)(ii)(I). *Cf. Wella Corp. v. Wella Graphics, Inc.* 874 F.Supp. 54, 56 (E.D.N.Y.1994) (finding the new mark "Wello" confusingly similar to the trademark "Wella").

D.   "Bad Faith Intent to Profit"

We next turn to the issue of whether Sporty's Farm acted with a "bad faith intent to profit" from the mark sporty's when it registered the domain name sportys.com. 15 U.S.C. § 1125(d)(1)(A)(i). The statute lists nine factors to assist courts in determining when a defendant has acted with a bad faith intent to profit from the use of a mark.[12] But we

---

12. These factors are:

(I) the trademark or other intellectual property rights of the person, if any, in the domain name;

(II) the extent to which the domain name consists of the legal name of the person or a

are not limited to considering just the listed factors when making our determination of whether the statutory criterion has been met. The factors are, instead, expressly described as indicia that "may" be considered along with other facts. *Id.* § 1125(d)(1)(B)(i).

We hold that there is more than enough evidence in the record below of "bad faith intent to profit" on the part of Sporty's Farm (as that term is defined in the statute), so that "no reasonable factfinder could return a verdict against" Sportsman's. *Norville v. Staten Island Univ. Hosp.*, 196 F.3d 89, 95 (2d Cir.1999). First, it is clear that neither Sporty's Farm nor Omega had any intellectual property rights in sportys.com at the time Omega registered the domain name. *See id.* § 1125(d)(1)(B)(i)(I). Sporty's Farm was not formed until nine months after the domain name was registered, and it did not begin operations or obtain the domain name from Omega until after this lawsuit was filed. Second, the domain name does not consist of the legal name of the party that registered it, Omega. *See id.* § 1125(d)(1)(B)(i)(II). Moreover, although the domain name does include part of the name of Sporty's Farm, that entity did not exist at the time the domain name was registered.

The third factor, the prior use of the domain name in connection with the bona fide offering of any goods or services, also cuts against Sporty's Farm since it did not use the site until after this litigation began, undermining its claim that the offering of Christmas trees on the site was in good faith. *See id.* § 1125(d)(1)(B)(i)(III). Further weighing in favor of a conclusion that Sporty's Farm had the requisite statutory bad faith intent, as a matter of law, are the following: (1) Sporty's Farm does

name that is otherwise commonly used to identify that person;

(III) the person's prior use, if any, of the domain name in connection with the bona fide offering of any goods or services;

(IV) the person's bona fide noncommercial or fair use of the mark in a site accessible under the domain name;

(V) the person's intent to divert consumers from the mark owner's online location to a site accessible under the domain name that could harm the goodwill represented by the mark, either for commercial gain or with the intent to tarnish or disparage the mark, by creating a likelihood of confusion as to the source, sponsorship, affiliation, or endorsement of the site;

(VI) the person's offer to transfer, sell, or otherwise assign the domain name to the mark owner or any third party for financial gain without having used, or having an intent to use, the domain name in the bona fide offering of any goods or services, or the

person's prior conduct indicating a pattern of such conduct;

(VII) the person's provision of material and misleading false contact information when applying for the registration of the domain name, the person's intentional failure to maintain accurate contact information, or the person's prior conduct indicating a pattern of such conduct;

(VIII) the person's registration or acquisition of multiple domain names which the person knows are identical or confusingly similar to marks of others that are distinctive at the time of registration of such domain names, or dilutive of famous marks of others that are famous at the time of registration of such domain names, without regard to the goods or services of the parties; and

(IX) the extent to which the mark incorporated in the person's domain name registration is or is not distinctive and famous within the meaning of subsection(c)(1) of section 43.

15 U.S.C. § 1125(d)(1)(B)(i).

not claim that its use of the domain name was "noncommercial" or a "fair use of the mark," *see id.* § 1125(d)(1)(B)(i)(IV), (2) Omega sold the mark to Sporty's Farm under suspicious circumstances, *see Sporty's Farm v. Sportsman's Market*, No. 96CV0756 (D.Conn. Mar. 13, 1998), reprinted in Joint Appendix at A277 (describing the circumstances of the transfer of sportys.com); 15 U.S.C. § 1125(d)(1)(B)(i)(VI), and, (3) as we discussed above, the *sporty's* mark is undoubtedly distinctive, *see id.* § 1125(d)(1)(B)(i)(IX).

The most important grounds for our holding that Sporty's Farm acted with a bad faith intent, however, are the unique circumstances of this case, which do not fit neatly into the specific factors enumerated by Congress but may nevertheless be considered under the statute. We know from the record and from the district court's findings that Omega planned to enter into direct competition with Sportsman's in the pilot and aviation consumer market. As recipients of Sportsman's catalogs, Omega's owners, the Hollanders, were fully aware that *sporty's* was a very strong mark for consumers of those products. It cannot be doubted, as the court found below, that Omega registered sportys.com for the primary purpose of keeping Sportsman's from using that domain name. Several months later, and after this lawsuit was filed, Omega created another company in an unrelated business that received the name Sporty's Farm so that it could (1) use the sportys.com domain name in some commercial fashion, (2) keep the name away from Sportsman's, and (3) protect itself in the event that Sportsman's brought an infringement claim alleging that a "likelihood of confusion" had been created by Omega's version of cybersquatting. Finally, the explanation given for Sporty's Farm's desire to use the domain name, based on the existence of the dog Spotty, is more amusing than credible. Given these facts and the district court's grant of an equitable injunction under the FTDA, there is ample and overwhelming evidence that, as a matter of law, Sporty's Farm's acted with a "bad faith intent to profit" from the domain name sportys.com as those terms are used in the ACPA. *See Luciano v. Olsten Corp.*, 110 F.3d 210, 214 (2d Cir.1997) (stating that, as a matter of law, judgment may be granted where "the evidence in favor of the movant is so overwhelming that 'reasonable and fair minded [persons] could not arrive at a verdict against [it].' " (quoting *Cruz v. Local Union No. 3*, 34 F.3d 1148, 1154 (2d Cir.1994) (alteration in original))).

E. *Remedy*

Based on the foregoing, we hold that under § 1125(d)(1)(A), Sporty's Farm violated Sportsman's statutory rights by its use of the sportys.com domain name. The question that remains is what remedy is Sportsman's entitled to. The Act permits a court to "order the forfeiture or cancellation of the domain name or the transfer of the domain name to the owner of the mark," § 1125(d)(1)(C) for any "domain name [ ] registered before, on, or after the date of the enactment of [the] Act," Pub.L. No. 106–113, § 3010. That is precisely what the district court did here, albeit under the pre-existing law, when it directed a) Omega and Sporty's Farm to release their interest in sportys.com and to transfer the name to Sportsman's, and b) permanently enjoined those entities from taking any action to prevent and/or hinder Sportsman's from obtaining the domain name. That relief remains appropriate under the ACPA. We therefore affirm the district court's grant of injunctive relief.

We must also determine, however, if Sportsman's is entitled to damages either under the ACPA or pre-existing law. Under the ACPA, damages are unavailable to Sportsman's since sportys.com was registered and used by Sporty's Farm prior to the passage of the new law. *See id.* (stating that damages can be awarded for violations of the Act but that they are not "available with respect to the registration, trafficking, or use of a domain name that occurs before the date of the enactment of this Act.").

But Sportsman's might, nonetheless, be eligible for damages under the FTDA since there is nothing in the ACPA that precludes, in cybersquatting cases, the award of damages under any pre-existing law. *See* 15 U.S.C § 1125(d)(3) (providing that any remedies created by the new act are "in addition to any other civil action or remedy otherwise applicable"). Under the FTDA, "[t]he owner of the famous mark shall be entitled only to injunctive relief unless the person against whom the injunction is sought *willfully* intended to trade on the owner's reputation or to cause dilution of the famous mark." *Id.* § 1125(c)(2) (emphasis added). Accordingly, where willful intent to dilute is demonstrated, the owner of the famous mark is—subject to the principles of equity—entitled to recover (1) damages (2) the dilutor's profits, and (3) costs. *See id.*; *see also id.* § 1117(a) (specifying remedies).

We conclude, however, that damages are not available to Sportsman's under the FTDA. The district court found that Sporty's Farm did not act willfully. We review such findings of "willfulness" by a district court for clear error. *See Bambu Sales, Inc. v. Ozak Trading Inc.*, 58 F.3d 849, 854 (2d Cir.1995). Thus, even assuming the *sporty's* mark to be famous, we cannot say that the district court clearly erred when it found that Sporty's Farm's actions were not willful. To be sure, that question is a very close one, for the facts make clear that, as a Sportsman's customer, Arthur Hollander (Omega's owner) was aware of the significance of the *sporty's* logo. And the idea of creating a Christmas tree business named Sporty's Farm, allegedly in honor of Spotty the dog, and of giving that business the sportys.com domain name seems to have occurred to Omega only several months after it had registered the name. Nevertheless, given the uncertain state of the law at the time that Sporty's Farm and Omega acted, we cannot say that the district court clearly erred in finding that their behavior did not amount to willful dilution. It follows that Sportsman's is not entitled to damages under the FTDA.

Sportsman's also argues that it is entitled to damages under state law. Because neither the FTDA nor the ACPA preempts state remedies such as CUTPA, damages under Connecticut law are not barred, and hence may be available to Sportsman's. *See* H.R.Rep. No. 104–374, at 4 (1995), *reprinted in* 1996 U.S.C.C.A.N. 1029, 1031; 15 U.S.C. § 1125(d)(3).

CUTPA, Conn. Gen.Stat. Ann. § 42–110b(a) (West Supp.1999), states that "[n]o person shall engage in unfair methods of competition and unfair or deceptive acts or practices in the conduct of any trade or commerce." In construing this statute, the Connecticut courts have applied the so-called "cigarette rule"[15] which asks:

> (1) [W]hether the practice, without necessarily having been previously considered unlawful, offends public policy as it has been established by statutes, the common law, or otherwise-whether, in other words, it is within at least the penumbra of some common law, statutory, or other established concept of unfairness; (2) whether it is immoral, unethical, oppressive, or unscrupulous; (3) whether it causes substantial injury to consumers [competitors or other businessmen]....

> All three criteria do not need to be satisfied to support a finding of unfairness. A practice may be unfair because of the degree to which it meets one of the criteria or because to a lesser extent it meets all three....

Saturn Const. Co. v. Premier Roofing Co., 238 Conn. 293, 310–11, 680 A.2d 1274, 1283 (1996) (internal quotation marks omitted).

We have no doubt that an ACPA violation meets the requirements of prong one of the cigarette rule test. But, despite our finding that Sporty's Farm acted with a bad faith intent, we do not think that its conduct meets prong two. While Sporty's Farm and Omega intended to do what they did, until today's holding interpreting the new ACPA, the line between business tactics with respect to domain name use that were unfair and those that, if hard-nosed, were nonetheless legitimate was blurry. Under the circumstances, we do not believe that the district court erred when it found that their conduct should not retrospectively be termed "immoral, unethical, oppressive, or unscrupulous." Moreover, prong three also cuts against a violation of CUTPA. Although the use of sportys.com and Sportsman's inability to use its trademark as a domain name injured Sportsman's, we cannot say that the record supports the

---

15. The "cigarette rule" was originally adopted by the Federal Trade Commission in 1964. *See* Statement of Basis and Purpose of Trade Regulation Rule 408, Unfair or Deceptive Advertising and Labeling of Cigarettes in Relation to the Health Hazards of Smoking, 29 Fed.Reg. 8324, 8355 (1964), *see also FTC v. Sperry & Hutchinson Co.*, 405 U.S. 233, 244–45 n. 5, 92 S.Ct. 898, 31 L.Ed.2d 170 (1972). This rule was later adopted by the Connecticut Supreme Court in *Conaway v. Prestia*, 191 Conn. 484, 464 A.2d 847 (1983), after the Connecticut legislature directed the Connecticut courts to "be guided by interpretations given by the Federal Trade Commission and the federal courts to Section 5(a)(1) of the Federal Trade Commission Act," when determining what constituted an unfair trade practice. Conn. Gen.Stat. Ann. § 42–110b(b) (West Supp.1999); *see McLaughlin Ford, Inc. v. Ford Motor Co.*, 192 Conn. 558, 567–68, 473 A.2d 1185, 1191 (1984).

additional contention that this injury was substantial enough to meet CUTPA's requirements.

This does not, however, end our inquiry since the three prongs of the cigarette rule test need not all be met to find that unfair competition took place. Nevertheless, after weighing the cigarette rule factors, we conclude—as the district court did—that the actions of Sporty's Farm and Omega did not contravene CUTPA. Although the removal of sportys.com from Sportsman's was designed to give Omega what we would now deem to be an unfair competitive advantage, we cannot say that this behavior was so unseemly at the time it occurred that Sporty's Farm and Omega should be found liable under state law.

In sum, then, we hold that the injunction issued by the district court was proper under the new anticybersquatting law, but that damages are not available to Sportsman's under the ACPA, the FTDA, or CUTPA.

* * *

CONCLUSION

The judgment of the district court is AFFIRMED in all particulars.

Note

Faber used "ballysucks.com" as the name of a domain devoted to criticism of the Bally health clubs. The holder of the "Bally" trademark sued for trademark infringement. The court held that Faber's use of the domain name was protected by First Amendment. *Bally Total Fitness Holding Corp. v. Faber,* 29 F.Supp.2d 1161, 1167 (C.D.Cal.1998). Although the *Bally* case occurred before the adoption of the Anticybersquatting Consumer Protection Act, the holding obviously is still good law, because the First Amendment, of course, would trump any act of Congress.

B. DOMAIN NAME ARBITRATION

Control of domain name registration was transferred in 1999 to the Internet Corporation for Assigned Names and Numbers. It was given the power to license organizations to become domain name registrars. It required these organizations to adhere to a "Uniform Domain Name Dispute Resolution Policy." This policy had provisions for arbitration of domain name disputes. The following case was among the first arbitrations under this policy.

OLLY'S B.V. v. CPS KOREA

WIPO Arbitration and Mediation Center, 2000.
Case No. D2000–0203 <http://arbiter.wipo.int>

GEORGE R. F. SOUTER, SOLE PANELIST

1. THE PARTIES

The complainant is Olly's B. V., a corporation organized under the laws of the Netherlands, whose principal place of business is 1822 BK

Alkmaar, Netherlands, represented by Edwin A. Getz, Tina D. Kourasis, and Liisa M. Thomas, of Gardner, Carton & Douglas, of 321 N. Clarke Street, Suite 3300, Chicago, IL 60610, USA.

The respondent is CPS Korea Corp, of Baekguang Bldg., 4th Floor, 946–5 Dogok-dong, Kangnam-gu, Seoul, Korea.

2. DOMAIN NAME AND REGISTRAR

The domain name at issue is <oilily.com>, and the registrar is Network Solutions, Inc., of 505 Huntmar Park Drive, Herndon, Virginia 20170, USA.

3. PROCEDURAL HISTORY

The complaint was submitted on March 23, 200. A timely response was submitted to and received by WIPO on April 17, 2000. George R. F. Souter was appointed as sole panelist on April 20, 2000.

4. FACTUAL BACKGROUND

The complainant claims to be the owner of all rights in and to the trademark OILILY, and to have obtained registrations throughout the world. Copies of the following registrations, all of which are still in force, were supplied: Benelux Registration No. 0460848; South Korean Registrations Nos. 216779, 217522, 219873, 221746, 221747, 225394 and 236539; Hong Kong Registrations Nos. 0958, 0959, B1755, 01888, 03118, 03796, and 03797; Indian Registrations Nos.543037, 543038 and 543039; Japanese Registrations Nos. 2036994 and 2464465; Singapore Registration Nos. 2441/90 and 2442/90; Nepalese Registration No. 10727/052; Taiwanese Registrations Nos. 642197 and 853718; Australian Registrations Nos. B545320 and A545321; United Kingdom Registrations Nos. 1270935 and 1513431; Canadian Registration No. TMA371731; and United States Registrations 1630912, 1634679 and 1665617.

Benelux Registration No. 0460848 covers goods in classes 3, 9, 16, 18, 24 and 25.

The South Korean Registrations mentioned above relate respectively to "Handbags, satchels, trunks, suitcases, rucksacks, purses, boxes, packing bags, closures of packing containers, bottles" (No 216779); "Dress coats, trousers, evening dresses, suits, skirts, children's clothes, overcoats, half coats, raincoats, cloaks, jumper, sweaters, cardigan jackets, waistcoats, white shirts, blouses, sportshirts, poloshirts, undershirts, pants, combinations, chemises, slips, pajamas, nightgowns, sportswear (uniform), hosieries, stockings (No. 217522); "Shoes, boots, lace up boots, leather shoes, gym shoes, baseball shoes, handball shoes" (No. 219873); "Letter paper, notebooks, sketchbooks, envelopes, cards, albums, seal materials" (No. 221746); "Ordinary spectacles, sunglasses, eyeglass case, frame" (No. 221747); "Magazines, picture postcards, calendars, dailies, other printed matters, writings and paintings, photographs" (No. 225394); and "Perfume, perfumed oil, general toilet water, skin lotion, hair cream and hair spray, compound perfumery, pomade, hair tonic (No. 236539).

The respondent registered the domain name <oilily.com> on September 28, 1998.

The complainant claims that it contacted the respondent on numerous occasions in an effort to amicably resolve the domain name dispute. On January 21, 2000, a Korean patent attorney representing CPS Korea, in response to previous correspondence, e-mailed the complainant, stating: "In principle, CPS Korea has a willingness to transfer the domain name if Olly's BV offers reasonable price." On February 2, 2000, the Korean patent attorney e-mailed the complainant, stating: "As I talked to the President of CPS Korea, Mr. Gary Koo, he is willing to transfer the domain name. Mr. Koo, his staffs of CPS and an appraiser thoroughly evaluated the reasonable price for the transfer of oilily.com. As a result, CPS Korea offers the transfer of the domain name for US$520,-000."

5. PARTIES' CONTENTIONS

A. *Complainant*

The complainant claims to be the deviser of the trademark OILILY, from the nickname, "Olly" of Willem Olsthoorn who, with Marieke Olsthoorn created the complainant company in 1963.

The complainant claims that it is a well known manufacturer and distributor of retail apparel, accessories and personal care products, and that the trademark OILILY has been in use for its products since at least as early as 1981, which products are now on sale in over 2000 retail stores in over 40 countries, including retail stores which trade under the trade name OILILY, including a store trading under that name in Seoul, to have generated over $100,000,000 in sales of its products under the trademark, and to have expended over $10,000,000 in marketing and advertising. Additionally, the complainant claims to have a "fan club" of over 80,000 members, operated through its web sites at <oililyusa.com> and <oilily.nl>.

The complainant alleges, "on information and belief", that the respondent obtained the domain name registration <oilily.com> with full knowledge of the complainant's long prior use and ownership of its OILILY trademark throughout the world, and in Korea, and to obtain financial gain from the extraordinarily valuable goodwill of its OILILY mark.

The complainant requests that the domain name <oilily.com> be transferred to them.

B. *Respondent*

The respondent claims that its main business is in the field of web-page designing businesses as well as providing general consulting services to clients in various business areas with respect to strategic planning and development of internet related operations. It claims that it is a corporation organized and registered to do business in Korea since 3 September 1998. Having stabilized its business, which was finally accomplished in the latter half of 1999, it claims to be in the process of diversifying into two new business areas, one of which relates to selling a variety of fresh produce and flowers through the internet. The respondent claims that, "with the unexpected difficulties in locating and establishing a business relationship with a suitable produce wholesaler, the fully fledged launching of the domain name . . .has been postponed up until today."

In connection with this proposed business, the respondent claims to have devised the domain name OILILY, "as a name which sounds unique and, at the same time coherent in relation to the business of selling fresh produce and flowers". The respondent claims that it derived the domain name from two words, namely "OI" and "LILY", the word "oi" dictated in English in the way it is pronounced in Korean meaning "cucumber", and the word "lily" pronounced in the same manner meaning the flower "lily".

The respondent claims that the complainant's trademark OILILY, "[g]iven the fact that the complainant does not advertise its products nor its trademark through the use of mass media such as television, radio nor daily newspapers in Korea", "is not a well-recognized trademark to the general public in Korea", and that the respondent, "as a member of the general public, did not know that the name "oilily" was a well known trademark prior to registering the domain name."

6. DISCUSSION AND FINDINGS

For the complainant to succeed, the Panel must, under Paragraph 4(a) of the Uniform Domain Name Dispute Resolution Policy, be satisfied:

(i) that the domain name registered by the respondent is identical or confusingly similar to a trademark or service mark in which the complainant has rights; and

(ii) that the respondent has no rights or legitimate interests in respect of the domain name; and

(iii) that the domain name has been registered and is being used in bad faith.

The language employed, namely the word "and" at the end of paragraphs (i) and (ii), makes it clear that the tests in all three paragraphs (i), (ii) and (iii) must be met for the complainant to succeed. Previous Administrative Panel Decisions have, uniformly, followed this interpretation. Further, the word "and" in paragraph (iii) requires that both the domain name registration has been registered in bad faith, and that it has been used in bad faith, and the Administrative Panel, in Case No. D99–0001 so decided.

In connection with Paragraph 4a(i), it is clear that this test has been met, as the complainant has extensive trademark rights in the identical word OILILY.

In connection with Paragraph 4a(ii), Paragraph 4c of the Uniform Domain Name Policy provides an aid to interpretation. Paragraph 4c(i) advises respondents that their rights or legitimate interests to a domain name for the purposes of Paragraph 4a(ii) would be demonstrated by "before any notice of the dispute, your use of, or demonstrable preparations to use, the domain name . . . in connection with bona fide offering of goods and services." Paragraph 4c(iii) alternatively advises respondents that their rights or legitimate interests to a domain name for the purposes of Paragraph 4a(ii) would be demonstrated by "making a legitimate . . . fair use of the domain name, without intent for commercial gain to misleadingly divert consumers"

In the Panel's opinion, the use of the expression "bona fide" in Paragraph 4c(i) is sufficient to prevent a respondent who knowingly adopted another's well known mark as a domain name from claiming the benefit of mere use of or demonstrable preparations to use the domain name in connection with the offering of goods or services prior to notice of a dispute.

The respondent's claim to have independently devised the word "oilily" as "coherent in relation to selling fresh produce and flowers" in connection with its intended use of the domain name in connection with its intended business in internet selling of fresh produce and flowers, is, in the Panel's opinion, plausible.

The complainant has not produced elucidation of the "information" which (together with "belief") leads to its allegation that the respondent obtained the domain name <oilily.com> "with full knowledge of Complainant's long prior use and ownership of its OILILY trademark throughout the world, and in Korea." Such elucidation might have swayed the Panel to an opposite conclusion as to the respondent's independent devising of the domain name, given the inherent improbability of the coincidence of name.

The respondent has provided some evidence of preparatory activity to launch its claimed proposed commercial activity, in the form of a "Memorandum of Understanding on Electronic Commerce", dated 26 December 1999, between itself and a Korean entity, known as Flora, which the respondent refers to as a "flower wholesaler", in addition to operating the web site <oilily.com> described below.

In the Panel's opinion, therefore, the respondent is entitled to take benefit of the advice given at Paragraph 4c(i) in connection with Paragraph 4a(ii).

The Panel notes that the selling of fresh produce and flowers is a different field of commerce to that of the complainant, and that a trademark clearance search in Korea, and elsewhere, in connection with the respondent's proposed business might very well have produced no reference to the complainant's registered trademarks.

In connection with the advice given in Paragraph 4c(iii), the fact that there is no commerce in common between the complainant's business and the respondent's proposed business, leads the Panel to the conclusion that "misleading diversion of consumers" is inherently unlikely. The fact that the respondent forwarded e-mails intended for the complainant addressed to the respondent's web site to the complainant reinforces this conclusion.

In connection with paragraph 4a(ii), consequently, the Panel decides that the test of absence of rights or legitimate interests in respect of the domain name has not been met, and that, accordingly, the complainant cannot succeed.

The Panel, nevertheless, feels that it should proceed to consider Paragraph 4a(iii), as it is in this paragraph that the protection of well known marks is specifically catered for. In this connection the Panel notes that, in "The Management of Internet Names and Addresses: Intellectual Property Issues" (Report of the WIPO Internet Domain Name Process), of 30 April 1999, at paragraph 262, the following statement appears:

> We consider that the administrative procedure in respect of bad faith, abusive registrations of domain names, . . . should provide an efficient means for suppressing many of the predatory and parasitical practices to which famous and well-known marks are subject.

In Case No. D2000–0102, the Panel considered the question of a well known mark in connection with the mark NOKIA, and concluded: "The trademark NOKIA is currently enjoying such fame internationally that it cannot reasonably be argued that Respondent could have been unaware of the trademark rights vested therein when registering the trade name." The Panel considers that, in spite of the alleged well known nature of the mark OILILY, it is not so well known that it cannot be reasonably argued that the respondent could not have been unaware of it when registering the domain name <oilily.com>. Accordingly, the Panel holds that the domain name was not registered in bad faith, for the reasons set out in its finding in connection with Paragraph 4a(ii).

The respondent has set up a web site, which is a single page, with illustrations of fresh produce and flowers, which in the Panel's opinion, is suggestive of the Respondent's claimed proposed commerce, together with a short Korean language text.

The page also has a "contact us" message, which, when accessed, merely provides an e-mail linkage to the respondent.

In the Panel's opinion, the content of this web site appears somewhat insubstantial, and the Panel notes that the Respondent did not take the opportunity to supply an English translation. The Panel is, accordingly, unconvinced that the use of the domain name to date could justify the very high value of US$520,000 as "assessed" by the respondent for the purposes of sale of the domain name to the complainant. Offers for sale of a domain name to a complainant has been considered a number of occasions by the Panel. The Panel in this case accepts reasoning of the Panel in Case No. D99–0001 to the effect that:

"Because respondent offered to sell the domain name to complainant 'for valuable consideration in excess of' any out of pocket costs directly related to the domain name, respondent has 'used' the domain name in bad faith as defined in the Policy." The Panel notes, in particular, that the absence of proof of any active trading under the domain name in connection with products or services in a different field of activity to that of the complainant, deprives the respondent of justification of the assessed value as arising from independently accumulated goodwill, and, in the Panel's opinion, the value assessed is, therefore, predatory, and, consequently, demonstrates use in bad faith.

This finding that the respondent has used the domain name in bad faith does not disturb the finding that the original registration of the domain name was not in bad faith. Consequently, the dual test of Paragraph 4a(iii) has not been met.

7. DECISION

The complainant has not satisfied the Panel that the respondent had no rights or legitimate interest in the domain name, nor that the domain name was registered in bad faith. Consequently, the respondent shall not be required to transfer the domain name <oilily.com> to the complainant.

WEBER–STEPHEN PRODUCTS CO. v. ARMITAGE HARDWARE AND BUILDING SUPPLY, INC.

United States District Court, N.D. Illinois, 2000.
54 U.S.P.Q.2d 1766, 2000 WL 562470.

ASPEN, CHIEF J.

Defendant Armitage Hardware (Armitage) owns a number of internet domain names that plaintiff Weber–Stephen Products Company (Weber) alleges intentionally and in bad faith use Weber's registered trademarks and service marks in a deceptive, confusing, and misleading manner. Weber initiated an administrative proceeding before the World Intellectual Property Organization (WIPO), pursuant to the Uniform Domain Name Dispute Resolution Policy of the Internet Corporation for Assigned Names and Numbers (ICANN Policy), requesting that the administrative panel issue a decision transferring Armitage's domain names to Weber or canceling Armitage's domain names. The following day, Weber also filed suit in this Court, alleging "cyberpiracy" as well as other claims, such as trademark infringement. Weber told this Court that it had commenced an ICANN proceeding to resolve the issue of whether Armitage was using its domain names in bad faith, which is the only issue that the ICANN administrative panel has power to decide under the Policy. Weber also said that because it expected a decision from the panel within 45 to 50 days from the filing of its ICANN complaint (the Policy provides for expedited review), it would not be seeking injunctive relief in this Court with respect to Armitage's registration of the Weber domain names unless the panel declines to cancel and/or to transfer the domain names to Weber.

We understand that the panel is scheduled to issue a decision as soon as May 5, 2000. Before us now is Armitage's motion to declare the administrative proceeding non-binding and to stay this case in favor of the administrative action, or alternatively—should we find the other proceeding to be binding—to stay it while we consider whether Armitage's participation in that proceeding can be compelled. Armitage's concern is that if the panel's arbitration decision is binding on this Court, Armitage will suffer irreparable harm because our review of the panel's decision will necessarily be circumscribed pursuant to the deference accorded arbitrators' decisions under the Federal Arbitration Act.

The ICANN is a new, quasi-governmental internet-regulating body, and its Policy (approved on October 24, 1999) provides for a "mandatory administrative proceeding" in disputes between domain name owners and trademark owners and purportedly applies to every domain name registrant who registers its domain names through an ICANN-accredited registrar.[1] Armitage contends that it did not agree to the administrative proceeding and thus cannot be compelled to participate in it. However, Armitage will participate if we declare that the proceeding is non-binding, that we owe no deference to the proceeding, and that WIPO, ICANN, and Network Solutions, Inc. (Armitage's ICANN-accredited registrar) cannot take any action adverse to Armitage until this matter is resolved in this Court.

No federal court has yet considered the legal effect of a WIPO proceeding. However, the ICANN Policy and its accompanying rules do contemplate the possibility of parallel proceedings in federal court. First, the Policy provides that ICANN will cancel or transfer domain name registrations upon "our receipt of an order from a court ... of competent jurisdiction, requiring such action; *and/or* ... our receipt of a decision of an Administrative Panel requiring such action in any administrative proceeding ... conducted under this Policy." ICANN Policy at ¶ 3. Also, the procedural rules governing the Policy provide that if legal proceedings are initiated prior to or during an administrative proceeding with regard to a domain name dispute that is the subject of the administrative complaint, the panel has the discretion to decide whether to suspend or terminate the administrative proceeding or whether to proceed and make a decision. Uniform Domain Name Dispute Resolution Rules, at ¶ 18.[2] And the language of the Policy suggests that the administrative panels' decisions are not intended to be binding on federal courts. For example, under the heading "Availability of Court Proceedings," the ICANN Policy provides:

---

1. The term "registrar" refers to the entity (such as Network Solutions, Inc. or America Online) through which a company or individual can register a domain name.

2. In this case, the panel has not yet suspended or terminated the ICANN proceedings.

The mandatory administrative proceeding requirements set forth in Paragraph 4 shall not prevent either you or the complainant from submitting the dispute to a court of competent jurisdiction for independent resolution before such mandatory administrative proceeding is commenced or after such proceeding is concluded. If an Administrative Panel decides that your domain name registration should be canceled or transferred, we will wait ten (10) business days ... before implementing that decision. We will then implement the decision unless we have received from you during that ten (10) business day period official documentation (such as a copy of a complaint, file-stamped by the clerk of the court) that you have commenced a lawsuit against the complainant in a jurisdiction to which the complainant has submitted ... If we receive such documentation within the ten (10) business day period, we will not implement the Administrative Panel's decision, and we will take no further action, until we receive (i) evidence satisfactory to us of a resolution between the parties; (ii) evidence satisfactory to us that your lawsuit has been dismissed or withdrawn; or (iii) a copy of an order from such court dismissing your lawsuit or ordering that you do not have the right to continue to use your domain name.

ICANN Policy at ¶ 4(k). Furthermore, Armitage's counsel sent an e-mail inquiry to <domain.disputes@wipo.int>, and the response from the WIPO Arbitration and Mediation Center said that the administrative panel's determination would be binding on the registrar of the domain name, but that "[t]his decision is not binding upon a court, and a court may give appropriate weight to the Administrative Panel's decision." Albeit a vague and rather unhelpful interpretation, Weber does not take issue with this WIPO statement.

We conclude that this Court is not bound by the outcome of the ICANN administrative proceedings. But at this time we decline to determine the precise standard by which we would review the panel's decision, and what degree of deference (if any) we would give that decision. Neither the ICANN Policy nor its governing rules dictate to courts what weight should be given to a panel's decision, and the WIPO e-mail message stating that "a court may give appropriate weight to the Administrative Panel's decision" confirms the breadth of our discretion.

Because both parties to this case have adequate avenues of recourse should they be unhappy with the administrative panel's imminent decision, we find no need to stay the pending ICANN administrative action. Instead, we hereby stay this case pending the outcome of those proceedings. It is so ordered.

C. MISAPPROPRIATION, PRODUCT STANDARDS, AND TRADEMARKS

As already discussed in earlier chapters, economic theory suggest there are two reasons why computer and Internet technology tends to move toward industry standards. Just to review what was discussed above, these standards have economic effects that are often called "network effects" and "switching costs." Network effects are the gains to be achieved if everyone uses the same standard—for instance if everyone's modem uses the same codes to communicate with other modems, or if everyone in the office uses the same word processor. Switching costs are the costs of changing standards, for instance the cost in training, time, and quality caused if an office switches brands of word processor. If a company can obtain strong intellectual property rights in something connected with substantial network effects or switching costs, it may expect huge profits. As indicated in a prior chapter, there are serious controversies concerning whether or not the owner of a copyright should be able to reap the extraordinary monopoly profits connected with the existence of network effects and switching costs. The cases below concern the use of trademark and misappropriation law in attempts to secure monopoly profits from an industry standard that was not protected by copyright or patent. Trademark conflicts arise because competitors not only would like to use the industry standard, they would like to advertise the fact that their product conforms to the industry standard by using the trademark that is generally applied to the standard.

UNITED STATES GOLF ASSOCIATION v. ST. ANDREWS SYSTEMS, DATA–MAX, INC.

United States Court of Appeals, Third Circuit, 1984.
749 F.2d 1028.

BECKER, CIRCUIT JUDGE.

This appeal presents two interesting questions in the law of intellectual property. It arises from a lawsuit brought by appellant, the United States Golf Association ("U.S.G.A."), the governing body of amateur golf in the United States. The U.S.G.A. has developed a system for deriving the "handicaps" of amateur golfers, the core of which is a mathematical formula. Appellee Data–Max, Inc., d/b/a St. Andrews Systems, markets small computers that are programmed to calculate a golfer's handicap based on the U.S.G.A. formula. The U.S.G.A. brought this suit to enjoin Data–Max from using its formula as the basis for its computerized handicap system.

The U.S.G.A. bases its claim for an injunction on two theories. The first is that the use of the U.S.G.A. formula by Data–Max amounts to a "false designation of origin," and thus violates both section 43(a) of the Lanham Act, 15 U.S.C. § 1125(a), and the New Jersey common law against unfair competition. The second theory is that the use of the formula is a "misappropriation" under the doctrine of *International News Service v. Associated Press*, 248 U.S. 215, 39 S.Ct. 68, 63 L.Ed. 211 (1918), as that doctrine has been adopted by New Jersey. * * *

We conclude that the U.S.G.A. handicap formula is "functional," and thus that the U.S.G.A. cannot enjoin the use of the formula either under section 43(a) of the Lanham Act or under state law on the basis of any association in the public mind between the formula and the U.S.G.A. We also conclude that the U.S.G.A.'s claim does not fall within the "misappropriation" doctrine as it has been adopted by the State of New Jersey, largely because in using the formula Data–Max will not compete directly with the U.S.G.A., and thus will not interfere with the economic incentives of the U.S.G.A. to maintain and update its handicap formula. Accordingly, we affirm the judgment of the district court.

I.   FACTS AND PROCEDURAL HISTORY

The U.S.G.A. has been the governing body of amateur golf in the United States since 1894. It seeks to promote the game of golf by numerous means, including the establishment of rules and regulations for play, the promotion of amateur tournaments, and the regulation of its member golf clubs. Among the services that the U.S.G.A. provides to amateur golfers is a "handicap" formula that allows golfers of different skill levels to compete with each other on an equal basis. The U.S.G.A. handicap system takes account of the difficulty of the course on which a round is played and provides "safeguards" against the inflation of handicaps by excluding particularly bad holes and by counting only the best ten of a golfer's last twenty rounds.[1]

The U.S.G.A. has developed the handicap formula over a period of eighty years. The first version of the system was published in 1897. A system based on a golfer's best three scores, first devised in 1904, was adopted by the U.S.G.A. in 1911. In later years, the basic formula was altered by the addition of several features: a "course rating system" and "net score" (score adjusted for course difficulty) method of handicapping; a "current ability" approach, in which only a golfer's most recent scores are counted; a system of "equitable stroke control" which disallows very high scores for individual holes; an upper limit on handicaps; and a "discounting" approach, in which a handicap is calculated based on a percentage, currently 96%, of the differentials between the player's score and the course difficulty. A single, nationwide system was pre-

---

1. The U.S.G.A. brief outlines the critical elements of the U.S.G.A. handicap formula:

The U.S.G.A. Handicap Formula uses a golfer's ten best adjusted scores out of his most recent twenty adjusted scores.* The U.S.G.A. Handicap Formula also reflects the difficulty of the golf course on which each score was achieved. The Formula averages the lowest ten handicap "differentials" ** among the golfer's last twenty scores,

multiplies the total by 96 percent, and then rounds off to the nearest whole number.

* A golfer's adjusted score reflects certain adjustments which are designed to eliminate aberrations caused by an unusually high score on a single hole.

** A differential represents the difference between a golfer's adjusted score and the course rating of the golf course on which the golfer achieved that score.

scribed by the U.S.G.A. in 1958. The most recent change of significance took place on January 1, 1976.

Data–Max was incorporated in 1980 for the purpose of providing golfers, primarily those who do not belong to U.S.G.A.-member clubs, with "instant handicaps." A computer program to calculate a handicap based on the U.S.G.A. formula is central to the products and services that Data–Max offers. Data–Max has sold or leased its computer to U.S.G.A.-member golf clubs, which use the computer in calculating handicaps.[2] Data–Max also markets a subscription telephone handicap service, which enables a golfer to call in a new score and immediately receive an updated handicap, and a computer that enables a golfer to directly enter a new score and receive an updated handicap.[3]

The U.S.G.A. filed a three count complaint in the United States District Court for the District of New Jersey, seeking relief for service mark infringement under the Lanham Act, 15 U.S.C. §§ 1051 *et seq.*; for service mark infringement, unfair competition, and misappropriation under the common law of New Jersey; and for unfair competition under Section 43(a) of the Lanham Act, 15 U.S.C. § 1125(a). Data–Max responded with a seven-count counterclaim. The two primary counterclaims sought declaratory judgments on the two critical issues in the case: Data–Max's right to use the U.S.G.A. formula in providing handicaps, and its right to advertise that use.

The district court considered these issues on Data–Max's motion for summary judgment on the counterclaims. The district court granted the motion on the first counterclaim mentioned above. The court held that the U.S.G.A. formula was not a "salable product," and thus not subject to "misappropriation" under the doctrine of *International News Service v. Associated Press*, 248 U.S. 215, 39 S.Ct. 68, 63 L.Ed. 211(1918), as adopted by the courts of New Jersey, and that, because the formula was "functional," it was not subject to protection under either federal or state law as a service mark. The court denied the summary judgment motion on the second counterclaim, holding that material issues of fact existed as to the "likelihood of confusion" if Data–Max continued to advertise that its handicaps were calculated by use of the U.S.G.A. formula. Having granted summary judgment on the first counterclaim, the court then entered a final judgment as to that claim under Rule 54(b). * * *

II. DISCUSSION

A. *Contentions of the Parties*

The U.S.G.A. advances two distinct legal theories to support its claim to an injunction. The first, which can be broadly characterized as

2. The U.S.G.A. has no objection to this aspect of Data–Max's business, since the handicap is ultimately provided by a member golf club. The U.S.G.A. objects to an unauthorized organization, such as Data–Max, providing handicaps derived by means of the U.S.G.A. formula directly to golfers.

3. This service operates on the same principle as electronic teller machines: a golfer puts his or her plastic "score card" into the machine and types in the new score. The machine then tells the golfer the new handicap.

"false designation of origin," is based on a branch of the law of unfair competition closely related to trademark law. The U.S.G.A. asserts that Data–Max, by using the U.S.G.A. formula, is misleading the golfing public into thinking that the U.S.G.A. endorses Data–Max's products and services. The second theory is "misappropriation." The U.S.G.A. argues that it has invested time, effort, and money in the creation of the formula, and therefore is entitled to protection against Data–Max's using the formula as the basis of its own products and services. As we have noted, the district court rejected both of the U.S.G.A.'s theories.

On appeal, the U.S.G.A. argues that the district court erred in both its conclusions. On the first theory, the U.S.G.A. argues that, on summary judgment, the district court was obligated to presume that the public associated the formula with the U.S.G.A., since the evidence would support such a conclusion. In addressing the district court's conclusion that the formula was functional, the U.S.G.A. argues that "even though a product or feature performs a function (*i.e.*, is useful), it can nevertheless acquire secondary meaning," and that other handicap formulas could easily be devised. From these two premises, the U.S.G.A. argues that the "functionality" doctrine was inapplicable. Alternatively, the U.S.G.A. argues that "the functionality doctrine . . . covers only matters of physical or visual design." On the misappropriation theory, the U.S.G.A. argues that the district court erred in concluding that the formula was not a "salable product," that it is undisputed that Data–Max used the U.S.G.A.'s formula without alteration, and that the misappropriation doctrine protects the "inventor" of a product or service from competition from a rival who merely takes that product or service and sells it as its own. U.S.G.A. also asserts that the fact that the formula was in the "public domain" is irrelevant to the applicability of the misappropriation doctrine.

In response, Data–Max raises two basic arguments with respect to the false designation of origin question. The first is that the formula can have no secondary meaning because it is neither "an object in commerce" nor an "identification for an object in commerce." Their second point is that the "use of the formula to compute does not exhibit it, and therefore [the formula] *could not be a designation of origin*," (emphasis in original) and hence could not be a *false* designation of origin. On the misappropriation question, Data–Max makes three points. First, it argues that any use of the misappropriation doctrine to effect "the monopolization of an arithmetic formula" is preempted by the exclusion of such formulas from the federal patent statutes. Second, Data–Max argues that, since the formula is "functional," it cannot acquire secondary meaning, and thus may not be misappropriated. Third, Data–Max argues that the efforts of the U.S.G.A. to publicize the formula over the years have made the formula part of the public domain, and thus not "salable."

Although we reach the result advocated by Data–Max, our reasoning differs substantially from that advanced by the parties. On the false designation of origin point, our reasoning parallels that of the district court. On the misappropriation question, our analysis proceeds from the policies that define the scope of the misappropriation doctrine rather than from a focus on the "salability" of the formula or on any of the arguments offered in the briefs. We take these matters up in turn.

B.   The "False Designation of Origin" Claim

Under both New Jersey law and federal law, the functional aspects of a product or service may not be protected under trademark law, or under the related unfair competition doctrines based on possible confusion as to the source of origin of the products or services.[6] This rule reflects a balancing of divergent social interests. The use of "non-functional" features of a product or service to identify its source is legally protected against imitation by competitors, because the value of such features in identifying the source of the goods or services outweighs the social interest in allowing competitors to copy them. Functional features, on the other hand, may not be legally protected methods of identification, regardless of their association with the original manufacturer, because their usefulness in identifying the source of the product or service is outweighed by the social interest in competition and improvements, which are advanced by giving competitors free access to those features.

The "functionality" of a feature of a product or service cannot be determined by the application of a mechanical test. Although various forms of the inquiry have been articulated, the essence of the question is whether a particular feature of a product or service is substantially related to its value *as a product or service, i.e.,* if the feature is part of the "function" served, or whether the primary value of a particular feature is the identification of the provider. Several courts have noted that the key policy served by barring the use of functional features for identification is the policy favoring competition, and that the "functionality" inquiry must be addressed in light of this policy.

The question of the "functionality" of the U.S.G.A. formula is not difficult. Its simple mathematical formula is the basic tool for deriving a handicap from a golfer's raw scores; as such, the formula is central to the "function" performed by the Data–Max products and services. The U.S.G.A., relying on *Ideal Toy Corp. v. Plawner Toy Manufacturing Corp.*, 685 F.2d 78 (3d Cir.1982), argues that the availability of numer-

---

6. The New Jersey and Lanham Act requirements for a finding of unfair competition are substantively similar. To establish "unprivileged imitation" of a competitor's product, under either the Lanham Act or New Jersey law, a plaintiff must establish both "non-functionality" and "secondary meaning."

A preliminary requirement of § 43(a) of the Lanham Act is that plaintiff establish a likelihood of damages. There must be "more than a mere subjective belief" that the plaintiff is likely to be harmed. It is not clear on the record developed thus far whether the handicap formula at issue had any commercial value for the U.S.G.A., and therefore, whether U.S.G.A. is likely to be injured by defendant's use of the formula. However, since none of the parties raised this issue at trial or on appeal, we will not hinge our result on this requirement. At all events, it has not been suggested that the U.S.G.A.'s interest in its formula is insufficient to create a "case or controversy" within the meaning of Article III.

ous alternative methods of designing a particular feature of a product or service defeats the functionality of any single method. This argument proceeds from an overly broad reading of *Plawner*. Although other formulas could be developed to serve the function of handicapping golfers, a particular method of serving that function may be superior to others. The feature at issue in *Plawner*, the color scheme of the Rubik's Cube, was held to be non-functional because the choice of colors was essentially arbitrary. If another aspect of the cube had been in issue, for instance, the internal design or the number of squares per side, a different result would probably have been reached. The manufacturer could not have asserted that these features were "non-functional" simply on the ground that other designs were conceivable because granting a monopoly over the "best" design of those features would have effectively excluded competition for the basic product—six-sided puzzles requiring that nine independent panels on each side be aligned in a single particular configuration.

When products or services of different providers are close substitutes for one another, the development of "industry standards" for certain aspects of the products or services will benefit consumers by facilitating comparability between and interchangeability among alternative products. The fact that any number of standards may be feasible and useful does not mean that the preferred standard is not "functional," since use of that standard promotes comparability and interchangeability. The U.S.G.A. formula is like an "industry standard": it allows the handicaps calculated by different providers to be compared with one another, much as the standard gauge of railroad track allows a locomotive of one company to run on the track of another. Allowing one provider to obtain exclusive rights in such a standard would enable it to exclude competitors desiring to provide the same product or service, particularly if the original provider, such as the U.S.G.A. in this case, starts with a virtual monopoly. To allow a monopoly over such a standard would defeat the policy of fostering competition that underlies the functionality doctrine.

The U.S.G.A. has raised no factual issues that would call into question a conclusion that the formula is "functional." Accordingly, we hold that the district court's entry of summary judgment on this aspect of the U.S.G.A.'s claim was appropriate.

C.   *The Misappropriation Claim*

The doctrine of "misappropriation," which is a distinct branch of the law of unfair competition, originated with the Supreme Court's decision in *International News Service v. Associated Press*, 248 U.S. 215, 39 S.Ct. 68, 63 L.Ed. 211(1918) ("*I.N.S.*"). The doctrine has been applied to a variety of situations in which the courts have sensed that one party was dealing "unfairly" with another, but which were not covered by the three established statutory systems protecting intellectual property:

copyright, patent, and trademark/deception as to origin.[9] The doctrine has also been the subject of considerable scholarly attention. Application of the misappropriation doctrine requires courts to contend with the basic problem of the law of intellectual property: balancing the rights of the creator of ideas or information to exploit them for commercial gain against the public's right to free access to those ideas.[10] Concomitantly, the dilemma posed by the doctrine can best be viewed as an attempt to provide the necessary incentives to the creators of intellectual property without unnecessarily restricting the public's free access to information.[11] The *I.N.S.* case illustrates the problem.

I.N.S., which was barred for political reasons by British censors from cabling its reports of the First World War to the United States, provided war coverage to the readers of its papers by buying early editions of A.P. papers and either copying or paraphrasing the A.P. reports in its own later editions. A.P. objected to this use of its stories, even though the stories were not copyrighted and even though A.P. had no protectible interest in the underlying facts it was reporting. The Court came down on the side of protecting A.P.'s investment of "labor, skill, and money" in reporting the news, against I.N.S.'s right to take that information and use it in direct competition with A.P. The Court noted that without such protection, A.P. would have little incentive to invest in newsgathering.

9. The broadest statements have gone so far as to say that any "unfair" use of an idea created by another is misappropriation. *E.g., Board of Trade v. Dow Jones & Co.,* 108 Ill.App.3d 681, 697, 64 Ill.Dec. 275, 286, 439 N.E.2d 526, 537 (1982), *aff'd,* 98 Ill.2d 109, 74 Ill.Dec. 582, 456 N.E.2d 84 (1983); *Metropolitan Opera Ass'n v. Wagner–Nichols Recorder Corp.,* 199 Misc. 786, 796, 101 N.Y.S.2d 483, 492 (1950), aff'd. 279 A.D. 632, 107 N.Y.S.2d 795 (1951). As noted below, the majority of courts has applied the doctrine more narrowly, as we do here.

10. The three statutory schemes of intellectual property law deal with this basic problem differently. Patent law preserves to the inventor the exclusive right to commercial exploitation of the invention for a limited period of time * * *. Copyright law preserves to an author the right to commercially exploit his or her works for a longer period of time * * * Substantive ideas, however, cannot be copyrighted; copyright attaches only to the form of the work. 17 U.S.C. § 102(b). Trademark law allows a business to use a mark or name to identify its products, but limits the type of mark or name which can be appropriated for that purpose. The law of false designation of origin discussed above is an offshoot of trademark law. *See* 15 U.S.C. § 1125(a). The doctrine of functionality, discussed in part II.B., limits the type of feature that can be protected for purposes of identification.

11. The dilemma can also be framed in terms of balancing the natural right of a producer in the fruits of his or her labor against the public's access right. *See* Baird, [Common Law Intellectual Property and the Legacy of International News Service v. Associated Press, 50 U.Chi.L.Rev. 411 (1983)] *supra* note 10. The constitutional provision authorizing copyrights and patents, and the statutes implementing it, are based on the "incentive" theory, in contrast to continental systems that are based on a "natural rights" theory. *I.N.S.,* however, explicitly recognized that the creator's interest is rooted in the "labor, skill and money" which has been devoted to the creation. Professor Baird believes there is little practical difference between relying on the "incentive" theory and relying on the "natural rights" theory. Baird, *supra* note 10, at 420–21. In our view, using the incentive theory to define the limits of misappropriation is more appropriate, since it is based on a "social" interest (incentives for creation) which can be balanced against another social interest (free access), while the natural rights theory requires a balancing of incommensurables.

The language of the *I.N.S.* opinion is very broad, and courts have struggled over the years to define the limits of the doctrine. The Second Circuit, under the leadership of Judge Learned Hand, sought to limit *I.N.S.* to its facts, because of the broad implications of the doctrine for limiting the use of copying in commercial competition. The doctrine survived, however, in the context of factual situations very close to that of *I.N.S. E.g., Associated Press v. KVOS, Inc.*, 80 F.2d 575 (9th Cir.1935) (radio broadcast of news taken from A.P. newspaper).

After the Supreme Court's decision in *Erie Railroad v. Tompkins*, 304 U.S. 64, 58 S.Ct. 817, 82 L.Ed. 1188 (1939), misappropriation became a question of state, rather than federal law. Although the *I.N.S.* doctrine was rejected by two federal courts interpreting the law of the state in which they were sitting, some state courts took a more expansive view of the scope of the misappropriation doctrine in the post-*Erie* era.

A federal aspect to the problem of the scope of the misappropriation doctrine was reintroduced by the Supreme Court's decisions in *Sears, Roebuck & Co. v. Stiffel Co.*, 376 U.S. 225, 84 S.Ct. 784, 11 L.Ed.2d 661 (1964), and *Compco Corp. v. Day–Brite Lighting, Inc.*, 376 U.S. 234, 84 S.Ct. 779, 11 L.Ed.2d 669 (1964). The Court held that the decision by Congress to exclude certain types of intellectual property from protection under the patent and copyright laws was a policy decision that the societal interest in free access to those ideas outweighed the need to provide incentives for their production, and that state law doctrines which protected such intellectual property were preempted by that policy decision. Subsequent decisions of the Supreme Court have made clear, however, that the misappropriation doctrine has not been completely eviscerated. The Court has not rejected the *Sears-Compro* doctrine, nor has it clearly defined where the power of the states to protect interests in intellectual property ends, and where the realm of federal preemption begins. The problem before us, therefore, is to apply the misappropriation doctrine as we believe the New Jersey courts would apply it, in light of the limitations which we believe federal preemption places on the permissible scope of state-law protection for intellectual property.

Two recent cases have grappled with these problems in a context analogous to this case. In *Board of Trade v. Dow Jones & Co.*, 98 Ill.2d 109, 74 Ill.Dec. 582, 456 N.E.2d 84 (1983), the Illinois Supreme Court upheld an injunction that barred the Chicago Board of Trade (the "CBT") from creating a stock index future contract based on the Dow Jones Industrial Average. The court based its decision on a number of factors: the fact that a significant part of the value of using the Dow Jones average is the association with Dow Jones; that "there are an infinite number of stock market indexes which could be devised" and that the CBT would be encouraged to develop a new index if it could not use Dow Jones's; and that, although Dow Jones was not licensing anyone to use its index as the basis for a stock index future at the time the CBT sought to use it, Dow Jones was entitled to protection against "misappropriation" of the index for that use. Justice Simon, joined by two of his colleagues, dissented. The dissent concentrated on the absence of "direct competition"—competition between the creator and copier in the creator's primary market—and argued that the majority's result "broadly expanded the tort of misappropriation in Illinois." 98 Ill.2d at 124, 74 Ill.Dec. at 589, 456 N.E.2d at 91.

In *Standard & Poor's Corp. v. Commodity Exchange, Inc.*, 683 F.2d 704 (2d Cir.1982), the Second Circuit, applying New York law, upheld a preliminary injunction against the Commodities Exchange ("Comex"), which was using the Standard & Poor's 500 ("S & P 500") as the basis of its stock index futures contract. In *Standard & Poor's*, the court relied on the "expenditure of time and money" in creating the index, and the competition between Comex and the Chicago Mercantile Exchange, which Standard & Poor's had licensed to create a stock market index future based on the S & P 500. Judges Newman and Knapp concurred in sustaining the preliminary injunction, deferring to the district court's analysis of the "public interest" considerations in maintaining the status quo pending trial, but declined to address the "different, novel and close" legal questions posed by Comex's use of the S & P 500 in competition with a licensee of Standard & Poor's.

This case is similar to the stock market index cases in a number of significant respects. As in the stock market index cases, the plaintiff here is seeking to exclude a rival from using a formula it has derived for commercial gain. The formulas in all three cases serve useful functions—in the stock market cases, the index is designed to track the general movement of the stock market; in this case, the formula is designed to indicate a golfer's level of competence. None of these formulas, however, is unique to its function. As a result of their creators' efforts, the respective formulas are generally accepted by the public as reliable means of performing their respective functions. Although the plaintiffs spend some time and effort updating their formulas, and also compute results by means of their formulas, the primary value of the results produced are not their inherent value in performing the underlying functions, but rather in the fact that they enable the public to discuss the underlying matters (*i.e.*, the direction of the stock market or the ability of golfers) by means of a common set of terms.

In determining whether the misappropriation doctrine should be applied in this case, however, we must keep in mind the basic policies that underlie the doctrine and its limits. In *I.N.S.*, the Court based its conclusion in substantial part on the fact that I.N.S. was using information which A.P. had developed in direct competition with A.P. in its primary market, the sale of newspapers. I.N.S.'s activity, if not checked, could have destroyed A.P.'s incentive to create the information involved, and this would not only have harmed A.P. but also would have left the public without the information. If, on the other hand, I.N.S. had used the information in a different manner—for instance, in writing a story on American correspondents covering the war—the use of A.P.'s information would not have affected A.P.'s incentive to gather the information. Although A.P. might have been better off if it had exclusive rights to such derivative uses of its information, providing legal protection might also harm the public, since A.P. might never have produced the story about correspondents covering the war. Indirect competition of this sort—use of information in competition with the creator outside of its primary market—falls outside the scope of the misappropriation doctrine, since the public interest in free access outweighs the public interest in providing an additional incentive to the creator or gatherer of information.

The competition in this case is indirect. The U.S.G.A. is not in the business of selling handicaps to golfers, but is primarily interested in the promotion of the game of golf, and in its own position as the governing body of amateur golf. The handicap formula was developed to further these two goals. A member of a golf club who obtains his handicap through his club does not pay for that service, and the U.S.G.A. is not directly affected by the number of official handicaps the clubs calculate each year or by the number of golfers who obtain handicaps. Data–Max, on the other hand, is in the business of providing "instant handicaps" to golfers, either by selling or leasing its computers to golf clubs, or by providing handicaps directly to golfers who cannot obtain "instant handicaps" through their clubs. The U.S.G.A. does not object to the sale or lease of Data–Max's computers, and does not attempt to provide the direct services which Data–Max provides to golfers. Thus, it is inconceivable that Data–Max's business will interfere with the U.S.G.A.'s incentive to maintain or update the handicap formula.

The absence of direct competition with the producer's primary use of the information was not viewed as dispositive by either the Illinois Supreme Court in *Dow Jones* or the Second Circuit in *Standard & Poor's*. The court in *Dow Jones* concluded that direct competition was unnecessary, and the court in *Standard & Poor's* found "direct competition" between S & P and Comex, even though the competition was outside S & P's primary market. Neither of these cases makes a persuasive argument for dispensing with the "direct competition" requirement. Since direct competition has generally been seen as necessary to a finding of misappropriation, and since it properly balances the competing concerns of providing incentives to producers of information while protecting free access, we believe that New Jersey would require direct competition in a misappropriation case, absent a substantial justification for making an exception.

A possible justification for dispensing with the direct competition requirement in this case, which was also present in *Dow Jones* and *Standard & Poor's*, is the fact that the information involved is so closely associated with the creator and has so little intrinsic value that the use of the information by the competitors is really an attempt to trade on the "good will" of the creator, and thus should be prohibited. The fact that the U.S.G.A. formula, like those involved in the stock market cases, is only one of a potentially large number of possible approaches to the underlying problem (quantifying the ability of golfers to enable them to compete with (and bet with) other golfers on an equitable basis) reduces the cost to the public of recognizing proprietary rights in the formula.

The presence of so many alternatives also indicates that the primary value to Data–Max of using the U.S.G.A. formula is the public acceptance that the U.S.G.A. has built up for it over the years. This public acceptance could be characterized as part of the U.S.G.A.'s "good will." We must determine, therefore, whether the New Jersey courts would interpret the misappropriation doctrine in such a way as to dispense with the "direct competition" requirement on the facts of this case.

We conclude that, at least on the facts of this case, New Jersey would not dispense with the requirement of direct competition. The public acceptance of the U.S.G.A.'s handicap formula stems from the golfing public's desire to have a uniform system of quantifying recent performances in a way that will allow equitable competition among golfers of differing abilities. The U.S.G.A., in furtherance of its role as the governing body of amateur golf, has provided such a system and, in the absence of a better system, the public has apparently accepted it. Under this state of affairs, the emergence of a single standard becomes largely a function of the need for uniformity. To require Data–Max to use a different formula would effectively destroy its ability to provide a handicapping service, since the U.S.G.A. formula is widely accepted by the golfing public. The purpose of a handicap is comparison between golfers, and handicaps based on different formulas cannot be readily compared.

We further note that expanding the misappropriation doctrine in such a way that it might give the creator of a particular idea or piece of information that has been made public a permanent monopoly over its commercial use could raise problems of preemption under the *Sears-Compco* doctrine. *See supra* notes 14–15 and accompanying text.

Because the U.S.G.A. formula is the equivalent of an "industry standard" for the golfing public, preventing other handicap providers from using it would effectively give the U.S.G.A. a national monopoly on the golf handicapping business.[24] Where such a monopoly is unnecessary to protect the basic incentive for the production of the idea or information involved, we do not believe that the creator's interest in its idea or

---

24. We note that this is a possible distinction of the stock market index cases. If a commodities exchange was to derive its own index, and if it could persuade a large enough group of investors that it performed the desired purpose better than any of the existing indices, the exchange could compete effectively with the Chicago Mercantile Exchange, which has the largest share of this business because it is licensed to use the S & P 500. There would be two obstacles to such a new index. First, since the availability of a deep and liquid market is probably more important to investors than the technical characteristics of the index which is the basis of the futures contract, a new index would probably have great difficulty competing with the CME. This same problem, however, would affect an exchange trying to set up a second market with a futures contract based on the S & P 500, and thus is extrinsic to the intellectual property question we are dealing with. Second, the Commodities Futures Trading Commission requires that such futures be based on an established index. Although this regulatory requirement might effectively give the established indices market power if they were granted the exclusive rights to use or license their own indices, we believe that this fact should have no impact on our analysis of the intellectual property questions involved in this case, but rather is a problem to be dealt with in the regulatory context. * * *

information justifies such an extensive restraint on competition. This case provides a good example of why such a restraint would harm the golfing public. Data–Max has expended time and creative energy in devising its own products and services. It has not only created the program used to calculate handicaps by computer, but has devised a handicapping service which improves on that provided by the U.S.G.A., at least to the extent that Data–Max provides a golfer with a fresh handicap faster than the U.S.G.A. does. In addition, the U.S.G.A. has not been completely deprived of the opportunity to be compensated for its "good will" in connection with the handicap formula. To the extent that the approval of the U.S.G.A. would enhance the value of "instant handicaps," the U.S.G.A. has an opportunity, if it wishes to exercise it, of offering either Data–Max or other companies the use of the U.S.G.A. name in marketing its products and services.

III. CONCLUSION

We hold that the U.S.G.A. has no legally protectible interest in its formula, and thus is not entitled to an injunction in this case. The U.S.G.A. formula is a functional aspect of its handicap system, and thus may not be protected as an identifying characteristic under either federal or New Jersey law. The false designation of origin claims are therefore legally insufficient. The "misappropriation" claim is also legally insufficient, because the use of the U.S.G.A. formula by Data–Max is not in direct competition with the U.S.G.A. We do not believe that New Jersey would dispense with the requirement of direct competition without a substantial reason, and we do not find such a reason on the facts of this case.

Accordingly, the judgment of the district court will be affirmed.

Note And Question

1. The United States Golf Association can exploit its name by making or endorsing a computer as, "The Only Computer Officially Approved by the United States Golf Association."

2. Could the United States Golf Association protect its formula by copyright? See the case below.

COMPAQ COMPUTER CORP. v. PROCOM TECHNOLOGY, INC.

United States District Court, S.D. Texas, 1995.
908 F.Supp. 1409.

HITTNER, DISTRICT JUDGE.

* * *

FACTUAL FINDINGS

[For a statement of facts see *Compaq Computer Corp. v. Procom Technology, Inc.*, above p. 47.]

* * *

F. *Procom's Products*

Procom distributes two products which are at issue in this lawsuit. The first product at issue is Procom's line of hard drives designed for use with the ProLiant server. Like Compaq, Procom purchases its drives from Seagate. Like Compaq, Procom offers a warranty program in which it agrees to replace its drives prior to failure. However, Procom did not develop its own prefailure notification system. Instead, after receiving drives from Seagate, Procom modifies the drives so that they access all features of CIM [Compaq Insight Manager], including the prefailure warnings.

Procom understood that its customers valued the features offered by CIM. Therefore, it set out to discover how it could modify its product to work in the same manner that Compaq drives work. In the early stages of developing drives that were compatible with CIM, Procom learned that it could access all features of CIM by modifying the firmware of the drives. When received from Seagate, the drives identified Seagate as the vendor in the vendor ID portion of the firmware. However, Procom discovered that by changing the vendor ID to Compaq, the requisite threshold values would be written to the drive, as described above. However, Procom decided not to market this drive because it was uncomfortable with the idea of shipping a product that incorrectly identified the vendor as Compaq.

* * *

After being sued, Procom reverted to the method of manufacture in which it changed the vendor ID in the firmware to specify Compaq as the vendor. This way, Procom did not actually copy any of the necessary data. The copying was done when the customer installed the drive and ran the EISA Config program. However, this alteration of the vendor ID has an unavoidable and unintentional consequence. When the network administrator runs CIM, a portion of the screen display identifies the vendor of the drive as Compaq. Had the drive been properly labeled as a Procom or a Seagate drive, those identifiers would appear on the screen. This result is of particular significance because the specific hard drive may not be located where it is easily accessible. Consequently, greater reliance may be placed on the screen display than would otherwise be the case if the user could simply reach over and pull the hard drive out of the server. * * *

LEGAL CONCLUSIONS

* * *

II. Procom's Second Drives

Compaq also takes issue with Procom's second, and current, line of hard drives. Procom's second line of drives differs from its first line in that these drives do not contain a copy of the M & P Partition from Compaq drives. However, the firmware of the drives has been modified to identify the vendor as Compaq rather than Procom or Seagate. Compaq contends that Procom's use of the word "Compaq" in the vendor ID portion of the drive firmware constitutes trademark infringement, counterfeiting, unfair competition, and contributory copyright infringement.

A. Trademark Infringement

Procom's use of the word "Compaq" in the vendor ID portion of a drive's firmware has two relevant consequences. First, it triggers the copying of Compaq's threshold data onto the drive where previously there had been no useful data. The second consequence is that a screen display in CIM identifies the drive as a Compaq product. As a result, Procom's use of the word Compaq in the vendor ID portion of its drives serves to incorrectly identify the vendor of the drives. Compaq contends that this misidentification constitutes trademark infringement in violation of the Lanham Act, § 32(1)(a); 15 U.S.C. § 1114(1)(a).

To prevail on its claim of trademark infringement, Compaq must demonstrate that Compaq is the owner of a valid trademark and that Procom's use of Compaq's registered trademark is likely to cause confusion. 15 U.S.C. § 1114(1)(a). Accordingly, even if there is a likelihood of confusion as to the source or vendor of Procom drives, for there to be trademark infringement, the Court must also find that Procom is the party responsible for that confusion. *Sega Enters. Ltd. v. Accolade, Inc.*, 977 F.2d 1510, 1529 (9th Cir.1992).

1. Source of Confusion

In *Sega*, Sega's "lockout code" had the secondary consequence of prompting a screen display of the Sega trademark. Both Sega and Accolade agreed that Accolade's use of Sega's lockout code was likely to cause confusion in the buyers of Accolade games. However, the Ninth Circuit found that Sega, not Accolade, was responsible for the confusion. *Sega*, 977 F.2d at 1529. In blaming Sega for the mislabeling problem, the court relied on two considerations. First, there was clear evidence that Accolade sought only to achieve compatibility with Sega's console and had no desire to represent its games as Sega products. *Id.* Second, the evidence also supported the conclusion that Sega's decision to use its trademark in connection with its lockout program was deliberate and in bad faith in that Sega intended "to lay the groundwork for the trademark prosecution of software pirates.... " *Id.*

Like Accolade, Procom did not seek to confuse its customers as to the source of the drives purchased. Although the use of the Compaq trademark was the first method by which Procom enabled prefailure warnings, it decided against using this method because it was uncomfortable with labeling its product with a competitor's name. Procom only turned to this method when it was sued for copyright infringement based on the direct copying of the threshold values. In addition, Procom labeled and packaged its products clearly to identify them as sourced from Procom. It is clear that Procom was not seeking to mislead its customers into believing they were buying Compaq hard drives.

Unlike Sega, there is no evidence that Compaq's decision to use the vendor ID portion of the drive to trigger copying of the threshold values was made with the desire to falsely label third parties products as Compaq's. The screen display which identifies Compaq as the vendor was not added to CIM in order to cause confusion or to establish a basis for a trademark infringement claim. Rather, the vendor screen display is informational—it apprises the user of who manufactured or sold the drive that is currently being used. However, Compaq did make the decision to use its trademark as the key to EISA Config. Compaq should have known the competitors would be discouraged from developing competitive products because of the risk of mislabeling. Compaq's decision to use the vendor ID portion of the drive to enable prefailure warnings had the effect of mislabeling other drives and thus, potentially excluding competitors from the market. Ultimately, the key consideration in this determination is the effect this particular use of the trademark rather than Compaq's intent. The effect of this use of the trademark is to limit competition.

2. Functionality

In addition to finding that Compaq is responsible for any potential confusion, the Court also finds that in this context, Compaq's trademark is not protectable because its use is purely functional. Functional features of a product are not protected under the Lanham Act. *Sega*, 977 F.2d at 1531. This is true even when the functional feature is a trademark. Compaq bears the burden of proving nonfunctionality.

A feature is functional if "it is essential to the use or purpose of the article or if it affects the cost or quality of the article." *Inwood Laboratories, Inc. v. Ives Laboratories, Inc.*, 456 U.S. 844, 850 n. 10, 102 S.Ct. 2182, 2187 n. 10, 72 L.Ed.2d 606 (1982). There are numerous factors the court can consider in making this assessment including the availability of alternative designs and the cost of producing those designs. *Sega*, 977 F.2d at 1531. An alternative method of production must be more than merely theoretical or speculative, it must be commercially feasible.

Part of the actual benefit that a drive purchaser wishes to buy is compatibility with CIM and its prefailure notification feature. The use of the word Compaq in the vendor ID position provides this compatibility. There is an alternative method to the use of the vendor ID and that is directly writing the threshold values to the drive. However, the Court has determined that this type of direct copying is a violation of Compaq's copyright of the threshold data. This type of alternative method cannot be considered commercially feasible since it violates copyright law.

Compaq has not established that there is any other commercially feasible method of achieving the desired result.

It is true that CIM will return prefailure warnings so long as data appears in the appropriate segment of the M & P Partition. However, the warnings have no value unless the underlying data is meaningful. While it is certainly conceivable that Procom could develop its own threshold data, there is no evidence in the record to show that this is commercially feasible. Accordingly, the use of Compaq's trademark has the functional aspect of locking out users from access to CIM.

B.   Other Trademark Claims

The Court has determined that Procom has not violated the Lanham Act and that Compaq is responsible for any confusion related to Procom's second line of drives. Accordingly, Procom is not liable for common law trademark infringement or unfair competition, nor has it violated of § 16.29 of the Texas Business and Commerce Code. * * *

IV.   Procom's Advertisements

Compaq alleges that two sets of Procom advertisements, one depicting a Compaq drive tray, and another referencing the compatibility of Procom drives with CIM, constitute false advertising in violation of section 43(a) of the Lanham Act. Section 43(a)(2) provides for a cause of action for what is commonly called false advertising.[18] When challenging a competitor's advertising under this section, a plaintiff must show that either "1) the challenged advertisement is literally false, or 2) while the advertisement is literally true it is nevertheless likely to mislead or confuse customers." *Johnson & Johnson Merck v. Smithkline Beecham Corp.*, 960 F.2d 294, 297 (2d Cir.1992); *see also Castrol Inc. v. Pennzoil Co.*, 987 F.2d 939, 943 (3d Cir.1993) (holding that in a false advertising claim, "a plaintiff must prove *either* literal falsity *or* consumer confusion, but not both.").

A.   Drive Tray Advertisements

The first set of advertisements that Compaq complains of involve hard drive trays. When these ads were first developed, they showed Procom hard drives mounted on trays displaying a Compaq logo. At the time the ad was prepared, it was neither false nor misleading. That is, Procom was able to deliver exactly what was depicted in the ad—Procom drives mounted on Compaq trays. However, some time after the ads

---

18.   Section 43(a) of the Lanham Act, as amended, codifies two major types of unfair competition: infringement on marks, names and trade dress, regardless of whether registered, and false advertising. The false advertising component of § 43(a) states:

(a) Any person who, on or in connection with any goods or services, or any container for goods, uses in commerce any word, term, name, symbol, or device, or any combination thereof, or any false designation of origin, false or misleading description of

fact, or false or misleading representation of fact, which—

. . .

(2) in commercial advertising or promotion, misrepresents the nature, characteristics, qualities, or geographic origin of his or her or another person's goods, services, or commercial activities, shall be liable in a civil action by any person who believes that he or she is or is likely to be damaged by such act.

were published, Procom began to use third party trays rather than Compaq trays. Shortly after this switch to third party trays, Procom modified its advertisement by overlaying a Procom logo on top of the Compaq logo. Despite this alteration, a thin straight line at the bottom of the Compaq logo remained visible on the face of the tray. The lag time between the tray switch and the ad modification was about forty days.

During the lag time between the switch to third party trays, and the alteration of the ads, the ads falsely represented that Procom was selling Compaq trays when it was not. This conduct violates the Lanham Act. However, this conduct was short-lived and has long since been discontinued. As Compaq is seeking only injunctive relief, the Court considers the grant of an injunction unnecessary.

Procom modified ads, displaying a Compaq tray with a Procom logo, are more problematic. In most situations, the use of a photograph of the plaintiff's product to advertise the defendant's product is a § 43(a) violation. This type of conduct includes situations, like the one presented here, where the defendant removes the plaintiff's logo and substitutes their own.

However, despite Procom's use of an altered Compaq tray in its ads, the Court does not believe that Procom violated section 43(a). It is true that the tray depicted in the challenged ads was a Compaq tray. However, the drive trays that Procom was selling at that time were virtually identical to the Compaq trays. So similar in fact, that Compaq asserted a trade dress infringement claim relative to Procom's trays. The differences between the trays are not easily observable when looking at the actual trays, and even less so when looking at a black and white photograph of them. Given that the differences between the displayed product and the actual product are slight, there is little chance that a customer could be misled by the photograph in Procom's ads. In the absence of any chance that customers will be deceived or misled by the false depiction, the ad does not violate the Lanham Act.

B. *Compatibility Advertisements*

The second group of Procom ads that Compaq takes issue with contain statements that Procom drives are "100% compatible" and "fully compatible" with CIM and the ProLiant server. Compaq asserts that both of these claims are false in violation of § 43 of the Lanham Act. Compaq bears the burden of proving that Procom's claims of compatibility are false or misleading. In the absence of an industry standard stating otherwise, the word "compatibility" has been defined as meaning "works with" or "functions with" another device. *Princeton Graphics Operating, L.P. v. NEC Home Electronics (U.S.A.), Inc.*, 732 F.Supp. 1258, 1261, 1262 n. 9 (S.D.N.Y.1990). This definition applies equally to the terms "100% compatible" and "fully compatible" as well merely "compatible," as no other meaning for the former terms has been demonstrated.

Compaq relies on the following evidence in support of its false advertising allegation. First, Procom's first drives contained prefailure threshold values that differed from Compaq's. Second, Procom's first drives did not have a cover to shield the drive from electrostatic discharge. Finally, Procom's first trays had large openings in the bottom that allowed the user to touch the exposed components of the drive. Without disputing this evidence, the Court nonetheless determines that it does not support a finding that Procom's ads were in violation of the Lanham Act.

Compaq does not deny that CIM will return the full range of outputs when run on a Procom drive. Rather, Compaq contends that Procom's claims of compatibility are false and misleading because the prefailure warnings occur at the wrong time. That is, Procom drives will trigger prefailure warnings at a different point in time than do Compaq drives. However, Compaq has not established there is a wrong time for the drive to be replaced. Clearly, a wrong time for prefailure replacement would be after the drives have actually failed. However, Compaq merely speculated that this could happen with the threshold values contained on Procom's drives. There is no evidence that this could in fact happen. Short of actual drive failure, it is not clear that there is a "right time" for prefailure warnings to issue. Since CIM returns the same range of outputs on Procom drives that it does with Compaq drives, Procom drives "work with" and "function with" CIM. Accordingly, the Court finds that Procom's ads are not literally false.

In addition, the Court find that Compaq has not established the misleading nature of Procom's claims. The appropriate reference point for this determination is the message conveyed by the challenged statements to the target audience. *Johnson & Johnson Merck*, 960 F.2d at 297–98; *Coca-Cola Co. v. Tropicana Prod. Inc.*, 690 F.2d 312, 317 (2d Cir.1982). Compaq did not present any evidence of how consumers interpret Procom's claims of 100% compatibility. It is conceivable that consumers view this message as a representation that Procom drives will trigger prefailure warnings at the same time that Compaq drives do. However, this is not the only possible interpretation of the statements, "100% compatible" and "fully compatible." Moreover, it is not for the Court to substitute its own opinion as to the meaning of these statements. In the absence of proof as to how the relevant market segment construed these representations, the Court cannot find that they were misleading.

Similarly, with respect to the differences between Compaq trays and Procom trays, Compaq has not shown that these differences make the representations of full compatibility false or misleading. The trays work with the ProLiant server in that drives mounted on these trays are hot-pluggable. Compaq has made no showing that 100% compatibility requires that Procom trays have an electrostatic discharge shield or smaller openings on the bottom of the tray. Aspects of Compaq's product which make it more desirable, and which are not featured in Procom's product are not necessarily required for a showing that Procom's product fully functions with the server. *B.H. Bunn Co. v. AAA Replacement Parts Co.*, 451 F.2d 1254, 1269 (5th Cir.1971). Therefore, the Court determines that Compaq has not made the requisite showing of falsity or misleading character necessary to sustain a claim under § 43(a). * * *

Notes

1. For many years each issue of Playboy Magazine has contained pictures of the "Playmate of the Month." Each year Playboy Magazine has selected a "Playmate of the Year." The defendant in the next case, Ms. Terri Welles, was Playboy Magazine's "Playmate of the Year" ("PMOY") for 1981.

2. The standard programming language for websites allows the insertion of "metatags." These contain information, which is not displayed on the screen but which is used by search engines, such as Altavista, Lycos, Excite, and Google, which index the Internet. When this casebook was published, the website of Terri Welles contained the following metatags.

<META NAME="keywords" CONTENT="terri, welles, playmate, playboy, * * *" >

The result of the inclusion of these "metatags" would be to lead web surfers who typed "playboy" or "playmate" into a search engine to Ms. Welles's homepage.

2. There are various other ways of coding webpages that will influence indexing. For instance, many search engines give high weight to the titles of pages. One of the pages on Ms. Welles's website, for instance, included the following line of code:

<TITLE>Terri Welles, PMOY '81</TITLE>

Search engines would pick up this code and would lead web surfers to Ms. Welles's website if they typed in "PMOY," the abbreviation of "Playmate of the Year."

PLAYBOY ENTERPRISES, INC.
v. TERRI WELLES, INC.

United States District Court, S.D. California, 1999.
78 F.Supp.2d 1066.

KEEP, J.

* * *

I. BACKGROUND

The following background facts are taken in large part from the court's April 22, 1998 order denying Plaintiff's motion for preliminary injunction:

Plaintiff Playboy Enterprises, Inc. (PEI) is an international publishing and entertainment company. Since 1953, PEI has published *Playboy* magazine, a widely popular magazine with approximately ten (10) million readers each month. PEI also publishes numerous specialty magazines such as *Playboy's Playmate Review*, *Playboy's Playmates of the Year*, and *Playboy's Calendar Playmates* among other publications. In addition to its publishing ventures, PEI produces television programming for cable and direct-to-home satellite transmission and sells and licenses various goods and services including videos.

PEI has established two websites. According to Plaintiff, its free website, http://www.playboy.com, has become one of the most popular sites on the Web and is used to promote its magazine, goods, and services. Its other website, called the "Playboy Cyber Club," http://www.cyber.playboy.com, is devoted to promoting current and former PEI models.

PEI owns federally registered trademarks for the terms *Playboy*, *Playmate*, *Playmate of the Month*, and *Playmate of the Year*. The term *Playmate of the Year* is sometimes abbreviated "PMOY." PEI does not have a federally registered trademark in the abbreviation "PMOY," although PEI argues that "PMOY" is worthy of trademark protection because it is a well-known abbreviation for the trademark *Playmate of the Year*.

Defendant Terri Welles is a self-employed model and spokesperson, who began her modeling career with *Playboy* magazine in 1980. In May of 1980, Ms. Welles appeared on the cover of *Playboy* magazine and was subsequently featured as the "Playmate of the Month" in the December 1980 issue. Ms. Welles received the "Playmate of the Year" award in June of 1981. Since 1980, Ms. Welles has appeared in no less than thirteen (13) issues of *Playboy* magazine and eighteen (18) newsstand specials published by PEI. Ms. Welles claims that since 1980 she has always referred to herself as a "Playmate" or "Playmate of the Year" with the knowledge of PEI.

On June 29, 1997, Ms. Welles opened a website, http://www.terriwelles.com, which includes photographs of herself and others (both nude and clothed), a fan club posting board, an autobiography section, and a listing of current events and personal appearances. The domain name for Defendant Welles' site is "terriwelles," the heading for the website is "Terri Welles—Playmate of the Year 1981," and the title of the link page is "Terri Welles—Playboy Playmate of the Year 1981." Each of the pages uses "PMOY '81" as a repeating watermark in the background. According to Defendant, eleven (11) of the fifteen (15) free web pages include a disclaimer at the bottom of the pages, in varying font sizes depending on the page, which indicates that the website is not endorsed by PEI; the disclaimer reads as follows: "This site is neither endorsed, nor sponsored by, nor affiliated with Playboy Enterprises, Inc. PLAYBOY, PLAYMATE OF THE YEAR and PLAYMATE OF THE MONTH are registered trademarks of Playboy Enterprises, Inc." Defendant Welles uses the terms *Playboy* and *Playmate* along with other terms within the keywords section of the meta tags, which constitutes the internal index of the website used by some search engines. The site contains link pages to other erotic, adult-oriented websites. It also contains advertising "banners" for some of those websites.

Since May of 1997, Ms. Welles has been in contact with Plaintiff about the design and creation of her website. Defendant claims that Plaintiff, through Marcia Terrones, the director of the "Rights and Permission" department at PEI, informed her that she could identify herself as the "Playmate of the Year 1981" but that she could not reproduce the rabbit head logo on her proposed website. Various communications between Defendant and Plaintiff ensued. According to Defendant, PEI, through Hugh Hefner, initially complimented her website and encouraged her use of the title "Playmate of the Year 1981." However, Mr. Hefner later informed Defendant that use of PEI's trademarks were restricted; instead, he invited Defendant to join PEI's new Cyber Club. Defendant refused this invitation, and PEI continued to demand that Defendant remove the "Playmate of the Year" title from the home page as well as remove the PMOY watermark from the background.

* * *

III. DISCUSSION

A. *Defendant Terri Welles, Terri Welles, Inc., and Pippi, Inc.*

1. *Counts I Through VII: Fair Use Defense*

Plaintiff alleges seven distinct trademark-related claims: 1) trademark infringement pursuant to 15 U.S.C. § 1114(1); 2) false designation of origin and unfair competition under 15 U.S.C. § 1125(a); 3) dilution of trademarks pursuant to 15 U.S.C. § 1125(c); 4) trademark infringement and unfair competition under California common law; 5) unfair competition in violation of Cal. Bus. & Prof.Code § 17200, *et seq.*; 6) trademark counterfeiting pursuant to 15 U.S.C. § 1114(1); and 7) dilution of trademark in violation of Cal. Bus. & Prof.Code § 14335. Defendant Welles asserts that she should be granted summary judgment on all seven claims because there is no dispute of material fact that Ms. Welles uses the terms "Playboy" and "Playmate" in a non-trademark manner to describe her status as a recipient of titles bestowed upon her by Plaintiff and to describe the content of her website. In other words, Defendant Welles argues that because her use of the terms "Playboy" and "Playmate" on her website is a "fair use" as a matter of law, she should be entitled to summary judgment as to all of Plaintiff's trademark-related claims against her.

A trademark is a "limited property right in a particular word, phrase, or symbol." *New Kids on the Block v. News America Publishing, Inc.*, 971 F.2d 302, 306 (9th Cir.1992). The purpose of a trademark is limited to the identification of the source of a good or service. *See id.* at 305. The "wrong protected against ... [has been] traditionally equally limited: [p]reventing producers from free-riding on their rivals' marks" and capitalizing on their rivals' investment of time, money, and resources. *Id.* Where a trademark also describes a person, place, or an attribute of a product, however, the "policies of free competition and free use of language dictate that trademark law cannot forbid the commercial use of terms in their descriptive sense." 1 J. MCCARTHY, TRADEMARKS AND

UNFAIR COMPETITION, § 11.45, at 82 (1999). Thus, trademark law, as embodied in the Lanham Act, recognizes a "fair use" defense—the concept that a trademark registrant or holder cannot "appropriate a descriptive term for his exclusive use and so prevent others from accurately describing a characteristic of their goods." *New Kids*, 971 F.2d at 306 (*quoting Soweco, Inc. v. Shell Oil Co.*, 617 F.2d 1178, 1185 (5th Cir.1980)).

Fair use is a defense to liability under the Lanham Act. *See* 15 U.S.C. §§ 1115(b)(4) and 1125(c)(4) (1999). The assertion by an alleged infringer that it is only using the contested term, mark, or designation at issue in a non-trademark, descriptive sense has become known as the "fair use" doctrine or defense. *See* 1 J. MCCARTHY, TRADEMARKS AND UNFAIR COMPETITION, § 11.45, at 80 (1999). Section 33(b)(4) of the Lanham Act codifies the fair use defense and states that the "right to use the registered mark . . . shall be subject to the . . . defense[ ] . . . [t]hat the use of the name, term, or device charged to be an infringement is a use, otherwise than as a mark . . . of a term or device which is descriptive of and used fairly and in good faith only to describe the goods or services of such party." 15 U.S.C. 1115(b) and (b)(4) (1999). A common law fair use defense incorporates the statutory elements of the Lanham Act § 33(b)(4) so that if the defendant's use is a fair use as against an assertion of a registered trademark, then it is also fair use as against a state statutory or common law count. *See* 1 J. MCCARTHY, TRADEMARKS AND UNFAIR COMPETITION, § 11.49, at 93–94 (1999) (*citing Sierra On–Line, Inc. v. Phoenix Software, Inc.*, 739 F.2d 1415, 1423 (9th Cir.1984) and *Zatarains, Inc. v. Oak Grove Smokehouse, Inc.*, 698 F.2d 786, 789 (5th Cir.1983)).

Section 33(b)(4) requires a defendant to prove three elements in order to establish a fair use defense:

1. Defendant's use of the term is not as a trademark or service mark.

2. Defendant uses the term "fairly and in good faith."

3. Defendant uses the term "*[o]nly* to describe" its goods or services.

1 J. MCCARTHY, TRADEMARKS AND UNFAIR COMPETITION, § 11.49, at 94 .1 (1999) (*quoting* 15 U.S.C. 1115(b)(4) (1999)).

Under element one, the only type of use which suffices as a "fair use" is use by a defendant of a term, mark, or symbol in a non-trademark sense. Under element two, a lack of good faith use may be inferred from: (1) a defendant's intentional breach of an agreement not to use the disputed mark; or (2) a defendant's use with the intent to "trade upon and dilute the good will" of a plaintiff's mark. *See* 1 J. MCCARTHY, TRADEMARKS AND UNFAIR COMPETITION, § 11.49, at 94.1 (1999). Finally, under element three, the statutory phrase "to describe the goods" is not restricted to words that describe a characteristic of the goods but rather the phrase can be applied to words that are descriptive in the broader sense.

Although Section 33(b)(4) makes no mention of a requirement that there be an absence of likelihood of confusion, the majority of courts, including the Ninth Circuit, have espoused the view that it is inconsistent to find both a likelihood of confusion and fair use. *See id.* at § 11.47, at 85–86. According to this reasoning, because the primary purpose of trademark law is to prevent likely confusion as to the origin, sponsor, or source of a mark, a showing of likely confusion bars a defendant's reliance on the fair use defense. *See Lindy Pen Co. v. Bic Pen Corp.*, 725 F.2d 1240 (9th Cir.1984), *cert. denied*, 469 U.S. 1188, 105 S.Ct. 955, 83 L.Ed.2d 962 (1985). Thus, in order to comply with the statutory requirement of § 33(b)(4) of the Lanham Act that "Defendant's use of the term is not as a trademark or service mark," 15 U.S.C. 1115(b)(4) (1999), the Ninth Circuit has held that a defendant invoking the fair use defense must also establish that its fair use is not likely to cause confusion or did not "lead to customer confusion as to the source of the goods or services." *Transgo, Inc. v. Ajac Transmission Parts Corp.*, 911 F.2d 363, 366 (9th Cir.1990) (*citing Zatarains, Inc. v. Oak Grove Smokehouse, Inc.* 698 F.2d 786, 791 (5th Cir.1983)). The Ninth Circuit has articulated an eight-factor test, known as the *Sleekcraft* test, which the court may consider in determining the likelihood of confusion: 1) the strength of the mark; 2) proximity or relatedness of the goods; 3) similarity in appearance, sound, and meaning of the marks; 4) evidence of actual confusion; 5) degree to which the marketing channels converge; 6) type of good and degree of care customers are likely to exercise in purchasing them; 7) evidence of the intention of defendant in selecting and using the alleged infringing name; and 8) likelihood that the parties will expand their product lines.

Notwithstanding the Ninth Circuit's clear adoption of the view that a fair use cannot simultaneously be a confusing use, it recently decided in 1991 in the case of *New Kids on the Block v. News America Publishing, Inc.* that there is a different type of fair use that "lies outside the strictures of trademark law" because it "does not implicate the source-identification function." *New Kids on the Block v. News America Publishing, Inc.*, 971 F.2d 302, 308 (9th Cir.1992). The court in *New Kids* described this type of fair use as a "nominative use of a mark—where the only word reasonably available to describe a particular thing is pressed into service." *Id.* Under the *New Kids* standard, a court does not conduct the traditional analysis of likelihood of confusion promulgated in *AMF, Inc. v. Sleekcraft Boats*, 599 F.2d 341, 351 (9th Cir.1979) that is used in the "classic fair use case" but rather conducts a special three-pronged analysis for the new type of fair use defense entitled "a nominative fair use defense." *Id.* The court in *New Kids* was clear in asserting that the *New Kids* analysis only governs in special, atypical cases and that it did not "purport to alter the test applicable in the paradigmatic fair use case." *Id.* In deciding whether Defendant Welles is entitled to summary judgment on Plaintiff's trademark claims, the court will consider whether this case falls under the classic fair use case or the non-paradigmatic nominative fair use case; the court's analysis of this question and the issue of likelihood of confusion will be discussed *infra*, in section III(A)(1)(a)(1)(iii), of this order.

Plaintiff alleges that Ms. Welles cannot invoke the fair use defense because her use of Plaintiff's trademarks on her website (1) is a trademark use; (2) which creates a likelihood of confusion; and (3) which "goes farther than, or is out of proportion to, a fair description of PEI or Ms. Welles on the website." Plaintiff's Opposition, at 15. Plaintiff makes these allegations in regards to four specific uses by Defendant Welles on her website: (i) use of the Playmate term in the visual title or masthead for the website; (ii) use of the abbreviation, "PMOY '81," as a repetitive, decorative watermark on pages throughout her site; (iii) use of the Playboy and Playmate terms in advertising banners on her site *and* in *other* websites to attract customers to click through to Welles' site; and (iv) use of the Playboy and Playmate terms in the HTML source code, including the HTML title, meta code description, and meta tag keywords. The HTML source code is the coding that is used for construction of a website's pages.

The court will address in turn each of these specific uses by Ms. Welles with respect to her invocation of the fair use defense. Because Plaintiff's analyses in its opposition papers regarding the uses specified in (I) (*sic*), (ii), and (iii) in the above paragraph are intimately interconnected, the court will group together for discussion in the first section, section (a), the visible uses of PEI trademarked terms in the title or masthead, in the repeating watermarks, and in the advertising banners. In the second section, section (b), the court will address the issue of the use of PEI trademarked terms in the HTML source code, including the source title and the metatags.

(a) *Visible Use of PEI Trademarked Terms: Title or Masthead, Watermarks, and Advertising Banners*

(1) *Overview of Plaintiff's Allegations*

This section summarizes Plaintiff's allegations. In support of its allegations, Plaintiff relies solely on the appearance of the website or on its expert witness' (James Sterne's) opinions regarding the website. Following this summary, in section (2), is an analysis of the sufficiency of Plaintiff's allegations in light of Defendant's summary judgment motion.

(i) *Title or Masthead*

The visual title at the top of Ms. Welles' website reads, "Terri Welles Playmate of the Year, 1981." *See* Decl. of Cynthia Johnston, PEI Legal Department Staff, Ex. J. The name "Terri Welles" is in large, filled-in block letters, overlapping and dwarfing the designation, "Playmate of the Year, 1981." *See id.* The words, "Playmate of the Year, 1981," are in slender, cursive script letters. *See id.* From the court's color copy of the exhibit, it appears that all the words in "Terri Welles Playmate of the Year, 1981" are of similar coloring, but that the words,

"Playmate of the Year, 1981," appear of a slightly lighter shade than the words "Terri Welles" so that they are visible under the overlapping block letters of the name "Terri Welles." *See id.* Plaintiff argues that Ms. Welles' "prominent, stylized and memorable use of PEI's trademarks operates to ... attract the attention of consumers to defendant's website," "borrow[s] from the cachet of the PEI marks," and "trade [s] off of the good will of those marks." Plaintiff further contends that Defendant Welles' trademark uses of the PEI marks are like "placing the marks on a sign above the entrance to a store, on the front of an advertising brochure, or on a product. They create source identification due to their context, prominence, location and stylization." Opposition, at 10 (*citing* Decl. of James Sterne ("Sterne Decl."), PEI Expert Witness, ¶ ¶ 7–9). Specifically, Plaintiff asserts, through its expert witness James Sterne and in its opposition briefs, that (1) Ms. Welles' site is a predominantly commercial site; (2) The visible title banner on the homepage is a prominent commercial use of the Playboy term; (3) The commercial theme is "Playboy Playmate of the Year"; (4) The visible use of the terms in the title banner and the subject headings along the left-hand side of the homepage (along with the repeating PMOY background watermark and the references in the HTML code and metatags) create a repetitive use of the Playboy and Playmate terms; (5) Title banners or mastheads at the top of a commercial website do not serve the same function as book titles, but rather serve to identify the "source" of the website and its products; (6) This "source identification effect" is a result of the context of the use (commercial), prominence of the use (repetition and size), the location of the use (in title banner, source code, advertising banner, and wallpaper), and the stylization of the use (in script letters as product name and repetition of PMOY). *See* Sterne Decl ., ¶ ¶ 8–11, at 4–5.

(ii) *Watermarks*

Plaintiff alleges that Defendant Welles' repeating background watermark, "PMOY '81" is a trademark use. PMOY is an abbreviation for Plaintiff's federally-registered trademark, "Playmate of the Year." It is undisputed that the abbreviation PMOY is not a registered trademark under state or federal law, although Plaintiff's application for registration of the PMOY trademark, filed on April 5, 1999, is currently pending in the United States Trademark and Patent Office. However, since "[i]t is not necessary that a trademark be registered in order for it to qualify for protection under the Lanham Act," *Metro Publishing v. San Jose Mercury News*, 987 F.2d 637 (9th Cir.1993), and since Section 33(b)(4) also allows the elements of a fair use defense to be asserted against an allegation of infringement of an *unregistered* mark brought into federal court under § 43(a) of the Lanham Act, *see* 1 J. MCCARTHY, TRADEMARKS AND UNFAIR COMPETITION, § 11.49, at 93–94 (1999) (emphasis added) (citations omitted), the court shall treat its discussion of Welles' fair use of PEI's unregistered trademarked term "PMOY" in the watermarks in the same manner as its discussion of PEI's registered terms "Playboy,"

"Playmate," and "Playmate of the Year" in other areas of Ms. Welles' website.

The "PMOY" abbreviation is used as a watermark on the homepage as well as on the other pages throughout the website. Specifically, Plaintiff contends that "PMOY" appears on the web pages on which Ms. Welles solicits paid subscriptions to the "Members Only" portion of her website, sells pictures of herself, and solicits paid promotional appearances. *See* Opposition, at 7. According to Plaintiff, rather than being related to any editorial comment or description of Ms. Welles or PEI, these watermarks are a "repetitive, prominent, and plainly commercial use of PEI's marks to identify defendant's business, goods, and services." *Id.*

(iii) *Advertising Banners*

Ms. Welles has created special advertising banners for her website: rectangular-shaped boxes which contain a photograph of Ms. Welles, the name "Terri Welles," and a designation that uses the term "Playmate" and/or "Playboy." There are two forms of the advertising banners; both contain a semi-nude photograph of Ms. Welles, and the title or name of the website. *See id.* One of the titles states, "Terri Welles Playboy Playmate of the Year '81," and the other states, "Playmate of the Year 1981 Terri Welles." *See id.* at Ex. D. In both of the banners, "Terri Welles" appears in script letters of a different coloring and of a larger size than the corresponding descriptors, "Playboy Playmate of the Year '81" and "Playmate of the Year 1981." *See id.* at Ex. D. These banners can be "borrowed" and "cut and pasted" by other website owners from her website to other websites. This process is accomplished by a user clicking on the banner on Ms. Welles' website and copying and transporting the underlying source code to the third party website. *See* Opposition, at 7.

Plaintiff makes several contentions regarding the use of the advertising banners: (1) Anyone can "grab" these banners from defendant's website, and by doing so, include PEI's trademarks on the face of their website and in the source code; (2) Defendant's motivation for these banners is to attract click through traffic from other adult websites and increase her ranking among search engines that rank, in part, on the basis of a number of links to a website; and (3) An internet user who clicks through to defendant's website by clicking on the advertising banner on a third party website will likely know nothing about Ms. Welles' site other than the references on the banner—adult entertainment, the PEI trademark, and Ms. Welles' identification as a Playmate. *See* Opposition, at 7–8.

(2) *Analysis*

* * *

The court finds that on the papers submitted to it on the summary judgment motion, Defendant Welles has met her burden in establishing sufficient facts to support a finding that she is entitled to a fair use defense. * * *

(i) *Only To Describe the Goods or Services*

There is no dispute as to the fact that the phrase "Playmate of the Year 1981" is descriptive of Ms. Welles and her on-line services in the sense that the title actually describes the product(s) being sold. Terri Welles was and is the "Playmate of the Year for 1981"—Plaintiff has conceded this fact. It was a title earned by and bestowed upon Ms. Welles as a Playboy model, a title which has become part of her identity and adds value and "prestige" to her name. Hugh Hefner, the owner and president of PEI, stated that becoming a Playboy Playmate was certainly "the first stepping stone" in establishing some women's fame and that the advantages of a woman becoming a Playmate are "celebrity, first and foremost." *See* Decl. of David Noonan, Defendant Welles' Counsel, Ex. 1 ("Deposition of Hugh Hefner") (hereafter, "Hefner Deposition"), at 7–8, 43. Furthermore, Mr. Hefner has admitted that PEI "has always encouraged Playmates or Playmates of the Year to use their fame to promote themselves or make a living in connection with television ... radio .. [a]nd movies." *Id.* at 54–55. Therefore, it is undisputed that the "Playmate" title of a Playmate model is a designation that either has, or is intended to have, public recognition.

Ms. Welles earned the title of "Playboy Playmate of the Year" in 1981 and has used that title ever since, without objection from PEI— until the inception of this lawsuit. Although it is undeniable that the term "Playboy" and "Playmate" are suggestive trademarks in which Plaintiff has a vested property right as the senior user, it is equally indisputable that the title has become part of Ms. Welles' identity to the public, in much the same way as her name identifies her to others. Not surprisingly, it has been noted that the fair use defense is founded upon the same principles as the defense of the right to use one's own personal name. *See* 1 J. MCCARTHY, TRADEMARKS AND UNFAIR COMPETITION, § 11.45, at 81 (1999). The concept that there should be some qualified right to use one's own name as a mark has resulted in a great reluctance of judges to issue an absolute injunction against any use, even trademark use, of a personal name mark. *See id.* at § 13.9, at 17. Courts have generally refused to "wholly forbid a man to do business in his own name" since "[t]o prevent all use of it [personal name] is to take away his identity; without it he cannot make known who he is to those who may wish to deal with him; and that is so grievous an injury that courts will avoid imposing it, if they possibly can." *Id.* at § 13.9, at 17 (citations omitted). As the Ninth Circuit stated in *New Kids,* "sometimes there is no descriptive substitute ... For example, one might refer to 'the two-time world champions' or 'the professional basketball team from Chicago,' but it's far simpler (and more likely to be understood) to refer to the Chicago Bulls." 971 F.2d at 306. Likewise, given that Ms. Welles is the "Playmate of the Year 1981," there is no other way that Ms. Welles can identify or describe herself and her services without venturing into absurd descriptive phrases. To describe herself as the "nude model selected by Mr. Hefner's magazine as its number-one prototypical woman for the year 1981" would be impractical as well as ineffectual in identifying Terri Welles to the public. This is especially true since, as Mr. Hefner has admitted, "most people around the world that are familiar with Playboy magazine would refer to these women as Playmates." Hefner Deposition, pp. 43–44. In such a case as this, use of the trademarks, "Playmate of the Year 1981," "Playboy Playmate of the Year 1981," and "PMOY '81," is purely *nominative* and "does not imply sponsorship or endorsement of the product because the marks are used only to describe the thing, rather than to identify its source." *Id*. Accordingly, the court finds that the use of the terms "Playmate of the Year 1981," "Playboy Playmate of the Year 1981," and "PMOY '81" in the visible portions of Defendant Welles' website is descriptive of Ms. Welles; it is her services and goods being described, and the public identifies her by the titles bestowed upon her by PEI.

(ii) *Used Fairly and in Good Faith*

Plaintiff correctly points out that bad faith can be inferred from evidence of an intent to "trade upon and dilute the good will" of a defendant's mark. *See Institute for Scientific Information, Inc. v. Gordon & Breach, Science Publishers, Inc.*, 931 F.2d 1002, (3d. Cir.1991), *cert. denied*, 502 U.S. 909, 112 S.Ct. 302, 116 L.Ed.2d 245 (1991)) (*sic*). Although Plaintiff implies that Ms. Welles is acting in bad faith when it asserts that she used its trademarked terms with the intent to "trade off of the good will" of PEI's marks, Opposition at 9, the court finds that Plaintiff has failed to identify any conduct of Ms. Welles that is sufficiently blameworthy. For example, Plaintiff has failed to state any facts which indicate that Ms. Welles' use of the PEI trademarked terms was improperly motivated. *Cf. Marcus v. Rowley, et al.*, 695 F.2d 1171, 1175 (9th Cir.1983) (in copyright infringement case, since fair use presupposes that the defendant has acted fairly and in good faith, the propriety of the defendant's conduct should also be weighed in analyzing the purpose and character of the use). Insofar as Plaintiff alleges that Defendant Welles' failure to seek written permission from PEI prior to her website use of PEI trademarked terms was evidence of bad faith, the court rejects this argument. The Supreme Court stated in *Campbell v. Acuff–Rose Music, Inc.* that being denied permission to use a work does not weigh against a finding of good faith fair use. *Campbell v. Acuff–Rose Music, Inc.*, 510 U.S. 569, 585, 114 S.Ct. 1164, 127 L.Ed.2d 500 (1994) (*citing Fisher v. Dees*, 794 F.2d 432, 437 (9th Cir.1986) The Supreme Court elaborated, "[W]e reject [plaintiff's] argument that [defendant's] request for permission to use the original should be weighed against a finding of fair use ... [The defendant's] actions do not necessarily suggest that they believed their version was not fair use; the offer may simply have been made in a good-faith effort to avoid this litigation. If the use is otherwise fair, then no permission need be sought or granted." *Id*. at 585, n. 18.

Contrary to Plaintiff's unsupported allegations of bad faith, Ms. Welles provides uncontroverted evidence that she sought to take precautions to ensure that her use of PEI's trademarked terms in her website was permitted by PEI. *See* Decl. of Terri Welles, ¶ ¶ 8–9, 17 and Exs. 2, 9–10. For example, in an effort to "avoid threatened litigation," Ms. Welles has removed some references per Plaintiff's request and made changes to her website consisting of: (1) adding disclaimers to the bottom of most pages of her website; (2) including a hyperlink from her website to www.playboy.com; (3) substituting the visual title of "Playboy Playmate of the Year 1981" to "Terri Welles, Playmate of the Year, 1981;" (4) removing the images of three Playboy covers; (5) removing any image which PEI contended was a PEI-copyrighted image. *See id.* at ¶ ¶ 19–20. Furthermore, it is undisputed that she does not use "Playboy" or "Playmate" in her domain name, she does not use in the "Playmate of the Year 1981" title a font recognizable as a Playboy magazine font, and she does not use the classic Playboy bunny logo. These factors indicate that Plaintiff has not intended to "misle[a]d or confuse[ ] [the consumer] as to the source of the different products or services." *WSM, Inc. v. Hilton*, 724 F.2d 1320, 1329 (8th Cir.1984) (holding that "the essential question in any case of alleged trademark infringement is whether purchasers are likely to be misled or confused as to the source of the different products or services"). Finally, the unavailability of other phrases to accurately describe Ms. Welles and her business bolsters the court's finding of good faith. *See Sierra On–Line, Inc. v. Phoenix Software, Inc.*, 739 F.2d 1415, 1423 (9th Cir.1984) (choice of the phrase "HiRes Adventure" when other phrases were available could indicate bad faith) (citations omitted). Therefore, the court finds that Ms. Welles has established sufficient evidence to show that under the Lanham Act § 33(b)(4), PEI's trademarked terms in her visible website are "used fairly and *in good faith* only to describe [her] goods or services." 15 U.S.C. 1115(b)(4) (1999) (emphasis added).

(iii) *"Otherwise Than as a Mark"*

The bulwark of Plaintiff's arguments are concentrated on this prong of the fair use defense: whether Ms. Welles' use of PEI terms is "otherwise than as a mark." The governing law in the Ninth Circuit is that in order to constitute a non-trademark, "fair use," the use cannot amount to a trademark infringement or unfair competition. *See Lindy Pen Co. v. Bic Pen Corp.*, 725 F.2d 1240, 1248 (9th Cir.1984), *cert. denied*, 469 U.S. 1188, 105 S.Ct. 955, 83 L.Ed.2d 962 (1985). The keystone of whether a use constitutes trademark infringement or unfair competition is the avoidance of a likelihood of confusion in the minds of the buying public. *See id.* at 1243; *see also* 1 J. McCarthy, Trademarks and Unfair Competition, § 2.8, at 15 (1999). Thus, the dispositive issue in deciding whether there is a genuine dispute of material fact as to Ms. Welles's non-trademark use of PEI trademarked terms in her website is the likelihood of confusion.

The Ninth Circuit has articulated an eight-factor test, known as the *Sleekcraft* test, which the court may consider in determining the likelihood of confusion: 1) the strength of the mark; 2) proximity or relatedness of the goods; 3) similarity in appearance, sound, and meaning of the marks; 4) evidence of actual confusion; 5) degree to which the marketing channels converge; 6) type of good and degree of care customers are likely to exercise in purchasing them; 7) evidence of the intention of defendant in selecting and using the alleged infringing name; and 8) likelihood that the parties will expand their product lines. *See AMF, Inc. v. Sleekcraft Boats*, 599 F.2d 341, 351 (9th Cir.1979). A party need not establish the existence of all eight factors in its favor in order to prevail on a finding of a likelihood of confusion (or lack thereof) since these factors are simply helpful guidelines for the determination of potential customer confusion, and no one factor is dispositive in every case. *See Metro Pub. Ltd. v. San Jose Mercury News*, 987 F.2d 637, 640 (9th Cir.1993). Additionally, although some factors will be much more significant than others, and the relative importance of each factor will be case-dependent, "it is often possible to reach a conclusion with respect to likelihood of confusion after considering only a subset of the factors." *Brookfield Communications, Inc. v. West Coast Entertainment Corp.*, 174 F.3d 1036, 1054 (9th Cir.1999).

Although Plaintiff offered as part of its evidence of likelihood of confusion its expert witness' opinion that there is a "likelihood of confusion," *see* Sterne Decl., ¶ ¶ 11, 13, 15, and 16, at 5–6, the court cannot rely on any of Plaintiff's expert witness' James Sterne's *ultimate conclusions* regarding whether there was a likelihood of confusion. Plaintiff's expert, James Sterne, makes the conclusory allegation that Defendant Welles' repetitive use of the contested terms throughout her website, "[i]nstead of being merely descriptive of her background . . . create[s] a commercial 'theme' for the website," and thus the "repetitive use of the Playboy marks will create confusion among a significant number of users regarding PEI's endorsement of or affiliation with the Welles Site." Sterne Decl., ¶ ¶ 9 and 11, at 5. In assessing whether there is a likelihood of confusion, this court first must consider the *Sleekcraft* factors and *then* determine whether there exists a likelihood of confusion. *See Alpha Industries, Inc. v. Alpha Steel Tube & Shapes, Inc.*, 616 F.2d 440, 443 (9th Cir.1980). With the analysis so structured, the determination of what is the state of affairs regarding each factor (a "foundational fact") is a finding of fact, *but the further determination of likelihood of confusion based on those factors is a legal conclusion. See id.*, 616 F.2d at 443 (emphasis added) (*citing J.B. Williams Co., Inc. v. Le Conte Cosmetics, Inc.* .), 523 F.2d 187, 191–92 (9th Cir.1975) and *AMF, Inc. v. Sleekcraft Boats*, 599 F.2d 341, 348–54 (9th Cir.1979). Federal Rules of Evidence 704 was not intended to allow experts to offer opinions embodying legal conclusions. See United States v. Scop, 846 F.2d 135, 139 (2d Cir.1988). Thus, Mr. Sterne's conclusion that Ms. Welles' use "create[s] confusion among a significant number of users regarding PEI's endorsement of or affiliation with the Welles Site," Sterne Decl., ¶ ¶ 9 and 11, at 5, renders a *legal opinion* which the court will not entitle any weight. Additionally, insofar as Mr. Sterne's conclusory statements render legal opinions regarding whether Ms. Welles' use of the contested terms is a "descriptive" or "fair use," or constitutes use as "Playboy [trade]marks," Sterne Decl., ¶ ¶ 9 and 11, at 5, the court likewise will not entitle them any weight. *See United States v. Scop*, 846 F.2d 135, 139 (2d Cir.1988) (holding that Fed.R. Evid. 704 was not intended to allow experts to offer opinions embodying legal conclusions). Expert testimony consisting of legal conclusions regarding the "likelihood of confusion" or Ms. Welles' "fair" or "descriptive" use are inappropriate subjects for expert testimony and as such, are inadmissible. *See Aguilar v. International Longshoremen's Union Local No. 10*, 966 F.2d 443, 447 (9th Cir.1992). However, for purposes of the motion for summary judgment, the court assumes as true the facts and opinions of Mr. Sterne (which are based upon his expertise) which are alleged in his declaration and from which he renders these conclusory statements. With respect to the foundational facts, Mr. Sterne's opinions are believed and "all justifiable inferences ... [are] drawn in his ... favor," *Anderson v. Liberty Lobby Inc.*, 477 U.S. 242, 255, 106 S.Ct. 2505, 91 L.Ed.2d 202 (1986), as long as Mr. Sterne goes beyond the pleadings to allege specific facts regarding "the state of affairs regarding each [*Sleekcraft*] factor," *Alpha Industries, Inc.*, 616 F.2d at 443, rather than merely assert a conclusory statement. *See Celotex Corp. v. Catrett*, 477 U.S. at 324. In other words, the court will assume as true Mr. Sterne's expert opinion on what is the state of affairs regarding each *Sleekcraft* factor, but the court will *not* allow Mr. Sterne to render a legal opinion on whether, based on all the *Sleekcraft* factors, there is a likelihood of confusion.

Applying the *Sleekcraft* test, the court finds that the totality of the *Sleekcraft* factors does not compel a finding of a likelihood of confusion. Plaintiff's mark is strong, the goods are related (online erotica), and the marketing channels (internet) converge. However, since the goods are related (online erotica), and the marketing channels (internet) converge, it is unnecessary to consider the eighth factor, whether the parties will expand their product lines so that there is even more competition; the fact that Plaintiff and Defendant Welles are in competition is not disputed. As for the sixth factor, the type of good and degree of care customers are likely to exercise in purchasing the goods, Plaintiff's expert states, without factual support, that "Internet users are easily frustrated," and "given the relatively inexpensive nature of these [online erotica] products, the degree of care one would expect consumers" to have "is low." Sterne Decl ., ¶ ¶ 15, 18, at 6–7. The court will assume without deciding that Plaintiff's expert's opinion is to be believed and that his opinion falls within his field of expertise in internet marketing. However, the court finds that the remaining three factors militate strongly in Defendant's favor: similarity in appearance, sound, and meaning of the marks, evidence of actual confusion, and evidence of the intention of defendant in selecting and using the alleged infringing name. As discussed *infra* in this section of the court's order, Ms. Welles' use of the trademarked terms and PEI's use of the trademark are certainly dissimilar in "appearance" of the marks: Ms. Welles does not use the PEI bunny logo, the PEI bunny theme, PEI trademark fonts, PEI trademark dress, or PEI trademark colors. Ms. Welles' use and PEI's use differ in meaning: Ms. Welles uses the contested terms in a non-trademark manner to describe herself and *not* to identify PEI as the source, sponsor, or affiliate of her goods; PEI's use is in a trademark manner to identify itself as the source of the goods. Therefore, the court finds that there is no "similarity in appearance . . . and meaning of the marks." The court's finding of dissimilarity under this *Sleekcraft* prong is not inconsistent with the fact that the words themselves used in Ms. Welles' website are identical to the words in PEI's trademarks. As the court explained in *Lindy Pen*, the "two marks viewed in isolation are indeed identical, but their similarity must be considered in light of the way the marks are encountered in the marketplace and the circumstances surrounding the purchase of the [products]." *Lindy Pen Co. v. Bic Pen Corp.*, 725 F.2d at 1245.

Plaintiff presents no "evidence of actual confusion," and the court is unaware of any evidence of actual confusion. In spite of Plaintiff's and Plaintiff's expert witness' conclusory allegations that consumers are likely to be confused, *PEI has presented no facts from which the court can infer that consumers have been confused or are likely to be confused.* Plaintiff has presented no empirical evidence (either anecdotal or survey) to show that there is actual confusion among consumers. Plaintiff's expert admits that there is no such evidence of which he is aware. *See* Reply Decl. of David J. Noonan, Ex. 2 ("Deposition of James Sterne—Volume I") ("Sterne Deposition"), at 117–118. The factors, e.g., prominence, repetition, location, and stylization, Plaintiff and Plaintiff's expert cite as causing consumer confusion as to the source or association of Ms. Welles' use of the contested terms will be discussed in more detail *infra* in this section. At this point, the court merely notes that for reasons discussed later, the court rejects Plaintiff's conclusions with respect to the factors of prominence, repetition, location, and stylization and holds that these factors as presented fail to raise a material issue of fact concerning Ms. Welles' fair use. Although actual confusion is not essential to a finding of infringement, a mere possibility is not enough: "There must be a *substantial* likelihood that the public will be confused." *WSM, Inc. v. Hilton*, 724 F.2d at 1329 (emphasis added); *see also Murray v. Cable National Broadcasting Co.*, 86 F.3d at 860–61 (confusion must be probable, not merely a possibility). The court finds that Plaintiff has failed to produce facts from which a "*substantial* likelihood that the public will be confused" can be inferred.

With respect to the "evidence of the intention of defendant in selecting and using the alleged infringing name" prong, the evidence weighs heavily in Ms. Welles' favor. As previously discussed in this order, there is an absence of evidence that Ms. Welles has acted in bad faith in her selection of PEI's trademarked terms in her website; on the contrary, there exists considerable evidence that Ms. Welles' acted in good faith and that her use was fair and not misleading. To summarize, Ms. Welles provides evidence that she sought to take precautions to ensure that her use of PEI's trademarked terms in her website was permitted by PEI, Ms. Welles has removed some references per Plaintiff's request and made changes to her website in order to placate some of Plaintiff's concerns, she does not use "Playboy" or "Playmate" in her domain name, she does not use in the "Playmate of the Year 1981" title a font recognizable as a Playboy magazine font, she does not use the classic Playboy bunny logo, and realistically, she is unable to identify herself as "Playmate of the Year" without using the title that PEI bestowed upon her. Thus, the court finds that notwithstanding Ms. Welles' selection and use of the contested PEI terms in the visible portion of her website, there is no evidence of bad faith or intent to infringe. And as this court has explained, Ms. Welles is the Playmate of the Year for 1981. Her celebrity status sprang from her repeated selections as a Playboy model. Her public persona is based on these titles, and although she uses these titles, these titles fairly and accurately describe her.

In short, the court's consideration of the factors in *Sleekcraft* affirms its finding with regards to Ms. Welles' fair-and-in-good-faith, nominative use of the PEI trademarked terms in the visible portion of her website. The court finds that Plaintiff has failed to present any facts to show a genuine issue as to the likelihood of confusion under *Sleekcraft. See, e.g., Lindy Pen Co. v. Bic Pen Corp.*, 725 F.2d at 1246 (affirming district court's finding of absence of likelihood of confusion based on factors of weakness of mark, dissimilarity, lack of actual confusion, and lack of bad faith).

Other Unnamed Variables Under the Sleekcraft Test

In its attempt to make a showing of likelihood of confusion, Plaintiff largely relies on its expert witness, James Sterne, to satisfy its burden that Ms. Welles' use of the contested terms is a use otherwise than as a trademark. The following discussion of the factors of location, commercial context, stylization, lettering, repetition, commercial theme, and prominence cannot neatly be categorized as an analysis of one, particular *Sleekcraft* factor, but arguably falls under the rubric of three *Sleekcraft* factors: similarity in appearance, sound, and meaning of the marks, degree to which the marketing channels converge, and evidence of the intention of defendant in selecting and using the alleged infringing name. The court need not decide whether its discussion of the factors of location, commercial context, stylization, lettering, repetition, commercial theme, and prominence strictly falls under the *Sleekcraft* eight-factor test. The Ninth Circuit has stated that the *Sleekcraft* test is a pliant one. *See Brookfield Communications, Inc. v. West Coast Entertainment Corp.*, 174 F.3d at 1053. In other words, "the foregoing list [of eight factors] does not purport to be exhaustive, and non-listed variables may often be quite important." *Id*.

With the pliant nature of the analysis of likelihood of confusion under *Sleekcraft* in mind, the court turns to a discussion of the factors enumerated by Plaintiff's expert witness as contributing to a likelihood of confusion regarding Ms. Welles' use of PEI trademarked terms. According to his declaration, Mr. Sterne has extensive experience in the field of marketing, both in relation to the Internet and to non-Internet forms. *See* Sterne Decl., ¶ 2. As discussed briefly in section

III(A)(1)(a)(1)(I), *supra*, of this order, Plaintiff's main "facts" supporting its allegations that Ms. Welles' "prominent, stylized and memorable use of PEI's trademarks operates to ... attract the attention of consumers to defendant's website," "borrow[s] from the cachet of the PEI marks," and "trade[s] off of the good will of those marks," Opposition at 9, are as follows:

(1) Ms. Welles' site is a predominantly commercial site; (2) The visible title banner on the homepage is a prominent commercial use of the Playboy term; (3) The commercial theme is "Playboy Playmate of the Year"; (4) The visible use of the terms in the title banner and the subject headings along the left-hand side of the homepage (along with the repeating PMOY background watermark and the references in the HTML code and metatags) create a repetitive use of the Playboy and Playmate terms; (5) Title banners or mastheads at the top of a commercial website do not serve the same function as book titles, but rather serve to identify the "source" of the website and its products; (6) This "source identification effect" is a result of the context of the use (commercial), prominence of the use (repetition and size), the location of the use (in title banner, source code, advertising banner, and wallpaper), and the stylization of the use (in script letters as product name and repetition of PMOY). *See* Decl. of James Sterne, PEI Expert Witness, ¶ ¶ 8–11, at 4–5.

In short, Plaintiff's expert contends that the prominence, location, stylization, and repetition of Ms. Welles' use of PEI terms in a commercial context creates a likelihood of confusion as to the source of the goods.

1) *Location and Commercial Context*

That Ms. Welles' site—and her use of the contested terms—are predominantly commercial is not contested. That the title or masthead is located at the top of the homepage and serves to identify the source of the website and its products is not disputed: Defendant Welles does not contest the location of the title or the fact that the visual title, "Terri Welles Playmate of the Year 1981," is meant to identify the source of her products and of her website. Neither does Ms. Welles dispute the location of the advertising banners (or the words contained therein) and that the words on both forms of the banner serve to identify the name or title of her website, or the "source" of her goods. The parties also do not dispute the location of the "PMOY '81" abbreviation used as watermarks on specific web pages. Even accepting as true Mr. Sterne's other assessments that the title and "PMOY '81" watermarks are "prominent" and appear "in script letters as [a] product name," and the combined repetitive use of the contested terms throughout the website create a "commercial theme" of "Playboy Playmate of the Year," this court holds that these facts, in combination with the factors of location (as a "sign above the entrance to a store") and of commercial use of the PEI terms, do not rebut Defendant Welles' showing that she has made a non-trademark use of the terms "Playboy Playmate of the Year 1981,"

"Playmate of the Year 1981," and "PMOY '81" in good faith merely to describe *her* products and services.

2) Stylization and Lettering

The fact that the font of the Playmate of the Year 1981 title is not recognizable as a Playboy magazine font evidences a reasonable use of the term and an absence of an intent to trick or mislead customers into implying sponsorship or endorsement by Plaintiff. *See Volkswagenwerk Aktiengesellschaft v. Church*, 411 F.2d 350, 352 (9th Cir.1969). The words "Terri Welles" are in *block* letters which overlap and partially cover the words, "Playmate of the Year 1981," which are in cursive *script* letters, in smaller size. *See* Decl. of Cynthia Johnston, PEI Legal Department Staff, Ex. J. It is undisputed that the title trademark for "Playboy" magazine is in *block*, not script letters. *See* Decl. of Martha Lindeman, PEI Senior Vice-President of Investor Relations and Corporate Communications, Ex. D; Second Amended Complaint, Ex. C, at 37. Plaintiff indicates nothing in particular about the stylization and lettering (size, coloring, font, etc.) of the "Playmate" term in the visual title, the "Playboy" and "Playmate" terms in the advertising banners, and the term "PMOY '81" in the watermarks which are either an imitation of PEI's trademark style or dress or an attempt to invoke the imagery—directly or indirectly—of PEI's well-recognized bunny logo. *See Volkswagenwerk Aktiengesellschaft v. Church*, 411 F.2d 350, 352 (9th Cir. 1969) ("Church did not use Volkswagen's distinctive lettering style or color scheme, nor did he display the encircled 'VW' emblem."). Rather, the undisputed facts indicate that Ms. Welles' use of PEI terms do not match PEI's use of its trademark in style, dress, or other manner. Also, it is undisputed that (1) the lettering of the name "Terri Welles" as it appears in the visual title of her homepage and in the advertising banners is *larger* than the lettering of the designation, "Playmate of the Year 1981" or "Playboy Playmate of the Year 1981" and (2) the picture of the *solo* Terri Welles appears on the homepage and in the advertising banners. Thus, despite Mr. Sterne's unsupported conclusions, there are no disputed facts that Ms. Welles' stylization and lettering of PEI terms in her website do not create a likelihood of confusion as to the source of the goods: Terri Welles.

Upon similar facts in the case of *Cosmetically Sealed Industries, Inc. v. Chesebrough–Pond's USA Co.*, the Second Circuit affirmed summary judgment and found that the defendant's use of the challenged trademarked terms was not a trademark infringement, but fair use. *Cosmetically Sealed*, 125 F.3d at 29–30. The court in *Cosmetically Sealed* noted that the defendant's product name, "Color Splash," and its own trademark, "Cutex," appeared in the center and top-center of the promotional display card in red *block* letters at least twice or three times the size of the lettering for the challenged phrase, "Seal it with a Kiss!!," which was in *script* type. *See id.* (emphasis added). The *Cosmetically Sealed* court held that "the non-trademark use of the challenged phrase and the defendant's good faith are both evidenced by the fact that the source of the defendants' product is clearly identified by the prominent display of defendant's own trademarks." *Id.* at 30. Likewise, the court here finds that Ms. Welles' use of PEI's terms in a style dissimilar to PEI's and in conjunction with the clear and prominent identification of her name and picture support a finding of a good-faith, non-trademark use.

3) *Repetition and Commercial Theme*

Mr. Sterne's conclusion that the repetitious use of PEI's terms creates a "commercial theme" of the "Playboy" or "Playmate" terms which is likely to confuse consumers is unsupported by the facts he puts forth. That the visible terms "Playboy" and "Playmate" in the title banner and the subject headings along the left-hand side of the site create a repetitive use of the Playboy and Playmate terms is, without more, irrelevant. Plaintiff has not asserted that the repeated use of "Playboy" and "Playmate" in the *subject headings* along the left-hand side of the homepage is anything other than a descriptive and/or editorial use of these terms. In fact, the use of these terms in her subject headings, "Playboy vs. Welles: Playboy Sues Playmate," "Autobiography: Learn More About My Playboy Days," and "Films & Videos/Magazines: Playboy Appearances and More," merely describe the contents of those web pages. Plaintiff's witness, James Sterne, also agreed: "Welles' non-commercial or *editorial* uses of the Playboy Marks are ... [for example] her 'Autobiography' page (describing her past association with PEI) ... [and] her 'Films & Videos/Magazines page' (listing her film roles and appearances in PEI publications)." Sterne Decl., ¶ 12 (emphasis added). Plaintiff has not cited one authority, nor is the court aware of any, where the repetitive use, without more, of a descriptive and/or editorial term creates a likelihood of confusion, reveals bad faith or an intent to imply sponsorship, or otherwise places into dispute a defendant's fair use.

Moreover, the holding in *Cosmetically Sealed* affirms that there is no legal impediment to use a contested term or mark as a "commercial theme" so long as it is used fairly to describe the defendant's goods. In *Cosmetically Sealed*, discussed *supra*, the Second Circuit affirmed the district court's grant of summary judgment of the plaintiff's trademark infringement and unfair competition claims, notwithstanding the defendant's use of "Seal it with a Kiss!!" (a variation of Plaintiff's trademark, "Sealed With a Kiss") as a commercial theme in its promotional display of its own lipstick products. The court in *Cosmetically Sealed* court stated that the district court ruled that the use of the challenged phrase was not a use as a "mark to identify its Color Splash lipsticks" with the plaintiff's product, but rather was a use of the words in their ordinary meaning, in "their 'descriptive sense'—to describe an action that the sellers hope consumers will take, using their product." *Cosmetically Sealed*, 125 F.3d at 30. Similarly, in this case, even if Ms. Welles use of PEI's terms amounts to a repetitious "commercial theme," the court finds that her use is a fair use of "Playmate of the Year 1981," "Playboy Playmate of the Year 1981," and "PMOY '81" for these terms *describe* her and her goods and services, and they are *not* used to identify her goods with PEI or to identify PEI as the source.

4) *Prominence*

Despite Plaintiff's contention that Ms. Welles' use of the PEI trademarked terms in the visual title, watermarks, and advertising banners are "prominent," Plaintiff provides little in the way of supporting facts to ground its allegation of prominence. In particular, the court finds problematic Plaintiff's failure to establish the "prominence" of the "PMOY" trademark—in either sense of the word prominent as "distinctly manifest to the senses," or "notable, leading, or eminent." Webster's Third New International Dictionary, p. 1815 (1976). In contrast to Plaintiff's evidence of (1) the registration of the terms "Playboy" and "Playmate of the Year;" and (ii) the trademark use of those terms for a substantial period of time, Plaintiff fails to provide evidence, with respect to "PMOY," of either the registration or of the prolonged or recognized use of "PMOY" as an abbreviation for the designation, "Playmate of the Year." Plaintiff has not brought to the court's attention anything in its voluminous exhibits which indicates the registration of "PMOY" or its recognized use. In fact, Defendant has pointed to uncontroverted evidence of Plaintiff's lack of registration of "PMOY." *See* Decl. of Susan O'Keefe Head, Defense Counsel's Paralegal, Ex. 2; *see also* Decl. of Martha Lindeman, PEI Senior Vice–President of Investor Relations and Corporate Communications, at 3, ¶ 3, and Ex. B. Consequently, the court declines to assume that the "PMOY" term is "prominent" in the sense of "notable, leading, or eminent." Furthermore, the court fails to see—and Plaintiff fails to explain—how a watermark is physically "prominent," especially in light of the fact that watermarks are usually located in the background and not the foreground of a page. In fact, Plaintiff's witness James Sterne's reference to the watermarks as "a decorative logo repeating in the *background* of the homepage," Sterne Decl., ¶ 10 (emphasis added), merely affirms the court's befuddlement at the oxymoronic meaning in the description of a watermark in the "background" as "prominent."

However, in spite of Plaintiff's lack of substantiation of its claim of "prominence" to describe the use of PEI terms in Ms. Welles' website, emphasis itself, without more, is not inconsistent with a finding of fair use and has never, in the court's knowledge, been held to bar a fair use defense. Although an infringing use can be evidenced by the employment of a challenged term as an "attention-getting symbol," the emphasis of a descriptive term on a label, packaging, or advertising does not necessarily mean that the term is being used in a trademark sense. *See* 1 J. McCarthy, Trademarks and Unfair Competition, § 11.49, at 94.1 (1999) (*citing Eli Lilly & Co. v. Revlon, Inc.*), 577 F.Supp. 477, 486 (S.D.N.Y. 1983). Surely, it would render the fair use defense meaningless if a defendant were permitted to make a descriptive use of a mark as long as its use of the mark is not "attention-getting" or not "emphasized" in the title or package. As the district court in *Eli Lilly & Co.* recognized: "Virtually every aspect of a product's trade dress is *intended* to catch the eye of the purchaser." *Eli Lilly & Co. v. Revlon, Inc.*, 577 F.Supp. at 486 (emphasis added). The court continued, "[u]nless attention is drawn to the particular word or term as being indicative of *source* of origin of that product, the term is *not* being used as a trademark." *Id.* As an appropriate analogy which the court finds equally apropos here, the court in *Eli Lilly & Co.* discussed the case of *Schmid Laboratories v. Youngs Drug Products Corp.*, 482 F .Supp. 14, 20–21 (D.N.J.1979) in which the *Schmid* court noted, "[W]hatever attention is drawn to 'RIBBED' serves only to inform the prospective purchaser what type of condom is contained within, not whose product it is ... It denotes the difference between this particular type of condom and ... several others ... " *Id.* Likewise in this case, the court finds that any *emphasis* on the PEI trademarked terms in the visual title, watermarks, and advertising banners in Ms. Welles' website serves only to inform the consumer "what type of [product] is contained within" (i.e., who Ms. Welles' is and what her products and services are likely to be), not whose product it is in the sense of the "source" of the goods.

Special Allegations Regarding the Advertising Banners

As briefly mentioned in section III(A)(1)(a)(iii), *supra*, of this order, Plaintiff makes three specific contentions regarding the use of the advertising banners:

> (1) Anyone can "grab" these banners from defendant's website, and by doing so, include PEI's trademarks on the face of their website and in the source code; (2) Defendant's motivation for these banners is to attract click through traffic from other adult websites and increase her ranking among search engines that rank, in part, on the basis of a number of links to a website; and (3) An internet user who clicks through to defendant's website by clicking on the advertising banner on a third party website will likely know nothing about Ms. Welles' site other than the references on the banner—adult entertainment, the PEI trademark, and Ms. Welles' identification as a Playmate. *See* Opposition, at 7–8.

Even assuming as true each of these contentions, none of these factors warrant a finding of a non-trademark use of the terms "Playboy Playmate of the Year 1981" or "Playmate of the Year 1981" by Ms. Welles. The fact that anyone else can reproduce Ms. Welles' advertising banner, with her permission, does not transform Ms. Welles' use of the terms "Playboy Playmate of the Year 1981" or "Playmate of the Year 1981" to a trademark use or a use that is other than a nominative, fair use of those terms. *See* discussion *supra*, section III(A)(1)(a)(2)(I). Since Plaintiff does not allege any facts which indicate that third party users are doing anything other than reproducing or "grabbing" from Defendant's site her advertising banners, the court fails to see how the placement of Ms. Welles' advertising banners on third party sites, without more, would convert what this court has otherwise found to be a fair, non-trademark use of PEI's terms in Ms. Welles' advertising banners into an infringing use. Moreover, no law is cited that would support this claim.

Plaintiff's second assertion, that Defendant's motivation for these banners is to "attract click through traffic from other adult websites and increase her ranking among search engines that rank, in part, on the basis of a number of links to a website," is equally irrelevant to Ms. Welles' fair use defense. Plaintiff offers as evidence a "Referring URLS" report which reveals that the Welles site does receive a significant amount of traffic from sites on which are posted banners or links that contain the Playboy marks. *See* Sterne Decl., Ex. E. Even assuming this is true, the court fails to see how this fact can support Plaintiff's conclusion that the "banner advertisements for the Welles' site confuses users." *Id.* at 12. It is undisputed that Ms. Welles' use of the "Playboy Playmate of the Year 1981" or "Playmate of the Year 1981" terms is a commercial use; it is therefore not surprising that she is motivated by a desire to increase her commercial popularity on the internet. She is legally permitted to do so, so long as she is not infringing upon PEI's trademarks by making a trademark use of the contested terms. As discussed previously in this order, Ms. Welles use in the advertising banners of the terms "Playmate of the Year 1981" and "Playboy Playmate of the Year '81" to truthfully identify herself and her services is a fair use. Given that Ms. Welles *is* the "Playmate of the Year 1981," there is no other way that Ms. Welles can fairly identify or describe herself and her services.

Finally, Plaintiff asserts that "an internet user who clicks through to defendant's website by clicking on the advertising banner on a third party website will likely know nothing about Ms. Welles' site other than the references on the banner—adult entertainment, the PEI trademark, and Ms. Welles' identification as a Playmate." Opposition, at 8. The court first notes that this statement is not factually accurate in the sense that in actuality the words "Playmate of the Year 1981" and "Playboy Playmate of the Year '81" appear, in smaller letters, directly below or above the name "Terri Welles" on the advertising banner, although these PEI *trademarked* terms do not necessarily appear in the style or dress of a PEI trademark. Plaintiff has not asserted that Ms. Welles is using the PEI bunny logo or that the fonts for the contested terms are the same or similar as the fonts used in PEI's trademarks. In fact, Plaintiff presents absolutely no evidence that there is any indication that PEI is sponsoring the website. Ms. Welles' use of the terms "Playboy Playmate of the Year 1981" or "Playmate of the Year 1981" in her advertising banners mirrors her use of these terms in the visual title of her homepage, with the exception of slight changes in the placement, font, size, and location. These banners are like mini-versions of her visual title or masthead in that they contain: (1) the lettering of the name "Terri Welles" in letters which are *larger* than the lettering of the designation, "Playmate of the Year 1981" or "Playboy Playmate of the Year 1981" and (2) a sole picture of the semi-nude Terri Welles. Like the visual title, the undisputed facts regarding and surrounding Ms. Welles' stylization and lettering of PEI terms in the advertising banners do not indicate a likelihood of confusion as to the source of the goods: Terri

Welles. Thus, the court cannot say that Ms. Welles took more than what was necessary to merely identify or describe herself or her goods. *Cf. Walt Disney Productions v. Air Pirates*, 581 F.2d 751, 758 (9th Cir.1978) (taking "more than was necessary" can defeat copyright fair use defense). Accordingly, the court finds that Plaintiff's specific allegations regarding Defendant's use of PEI trademarked terms in the advertising banners do not create a dispute of material fact as to Ms. Welles' non-trademark, fair use of those terms.

The Non–Paradigmatic Fair Use Case: The New Kids Standard

As stated previously in section III(A)(1)(a)(2)(iii), *supra*, of this order, the governing law in this circuit regarding the classic fair use case is that a junior user's use should be deemed a fair, non-trademark use only if it is non-confusing. *See New Kids*, 971 F.2d at 308; *Lindy Pen Co. v. Bic Pen Corp.*, 725 F.2d 1240 (9th Cir.1984), *cert. denied*, 469 U.S. 1188, 105 S.Ct. 955, 83 L.Ed.2d 962 (1985). In *New Kids*, however, the Ninth Circuit articulated a different kind of fair use: "Such a nominative use of a mark—where the only word reasonably available to describe a particular thing is pressed into service—lies outside the strictures of trademark law" because "it does not implicate the source-identification function that is the purpose of trademark" and because it "does not imply sponsorship or endorsement by the trademark holder." *See New Kids*, 971 F.2d at 308. In such non-paradigmatic cases of "nominative use", the court held that a commercial defendant is entitled to a nominative fair use defense provided it meets the following three requirements: (1) the product or service in question must be one not readily identifiable without use of the trademark; (2) only so much of the mark or marks may be used as is reasonably necessary to identify the product or service; and (3) the defendant must do nothing that would, in conjunction with the mark, suggest sponsorship or endorsement by the trademark holder. *See id.* Under the *New Kids* standard, a court does not reach the question of likelihood of confusion, apart from any analysis of a likelihood of confusion that is implied in the third *New Kids* prong. *See Mattel, Inc. v. MCA Records, Inc.*, 28 F.Supp.2d 1120, 1143 (C.D.Cal. 1998).

This court has previously discussed reasons why Ms. Welles' use of PEI terms in her website constitutes a fair use under the Lanham Act § 33(b)(4), i.e., why her descriptive use was fair and in good faith and was used only to describe her goods and services in a non-trademark manner. *See* 15 U.S.C. § 1115(b)(4) (1999). The court, however, additionally holds that Ms. Welles' use of the words "Playmate of the Year 1981" in her title on her homepage, "PMOY '81" in the watermarks, and "Playboy Playmate of the Year 1981" and "Playmate of the Year 1981" in her advertising banners falls within the non-paradigmatic line of cases established under *New Kids*. All three of the *New Kids* requirements have been met. As discussed previously in this order, 1) Ms. Welles has no viable alternative to the use of the term, "Playmate of the Year 1981," or "PMOY '81," 2) she references the contested terms only to the extent necessary to identify herself and doesn't use the distinctive Bunny logo or anything else that isn't needed to make the website intelligible and identifiable to consumers, and 3) she does nothing to suggest or imply sponsorship or endorsement of her website by PEI. On the contrary, she has disclaimers on her web pages and prominently displays as one of her subject headings, "Playboy vs. Welles: Playboy Sues Playmate." Moreover, she has links to and references about articles regarding the litigation on her website, and sometimes makes critical, albeit editorial, comments about Playboy. As the court stated in *Patmont Motor Werks, Inc. v. Gateway Marine, Inc.*, 1997 WL 811770, * 4 (N.D.Cal.1997), the court "would find incredible any argument to the contrary [of the finding of no sponsorship given the website's disparagement" of PEI.] The court finds that there is no genuine dispute of material fact as to Ms. Welles' nominative fair use of the PEI contested terms in the visual title, watermarks, or advertising banners of her website. Accordingly, the court finds that Defendant Welles has established a fair use defense under the *New Kids* standard for her use of the words "Playmate of the Year 1981" in her title on her homepage, "PMOY '81" in the watermarks, and "Playboy Playmate of the Year 1981" and "Playmate of the Year 1981" in her advertising banners. Summary judgment for Ms. Welles is proper as to all Plaintiff's trademark claims with respect to the visible portion of her website.

(3) *Conclusion*

Viewing the facts and evidence in the light most favorable to Plaintiff, the court finds as a matter of law that Ms. Welles' has made a fair use of the terms "Playboy Playmate of the Year 1981," "Playmate of the Year 1981," and "PMOY '81" to describe and identify herself and her goods in the visual title, watermarks, and advertising banners on her website. Accordingly, granting of summary judgment is proper as to as to all Plaintiff's trademark claims, in Counts I through VII of the Second Amended Complaint, against Defendant Welles with respect to the use of use of the terms "Playboy Playmate of the Year 1981," "Playmate of the Year 1981," and "PMOY '81" in the visual title, watermarks, and advertising banners on her website.

(b) *HTML Source Code: The Non–Visible Title, Meta Code Description, and Meta Tag Keywords*

(1) *Factual and Technical Background*

The HTML source code is the coding that is used for construction of a website's pages. All visible text that a user sees when viewing a web page is contained in the HTML source code. The HTML coding language also allows non-visible information about a web page to be recorded in the source code. Plaintiff alleges that Ms. Welles' use of its trademarks, "Playboy," "Playmate," and "Playmate of the Year" in the HTML source code of her website constitutes an infringing and diluting trademark use of its marks. The domain name of Ms. Welles' site is "www.terriwelles.com." The HTML code for the title of Ms. Welles' site currently reads, "Terri Welles Erotica." The description of Ms. Welles' site as it appears in the meta code is "Playboy Playmate of the Year 1981 Terri Welles website featuring erotic nude photos, semi-nude photos, softcore and exclusive Members Club." *See* Opposition, at 8 and Ex. E. The metatag keywords on Ms. Welles' website reads, "terri, welles, playmate, playboy, model, models, semi-nudity, naked, breast, breasts, tit, tits, nipple, nipples, ass, butt." *See id.* at Ex. E.

The Internet is an international, complex network connecting millions of individual computer networks and computers. Although the Internet is widely known, as the "World Wide Web," for its almost endless capacity for presenting and disseminating information, the Internet supports many other forms of communication in addition to the Web, such as e-mail, bulletin board services, news groups, and numerous others. *See Lockheed Martin Corp. v. Network Solutions, Inc.*, 985 F.Supp. 949, 951 (C.D.Cal.1997), *aff'd*, 194 F.3d 980 (9th Cir.1999). Because of its capabilities, "[f]or commercial users, the Web is the most important part of the Internet" and "has become a popular medium for advertising and for direct consumer access to goods and services." *Id.* However, simultaneously, the Web remains an important medium of *non-commercial* communications and has made it easier for individuals and small groups or organizations to publish information to the general public as well as obtain information. *See id.*

The following technical facts regarding how the Internet and Web operate are undisputed by the parties. Internet communication is premised on the use of domain names to locate specific computers and networks in cyberspace. A link, or hyperlink, is an image or section of text referring to another document on the Web and is in essence a system which takes people between websites or web pages. *See* Decl. of Danny Sullivan ("Sullivan Decl."), Defendant Welles' Expert Witness, ¶ 9, at 4. Web pages display words and pictures about a particular topic, in much the same way that a printed page from a magazine or a book might display words and pictures. *See id.* at ¶ 4. And just as a magazine or book is a collection of interconnected pages unified by one or more subjects or themes, a website is a collection of interconnected web pages with one or more common themes or topics. *See id.*

Users searching for a specific website can either type it into a web browser to access the site directly, or they can utilize a "search engine" available on the Web to search for a specific website by keywords and phrases. Listings or results are the end product of a search. There are two basic types of search engines: human powered and web-crawler. Human-powered search engines produce human-compiled listings which have been approved and categorized by human search engine editors, much like how a librarian might catalog books in the library. *See id.* at ¶ 13. Changes to a website's meta tag descriptors, keywords, or HTML title have no impact on human-compiled listings or search results unless a human editor decides to follow or endorse these changes. *See id.* However, due to the inordinate amount of websites, human editors cannot classify everything, and consequently, some search engines are more reliant on the web-crawler than the human-powered engines, or human editors. *See id.* at ¶ 16.

Web crawlers "read" individual web pages by reading much of the text in the HTML source code and store in cyberspace memory the text they find on each page. *See id.* at ¶ 15. In addition to providing a listing of search results which was initiated by the consumer's typing of keywords or phrases into a browser, search engines enable consumers to sort through their listings by ranking pages so that the pages which best match their relevancy criteria are listed first, then continuing in chronological order. *See id.* at ¶ 17. The criteria or algorithm used by search engines to rank search results in response to a particular search query varies among different search engines and even within search engines, as these formula continue to change from time to time. *See id.* at ¶ ¶ 17–24; *see also* Sterne Decl., ¶ 31, at 11. These criteria or algorithms are a combination of many various factors, including but not limited to, the frequency of words on a page, the location of words, the HTML title, and metatags (meta descriptors and meta keywords). *See* Sullivan Decl., at ¶ ¶ 17–24. The title tag is text that is used as the title of a web page in the listings of a crawler-based search engine. *See id.* at ¶ 20. Metatags are mostly used to provide additional information about a web page and are not ordinarily viewed by users. *See id.* at ¶ 21. The meta descriptors allows web page authors to state the exact description they would like to have for their web pages as listed in the search results of a web crawler search engine, and the meta keyword tags allow page authors, at least in theory, to identify or add words to their pages in order to better define or accurately relate the contents of the page for the web crawler search engine. *See id.* at ¶ 23.

(2) *Analysis*

Plaintiff relies on *Brookfield Communications, Inc. v. West Coast Entertainment Corp.*, 174 F.3d 1036 (9th Cir.1999), to support its contention in this case that Defendant's use of PEI's trademarks in the metatags in her website infringes on its trademark by causing "likelihood of confusion ... shown on the basis of initial interest confusion." Opposition, at 12. The metatag use at issue is the use of the terms "Playboy Playmate of the Year 1981" in the meta code descriptor and the terms "playboy" and "playmate" in the metatag keywords. The court will simultaneously refer to the use of these terms in the metatags as "the use of PEI terms." Although Plaintiff is correct in citing *Brookfield* for the proposition that "likelihood of confusion can be shown on the basis of initial interest confusion," Plaintiff's reliance on *Brookfield* is misplaced as applied to Ms. Welles' case.

In *Brookfield*, the Ninth Circuit has noted that "the few courts to consider whether the use of another's trademark in one's metatags constitutes trademark infringement have ruled in the affirmative." *Brookfield Communications, Inc.*, 174 F.3d at 1064 (discussing *Playboy Enterprises, Inc. v. Asiafocus Int'l, Inc.*, 1998 WL 724000, at *3, * 6–*7 (E.D.Va.Apr.10, 1998), *Playboy Enterprises, Inc. v. Calvin Designer La-*

bel, 985 F.Supp. 1220, 1221 (N.D.Cal.1997), and *Niton Corp. v. Radiation Monitoring Devices, Inc.*, 27 F.Supp.2d 102, 104 (D.Mass.1998)). None of the cases which *Brookfield* discusses, however, involved the fair use defense or a use of trademarks in the metatags which accurately and fairly describe the contents of the web page or website. And although *Brookfield* concerned the use of the plaintiff's trademarked terms in the metatags of the defendant's website, it did *not* involve the use of the fair use defense within the metatags context. In other words, *Brookfield* is distinguishable from the present case since here *both* the (1) fair use defense; *and* (2) the use of trademarks in the metatags are involved, a situation which is unlike the scenario before the *Brookfield* court.

The court in *Brookfield*, however, did not entirely overlook the possibility of such a situation as Ms. Welles finds herself in here. In *Brookfield*, the Ninth Circuit held that the defendant video store chain's use of Plaintiff's trademark, "MovieBuff," would create a likelihood of confusion even though the defendant had a protected trademark in the words, "The Movie Buff's Movie Store." In so holding, the court stated that "we are not in any way restricting [the defendant's] right to use terms in a manner which would constitute fair use under the Lanham Act." *Brookfield Communications, Inc.*, 174 F.3d at 1065 (*citing New Kids*, 971 F .2d at 306–309). Coincidentally, the court cited an earlier opinion in this case denying preliminary injunction as an example that a defendant's use of trademarks in a website's metatags in a descriptive manner can be a permissible, non-infringing fair use. *See id.* at 1065–66 (*citing Playboy Enterprises, Inc. v. Welles*, 7 F.Supp.2d 1098, 1100 (S.D.Cal.1998)). Thus, the court finds that insofar as Plaintiff relies on *Brookfield* to support its position, *Brookfield* is distinguishable since the defendant's use in *Brookfield* of the word "MovieBuff" was found *not* to have been a descriptive use (although the court noted that the term "Movie Buff" (*with* a single space) *is* a descriptive term and that the difference was pivotal). *See id.* at 1066.

Although *Brookfield* is distinguishable in the above-described manner, the court must nevertheless address the issue of whether there is a likelihood of confusion, the keystone of whether a use constitutes trademark infringement or unfair competition. *See Lindy Pen Co.*, 725 F.2d at 1243. As the court stated earlier in section III(A)(1)(a)(2)(iii) of this order, the governing law in the Ninth Circuit is that in order to constitute a non-trademark, "fair use," the use cannot amount to a trademark infringement or unfair competition. *See id.* at 1248. As this court has also noted on several prior occasions, however, this case is not a standard trademark case and does not lend itself to the systematic application of the eight factors in *Sleekcraft*. This particular difficulty was acknowledged by the *Brookfield* court, wherein that court noted that "the traditional eight-factor test is not well-suited for analyzing the metatags issue." *Id.* at 1062, fn. 24. The reasons the *Brookfield* court cited for distinguishing "metatags" cases from other trademark cases, *even* those involving closely-related issues of trademark infringement on the internet, such as in the case of domain names, concerned the special nature of confusion in the context of Internet searches via Internet search engines. *See id.* at 1062. Specifically, the court noted that the results listings produced by a search engine after a web user's inputting of the contested trademark (e.g., "MovieBuff") is likely to include both the defendant's and the plaintiff's websites, and in reviewing such a list, the web user "will often be able to find the particular web site he is seeking." *Id.* In addition, the court noted that even if a web user clicks on the website belonging to the defendant, he will see that the domain name of the website he has selected is the defendant's domain name (e.g., "westcoastvideo.com"), not the plaintiff's, and that the initial web page will feature the defendant's, not the plaintiff's business name. *See id.* Consequently, the *Brookfield* court concluded that in the context of metatags, it is "difficult to say that a consumer is likely to be confused about whose site he has reached or to think that somehow [the plaintiff] sponsors [the defendant's] web site." *Id.* The *Brookfield* court's reasoning with respect to the inadequacy of the *Sleekcraft* analysis in the metatags context is pertinent to this case; this court will therefore consider whether there is a likelihood of confusion in this case without attempting to justify its analysis under all of the *Sleekcraft* factors.

Here, Defendant has used the terms "playboy," and "playmate" in the meta tag keywords and the term "Playboy Playmate of the Year 1981," in the meta code descriptor for her site so that those using search engines on the Web can find her website if they are looking for a Playboy Playmate. Plaintiff's only evidence regarding likelihood of confusion with respect to Defendant's use of PEI terms in her metatags (other than the evidence of prominence, repetition, location, commercial theme, etc. which was previously discussed and rejected in section III(A)(1)(a)(2) of this order) concerns the theory of initial interest confusion: a confusion of "consumer attention, even though no actual sale is finally completed as a result of the confusion" and even though, once reaching the site, the consumer is not actually confused or is not likely to be confused as to the correct sponsor of the site to which he or she was led initially. *See Dr. Seuss Enters. v. Penguin Books USA, Inc.*, 109 F.3d 1394, 1405 (9th Cir.1997), *cert. denied*, 521 U.S. 1146, 118 S.Ct. 27, 138 L.Ed.2d 1057 (1997). Plaintiff presents some circumstantial evidence, and both parties' experts agree, that an "appreciable number" of people who plug in one of Plaintiff's trademark terms into a web browser search engine are "looking for Playboy's official site." *See* Decl. of Ross Hyslop (Hyslop Decl.), Plaintiff's co-counsel, ¶ 3, at 2, and Ex. B ("Deposition of Danny Sullivan, Defendant's Expert Witness") ("Sullivan Deposition"). This indicates that there is at least a showing of some "initial interest confusion."

Dr. Seuss, like *Brookfield*, held that initial interest confusion is actionable under the Lanham Act, *not* that a finding of initial interest confusion compelled a finding of trademark infringement or barred a finding of fair use. In other words, both cases held that a finding of initial interest confusion *can* be a basis for a finding of likelihood of confusion, but the presence of initial interest confusion does not necessarily support a finding of likelihood of confusion. To the contrary, the *Brookfield* court stated that their holding did not "in any way restrict[ ] [the defendant's] right to use terms in a manner which would constitute fair use under the Lanham Act." *Id.* at 1065.

Other courts cited by the *Brookfield* court which acknowledged initial interest confusion as being actionable under the Lanham Act have indicated that other factors are relevant in a finding of a confusing trademark use, or infringement. Among these are: (1) evidence of the initial interest confusion as being "damaging and wrongful," *Koppers Co. v. Krupp–Koppers GmbH*, 517 F.Supp. 836, 844 (W.D.Pa.1981); (2) evidence that confusion between two products "will mistakenly lead the consumer to believe there is some connection between the two and therefore develop an interest in the [defendant's] line that it would otherwise not have," *Kompan A.S. v. Park Structures, Inc.*, 890 F.Supp. 1167, 1180 (N.D.N.Y.1995); or (3) evidence that the "situation offers an opportunity for sale not otherwise available by enabling defendant to interest prospective customers by confusion with the plaintiff's product." *Sara Lee Corp. v. Kayser–Roth Corp.*, 1992 WL 436279, at *24 (W.D.N.C. Dec.1, 1992). In the present case, Plaintiff has failed to present any facts indicating 1) any initial interest confusion was "damaging and wrongful"; 2) anyone believes or is likely to believe there is a connection between PEI's and Ms. Welles' site; 3) Ms. Welles received "opportunit[ies] for sale not otherwise available" by confusing web users; or 4) any of Ms. Welles' actual customers were in the "appreciable number," or majority of people who when plugging in one of Plaintiff's trademark terms into a web browser search engine, was "looking for Playboy's official site." *See* Hyslop Decl.¶ 3, at 2, and Ex. B ("Sullivan Deposition"). Furthermore, there is no evidence in this case that Ms. Welles— has intended to divert Plaintiff's customers to her website by trading on PEI's goodwill. *See supra*, section III(A)(1)(a)(2)(ii) of this order. This intent is relevant since the court in *Brookfield* stated that "in *Dr. Seuss*, the Ninth Circuit explicitly recognized that the use of another's trademark in a manner *calculated* 'to capture initial consumer attention, even though no actual sale is finally completed as a result of the confusion, *may* be still an infringement.'" *Brookfield Communications, Inc.*, 174 F.3d at 1062 (citing *Dr. Seuss*, 109 F.3d at 1405) (emphasis added).

The Ninth Circuit warned in *Brookfield*: "We must be acutely aware of excessive rigidity when applying the law in the Internet context; emerging technologies require a flexible approach." *Id.* at 1054. As this court previously stated, the Internet is an international, complex network connecting millions of individual computer networks and computers, thus earning the denomination of "information superhighway." The Internet is constantly evolving, as is the new field of cyberspace law. The novelty of this area, especially in the area of trademark infringement, is evidenced by the few courts that have considered the precise issues that are raised before the court in this case. In rendering an analysis which is flexible and reflective of "emerging technologies," this court is also mindful that it must not lose sight of either common sense or the important, foundational and underlying principles of trademark law. Finding that Ms. Welles' use of PEI's trademarked terms in the meta-tags of her website is a fair use comports with the fact web users must utilize identifying words to find their intended site. Not all web searches utilizing the words "Playboy," "Playmate," and "Playboy Playmate of the Year 1981" are intended to find "Playboy" goods or the official "Playboy" site. Plaintiff has not addressed the fact that Ms. Welles' fame and recognition derive from her popularity as a Playboy model and Playmate of the Year. If a consumer cannot remember her name, the logical way to find her site on the web is by using key words that identify her source of recognition to the public: "Playboy Playmate of the Year 1981," "Playboy," and "Playmate." These are the words to which PEI objects. PEI, however, fails to suggest alternative, non-offending words to locate Ms. Welles' website. The World Wide Web is a commercial marketplace and a free speech marketplace. To give consumers access to it, the court must also be careful to give consumers the freedom to locate desired sites while protecting the integrity of trademarks and trade names. The court stresses that the underlying or foundational purpose of trademark protection is *not* to create a property interest in *all* words used in a commercial context, but rather "[t]he policies of free competition and free use of language dictate that trademark law cannot forbid the commercial use of terms in their descriptive sense ." 1 J. MCCARTHY, TRADEMARKS AND UNFAIR COMPETITION, § 11.45, at 82 (1999). As Justice Holmes in *Prestonettes v. Coty*, 264 U.S. 359, 368, 44 S.Ct. 350, 68 L.Ed. 731 (1924), put more eloquently, "[w]hen the mark is used in a way that does not deceive the public we see no such sanctity in the word as to prevent its being used to tell the truth."

(3) *Conclusion*

In summary, the court finds in this case that Plaintiff's presentation of evidence regarding initial interest confusion is insufficient under *Dr. Seuss* and *Brookfield* to establish a material issue of fact as to whether Ms. Welles' use of PEI terms in the metatags of her website was a trademark infringement or amounted to unfair competition under the Lanham Act. Furthermore, in light of the fact that there is no evidence of an intent by Ms. Welles to trade upon the goodwill of Plaintiff's marks by falsely implying sponsorship by or affiliation with PEI, and there is no evidence of actual consumer confusion or likelihood of confusion regarding any implied PEI endorsement, and in light of the court's discussion in section III(A)(1)(a)(2), *supra*, of this order, regarding Ms. Welles' nominative, fair use of the terms to describe her goods and services, the court holds that Plaintiff has failed to raise a material issue of fact concerning the fair use of PEI terms in her metatags. Accordingly, the court grants Defendant Welles' motion for summary judgment on all Plaintiff's trademark claims against her with respect to the use of the terms "Playboy," "Playmate," and "Playmate of the Year 1981," in the HTML source code of her website.

2. *Counts III and VII: Trademark Dilution*

Dilution is defined as "the lessening of the capacity of a famous mark to identify and distinguish goods or services, regardless of the presence or absence of ... (2) likelihood of confusion, mistake, or deception." 15 U.S.C. § 1127 (1999). Under the Federal Trademark Dilution Act, a dilution claim is not actionable if there is a "[f]air use of a famous mark by another person in comparative commercial advertising or promotion to identify the competing goods or services of the owner of the famous mark." 15 U.S.C. § 1125(c)(4)(A) (1999). Similarly, under California Business and Professions Code § 14335, a claim for dilution cannot lie where a person uses a mark "in an otherwise non-infringing manner, either on the person's own goods or services or to describe the person's own goods or services." Cal. Bus. & Prof.Code § 14335 (1999).

The court has found in this order that Ms. Welles' use of the terms "Playboy Playmate of the Year 1981," "Playmate of the Year 1981," and "PMOY '81" in her website constitute identification of herself: a nominative fair use. The use of those terms in the visible portion of her website and the terms, "Playboy Playmate of the Year 1981," "Playboy," and "Playmate," in the meta tags, allows web surfers and potential customers correctly to identify her site and locate her services. In cases where the trademarked term must be used to identify the individual or a good, infringement and dilution laws do not apply. *See New Kids*, 971 F.2d at 306. Since the court has found that Defendant is entitled to the "fair use" defense pursuant to the Lanham Act, 15 U.S.C. § 1115(b)(4), as to Plaintiff's trademark infringement and unfair competition claims, the court also finds that Defendant is entitled to the "fair use" defense on Plaintiff's federal dilution claims under the Lanham Act, 15 U.S.C. § 1125(c)(4)(A). In addition, since a common law fair use defense incorporates the statutory elements of Lanham Act § 33(b)(4), this court's finding as a matter of law of a fair use defense as to Plaintiff's trademark infringement, dilution, and unfair competition claims under the Lanham Act also applies to Plaintiff's dilution claims under California state and common law. *See Sierra On–Line, Inc. v. Phoenix Software, Inc.*, 739 F.2d 1415, 1423 (9th Cir.1984). Accordingly, the court finds as a matter of law that Defendant Welles' use of the terms "Playboy Playmate of the Year 1981," "Playmate of the Year 1981," "PMOY '81," "Playmate," and "Playboy" does not dilute PEI's trademarks.

3. *Count VIII: Breach of Contract Claim*

* * *

IV. CONCLUSION

Based on the foregoing analysis, the court, hereby **GRANTS** Defendant Terri Welles,' Terri Welles, Inc, Pippi, Inc.'s, Defendant Mihalko's, and Defendant Huntington's Motion For Summary Judgement as to all Plaintiff's claims in Counts I through VIII of the Second Amended Complaint. The court also **DENIES** Plaintiff's evidentiary objections as moot. The court **DENIES** Defendant Welles' evidentiary objections to

Plaintiff's Expert Witness James Sterne's Declaration and **DENIES** Defendant Welles' remaining evidentiary objections as moot.

IT IS SO ORDERED.

Note

The above case is the leading case on the way another's trademark can be used on the Internet without infringement.

PLAYBOY ENTERPRISES, INC. v. NETSCAPE COMMUNICATIONS CORP.

PLAYBOY ENTERPRISES, INC. v. EXCITE, INC.

United States District Court, C.D. California, 1999.
55 F.Supp.2d 1070, *aff'd* 202 F.3d 278 (9th Cir. 1999).

STOTLER, DISTRICT JUDGE.

I.

PROCEDURAL BACKGROUND

On April 15, 1999, plaintiff Playboy Enterprises, Inc. ("PEI") filed a Motion for Preliminary Injunction against defendant Netscape Communications Corp. and against defendant Excite, Inc. On May 10, 1999, defendants filed a joint opposition. PEI filed its reply on May 17, 1999. The Court heard oral argument on the motion on May 24, 1999. At the end of the hearing, the Court took the matter under advisement, and ordered the parties to lodge proposed Findings of Fact and Conclusions of Law. Plaintiff lodged its proposed Findings on June 1, 1999; defendants lodged theirs on June 8, 1999. The Court has considered all of the parties' submissions, as well as arguments presented at the hearing.

II.

FACTUAL BACKGROUND

Defendants operate search engines on the Internet. When a person searches for a particular topic in either search engine, the search engine compiles a list of sites matching or related to the user's search terms, and then posts the list of sites, known as "search results."

Defendants sell advertising space on the search result pages. Known as "banner ads," the advertisements are commonly found at the top of the screen. The ads themselves are often animated and whimsical, and designed to entice the Internet user to "click here." If the user does click on the ad, she is transported to the web site of the advertiser.

As with other media, advertisers seek to maximize the efficacy of their ads by targeting consumers matching a certain demographic profile. Savvy web site operators accommodate the advertisers by "keying" ads to search terms entered by users. That is, instead of posting ads in a random rotation, defendants program their servers to link a pre-selected set of banner ads to certain "key" search terms. Defendants market this context-sensitive advertising ability as a value-added service and charge a premium.

Defendants key various adult entertainment ads to a group of over 450 terms related to adult entertainment, including the terms "playboy" and "playmate." Plaintiff contends that inclusion of those terms violates plaintiff's trademarks rights in those words.

III.

PARTIES' CONTENTIONS

Plaintiff has a trademark on "Playboy®" and "Playmate®." Plaintiff contends that defendants are infringing and diluting its trademarks (1) by marketing and selling the group of over 450 words, including "playboy" and "playmate," to advertisers, (2) by programming the banner ads to run in response to the search terms "playboy" and "playmate" (i.e., "keying"), and (3) by actually displaying the banner ad on the search results page. As a result, plaintiff contends, Internet users are diverted from plaintiff's official web site and web sites sponsored or approved by plaintiff, which generally will be listed as search results, to other adult entertainment web sites. Plaintiff further argues that defendants intend to divert the users to the non-PEI sites. Plaintiff does not contend, however, that defendants infringe or dilute the marks when defendants' search engines generate a list of Web sites related to "playboy" or "playmate."

Defendants respond that while plaintiff may have a trademark on "Playboy®" and "Playmate®," defendants do not actually "use" the trademarks qua trademarks. Moreover, even if defendants do use the trademarks, defendants argue that a trademark does not confer an absolute property right on all uses of the protected terms, and that defendants' use of the terms is permitted. Finally, defendants dispute that they have any intent to divert users from clicking on search results (such as PEI's sites) to clicking on banner ads.

IV.

DISCUSSION

* * *

B.   *Law and the Internet*

"The Internet is 'a unique and wholly new medium of worldwide human communication.'" *Reno v. ACLU*, 521 U.S. 844, 117 S.Ct. 2329, 2334, 138 L.Ed.2d 874 (1997) (citation omitted). The parties and the Court are conversant with the workings of the Internet, as well as with the constantly expanding body of law that seeks to craft a legal contour for it. The Court is mindful of the difficulty of applying well-established doctrines to what can only be described as an amorphous situs of information, anonymous messenger of communication, and seemingly endless stream of commerce. Indeed, the very vastness, and manipulability, of the Internet forms the mainspring of plaintiff's lawsuit.

C. Trademark Use

Integral to plaintiff's success on the merits of its case, on either the infringement or dilution theory, is a showing that defendants use plaintiff's trademarks in commerce. *See* Memorandum of Points & Authorities [Excite], pg. 13 (e.g., "Excite is deriving substantial and direct revenue by selling banner advertisements keyed to the PEI marks"); Memorandum of Points and Authorities [Netscape], pg. 14 (same). Plaintiff does not so show. Rather, plaintiff can only contend that the use of the words "playboy" and "playmate," as keywords or search terms, is equivalent to the use of the trademarks "Playboy (R)" and "Playmate®." However, it is undisputed that an Internet user cannot conduct a search using the trademark form of the words, i.e., Playboy® and Playmate®. Rather, the user enters the generic word "playboy" or "playmate." It is also undisputed that the words "playboy" and "playmate" are English words in their own right, and that there exist other trademarks on the words wholly unrelated to PEI. Thus, whether the user is looking for goods and services covered by PEI's trademarks or something altogether unrelated to PEI is anybody's guess. Plaintiff guesses that most users searching the Web for "playboy" and "playmate" are indeed looking for PEI sites, goods and services. Based on that theory, plaintiff argues that since defendants also speculate that users searching for "playboy" and "playmate" are looking for things related to Playboy® and Playmate®, defendants use the trademarks when they key competing adult entertainment goods and services to the generic "playboy" and "playmate."

Plaintiff has not shown that defendants use the terms in their trademark form, i.e., Playboy® and Playmate®, when marketing to advertisers or in the algorithm that effectuates the keying of the ads to the keywords. Thus, plaintiff's argument that defendants "use" plaintiff's trademarks falls short.

D. Trademark Infringement and Dilution

Even if use of the generic "playboy" and "playmate" were construed to be use the trademark terms Playboy® Playmate®, plaintiff still must show that the use violates trademark law. Plaintiff has asserted two theories, trademark infringement and trademark dilution.

1. Infringement

"The core element of trademark infringement is the likelihood of confusion, i.e., whether the similarity of the marks is likely to confuse customers about the source of the products." *Official Airline Guides, Inc. v. Goss*, 6 F.3d 1385, 1391 (9th Cir.1993). Assuming arguendo that defendants' use of "playboy" and "playmate" is use of plaintiff's marks, plaintiff must still show that confusion is likely to result from that use. Plaintiff has not so shown.

Rather, plaintiff relies on the recent case from the Court of Appeals for the Ninth Circuit, *Brookfield Communications, Inc. v. West Coast Entertainment Corp.*, 174 F.3d 1036, 1062–64 (9th Cir.1999), for the proposition that defendants cause "initial interest confusion" by the use of the words "playboy" and "playmate." Initial interest confusion, as coined by the Ninth Circuit, is a brand of confusion particularly applicable to the Internet. Generally speaking, initial interest confusion may result when a user conducts a search using a trademark term and the results of the search include web sites not sponsored by the holder of the trademark search term, but rather of competitors. *Id.* The Ninth Circuit reasoned that the user may be diverted to an un-sponsored site, and only realize that she has been diverted upon arriving at the competitor's site. Once there, however, even though the user knows she is not in the site initially sought, she may stay. In that way, the competitor has captured the trademark holder's potential visitors or customers. *Id.*

Brookfield is distinguishable from this case, and where applicable, supportive of defendants' position.

First, the trademark at issue in *Brookfield* was not an English word in its own right. In *Brookfield*, the Court compared Brookfield's trademark "MovieBuff" with competitor West Coast's use of the domain name "moviebuff.com," and found them to be "essentially identical" despite the differences in capitalization, which the Court considered "inconsequential in light of the fact that Web addresses are not capssensitive ... " *Id.* at 1054. However, the Court held that West Coast could use the term "Movie Buff" (or, presumably, "movie buff") with the space, as such is the "proper term for the 'motion picture enthusiast'.... It cannot, however, omit the space." *Id.* at 1065. On the other hand, "[i]n light of the fact that it is not a word in the English language, when the term 'MovieBuff' is employed, it is used to refer to Brookfield's products and services, rather than to mean 'motion picture enthusiast.' " *Id.* at 1065.

As English words, "playboy" and "playmate" cannot be said to suggest sponsorship or endorsement of either the web sites that appear as search results (as in *Brookfield*) or the banner ads that adorn the search results page. Although the trademark terms and the English language words are undisputedly identical, which, presumably, leads plaintiff to believe that the use of the English words is akin to use of the trademarks, the holder of a trademark may not remove a word from the English language merely by acquiring trademark rights in it. *Id.*

Second, the use by defendant of plaintiff's trademark in *Brookfield* was more suspect because the parties compete in the same market—as online providers of film industry information. *See Id.*, at 1056–57 ("[n]ot only are they not non-competitors, the competitive proximity of their products is actually quite high"). The Ninth Circuit analogized the capture of unsuspecting Internet users by a competitor to highways and billboards:

Suppose West Coast's competitor ... puts up a billboard on a highway reading—"West Coast Video: 2 miles ahead at Exit 7"— where West Coast is really located at Exit 8 but Blockbuster is located at Exit 7. Customers looking for West Coast's store will pull off at Exit 7 and drive around looking for it. Unable to locate West, Coast, but seeing the Blockbuster store right by the highway entrance, they may simply rent there.

Brookfield, at 1064. Although the customer is not confused as to where she ultimately rents a video, Blockbuster has misappropriated West Coast's goodwill through causing initial consumer confusion. *Id*. The customer has been captured by the competitor in much the same way that defendant in *Brookfield* captures Internet users looking for plaintiff's web site.

Here, the analogy is quite unlike that of a devious placement of a road sign bearing false information. This case presents a scenario more akin to a driver pulling off the freeway in response to a sign that reads "Fast Food Burgers" to find a well-known fast food burger restaurant, next to which stands a billboard that reads: "Better Burgers: 1 Block Further." The driver, previously enticed by the prospect of a burger from the well-known restaurant, now decides she wants to explore other burger options. Assuming that the same entity owns the land on which both the burger restaurant and the competitor's billboard stand, should that entity be liable to the burger restaurant for diverting the driver? That is the rule PEI contends the Court should adopt.

2. *Dilution*

Trademark dilution is defined as "the lessening of the capacity of a famous mark to identify and distinguish goods or services." 15 U.S.C. § 1127. However, dilution is "not intended to serve as a mere fallback protection for trademark owners unable to prove trademark infringement." *I.P. Lund Trading ApS v. Kohler Co.*, 163 F.3d 27, 48 (1st Cir.1998).

To establish dilution, plaintiff must show that "(1) [defendants have] made use of a junior mark sufficiently similar to the famous mark to evoke in a relevant universe of consumers a mental association of the two that (2) has caused (3) actual economic harm to the famous mark's economic value by lessening its former selling power as an advertising agent for its goods and services." *Ringling Bros.-Barnum & Bailey Combined Shows, Inc. v. Utah Div'n of Travel Dev.*, 170 F.3d 449, 459 (4th Cir.1999). Dilution generally occurs through the blurring of a famous mark or tarnishment of the mark, but is not limited to these categories. *See Panavision Int'l, L.P. v. Toeppen*, 141 F.3d 1316, 1326 (9th Cir.1998). Plaintiff has not shown blurring of its marks, which would occur if defendants used the marks to identify defendants' goods or services. *Id*. at 1326 n. 7. First, as discussed *supra*, plaintiff has not shown that defendant use its marks Playboy® and Playmate®. Further, plaintiff has not presented any evidence that defendants' use of the words "playboy" and "playmate" causes any severance of the association between plaintiff and its marks Playboy® and Playmate®, much less in the minds of Internet users.

Plaintiff has also failed to show tarnishment, which occurs when a famous mark is associated improperly with an inferior or offensive product or service. *Id.* at 1326 n. 7. Plaintiff contends that because the content of the banner ads is more sexually explicit that PEI's content, PEI's marks are being tarnished. Again, plaintiff's argument is based on the incorrect assumption that defendants use plaintiff's marks, rather than the generic words "playboy" and "playmate." But even if the defendants could be said to use plaintiff's marks, plaintiff would still be required to show that associating marks admittedly famous for adult entertainment with other purveyors of adult entertainment somehow harms plaintiff's marks. Whether PEI is a cut above the rest, as it contends, is undercut by the fact that PEI's marks are associated with other purveyors of adult entertainment in other marketing channels, as defendants' exhibits graphically establish. Adoption of plaintiff's tarnishment would secure near-monopoly control of the placement of plaintiff's marks and the associated goods and services on the Internet, where, arguably, "placement" is a nebulous concept. A greater showing of harm is required.

V.

CONCLUSION

Accordingly, and for the foregoing reasons, the plaintiff's motion is denied. * * *

D. INTERFERING WITH INTERNET COMMUNICATIONS

AMERICA ONLINE, INC. v. LCGM, INC.

United States District Court, E.D. Virginia 1998.
46 F.Supp.2d 444.

LEE, DISTRICT JUDGE.

This matter is before the Court on plaintiff's Motion for Summary Judgment as to each of the seven counts in the complaint. Plaintiff America Online, Inc. (AOL) complains that defendants sent large numbers of unauthorized and unsolicited bulk e-mail advertisements ("spam") to its members (AOL members).[1] AOL's complaint has seven counts: Count I (False Designation of Origin under the Lanham Act);

---

1. "Spam" is unsolicited commercial bulk e-mail akin to "junk mail" sent through the postal mail. The transmission of spam is a practice widely condemned in the Internet Community. *Hotmail Corp. v. Van$ Money Pie Inc., et al.*, 47 U.S.P.Q.2d 1020, 1998 WL 388389 (N.D.Cal.1998). For a discussion of spamming and the emerging case law in this area, *see generally* Susan E. Gindin, *Lost and Found in Cyberspace: Informational Privacy in the Age of the Internet*, 32 San Diego L.Rev. 1153 (1997); Anne E. Hawley, Comment, *Taking Spam Out of Your Cyberspace Diet: Common Law Applied to Bulk Unsolicited Advertising Via Electronic Mail*, 66 UMKC L.Rev. 381 (1997).

Count II (Dilution of Interest in Service Marks under the Lanham Act); Count III (Exceeding Authorized Access in Violation of the Computer Fraud and Abuse Act); Count IV (Impairing Computer Facilities in Violation of the Computer Fraud and Abuse Act); Count V (Violations of the Virginia Computer Crimes Act); Count VI (Trespass to Chattels under the Common Law of Virginia); and Count VII (Common Law Conspiracy to Commit Trespass to Chattels and Violate Federal and Virginia Statutes). Plaintiff seeks compensatory and punitive damages, attorney's fees, costs, and permanent injunctive relief. After reviewing the evidence appropriately before this Court, the Court concludes that there are no genuine issues of material fact in regard to Counts I, II, III, IV, V, and VI, but that such issues remain as to Count VII as well as the issue of damages. Therefore, the Court grants summary judgment in favor of plaintiff on Counts I through VI and denies plaintiff's motion on Count VII and on the issue of damages for the reasons that follow.

* * *

II. Findings of Fact and Conclusions of Law

AOL, an Internet service provider located in the Eastern District of Virginia, provides a proprietary, content-based online service that provides its members (AOL members) access to the Internet and the capability to receive as well as send e-mail messages. AOL registered "AOL" as a trademark and service mark in 1996 and has registered its domain name "aol.com" with the InterNIC. At the time this cause of action arose, defendant LCGM, Inc. was a Michigan corporation which operated and transacted business from Internet domains offering pornographic web sites. Plaintiff alleges that defendant Web Promo is a d/b/a designation for FSJD, Inc., a Michigan corporation that operates Internet domains offering pornographic web sites. Defendant Francis Sharrak was the vice-president of Web Promo and the sole shareholder and president of LCGM. Defendant James Drakos was the president of Web Promo. Defendants Francis Sharrak and James Drakos have participated in the transmission of the bulk e-mails. *See LCGM and Web Promo's Response to Interrogatory 22.*

AOL alleges that defendants, in concert, sent unauthorized and unsolicited bulk e-mail advertisements ("spam") to AOL customers. AOL's Unsolicited Bulk E-mail Policy and its Terms of Service bar both members and nonmembers from sending bulk e-mail through AOL's computer systems. Plaintiff estimates that defendants, in concert with their "site partners," transmitted more than 92 million unsolicited and bulk e-mail messages advertising their pornographic Web sites to AOL members from approximately June 17, 1997 to January 21, 1998. Plaintiff bases this number on defendants' admissions that they sent approximately 300,000 e-mail messages a day at various intervals from their Michigan offices. *See LCGM and Web Promo's Answers to Document Request 12; Sharrak and Drakos' Answers to Document Request 16.* Plaintiff asserts that defendants provided AOL with computer disks containing a list of the addresses of 820,296 AOL members to whom defendants admitted to transmitting bulk e-mail.

Plaintiff alleges that defendants harvested, or collected, the e-mail addresses of AOL members in violation of AOL's Terms of Service. Defendants have admitted to maintaining AOL memberships to harvest or collect the e-mail addresses of other AOL members. *See Defendants' Answer*, para. 63. Defendants have admitted to maintaining AOL accounts and to using the AOL Collector and E-mail Pro/Stealth Mailer extractor programs to collect the e-mail addresses of AOL members, alleging that they did so in targeted adult AOL chat rooms. *See LCGM and Web Promo's Answers to Document Request 3. See Sharrak and Drakos' Answers to Document Requests 4 and 20*. Defendants have admitted to using this software to evade AOL's filtering mechanisms. *See Sharrak and Drakos' Answers to Document Request 16*.

Plaintiff alleges that defendants forged the domain information "aol.com" in the "from" line of e-mail messages sent to AOL members. Defendants have admitted to creating the domain information "aol.com" through an e-mail sending program, and to causing the AOL domain to appear in electronic header information of its commercial e-mails. *See LCGM and Web Promo's Answers to Document Request 17; Sharrak and Drakos' Answers to Document Requests 13 and 21. LCGM and Web Promo's Answers to Interrogatory 14*. Plaintiffs assert that as a result, many AOL members expressed confusion about whether AOL endorsed defendants' pornographic Web sites or their bulk e-mailing practices. Plaintiff also asserts that defendants e-mail messages were sent through AOL's computer networks. Defendants have admitted to sending e-mail messages from their computers through defendants' network via e-mail software to AOL, which then relayed the messages to AOL members. *See LCGM and Web Promo's Answers to Document Request 14*.

Plaintiff alleges that AOL sent defendants two cease and desist letters, dated respectively December 8, 1997 and December 30, 1997, but that defendants continued their e-mailing practices to AOL members after receiving those letters. Defendants have admitted to receiving those letters, contending that any e-mails sent after such receipt were "lawful." *See Defendants Answer*, para. 46–47.

Plaintiff alleges that defendants paid their "site partners" to transmit unsolicited bulk e-mail on their behalf and encouraged these site partners to advertise. Plaintiff further alleges that defendants conspired with CN Productions, another pornographic e-mailer, to transmit bulk e-mails to AOL members. Plaintiff alleges that many e-mails sent by defendants contained Hyper–Text Links both to defendants' web sites and CN Production's web sites.

Plaintiff alleges that defendants' actions injured AOL by consuming capacity on AOL's computers, causing AOL to incur technical costs, impairing the functioning of AOL's e-mail system, forcing AOL to upgrade its computer networks to process authorized e-mails in a timely manner, damaging AOL's goodwill with its members, and causing AOL to lose customers and revenue. Plaintiff asserts that between the months of December 1997 and April 1998, defendants' unsolicited bulk e-mails generated more than 450,000 complaints by AOL members.

Count I: False Designation of Origin Under the Lanham Act

The undisputed facts establish that defendants violated 15 U.S.C. § 1125(a)(1) of the Lanham Act, which makes it unlawful to use in commerce:

> any false designation of origin ... which ... is likely to cause confusion, or to cause mistake, or to deceive as to the affiliation, connection, or association of such person with another person, or as to the origin, sponsorship, or approval of his or her goods, services, or commercial activities by another person.

The unauthorized sending of bulk e-mails has been held to constitute a violation of this section of the Lanham Act. *America Online, Inc. v. IMS, et al.*, Civil Action No. 98–11–A (E.D.Va.1998); *See also Hotmail Corp. v. Van$ Money Pie Inc., et al.*, 47 U.S.P.Q.2d 1020, 1998 WL 388389 (N.D.Cal.1998) (granting injunction where plaintiff was likely to prevail on the merits under the Lanham Act). The elements necessary to establish a false designation violation under the Lanham Act are as follows: (1) a defendant uses a designation; (2) in interstate commerce; (3) in connection with goods and services; (4) which designation is likely to cause confusion, mistake or deception as to origin, sponsorship, or approval of defendant's goods or services; and (5) plaintiff has been or is likely to be damaged by these acts. *See First Keystone Federal Savings Bank v. First Keystone Mortgage, Inc.* 923 F.Supp. 693, 707 (E.D.Pa. 1996).

Each of the false designation elements has been satisfied. First, defendants clearly used the "aol.com" designation, incorporating the registered trademark and service mark AOL in their e-mail headers. Second, defendants' activities involved interstate commerce because all e-mails sent to AOL members were routed from defendants' computers in Michigan through AOL's computers in Virginia. Third, the use of AOL's designation was in connection with goods and services as defendants' e-mails advertised their commercial web sites. Fourth, the use of "aol.com" in defendants' e-mails was likely to cause confusion as to the origin and sponsorship of defendants' goods and services. Any e-mail recipient could logically conclude that a message containing the initials "aol.com" in the header would originate from AOL's registered Internet domain, which incorporates the registered mark "AOL." *AOL v. IMS*, CA 98–11–A. The recipient of such a message would be led to conclude the sender was an AOL member or AOL, the Internet Service Provider. Indeed, plaintiff alleges that this designation did cause such confusion among many AOL members, who believed that AOL sponsored and authorized defendants' bulk e-mailing practices and pornographic web sites. Finally, plaintiff asserts that these acts damaged AOL's technical capabilities and its goodwill. The defendants are precluded from opposing these claims due to their failure to comply with discovery orders.

Therefore, there is no genuine issue of material fact in regards to this Count, and the Court holds the plaintiff is entitled to summary judgment on Count I.

Count II: Dilution of Interest in Service Marks Under the Lanham Act

The undisputed facts establish that defendants violated 15 U.S.C. § 1125(c)(1) of the Lanham Act, also known as the Federal Trademark Dilution Act of 1995, which provides relief to an owner of a mark whose mark or trade name is used by another person in commerce "if such use begins after the mark has become famous and causes dilution of the distinctive quality of the mark." The legislative history of the Act indicates that it was intended to address Internet domain name issues. *Intermatic Inc. v. Toeppen*, 947 F.Supp. 1227, 1238 (N.D.Ill.1996) (granting summary judgment to Intermatic, Inc. on its Lanham Act dilution claim against defendant who had registered "intermatic.com" as its domain name). United States Senator Leahy, in discussing the Act, stated that

> ... it is my hope that this antidilution statute can help stem the use of *deceptive Internet addresses* taken by those who are choosing marks that are associated with the products and reputations of others [emphasis added].

Id. (quoting 141 Cong.Rec. S19312–01 (daily ed. December 29, 1995) (statement of Senator Leahy)). Moreover, this Court has found the unauthorized sending of bulk e-mails constitutes a violation of Section 1125(c)(1) of the Lanham Act. *AOL v. IMS*, CA 98–11–A; *see also Hotmail*, 47 U.S.P.Q.2d 1020, 1998 WL 388389 (court granted injunction, finding plaintiffs were likely to prevail on the merits under this section of the Act).

Plaintiff has satisfied the two elements necessary to establish a dilution claim: "(1) the ownership of a distinctive mark, and (2) a likelihood of dilution." *Hormel Foods Corp. v. Jim Henson Productions, Inc.*, 73 F.3d 497, 506 (2d Cir.1996) (applying New York's anti-dilution statute). Plaintiff's "AOL" mark qualifies as a distinctive mark. The "AOL" mark is registered on the principal register of the United States Patent and Trademark Office. Furthermore, the mark is recognized throughout the world in association with AOL's online products and services. Dilution can be established by "tarnishment." "The sine qua non of tarnishment is a finding that plaintiff's mark will suffer negative associations through defendant's use." *Id.* at 507. Plaintiff contends that the "AOL" mark is a valuable business asset to plaintiff. Plaintiff argues that the "AOL" mark is tarnished, and thus diluted, by association with defendants' bulk e-mail practices and submits thousands of member complaints about defendants' e-mails as evidence of tarnishment.

Count III: Exceeding Authorized Access in Violation
of the Computer Fraud and Abuse Act

The facts before the Court establish that defendants violated 18 U.S.C. § 1030(a)(2)(C) of the Computer Fraud and Abuse Act, which prohibits individuals from "intentionally access[ing] a computer without authorization or exceed[ing] authorized access, and thereby obtain[ing] information from any protected computer if the conduct involved an interstate or foreign communication." Defendants' own admissions satisfy the Act's requirements. Defendants have admitted to maintaining an AOL membership and using that membership to harvest the e-mail addresses of AOL members. Defendants have stated that they acquired these e-mail addresses by using extractor software programs. Defendants' actions violated AOL's Terms of Service, and as such was unauthorized. Plaintiff contends that the addresses of AOL members are "information" within the meaning of the Act because they are proprietary in nature. Plaintiff asserts that as a result of defendants' actions, it suffered damages exceeding $5,000, the statutory threshold requirement.

Count IV: Impairing Computer Facilities In Violation of the Computer Fraud and Abuse Act

The undisputed facts establish that defendants violated 18 U.S.C. § 1030(a)(5)(C) of the Computer Fraud and Abuse Act, which prohibits anyone from "intentionally access[ing] a protected computer without authorization, and as a result of such conduct, causes damage." Another court found that spamming was an actionable claim under this Act. *See Hotmail*, 47 U.S.P.Q.2d 1020, 1998 WL 388389 (granting injunction to Hotmail because it was likely to prevail on the merits under this statute). Defendants have admitted to utilizing software to collect AOL members' addresses. These actions were unauthorized because they violated AOL's Terms of Service. Defendants' intent to access a protected computer, in this case computers within AOL's network, is clear under the circumstances. Defendants' access of AOL's computer network enabled defendants to send large numbers of unsolicited bulk e-mail messages to AOL members.

In addition to defendants' admissions, plaintiff alleges that by using the domain information "aol.com" in their e-mails, defendants and their "site partners" camouflaged their identities, and evaded plaintiff's blocking filters and its members' mail controls. Defendants have admitted to using extractor software to evade AOL's filtering mechanisms. As a result of these actions, plaintiff asserts damages to its computer network, reputation and goodwill in excess of the minimum $5,000 statutory requirement.

Count V: Violations of the Virginia Computer Crimes Act

The facts presented to the Court establish that defendants violated the Virginia Computer Crimes Act, Va.Code § 18.2–152.3(3), which provides that "[a]ny person who uses a computer or computer network without authority and with the intent to [c]onvert the property of another shall be guilty of the crime of computer fraud." Section 18.2–152.12 authorizes a private right of action for violations of the Act. Defendants have admitted to causing "aol.com" to appear in the electronic header information of e-mail messages which they sent. Sending such messages through AOL's computer network was unauthorized. Plaintiff alleges that defendants intended to obtain services by false pretenses and to convert AOL's property. Plaintiff alleges that the inclusion of false domain information in defendants' e-mails enabled defendants to escape detection by plaintiff's blocking filters and its members' mail controls. Plaintiff argues that as a result, defendants illegitimately obtained the unauthorized service of plaintiff's mail delivery system and obtained free advertising from AOL because AOL, not defendants, bore the costs of sending these messages. There are no genuine issues for trial with respect to this Count. As such, plaintiff's Motion for Summary Judgment must be granted on Count V.

COUNT VI: TRESPASS TO CHATTELS UNDER THE COMMON LAW OF VIRGINIA

The undisputed facts establish that defendants' actions constituted a trespass to chattels under Virginia common law. Courts have recognized that the transmission of unsolicited bulk e-mails can constitute a trespass to chattels. *See AOL v. IMS*, CA 98–11–A (finding that spammers committed a trespass to chattels in violation of Virginia Common Law at summary judgment stage); *Hotmail*, 47 U.S.P.Q.2d 1020, 1998 WL 388389 (granting a preliminary injunction because plaintiff was likely to succeed on the merits on a theory of trespass to chattels); *CompuServe, Inc. v. Cyber Promotions, Inc.*, 962 F.Supp. 1015 (S.D.Ohio 1997). Case law suggests that trespass to chattels is actionable in Virginia. *See AOL v. IMS*, CA 98–11–A (citing *Vines v. Branch*, 244 Va. 185, 418 S.E.2d 890, 894 (1992)).

A trespass to chattels occurs when one party intentionally uses or intermeddles with personal property in rightful possession of another without authorization. *AOL v. IMS*, CA 98–11–A (citing RESTATEMENT (SECOND) OF TORTS § 217(b)). One who commits a trespass to chattel is liable to the possessor of the chattel if the chattel is impaired as to its "condition, quality, or value." *Id.* (citing RESTATEMENT (SECOND) OF TORTS § 218(b)). As articulated in *CompuServe*,

> [t]o the extent that defendants' multitudinous electronic mailings demand the disk space and drain the processing power of plaintiff's computer equipment, those resources are not available to serve [plaintiff] subscribers. Therefore, the value of that equipment to [plaintiff] is diminished even though it is not physically damaged by defendants' conduct.

962 F.Supp. at 1022. Plaintiff asserts that defendants intentionally used AOL's computers and computer network, which are tangible personal property. The transmission of electrical signals through a computer network is sufficiently "physical" contact to constitute a trespass to property. *See CompuServe*, 962 F.Supp. at 1021. Because AOL's Unsolicited Bulk E-mail Policy and Terms of Service prohibit the sending of such e-mails, defendants' actions were unauthorized. Plaintiff asserts that its possessory interest in its computer equipment and business goodwill has been injured by defendants' unauthorized use of AOL's computers.

COUNT VII: COMMON LAW CONSPIRACY TO COMMIT TRESPASS TO
CHATTELS AND VIOLATE FEDERAL AND VIRGINIA STATUTES

The elements necessary to establish the existence of a civil conspiracy are: (1) that two or more persons engaged in concerted action; (2) to accomplish some criminal or unlawful purpose, or some lawful purpose by some criminal and unlawful means; and (3) that actual damages resulted from something done by one or more of the conspirators in furtherance of the object of the conspiracy. *See Blackwelder v. Millman*, 522 F.2d 766 (4th Cir.1975).

Plaintiff alleges that defendants engaged in a conspiracy with one another, their site partners and another pornographic spammer (CN Productions and its president Jay Nelson) to commit trespass to chattels by transmitting unauthorized and unsolicited e-mail messages to AOL members. Plaintiff alleges that defendants' "site partners" program promised compensation to individuals who drove customers to defendants' Web sites and urged them to exploit the fact that the transmission of bulk e-mail is free to its sender. Plaintiff alleges that after conspiring with their "site partners," defendants attempted to "look the other way" while the site partners sent AOL members millions of unsolicited e-mail messages. Plaintiff alleges that defendants knowingly paid these site partners thousands of dollars for such transmissions. Plaintiff cites as evidence of this the fact that defendant LCGM paid a third party thousands of dollars and noted on checks made out to that party "5 million bulk e-mail" and "partial payment bulk email." Plaintiff argues that defendants' conspiracy with CN Productions is evidenced by Hyper–Text Links to CN Production's web sites in some of defendants' e-mails sent to AOL members. Plaintiff also contends that defendants purchased airplane tickets for CN Productions personnel to visit defendants' offices. Despite Judge Poretz' ruling, the facts are in dispute with respect to Count VII. Thus, the Court denies plaintiff's Motion for Summary Judgment on Count VII.

DAMAGES

AOL's claim for damages is unliquidated and therefore the Court must determine the issue at trial. Thus, the Court denies plaintiff's Motion for Summary Judgment on the issue of damages. However, the Court finds that AOL is entitled to injunctive relief preventing defendants from further distributing unsolicited bulk e-mail messages to AOL members. Defendants are further enjoined from using "aol.com" to send and distribute e-mail messages and from using the AOL network for the purpose of harvesting the addresses of AOL members. Defendants are to terminate any AOL membership. At trial, the Court can consider the parties' evidence and arguments regarding the appropriate terms of the injunction. In addition, pursuant to 15 U.S.C. § 1117(a), the Court may consider awarding attorney's fees for the Counts arising under the Lanham Act.

CONCLUSION

For the reasons discussed fully in this Opinion, the Court grants plaintiff's Motion for Summary Judgment with respect to Counts I, II, III, IV, V, and VI. The Court denies plaintiff's Motion for Summary Judgment as to Count VII and as to the issue of damages, but finds that plaintiff is entitled to injunctive relief.

An appropriate Order will issue.

Note

As this casebook was being prepared for publication, the House of Representatives had passed and the Senate was considering the "Unsolicited Electronic Mail Act." This act would require unsolicited commercial e-mail to have valid routing information and include a valid e-mail address to which the recipient could reply so as to be removed from the mailing list. It would create criminal penalties for continuing to send e-mail to recipients who asked to be removed from mailing lists. It would also provide Internet service providers the right to recover substantial statutory damages (without proof of actual damages) for the burden placed on their servers by unauthorized unsolicited e-mail.

HARTFORD HOUSE, LTD v. MICROSOFT CORP.

Superior Court of California County of Santa Clara, 1988.
CASE NO.: CV778550.

TEMPORARY RESTRAINING ORDER AND ORDER TO SHOW CAUSE

The application of plaintiff Hartford House, Ltd. d.b.a. Blue Mountain Arts ("Blue Mountain") for a Temporary Restraining Order and an Order to Show Cause came on for hearing on December 17 and 18, 1998. After consideration of all of the materials submitted by the parties in this action and the oral arguments of counsel, IT IS HEREBY ORDERED THAT Blue Mountain's application is GRANTED. Defendant Microsoft Corporation ("Microsoft") shall appear before this Court on Thursday January 21, 1999 at 2:00 p.m. to show cause, if any it has, as to why the injunctive relief requested ex parte as well as following provisions should not be incorporated into a Preliminary Injunction to last throughout this action:

1. Microsoft Corporation shall make available to Blue Mountain that minimum information necessary to enable Blue Mountain to design its electronic mail ("e-mail") notification messages and e-mail greeting cards so that they are received by the intended recipient in their standard e-mail in-box and are not relegated to the "Junk" mail folder when the junk mail filter contained in Outlook Express, available from the downloadable version of Internet Explorer 5.0, beta version 5 is enabled on the default setting or any less restrictive setting. For purposes of the Order, the "default setting" is currently the middle of the five settings available to the user of the junk mail filter. Any confidential information shared by Microsoft with Blue Mountain about the filter

shall be disclosed pursuant to a standard non-disclosure agreement entered into between Microsoft and Blue Mountain.

2. At least 15 days in advance of any changes, modifications or redesigns that Microsoft intends to make to the above-noted junk mail filter in any subsequent beta version or commercially available version, which would affect the delivery of Blue Mountain e-mail notification messages and e-mail greeting cards to the standard in-box when the filter is set to its default setting or any less restrictive setting, Microsoft shall inform Blue Mountain of such changes, and provide to Blue Mountain that minimum information necessary to enable Blue Mountain to design its electronic mail ("e-mail") notification messages and e-mail greeting cards so that they are received by the intended recipient in their standard e-mail in-box when the junk mail filter is enabled on the default setting or any less restrictive setting.

3. Microsoft shall post a clear and conspicuous warning which is displayed to every Internet user that chooses to download the current, and any future, beta or commercial release of Internet Explorer 5.0 containing a version of Outlook Express with a junk mail filter that states as follows:

> "WARNING: Users are advised that Outlook Express comes equipped with a 'junk' e-mail filter which, when turned on, may relegate legitimate e-mails, such as electronic greeting cards from family or friends to the junk mail folder, and dispose of them according to the user's preferences."

Microsoft has further agreed to the date for the hearing on the Order to Show Cause, notwithstanding the provisions of C.C.P. Section 527(d). The parties shall agree upon mutually acceptable schedules for briefing and discovery to take place in advance of the hearing.

The Court finds that good cause exists for a TEMPORARY RE-STRAINING ORDER to issue pending the resolution of the Order to Show Cause, pursuant to Code of Civil Procedure Sections 526(a)(1)–526(a)(5).

Accordingly, IT IS FURTHER ORDERED THAT:

1. By no later than December 22, 1998, Microsoft shall make available to Blue Mountain that minimum information necessary to enable Blue Mountain to design its electronic mail ("e-mail") notification messages and e-mail greeting cards so that they are received by the intended recipient in their standard e-mail in-box and are not relegated to the "Junk" mail folder when the junk mail filter contained in Outlook Express, available from the downloadable version of Internet Explorer 5.0, beta version 5 is enabled on the default setting or any less restrictive setting. For purposes of the Order, the "default setting" is currently the middle of the five settings available to the user of the junk mail filter. Any confidential information shared by Microsoft with Blue Mountain about the filter shall be disclosed pursuant to a standard non-disclosure agreement entered into between Microsoft and Blue Mountain.

2. At least 15 days in advance of any changes, modifications or redesigns that Microsoft intends to make to the above-noted junk mail filter in any subsequent beta version or commercially available version, which would affect the delivery of Blue Mountain e-mail notification messages and e-mail greeting cards to the standard in-box when the filter is set to its default setting or any less restrictive setting, Microsoft shall inform Blue Mountain of such changes, and provide to Blue Mountain that minimum information necessary to enable Blue Mountain to design its electronic mail ("e-mail") notification messages and e-mail greeting cards so that they are received by the intended recipient in their standard e-mail in-box when the junk mail filter is enabled on the default setting or any less restrictive setting.

3. By Wednesday, December 23, 1998 at 6:00 a.m. PST., Microsoft shall post a clear and conspicuous warning which is displayed to every Internet user that chooses to download the current, and any future, beta or commercial English-language release of Internet Explorer 5.0 containing a version of Outlook Express with a junk mail filter that states as follows: "WARNING: Users are advised that Outlook Express comes equipped with a 'junk' e-mail filter which, when turned on, may relegate legitimate e-mails, such as electronic greeting cards from family or friends to the junk mail folder, and dispose of them according to the user's preferences."

Microsoft has waived service of this Order and has already received notice of it. Blue Mountain shall nevertheless serve of a copy of this Order on Microsoft within three days of the date of entry of the Order.

IT IS FURTHER ORDERED THAT Blue Mountain shall post, by not later than 4 p.m. on December 22, 1998, a bond in the amount of $5,000, which the Court finds is an appropriate undertaking.

Note

At the time this book was prepared for publication, the text of the above court order was available at: <http://www.bluemountain.com/home/courtorder122198.html>, and other court orders in the same case were also at the bluemountain.com website, where they could be located by using an Internet search engine to search for the word "Microsoft" at the host "bluemountain.com".

Chapter V

INTERNET JURISDICTION

A. REACH OF "LONG–ARM" STATUTES

BENSUSAN RESTAURANT CORP. v. KING

United States Court of Appeals, Second Circuit, 1997.
126 F.3d 25.

Van Graafeiland, Circuit Judge.

Bensusan Restaurant Corporation, located in New York City, appeals from a judgment of the United States District Court for the Southern District of New York (Stein, J.) dismissing its complaint against Richard B. King, a Missouri resident, pursuant to Fed.R.Civ.P. 12(b)(2) for lack of personal jurisdiction. We affirm.

Columbia, Missouri is a small to medium size city far distant both physically and substantively from Manhattan. It is principally a white-collar community, hosting among other institutions Stephens College, Columbia College and the University of Missouri. It would appear to be an ideal location for a small cabaret featuring live entertainment, and King, a Columbia resident, undoubtedly found this to be so. Since 1980, he has operated such a club under the name "The Blue Note" at 17 North Ninth Street in Columbia.

Plaintiff alleges in its complaint that it is "the creator of an enormously successful jazz club in New York City called 'The Blue Note,'" which name "was registered as a federal trademark for cabaret services on May 14, 1985." Around 1993, a Bensusan representative wrote to King demanding that he cease and desist from calling his club The Blue Note. King's attorney informed the writer that Bensusan had no legal right to make the demand.

Nothing further was heard from Bensusan until April 1996, when King, at the suggestion of a local web-site design company, ThoughtPort Authority, Inc., permitted that company to create a web-site or cyberspot on the internet for King's cabaret. This work was done in Missouri. Bensusan then brought the instant action in the Southern District of New York, alleging violations of sections 32(1) and 43(a) of the Lanham Act, 15 U.S.C. §§ 1114(1) & 1125(a), and section 3(c) of the Federal Trademark Dilution Act of 1995, 15 U.S.C. § 1125(c), as well as common law unfair competition.

In addition to seeking trebled compensatory damages, punitive damages, costs and attorney's fees, Bensusan requests that King be enjoined from:

> using the mark "The Blue Note", or any other indicia of the Blue Note in any manner likely to cause confusion, or to cause mistake, or to deceive, or from otherwise representing to the public in any way that [King's club] is in any way sponsored, endorsed, approved, or authorized by, or affiliated or connected with, Plaintiff or its CABARET, by means of using any name, trademark, or service mark of Plaintiff or any other names whatsoever, including but not limited to removal of Defendant's website....

The web-site describes King's establishment as "Mid–Missouri's finest live entertainment venue, ... [l]ocated in beautiful Columbia, Missouri," and it contains monthly calendars of future events and the Missouri telephone number of King's box office. Initially, it contained the following text:

> The Blue Note's CyberSpot should not be confused with one of the world's finest jazz club Blue Note, located in the heart of New York's Greenwich Village. If you should ever find yourself in the big apple give them a visit.

This text was followed by a hyperlink that could be used to connect a reader's computer to a web-site maintained by Bensusan. When Bensusan objected to the above-quoted language, King reworded the disclaimer and removed the hyperlink, substituting the following disclaimer that continues in use:

> The Blue Note, Columbia, Missouri should not be confused in any way, shape, or form with Blue Note Records or the jazz club, Blue Note, located in New York. The CyberSpot is created to provide information for Columbia, Missouri area individuals only, any other assumptions are purely coincidental.

The district court dismissed the complaint in a scholarly opinion that was published in 937 F.Supp. 295 (1996). Although we realize that attempting to apply established trademark law in the fast-developing world of the internet is somewhat like trying to board a moving bus, we believe that well-established doctrines of personal jurisdiction law support the result reached by the district court.

In diversity or federal question cases the court must look first to the long-arm statute of the forum state, in this instance, New York. *PDK Labs, Inc. v. Friedlander*, 103 F.3d 1105, 1108 (2d Cir.1997). If the exercise of jurisdiction is appropriate under that statute, the court then must decide whether such exercise comports with the requisites of due process. *See Metropolitan Life Ins. Co. v. Robertson–Ceco Corp.*, 84 F.3d 560, 567 (2d Cir.), *cert. denied*, ___ U.S. ___, 117 S.Ct. 508, 136 L.Ed.2d 398 (1996). Because we believe that the exercise of personal jurisdiction in the instant case is proscribed by the law of New York, we do not address the issue of due process.

The New York law dealing with personal jurisdiction based upon tortious acts of a non-domiciliary who does not transact business in New York is contained in sub-paragraphs (a)(2) and (a)(3) of CPLR § 302, and Bensusan claims jurisdiction with some degree of inconsistency under both sub-paragraphs. Because King does not transact business in New York State, Bensusan makes no claim under section 302(a)(1). The legislative intent behind the enactment of sub-paragraphs (a)(2) and (a)(3) best can be gleaned by reviewing their disparate backgrounds. Sub-paragraph (a)(2), enacted in 1962, provides in pertinent part that a New York court may exercise personal jurisdiction over a non-domiciliary who "in person or though an agent" commits a tortious act *within* the state. The New York Court of Appeals has construed this provision in several cases. In *Feathers v. McLucas*, 15 N.Y.2d 443, 458, 261 N.Y.S.2d 8, 209 N.E.2d 68 (1965), the Court held that the language "commits a tortious act within the state," as contained in sub-paragraph (a)(2), is "plain and precise" and confers personal jurisdiction over non-residents *"when they commit acts within the state." Id.* at 460, 261 N.Y.S.2d 8, 209 N.E.2d 68 (internal quotation marks omitted). *Feathers* adopted the view that CPLR § 302(a)(2) reaches only tortious acts performed by a defendant who was physically present in New York when he performed the wrongful act. The official Practice Commentary to CPLR § 302 explains that "if a New Jersey domiciliary were to lob a bazooka shell across the Hudson River at Grant's tomb, *Feathers* would appear to bar the New York courts from asserting personal jurisdiction over the New Jersey domiciliary in an action by an injured New York plaintiff." C302:17. The comment goes on to conclude that:

> As construed by the *Feathers* decision, jurisdiction cannot be asserted over a nonresident under this provision unless the nonresident commits an *act* in this state. This is tantamount to a requirement that the defendant or his agent be physically present in New York.... In short, the failure to perform a duty in New York is not a tortious act in this state, under the cases, unless the defendant or his agent enters the state.

* * *

* * * As recently as 1996, another of our district judges flatly stated:

> To subject non-residents to New York jurisdiction under § 302(a)(2) the defendant must commit the tort while he or she is physically in New York State.

Carlson v. Cuevas, 932 F.Supp. 76, 80 (S.D.N.Y.1996)(Baer, J.).

Like the district court in *Bulk Oil, supra*, 584 F.Supp. 36, 41 (S.D.N.Y.1983), we recognize that the interpretation of sub-paragraph (a)(2) in the line of cases above cited has not been adopted by every district judge in the Second Circuit. However, the judges who differ are in the minority. In the absence of some indication by the New York Court of Appeals that its decisions in *Feathers* and *Platt*, as interpreted and construed in the above-cited majority of cases, no longer represent the law of New York, we believe it would be impolitic for this Court to hold otherwise. Applying these principles, we conclude that Bensusan has failed to allege that King or his agents committed a tortious act in New York as required for exercise of personal jurisdiction under CPLR § 302(a)(2). The acts giving rise to Bensusan's lawsuit—including the authorization and creation of King's web site, the use of the words "Blue Note" and the Blue Note logo on the site, and the creation of a hyperlink to Bensusan's web site—were performed by persons physically present in Missouri and not in New York. Even if Bensusan suffered injury in New York, that does not establish a tortious act in the state of New York within the meaning of § 302(a)(2). *See Feathers,* 15 N.Y.2d at 460, 261 N.Y.S.2d 8, 209 N.E.2d 68.

Bensusan's claims under sub-paragraph (a)(3) can be quickly disposed of. Sub-paragraph (a)(2) left a substantial gap in New York's possible exercise of jurisdiction over non-residents because it did not cover the tort of a non-resident that took place outside of New York but caused injury inside the state. Accordingly, in 1966 the New York Legislature enacted sub-paragraph (a)(3), which provides in pertinent part that New York courts may exercise jurisdiction over a non-domiciliary who commits a tortious act without the state, causing injury to person or property within the state. However, once again the Legislature limited its exercise of jurisdictional largess. Insofar as is pertinent herein it restricted the exercise of jurisdiction under sub-paragraph (a)(3) to persons who expect or should reasonably expect the tortious act to have consequences in the state and in addition derive substantial revenue from interstate commerce. To satisfy the latter requirement, Bensusan relies on the arguments that King participated in interstate commerce by hiring bands of national stature and received revenue from customers—students of the University of Missouri—who, while residing in Missouri, were domiciliaries of other states. These alleged facts were not sufficient to establish that substantial revenues were derived from interstate commerce, a requirement that "is intended to exclude non-domiciliaries whose business operations are of a local character." Report of the Administrative Board of the Judicial Conference of the State of New York for the Judicial Year July 1, 1965 through June 30, 1966, Legislative Document (1967) No. 90. *See United Bank of Kuwait v. James M. Bridges, Ltd.,* 766 F.Supp. 113, 117–18 (S.D.N.Y.1991); *Markham v. Gray,* 393 F.Supp. 163, 166 (W.D.N.Y.1975). King's "Blue Note" cafe was unquestionably a local operation.

For all the reasons above stated, we affirm the judgment of the district court.

Note

As indicated by the court in the above case, the first issue in Internet jurisdiction cases is the reach of the relevant state "long-arm" statute. Since these statutes vary widely, it is impossible to make any generally-true statements about whether or not particular types of Internet behavior will fall under state long-arm statutes. If the behavior is within the reach of the long-arm statute, the next question is whether or not the statute has reached beyond Constitutional limits. This is an area in which general principles can be found, because of the large number of Supreme Court cases on the Constitutional limits of jurisdiction. Courts have struggled, however, with the application of these general principles to the Internet. The following case deals with this Constitutional issue.

B. CONSTITUTIONAL LIMITS ON THE REACH OF LONG–ARM STATUTES

CYBERSELL, INC. v. CYBERSELL, INC.

United States Court of Appeals, Ninth Circuit, 1997.
130 F.3d 414.

RYMER, CIRCUIT JUDGE.

We are asked to hold that the allegedly infringing use of a service mark in a home page on the World Wide Web suffices for personal jurisdiction in the state where the holder of the mark has its principal place of business. Cybersell, Inc., an Arizona corporation that advertises for commercial services over the Internet, claims that Cybersell, Inc., a Florida corporation that offers web page construction services over the Internet, infringed its federally registered mark and should be amenable to suit in Arizona because cyberspace is without borders and a web site which advertises a product or service is necessarily intended for use on a world wide basis. The district court disagreed, and so do we. Instead, applying our normal "minimum contacts" analysis, we conclude that it would not comport with "traditional notions of fair play and substantial justice," *Core-Vent Corp. v. Nobel Indus. AB*, 11 F.3d 1482, 1485 (9th Cir.1993) (quoting *International Shoe Co. v. Washington*, 326 U.S. 310, 316, 66 S.Ct. 154, 158, 90 L.Ed. 95 (1945)), for Arizona to exercise personal jurisdiction over an allegedly infringing Florida web site advertiser who has no contacts with Arizona other than maintaining a home page that is accessible to Arizonans, and everyone else, over the Internet. We therefore affirm.

I

Cybersell, Inc. is an Arizona corporation, which we will refer to as Cybersell AZ. It was incorporated in May 1994 to provide Internet and web advertising and marketing services, including consulting. The principals of Cybersell AZ are Laurence Canter and Martha Siegel, known among web users for first "spamming" the Internet.[1] Mainstream print media carried the story of Canter and Siegel and their various efforts to commercialize the web.

---

1. Spamming refers to the posting indiscriminately of advertisements to news groups on the web. Unlike crossposting, spamming individually posts the advertisement to each news group, requiring the recipient to delete the message from each news group to which she has subscribed.

On August 8, 1994, Cybersell AZ filed an application to register the name "Cybersell" as a service mark. The application was approved and the grant was published on October 30, 1995. Cybersell AZ operated a web site using the mark from August 1994 through February 1995. The site was then taken down for reconstruction.

Meanwhile, in the summer of 1995, Matt Certo and his father, Dr. Samuel C. Certo, both Florida residents, formed Cybersell, Inc., a Florida corporation (Cybersell FL), with its principal place of business in Orlando. Matt was a business school student at Rollins College, where his father was a professor; Matt was particularly interested in the Internet, and their company was to provide business consulting services for strategic management and marketing on the web. At the time the Certos chose the name "Cybersell" for their venture, Cybersell AZ had no home page on the web nor had the PTO granted their application for the service mark.

As part of their marketing effort, the Certos created a web page at http:// www.cybsell.com/cybsell/index.htm. The home page has a logo at the top with "CyberSell" over a depiction of the planet earth, with the caption underneath "Professional Services for the World Wide Web" and a local (area code 407) phone number. It proclaims in large letters "Welcome to CyberSell!" A hypertext link allows the browser to introduce himself, and invites a company not on the web—but interested in getting on the web—to "Email us to find out how!"

Canter found the Cybersell FL web page and sent an e-mail on November 27, 1995 notifying Dr. Certo that "Cybersell" is a service mark of Cybersell AZ. Trying to disassociate themselves from Canter and Siegel, the Certos changed the name of Cybersell FL to WebHorizons, Inc. on December 27 (later it was changed again to WebSolvers, Inc.) and by January 4, 1996, they had replaced the CyberSell logo at the top of their web page with WebHorizons, Inc. The WebHorizons page still said "Welcome to CyberSell!"

Cybersell AZ filed the complaint in this action January 9, 1996 in the District of Arizona, alleging trademark infringement, unfair competition, fraud, and RICO violations. On the same day Cybersell FL filed suit for declaratory relief with regard to use of the name "Cybersell" in the United States District Court for the Middle District of Florida, but that action was transferred to the District of Arizona and consolidated with the Cybersell AZ action. Cybersell FL moved to dismiss for lack of personal jurisdiction. The district court denied Cybersell AZ's request for a preliminary injunction, then granted Cybersell FL's motion to dismiss for lack of personal jurisdiction Cybersell AZ timely appealed.

II

The general principles that apply to the exercise of personal jurisdiction are well known. As there is no federal statute governing personal jurisdiction in this case, the law of Arizona applies. Under Rule 4.2(a) of the Arizona Rules of Civil Procedure, an Arizona court may exercise personal jurisdiction over parties, whether found within or outside the state, to the maximum extent permitted by the Constitution of this state and the Constitution of the United States.

The Arizona Supreme Court has stated that under Rule 4.2(a), "Arizona will exert personal jurisdiction over a nonresident litigant to the maximum extent allowed by the federal constitution." *Uberti v. Leonardo*, 181 Ariz. 565, 569, 892 P.2d 1354, 1358, *cert. denied*, ___ U.S. ___, 116 S.Ct. 273, 133 L.Ed.2d 194 (1995). Thus, Cybersell FL may be subject to personal jurisdiction in Arizona so long as doing so comports with due process.

A court may assert either specific or general jurisdiction over a defendant. *See Helicopteros Nacionales de Colombia, S.A. v. Hall*, 466 U.S. 408, 414, 104 S.Ct. 1868, 1872, 80 L.Ed.2d 404 (1984). Cybersell AZ concedes that general jurisdiction over Cybersell FL doesn't exist in Arizona, so the only issue in this case is whether specific jurisdiction is available.

We use a three-part test to determine whether a district court may exercise specific jurisdiction over a nonresident defendant:

> (1) The nonresident defendant must do some act or consummate some transaction with the forum or perform some act by which he purposefully avails himself of the privilege of conducting activities in the forum, thereby invoking the benefits and protections[;] (2)[t]he claim must be one which arises out of or results from the defendant's forum-related activities[; and] (3)[e]xercise of jurisdiction must be reasonable.

Ballard v. Savage, 65 F.3d 1495, 1498 (9th Cir.1995) (citations omitted).

Cybersell AZ argues that the test is met because trademark infringement occurs when the passing off of the mark occurs, which in this case, it submits, happened when the name "Cybersell" was used on the Internet in connection with advertising. Cybersell FL, on the other hand, contends that a party should not be subject to nationwide, or perhaps worldwide, jurisdiction simply for using the Internet.

A

Since the jurisdictional facts are not in dispute, we turn to the first requirement, which is the most critical. As the Supreme Court emphasized in *Hanson v. Denckla*, "it is essential in each case that there be some act by which the defendant purposefully avails itself of the privilege of conducting activities within the forum State, thus invoking the benefits and protections of its laws." 357 U.S. 235, 253, 78 S.Ct. 1228, 1239, 2 L.Ed.2d 1283 (1958). We recently explained in *Ballard* that

> the "purposeful availment" requirement is satisfied if the defendant has taken deliberate action within the forum state or if he has created continuing obligations to forum residents. "It is not required that a defendant be physically present within, or have physical

contacts with, the forum, provided that his efforts 'are purposefully directed' toward forum residents."

Ballard, 65 F.3d at 1498 (citations omitted).

We have not yet considered when personal jurisdiction may be exercised in the context of cyberspace, but the Second and Sixth Circuits have had occasion to decide whether personal jurisdiction was properly exercised over defendants involved in transmissions over the Internet, *see CompuServe, Inc. v. Patterson*, 89 F.3d 1257 (6th Cir.1996); *Bensusan Restaurant Corp. v. King*, 937 F.Supp. 295 (S.D.N.Y.1996), *aff'd*, 126 F.3d 25 (2d Cir.1997), as have a number of district courts. Because this is a matter of first impression for us, we have looked to all of these cases for guidance. Not surprisingly, they reflect a broad spectrum of Internet use on the one hand, and contacts with the forum on the other. As *CompuServe* and *Bensusan* seem to represent opposite ends of the spectrum, we start with them.[4]

CompuServe is a computer information service headquartered in Columbus, Ohio, that contracts with individual subscribers to provide access to computing and information services via the Internet. It also operates as an electronic conduit to provide computer software products to its subscribers. Computer software generated and distributed in this way is often referred to as "shareware." Patterson is a Texas resident who subscribed to CompuServe and placed items of "shareware" on the CompuServe system pursuant to a "Shareware Registration Agreement" with CompuServe which provided, among other things, that it was "to be governed by and construed in accordance with" Ohio law. During the course of this relationship, Patterson electronically transmitted thirty-two master software files to CompuServe, which CompuServe stored and displayed to its subscribers. Sales were made in Ohio and elsewhere, and funds were transmitted through CompuServe in Ohio to Patterson in Texas. In effect, Patterson used CompuServe as a distribution center to market his software. When Patterson threatened litigation over allegedly infringing CompuServe software, CompuServe filed suit in Ohio seeking a declaratory judgment of noninfringement. The court found that Patterson's relationship with CompuServe as a software provider and marketer was a crucial indicator that Patterson had knowingly reached out to CompuServe's Ohio home and benefitted from CompuServe's handling of his software and fees. Because Patterson had chosen to transmit his product from Texas to CompuServe's system in Ohio, and that system provided access to his software to others to whom he advertised and sold his product, the court concluded that Patterson purposefully availed himself of the privilege of doing business in Ohio.

4. Since *Bensusan* was decided on the basis of New York's long-arm statute (which requires presence in the forum and is therefore more stringent than due process), its holding is not instructive, but the district court's analysis is. The district court dismissed for lack of personal jurisdiction under the long-arm statute as well as on due process grounds, while the Second Circuit affirmed on the statute and did not discuss the constitutional issue.

By contrast, the defendant in *Bensusan* owned a small jazz club known as "The Blue Note" in Columbia, Missouri. He created a general access web page that contained information about the club in Missouri as well as a calendar of events and ticketing information. Tickets were not available through the web site, however. To order tickets, web browsers had to use the names and addresses of ticket outlets in Columbia or a telephone number for charge-by-phone ticket orders, which were available for pick-up on the night of the show at the Blue Note box office in Columbia. Bensusan was a New York corporation that owned "The Blue Note," a popular jazz club in the heart of Greenwich Village. Bensusan owned the rights to the "The Blue Note" mark. Bensusan sued King for trademark infringement in New York. The district court distinguished King's passive web page, which just posted information, from the defendant's use of the Internet in *CompuServe* by observing that whereas the Texas Internet user specifically targeted Ohio by subscribing to the service, entering into an agreement to sell his software over the Internet, advertising through the service, and sending his software to the service in Ohio,

> King has done nothing to purposefully avail himself of the benefits of New York. King, like numerous others, simply created a Web site and permitted anyone who could find it to access it. Creating a site, like placing a product into the stream of commerce, may be felt nationwide-or even worldwide-but, without more, it is not an act purposefully directed toward the forum state.

Bensusan, 937 F.Supp. at 301 (citing the plurality opinion in *Asahi Metal Indus. Co. v. Superior Court*, 480 U.S. 102, 112, 107 S.Ct. 1026, 1032, 94 L.Ed.2d 92 (1987)). Given these facts, the court reasoned that the argument that the defendant "should have foreseen that users could access the site in New York and be confused as to the relationship of the two Blue Note clubs is insufficient to satisfy due process." *Id.* at 301.

"Interactive" web sites present somewhat different issues. Unlike passive sites such as the defendant's in *Bensusan*, users can exchange information with the host computer when the site is interactive. Courts that have addressed interactive sites have looked to the "level of interactivity and commercial nature of the exchange of information that occurs on the Web site" to determine if sufficient contacts exist to warrant the exercise of jurisdiction. *See, e.g., Zippo Mfg. Co. v. Zippo Dot Com, Inc.*, 952 F.Supp. 1119, 1124 (W.D.Pa.1997) (finding purposeful availment based on Dot Com's interactive web site and contracts with 3000 individuals and seven Internet access providers in Pennsylvania allowing them to download the electronic messages that form the basis of the suit); *Maritz, Inc. v. Cybergold, Inc.*, 947 F.Supp. 1328, 1332–33 (E.D.Mo.) (browsers were encouraged to add their address to a mailing list that basically subscribed the user to the service), *reconsideration denied*, 947 F.Supp. 1338 (1996).

Cybersell AZ points to several district court decisions which it contends have held that the mere advertisement or solicitation for sale of goods and services on the Internet gives rise to specific jurisdiction in the plaintiff's forum. However, so far as we are aware, no court has ever held that an Internet advertisement alone is sufficient to subject the advertiser to jurisdiction in the plaintiff's home state. *See, e.g., Smith v. Hobby Lobby Stores*, 968 F.Supp. 1356 (W.D.Ark.1997) (no jurisdiction over Hong Kong defendant who advertised in trade journal posted on the Internet without sale of goods or services in Arkansas). Rather, in each, there has been "something more" to indicate that the defendant purposefully (albeit electronically) directed his activity in a substantial way to the forum state.

Inset Systems, Inc. v. Instruction Set, Inc., 937 F.Supp. 161 (D.Conn. 1996), is the case most favorable to Cybersell AZ's position. Inset developed and marketed computer software throughout the world; Instruction Set, Inc. (ISI) provided computer technology and support. Inset owned the federal trademark "INSET"; but ISI obtained "INSET.COM" as its Internet domain address for advertising its goods and services. ISI also used the telephone number "1–800–US–INSET." Inset learned of ISI's domain address when it tried to get the same address, and filed suit for trademark infringement in Connecticut. The court reasoned that ISI had purposefully availed itself of doing business in Connecticut because it directed its advertising activities via the Internet and its toll-free number toward the state of Connecticut (and all states); Internet sites and toll-free numbers are designed to communicate with people and their businesses in every state; an Internet advertisement could reach as many as 10,000 Internet users within Connecticut alone; and once posted on the Internet, an advertisement is continuously available to any Internet user.

Cybersell AZ further points to the court's statement in *EDIAS Software International, L.L.C. v. BASIS International Ltd.*, 947 F.Supp. 413 (D.Ariz.1996), that a defendant "should not be permitted to take advantage of modern technology through an Internet Web page and forum and simultaneously escape traditional notions of jurisdiction." *Id.* at 420. In that case, EDIAS (an Arizona company) alleged that BASIS (a New Mexico company) sent advertising and defamatory statements over the Internet through e-mail, its web page, and forums. However, the court did not rest its minimum contacts analysis on use of the Internet alone; in addition to the Internet, BASIS had a contract with EDIAS, it made sales to EDIAS and other Arizona customers, and its employees had visited Arizona during the course of the business relationship with EDIAS.

Some courts have also given weight to the number of "hits" received by a web page from residents in the forum state, and to other evidence that Internet activity was directed at, or bore fruit in, the forum state. *See, e.g., Heroes, Inc. v. Heroes Found.*, 958 F.Supp. 1 (D.D.C.1996) (web page that solicited contributions and provided toll-free telephone number along with the defendant's use on the web page of the allegedly infringing trademark and logo, along with other contacts, provided sustained contact with the District), *amended by* No. Civ.A. 96–1260(TAF) (1997);

Pres-Kap, Inc. v. System One, Direct Access, Inc., 636 So.2d 1351 (Fla. Dist.Ct.App.1994) (declining jurisdiction where defendant consumer subscribed to plaintiff's travel reservation system but was solicited and serviced instate by the supplier's local representative).

In sum, the common thread, well stated by the district court in *Zippo*, is that "the likelihood that personal jurisdiction can be constitutionally exercised is directly proportionate to the nature and quality of commercial activity that an entity conducts over the Internet." *Zippo*, 952 F.Supp. at 1124.

B

Here, Cybersell FL has conducted no commercial activity over the Internet in Arizona. All that it did was post an essentially passive home page on the web, using the name "CyberSell," which Cybersell AZ was in the process of registering as a federal service mark. While there is no question that anyone, anywhere could access that home page and thereby learn about the services offered, we cannot see how from that fact alone it can be inferred that Cybersell FL deliberately directed its merchandising efforts toward Arizona residents.

Cybersell FL did nothing to encourage people in Arizona to access its site, and there is no evidence that any part of its business (let alone a continuous part of its business) was sought or achieved in Arizona. To the contrary, it appears to be an operation where business was primarily generated by the personal contacts of one of its founders. While those contacts are not entirely local, they aren't in Arizona either. No Arizonan except for Cybersell AZ "hit" Cybersell FL's web site. There is no evidence that any Arizona resident signed up for Cybersell FL's web construction services. It entered into no contracts in Arizona, made no sales in Arizona, received no telephone calls from Arizona, earned no income from Arizona, and sent no messages over the Internet to Arizona. The only message it received over the Internet from Arizona was from Cybersell AZ. Cybersell FL did not have an "800" number, let alone a toll-free number that also used the "Cybersell" name. The interactivity of its web page is limited to receiving the browser's name and address and an indication of interest—signing up for the service is not an option, nor did anyone from Arizona do so. No money changed hands on the Internet from (or through) Arizona. In short, Cybersell FL has done no act and has consummated no transaction, nor has it performed any act by which it purposefully availed itself of the privilege of conducting activities, in Arizona, thereby invoking the benefits and protections of Arizona law.

We therefore hold that Cybersell FL's contacts are insufficient to establish "purposeful availment." Cybersell AZ has thus failed to satisfy the first prong of our three-part test for specific jurisdiction. We decline to go further solely on the footing that Cybersell AZ has alleged trademark infringement over the Internet by Cybersell FL's use of the registered name "Cybersell" on an essentially passive web page advertisement. Otherwise, every complaint arising out of alleged trademark infringement on the Internet would automatically result in personal jurisdiction wherever the plaintiff's principal place of business is located. That would not comport with traditional notions of what qualifies as purposeful activity invoking the benefits and protections of the forum state. *See Peterson v. Kennedy*, 771 F.2d 1244, 1262 (9th Cir.1985) (series of phone calls and letters to California physician regarding plaintiff's injuries insufficient to satisfy first prong of test).

III

Cybersell AZ also invokes the "effects" test employed in *Calder v. Jones*, 465 U.S. 783, 104 S.Ct. 1482, 79 L.Ed.2d 804 (1984), and *Core-Vent Corp. v. Nobel Industries*, 11 F.3d 1482 (9th Cir.1993), with respect to intentional torts directed to the plaintiff, causing injury where the plaintiff lives. However, we don't see this as a *Calder* case. Because Shirley Jones was who she was (a famous entertainer who lived and worked in California) and was libeled by a story in the National Enquirer, which was published in Florida but had a nationwide circulation with a large audience in California, the Court could easily hold that California was the "focal point both of the story and of the harm suffered" and so jurisdiction in California based on the "effects" of the defendants' Florida conduct was proper. *Calder*, 465 U.S. at 789, 104 S.Ct. at 1486. There is nothing comparable about Cybersell FL's web page. Nor does the "effects" test apply with the same force to Cybersell AZ as it would to an individual, because a corporation "does not suffer harm in a particular geographic location in the same sense that an individual does." *Core-Vent*, 11 F.3d at 1486. Cybersell FL's web page simply was not aimed intentionally at Arizona knowing that harm was likely to be caused there to Cybersell AZ.

IV

We conclude that the essentially passive nature of Cybersell FL's activity in posting a home page on the World Wide Web that allegedly used the service mark of Cybersell AZ does not qualify as purposeful activity invoking the benefits and protections of Arizona. As it engaged in no commercial activity and had no other contacts via the Internet or otherwise in Arizona, Cybersell FL lacks sufficient minimum contacts with Arizona for personal jurisdiction to be asserted over it there. Accordingly, its motion to dismiss for lack of personal jurisdiction was properly granted.

AFFIRMED.

Note

The cases have quite rapidly established two extremes on the Constitutional question. First, a court cannot establish jurisdiction over a potential defendant if the defendant's only contact with that state is a website that happens to be accessible in the state. Second, if the defendant has done any additional activity along with the website, including active marketing or interaction with customers in the state the courts generally hold that jurisdiction has been established over the defendant. Future issues will concern where the line is drawn in the middle ground, by determining the amount of customer interaction that a court will require in order for it to obtain jurisdiction Constitutionally.

C. IN REM JURISDICTION OVER DOMAIN NAMES

LUCENT TECHNOLOGIES, INC. v. LUCENTSUCKS.COM

United States District Court, E.D. Virginia, 2000.
95 F.Supp.2d 528.

BRINKEMA, DISTRICT JUDGE.

Before the Court is the Motion of Defendant lucentsucks.com's [sic] to Dismiss the Complaint, in which defendant argues that plaintiff's failure to comply with the requirements of the recently enacted Anti–Cybersquatting Consumer Protection Act mandates dismissal of the complaint. For the reasons stated below, the motion will be granted.

I. BACKGROUND

Plaintiff Lucent Technologies, Inc. is a Delaware Corporation with its principal place of business in Murray Hill, New Jersey. It has filed this *in rem* action against the domain name lucentsucks.com under the Anti–Cybersquatting Consumer Protection Act ("ACPA"), 15 U.S.C. § 1125.

Plaintiff alleges that, on November 30, 1995, its predecessor filed an application with the United States Patent and Trademark Office ("PTO") to register LUCENT as a trademark. Since 1996, plaintiff has manufactured, marketed and sold telecommunications equipment and services under the marks LUCENT and LUCENT TECHNOLOGIES. It has registered and applied to register LUCENT marks with the PTO for a variety of goods and services. Plaintiff alleges that the money and effort it has expended on advertising and promoting its products and services under these marks has created valuable goodwill in the marks.

According to plaintiff, on August 2, 1998, Russell Johnson registered the domain name lucentsucks.com through Network Solutions, Inc. ("NSI"), located in Herndon, Virginia. Plaintiff alleges that the website at this domain name contains pornographic photographs and services for sale.

Plaintiff advances two causes of action: Count I, Trademark Infringement, 15 U.S.C. § 1114(1) and 15 U.S.C. § 1125(a); and Count II, dilution, Section 43(c) of the Lanham Act, 15 U.S.C. § 1125(c). Plaintiff seeks court order directing NSI to transfer registration of lucentsucks.com to Lucent.

II. DISCUSSION

Lucentsucks.com raises several arguments in support of its argument to dismiss the complaint: plaintiff did not satisfy the *in rem* jurisdictional requirements of the ACPA; an internet domain name is not "property," for purposes of obtaining *in rem* jurisdiction; and First Amendment principles would be violated if plaintiff could force forfeiture of defendant domain name. We find for the reasons discussed below that plaintiff failed to satisfy the jurisdictional requirements of the ACPA, and therefore will dismiss the complaint on that basis. Because the ACPA is a new statute, and is still the source of some confusion, we also briefly address some of defendant's other arguments.

A. *The ACPA*

On November 29, 1999, the Anticybersquatting Consumer Protection Act ("ACPA"), Pub.L. No. 106–113, 113 Stat. 1501 (codified as amended at 15 U.S.C. §§ 1114, 1116, 1117, 1125, 1127, 1129 (1999)), went into effect as an amendment to the Trademark Act. Congress enacted the ACPA to address the growing phenomenon of "cyberpiracy or cybersquating," which involves "registering, trafficking in, or using domain names (Internet addresses) that are identical or confusingly similar to trademarks with the bad-faith intent to profit from the goodwill of trademarks." H.R.Rep. No. 106–412, at 7 (1999).

Supporters of the ACPA were particularly concerned about anonymous trademark violators on the Internet. That is, they were troubled by the increasing trend of individuals registering domain names in violation of trademark rights and then eluding trademark enforcement because they could not be found. The Senate Judiciary Committee observed:

> A significant problem faced by trademark owners in the fight against cybersquatting is the fact that many cybersquatters register domain names under aliases or otherwise provide false information in their registration applications in order to avoid identification and service of process by the mark owner.

Sen. Rep. No. 106–140, at 4 (1999). The Judiciary Committee believed that including an in rem provision in the ACPA would alleviate the problem of anonymous cybersquatters, by allowing a mark owner to file an action against the domain name itself, provided it satisfied the court that it exercised due diligence in trying to locate the owner of the domain name but could not do so. *Id.*

B. *Plaintiff's Efforts to Comply with the In Rem Provision*

Once plaintiff learned of lucentsucks.com, its in-house counsel sought the name and address of the registrant for that domain name from NSI, the registry. NSI's records showed a registrant by the name of Russell Johnson. On November 11, 1999, plaintiff's in-house counsel sent a letter via Federal Express to Johnson at the address listed with NSI. In it, plaintiff demanded that Johnson "immediately cease and desist from engaging in or permitting any further or future use of the

Lucent Marks ... '' (Opp. to Def. Ex. D.) The letter was returned by Federal Express as undeliverable.

Plaintiff contacted NSI to determine whether Johnson had changed his address on the lucentsucks.com registration. Although NSI's agreement with registrants requires that they maintain current mail and e-mail addresses, no changes of address were noted for Johnson. Plaintiff then sent another demand letter on December 8, 1999, to the addresses listed with NSI. This letter, however, was sent first class United States Postal Service mail and e-mail. In the letter, plaintiff referred to the *in rem* provision of the just-enacted ACPA:

> Because we have not been able to reach you, Lucent Technologies Inc. intends to proceed with filing an in rem civil action against your domain name registration Lucentsucks.com pursuant to Section 43(d)(2)(A) of the Lanham Act, 15 U.S.C. § 1125(d)(2)(A).

(Opp. to Def. Ex. E.) The e-mail was returned as undeliverable. However, the letter sent via first class mail was successfully delivered to Johnson. The record shows that Johnson had moved after registering the domain name with NSI, and that he left a forwarding address with the United States Postal Service ("U.S.P.S").

On December 16, 1999, eight days after the second demand letter was mailed and e-mailed, plaintiff filed this action. On December 21, 1999, thirteen days after the second demand letter was sent, Johnson called Lucent's outside counsel. Counsel informed Johnson that an *in rem* suit had been filed, and Johnson provided counsel a pager number. On December 22, 1999, Johnson called counsel again, allegedly asking for money in exchange for releasing the domain name. Counsel called Johnson later that day to reject the offer. Johnson gave counsel his new address during that call, and counsel sent a copy of the complaint to that address.

Although plaintiff now knew the location of the registrant, it continued to prosecute its *in rem* action under the ACPA. Plaintiff moved for Entry of Order to Publish Notice of Action on January 7, 2000. The ordered was entered and plaintiff published a notice of the action in *The Washington Post* for two consecutive weeks. It also mailed copies of the Order and the complaint to registrant's address as provided by NSI and as provided by Johnson. Plaintiff filed an affidavit of compliance on February 11, 2000.

C. *Plaintiff has not Satisified (sic) the Requirements of the In Rem Provision*

By the express terms of Section 1125(d)(2)(A)(ii) of the ACPA, a plaintiff may proceed with an *in rem* action against a domain name if and only if the Court finds either that the plaintiff is unable to obtain *in personam* jurisdiction over the domain name registrant, or that the plaintiff is unable to find the domain name registrant. Plaintiff does not base *in rem* jurisdiction on an inability to assert *in personam* jurisdiction. Instead, it rests its case on Section 1125(d)(2)(A)(ii)(II), which states, in pertinent part:

> The owner of a mark *may* file an in rem civil action against a domain name in the judicial district in which the domain name registrar . . . that registered or assigned the domain name is located if . . . (ii) *the court finds* that the owner . . . (II) through *due diligence* was not able to find a person who would have been a defendant in a civil action under paragraph (1) by-(aa) *sending notice* of the alleged violation and intent to proceed under this paragraph to the registrant of the domain name at the postal and e-mail address provided by the registrant to the registrar; *and* (bb) publishing notice of the action as the court may direct promptly after filing the action.

15 U.S.C. § 1125(d)(2)(A)(emphasis added).

We find that, based on the allegations in plaintiff's complaint, Russell Johnson, the listed registrant of defendant lucentsucks.com would be "a person who would have been a defendant in a civil action under paragraph (1)." Therefore, proceeding any further *in rem* is not appropriate. We also find that plaintiff failed to satisfy the due diligence clause, Section 1125(d)(2)(A)(ii)(II)(aa), because it did not allow a reasonable time for Johnson to respond to its December 8, 1999 notice before filing the *in rem* complaint

1. *Due Process Requires Reasonable Time*

Plaintiff's counsel waited only eight days between sending the December 8, 1999 letter via mail and e-mail and filing this action. Plaintiff contends that these actions satisfied the express terms of the ACPA *in rem* provision and should therefore the complaint should go forward. However, to find, as plaintiff urges, that an eight-day waiting period between sending notice of an intent to proceed *in rem* and filing an *in rem* action, is sufficient, would run afoul of Due Process. It is true that Congress did not specify the waiting period. In the face of this ambiguity, we must interpret the ACPA *in rem* provision consistently with Due Process requirements. *NLRB v. Catholic Bishop of Chicago*, 440 U.S. 490, 500, 99 S.Ct. 1313, 59 L.Ed.2d 533 (1979) ("an Act of Congress ought not be construed to violate the Constitution if any other possible construction remains available"). Furthermore, for an *in rem* action to proceed pursuant to Section 1125(d)(2)(A)(ii)(II), the ACPA requires the Court to find that plaintiff used "due diligence" when attempting to notify registrant. 15 U.S.C. § 1125(d)(2)(A)(ii)(II). We find that a waiting period of merely eight days does not demonstrate the requisite "due diligence."

The seminal case addressing the notice aspect of procedural Due Process is *Mullane v. Central Hanover Bank & Trust Co.*, 339 U.S. 306, 70 S.Ct. 652, 94 L.Ed. 865 (1950). In it, the Supreme Court observed:

> An elementary and fundamental requirement of due process in any proceeding which is to be accorded finality is notice, reasonably

calculated, under all the circumstances, to apprise interested parties of the pendency of the action and afford them an opportunity to present their objections.... The notice must of be such nature as reasonably to convey the required information, and *it must afford a reasonable time for those interested to make their appearance.*

Id. at 314, 70 S.Ct. 652 (citations omitted) (emphasis added); * * *

There are few cases specifically addressing what length of time is a "reasonable time" between notification of a possible or pending court action and the action. However, we are certain that eight days is insufficient. The notice provided must be more than "mere gesture." *Mullane*, 339 U.S. at 315, 70 S.Ct. 652. We note that potential parties to a court action share the same tendency as the rest of us to take vacations of two weeks or more without leaving a forwarding address, and that, when they make a permanent change of residence, mail forwarded by the United States Postal Service arrives more slowly than mail addressed directly to the new residence. Furthermore, the Due Process requirements contemplate the time reasonably necessary to digest the notice and to find an attorney. *See Grunin v. International House of Pancakes*, 513 F.2d 114, 121 (8th Cir.1975) (due process satisfied where notice of proposed settlement was mailed to class members 19 days before hearing, especially in light of "continuing notice" afforded members because litigation was two years ongoing and all counsel appearing at earlier settlement hearing were kept informed of all subsequent developments in case).

* * *

III. CONCLUSION

Because we find that plaintiff instituted this *in rem* action too hastily after mailing and e-mailing the notice of a proposed *in rem* action to the registrant of lucentsucks.com, we cannot make the necessary prerequisite findings to permit an *in rem* action to proceed pursuant to Section 1125(d)(2)(A)(ii)(II) of the ACPA. Therefore, defendant's motion will be granted, and plaintiff's *in rem* action will be dismissed by an appropriate order.

The Clerk is directed to forward copies of this Memorandum Opinion to counsel of record.

Note

Network Solutions, Inc., the former sole registrar, lobbied for the creation of an in rem action. Before this action was available, Network Solutions, Inc. had been named as defendant in a number of suits brought be trademark owners. It wanted to be spared the time and expense of defending these suits. Trademark owners had also pressed for the in rem action, because of the difficulty of suing defendants who did not keep the domain name registrar informed of their current addresses.

D. JURISDICTION OVER PERSONS NOT DOING BUSINESS ON THE INTERNET

BOCHAN v. LA FONTAINE

United States District Court, E.D. Virginia, 1999.
68 F.Supp.2d 692.

ELLIS, DISTRICT JUDGE.

This is an Internet libel case. Plaintiff, a Virginia resident, alleges that defendants, Texas and New Mexico residents, defamed him in Virginia and elsewhere by posting libelous messages from Texas and New Mexico on an Internet newsgroup. At issue is whether there is personal jurisdiction over defendants in Virginia. For the reasons that follow, defendants' alleged activities are sufficient to warrant personal jurisdiction.

I.

Plaintiff, a devote of John F. Kennedy (JFK) conspiracy theories, is the district manager of a group of theaters in Northern Virginia. Journalists Ray and Mary La Fontaine are Texas residents who wrote a book on the JFK assassination entitled *Oswald Talked: The New Evidence in the JFK Assassination.* * * *

Plaintiff purchased the La Fontaines' book at Borders Bookstore in Fairfax, Va. sometime after it was published in 1996. He became a vocal critic of the book, often expressing his criticisms via the Internet, specifically by posting his critiques to the interactive newsgroup *alt.conspiracy.jfk*.[2] These postings provoked defendants to post responses to the newsgroup, which responsive postings are the alleged defamations in this action.

The principal precipitating event occurred on October 12, 1998, when plaintiff posted a message to the La Fontaines that contained the following quote from the acknowledgments of the La Fontaine's book: " 'We thank Charlotte and Eugenia for putting up with weird parents.' "[3] The next day, Ray La Fontaine responded from Dallas, Texas,

---

2. This newsgroup is described by Bochon's proffered expert in computer network technology as a "USENET newsgroup," which a recent federal case concerning obscenity on the Internet correctly described in the following terms:

USENET newsgroups are disseminated using ad hoc, peer to peer connections between approximately 200,000 computers (called USENET "servers") around the world. For unmoderated newsgroups, when an individual user with access to a USENET server posts a message to a newsgroup, the message is automatically forwarded to all adjacent USENET servers that furnish access to the newsgroup, and it is then propagated to the servers adjacent to those servers, etc. The messages are temporarily stored on each receiving server, where they are available for review and response by individual users. The messages are automatically and periodically purged from each system after a time to make room for new messages. . . .

See Reno, 929 F.Supp. at 834–35.

3. Charlotte and Eugenia are the La Fontaines' daughters.

by posting a message to *alt.conspiracy.jfk*.[4] This October 13, 1998 posting was labeled "The scum posts of Bochan," and stated, "I know you like kids, Bochan, but I suggest you limit your interest to trolling in *alt.sex.festish.tinygirls* and leave our children out of it." La Fontaine then went on in this posting to provide "for anyone interested" what La Fontaine claimed was Bochan's October 1997 author profile with Deja News, an Internet discussion network. This author profile, as provided by Bochan, listed 238 articles,[6] allegedly posted by Bochan, identifying the individual newsgroups to which each article was posted. The majority of the articles were listed as posted to various conspiracy theory sites, but according to La Fontaine's version of the author profile, Bochan also posted articles to three apparently pornographic sites: *alt.sex.fetish.tinygirls*, *alt.sex.pictures.male*, and *alt.sex.snuff.cannibalism*. La Fontaine followed the alleged profile with the following additional editorial comment directed to Bochan: "How come you only posted once to *alt.sex.fetish.tinygirls* and *alt.sex.pictures.male*, Bochan? Did you get lucky the first time around?"

The matter did not end with Ray La Fontaine's seemingly unsavory posting. On October 14, 1998, Mary La Fontaine posted a message on *alt.conspiracy.jfk* to a friend of Bochan's, which defended the La Fontaines' actions in posting the alleged profile from Deja News.[7] In this posting, Mary La Fontaine asserted that her husband had downloaded the profile directly from Deja News, and that she and her husband had decided to "reveal the truth" about the 1997 profile, then roughly a year old, because of the "not-so veiled attempt at intimidation" contained in the reference to the La Fontaines' children in Bochan's October 12, 1998 posting. Not content simply to defend the La Fontaine Deja News profile posting, Mary La Fontaine went on to suggest that Bochan's friend would be derelict as a mother were she to allow her children to associate with Bochan.[8]

* * *

On the basis of these postings, Bochan sues * * * the La Fontaines * * * in the Eastern District of Virginia for defamation and for inten-

---

4. La Fontaine posted the message using the La Fontaines' America OnLine (AOL) account, accessing the Internet through their Internet service provider, Earthlink.net. AOL is located in Herndon, Virginia; Earthlink.net is located in Pasadena, California. The La Fontaines' AOL account is an auxiliary service that the La Fontaines used to screen responses to their posts; the AOL account does not provide access to the Internet, but instead specifically requires that the subscriber provide its own access to the Internet through another Internet service provider, such as Earthlink.net.

6. "Articles" on Internet newsgroups are essentially analogous to email messages, except that, like print articles, they are

published, i.e., they are on the Internet and generally available to anyone accessing the newsgroup.

7. This message was also posted through the La Fontaines' AOL account by way of Earthlink.net.

8. Specifically, Mary La Fontaine wrote in her posting, "It concerns me as a mother, Ms. Junkkarinen, that you may have young children who have spent time with Mr. Bochan. I hope you give this some thought. You are obviously a loyal friend of this man. Perhaps he fulfills some need for you. But I cannot help but believe that your children should come before anything else, just as mine do."

tional infliction of emotional distress, alleging that * * * defendants have publicly accused him of being a pedophile. At the threshold, defendants assert a lack of personal jurisdiction. In support of this contention, the La Fontaines state that they i) have not been in Virginia since 1993, when they drove from National Airport to the District of Columbia, ii) have not participated in any book promotions in Virginia, iii) receive no royalties from Virginia sales as they do not directly sell their book in Virginia, nor do they directly receive royalties on books sold by others in Virginia, but rather receive royalties on the total books sold by their publisher to national chains, and iv) have never derived any revenue that they are aware of from Virginia. Moreover, they note as significant that they i) do not have their own website, ii) do not conduct commercial activity over the Internet, and iii) made the allegedly defamatory postings by accessing the Internet through a California-based Internet service provider.

* * *

Bochan responds that the La Fontaines posted the allegedly defamatory messages using an account with AOL, a Virginia-based company, and moreover, that the La Fontaines have advertised, promoted and sold their book in Virginia. * * *

II.

* * * [D]efendants move to dismiss the complaint pursuant to Rule 12(b)(2), Fed.R.Civ.P., for lack of personal jurisdiction. When the exercise of personal jurisdiction is challenged pursuant to Rule 12(b)(2), Fed.R.Civ.P., the question "is one for the judge, with the burden on the plaintiff ultimately to prove the existence of a ground for jurisdiction by the preponderance of the evidence." *See Combs v. Bakker*, 886 F.2d 673, 676 (4th Cir.1989). When a court rules on this issue in reliance upon the complaint and affidavits alone, a plaintiff need only make a *prima facie* showing of a sufficient jurisdictional basis to survive the jurisdictional challenge. *Id.* Specifically, a plaintiff in Virginia must make a *prima facie* showing that first, Virginia's long-arm statute reaches the non-resident defendant given the cause of action alleged and the nature of the defendant's Virginia contacts, and second, that the exercise of personal jurisdiction in the circumstances is consistent with due process, that is, that the long-arm statute's reach in the circumstances does not exceed its constitutional grasp. *See DeSantis v. Hafner Creations, Inc.*, 949 F.Supp. 419, 422 (E.D.Va.1996); *see also Peanut Corp. of Am. v. Hollywood Brands, Inc.*, 696 F.2d 311, 313 (4th Cir.1982). Although Virginia's long-arm statute extends personal jurisdiction "to the outmost perimeters of due process,"[16] it nonetheless appears that it is possible "for the

16. *.See Peanut*, 696 F.2d at 313. Some states, like California, have enacted long-arm statutes that actually collapse the statutory inquiry into the constitutional inquiry. *See Calder v. Jones*, 465 U.S. 783, 786 n. 5, 104 S.Ct. 1482, 79 L.Ed.2d 804 (1984) ("California's 'long-arm' statute permits an assertion of jurisdiction over a nonresident whenever permitted by the state and federal Constitutions."); Cal.Civ.Proc.Code § 410.10 (West 1973) ("A court of this state may exercise jurisdiction on any basis not

contacts of a non-resident defendant to satisfy due process but not meet the specific grasp of a Virginia long-arm statute provision."[17]

Bochan contends that jurisdiction exists over all defendants on the basis of two separate prongs of Virginia's long arm statute, Va.Code § 8.01–328.1(A)(3), and § 8.01–328.1(A)(4). Under § 8.01–328.1(A)(3), a court may exercise personal jurisdiction over a defendant who causes "tortious injury by an act or omission in this Commonwealth." *See* Va.Code § 8.01–328.1(A)(3). Under § 8.01–328.1(A)(4), a court may exercise personal jurisdiction over a defendant who causes "tortious injury in this Commonwealth by an act or omission outside this Commonwealth" if that defendant i) regularly does or solicits business in Virginia, ii) engages in any other persistent course of conduct in Virginia, or iii) derives substantial revenue from goods used or consumed or services rendered, in Virginia. *See* Va.Code § 8.01–328.1(A)(4). As defendants contend that neither prong of the long-arm reaches them, each defendant's contacts with the forum must be analyzed in turn under the relevant prongs of the long-arm.

A. The La Fontaine Defendants

Analysis properly begins with the question whether the La Fontaines' conduct fits within the reach of § 8.01–328.1(A)(3). Put more concretely, the question is whether the La Fontaines committed a tort (*i.e.* libel) in Virginia by posting certain messages to an Internet newsgroup via AOL and Earthlink.net. This, as it happens, is a novel question in Virginia and there do not appear to be any decisions from other jurisdictions that are factually identical. There are, however, factually analogous cases that shed some light on how the Supreme Court of Virginia would analyze this issue. In *Krantz v. Air Line Pilots Association, Int'l*, 427 S.E.2d 326, 245 Va. 202 (1993), the defendant airline pilot posted a message from New York to ACCESS, a computer bulletin board physically located in Virginia. This message called for other pilots to pass the word that plaintiff was a "scab," apparently in an attempt to sabotage plaintiff's prospective employment at another airline. The Supreme Court of Virginia concluded that defendant's use of a bulletin board based in a Virginia facility satisfied § 8.01–328.1(A)(3). In reaching this conclusion, the court stated that "[w]ithout the use of ACCESS, a Virginia facility, [defendant] could not have obtained those recruits, and there would have been no interference with [plaintiff's] prospective contract, the third required element for a prima facie showing of this sort." *See Krantz*, 427 S.E.2d at 328.

Several federal district courts have applied the principles enunciated in *Krantz* to cases alleging Internet torts. In *TELCO Communications v. An Apple A Day*, 977 F.Supp. 404 (E.D.Va.1997), the court, in dicta, concluded that jurisdiction existed under § 8.01–328.1(A)(3) on the

inconsistent with the Constitution of this state or of the United States.").

17. *See TELCO Communications v. An Apple A Day*, 977 F.Supp. 404, 405 (E.D.Va.

1997) (citing *DeSantis v. Hafner Creations, Inc.*, 949 F.Supp. 419, 423 (E.D.Va.1996)).

ground that "[b]ut for the Internet service providers [AOL] and users present in Virginia, the alleged tort of defamation would not have occurred in Virginia." Thus, the court concluded that those defendants fell "under the jurisdictional net cast by *Krantz*." In contrast, the court in *Mitchell v. McGowan*, Civ. No. 98–1026–A, 1998 U.S. Dist. LEXIS 18587 (E.D.Va. September 18, 1998) (unpublished disposition), concluded that the defendant "appears to escape [the 'net' cast by *Krantz*] because the computer bulletin board he accessed is based in Texas," noting that this distinction, though rather "fine," was dispositive. Thus, since *Krantz* courts have focused in large measure on the location of the Internet service provider or the server on which the bulletin board is stored and the role played by this service or hardware in facilitating the alleged tort.

Under this analysis, a *prima facie* showing of a sufficient act by the La Fontaines in Virginia follows from their use of the AOL account, a Virginia-based service, to publish the allegedly defamatory statements. According to Bochan's expert, because the postings were accomplished through defendant's AOL account, they were transmitted first to AOL's USENET server hardware, located in Loudon County, Virginia. There, the message was apparently both stored temporarily and transmitted to other USENET servers around the world. Thus, as to the La Fontaines, because publication is a required element of defamation, and a *prima facie* showing has been made that the use of USENET server in Virginia was integral to that publication, there is a sufficient act in Virginia to satisfy § 8.01–328.1(A)(3).

* * *

III.

Given that § 8.01–328.1(A)(3) reaches the La Fontaines * * *, the next question is whether * * * [this reach exceeds the constitutional grasp of the provision]. In this regard, the Due Process Clause requires that no defendant shall be haled into court unless defendant has "certain minimum contacts [with the state] ... such that the maintenance of the suit does not offend traditional notions of fair play and substantial justice." *International Shoe Co. v. Washington*, 326 U.S. 310, 316, 66 S.Ct. 154, 90 L.Ed. 95 (1945). * * *. The statements made by * * * defendants posted on the Internet concerned the presumably local activities of an individual each knew was a Virginia citizen. Bochan, and several of his Virginia friends, accessed the postings in Virginia, and the reputational harm resulting from defendants' actions and allegations of pedophilia and sexual deviancy, if any, has been primarily suffered in Virginia, where Bochan lives and works. Under these circumstances, because the predominant "effects" of the La Fontaines' and Harris's conduct are in Virginia, these defendants could reasonably foresee being haled into court in this jurisdiction. *See Calder v. Jones*, 465 U.S. 783, 789–90, 104 S.Ct. 1482, 79 L.Ed.2d 804 (1984) (holding that California court's assertion of personal jurisdiction over Florida-based reporters did not violate due process when allegedly defamatory article that was the basis of the suit focused on the California activities of California residents); *First American First, Inc. v. National Ass'n of Bank Women*, 802 F.2d 1511, 1517 (4th Cir.1986) (concluding that Virginia court's exercise of jurisdiction did not violate Constitution when defendant knew or should have known that its alleged defamation would inflict the greatest injury upon plaintiff in Virginia, the state where he lived and conducted his business); *TELCO*, 977 F.Supp. at 407 (noting that assertion of jurisdiction was supported by the fact that the effect of the challenged communication would be felt in Virginia). Thus, the constitutional prong of the inquiry is satisfied as to all defendants.

IV.

Based on the affidavits before the Court at this time, Bochan has made a *prima facie* case for jurisdiction over all defendants. Thus, defendants' motions to dismiss must be denied. * * *

Notes

1. At the relevant time America OnLine (AOL) offered two types of subscriber accounts: (1) a regular account including a local internet access telephone number, and (2) a much cheaper "bring your own Internet" account, not offering an access telephone number but allowing access over the Internet to all the features of AOL. The La Fontaines had the second type of account—they used a non-Virginia-based Internet service provider for access to the Internet. Thus the role of AOL and the La Fontaines' contact with Virginia was quite limited.

2. If John Doe defames Jane Roe in an AOL chat room, can Jane get jurisdiction over AOL in Virginia? Note that the procedural question of jurisdiction is a very separate question from the substantive question of whether or not AOL is civilly liable for defamatory statements in its chat room.

CHAPTER VI

E–COMMERCE AND SOFTWARE CONTRACTS

A. OLD LAW AND NEW SITUATIONS

The following case demonstrates the kind of problems that can arise in trying to make new trends in technology fit under legal rules designed for more traditional forms of commerce.

WALGREEN v. WISCONSIN PHARMACY EXAMINING BOARD

Court of Appeals of Wisconsin, 1998.
217 Wis.2d 290, 577 N.W.2d 387.

NOTICE: UNPUBLISHED OPINION. RULE 809.23(3), RULES OF CIVIL PROCEDURE, PROVIDE THAT UNPUBLISHED OPINIONS ARE OF NO PRECEDENTIAL VALUE AND MAY NOT BE CITED EXCEPT IN LIMITED INSTANCES.

EICH, CHIEF JUDGE.

The Wisconsin Pharmacy Examining Board appeals from an order reversing its ruling that the Walgreen Company, the owner and operator of several pharmacies in Wisconsin, violated various regulatory statutes and administrative rules relating to pharmacies when, as part of a test program, it accepted prescription orders from physicians via a computer electronic mail system, and provided used computers for some of the physicians participating in the test. The board concluded that: (1) the use of computer-transmitted prescriptions violated § 450.11(1), Stats., which requires written prescription orders to be signed by the prescribing physician;[1] and (2) Walgreen's provision of computers to some of the participating physicians violated Wis. Adm.Code § Phar 10.03(14), which prohibits pharmacies from participating in "rebate or fee-splitting arrangements" with physicians. The statute uses the term "practitioner" rather than "physician," defining the former as "a person licensed in

---

1. Section 450.11(1), Stats., provides:

(1) DISPENSING. No person may dispense any prescribed drug or device except upon the prescription order of a [physician]. All prescription orders shall specify the date of issue, the name and address of the patient, the name and address of the [physician], the name and quantity of the drug ... prescribed, directions for the use of the drug ... and, if the order is written by the [physician], the signature of the [physician]. Any oral prescription order shall be immediately reduced to writing by the pharmacist and filed.... (Emphasis added.??)

495

this state to prescribe and administer drugs." See § 450.01(17), Stats. For simplicity, we use the term "physician."

While we pay due deference to the board's decision, we are satisfied that its interpretation of § 450.11(1), Stats., while reasonable, is overcome by a more reasonable interpretation and that its determination that Walgreen's program violated the "rebate" rule lacks any reasonable basis in the record. We therefore reverse the board's decision and affirm the circuit court's order.

The facts are not in dispute. Walgreen tested a computer system it had developed whereby ten physicians electronically transmitted prescriptions to a Walgreen pharmacy. Each electronically transmitted prescription contained the same information as a written or faxed prescription but did not include the physician's signature. Walgreen provided the necessary software to the ten participating physicians and also supplied six of them with used computers and modems at no cost.

In determining that Walgreen's program violated § 450.11(1), Stats., the board reasoned that, because the statute does not specifically mention electronic transmissions, but rather defines a "prescription order" as simply "a written or oral order by a [physician] for a drug or device for a particular patient," § 450.01(21), Stats., an electronic transmission is the equivalent of a written order and thus subject to the signature requirement of the statute. The board determined that the program also violated the "rebate" rule because Walgreen received a financial benefit by providing free computer equipment to several of the participating physicians—although it never estimated either the value of the equipment or the nature of the "benefit" to Walgreen. Having so found, the board assessed a forfeiture of $89,200 against Walgreen.

Walgreen sought judicial review of the board's decision and the circuit court reversed, concluding with respect to the § 450.11(1), Stats., violation that prescriptions transmitted electronically were more analogous to prescriptions ordered by telephone, which, under the statute, a physician need not sign. The court also rejected the board's determination that Walgreen's program violated the "rebate" rule because the board failed to determine the extent of any financial benefit to either Walgreen or the participating physicians.

The board appeals, reasserting the arguments it raised before the trial court. * * *

II. THE STATUTORY VIOLATION

Emphasizing that § 450.11(1), Stats., on its face, deals with only written and "oral" prescriptions, the board maintains that a computer electronic mail system is more analogous to a written prescription order than an oral one because "the communication between the doctor and the pharmacist is textual," involving the use of letters and numbers typed at one computer and read on another computer. Thus, according to the board, because a computer transmission lacks the prescribing physician's signature, Walgreen's system violates § 450.11(1).

It is in the nature of things that statutes must at times be applied to situations unforeseen at the time of their enactment. When this occurs, the statute can and should be considered in terms of its manifest intent to see, in Professor Hurst's words, whether the "pictures actually drawn by the statutory text ... [are] sufficient to cover the new type of situation that the course of events ha[s] produced." James W. Hurst, Dealing with Statutes 35 (1982). According to Hurst, if the legislature has supplied "sufficient specifications to provide a discernible frame of reference within which the situation now presented quite clearly fits, even though it represents in some degree a new condition of affairs unknown to the lawmakers," the statute may be interpreted accordingly. *Id.*

The circuit court, disagreeing with the board's conclusion that a computer-transmitted prescription was so analogous to a written prescription that it must be treated as such under the statute, ruled that it was more closely akin to a prescription transmitted orally—by telephone—which the legislature, in the concluding lines of § 450.11(1), Stats., expressly stated may be filled without being signed. That is, to us, a more reasonable interpretation than the board's in light of the simple facts of computer transmission: The prescription is put into a computer as text and the message is then electronically transmitted to the pharmacy's terminal, much as a telephone call—or a facsimile—would be.[8]

The board asserts that "security considerations" should bar us from considering a computer transmission as analogous to a telephone order. The board suggests in its brief that pharmacists can recognize the caller's voice over the telephone, and thus verify his or her identity, while "[a] computer, on the other hand, is more anonymous," creating a danger that the prescription information "will fall into the wrong hands." And, it maintains that we should defer to such concerns. The board failed to expressed such concerns, however, and we have not been pointed to any evidence in the record, or any findings or determinations made by the board, that touch on this point. The board's attorneys raise this unsupported argument for the first time on appeal. We owe the assertion no deference and we are not persuaded by the argument. We agree with Walgreen that the unsubstantiated statement that the pharmacists' ability to recognize prescribing physicians' voices—especially pharmacies in large metropolitan areas such as Milwaukee or Madison—will ensure that prescriptions are not pirated pales when contrasted with the benefits Walgreen's system has over written, faxed or telephone orders. As the trial court noted, and as the parties agreed in their stipulation of facts, such benefits include savings in time for both physician and pharmacist, elimination of the need to interpret physicians' handwriting, and removing the opportunity for patients to alter prescriptions.

---

8. Indeed, computer transmission presents an advantage over an oral prescription order—where the listener must record the order on paper—by greatly reducing the risk of misunderstanding because the prescription appears in written form on the pharmacy's terminal.

Finally, we note that the circuit court's interpretation appears to be consistent with the board's own rule allowing electronic transmission of renewal prescription orders on a one-time basis between two pharmacies. See WIS. ADM.CODE § PHAR 7.05(3) and (5).

We are thus satisfied that the circuit court properly reversed the board's conclusion that Walgreen's test program violated § 450.11(1), Stats.

* * *

By the Court.-Order affirmed.

Recommended for publication in the official reports.

B. PAPERFREE TRANSACTIONS

Computerization of a wide variety of transactions offers huge savings both for businesses and consumers. Business save the cost of buying, shipping, storing, and handling masses of paper. Consumers can enjoy increased competition by choosing from numerous competitors on the Internet rather than being limited to those who can offer local facilities for signing papers. The National Council of Commissioners on Uniform State Laws ("NCCUSL") in 1999 approved the Uniform Electronic Transactions Act ("UETA"), 7A, Part I, U.L.A. 17 (Supp.2000), to authorize the use of electronic documents and electronic signatures instead of paper documents and paper signatures. The Uniform Computer Information Transactions Act ("UCITA"), <http://www.law.upenn.edu/bll/ulc/ulc_frame.htm>, also approved by NCCUSL in 1999, among other provisions includes articles validating electronic transactions for what it calls "licensing" of computer data. Disappointed with the slow pace of adoption of UETA, Congress in 2000 enacted the "Electronic Signatures in Global and National Commerce Act." Pub. L. No. 106–229, 114 Stat. 464 (2000). The title "Electronic Signatures" is misleading. In fact the Act not only authorizes the use of electronic signatures, it authorizes the use of electronic records in place of paper records. It contains a very limited number of exceptions, for instance paper may still be required for wills and utility shutoff notices. To the extent Congress's power to regulate interstate commerce allows, the Act overrides conflicting state legislation.

One type of paperfree transaction that Congress has not moved to encourage is the use of "digital cash." A number of computerized payment systems have been used successfully for years, including ATM's, electronic funds transfer systems, and Internet home banking services. All these systems leave some sort of audit trail. There are emerging technologies, however, that leave no audit trail. These include smart card technology and electronic money systems, known collectively as digital cash. The possible emergence of "digital cash" is perceived by law enforcement officials as presenting a serious threat to their mission. Crime does pay, and one of the major methods of fighting crime is the detection of the flow of cash or bank transfers that reflect the profits of criminal activity. Customs officials can catch suspicious travelers with suitcases full of cash. Federal law enforcement official can and do analyze reports that banks much submit on all large money transfers. Authorities fear, however, that digital cash, consisting of encrypted information, could be transferred internationally over the Internet in unlimited quantities without detection.

PREFATORY NOTE TO THE UNIFORM ELECTRONIC TRANSACTIONS ACT

7A, Part I, U.L.A. 17 (Supp. 2000).
© 1999 National Council of Commissioners on
State Laws; reprinted with permission.

With the advent of electronic means of communication and information transfer, business models and methods for doing business have evolved to take advantage of the speed, efficiencies, and cost benefits of electronic technologies. These developments have occurred in the face of existing legal barriers to the legal efficacy of records and documents which exist solely in electronic media. Whether the legal requirement that information or an agreement or contract must be contained or set forth in a pen and paper writing derives from a statute of frauds affecting the enforceability of an agreement, or from a record retention statute that calls for keeping the paper record of a transaction, such legal requirements raise real barriers to the effective use of electronic media.

One striking example of electronic barriers involves so called check retention statutes in every State. A study conducted by the Federal Reserve Bank of Boston identified more than 2500 different state laws which require the retention of canceled checks by the issuers of those checks. These requirements not only impose burdens on the issuers, but also effectively restrain the ability of banks handling the checks to automate the process. Although check truncation is validated under the Uniform Commercial Code, if the bank's customer must store the canceled paper check, the bank will not be able to deal with the item through electronic transmission of the information. By establishing the equivalence of an electronic record of the information, the Uniform Electronic Transactions Act (UETA) removes these barriers without affecting the underlying legal rules and requirements.

It is important to understand that the purpose of the UETA is to remove barriers to electronic commerce by validating and effectuating electronic records and signatures. It is NOT a general contracting statute–the substantive rules of contracts remain unaffected by UETA. Nor is it a digital signature statute. To the extent that a State has a Digital Signature Law, the UETA is designed to support and compliment that statute.

A. Scope of the Act and Procedural Approach. The scope of this Act provides coverage which sets forth a clear framework for covered transactions, and also avoids unwarranted surprises for unsophisticated parties dealing in this relatively new media. The clarity and certainty of the scope of the Act have been obtained while still providing a solid legal framework that allows for the continued development of innovative technology to facilitate electronic transactions.

With regard to the general scope of the Act, the Act's coverage is inherently limited by the definition of "transaction." The Act does not apply to *all* writings and signatures, but only to electronic records and signatures relating to a transaction, defined as those interactions between people relating to business, commercial and governmental affairs. In general, there are few writing or signature requirements imposed by law on many of the "standard" transactions that had been considered for exclusion. A good example relates to trusts, where the general rule on creation of a trust imposes no formal writing requirement. Further, the writing requirements in other contexts derived from governmental filing issues. For example, real estate transactions were considered potentially troublesome because of the need to file a deed or other instrument for protection against third parties. Since the efficacy of a real estate purchase contract, or even a deed, between the parties is not affected by any sort of filing, the question was raised why these transactions should not be validated by this Act if done via an electronic medium. No sound reason was found. Filing requirements fall within Sections 17–19 on governmental records. An exclusion of all real estate transactions would be particularly unwarranted in the event that a State chose to convert to an electronic recording system, as many have for Article 9 financing statement filings under the Uniform Commercial Code.

The exclusion of specific Articles of the Uniform Commercial Code reflects the recognition that, particularly in the case of Articles 5, 8 and revised Article 9, electronic transactions were addressed in the specific contexts of those revision processes. In the context of Articles 2 and 2A the UETA provides the vehicle for assuring that such transactions may be accomplished and effected via an electronic medium. At such time as Articles 2 and 2A are revised the extent of coverage in those Articles/Acts may make application of this Act as a gap-filling law desirable. Similar considerations apply to the recently promulgated Uniform Computer Information Transactions Act ("UCITA").

The need for certainty as to the scope and applicability of this Act is critical, and makes any sort of a broad, general exception based on notions of inconsistency with existing writing and signature requirements unwise at best. The uncertainty inherent in leaving the applicability of the Act to judicial construction of this Act with other laws is unacceptable if electronic transactions are to be facilitated.

Finally, recognition that the paradigm for the Act involves two willing parties conducting a transaction electronically, makes it necessary to expressly provide that some form of acquiescence or intent on the part of a person to conduct transactions electronically is necessary before the Act can be invoked. Accordingly, Section 5 specifically provides that the Act only applies between parties that have agreed to conduct transactions electronically. In this context, the construction of the term agreement must be broad in order to assure that the Act applies whenever the circumstances show the parties intention to transact electronically, regardless of whether the intent rises to the level of a formal agreement.

B. Procedural Approach. Another fundamental premise of the Act is that it be minimalist and procedural. The general efficacy of existing law in an electronic context, so long as biases and barriers to the medium are removed, validates this approach. The Act defers to existing substantive law. Specific areas of deference to other law in this Act include: (1) the meaning and effect of "sign" under existing law, (2) the method and manner of displaying, transmitting and formatting information in Section 8, (3) rules of attribution in Section 9, and (4) the law of mistake in Section 10.

The Act's treatment of records and signatures demonstrates best the minimalist approach that has been adopted. Whether a record is attributed to a person is left to law outside this Act. Whether an electronic signature has any effect is left to the surrounding circumstances and other law. These provisions are salutary directives to assure that records and signatures will be treated in the same manner, under currently existing law, as written records and manual signatures.

The deference of the Act to other substantive law does not negate the necessity of setting forth rules and standards for using electronic media. The Act expressly validates electronic records, signatures and contracts. It provides for the use of electronic records and information for retention purposes, providing certainty in an area with great potential in cost savings and efficiency. The Act makes clear that the actions of machines ("electronic agents") programmed and used by people will bind the user of the machine, regardless of whether human review of a particular transaction has occurred. It specifies the standards for sending and receipt of electronic records, and it allows for innovation in financial services through the implementation of transferable records. In these ways the Act permits electronic transactions to be accomplished with certainty under existing substantive rules of law.

ELECTRONIC SIGNATURES IN GLOBAL AND NATIONAL COMMERCE ACT

Pub. L. No. 106–229, 114 Stat. 464.

SECTION 1. SHORT TITLE.

This Act may be cited as the "Electronic Signatures in Global and National Commerce Act".

TITLE I—ELECTRONIC RECORDS AND SIGNATURES IN COMMERCE

SEC. 101. GENERAL RULE OF VALIDITY.

(a) IN GENERAL.—Notwithstanding any statute, regulation, or other rule of law (other than this title and title II), with respect to any transaction in or affecting interstate or foreign commerce—

(1) a signature, contract, or other record relating to such transaction may not be denied legal effect, validity, or enforceability solely because it is in electronic form; and

(2) a contract relating to such transaction may not be denied legal effect, validity, or enforceability solely because an electronic signature or electronic record was used in its formation.

(b) PRESERVATION OF RIGHTS AND OBLIGATIONS.—This title does not—

(1) limit, alter, or otherwise affect any requirement imposed by a statute, regulation, or rule of law relating to the rights and obligations of persons under such statute, regulation, or rule of law other than a requirement that contracts or other records be written, signed, or in nonelectronic form; or

(2) require any person to agree to use or accept electronic records or electronic signatures, other than a governmental agency with respect to a record other than a contract to which it is a party.

Note

There has been some controversy about UETA and the Electronic Signatures in Global and National Commerce Act because they would remove certain writing requirements designed for consumer protection. There is even more controversy about contractual consent provisions of the Uniform Computer Information Transactions Act ("UCITA"), which is discussed below.

THE UNIFORM COMPUTER INFORMATION TRANSACTIONS ACT

http://www.law.upenn.edu/bll/ulc/ulc_frame.htm

The Uniform Computer Information Transactions Act ("UCITA") was promulgated in 1999 by the National Council of Commissioners on Uniform State Laws ("NCCUSL"). The act governs contracting procedures for "licensing" of and access to computer information, a concept that is defined very broadly. The Act originated as a draft Article 2B for the Uniform Commercial Code. Opposition within the American Law Institute ("ALI"), which shares responsibility with NCCUSL for revision of the Uniform Commercial Code, led to the withdrawal of ALI from the project. (One of the authors of this casebook was among those active in opposing Article 2B in the ALI.) NCCUSL then adopted UCITA as a Uniform Act and recommended its adoption to the states. At the time of printing of this casebook, several states had adopted UCITA. UCITA, has remained quite controversial. Below are printed an explanation and defense of the act from the official NCCUSL website, followed by an attack upon the act from the Federal Trade Commission.

SUMMARY OF THE UNIFORM COMPUTER INFORMATION TRANSACTIONS ACT

© 2000 National Council of Commissioners on Uniform
State Laws; reprinted with permission.
http://www.nccusl.org/uniformact_summaries/uniformacts-s-ucita.htm.

The National Conference of Commissioners on Uniform State Laws promulgated the Uniform Computer Information Transactions Act (UCI-TA) in 1999. This act provides a comprehensive set of rules for licensing computer information, whether computer software or other clearly identified forms of computer information. Computerized databases and computerized music are other examples of computer information that would be subject to UCITA. It would also govern access contracts to sites containing computer information, whether on or off the Internet. UCITA would also apply to storage devices, such as disks and CD's that exist only to hold computer information. Other kinds of goods which contain computer information as a material part of the subject matter of a transaction may also be made subject to UCITA by express reference in a contract. Otherwise, other law would apply, such as the law of sales or leases for most transactions. UCITA would not govern contracts, even though they may be licensing contracts, for the traditional distribution of movies, books, periodicals, newspapers, or the like.

For the most part, the rules governing computer information contracts in UCITA are default rules. This means that they may be waived or varied by contract, and that in almost all cases the terms of a contract will prevail over a contrary rule in UCITA. Rules generally relating to fairness of the contract process are not default rules, and cannot be disclaimed by contract. Included in the rules that may not be disclaimed are the obligation of good faith, diligence, and reasonableness; limitations on enforcement imposed by unconscionability and fundamental public policy; and any standard of care prescribed in UCITA. Express rules for consumers, also, may not generally be disclaimed.

UCITA's rules govern licensing of contracts for computer information from formation through performance, including remedies if there is a breach of contract. Included in UCITA are rules for warranties, both implied and express, and rules pertaining to risk of loss in a computer information transaction. Most of the rules in UCITA are the traditional and familiar rules of contract from the law of sales and from the common law, but adapted to the special nature of computer information licensing contracts. Freedom of contract is a dominating underlying policy for UCITA, exactly as that principle is the foundation for the law of commercial transactions, generally, and exactly as that law has served all commercial transactions in the United States and has contributed to the economic growth and health of the United States.

A licensing contract involves transferring computer information such as software or other computerized information, from vendor (called licensor) to recipient (called licensee). A license grants informational rights to the licensee. Informational rights include any intellectual property rights derived from copyright, patents and the like, but also all other rights in information that any other law provides to a person that allows control of the information or restriction on the use of the information by other persons. The difference between a licensing contract and a sale contract is that the license generally contains restrictions on use and transfer of the computer information by the licensee during the life of the contract, and it may or may not transfer title to the licensee. A breach of express restrictions on use and transfer in the contract provides a remedy to the licensor.

A license under UCITA is not fundamentally rooted in intellectual property law such as patent or copyright law. A license under UCITA is simply a commercial contract, dependent wholly on the parties' ability to enter into a normal, commercial contract, just as a contract of sale or lease is simply and wholly a commercial contract. However, intellectual property rights may be licensed in a contract subject to UCITA. UCITA may not be used to vary or extend informational rights that are intellectual property rights, and expressly recognizes preemption by copyright, patent, or other federal intellectual property law in Section 105(b).

Like the law of sales and leases, in general, the right to contract is constrained by principles of unconscionability, good faith and fair dealing, UCITA has an additional restraint, an express power for a court to deny enforcement of a provision in a licensing contract that violates fundamental public policy. This public policy defense is unique in UCITA. An essential purpose of this defense is to give courts some latitude in reconciling commercial licensing law with the principles of intellectual property law. Most intellectual property law is federal, and UCITA expressly recognizes the preemptive effect of that federal law. But the public policy defense gives courts an additional power to consider intellectual property principles purely within the context commercial law.

Why is there a need for licensing contracts, rather than sale contracts for computer information? Computer information is peculiarly vulnerable to dissipation of its value by copying. The genius of computers is their ability to retain and copy information. Copies of information look just like their originals. In fact, everything is a copy. There are no true originals. Copies can be duplicated in huge numbers and disseminated to millions of users in times measured in less than seconds. Therefore, those who invest capital, intellectual effort and labor into the creation of valuable computer information may lose the economic value of their products in seconds. Without the ability to control copying and dissemination of computer information, vendors risk losing everything. The risk is so great that without licensing, the development of computer information products could become uneconomical and the great economic benefit of computer information products could be lost.

The term "copy" is, in fact, defined in UCITA as the "medium on which information is fixed on a temporary or permanent basis and from which it can be perceived, reproduced, used, or communicated, either directly or with the aid of a machine or device." Transfer of a copy is the basis of a licensing transaction. UCITA clearly separates transfer of a copy from transfer of ownership of informational rights. Title of a copy is separate from title to the informational rights, and may be transferred separately. A licensee's rights are not dependent upon transfer of title to the informational rights, although a license contract may expressly transfer title to informational rights and/or title to a copy. Transfers under UCITA are basically transfers of copies. The basic restrictions in licensing contracts are usually restrictions on creating further copies.

Licensing of information is the standard of the computer information business today. The huge bulk of vendors license their computer information products. UCITA, therefore, does not originate licensing contracts. UCITA was developed to provide basic, recognizable default rules for the existing licensing activity that goes on and expands as commerce in computer information expands. That expansion is the primary source of economic development in the United States and is projected to be the economic mainstay of the United States for the foreseeable future. UCITA, therefore, is responding to existing economic activity and a mode of contract upon which the computer information industry, itself, has come to rely. Firming the law and establishing some certainty with respect to the rules that apply, and that apply uniformly, is the modest goal of UCITA. It is not a radical, destabilizing proposal. It is familiar law adapted to ongoing economic activity that can use stable, predictable law that otherwise does not now exist.

These are some highlights of UCITA:

Mass market license. Traditionally, contract formation contemplates some negotiation and arms-length give and take between contracting parties. Commercial contract law has long-since abandoned this image of contracting activity as the only image. Article 2 of the Uniform Commercial Code has long had rules governing contracts that do not form in the traditional image, and has legitimized form contracts for sales of goods for nearly half-a-century. The mass-market license is an electronic form contract for computer information licensing, exactly as there have been form contracts for the sales of goods for a very long time. The difference is that a mass-market license is often presented with the package for the computer information found in retail stores, and, more importantly as electronic commerce grows, as part of the transfer of computer information, electronically, from computer to computer. Whether called "shrink-wrap" or "click-wrap," these are mass-market licenses. UCITA treats mass-market licenses differently from negotiated licenses. A mass-market license is not enforceable against the licensee unless the terms to be enforced are readily available to the licensee and until the licensee has had a appropriate time to review them. If, upon review, the licensee does not like the license contract or any part of it, the copy of the computer information may be returned to the vendor for a refund, plus reasonable expenses for making a rightful return and compensation for damages to a processing system by the removal of the information from that system. This right of return may not be waived or disclaimed in a contract. Nowhere else in the commercial law is there such a no-fault return policy for rejecting or repudiating a contract.

Warranties of license are incorporated into UCITA, based on the warranty provisions for sale of goods under Article 2 of the Uniform Commercial Code. But computer information requires special implied warranties. One is the warranty of compatibility of computer systems under Section 405(b). The licensor has an implied warranty, if the licensee is relying upon the licensor for skill and judgment in selecting components of a computer system, that the components will function together as a system.

Implied warranties may be disclaimed. Disclaimers in mass-market contracts must be conspicuous. Any affirmation of fact or promise made by a licensor as part of the basis of the bargain, becomes an express warranty of the licensor.

There are special rules for communication of computer information in electronic form. Since these transactions are almost all electronic, and faceless, it is necessary to have rules governing the attribution of electronic signatures, and the accuracy of electronic messages. Part 2, Subpart B is largely devoted to these communications rules. The term "authenticate" is the basis for these rules. A signature or its electronic equivalent is the basic means of authentication under UCITA. That "authentication" is attributed to the person whose intentional act that "authentication" is. A party relying upon that authentication has the burden of establishing attribution, which may be shown in any manner, including evidence of the efficacy of any "attribution procedure" used in the communication. An "attribution procedure" is any procedure that provides greater assurance than a simple transmission of information that the "authentication" is that of the party to which it is attributed. There are both simple and complex attribution procedures available for identifying the person who sends an electronic communication, and persons may choose the procedures that suit their particular transactions.

Attribution procedures may have impact on message content in an electronic communication. If a procedure is in place to detect errors or changes in the message communicated, a party that conforms to the procedure is not bound by an error or change that results because the other party does not conform to the procedure. There is a special rule for consumers. Consumers who make errors while entering automated transactions are not bound by the unintended erroneous message, so long as the consumer notifies the other party of the error promptly after it is identified, properly returns the computer information received and has not obtained value or benefit from using the information.

An "access contract" is a contract to enter the information system (read computer) of another to obtain information, or use that information system for specific purposes. Most current computer users have access contracts, if for no other reason than to use the Internet. UCITA governs these contracts with special rules relating to rights of access in Section 61.

UCITA also governs support contracts, and service contracts for the correction of performance problems. No licensor of information is required to provide such contracts (computer software support services are common), but if it does, it is subject to the express terms of the contract, or if silent, to what is "reasonable in light of ordinary standards of the business, trade, or industry . . . "

In Section 816, UCITA allows a licensor to disable computer information subject to a license and in use by a licensee for breach of contract. There are substantial limitations upon the exercise of this remedy. The remedy is not available unless the licensee has manifested assent to the specific part of the licensing contract that permits exercise of the remedy. There must be notice to the licensee at least 15 days prior to the exercise of the remedy. This notice gives the licensee the opportunity to cure the breach. The licensor may not exercise the remedy if it knows that exercise "will result in substantial injury or harm to the public health or safety or grave harm to the public interest substantially affecting third parties not involved in the dispute" (between licensor and licensee). The conditions for exercise of the remedy in Section 816 may not be waived or varied by contract.

These are some of the provisions in the Uniform Computer Information Transactions Act. It is a comprehensive act, so that the above-cited provisions are merely highlights. This Act is a very important contribution to computer information law, and should receive serious attention in every state.

LETTER FROM THE FEDERAL TRADE COMMISSION BUREAU OF CONSUMER PROTECTION, BUREAU OF COMPETITION, AND POLICY PLANNING OFFICE

http://www.ftc.gov/be/v990010.htm

July 9, 1999.

Mr. John L. McClaugherty
Chair, Executive Committee
National Conference of Commissioners on Uniform State Laws
211 E. Ontario Street, Suite 1300
Chicago, Illinois 60611

Dear Mr. McClaugherty:

As the National Conference of Commissioners on Uniform State Laws (NCCUSL) prepares to consider adoption of the Uniform Computer Information Transactions Act (UCITA), the staff of the Bureaus of Consumer Protection and Competition and of the Policy Planning office of the Federal Trade Commission (FTC) wishes to express the same consumer welfare concerns that it raised in its October 30, 1998 letter to Carlyle C. Ring and Professor Geoffrey Hazard, Jr. about UCITA's predecessor, Uniform Commercial Code Article 2B (August 1, 1998 draft).[1] Those concerns, with one exception, have not been addressed in any significant respect in UCITA.[2] We briefly summarize the October 30, 1998 letter and have attached a copy for your convenience.

Although UCITA Section 105(b) now includes a public policy preemption provision, the language of the provision creates additional barriers to enforcing this public policy preemption that were not proposed in the August 1, 1998 draft of Article 2B. Indeed, the new language of 105(b) only enhances the staff concerns enumerated in the October 30, 1998 letter.

UCITA endorses a license model for "computer information transactions."[3] For example, under UCITA a license to use software (rather than the sale of the software itself) would allow the licensor to limit or control how the licensee uses the software, even where the software has been mass-marketed to consumers. Examples of these limits or controls include restrictions on a consumer's right to sue for a product defect, to use the product, or even to publicly discuss or criticize the product.[4]

Unlike the law governing sales of goods, UCITA departs from an important principle of consumer protection that material terms must be disclosed prior to the consummation of the transaction. UCITA does not require that licensees be informed of licensing restrictions in a clear and conspicuous manner prior to the consummation of the transaction.[5] For

1. This letter represents the views of the Bureaus of Consumer Protection and Competition and of the Policy Planning office and does not necessarily represent the views of the FTC or any individual Commissioner. The FTC, however, has authorized the staff to submit this letter.

2. The one exception is UCITA Section 816, which had no counterpart in Article 2B, that does address the staff's notice concerns about the use of electronic self-help by a licensor.

3. The Prefatory Note to UCITA defines "computer information transactions" to include transactions involving computer software, multimedia interactive products, computer data and databases, and Internet and online information.

4. Although the actual provisions of UCITA itself do not expressly preempt or supplant any existing federal or state con-sumer protection laws and policies, the effect of these provisions is to allow licensors to enforce contract use restrictions in a mass market license that supplant many traditional terms of a contract that ordinarily are set by state and federal law.

5. Under Section 5 of the FTC Act, a misleading omission occurs "when qualifying information necessary to prevent a practice, claim, representation, or reasonable expectation or belief from being misleading is not disclosed." Federal Trade Commission Policy Statement on Deception, appended to *Cliffdale Associates, Inc.*, 103 F.T.C. 110, 174 (note 4). This qualifying information must be made prior to purchase. The test of whether a misleading omission violates Section 5 of the FTC Act is whether "the omitted information would be a material factor in the consumer's decision to purchase the product." *Id.*, note 44.

example, UCITA allows licensors of software to disclose these restrictions after the transaction has been completed, such as when the licensee opens the software box and discovers the terms of the license. Thus, in effect there may be no "meeting of the minds" prior to the consummation of the transaction. Moreover, UCITA adopts a definition of the term "conspicuous" that has the effect of allowing material license terms not to be disclosed clearly and conspicuously at any point before or after the transaction is completed.[6]

In addition, in its effort to establish a legal framework to facilitate electronic commerce, UCITA allocates significant risks to consumers in the event of unauthorized transactions. This, in turn, might deter, rather than advance, development of electronic commerce.

Further, UCITA expands the scope and power of contracts, particularly contracts designed by software vendors and intellectual property owners. The effect of such a change is potentially to provide state contract law with primacy over federal intellectual property laws in those cases where the licensor seeks to acquire or restrict rights beyond what federal or state law permits. For example, if a state were to adopt UCITA, state law could permit licensors to include anticompetitive grantback terms in a license that reduce the licensee's incentive to engage in research and development, unless the licensee took on the uncertain task of challenging the term subject to UCITA Section 105.[7] By doing so, this could upset the delicate balance between intellectual property and competition policy, which has been carefully calibrated to recognize certain limits on intellectual property so as not to stifle competition or innovation. By allowing licensors of computer information to expand their rights, there is a possibility that these state-enforced contracts could restrain trade in violation of the antitrust laws, consti-

Under FTC law, a deceptive act or practice prior to purchase cannot be cured by a post-purchase money-back guarantee. See *e.g.*, *In the Matter of Thompson Medical Company, Inc.*, 104 F.T.C. 648 (1984) (money back guarantee is not a defense to the charge of deceptive advertising); *Montgomery Ward & Co. v. FTC*, 379 F.2d 666, 671 (1967) (defendant cannot rely on a money-back guarantee policy to defend deceptive advertising practice because such a defense "would make the false advertising prohibitions of the [FTC] Act a nullity."). For a specific example of this same principle, see FTC Telemarketing Sales Rule, 16 C.F.R. § 310.3(a)(1) (1998).

6. UCITA's approach to "conspicuous" disclosure fails to take into consideration the context in which the disclosure is given. For example, UCITA includes several broad safe harbors in its definition of "conspicuous," so that, for example, a disclosure which is "in capitals in a size equal to or greater than, or in contrasting type, font, or color to, the surrounding text" (UCITA § 102(a)(15)(A)) would be considered conspicuous regardless of the context of the disclosure. Thus, under UCITA a disclosure would be considered "conspicuous" even if such a disclosure were buried amid boilerplate license text, or were printed on one of many different leaflets enclosed within a software box. This is the opposite approach the FTC has used to fulfil its law enforcement responsibilities. The term "clear and conspicuous" in FTC law refers to a general standard of effective communication. This standard is central to much of the case law that has developed under Section 5 of the FTC Act, 15 U.S.C. § 45, which empowers the FTC to take enforcement action against deceptive commercial practices. In order to determine whether this standard has been met, "the Commission considers the disclosure in the context of all the elements of the advertisement." FTC Request for Comment, Interpretation of Rules and Guides for Electronic Media, 63 Fed. Reg. 24996, 25002 (1998) (footnote omitted).

7. See fn 2, *supra*.

tute misuse of intellectual property, and/or violate state trade secret statutes. As a result, UCITA may not have a neutral effect on competition policy.

In sum, we question whether it is appropriate to depart from these consumer protection and competition policy principles in a state commercial law statute, especially since many of these same principles are now being included as core elements in international e-commerce discussions. UCITA proposes these changes based on the implicit assumption that there is something unique about the technology involved (software and information access) that necessitates this departure from the traditional law of sales. If this is the case, we believe it would be more appropriate to seek a change to the underlying laws that are deemed to be inappropriate to software and other UCITA products. If a license model is deemed most appropriate nonetheless, the FTC staff in its October 30, 1998 letter recommended a number of changes to an earlier draft of UCITA which would help alleviate the staff's concerns.

It is our hope that the NCCUSL membership will consider the issues raised in the attached letter during deliberations over whether to adopt UCITA.

Respectfully submitted,

Joan Z. Bernstein, Director
Adam G. Cohn, Attorney
Division of Marketing Practices
Bureau of Consumer Protection

William J. Baer, Director
David A. Balto, Assistant Director for Policy and Evaluation
Bureau of Competition

Susan S. DeSanti, Director
Michael S. Wroblewski, Advocacy Coordinator
Policy Planning

FEDERAL TRADE COMMISSION
600 Pennsylvania Ave., NW
Washington, DC 20580

cc: NCCUSL Members

Attachment

C. AUTHENTICATION OF SIGNATURES

Authentication of a signature is sometimes demanded by a party to a transaction or required by law. Various traditional methods exist for authenticating signatures, for instance attestation and notarization in connection with a real estate transaction or a bank or broker guaranty of a signature on a stock transfer document. UETA and the Electronic Signatures in Global and National Commerce Act allow the signature of a notary public or guarantor to be in the form of an electronic signature.

On the Internet, there are also various methods of authentication of signatures. No verification is usually required if a prospective customer wants to be put on an e-mail mailing list for "free information about exiting new products." Online shops usually want a credit card number and the customer's billing address so that they can compare these to credit card company records. Online car rental may also require a driver's license number. More elaborate authentication and special access codes may be required for making large money transfers from banks or for buying and selling stock online. For most types of transactions, the approach of the legal system has been to let the market decide what form of authentication the parties to a particular transaction will demand.

A problem common to all forms of signature authentication is that of ensuring that the person or organization that authenticates the signature is competent and trustworthy. In the case of notaries public, the state performs (at least in theory) an important function in checking the identity and qualifications of prospective notaries and of dismissing dishonest notaries. If in doubt about a notary's commission, one can contact the state authorities and check. Some states now offer a similar service with respect to digital signatures. Unlike the term "electronic signature," which is used in UETA and the Electronic Signatures in Global and National Commerce Act to refer to any identifying information in electronic form, "digital signature" is usually used to refer to a technique that uses cryptography to provide security against forgery. The most common type of digital signature involves the use of cryptography to create digital data derived from the text of and signature to a message. A private certification organization holds the key to decrypt the digital signature. On demand it will decrypt the signature and certify the authenticity of the signature and the integrity of the attached document. Legislation in some states provides for official public certification of reliable certifying organizations, much the way the state only appoints (or only should appoint) reliable people to be notaries public.

Question

A number of states passed legislation in the late 1990s that not only provided for approval of digital signature certification entities but also required specific cryptographic techniques for digital signatures and gave special force to digital signatures using these techniques. To what extent is such legislation preempted by the Electronic Signatures in Global and National Commerce Act? See the material below.

ELECTRONIC SIGNATURES IN GLOBAL AND NATIONAL COMMERCE ACT
Pub. L. No. 106–229, 114 Stat. 464

SECTION 1. SHORT TITLE.

This Act may be cited as the "Electronic Signatures in Global and National Commerce Act".

TITLE I—ELECTRONIC RECORDS AND SIGNATURES IN COMMERCE

SEC. 101. GENERAL RULE OF VALIDITY.

(a) IN GENERAL.—Notwithstanding any statute, regulation, or other rule of law (other than this title and title II), with respect to any transaction in or affecting interstate or foreign commerce—

(1) a signature, contract, or other record relating to such transaction may not be denied legal effect, validity, or enforceability solely because it is in electronic form; and

(2) a contract relating to such transaction may not be denied legal effect, validity, or enforceability solely because an electronic signature or electronic record was used in its formation.

SEC. 102. EXEMPTION TO PREEMPTION.

(a) IN GENERAL.—A State statute, regulation, or other rule of law may modify, limit, or supersede the provisions of section 101 with respect to State law only if such statute, regulation, or rule of law—

(1) constitutes an enactment or adoption of the Uniform Electronic Transactions Act as approved and recommended for enactment in all the States by the National Conference of Commissioners on Uniform State Laws in 1999, except that any exception to the scope of such Act enacted by a State under section 3(b)(4) of such Act shall be preempted to the extent such exception is inconsistent with this title or title II, or would not be permitted under paragraph (2)(A)(ii) of this subsection; or

(2)(A) specifies the alternative procedures or requirements for the use or acceptance (or both) of electronic records or electronic signatures to establish the legal effect, validity, or enforceability of contracts or other records, if—

(i) such alternative procedures or requirements are consistent with this title and title II; and

(ii) such alternative procedures or requirements do not require, or accord greater legal status or effect to, the implementation or application of a specific technology or technical specification for performing the functions of creating, storing, generating, receiving, communicating, or authenticating electronic records or electronic signatures; and

(B) if enacted or adopted after the date of the enactment of this Act, makes specific reference to this Act.

* * *

SEC. 106. DEFINITIONS.

* * *

(5) ELECTRONIC SIGNATURE.—The term "electronic signature" means an electronic sound, symbol, or process, attached to or logically associat-

ed with a contract or other record and executed or adopted by a person with the intent to sign the record.

UNIFORM ELECTRONIC TRANSACTIONS ACT

7A, Part I, U.L.A. 17 (Supp. 2000).
© 1999 National Council of Commissioners on
State Laws; reprinted with permission.

SECTION 1. SHORT TITLE. This [Act] may be cited as the Uniform Electronic Transactions Act.

SECTION 2. DEFINITIONS. In this [Act]:

* * *

(5) "Electronic" means relating to technology having electrical, digital, magnetic, wireless, optical, electromagnetic, or similar capabilities.

* * *

(8) "Electronic signature" means an electronic sound, symbol, or process attached to or logically associated with a record and executed or adopted by a person with the intent to sign the record.

SECTION 7. LEGAL RECOGNITION OF ELECTRONIC RECORDS, ELECTRONIC SIGNATURES, AND ELECTRONIC CONTRACTS.

(a) A record or signature may not be denied legal effect or enforceability solely because it is in electronic form.

(b) A contract may not be denied legal effect or enforceability solely because an electronic record was used in its formation.

(c) If a law requires a record to be in writing, an electronic record satisfies the law.

(d) If a law requires a signature, an electronic signature satisfies the law.

D. APPLICABLE LAW

If the transaction is governed by the law of a state that has adopted UCITA, the following provisions of UCITA will determine if UCITA or some other law applies:

UNIFORM COMPUTER INFORMATION TRANSACTIONS ACT

http://www.law.upenn.edu/bll/ulc/ulc_frame.htm
© 1999 National Council of Commissioners on
State Laws; reprinted with permission.

SECTION 102. DEFINITIONS.

* * *

(9) "Computer" means an electronic device that accepts information in digital or similar form and manipulates it for a result based on a sequence of instructions.

(10) "Computer information" means information in electronic form which is obtained from or through the use of a computer or which is in a form capable of being processed by a computer. The term includes a copy of the information and any documentation or packaging associated with the copy.

(11) "Computer information transaction" means an agreement or the performance of it to create, modify, transfer, or license computer information or informational rights in computer information. The term includes a support contract under Section 612. The term does not include a transaction merely because the parties' agreement provides that their communications about the transaction will be in the form of computer information.

* * *

(43) "Mass-market license" means a standard form used in a mass-market transaction.

(44) "Mass-market transaction" means a transaction that is:

(A) a consumer contract; or

(B) any other transaction with an end-user licensee if:

(i) the transaction is for information or informational rights directed to the general public as a whole, including consumers, under substantially the same terms for the same information;

(ii) the licensee acquires the information or informational rights in a retail transaction under terms and in a quantity consistent with an ordinary transaction in a retail market; and

(iii) the transaction is not:

(I) a contract for redistribution or for public performance or public display of a copyrighted work;

(II) a transaction in which the information is customized or otherwise specially prepared by the licensor for the licensee, other than minor customization using a capability of the information intended for that purpose;

(III) a site license; or

(IV) an access contract.

SECTION 103. SCOPE; EXCLUSIONS.

(a) This [Act] applies to computer information transactions.

(b) Except for subject matter excluded in subsection (d) and as otherwise provided in Section 104, if a computer information transaction includes subject matter other than computer information or subject matter excluded under subsection (d), the following rules apply:

(1) If a transaction includes computer information and goods, this [Act] applies to the part of the transaction involving computer information, informational rights in it, and creation or modification of it. However, if a copy of a computer program is contained in and sold or leased as part of goods, this [Act] applies to the copy and the computer program only if:

    (A) the goods are a computer or computer peripheral; or

    (B) giving the buyer or lessee of the goods access to or use of the program is ordinarily a material purpose of transactions in goods of the type sold or leased.

(2) In all other cases, this [Act] applies to the entire transaction if the computer information and informational rights, or access to them, is the primary subject matter, but otherwise applies only to the part of the transaction involving computer information, informational rights in it, and creation or modification of it.

(c) To the extent of a conflict between this [Act] and [Article 9 of the Uniform Commercial Code], [Article 9] governs.

(d) This [Act] does not apply to:

(1) a financial services transaction;

(2) an agreement to create, perform or perform in, include information in, acquire, use, distribute, modify, reproduce, have access to, adapt, make available, transmit, license, or display:

    (A) audio or visual programming that is provided by broadcast, satellite, or cable as defined or used in the Federal Communications Act and related regulations as they existed on July 1, 1999, or by similar methods of delivering that programming; or

    (B) a motion picture, sound recording, musical work, or phonorecord as defined or used in Title 17 of the United States Code as of July 1, 1999, or an enhanced sound recording.

(3) a compulsory license; or

(4) a contract of employment of an individual, other than an individual hired as an independent contractor to create or modify computer information, unless the independent contractor is a freelancer in the news reporting industry as that term is commonly understood in that industry;

(5) a contract that does not require that information be furnished as computer information or a contract in which, under the agreement, the form of the information as computer information is otherwise insignificant with respect to the primary subject matter of the part of the transaction pertaining to the information; or

(6) subject matter within the scope of [Article 3, 4, 4A, 5, [6,] 7, or 8 of the Uniform Commercial Code].

(e) As used in subsection (d)(2)(B), "enhanced sound recording" means a separately identifiable product or service the dominant character of which consists of recorded sounds but which includes (i) statements or instructions whose purpose is to allow or control the perception, reproduction, or communication of those sounds or (ii) other information so long as recorded sounds constitute the dominant character of the product or service despite the inclusion of the other information.

SECTION 104. MIXED TRANSACTIONS: AGREEMENT TO OPT–IN OR OPT–OUT.

The parties may agree that this [Act], including contract-formation rules, governs the transaction, in whole or part, or that other law governs the transaction and this [Act] does not apply, if a material part of the subject matter to which the agreement applies is computer information or informational rights in it that are within the scope of this [Act], or is subject matter within this [Act] under Section 103(b), or is subject matter excluded by Section 103(d)(1) or (2). However, any agreement to do so is subject to the following rules:

(1) An agreement that this [Act] governs a transaction does not alter the applicability of any rule or procedure that may not be varied by agreement of the parties or that may be varied only in a manner specified by the rule or procedure, including a consumer protection statute [or administrative rule]. In addition, in a mass-market transaction, the agreement does not alter the applicability of a law applicable to a copy of information in printed form.

(2) An agreement that this [Act] does not govern a transaction:

(A) does not alter the applicability of Section 214 or 816; and

(B) in a mass-market transaction, does not alter the applicability under [this Act] of the doctrine of unconscionability or fundamental public policy or the obligation of good faith.

(3) In a mass-market transaction, any term under this section which changes the extent to which this [Act] governs the transaction must be conspicuous.

(4) A copy of a computer program contained in and sold or leased as part of goods and which is excluded from this [Act] by Section 103(b)(1) cannot provide the basis for an agreement under this section that this [Act] governs the transaction.

Notes And Question

1. While this casebook was in the process of publication, a number of amendments to Article 103 of UCITA were under consideration. Check at <http://www.law.upenn.edu/bll/ulc/ulc_frame.htm> for the latest version of UCITA.

1. Does UCITA apply in the following cases: (1) a consumer buys an automobile with a computer-controlled brake system; (2) a law firm subscribes to an on-line data service; (3) a sole practitioner buys a computer that comes bundled with what is advertised as "$2000 worth of software"?

2. If UCITA does apply to a transaction, the seller will be able to take advantage of UCITA's strong pro-seller slant. The default provisions of

UCITA provide more limited rights to the buyer to reject or revoke and more limited warranty protection. Through the "shrinkwrap" provisions of UCITA, the seller will be able to impose contract terms on the buyer even in the absence of traditional forms of consent.

3. If a state has not enacted UCITA or if UCITA is inapplicable by its terms, the question arises whether the transaction is covered by Article 2 of the Uniform Commercial Code or by the common law. Article 2 provides better protection for buyers than does either UCITA or the common law. Article 2, of course, was drafted before computers were important. It included a scope provision, § 2–102, which provided "Unless the context otherwise requires, this Article applies to transactions in goods * * *." Section 2–105 defined "Goods" as meaning "all things (including specially manufactured goods) which are movable at the time of identification to the contract for sale * * *." Discussions were underway as this casebook went to press on the possibility of revising Article 2 to exclude some types of transactions involving software and information. Unless and until this occurs and states adopt the revisions, the existing case law on the applicability of Article 2 will remain important in those states that have not adopted UCITA. Check at <http://www.law.upenn.edu/bll/ulc/ulc_frame.htm> for the latest version of the Uniform Commercial Code.

4. When a contract contains a mixture of goods and services, the tests used to classify these mixed contracts differ from state to state. For example, Michigan courts apply a "predominant factor test," which looks at whether the purchasers ultimate goal is to acquire a product or service. *See Dahlmann v. Sulcus Hospitality Technologies, Corp.*, 63 F.Supp.2d 772, 774 (E.D.Mich.1999). Similar, but not quite the same is the "predominant purpose test." If the predominant purpose of the contract is to sell goods, it is governed by the U.C.C. "However, if service predominates and the transfer of title to personal property is an incidental feature of the transaction, the contract does not fall within the ambit of the Code." *Novamedix, Ltd. v. NDM Acquisition Corp.*, 166 F.3d 1177, 1182 (Fed.Cir.1999).

5. In *Micro-Managers v. Gregory*, 434 N.W.2d 97 (Wis.Ct.App.1988), plaintiff Micro-Managers sued Gregory for breach of contract. Gregory refused to pay for a computer program designed for him by plaintiff. The court held that the contract for the program was mainly one for services, and therefore not covered by the U.C.C. The contract between the parties was unarguably a mixed contract—for goods and services. The issue for the court was whether the contract was predominately for goods, or services. "The test for inclusion or exclusion [within the U.C.C.] is not whether [contracts] are mixed, but, granting that they are mixed, whether their predominant factor, their thrust, their purpose, reasonably stated, is the rendition of service, with goods incidentally involved (e.g., contract with artist for painting) or is a transaction of sale, with labor incidentally involved (e.g., installation of a water heater in a bathroom)." The court relied in part on billing records to determine the issue. Labor costs accounted for over ninety percent of the bill, for things such as development, time, and design. "These words connote the rendition of services and not a sales transaction."

6. In *Delorise Brown, M.D., Inc. v. Allio*, 620 N.E.2d 1020 (Ohio Ct.App.1993), the plaintiff Brown sued Allio for breach or contract, on the grounds that Allio failed to completely deliver hardware, and perform the

necessary training, for a computer system Brown purchased for her office. The court applied a predominate purpose test, and concluded that the contract was primarily for the acquisition of a computer system, and that the labor aspect was incidental to that primary purpose.

E. TORT AS AN ALTERNATIVE TO CONTRACT CLAIMS

A.T. KEARNEY, INC. v. INTERNATIONAL BUSINESS MACHINES CORP.

United States Court of Appeals, Ninth Circuit, 1995.
73 F.3d 238.

T.G. Nelson, Circuit Judge:

A.T. Kearney, Inc. ("Kearney"), A management consulting firm with expertise in systems technology, was retained by Fred Meyer ("FM") to develop a management information system ("MIS" or "The System") for FM stores. The MIS devised by Kearney employed International Business Machines Corporation ("IBM") mid-size computers. When new FM management decided the system was a failure, FM sued Kearney. The parties eventually settled. While the action was pending, Kearney brought suit against IBM in state court alleging negligence and negligent misrepresentation to itself and FM and claiming contribution and indemnity from IBM. IBM successfully petitioned for removal to federal court, where it moved for, and was granted, summary judgment. Kearney timely appeals the dismissal of its negligence and contribution claims. We have jurisdiction under 28 U.S.C. § 1291, and we affirm.

Factual and Procedural Background

In 1989, FM, a retailer offering consumers the convenience of "one-stop shopping" for a wide range of goods, hired Kearney, an information systems consultant, to advise it in overhauling its computer system. FM's then-CEO, Steve Stevens, sought with Kearney's help to implement a new, decentralized management system at FM. FM and Kearney took bids from a number of computer hardware vendors in May 1989, including IBM. IBM submitted a proposal which included use of a mainframe computer at FM headquarters, but FM and Kearney rejected this proposal as not in keeping with its decentralized plan.

In October 1989, Kearney suggested FM use a "distributed" MIS architecture, which did not include use of a mainframe. It advised FM to install IBM AS/400 mid-size computers at the stores and headquarters, a decision which Kearney admits was "unusual because large companies such as Fred Meyer always used mainframe computers, rather than mid-size computers, to handle headquarters operations." However, Kearney assured FM that the System would be viable and cost-efficient. At least two IBM employees questioned the decision to use only mid-size computers in the System, but they did not disclose their reservations to FM or to Kearney.

FM accordingly purchased approximately one hundred AS/400 computers from IBM under the provisions of a twenty-three page contract. The sales contract explicitly excluded "warranties of merchantability and fitness for a particular purpose." IBM and Kearney had no contractual relationship. Incident to the sale, IBM provided FM with installation assistance, technical support and the benefit of its expertise. Thirteen IBM employees were installed at FM headquarters for the purpose of helping Kearney and FM get the System up and running. The parties agree that IBM was compensated only for the purchase price of the computers and that IBM neither sought nor received compensation for consultation or any other services.

In January 1991, Steve Stevens was removed as FM's CEO. FM's new management team reviewed the MIS and found it wanting. FM subsequently ended its relationship with Kearney and installed an IBM mainframe computer at its headquarters. In September 1991, FM sued Kearney for $14 million in damages for breach of contract, negligence, negligent misrepresentation and breach of fiduciary duty. In October 1992, FM amended its complaint to seek $110 million in damages. Kearney admitted no wrong, but settled with FM in December 1992 for $13.25 million.

While the dispute with FM was ongoing, Kearney filed an indemnity suit against IBM in Oregon state court. IBM removed the case to federal court, and later moved for summary judgment. The district court granted summary judgment to IBM and dismissed as moot Kearney's cross-motion for summary judgment and IBM's motion to strike certain evidence. *See A.T. Kearney, Inc. v. International Business Machines Corp.*, 867 F.Supp. 943 (Or. 1994). Kearney timely appeals.

ANALYSIS

We review a grant of summary judgment *de novo*. Our review is governed by the same standard used by the trial court under Fed. R.Civ.P. 56(c). We must determine, viewing the evidence in the light most favorable to Kearney, whether there are any genuine issues of material fact and whether the district court correctly applied the relevant substantive law.

Oregon statutory law allows for contribution "where two or more persons become jointly or severally liable in tort for the same injury to person or property.... " Ore.Rev.Stat. § 18.440(1). Citing this statute, Kearney states at the beginning of its argument that its contribution claim against IBM "depends upon establishing IBM's liability in tort to Fred Meyer." However, Kearney also predicates its case on IBM's liability to Kearney under a "special relationship" theory.

Kearney argues that IBM is liable in tort to FM, and thus liable for contribution to Kearney, based on its negligent failure to inform FM of its doubts concerning the suitability of its mid-size computers for FM's purposes. Kearney further argues that IBM had a duty to inform Kearney of its doubts because of the special relationship between them. Thus, Kearney has both a derivative claim based on IBM's alleged duty to FM, and a direct claim based on IBM's alleged duty to Kearney. In its briefs, Kearney stressed the derivative claim: "The real issue before this court ... is whether a company that provides a range of goods and services in connection with a multi-million dollar information systems project has a duty to avoid making misrepresentations to its customers." At oral argument, however, Kearney clarified the dual nature of its claims. We consider both claims subsequent to our review of pertinent Oregon law.

As a preliminary matter, we observe that IBM's alleged liability in tort rests on the issue of whether or not it owed a duty to either FM or to Kearney to avoid negligent misrepresentation. Because we find IBM owed no such duty to either FM or Kearney, we do not reach the question of breach. The Oregon Supreme Court has held that duty is a legal issue to be decided by the court. We therefore reject Kearney's assertion that the issue must be sent to a jury. We also reject Kearney's argument that the existence of a special relationship is a factual issue separate from the issue of duty, requiring a decision by a jury.

Under Oregon common law, as set out by the Oregon Supreme Court in the seminal case of *Onita Pacific Corp. v. Trustees of Bronson*, tort claims for purely economic loss "must be predicated on some duty of the negligent actor to the injured party beyond the common law duty to exercise reasonable care to prevent foreseeable harm." 315 Or. 149, 843 P.2d 890, 896 (1992) (In Banc). The Oregon Supreme Court held that while one " 'ordinarily is not liable for negligently causing a stranger's purely economic loss without injuring his person or property,' " *id.* (quoting *Hale v. Groce*, 304 Or. 281, 283, 744 P.2d 1289 (1987)), "under some circumstances, one may be liable for economic loss sustained by others who rely on one's representations negligently made." *Id.* The court defined "economic losses" as "financial losses such as indebtedness incurred and return of monies paid, as distinguished from damages for injury to person or property.".

Rather than adopt a black letter rule on the issue of when to ascribe tort liability in cases of economic loss, the Oregon Supreme Court "opt[ed] to develop the scope of the duty and the scope of recovery on a case-by-case basis." Questions of liability are to be resolved by "examin[ing] the nature of the parties' relationship and compar[ing] that relationship to other relationships in which the law imposes a duty on parties to conduct themselves reasonably, so as to protect the other parties to the relationship."

The court listed the following as examples of relationships to which the Oregon common law ascribes a special duty of care: attorney-client, engineers or architects to their beneficiaries, agent-principal, and primary insurer to excess insurer and insured. The court also indicated that "nongratuitous suppliers of information owe a duty to their clients or employers or to intended third-party beneficiaries of their contractual, professional, or employment relationship to exercise reasonable care to avoid misrepresenting facts."

In such relationships, which might be termed "special relationships," the professional who owes a duty of care "is, at least in part, acting to further the economic interests of the 'client,' the person owed the duty of care." At the other end of the spectrum are relationships involving "two adversarial parties negotiating at arm's length to further their own economic interests." In the latter situation, "economic losses arising from a negligent misrepresentation are *not* actionable."

The court characterized "arm's length" adversaries not as hostile or aggrieved parties, but as "business adversaries in the commercial sense." To explain its reasoning, the court cited Professor Alfred Hill, distinguishing between commercial adversaries and suppliers of information to the general public:

> "When the aggrieved person is a buyer, who does not complain of the negligent performance of a service but rather of misrepresentation by a seller inducing the making of a contract, the conceptual mold has been different from the inception of modern contract law: the options have been to sue on the contract or to sue in deceit, without a middle ground consisting of actionable negligence."

Id., 843 P.2d at 898 (quoting Hill, Damages for Innocent Misrepresentation, 73 Column.L.Rev. 679, 688 (1973)). The court agreed with Professor Hill that "allowing recovery for negligent misrepresentations made in the bargaining process would undermine the law of contracts...."

IBM maintains, and the district court held as a matter of law, that its role was purely that of vendor, or commercial adversary. As such, IBM owed FM no duty beyond that specified in the contract, which disclaims, inter alia, warranty of fitness for a particular purpose. Kearney argues that IBM, FM and Kearney were "partners," not "adversaries"; that Kearney was an intended third-party beneficiary of the IBM–FM contract; and that IBM was not merely a vendor in the transaction but also a provider of information and services, and as such had a "special relationship" with FM and with Kearney.

Though IBM frequently declared itself FM's and Kearney's "partner," it clearly was not involved in a true partnership agreement with either party. Nor can it be said that Kearney was an intended third-party beneficiary of the contract between FM and IBM. Of the three categories of third-party beneficiary recognized by Oregon—donee, creditor, and incidental—Kearney is at best an incidental beneficiary, and thus has no enforceable rights under the contract.

Kearney's claims concerning partnership and beneficiary duties are better understood in light of its argument that IBM's relationships with FM and with Kearney are analogous to those described in Onita and progeny as giving rise to an exceptional duty of care. We are asked to determine whether the relationships in question are best characterized as belonging to the commercial adversary or to the special relationship end of the continuum suggested by Onita.

Kearney argues that two recent Oregon cases, *Lindstrand v. Transamerica Title Ins. Co.*, 127 Or.App. 693, 874 P.2d 82 (1994), and *Meininger v. Henris Roofing & Supply of Klamath County, Inc.*, 137 Or.App. 451, 905 P.2d 861 (1995), evince the state court's intent to extend the duty to avoid negligent misrepresentation to defendants in positions similar to IBM's vis-a-vis both FM and Kearney.

According to Kearney, *Lindstrand* expands on *Onita* by holding, in Kearney's words, that "neutral parties who elect to provide information" are subject to a heightened duty of care. We are not persuaded by this argument. In *Lindstrand*, the Oregon Court of Appeals held that a jury could find that an escrow company which provided deed information extracontractually to residential owners was a "nongratuitous supplier of information," and was bound as such to exercise due care in supplying the information. If the jury were to find that the escrow company "supplied the document about the restriction as an adjunct to the performance of its other duties," it would follow as a matter of law that the company "had a duty to exercise due care in providing the restriction."

Similarly, in *Meininger*, the Court of Appeals considered whether "a roof inspector hired by the sellers' agent to inspect a roof in contemplation of the sale of a house has a duty to avoid negligently misrepresenting the condition of the roof." As a nongratuitous supplier of information, the court held, the roof inspector owes a duty of care to the buyers as intended beneficiaries of the contractual relationship.

The Court of Appeals explained that:

> "The common thread in the special relationships that the [Oregon] Supreme Court has recognized as giving rise to a duty of care to protect against purely economic loss is that the professional is acting, at least in part, to further the economic interests of the person to whom the duty is owed."

In *Lindstrand*, the relation between the parties was of insurer to insured; in *Meininger*, the relation was also a fiduciary one—the roof inspector was hired to act in the economic interest of the buyer. There was no arm's length adversarial relationship in either case. Here, by contrast, the relationship of IBM and FM was clearly buyer-seller, as defined by the contract. We do not agree with Kearney that IBM acquired extracontractual obligations to FM based on its statements or assistance in installing the hardware.

We hold that neither IBM's friendliness, nor its self-interest, nor its aggressive sales tactics, altered the essentially commercial nature of its relationship with FM. We therefore hold that IBM owed no extracontractual duty to FM based on a special relationship; Kearney's derivative claim against IBM accordingly fails.

Nor do we agree that Oregon case law supports Kearney's proposition that IBM owed a duty of care to Kearney on this basis. FM was the customer; Kearney was the expert hired to devise a computer system to meet FM's needs. We are unable to infer a source of duty on the part of IBM to look out for Kearney's economic interest under the circumstances.

Finally, Kearney urges us to find as a matter of law that "a seller of sophisticated computer equipment assumes a duty of care to provide assistance and support that exists independent of the terms of the contract." Kearney offers no case or statute in support of this claim, but proffered to the district court expert testimony to the effect that computer hardware manufacturers generally, and IBM specifically, provide information, resources and support beyond the norm of the ordinary seller. IBM does not dispute that it provides significant assistance to purchasers of hardware, especially when the purchase is as large as the one in question here. However, IBM would characterize the support it offers as quantitatively, but not qualitatively, different than that provided by a seller of stereophonic or other kinds of technological equipment.

Kearney's argument that contracts for computer hardware differ from ordinary sales contracts is contradicted by case law. IBM cites *Triangle Underwriters, Inc. v. Honeywell, Inc.* 604 F.2d 737, 742–743 (2d Cir. 1979), holding that a contract for a sale of computer hardware remains a contract for a sale of goods, not services, regardless of any assistance provided by the manufacturer in installing the equipment. Kearney responds that Triangle is inapposite, because it deals with characterization of a contract for statute of limitations purposes, rather than for liability for negligence. In other words, Kearney maintains that the court in Triangle was forced in choosing between statutes of limitations to find that the contract was for either goods or services; it could not have found the contract to be for both. While this argument is questionable—the court in Triangle did not equivocate in deciding the contract was clearly for goods—a recent case of this circuit offers better authority and support for IBM's position.

In *Apollo Group, Inc. v. Avnet, Inc.*, we reviewed a computer hardware contract similar to the one between IBM and FM and held the agreement was for sales, not services, in spite of the manufacturer's proffer of technical advice to the buyer. 58 F.3d 477, 480 (9th Cir.1995). Though the dispute involved Arizona law, we looked to federal law for guidance because Arizona courts—like Oregon courts—have yet to formulate a test for determining whether a contract is for sales or services. Under federal law, " '[w]hen a sale predominates, incidental services provided do not alter the basic transaction.' " *Id.* (quoting *RRX Indus., Inc. v. Lab–Con, Inc.*), 772 F.2d 543, 546 (9th Cir.1985).

Because the "heart of the transaction was the sale of computer hardware," and the computer manufacturer was not paid for its consulting advice, but was remunerated only for the equipment itself, we held the agreement was to be construed as a sales contract. As in Apollo, the agreement between IBM and FM was for the purchase of machines, bore a disclaimer of warranty of fitness for a particular purpose, and contained no consultation provisions. Like the computer vendor in Apollo, IBM was not paid for consulting. Furthermore, FM's president, its CEO, and Kearney's managing director testified that they considered IBM to be a vendor, and not a consultant, either to FM or to Kearney.

Because we find no evidence of a special relationship between IBM and either FM or Kearney, and because we decline the invitation in this instance to find computer sales contracts different from other sales contracts as a matter of law, we affirm the district court's decision.

AFFIRMED.

Note

In *Apollo Group v. Avnet*, 58 F.3d 477 (9th Cir.1995), plaintiff Apollo sued Avnet for, among other things, negligent misrepresentation. Apollo contracted with Avnet to design a hardware system to run database and accounting software that Apollo purchased from Oracle Corporation. After the machine was installed, plaintiff found that it did not have the power to run the Oracle software, evidenced by the length of time—measured in days—that were required to process a single report, and the two to ten minute response time for even routine tasks. Plaintiff sought to replace the machine with a more powerful model. Apollo requested that Avnet accept the return of the original machine or allow Apollo to trade it for a more powerful model. Avnet refused to accept the return of the original computer.

Under its claim of negligent misrepresentation, Apollo sought recovery for pecuniary injuries. "Generally, under the 'economic loss' rule, a plaintiff who suffers only pecuniary injury as a result of the conduct of another cannot recover those losses in tort. Instead, the claimant is limited to recovery under the law of contract." In a matter of first impression, the court analyzed whether, as Apollo claimed, negligent misrepresentation falls outside the economic loss rule. The court concluded that the economic loss rule was to be given a broad reading. Additionally, the court pointed to the "safety rationale" underlying tort law. "Where the potential for danger to person or property is absent, tort principles need not be invoked because the safety incentive policy of tort liability is not implicated." Therefore, Apollo was barred from recovering under a tort theory, and was limited to contractual remedies.

GLOVATORIUM, INC. v. NCR CORP.

United States Court of Appeals, Ninth Circuit, 1982.
684 F.2d 658.

ALARCON, CIRCUIT JUDGE:

Glovatorium filed this action against NCR Corporation (NCR) in state court alleging breach of contract, intentional and negligent misrepresentation, breach of warranty, and fraud for conversion of equipment. NCR removed the action to the federal district court on the basis of diversity of citizenship. After a jury trial, Glovatorium was awarded compensatory damages for intentional misrepresentation, breach of warranty, and breach of the implied covenant of good faith. Punitive damages were also awarded.

I. Sufficiency of the Evidence of Fraud by NCR

NCR contends that the evidence adduced at trial did not establish that it acted fraudulently in the sale of the SPIRIT/8200 computer system to Glovatorium. Under California law, fraud is established when a misrepresentation is knowingly made with the intent to induce reliance, and justifiable reliance results, causing plaintiff damage. Review of whether there is sufficient evidence to support the finding of fraud is, however, a procedural matter in which we must apply federal law. This court will not disturb a jury verdict unless the evidence is such "that no reasonable man would accept it as adequate to establish the existence of each fact essential to the liability." *Kunz v. Utah Power & Light Co.*, 526 F.2d 500, 504 (9th Cir.1975). It is the function of the jury, not of this court, to weigh conflicting evidence and judge the credibility of witnesses. *Standard Oil Co. v. Perkins*, 347 F.2d 379, 383 (9th Cir.1965).

A.

Glovatorium. sought to show fraud by NCR in that NCR sold the SPIRIT system with knowledge of its defects. Review of the record indicates that the evidence supports the claim that NCR had knowledge of the defects. First, Norman Cohen, a former district manager for NCR, testified that he notified the SPIRIT support group in Dayton, Ohio of problems with the system. He also stated that he advised "headquarters" about these problems. Second, NCR's own witness, Peter Ford, who was associated with the SPIRIT support group stated that as project leader for the SPIRIT development team, he "was responsible for the time and delivery of the system and *reporting progress to management at NCR.*" (emphasis added). It can reasonably be inferred that as project leader he knew of the problems and that as part of his report to NCR management about the progress of the system, he advised them of the problems with the system. Third, there was evidence that NCR "corporate" attempted to cover up defects in the system. For instance, one of the problems experienced with the system was that it was so slow that many clients found they could accomplish the same task faster if it were done manually rather than using the SPIRIT system. NCR, however, developed and distributed a demonstrator model for the system to be used as a sales tool that "was specifically designed to function very, very effectively, and very fast, much more so than the actual SPIRIT programs did." Thus, it is reasonable to infer knowledge of this defect on the part of NCR since the demonstrator was specifically designed to cover it up.

B.

Fraud on the part of NCR was also claimed with regard to the sales representations made to Glovatorium concerning the route accounting system.

Under California law, fraud is properly inferred from the immediate failure to perform a promise. *Kaylor v. Crown Zellerbach, Inc.,* 643 F.2d 1362, 1368 (9th Cir.1981). In the matter before us, it was represented to Glovatorium that the computer would perform route accounting functions and that it would be delivered with the system by September, 1975. The computer was delivered in September, 1975, but could not be used for any route accounting functions. The payroll function was not operating until late 1975 or early 1976, and once in operation, it never ran properly. The route accounting system (without the other systems) was not available until March, 1976. Only one of Glovatorium's five routes was ever put on the computer because of problems with the system. The accounts payable and general ledger systems were *never* installed because of problems. Under Kaylor, the immediate failure to perform in terms of the installation and the operation of the computer systems for which Glovatorium, contracted is evidence from which fraud on the part of NCR is properly inferred.

Further evidence of fraud is shown by Warman's testimony that the 8200/SPIRIT system was never designed to perform a route accounting function. Yet, Glovatorium was sold the 8200/SPIRIT system to perform a route accounting function. Moreover, NCR had also determined that the SPIRIT system should not be modified. Yet, Glovatorium was sold a modified version of SPIRIT.[3]

C.

NCR contends that even if the above evidence shows fraud on the part of NCR employees, there is no evidence to establish fraud by NCR.

California law provides for corporate liability where "the advance knowledge, ratification, or act of oppression, fraud, or malice [is] * * * on the part of an officer, director, or managing agent of the corporation." Cal.Civil Code § 3294(b). The key inquiry in the determination of whether an employee is a managing agent is "the degree of discretion the employees possess in making decisions that will ultimately determine corporate policy." *Egan v. Mutual of Omaha Insurance Co.,* 24 Cal.3d 809, 822–23, 620 P.2d 141, 148, 169 Cal.Rptr. 691, 698 (1979), *cert. denied & appeal denied,* 445 U.S. 912, 100 S.Ct. 1271, 63 L.Ed.2d 597(1980).

Warman testified that his conduct in connection with the Glovatorium. sales transaction was, to his knowledge, "consistent * * * with NCR's *general policies and practices.*" (emphasis added). Indeed, the record demonstrates fraudulent acts by several NCR employees. First, Warman made the sale to Glovatorium of the computer system with the

---

3. NCR Corporate headquarters rejected the original contracts signed by Glovatorium which indicated a modification of SPIRIT. Thomas Warman, the NCR salesman, then prepared the contracts in such a way that the proposed modification was not apparent on the face of the contracts and they were approved. Information concerning the anticipated volume of transactions, referred to as a configurator, was also sent with both sets of contracts. The configurator sent with the second set of contracts, however, was one in which the volume of transactions had been falsely reduced so that it had no relationship to the Glovatorium installation.

knowledge that it was not designed to perform the functions for which it was sold. Second, the Oakland office manager for NCR and his assistant told one of their employees to switch the serial numbers on the drive from a loaner with the serial numbers on the Glovatorium drive. Glovatorium, however, had been told that the loaner was temporary.

There is also, as discussed above, evidence of fraudulent sales practices regarding the SPIRIT system at the direction of NCR headquarters. NCR seeks to distinguish such alleged fraud from the sales representations made to Glovatorium. The evidence of directions from headquarters is, however, probative of intent and, therefore establishes lack of good faith on the part of NCR and its sales personnel in the representations made concerning the route accounting systems. Even in criminal cases, probative evidence of willingness to participate in similar crimes is admissible.

The above evidence and the inferences that can reasonably be drawn from it are adequate to support the jury's conclusion that someone at NCR who was an officer or a director or who qualified as a managing agent participated in or ratified the fraudulent sale representations made to Glovatorium. This is particularly true in light of the fact that NCR offered no evidence to rebut such an inference. A reasonable person might accept the above evidence as adequate to establish NCR's liability; we will not disturb the jury verdict.

II. REQUESTED JURY INSTRUCTION DEFINING MANAGING AGENT

Appellant claims prejudicial error in the refusal of the trial court to give its requested instruction which would have defined the term "managing agent."

NCR requested that the judge instruct the jury that corporate liability existed, inter alia, if a managing agent "having power to bind the corporation" was involved in the fraud. No error existed in the trial judge's refusal to give the proffered instruction because the definition of a managing agent is not restricted to those who have power to bind the corporation. As discussed above, the California Supreme Court has held that focus in determining whether one is a managing agent is the degree of discretion the employee has to make decisions that will ultimately determine corporate policy. *Egan,* 24 Cal.3d at 822–23, 620 P.2d at 148, 169 Cal.Rptr. at 698. NCR's reliance on *Toole v. Richardson-Merrell, Inc.,* 251 Cal.App.2d 689, 711, 60 Cal.Rptr. 398, 414 (1967), as support for its requested instruction is misplaced. The court in *Toole* did not define a managing agent as one having power to bind the corporation; it referred only to "corporate officials having power to bind the corporation." *Id.* Moreover, even if the *Toole* court meant to define a managing agent as such, the more recent decision of the California Supreme Court in *Egan is* controlling.

The trial court's instruction on this point gave adequate guidance to the jury. The court, in effect, required that a person in the corporate hierarchy other than the salesman must have approved or aided the fraud, before punitive damages could be awarded. The relevant language given was: "you would have to find that an officer, director, or managing agent other than Mr. Warman, either over ratified or approved or confirmed these acts of fraud, oppression or the character of those acts, or that such a person personally participated in the acts of fraud, oppression or malice." No better or more complete instruction was proffered by NCR and, on the facts of this case, none was needed.

It is also clear from NCR's closing argument that it did not base its theory of defense on the grounds that any fraudulent acts that occurred were committed by employees who were not of the level of managing agents and that no one in authority at NCR knew about or ratified such acts. In speaking to the jury about intentional fraud, NCR stated that the issue "gets down to Mr. Warman, and it gets down to NCR." RT: 1520. NCR then discusses Warman's credibility, RT: 1521, and the fact that he had no incentive to make intentional misrepresentations. RT: 1523–25. With regard to NCR itself, Appellant claims that NCR acted in good faith and that "there was nothing nefarious, or underhanded, or fraudulent about the whole transaction." RT: 1533. NCR did not argue that if any fraud took place, there was insufficient evidence upon which to hold NCR liable under Cal.Civil Code § 3294. It is difficult to find prejudice due to an error based upon a theory that NCR did not argue to the jury.

Based on the foregoing, we conclude that any error committed by the trial judge was not prejudicial.

III. THE PUNITIVE DAMAGE AWARD

NCR argues that the punitive damages awarded to Glovatorium by the jury were excessive and must be reversed. An award of punitive damages that is approved by the district court will not be disturbed by the appellate court "unless it appears that the jury was influenced by passion or prejudice." *Moore v. Greene,* 431 F.2d 584, 593–94 (9th Cir.1970). NCR contends that the award is unjustifiable punishment because it was based "upon a fraud judgment absent any malice, reprehensible or outrageous conduct, or evidence of wilful disregard of plaintiffs interest." They also point to the fact that the punitive damage award exceeded the compensatory damage award by 9.1 times. These claims fail to demonstrate that the jury was influenced by passion or prejudice.

As discussed in section I, *supra,* there is adequate evidence in the record to support the jury's finding of fraud on the part of NCR. There is no requirement under Cal.Civil Code § 3294 that malice, reprehensible or outrageous conduct or wilful disregard be shown in addition to the fraud. *Horn v. Guaranty Chevrolet Motors,* 270 Cal.App.2d 477, 484, 75 Cal.Rptr. 871, 875–76 (1969). Thus, only the fact that the punitive damages were 9.1 times the compensatory damages remains. Without anything more, this is not an adequate basis for this court to find that the jury was impassioned or prejudiced.

IV.   THE COMPENSATORY DAMAGE AWARD

NCR claims that the jury awarded over $32,000 in damages that were not proved at trial and that damages were improperly awarded for Glovatorium's lost profits.

We must determine whether the verdict is grossly excessive or monstrous absent a total lack of evidence on all or certain portions of the case and absent prejudice. *Barzelis v. Kulikowski,* 418 F.2d 869, 870 (9th Cir.1969).

A.

NCR focuses its argument that excessive damages were awarded on the fact that, during closing argument, Glovatorium requested $253,000 in damages, *see, e.g.,* Reply Brief for Appellant at 18, while the jury awarded over $32,000 more. This fact, however, is not an adequate basis upon which to disturb the jury verdict. The jury was entitled to disregard the amount asked for when there was other evidence from which the jurors could draw their own conclusions. *Luria Brothers & Co. v. Pielet Brothers Scrap Iron & Metal, Inc.,* 600 F.2d 103, 115 (9th Cir. 1979). In the case before us, there was such evidence. For instance, the president of Glovatorium testified that lost profits could have been as high as $150,000. *See* RT: 565. To be conservative, however, he asked only for $24,000 in lost profits. *Id.* This evidence alone is enough to support the amount awarded by the jury.

B.

NCR contends that damages were improperly awarded on the basis of Glovatorium's lost profits. NCR, however, failed to raise any objection at trial to the instruction by the court that lost profits constituted a proper element of damages. NCR thereby waived its objection.

CONCLUSION

Based on the foregoing, the judgment entered by the district court is Affirmed.

Notes and Questions

1.   If neither the UCC nor UCITA apply to a computer-related contract, the parties may rely upon common law contract law, and, if the appropriate conditions are present, tort law.

2.   In *Glovatorium* the plaintiff acquired a defective software program from the defendant. The contract did not require the defendant to provide services. Was this a sale of a good? Why did the plaintiff sue in tort rather than contract?

3.   *Glovatorium* is a good example of a small-business plaintiff and a large, deep-pocket defendant. Although the actual damages were $253,000, the defendant won $2,073,000 in punitive damages. This case shows the importance for the vendor to keep a record of all representations and actions

of sales representatives. What could NCR's counsel have done during the contract negotiations to have reduced the possibility of such a large punitive damage award? See the unreported oral decision in Bigelow, Robert P., *Computer Contracts: Negotiating and Drafting Guide*, (Vol. 3) (April 1987) (8 CLSR 171).

F. BANKRUPTCY–PROTECTING SOFTWARE USERS

Inevitably some software licensors will fail. Normally, under bankruptcy law, the trustee in bankruptcy may "reject" a contract and stop performing it, leaving the other party to the contract to claim any relevant damages against the bankrupt estate. If, however, a trustee were to stop the effect of a software license, the effect on a software licensee could be catastrophic. Therefore, Congress amended the Bankruptcy Act to provide some special rules for protection of software licensees.

BANKRUPTCY CODE

11 U.S.C. § 365.

(n)(*l*) If the trustee rejects an executory contract under which the debtor is a licensor of a right to intellectual property, the licensee under such contract may elect-

(A) to treat such contract as terminated by such rejection if such rejection by the trustee amounts to such a breach as would entitle the licensee to treat such contract as terminated by virtue of its own terms, applicable nonbankruptcy law, or an agreement made by the licensee with another entity; or

(B) to retain its rights (including a right to enforce any exclusivity provision of such contract, but excluding any other right under applicable nonbankruptcy law to specific performance of such contract) under such contract and under any agreement supplementary to such contract, to such intellectual property (including any embodiment of such intellectual property to the extent protected by applicable nonbankruptcy law), as such rights existed immediately before the case commenced, for—

(i) the duration of such contract; and

(ii) any period for which such contract may be extended by the licensee as of right under applicable nonbankruptcy law.

(2) If the licensee elects to retain its rights, as described in paragraph (1)(B) of this subsection, under such contract—

(A) the trustee shall allow the licensee to exercise such rights;

(B) the licensee shall make all royalty payments due under such contract for the duration of such contract and for any period described in paragraph (1)(B) of this subsection for which the licensee extends such contract; and

(C) the licensee shall be deemed to waive—

(i) any right of setoff it may have with respect to such contract under this title or applicable nonbankruptcy law; and

(ii) any claim allowable under section 503(b) of this title arising from the performance of such contract.

(3) If the licensee elects to retain its rights, as described in paragraph (1)(B) of this subsection, then on the written request of the licensee the trustee shall—

(A) to the extent provided in such contract, or any agreement supplementary to such contract, provide to the licensee any intellectual property (including such embodiment) held by the trustee; and

(B) not interfere with the rights of the licensee as provided in such contract, or any agreement supplementary to such contract, to such intellectual property (including such embodiment) including any right to obtain such intellectual property (or such embodiment) from another entity.

(4) Unless and until the trustee rejects such contract, on the written request of the licensee the trustee shall—

(A) to the extent provided in such contract or any agreement supplementary to such contract—

(i) perform such contract; or

(ii) provide to the licensee such intellectual property (including any embodiment of such intellectual property to the extent protected by applicable nonbankruptcy law) held by the trustee; and

(B) not interfere with the rights of the licensee as provided in such contract, or any agreement supplementary to such contract, to such intellectual property (including such embodiment), including any right to obtain such intellectual property (or such embodiment) from another entity.

* * *

G. SELF–HELP

CLAYTON X–RAY CO. v. PROFESSIONAL SYSTEMS CORP.

Missouri Court of Appeals, Western District, 1991.
812 S.W.2d 565.

KENNEDY, PRESIDING JUDGE.

Clayton X–Ray Company was in the business of selling x-ray machines, x-ray film and chemicals used to develop the film to doctors and hospitals. It entered into a contract for the purchase of a computer system from Professional Systems Corporation, including the machine itself and software for the management and control of Clayton X–Ray Company business operations.

The written contract, entitled "Agreement to Purchase" was actually signed by John Clayton, Clayton X–Ray's president, in February, 1983. He had had the contract in his possession, however, since March 15, 1982, and the computer system had been delivered to Clayton X–Ray in May, 1982, and was in use well before Mr. Clayton signed the purchase agreement.

The contract price was $42,800, including $32,800 for equipment and $10,000 for software. Clayton made a down payment of $4,280, and later, in mid–1982, paid $30,000. The $10,000 balance was never paid, and PSC recovered judgment on a counterclaim for that amount in this lawsuit.

After the installation of the equipment and part of the software, a PSC employee, over a space of two years, worked 1100 hours at the Clayton X–Ray premises in an effort to get the bugs out of the software and adapt it to Clayton X–Ray operations. In early 1984 PSC informed Clayton X–Ray that it would not work on the computer any more. Bugs continued to cause difficulties and in 1985 PSC began once more to work on the system to correct 119 bugs that had appeared. In a January, 1986, letter, PSC told Clayton X–Ray that most of the bugs had been fixed.

PSC did additional work on the computer from April 15, 1986, to July, 1986. In July, PSC wrote to Clayton that the situation had "moved past the bug-fixing phase into a standard support and possible modification-need phase." This letter also reminded Clayton X–Ray of its unpaid account of $11,628.06, which included $10,000 of the original purchase price.

Clayton did not pay its bill. PSC, unknown to Clayton, put into the computer system a lockup program which at a pre-set time, October 31, 1986, locked up the computer programs so that Clayton could not access its files. The message on the computer was "Call Professional Systems Corporation About Your Bill." Clayton hired a person who was able to unlock the system and give Clayton access to its files.

Clayton brought suit against PSC for damages due to PSC's alleged breach of express warranty and, in another count, for actual and punitive damages for conversion in its lock up of the computer programs.

PSC counterclaimed for $11,628.06, which included the $10,000 balance owing on the original contract, and $1,628.06 for other goods.

The jury returned verdicts in favor of Clayton and against PSC on the breach of warranty claim for $60,000 and on the conversion claim for $1,050 actual damages and $10,000 punitive damages. As noted above, the jury returned a verdict for $10,000 on PSC's counterclaim and judgment was entered therefor.

Both of the parties' motions for a new trial were overruled, and both parties have appealed from the judgment.

* * *

We turn now to PSC's appeal from the $60,000 breach of warranty judgment, and the $1050 actual damages and $10,000 punitive damages judgment on the conversion claim. PSC says the verdicts are inconsistent and mutually destructive which give PSC $10,000 upon its contract claim against Clayton and also give Clayton damages upon its breach of warranty claim against PSC. This inconsistency—or rather the trial court's acceptance of the verdicts, and its failure to instruct the jury to deliberate further (MAI 2.06)—entitles it, says PSC, to a new trial.

When the verdicts were returned and their inconsistency suggested, PSC did not ask that the jury be instructed to deliberate further, and in fact objected to that course, PSC thereby waived any error based upon inconsistency of verdicts. *Douglass v. Safire*, 712 S.W.2d 373, 374 (Mo. banc 1986); *Holmes v. Drakey*, 759 S.W.2d 610, 611 (Mo.App.1988). We do not, of course, hold the two verdicts were inconsistent and mutually destructive.

PSC says the evidence makes no submissible case of conversion, nor a submissible case for punitive damages on Clayton's conversion claim. PSC does not present any argument or authority for the statement that the evidence did not support the conversion submission. It argues, though, that the evidence does not show defendant's conduct was outrageous because of "defendant's evil motive or reckless indifference to the rights of others" in its lock up of Clayton's computer system. See *Walker v. Gateway Nat. Bank*, 799 S.W.2d 614, 617 (Mo.App.1990); MAI No. 10.01. If PSC is correct in this position, it would follow that the punitive damages verdict on the conversion claim was unsupported by the evidence.

We hold, however, that the evidence was sufficient for the submission of punitive damages. PSC had no legal right, or any colorable legal right, to lock up Clayton's computer system. PSC's president had told a PSC employee to take a disk to Clayton's place of business, to tell the people at Clayton that there were some program changes that needed to be done, but then to load the computer instead with instructions to lock up on October 31, 1986. The effect of the lockup was to prevent Clayton's access to the records of its business. Only by the fortuity of being able to enlist the aid of a former employee of PSC was Clayton able to regain access to the records of its business in fairly short order, and PSC's stratagem did not accomplish the intended paralysis of Clayton's business. This evidence made a submissible case for punitive damages.

The judgment is affirmed.

All concur.

UNIFORM COMPUTER INFORMATION TRANSACTIONS ACT § 816

http://www.law.upenn.edu/bll/ulc/ulc_frame.htm.
© 1999 National Council of Commissioners on
State Laws; reprinted with permission.

SECTION 816. LIMITATIONS ON ELECTRONIC SELF–HELP.

(a) In this section, "electronic self-help" means the use of electronic means to exercise a licensor's rights under Section 815(b).

(b) On cancellation of a license, electronic self-help is not permitted, except as provided in this section.

(c) A licensee shall separately manifest assent to a term authorizing use of electronic self-help. The term must:

(1) provide for notice of exercise as provided in subsection (d);

(2) state the name of the person designated by the licensee to which notice of exercise must be given and the manner in which notice must be given and place to which notice must be sent to that person; and

(3) provide a simple procedure for the licensee to change the designated person or place.

(d) Before resorting to electronic self-help authorized by a term of the license, the licensor shall give notice in a record to the person designated by the licensee stating:

(1) that the licensor intends to resort to electronic self-help as a remedy on or after 15 days following receipt by the licensee of the notice;

(2) the nature of the claimed breach that entitles the licensor to resort to self-help; and

(3) the name, title, and address, including direct telephone number, facsimile number, or e-mail address, to which the licensee may communicate concerning the claimed breach.

(e) A licensee may recover direct and incidental damages caused by wrongful use of electronic self-help. The licensee may also recover consequential damages for wrongful use of electronic self-help, whether or not those damages are excluded by the terms of the license, if:

(1) within the period specified in subsection (d)(1), the licensee gives notice to the licensor's designated person describing in good faith the general nature and magnitude of damages;

(2) the licensor has reason to know the damages of the type described in subsection (f) may result from the wrongful use of electronic self-help; or

(3) the licensor does not provide the notice required in subsection (d).

(f) Even if the licensor complies with subsections (c) and (d), electronic self-help may not be used if the licensor has reason to know that its use will result in substantial injury or harm to the public health or safety or grave harm to the public interest substantially affecting third persons not involved in the dispute.

(g) A court of competent jurisdiction of this State shall give prompt consideration to a petition for injunctive relief and may enjoin, temporarily or permanently, the licensor from exercising electronic self-help even if authorized by a license term or enjoin the licensee from misappropriation or misuse of computer information, as may be appropriate, upon consideration of the following:

(1) grave harm of the kinds stated in subsection (f), or the threat thereof, whether or not the licensor has reason to know of those circumstances;

(2) irreparable harm or threat of irreparable harm to the licensee or licensor;

(3) that the party seeking the relief is more likely than not to succeed under its claim when it is finally adjudicated;

(4) that all of the conditions to entitle a person to the relief under the laws of this State have been fulfilled; and

(5) that the party that may be adversely affected is adequately protected against loss, including a loss because of misappropriation or misuse of computer information, that it may suffer because the relief is granted under this [Act].

(h) Before breach of contract, rights or obligations under this section may not be waived or varied by an agreement, but the parties may prohibit use of electronic self-help, and the parties, in the term referred to in subsection (c), may specify additional provisions more favorable to the licensee.

(i) This section does not apply if the licensor obtains possession of a copy without a breach of the peace and the electronic self-help is used solely with respect to that copy.

H. CONSUMER PROTECTION BY THE FEDERAL TRADE COMMISSION

The Federal Trade Commission (FTC) has become the primary agent of government enforcement and consumer protection on the Internet. The following case is an enforcement action taken against an online scheme that cleverly used the Internet to defraud customers.

IN RE BEYLEN TELECOM, LTD.

United States Federal Trade Commission, 1997.
No. 972–3128 http://www.ftc.gov/os/1997/9711/Bylnadmfcmp.htm

Westlaw, Federal Antitrust & Trade Regulation-Combined Antitrust & Trade Regulation Materials (FATR–ALL)

[DRAFT]   COMPLAINT

The Federal Trade Commission, having reason to believe that Beylen Telecom, Ltd. and NiteLine Media, Inc., corporations, and Ron Tan, individually and as an officer of NiteLine Media, Inc. ("the Respondents"), have violated the provisions of the Federal Trade Commission Act, and it appearing to the Commission that this proceeding is in the public interest, alleges:

1.   Beylen Telecom, Ltd., ("BTL") is a corporation organized, existing and doing business under and by virtue of the laws of the Cayman Islands with its principal office or place of business at Genesis Building, PS Box 2097, Grand Cayman, Cayman Islands, British West Indies.

2.   NiteLine Media, Inc. ("NiteLine") is a corporation doing business under and by virtue of the laws of the State of New York with its principal office or place of business at 7302 19th Avenue, Brooklyn, New York 11204.

3.   Ron Tan a/k/a Roeun Tan ("Tan") is an officer and shareholder of corporate respondent NiteLine Media, Inc. Individually or in concert with others, he has formulated, directed, controlled or participated in the acts or practices of the corporation, including the acts or practices alleged in this complaint. His principal office or place of business is the same as that of NiteLine Media, Inc.

4.   At all times relevant to this complaint, the Respondents have maintained a substantial course of trade, advertising, offering for sale and selling computer-stored images via both the Internet and international and interstate telephone lines, in or affecting commerce, as "commerce" is defined in Section 4 of the FTC Act, 15 U.S.C. § 44.

Course of Business

5.   From at least December 1996 through January 1997, the Respondents Tan and NiteLine posted messages to newsgroups and operated and promoted one or more World Wide Web sites, including the web sites located at "www.erotic2000.com" and "www.erotica2000.com." Through newsgroup messages and these web sites, Respondents Tan and NiteLine represented, expressly or by implication, that consumers could view "adult" images for free at sites on the Internet. A newsgroup is a collection of electronic messages, purportedly about a given topic, that consumers may read on the Internet. The World Wide Web or Web is a system used on the Internet for cross-referencing and retrieving information. A web site is a set of electronic documents, usually a home page and subordinate pages, readily viewable on computer by anyone with

access to the Web, standard software, and knowledge of the web site's location or address.

6. At one or more of the web sites operated by Respondents Tan and NiteLine and in one or more of their newsgroup messages, Respondents Tan and NiteLine stated that they offered "FREE XXX Images" for viewing at "FREE ADULT SITES." In addition, at one or more of their web sites, the Respondents Tan and NiteLine stated that the international sites they offered entailed:

NO MEMBERSHIP FEES!
NO CREDIT CARDS NEEDED!
NO 900#CHARGES!

7. Web sites operated by Respondents Tan and NiteLine instructed consumers that to view the "adult" images offered, the consumer had to first "download a special image viewer." This "image viewer" was a software program, which was identified as "david.exe," or "david7.exe," or other similar names.

8. Contrary to the clear implication of the term "image viewer" that Respondents Tan and NiteLine used on their web sites to describe this software program, the "david.exe" (or similarly named software) was not merely a means for reading computer data and converting such data into visual images. Instead, this software, if downloaded, installed, and activated, would, without any explanations or adequate disclosures: (a) automatically terminate the consumer's computer modem connection to the consumer's local Internet service provider while maintaining the appearance that the computer modem remained connected to such local Internet service provider; (b) automatically direct the consumer's computer modem to dial an international telephone number to re-connect to the Internet; (c) maintain the international long distance telephone connection thus established unless and until the consumer turned off the power switch to his computer or modem, or took other unusual action to terminate the telephone connection; and (d) caused the consumer to incur international long distance telephone charges on his telephone bill at rates in excess of $2.00 per minute for as long as the international long distance telephone connection was maintained. One of the techniques that this software employed to maintain the appearance that the computer modem remained connected to the consumer's local Internet service provider was to automatically turn off the speaker on the consumer's modem before dialing, thus preventing the consumer from hearing the sound of the international number being automatically dialed.

9. Prior to about January 23, 1997, Respondents Tan and NiteLine, at one or more of their web sites and in newsgroup messages, failed to disclose any of the events, described above in Paragraph 8, that automatically followed if one downloaded, installed and activated the purported "viewer" software.

10. Respondents Tan and NiteLine changed one or more of their web sites on or about January 23, 1997. Nevertheless, after that date, their

web sites and newsgroup messages continued to fail to disclose that once a consumer downloaded, installed and activated the "viewer" software, it caused consumers to incur international long distance telephone charges at rates in excess of $2.00 per minute. In addition, web sites and news group messages posted by Respondents Tan and NiteLine continued to fail to disclose that the consumer's computer modem would maintain the international long distance telephone connection unless and until the consumer turned off the power switch to his computer or modem or took other unusual action to terminate the telephone connection.

11. After about January 10, 1997, one or more of Respondents' web sites stated if consumers downloaded their "viewer" software, the consumers' computer modems would be connected to a site in Moldova, a former constituent state of the now-defunct Soviet Union. However, the computer modems of consumers who downloaded the software were not connected to a site located in Moldova, but rather were connected to a site located in Canada. Thus, even though the automatic telephone call generated by the "viewer" software went to Canada, the consumer was charged at the comparatively much higher per-minute rates for a call to Moldova.

12. Once a consumer had downloaded, installed and activated the purported "viewer" software offered by Respondents Tan and NiteLine, the consumer continued to incur international long distance telephone charges for as long as his computer modem was connected to the international long distance number and even after the consumer had exited Respondents Tan and NiteLine's "adult" sites.

13. Respondents Tan and NiteLine's promises of "free" Internet viewing of computer-stored images lured consumers from the U.S. and foreign countries into incurring hundreds of thousands of dollars in international long distance telephone charges.

14. Respondent BTL is a service bureau that provides telecommunications and other services to entities that promote international pay-per-call programs. In that capacity, Respondent BTL assigned Moldovan telephone numbers to Respondent NiteLine, as well as to Internet Girls, Inc.—a defendant in the federal court action, *FTC v. Audiotex Connection, Inc.* CV–97 0726 (DRH) (E.D.N.Y. filed Feb. 13, 1997). Directly or indirectly, Respondent BTL also provided NiteLine and Internet Girls with the following services: a) daily telephone traffic and billing reports; b) the "david.exe" (or similarly named software) program and technical support for this "viewer" software program described above; c) text or graphics to use in soliciting consumers on the Internet, including information that Tan or NiteLine incorporated into newsgroup messages or that Tan, NiteLine, or *Audiotex* defendants William Gannon or Internet Girls incorporated into the web sites "www.erotic2000.com," "www.erotica2000.com," "www.sexygirls.com," "www.1adult.com," or "www.beavisbutthead.com"; and d) a termination point for audiotext calls, namely a site in Canada containing computer images for viewing.

15. A foreign telephone carrier contracted to pay Respondent BTL a portion of the revenues received from consumers for calls placed to specific international telephone numbers. Respondent BTL, in turn, contracted to pay Respondent NiteLine a per-minute rate for calls they generated to those specific international telephone numbers. (Respondent BTL contracted to pay defendant Internet Girls on a similar basis). Thus, Respondents BTL, Tan, and NiteLine were to receive a portion of the amount of international telephone charges incurred by consumers.

Viewing Cost

16. In numerous instances, in the course of advertising, offering, offering for sale, or selling certain computer-stored images located at Internet sites, Respondents Tan and NiteLine represented to consumers, expressly or by implication, that consumers could view the images without cost by downloading, installing and activating purported "viewer" software.

17. In truth and in fact, once a consumer downloaded, installed and activated the purported "viewer" software to view computer-stored images located at Internet sites, the consumer incurred costs for an international long distance telephone call.

18. Therefore, the representations of Respondents Tan and NiteLine, as set forth in Paragraph 16, above, were false and deceptive, in violation of Section 5 of the FTC Act, 15 U.S.C. s 45.

Software for Downloading

19. In numerous instances, in the course of advertising, offering, offering for sale, or selling certain computer-stored images located at Internet sites, Respondents Tan and NiteLine represented to consumers, expressly or by implication, that consumers could view the images by downloading, installing and activating purported "viewer" software.

20. In numerous instances, Respondents Tan and NiteLine failed to disclose or disclose adequately to consumers the material facts that, by downloading, installing, and activating the purported "viewer" software, the following would result:

    a. The consumer's computer would terminate its modem connection to the consumer's usual local Internet service provider;

    b. The consumer's modem would dial an international long distance telephone number and establish a long-distance telephone connection with an Internet service provider at some remote location outside the United States;

    c. The consumer would likely incur international long distance telephone charges at rates in excess of $2.00 per minute for as long as the long-distance telephone connection with the remote Internet service provider was maintained; and

    d. The consumer's computer modem would not terminate the international long distance telephone connection to the remote Internet service provider unless and until the consumer turned off the power switch to his computer or modem or took other unusual action to terminate the telephone connection.

21.   In view of representations by Respondents Tan and NiteLine that consumers could view certain images located at Internet sites by downloading, installing and activating purported "viewer" software, as set forth in Paragraph 19, above, Respondents Tan and NiteLine's failure to disclose or disclose adequately the material information set forth in Paragraph 20, above, was deceptive, in violation of Section 5 of the FTC Act, 15 U.S.C. s 45.

22.   By providing Respondent NiteLine (and defendant Internet Girls) with telephone numbers, and by directly or indirectly providing the "viewer" software, text or graphics, or other goods or services described in Paragraphs 14 and 15, above, for the purpose of inducing consumers to call international telephone numbers, Respondent BTL provided the means and instrumentalities to others, and thereby acted in concert with others or knowingly and substantially assisted others, to engage in the deceptive acts and practices alleged in Paragraphs 16 through 21, above, in violation of Section 5 of the FTC Act, 15 U.S.C. s 45.

Telephone Billing

23.   In numerous instances, in the course of advertising, offering, offering for sale, or selling certain computer-stored images located at Internet sites, Respondents directly or through an intermediary caused charges for long distance calls to Moldova to appear on the telephone billing statements of consumers who downloaded, installed and activated Respondents' purported "viewer" software.

24.   In truth and in fact, the call that a consumer's computer modem dialed when the consumer downloaded, installed and activated Respondents' purported "viewer" software did not go to Moldova, which has high per-minute long distance telephone rates for calls from the United States, but instead went to Canada, which has comparatively much lower long distance rates for calls from the United States.

25.   Therefore, Respondents' practice of causing charges for long distance calls to Moldova to appear on the telephone billing statements of consumers who had downloaded, installed and activated Respondents' purported "viewer" software, as set forth in Paragraph 23, above, was deceptive, in violation of Section 5 of the FTC Act, 15 U.S.C. s 45.

26.   The acts and practices of Respondents as alleged in this complaint constitute unfair or deceptive acts or practices in or affecting commerce in violation of Section 5(a) of the Federal Trade Commission Act.

THEREFORE, the Federal Trade Commission this day of October, 1997 has issued this complaint against Respondents.

Note

1.   Beylen Telecom, Ltd. agreed to a Federal Trade Commission consent order, requiring it to cease the practices mentioned in the complaint and to

provide funds to leading long distance companies for them to distribute to victimized consumers. *In re Beylen Telecom*, Ltd., United States Federal Trade Commission, File No. 972–3128 (1997), <http://www.ftc.gov/os/1997/9711/Adtxprmford.htm>, Westlaw, Federal Antitrust & Trade Regulation—Combined Antitrust & Trade Regulation Materials (FATR–ALL).

I. TAXATION

The following Supreme Court case did not involve sales over the Internet, but rather sales through mail order catalogs. The case, however, is directly relevant to taxation issues that are now being discussed with regard to Internet sales, and is currently the starting point for state and federal government discussions of Internet taxation.

QUILL CORPORATION v. NORTH DAKOTA

Supreme Court of the United States, 1992.
504 U.S. 298, 112 S.Ct. 1904, 119 L.Ed.2d 91.

JUSTICE STEVENS delivered the opinion of the Court.

This case, like *National Bellas Hess, Inc. v. Department of Revenue of Ill.*, 386 U.S. 753, 87 S.Ct. 1389, 18 L.Ed.2d 505 (1967), involves a State's attempt to require an out-of-state mail-order house that has neither outlets nor sales representatives in the State to collect and pay a use tax on goods purchased for use within the State. In *Bellas Hess* we held that a similar Illinois statute violated the Due Process Clause of the Fourteenth Amendment and created an unconstitutional burden on interstate commerce. In particular, we ruled that a "seller whose only connection with customers in the State is by common carrier or the United States mail" lacked the requisite minimum contacts with the State. *Id.*, at 758, 87 S.Ct., at 1392.

In this case, the Supreme Court of North Dakota declined to follow *Bellas Hess* because "the tremendous social, economic, commercial, and legal innovations" of the past quarter-century have rendered its holding "obsole[te]." 470 N.W.2d 203, 208 (1991). Having granted certiorari, 502 U.S. 808, 112 S.Ct. 49, 116 L.Ed.2d 27, we must either reverse the State Supreme Court or overrule *Bellas Hess*. While we agree with much of the state court's reasoning, we take the former course. * * *

[T]he underlying issue is not only one that Congress may be better qualified to resolve, but also one that Congress has the power to resolve. * * * Congress is now free to decide whether, and to what extent the States may burden interstate mail-order concerns with a duty to collect use taxes. * * *

The judgment of the Supreme Court of North Dakota is reversed, and the case is remanded for further proceedings not inconsistent with this opinion.

It is so ordered.

Notes

1. States have been free to charge a "use tax" to consumers who buy goods from out of state sellers and avoid paying the sales tax. States that have sales taxes generally also have use taxes. However, enforcement, with some exceptions, is impossible. Automobiles are an exception, because the destination state can require payment of the use tax as a precondition to issuing a license plate. There are some interstate compacts concerning mutual reporting of out of state sales, but these are relatively ineffective.

2. Mail-order, phone order, and Internet sellers naturally like the price advantage of not having to charge tax. They argue that they do not use the local fire and police services that are supported by sales tax. They also use the argument that there are tens of thousands of state, city, and local taxing districts in the United States, each with its own list of rates for various kinds of items. They argue that it is not practical for them to collect the tax unless there is a single national tax schedule. Congress enacted a temporary sales tax moratorium, called the Internet Tax Freedom Act in 1997, P.L. 105–277. However, renewal of the moratorium met with strong opposition in 2000. It is likely that a compromise will be reached, under which states will simplify their use taxes and out-of-state Internet sellers will be forced to collect the use tax on interstate sales.

J. RESTRICTING E–COMPETITION

Certain types of businesses have been successful in obtaining state legislation or court decisions limiting Internet-based competition. These businesses are greatly threatened by the Internet, which threatens to bring out-of-state competitors into local customers' homes. So that they may continue to exploit consumers and earn monopoly profits, these businesses have lobbied for enforcement of existing legislation against Internet competitors and also for the passage of new legislation to head off Internet competition not covered by existing legislation. The most prominent businesses seeking protection from Internet competition are: (1) alcoholic beverage dealers and wholesalers; (2) automobile dealers; (3) state lotteries; and (4) doctors and lawyers. Of course, some of those seeking restrictions on Internet transactions have higher motives. The Internet could allow minors to obtain alcohol and hypochondriacs to obtain medicines that they should not have. Out-of-state legal advisors could escape the enforcement of ethical rules. Many states would have trouble financing education without the money that their less educated and less affluent citizens lose playing the very poor odds in state lotteries. Country clubs would have difficulty maintaining golf courses without the dues paid by automobile dealers, doctors, and lawyers.

STATE v. AMOROSO

Court of Appeals of Utah, 1999.

975 P.2d 505, *cert. denied*, 994 P.2d 1271.

BILLINGS, JUDGE:

¶ 1 Appellant, the State of Utah, appeals an order dismissing a criminal prosecution against Appellees Louis A. Amoroso and Beer Across America (BAA) involving several violations of Utah liquor laws. We reverse and remand.

FACTS

¶ 2 BAA is a national marketer of several products, including "heavy" beer, which qualifies as "liquor" under Utah liquor laws. BAA is located in Illinois. It has no property in Utah, maintains no representatives here, nor does it directly solicit sales in Utah. However, BAA advertises nationally, including in Utah, via the Internet and newsletters.

¶ 3 BAA's customers purchase BAA products by mail, telephone 800 number, or the Internet. All orders must be prepaid by the purchaser, including freight and handling charges, before any purchases are delivered to the shipper. The purchases are then delivered to a shipper in Illinois "freight paid" for delivery to the customer in accordance with the customer's instructions. BAA collects and pays sales tax to Illinois on all purchases. Since 1992, BAA has shipped alcoholic beverages to several hundred Utah customers.

¶ 4 BAA was charged with the following criminal violations:

Count I: Unlawful importation of alcoholic product, a class B misdemeanor, in violation of Utah Code Ann. § 32A–12–503 (1994);

Count II: Unlawful sale or supply of alcoholic beverage or product, a class B misdemeanor, in violation of Utah Code Ann. § 32A–12–201 (1994);

Count III: Unlawful warehousing, distribution, and transportation of liquor, a class B misdemeanor, in violation of Utah Code Ann. § 32A–9–101(2) (1994);

Count IV: Unlawful sale or supply of alcoholic beverage to minors, a class A misdemeanor, in violation of Utah Code Ann. § 32A–12–203 (Supp.1996);

Count V: Pattern of unlawful activity, a second degree felony, in violation of Utah Code Ann. § 76–10–1601 and § 76–10–1603.5 (1995) et seq.

¶ 5 On June 11, 1997, BAA filed Motions to Dismiss the charges. The trial court dismissed counts I, II, III, and V for lack of jurisdiction. Additionally, the court concluded that prosecuting BAA would violate the Commerce Clause of the United States Constitution. See U.S. Const. art.

I, § 8, cl. 3. Although the trial court did not dismiss count IV, the State voluntarily dismissed this count without prejudice. This appeal followed.

ANALYSIS

* * *

¶ 11 The rule is well-settled that civil "minimum contacts" analysis has no place in determining whether a state may assert criminal personal jurisdiction over a foreign defendant. *See, e.g., Boyd v. Meachum*, 77 F.3d 60, 66 (2d Cir.1996) (federal constitutional requirements of civil personal jurisdiction do not apply in a criminal case); *State v. McCormick*, 273 N.W.2d 624, 628 (Minn.1978) (criminal cases "not subject to the same flexibility enjoyed by the more elastic rules governing extraterritorial jurisdiction in civil cases"); *State v. Taylor*, 838 S.W.2d 895, 897 (Tex.App.1992) (citing *Ex parte Boetscher*, 812 S.W.2d 600, 602 (Tex. Crim.App.1991) ("A 'minimum contacts' analysis is not applicable to establish jurisdiction in criminal prosecutions.")); *Rios v. State*, 733 P.2d 242, 244 (Wyo.1987) ("the concept of minimum contacts ... has no application to criminal cases").

¶ 12 We conclude the trial court erred in applying a civil minimum contacts analysis in this criminal prosecution. BAA, by way of Louis Amoroso, was physically present at the proceedings below. Thus, the trial court erred when it failed to assert criminal personal jurisdiction over BAA.

B. Subject Matter Jurisdiction

¶ 13 The State argues BAA is subject to prosecution in Utah because its "conduct [in Illinois] caused an unlawful result within this state," and thus BAA committed the charged offenses partly within Utah. In opposition, BAA, by way of a tortured reading of section 76–1–201, argues the State improperly relies solely on a "result" test.

¶ 14 Utah's Criminal Jurisdiction Statute provides

(1) A person is subject to prosecution in this state for an offense which he commits, while either within or outside the state, by his own conduct or that of another for which he is legally accountable, if:

    (a) the offense is committed either wholly or partly within the state;

    . . . .

(2) An offense is committed partly within this state if either the conduct which is any element of the offense, or the result which is such an element, occurs within this state.

Utah Code Ann. § 76–1–201(1)-(2) (Supp.1998).

¶ 15 As early as 1911, the United States Supreme Court implicitly endorsed the State's interpretation of the statute. *Strassheim v. Daily*, 221 U.S. 280, 31 S.Ct. 558, 55 L.Ed. 735 (1911), supports the proposition that Utah may apply its criminal statute to conduct occurring entirely outside its borders. In Strassheim, the Supreme Court held that Michigan could prosecute a defendant charged with defrauding the Michigan state government even though the defendant committed the fraudulent acts entirely outside of Michigan and never entered Michigan until the fraud was complete. *See id.* at 281–83, 31 S.Ct. at 559.

¶ 16 This principle of extraterritoriality is codified in Utah Code Ann. § 76–1–201 (Supp.1998). Under this statute, if conduct or a result of conduct constituting any element of the offense occurs within the state, the State has jurisdiction to prosecute the offense. See *State v. Sorenson*, 758 P.2d 466, 470 (Utah Ct.App.1988). In Sorenson, an issue raised was whether Utah had jurisdiction arising from a charge of possession of alcohol pursuant to Utah Code Ann. § 32A–12–13(1) (1986), which prohibited the purchase, possession, or consumption of alcohol by a person under the age of 21. *Id.* at 467. Sorenson was stopped for speeding in St. George, Utah, but a search of his car revealed he was not in possession of any alcohol. *Id.* We noted that "Sorenson's conviction of the offense of consumption necessarily requires proof of the jurisdictional factor that at least some alcohol was consumed in Utah." *Id.* at 470 (citing Utah Code Ann. § 76–1–201 (1978)).

¶ 17 BAA is subject to prosecution in Utah for conduct committed in Illinois because its conduct caused an unlawful result in Utah. In sum, the information alleges conduct that resulted in unlawful importation of alcohol into Utah; unlawful sale or supply of alcohol in Utah;[6] unlawful warehousing, distribution, or transportation of alcohol to Utah; unlawful supplying of alcohol to persons within Utah; and unlawful distribution or transportation for sale or resale to retail customers within Utah without a license.

¶ 18 Accordingly, the trial court erred when it concluded that Utah could not assert subject matter jurisdiction over BAA.

III. COMMERCE CLAUSE

¶ 19 The trial court concluded, and BAA asserts on appeal, that even if Utah has jurisdiction over BAA, this prosecution runs afoul of the Commerce Clause, and is therefore unconstitutional. The State argues that under the Twenty–First Amendment, this prosecution is proper and is not barred by the Commerce Clause.

¶ 20 "Constitutional interpretation is a question of law which we review for correctness, giving no deference to the trial court's conclu-

---

6. The proper definition for "sale" in this case is not the UCC definition (as the magistrate erroneously concluded), but the Utah Alcoholic Beverage Control Act (ABCA) definition. The ABCA broadly defines "sale" to include "any transaction ... whereby, for any consideration, an alcoholic beverage is either directly *or indirectly* *transferred, solicited, ordered, delivered for value,* or by any means or under any pretext *is promised or obtained, whether done by a person as a principal, proprietor, or as an agent, servant, or employee.*" Utah Code. Ann. § 32A–1–105(47) (Supp.1998) (emphasis added).

sion." *State v. Davis*, 903 P.2d 940, 943 (Utah Ct.App.1995) (citing *State v. Contrel*, 886 P.2d 107, 111 (Utah Ct.App.1994)).

¶ 21 The State relies on Section Two of the Twenty–First Amendment: "The *transportation* or *importation* into any State, Territory, or possession of the United States for delivery or use therein of intoxicating liquors, in violation of the laws thereof, is hereby prohibited." U.S. Const. amend. XXI § 2, (emphasis added). Historically, the Twenty–First Amendment "subordinat[ed Congress'] rights under the Commerce Clause to the power of a State to control, and to control effectively, the traffic in liquor within its borders." *United States v. Frankfort Distilleries, Inc.*, 324 U.S. 293, 300, 65 S.Ct. 661, 665, 89 L.Ed. 951 (1945) (Frankfurter, J., concurring). Thus, States were "freed from the restrictions upon state power which the Commerce Clause implies as to ordinary articles of commerce." *Id.*

¶ 22 A review of more recent Supreme Court case law dealing with the interaction between the Twenty–First Amendment and the Commerce Clause is helpful. In *Hostetter v. Idlewild Bon Voyage Liquor Corp.*, 377 U.S. 324, 84 S.Ct. 1293, 12 L.Ed.2d 350 (1964), the New York State Liquor Authority claimed authority to prohibit an arrangement whereby defendant sold liquor to international airline travelers in a New York airport. *Id.* at 325, 84 S.Ct. at 1294. The customers collected the purchased liquor only after their flights (on which the liquor purchases also traveled) touched down in a foreign city. The issue before the Court was "whether the Twenty–First Amendment so far obliterates the Commerce Clause as to empower New York to prohibit absolutely the passage of liquor through its territory, under the supervision of the United States Bureau of Customs acting under federal law, for delivery to consumers in foreign countries." *Id.* at 329, 84 S.Ct. at 1296.

¶ 23 The Court held New York exceeded its authority, writing "[h]ere, ultimate delivery and use is not in New York, but in a foreign country.... [T]his case does not involve measures aimed at preventing unlawful diversion or use of alcoholic beverages within New York." *Id.* at 333–34, 84 S.Ct. at 1299 (emphasis added) (internal quotations omitted). Thus, since New York was attempting to regulate delivery and use of liquor transported outside of New York, the Commerce Clause trumped the Twenty–First Amendment, and the state law had to give way. *See id.* However, the Court made clear that "a State is totally unconfined by traditional Commerce Clause limitations when it restricts the importation of intoxicants destined for *use, distribution, or consumption within its borders." Id.* at 330, 84 S.Ct. at 1297 (emphasis added).

¶ 24 In *Brown-Forman Distillers v. New York State*, 476 U.S. 573, 106 S.Ct. 2080, 90 L.Ed.2d 552 (1986), the Court struck down, again under the Commerce Clause, New York's "affirmation law" that required distillers to affirm that they were selling to New York wholesalers at a price "no higher than the lowest price the distiller charges wholesalers anywhere else in the United States." *Id.* at 476 U.S. at 575, 106 S.Ct. at 2082. The Court noted the Twenty-First Amendment "speaks only to state regulation of the 'transportation or importation into any State ... for delivery or use therein' of alcoholic beverages." *Id.* at 585, 106 S.Ct. at 2087. The Court concluded "that [the fact that] New York has attempted to regulate sales in other States of liquor that will be consumed in other States therefore disposes of the Twenty–First Amendment issue." *Id.*

¶ 25 Unlike Hostetter and Brown–Forman, the liquor at issue in this case was shipped to be consumed by Utah residents in Utah. Utah is not attempting to regulate the sale of alcohol that will be consumed in another state. Instead, Utah seeks to regulate the "transportation or importation into" Utah "for delivery or use therein of intoxicating liquors, in violation of the laws thereof." These goals are at the core of the Twenty–First Amendment.

¶ 26 BAA also relies on *Capital Cities Cable, Inc. v. Crisp*, 467 U.S. 691, 104 S.Ct. 2694, 81 L.Ed.2d 580 (1984). In that case, an Oklahoma statute prohibited the advertising of alcoholic beverages, except by means of strictly regulated on-premises signs. The Oklahoma Attorney General determined that this ban prohibited cable television systems operating in Oklahoma from retransmitting out-of-state signals containing alcoholic beverage commercials. Petitioners, operators of cable television systems in Oklahoma—who, with other such operators, had been warned by the Director of the Oklahoma Alcoholic Beverage Control Board that they would be criminally prosecuted if they carried out-of-state wine advertisements—filed suit, alleging that Oklahoma's policy violated various provisions of the Federal Constitution, including the Supremacy Clause and the First Amendment. See *id.* at 695–96, 104 S.Ct. at 2698–99.

¶ 27 The Supreme Court struck down the law and held:

> In rejecting the claim that the Twenty–First Amendment ousted the Federal Government of all jurisdiction over interstate traffic in liquor, we have held that when a State has not attempted directly to regulate the sale or use of liquor within its borders—the core § 2 power—a conflicting exercise of federal authority may prevail.

Id. at 713, 104 S.Ct. at 2707.

¶ 28 The Court further stated:

> [W]e hold that when, as here, a state regulation squarely conflicts with the accomplishment and execution of the full purposes of federal law, and the State's central power under the Twenty–First Amendment of regulating the times, places, and manner under which liquor may be imported and sold is not directly implicated, the balance between state and federal power tips decisively in favor of the federal law, and enforcement of the state statute is barred by the Supremacy Clause.

Id. at 716, 104 S.Ct. at 2709.

¶ 29 Further, in 1980, the Court found unconstitutional California's minimum wine-pricing mechanism, which prohibited liquor manufacturers from selling at below the price prescribed in a minimum price schedule. *See California Retail Liquor Dealers Ass'n v. Midcal Aluminum, Inc.*, 445 U.S. 97, 100 S.Ct. 937, 63 L.Ed.2d 233 (1980). In that case, the Court conceded that as to core Twenty–First Amendment powers (i.e., liquor importation and distribution), California's authority was virtually unlimited, but stated that when states attempt to exercise their "substantial discretion" over other areas of liquor control, "those controls may be subject to the federal commerce power in appropriate situations." *Id.* at 110, 100 S.Ct. at 946. The Court held that the federal interest in preventing restraints on trade via the Sherman Act prevailed and struck the law. *See id.* at 113–14, 100 S.Ct. at 947.

¶ 30 We note that in *Capital Cities Cable, Inc.* and *California Retail Liquor Dealers Ass'n*, the attempted state regulation of alcohol under the Twenty–First Amendment was in direct violation of other federal statutory or constitutional law, unlike the case before us. These cases are further distinguishable in that they did not involve core powers under the Twenty–First Amendment (i.e., the power to ban importation of liquor that will be consumed by state residents).

¶ 31 We conclude that Utah's prosecution is valid under the Twenty–First Amendment, and does not run afoul of the Commerce Clause. We note that Utah's attempt to enforce its liquor laws does not conflict with any federal statute or constitutional provision other than the alleged violation of the Commerce Clause. Even if we assume for purposes of argument that another federal law was implicated in this case (and BAA has directed our attention to none), we note that "the interests implicated by [Utah's ABCA] are so closely related to the powers reserved by the Twenty–First Amendment that the regulation may prevail, notwithstanding that its requirements directly conflict with express federal policies." *Capital Cities Cable, Inc.*, 467 U.S. at 714, 104 S.Ct. at 2708. In sum, we conclude that Utah's ABCA derives from a core Twenty–First Amendment power. Namely, the statute seeks to regulate the consumption, importation, manufacture, and transportation of liquor in or to Utah, and is therefore constitutional.

CONCLUSION

¶ 32 First, we hold that the State's arguments were properly preserved. Next, we hold that Utah has personal and subject matter jurisdiction over BAA. Finally, we conclude that Utah's prosecution of these ABCA offenses are proper under the Twenty–First Amendment and do not run afoul of the Commerce Clause. We therefore reverse and remand for proceedings consistent with this opinion.

ARIZONA REVISED STATUTES § 28–4460

2000 Ariz. Legis. Serv. 102 (West).

§ 28–4460. Factories; competition or unfair discrimination prohibited; definitions

A.   A factory shall not directly or indirectly compete with or unfairly discriminate among its dealers.

B. Competing with or unfair discrimination includes any one of the following:

1. The factory having an ownership interest or franchise interest in, or operating or acting in the capacity of, a new motor vehicle dealer or a used motor vehicle dealer, except that:

(a) A factory is not prohibited from owning or operating as a new motor vehicle dealer for a temporary period of not more than twelve months during the transition from one dealer to another dealer if the dealership is for sale and is being actively marketed by the factory at a bona fide reasonable price and on reasonable terms and conditions to any independent qualified buyer. On good cause shown by the factory, the temporary period may be extended by up to six months. For recreational vehicle manufacturers, the temporary period may be extended in one year increments for a maximum total extension of not more than five years, if good cause is shown.

* * *

2. The factory selling, leasing or providing, or offering to sell, lease or provide, vehicles or products, services or financing to any retail consumer or lead. This paragraph does not:

(a) Prohibit a Factory from advertising to sell, lease or provide vehicles or products, services or financing through its dealers.

(b) Prohibit a factory from selling, leasing or providing or offering to sell, lease or provide vehicles or products, services or financing through its dealers.

* * *

3. The factory controlling any aspect of the final amount charged, the final sales price or the final lease price for any of the vehicles or products, trade-ins, services or financing offered, offered for sale or offered for lease to retail consumers in a dealer's area of responsibility without the written consent of the dealer. The dealer's consent may be withdrawn on thirty days' notice without retribution or the threat of retribution from the factory. this paragraph does not prohibit a factory from:

(a) Changing dealer cost or establishing manufacturer's suggested retail price pursuant to 15 United States Code section 1232.

(b) Establishing from time to time reasonable sales, lease or financing promotions of reasonable and limited duration.

(c) Establishing reasonable standard feature option packages or vehicle option content in any way.

(d) Establishing the terms of any vehicle warranty.

* * *

4. The factory refusing to unconditionally offer and provide to its same line-make dealers all models or series manufactured and publicly

advertised for that line-make at prices that are, or by the effect of any device or program at prices that are, no greater than any other dealer in the United States would pay for the same model vehicle that is similarly equipped. The failure to deliver any motor vehicles shall not be considered a violation of this paragraph if the failure is caused by a condition over which the factory has no control. A factory may require a dealer to purchase reasonable quantities of advertising materials, purchase reasonable quantities of special tools required to properly service a motor vehicle and undertake reasonable salesperson or service person training related to the motor vehicle as a condition of receiving a motor vehicle. * * *

* * *

5. The factory providing or directing less than all leads of prospective retail consumers of vehicles or products, services or financing of a particular line-make to the dealer of the same line-make in whose assigned area of responsibility the lead resides or, in the event of a commercial lead, the primary local business address. the factory is only responsible for providing to the dealer information that it possesses concerning the lead. The factory is not precluded from providing or directing leads to other dealers of the same line-make. All leads shall be provided or directed in a fair, nondiscriminatory, equitable and timely manner and without charging a fee for those leads.

* * *

Note

The above provisions were passed by the Arizona legislature in 2000. They are clearly aimed against Internet sales by automobile manufacturers. They are also of dubious constitutionality, because state regulation of automobile sales, unlike state regulation of alcoholic beverage sales, enjoys no special exemption from the Commerce Clause.

PEOPLE v. WORLD INTERACTIVE GAMING CORPORATION

Supreme Court, New York County, New York, 1999.
1999 WL 591995.

NOT APPROVED BY REPORTER OF DECISIONS FOR REPORTING IN STATE REPORTS. NOT REPORTED IN N.Y.S.2d.

Ramos, J.S.C.

This proceeding is brought by the Attorney General of the State of New York (the "Attorney General" or the "State of New York"), pursuant to New York's Executive Law § 63(1.2) and General Business Law Article 23–A, to enjoin the respondents, World Interactive Gaming Corporation ("WIGC"), Golden Chips Casino, Inc. ("GCC"), and their principals, officers, and directors from operating within or offering to residents of the State of New York State gambling over the Internet. The State also seeks to enjoin respondents from selling unregistered securities in violation of New York State's General Business Law § 352 (also known as "The Martin Act").

The central issue here is whether the State of New York can enjoin a foreign corporation legally licensed to operate a casino offshore from offering gambling to Internet users in New York. At issue is Section 9(1), Article 1 of the New York State Constitution which contains an express prohibition against any kind of gambling not authorized by the state legislature. The prohibition represents a deep-rooted policy of the. state against unauthorized gambling (*Intercontinental Hotels Corp. v. Golden*, 18 A.D.2d 45 [1st Dept 1963]; *rev'd on other grounds*, 15 N.Y.2d 9 [1964]),

WIGC is a Delaware corporation that maintains corporate offices in New York. WIGC wholly owns GCC, an Antiguan subsidiary corporation which acquired a license from the government of Antigua to operate a land-based casino. Through contracts executed by WIGC, GCC developed interactive software, and purchased computer servers which were installed in Antigua to allow users around the world to gamble from their home computers. GCC promoted its casino at its website, advertised on the Internet and in a national gambling magazine. The promotion was targeted nationally and was viewed by New York residents. * * *

In June 1998, the Attorney General furthered its investigation by logging onto respondents' website, downloading the gambling software, and in July 1998, placed the first of several bets. Users who wished to gamble in the GCC Internet casino were directed to wire money to open a bank account in Antigua and download additional software from GCC's website. In opening an account, users were asked to enter their permanent address. A user which submitted a permanent address in a state that permitted land-based gambling, such as Nevada, was granted permission to gamble. Although a user which entered a state such as New York, which does not permit land-based gambling, was denied permission to gamble, because the software does not verify the user's actual location, a user initially denied access, could easily circumvent the denial by changing the state entered to that of Nevada, while remaining physically in New York State. The user could then log onto the GCC casino and play virtual slots, blackjack or roulette. This raises the question if this constitutes a good faith effort not to engage in gambling in New York.

The Attorney General commenced this action pursuant to Executive Law § 63(12) and General Business Law Article 23–A. Petitioner seeks: (1) to enjoin respondents from conducting a business within the State of New York until they are properly registered with the Secretary of State to conduct business in New York; (2) to enjoin respondents from running any aspect of their Internet gambling Business within the State of New York; (3) to be awarded restitution and damages to injured investors; and (4) to be awarded penalties and costs to the State of New York for violations of New York State's Securities Law (GBL § 352 also known as

"The Martin Act"), federal and state laws prohibiting gambling, and New York State's Executive Law.

Respondents move to dismiss the petition on the grounds that (1) the Attorney General lacks the authority to bring a proceeding under Executive Law 5 63(12), where a pattern of repeated or persistent fraud or illegal conduct is absent; (2) lack of personal jurisdiction over WIGC and GCC; and (3) lack of subject matter jurisdiction to prosecute alleged violations of the Federal Interstate Wire Act 18 USC § 1084(a) ("The Wire Act"), the Interstate and Foreign Travel or Transportation in Aid of Racketeering Enterprising Act 18 USC § 1952("The Travel Act"), and the Wagering and Paraphernalia Act 18 USC § 1953 ("The Paraphernalia Act").

Respondents contend that the transactions occurred offshore and that no state or federal law regulates Internet gambling. They claim that they were operating a duly licensed legitimate business fully authorized by the government of Antigua and in compliance with that country's rules and regulations of a land-based casino. They further argue that the federal and state laws upon which the State relies either do not apply to the activities of WIGC or are too vague and ambiguous to criminalize the activity of Internet gambling, when such activity is offshore in Antigua.

Executive Law

Executive Law § 63(12) authorizes the Attorney General to bring a special proceeding against a person or business committing repeated or persistent fraudulent or illegal acts. Any conduct which violates state or federal law or regulation is actionable under this provision (See *State v. Ford*, 74 N.Y.2d 495 [1989]). Under Executive Law § 63(12), fraud has been interpreted broadly requiring only a showing that the action has a potential to deceive (See *People v. Apple Health & Sports Clubs*, 206 A.D.2d 266, 267 [1st Dept. 1994]). in order for fraudulent or illegal acts to be actionable under Executive Law § 63(12), respondents, activities must be repeated, (See *State v. Princess Prestige Co.*, Inc., 42 N.Y.2d 104, 107–108 [1977] finding that Executive Law § 63(12) does not require a large number of repeated illegal or fraudulent acts).

* * * Respondents have failed to submit evidence of any probative value to refute the allegation of the petition.

Personal Jurisdiction Over WIGC and GCC

[The court found that there was personal jurisdiction over WIGC and GCC]

Subject Matter Jurisdiction and Application of New York Law

Respondents argue that the Court lacks subject matter jurisdiction, and that Internet gambling falls outside the scope of New York state gambling prohibitions, because the gambling occurs outside of New York state. However, under New York Penal Law, if the person engaged in gambling is located in New York, then New York is the location where. the gambling occurred [See, Penal Law § 225.00(2)]. Here, some or all of those funds in an Antiguan bank account are staked every time the

New York user enters betting information into the computer. It is irrelevant that Internet gambling is legal in Antigua. The act of entering the bet and transmitting the information from New York via the Internet is adequate to constitute gambling activity within the New York state.

Wide range implications would arise if this Court adopted respondents' argument that activities or transactions which may be targeted at New York residents are beyond the state's jurisdiction. Not only would such an approach severely undermine this state's deep-rooted policy against unauthorized gambling, it also would immunize from liability anyone who engages in any activity over the Internet which is otherwise illegal in this state. A computer server cannot be permitted to function as a shield against liability, particularly in this case where respondents actively targeted New York as the location where they conducted many of their allegedly illegal activities. Even though gambling is legal where the bet was accepted, the activity was transmitted from New York. Contrary to respondents' unsupported allegation of an Antiguan management company managing GCC, the evidence also indicates that the individuals who gave the computer commands operated from WIGC's New York office. The respondents enticed Internet users, including New York residents, to play in its casino.

As for respondents' claim that none of the federal statutes apply to operation of an Internet casino licensed by a foreign government, there is nothing in the record or the law to support their contentions. To the contrary, the Wire Act, Travel Act and Wagering Paraphernalia Act all apply despite the fact that the betting instructions are transmitted from outside the United States over the Internet. The scope of each of these statutes clearly extends to the transmission of betting information to a foreign country (See, the Wire Act which prohibits "use of a wire communication facility for the transmission in interstate or foreign commerce of bets or wagers ..." [18 USC § 1084(a)]; the Travel Act which prohibits the use of "any facility in interstate or foreign commerce" with intent to promote any unlawful activity [18 USC 51952]). Nor can it be convincingly argued by respondents that the federal statutes are unconstitutionally vague (See, *Turf Center. Inc. v. US*, 325 F.2d 793, 795 [9th Cir.1963], *Katz v. United States*, 369 F.2d 130, 135 [9th Cir.1966], *United States v. Mendelsohn*, 896 F.2d 1183, 1186 [9th Cir.1989]). Because the Wire act, the Travel Act and the Wagering Paraphernalia Act have all been found to be constitutionally valid, and have been found not to be overly broad or vague, and because respondents' conduct falls within the scope of New York's prohibition against gambling, all of these statutes apply to respondents' activities.

The evidence demonstrates that respondents have violated New York Penal law which states that "a person is guilty of promoting gambling .. when he knowingly advances or profits from unlawful gambling activity" (Penal Law § 225.05). By having established the gambling enterprise, advertised, solicited investors to buy its stock, to gamble through its on-line casino, respondents have "engage[d] in conduct which materially aids gambling activity'', in violation of New York law (Penal Law § 225.00(4) which states "conduct includes but is not limited to conduct directed toward the creation or establishment of a particular game, contest, scheme, device ... [or] toward the solicitation or inducement of persons to participate therein"). Moreover, this Court rejects respondents' argument that it unknowingly accepted bets from New York residents. New York users can easily circumvent the casino software in order to play by the simple expedient of entering an out-of-state address. Respondents' violation of the Penal Law is that they persisted in continuous illegal conduct directed toward the creation, establishment, and advancement of unauthorized gambling. The violation had occurred long before a New York resident ever staked a bet. Because all of respondents' activities illegally advanced gambling, this Court finds that they have knowingly violated Penal Law § 225.05.

Not only are respondents guilty of violating New York state's gambling laws but they have also violated several federal laws. Like the great majority of states, federal law also proscribes gambling. Statutes such as the Wire Act, the Travel Act and the Interstate Transportation of Wagering Paraphernalia Act are just three examples of the federal government's policy against gambling. As the Wire Act's legislative history states:

> "The purpose of the bill is to assist various States and the District of Columbia in the enforcement of their laws pertaining to gambling, bookmaking, and like offenses and to aid in the suppression of organized gambling activities by prohibiting the use of wire communication facilities which are or will be used for the transmission of bets or wagers and gambling information in interstate and foreign commerce."

H.R.Rep. No. 967, 87th Cong. 1st Sess. (1961), U.S.Code Congressional and Administrative News 1961, p 26311 see also *Telephone News System, Inc. v. Illinois Bell Tel. Co.*, 220 F.Supp. 621 (1963), *affirmed* 376 U.S. 782.

The Wire Act bars citizens from engaging "[i]n the business of betting or wagering knowingly using a wire communication for the transmission of interstate or foreign commerce of bets or wagers or information assisting in the placing of bets or wagers." 18 U.S.C. 1084(a). A Wire Act violation occurs when a defendant is in the business of betting or wagering (See *U.S. v. Anderson*. C.A. Wisconsin, 542 F.2d 428 [7th Cir.1976]).

Furthermore, the Travel Act, 18 U.S.C. § 1952, proscribes similar interstate gambling activity by stating:

> " ... the use of any facility in interstate or foreign commerce, including the mail, with intent to (1) distribute the records of any unlawful activity or (3) otherwise promote, manage, establish carry on or facilitate the promotion, management, establishment or carrying on, of any unlawful activity ... shall be fined not more than $10,000 or imprisoned for not more than five years or both."

Respondents' interstate use of the Internet to conduct their illegal gambling business violates federal law. As the legislative history behind the Wire Act indicates, the purpose of these federal controls is to aid the states in controlling gambling. Like a prohibited telephone call from a gambling facility, the Internet is accessed by using a telephone wire. When the telephone wire is connected to a modem attached to a user's computer, the user's phone line actually connects the user to the Internet server and then the user may log onto this illegal gambling website from any location in the United States. After selecting from the multitude of illegal games offered by respondent, the information is transmitted to the server in Antigua. Respondents' server then transmits betting information back to the user which is against the Wire Act. The Internet site creates a virtual casino within the user's computer terminal. By hosting this casino and exchanging betting information with the user, an illegal communication in violation of the Wire Act and the Travel Act has occurred.

Respondents attempt to circumvent federal law by asserting that none of these statutes apply to the operation of an Antiguan casino. Moreover, they allege the federal government has not explicitly ruled on Internet gambling therefore it is an unregulated field. Respondents disregard that the Interstate Commerce Clause gives Congress the plenary power to regulate illegal gambling conducted between a U.S. and a foreign location. (See *Champion v. Ames*, 188 U.S. 321, 334 [1903]). Gambling conducted via the Internet from New York to Antigua is indistinguishable from any other form of gambling since both the Wire and Travel Act apply to the transmission of information into a foreign country. See 18 U.S.C. 1084(a); 18 U.S.C.1953(a). Therefore, the respondents are culpable for violating the Wire Act and the Travel Act.

Additionally, respondents violated The Interstate Transportation of Wagering Paraphernalia Act. Under this act:

> "[w]hoever, except a common carrier in the usual course of business, knowingly carries or sends in interstate or foreign commerce any record, paraphernalia, ticket, certificate, bills slip, token, paper, writing or other device under, or to be used, or adapted, devised, designed for use in (a) bookmaking; or (b) wagering pools with respect to a sporting event or (c) in a numbers, policy, bolita, or similar game shall be fined not more than $10,000 or imprisoned for more than five years, or both." [18 USC § 1953(a)]

The respondents intentionally sent records of gambling activity from the GCC location in Antigua through international and interstate commerce into various United States locations, among them New York. When respondents solicited perspective investors, they sent them a multitude of materials which were specifically to be utilized for the setting up and advancing of the Internet gambling business through U.S. mail. Furthermore, the actual computers which would be used for gambling between the United States and Antigua was bought and delivered through U.S. mail from Florida to GCC's location in Antigua.

The respondent's total activities unambiguously advance gambling in direct violation of the explicit safeguards that New York and the federal laws have placed against unauthorized gambling activity.

In addition, several of New York's registration requirements have been violated. For instance, under BCL § 1301(a), a "foreign corporation shall not do business in this state until it has been authorized to do so . . . " by submitting an application to the Department of State. WIGC is a foreign corporation, incorporated in Delaware, operating out of offices in Bohemia, New York. Since WIGC failed to apply for approval from the Department of State, the respondents were repeatedly operating illegally in New York State. * * *

* * * Furthermore, although a company failing to register is normally penalized with a fine and subsequently the company is often allowed to file for registration, the violation still constitutes a fraudulent practice under New York law (See, GBL § 359–e(14)(1)).

Because of the clear illegality present in respondents' actions, and absence of any triable issue of fact, respondents are found liable under Executive Law § 63(12) for their state and federal law violations.

Remedies

The Attorney General is entitled to injunctive relief which is routinely granted in special proceedings under Executive Law 5 63(12) (*People v. Apple Health Sports Clubs, Ltd., Inc.*, 206 A.D.2d 266 [1st Dept 1994], aff'd, 84 N.Y.2d 1004 [1994]). The requirement of a bond to assure future proper behavior on the part of an enjoined party traditionally accompanies such an injunction (see, *People v. Empvre Inground Pool*, 227 A.D.2d 731 [3d Dept. 1996]; *People v. Helena VIP Personal Introductions Servs.*, 199 A.D.2d 186. [1st Dept. 1993]). This Court finds the request for an injunction warranted, and directs fixing of the amount be incorporated in an order to be settled.

As for the Attorney General's request for restitution, penalties, and costs, which are available under Executive Law § 63(12) and GBL § 353(3), this Court finds the circumstances warrant awarding them in this case. The manner of the accounting, the mechanism for restitution, and the amount in penalties and costs to be awarded shall be resolved at a hearing.

Because each respondent is individually liable for the actions conducted by both WIGC and GCC WIGC's (see, *e.g.*, *Matter of State of New York v. Daro Chartours*, 72 A.D.2d 872, 873 [3rd Dept. 1979]; see also, *Marine Midland Bank v, Russo Produce Co.*, 50 N.Y.2d 31, 44 [1980] finding that corporate veil can be pierced to hold corporate officers liable for a tort regardless of whether they acted in conjunction with the corporation and in the course of their corporate duties), and shall be fined appropriately, all parties including individual respondents are directed to appear for a preliminary conference before this Court on September 9, 1999, at 9:30 a.m., to resolve any issues regarding, the scope of the accounting, discovery, or scheduling of the hearing.

Respondents are further directed not to destroy any personal or business records relating to this matter.

This constitutes the decision and order of this Court. Settle order on notice.

Questions

1. Suppose a wholly offshore Internet gambling website is set up with no contact whatsoever with New York State except that New York residents gamble at the website. Is there anything that New York can do to prevent the website from accepting patronage by New York residents?

2. Legislation was before Congress as this casebook went to press that would simultaneously expand the rights of U.S.-based gambling operations to use the Internet and restrict use of the Internet by their foreign competitors. This legislation may be in violation of United States obligations to provide a level playing field for domestic and foreign businesses under World Trade Organization rules.

UNAUTHORIZED PRACTICE OF LAW COMMITTEE v. PARSONS TECHNOLOGY, INC.

United States District Court, N.D. Texas, 1999.
1999 WL 47235.

SANDERS, SENIOR J.

* * *Having considered the motions, briefs, and arguments of both parties, and for the reasons set forth below, the Court concludes that there are no genuine issues of material fact and that Plaintiff Unauthorized Practice of Law Committee is entitled to judgment as a matter of law. Therefore, Plaintiff's Motion for Summary Judgment is granted and Defendant's Motion for Summary Judgment is denied.

I. BACKGROUND

The Plaintiff, the Unauthorized Practice of Law Committee ("the UPLC"), is comprised of six Texas lawyers and three lay citizens appointed by the Supreme Court of Texas. The UPLC is responsible for enforcing Texas' unauthorized practice of law statute, TEX. GOV'T CODE §§ 81.101–106 (Vernon's 1998) ("the Statute").[1]

The Defendant, Parsons Technology, Inc., ("Parsons") is a California corporation, whose principal place of business is Iowa, and is engaged

---

1. TEX GOV'T CODE § 81.101 defines the practice of law, as follows:

(a) In this chapter the "practice of law" means the preparation of a pleading or other document incident to an action or special proceeding or the management of the action or proceeding on behalf of a client before a judge in court as well as a service rendered out of court, including the giving of advice or the rendering of any service requiring the use of legal skill or knowledge, such as

preparing a will, contract, or other instrument, the legal effect of which under the facts and conclusions involved must be carefully determined.

(b) The definition in this section is not exclusive and does not deprive the judicial branch of the power and authority under both this chapter and the adjudicated cases to determine whether other services and acts not enumerated may constitute the practice of law.

in the business of developing, publishing and marketing software products, such as *Quicken Financial Software*, Turbo Tax, and *Webster's Talking Dictionary*. Parsons has published and offered for sale through retailers in Texas a computer software program entitled *Quicken Family Lawyer*, version 8.0, and its updated version *Quicken Family Lawyer '99* ("QFL").

QFL is the product at the center of this controversy. In its most recent version, QFL offers over 100 different legal forms (such as employment agreements, real estate leases, premarital agreements, and seven different will forms) along with instructions on how to fill out these forms. QFL's packaging represents that the product is "valid in 49 states including the District of Columbia;" is "developed and reviewed by expert attorneys;" and is "updated to reflect recent legislative formats." (Pl's Ex. 1, p. 8.) The packaging also indicates that QFL will have the user "answer a few questions to determine which estate planning and health care documents best meet [the user's] needs;" (Pl's Ex. 1, p. 9), and that QFL will "interview you in a logical order, tailoring documents to your situation." (Pl's Ex. 1, p. 8.) Finally, the packaging reassures the user that "[h]andy hints and comprehensive legal help topics are always available." (Pl's Ex. 1, p. 8.)

The first time a user accesses QFL after installing it on her computer the following disclaimer appears as the initial screen:

> This program provides forms and information about the law. We cannot and do not provide specific information for your exact situation.

> For example, we can provide a form for a lease, along with information on state law and issues frequently addressed in leases. But we cannot decide that our program's lease is appropriate for you.

> Because we cannot decide which forms are best for your individual situation, you must use your own judgment and, to the extent you believe appropriate, the assistance of a lawyer.

This disclaimer does not appear anywhere on QFL's packaging. Additionally, it does not appear on subsequent uses of the program unless the user actively accesses the "Help" pull-down menu at the top of the screen and then selects "Disclaimer."

On the initial use of QFL, or anytime a new user name is created, QFL asks for the user's name and state of residence. It then inquires whether the user would like QFL to suggest documents to the user. If the user answers "Yes," QFL's "Document Advisor" asks the user a few short questions concerning the user's marital status, number of children, and familiarity with living trusts.[3] QFL then displays the entire list of available documents, but marks a few of them as especially appropriate for the user based on her responses.

---

3. If the user answers "Yes" to the question concerning living trusts, she is asked one additional question concerning the amount of effort the user is willing to put into her estate plan.

When the user accesses a document, QFL asks a series of questions relevant to filling in the legal form. With certain questions, a separate text box explaining the relevant legal considerations the user may want to take into account in filling out the form also appears on the screen. As the user proceeds through the questions relevant to the specific form, QFL either fills in the appropriate blanks or adds or deletes entire clauses from the form. For example, in the "Real Estate Lease—Residential" form, depending on how the user answers the question regarding subleasing the apartment, a clause permitting subleasing with the consent of the landlord is either included or excluded from the form.

If a user selects a "health care document" (i.e., a living will, an advance health care directive, or a health care power of attorney) the following screen appears:

Health Care laws vary from state to state. Your state may not offer every type of health care document.

Family Lawyer assumes that you wish to have a health care document based on the laws of your state.

When you select a living will, health care power of attorney, or advance health care directive, Family Lawyer will open the appropriate document based on your state.

When a Texas user selects a health care document a form entitled "Directive to Physicians and Durable Power of Attorney for Health Care" appears.

In addition to the separate text boxes providing question and form specific information, at any time throughout the program, the user may access various other help features which provide additional legal information. One such feature is "Ask Arthur Miller," where the user selects a general topic and then a specific question,[4] after which either a text-

---

4. The "Ask Arthur Miller" feature answers a number of predetermined frequently asked legal questions in the general topics of estate planning, family and personal, powers of attorney, health and medical, real estate, employment, financial, corporate, consumer and credit, and common questions. Some of the specific questions contained within these general topics are "What if I have a dispute, but don't want to go to the expense and delay of bringing a law suit?", "Why should I go to the trouble of writing a will?", "What is probate?", and "Doesn't a Premarital agreement take the romance out of marriage?". After the user clicks on the general question, a general response to the question appears. For instance, the response to the question, "Should a real estate lease be in writing?" is:

No matter how friendly the landlord-tenant relationship seems to be, it's usually best to have a written lease. In most states,

an agreement to lease property must be in writing if the term of the lease is longer than one year. But even for shorter leases, a written lease can be very helpful in resolving issues that might arise later. Such issues might include the length of the lease, the amount of the rent, late charges, return of the security deposit, who pays for utilities and repairs, and whether pets are allowed. On the other hand, an oral lease may allow either party to terminate the lease upon much shorter notice.

In addition, it is important to remember that most states have laws regarding the rights and obligations of landlords and tenants. These laws may limit the amount of rent or security deposit that can be charged. They may also spell out the required procedures for removing a tenant, and explain the procedures that must be followed by the landlord before claiming all or a portion of the security deposit. Be sure

based answer is provided or, if the user's computer has a CD–ROM player, a sound card and a video card, a sound and video image of Arthur Miller answering the question appears.

The UPLC filed this action in state court alleging that the selling of QFL violates Texas' unauthorized practice of law statute, TEX. GOV'T CODE § 81.101 and seeking, among other things, to enjoin the sale of QFL in Texas. Parsons subsequently removed this case to this Court. Both parties now seek summary judgment. The UPLC argues that Parsons has violated the Statute as a matter of law. Parsons responds that the mere selling of books or software cannot violate the statute because some form of personal contact beyond publisher-consumer is required by a plain reading of the Statute. Alternatively, if the statute is not construed to require some form of personal relationship, Parsons argues that the application of the Statute to the mere sale and distribution of QFL would infringe upon Parsons' speech rights under the United States and Texas Constitutions. Parsons also argues that the Statute, if utilized to prevent the sale and distribution of QFL, should be void for vagueness. * * *

III.   ANALYSIS

* * *

B.   The Violation of the Texas Unauthorized Practice of Law Statute.

The UPLC moves for summary judgment because it claims, as a matter of law, the sale and distribution of QFL violates the Statute. The UPLC argues that QFL gives advice concerning legal documents and selects legal documents for users, both of which involve the use of legal skill and knowledge, and this constitutes the practice of law. Additionally, the UPLC argues that the Defendant's forms are misleading and incorrect. (Pl's Brief in Supp. of Mot. for Summ. J. at 5). In sum, the UPLC alleges that QFL acts as a "high tech lawyer by interacting with its 'client' while preparing legal instruments, giving legal advice, and suggesting legal instruments that should be employed by the user." (Pl.'s Reply to Def's Resp. to Pl's Mot. at 3.). In other words, QFL is a "cyber-lawyer."

No one disputes that the practice of law encompasses more than the mere conduct of cases in the courts. See *In re Duncan*, 65 S.E. 210 (S.C.1909) (finding that the practice of law includes "the preparation of legal instruments of all kinds, and, in general, all advice to clients, and all action taken for them in matters connected with the law."). However, a comprehensive definition of just what qualifies as the practice of law is "impossible," and "each case must be decided upon its own particular facts." *Palmer v. Unauthorized Practice of Law Committee*, 438 S.W.2d 374, 376 (Tex.App.—Houston 1969, no writ); see also *State Bar of Michigan v. Cramer*, 249 N.W.2d 1, 7 (Mich.1976) ("any attempt to

you understand your state's landlord and
tenant laws.

formulate a lasting, all encompassing definition of 'practice of law' is doomed to failure.'').

The UPLC, in arguing that the publication and sale of QFL constitutes the unauthorized practice of law, relies on two Texas Court of Appeals cases, *Palmer v. Unauthorized Practice of Law Committee*, 438 S.W.2d 374 (Tex.App.—Houston 1969, no writ), and *Fadia v. Unauthorized Practice of Law Committee*, 830 S.W.2d 162 (Tex.App.—Dallas 1992, writ denied).

Palmer held that the sale of will forms containing blanks to be filled in by the user, along with instructions, constituted the unauthorized practice of law. The *Palmer* court observed that the form sold by Mr. Palmer was "almost a will itself" and that the form purported to make specific testamentary bequests. The court feared that the unsuspecting layman "by reading defendants' advertisements, by reading the will form, and by reading the definitions that are attached, . . . [would be] led to believe that defendants' will 'form' is in fact only a form and that all testamentary dispositions may be thus standardized." *Id.* at 376. The *Palmer* court held that the preparation of legal instruments of all kinds involves the practice of law. *Palmer* at 376 (citing *Stewart Abstract Co. v. Judicial Commission*, 131 S.W.2d 686 (Tex.App.—Beaumont 1939, no writ)). The *Palmer* court further held that the exercise of judgment in the proper drafting of legal instruments, or even the selecting of the proper form of instrument, necessarily affects important legal rights, and thus, is the practice of law. *Palmer* at 377 (citing *Cape May County Bar Ass'n v. Ludlam*, 211 A.2d 780, 782 (N.J.1965) (per curiam)).

In *Fadia*, the pro se defendant sold and distributed a manual entitled "You and Your Will: A Do–It–Yourself Manual." The defendant in *Fadia* attempted to get around *Palmer's* conclusion that the selling of a will manual constitutes the unauthorized practice of law, by arguing that the court should reject *Palmer* in light of recent state court decisions requiring some form of personal contact or relationship between the alleged unauthorized lawyer and the putative client in order to violate the unauthorized practice of law statute. The court rejected the defendant's argument, stating that it would not overrule *Palmer* and if there were to be a pre-requisite of personal contact between the parties, such a change to the Statute would have to come from the legislature and not the courts. *Fadia*, 830 S.W.2d at 164. The *Fadia* court went on to hold that because a will secures legal rights and its drafting involves the giving of advice requiring the use of legal skill or knowledge, the preparation of a will involves the practice of law. *Id.* Since the selection of the proper legal form also affects important legal rights, the court reasoned that it too constituted the practice of law. *Id.* at 165. Therefore, since the will manual both purported to advise a layman on how to draft a will and selected a specific form for the layman to use, the court determined that the Defendant's selling of a will manual qualified as the unauthorized practice of law. *Id.*

As already mentioned, the *Palmer* court found that the preparation of legal instruments of all kinds involves the practice of law. *Palmer* 438 S.W.2d at 376. The Texas Supreme Court has since held that the mere advising of a person as to whether or not to file a form requires legal skill and knowledge, and therefore, would be the practice of law. *Unauthorized Practice of Law Committee v. Cortez*, 692 S.W.2d 47, 50 (Tex. 1985).

Based on the interpretations of the Statute by the Texas courts, QFL falls within the range of conduct that Texas courts have determined to be the unauthorized practice of law. For instance, QFL purports to select the appropriate health care document for an individual based upon the state in which she lives. QFL customizes the documents, by adding or removing entire clauses, depending upon the particular responses given by the user to a set of questions posed by the program. The packaging of QFL represents that QFL will "interview you in a logical order, tailoring documents to your situation." Additionally, the packaging tells the user that the forms are valid in 49 states and that they have been updated by legal experts. This creates an air of reliability about the documents, which increases the likelihood that an individual user will be misled into relying on them. This false impression is not diminished by QFL's disclaimer. The disclaimer only actively appears the first-time the program is used after it is installed, and there is no guarantee that the person who initially uses the program is the same person who will later use and rely upon the program.

QFL goes beyond merely instructing someone how to fill in a blank form. While no single one of QFL's acts, in and of itself, may constitute the practice of law, taken as a whole Parsons, through QFL, has gone beyond publishing a sample form book with instructions, and has ventured into the unauthorized practice of law.

Parsons attempts to avoid the conclusion that it is guilty of the unauthorized practice of law by arguing that the Statute requires personal contact or a lawyer-client relationship. Parsons bases its argument first on the language of the Statute, which it contends requires that the prohibited services must be provided "on behalf of a client" in order to be the practice of law.

Even assuming that Parsons is correct that paragraph (a) of the Statute requires the prohibited services to be completed "on behalf of" a client, paragraph (a) of the Statute is not an exclusive definition of the unauthorized practice of law. Paragraph (b) of the Statute gives the Court the authority to determine that other acts constitute the unauthorized practice of law. Therefore, a judge could legitimately determine, under the authority granted in paragraph (b), that services provided to the public as a whole, as opposed to a singular client, qualify as the practice of law.

Next, Parsons argues that this Court should require a personal relationship between the party charged with the unauthorized practice of law and the party who benefits from the "advice" since this is the logic of almost every other court to consider the issue. (See Def's. Resp. to Pl's Mot. for Summ. J. at 6); see also, e .g., *New York County Lawyers' Association v. Dacey*, 283 N.Y.S.2d 984, 999 (N.Y.App.Div.) *overruled and dissenting opinion adopted by*, *New York County Lawyers' Association v. Dacey*, 234 N.E.2d 459 (N.Y.1967). However, as noted above, the pro se defendant in *Fadia* made this exact argument and the Texas Court of Appeals rejected it. *Fadia*, 830 S.W.2d at 164.

Nonetheless, Parsons contends that if the Texas Supreme Court were to consider the issue it would follow the lead of the other states. Although this Court is not Erie bound to follow the *Fadia* decision, it believes the Texas Supreme Court would find the *Fadia* decision a persuasive precedent. See *Hall v. Dow Corning Corp.*, 114 F.3d 73, 77 (5th Cir.1997). For this Court to be the first to impose a new interpretation of a state statute which has been on the books in its current form since 1987, and some form since 1939, would fly in the face of generally accepted notions of federal-state comity. If Parsons believes such a personal contact requirement should be included in the Statute, it should address these concerns to the Texas legislature. It is not appropriate for this Court to be the first to read such a requirement into the Statute.

Parsons' arguments to the contrary notwithstanding, QFL is far more than a static form with instructions on how to fill in the blanks. For instance, QFL adapts the content of the form to the responses given by the user. QFL purports to select the appropriate health care document for an individual based upon the state in which she lives. The packaging of QFL makes various representations as to the accuracy and specificity of the forms. In sum, Parsons has violated the unauthorized practice of law statute.

C.   Does the Statute Withstand Scrutiny Under the United States Constitution?

Having determined that the publication of QFL violates the Texas unauthorized practice of law statute, the Court must now examine whether applying the Statute in such a manner infringes upon the rights guaranteed by the First Amendment of the United States Constitution. The First Amendment is plainly implicated by the UPLC's desire to halt the sale of QFL in the state of Texas. While there is no right of unlicensed laymen to represent another under the First Amendment's guarantees of freedom of association and freedom to petition one's government, *Turner v. American Bar Ass'n*, 407 F.Supp. 451, 478 (N.D.Tex.1975), Parsons' rights under the First Amendment's protections of a free press still apply.

1.   Determining the Appropriate Level of Scrutiny: Content–Neutral v. Content-Based

The Court's initial First Amendment inquiry is to determine whether the Statute is a content-neutral or content-based restriction of speech because this answer will determine the level of scrutiny to which the Statute and its application will be subjected. If the Statute is determined to prevent speech based on its content, it is subject to strict scrutiny. If the Statute is merely a content-neutral restriction on speech, it is subject only to intermediate scrutiny.

The principal inquiry in determining content neutrality in speech cases is whether the government has adopted a regulation of speech because of disagreement with the message it conveys. *Ward v. Rock Against Racism*, 491 U.S. 781, 791 (1989). If the answer is "no," then the statute is content-neutral and subject only to intermediate scrutiny. The government's purpose is the controlling consideration in this inquiry. A regulation that serves purposes unrelated to the content of the expression is deemed neutral, even if it has an incidental effect on some speakers or messages but not others. *Id.*, at 791.

Parsons vehemently asserts that the Statute's prohibition is a content-based restriction on speech. It bases this assertion, not on the general purpose of the Statute, but on the deposition testimony of the UPLC's designated representative that the UPLC would not prosecute Parsons for the publication of its non-legal software titles. (Def's Mot. for Summ. J. at 14 & Exhibit 2, pp. 75–76, 78–80). Thus, according to Parsons, since only its legal titles are subject to restriction, the Statute is based on the content of the software title, and therefore, the Statute is subject to strict scrutiny.

However, it is not what specific speech (or conduct) the Statute prohibits, but whether the government is evidencing a disagreement with the speaker's message, as well as the underlying purpose behind the statute, which determines content-neutrality. The mere fact that the Statute sanctions speech-based conduct does not make the Statute content-based. See *Ohralik v. Ohio State Bar Ass'n*, 436 U.S. 447, 456 (1978) ("it has never been deemed an abridgment of freedom of speech or press to make a course of conduct illegal merely because the conduct was in part initiated, evidenced, or carried out by means of language, either spoken, written, or printed.")

The Statute at issue is aimed at eradicating the unauthorized practice of law. The Statute's purpose has nothing to do with suppressing speech. The UPLC's decision to challenge some of Parsons' software titles but not others has less to do with their content than with the likelihood that the title has possibly violated the unauthorized practice of law statute. Of course, the UPLC would not subject Parson's non-legal titles to scrutiny under the Statute, it is unlikely that the Life Application Bible engages in the prohibited conduct of practicing law without a license. Such discrimination between products does not evidence a disagreement with the message of Parsons' software.

There being no other arguments that the Statute is anything but content-neutral, the Court finds that the Statute is aimed at the non-communicative impact of Parsons' speech, and therefore, is a content-neutral regulation which only incidentally affects speech and therefore is subject only to intermediate scrutiny.

2. Determining Whether a Content–Neutral Statute Overburdens Protected Speech Rights

Having determined that the Statute is content-neutral, the Court must still decide whether the Statute nonetheless overburdens protected speech. To make this determination, the Court subjects the Statute to intermediate scrutiny and the four part test of *United States v. O'Brien*, 391 U.S. 367 (1968).[8] Under *O'Brien*, the UPLC must establish that:

1) The regulation is within the constitutional power of the state;

2) It furthers an important or substantial government interest;

3) The government interest is unrelated to the suppression of free expression; and

4) The incidental restriction of speech is no greater than is essential to the furtherance of that interest.

The Court will examine each of the *O'Brien* factors in turn.

a.   Is the Statute is Within the Constitutional Power of the State?

The first prong of *O'Brien* requires that the government have the constitutional power to enact the regulation in question. *O'Brien*, 391 U.S. at 371. Parsons does not dispute that the state of Texas has the power to prohibit the unauthorized practice of law. Therefore, the first prong of *O'Brien* is satisfied.

b.   Does the Statute Further an Important Government Interest?

The State has a significant interest in regulating the practice of law and protecting its citizens from being mislead. The Supreme Court has said that states have a "substantial interest in regulating the practice of law within the State." Sperry v. Florida, 373 U.S. 379, 383 (1963). Therefore, the second prong of O'Brien is satisfied.

c.   Is the government interest unrelated to the suppression of free expression?

A regulation satisfies O'Brien's third criterion if it can be justified without reference to the content of the regulated speech. J & B Entertainment v. City of Jackson, 152 F.3d 362, 376 (5th Cir.1998). This criterion is essentially no different than the initial test to establish if the regulation was content-neutral. Since the Statute can be justified on the need to prevent people who are not lawyers from giving legal advice and

---

8. The Supreme Court has identified seven different tests for determining the constitutionality of content-neutral regulations of speech. Geoffrey Stone, Content–Neutral Restrictions, 54 U. Chi. L.Rev. 46, 49 (1987). Other than the 4–part **O'Brien** test, courts most often describe the test for intermediate scrutiny as a 3–part test: (1) Are the restrictions justified without reference to the content of regulated speech; (2) Are they narrowly tailored to serve a significant government interest; and (3) Do the regulations leave open ample alternative channels of communication. This is specifically the test for a time, place or manner restriction. The Supreme Court has held that the *O'Brien* test "in the last analysis is little, if any, different from the standard applied to time, place, or manner restrictions." *Clark v. Community for Creative Non–Violence*, 468 U.S. 288, 298 (1984). The *O'Brien* test is generally used for regulations which prohibit conduct with a speech element. Additionally, it is hard to argue that the unauthorized practice of law statute is a time, place, or manner restriction. Therefore, the Court will utilize the *O'Brien* test in determining the constitutionality of the Statute.

harming the citizens of Texas, the Statute satisfies the third prong of O'Brien.

d.   Is the incidental restriction of speech no greater than is essential to the furtherance of the governmental interest?

A regulation satisfies the final prong, often referred to as "the narrow tailoring requirement," "so long as the ... regulation promotes a substantial government interest that would be achieved less effectively absent the regulation." *United States v. Albertini*, 472 U.S. 675, 689 (1985). The regulation must also "not burden substantially more speech than is necessary to further the government's legitimate interest." *Ward*, 491 U.S. at 799.

The version of the narrow tailoring requirement for intermediate scrutiny does not require the government to chose the "least-restrictive alternative" in achieving its interests. *Ward*, 491 U.S. at 798. Furthermore, a court should not invalidate the government's preferred remedial scheme because some alternative solution is marginally less intrusive on a speaker's First Amendment interests. *Turner Broadcasting System, Inc. v. F.C.C.*, 117 S.Ct. 1174, 1200 (1997) (*Turner II*). A statute should be struck down under intermediate scrutiny only when a "substantial portion of the burden on speech does not serve to advance [the State's content-neutral goals]." *Simon & Schuster v. New York Crime Victims Bd.*, 502 U.S. at 122 n.* (quoting Ward, 491 U.S. at 799).

While the Court recognizes that the issue is close, it is of the opinion that the Statute does not "substantially burden" more speech than necessary, and that the government's interest would be achieved less effectively absent the regulation. Absent the regulation, as it is being applied in this case, the State's ability to combat the unauthorized practice of law in the computer age would be hindered. The State possesses an interest in protecting the uninformed and unwary from overly-simplistic legal advice. The UPLC does not seek to prevent the simple provision of information concerning legal rights; rather, it seeks to prevent the citizens of Texas from being lulled into a false sense of security that if they use QFL they will have a "legally valid" document that's "tailored to [their] situation" and "best meets their needs." If the UPLC is prevented from prosecuting Parsons, the State's interests in preventing those who are not authorized to practice law from giving legal advice would be less effectively achieved. Additionally, while the Statute burdens some speech, that burden does not rise to the level of a substantial burden. Moreover, the burden which the Statute does place on speech is necessary to serve the State's legitimate content-neutral interests. Thus, the Statute satisfies the fourth prong of *O'Brien*.

Since the Statute meets all four of O'Brien's requirements, it survives review under intermediate scrutiny. The Statute does not violate the First Amendment to the United States Constitution.

D.   Speech Rights Under the Texas Constitution

Parsons also alleges that the UPLC's actions in enforcing the Statute against it violates Parsons' rights to free speech under Article I, Section 8 of the Texas Constitution.[9] It does not. Granted, *Davenport v. Garcia*, 834 S.W.2d 4 (Tex.1992), requires a showing of immediate and irreparable harm before issuing an injunction. This test is more stringent than the test under federal law. However, the cases since Davenport have limited this higher standard under the Texas Constitution to cases which "have involved prior restraints in the form of court orders prohibiting or restricting speech." *Commission for Lawyer Discipline v. Benton*, 980 S.W.2d 425, 434 (Tex.1998). Furthermore, the Fifth Circuit has refused to expand the Davenport's heightened standard outside of the narrow areas specifically addressed by the Texas Supreme Court, *Woodall v. City of El Paso*, 49 F.3d 1120 (5th Cir.1995), and the Court will not do so here. Furthermore, the UPLC has made a sufficient showing of immediate and irreparable harm to the citizens of Texas from the sale and publication of QFL that the heightened standard of Davenport has been satisfied.

Since the injunction this Court will issue will be limited to only Quicken Family Lawyer, version 8.0, and Quicken Family Lawyer '99, which have already been published, the injunction is not a "prior restraint," and the heightened standards of Davenport should not apply. "Not all injunctions that may incidentally affect expression are 'prior restraints.'" *Madsen v. Women's Health Center, Inc.*, 512 U.S. 753, 763 n. 2 (1994). When an injunction issues "not because of the content of petitioners' expression ... but because of their prior unlawful conduct," it is not a prior restraint. *Id.*; see also *Securities & Exchange Commission v. Wall Street Publishing, Inc.*, 851 F.2d 365, 370 (D.C.Cir.1988) (finding that the prior restraint doctrine is the wrong analytical framework if the injunction is imposed only after full judicial review on the merits). The injunction that will issue in accordance with this Memorandum Opinion and Order will not be the broad relief sought by the UPLC. Rather, this Court will limit relief to enjoining the sale and distribution of Quicken Family Lawyer, version 8.0, and Quicken Family Lawyer '99 within the state of Texas.

Thus, enforcement of the Statute here does not violate the Texas Constitution.

E. Is the Statute Unconstitutionally Vague as Applied to Parsons?

Finally, Parsons challenges the Statute as being impermissibly vague as it is being applied to them. This challenge also fails.

---

9. Article 1, Section 8 of the Texas Constitution states:

Every person shall be at liberty to speak, write or publish his opinions on any subject, being responsible for the abuse of that privilege; and no law shall ever be passed curtailing the liberty of speech or of the press. In prosecutions for the publication of papers, investigating the conduct of officers, or men in public capacity, or when the matter published is proper for public information, the truth thereof may be given in evidence. And in all indictments for libels, the jury shall have the right to determine the law and the facts, under the direction of the court, as in other cases.

Vagueness is a constitutional infirmity rooted in due process. "An enactment is void for vagueness if its prohibitions are not clearly defined." *J & B Entertainment*, 152 F.3d at 367 (quoting *Grayned v. City of Rockford*, 408 U.S. 104, 109 (1972)); see also *Posters 'N' Things, Ltd. v. United States*, 511 U.S. 513, 525 (1994) (upholding federal drug paraphernalia law against a void-for-vagueness challenge). Vague laws are prohibited because they do not give citizens fair warning that their conduct is illegal. In determining whether a statute is vague, we view the law from the standpoint of a person of ordinary intelligence. *J & B Entertainment*, 152 F.3d at 367.

This Statute was challenged for vagueness in *Drew v. Unauthorized Practice of Law Comm.*, 970 S.W.2d 152 (Tex.App.—Austin 1998, writ denied). Mr. Drew, a non-lawyer, had filed habeas corpus petitions on behalf of people who believed they had been denied their rights. An order was entered enjoining Mr. Drew from practicing law. On appeal, he challenged the Statute as being void for vagueness. The Court of Appeals concluded that "the statute is sufficiently specific as concerns the actions the court enjoined, including preparation of pleadings, giving legal advice, preparing legal documents, and attempting to appear before a judge on behalf of another." *Id.* at 155. This holding is consistent with every other court which has considered a vagueness challenge to a state's unauthorized practice law. See *State v. Rogers*, 705 A.2d 397, 401 (N.J.Sup.Ct.1998) (citing cases upholding unauthorized practice of law statutes against vagueness challenges); see also *Lawline v. American Bar Assn.* 956 F.2d 1378 (7th Cir.1992) (upholding against a vagueness challenge state ethical rule prohibiting lawyers from assisting others in the unauthorized practice of law).

While the Statute is not a model of clarity, "condemned to the use of words, we can never expect mathematical certainty from our language." *Grayned*, 408 U.S. at 110. The Statute and the surrounding case law set forth a core of prohibited conduct with sufficient definiteness to guide those who must interpret it. The Statute speaks of the preparation of a will or contract or other legal instrument as being potentially prohibited conduct. This should have put Parsons or anyone else who assists others in the preparation of a legal document on notice that they may run afoul of the unauthorized practice of law statute. Moreover, while Parsons may believe it to be wrongly decided, *Fadia v. Unauthorized Practice of Law Comm.*, 830 S.W.2d 162 (Tex.App.—Dallas 1992, writ denied), should have also placed Parsons on notice that in Texas the selling of forms, without more, may be considered the unauthorized practice of law. The acts prohibited by the Statute were sufficiently defined that Parsons had fair warning that the publication and sale of QFL was potentially illegal in Texas. Consequently, Parsons' claim that the Statute is unconstitutionally vague as applied fails.

III. CONCLUSION

Plaintiff's Motion for Summary Judgment is GRANTED. Defendant's Motion for Summary Judgment is DENIED. * * *

UNAUTHORIZED PRACTICE OF LAW COMMITTEE v. PARSONS TECHNOLOGY, INC.

United States Court of Appeals, Fifth Circuit, 1999.
179 F.3d 956.

PER CURIAM:

Defendant-appellant Parsons Technology, Inc. appeals the district court's grant of summary judgment in favor of plaintiff-appellee, The Unauthorized Practice of Law Committee, and the court's subsequent order permanently enjoining defendant-appellant from selling and distributing its software programs, Quicken Family Lawyer Version 8.0 and Quicken Family Lawyer '99, within the state of Texas. The district court based its decision on its determination that the sale and distribution of the software constitutes the "practice of law" under Texas Government Code Annotated § 81.101 (1998). See *Unauthorized Practice of Law Committee v. Parsons Technology, Inc.*, No. Civ.A.3:97:CV-2859H, 1999 WL 47235, at *6 (N.D. Tex. Jan. 22, 1999); *see also* TEX. GOV'T CODE ANN. § 81.101(a) (1998) (stating that the "practice of law" includes, *inter alia*, "the giving of advice or the rendering of any service requiring the use of legal skill or knowledge, such as preparing a will, contract, or other instrument, the legal effect of which under the facts and conclusions involved must be carefully determined").

Subsequent to the filing of this appeal, however, the Texas Legislature enacted an amendment to § 81.101 providing that "the 'practice of law' does not include the design, creation, publication, distribution, display, or sale ... [of] computer software, or similar products if the products clearly and conspicuously state that the products are not a substitute for the advice of an attorney," effective immediately. H.B. 1507, 76th Leg., Reg. Sess. (Tex.1999). We therefore VACATE the injunction and judgment in favor of plaintiff-appellee and REMAND to the district court for further proceedings, if any should be necessary, in light of the amended statute. Each party shall bear its own costs.

Note And Questions

1.   This case concerned software sold to individual computer users. But obviously an Internet website could run an identical program and give similar advice on legal problems.

2.   Does the public need protection against software or Internet sites that give legal advice? Medical advice? Should there be any restrictions on such computerized advice? With the advance of artificial intelligence techniques is it more appropriate to apply to interactive software the legal standards for books or the legal standards for human advice? Should it make any difference whether the software runs on home computers, business computers, or an Internet site? Does the warning required by the amendment to the Texas Statute provide any real protection to the public?

Chapter VII

TELECOMMUNICATIONS
AND THE INTERNET
A. INTRODUCTION

As computers have become ubiquitous in our personal and professional lives, our appreciation of their networking capabilities has grown proportionally. Networking technology has relied primarily on the existing telecommunications infrastructures as the conduit for information transfer. Most private individuals access the Internet via their telephone lines, while a growing number access the Internet through their cable lines. Existing legislation regulating telephone and cable services does not provide clear answers in the unprecedented situations that are arising with respect to the Internet.

B. LINE SHARING

Given the increasing popularity of the Internet, and the desire for higher speed connections, a number of companies were formed to sell high speed Internet connections. These companies sought to force local telephone companies to provide access to their lines so that the companies could use existing local telephone lines to provide high speed internet services. The following ruling of the Federal Communications Commission deals with this question of access.

BEFORE THE FEDERAL COMMUNICATIONS COMMISSION IN THE MATTERS OF DEPLOYMENT OF WIRELINE SERVICES OFFERING ADVANCED TELECOMMUNICATIONS CAPABILITY AND IMPLEMENTATION OF THE LOCAL COMPETITION PROVISIONS OF THE TELECOMMUNICATIONS ACT OF 1996

Federal Communications Commission Third Report and Order
in Cc Docket No. 98–147. Fourth Report and Order in Cc
Docket No. 96–98 adopted November 18, 1999.
14 F.C.C.R. 20,912, 1999 WL 1124073.

I. Introduction and Overview

1. Among the fundamental goals of the Telecommunications Act of 1996 (1996 Act) is the promotion of innovation, investment, and compe-

tition among all participants and for all services in the telecommunications marketplace, including advanced services. The Commission has issued three orders in this proceeding to date, and has issued other decisions intended to promote competition in the advanced services market. In this Third Report and Order we take additional, important steps toward implementing Congress's goals for the deployment of competitive advanced services by instituting line sharing obligations for incumbent LECs, and establishing spectrum management policies and rules.

2. Carriers are increasingly transmitting electronic communications in digital, rather than analog form, and by means of "packet switching." Packet-switched transmission of information promises a revolution in information services, communications services, and entertainment by offering businesses, residential users, schools and libraries, and other end users the ability to access and send large amounts of information quickly, reliably, and at low cost across the street or across the globe. Moreover, for wireline carriers, digital subscriber line technologies are making it possible for ordinary citizens to access various networks, such as the Internet, corporate networks, and governmental networks, at high speeds through the existing copper telephone lines that connect their residences or businesses to the incumbent local exchange carriers' (LEC's) central office. The existing infrastructure is beginning to be used in new ways that make available to average citizens a variety of new services and vast improvements to existing services. The ability of all Americans to access these high-speed, packet-switched networks will spur the growth and development of our nation.

3. Incumbent and competitive LECs are beginning to provide xDSL-based services to customers in major markets nationwide. These xDSL-based services provide high-speed connections between subscribers and packet switched networks, over ordinary copper telephone "loops." Because the advanced services market is still in its developmental stage, robust competition among xDSL providers is just beginning to emerge in many markets. The economic realities of providing advanced services have also caused most xDSL providers to market primarily to large business customers. Nevertheless, both incumbent and competitive carriers appear to have recently begun to make some of the technological investment necessary to compete in the provision of advanced services to residential and small business consumers.

4. In this Order we adopt measures to promote the availability of competitive broadband xDSL-based services, especially to residential and small business customers. We amend our unbundling rules to require incumbent LECs to provide unbundled access to a new network element, the high frequency portion of the local loop. This will enable competitive LECs to compete with incumbent LECs to provide to consumers xDSL-based services through telephone lines that the competitive LECs can share with incumbent LECs. The provision of xDSL-based service by a competitive LEC and voiceband service by an incumbent LEC on the same loop is frequently called "line sharing." In addition, we adopt

spectrum management policies and rules to facilitate the competitive deployment of advanced services.

5. The record shows that lack of access to the high frequency portion of the local loop materially diminishes the ability of competitive LECs to provide certain types of advanced services to residential and small business users, delays broad facilities-based market entry, and materially limits the scope and quality of competitor service offerings. The record reveals no evidence of substantial technical, economic, operational, or practical barriers to incumbent LEC line sharing with competitors. We believe that line sharing is vital to the development of competition in the advanced services market, especially for residential and small business consumers. We believe that unbundled access to the high frequency portion of the loop can be implemented rapidly and in an equitable manner that balances the needs of both potential competitors and incumbent LECs.

6. In addition, we adopt rules in this Order that apply to spectrum compatibility and management. These rules will significantly benefit the rapid and efficient deployment of xDSL-based technologies. Specifically, we seek to encourage the voluntary development of industry standards while limiting the ability of any one class of carriers to impose unilateral and potentially anti-competitive spectrum management or compatibility rules on other xDSL providers. We believe that the spectrum policies we adopt in this Order will ensure the compatibility of technologies and minimize the risk of harmful spectrum interference among transmission services. As such, these policies will ensure that American consumers will not face undue delay in receiving the benefits of technological innovation.

* * *

Note

Line sharing is one approach for new entrants into the high speed Internet access market. New entrants do not have the economic resources to replicate the entire telecommunications network and thus want to be able to share lines belonging to the existing telephony providers. There is obvious tension between new entrants, who want access at low rates, and the existing telephony provider, who wants to ensure that its investment is appropriately compensated. The order above is an example of Federal Communications Commissions intervention in this struggle.

C. INTERNET ACCESS OVER CABLE TELEVISION FACILITIES

Technology continues to move forward. A major battle in coming years will be between the two communications providers—traditional local telephone companies and cable television companies—that now provide service over the "last mile" to enable consumers to have high speed Internet access. As they compete with one another, other companies will struggle to share the only two existing systems of lines that extend over the "last mile" to customers homes.

AT&T CORP. v. CITY OF PORTLAND

United States Court of Appeals, Ninth Circuit, 2000.
216 F.3d 871.

THOMAS, CIRCUIT JUDGE.

This appeal presents the question of whether a local cable franchising authority may condition a transfer of a cable franchise upon the cable operator's grant of unrestricted access to its cable broadband transmission facilities for Internet service providers other than the operator's proprietary service. We conclude that the Communications Act prohibits a franchising authority from doing so and reverse the judgment of the district court.

I

Distilled to its essence, this is a struggle for control over access to cable broadband technology. In broadband data transmission, a single medium carries multiple communications at high transmission speeds. The allure of broadband technology is that it allows users to access the Internet at speeds fifty to several hundred times faster than those available through conventional computer modems connected to what is commonly referenced in the telecommunications industry as "plain old telephone service." Broadband allows transmission, or "streaming," of live video and audio communications, as well as video and audio data files. To satisfy consumer demand for broadband Internet access, cable television operators have replaced coaxial wires with fiber-optic cable, telephone companies have initiated high-frequency digital subscriber line ("DSL") services over standard twisted-pair copper wires, fixed wireless providers have upgraded their microwave transmission capacities, satellite providers have launched global two-way digital networks, and researchers have explored the use of quantum communication methods.

The race to acquire broadband transmission systems has, in part, prompted a number of corporate mergers. This appeal concerns the merger between AT&T, at the time the nation's largest long distance telephone provider, and Telecommunications, Inc. ("TCI"), one of the nation's largest cable television operators. In addition to providing traditional cable television programming, TCI provided cable broadband Internet access to consumers in certain geographic areas. Since acquiring TCI, AT&T has continued to offer cable broadband access as part of its "@Home" service, which bundles its cable conduit with Excite, an Internet service provider ("ISP") under an exclusive contract. Like many other ISPs, @Home supplements its Internet access with user e-mail accounts and a Web portal site, a default home page gateway offering Internet search capabilities and proprietary content devoted to chat groups, interactive gaming, shopping, finance, news, and other topics. @Home subscribers also may "click-through" to other free Web portal sites, and may access other Internet service providers if they are willing to pay for an additional ISP; however, subscribers cannot purchase cable broadband access separately from an unaffiliated ISP, and have no choice over terms of Internet service such as content and bandwidth restrictions.

The @Home cable broadband infrastructure differs from that of most ISPs. A typical ISP connects with the Internet via leased telecommuncations lines, which its consumers access through "dial-up" connections over ordinary telephone lines. @Home operates a proprietary national "backbone," a high-speed network parallel to the networks carrying most Internet traffic, which connects to those other Internet conduits at multiple network access points. This backbone serves regional data hubs which manage the network and deliver Excite's online content and services, including multimedia content that exploits broadband transmission speeds. Each hub connects to local "headend" facilities, cable system transmission plants that receive and deliver programming, where "proxy" servers cache frequently requested Internet data, such as Web sites, for local delivery. Each headend connects to cable nodes in neighborhoods, each of which in turn connects via coaxial cable to the user's cable modem and computer.

To effect the merger, AT&T and TCI sought three types of regulatory approval. The Department of Justice approved the merger on antitrust grounds, subject to TCI's divestiture of its interest in Sprint PCS wireless services. *See United States v. AT&T Corp. and Tele-Communications Inc.*, No. CIV. 98 CV03170, 1999 WL 1211462 (D.D.C. Aug.23, 1999) (final judgment). The Federal Communications Commission ("FCC") approved the transfer of federal licenses from TCI to AT&T, after addressing public interest concerns in four service areas, including residential Internet access. *See Application for Consent to the Transfer of Licenses and Section 214 Authorizations from TCI to AT&T*, 14 F.C.C.R. 3160 (1999) ("Transfer Order ").

One of the issues that the FCC considered forms the undercurrent of the present controversy: whether to impose a requirement of open access to cable broadband facilities. A variety of interest groups and competitors argued that allowing AT&T to restrict cable broadband access to the proprietary @Home service would harm competition and reduce consumer choice. In its order approving the license transfer, the FCC rejected any open access condition, citing the emergence of competing methods of high-speed Internet access, and @Home customers' "ability to access the Internet content or portal of his or her choice." It found "that the equal access issues raised by parties to this proceeding do not provide a basis for conditioning, denying, or designating for hearing any of the requested transfers of licenses and authorizations." Transfer Order at ¶ 96. The FCC concluded that "while the merger is unlikely to yield anti-competitive effects, we believe it may yield public interest benefits to consumers in the form of a quicker roll-out of high-speed Internet access services." Transfer Order at ¶ 94.

The last regulatory hurdle that AT&T and TCI faced was the approval of local franchising authorities where required by local franchising agreements. *See* 47 U.S.C. § 537 (permitting franchising authority approval of cable system sales when the franchise agreement so requires). TCI's franchises with Portland and Multnomah County (collectively, "Portland") permitted the city to "condition any Transfer upon such conditions, related to the technical, legal, and financial qualifications of the prospective party to perform according to the terms of the Franchise, as it deems appropriate." This language parallels the text of 47 U.S.C. § 541(a)(4)(C), which describes the conditions a locality may impose on a franchise.

Portland referred the transfer application for recommendation by the Mount Hood Cable Regulatory Commission, an intergovernmental agency overseeing cable affairs in the Portland region. In response to Portland's preliminary questions, AT&T confirmed that TCI was in the process of upgrading its cable system to support @Home over cable broadband, and maintained that @Home was a proprietary product "not subject to common carrier obligations." At public hearings, the incumbent local telephone exchange carrier U.S. WEST and the Oregon Internet Service Providers Association called for open access to TCI's cable broadband network, citing-in addition to consumer welfare-the need for "a level playing field" with U.S. WEST's common carrier obligations and a "very real potential that consumer [Internet] access businesses could go out of business." The Mount Hood Commission recommended that the city and county approve the transfer of franchise control subject to an open access requirement.

On December 17, 1998, Portland and Multnomah County voted to approve the transfer, subject to an open access condition expressed in a written acceptance:

> Non-discriminatory access to cable modem platform. Transferee shall provide, and cause the Franchisees to provide, non-discriminatory access to the Franchisees' cable modem platform for providers of Internet and on-line services, whether or not such providers are affiliated with the Transferee or the Franchisees, unless otherwise required by applicable law. So long as cable modem services are deemed to be "cable services," as provided under Title VI of the Communications Act of 1934, as amended, Transferee and the Franchisees shall comply with all requirements regarding such services, including but not limited to, the inclusion of revenues from cable modem services and access within the gross revenues of the Franchisees' cable franchises, and commercial leased access requirements.

AT&T refused the condition, which resulted in a denial of the request to transfer the franchises. AT&T then brought this action, seeking declarations that the open access condition violated the Communications Act of 1934, as amended by the Telecommunications Act of 1996, Pub.L. No. 104–104, 110 Stat. 56 (1996), codified at 47 U.S.C.

§ 151, et seq. (collectively, the "Communications Act"), the franchise agreements, and the Constitution's Commerce Clause, Contract Clause, and First Amendment. The district court rejected all of AT&T's claims and granted summary judgment to Portland. *See AT&T Corp. v. City of Portland*, 43 F.Supp.2d 1146 (D.Or.1999). We review de novo a grant of summary judgment; there being no disputed factual issues, we face only a question of statutory interpretation. *See Fort Belknap Indian Community v. Mazurek*, 43 F.3d 428, 432 (9th Cir.1994).

II

The parties, and numerous amici, forcefully urge us to consider what our national policy should be concerning open access to the Internet. However, that is not our task, and in our quicksilver technological environment it doubtless would be an idle exercise. The history of the Internet is a chronicle of innovation by improvisation, from its genesis as a national defense research network, to a medium of academic exchange, to a hacker cyber-subculture, to the commercial engine for the so-called "New Economy." Like Heraclitus at the river, we address the Internet aware that courts are ill-suited to fix its flow; instead, we draw our bearings from the legal landscape, and chart a course by the law's words. To that end, "we look first to the plain language of the statute, construing the provisions of the entire law, including its object and policy." *United States v. Mohrbacher*, 182 F.3d 1041, 1048 (9th Cir.1999) (citation omitted). We note at the outset that the FCC has declined, both in its regulatory capacity and as amicus curiae, to address the issue before us. Thus, we are not presented with a case involving potential deference to an administrative agency's statutory construction pursuant to the Chevron doctrine. See *Food and Drug Administration v. Brown & Williamson Tobacco Corp.*, 120 S.Ct. 1291, 1300–01 (2000).

A

Because Portland premised its open access condition on its position that @Home is a "cable service" governed by the franchise, we begin with the question of whether the @Home service truly is a "cable service" as Congress defined it in the Communications Act. We conclude that it is not.

Subject to limited exceptions, the Communications Act provides that "a cable operator may not provide cable service without a franchise." 47 U.S.C. § 541(b)(1). The Act defines "cable service" as "(A) the one-way transmission to subscribers of (i) video programming, or (ii) other programming service, and (B) subscriber interaction, if any, which is required for the selection or use of such video programming or other programming service." 47 U.S.C. § 522(6). For the purposes of this definition, "video programming" means "programming provided by, or generally considered comparable to programming provided by, a television broadcast station," 47 U.S.C. § 522(20), and "other programming service" means "information that a cable operator makes available to all subscribers generally." 47 U.S.C. § 522(14). The essence of cable service, therefore, is one-way transmission of programming to subscribers generally.

This definition does not fit @Home. Internet access is not one-way and general, but interactive and individual beyond the "subscriber interaction" contemplated by the statute. Accessing Web pages, navigating the Web's hypertext links, corresponding via e-mail, and participating in live chat groups involve two-way communication and information exchange unmatched by the act of electing to receive a one-way transmission of cable or pay-per-view television programming. And unlike transmission of a cable television signal, communication with a Web site involves a series of connections involving two-way information exchange and storage, even when a user views seemingly static content. Thus, the communication concepts are distinct in both a practical and a technical sense. Surfing cable channels is one thing; surfing the Internet over a cable broadband connection is quite another.

Further, applying the carefully tailored scheme of cable television regulation to cable broadband Internet access would lead to absurd results, inconsistent with the statutory structure. For example, cable operators like AT&T may be required by a franchising authority to set aside cable channels for public, educational or governmental use, see 47 U.S.C. § 531, must designate some of their channels for commercial use by persons unaffiliated with the operator, see 47 U.S.C. § 532, and must carry the signals of local commercial and non-commercial educational television stations, see 47 U.S.C. §§ 534 & 535. We cannot rationally apply these cable television regulations to a non-broadcast interactive medium such as the Internet. As our sister circuit concluded in the context of the abortive "video dialtone" common carrier television technology, regulating @Home as a cable service "simply makes no sense in any respect, and would be infeasible in many respects." *National Cable Television Ass'n. v. FCC*, 33 F.3d 66, 75 (D.C.Cir.1994).

Thus, because the Internet services AT&T provides through @Home cable modem access are not "cable services" under the Communications Act, Portland may not directly regulate them through its franchising authority.

B

Although we conclude that a cable operator may provide cable broadband Internet access without a cable service franchise, we must also determine whether Portland may condition AT&T's provision of standard cable service upon its opening access to the cable broadband network for competing ISPs. To do so, we must determine how the Communications Act defines @Home.

Under the statute, Internet access for most users consists of two separate services. A conventional dial-up ISP provides its subscribers access to the Internet at a "point of presence" assigned a unique Internet address, to which the subscribers connect through telephone lines. The telephone service linking the user and the ISP is classic "telecommunications," which the Communications Act defines as "the transmission, between or among points specified by the user, of information of the user's choosing, without change in the form or content of the information as sent and received." 47 U.S.C. § 153(43). A provider of telecommunications services is a "telecommunications carrier," which the Act treats as a common carrier to the extent that it provides telecommunications to the public, "regardless of the facilities used." 47 U.S.C. § 153(44) & (46).

By contrast, the FCC considers ISP itself as providing "information services" under the Act, defined as "the offering of a capability for generating, acquiring, storing, transforming, processing, retrieving, utilizing, or making available information via telecommunications." 47 U.S.C. § 153(20) (1996). As the definition suggests, ISPs are themselves users of telecommunications when they lease lines to transport data on their own networks and beyond on the Internet backbone. However, in relation to their subscribers, who are the "public" in terms of the statutory definition of telecommunications service, they provide "information services," and therefore are not subject to regulation as telecommunications carriers. See Federal–State Joint Board on Universal Service, 13 F.C.C.R. 11501, ¶ ¶ BM, CB (1998) (report to Congress); cf. Child Online Protection Act, Pub.L. No. 105–277, § 1403(e)(4), 112 Stat. 2681 (1998) (codified at 47 U.S.C. § 231(e)(4)) & Internet Tax Freedom Act, Pub.L. No. 105–277, § 1101(e), 112 Stat. 2681 (1998) (reproduced at note to 47 U.S.C. § 151(e) (1998)) (defining Internet access services as: "a service that enables users to access content, information, electronic mail, or other services offered over the Internet, and may also include access to proprietary content, information, and other services as part of a package of services offered to consumers. Such term does not include telecommunications services."). Indeed, "information services"-the codified term for what the FCC first called "enhanced services"-have never been subject to regulation under the Communications Act. See Howard v. America Online, Inc., 208 F.3d 741, 752–53 (9th Cir.2000); see also 47 C.F.R. § 64.702(a); California v. FCC, 905 F.2d 1217, 1223–25 (9th Cir.1990) (discussing history of "enhanced services" non-regulation).

Like other ISPs, @Home consists of two elements: a "pipeline" (cable broadband instead of telephone lines), and the Internet service transmitted through that pipeline. However, unlike other ISPs, @Home controls all of the transmission facilities between its subscribers and the Internet. To the extent @Home is a conventional ISP, its activities are one of an information service. However, to the extent that @Home provides its subscribers Internet transmission over its cable broadband facility, it is providing a telecommunications service as defined in the Communications Act.

Under this taxonomy, the Communications Act bars Portland from conditioning the franchise transfer upon AT&T's provision of the @Home transmission element that constitutes telecommunications:

(3)(A) If a cable operator or affiliate thereof is engaged in the provision of telecommunications services-

(i) such cable operator or affiliate shall not be required to obtain a franchise under this title for the provision of telecommunications services; and

(ii) the provisions of this title shall not apply to such cable operator or affiliate for the provision of telecommunications service

(B) A franchising authority may not impose any requirement under this title that has the purpose or effect of prohibiting, limiting, restricting, or conditioning the provision of a telecommunications service by a cable operator or an affiliate thereof.

(C) A franchising authority may not order a cable operator or affiliate thereof-

(i) to discontinue the provision of a telecommunications service, or

(ii) to discontinue the operation of a cable system, to the extent such cable system is used for the provision of a telecommunications service, by reason of the failure of such cable operator or affiliate thereof to obtain a franchise or franchise renewal under this title with respect to the provision of such telecommunications service.

(D) Except as otherwise permitted by sections 611 and 612, a franchising authority may not require a cable operator to provide any telecommunications service or facilities, other than institutional networks, as a condition of the initial grant of a franchise, a franchise renewal, or a transfer of a franchise.

Pub.L. No. 104–104, § 303(a), 110 Stat. 56, 124–25 (1996), codified at 47 U.S.C. § 541(b)(3); see also § 101(a), 110 Stat. at 70, codified at 47 U.S.C. § 253(a) ("No State or local statute or regulation, or other State or local legal requirement, may prohibit or have the effect of prohibiting the ability of any entity to provide any interstate or intrastate telecommunications service."). Subsection 541(b)(3) expresses both an awareness that cable operators could provide telecommunications services, and an intention that those telecommunications services be regulated as such, rather than as cable services.

The Communications Act includes cable broadband transmission as one of the "telecommunications services" a cable operator may provide over its cable system. Thus, AT&T need not obtain a franchise to offer cable broadband, see 47 U.S.C. § 541(b)(3)(A); Portland may not impose any requirement that has "the purpose or effect of prohibiting, limiting, restricting or conditioning" AT&T's provision of cable broadband, see 47 U.S.C. § 541(b)(3)(B); Portland may not order AT&T to discontinue cable broadband, see 47 U.S.C. § 541(b)(3)(C); and Portland may not require AT&T to provide cable broadband as a condition of the franchise transfer, see 47 U.S.C. § 541(b)(3)(D). Therefore, under the several provisions of § 541(b)(3), Portland may not regulate AT&T's provision of @Home in its capacity as a franchising authority, and the open access condition contained in the franchise transfer agreement is void.

C

Beyond the domain of cable-specific regulation, the definition of cable broadband as a telecommunications service coheres with the over-all structure of the Communications Act as amended by the Telecommunications Act of 1996, and the FCC's existing regulatory regime. Elsewhere, the Communications Act contemplates the provision of telecommunications services by cable operators over cable systems. See, e.g., 47 U.S.C. § 224(d)(3) (authorizing FCC utility pole attachment rate-setting "for any pole attachment used by a cable system ... to provide any telecommunications service."). In the Telecommunications Act, Congress defined advanced telecommunications capability "without regard to any transmission media or technology," in terms that describe cable broadband: "high-speed, switched, broadband telecommunications capability that enables users to originate and receive high-quality voice, data, graphics, and video telecommunications using any technology." Pub.L. 104–104, § 706(c)(1), 110 Stat. 56, 153 (1996) (reproduced at note under 47 U.S.C. § 157). Consistent with our view, the FCC regulates DSL service, a high-speed competitor to cable broadband, as an advanced telecommunications service subject to common carrier obligations. See GTE Operating Companies Tariff No. 1, 13 F.C.C.R. 22466 (1998).

Among its broad reforms, the Telecommunications Act of 1996 enacted a competitive principle embodied by the dual duties of nondiscrimination and interconnection. See 47 U.S.C. § 201(a) ("It shall be the duty of every common carrier engaged in interstate or foreign communication by wire or radio to furnish such communication service upon reasonable request therefor"); 47 U.S.C. § 251(a)(1) ("Each telecommunications carrier has the duty ... to interconnect directly or indirectly with the facilities and equipment of other telecommunications carriers"). Together, these provisions mandate a network architecture that prioritizes consumer choice, demonstrated by vigorous competition among telecommunications carriers. As applied to the Internet, Portland calls it "open access," while AT&T dysphemizes it as "forced access." Under the Communications Act, this principle of telecommunications common carriage governs cable broadband as it does other means of Internet transmission such as telephone service and DSL, "regardless of the facilities used." 47 U.S.C. § 153(46). The Internet's protocols themselves manifest a related principle called "end-to-end": control lies at the ends of the network where the users are, leaving a simple network that is neutral with respect to the data it transmits, like any common carrier. On this rule of the Internet, the codes of the legislator and the programmer agree.

Thus far, the FCC has not subjected cable broadband to any regulation, including common carrier telecommunications regulation. We note that the FCC has broad authority to forbear from enforcing the telecommunications provisions if it determines that such action is unnecessary to prevent discrimination and protect consumers, and is consistent with the public interest. See 47 U.S.C. § 160(a). Congress has reposed the details of telecommunications policy in the FCC, and we will not impinge on its authority over these matters.

III

We hold that subsection 541(b)(3) prohibits a franchising authority from regulating cable broadband Internet access, because the transmission of Internet service to subscribers over cable broadband facilities is a telecommunications service under the Communications Act. Therefore, Portland may not condition the transfer of the cable franchise on nondiscriminatory access to AT&T's cable broadband network. We need not reach AT&T's other statutory and constitutional arguments.

REVERSED.

Note

The picture is complicated by the emergence of other high speed Internet access techniques, such as satellite, fixed wireless, and mobile wireless. As the number of competing technologies, the arguments for government intervention must be reexamined.

Chapter VIII

ANTITRUST

A. INTRODUCTION

The computer industry has witnessed a number of antitrust suits. The need for product compatibility meant that companies that established an early position in the market tended to keep and expand their market shares and that makers of different products had difficulty in entering such markets. These would-be competitors have had some successes in challenging the actions of dominant companies as being in violation of antitrust law. The most significant antitrust case has been one in which the United States government and the states joined in a suit against Microsoft, accusing it of using improper means to maintain a monopolistic position in the market for operating systems and Internet browsers.

The primary goal of antitrust laws is to ensure that competitive markets are maintained to protect the consumer. (Some see as secondary goals the preserving of small businesses and avoiding undue concentration of economic power.) Section One of the Sherman Act prohibits "every contract, combination . . . or conspiracy in restraint of trade." 15 U.S.C. § 1 (1994). The courts however have interpreted this section as prohibiting not all, but only "unreasonable" restraints of trade. Section Two of the Sherman Act prohibits monopolization, attempted monopolization, and conspiracies to monopolize. 15 U.S.C. § 2 (1994). Monopolization has two elements: monopoly power and the unlawful acquisition or maintenance of that power. Monopoly or market power is defined as the power to control market prices or exclude competition. The Clayton Act prohibits mergers and acquisitions where the effect may be to substantially lessen competition or "to tend to create a monopoly." 15 U.S.C. § 18 (1994).

The Supreme Court has developed two approaches to the determination of whether or not a violation has occurred: "per se" and "rule of reason." Some activities, called "per se" violations, have been held by the Supreme Court to always constitute violations of the antitrust laws. These include fixing minimum prices, certain types of agreements on market division and exclusive dealing, group boycotts, and certain types of arrangements where the purchase of one type of goods is tied to the purchase of another. To other situations, the Supreme Court applies the "rule of reason," balancing the pro-competitive benefits of the challenged activity against the anticompetitive effects to ensure that competition is being maintained or strengthened rather than restrained.

B. TIE–IN SALES

The most significant Internet and computer related antitrust litigation has involved "tie-in sales." These are situations where a company with a monopoly on one product, the "tying" product, has used this monopoly to force customers who want the tying product to buy another product, the "tied" product, from the same company. The courts have long been hostile to tie-ins and have often found tie-ins to be in violation of the antitrust laws. For decades, however, economists, with few exceptions, have regarded tie-in sales as generally harmless and often beneficial. *E.g*, Richard A. Posner, Antitrust Law: An Economic Perspective, at 172–173, 181–183 (Chicago, 1976); Robert H. Bork, The Antitrust Paradox, at 380–381(Basic Books, 1978). Despite the economists' views, the United States Supreme Court reaffirmed the illegality of some types of tie-in sales in a leading case, *Eastman Kodak Co. v. Image Technical Services, Inc.*, 504 U.S. 451, 112 S.Ct. 2072, 119 L.Ed.2d 265 (1992).

Kodak, the petitioner, manufactured and sold photocopiers and micrographic equipment. Kodak also sold service and replacement parts for its equipment. Kodak's replacement parts and equipment were not compatible with those of other manufacturers. The respondents were 18 Independent Service Organizations (ISO's) that repaired and serviced Kodak copying and micrographic equipment; sold parts; and reconditioned and sold used Kodak equipment. The ISO's claimed that Kodak violated § 1 of the Sherman Act by tying the sale of service for Kodak machines to the sale of Kodak parts and that Kodak violated § 2 of the Sherman Act by monopolizing or attempting to monopolize the sale of service for Kodak machines.

The issue before the Court was whether Kodak's "lack of market power in the primary equipment market precludes—as a matter of law— the possibility of market power in derivative aftermarkets" for Kodak parts and service. The Court decided this issue based on the premise that competition existed in the equipment market.

In ruling on the § 1 claim, the Court found that the ISO's had presented sufficient evidence of a tie between service and parts to defeat the summary judgment motion. The Court noted that the ISOs alleged a tie between service and parts rather than between equipment and service or parts.

The Court also found that a factual issue existed regarding Kodak's economic power in the tying (parts) market. Kodak argued that even if it had a monopoly share of the parts market, "any increase in profits from a higher price in the aftermarkets" would be offset by a corresponding decrease in profits from lower sales in the competitive equipment market. The Court rejected Kodak's argument and refused to adopt a substantive legal rule that the existence of competition in a primary equipment market precludes, as a matter of law, a finding of monopoly power in the derivative aftermarkets of parts and services for the equipment. The Court found that "there is a question of fact whether information costs and switching costs foil the simple assumption that the equipment and service markets act as pure complements to one another."

The Court also rejected Kodak's argument that its policy is procompetitive, stating that "[w]e note only that Kodak's service and parts policy is simply not one that appears always or almost always to enhance competition, and therefore to warrant a legal presumption without any evidence of its actual economic impact."

The Court refused to grant summary judgment on the Sherman Act § 2 claim as well. The Court held that the ISO's had presented sufficient evidence that Kodak possessed the required amount of monopoly power and that Kodak "took exclusionary action to maintain its parts monopoly and used its control over parts to strengthen its monopoly share of the Kodak service market." The Court ruled that factual questions existed about the validity and sufficiency of Kodak's three proffered "valid business justifications" for its actions: "(1) to promote interbrand equipment by allowing Kodak to stress the quality of its service; (2) to improve asset management by reducing Kodak's inventory costs; and (3) to prevent ISO's from free riding on Kodak's capital investment in equipment, parts and service."

CALDERA, INC. v. MICROSOFT CORP.

United States District Court, D. Utah, 1999.
72 F.Supp.2d 1295.

BENSON, DISTRICT JUDGE.

I. INTRODUCTION

Presently before the Court are four motions for partial summary judgment brought by defendant, Microsoft Corporation. In its complaint, plaintiff, Caldera, Inc., alleges that Microsoft engaged in anticompetitive conduct in violation of §§ 1 and 2 of the Sherman Antitrust Act, 15 U.S.C. §§ 1, 2, as well as § 3 of the Clayton Act, 15 U.S.C. § 14. Microsoft has attempted to separate what it believes are Caldera's individual claims by filing the following nine motions for partial summary judgment on: (1) "Plaintiff's Preannouncement Claim," (2) "Plaintiff's Product Disparagement Claim," (3) "Plaintiff's Claim Regarding Microsoft's Licensing Practices," (4) "Plaintiff's Perceived Incompatibilities Claim," (5) "Plaintiff's Intentional Incompatibilities Claim," (6) "Plaintiff's 'Predisclosure' Claim," (7) "Plaintiff's Technological Tying Claim," (8) "Plaintiff's European & Japanese Claims," and (9) "Plaintiff's State Law Tortious Interference Claims." In addition to responding to each of Microsoft's motions for partial summary judgment, Caldera filed its own "Motion to Strike Microsoft's Partial Summary Judgment Briefs Relating to Substantive Antitrust Violations."

* * *

II.   Background & Description of Plaintiff's Claims

This case finds its genesis in the mid–1970s with the advent of the personal computer. Critical to the evolution of the personal computer was the development of the computer operating system. An operating system functions as the control center of the computer. It controls the computer's interaction with peripheral hardware such as keyboards, modems, and printers and also serves as the underlying support structure for software applications. An operating system functions as the interface between the computer and the software applications. Independent software venders (ISVs) write software application programs, such as games, spreadsheets, and wordprocessors, that rely for their operation on certain general functions written into the operating system.

* * *

Caldera claims that Microsoft, alarmed at this positive reception of DR DOS 5.0 the computer industry and concerned about losing its DOS monopoly, began to engage in a series of practices to eliminate the threat DR DOS posed to Microsoft's market dominance. Initially, rather than competing with DRI, Microsoft attempted to bargain for DRI's exit out of the market. In essence, as plaintiff alleges, Microsoft offered DRI a certain amount of money for the use of DR DOS technology. Microsoft was proposing that DRI market MS–DOS instead of DR DOS and that each company license rights in the other's product. DRI, uninterested in a long-term relationship with Microsoft, offered DR DOS technology to Microsoft for $30 to $40 million. Microsoft refused.

Plaintiff alleges that beginning in approximately the latter half of 1990 with the introduction of DR DOS 5.0 into the marketplace, Microsoft began its improper campaign to eliminate DR DOS as a competitor and to illegally maintain its operating systems monopoly. By this time, DR DOS had captured approximately six percent of the operating systems worldwide market. Among the first of these allegedly improper actions was Microsoft's use of preemptive false and misleading announcements of forthcoming, competitive MS–DOS and Windows products. This practice of preannouncing upcoming products is known in the industry as "vaporware." Caldera claims that beginning in April 1990, Microsoft began making knowingly false and misleading preannouncements relating to the forthcoming MS–DOS 5.0, an allegedly comparable product to DR DOS 5.0. Plaintiff claims Microsoft knowingly misled the public by stating MS–DOS 5.0 would be available to OEMs by September 1990, a full nine months before it was actually on the market.

Following DRI's April 26, 1990 announcement at an England trade show that DR DOS 5.0 would be available in eight weeks, Microsoft immediately announced to the trade press its development of MS–DOS 5.0. An e-mail sent by Mark Chestnut, then a product manager of MS–DOS 5.0, to a number of Microsoft executives on May 2, 1990, stated:

> On the PR side, we have begun an "aggressive leak" campaign for MS–DOS 5.0. The goal is to build an anticipation for MS–DOS 5.0

and diffuse potential excitement/momentum from the DR DOS 5.0 announcement. At this point, we are telling the press that a major new release from Microsoft is coming this year which will provide significant memory relief and other important features. This was picked up by the major weeklies in the U.S. and was the page 1 story in PC Week on 4/30.

Additionally, Chestnut himself flew to several countries, meeting with dozens of OEMs and telling them that they could expect MS–DOS 5.0 by September 1990. Plaintiff alleges that Chestnut's representations caused these OEMs to postpone any decision to switch to DR DOS.

Caldera argues that the purpose behind Microsoft's preannouncements was to prevent OEMs from entering into licensing agreements with DR DOS 5.0. and that Microsoft knew it could not possibly comply with the schedule it was announcing to the public. Caldera's expert states that such an aggressive schedule was objectively unattainable. For one thing, a release date of September 1990 would only allow for a three-month beta test cycle, which, according to Caldera, is an unacceptably short beta testing period. Plaintiff argues that by the end of 1990, however, Microsoft was aware that its tactics were working. In a performance self-evaluation, Chestnut wrote "virtually all of our OEMs worldwide were informed about DOS 5, which diffused DRI's ability to capitalize on a window of opportunity with these OEMs." (Pl.'s Exhibit 62).

By mid-October 1990, the media became concerned about the veracity of Microsoft's preemptive remarks directed at DR DOS 5.0. Such media pressure was not taken lightly. Following an interview with *PC Week*, a trade magazine, regarding the release of MS–DOS 5.0, Chestnut wrote to other Microsoft employees on October 17, 1990:

> I'm afraid that this guy [Paul Sherer of *PC Week*] is going to write that we are being open about DOS 5 beta because we are trying to pre-empt DR DOS 5 sales. I tried real hard to present a different point of view, but I don't think he bought it. I'm concerned that this article may make us look bad. Can you guys follow up and see if we need to do some damage control?

> This was the toughest interview I've ever done, I felt like Richard Nixon giving his "I am not a crook" speech.

(Pl.'s Exhibit 87).

In addition to Microsoft's "vaporware" strategies, Caldera alleges that following the launch of DR DOS 5.0 Microsoft refined and dramatically expanded a campaign of "fear, uncertainty, and doubt" (FUD) against DRI and all of its forthcoming versions of DR DOS. Plaintiff alleges that account managers were directed to share purported "serious problems" with OEMs considering a switch to DR DOS 5.0. Caldera asserts that Microsoft deliberately withheld from these same OEMs independent tests confirming DR DOS 5.0 compatibility with MS–DOS and Windows, while creating its own tests to give the appearance of "incompatibility."

In addition to its improper vaporware and FUD campaigns, Caldera alleges that Microsoft also forced OEMs away from DR DOS 5.0 by what plaintiff refers to as the "licensing triple-whammy," which refers to (1) per processor licenses, (2) minimum commitments subject to forfeiture, and (3) increased license duration. Per processor licensing agreements required an OEM to pay Microsoft a royalty on every machine the OEM shipped regardless whether the machine contained MS–DOS or a different operating system. This is in contrast to a per system licensing agreement, which required OEMs to pay a royalty on only those computers shipped with MS–DOS installed. The use of per processor agreements is argued by plaintiff to be Microsoft's most effective single weapon against DR DOS. Plaintiff alleges that DRI had no realistic chance to license DR DOS to OEMs under a per processor license with Microsoft. It would make no sense for an OEM to install DR DOS when it had already paid for MS–DOS on every machine. Microsoft contends that OEMs were free to depart from the per processor licensing scheme, and that price differentials between license types were "relatively minor." However, plaintiff points to the depositions of several OEM executives who testified that even slight price differentials between the per processor and per system licenses meant that only the per processor license was financially viable.

Plaintiff also asserts that Microsoft's use of minimum commitments with prepaid balances raised the costs to OEMs who may have wanted to switch to an alternative operating system. As alleged, during the life of a Microsoft contract, OEMs could find themselves over-committed with respect to units of Microsoft products. Plaintiff claims that given the nature of Microsoft's mandatory, nonrefundable minimum commitment payments, OEMs faced the prospect of either forfeiting their prepaid balance or signing a new agreement with Microsoft to partially recoup the prepaid balance. The rationale, plaintiff asserts, behind Microsoft's minimum commitments policy was not just to provide an OEM an opportunity to recoup the prepaid balance, but rather to sign a new license agreement so that the OEM would continue to distribute only MS–DOS.

Microsoft's final licensing tactic aimed at DR DOS, as plaintiff alleges, was increased license duration. Microsoft began increasing its licensing agreements from two-year to three-year terms and gave OEMs a small price break for agreeing to the longer term. Caldera claims that the increased licensing time was implemented only after DR DOS became a threat to MS–DOS's monopoly position, and that Microsoft deliberately increased the term length as part of its illegal scheme to drive DRI from the market. The strategy, plaintiff alleges, foreclosed DR DOS from effectively competing for existing OEM business.

In late September 1991, Novell released DR DOS 6.0. Plaintiff alleges with this release, Microsoft adhered to the same pattern of attack, vaporware, FUD, and per processor licensing agreements, but with more intensity. Microsoft executives were aware of the threat Novell/DRI and the new DR DOS 6.0 posed. Jim Allchin wrote on September 9, 1991:

> We must slow down Novell.... As you said Bill, it has to be dramatic.... We need to slaughter Novell before they get stronger.

(Pl.'s Exhibit 175). * * *

To assure DR DOS's incompatibility with Windows, plaintiff alleges that Microsoft placed DRI on a "beta blacklist." According to plaintiff, Microsoft knew that if the DR DOS development team had access to a Windows 3.1 beta, it would allow them to make DR DOS compatible and consequently allay public fears of incompatibility. DRI submitted a formal request to become a beta site. The request was denied on August 2, 1991. Being placed on Microsoft's beta blacklist had an alleged direct effect on DR DOS sales. One corporation notifying DRI of its decision to reject DR DOS 6.0, stated that

> the most important factor, however, is the rift developing between Digital Research and Microsoft. By this I mean Microsoft not allowing you to beta test Windows 3.1. Since the users who would be most inclined to switch to DR DOS are also using Windows, this one factor is of particular concern.

(Pl.'s Exhibit 266).

According to Caldera, Microsoft continued its attacks on DRI by intentionally making Windows 3.1 incompatible with DR DOS, not for any technologically significant reason, but for the sole purpose of eliminating DR DOS as a competitor. Caldera supports its claim with internal Microsoft statements, such as these written by David Cole and Phil Barrett on September 30, 1991, respectively: "It's pretty clear we need to make sure Windows 3.1 only runs on top of MS DOS or an OEM version of it," and "[t]he approach we will take is to detect dr 6 and refuse to load. The error message should be something like 'Invalid device driver interface.' "(Pl.'s Exhibits 205 and 206). Microsoft developers discussed reliable DR DOS detection mechanisms, and allegedly incorporated "Bambi," Microsoft's code name for its updated disc cache utility, which among other things detects DR DOS and refuses to load, in Windows 3.1.

* * *

Through Microsoft's alleged use of vaporware, per processor licensing agreements, FUD, beta blacklisting, and the insertion of incompatibilities between Windows and DR DOS, Caldera claims that Microsoft was essentially forcing OEMs to purchase both MS–DOS and Windows. By this method Microsoft, Caldera asserts, was using its monopoly in the GUI (i.e. Windows) market, to illegally maintain its monopoly in the operating systems market. One OEM, an alleged leading proponent of DR DOS, stated: "[Microsoft] just said they had changed the way in which they market the product, instead of it being available as two separate packages it now came as an integrated package, which was DOS and Windows 3.11 or DOS and Windows for Workgroups 3.11, take it or leave it.'' (Harvey Depo. at 33).

* * *

In August 1995, Microsoft released Windows 95. For ten years prior thereto, Microsoft had sold MS–DOS and Windows separately. However, Windows 95 combined the functions of Windows and DOS into one product. Microsoft touts Windows 95 as one of the most popular software products in history, selling within four months after its release nearly eleven million copies through OEM channels and nearly five million copies through retail channels. After its release, virtually all new personal computers came with Windows 95 preinstalled by OEMs. With the release of Windows 95, users of the Intel-based personal computer had a totally integrated (from boot-up to shutdown) graphical operating system for the first time. Microsoft claims that Windows 95 offered many new features of functionality over that provided by the combination of MS–DOS 6.0 and Windows 3.0 when those products were installed separately on a personal computer. Caldera, however, alleges that in reality Windows 95 is not an integrated software product, but rather two products— MS–DOS 7.0 and Windows 4.0, which Caldera asserts are merely updated versions of both MS–DOS 6.22 and Windows 3.1—packaged together using a common installation program with blue cloud graphics to make them appear to be a single product. Plaintiff claims that MS–DOS 7.0 and Windows 4.0 can be easily isolated and sold as separate products. Since the release of Windows 95, updated versions of Windows and MS–DOS were not sold separately. Plaintiff claims Novell would have been able to compete with Microsoft but for Microsoft's prior conduct and ultimately this illegal tying arrangement of, Windows 95, which plaintiff argues was the coup de grace for DR DOS.

On July 23, 1996, Caldera acquired DRI from Novell. Included in the purchase was the right to bring this lawsuit against Microsoft. Based on the foregoing, Caldera filed its complaint against Microsoft, alleging the improper use and maintenance of monopoly power in violation of § 2 of the Sherman Act and for the illegal restraint of trade in violation of § 1 of the Sherman Act. Caldera supports its § 1 claim by arguing that Windows 95 constitutes an illegal tie of two separate products formerly sold as MS–DOS and Windows. Caldera supports its § 2 claim, as aforementioned, by alleging that Microsoft engaged in an anticompetitive scheme, the factual components of which consist of, improper licensing arrangements, improper preannouncements, improper intentional and perceived incompatibilities, beta blacklisting, the improper creation of fear, uncertainty, and doubt, and the illegal tying together of its products. Caldera acknowledges that each instance of alleged misconduct taken alone may not amount to a violation of § 2. However, when viewed in totality, Caldera asserts that Microsoft has engaged in an unlawful, anticompetitive scheme to illegally maintain its monopoly in the operating systems market.

III. DISCUSSION

In 1890, Congress passed the Sherman Antitrust Act in an effort to protect competition and prevent monopolies. Section 1 of the Sherman Act prohibits "[e]very contract, combination ..., or conspiracy, in restraint of trade or commerce." 15 U.S.C. § 1. Despite this broad language, almost from its inception the Sherman Act has been read to prohibit only those restraints of trade that are unreasonable. *Board of Trade v. United States*, 246 U.S. 231, 238, 38 S.Ct. 242, 62 L.Ed. 683 (1918) (recognizing that because every agreement involving trade is a restraint on trade in some form, the proper inquiry is whether the restraint suppresses or destroys competition). Courts have also developed a doctrine of per se violations to cover those business relationships that "because of their pernicious effect on competition and lack of any redeeming virtue are conclusively presumed to be unreasonable and therefore illegal without elaborate inquiry as to the precise harm they have caused or the business excuse for their use." *Northern Pac. Ry. Co. v. United States*, 356 U.S. 1, 5, 78 S.Ct. 514, 2 L.Ed.2d 545 (1958). Section 2 of the Sherman Act condemns "[e]very person who shall monopolize, or combine or conspire with any other person or persons, to monopolize any part of the trade or commerce among the several States or with foreign nations." 15 U.S.C. § 2. The Supreme Court has determined that "the offense of monopoly under § 2 of the Sherman Act has two elements: (1) the possession of monopoly power in the relevant market and (2) the willful acquisition or maintenance of that power as distinguished from growth or development as a consequence of a superior product, business acumen, or historic accident." *United States v. Grinnell Corp.*, 384 U.S. 563, 570–71, 86 S.Ct. 1698, 16 L.Ed.2d 778 (1966).

Although by enacting the Sherman Act Congress expressed an inherent distrust of monopolies and their possible adverse effects on competition, it did not declare monopolies illegal per se. Antitrust laws are designed to protect and foster competition, even when the competitor is a monopolist. In general, a monopolist is free to market its products, engage in research and development to improve its products, and engage in any other business practice that is procompetitive. If smaller businesses find themselves unable to compete on the merits of their products against a procompetitive monopolist, there is nothing in the antitrust laws to protect them. Antitrust laws protect the competitive process; they do not protect individual competitors.

Notwithstanding, § 2 does proscribe a monopolist from engaging in business practices that are anticompetitive or exclusionary. Congress, recognizing that "it is difficult to define in legal language the precise line between lawful and unlawful combination[,]" left to the courts the responsibility of defining the parameters of anticompetitive conduct. 21 Cong. Rec. 2460 (1890). Anticompetitive conduct describes a wide variety of behavior including espionage, sabotage, predatory pricing, fraud, price discrimination, price-fixing, bid-rigging, illegal tying arrangements, product disparagement and a host of other activities that improperly stifle competition. Section 2 prohibits a monopolist from engaging in anticompetitive practices that are designed to deter potential rivals from entering the market or from preventing existing rivals from increasing their output, no matter how flagrant or subtle the violation. A monopoly may not improperly "wield [its] resulting power to tighten its hold on the market." *Berkey Photo, Inc. v. Eastman Kodak Co.*, 603 F.2d 263, 275 (2d Cir.1979). Perhaps the clearest way to explain what a monopolist may legally do is to say that the monopolist may engage in all of the same procompetitive activities that allowed it to become a legal monopolist in the first place. These would include building a better or less expensive product, engaging in better public relations, employing effective (and honest) advertising campaigns, and developing aggressive and effective marketing techniques. If these activities result in even more market share, and drive competitors out of the market, the monopolist is nevertheless fully entitled to such expansion, and its conduct is not a violation of the Sherman Act. Conversely, a monopolist may not engage in any activities other than those that are procompetitive, as generally described above.

* * *

B. *Microsoft's Motions for Partial Summary Judgment*

* * *

4. *Technological Tying*

Caldera next alleges pursuant to §§ 1 and 2 of the Sherman Act and § 3 of the Clayton Act that Microsoft's development of Windows 95 as an integrated, graphical operating system constitutes an illegal tying arrangement of products formerly sold as MS–DOS and Windows. Microsoft contends, however, that Windows 95 is far from a tied together version of MS–DOS and Windows, but rather a new product with vast technological improvements over the prior products. Accordingly, Microsoft argues that the requirements for an unlawful "technological tying" arrangement have not been satisfied and should be dismissed as a matter of law.

"A tying arrangement is an agreement by a party to sell one product—the 'tying product'—only on condition that the buyer also purchase a second product—the 'tied product'—or at least agree not to buy that product from another supplier." *Multistate Legal Studies v. Harcourt Brace Jovanovich Legal & Professional Publications, Inc.*, 63 F.3d 1540, 1546 (10th Cir.1995) (citing *Eastman Kodak Co. v. Image Technical Services, Inc.*, 504 U.S. 451, 461–462, 112 S.Ct. 2072, 119 L.Ed.2d 265 (1992)). In the instant case, Caldera alleges that Microsoft is involved in an illegal tying arrangement by tying Windows 4.0, the tying product, and MS–DOS 7.0, the tied product, together and selling them as one product known as Windows 95. This allegation is based on the claim that Microsoft used its monopoly power in the Windows market to force consumers to use MS–DOS by tying these products together into one product. "A tie-in constitutes a per se section 1 violation if the seller has appreciable economic power in the tying product market and if the arrangement affects a substantial volume of commerce in the tied product." *Id.* For purposes of this motion, Microsoft concedes that it has monopoly power in the personal computer operating system market.

Several economic reasons exist for outlawing anticompetitive tying. Indeed, the law forbids a manufacturer who has market power in a certain area to gain advantage in another area by requiring consumers to buy another product. *See Jefferson Parish Hospital v. Hyde,* 466 U.S. 2, 104 S.Ct. 1551, 80 L.Ed.2d 2 (1984). If market "power is used to impair competition on the merits in another market, a potentially inferior product may be insulated from competitive pressures. This impairment could either harm existing competitors or create barriers to entry of new competitors in the market for the tied product." *Id.* at 14, 104 S.Ct. 1551. The Supreme Court captured Congress' concern about the anticompetitive character of tying arrangements when it recognized that tying arrangements have the power to "completely shut[ ] out competitors, not only from trade in which they are already engaged, but from the opportunities to build up trade in any community where these great and powerful combinations are operating under this system and practice." *Id.* at 10 n. 14, 104 S.Ct. 1551 (quoting H.R. Rep. No 63–627, 63d Cong.2d Sess., 12–13 (1914) and noting that congressional findings "concerning the competitive consequences of tying is illuminating, and must be respected").

The Supreme Court has recognized that "every refusal to sell two products separately cannot be said to restrain competition." *Id.* at 11–12, 104 S.Ct. 1551 (finding that "buyers often find package sales attractive; a seller's decision to offer such packages can merely be an attempt to compete effectively"). Nevertheless, the Supreme Court has established that upon meeting certain criteria, a tying arrangement may constitute a per se § 1 violation. "[T]he essential characteristic of an invalid tying arrangement lies in the seller's exploitation of its control over the tying product that the buyer either did not want at all, or might have preferred to purchase elsewhere on different terms." *Id.* at 12, 104 S.Ct. 1551. The Court continued: "When such 'forcing' is present, competition on the merits in the market for the tied item is restrained and the Sherman Act is violated." *Id.* at 12, 104 S.Ct. 1551. In sum, "[t]ying arrangements need only be condemned if they restrain competition on the merits by forcing purchases that would not otherwise be made." *Id.* at 27, 104 S.Ct. 1551.

a. Caldera's Standing to Bring a Tying Claim

As a preliminary manner, the Court first addresses Microsoft's argument that Caldera lacks standing to raise any tying claim concerning Windows 95 because neither Caldera nor its predecessors, DRI or Novell, ever produced a substitute for the allegedly tied product that would have enabled Caldera to compete with Microsoft. Specifically, Microsoft contends that Caldera was not an actual or potential participant in the business from which Caldera alleges they were foreclosed from competition.

While acknowledging that Novell stopped its development work on DR DOS in 1994 and never developed a Windows-like (GUI) program, Caldera argues that it cannot be precluded from bringing a claim on the basis of standing. Caldera claims that it could not participate because Microsoft foreclosed the competition in the DOS market by tying together in Windows 95 two functionally distinct products, Windows 4.0 and MS–DOS 7.0. Through this tie, Caldera argues, Microsoft used its monopoly power in the Windows market to effectively prevent further competition in the DOS market by completely closing that market to outside competition. Consequently, any further development of a DOS program would have been futile since Windows was no longer sold separately. Caldera's claim is based on the fact that after 1995 consumers could not buy Windows 4.0 alone. The fundamental premise of Caldera's tying claim is that it and its predecessors would have, and could have, made a version of DR DOS that would have been compatible with Windows 4.0 and fully competitive with MS–DOS 7.0.

Caldera alleges that Microsoft developed Windows 95 as an attempt to destroy its DOS competition. Such allegations are supported by internal Microsoft documents. For example, in a 1992 internal strategy document, Microsoft, referring to Windows 95 by its code name "Chicago," stated:

> Novell is after the desktop. As you know, they have acquired Digital Research and are now working hard to tightly integrate DR–DOS with Netware. We should also assume they are working on a Windows clone and/or that they are working on a virtualized DOS environment which will run standard mode Windows as a client. This is perhaps our biggest threat. We must respond in a strong way by making Chicago a complete Windows operating system, from boot-up to shutdown. There will be no place or need on a Chicago machine for DR–DOS (or any DOS).

(Pl.'s Exhibit 309). Caldera argues that Microsoft did exactly as it planned, and were it not for Microsoft's tying Windows to DOS, Caldera would still be a viable competitor in the DOS business. Indeed, as inferred from the following e-mail, Caldera asserts that but for Microsoft's deliberate anticompetitive conduct aimed at Novell, DR DOS would still be alive. In 1993, Microsoft executives further stated: "If you're going to kill someone there isn't much reason to get all worked up about it and angry—you just pull the trigger.... We need to smile at Novell while we pull the trigger." (Pl.'s Exhibit 384).

Caldera has alleged facts sufficient to persuade the Court that Caldera has standing as an actual and potential competitor to bring its tying claim. Novell was an actual competitor to Microsoft in the DOS market in 1994. Novell ceased its active development and marketing of its DOS product based on the imminent release of Windows 95, which eliminated the need for a separate DOS program. Additionally, Caldera has alleged sufficient facts that it had the financial resources, the engineering talent, and the marketing capability to continue upgrading Novell DOS, as it had done in the past with DR DOS, so that it would continue to be a marketable component to Windows. *See Curtis v. Campbell–Taggart, Inc.*, 687 F.2d 336, 338 (10th Cir.1982) (holding that a potential competitor may have standing under the antitrust laws "if he has manifested an intention to enter the business and has demonstrated his preparedness to do so"). Certainly Caldera has demonstrated that it was foreclosed from a market in which it would otherwise have competed. It is hard to imagine that Caldera does not have standing to sue under these alleged facts. Accordingly, the Court finds that as an actual competitor to MS–DOS 6.22, and as a potential competitor to the allegedly tied product, MS–DOS 7.0, Caldera has the requisite standing to pursue its tying claim against Microsoft.

b. *Technological Tying Arrangements*

Microsoft contends that so long as the integrated design of Windows 95 offers any technological benefit, its design is immune to judicial review under the antitrust laws. Because the tying cases that are binding upon this Court involve nontechnical products such as bar review courses, *Multistate Legal Studies v. Harcourt Brace Jovanovich Legal & Professional Publications, Inc.*, 63 F.3d 1540 (10th Cir.1995), and medical services, *Jefferson Parish Hospital Dist. v. Hyde*, 466 U.S. 2, 104 S.Ct. 1551, 80 L.Ed.2d 2 (1984), Microsoft argues that the Court should apply the reasoning used by the United States Court of Appeals for the District of Columbia Circuit in *United States v. Microsoft Corp.*, 147 F.3d 935 (D.C.Cir.1998). Microsoft relies heavily on this case in support of its present motion, premising its argument on the contention that technically integrated products are immune from per se § 1 liability. As with the case at bar, the case before the D.C. Circuit arose from Microsoft's practices in marketing Windows 95. In that case, the D.C. Circuit considered whether the district court erred in entering a preliminary injunction prohibiting Microsoft from requiring computer manufacturers who license its operating system software to license its internet browser, Internet Explorer, as well. *Id.* at 938. The preliminary injunction turned on the court's interpretation of a consent decree between the Department of Justice (DOJ) and Microsoft, which in relevant part reads:

> Microsoft shall not enter into any License Agreement in which the terms of that agreement are expressly or impliedly conditioned upon:
>
> (i) the licensing of any other Covered Product, Operating System Software product or other product (provided, however, that this provision in and of itself shall not be construed to prohibit Microsoft from developing integrated products).

Id. at 125 (quoting section IV(E) of the Consent Decree). * * *

After debating whether Windows 95 and its Internet Explorer were an "integrated product" under the consent decree, the D.C. Circuit determined that it should ask the question "not whether the integration is a net plus but merely whether there is a plausible claim that it brings some advantage." *Id.* at 950. Microsoft now urges the Court to adopt this standard and reject Caldera's challenge to Microsoft's integrated product design of Windows 95 so long as Microsoft has a plausible claim of technological improvement that brings some advantage. Upon announcing this standard the D.C. Circuit acknowledged that "[w]hether or not this is the appropriate test for antitrust law generally, we believe it is the only sensible reading of § IV(E)(i)." *Id.* This Court finds that such a test is not the appropriate standard to determine whether an illegal tie has taken place under antitrust law. Simply determining whether a "facially plausible benefit" has been ascribed to justify an integrated product that is alleged to constitute an illegal tying arrangement falls short of satisfying the antitrust laws, as well as existing antitrust authority. This Court agrees with Judge Wald's dissenting opinion in *Microsoft*, that the majority's standard allows Microsoft "too safe a harbor with too easily navigable an entrance." *Id.* at 957. Just as the dissent recognized that Microsoft could require OEMs to install "integrated" software without fear of running aground on the main prohibition of section IV(E)(i) so long as Microsoft has created a design to combine functionality in a way that offers the ultimate user some "plausible" advantage otherwise unavailable, this Court finds that if the same standard were applied in the case at bar, Microsoft could similarly avoid § 1 violations and tie whatever products it wanted by simply pointing to some "plausible advantage." Furthermore, as Judge Wald stated: "It is difficult to imagine how Microsoft could not conjure up some technological advantage for any currently separate software product it wished to 'integrate' into the operating system." *Id.* at 961. Were this Court to adopt in this case the standard the D.C. Circuit articulated in the narrow context of the D.C. case, the Court would be adopting a broad standard of allowing a showing of "plausible" product improvement functionality, whatever that means, as an absolute defense to a § 1 tying claim. The Court is not willing to do so and would find such a standard to be inconsistent with existing legal precedent. *See, e.g., Eastman Kodak Co. v. Image Technical Services, Inc.* 504 U.S. 451, 112 S.Ct. 2072, 119 L.Ed.2d 265 (1992); *Jefferson Parish Hospital Dist. v. Hyde*, 466 U.S. 2, 104 S.Ct. 1551, 80 L.Ed.2d 2 (1984); *Multistate Legal Studies v. Harcourt Brace Jovanovich Legal & Professional Publications, Inc.*, 63 F.3d 1540 (10th Cir.1995).

This is a case dealing with technology, and the Court recognizes the need to promote pro-competitive conduct in the technology world. Indeed, technological innovation is an important defense in defending antitrust allegations. As the D.C. Circuit noted, "[a]ntitrust scholars have long recognized the undesirability of having courts oversee product design, and any dampening of technological innovation would be at cross-purposes with antitrust law." *Microsoft* 147 F.3d at 948. Thus, acknowledging the importance of promoting technological innovation, the Court is cautious in completely relying on the analysis contained in cases such as *Jefferson Parish* and *Multistate Legal Studies*, which involved medical services and bar-review courses. However, the Court finds that the D.C. Circuit has given too much deference to the technology argument and not enough to current antitrust law. Certainly a company should be allowed to build a better mousetrap, and the courts should not deprive a company of the opportunity to do so by hindering technological innovation. Yet, antitrust law has developed for good reason, and just as courts have the potential to stifle technological advancements by second guessing product design, so too can product innovation be stifled if companies are allowed to dampen competition by unlawfully tying products together and escape antitrust liability by simply claiming a "plausible" technological advancement.

Microsoft requests the Court do as other courts have and apply a more deferential standard to technically integrated products. *See, e.g., Response of Carolina, Inc. v. Leasco Response, Inc.*, 537 F.2d 1307, 1330 (5th Cir.1976) (holding that an antitrust "violation must be limited to those instances where the technological factor tying the hardware to the software has been designed for the purpose of tying the products, rather than to achieve some technologically beneficial result"); *Innovation Data Processing, Inc. v. IBM*, 585 F.Supp. 1470, 1476 (D.N.J.1984) (finding that the integration of a "dump-restore" utility into mainframe operating system was a lawful package of technologically interrelated components); *ILC Peripherals Leasing Corp. v. IBM*, 448 F.Supp. 228 (N.D.Cal. 1978) (finding that disk drives and head/disk assembly combination were lawful), *aff'd per curiam sub nom., Memorex Corp. v. IBM*, 636 F.2d 1188 (9th Cir.1980); *Telex Corp. v. IBM*, 367 F.Supp. 258 (N.D.Okla.1973) (denying a claim that IBM's integration of additional memory and control functions into its CPU constituted unlawful tying), *rev'd on other grounds*, 510 F.2d 894 (10th Cir.1975). These cases, upon which Microsoft relies, arose from an era when IBM was accused of tying its central processing unit to various peripheral devices such as disk drives. The courts addressing this issue generally concluded that IBM's integrations did not amount to illegal tying arrangements due to the fact that the computers were considered a single product, and the integration of related devices could not be regarded as predatory within the contemplation of antitrust policy. See *Telex*, 367 F.Supp. at 342. However, as noted by the D.C. District Court, on remand in the Internet Explorer case, Microsoft has taken an additional step beyond the defendants in the IBM cases by not only bundling two products together, but also by prohibiting the unbundling of the two. *See United States v. Microsoft Corp.*, No. Civ. A. 98–1232, 1998 WL 614485 at *8–*9 (D.D.C. Sept.14 1998). In the instant case, unlike the *IBM* cases, Microsoft ceased selling Windows and DOS separately after the release of Windows 95. Furthermore, Caldera argues that the Court should not look to these cases because they were decided prior to the Supreme Court's decisions in *Jefferson Parish* and *Eastman Kodak* and have been preempted by the Court's "separate product analysis."

Although not "technology" cases, *Jefferson Parish* and *Eastman Kodak* both involved integrated products and services where the defendants claimed that a functionally integrated package of services existed. In order to determine whether an unlawful tying arrangement had taken place, the *Jefferson Parish* Court considered whether anesthesiological services, which a hospital had required patients to take only from certain anesthesiologists, were in fact separate products from the other services provided by the hospital or, rather, were part of what the hospital claimed was a "functionally integrated package of services." *Id.* at 19, 104 S.Ct. 1551. In its analysis the Court asked the fundamental question: Are there two separate products? This was not a question of function, but rather one assessing whether there was a market for two separate products. *Id.* at 21, 104 S.Ct. 1551 (holding that "a tying arrangement cannot exist unless two separate product markets have been linked"). The Court found that no tying arrangement could exist unless there was sufficient demand for the purchase of anesthesiological services separate from hospital services to identify a distinct product market in which it is efficient to offer anesthesiological services separately from hospital services. *Id.* at 21–22, 104 S.Ct. 1551. The *Jefferson Parish* test is actually consistent with the *IBM* cases in that the market should determine whether an integration is desirable—not Microsoft. The market can only make that decision if the two integrated products are, as a practical matter, available individually, as they were in the *IBM* cases.

The Tenth Circuit has also applied the *Jefferson Parish* tying analysis in *Multistate Legal Studies v. Harcourt Brace Jovanovich Legal & Professional Publications, Inc.*, 63 F.3d 1540 (10th Cir.1995). The court was faced with the task of determining whether an unlawful tying arrangement was created when a bar review provider bundled its multistate bar review workshop with its full-service bar review course and required customers to purchase the workshop if they wanted the full-service course. In making such a determination, the Tenth Circuit articulated that the following elements were necessary in order to find a per se tying violation: "(1) two separate products, (2) a tie—or conditioning of the sale of one product on the purchase of another, (3) sufficient economic power in the tying product market, and (4) a substantial volume of commerce affected in the tied product market." *Id.* at 1546. In determining whether the first prong of its analysis was satisfied, the Tenth Circuit stated that "[t]he Supreme Court has made clear that the test for determining whether two components are separate products turns not on their function, but on the nature of any consumer demand for them." *Id.* at 1547. In essence the Tenth Circuit requires an inquiry as to whether the market wants two separate products. In its analysis the court held "there must be sufficient consumer demand so that it is efficient for a firm to provide [one] separate from [the other]." *Id.* (quoting *Eastman Kodak Co. v. Image Technical Services, Inc.*, 504 U.S. 451, 462, 112 S.Ct. 2072, 119 L.Ed.2d 265 (1992)).

* * *

The Court's standard is consistent with what the Tenth Circuit said when it stated that "a product improvement motivation—at least without something more, such as demonstrated efficiencies—will not save an otherwise illegal tying arrangement under § 1." *Multistate*, 63 F.3d at 1551 n. 9 (citing *Jefferson Parish*, 466 U.S. at 25 n. 41, 104 S.Ct. 1551). Accordingly, the technological improvements must have demonstrated efficiencies. This is more than just a "plausible claim that brings some advantage." *Microsoft*, 147 F.3d at 950. Any other standard would have the potential to allow illegal tying arrangement to deter, or even eliminate, effective competition, which in turn could hurt consumers not just because of higher prices, but because of a lack of technologically improved products.

In determining whether a technological advance has essentially created a new product through integration, the two products that have been integrated must be joined for technological reasons. In other words, in the spirit of *Jefferson Parish*, this analysis requires the integration to be driven by technology rather than by marketing. *See Jefferson Parish*, 466 U.S. at 21, 104 S.Ct. 1551. Evidence that consumers prefer an integrated product may not be enough, especially where the two previous products have essentially ceased to exist as separate commodities, as is the case here. Caldera asserts that the Windows 95 package consists of two separate products to which the link is no stronger than it was between the prior products and can be easily separated. (Pl.'s Expert, Dr. Hollaar's Report at 20–26). When asked about the integration of Windows and DOS in Windows 95, one of Microsoft's software engineers acknowledged that DOS and Windows were basically "stuck together with baling wire and bubble gum." (Barrett Depo. at 60–61). Based on this contention, Caldera argues that Microsoft's decision to combine them into Windows 95 turned on marketing decisions (and anticompetitive ones) rather than technological reasons. For example, Caldera again cites to the 1992 internal strategy document, where Microsoft, referring to Windows 95 by its code name "Chicago," stated:

> While Chicago is being developed as a single integrated Windows operating system, it's being designed and built so that 3 specific retail products can be packaged up and sold separately. Which products actually ship other than full Chicago is a marketing issue.

(Pl.'s Exhibit 309). Microsoft never released separate updated versions of DOS or Windows subsequent to the release of Windows 95. Accordingly, this evidence supports Caldera's contention that Windows 95 consists of separate DOS and Windows products and was integrated not for technological reasons but rather for marketing reasons to gain market power. Such allegations, together with Dr. Hollaar's report, support Caldera's claim that genuine issues of material fact exist as to any alleged technological advantage of Windows 95.

Microsoft, however, responds with evidence that Windows 95 is more than two separate products tied together and that any integration was done for technological reasons and achieved legitimate technological advantages. Indeed, Microsoft argues that incorporating a real-mode DOS component into Windows 95 resulted in several significant benefits, including the benefit of integration itself, sparing users the uncertainties of combining two products from different companies and giving users more confidence in the product, as well as the benefit of a single installation program, requiring users to only install one software program rather than two. Additionally, Microsoft argues that the integration provided several technological benefits that were not present in MS-DOS 6.22 or Windows 3.1, including the ability to (1) use long file names; (2) protect against incompatible utilities; (3) support plug-and-play devices so that notebook computers using docking stations will function properly; (4) use a "safe mode" boot-up process to determine if the boot-up process was completed properly, and if not, shift the computer into safe mode when the computer is restarted; (5) detect incompatible device drivers; and (6) obscure boot noise with an blue cloud image so users do not see the series of confusing messages that appear on the screen during the DOS boot-up sequence.

There appears to be no question that Windows 95, as Microsoft argues, is greater than the sum of Windows 3.1 and MS-DOS 6.22 and contains features that the previous products did not contain. However, the question that must be addressed is whether the technological improvements were in reality improvements to the prior products, ultimately creating Windows 4.0 and MS-DOS 7.0, under the guise of a new technologically advanced product, Windows 95. Caldera claims that none of the improvements offered in Windows 95 required—or even resulted from—the MS-DOS/Windows integration. Caldera's expert, Dr. Hollaar, argues this position. (Hollaar Report at 21–26). Dr. Hollaar claims that no shared software code exists between the underlying products in Windows 95 and that the two products can be easily separated and work properly once separated. *See id.* Thus, Caldera contends that the relationship between MS-DOS 7.0 and Windows 4.0 in Windows 95 is the same relationship that existed between Windows 3.1 and MS-DOS 6.22. Furthermore, Caldera alleges that but for Microsoft's anticompetitive conduct, Caldera would have and could have produced a DOS system that would support Windows 4.0, and thus would have all of the same technological benefits advanced by Windows 95.

The Supreme Court has instructed that "any inquiry into the validity of a tying arrangement must focus on the market or markets in which the two products are sold, for that is where the anticompetitive forcing has its impact." *Jefferson Parish*, 466 U.S. at 18, 104 S.Ct. 1551. Thus, the Court explained, "the answer to the question whether one or two products are involved turns not on the functional relation between them, but rather on the character of the demand for the two items." *Id.* at 19, 104 S.Ct. 1551. The alleged fact that Microsoft could have produced the products separately is not enough. "There must be sufficient consumer demand so that it is efficient for a firm to provide separately [its products]." *Eastman Kodak v. Image Tech. Services*, 504 U.S. 451, 462, 112 S.Ct. 2072, 119 L.Ed.2d 265 (1992). Caldera argues that there exists a demand for separate Windows and DOS products. Certainly a demand existed prior to the release of Windows 95, when for ten years DOS and Windows were marketed separately. Caldera claims that some OEMs would prefer Windows and DOS to still be offered separately. Indeed, in a 1991 PC User interview when asked about giving GUI users a single operating system, Microsoft executive Steve Ballmer stated:

> [w]e'll certainly be providing OEMs with an installation program that installs DOS and Windows as if they were one product. But not all hardware vendors want to sell Windows and not all end-users want to run Windows. And there is nothing we give up technically by offering Windows and DOS separately.

(Engel Declaration, Exhibit 3). Caldera's claim that there is a demand for separate products is further buttressed by the fact that Microsoft continued to sell old versions of MS–DOS and Windows separately. While these sales are relatively small and relate largely to obsolete products, they illustrate that some level of consumer demand exists even after the introduction of Windows 95.

Based on the fact that Caldera's expert has opined that Windows 95 is in reality nothing more than updated versions of Windows and MS–DOS, that these products could be separated, that any improvements in Windows 95 did not result from the integration of its underlying products, and that but for the tying of Windows 95 a market would exist for other DOS products, this Court finds that drawing all inferences in the light most favorable to the nonmoving party, genuine issues of material fact exist as to whether a valid, not insignificant, technological improvement have been advanced by integrating Windows and DOS into what would constitute one superior technological product. While in the end Microsoft may be able to satisfy a jury that Windows 95 constitutes a significant technological improvement over the prior products, at this point, based on Caldera's expert testimony and on Microsoft's own admissions, the Court will allow these factual disputes to be presented to a fact finder. Indeed, this is not the time to assess the strength of Caldera's case, but the time to determine whether there is enough evidence to allow a jury to make such an assessment. Even the D.C. District Court upon remand from the D.C. Circuit found that under the D.C. Circuit's rigid standard there were enough disputed facts that summary judgment should be denied in relation to the alleged tie of Microsoft's Internet Explorer to Windows 98, the latest update of Windows 95. *See United States v. Microsoft Corp.*, No. Civ. A. 98–1232, 1998 WL 614485 at *10 (D.D.C. Sept.14 1998). Based on these findings the Court concludes that Microsoft's motion for partial summary judgment on its "technological tying" claim must fail. Accordingly, Caldera will be allowed to present its § 1 tying claim to a jury.

c.   Caldera's § 2 Tying Claim

Furthermore, in addition to presenting its § 1 tying claim to the jury, Caldera will be allowed to present to the jury Microsoft's alleged unlawful tying arrangement of Windows 4.0 and MS–DOS 7.0 as part of Caldera's evidence in support of its § 2 claim for anticompetitive conduct. "Illegal tie-ins . . . under section 1 may also qualify as anticompetitive conduct for section 2 purposes." *Multistate Legal Studies v. Harcourt Brace Jovanovich Legal & Professional Publications, Inc.*, 63 F.3d 1540, 1550 (10th Cir.1995).

IV. Conclusion

For the foregoing reasons, the Court finds that plaintiff's "Motion to Strike Microsoft's Partial Summary Judgment Briefs Relating to Substantive Antitrust Violations" is DENIED, and defendant's Motions for Partial Summary Judgment on "Plaintiff's Claim of Predisclosure," "Plaintiff's Claim of Perceived Incompatibilities," "Plaintiff's Claim of Intentional Incompatibilities," and "Plaintiff's Claim of Technological Tying" are DENIED.

Note

1. This is a typical private antitrust suit. While the plaintiff's principal theory turns on tie-in sales, plaintiff's counsel have thought of a number of other plausible theories as well.

2. Consider each of plaintiff's theories. Is it a tie-in sale theory or some other type of monopolization theory? If it is a tie-in theory, consider the following questions: (1) what is the tying product? (2) did Microsoft face competition for the tying product? (3) what is the tied product? (4) what was Microsoft's likely motive for the tying?

3. Another problem with tie-in theories is that of determining whether there is just one product or there are two different products. Suppose X Corporation has 80% of the market for processor chips for personal computers. Now suppose X Corporation starts selling only processor chips that include so much memory that computer makers no longer buy memory chips from anyone else. Is X Corporation violating the antitrust laws? Does it make a difference if computers are faster and more reliable if the processor and the memory are on the same chip? The next two cases may throw some light on the answer to this question.

UNITED STATES v. MICROSOFT CORPORATION

United States Court of Appeals, District of Columbia Circuit, 1998.
147 F.3d 935.

Stephen F. Williams, Circuit Judge.

The district court entered a preliminary injunction prohibiting Microsoft Corporation from requiring computer manufacturers who license its operating system software to license its internet browser as well. In granting the preliminary injunction the court also referred the government's motion for a permanent injunction to a special master. Microsoft appeals the preliminary injunction and applies for a writ of mandamus revoking the reference to a master. We find that the district court erred procedurally in entering a preliminary injunction without notice to Microsoft and substantively in its implicit construction of the consent decree on which the preliminary injunction rested. We also grant the petition for mandamus and direct the district court to revoke or revise its reference.

I.

This case arises from Microsoft's practices in marketing its Windows 95 operating system. An operating system is, so to speak, the central nervous system of the computer, controlling the computer's interaction with peripherals such as keyboards and printers. Windows 95 is an operating system that integrates a DOS shell with a graphical user interface, i.e., a technology by which the operator performs functions not by typing at the keyboard but by clicks of his mouse. Operating systems also serve as "platforms" for application software such as word processors. As the word "platform" suggests, the operating system provides a basic support structure for an application via "application programming interfaces" ("APIs"), which provide general functions on which applications can rely. Each operating system's APIs are unique; hence applications tend to be written for particular operating systems. The primary market for operating systems consists of original equipment manufacturers ("OEMs"), which make computers, install operating systems and other software that they have licensed from vendors such as Microsoft, and sell the package to end users. These may be either individual consumers or businesses.

In an earlier opinion, also arising from litigation generated by the Justice Department's 1994 antitrust suit against Microsoft, we briefly described Microsoft's role in the software industry and some of the industry's economics. *United States v. Microsoft Corp.*, 56 F.3d 1448, 1451–52 (D.C.Cir.1995). Because IBM chose to install Microsoft's operating system on its personal computers, Microsoft acquired an "installed base" on millions of IBM and IBM-compatible PCs. That base constituted an exceptional advantage, and created exceptional risks of monopoly, because of two characteristics of the software industry—increasing returns to scale and network externalities. First, because most of the costs of software lie in the design, marginal production costs are negligible. Production of additional units appears likely to lower average costs indefinitely. (I.e., the average cost curve never turns upward.) Second, an increase in the number of users of a particular item of software increases the number of other people with whom any user can share work. As a result, Microsoft's large installed base increases the incentive for independent software vendors to write compatible applications and thereby increases the value of its operating system to consumers.

The Department's 1994 complaint alleged a variety of anticompetitive practices, chiefly in Microsoft's licensing agreements with OEMs. Along with it, the Department filed a proposed consent decree limiting Microsoft's behavior, the product of negotiations between Microsoft, the

Department and European competition authorities. Most relevant here is § IV(E) of the decree:

> Microsoft shall not enter into any License Agreement in which the terms of that agreement are expressly or impliedly conditioned upon:
>
>> (i) the licensing of any other Covered Product, Operating System Software product or other product (provided, however, that this provision in and of itself shall not be construed to prohibit Microsoft from developing integrated products); or
>>
>> (ii) the OEM not licensing, purchasing, using or distributing any non-Microsoft product.

The Department sees a violation of § IV(E)(i) in Microsoft's marketing of Windows 95 and its web browser, Internet Explorer ("IE").

The Internet is a global network that links smaller networks of computers. The World Wide Web ("the Web") is the fastest-growing part of the Internet, composed of multimedia "pages" written in Hypertext Markup Language ("HTML") and connected to other pages by hypertext links. Browsers enable users to navigate the Web and to access information.

Most browsers are designed according to a "multi-platform" approach, with different versions for each of a variety of different operating systems. Joint Appendix ("J.A.") 81. Browsers also have the potential to serve as user interfaces and as platforms for applications (which could then be written for the APIs of a particular browser rather than of a particular operating system), providing some of the traditional functions of an operating system. Widespread use of multi-platform browsers as user interfaces has some potential to reduce any monopoly-increasing effects of network externalities in the operating system market. Browsers can enable the user to access applications stored on the Internet or local networks, or to operate applications that are independent of the operating system.

Microsoft has developed successive versions of IE, the first of which was initially released with Windows 95 in July 1995. Microsoft's Windows 95 license agreements have required OEMs to accept and install the software package as sent to them by Microsoft, including IE, and have prohibited OEMs from removing any features or functionality, i.e., capacity to perform functions such as browsing. J.A. 86–89.

The first three versions of IE were actually included on the Windows 95 "master" disk supplied to OEMs. Department Br. at 4; J.A. 1277–78. IE 4.0, by contrast, was initially distributed on a separate CD–ROM and OEMs were not required to install it. Microsoft intended to start requiring OEMs to preinstall IE 4.0 as part of Windows 95 in February 1998. On learning of Microsoft's plans, the Department became concerned that this practice violated § IV(E)(i) by effectively conditioning the license for Windows 95 on the license for IE 4.0, creating (in its view) what antitrust law terms a "tie-in" between the operating system and the browser.[2] (It is not clear why extension of Microsoft's established IE policy to IE 4.0 aroused the Department's concern.) It filed a petition seeking to hold Microsoft in civil contempt for its practices with respect to IE 3.0, and requesting "further" that the court explicitly order Microsoft not to employ similar agreements with respect to any version of IE.

A party seeking to hold another in contempt faces a heavy burden, needing to show by "clear and convincing evidence" that the alleged contemnor has violated a "clear and unambiguous" provision of the consent decree. *Armstrong v. Executive Office of the President*, 1 F.3d 1274, 1289 (D.C.Cir.1993). Finding § IV(E)(i) ambiguous, the district court denied the Department's contempt petition. But that left open the possibility that Microsoft's practices might in fact violate the consent decree (though not so clearly as to justify contempt), and the district court continued the proceedings in order to answer that question, appointing a special master not only to oversee discovery but also to propose findings of fact and conclusions of law. For the meantime, the court entered a preliminary injunction forbidding Microsoft

> from the practice of licensing the use of any Microsoft personal computer operating system software (including Windows 95 or any successor version thereof) on the condition, express or implied, that the licensee also license and preinstall any Microsoft Internet browser software (including Internet Explorer 3.0, 4.0, or any successor versions thereof).

J. A. 1300.

A detour is necessary to explore what this injunction meant. In some of its papers before the court the Department had argued for an order barring Microsoft from "forcing OEMs to accept and preinstall the software code" that it separately distributes at retail as IE 3.0. J.A. 996. Microsoft had responded that a Windows 95 operating system without IE software code simply would not function. The government characterized that assertion as "greatly overblown." J.A. 1237. The district court, in its justifying memorandum, referred to the injunction as barring Microsoft from "forcing OEMs to accept and preinstall the software code" separately distributed as IE 3.0, J.A. 1296–97; i.e., it employed the Department's exact words on the subject. After the injunction was issued, Microsoft and the Department had further consultations, at the end of which they entered a stipulation that Microsoft would be in compliance with the injunction if it extended to OEMs the options of (1) running the Add/Remove Programs utility with respect to IE 3.x and (2)

2. The Department's language suggests that two products, and indeed, two license agreements are at issue. See, e.g., the Department Br. at 4 ("Microsoft conditioned its OEM licenses to Windows 95 on OEMs' licensing Internet Explorer.") It is undisputed that OEMs enter into only one license agreement, which covers IE as part of Windows 95. J.A. 1274. Microsoft's central argument, of course, is that there is only one product. The terminology used in our introductory recitation of facts is of course not intended to resolve, or to reflect any resolution of, contested issues, and no inference as to those issues should be drawn from the wording of this section.

removing the IE icon from the desktop and from the Programs list in the Start menu and marking the file IEXPLORE.EXE "hidden." J.A. 1780–81. It appears not to be disputed that these alternate modes of compliance do not remove the IE software code, which indeed continues to play a role in providing non-browser functionality for Windows. In fact, browser functionality *itself* persists, and can be summoned up either by entering four lines of code or by running any application (such as Quicken) that contains the code necessary to invoke the functionality. J.A. 1649–55. The agreed-upon means of compliance simply enable the OEMs to make user access to IE more difficult.[3]

Microsoft appealed, as authorized by 28 U.S.C. § 1292(a)(1), and also sought mandamus directing the district court to revoke the reference to the special master.

II.

Microsoft claims at the outset that the district court, after finding no contempt, should simply have dismissed the Department's petition. But although the petition was styled simply as one for an order to show cause "Why Respondent Microsoft Corporation Should Not Be Held in Civil Contempt," its prayer for relief sought not only pure contempt remedies (such as the attention-grabbing request for $1,000,000 a day in damages), but also an order directing Microsoft to cease and desist from requiring "OEMs to license any version of Internet Explorer as an express or implied condition of licensing Windows 95." J.A. 41. This was plainly a request for clarification of the consent decree, pinning down its application to the browser issue. Such a clarification may properly take the form of an injunction. See *Brewster v. Dukakis*, 675 F.2d 1, 3–4 (1st Cir.1982). Indeed, as a consent decree contains an injunction already, a clarification naturally acquires the same character. (Of course, if the supplementary language goes beyond the consent decree, it is a modification rather than a clarification, and is governed by different standards. See, e.g., *United States v. Western Elec.* Co., 894 F.2d 430, 435 (D.C.Cir. 1990) (*"Manufacturing Appeal"*).) Although the framing of this request as part of a *remedy* for contempt may have been odd, Microsoft does not contest that the proceeding put in controversy the meaning of § IV(E)(i) as applied to its browser technology.

* * *

IV.

Section IV(E) arose from a 1993 complaint filed with the Directorate General IV of the European Union ("DG IV") (the principal competition authority in Europe). Novell, a rival software vendor, alleged that Microsoft was tying its MS–DOS operating system to the graphical user interface provided by Windows 3.11. Before the introduction of Windows

---

3. Additionally, by allowing OEMs to conceal IE, rather than to refuse it, the remedy fits poorly with the Department's tying theory. A tie-in is not affected by the purchaser's ability to discard the tied good.

95, which integrated the two, Microsoft marketed the DOS component and the Windows component of the operating system separately, and Windows 3.11 could be operated with other DOS products. But Novell, which marketed a competing DOS product, DR–DOS, complained that by means of specific marketing practices—particularly "per processor and per system licenses," J.A. 754—Microsoft was creating economic incentives for OEMs to preinstall MS–DOS as well as Windows 3.11, thereby using its power in the market for DOS-compatible graphical user interfaces (where it commanded a near 100% market share) to affect OEM choice in the DOS market.

During June 1994 negotiations with the Department, Microsoft proposed the possibility of a joint settlement, and representatives of DG IV participated in meetings in Brussels and later in Washington, D.C. On July 15, 1994, the three sides reached agreement and Microsoft and the Department signed a stipulation agreeing to entry of the consent decree, including § IV(E). Both Microsoft and the Department characterize § IV(E) as an "anti-tying" provision.

Microsoft and the Department engage in a brief battle over the extent to which antitrust law may be relevant to this dispute. Without wasting time on the parties' somewhat exaggerated positions, we can simply say that Microsoft is clearly right that the decree does not embody either the entirety of the Sherman Act or even all "tying" law under the Act, and the Department is equally right to point out that the consent decree emerged from antitrust claims, unresolved though they were, so that we must keep procompetitive goals in mind in the interpretive task.

As *[United States v.] Armour [& Co.]* makes clear, however, an antitrust consent decree cannot be read as though its animating spirit were solely the antitrust laws. "[T]he decree itself cannot be said to have a purpose; rather the parties have purposes, generally opposed to each other, and the resultant decree embodies as much of those opposing purposes as the respective parties have the bargaining power and skill to achieve." 402 U.S. 673, 681–82, 91 S.Ct. 1752, 29 L.Ed.2d 256 (1971).

The court's task, then, is to discern the bargain that the parties struck; this is the sense behind the proposition that consent decrees are to be interpreted as contracts. See, *e.g., [United States v.] ITT Continental Baking Co.*, 420 U.S. 223, 236–37, 95 S.Ct. 926, 43 L.Ed.2d 148 (1975); *Richardson [v. Edwards]*, 127 F.3d 97, 101 (D.C.Cir.1997); *United States v. Western Elec. Co.*, 894 F.2d 1387, 1390 (D.C.Cir.1990). To find the meaning of an ambiguous provision we look for the intent of the parties, just as we would with a contract. See *Western Elec. Co.*, 12 F.3d at 231–32 (reading ambiguous provision of consent decree "in light of the parties' jointly intended purpose" (internal quotation omitted)); *NRM Corp. v. Hercules, Inc.*, 758 F.2d 676, 681–82 (D.C.Cir.1985) (contract interpretation). In that quest we may rely on the same aids to construction as we would when interpreting an ambiguous contract, including "the circumstances surrounding the formation of the consent order." See *ITT*, 420 U.S. at 238, 95 S.Ct. 926.

Section IV(E)(i) represented the parties' agreed "solution" to the problem posed by the Novell complaint. The practices complained of there, coupled with the decree's explicit acceptance of Windows 95, establish the competing models that guide our resolution of the present dispute. Whatever else § IV(E)(i) does, it must forbid a tie-in between Windows 3.11 and MS–DOS, and it must permit Windows 95. Thus if the relation between Windows 95 and IE is similar to the relation between Windows 3.11 and MS–DOS, the link is presumably barred by § IV(E)(i). On the other hand, a counter-analogy is Windows 95 itself, which the decree explicitly recognizes as a single "product" (it defines it as a "Covered Product," § II(1)(v)), even though, as we have said, Windows 95 combines the functionalities of a graphical interface and an operating system. If the Windows 95/IE combination is like the MS-DOS/graphical interface combination that comprises Windows 95 itself, then it must be permissible.

The parties offer us little help in picking the correct analogy. Both propose readings of § IV(E)(i) that fail to reconcile its language with the facts of the Novell complaint and the later permissible release of Windows 95. The Department claims that § IV(E)(i) prohibits Microsoft from bundling together a Covered Product and anything that "Microsoft simultaneously treats" and "antitrust law regards" as "a distinct commercial product." Department Br. at 37–38. It says that the browser-Windows pair is caught in the first filter (Microsoft's treatment of IE as a separate product) because Microsoft provides it separately to end users, sells versions of IE 4 for different operating systems, advertises IE 4, tracks its performance in a "browser market," and distributes it on a separate CD–ROM. J.A. 32–37. For antitrust criteria, the Department draws on *Jefferson Parish Hosp. District No. 2 v. Hyde*, 466 U.S. 2, 104 S.Ct. 1551, 80 L.Ed.2d 2 (1984), for the proposition that products are distinct for tying purposes if consumer demand exists for each separately. (The Department notes correctly that this does not require demand for one product without the other but simply demand for the two products from different sellers. See *id.* at 19 & n. 30, 104 S.Ct. 1551.)

We are not convinced that these indicia necessarily point to separateness, especially those that depend on Microsoft's treatment. Microsoft plausibly characterizes the IE that it provides to end users as an operating system upgrade, as does its rival Netscape, and the Department offers no means of distinguishing an upgrade from a separate product. Versions developed for different operating systems may be better understood as different products altogether; hence, their relevance to separateness is obscure. Distribution of software code on a separate CD–ROM shows nothing at all about whether the code is integrated into an operating system (software for an operating system that is clearly a single product may take up many disks).

The Department's interpretation of the "integrated products" proviso does nothing to remedy its reading of the body of § IV(e)(i). On the Department's account, the proviso allows Microsoft to incorporate new features into an operating system and offer the package to OEMs—as long as it and antitrust law do not simultaneously treat those features as "a distinct commercial product." Department Br. at 37–38. But these are just the criteria deployed to argue that IE is an "other product"; if the proviso merely reiterates them (to say that what is not an "other product" is "integrated"), it does nothing. And while the Department says that the proviso would protect Microsoft from a charge that it had violated the decree by adopting a technology incompatible with other firms' products, Department Br. at 37 n.17, it is not apparent how § IV(E)(i)'s ban might prohibit such conduct nor how, if it did, the proviso on integration would help it. In short, the Department effectively reads the proviso out of § IV(e)(i).

But the most immediate problem with this reading is that it produces the wrong result on the Novell allegations. In its attempts to define the "product" IE, the Department consistently invokes the concept of "browser functionality." Department Br. at 10; Department Motion for Contempt, J.A. 1317–19; Department Reply Memorandum in Support of Motion for Contempt, J.A. 1424, 1429. But if functionality is the criterion of identity (which the Department asserts so as to claim that the "browser functionality" in Windows 95 is the same product as IE 4 for other operating systems), Windows 95 looks like a tie-in of two products (MS–DOS and Windows 3.11) that were sold separately in the market: it contains the functionalities of both. On the Department's reading, it should thus be prohibited unless Microsoft refrains from marketing MS–DOS separately. There is some suggestion that Microsoft has in fact continued to license MS–DOS separately, at least to end users. Microsoft Reply Br. at 15–16. More significantly, the consent decree does not condition its approval of Windows 95 on Microsoft's marketing behavior with respect to MS–DOS. The failure to produce the right result when applied to Windows 95, one of the situations clearly resolved by the decree, is a fatal flaw.

* * *

Curiously, in both parties' readings Microsoft's behavior determines the permissibility of conditioned licensing. This would be no defect if the behavior were in some way relevant to the economic principles of tie-ins. But it is not. The Department offers no theory as to how a seller's abstaining from separate marketing of the tied good might blunt the possible anticompetitive effects of bundling.[10] It seems especially beside the point where the goods are complements used in fixed proportions. A monopolist who ties two such goods has no obvious reason to market the tied good separately: since all buyers of the tying good will also take the

---

10. The hospital in *Jefferson Parish* surely did not offer the tied good (anesthesia) separately from the tying good (surgery), but this fact played no role in the Court's decision.

tied good, the residual market for the tied good will be minimal. If the concern is that the tie-in makes it more difficult for competitors to enter the market for the *tying* good (because they must also offer the tied good), see *Grappone, Inc. v. Subaru of New England*, 858 F.2d 792, 795–96 (1st Cir.1988) (Breyer, J.), separate marketing of the tied good actually mitigates the posited harm by facilitating new entry into the market for the tying good. Thus both readings allow legitimation by behavior that is either irrelevant or actively harmful.

We think it quite possible, however, to find a construction of § IV(E)(i) that is consistent with the antitrust laws and accomplishes the parties' evident desires on entering the decree. The Department and DG IV were concerned with the alleged anticompetitive effects of tie-ins. Microsoft's goal was to preserve its freedom to design products that consumers would like. Antitrust scholars have long recognized the undesirability of having courts oversee product design, and any dampening of technological innovation would be at cross-purposes with antitrust law. Thus, a simple way to harmonize the parties' desires is to read the integration proviso of § IV(E)(i) as permitting any genuine technological integration, regardless of whether elements of the integrated package are marketed separately.

This reading requires us, of course, to give substantive content to the concept of integration. We think that an "integrated product" is most reasonably understood as a product that combines functionalities (which may also be marketed separately and operated together) in a way that offers advantages unavailable if the functionalities are bought separately and combined by the purchaser.

The point of the test is twofold and may be illustrated by its application to the paradigm case of the Novell complaint and the subsequent release of Windows 95. First, "integration" suggests a degree of unity, something beyond merely placing disks in the same box. If an OEM or end user (referred to generally as "the purchaser") could buy separate products and combine them himself to produce the "integrated product," then the integration looks like a sham. If Microsoft had simply placed the disks for Windows 3.11 and MS–DOS in one package and covered it with a single license agreement, it would have offered purchasers nothing they could not get by buying the separate products and combining them on their own.[11]

---

11. The same analysis would apply to peripherals. If, for example, Microsoft tried to bundle its mouse with the operating system, it would have to show that the mouse/operating system package worked better if combined by Microsoft than it would if combined by OEMs. This is quite different from showing that the mouse works better with the operating system than other mice do. Compare Sep. Op. at 957. See X Areeda, Elhauge & Hovenkamp, *Antitrust Law* ¶ 1746b. Problems seem unlikely to arise with peripherals, because their physical existence makes it easier to identify the act of combination. It seems unlikely that a plausible claim could be made that a mouse and an operating system were integrated in the sense that neither could be said to exist separately. An operating system used with a different mouse does not seem like a different product. But Windows 95 without IE's code will not boot, J.A. 1623, and adding a rival browser will not fix this. If the add/remove utility is run to hide the IE 4 technologies, Windows 95

Windows 95, by contrast, unites the two functionalities in a way that purchasers could not; it is not simply a graphical user interface running on top of MS–DOS. Windows 95 is integrated in the sense that the two functionalities—DOS and graphical interface—do not exist separately: the code that is required to produce one also produces the other. Of course one can imagine that code being sold on two different disks, one containing all the code necessary for an operating system, the other with all the code necessary for a graphical interface. But as the code in the two would largely overlap, it would be odd to speak of either containing a discrete functionality. Rather, each would represent a disabled version of Windows 95. The customer could then "repair" each by installing them both on a single computer, but in such a case it would not be meaningful to speak of the customer "combining" two products. Windows 95 is an example of what Professor Areeda calls "physical or technological inter-linkage that the customer cannot perform." X Areeda, Elhauge & Hovenkamp, *Antitrust Law* § 1746b at 227, 228 (1996).

So the combination offered by the manufacturer must be different from what the purchaser could create from the separate products on his own. The second point is that it must also be better in some respect; there should be some technological value to integration. Manufacturers can stick products together in ways that purchasers cannot without the link serving any purpose but an anticompetitive one. The concept of integration should exclude a case where the manufacturer has done nothing more than to metaphorically "bolt" two products together, as would be true if Windows 95 were artificially rigged to crash if IEXP-LORE.EXE were deleted. Cf. *ILC Peripherals Leasing Corp. v. International Business Machines Corp.*, 448 F.Supp. 228, 233 (N.D.Cal.1978) ("If IBM had simply bolted a disk pack or data module into a drive and sold the two items as a unit for a single price, the 'aggregation' would clearly have been an illegal tying arrangement.") *aff'd per curiam sub nom. Memorex Corp. v. International Business Machines Corp.*, 636 F.2d 1188 (9th Cir.1980); X Areeda, Elhauge & Hovenkamp, *Antitrust Law* ¶ 1746 at 227 (discussing literal bolting). Thus if there is no suggestion that the product is superior to the purchaser's combination in some respect, it cannot be deemed integrated.

It might seem difficult to put the two elements discussed above together. If purchasers cannot combine the two functionalities to make Windows 95, it might seem that there is nothing to test Windows 95 against in search of the required superiority. But purchasers can combine the functionalities in their stand-alone incarnations. They can install MS–DOS and Windows 3.11. The test for the integration of Windows 95 then comes down to the question of whether its integrated design offers benefits when compared to a purchaser's combination of corresponding stand-alone functionalities. The decree's evident embrace of Windows 95 as a permissible single product can be taken as manifesting the parties' agreement that it met this test.

reverts to an earlier version, OEM service release ("OSR") 2.0. J.A. 1660–61.

The short answer is thus that integration may be considered genuine if it is beneficial when compared to a purchaser combination. But we do not propose that in making this inquiry the court should embark on product design assessment. In antitrust law, from which this whole proceeding springs, the courts have recognized the limits of their institutional competence and have on that ground rejected theories of "technological tying." A court's evaluation of a claim of integration must be narrow and deferential. As the Fifth Circuit put it, "[S]uch a violation must be limited to those instances where the technological factor tying the hardware to the software has been designed for the purpose of tying the products, rather than to achieve some technologically beneficial result. Any other conclusion would enmesh the courts in a technical inquiry into the justifiability of product innovations." *Response of Carolina, Inc. v. Leasco Response, Inc.*, 537 F.2d 1307, 1330 (5th Cir.1976).

In fact, Microsoft did, in negotiations, suggest such an understanding of "integrated." In response to the Department and DG IV's statement of concern about tying, it asserted its right to "continue to develop integrated products like [Windows 95] *that provide technological benefits to end users*." J.A. 756 (emphasis added). Microsoft later withdrew this qualifying phrase, J.A. 760, in order, it claims, to avoid the application of "vague or subjective criteria"—though why the absence of criteria should cure a vagueness problem is unclear. But we do not think that removing the phrase can drain the word "integrated" of all meaning, and we do not accept the suggestion that the Department and DG IV bargained for an "integrated products" proviso so boundless as to swallow § IV(E)(i). Significantly, Microsoft assured the Department and DG IV that the elimination of the qualifying phrase "did not represent a substantive change." J.A. 761.

We believe this understanding is consistent with tying law. The Court in *Eastman Kodak Co. v. Image Tech. Servs.*, 504 U.S. 451, 112 S.Ct. 2072, 119 L.Ed.2d 265 (1992), for example, found parts and service separate products because sufficient consumer demand existed to make separate provision efficient. See *id.* at 462, 112 S.Ct. 2072. But we doubt that it would have subjected a self-repairing copier to the same analysis; i.e., the separate markets for parts and service would not suggest that such an innovation was really a tie-in. (The separate opinion, we take it, makes roughly the same point by its observation about digital cameras. See Sep. Op. at 958.) Similarly, Professor Areeda argues that new products integrating functionalities in a useful way should be considered single products regardless of market structure. See X Areeda, Elhauge & Hovenkamp, *Antitrust Law* ¶ 1746b.

We emphasize that this analysis does not require a court to find that an integrated product is superior to its stand-alone rivals. See *ILC Peripherals Leasing Corp. v. International Business Machines Corp.*, 458 F.Supp. 423, 439 (N.D.Cal.1978) ("Where there is a difference of opinion as to the advantages of two alternatives which can both be defended from an engineering standpoint, the court will not allow itself to be enmeshed 'in a technical inquiry into the justifiability of product innovations.' ") (quoting *Leasco*, 537 F.2d at 1330), *aff'd per curiam sub nom. Memorex Corp. v. IBM Corp.*, 636 F.2d 1188 (9th Cir.1980). We do not read § IV(E)(i) to "put[ ] judges and juries in the unwelcome position of designing computers." IX Areeda, *Antitrust Law* ¶ 1700j at 15 (1991). The question is not whether the integration is a net plus but merely whether there is a plausible claim that it brings some advantage. Whether or not this is the appropriate test for antitrust law generally, we believe it is the only sensible reading of § IV(E)(i).

On the facts before us, Microsoft has clearly met the burden of ascribing facially plausible benefits to its integrated design as compared to an operating system combined with a stand-alone browser such as Netscape's Navigator. Incorporating browsing functionality into the operating system allows applications to avail themselves of that functionality without starting up a separate browser application. J.A. 944, 965. Further, components of IE 3.0 and even more IE 4—especially the HTML reader—provide system services not directly related to Web browsing, enhancing the functionality of a wide variety of applications. J.A. 607–22, 1646–48. Finally, IE 4 technologies are used to upgrade some aspects of the operating system unrelated to Web browsing. For example, they are used to let users customize their "Start" menus, making favored applications more readily available. J.A. 490–95; 1662–64. They also make possible "thumbnail" previews of files on the computer's hard drive, using the HTML reader to display a richer view of the files' contents. J.A. 1664–69. Even the Department apparently concedes that integration of functionality into the operating system can bring benefits; responding to a comment on the proposed 1994 consent decree (which the Department published in the Federal Register as required by the Tunney Act), it stated that "a broad injunction against such behavior generally would not be consistent with the public interest." 59 Fed.Reg. 59426, 59428 (Nov. 17, 1994).

The conclusion that integration brings benefits does not end the inquiry we have traced out. It is also necessary that there be some reason Microsoft, rather than the OEMs or end users, must bring the functionalities together. See X Areeda, Elhauge & Hovenkamp, *Antitrust Law* ¶ 1746b at 227; ¶ 1747 at 229. Some more subtleties emerge at this stage, parallel to those encountered in determining the integrated status of Windows 95. Microsoft provides OEMs with IE 4 on a separate CD–ROM (a fact to which the Department attaches great significance). It might seem, superficially, that the OEM is just as capable as Microsoft of combining the browser and the operating system.

But the issue is not which firm's employees should run particular disks or CD–ROMs. A program may be provided on three disks—Windows 95 certainly could be—but it is not therefore three programs which the user combines. Software code by its nature is susceptible to division and combination in a way that physical products are not; if the feasibility of installation from multiple disks meant that the customer was doing the combination, no software product could ever count as integrated. The idea that in installing IE 4 an OEM is combining two stand-alone products is defective in the same way that it would be nonsensical to say that an OEM installing Windows 95 is itself "combining" DOS functionality and a graphical interface. As the discussion above indicates, IE 3 and IE 4 add to the operating system features that cannot be included without also including browsing functionality. See J.A. 1661–68. Thus, as was the case with Windows 95, the products—the full functionality of the operating system when upgraded by IE 4 and the "browser functionality" of IE 4—do not exist separately. This strikes us as an essential point. If the products have no separate existence, it is incorrect to speak of the purchaser combining them. Purchasers who end up with the Windows 95/IE package may have installed code from more than one disk; they may have taken the browser out of hiding;[18] they may have upgraded their operating system—indeed, Netscape characterizes the installation of IE 4 as "really an OS [operating system] upgrade." J.A. 589. But they have not combined two distinct products.

What, then, counts as the combination that brings together the two functionalities? Since neither fully exists separately, we think the only sensible answer is that the act of combination is the creation of the design that knits the two together. OEMs *cannot* do this: if Microsoft presented them with an operating system and a stand-alone browser application, rather than with the interpenetrating design of Windows 95 and IE 4, the OEMs could not combine them in the way in which Microsoft has integrated IE 4 into Windows 95. They could not, for example, make the operating system use the browser's HTML reader to provide a richer view of information on the computer's hard drive, J.A. 1665—not without changing the code to create an integrated browser. This reprogramming would be absurdly inefficient. Consequently, it seems clear that there is a reason why the integration must take place at Microsoft's level. This analysis essentially replays our comparison of Windows 95 to a bundle of MS–DOS and Windows 3.11 and concludes that the Windows 95/IE package more closely resembles Windows 95 than it does the bundle. The factual conclusion is, of course, subject to reexamination on a more complete record. On the facts before us, however, we are inclined to conclude that the Windows 95/IE package is a genuine integration; consequently, § IV(E)(i) does not bar Microsoft from offering it as one product.

* * *

A few words with respect to our colleague's separate opinion may clarify our position. Judge Wald suggests that "the prohibition and the proviso could reasonably be construed to state that Microsoft may offer

---

18. The preliminary injunction, as construed by the parties' later stipulation, treats Microsoft as in compliance if it allows the options of (1) running the Add/Remove Programs utility with respect to IE 3.x and (2) removing the IE icon from the desktop and from the Programs list in the Start menu and marking the file IEXP-LORE.EXE "hidden." See above at p. 7. The injunction's evidently unique status as a remedy for a "tying" complaint, requiring the defendant merely to allow an intermediary to hide the allegedly tied product, suggests the oddity of treating as separate products functionalities that are integrated in the way that Windows 95 and IE are.

an 'integrated' product to OEMs under one license only if the integrated product achieves synergies great enough to justify Microsoft's extension of its monopoly to an otherwise distinct market." Sep. Op. at 958. We are at a loss to understand how a section that (1) articulates a prohibition and (2) sets a limit on the reach of the prohibition can be read to state a balancing test. Apart from the lack of textual support, we think that a balancing test that requires courts to weigh the "synergies" of an integrated product against the "evidence of distinct markets," Sep. Op. at 959, is not feasible in any predictable or useful way. Courts are ill equipped to evaluate the benefits of high-tech product design,[20] and even could they place such an evaluation on one side of the balance, the strength of the "evidence of distinct markets," proposed for the other side of the scale, seems quite incommensurable. Both *Jefferson Parish* and *Eastman Kodak* use their "distinct markets" analysis in a binary fashion: markets are distinct or they are not. See 466 U.S. at 21–22, 104 S.Ct. 1551, 504 U.S. at 462, 112 S.Ct. 2072. If, as the record suggests, Microsoft proposed modification of the integration proviso because of concern about "vague or subjective criteria," J.A. 760, an interpretation requiring courts to weigh evidence that establishes distinctness (or does not) against a sliding scale of net synergistic value looks like the most total transvaluation one can imagine.

Institutional competence may not have been foremost in the parties' minds in drafting the consent decree, and judicial inability to apply a test does not ipso facto mean that the parties did not intend it. But if they did intend a balancing test, they kept that intent well hidden. Nothing in their contemporaneous conduct (or in the conduct of anyone, at any time) suggests that they contemplated a balancing inquiry. Windows 95 was not subjected to any such analysis, though the markets it unified were substantial and obviously distinct. J.A. 790–96. Indeed, one might think that an especially compelling case would be required to "justify Microsoft's extension of its monopoly," Sep. Op. at 958, via Windows 95. Windows 95 leveraged Microsoft's Windows 3.11 market power into the operating system market, where network externalities are most apparent. See *Microsoft*, 56 F.3d at 1451. According to the separate opinion, Windows 95 should have required the utmost justification. But nothing suggests that it was analyzed that way, and it seems more likely that it passed muster not because the synergies of its integration outweighed the evidence of distinct markets but because it was, simply, integrated.

The view expressed in the separate opinion seems sure to thwart Microsoft's legitimate desire to continue to integrate products that had been separate—and hence necessarily would have been provided in distinct markets. By its very nature "integration" represents a change from a state of affairs in which products were separate, to one in which

---

20. Our colleague seems to hint that one way to perform this evaluation is to examine whether the integrated product "overwhelm[s]" the separate market. Sep. Op. at 961. But data on market perfor- mance will obviously not be available when the new product is introduced, and in any case, the overwhelming of the separate market is precisely what is feared and may simply indicate anticompetitive practices.

they are no longer. By focusing on the historical fact of separate provision, the separate opinion puts a thumb on the scale and requires Microsoft to counterbalance with evidence courts are not equipped to evaluate. We do not think that this makes sense in terms of the text of the consent decree, the evidence of the parties' intents, the values the decree was presumably intended to promote, or the competence of the judiciary.

* * *

At this stage, then, the Department has not shown a reasonable probability of success on the merits. Given this failure, there is no reason to allow the preliminary injunction to remain in effect pending a proper hearing, and we reverse the district court's grant.

* * *

WALD, CIRCUIT JUDGE, concurring in part and dissenting in part:

I depart from my colleagues only as to their interpretation of the consent decree, which I believe unnecessarily narrows the scope of the inquiry that the district court may conduct on remand. First, the majority opinion appears to decide that there is only one reasonable interpretation of section IV(E)(i), notwithstanding the fact that we are remanding for further factual development that may well be relevant to the most faithful interpretation of the section. Second, although the majority claims to have rooted its interpretation in antitrust law in accordance with the intent of the parties, it interprets section IV(E)(i) in a way that is, in fact, inconsistent with at least some governing precedent. For these reasons, I write separately to suggest that there may be an interpretation of section IV(E)(i) more consonant with the intent of the drafters and the weight of antitrust law. If facts are found on remand to support such an alternative interpretation, it should not be foreclosed by the majority opinion.

Under the majority's interpretation, the proviso of section IV(E)(i), which says that section IV(E)(i) "in and of itself shall not be construed to prohibit Microsoft from developing integrated products," is too safe a harbor with too easily navigable an entrance: So long as Microsoft has created a design to combine functionalities in a way that offers the ultimate user some "plausible" advantage otherwise unavailable, Microsoft may require OEMs to install the resulting creation in its entirety, without fear of running aground on the main prohibition of section IV(E)(i) (which prohibits Microsoft from entering into any license agreement "in which the terms of that agreement are expressly or impliedly conditioned upon" the licensing of any "other product"). To my mind, this reading does not impose nearly enough scrutiny on "integration" and renders the central prohibition of section IV(E)(i) largely useless.
* * *

Another—some might say more—reasonable reading of section IV(E)(i) would give much greater weight to the main prohibition of the section. On its face, that prohibition forbids Microsoft from requiring

OEMs to accept under one agreement any offering that is in reality two products: a "Covered Product" and, for purposes of this case, an "other product." The proviso, on the other hand, permits Microsoft to develop and license "integrated" products. Read together, I think the prohibition and the proviso could reasonably be construed to state that Microsoft may offer an "integrated" product to OEMs under one license only if the integrated product achieves synergies great enough to justify Microsoft's extension of its monopoly to an otherwise distinct market.

As I explain below, and as I read the majority opinion to agree, the consent decree was drafted against a backdrop of antitrust law. Under antitrust law, two products are considered distinct if there exists "sufficient consumer demand so that it is efficient for a firm to provide [the first product] separately from [the second]." *Eastman Kodak Co. v. Image Technical Servs., Inc.,* 504 U.S. 451, 462, 112 S.Ct. 2072, 119 L.Ed.2d 265 (1992). The difficulty in this case is that technological evolution can change the boundaries of what is "efficient." For example, *Eastman Kodak* cites cameras and film as examples of two functionally linked products for which there exist separate markets. *See id.* at 463, 112 S.Ct. 2072. But antitrust law presumably would not bar the development of digital cameras, which do not require film in any conventional sense.

Thus, antitrust law cannot avoid determining whether a particular technological development has occurred because it is efficient or merely because it permits a monopolist to extend its monopoly to a new market. Software code is a particularly stark example of why such analysis is essential if antitrust concepts are to survive at all. Here, the majority effectively exempts software products from antitrust analysis by stating that "[s]oftware code by its nature is susceptible to division and combination in a way that physical products are not." Maj. Op. at 948. But this to me is an argument for closer, rather than more relaxed, scrutiny of Microsoft's claims of integration. An operating-system designer who wished to turn two products into one could easily commingle the code of two formerly separate products, arranging it so that "Windows 95 without IE's code will not boot," *id.* at 949 n. 11, so that Windows 95 without Internet Explorer would "represent a disabled version of Windows 95," *id.* at 948, and so that Internet Explorer instructs the Add/Remove function to leave so much of that program in place that "four lines of programming" will suffice to activate it, *see id.* at 952 n. 17. This is not to say that commingling of code is *per se* pernicious or even suspicious. Rather, the point is that commingling alone is not sufficient evidence of true integration; the courts must consider whether the resulting product confers benefits on the consumer that justify a product's bridging of two formerly separate markets.

Although this task is difficult, it is by no means the impossible project that the majority suggests. As I explain below, traditional antitrust analysis, and the usual methods of the law, provide the courts with a range of ways to address the ultimate question of efficiency. *See, e.g., PSI Repair Servs., Inc. v. Honeywell, Inc.,* 104 F.3d 811, 817 (6th

Cir.1997), *cert. denied,*——U.S.——, 117 S.Ct. 2434, 138 L.Ed.2d 195 (1997) (citation omitted) ("While we are mindful of the various efficiency gains that can accrue to both suppliers and consumers from bundling certain products together, we are confident that the antitrust laws provide the tools to distinguish between meritorious and non-meritorious claims."). As I see it, the efficiency calculus takes two factors into account. The first is evidence that there are real benefits to the consumer associated with integrating two software products; I call these benefits "synergies."[3] The second is independent evidence, of the type that is usually employed in antitrust analysis, that a genuine market exists for the two products provided separately. For example, Windows 95 includes a built-in calculator program with relatively few functions. Although there may be few synergies associated with building this program into the operating system, there is also not likely to be much of a market for this program provided separately, and this factor must be taken into account. Market evidence of demand for independent products will spare the courts from the need to speculate in the abstract about considerations of efficiency.

Taken together, then, these two factors generate a balancing test. The greater the evidence of distinct markets, the more of a showing of synergy Microsoft must make in order to justify incorporating what would otherwise be an "other" product into an "integrated" whole. If the evidence of distinct markets is weak, then Microsoft can get by with a fairly modest showing (although perhaps not the minimal showing required by the majority). But if there are clearly two distinct markets, then Microsoft would need to demonstrate substantial synergies in order to compel OEMs to accept a new "integrated" product that bridges those markets. In other words, the decree does not purport to chill Microsoft's technological development of its products by prohibiting a product outright merely because it incorporates new features—the proviso makes clear that Microsoft is free to design such products and to market their benefits to OEMs such that OEMs overwhelmingly choose the new product over a competitor's product. The proviso thus becomes a safe harbor only for those integrations in which the "other product" has been (legitimately) technologically subsumed in a greater whole.

Thus, the real question for purposes of determining if a violation of the degree has taken place is whether a new combination of formerly separate functionalities still contains an "other product" or if the two functionalities have been legitimately blended, or "integrated," and so

---

3. The majority questions the institutional competence of the courts to judge the level of synergy provided by an "integrated" product. *See* Maj. Op. at 949–50. By no means do I endorse routine judicial intervention in the details of product design. But I also do not endorse (as the majority comes close to doing) judicial abdication in the face of complexity. The courts are certainly capable of determining whether a particular integration offers any synergistic benefits at all and whether these benefits are minimal, significant, or great. As this is a factual determination, they may be guided in this effort by, for example, affidavits, consumer surveys, and other evidence presented by the parties as well as testimony from experts selected by the parties or by the court. Certainly this approach is preferable to the majority's proposal, under which antitrust law surrenders to any bona fide assertion of a "plausible" benefit of integration.

have lost their former identities and become one product to which the prohibition no longer applies. (This, of course, is a factual question to be explored on remand.) As I have already suggested, and as the majority agrees, given the context in which section IV(E)(i) arose, it is appropriate to look to antitrust law as a guide to determining when such integration occurs. Although the majority opinion claims that its construction is consistent with antitrust law, *see* Maj. Op. at 951, it does not, in my view, give due weight to the Supreme Court's holding in *Jefferson Parish Hospital District No. 2 v. Hyde*, 466 U.S. 2, 104 S.Ct. 1551, 80 L.Ed.2d 2 (1984), the leading guide to the separate product determination. * * *

The tying analysis is, of course, a pragmatic one. For example, no one would claim that tying law was violated by the practice of selling shoes in pairs despite the possible existence of some market for only left shoes (among those with only one foot, for example, or with differently sized feet). Likewise, it is in all likelihood not a tying violation for *Jefferson Parish*'s hospital to require that patients accept the hospital's receptionists (instead of bringing their own) and accept the cleaning services and meals provided in their rooms (instead of making other arrangements) and to charge patients for these services. This is so even though there might be a limited group of patients who would prefer to make their own arrangements for receptionists, cleaning, and meals. *Cf. Jefferson Parish.*, 466 U.S. at 22 n. 36, 104 S.Ct. 1551 (noting that the antitrust analysis might differ for "radiologists, pathologists, and other types of hospital-based physicians"); *see also Jack Walters & Sons Corp. v. Morton Bldg., Inc.*, 737 F.2d 698, 703 (7th Cir.1984) (noting that "[t]he practice has been to classify a product as a single product if there are rather obvious economies of joint provision"). In the case of the shoes, the receptionist, and the cleaning, a judgment is made that the benefits of joint provision clearly predominate over what is undoubtedly a minimal separate market (if one can be said to exist at all). In the case of the anesthesiologist, by contrast, the Court found that the claimed benefits—24–hour anesthesiology coverage, flexible scheduling, and facilitation of work routine, professional standards, and equipment maintenance—were not sufficient to justify joint provision because there was a very substantial market for anesthesiologists' services and because these benefits could be achieved without the forced tie (by, for example, promoting the benefits of the hospital's anesthesiologists to patients and setting standards of compatibility). *See Jefferson Parish*, 466 U.S. at 25 n. 42, 104 S.Ct. 1551. Under this doctrine, then, an "integrated" product cannot simply be one where *some* benefit exists as a result of joint provision, since the hospital easily met this standard. Rather, "integration" must mean something more: a combination of functionalities in which the synergies created predominate over the existence of a separate market—in other words, where the benefits of the combination dissuade consumers from seeking and suppliers from providing the alleged "tied" product.

* * *

Note

Having failed in its attack upon Microsoft's practice of incorporating its Internet Explorer browser in Windows on the theory of violation of the consent decree, the Justice Department filed an antitrust suit to attack the same practice and related practices on the theory of violation of the Sherman Act. Nineteen states and the District of Columbia joined as plaintiffs. The District Court's "Findings of Fact" in this case are below.

UNITED STATES v. MICROSOFT CORP.

NEW YORK v. MICROSOFT CORP.

United States District Court, District of Columbia, 1999.
84 F.Supp.2d 9.

JACKSON, DISTRICT JUDGE.

FINDINGS OF FACT

These consolidated civil antitrust actions alleging violations of the Sherman Act, §§ 1 and 2, and various state statutes by the defendant Microsoft Corporation were tried to the Court, sitting without a jury, between October 19, 1998, and June 24, 1999. The Court has considered the record evidence submitted by the parties, made determinations as to its relevancy and materiality, assessed the credibility of the testimony of the witnesses, both written and oral, and ascertained for its purposes the probative significance of the documentary and visual evidence presented. Upon the record before the Court as of July 28, 1999, at the close of the admission of evidence, pursuant to Fed.R.Civ.P. 52(a), the Court finds the following facts to have been proved by a preponderance of the evidence. * * *

* * *

The debut of Internet Explorer and its rapid improvement gave Netscape an incentive to improve Navigator's quality at a competitive rate. The inclusion of Internet Explorer with Windows at no separate charge increased general familiarity with the Internet and reduced the cost to the public of gaining access to it, at least in part because it compelled Netscape to stop charging for Navigator. These actions thus contributed to improving the quality of Web browsing software, lowering its cost, and increasing its availability, thereby benefitting consumers.

To the detriment of consumers, however, Microsoft has done much more than develop innovative browsing software of commendable quality and offer it bundled with Windows at no additional charge. As has been shown, Microsoft also engaged in a concerted series of actions designed to protect the applications barrier to entry, and hence its monopoly power, from a variety of middleware threats, including Netscape's Web browser and Sun's implementation of Java. Many of these actions have harmed consumers in ways that are immediate and easily discernible.

They have also caused less direct, but nevertheless serious and far-reaching, consumer harm by distorting competition.

* * *

Many of the tactics that Microsoft has employed have also harmed consumers indirectly by unjustifiably distorting competition. The actions that Microsoft took against Navigator hobbled a form of innovation that had shown the potential to depress the applications barrier to entry sufficiently to enable other firms to compete effectively against Microsoft in the market for Intel-compatible PC operating systems. That competition would have conduced to consumer choice and nurtured innovation. The campaign against Navigator also retarded widespread acceptance of Sun's Java implementation. This campaign, together with actions that Microsoft took with the sole purpose of making it difficult for developers to write Java applications with technologies that would allow them to be ported between Windows and other platforms, impeded another form of innovation that bore the potential to diminish the applications barrier to entry. There is insufficient evidence to find that, absent Microsoft's actions, Navigator and Java already would have ignited genuine competition in the market for Intel-compatible PC operating systems. It is clear, however, that Microsoft has retarded, and perhaps altogether extinguished, the process by which these two middleware technologies could have facilitated the introduction of competition into an important market.

Most harmful of all is the message that Microsoft's actions have conveyed to every enterprise with the potential to innovate in the computer industry. Through its conduct toward Netscape, IBM, Compaq, Intel, and others, Microsoft has demonstrated that it will use its prodigious market power and immense profits to harm any firm that insists on pursuing initiatives that could intensify competition against one of Microsoft's core products. Microsoft's past success in hurting such companies and stifling innovation deters investment in technologies and businesses that exhibit the potential to threaten Microsoft. The ultimate result is that some innovations that would truly benefit consumers never occur for the sole reason that they do not coincide with Microsoft's self-interest.

* * *

Note

In related proceedings, the court went on to find that Microsoft had violated the antitrust laws and ruled that Microsoft should be broken up into two companies—an operating systems company and an applications software company. 87 F.Supp.2d 30 (2000); 97 F.Supp.2d 59 (2000). The Court also ruled that Microsoft should stop a number of specific practices that it found to be in violation of the antitrust law. Microsoft promptly appealed. The appeal has gone to the D.C. Circuit because the Supreme Court denied the request of the Justice Department to take the case directly. 2000 WL 1052937. Microsoft's appeal had not been decided as this book went to press.

C. AGREEMENTS IN VIOLATION OF THE ANTITRUST LAWS

IN RE INTEL CORP.

Federal Trade Commission, March, 1999.
Docket No. 9288 (Westlaw, Federal Antitrust & Trade Regulation Combined Antitrust & Trade Regulation Materials (FATR–ALL))
http://www.ftc.gov/os/1999/9903/d09288intelagreement.htm

AGREEMENT CONTAINING CONSENT ORDER

The Agreement herein, by and between Intel Corporation, a corporation, by its duly authorized officer, herein sometimes referred to as respondent, and its attorney, and counsel for the Federal Trade Commission, is entered into in accordance with the Commission's Rule governing consent order procedures. In accordance therewith the parties hereby agree that:

1. Respondent Intel Corporation is a corporation organized, existing and doing business under and by virtue of the laws of the State of Delaware with its office and principal place of business located at Mission College Boulevard, Santa Clara, California 95052.

2. Respondent has been served with a copy of the complaint issued by the Federal Trade Commission charging it with violation of section 5 of the Federal Trade Commission Act, 15 U.S.C. 45, and has filed answers to said complaint denying said charge.

3. Respondent admits all the jurisdictional facts set forth in Paragraphs 1 and 3 of the Commission's complaint in this proceeding.

4. Respondent waives:

    a.   any further procedural steps;

    b.   the requirement that the Commission's Decision contain a statement of findings of fact and conclusions of law;

    c.   all rights to seek judicial review or otherwise to challenge or contest the validity of the order entered pursuant to this Agreement; and

    d.   any claim under the Equal Access to Justice Act.

5. Respondent shall submit, within thirty (30) days of the date this agreement is signed by Respondent, an initial report, pursuant to 2.33 of the Commission's Rules, signed by the Respondent, setting forth in detail the manner in which the Respondent will comply with the Order when and if entered. Such report will not become part of the public record unless and until the accompanying agreement and order are accepted by the Commission for public comment.

6. This Agreement shall not become part of the public record of the proceeding unless and until it is accepted by the Commission. If this Agreement is accepted by the Commission it will be placed on the public

record for a period of sixty (60) days and information in respect thereto publicly released. The Commission thereafter may either withdraw its acceptance of this Agreement and so notify the Respondent, in which event it will take such action as it may consider appropriate, or issue and serve its Decision, in disposition of the proceeding.

7. This Agreement is for settlement purposes only and does not constitute an admission by Respondent that the law has been violated as alleged in the Complaint, or that the facts as alleged in the Complaint, other than the jurisdictional facts set forth in Paragraphs 1 and 3 of the Complaint, are true.

8. This Agreement contemplates that, if it is accepted by the Commission, and if such acceptance is not subsequently withdrawn by the Commission pursuant to the provisions of section 3.25(f) of the Commission's Rules, the Commission may, without further notice to Respondent, (1) issue its Decision containing the following Order to cease and desist in disposition of the proceeding, and (2) make information public with respect thereto. When so entered, the Order to cease and desist shall have the same force and effect and may be altered, modified or set aside in the same manner and within the same time provided by statute for other orders. The Order shall become final upon service. Delivery by the U.S. Postal Service of the Decision containing the agreed-to Order to Respondent's address as stated in this Agreement shall constitute service. Respondent waives any right it may have to any other manner of service. The complaint may be used in construing the terms of the Order, and no agreement, understanding, representation, or interpretation not contained in the Order or the Agreement may be used to vary or contradict the terms of the Order.

9. Respondent has read the complaint and the Order contemplated hereby. Respondent understands that once the Order has been issued, it will be required to file one or more compliance reports showing how it is complying and has complied with the Order. Respondent further understands that it may be liable for civil penalties in the amount provided by law for each violation of the Order after it becomes final.

ORDER

I

IT IS ORDERED that, as used in this Order, the following definitions shall apply: * * *

II.

IT IS FURTHER ORDERED that,

A. Except as otherwise provided in Paragraph II.B. below, for a period of ten (10) years from the date this Order becomes final, subject to the proviso set forth in this paragraph, Respondent shall cease and desist from taking the following actions or threatening to take the following actions: (1) impeding, altering, suspending, withdrawing, withholding or refusing to provide access by any microprocessor customer to AT Information for reasons related to an Intellectual Property Dispute with such customer if at the time of such IP Dispute such customer is receiving AT Information from Respondent or (2) basing any supply decisions for general purpose microprocessors upon the existence of an IP Dispute. *Provided, however*, that any obligation set forth in this Paragraph II.A. shall be inapplicable with regard to any AT Information or product supply decision specific to any Intel microprocessor that the customer has asserted is infringing its patent, copyright or trade secret rights unless that customer agrees in writing not to seek an injunction against the manufacture, use, sale, offer to sell, or importation of all Intel microprocessors that are based upon the same core microarchitecture (e.g. P5, P6) as the Intel microprocessor that is the subject of the assertion of infringement; provided further, however, that Respondent shall not take action prohibited in this Paragraph II.A. for the reason that such customer is seeking or has sought compensation, damages or any other legal or equitable remedies other than injunction as herein provided.

B.   Nothing in Paragraph II.A. of this Order shall be construed to:

1.   prohibit Respondent from seeking all available legal or equitable remedies with regard to any of its patent, copyright, trade secrets, mask work, trademark, or other intellectual property; provided that a dispute as to such remedies or compensation sought for the AT Information shall not affect Respondent's obligation to continue to provide the AT Information to a customer as provided in Paragraph II.A. above;

2.   prohibit Respondent from withholding AT Information or demanding the return of previously provided AT Information from a customer based on business considerations unrelated to the existence of the IP Dispute, including but not limited to a customer's breach of an agreement between the customer and Respondent regarding the disclosure or use of the AT Information;

3.   limit Respondent's right to make product (including sample) supply decisions based upon business considerations unrelated to the existence of the IP Dispute, including but not limited to constrained product (including sample) supply, customer's order rate and payment history, or customer's breach of an agreement between the customer and Respondent regarding the supply or use of such products;

4.   require Respondent to provide AT Information or supply general purpose microprocessors to a customer to facilitate the design or development of a type of system (e.g., server, workstation, desktop, mobile unit) that such customer has not designed or developed or demonstrated plans to design or develop within the preceding year;

5.   prohibit Respondent from restricting the use of AT Information to the customer's design and development of computer systems that incorporate the microprocessor to which the AT Information pertains;

6. require Respondent to disclose AT Information or supply general purpose microprocessors, when such AT Information or products (including samples) are not otherwise available for disclosure or supply to Respondent's customers; or

otherwise limit Respondent's intellectual property rights, including the disposition of those rights.

III.

IT IS FURTHER ORDERED that:

A. Within five (5) days of the date this Order becomes final, and for a period of thirty (30) days thereafter, Respondent shall publish this Order on its World Wide Web site. Notice of such publication shall be made in a manner calculated to be viewed by all of Respondent's customers. For purposes of this provision, notice will be deemed satisfactory if it is made by providing a direct link to the Order from a notice in the following language: "FTC and Intel Settle Antitrust Litigation" posted as the first link under the "In the News" section of the "developer's" page (developer.Intel.com) as the Intel site is constituted on the date this Order is signed. In the event that Intel changes its site structure, an equivalent notice in terms of ease of access and conspicuousness must be provided. After such thirty (30) day period, Respondent shall maintain a link from the "developer's" page (or its equivalent) to the Order in a manner that provides reasonable notice to interested parties.

B. Within ten (10) days after the date on which any person becomes a director or corporate officer, Respondent shall provide a copy of this Order to such person.

C. Within sixty (60) days after the date this Order becomes final, Respondent shall file with the Commission a verified written report setting forth in detail the manner and form in which Respondent is complying and has complied with this Order.

D. One (1) year from the date this Order becomes final, annually for the next five (5) years on the anniversary of the date this Order becomes final, and at such other times as the Commission may require, Respondent shall file a verified written report with the Commission setting forth in detail the manner and form in which it has complied and is complying with this Order, and setting forth in detail any action taken in connection with the activities covered by this Order.

E. For a period of five (5) years after the date this Order becomes final, Respondent shall maintain and make available to the Federal Trade Commission staff for inspection and copying, upon reasonable notice, records adequate to describe in detail any action taken in connection with the activities covered by Paragraph II. of this Order.

IV.

IT IS FURTHER ORDERED that Respondent shall notify the Commission at least thirty (30) days prior to any proposed change in the Respondent such as dissolution, assignment, sale, or reorganization resulting in the emergence of a successor corporation or association, or the creation or dissolution of subsidiaries or any other change in the corporation that may affect compliance obligations arising out of this Order.

V.

IT IS FURTHER ORDERED that, for the purpose of determining or securing compliance with this Order, upon written request, Respondent shall permit any duly authorized representative of the Commission:

A. Access, during office hours and in the presence of counsel, to all facilities and access to inspect and copy all books, ledgers, accounts, correspondence, memoranda and other records and documents in the possession or under the control of Respondent relating to any matters contained in this Order; and

B. Upon five days' notice to Respondent and without restraint or interference from them, to interview officers, directors, or employees of Respondent, who may have counsel present.

IT IS FURTHER ORDERED that this Order shall terminate ten (10) years after the date on which it is issued.

Note

The Federal Trade Commission, as well as the Department of Justice, has authority to enforce the antitrust laws.

BUSINESS ELECTRONICS CORPORATION v. SHARP ELECTRONICS CORPORATION

United States Supreme Court, 1988.
485 U.S. 717, 108 S.Ct. 1515, 99 L.Ed.2d 808.

JUSTICE SCALIA delivered the opinion of the Court.

Petitioner Business Electronics Corporation seeks review of a decision of the United States Court of Appeals for the Fifth Circuit holding that a vertical restraint is *per se* illegal under § 1 of the Sherman Act, 26 Stat. 209, as amended, 15 U.S.C. § 1, only if there is an express or implied agreement to set resale prices at some level. 780 F.2d 1212, 1215–1218 (1986). We granted certiorari, 482 U.S. 912, 107 S.Ct. 3182, 96 L.Ed.2d 671 (1987), to resolve a conflict in the Courts of Appeals regarding the proper dividing line between the rule that vertical price restraints are illegal *per se* and the rule that vertical nonprice restraints are to be judged under the rule of reason.

I

In 1968, petitioner became the exclusive retailer in the Houston, Texas, area of electronic calculators manufactured by respondent Sharp Electronics Corporation. In 1972, respondent appointed Gilbert Hartwell as a second retailer in the Houston area. During the relevant period, electronic calculators were primarily sold to business customers for prices up to $1,000. While much of the evidence in this case was conflicting—in particular, concerning whether petitioner was "free riding" on Hartwell's provision of presale educational and promotional services by providing inadequate services itself—a few facts are undisputed. Respondent published a list of suggested minimum retail prices, but its written dealership agreements with petitioner and Hartwell did not obligate either to observe them, or to charge any other specific price. Petitioner's retail prices were often below respondent's suggested retail prices and generally below Hartwell's retail prices, even though Hartwell too sometimes priced below respondent's suggested retail prices. Hartwell complained to respondent on a number of occasions about petitioner's prices. In June 1973, Hartwell gave respondent the ultimatum that Hartwell would terminate his dealership unless respondent ended its relationship with petitioner within 30 days. Respondent terminated petitioner's dealership in July 1973.

Petitioner brought suit in the United States District Court for the Southern District of Texas, alleging that respondent and Hartwell had conspired to terminate petitioner and that such conspiracy was illegal *per se* under § 1 of the Sherman Act. The case was tried to a jury. The District Court submitted a liability interrogatory to the jury that asked whether "there was an agreement or understanding between Sharp Electronics Corporation and Hartwell to terminate Business Electronics as a Sharp dealer because of Business Electronics' price cutting." Record, Doc. No. 241. The District Court instructed the jury at length about this question:

> "The Sherman Act is violated when a seller enters into an agreement or understanding with one of its dealers to terminate another dealer because of the other dealer's price cutting. Plaintiff contends that Sharp terminated Business Electronics in furtherance of Hartwell's desire to eliminate Business Electronics as a price-cutting rival.

> "If you find that there was an agreement between Sharp and Hartwell to terminate Business Electronics because of Business Electronics' price cutting, you should answer yes to Question Number 1.

> * * *

> "A combination, agreement or understanding to terminate a dealer because of his price cutting unreasonably restrains trade and cannot be justified for any reason. Therefore, even though the combination, agreement or understanding may have been formed or engaged in ... to eliminate any alleged evils of price cutting, it is still unlawful ...

> "If a dealer demands that a manufacturer terminate a price cutting dealer, and the manufacturer agrees to do so, the agreement

is illegal if the manufacturer's purpose is to eliminate the price cutting." App. 18–19.

The jury answered Question 1 affirmatively and awarded $600,000 in damages. The District Court * * * entered judgment for petitioner for treble damages plus attorney's fees.

The Fifth Circuit reversed, holding that the jury interrogatory and instructions were erroneous, and remanded for a new trial. It held that, to render illegal *per se* a vertical agreement between a manufacturer and a dealer to terminate a second dealer, the first dealer "must expressly or impliedly agree to set its prices at some level, though not a specific one. The distributor cannot retain complete freedom to set whatever price it chooses." 780 F.2d, at 1218.

II

A

Section 1 of the Sherman Act provides that "[e]very contract, combination in the form of trust or otherwise, or conspiracy, in restraint of trade or commerce among the several States, or with foreign nations, is declared to be illegal." 15 U.S.C. § 1. Since the earliest decisions of this Court interpreting this provision, we have recognized that it was intended to prohibit only unreasonable restraints of trade. Ordinarily, whether particular concerted action violates § 1 of the Sherman Act is determined through case-by-case application of the so-called rule of reason—that is, "the factfinder weighs all of the circumstances of a case in deciding whether a restrictive practice should be prohibited as imposing an unreasonable restraint on competition." *Continental T.V., Inc. v. GTE Sylvania Inc.*, 433 U.S. 36, 49, 97 S.Ct. 2549, 2557, 53 L.Ed.2d 568 (1977). Certain categories of agreements, however, have been held to be *per se* illegal, dispensing with the need for case-by-case evaluation. We have said that *per se* rules are appropriate only for "conduct that is manifestly anticompetitive," *id.*, at 50, 97 S.Ct., at 2557, that is, conduct " 'that would always or almost always tend to restrict competition and decrease output.' "*Northwest Wholesale Stationers, Inc. v. Pacific Stationery & Printing Co.*, 472 U.S. 284, 289–290 (1985), quoting *Broadcast Music, Inc. v. Columbia Broadcasting System, Inc.*, 441 U.S. 1, 19–20 (1979). * * *

Although vertical agreements on resale prices have been illegal *per se* since *Dr. Miles Medical Co. v. John D. Park & Sons Co.*, 220 U.S. 373, 31 S.Ct. 376, 55 L.Ed. 502 (1911), we have recognized that the scope of *per se* illegality should be narrow in the context of vertical restraints. In *Continental T.V., Inc. v. GTE Sylvania Inc.*, *supra*, we refused to extend *per se* illegality to vertical nonprice restraints, specifically to a manufacturer's termination of one dealer pursuant to an exclusive territory agreement with another. We noted that especially in the vertical restraint context "departure from the rule-of-reason standard must be based on demonstrable economic effect rather than . . . upon formalistic line drawing." *Id.*, 433 U.S., at 58–59, 97 S.Ct., at 2562. We concluded that vertical nonprice restraints had not been shown to have such a " 'pernicious effect on competition' " and to be so " 'lack[ing] [in] . . . redeeming value' " as to justify *per se* illegality. Rather, we found, they had real potential to stimulate interbrand competition, "the primary concern of antitrust law". * * *

Moreover, we observed that a rule of *per se* illegality for vertical nonprice restraints was not needed or effective to protect *intra*brand competition. First, so long as interbrand competition existed, that would provide a "significant check" on any attempt to exploit intrabrand market power. In fact, in order to meet that interbrand competition, a manufacturer's dominant incentive is to lower resale prices. *Id.*, at 56, and n. 24, 97 S.Ct., at 2560, and n. 24. Second, the *per se* illegality of vertical restraints would create a perverse incentive for manufacturers to integrate vertically into distribution, an outcome hardly conducive to fostering the creation and maintenance of small businesses. *Id.*, at 57, n. 26, 97 S.Ct., at 2561, n. 6.

Finally, our opinion in *GTE Sylvania* noted a significant distinction between vertical nonprice and vertical price restraints. That is, there was support for the proposition that vertical price restraints reduce *inter*brand price competition because they " 'facilitate cartelizing.' " The authorities cited by the Court suggested how vertical price agreements might assist horizontal price fixing at the manufacturer level (by reducing the manufacturer's incentive to cheat on a cartel, since its retailers could not pass on lower prices to consumers) or might be used to organize cartels at the retailer level. Similar support for the cartel-facilitating effect of vertical nonprice restraints was and remains lacking.

We have been solicitous to assure that the market-freeing effect of our decision in *GTE Sylvania* is not frustrated by related legal rules. In *Monsanto Co. v. Spray–Rite Service Corp.*, 465 U.S. 752, 763, 104 S.Ct. 1464, 1470, 79 L.Ed.2d 775 (1984), which addressed the evidentiary showing necessary to establish vertical concerted action, we expressed concern that "[i]f an inference of such an agreement may be drawn from highly ambiguous evidence, there is considerable danger that the doctrin[e] enunciated in *Sylvania* . . . will be seriously eroded." We eschewed adoption of an evidentiary standard that "could deter or penalize perfectly legitimate conduct" or "would create an irrational dislocation in the market" by preventing legitimate communication between a manufacturer and its distributors. * * *

Our approach to the question presented in the present case is guided by the premises of *GTE Sylvania* and *Monsanto*: that there is a presumption in favor of a rule-of-reason standard; that departure from that standard must be justified by demonstrable economic effect, such as the facilitation of cartelizing, rather than formalistic distinctions; that interbrand competition is the primary concern of the antitrust laws; and that rules in this area should be formulated with a view towards protecting the doctrine of *GTE Sylvania*. These premises lead us to conclude that the line drawn by the Fifth Circuit is the most appropriate one.

There has been no showing here that an agreement between a manufacturer and a dealer to terminate a "price cutter," without a further agreement on the price or price levels to be charged by the remaining dealer, almost always tends to restrict competition and reduce output. Any assistance to cartelizing that such an agreement might provide cannot be distinguished from the sort of minimal assistance that might be provided by vertical nonprice agreements like the exclusive territory agreement in *GTE Sylvania*, and is insufficient to justify a *per se* rule. Cartels are neither easy to form nor easy to maintain. Uncertainty over the terms of the cartel, particularly the prices to be charged in the future, obstructs both formation and adherence by making cheating easier. Without an agreement with the remaining dealer on price, the manufacturer both retains its incentive to cheat on any manufacturer-level cartel (since lower prices can still be passed on to consumers) and cannot as easily be used to organize and hold together a retailer-level cartel.

The District Court's rule on the scope of *per se* illegality for vertical restraints would threaten to dismantle the doctrine of *GTE Sylvania*. Any agreement between a manufacturer and a dealer to terminate another dealer who happens to have charged lower prices can be alleged to have been directed against the terminated dealer's "price cutting." In the vast majority of cases, it will be extremely difficult for the manufacturer to convince a jury that its motivation was to ensure adequate services, since price cutting and some measure of service cutting usually go hand in hand. Accordingly, a manufacturer that agrees to give one dealer an exclusive territory and terminates another dealer pursuant to that agreement, or even a manufacturer that agrees with one dealer to terminate another for failure to provide contractually obligated services, exposes itself to the highly plausible claim that its real motivation was to terminate a price cutter. Moreover, even vertical restraints that do not result in dealer termination, such as the initial granting of an exclusive territory or the requirement that certain services be provided, can be attacked as designed to allow existing dealers to charge higher prices. Manufacturers would be likely to forgo legitimate and competitively useful conduct rather than risk treble damages and perhaps even criminal penalties.

We cannot avoid this difficulty by invalidating as illegal *per se* only those agreements imposing vertical restraints that contain the word "price," or that affect the "prices" charged by dealers. Such formalism was explicitly rejected in *GTE Sylvania*. As the above discussion indicates, all vertical restraints, including the exclusive territory agreement held not to be *per se* illegal in *GTE Sylvania*, have the potential to allow dealers to increase "prices" and can be characterized as intended to achieve just that. In fact, vertical nonprice restraints only accomplish the benefits identified in *GTE Sylvania* because they reduce intrabrand price competition to the point where the dealer's profit margin permits provision of the desired services. As we described it in *Monsanto*: "The manufacturer often will want to ensure that its distributors earn sufficient profit to pay for programs such as hiring and training additional salesmen or demonstrating the technical features of the product, and will want to see that 'free-riders' do not interfere." 465 U.S., at 762–763.

* * *

Finally, we do not agree with petitioner's contention that an agreement on the remaining dealer's price or price levels will so often follow from terminating another dealer "because of [its] price cutting" that prophylaxis against resale price maintenance warrants the District Court's *per se* rule. Petitioner has provided no support for the proposition that vertical price agreements generally underlie agreements to terminate a price cutter. That proposition is simply incompatible with the conclusion of *GTE Sylvania* and *Monsanto* that manufacturers are often motivated by a legitimate desire to have dealers provide services, combined with the reality that price cutting is frequently made possible by "free riding" on the services provided by other dealers. The District Court's *per se* rule would therefore discourage conduct recognized by *GTE Sylvania* and *Monsanto* as beneficial to consumers.

B

In resting our decision upon the foregoing economic analysis, we do not ignore common-law precedent concerning what constituted "restraint of trade" at the time the Sherman Act was adopted. But neither do we give that pre–1890 precedent the dispositive effect some would. The term "restraint of trade" in the statute, like the term at common law, refers not to a particular list of agreements, but to a particular economic consequence, which may be produced by quite different sorts of agreements in varying times and circumstances. The changing content of the term "restraint of trade" was well recognized at the time the Sherman Act was enacted.

The Sherman Act adopted the term "restraint of trade" along with its dynamic potential. It invokes the common law itself, and not merely the static content that the common law had assigned to the term in 1890. If it were otherwise, not only would the line of *per se* illegality have to be drawn today precisely where it was in 1890, but also case-by-case evaluation of legality (conducted where *per se* rules do not apply) would have to be governed by 19th-century notions of reasonableness. It would make no sense to create out of the single term "restraint of trade" a chronologically schizoid statute, in which a "rule of reason" evolves with new circumstances and new wisdom, but a line of *per se* illegality remains forever fixed where it was.

Of course the common law, both in general and as embodied in the Sherman Act, does not lightly assume that the economic realities underlying earlier decisions have changed, or that earlier judicial perceptions of those realities were in error. It is relevant, therefore, whether the common law of restraint of trade ever prohibited as illegal per se an agreement of the sort made here, and whether our decisions under § 1 of the Sherman Act have ever expressed or necessarily implied such a prohibition.

With respect to this Court's understanding of pre-Sherman Act common law, petitioner refers to our decision in *Dr. Miles Medical Co. v. John D. Park & Sons Co.*, *supra*. Though that was an early Sherman Act case, its holding that a resale price maintenance agreement was *per se* illegal was based largely on the perception that such an agreement was categorically impermissible at common law. As the opinion made plain, however, the basis for that common-law judgment was that the resale restriction was an unlawful restraint on alienation. * * * "*[D]r. Miles* . . . decided that under the general law the owner of movables . . . could not sell the movables and lawfully by contract fix a price at which the product should afterwards be sold, because to do so would be at one and the same time to sell and retain, to part with and yet to hold, to project the will of the seller so as to cause it to control the movable parted with when it was not subject to his will because owned by another." [*Boston Store of Chicago v. American Graphophone Co.*, 246 U.S. 8, 21–22 (1918).] In the present case, of course, no agreement on resale price or price level, and hence no restraint on alienation, was found by the jury, so the common-law rationale of *Dr. Miles* does not apply.

Petitioner's principal contention has been that the District Court's rule on *per se* illegality is compelled not by the old common law, but by our more recent Sherman Act precedents. First, petitioner contends that since certain horizontal agreements have been held to constitute price fixing (and thus to be *per se* illegal) though they did not set prices or price levels, see, *e.g.*, *Catalano, Inc. v. Target Sales, Inc.*, 446 U.S. 643, 647–650, 100 S.Ct. 1925, 1927–29, 64 L.Ed.2d 580 (1980) *(per curiam)*, it is improper to require that a vertical agreement set prices or price levels before it can suffer the same fate. This notion of equivalence between the scope of horizontal *per se* illegality and that of vertical *per se* illegality was explicitly rejected in *GTE Sylvania*, as it had to be, since a horizontal agreement to divide territories is *per se* illegal, while *GTE Sylvania* held that a vertical agreement to do so is not.

Second, petitioner contends that *per se* illegality here follows from our two cases holding *per se* illegal a group boycott of a dealer because of its price cutting. This second contention is merely a restatement of the first, since both cases involved horizontal combinations * * *.

Third, petitioner contends, relying on *Albrecht v. Herald Co.*, 390 U.S. 145, 88 S.Ct. 869, 19 L.Ed.2d 998 (1968), and *United States v. Parke, Davis & Co.*, 362 U.S. 29, 80 S.Ct. 503, 4 L.Ed.2d 505 (1960), that our vertical price-fixing cases have already rejected the proposition that *per se* illegality requires setting a price or a price level. We disagree. In *Albrecht*, the maker of the product formed a combination to force a retailer to charge the maker's advertised retail price. This combination had two aspects. Initially, the maker hired a third party to solicit customers away from the noncomplying retailer. This solicitor "was aware that the aim of the solicitation campaign was to force [the noncomplying retailer] to lower his price" to the suggested retail price. Next, the maker engaged another retailer who "undertook to deliver [products] at the suggested price" to the noncomplying retailer's customers obtained by the solicitor. *Ibid.* This combination of maker, solicitor, and new retailer was held to be *per se* illegal. It is plain that the combination involved both an explicit agreement on resale price and an agreement to force another to adhere to the specified price.

In *Parke, Davis,* a manufacturer combined first with wholesalers and then with retailers in order to gain the "retailers' adherence to its suggested minimum retail prices." The manufacturer also brokered an agreement among its retailers not to advertise prices below its suggested retail prices, which agreement was held to be part of the *per se* illegal combination. This holding also does not support a rule that an agreement on price or price level is not required for a vertical restraint to be *per se* illegal—first, because the agreement not to advertise prices was part and parcel of the combination that contained the price agreement, *id.*, at 35–36, 80 S.Ct., at 507, and second because the agreement among retailers that the manufacturer organized was a *horizontal* conspiracy among competitors. * * *

In sum, economic analysis supports the view, and no precedent opposes it, that a vertical restraint is not illegal *per se* unless it includes some agreement on price or price levels. Accordingly, the judgment of the Fifth Circuit is

Affirmed.

Note

Note that in *Sharp* the Court required direct evidence of an agreement between manufacturer/developer and remaining distributor to raise prices, for the terminated distributor to succeed in a § 1 complaint.

D. HORIZONTAL RESTRAINTS

Successful operation of a price-fixing cartel in any industry requires regular communication of price information among members of the cartel and the catching and "punishing" of "cheaters" who undercut cartel prices. Government investigators can detect such interfirm communications more easily than intrafirm communications. Therefore, government antitrust enforcers often focus on such communications. In the old days conspirators talked by telephone or met in smoke-filled rooms. But starting years ago, they began communicating by computer. Edwin McDowell, "9 Airlines Face Suit on Prices," *New York Times*, August 8, 1991, p. C1; Asra Q. Nomani, "Fare Game; Coding of Tariffs/Can Tell Rivals of One's Intentions; U.S. Begins Investigation; Signaling an Attack on a Hub," *Wall Street Journal*, June 28, p. 1, col. 6. Particularly worrisome are joint Internet purchase and sales websites, which a number of industries have created .. David Leonhardt, "Business Exchange Sites Raise Questions for Regulators," *New York Times*, July 7, 2000, p. 1.

Chapter IX

PRIVACY

A. INTRODUCTION

Before the computer age, the greatest protection of individual privacy was the inefficiency of the data collection and distribution system. In the nineteenth century, an American could start a new life on the Western frontier. The quality of record-keeping and communications was such that there was little chance of being haunted by true or false reports about the past. Record-keeping and distribution systems improved gradually over the first half of the twentieth century. Then, in the 1960s, the introduction of computer data banks caused a sudden, dramatic improvement in the keeping and distribution of records about individuals. The advent of the Internet suddenly empowered everyone to distribute information true or false to the world. Absent change in the law, these technological developments would have meant a dramatic decrease in privacy and a drastic increase in the risk of harm from false information. At the same time there were clear benefits. Families with good credit records could get instant approval for home mortgages. People could find long-lost friends and relatives. Free Internet service providers and free websites lowered the cost of expression of opinion for ordinary Americans virtually to zero.

Congress enacted a variety of legislation in response to the problems posed by improvements in the collection and distribution of information about individuals. State legislatures and the courts have also contributed to the development of the law in this area. This and the next two chapters deal with the particular ways in which this new area of the law affects computer storage and transmission of information. Computer data banks threatened to make it impossible for individuals ever to escape past misdeeds, by recording and distributing information about them with computerized efficiency. The law of computer privacy, the subject of Chapter IX, attempts to curb this threat to individuals. The efficiency of the computer is more dangerous when the information it stores and distributes is false. Chapter X deals with legal remedies designed to ensure that the information stored and distributed is true. Information is power. Chapter XI covers legislation aimed at forcing those with information in computers to share it with those who need the information.

In analyzing a violation of privacy rights privacy, it is convenient to look at the following questions in order: Was the private information obtained through unlawful government compulsion or unlawful private action? Was the information unlawfully used by the entity that obtained it? Was the information unlawfully disclosed to third parties.

B. RESTRICTING THE POWER OF GOVERNMENT TO USE COMPULSION TO FORCE DISCLOSURE OF PERSONAL INFORMATION

WHALEN v. ROE

Supreme Court of the United States, 1977.
429 U.S. 589, 97 S.Ct. 869, 51 L.Ed.2d 64.

MR. JUSTICE STEVENS delivered the opinion of the Court.

The constitutional question presented is whether the State of New York may record, in a centralized computer file, the names and addresses of all persons who have obtained, pursuant to a doctor's prescription, certain drugs for which there is both a lawful and an unlawful market.

The District Court enjoined enforcement of the portions of the New York State Controlled Substances Act of 1972 which require such recording on the ground that they violate appellees' constitutionally protected rights of privacy. We noted probable jurisdiction of the appeal by the Commissioner of Health, 424 U.S. 907, 96 S.Ct. 1100, 47 L.Ed.2d 310, and now reverse.

Many drugs have both legitimate and illegitimate uses. In response to a concern that such drugs were being diverted into unlawful channels, in 1970 the New York Legislature created a special commission to evaluate the State's drug-control laws. The commission found the existing laws deficient in several respects. There was no effective way to prevent the use of stolen or revised prescriptions, to prevent unscrupulous pharmacists from repeatedly refilling prescriptions, to prevent users from obtaining prescriptions from more than one doctor, or to prevent doctors from over-prescribing, either by authorizing an excessive amount in one prescription or by giving one patient multiple prescriptions. In drafting new legislation to correct such defects, the commission consulted with enforcement officials in California and Illinois where central reporting systems were being used effectively

The new New York statute classified potentially harmful drugs in five schedules. Drugs, such as heroin, which are highly abused and have no recognized medical use, are in Schedule I; they cannot be prescribed. Schedules II through V include drugs which have a progressively lower potential for abuse but also have a recognized medical use. Our concern is limited to Schedule II which includes the most dangerous of the legitimate drugs.

With an exception for emergencies, the Act requires that all prescriptions for Schedule II drugs be prepared by the physician in triplicate on an official form. The completed form identifies the prescribing physician; the dispensing pharmacy; the drug and dosage; and the name, address, and age of the patient. One copy of the form is retained by the physician, the second by the pharmacist, and the third is forwarded to the New York State Department of Health in Albany. A prescription made on an official form may not exceed a 30–day supply, and may not be refilled.

The District Court found that about 100,000 Schedule II prescription forms are delivered to a receiving room at the Department of Health in Albany each month. They are sorted, coded, and logged and then taken to another room where the data on the forms is recorded on magnetic tapes for processing by a computer. Thereafter, the forms are returned to the receiving room to be retained in a vault for a five-year period and then destroyed as required by the statute. The receiving room is surrounded by a locked wire fence and protected by an alarm system. The computer tapes containing the prescription data are kept in a locked cabinet. When the tapes are used, the computer is run "off-line," which means that no terminal outside of the computer room can read or record any information. Public disclosure of the identity of patients is expressly prohibited by the statute and by a Department of Health regulation. Willful violation of these prohibitions is a crime punishable by up to one year in prison and a $2,000 fine At the time of trial there were 17 Department of Health employees with access to the files; in addition, there were 24 investigators with authority to investigate cases of overdispensing which might be identified by the computer. Twenty months after the effective date of the Act, the computerized data had only been used in two investigations involving alleged overuse by specific patients.

A few days before the Act became effective, this litigation was commenced by a group of patients regularly receiving prescriptions for Schedule II drugs, by doctors who prescribe such drugs, and by two associations of physicians. After various preliminary proceedings, a three-judge District Court conducted a one-day trial. Appellees offered evidence tending to prove that persons in need of treatment with Schedule II drugs will from time to time decline such treatment because of their fear that the misuse of the computerized data will cause them to be stigmatized as "drug addicts."

The District Court held that "the doctor-patient relationship intrudes on one of the zones of privacy accorded constitutional protection" and that the patient-identification provisions of the Act invaded this zone with "a needlessly broad sweep," and enjoined enforcement of the provisions of the Act which deal with the reporting of patients' names and addresses.

I

The District Court found that the State had been unable to demonstrate the necessity for the patient-identification requirement on the basis of its experience during the first 20 months of administration of the new statute. There was a time when that alone would have provided a basis for invalidating the statute. *Lochner v. New York*, 198 U.S. 45, 25

S.Ct. 539, 49 L.Ed. 937, involved legislation making it a crime for a baker to permit his employees to work more than 60 hours in a week. In an opinion no longer regarded as authoritative, the Court held the statute unconstitutional as "an unreasonable, unnecessary and arbitrary interference with the right of the individual to his personal liberty. . . . " *Id.,* at 56, 25 S.Ct., at 543.

The holding in *Lochner* has been implicitly rejected many times. State legislation which has some effect on individual liberty or privacy may not be held unconstitutional simply because a court finds it unnecessary, in whole or in part For we have frequently recognized that individual States have broad latitude in experimenting with possible solutions to problems of vital local concern.

The New York statute challenged in this case represents a considered attempt to deal with such a problem. It is manifestly the product of an orderly and rational legislative decision. It was recommended by a specially appointed commission which held extensive hearings on the proposed legislation, and drew on experience with similar programs in other States. There surely was nothing unreasonable in the assumption that the patient-identification requirement might aid in the enforcement of laws designed to minimize the misuse of dangerous drugs. For the requirement could reasonably be expected to have a deterrent effect on potential violators as well as to aid in the detection or investigation of specific instances of apparent abuse. At the very least, it would seem clear that the State's vital interest in controlling the distribution of dangerous drugs would support a decision to experiment with new techniques for control. For if an experiment fails if in this case experience teaches that the patient-identification requirement results in the foolish expenditure of funds to acquire a mountain of useless information the legislative process remains available to terminate the unwise experiment. It follows that the legislature's enactment of the patient-identification requirement was a reasonable exercise of New York's broad police powers. The District Court's finding that the necessity for the requirement had not been proved is not, therefore, a sufficient reason for holding the statutory requirement unconstitutional.

II

Appellees contend that the statute invades a constitutionally protected "zone of privacy." The cases sometimes characterized as protecting "privacy" have in fact involved at least two different kinds of interests One is the individual interest in avoiding disclosure of personal matters, and another is the interest in independence in making certain kinds of important decisions Appellees argue that both of these interests are impaired by this statute. The mere existence in readily available form of the information about patients' use of Schedule II drugs creates a genuine concern that the information will become publicly known and that it will adversely affect their reputations. This concern makes some patients reluctant to use, and some doctors reluctant to prescribe, such drugs even when their use is medically indicated. It follows, they argue, that the making of decisions about matters vital to the care of their health is inevitably affected by the statute. Thus, the statute threatens to impair both their interest in the nondisclosure of private information and also their interest in making important decisions independently.

We are persuaded, however, that the New York program does not, on its face, pose a sufficiently grievous threat to either interest to establish a constitutional violation.

Public disclosure of patient information can come about in three ways. Health Department employees may violate the statute by failing, either deliberately or negligently, to maintain proper security. A patient or a doctor may be accused of a violation and the stored data may be offered in evidence in a judicial proceeding. Or, thirdly, a doctor, a pharmacist, or the patient may voluntarily reveal information on a prescription form.

The third possibility existed under the prior law and is entirely unrelated to the existence of the computerized data bank. Neither of the other two possibilities provides a proper ground for attacking the statute as invalid on its face. There is no support in the record, or in the experience of the two States that New York has emulated, for an assumption that the security provisions of the statute will be administered improperly. And the remote possibility that judicial supervision of the evidentiary use of particular items of stored information will provide inadequate protection against unwarranted disclosures is surely not a sufficient reason for invalidating the entire patient-identification program.

Even without public disclosure, it is, of course, true that private information must be disclosed to the authorized employees of the New York Department of Health. Such disclosures, however, are not significantly different from those that were required under the prior law. Nor are they meaningfully distinguishable from a host of other unpleasant invasions of privacy that are associated with many facets of health care. Unquestionably, some individuals' concern for their own privacy may lead them to avoid or to postpone needed medical attention. Nevertheless, disclosures of private medical information to doctors, to hospital personnel, to insurance companies, and to public health agencies are often an essential part of modern medical practice even when the disclosure may reflect unfavorably on the character of the patient. Requiring such disclosures to representatives of the State having responsibility for the health of the community, does not automatically amount to an impermissible invasion of privacy.

Appellees also argue, however, that even if unwarranted disclosures do not actually occur, the knowledge that the information is readily available in a computerized file creates a genuine concern that causes some persons to decline needed medication. The record supports the conclusion that some use of Schedule II drugs has been discouraged by that concern; it also is clear, however, that about 100,000 prescriptions for such drugs were being filled each month prior to the entry of the

District Court's injunction. Clearly, therefore, the statute did not deprive the public of access to the drugs.

Nor can it be said that any individual has been deprived of the right to decide independently, with the advice of his physician, to acquire and to use needed medication. Although the State no doubt could prohibit entirely the use of particular Schedule II drugs, it has not done so. This case is therefore unlike those in which the Court held that a total prohibition of certain conduct was an impermissible deprivation of liberty. Nor does the State require access to these drugs to be conditioned on the consent of any state official or other third party. Within dosage limits which appellees do not challenge, the decision to prescribe, or to use, is left entirely to the physician and the patient.

We hold that neither the immediate nor the threatened impact of the patient-identification requirements in the New York State Controlled Substances Act of 1972 on either the reputation or the independence of patients for whom Schedule II drugs are medically indicated is sufficient to constitute an invasion of any right or liberty protected by the Fourteenth Amendment.

III

The appellee doctors argue separately that the statute impairs their right to practice medicine free of unwarranted state interference. If the doctors' claim has any reference to the impact of the 1972 statute on their own procedures, it is clearly frivolous. For even the prior statute required the doctor to prepare a written prescription identifying the name and address of the patient and the dosage of the prescribed drug. To the extent that their claim has reference to the possibility that the patients' concern about disclosure may induce them to refuse needed medication, the doctors' claim is derivative from, and therefore no stronger than, the patients'. Our rejection of their claim therefore disposes of the doctors' as well.

IV

A final word about issues we have not decided. We are not unaware of the threat to privacy implicit in the accumulation of vast amounts of personal information in computerized data banks or other massive government files. The collection of taxes, the distribution of welfare and social security benefits, the supervision of public health, the direction of our Armed Forces, and the enforcement of the criminal laws all require the orderly preservation of great quantities of information, much of which is personal in character and potentially embarrassing or harmful if disclosed. The right to collect and use such data for public purposes is typically accompanied by a concomitant statutory or regulatory duty to avoid unwarranted disclosures. Recognizing that in some circumstances that duty arguably has its roots in the Constitution, nevertheless New York's statutory scheme, and its implementing administrative procedures, evidence a proper concern with, and protection of, the individual's interest in privacy. We therefore need not, and do not, decide any question which might be presented by the unwarranted disclosure of accumulated private data whether intentional or unintentional or by a system that did not contain comparable security provisions. We simply hold that this record does not establish an invasion of any right or liberty protected by the Fourteenth Amendment.

Reversed.

Note

The spouse of one of the authors works in a medical laboratory. Once a patient is diagnosed with HIV, the data is maintained on a state and federal level following the principles of *Whalen v. Roe.*

ELECTRONIC COMMUNICATIONS PRIVACY ACT § 2703

18 U.S.C. § 2703.

§ 2703. Requirements for governmental access

(a) Contents of electronic communications in electronic storage.—A governmental entity may require the disclosure by a provider of electronic communication service of the contents of an electronic communication, that is in electronic storage in an electronic communications system for one hundred and eighty days or less, only pursuant to a warrant issued under the Federal Rules of Criminal Procedure or equivalent State warrant. A governmental entity may require the disclosure by a provider of electronic communications services of the contents of an electronic communication that has been in electronic storage in an electronic communications system for more than one hundred and eighty days by the means available under subsection (b) of this section.

(b) Contents of electronic communications in a remote computing service.—(1) A governmental entity may require a provider of remote computing service to disclose the contents of any electronic communication to which this paragraph is made applicable by paragraph (2) of this subsection—

(A) without required notice to the subscriber or customer, if the governmental entity obtains a warrant issued under the Federal Rules of Criminal Procedure or equivalent State warrant; or

(B) with prior notice from the governmental entity to the subscriber or customer if the governmental entity—

(i) uses an administrative subpoena authorized by a Federal or State statute or a Federal or State grand jury or trial subpoena; or

(ii) obtains a court order for such disclosure under subsection (d) of this section;

except that delayed notice may be given pursuant to section 2705 of this title.

(2) Paragraph (1) is applicable with respect to any electronic communication that is held or maintained on that service—

(A) on behalf of, and received by means of electronic transmission from (or created by means of computer processing of communications received by means of electronic transmission from), a subscriber or customer of such remote computing service; and

(B) solely for the purpose of providing storage or computer processing services to such subscriber or customer, if the provider is not authorized to access the contents of any such communications for purposes of providing any services other than storage or computer processing.

(c) Records concerning electronic communication service or remote computing service.—(1)(A) Except as provided in subparagraph (B), a provider of electronic communication service or remote computing service may disclose a record or other information pertaining to a subscriber to or customer of such service (not including the contents of communications covered by subsection (a) or (b) of this section) to any person other than a governmental entity.

(B) A provider of electronic communication service or remote computing service shall disclose a record or other information pertaining to a subscriber to or customer of such service (not including the contents of communications covered by subsection (a) or (b) of this section) to a governmental entity only when the governmental entity—

(i) obtains a warrant issued under the Federal Rules of Criminal Procedure or equivalent State warrant;

(ii) obtains a court order for such disclosure under subsection (d) of this section;

(iii) has the consent of the subscriber or customer to such disclosure; or

(iv) submits a formal written request relevant to a law enforcement investigation concerning telemarketing fraud for the name, address, and place of business of a subscriber or customer of such provider, which subscriber or customer is engaged in telemarketing (as such term is defined in section 2325 of this title).

(C) A provider of electronic communication service or remote computing service shall disclose to a governmental entity the name, address, local and long distance telephone toll billing records, telephone number or other subscriber number or identity, and length of service of a subscriber to or customer of such service and the types of services the subscriber or customer utilized, when the governmental entity uses an administrative subpoena authorized by a Federal or State statute or a Federal or State grand jury or trial subpoena or any means available under subparagraph (B).

(2) A governmental entity receiving records or information under this subsection is not required to provide notice to a subscriber or customer.

(d) Requirements for court order.—A court order for disclosure under subsection (b) or (c) may be issued by any court that is a court of competent jurisdiction described in section 3127(2)(A) and shall issue only if the governmental entity offers specific and articulable facts showing that there are reasonable grounds to believe that the contents of a wire or electronic communication, or the records or other information sought, are relevant and material to an ongoing criminal investigation. In the case of a State governmental authority, such a court order shall not issue if prohibited by the law of such State. A court issuing an order pursuant to this section, on a motion made promptly by the service provider, may quash or modify such order, if the information or records requested are unusually voluminous in nature or compliance with such order otherwise would cause an undue burden on such provider.

(e) No cause of action against a provider disclosing information under this chapter.—No cause of action shall lie in any court against any provider of wire or electronic communication service, its officers, employees, agents, or other specified persons for providing information, facilities, or assistance in accordance with the terms of a court order, warrant, subpoena, or certification under this chapter.

(f) Requirement to preserve evidence.—

(1) In general.—A provider of wire or electronic communication services or a remote computing service, upon the request of a governmental entity, shall take all necessary steps to preserve records and other evidence in its possession pending the issuance of a court order or other process.

(2) Period of retention.—Records referred to in paragraph (1) shall be retained for a period of 90 days, which shall be extended for an additional 90–day period upon a renewed request by the governmental entity.

Note

Consider the above legislation and the cases below. If you are thinking of exchanging illicit materials by e-mail, would you be safe storing this material: (1) on the computer of your Internet service provider, (2) on your employer's computer, (3) on your home computer, or (4) nowhere?

UNITED STATES v. CHARBONNEAU

United States District Court, S.D. Ohio, Eastern Division, 1997.
979 F.Supp. 1177.

KINNEARY, DISTRICT JUDGE.

* * * Defendant moves the Court to suppress (1) any statements made by Defendant while on the Internet using the America OnLine

("AOL") computer service; (2) any physical evidence seized during a search of Defendant's residence; and (3) any physical evidence resulting from Defendant's "conversations" while using AOL. The Court held an evidentiary hearing on these motions on September 17, 1997. * * * The Court DENIES Defendant's * * * motion to suppress statements and physical evidence because the Court finds that Defendant had no reasonable expectation of privacy while using AOL and because the items seized at Defendant's residence would have been inevitably discovered.

I. FACTS

In making its decision, the Court finds the following facts. Early in 1994, federal law enforcement agents began an investigation into child pornography on the Internet. The investigators included D. Douglas Rehman of the Florida Department of Law Enforcement assigned to an FBI task force in Orlando, Florida. Agent Rehman would "go on-line," using the America OnLine Internet service, and pose as a pedophile. Using the screen or user name of "Mikey1L", Agent Rehman would enter private AOL chat rooms and observe the on-line conversations between users. Agent Rehman operated primarily in the private chat rooms, "BOYS" and "PRETEEN." Both private chat rooms (maintained by private users and not by AOL) contained many users interested in trading graphic files with pictures of child pornography.

After entering a chat room, Agent Rehman would "record" the "conversations" as they occurred in the private room. The government offered Exhibit 4 as an example of one such conversation. Agent Rehman was not active in these conversations but passively "sat" in the rooms as an observer. In the course of his investigation, Agent Rehman observed the transmission of numerous graphic pictures containing child pornography

The child pornography was distributed by one user using a "list." A user generally would create the list by identifying all users in a private room; the user then would enter the screen names of the identified users onto an "e-mail" message and create a list of recipients. The sender of the pornographic pictures would next send an e-mail to the recipients identified on the list. The e-mail often would contain a brief message and an attached graphic file containing child pornography. Recipients frequently recycled the list so that every user on a list could trade graphic files with each other. Because Agent Rehman was present in the private chat rooms, users would include his screen name on such lists. Agent Rehman then would receive the same pornographic pictures of children as the other recipients on the list.

One of the users that Agent Rehman observed sending child pornography was a user identified as "Charbyq." (Tr. at 49.) Through the use of a search warrant, the FBI in Virginia identified this user as Defendant. Consequently, the FBI learned that Defendant lived in the Columbus area and referred the investigation to its Columbus office. Special Agent Bevin Staufer of the Columbus office led the investigation for the FBI using the Violent Crime/Safe Streets Task Force. The task force consisted of various local and federal law enforcement officials. With all of the information about Defendant's activities on AOL, on December 10, 1996, Agent Staufer sought a search warrant for Defendant's residence at 5686 Wilcox Road, Dublin, Ohio.

The next day, December 11, the task force, armed with the search warrant, went to Defendant's residence; however, neither Mrs. Charbonneau nor her husband were home. At least six agents then proceeded to Dublin Coffman High School; Defendant's eighteen year old son Brent attended this school. When the agents arrived, they also discovered that Debra Charbonneau, Defendant's wife, worked at the school. Agents, dressed in jeans and t-shirts, then located Brent and Debra and questioned the two in separate rooms about Defendant's activities.

Agent Staufer and another agent interviewed Debra. Agent Staufer told Mrs. Charbonneau that her husband had committed the crime of transmitting child pornography and that she was not under suspicion. Agent Staufer also told Mrs. Charbonneau that the FBI had a search warrant that would be executed if she did not sign a consent-to-search form. Agents spoke with Mrs. Charbonneau for approximately an hour and a half. During the course of the interview, Mrs. Charbonneau learned that the agents were also questioning her son, Brent. Brent was not able to speak to his mother, however, until after the interview concluded. Although Agent Staufer testified that Mrs. Charbonneau was not upset, Mrs. Charbonneau testified that she was very upset and cried. Agent Staufer also testified that Mrs. Charbonneau understood that she could refuse to sign the consent-to-search form. Mrs. Charbonneau testified that the agents told her that they would "go easier" on her and her husband if she signed. Further, the agents told her that, in order to execute the search warrant, they would have to break down her door if she did not sign the consent form. Sometime during the course of the questioning, Mrs. Charbonneau signed the consent form.

At the conclusion of the interview, agents told Debra to drive her car to her home and wait for the agents to arrive. Upon the agents' arrival, Mrs. Charbonneau let them inside her home. Though the agents still had the search warrant, they never executed it. Instead, the agents relied on Mrs. Charbonneau's signed consent form as their justification to enter the Charbonneau residence. In an apparent show of force, six agents scoured the house for more than an hour. During the search, agents recovered two computers and a number of disks containing child pornography. After giving Debra a written list of all the items taken in the search, agents left the Charbonneau residence.

* * *

III. MOTION TO SUPPRESS STATEMENTS AND PHYSICAL EVIDENCE

In Defendant's motion to suppress physical evidence and statements, Defendant requests that this Court suppress three different items. First, Defendant moves to suppress any statements made by Defendant while on the Internet using the AOL computer service.

Defendant claims that the government violated his First and Fourth Amendment rights relating to both the expectation of privacy and the right of free speech while using AOL. Second, Defendant moves to suppress any physical evidence seized during a search of Defendant's residence on the Fourth Amendment ground that the evidence was obtained by an illegal seizure. Third, Defendant moves to suppress any physical evidence resulting from Defendant's "conversations" using AOL on First and Fourth Amendment grounds relating to (A) free speech on AOL, (B) the illegal seizure of the conversations, and (C) the expectation of privacy while on AOL. Because the first and third requests are so interrelated, the Court will examine the issues relating to AOL at the same time.

In response to Defendant's AOL claims, the government claims that Defendant's conversations on AOL were not private and should not be afforded any constitutional protection. In response to Defendant's illegal seizure claims, the government claims that Mrs. Charbonneau voluntarily consented to a search of the Charbonneau residence; further, even if her consent was involuntary, the government claims that agents would have inevitably discovered the incriminating evidence.

The Court finds that, with respect to Defendant's AOL claims, first Defendant had no First Amendment rights when using AOL to transmit child pornography. Second, Defendant did not have a reasonable expectation of privacy while using AOL. The Court also finds that the search of Defendant's home was illegal but the evidence seized during that search is admissible under the doctrine of inevitable discovery.

A.   Statements on AOL

Before analyzing Defendant's Fourth Amendment grounds, the Court will examine Defendant's First Amendment free speech claim. As Defendant's First Amendment claims were not adequately supported by case law, the Court dismisses Defendant's First Amendment claims as meritless.

The Court will next examine Defendant's Fourth Amendment grounds for challenging the seizure of Defendant's AOL conversations. A person challenging the validity of a search or seizure may only assert a "reasonable" "subjective expectation of privacy." As another court addressing a very similar issue found, this Court finds that Defendant possessed a limited reasonable expectation of privacy in the e-mail messages he sent and/or received on AOL. E-mail is almost equivalent to sending a letter via the mails. When an individual sends or mails letters, messages, or other information on the computer, that Fourth Amendment expectation of privacy diminishes incrementally. Furthermore, the openness of the "chat room" diminishes Defendant's reasonable expectation of privacy.

As the *Maxwell* court noted:

E-mail transmissions are not unlike other forms of modern communication. We can draw parallels from these other mediums.

For example, if a sender of first-class mail seals an envelope and addresses it to another person, the sender can reasonably expect the contents to remain private and free from the eyes of the police absent a search warrant founded upon probable cause. However, once the letter is received and opened, the destiny of the letter then lies in the control of the recipient of the letter, not the sender, absent some legal privilege.

Similarly, the maker of a telephone call has a reasonable expectation that police officials will not intercept and listen to the conversation; however, the conversation itself is held with the risk that one of the participants may reveal what is said to others.

Drawing from these parallels, we can say that the transmitter of an e-mail message enjoys a reasonable expectation that police officials will not intercept the transmission without probable cause and a search warrant. However, once the transmissions are received by another person, the transmitter no longer controls its destiny.

United States v. Maxwell, 45 M.J. 406, 418 (Armed Forces 1996). Thus an e-mail message, like a letter, cannot be afforded a reasonable expectation of privacy once that message is received.

Moreover, a sender of e-mail runs the risk that he is sending the message to an undercover agent. In *Hoffa v. United States*, 385 U.S. 293, 87 S.Ct. 408, 17 L.Ed.2d 374 (1966), the Supreme Court held that statements made to undercover agents are not protected by the Fourth Amendment. In *Hoffa*, labor leader James "Jimmy" Hoffa admitted guilt in a conversation overheard by the government's undercover informant. The Court found that no Fourth Amendment rights exist where "a wrongdoer's misplaced belief that a person to whom he voluntarily confides his wrongdoing will not reveal it." *Id.* at 302, 87 S.Ct. at 413. Indeed, "The risk of being overheard by an eavesdropper . . . or deceived as to the identity of one with whom one deals is probably inherent in the conditions of human society. It is the kind of risk we necessarily assume whenever we speak." *Id.* at 303, 87 S.Ct. at 414.

The expectations of privacy in e-mail transmissions depend in large part on both the type of e-mail sent and recipient of the e-mail .. E-mail messages sent to an addressee who later forwards the e-mail to a third party do not enjoy the same reasonable expectations of privacy once they have been forwarded. Similarly, "Messages sent to the public at large in the 'chat room' or e-mail that is 'forwarded' from correspondent to correspondent lose any semblance of privacy." *Maxwell*, 45 M.J. at 419.

In this case, Defendant wishes to suppress all of the statements made in AOL chat rooms. All of the evidence gathered by the FBI from the chat rooms resulted from the presence of undercover agents in the rooms. Clearly, when Defendant engaged in chat room conversations, he ran the risk of speaking to an undercover agent. Furthermore, Defendant could not have a reasonable expectation of privacy in the chat rooms. Accordingly, the e-mail sent by Defendant to others in a "chat room" is not afforded any semblance of privacy; the government may present the evidence at trial. In addition, all e-mail sent or forwarded to the undercover agents is not protected by the Fourth Amendment. Therefore, the Court **DENIES** Defendant's motion to suppress as it relates to any statements made on AOL and any physical evidence that resulted from transmissions made by Defendant on AOL.

B. *Evidence Seized at Defendant's Residence*

The Court will next examine Defendant's motion to suppress as it relates to the evidence seized at Defendant's residence. It is well-settled law that a search conducted without the execution of a warrant is "per se unreasonable" and "subject only to a few specifically established and well-delineated exceptions. Further, one of the specifically established exceptions to the requirements of both a warrant and probable cause is a search that is conducted pursuant to consent. When the government seeks, however, to 'rely upon consent to justify the lawfulness of a search, [the government] has the burden of proving that the consent was, in fact, freely and voluntarily given.' "

The Supreme Court defined the test for whether a person's consent was voluntary by referencing a prior holding defining a "voluntary" confession. Quoting an earlier case, the Supreme Court stated:

> The ultimate test remains that which has been the only clearly established test in Anglo–American courts for two hundred years: the test of voluntariness. Is the confession the product of an essentially free and unconstrained choice by its maker? If it is, if he has willed to confess, it may be used against him. If it is not, if his will has been overborne and his capacity for self-determination critically impaired, the use of his confession offends due process.

Bumper v. North Carolina, 391 U.S. 543, 548, 88 S.Ct. 1788, 1792, 20 L.Ed.2d 797 (1968) (quoting *Culombe v. Connecticut*, 367 U.S. 568, 602, 81 S.Ct. 1860, 1879, 6 L.Ed.2d 1037 (1961)).

Similarly, the Supreme Court has used the totality of the circumstances test to determine whether a consent was voluntary. "[I]t is only by analyzing all the circumstances of an individual consent that it can be ascertained whether in fact it was voluntary or coerced." Some of the factors to consider in using the totality of the circumstances include: the age, education, intelligence of the person consenting; the presence of physical punishment or credible threats of violence; overreaching by the police; whether the defendant was under the influence of drugs or alcohol; and whether defendant was informed of his constitutional rights. The presence or absence of a single consensual or coercive factor is not of itself controlling as a matter of law. Instead, the court must "carefully sift the unique facts and circumstances of the case before it to determine whether the coercive factors ... outweigh the noncoercive ones."

In this case, the Court finds that the coercive factors outweigh the noncoercive factors. Specifically, the factors tending to establish an involuntary and coercive consent include: (a) the presence of over six agents at Dublin Coffman High School to question Debra Charbonneau and Brett Charbonneau; (b) the interrogation of Mrs. Charbonneau and her state of mind during the interrogation; (c) the threats made by the agents that they would have to forcibly enter her home by breaking down her front door if she failed to consent to the search; (d) the length of the interrogation of Mrs. Charbonneau by the agents; and (e) the simultaneous interrogation of her son Brent in a nearby room.

When a court examines the totality of the circumstances to determine whether a consent was voluntary, the Supreme Court counseled that "account must be taken of subtly coercive police questions, as well as the possibly vulnerable subjective state of the person who consents." Further, the evidence of voluntary consent must be "proved by clear and positive testimony" and "must be unequivocal, specific, and intelligently given, uncontaminated by any duress or coercion."

From all of the evidence presented, the Court finds that the government has failed to show that Debra Charbonneau's consent was "unequivocal, specific, and intelligently given, uncontaminated by any duress or coercion."

The government contends that even if Mrs. Charbonneau's consent was not voluntary, under the doctrine of inevitable discovery, the search was nonetheless valid. The inevitable discovery doctrine is a means by which the government can show that evidence that might be excluded because of some unconstitutional conduct nonetheless should be admissible. The inevitable discovery doctrine requires the court to speculate as to what would have occurred absent the illegal conduct. "Speculation, however, must be kept to a minimum; courts must focus on 'demonstrated historical facts capable of ready verification or impeachment.'" The burden of proof is on the government to establish that illegal evidence "would have been discovered by lawful means."

In *United States v. Kennedy*, 61 F.3d 494, 498–500 (6th Cir.1995) *cert. denied*, ___ U.S. ___ , 116 S.Ct. 1351, 134 L.Ed.2d 520 (1996), the Sixth Circuit discussed the doctrine of inevitable discovery. The doctrine applies when the "government can demonstrate either the existence of an independent, untainted investigation that inevitably would have uncovered the same evidence or other compelling facts establishing that the disputed evidence would have inevitably been discovered." *Id.* at 499. In other words, the Court must determine "what would have happened had the unlawful search never occurred."

In *Kennedy*, the Sixth Circuit held that the government can meet its burden of showing that the tainted evidence would be discovered through lawful means by showing that routine or standard police practices would have revealed the evidence. In this case, the Court finds that the items seized would have been inevitably discovered through the execution of the search warrant. Although this Court believes that the FBI agents did not behave in an appropriate manner when they dealt with Mrs. Charbonneau, the fact remains that the agents did have a search warrant that they could have executed upon their arrival at the

Charbonneau residence. Defendant does not challenge the sufficiency of that warrant and the Court sees no reason to conclude that the warrant is deficient. Executing a valid search warrant is a routine police practice. Therefore, even if Mrs. Charbonneau had not consented to a search, the agents would have legally discovered the evidence by executing the warrant.

Consequently, the evidence seized at the Charbonneau residence is admissible pursuant to the inevitable discovery exception to the exclusionary rule. Therefore, the Court **DENIES** Defendant's motion to suppress as it relates to any evidence seized at Defendant's residence.

IV. CONCLUSION

Upon consideration and being duly advised, the Court **GRANTS** Defendant's motion to suppress the oral statements made at the airport and **DENIES** Defendant's motion to suppress statements and physical evidence.

IT IS SO ORDERED.

C. RESTRICTING NON–GOVERNMENTAL COLLECTION OF INFORMATION

CHILDREN'S ONLINE PRIVACY PROTECTION ACT

15 U.S.C. § 6501 *et seq.*

§ 6502. Regulation of unfair and deceptive acts and practices in connection with the collection and use of personal information from and about children on the internet

(a) Acts prohibited

(1) In general

It is unlawful for an operator of a website or online service directed to children, or any operator that has actual knowledge that it is collecting personal information from a child, to collect personal information from a child in a manner that violates the regulations prescribed under subsection (b).

(2) Disclosure to parent protected

Notwithstanding paragraph (1), neither an operator of such a website or online service nor the operator's agent shall be held to be liable under any Federal or State law for any disclosure made in good faith and following reasonable procedures in responding to a request for disclosure of personal information under subsection (b)(1)(B)(iii) to the parent of a child.

(b) Regulations

(1) In general

Not later than 1 year after October 21, 1998, the Commission shall promulgate under section 553 of Title 5, regulations that—

(A) require the operator of any website or online service directed to children that collects personal information from children or the operator of a website or online service that has actual knowledge that it is collecting personal information from a child—

(i) to provide notice on the website of what information is collected from children by the operator, how the operator uses such information, and the operator's disclosure practices for such information; and

(ii) to obtain verifiable parental consent for the collection, use, or disclosure of personal information from children;

(B) require the operator to provide, upon request of a parent under this subparagraph whose child has provided personal information to that website or online service, upon proper identification of that parent, to such parent—

(i) a description of the specific types of personal information collected from the child by that operator;

(ii) the opportunity at any time to refuse to permit the operator's further use or maintenance in retrievable form, or future online collection, of personal information from that child; and

(iii) notwithstanding any other provision of law, a means that is reasonable under the circumstances for the parent to obtain any personal information collected from that child;

(C) prohibit conditioning a child's participation in a game, the offering of a prize, or another activity on the child disclosing more personal information than is reasonably necessary to participate in such activity; and

(D) require the operator of such a website or online service to establish and maintain reasonable procedures to protect the confidentiality, security, and integrity of personal information collected from children.

(2) When consent not required

The regulations shall provide that verifiable parental consent under paragraph (1)(A)(ii) is not required in the case of—

(A) online contact information collected from a child that is used only to respond directly on a one-time basis to a specific request from the child and is not used to recontact the child and is not maintained in retrievable form by the operator;

(B) a request for the name or online contact information of a parent or child that is used for the sole purpose of obtaining parental consent or providing notice under this section and where such information is not maintained in retrievable form by the operator if parental consent is not obtained after a reasonable time;

(C) online contact information collected from a child that is used only to respond more than once directly to a specific request from the child and is not used to recontact the child beyond the scope of that request—

(i) if, before any additional response after the initial response to the child, the operator uses reasonable efforts to provide a parent notice of the online contact information collected from the child, the purposes for which it is to be used, and an opportunity for the parent to request that the operator make no further use of the information and that it not be maintained in retrievable form; or

(ii) without notice to the parent in such circumstances as the Commission may determine are appropriate, taking into consideration the benefits to the child of access to information and services, and risks to the security and privacy of the child, in regulations promulgated under this subsection;

(D) the name of the child and online contact information (to the extent reasonably necessary to protect the safety of a child participant on the site)—

(i) used only for the purpose of protecting such safety;

(ii) not used to recontact the child or for any other purpose; and

(iii) not disclosed on the site,

if the operator uses reasonable efforts to provide a parent notice of the name and online contact information collected from the child, the purposes for which it is to be used, and an opportunity for the parent to request that the operator make no further use of the information and that it not be maintained in retrievable form; or

(E) the collection, use, or dissemination of such information by the operator of such a website or online service necessary—

(i) to protect the security or integrity of its website;

(ii) to take precautions against liability;

(iii) to respond to judicial process; or

(iv) to the extent permitted under other provisions of law, to provide information to law enforcement agencies or for an investigation on a matter related to public safety.

(3) Termination of service

The regulations shall permit the operator of a website or an online service to terminate service provided to a child whose parent has refused, under the regulations prescribed under paragraph

(1)(B)(ii), to permit the operator's further use or maintenance in retrievable form, or future online collection, of personal information from that child.

(c) Enforcement

Subject to sections 6503 of this title and 6505 of this title, a violation of a regulation prescribed under subsection (a) shall be treated as a violation of a rule defining an unfair or deceptive act or practice prescribed under section 18(a)(1)(B) of the Federal Trade Commission Act (15 U.S.C. 57a(a)(1)(B)).

(d) Inconsistent State law

No State or local government may impose any liability for commercial activities or actions by operators in interstate or foreign commerce in connection with an activity or action described in this chapter [15 U.S.C.A. § 6501 et seq.] that is inconsistent with the treatment of those activities or actions under this section.

IN RE LIBERTY FINANCIAL COMPANIES, INC.

Federal Trade Commission, May, 1999.

File No. 982 3522 (Westlaw, Federal Antitrust & Trade Regulation–Combined Antitrust & Trade Regulation Materials (FATR–ALL))

AGREEMENT CONTAINING CONSENT ORDER

The Federal Trade Commission has conducted an investigation of certain acts and practices of Liberty Financial Companies, Inc., a corporation ("proposed respondent"). Proposed respondent, having been represented by counsel, is willing to enter into an agreement containing a consent order resolving the allegations contained in the attached draft complaint. Therefore,

IT IS HEREBY AGREED by and between Liberty Financial Companies, Inc., by its duly authorized officer, and counsel for the Federal Trade Commission that:

* * *

ORDER

* * *

I.

IT IS ORDERED that respondent, directly or through any corporation, subsidiary, division, or other device, in connection with any online collection of personal information from children and/or consumers age thirteen (13) through seventeen (17), in or affecting commerce, shall not make any misrepresentation, in any manner, expressly or by implication:

A. That the information collected is maintained in an anonymous manner;

B. That children and/or consumers age thirteen (13) through seventeen (17) who submit such information will receive an e-mail newsletter or any other represented product or service;

C. That children and/or consumers age thirteen (13) through seventeen (17) who submit such information are eligible to win prizes in respondent's drawing or contest; or

D. Regarding the collection or use of personal information from or about children and/or consumers age thirteen (13) through seventeen (17).

II.

IT IS FURTHER ORDERED that respondent, directly or through any corporation, subsidiary, division, or other device, in connection with the online collection of personal information at a website directed to children, or at any commercial website where respondent has actual knowledge that it is collecting personal information from a child, in or affecting commerce, shall not collect personal information from any child if respondent has actual knowledge that such child does not have his or her parent's permission to provide the information to respondent. For purposes of Parts II, III, IV, and V of this order, respondent shall not be deemed to have actual knowledge if the child has falsely represented that (s)he is not a child and respondent does not knowingly possess information that such representation is false.

III.

IT IS FURTHER ORDERED that respondent, directly or through any corporation, subsidiary, division, or other device, in connection with the online collection of personal information from children, at a website directed to children, or at any commercial website where respondent has actual knowledge that it is collecting personal information from a child, in or affecting commerce, shall provide clear and prominent notice with respect to respondent's practices regarding its collection and use of personal information. Such notice shall include:

A. what information is being collected (e.g., "name," "home address," "e-mail address," "age," "interests");

B. how respondent uses such information;

C. respondent's disclosure practices for such information (e.g., parties to whom it may be disclosed, such as "advertisers of consumer products," "mailing list companies," "the general public");

D. a description of a means that is reasonable under the circumstances by which a parent whose child has provided personal information may obtain, upon request and upon proper identification, (i) a description of the specific types of personal information collected from the child by respondent, (ii) the opportunity at any time to refuse to permit the respondent's further use or maintenance in retrievable form, or future online collection, of personal information from that child, and (iii) any personal information collected from the child.

Such notice shall appear on the home page of respondent's website(s) directed to children, or at any commercial website where respondent has actual knowledge that it is collecting personal information from a child, and at each location on the site(s) at which such information is collected.

Provided, however, that for purposes of this Part, compliance with all of the following shall be deemed adequate notice: (a) placement of a clear and prominent hyperlink or button labeled **PRIVACY NOTICE** on the home page(s), which directly links to the privacy notice screen(s); (b) placement of the information required in this Part clearly and prominently on the privacy notice screen(s), followed on the same screen(s) with a button that must be clicked on to make it disappear; and (c) at each location on the site at which any personal information is collected, placement of a clear and prominent hyperlink on the initial screen on which the collection takes place, which links directly to the privacy notice and which is accompanied by the following statement in bold typeface:

NOTICE: We collect personal information on this site. To learn more about how we use your information click here.

IV.

IT IS FURTHER ORDERED that respondent, directly or through any corporation, subsidiary, division, or other device, in connection with the online collection of personal information from children at a website directed to children, or at any commercial website where respondent has actual knowledge that it is collecting personal information from a child, in or affecting commerce, shall maintain a procedure by which it obtains verifiable parental consent for the collection, use or disclosure of such information from children.

V.

IT IS FURTHER ORDERED that respondent Liberty Financial Companies, Inc., and its successors and assigns, shall delete from its website(s) directed to children, and at any commercial website(s) where respondent has actual knowledge that it is collecting personal information from a child, all personal information collected from children prior to the date of service of the order.

* * *

Notes and Questions

1. The FTC recently brought a case against James and Regana Rapp, owners of Touch Tone Information, Inc. for trafficking in private information. *See* Complaint, File No. 9823619, April 21, 1999, <http://www.ftc.gov/os/1999/9904/touchtonecomplaint.htm>; *see also* "Consumers' Private Financial Information Obtained and Sold Illegally; FTC

Alleges," FTC News Release April 22, 1999, 1999 WL 235845. This particular case gained a great deal of attention because the company was allegedly selling private information about the parents of the murdered child Jon–Benet Ramsey. These were data brokers calling themselves legitimate private investigators and providing a service to clients such as lawyers and employers who are looking for information about litigants, employees and job applicants. But the FTC claimed that these data brokers were engaging in deceptive and unfair practices which are invading consumer privacy. For example, according to the FTC, these data brokers started a search in public databases where they obtain some private information, then they make phone calls to banks pretending to be an account holder, in order to obtain more sensitive information about the real owner's account.

2.   Do you think it is appropriate for private investigators to obtain private information in this way? Should such practices be forbidden by specific legislation such as was before Congress as this book was being prepared? Should people who conduct ruses as described above be treated as criminals or rewarded for their ingenuity? Do you think the FTC is the appropriate agency to deal with this situation?

3.   The following discussion is based upon various sources on the Internet. Due to transitory nature of Internet pages, citations to sources are omitted.

In January 1999 Intel introduced the Pentium III chip for personal computers. Hardwired into each chip is a unique 96 bit number known as a Processor Serial Number (PSN), which Intel claims will enhance security for e-commerce and help corporate IT officials manage PCs and software. But privacy advocates immediately cried foul, claiming that the i.d. is a "super cookie" that web masters can use to track your every move online, and use the information to inundate you with unwanted spam or target online advertising to you based on your web habits.

In response to the criticism, and anticipating it, Intel announced that the chip would be shipped with the number turned on, and a utility that would allow users to turn it off. Based on significant negative feedback, Intel changed its policy and recommended that manufacturers ship PCs with the chip turned off. The company is also recommending that web sites mask user's PSN's, and is working with web sites to ensure that PSN's are used responsibly. Privacy advocates said this was not sufficient. For one thing, web sites could block users whose PSN's are turned off. Complaints have been lodged with the FTC, and states and some congressmen are considering legislation to counter what they see as invasion of privacy.

A privacy firm demonstrated in May 1999 that 'malicious code' could steal the PSN from a Pentium III PC without the user's knowledge. The purpose was to illustrate the vulnerability of personal information. Some are now concerned that this program could be made available on the Internet and cause additional malicious problems. This program is now included on a list of malicious programs in Symantec's Norton Antivirus software.

Was the Pentium III a threat to privacy?

Intel's website has made the following statement about the PSN:

The Pentium III processor was designed with the Internet in mind. One of the new security features designed to enhance your Internet experience is the "processor serial number," an electronic number that will be incorporated into the new Pentium III processor. The processor serial number is built into the silicon chip during the manufacturing process... If the user chooses, the processor serial number can serve as a means of identifying his or her system. System identification can enable certain benefits, such as authenticating participants in a secure chat room or enhanced security in e-commerce situations. For business users, processor serial number identification will allow Information Technology departments to provide better information management or improved management of corporate PC assets...We at Intel believe that protecting user privacy is very important, and we have taken a number of steps to give PC users choices on how they permit Internet websites to access their processor serial number. These steps include:

The ability of the processor hardware to turn off the feature so the serial number cannot be read. An Intel-developed control utility that gives users the option of enabling or disabling the processor serial number feature. The default setting of the control utility is to turn the processor serial number feature "OFF". This software will be made widely available free of charge on our website and other locations when the processor becomes available publicly.

Intel will not maintain a database that correlates processor serial numbers with consumers.

In general, if the processor serial number feature is turned "ON," a user will still need to explicitly allow the reading of the processor serial number by a website. In order to read the processor serial number, a website will need to run a program on a user's system. The default security setting of popular web browsers alerts a user before permitting a program to be executed...

Does the above statement change your opinion about the Pentium III?

When Microsoft released Windows 98, it contained a 'bug' in which anyone who registered the product online ended up putting a great deal of personal information on the Windows Registry that could be accessed by websites. This was done without the knowledge of the registrant. Microsoft offered on its website a download to remove this information, thus admitting that it created a security flaw. At least Microsoft offered a fix.

4. The operator of a web-advertising company, DoubleClick Inc., has faced at least six lawsuits for invasion of privacy. The lawsuits challenged the way the company handled data that it collects from individuals who surf the Web. It obtained this information via cookies, files of information stored on an individuals computer, and retrievable by website software. Concern grew when DoubleClick obtained a database of 90 million individual purchasing profiles that could then be matched to the numerous anonymous profiles of people who had visited the websites hosting its advertisement. Double-Click claimed that it obtained this information in order to customize the advertisements displayed for individuals based on their web surfing habits. Many of the lawsuits alleged that DoubleClick did not provide adequate notice of its use of personal information, because the privacy policies of the

host websites did not include notice that Double Click would use data collected from these sites. As a result of the complaints, DoubleClick shelved some of its plans to use the information it collected.

ELECTRONIC COMMUNICATIONS PRIVACY ACT § 2701

18 U.S.C. § 2701.

§ 2701. Unlawful access to stored communications

(a) Offense.—Except as provided in subsection (c) of this section whoever—

(1) intentionally accesses without authorization a facility through which an electronic communication service is provided; or

(2) intentionally exceeds an authorization to access that facility; and thereby obtains, alters, or prevents authorized access to a wire or electronic communication while it is in electronic storage in such system shall be punished as provided in subsection (b) of this section.

(b) Punishment. * * *

(c) Exceptions.—Subsection (a) of this section does not apply with respect to conduct authorized–

(1) by the person or entity providing a wire or electronic communications service;

(2) by a user of that service with respect to a communication of or intended for that user; or

(3) in section 2703, 2704 or 2518 of this title.

D. RESTRICTING USE BY THE GOVERNMENT OF INFORMATION IN GOVERNMENT RECORDS

PIPPINGER v. RUBIN

United States Court of Appeals, Tenth Circuit, 1997.
129 F.3d 519.

EBEL, CIRCUIT JUDGE.

Because of a romantic relationship with a subordinate, Plaintiff–Appellant John Pippinger was temporarily suspended from his job as an Internal Revenue Service ("IRS") branch manager. Several IRS employees were involved in helping the local IRS District Director reach the decision to suspend Pippinger. Eventually, many IRS employees in the district knew why Pippinger was suspended.

Before Pippinger's suspension was carried out, Pippinger's supervisor Patrick Schluck got into trouble with the IRS because he too had a romantic relationship with a subordinate. During the depositions and proceedings pertaining to Schluck's case, Pippinger's case was discussed and the IRS disclosed information from records of Pippinger's case to Schluck and his attorneys.

Pippinger sued the IRS, alleging violations of the Privacy Act of 1974, 5 U.S.C. § 552a (1994). The district court granted summary judgment in favor of the IRS. Pippinger appeals. Because we agree with the district court that Pippinger's rights under the Privacy Act were not violated, we affirm.

* * *

In April 1994, Pippinger was granted a hearing by the Regional Commissioner's office. Around that time, Pippinger learned that his case had been discussed, and his and Boak's identities revealed, during discovery in Schluck's MSPB proceeding. At that time, Pippinger also learned that the IRS had been maintaining a computer database known as the "Automated Labor Employee Relations Tracking System" ("ALERTS"). The nationwide ALERTS system was used by the IRS permanently to record all disciplinary action proposed or taken against any IRS employee.

The ALERTS system contained two separate entries on Pippinger: one describing Pippinger's alleged misconduct and his proposed two-day suspension; the other documenting Pippinger's appeal through the agency's grievance process. Information from the ALERTS entry pertaining to Pippinger's misconduct and suspension had been disclosed in depositions taken during Schluck's MSPB proceedings.

In May 1994, the Regional Commissioner upheld Pippinger's suspension. Pippinger then requested the appointment of an IRS Grievance Examiner. On November 2, 1994, the Grievance Examiner issued a Report of Findings and Recommendations upholding Pippinger's suspension.

On January 19, 1995, Pippinger sued the Secretary of the Treasury (also referred to in this opinion as the "IRS"), alleging that the IRS had violated the Privacy Act of 1974, 5 U.S.C. § 552a (1994), by maintaining disciplinary records on Pippinger in the allegedly unlawful ALERTS database and also by allegedly disclosing information from those records on several occasions. In a second count, Pippinger also claimed that the IRS had violated his First, Fourth and Fifth Amendment rights to Due Process and Privacy.

The IRS moved pursuant to Fed.R.Civ.P. 12(b)(6) to dismiss Pippinger's constitutional claims, and moved for summary judgment with respect to Pippinger's Privacy Act claims. Before ruling on the IRS's motions, the district court allowed discovery to proceed.

* * *

Discussion

I. Maintenance of Disciplinary Records

As a threshold matter, Pippinger claims that the Privacy Act of 1974, 5 U.S.C. § 552a (1994), prohibits the IRS from maintaining disciplinary records of its employees in the ALERTS system, because the ALERTS system is not adequately described in the Federal Register. In support of this claim, Pippinger cites 5 U.S.C. § 552a(e)(4) (1994), which provides that:

> Each agency that maintains a system of records shall . . . publish in the Federal Register upon establishment or revision a notice of the existence and character of the system of records, which notice shall include—
>
> (A) the name and location of the system;
>
> (B) the categories of individuals on whom records are maintained in the system;
>
> (C) the categories of records maintained in the system;
>
> (D) each routine use of the records contained in the system, including the categories of users and the purpose of such use;
>
> (E) the policies and practices of the agency regarding storage, retrievability, access controls, retention, and disposal of the records;
>
> (F) the title and business address of the agency official who is responsible for the system of records;
>
> (G) the agency procedures whereby an individual can be notified at his request if the system of records contains a record pertaining to him;
>
> (H) the agency procedures whereby an individual can be notified at his request how he can gain access to any record pertaining to him contained in the system of records, and how he can contest its content; and
>
> (I) the categories of sources of records in the system.

In particular, Pippinger claims that the IRS failed to comply with subsections (A) through (E) of 5 U.S.C. § 552a(e)(4) (1994). With respect to subsections (B) through (E), Pippinger's claim is predicated on his factual misconception that the IRS never published any notice regarding the keeping of records on disciplinary actions taken against employees. This assertion is simply incorrect.

* * *

Pippinger does, however, state one facially valid claim against the legality of the ALERTS system. He correctly notes that the name and location of the ALERTS system have never been published in the Federal Register, which he claims is in violation of 5 U.S.C. § 552a(e)(4)(A) (1994). Thus, we must decide whether the abstraction of certain individual records from a "system of records," or the transcription of such an abstract from paper to computer or electronic storage media, constitutes the creation of a new "system of records" under 5 U.S.C. § 552a(a)(5) (1994), where, as here, the electronic abstract may be accessed only by the same users, and only for the same purposes, as the original "system of records."

Although no court, to our knowledge, has addressed these questions directly, there is limited case authority consistent with the proposition that abstraction of individual records from a "system of records" does not by itself create a new system of records. In *Henke v. United States Dep't of Commerce*, 83 F.3d 1453, 1459–61 (D.C.Cir.1996), the court addressed whether an agency can be deemed to maintain a computerized "system of records" where it has the capability to retrieve information about an individual by name, but not the practice of doing so. Although this is not the question before us, the approach of the *Henke* court to determining the meaning of a "system of records" under 5 U.S.C. § 552a(a)(5) is instructive.

In holding that the records at issue there did not constitute a "system of records" under the Privacy Act, the *Henke* court noted that the phrase "system of records" should be narrowly construed, because under an expansive reading of the phrase:

an agency faces the threat of being found retrospectively to be maintaining a system of records it did not even know existed, simply by dint of a potential use it neither engaged in nor contemplated. This in turn would create serious compliance problems for the agency, because if it had not recognized that it maintained a system of records and had therefore not published notice of its system in the Federal Register, then neither would it have followed the procedures necessary [under the Privacy Act]. . . .

Henke, 83 F.3d at 1461;

The *Henke* court expressly disclaimed suggesting "that an agency may simply refuse to acknowledge that it maintains a system of records and thereby insulate itself from the reach of the Privacy Act." However, it opined that a major factor in determining whether a "system of records" exists "is the *purpose* for which the information on individuals is being gathered, an approach which is consistent with Congress' distinction between a mere group of records and a *system* of records." *Id.* (emphasis in original).

In the present case, Pippinger has presented no evidence suggesting that the records abstracted from the Appeals, Grievance, and Complaint System and the General Personnel and Payroll Records System and stored in the ALERTS computer system were used for any purposes other than the purposes, published in the Federal Register, for which those records were intended. Similarly, he has presented no evidence that the abstracted records could be accessed via the ALERTS system by anyone not identified in the Federal Register as an authorized user of the same records contained in the Appeals, Grievance, and Complaint System or the General Personnel and Payroll Records System. Thus, consistent with *Henke*, a properly "narrow" construction of 5 U.S.C. § 552a(a)(5) leads to the conclusion that ALERTS is not a "system of records."

We turn then to the question of whether transcription of a system of records from paper to computer or electronic storage media necessarily constitutes the creation of a new "system of records" under 5 U.S.C. § 552a(a)(5) (1994). In addition to requiring publication of the establishment and existence of a government-maintained "system of records," the Privacy Act also requires government agencies to publish in the Federal Register notice of revisions in the *character* of existing systems of records. For this reason, one circuit court recently remanded a Privacy Act case to the district court to determine whether a government agency had, in fact, transferred a system of records stored in paper documents to a digitally stored format. *Williams v. Department of Veterans Affairs*, 104 F.3d 670, 676 (4th Cir.1997). In doing so, the *Williams* court suggested the possibility that if such a change had occurred without proper publication, 5 U.S.C. § 552a(e)(4) would have been violated. *Id.*

We need not, in the present case, decide whether or not we agree with the *Williams* court that routine transcription of records from paper to computer or electronic storage media always necessitates publication in the Federal Register. Here, unlike in *Williams*, the IRS properly published the fact that records maintained in both the Appeals, Grievances and Complaint System and the General Personnel and Payroll Records System would be stored on "magnetic media." Because the transcription of records stored in the Appeals, Grievances and Complaint System and the General Personnel and Payroll Records System to "magnetic media" was contemplated and announced in the Federal Register, the "character" of the records was not revised when the records were in fact transcribed to the ALERTS system.

In addition, even if the ALERTS system were a separate "system of records" under 5 U.S.C. § 552a(e) (1994), Pippinger would lack standing to challenge the IRS's failure to publish the ALERTS system's name and location in the Federal Register. In its "civil remedies" subsection, the Privacy Act provides that:

> Whenever any agency ... fails to comply with [5 U.S.C. § 552a], ... *in such a way as to have an adverse effect on an individual*, the individual may bring a civil action against the agency....

5 U.S.C. § 552a(g)(1)(D) (1994) (emphasis added).

Here, Pippinger has introduced no evidence tending to suggest that the mere maintenance in the ALERTS system of records that could be lawfully maintained by the IRS in other systems of records "adversely affected" him in any way. Indeed, when Pippinger requested copies of all IRS records pertaining to him, the ALERTS system *assisted* the IRS in locating Pippinger's two records—which were kept in two different systems—in order to provide them to him. Thus, even if the ALERTS system were a "system of records" subject to the publication requirements of 5 U.S.C. § 552a(e)(4)(A) (1994), Pippinger would not recover for the IRS's technical failure to comply with those requirements.

II. *Disclosure of Disciplinary Records*

The Privacy Act of 1974 limits the circumstances under which government agencies, including the IRS, may disclose information contained in their records. In general, the Act provides that:

No agency shall disclose any record which is contained in a system of records by any means of communication to any person, or to another agency, except pursuant to a written request by, or with the prior written consent of, the individual to whom the record pertains

. . . .

5 U.S.C. § 552a(b) (1994); accord 5 C.F.R. § 297.401 (1996) However, the Act goes on to enumerate twelve exceptions to this general prohibition. *See id.*

Pippinger, who did not consent to any disclosure, claims that the IRS unlawfully disclosed his employment records on three different occasions. In analyzing each of these three claims, we must decide whether a record was "disclosed," and, if so, whether it was disclosed pursuant to an exception enumerated in 5 U.S.C. § 552a(b).

Although "disclosure" is not defined in the text of the Privacy Act, the Office of Personnel Management ("OPM") has defined "disclosure" under the Privacy Act to mean "providing personal review of a record, or a copy thereof, to someone other than the data subject or the data subject's authorized representative...." 5 C.F.R. § 297.102 (1997). Although the OPM's definition of "disclosure" would appear to be limited to disclosures of the physical records themselves (or mechanical reproductions thereof), this court and other courts have assumed or held that the Privacy Act more broadly prohibits disclosure of information directly or indirectly derived from an agency system of records, even where the physical records are not disclosed. *See Wilborn v. Department of Health and Human Servs.,* 49 F.3d 597, 600 (9th Cir.1995).

As the *Wilborn* court explained:

the Privacy Act applies to a situation where an agency official uses the government's sophisticated information collecting methods to acquire personal information for inclusion in a record, and then discloses that information in an unauthorized fashion *without actually physically retrieving* it from the record system.

Id. at 601 (quoting *Bartel v. FAA),* 725 F.2d 1403, 1410 (D.C.Cir.1984) (emphasis in *Wilborn*). The courts' broad interpretation of the Privacy Act's prohibition against disclosure is clearly consistent with Congressional intent. As the Joint House and Senate Report explained, a primary purpose of 5 U.S.C. § 552a(b) is to:

require employees to refrain from disclosing records *or personal data in them*, within the agency other than to officers or employees who have a need for such record or data in the performance of their duties for the agency.

This section is designed to prevent the office gossip, interoffice and interbureau leaks of information about persons of interest in the agency or community, or such actions as the publicizing of information of a sensational or salacious nature or of that detrimental to character or reputation.

S.Rep. No. 93–1183, H.Rep. No. 93–1416, at 51 (1974) (emphasis added), *reprinted in* 1974 U.S.C.C.A.N. 6916, 6966, *and quoted in part in Parks v. Internal Revenue Service*, 618 F.2d 677, 681 n. 1 (10th Cir.1980).

With these broad purposes in mind, we proceed to analyze Pippinger's claim that improper disclosures were made on three occasions.

* * *

[The court held that the disclosures were authorized and had no adverse effect upon Pippinger.]

For these reasons, we hold that the district court did not abuse its discretion by ruling on the IRS's substantive motions on April 10, 1996.

CONCLUSION

The judgment of the district court is AFFIRMED in all respects.

Note

Major changes are taking place in computerized record keeping. Originally, most government and private organizations kept a number of separate records systems. For instance a law school might keep a records system for admissions applications, another for grades, another for alumni affairs, another for personnel, another for event planning, etc. Increasingly the trend has been to develop software that can combine data from various records systems for analysis. For instance the law school fundraising office might be able use this software to identify, with a single query, alumni who were on the waiting list when they had applied for admission, received good grades from Professor Smith, and were regular donors so as to seat them at Professor Smith's table and not at the admission director's table at an alumni luncheon. In the context of such software, the idea that an agency maintains separate "systems of records" may make little sense.

BOHACH v. CITY OF RENO

United States District Court, D. Nevada, 1996.
932 F.Supp. 1232.

EDWARD C. REED, JR., DISTRICT JUDGE.

Mr. Bohach and Mr. Catalano are officers of the Reno Police Department. In early 1996, they sent messages to one another, and to another member of the Department, over the Department's "Alphapage" message system. Faced with an internal affairs investigation based on the contents of those messages, they filed this lawsuit, claiming that both the storage of the messages by the Department's computer network, and their subsequent retrieval from the computer's files, were violations of the federal wiretapping statutes and of their constitutional right to privacy. They sought to stop the investigation and to bar any disclosure of the contents of the messages As they were to be interrogated almost immediately, we issued a temporary restraining order. After a hearing, we dissolved the restraining order and refused to issue a preliminary injunction.

Officers Bohach and Catalano have taken an interlocutory appeal and ask that the court's decision denying the injunction be suspended under Rule 62(c). That amounts to a request that their motion for an injunction, having been denied, in effect be granted pending resolution of the appeal. This would bar the Reno Police Department from conducting an internal affairs investigation, and interference by a federal court in the internal operations of a state or local government is an exceptional matter. We therefore gave the City an opportunity to respond to the plaintiffs' Rule 62 motion, and it has done so.

I. FACTS

According to Patricia Marcuerquiaga, the Reno Police Department's computer administrator, "Alphapage" is a software program, installed on the Reno Police Department's Local Area Network ("LAN") computer system, which allows the transmission of brief alphanumeric messages to visual display pagers. The software, formally styled the "Alphapage Media Notification System," was installed on the system in mid–1994. According to a standing order issued at that time by Richard Kirkland, who was then Chief of the Reno Police Department, , the purpose was to allow the broadcast of "mini news releases" and other "timely information" to the media by means of the pagers and thus to free up the Department's regular telephone lines. The order warned all users that "[e]very Alphapage message is logged on the network," and prohibited some types of messages (e.g., those containing comment on Department policy, and those whose contents violated the Department's anti-discrimination policy).

The system's mechanical details are fairly simple, at least from the user's standpoint. Alphanumeric or voice messages can be sent on the Alphapage system by telephone, by "stand-alone" keyboard, or by means of the LAN computer system. We pass over the first two methods of transmission and the matter of voice messages. All the messages at issue in this case were alphanumeric (no human voice was involved). And all, it seems, were sent to the recipient's pager from a computer terminal, rather than by telephone or "stand-alone" keyboard; we assume that this is so because the latter methods of transmission, according to the City's expert, would have left no permanent record in the computer.

Use of the Alphapage system by means of the computer system proceeds roughly as follows. The user logs on to any Reno Police Department computer terminal and selects Alphapage from the menu of available functions, and then selects, from a list of all persons to whom pagers have been issued, the name of the person to whom the message is to be sent. The user then types the message and hits the "send" key. The message is sent to the computer system's "Inforad Message Directory," where it is stored in a server file, and the user receives a message on the computer screen indicating that the page is being processed. The computer then dials the commercial paging company, sends the message to the company by modem, and disconnects. The user receives a "page sent" message on the computer screen, and the paging company takes over, sending the message to the recipient pager by radio broadcast.

II.   FOURTH AMENDMENT

Officers Bohach and Catalano can succeed on their § 1983 fourth amendment claim only if, at a minimum, they demonstrate that they had a reasonable expectation of privacy in their use of the Alphapage system. We assume that they did indeed have a subjective expectation of privacy, if only because we cannot believe that, had they thought otherwise, they would ever have sent over the system the sorts of messages they did send. The question is whether their expectation was objectively reasonable. Based on the evidence now available, we think that is most unlikely.

To begin with, all messages are recorded and stored not because anyone is "tapping" the system, but simply because that's how the system works. It is an integral part of the technology, and in this respect Alphapage is like most pager systems, which store messages in a central computer until they are retrieved by, or sent to, the intended recipient. Moreover, while one phase of an Alphapage transmission (from the pager company to the recipient pager) may involve a radio broadcast, the earlier phase at issue here (from the user's keyboard to the computer) is essentially electronic mail—and e-mail messages are, by definition, stored in a routing computer.

That only a diminished expectation of privacy would be reasonable in this case is also suggested by then-Chief of Police Kirkland's order, issued when Alphapage was first installed and long before the messages in this case were sent, notifying all users that their messages would be "logged on the network" and that certain types of messages (e.g., those violating the Department's antidiscrimination policy) were banned from the system. Now, that is not the same thing as saying that the contents of all messages will be recorded and retained, but it suggests that one should expect less privacy on Alphapage than on, say, a private telephone line. We note, also, that Alphapage is accessible to anyone with access to, and a working knowledge of, the Department's computer system. No special password or clearance is needed. The current Chief of the Reno Police Department, James Weston, testified that the Department's janitor, if he had general access to the computer system, could roam at will through Alphapage.

Finally, and more generally, we note that police stations often record all outgoing and incoming phone calls, "for a variety of reasons: to make sure that their dispatches are accurate, to verify information, and to keep a log of emergency and nonemergency calls." This may or may not violate the wiretapping statutes, depending upon how it is done. For fourth amendment purposes, however, the point is that the practice is part of the "ordinary course of business" for police departments, and it is all the more reasonable in this case in light of Alphapage's purpose and limitations. Unlike a telephone, the system is not designed to communicate with the public generally. It was installed to allow communications among police personnel, and between police personnel and the press, about police matters; that it can be used to send private communications between police personnel is incidental to its primary function. Further, unlike a telephone line, Alphapage can be used to communicate only with a recipient who has an Alphapage pager, i.e., a member of the Department or the press. So, while officers Bohach and Catalano attempt liken their communications to private telephone calls, we think that some aspects of the system (its primary though not exclusive purpose, the restrictions placed on the contents of messages, the limited number of persons with whom one can communicate using it, and the fact that police departments routinely and properly record their communications with the public) suggest that one should expect, when using it, less privacy than one might expect when, say, making a private telephone call, even from a police station.

III. STATUTORY CLAIMS

The federal wiretapping statutes cover "wire," "oral" and "electronic" communications. The messages at issue here were "electronic" communications within the meaning of 18 U.S.C. § 2510(12). (They did not involve a human voice and thus were not "wire" or "oral" communications). An "electronic communication" consists of the "transfer" of the signals, data, and other items listed at § 2510(12), but does not include their "electronic storage." An electronic communication may be put into electronic storage, but the storage is not itself a part of the communication. The statutes therefore distinguish the "interception" of an electronic communication at the time of transmission from the retrieval of such a communication after it has been put into "electronic storage." Interceptions are covered by §§ 2510–22, and access to information in electronic storage by §§ 2701–11.

Section 2511(1)(a) forbids, among other things, the interception of electronic communications. An "interception" is the "acquisition of the contents of any . . . electronic . . . communication through the use of any electronic, mechanical or other device." § 2510(4). One might ask how any "interception," as the word is usually understood, could be thought to have occurred here. After all, no computer or phone lines have been tapped, no conversations picked up by hidden microphones, no duplicate pager "cloned" to tap into messages intended for another recipient.

This view is supported by both the statute and the nature of the pager system's operation. To begin with, we think no one would object if the computer were just a passive conduit for a communication, on its way from the sender's keyboard to the pager company and on to recipient's pager. After all, if the computer received an electronic communication from a terminal and passed it on to the pager company, but did *not* store or otherwise record its contents, it would not have acquired "information concerning the [communication's] substance, purport, or meaning," and therefore no "intercept" would have taken place. (And if there were an intercept, consent would likely be implied under

§ 2511(2)(c), for one who sends a message using a computer surely must understand that the message will pass through the computer.)

Indeed, we do not understand the plaintiffs to object to the mere passage of their messages through the computer. Their complaint, as we understand it, is that the computer stored (or recorded, or downloaded) the contents of those messages. And that, we think, is where their argument breaks down. The computer's storage of an electronic communication, whether that storage was "temporary" and "intermediate" and "incidental to" its impending "electronic transmission," or more permanent storage for backup purposes, was "electronic storage." An "electronic communication," by definition, cannot be "intercepted" when it is in "electronic storage," because only "communications" can be "intercepted," and, as the Fifth Circuit held in *Steve Jackson Games Inc. v. United States Secret Service*, 36 F.3d 457 (5th Cir.1994), the "electronic storage" of an "electronic communication" is by definition not part of the communication. The treatment of messages in "electronic storage" is governed by §§ 2701–11, not by the restrictions on "interception" set out at §§ 2501–22.

This leads us to the plaintiffs' claim that the City acted unlawfully when, months after the messages were sent, it accessed and retrieved them from storage in the computer. The problem with the claim is simple. The City is the "provider" of the "electronic communications service" at issue here: the Reno Police Department's terminals, computer and software, and the pagers it issues to its personnel, are, after all, what provide those users with "the ability to send or receive" electronic communications. But § 2701(c)(1) allows service providers to do as they wish when it comes to accessing communications in electronic storage. Because the City is the provider of the "service," neither it nor its employees can be liable under § 2701.

IV. CONCLUSION

The plaintiffs have not established that they had an objectively reasonable expectation of privacy in the messages at issue. To the extent that the computer acted as a mere conduit of their messages to one another, we do not understand the plaintiffs to complain, and in any event we that think no "interception" occurred; even if there had been an interception, we would likely find implied consent in light of the plaintiffs' decision to send those messages via the computer. We understand the plaintiffs' real complaint to be that their messages were recorded and stored in, and later retrieved from, the computer. But the initial act of storage was "electronic storage," and the applicable statutes are therefore §§ 2701–11 rather than §§ 2501–22. Under those statutes, the City, as the system provider, was free to access the stored messages as it pleased. The injunction was properly denied, and there is no reason to suspend that denial pending resolution of the plaintiffs' appeal.

IT IS THEREFORE HEREBY ORDERED that the plaintiffs' **motion** pursuant to Fed.R.Civ.P. 62 is **DENIED**.

IT IS FURTHER ORDERED that the court's prior **order**, enjoining the City's actions pending further order of this court, is **VACATED**, and the City is free to proceed.

E. RESTRICTING USE BY PRIVATE PARTIES OF INFORMATION IN PRIVATE RECORDS

SMYTH v. PILLSBURY

United States District Court, E.D. Pennsylvania, 1996.
914 F.Supp. 97.

WEINER, DISTRICT JUDGE.

In this diversity action, plaintiff, an at-will employee, claims he was wrongfully discharged from his position as a regional operations manager by the defendant. Presently before the court is the motion of the defendant to dismiss pursuant to Rule 12(b)(6) of the Federal Rules of Civil Procedure. For the reasons which follow, the motion is granted.

* * *

Defendant maintained an electronic mail communication system ("e-mail") in order to promote internal corporate communications between its employees. Defendant repeatedly assured its employees, including plaintiff, that all e-mail communications would remain confidential and privileged. Defendant further assured its employees, including plaintiff, that e-mail communications could not be intercepted and used by defendant against its employees as grounds for termination or reprimand.

In October 1994, plaintiff received certain e-mail communications from his supervisor over defendant's e-mail system on his computer at home. In reliance on defendant's assurances regarding defendant's e-mail system, plaintiff responded and exchanged e-mails with his supervisor. At some later date, contrary to the assurances of confidentiality made by defendant, defendant, acting through its agents, servants and employees, intercepted plaintiff's private e-mail messages made in October 1994. On January 17, 1995, defendant notified plaintiff that it was terminating his employment effective February 1, 1995, for transmitting what it deemed to be inappropriate and unprofessional comments over defendant's e-mail system in October, 1994.

As a general rule, Pennsylvania law does not provide a common law cause of action for the wrongful discharge of an at-will employee such as plaintiff. Pennsylvania is an employment at-will jurisdiction and an employer "may discharge an employee with or without cause, at pleasure, unless restrained by some contract."

However, in the most limited of circumstances, exceptions have been recognized where discharge of an at-will employee threatens or violates a clear mandate of public policy. To date, the Pennsylvania Superior Court has only recognized three such exceptions. * * *

First, an employee may not be fired for serving on jury duty. *Reuther v. Fowler & Williams, Inc.*, 255 Pa.Super. 28, 386 A.2d 119 (1978). The Reuther court cited the Pennsylvania constitution as well as the Pennsylvania statutes in concluding that "the necessity of having citizens freely available for jury service is just the sort of 'recognized facet of public policy' alluded to by our Supreme Court in Geary."

Second, an employer may not deny employment to a person with a prior conviction. *Hunter v. Port Authority of Allegheny County*, 277 Pa.Super. 4, 419 A.2d 631 (1980). The *Hunter* court relied on federal court decisions as well as Pennsylvania statutes and Pennsylvania court decisions before concluding that the defendant violated the Pennsylvania constitution and "the deeply ingrained public policy of this State ... to avoid unwarranted stigmatization of and unreasonable restrictions upon former offenders."

And finally, an employee may not be fired for reporting violations of federal regulations to the Nuclear Regulatory Commission. *Field v. Philadelphia Electric Company*, 388 Pa.Super. 400, 565 A.2d 1170, 1180 (1989). That court held that the alleged discharge was against public policy because federal law required the employee to report violations and he was an expert in the area and there was no evidence that he bypassed any internal chain of command.

As evidenced above, a public policy exception must be clearly defined. The sources of public policy can be found in "legislation, administrative rules, regulation, or decision; and judicial decisions ... Absent legislation, the judiciary must define the cause of action in case by case determinations."

Plaintiff claims that his termination was in violation of "public policy which precludes an employer from terminating an employee in violation of the employee's right to privacy as embodied in Pennsylvania common law." In support for this proposition, plaintiff directs our attention to a decision by our Court of Appeals in *Borse v. Piece Goods Shop, Inc.*, 963 F.2d 611 (3d Cir.1992). In *Borse*, the plaintiff sued her employer alleging wrongful discharge as a result of her refusal to submit to urinalysis screening and personal property searches at her work place pursuant to the employer's drug and alcohol policy. After rejecting plaintiff's argument that the employer's drug and alcohol program violated public policy encompassed in the United States and Pennsylvania Constitutions, our Court of Appeals stated "our review of Pennsylvania law reveals other evidence of a public policy that may, under certain circumstances, give rise to a wrongful discharge action related to urinalysis or to personal property searches. Specifically, we refer to the Pennsylvania common law regarding tortious invasion of privacy." *Id.* at 620.

The Court of Appeals in *Borse*, observed that one of the torts which Pennsylvania recognizes as encompassing an action for invasion of privacy is the tort of "intrusion upon seclusion." As noted by the Court of Appeals, the Restatement (Second) of Torts defines the tort as follows:

One who intentionally intrudes, physically or otherwise, upon the solitude or seclusion of another or his private affairs or concerns, is subject to liability to the other for invasion of his privacy, if the intrusion would be highly offensive to a reasonable person.

Restatement (Second) of Torts § 652B. Liability only attaches when the "intrusion is substantial and would be highly offensive to the 'ordinary reasonable person.' " *Borse*, 963 F.2d at 621 (citation omitted). Although the Court of Appeals in *Borse* observed that "[t]he Pennsylvania courts have not had occasion to consider whether a discharge related to an employer's tortious invasion of an employee's privacy violates public policy", the Court of Appeals predicted that in any claim where the employee claimed that his discharge related to an invasion of his privacy "the Pennsylvania Supreme Court would examine the facts and circumstances surrounding the alleged invasion of privacy. If the court determined that the discharge was related to a substantial and highly offensive invasion of the employee's privacy, [the Court of Appeals] believe that it would conclude that the discharge violated public policy." *Id.* at 622. In determining whether an alleged invasion of privacy is substantial and highly offensive to a reasonable person, the Court of Appeals predicted that Pennsylvania would adopt a balancing test which balances the employee's privacy interest against the employer's interest in maintaining a drug-free workplace. Because the Court of Appeals in *Borse* could "envision at least two ways in which an employer's drug and alcohol program might violate the public policy protecting individuals from tortious invasion of privacy by private actors" *id.* at 626, the Court vacated the district court's order dismissing the plaintiff's complaint and remanded the case to the district court with directions to grant Borse leave to amend the Complaint to allege how the defendant's drug and alcohol program violates her right to privacy.

Applying the Restatement definition of the tort of intrusion upon seclusion to the facts and circumstances of the case *sub judice*, we find that plaintiff has failed to state a claim upon which relief can be granted. In the first instance, unlike urinalysis and personal property searches, we do not find a reasonable expectation of privacy in e-mail communications voluntarily made by an employee to his supervisor over the company e-mail system notwithstanding any assurances that such communications would not be intercepted by management. Once plaintiff communicated the alleged unprofessional comments to a second person (his supervisor) over an e-mail system which was apparently utilized by the entire company, any reasonable expectation of privacy was lost. Significantly, the defendant did not require plaintiff, as in the case of an urinalysis or personal property search to disclose any personal information about himself. Rather, plaintiff voluntarily communicated the alleged unprofessional comments over the company e-mail system. We find no privacy interests in such communications.

In the second instance, even if we found that an employee had a reasonable expectation of privacy in the contents of his e-mail communications over the company e-mail system, we do not find that a reasonable person would consider the defendant's interception of these communications to be a substantial and highly offensive invasion of his privacy. Again, we note that by intercepting such communications, the company is not, as in the case of urinalysis or personal property searches, requiring the employee to disclose any personal information about himself or invading the employee's person or personal effects. Moreover, the company's interest in preventing inappropriate and unprofessional comments or even illegal activity over its e-mail system outweighs any privacy interest the employee may have in those comments.

In sum, we find that the defendant's actions did not tortiously invade the plaintiff's privacy and, therefore, did not violate public policy. As a result, the motion to dismiss is granted.

Notes and Questions

In *McLaren v. Microsoft*, 1999 WL 339015, Court of Appeals of Texas, Dallas, 1999, a former employee of the company argued for a cause of action for invasion of privacy because his employer reviewed and disseminated electronic mail that had been stored in a "personal folder" on his office computer. In this case, the court did not find facts sufficient to state a cause of action for invasion of privacy. What facts in this case and the other cases in this section suggest that it is difficult for employees to bring invasion of privacy actions against their employers with regard to email.

F. RESTRICTING DISCLOSURE BY THE GOVERNMENT OF INFORMATION IN GOVERNMENT RECORDS

RENO v. CONDON

Supreme Court of the United States, 2000.
528 U.S. 141, 120 S.Ct. 666, 145 L.Ed.2d 587.

CHIEF JUSTICE REHNQUIST delivered the opinion of the Court.

The Driver's Privacy Protection Act of 1994 (DPPA or Act), 18 U.S.C. §§ 2721–2725 (1994 ed. and Supp. III), regulates the disclosure of personal information contained in the records of state motor vehicle departments (DMVs). We hold that in enacting this statute Congress did not run afoul of the federalism principles enunciated in *New York v. United States*, 505 U.S. 144, 112 S.Ct. 2408, 120 L.Ed.2d 120 (1992), and *Printz v. United States*, 521 U.S. 898, 117 S.Ct. 2365, 138 L.Ed.2d 914 (1997).

The DPPA regulates the disclosure and resale of personal information contained in the records of state DMVs. State DMVs require drivers and automobile owners to provide personal information, which may include a person's name, address, telephone number, vehicle description, Social Security number, medical information, and photograph, as a condition of obtaining a driver's license or registering an automobile.

Congress found that many States, in turn, sell this personal information to individuals and businesses. These sales generate significant revenues for the States.

The DPPA establishes a regulatory scheme that restricts the States' ability to disclose a driver's personal information without the driver's consent. The DPPA generally prohibits any state DMV, or officer, employee, or contractor thereof, from "knowingly disclos[ing] or otherwise mak[ing] available to any person or entity personal information about any individual obtained by the department in connection with a motor vehicle record." 18 U.S.C. § 2721(a). The DPPA defines "personal information" as any information "that identifies an individual, including an individual's photograph, social security number, driver identification number, name, address (but not the 5–digit zip code), telephone number, and medical or disability information," but not including "information on vehicular accidents, driving violations, and driver's status." § 2725(3). A "motor vehicle record" is defined as "any record that pertains to a motor vehicle operator's permit, motor vehicle title, motor vehicle registration, or identification card issued by a department of motor vehicles." § 2725(1).

The DPPA's ban on disclosure of personal information does not apply if drivers have consented to the release of their data. When we granted certiorari in this case, the DPPA provided that a DMV could obtain that consent either on a case-by-case basis or could imply consent if the State provided drivers with an opportunity to block disclosure of their personal information when they received or renewed their licenses and drivers did not avail themselves of that opportunity. § 2721(b)(11), (13), and (d). However, Public Law 106–69, 113 Stat. 986, which was signed into law on October 9, 1999, changed this "opt-out" alternative to an "opt-in" requirement. Under the amended DPPA, States may not imply consent from a driver's failure to take advantage of a state-afforded opportunity to block disclosure, but must rather obtain a driver's affirmative consent to disclose the driver's personal information for use in surveys, marketing, solicitations, and other restricted purposes.

The DPPA's prohibition of nonconsensual disclosures is also subject to a number of statutory exceptions. For example, the DPPA *requires* disclosure of personal information "for use in connection with matters of motor vehicle or driver safety and theft, motor vehicle emissions, motor vehicle product alterations, recalls, or advisories, performance monitoring of motor vehicles and dealers by motor vehicle manufacturers, and removal of non-owner records from the original owner records of motor vehicle manufacturers to carry out the purposes of titles I and IV of the Anti Car Theft Act of 1992, the Automobile Information Disclosure Act, the Clean Air Act, and chapters 301, 305, and 321–331 of title 49." The DPPA *permits* DMVs to disclose personal information from motor vehicle records for a number of purposes.

The DPPA's provisions do not apply solely to States. The Act also regulates the resale and redisclosure of drivers' personal information by private persons who have obtained that information from a state DMV. 18 U.S.C. § 2721(c) (1994 ed. and Supp. III). In general, the Act allows private persons who have obtained drivers' personal information for one of the aforementioned permissible purposes to further disclose that information for any one of those purposes. *Ibid.* If a State has obtained drivers' consent to disclose their personal information to private persons generally and a private person has obtained that information, the private person may redisclose the information for any purpose. *Ibid.* Additionally, a private actor who has obtained drivers' information from DMV records specifically for direct-marketing purposes may resell that information for other direct-marketing uses, but not otherwise. *Ibid.* Any person who rediscloses or resells personal information from DMV records must, for five years, maintain records identifying to whom the records were disclosed and the permitted purpose for the resale or redisclosure. *Ibid.*

The DPPA establishes several penalties to be imposed on States and private actors that fail to comply with its requirements. The Act makes it unlawful for any "person" knowingly to obtain or disclose any record for a use that is not permitted under its provisions, or to make a false representation in order to obtain personal information from a motor vehicle record. §§ 2722(a) and (b). Any person who knowingly violates the DPPA may be subject to a criminal fine, §§ 2723(a), 2725(2). Additionally, any person who knowingly obtains, discloses, or uses information from a state motor vehicle record for a use other than those specifically permitted by the DPPA may be subject to liability in a civil action brought by the driver to whom the information pertains. § 2724. While the DPPA defines "person" to exclude States and state agencies, § 2725(2), a state agency that maintains a "policy or practice of substantial noncompliance" with the Act maybe subject to a civil penalty imposed by the United States Attorney General of not more than $5,000 per day of substantial noncompliance. § 2723(b).

South Carolina law conflicts with the DPPA's provisions. Under that law, the information contained in the State's DMV records is available to any person or entity that fills out a form listing the requester's name and address and stating that the information will not be used for telephone solicitation. S.C.Code Ann. §§ 56–3–510 to 56–3–540 (Supp. 1998). South Carolina's DMV retains a copy of all requests for information from the State's motor vehicle records, and it is required to release copies of all requests relating to a person upon that person's written petition. § 56–3–520. State law authorizes the South Carolina DMV to charge a fee for releasing motor vehicle information, and it requires the DMV to allow drivers to prohibit the use of their motor vehicle information for certain commercial activities. §§ 56–3–530, 56–3–540.

Following the DPPA's enactment, South Carolina and its Attorney General, respondent Condon, filed suit in the United States District Court for the District of South Carolina, alleging that the DPPA violates the Tenth and Eleventh Amendments to the United States Constitution. The District Court concluded that the Act is incompatible with the principles of federalism inherent in the Constitution's division of power between the States and the Federal Government. The court accordingly granted summary judgment for the State and permanently enjoined the Act's enforcement against the State and its officers. The Court of Appeals for the Fourth Circuit affirmed, concluding that the Act violates constitutional principles of federalism.

We of course begin with the time-honored presumption that the DPPA is a "constitutional exercise of legislative power."

The United States asserts that the DPPA is a proper exercise of Congress' authority to regulate interstate commerce under the Commerce Clause, U.S. Const., Art. I, § 8, cl. 3. The United States bases its Commerce Clause argument on the fact that the personal, identifying information that the DPPA regulates is a "thin[g] in interstate commerce," and that the sale or release of that information in interstate commerce is therefore a proper subject of congressional regulation. *United States v. Lopez*, 514 U.S. 549, 558–559, 115 S.Ct. 1624, 131 L.Ed.2d 626 (1995). We agree with the United States' contention. The motor vehicle information which the States have historically sold is used by insurers, manufacturers, direct marketers, and others engaged in interstate commerce to contact drivers with customized solicitations. The information is also used in the stream of interstate commerce by various public and private entities for matters related to interstate motoring. Because drivers' information is, in this context, an article of commerce, its sale or release into the interstate stream of business is sufficient to support congressional regulation. We therefore need not address the Government's alternative argument that the States' individual, intrastate activities in gathering, maintaining, and distributing drivers' personal information has a sufficiently substantial impact on interstate commerce to create a constitutional base for federal legislation.

But the fact that drivers' personal information is, in the context of this case, an article in interstate commerce does not conclusively resolve the constitutionality of the DPPA. In *New York* and *Printz*, we held federal statutes invalid, not because Congress lacked legislative authority over the subject matter, but because those statutes violated the principles of federalism contained in the Tenth Amendment. In *New York*, Congress commandeered the state legislative process by requiring a state legislature to enact a particular kind of law. We said:

> "While Congress has substantial powers to govern the Nation directly, including in areas of intimate concern to the States, the Constitution has never been understood to confer upon Congress the ability to the require the States to govern according to Congress' instructions."

In *Printz*, we invalidated a provision of the Brady Act which commanded "state and local enforcement officers to conduct background check on prospective handgun purchasers,'' 521 U.S., at 902, 117 S.Ct. 2365. We said:

> "We held in *New York* that Congress cannot compel the States to enact or enforce a federal regulatory program. Today we hold that Congress cannot circumvent that prohibition by conscripting the States' officers directly. The Federal Government may neither issue directives requiring the States to address particular problems, nor command the States' officers, or those of their political subdivisions, to administer or enforce a federal regulatory program." *Id.*, at 935, 117 S.Ct. 2365.

South Carolina contends that the DPPA violates the Tenth Amendment because it "thrusts upon the States all of the day-to-day responsibility for administering its complex provisions," Brief for Respondents 10, and thereby makes "state officials the unwilling implementors of federal policy," *id.*, at 11. South Carolina emphasizes that the DPPA requires the State's employees to learn and apply the Act's substantive restrictions, which are summarized above, and notes that these activities will consume the employees' time and thus the State's resources. South Carolina further notes that the DPPA's penalty provisions hang over the States as a potential punishment should they fail to comply with the Act.

We agree with South Carolina's assertion that the DPPA's provisions will require time and effort on the part of state employees, but reject the State's argument that the DPPA violates the principles laid down in either *New York* or *Printz*. We think, instead, that this case is governed by our decision in *South Carolina v. Baker*, 485 U.S. 505, 108 S.Ct. 1355, 99 L.Ed.2d 592 (1988). In *Baker*, we upheld a statute that prohibited States from issuing unregistered bonds because the law "regulate[d] state activities," rather than "seek[ing] to control or influence the manner in which States regulate private parties." We further noted:

> "The NGA [National Governor's Association] nonetheless contends that § 310 has commandeered the state legislative and administrative process because many state legislatures had to amend a substantial number of statutes in order to issue bonds in registered form and because state officials had to devote substantial effort to determine how best to implement a registered bond system. Such 'commandeering' is, however, an inevitable consequence of regulating a state activity. Any federal regulation demands compliance. That a State wishing to engage in certain activity must take administrative and sometimes legislative action to comply with federal standards regulating that activity is a commonplace that presents no constitutional defect."

Like the statute at issue in *Baker*, the DPPA does not require the States in their sovereign capacity to regulate their own citizens. The DPPA regulates the States as the owners of databases. It does not require the South Carolina Legislature to enact any laws or regulations, and it does not require state officials to assist in the enforcement of federal statutes regulating private individuals. We accordingly conclude that the DPPA is consistent with the constitutional principles enunciated in *New York* and *Printz*.

As a final matter, we turn to South Carolina's argument that the DPPA is unconstitutional because it regulates the States exclusively. The essence of South Carolina's argument is that Congress may only regulate the States by means of "generally applicable" laws, or laws that apply to individuals as well as States. But we need not address the question whether general applicability is a constitutional requirement for federal regulation of the States, because the DPPA is generally applicable. The DPPA regulates the universe of entities that participate as suppliers to the market for motor vehicle information—the States as initial suppliers of the information in interstate commerce and private resellers or redisclosers of that information in commerce.

The judgment of the Court of Appeals is therefore

Reversed.

Note

The result of this case will not be to eliminate the existence of private databanks of driver's license records. Various companies obtained complete copies of the motor vehicle and driver's license registries of those states that sold them. While these records are gradually becoming obsolete, they may be updated from such sources as auto loan applications, auto dealers' sales records, and rental car company files.

G. RESTRICTION OF DISCLOSURE BY PRIVATE PARTIES OF INFORMATION IN THEIR RECORDS

IN RE TRANS UNION CORP.

Federal Trade Commission, February 10, 2000.
Docket No. 9255 (Westlaw, Federal Antitrust & Trade Regulation–Combined
Antitrust & Trade Regulation Materials (FATR–ALL))

FINAL ORDER

This matter has been heard by the Commission upon the appeal of respondent Trans Union Corporation from the Initial Decision and Order on remand, and upon briefs and oral argument in support of and in opposition to the appeal. For the reasons stated in the accompanying Opinion, the Commission has determined to adopt the Administrative Law Judge's findings and conclusions to the extent that they are consistent with those set forth in the accompanying Opinion. Accordingly, the Commission enters the following order:

IT IS HEREBY ORDERED that, consistent with the terms of this opinion, respondent Trans Union Corporation, and its successors and assigns:

a) Cease and desist from distributing or selling consumer reports, including those in the form of target marketing lists, to any person unless respondent has reason to believe that such person intends to use the consumer report for purposes authorized under Section 604 of the FCRA.

* * *

OPINION OF THE COMMISSION

By THOMPSON, COMMISSIONER:

I.   INTRODUCTION

In this information age, technological advances in information gathering and dissemination have generated substantial benefits for American consumers by providing them with, among other things, the strongest and most efficient credit markets in the world. In 1970, Congress recognized the importance of personal financial data to these markets when it enacted the Fair Credit Reporting Act ("FCRA" or "Act"). Congress expressly noted in the Act's findings and statement of purpose that the "banking system is dependent upon fair and accurate credit reporting" and acknowledged the "vital role" of credit bureaus (called "consumer reporting agencies" under the Act) "in assembling and evaluating consumer credit and other information on consumers." 15 U.S.C. s 1681(a)(l)and(3).

Under the U.S. credit reporting system, consumer reporting agencies (hereinafter "CRAs") collect consumer credit information from credit grantors and other sources, compile the information into credit reports, and then sell the reports to banks and other lenders, as well as to employers and insurance companies. Credit grantors have an incentive to provide data to CRAs because they benefit from the credit reporting system as well. The effectiveness of this system depends upon a constant flow of consumers' credit information into large databases maintained by CRAs. It also depends on accuracy and timeliness. As a result, CRAs, unlike other data providers, have access to a broad range of continually-updated, detailed information about millions of consumers' personal credit histories. This information includes, for example, consumers' delinquencies and defaults, the types of credit accounts they have, when they obtained credit, and additional information that banks and other lenders often use in determining whether to extend credit.

Although Congress understood the importance of CRAs access to such information regarding millions of consumers, it also recognized the importance of protecting consumers' financial privacy. In fact, legislative history reveals that one of the FCRA's principal goals was to protect the privacy of individuals whose sensitive credit and financial data are collected, used, reviewed and transmitted by CRAs. Thus, in enacting the FCRA, Congress struck a balance between these competing interests. While Congress did not disturb the ability of CRAs to collect personal credit information, it did provide safeguards designed to protect the confidentiality of these data. Specifically, Section 604 of the FCRA limits the circumstances under which a CRA may disclose a "consumer report"[2]—the statutory term for information commonly referred to as a credit report. For instance. Section 604 allows a CRA to furnish consumer reports to, *inter alia*, persons with certain "permissible purposes." These permissible purposes include: (1) the extension of credit; (2) employment purposes; (3) underwriting of insurance; (4) determination of license eligibility; (5) risk assessment for an existing credit obligation; and (6) legitimate business need for the information. 15 U.S.C. § 1681b. Section 607 of the Act also requires CRAs to maintain reasonable procedures to ensure that they only furnish consumer reports for the purposes set forth in Section 604. *See* 15 U.S.C. § 81e(a).

After careful consideration of the parties' arguments and thorough review of the substantial record in this case, the Commission concludes that Trans Union Corporation ("Trans Union"), a CRA, violates or has violated Sections 604 and 607 of the FCRA through the activities of its target marketing business. In connection with its consumer reporting business, Trans Union receives various types of personal, credit information about consumers. Much of this information constitutes a "consumer report" as that term is defined by Section 603(d). Trans Union's sale of consumer reports to target marketers without a "permissible purpose" under the FCRA is a violation of the Act.

* * *

IV. FACTUAL BACKGROUND

A. *Trans Union's Business*

Trans Union is a Delaware corporation whose principal place of business is located at 555 West Adams Street, Chicago. IL 60661. Trans Union's primary business is credit reporting and it is a CRA under Section 603(f) of the Act. As a CRA, Trans Union collects credit information about millions of American consumers from numerous credit grantors and others, compiles this information into credit reports and sells the reports to credit grantors nationwide. Trans Union's main competitors in the credit reporting business are Experian (formerly TRW) and Equifax. These companies are also CRAs.

The millions of pieces of consumer information Trans Union receives every month are maintained in an extensive database called CRONUS. The information in CRONUS comes from credit grantors—including banks, mortgage companies, credit unions and auto dealers—collection agencies, public records and others. The information is very current as Trans Union receives new data every day and updates

---

2. Section 603(d) of the FCRA defines "consumer report" as: "[a]ny written, oral, or other communication of any information by a consumer reporting agency bearing on a consumer's credit worthiness, credit standing, credit capacity, character, general reputation, personal characteristics, or mode of living which is used or expected to be used or collected in whole or in part for the purpose of serving as a factor in establishing a consumer's eligibility for ... credit or insurance ... [or] employment ... " 15 U.S.C. § 1681a(d).

CRONUS weekly. Information compiled on a specific consumer within CRONUS is called a consumer file.

In addition to its credit reporting business, Trans Union also sells a variety of target marketing products through its subsidiary, Performance Data (formerly Trans Mark and Trans Union Lists). Performance Data creates lists of the names and addresses of specific classes of consumers and sells them to target marketers who in turn solicit the consumers to purchase goods and services. * * *

As a CRA, Trans Union is in a special position. Trans Union has access to a vast array of very current and detailed consumer information from its credit reporting business which affords it a distinct advantage as a target marketer. Trans Union takes consumer information from CRO-NUS to create two primary As a CRA, Trans Union is in a special position. Trans Union has access to a vast array of very current and detailed consumer information from its credit reporting business which affords it a distinct advantage as a target marketer. Trans Union takes consumer information from CRONUS to create two primary databases called the Master File and the Standard Characteristics database. Trans Union offers different target marketing products based upon the information gathered in these two databases as well as data taken directly from CRONUS. * * * [T]he fact that Trans Union uses CRONUS information in its target marketing business is significant because CRO-NUS information is far richer and more detailed than the data collected and used by non-CRA competitors who sell target marketing lists. Trans Union is also the only CRA that sells to target marketers an array of personal credit information obtained from its credit reporting database.

1. The Master File

The CRONUS-derived Master File is one of the databases Trans Union uses for target marketing. It contains information on 160 million people and 105–110 million households. * * *

In order for Trans Union to include a CRONUS consumer file in the Master File, thereby making the consumer's name and address available for target marketing purposes, the consumer file must satisfy several minimum criteria. These criteria have changed over time. Prior to January 1998, each CRONUS consumer file had to show at least two open tradelines with one of the tradelines verified—i.e., that some reported activity took place—during the preceding 12 months. In addition, a qualifying tradeline could not be closed or an account about which there was a consumer dispute, and could not be a collection record or public record . .

In January 1998, in order to be included in the Master File, Trans Union began to require CRONUS consumer files to contain two trade-lines active within the last six months or one tradeline active in the last six months with an address confirmed by an outside source. * * *

Trans Union claims that the two tradeline, pre–1998 Minimum Criteria did not reveal consumer credit information and that the two tradeline minimum was only important because it confirmed, by two sources, the subject's current name and address. Statements made by Trans Union during the relevant time and in its regular course of business, however, belie this simple characterization. For instance, Trans Union's promotions boasted that the Master File is a list of "135 million *financially active individuals*" (emphasis added), that "[a]ny adult with at least two active tradelines is represented," and that a person with no activity in a 12 month period—*i.e.*, making payments or establishing credit—is dropped from the Master File. We agree with Trans Union's written characterizations and find that the "two-tradeline minimum" criterion indicates more than just a confirmed address. It instead reveals a significant fact about consumers in the Master File, *i.e.*, that they are current, at least somewhat active users of credit.

2. *Trans Union's "Master File/Selects" Product*

While the Master File contains names, addresses and other demographic information on people who meet the Minimum Criteria discussed above, it also is frequently enhanced with the addition of other personal, often credit-related, information on each individual. This enhancement enables Trans Union to offer its target marketing customers the opportunity to select, from the 160 million consumer files in the Master File, names and addresses of a smaller set of consumers who meet certain criteria specified by the target marketing customer. The criteria Trans Union uses to create these subsets are called "indicators" or "selects," and Trans Union generates half of them from its consumer reporting database CRONUS.

Trans Union's target marketing customers use the Master File/Selects product in two ways. Some customers provide a list of consumers to Trans Union and purchase Master File select information regarding those customers. Other customers request that Trans Union *extract* from the Master File names and addresses of those consumers who satisfy criteria selected by the customer. In other words. Trans Union's target marketing customers can choose from a menu of selects and ask for a tailored list of consumers' names and addresses who, for example, have a bank card, an open mortgage, but never have obtained short term (30/60/90 day) financing. Trans Union sells these lists for one-time use by its customers either by rental or by license and charges a "base price" per thousand names, with additional charges per thousand based on the selects that the customer has chosen.

Prior to October 1997, when it made certain changes in its business practices Trans Union permitted its target marketing customers to order from the Master File lists of the names and addresses of consumers who had the following types of credit accounts * * *.

The record contains ample evidence of how Trans Union's customers used the Master File/Selects product. For example, Mercantile Mortgage Co. obtained information from Trans Union to advance its telemarketing promotion which offered homeowners who had been denied credit elsewhere the opportunity to reduce their monthly mortgage rates by refinancing their mortgage, thereby freeing up funds for "home improvements," a "new car," or a "dream vacation." Mercantile purchased from Trans Union a list of consumers in Mercantile's area of business (Ohio), with telephone numbers (necessary for telemarketing promotion), who also had single or multiple mortgages (an important minimum eligibility factor) and credit with a finance company.

* * *

The record in this case includes substantial evidence of factors important to credit scoring and prescreening criteria. The record demonstrates that much of the information Trans Union discloses in its target marketing lists—including the Master File/Selects, proprietary models, and TransLink/reverse append products—is the same information that credit grantors, such as Wachovia Bank Card Services, Inc. ("Wachovia"), First Card First Chicago NBD ("First Card"), the Northern Trust Company ("Northern Trust"), Discover Card Brand, Novus Services, Inc. ("Discover"), and Chase Manhattan Bank ("Chase Manhattan"), *use* in credit eligibility determinations. Moreover, the record shows that Trans Union *expected* its credit grantor customers to *use* the information as factors in such determinations.

* * *

VI. CONSTITUTIONAL ANALYSIS

Trans Union raises two constitutional defenses in this matter. Trans Union first asserts that, by barring it from selling target marketing lists, the FCRA violates the First Amendment of the United States Constitution. Second, Trans Union claims that the FCRA's definition of consumer report is unconstitutionally vague under the Fifth Amendment. We disagree with both arguments.

A. The FCRA Is a Constitutionally Permissible Restriction on Speech

The First Amendment states that "Congress shall make no law . . . abridging the freedom of speech. . . ." The right to free speech, however, is not unfettered and it is well settled that different types of speech merit different levels of constitutional protection. Specifically, courts apply the highest degree of protection to speech related to issues of public concern such as political or social change or artistic or scientific expression. *See, e.g., Dun & Bradstreet, Inc. v. Greenmoss Builders, Inc.,* 472 U.S. 749, 758–59 (1985) (plurality opinion). Such fully protected speech may be called "pure" speech. *American Future Systems, Inc. v. Pennsylvania State Univ.,* 752 F.2d 854, 861 (3d Cir. 1984). By contrast, courts apply a reduced or intermediate level of protection to "commercial" speech—speech, such as advertising, that is related to a commercial transaction. *See, e.g .. Central Hudson Gas & Electric Corp. v. Public Serv. Comm. 'n of New York,* 447 U.S. 557, 561–63 (1980). Courts have also recognized that the First Amendment does not protect certain types of speech, such as obscenity and "fighting words," *Dun & Bradstreet,* 472 U.S. at 758–59, n.5, or conduct that does not constitute speech,

Michael Barnes, et al. v. Glen Theatre, Inc., et al., 501 U.S. 560, 570 (1991). For the reasons discussed below, we find that Trans Union's consumer reports are entitled to intermediate First Amendment protection. Accordingly, we analyze the FCRA under the standard established by the Supreme Court in *Central Hudson* and its progeny and conclude that the Act does not violate the First Amendment by prohibiting Trans Union from selling consumer reports to target marketers.

* * *

[I]t is evident that the FCRA's restriction on Trans Union's target marketing lists is sufficiently narrowly tailored to achieve the goal of protecting the privacy of consumers' personal credit information. We therefore conclude that the provisions of the FCRA at issue here do not violate the First Amendment.

* * *

[W]e conclude that the term "eligibility for credit" in the FCRA's definition of a "consumer report" is not too vague to provide adequate notice to Trans Union of the conduct proscribed under the FCRA. We also believe that the term is sufficiently clear to prevent arbitrary and discriminatory enforcement. This is true even though the Act has some impact upon Trans Union's First Amendment right to freedom of expression.

* * *

[W]e conclude that the definition of "consumer report," including the term "eligibility," under Section 603(d) of the FCRA gives regulated parties like Trans Union adequate notice of what conduct is proscribed and is sufficiently clear to avoid risk of discriminatory enforcement. [FN93] For these reasons, the FCRA is not unconstitutionally vague.

VII. CONCLUSION

Based on the foregoing, as well as the thorough and substantial record in this case, we find that Trans Union violated Sections 604 and 607(a) of the FCRA because its target marketing lists are "consumer reports" that were disclosed without a "permissible purpose." We also find that the FCRA, as applied in this case, passes constitutional muster.

ELECTRONIC COMMUNICATIONS PRIVACY ACT § 2702

18 U.S.C. § 2701 *et seq.*

§ 2701. Unlawful access to stored communications

(a) Offense.—Except as provided in subsection (c) of this section whoever

(1) intentionally accesses without authorization a facility through which an electronic communication service is provided; or

(2) intentionally exceeds an authorization to access that facility; and thereby obtains, alters, or prevents authorized access to a wire or electronic communication while it is in electronic storage in such system shall be punished as provided in subsection (b) of this section.

* * *

§ 2702.　Disclosure of contents

(a) Prohibitions.—Except as provided in subsection (b)—

(1) a person or entity providing an electronic communication service to the public shall not knowingly divulge to any person or entity the contents of a communication while in electronic storage by that service; and

(2) a person or entity providing remote computing service to the public shall not knowingly divulge to any person or entity the contents of any communication which is carried or maintained on that service—

(A) on behalf of, and received by means of electronic transmission from (or created by means of computer processing of communications received by means of electronic transmission from), a subscriber or customer of such service; and

(B) solely for the purpose of providing storage or computer processing services to such subscriber or customer, if the provider is not authorized to access the contents of any such communications for purposes of providing any services other than storage or computer processing.

* * *

§ 2703.　Requirements for governmental access

(a) Contents of electronic communications in electronic storage.—A governmental entity may require the disclosure by a provider of electronic communication service of the contents of an electronic communication, that is in electronic storage in an electronic communications system for one hundred and eighty days or less, only pursuant to a warrant issued under the Federal Rules of Criminal Procedure or equivalent State warrant. A governmental entity may require the disclosure by a provider of electronic communications services of the contents of an electronic communication that has been in electronic storage in an electronic communications system for more than one hundred and eighty days by the means available under subsection (b) of this section.

* * *

H. THE EFFECT OF EUROPEAN UNION PRIVACY LAW

DIRECTIVE ON THE PROTECTION OF INDIVIDUALS WITH REGARD TO THE PROCESSING OF PERSONAL DATA AND ON THE FREE MOVEMENT OF SUCH DATA

Directive 95/46/EC of the European Parliament
and of the Council of October 24, 1995.
1995 O.J. (L 281) 31.

CHAPTER 1

General Provisions

Article 1

Object of the Directive

1. In accordance with this Directive, Member States shall protect the fundamental rights and freedoms of natural persons, and in particular their right to privacy, with respect to the processing of personal data.

* * *

Article 6

1. Member States shall provide that personal data must be:

(a) processed fairly and lawfully;

(b) collected for specified, explicit and legitimate purposes and not further processed in a way incompatible with those purposes. Further processing of data for historical, statistical or scientific purposes shall not be considered as incompatible provided that Member States provide appropriate safeguards;

(c) adequate, relevant and not excessive in relation to the purposes for which they are collected and/or for which they are further processed;

(d) accurate and, where necessary, kept up to date; every reasonable step must be taken to ensure that data which are inaccurate or incomplete, having regard to the purposes for which they were collected or for which they are further processed, are erased or rectified;

(e) kept in a form which permits identification of data subjects for no longer that is necessary for the purposes for which the data were collected or for which they are further processed. Member Sates shall lay down appropriate safeguards for personal data stored for longer periods for historical, statistical or scientific use.

2. It shall be for the controller to ensure that paragraph 1 is complied with.

* * *

Article 7

Member States shall provide that personal data may be processed only if:

(a) the data subject has given his consent unambiguously; or

(b) processing is necessary for the performance of a contract to which the data subject is party or in order to take steps at the request of the data subject entering into a contract.; or

(c) processing is necessary for compliance with a legal obligation to which the controller is subject; or

(d) processing is necessary in order to protect the vital interests of the data subject; or

(e) processing is necessary for the performance of a task carried out in the public interest or in the exercise of official authority vested in the controller or in a third party to whom the data are disclosed; or

(f) processing is necessary for the purposes of the legitimate interests pursued by the controller or by the third party or parties to whom the data are disclosed, except where such interests are overridden by the interests or fundamental rights and freedoms of the data subject which require protection under Article 1(1).

* * *

Article 12

Right of access

Member States shall guarantee for every data subject the right to obtain from the controller:

(a) without constraint at reasonable intervals and without excessive delay or expense:

— confirmation as to whether or not data relating to him are processed and information at least as to the purposes of the processing, the categories of data concerned, and the recipients or categories of recipients to whom the data are disclosed;

— communication to him in an intelligible form of the data undergoing processing and of any available information as to their source;

— knowledge of the logic involved in any automatic processing of data concerning him at least in the case of the automated decisions referred to in Article 15(1);

(b) as appropriate the rectification, erasure or blocking of data, the processing of which does not comply with the provisions of this Directive, in particular because of the incomplete or inaccurate nature of the data;

(c) notification to third parties to whom the data have been disclosed of any rectification, erasure or blocking carried out in compliance with paragraph 2, unless this proves impossible or involves a disproportionate effort.

* * *

CHAPTER IV

Transfer of Personal Data to Third Countries

Article 25

Principles

1.   Member States shall provide that the transfer to a third country of personal data which are undergoing processing or are intended for processing after transfer may take place only if, without prejudice to compliance with the national provisions adopted pursuant to the other provisions of this Directive, the third country in question ensures an adequate level of protection.

2.   The adequacy of the level of protection afforded by a third country shall be assessed in the light of all the circumstances surrounding a data transfer operation or set of data transfer operations; particular consideration shall be given to the nature of the data, the purpose and duration of the proposed processing operation or operations, the country of origin and country of final destination, the rules of law, both general and sectoral, in force in the third country in question and the professional rules and security measures which are complied with in those countries.

3.   Member States and the Commission shall inform each other of cases where the consider that a third country does not ensure an adequate level of protection within the meaning of paragraph 2.

4.   Where the Commission finds, under the procedure provided for in Article 31(2), that a third country does not ensure an adequate level of protection within the meaning of paragraph 2 of this Article Member States shall take the measures necessary to prevent the transfer of data of the same type to the third country in question.

5.   At the appropriate time, the Commission shall enter into negotiations with a view to remedying the situation resulting from the funding made pursuant to paragraph 4.

6.   The Commission may find, in accordance with the procedure referred to in Article 31(2), that a third country ensures an adequate level of protection within the meaning of paragraph 2 of this Article, by reason of its domestic law or of the international commitments it has entered into, particularly upon conclusion of the negotiations referred to in paragraph 5, for the protection of the private lives and basic freedoms and rights of individuals.

Member States shall take the measures necessary to comply with the Commission's decision.

Article 26

Derogations

1. By way of derogation from Article 25 and save where otherwise provided by domestic law governing particular cases, Member States shall provide that a transfer or a set of transfers of personal data to a third country which does not ensure an adequate level of protection within the meaning of Article 25(2) may take place on condition that:

(a) the data subject has given his consent unambiguously to the proposed transfer, or

(b) the transfer is necessary for the performance of a contract between the data subject and the controller or the implementation of precontractual measures taken in response to the data subject's request, or

(c) the transfer is necessary for the conclusion or for the performance of a contract concluded in the interest of the data subject between the controller and a third party, or

(d) the transfer is necessary or legally required on important public interest grounds, or for the establishment, exercise or defence of legal claims, or

(e) the transfer is necessary in order to protect the vital interests of the data subject, or

(f) the transfer is made from a register which according to laws or regulations is intended to provide information to the public and which is open to consultation either by the public in general or by any person who can demonstrate legitimate interest, to the extent that the conditions laid down in law for consultation are fulfilled in the particular case.

2. Without prejudice to paragraph 1, a Member State may authorize a transfer or a set of transfers of personal data to a third country which does not ensure an adequate level of protection within the meaning of Article 25(2), where the controller adduces sufficient guarantees with respect to the protection of the privacy and fundamental rights and freedoms of individuals and as regards the exercise of the corresponding rights; such guarantees may in particular result from appropriate contractual clauses.

3. The Member State shall inform the Commission and the other Member States of the authorizations granted pursuant to paragraph 2.

If a Member State or the Commission objects on justified grounds involving the protection of the privacy and fundamental rights and freedoms of individuals, the Commission shall take appropriate measures in accordance with the procedure laid down in Article 31(2).

Member States shall take the necessary measures to comply with the Commission's decision.

4. Where the Commission decides, in accordance with the procedure referred to in Article 31(2), that certain standard contractual clauses offer sufficient guarantees required by paragraph 2, Member States shall take the necessary measures to comply with the Commission's decision.

Note

Article 25 poses special problems for companies in countries (such as the United States) with weaker privacy protection laws than those of the European Union. If such companies kept data on Europeans in the same way that they keep data on United States residence, it would be illegal to export data to them from Europe. After extensive negotiations, the United States and the European Union came to an agreement that will allow companies on both sides to continue to conduct business with each other. What follows is a set of principles reflecting the agreement.

SAFE HARBOR PRINCIPLES

U.S. Department of Commerce, July 21, 2000.
http://www.ita.doc.gov/td/ecom/menu.html

The European Union's comprehensive privacy legislation, the Directive on Data Protection (the Directive), became effective on October 25, 1998. It requires that transfers of personal data take place only to non-EU countries that provide an "adequate" level of privacy protection. While the United States and the European Union share the goal of enhancing privacy protection for their citizens, the United States takes a different approach to privacy from that taken by the European Community. The United States uses a sectoral approach that relies on a mix of legislation, regulation, and self regulation. Given those differences, many U.S. organizations have expressed uncertainty about the impact of the EU-required "adequacy standard" on personal data transfers from the European Community to the United States.

To diminish this uncertainty and provide a more predictable framework for such data transfers, the Department of Commerce is issuing this document and Frequently Asked Questions (the Principles) under its statutory authority to foster, promote, and develop international commerce. The Principles were developed in consultation with industry and the general public to facilitate trade and commerce between the United States and European Union. They are intended for use solely by U.S. organizations receiving personal data from the European Union for the purpose of qualifying for the safe harbor and the presumption of "adequacy" it creates. Because the Principles were solely designed to serve this specific purpose, their adoption for other purposes may be inappropriate. The Principles cannot be used as a substitute for national provisions implementing the Directive that apply to the processing of personal data in the Member States.

Decisions by organizations to qualify for the safe harbor are entirely voluntary, and organizations may qualify for the safe harbor in different ways. Organizations that decide to adhere to the Principles must comply with the Principles in order to obtain and retain the benefits of the safe harbor and publicly declare that they do so. For example, if an organization joins a self regulatory privacy program that adheres to the Principles, it qualifies for the safe harbor. Organizations may also qualify by developing their own self regulatory privacy policies provided that they conform with the Principles. Where in complying with the Principles, an organization relies in whole or in part on self regulation, its failure to comply with such self regulation must also be actionable under Section 5 of the Federal Trade Commission Act prohibiting unfair and deceptive acts or another law or regulation prohibiting such acts. *(See annex 1 for the list of U.S. statutory bodies recognized by the EU.)* In addition, organizations subject to a statutory, regulatory, administrative or other body of law (or of rules) that effectively protects personal privacy may also qualify for safe harbor benefits. In all instances, safe harbor benefits are assured from the date on which each organization wishing to qualify for the safe harbor self-certifies to the Department of Commerce (or its designee) its adherence to the Principles in accordance with the guidance set forth in the Frequently Asked Question on Self Certification.

Adherence to these Principles may be limited: (a) to the extent necessary to meet national security, public interest, or law enforcement requirements; (b) by statute, government regulation, or case law that create conflicting obligations or explicit authorizations, provided that, in exercising any such authorization, an organization can demonstrate that its non-compliance with the Principles is limited to the extent necessary to meet the overriding legitimate interests furthered by such authorization; or (c) if the effect of the Directive or Member State law is to allow exceptions or derogations, provided such exceptions or derogations are applied in comparable contexts. Consistent with the goal of enhancing privacy protection, organizations should strive to implement these Principles fully and transparently, including indicating in their privacy policies where exceptions to the Principles permitted by (b) above will apply on a regular basis. For the same reason, where the option is allowable under the Principles and/or U.S. law, organizations are expected to opt for the higher protection under U.S. law where possible.

Organizations may wish for practical or other reasons to apply the Principles to all their data processing operations, but they are only obligated to apply them to data transferred after they enter the safe harbor. To qualify for the safe harbor, organizations are not obligated to apply these Principles to personal information in manually processed filing systems. Organizations wishing to benefit from the safe harbor for receiving information in manually processed filing systems from the EU must apply the Principles to any such information transferred after they enter the safe harbor. An organization that wishes to extend safe harbor benefits to human resources personal information transferred from the EU for use in the context of an employment relationship must indicate this when it self-certifies to the Department of Commerce (or its designee) and conform to the requirements set forth in the Frequently Asked Question on Self Certification. Organizations will also be able to provide the safeguards necessary under Article 26 of the Directive if they include the Principles in written agreements with parties transferring data from the EU for the substantive privacy provisions, once the other provisions for such model contracts are authorized by the Commission and the Member States.

U.S. law will apply to questions of interpretation and compliance with the Safe Harbor Principles (including the Frequently Asked Questions) and relevant privacy policies by safe harbor organizations, except where organizations have committed to cooperate with European Data Protection Authorities. Unless otherwise stated, all provisions of the Safe Harbor Principles and Frequently Asked Questions apply where they are relevant.

"Personal data" and "personal information" are data about an identified or identifiable individual that are within the scope of the Directive, received by a U.S. organization from the European Union, and recorded in any form.

NOTICE: An organization must inform individuals about the purposes for which it collects and uses information about them, how to contact the organization with any inquiries or complaints, the types of third parties to which it discloses the information, and the choices and means the organization offers individuals for limiting its use and disclosure. This notice must be provided in clear and conspicuous language when individuals are first asked to provide personal information to the organization or as soon thereafter as is practicable, but in any event before the organization uses such information for a purpose other than that for which it was originally collected or processed by the transferring organization or discloses it for the first time to a third party.[1]

CHOICE: An organization must offer individuals the opportunity to choose (opt out) whether their personal information is (a) to be disclosed to a third party or (b) to be used for a purpose that is incompatible with the purpose(s) for which it was originally collected or subsequently authorized by the individual. Individuals must be provided with clear and conspicuous, readily available, and affordable mechanisms to exercise choice.

For sensitive information (i.e. personal information specifying medical or health conditions, racial or ethnic origin, political opinions, religious or philosophical beliefs, trade union membership or information specifying the sex life of the individual), they must be given affirmative or explicit (opt in) choice if the information is to be disclosed to a third party or used for a purpose other than those for which it was originally collected or subsequently authorized by the individual through the exercise of opt in choice. In any case, an organization should treat as sensitive any information received from a third party where the third party treats and identifies it as sensitive.

ONWARD TRANSFER: To disclose information to a third party, organizations must apply the notice and choice Principles. Where an

1. It is not necessary to provide notice or choice when disclosure is made to a third party that is acting as an agent to perform task(s) on behalf of and under the instruc-tions of the organization. The onward transfer principle, on the other hand, does apply to such disclosures.

organization wishes to transfer information to a third party that is acting as an agent, as described in the endnote, it may do so if it first either ascertains that the third party subscribes to the Principles or is subject to the Directive or another adequacy finding or enters into a written agreement with such third party requiring that the third party provide at least the same level of privacy protection as is required by the relevant Principles. If the organization complies with these requirements, it shall not be held responsible (unless the organization agrees otherwise) when a third party to which it transfers such information processes it in a way contrary to any restrictions or representations, unless the organization knew or should have known the third party would process it in such a contrary way and the organization has not taken reasonable steps to prevent or stop such processing.

SECURITY: Organizations creating, maintaining, using or disseminating personal information must take reasonable precautions to protect it from loss, misuse and unauthorized access, disclosure, alteration and destruction.

DATA INTEGRITY: Consistent with the Principles, personal information must be relevant for the purposes for which it is to be used. An organization may not process personal information in a way that is incompatible with the purposes for which it has been collected or subsequently authorized by the individual. To the extent necessary for those purposes, an organization should take reasonable steps to ensure that data is reliable for its intended use, accurate, complete, and current.

ACCESS: Individuals must have access to personal information about them that an organization holds and be able to correct, amend, or delete that information where it is inaccurate, except where the burden or expense of providing access would be disproportionate to the risks to the individual's privacy in the case in question, or where the rights of persons other than the individual would be violated.

ENFORCEMENT: Effective privacy protection must include mechanisms for assuring compliance with the Principles, recourse for individuals to whom the data relate affected by non-compliance with the Principles, and consequences for the organization when the Principles are not followed. At a minimum, such mechanisms must include (a) readily available and affordable independent recourse mechanisms by which each individual's complaints and disputes are investigated and resolved by reference to the Principles and damages awarded where the applicable law or private sector initiatives so provide; (b) follow up procedures for verifying that the attestations and assertions businesses make about their privacy practices are true and that privacy practices have been implemented as presented; and (c) obligations to remedy problems arising out of failure to comply with the Principles by organizations announcing their adherence to them and consequences for such organizations. Sanctions must be sufficiently rigorous to ensure compliance by organizations.

Chapter X

RIGHT TO ACCURACY
OF INFORMATION

A. DEFAMATION

The common law of defamation has long protected individuals against the dissemination of derogatory, inaccurate information. The Internet and computerized databanks are extremely dangerous if they contain inaccurate information, because they can spread this information to the world. In the old days, an individual could say something bad about someone else, but only those in the immediate vicinity could hear. Now anyone can easily disseminate derogatory information about another person throughout the Internet. Merchants have always kept credit data about their customers. Until computers became widespread, however, this data was kept by individual merchants, with the result that mistakes had only very limited effects. Computers allowed the pooling of data and the sharing of the expense of data-gathering. The result was that they rapidly replaced the traditional credit systems. But as a result, mistakes became much more serious, since an error in a credit file could taint someone's credit everywhere and always. Police have always kept data on wanted criminals. Today such data goes into a nationwide databank, creating a huge problem for anyone wrongly described as a wanted suspect. This huge expansion in the harm that errors could cause has led to significant changes in the legal rules governing the keeping and dissemination of information related to individuals.

Even if information is not released to the public, private parties and government agencies can cause harm by acting on the basis of inaccurate information.

ANDREWS v. TRW, INC.

United States Court of Appeals, Ninth Circuit, 2000.
225 F.3d 1063, 2000 WL 973260.

NOONAN, CIRCUIT JUDGE.

Adelaide Andrews (Andrews) appeals the judgment by the district court in her suit against TRW, Inc. The case involves the rights under the Fair Credit Reporting Act, 15 U.S.C. §§ 1681–1681u (1994 & Supp. II) (FCRA), and Cal. Bus. & Prof.Code § 17200 et. seq. (1996), of a person claiming to be damaged by the disclosure of inaccurate credit information by a consumer credit reporting agency such as TRW.

We hold that Andrews's suit was not barred by § 1681p. We further hold that it was not a question of law but a question to be resolved by the jury as to whether TRW had reason to believe that it was furnishing information in connection with a consumer transaction involving Andrews. For these reasons we reverse the partial summary judgments awarded TRW on the first of Andrews's claims. As to the claims that did go to trial and ended in judgment against her after trial, we find no harmful error and affirm.

FACTS

In June 1993, Andrea Andrews (hereafter the Imposter) obtained the social security number and California driver's license number of Adelaide Andrews (hereafter the Plaintiff). The Imposter did so simply by misusing her position as a doctor's receptionist and copying the information that the Plaintiff, as a patient in that office, supplied to the doctor.

In 1994–1995 the Imposter applied for credit to four companies subscribing to TRW's credit reports. For example, on July 25, 1994, to First Consumers National Bank (FCNB), the Imposter applied as Andrea A. Andrews, 3993–1/2 Harvard Blvd., Los Angeles, CA, 90062, phone 213–312–0605, employed at Spensor Robbyns Products, Los Angeles. The Imposter gave the birth date and social security number of the Plaintiff.

In this application the only misinformation was the Imposter's use of the Plaintiff's social security number and date of birth. On October 28, 1994 to Express Department Stores the Imposter made a comparable credit application, using her own identity except for the Plaintiff's social security number. Again, in January 1995, to Commercial Credit the Imposter applied for credit, using her own identity, except for Plaintiff's social security number and a clumsy misspelling of her first name as "Adeliade."

TRW responded to the credit inquiries of the three companies by treating the applications as made by the Plaintiff. TRW furnished the information in its file on the Plaintiff and added the three inquiries to the Plaintiff's file.

Each of the credit applications applied for by the Imposter was turned down by the company getting the TRW report. In addition, the Imposter applied for cable service to a public utility, Prime Cable of Las Vegas, which was required by law to provide cable services but nonetheless asked for a TRW report. The Imposter applied as Andrea Andrews, 4201 S. Decatur #2202, Las Vegas, NV, 89103, Phone 248–6352. The Imposter used the social security number of the Plaintiff, which was the only stolen item of identity provided. This account became delinquent and was referred to a collection agency.

The Plaintiff, however, became aware of the Imposter only on May 31, 1995 when she sought to refinance the mortgage on her home. The bank from which the financing was sought received a report from Chase Credit Research, not a party to this case, whose report combined information from TRW and two other credit reporting agencies. Now aware of the fraud, Andrews contacted TRW and requested deletion from her file of all reference to the Imposter's fraudulent activities. TRW complied.

PROCEEDINGS

On October 21, 1996, the Plaintiff filed this suit in the district court. In her first claim she alleged that TRW had furnished credit reports without "reasonable grounds for believing" that she was the consumer whom the credit applications involved, contrary to 15 U.S.C. § 1681b, and that as a consequence she had suffered damages including an expenditure of time and money and "commercial impairment, inconvenience, embarrassment, humiliation, and emotional distress including physical manifestations." In her second claim, she alleged that TRW had violated § 1681e by not maintaining the "reasonable procedures" required by that statute in order "to assure maximum possible accuracy of the information concerning the individual about whom the report relates." 15 U.S.C. § 1681e(b). She alleged the same damages. She asserted that both violations were willful and that both also violated Cal. Bus. & Prof.Code § 17200 et. seq. She sought actual and punitive damages and an injunction requiring TRW to comply with the Fair Credit Reporting Act by "requiring a sufficient number of corresponding points of reference" before disseminating an individual's credit history or attributing information to an individual's credit file.

On May 28, 1998, the district court granted partial summary judgment to TRW. The court held that the two year statute of limitations provided by § 1681p began to run at the time the alleged wrongful disclosures of credit information were made to the requesting companies. By this test the complaint was too late as to the disclosures made to FCNB and to Prime Cable. As to the disclosures made to Express and Commercial, the court ruled that they were made for a purpose permissible under § 1681b(a)(3)(A), because the Plaintiff, even against her will, was "involved" in the credit transaction initiated by the Imposter. Any other rule, the court said, would place "too heavy a burden on credit reporting agencies." In addition, the court ruled that TRW had used the "reasonable procedures" required by § 1681e(a) to limit disclosures to permissible purposes. For these several reasons, the court granted summary judgment to TRW on the Plaintiff's first claim.

The court also struck Plaintiff's claim for punitive damages on both her first and second causes of action. The court ruled that the Plaintiff had produced no evidence of TRW's conscious disregard of reasonable procedures. In so ruling, the court did not consider the testimony of Evan Hendricks, the Plaintiff's expert on computers and on the prevalence of identity theft.

TRW then moved in limine to bar from testifying at trial the Plaintiff's witness Douglas Stott Parker, offered as an expert on the Plaintiff's second claim that TRW's procedures were not reasonable in assuring maximum possible accuracy. Relying in part on its earlier rulings, the district court ordered that Parker not testify as to procedures leading to inaccuracy in TRW disclosing the Plaintiff's information upon the Impostor's applications.

The case proceeded to trial on the Plaintiff's second and third claims. The jury returned a verdict for TRW. The Plaintiff appeals the consequent judgment on all her claims.

ANALYSIS

The Statute of Limitations. Liability under the statute arises when a consumer reporting agency fails to comply with § 1681e(b). *Guimond v. Trans Union Credit Information Co.*, 45 F.3d 1329 (9th Cir.1995). The question is presented whether Andrews's claims are barred as to those alleged failures to comply which occurred before October 21, 1994. 15 U.S.C. § 1681p reads:

> An action to enforce any liability created under this title may be brought in any appropriate United States district court without regard to the amount in controversy, or in any other court of competent jurisdiction, within two years from the date on which the liability arises, except that where a defendant has materially and willfully misrepresented any information required under this subchapter to be disclosed to an individual and the information so misrepresented is material to the establishment of the defendant's liability to that individual under this title, the action may be brought at any time within two years after discovery by the individual of the misrepresentation.

The general federal rule is that a federal statute of limitations begins to run when a party knows or has reason to know that she was injured. *Norman-Bloodsaw v. Lawrence Berkeley Lab.*, 135 F.3d 1260, 1266 (9th Cir.1998). By this test none of the Plaintiff's injuries were stale when suit was brought.

The district court relied on what it saw as the implication of the statute explicitly referencing a discovery time limit where a defendant had wilfully misrepresented information "required to be disclosed to an individual." The creation of this exception, the court reasoned, implied an exclusion of a general discovery rule. *Accord, Rylewicz v. Beaton Services, Ltd.*, 888 F.2d 1175 (7th Cir.1989); *Houghton v. Insurance Crime Prevention Inst.*, 795 F.2d 322 (3d Cir.1986); *Clay v. Equifax, Inc.*, 762 F.2d 952, 961 (11th Cir.1985). It is argued, to the contrary, that neither the language of the statute nor its interpretation by other respected circuit courts of appeals is a warrant for disregarding the teaching of the Supreme Court: unless Congress has expressly legislated otherwise, the equitable doctrine of discovery "is read into every federal statute of limitations." *Holmberg v. Armbrecht*, 327 U.S. 392, 397, 66 S.Ct. 582, 90 L.Ed. 743 (1946); *see also Lampf v. Gilbertson*, 501 U.S. 350, 363, 111 S.Ct. 2773, 115 L.Ed.2d 321 (1991). We have followed this approach in interpreting an analogous statute. *See Englerius v. Veterans Admin.*, 837 F.2d 895, 898 (9th Cir.1988). We are not persuaded to depart from the general rule or the analogy. Andrews's claims were not barred.

Disclosure Without Reasonable Belief. Under § 1681b TRW could only furnish a report on a consumer to a customer which it had "reason to believe" intended to use the information in connection with "a credit transaction involving the consumer on whom the information is to be furnished." 15 U.S.C. § 1681b(a)(3). Did TRW have a reasonable belief that the Plaintiff was the consumer involved in the credit transactions as to which the four companies sought a report from TRW? As the district court observed, there are 250,000,000 persons in the United States (not all of them having Social Security numbers) and 1,000,000,000 possibilities as to what any one Social Security number may be. The random chance of anyone matching a name to a number is very small. If TRW could assume that only such chance matching would occur, it was reasonable as a matter of law in releasing the Plaintiff's file when an application matched her last name and the number. But we do not live in a world in which such matches are made only by chance.

We take judicial notice that in many ways persons are required to make their social security numbers available so that they are no longer private or confidential but open to scrutiny and copying. Not least of these ways is on applications for credit, as TRW had reason to know. In a world where names are disseminated with the numbers attached and dishonest persons exist, the matching of a name to a number is not a random matter. It is quintessentially a job for a jury to decide whether identity theft has been common enough for it to be reasonable for a credit reporting agency to disclose credit information merely because a last name matches a social security number on file.

In making that determination the jury would be helped by expert opinion on the prevalence of identity theft, as the district court would have been helped if it had given consideration to the Plaintiff's witness on this point before giving summary judgment.

The reasonableness of TRW's responses should also have been assessed by a jury with reference to the information TRW had indicating that the Imposter was not the Plaintiff. TRW argues that people do use nicknames and change addresses. But how many people misspell their first name? How many people mistake their date of birth? No rule of law answers these questions. A jury will have to say how reasonable a belief is that let a social security number trump all evidence of dissimilarity between the Plaintiff and the Imposter.

The district court held that the Plaintiff was involved in the transaction because her number was used. The statutory phrase is "a credit transaction involving the consumer." 15 U.S.C. § 1681b(a)(3)(A). "Involve" has two dictionary meanings that are relevant: (1) "to draw in as a participant" or (2) "to oblige to become associated." The district court understood the word in the second sense. We are reluctant to conclude that Congress meant to harness any consumer to any transaction where any crook chose to use his or her number. The first meaning of the statutory term must be preferred here. In that sense the Plaintiff was not involved.

Another consideration for the district court was that a different rule would impose too heavy a cost on TRW. The statute, however, has already made the determination as to what is a bearable cost for a credit reporting agency. The cost is what it takes to have a reasonable belief. In this case that belief needed determination by a jury not a judge.

We reinstate the Plaintiff's first claim together with her request for punitive damages based upon it.

Reasonable Procedures To Assure Accuracy. The statutory command is clear: "Whenever a consumer reporting agency prepares a consumer report it shall follow reasonable procedures to assure maximum possible accuracy of the information concerning the individual about whom the report relates." 15 U.S.C § 1681e(b). It would normally not be easy for a court as a matter of law to determine whether a given procedure was reasonable in reaching the very high standard set by the statute as to each individual reported upon. "The reasonableness of the procedures and whether the agency followed them will be jury questions in the overwhelming majority of cases." *Guimond*, 45 F.3d at 1333. The expert testimony to be offered by Dr. Parker on "automated procedures for connecting and resolving inaccuracies in credit reports" was germane to a jury determination of this question.

The district court ruled that it was already the law of the case, as a result of its summary judgment rulings, that it was permissible for TRW to disclose the Plaintiff's file after an application by the Imposter. In ruling on what Dr. Parker could testify to, the district court expanded that ruling to include the permissibility of TRW disclosing the Imposter's file when the Plaintiff applied for credit. On the basis of this expanded position, the district court ruled that Dr. Parker could not testify as to the availability of computer software that could have kept the Imposter's data and the Plaintiff's data from being merged in a TRW report. As we have already held, it was not a question of law for the court to decide whether TRW had a reasonable belief permitting disclosure. The court's legal error infected its ruling on the scope of Dr. Parker's testimony.

Despite its in limine ruling, the district court permitted Andrews to examine Dr. Parker on the basis of a TRW report to Strategic Mortgage Services made on June 5, 1995. This report attributed to the Plaintiff the Dillard's account opened by the Imposter. Dr. Parker testified that TRW could have had in place "an integrity restraint" that would have prevented this error. He described an integrity restraint as a watchdog that would have looked for problems or anomalies of the kind that TRW failed to detect with the result that the Imposter's applications to FCNB, Express, and Commercial Credit, and her Prime Cable connection were attributed to the Plaintiff. Dr. Parker testified that such integrity restraints were available in the relevant period, 1994–1996. In the light of this testimony it is difficult to conclude that the Plaintiff was harmed at trial by the court's initial ruling.

Conclusion: Judgment on Plaintiff's first cause of action is RE-VERSED and and the case is REMANDED for trial. Judgment on Plaintiff's second and third causes of action is AFFIRMED. Each party should bear its own costs.

Note

The increasing availability on the Internet of information about individuals is making identity theft easier. See the warnings on identity theft at <http://www.ftc.gov>.

ROGAN v. CITY OF LOS ANGELES

United States District Court, Central District of California, 1987.
668 F.Supp. 1384.

KELLEHER, SENIOR DISTRICT JUDGE.

I.   INTRODUCTION

This is an action under 42 U.S.C. section 1983 for money damages, declaratory relief, litigation costs and attorneys' fees against: (a) the City of Los Angeles ("the Defendant City"); and (b) two police officers employed by the city, Defendant Crotsley and Defendant Slack (referred to hereinafter collectively as "the Defendant Officers"). The action arises out of the alleged deprivation of Plaintiff Terry Dean Rogan's constitutional rights resulting from his mistaken arrests for robbery and murder. * * *

1.   Deprivation of a Constitutionally Protected Interest.

a.   Relevant Facts.

During 1981, Bernard McKandes ("McKandes"), an escapee from an Alabama state prison, started using Plaintiff's name after he obtained Plaintiff's birth certificate. * * *

After obtaining Plaintiff's birth certificate, McKandes proceeded to California. McKandes there used Plaintiff's birth certificate to obtain a California driver's license and various other identification documents in Plaintiff's name.

Sometime during 1982, McKandes was arrested by the Los Angeles Police Department ("LAPD") on suspicion of murder. McKandes was using the false identification in Plaintiff's name at the time of his arrest. The LAPD released McKandes for reasons presently unknown.

Approximately three months later, but still during 1982, McKandes left Los Angeles and stopped using the identification in Plaintiff's name.

On or about April 20, 1982, Defendant Crotsley caused an arrest warrant to issue in the name of Terry Dean Rogan, charging him with two robbery-murders which occurred in Los Angeles that month. Said warrant listed Plaintiff's name and an alias, but did not contain McKandes' known physical characteristics (e.g., scars, tattoos, height, weight, etc.).

On approximately May 10, 1982, Defendant Slack caused the warrant information to be placed into the national computer arrest warrant notification system known as the National Crime Information Center ("NCIC"). Entry of said information into the NCIC system ensured that any police officer in the United States having access to the system would be made aware that a robbery-murder warrant in the name of Terry Dean Rogan was outstanding in California. Like the warrant upon which it was based, said information set forth Plaintiff's name and an alias, but did not contain McKandes' known physical characteristics.

On or about June 7, 1982, Defendant Crotsley requested that an official police bulletin be completed and forwarded to certain police departments through official channels. Said bulletin contained, inter alia: (a) Plaintiff's name; (b) three aliases, one of which contained McKandes' correct surname; (c) McKandes' photograph; (d) McKandes' fingerprint; (e) McKandes' height; (f) McKandes' weight; and (g) notice that the suspect had the tattoo "Connie" on the right side of his chest. The bulletin also stated that the suspect should be considered armed and extremely dangerous. The bulletin's widest area of distribution was achieved by or about March 21, 1983, at which time it was sent to: (a) Chicago, Illinois; (b) Mobile, Alabama; and (c) Detroit, Michigan. None of Plaintiff's arrests at issue herein were made by police departments which relied upon the bulletin or had it in their possession.

During July, 1982, Defendant Slack reentered the pertinent NCIC record without modification or amendment.

On or about October 31, 1982, Plaintiff came into contact with officers of the Carrollton Township Police Department in Saginaw County, Michigan, during the course of a trespassing dispute. Plaintiff was arrested on a charge of resisting arrest. The police officers made an inquiry of the NCIC system. The resulting computer report reflected the existence of the California robbery-murder warrant in Plaintiff's name.

On or about November 1, 1982, the Carrollton police contacted LAPD about the California arrest warrant. The Carrolton police established four days later through fingerprint comparison and Plaintiff's lack of certain scars and tattoos that were visible on the body of the wanted suspect, McKandes, that Plaintiff was not the man wanted by the LAPD. Plaintiff then pleaded (either guilty or *nolo contendere*, the record does not reveal which) to the charge of resisting arrest and was sentenced to "time served" of five days, and released. Upon Plaintiff's initial arrest, the NCIC record regarding the California warrant was automatically removed from the NCIC system.

Later during November, 1982, Defendant Crotsley caused the arrest warrant information in Plaintiff's name to be reentered into the NCIC system without modifying same to reflect either the suspect's (i.e., McKandes') known unique physical characteristics (i.e., scars, tattoos) or the duplicate name-misidentification problem. As reflected by the relevant NCIC data entry form, a NCIC computer record contains a miscellaneous field that allows for the entry of up to 121 characters of information regarding identifying physical characteristics or possible mistaken identity-duplicate name situations.

During February or March, 1983, Plaintiff was a passenger in an automobile which was stopped by Bay County sheriff's deputies outside of Saginaw, Michigan, for failure to use a turn signal. The officers ran a computer check on Plaintiff after he showed the officers his identification. The California robbery-murder warrant was reported back to the officers in response to their computer check. As a result, Plaintiff was ordered out of the car at gunpoint, searched, handcuffed, and transported to the jail in Bay City, Michigan. Plaintiff was there handcuffed to metal bars while the sheriff's deputies made telephone calls to the Saginaw police and the LAPD in order to determine Plaintiff's status. Plaintiff was released after being held in jail for approximately two hours.

During early 1983, Plaintiff was stopped for a traffic offense by Saginaw police officers and was again detained until the California robbery-murder warrant problem could be clarified. Plaintiff testified that he did not recall the details of this encounter.

Plaintiff then sought the assistance of the local Federal Bureau of Investigation ("FBI") office in Saginaw. A FBI agent confirmed the existence of a murder warrant in Plaintiff's name in the NCIC system, but informed Plaintiff that only the originating state agency (i.e., the LAPD) could delete, amend, or correct the computer warrant entry.

During July, 1983, Plaintiff traveled from Michigan to Hugo, Oklahoma to visit relatives and to look for employment there and in Kolleen, Texas. On or about July 18, 1983, while driving through Denton County, Texas, Plaintiff was stopped by the police for speeding. The officer's inquiry to the NCIC system again revealed the existence of the outstanding robbery-murder warrant in Plaintiff's name. As a result, Plaintiff was arrested at gunpoint, handcuffed and taken to the nearest jail facility, where he was held for investigation of his true identity. Plaintiff was released after being held in custody for approximately three hours when the relevant finger prints were transmitted to Texas.

Also on or about July 18, 1983, Defendant Crotsley again reactivated the NCIC file in Plaintiff's name without modification.

On or about January 14, 1984, Plaintiff was stopped while driving his car in Saginaw, Michigan, by a county deputy for not having his headlights on. The resulting inquiry into the NCIC system again revealed the existence of the California robbery-murder warrant. Two or three more police cars arrived, including officers armed with shotguns. Plaintiff was apprehended at gunpoint, searched, handcuffed, and taken to the county jail. Plaintiff was then released after officers there on duty vouched for his true identity.

During January, 1984, a reporter for the Saginaw News informed Defendant Crotsley that McKandes, who was by then again incarcerated in an Alabama prison, was the person actually wanted for the robbery-murders in Los Angeles. A FBI agent verified that the fingerprints of the suspect wanted in Los Angeles were those of McKandes.

On January 23, 1984, Defendant Crotsley forwarded the suspect's fingerprints to the Alabama Department of Corrections, and removed the NCIC record in Plaintiff's name.

McKandes was later convicted of the California robbery and murder charges.

During the period of their investigation, the Defendant Officers tried to check the NCIC system at least once per month, and more often if possible, to make sure that the warrant information was still in the system.

* * *

2. CAUSATION OF THE DEVIATION BY OFFICIAL POLICY, CUSTOM OR USAGE

a. *The Law*

It is well settled that inadequate training or supervision can constitute an actionable policy or custom under the second prong of the Monell municipal liability test. *Bergquist v. County of Cochise*, 806 F.2d 1364, 1370 (9th Cir.1986). However, mere negligence does not give rise to section 1983 liability. *Daniels v. Williams*, 474 U.S. 327, 106 S.Ct. 662, 666–67, 88 L.Ed.2d 662 (1986); *Bergquist*, 806 F.2d at 1370. Conversely, a "policy" of *gross* negligence in training or supervision gives rise to section 1983 liability. Thus, a city may be held liable either for the grossly negligent failure to implement a training program for its officers or for implementing a program grossly inadequate to prevent the type of harm suffered. *Id.* Such gross negligence must manifest deliberate indifference to the resulting violations of the citizen's constitutional rights. * * *

The requisite policy, custom or usage may not be proved through reference to a single unconstitutional incident unless "proof of the incident includes proof that it was caused by an existing unconstitutional ... policy." *City of Oklahoma v. Tuttle*, 471 U.S. 808, 105 S.Ct. 2427, 2436, 85 L.Ed.2d 791 (1985); *Bergquist*, 806 F.2d at 1370 n. 1. In contrast, it is sufficient to show a pattern of similar incidents in which citizens were injured or endangered by intentional or negligent police misconduct or that serious incompetence or misbehavior was general or widespread throughout the police force. *Languirand*, 717 F.2d at 228.

b. *Relevant Facts.*

Information in the NCIC system can be withdrawn, added to, corrected, or amended by the law enforcement agency that originally inserted same. However, neither Defendant Slack nor Defendant Crotsley received any training in the procedures for or the necessity of amending information that had been entered into the NCIC system when additional or more accurate information becomes available. The Defendant Officers did not discuss the possibility of adding information to the NCIC record in response to Plaintiff's original misidentification as the suspect.

Defendant Slack has placed information into the NCIC system at least several hundred times during his career as a police officer. Defendant Slack never amended a NCIC file record when more complete or accurate information became available. Moreover, Defendant Slack did not know for sure if it was possible to do so.

Similarly, Defendant Crotsley never considered whether it was possible to insert information into the NCIC system that would alert the officers using the system about the misidentification-dual name problem. Defendant Crotsley was not aware of any LAPD policy addressing dual name-misidentification situations. Defendant Crotsley's policy in such situations was to give the innocent person a computer printout of the warrant and his business card as evidence of the person's innocence only if the person came to Los Angeles and picked the items up personally. Defendant Crotsley testified that he had followed this procedure on four prior occasions, and that "quite a few other police officers" followed the same procedure. During the seventeen years Defendant Crotsley was a police officer it was not the custom for investigators to obtain their superior's approval prior to inserting information into the system. Defendant Crotsley received no instructions or supervision from his superiors regarding the information to be inserted into the NCIC system in this case. However, Defendant Crotsely's superiors were aware of his reactivation of the NCIC entry after Plaintiff's initial misidentification.

LAPD's NCIC operators and supervisors do not make any independent decisions regarding the information inserted into the system, but instead follow the investigators' instructions.

There is one and only one reasonable and permissible factual inference possible given this uncontroverted evidence. See: n. 2, *supra*. Said inference is that the Defendant City (i) failed to adopt any policy, (ii) to train, and (iii) to supervise the Defendant Officers regarding: (a) the Fourth Amendment requirement that both the arrest warrant and the initial NCIC record describe the suspect with particularity; and (b) the procedures for and the necessity of amending the NCIC record when additional or more accurate descriptive information became available.

c. *Application of the Law to the Facts*

(i) The Defendant Officers' Failure to Adequately Describe the Suspect in the Warrant and the NCIC Record Created Pursuant thereto

* * * The Defendant Officers tried to check the NCIC system at least once per month to make sure that the entry was still in the system. Moreover, the Defendant Officers reactivated the erroneous and incomplete NCIC record three times (i.e., once before Plaintiff's initial misidentification and twice afterward). Defendant Crotsley was aware of at least four prior occasions where such problems arose. Similarly, Defendant Crotsley testified that "quite a few other police officers" had dealt with the same problem in the same way in which he did. The only reasonable and permissible inference given the uncontroverted facts set forth in Section II.A.2.b. above (See, n. 2, supra.) is that the insufficiently descriptive warrant and NCIC record were: (i) systemic in nature; and (ii) the result of the Defendant City's grossly negligent and indifferent failure to adequately train and/or supervise the Defendant Officers, or to even adopt and make known appropriate policy.

(ii) The Defendant's Maintenance and Reentry of the Inadequately Descriptive NCIC Record After Receiving Notice of Plaintiff's Initial Misidentification as the Suspect

* * * Moreover, as previously noted, the relevant NCIC policy statement requires that state agencies "adopt a careful and permanent program of data verification including * * * tak[ing] immediate action to correct or complete the NCIC record as well as its own state records" when "errors or points of incompleteness are detected." *See: Mackey*, 387 F.Supp. at 1123; *Cf*. 28 C.F.R. 20.37 (1986). The purpose of this requirement is obviously to protect innocent persons. *See: Mackey*, 387 F.Supp. at 1123 ("In a national system . . . individual users are responsible for the accuracy, validity, and completeness of their record entries . . . and more stringent controls with respect to system discipline are required." Quoting "National Crime Information History Center (NCIC) Computerized History Program Background, Concept and Policy," approved June 11, 1974, at 3.). Thus, the Defendant City's failure to adopt such a program was negligent per se. * * *

Most importantly, the breach of an official policy constitutes reckless disregard for the safety of those for whose protection it is adopted when omission of the required precautions involves a high degree of probability that serious harm will result. Restatement (Second) of Torts, section 500 comment e (1965); W. Keeton, D. Dobbs, R. Keeton & D. Owen, *Prosser and Keeton on the Law of Torts*, section 34, at 214 (5th Ed.1984); *see, e.g., Lewis v. Zell*, 279 Ala. 33, 181 So.2d 101 (1965). Such is the case here. Plaintiff was subjected to the pain and humiliation of being arrested, handcuffed, searched, booked, and incarcerated. Moreover, as Chief Judge Bazelon recognized, an arrest record creates a continuing disability:

> Information denominated a record of arrests, if it becomes known, may subject an individual to serious difficulties. Even if no direct economic loss is involved, the injury to an individual's reputation may be substantial. Economic losses themselves may be both direct and serious. Opportunities for schooling, employment, or professional licenses may be restricted or nonexistent as a consequence of the mere fact of an arrest, even if followed by acquittal or complete exoneration of the charges involved. An arrest record may be used by the police in determining whether subsequently to arrest the individual concerned, or whether to exercise their discretion to bring

formal charges against an individual already arrested. Arrest records have been used in deciding whether to allow a defendant to present his story without impeachment by prior convictions, and as a basis for denying release prior to trial or an appeal; or then may be considered by a judge in determining the sentence to be given a convicted offender.

Menard v. Mitchell, 430 F.2d 486, 490, 491 (D.C.Cir.1970). Most compellingly, Plaintiff's life was endangered each time he was apprehended at gunpoint by police officers who believed that he was an armed and dangerous murder suspect. Said danger of serious harm was both highly probable and foreseeable. Such reckless conduct, if not less, constitutes "gross negligence." *See: Languirand*, 717 F.2d at 220; *Owens*, 601 F.2d at 1246; Restatement (Second) of Torts, section 282 comment e (1965); W. Keeton, D. Dobbs, R. Keeton & D. Owen, *Prosser and Keeton on the Law of Torts*, section 34, at 212–214 (5th Ed.1984); 2 F. Harper & F. James, Jr., *The Law of Torts*, section 15.15, at 953–59 (1956). Thus, the Defendant City's above-defined failure to train or supervise its police officers satisfies the gross negligence test. * * *

(iii) Summary

The Court finds that the Defendant City's failure to (i) adopt any policy, (ii) train, and (iii) supervise its police officers regarding: (a) the Fourth Amendment requirement that the arrest warrant and the NCIC record created pursuant thereto describe the suspect with particularity; and (b) the procedures for and the necessity of amending the NCIC record when additional or more accurate descriptive information became available were both grossly negligent and systemic in nature.

3. Conclusion

For the reasons stated, the Court holds that there is no material question of fact and that Plaintiff is entitled to judgment against the City of Los Angeles on the 42 U.S.C. section 1983 liability issue as a matter of law. *See:* Fed.R.Civ.P. 56(c). The Court, however, believes it is appropriate to emphasize the limited scope of said holding.

The Court recognizes that: (i) the Defendant Officers were diligently seeking to apprehend a dangerous murder suspect; (ii) the suspect, McKandes, had used Plaintiff's name; and (iii) said officers had probable cause to place Plaintiff's name on the arrest warrant and the NCIC record created pursuant thereto (*See: Powe*, 664 F.2d at 647.). However, Defendants mistakenly contend that the officers were faced with the choice of either proceeding as they did or not acting at all. Defendants fail to recognize the third option which would allow the officers to discharge their duties to apprehend McKandes and to respect Plaintiff's constitutional rights. This option was to: (1) insert the additional descriptive information concerning McKandes (re: scars, tattoos, etc.) into the arrest warrant and NCIC record; and (2) amend same to reflect the misidentification-duplicate name problem after Plaintiff's initial misidentification. * * *

Notes and Questions

1. In *Arizona v. Evans*, 514 U.S. 1, 115 S.Ct. 1185, 131 L.Ed.2d 34 (1995), defendant was arrested on the basis of a quashed warrant that was erroneously indicated in the police computer system as still being valid. Defendant Evans moved to suppress marijuana found in his car at the time of his arrest. A majority of the Supreme Court held that since the unlawful arrest was caused by a clerical error in the computer system, the evidence was admissible under the "good faith" exception to the exclusionary rule.

2. In *Pippinger v. Rubin*, 129 F.3d. 519 (10th Cir.1997), plaintiff sought to use the Privacy Act to prevent disclosure and use of true information in government databanks about his improper behavior. In *Fisher v. National Institute of Health*, 934 F.Supp. 464 (D.D.C.1996), *aff'd*, 107 F.3d 922, 323 U.S.App.D.C. 289 (D.C.Cir.1996), the plaintiff sought to use the Privacy Act to prevent dissemination of false statements wrongly suggesting he had behaved improperly. Plaintiff, Dr. Fisher, a medical school professor, charged that the National Institutes of Health had violated the Privacy Act. The Office of Research Integrity of the United States Department of Health and Human Services had investigated a government-financed research project that Dr. Fisher had administered. While another doctor was found to have engaged in scientific misconduct, plaintiff Dr. Fisher was not. Several computerized databases maintained by the National Institutes of Health contain articles published in medical journals. These databases contain bibliographic information about the articles including the author's or authors' names. Articles for which Dr. Fisher was listed as author were annotated in the databases with statements such as "scientific misconduct—data to be reanalyzed." When Dr. Fisher was unable to get the annotations removed from the articles after he was cleared, he brought this action. The doctor contended that the annotations violated the Privacy Act. The doctor also argued that the data collected by the Office of Research Integrity in its investigation was disclosed in violation of the Privacy Act.

Defendants National Institutes of Health argued that the database files were not covered by the Privacy Act for two reasons: (1) they were exempt from coverage because they are library reference materials, and (2) they did not qualify as "records" under the Act. The court was not persuaded by the first argument, but did agree that the database files were not records as defined by the Act, because the databases were not a system of records "about" the doctor, so they were not subject to the Privacy Act. (This exceedingly narrow interpretation of "records" was rejected in *Bechhoefer v. U.S. Dept. of Justice D.E.A.*, 209 F.3d 57 [2d Cir. 2000].) The court in *Fisher* also said that even if the ORI files were covered by the Privacy act, that Dr. Fisher had failed to demonstrate with evidence the necessary connection between the disclosures and the files.

B. IMMUNITY OF INTERNET SERVICE PROVIDERS

ZERAN v. AMERICA ONLINE, INC.

United States Court of Appeals, Fourth Circuit, 1997.
129 F.3d 327.

WILKINSON, CHIEF JUDGE:

Kenneth Zeran brought this action against America Online, Inc. ("AOL"), arguing that AOL unreasonably delayed in removing defamatory messages posted by an unidentified third party, refused to post retractions of those messages, and failed to screen for similar postings thereafter. The district court granted judgment for AOL on the grounds that the Communications Decency Act of 1996 ("CDA")—47 U.S.C. § 230—bars Zeran's claims. Zeran appeals, arguing that § 230 leaves intact liability for interactive computer service providers who possess notice of defamatory material posted through their services. He also contends that § 230 does not apply here because his claims arise from AOL's alleged negligence prior to the CDA's enactment. Section 230, however, plainly immunizes computer service providers like AOL from liability for information that originates with third parties. Furthermore, Congress clearly expressed its intent that § 230 apply to lawsuits, like Zeran's, instituted after the CDA's enactment. Accordingly, we affirm the judgment of the district court.

I.

"The Internet is an international network of interconnected computers," currently used by approximately 40 million people worldwide. *Reno v. ACLU*, ___ U.S. ___ , ___ , 117 S.Ct. 2329, 2334, 138 L.Ed.2d 874 (1997). One of the many means by which individuals access the Internet is through an interactive computer service. These services offer not only a connection to the Internet as a whole, but also allow their subscribers to access information communicated and stored only on each computer service's individual proprietary network. *Id.* AOL is just such an interactive computer service. Much of the information transmitted over its network originates with the company's millions of subscribers. They may transmit information privately via electronic mail, or they may communicate publicly by posting messages on AOL bulletin boards, where the messages may be read by any AOL subscriber.

The instant case comes before us on a motion for judgment on the pleadings, see Fed.R.Civ.P. 12(c), so we accept the facts alleged in the complaint as true. *Bruce v. Riddle*, 631 F.2d 272, 273 (4th Cir.1980). On April 25, 1995, an unidentified person posted a message on an AOL bulletin board advertising "Naughty Oklahoma T–Shirts." The posting described the sale of shirts featuring offensive and tasteless slogans related to the April 19, 1995, bombing of the Alfred P. Murrah Federal Building in Oklahoma City. Those interested in purchasing the shirts were instructed to call "Ken" at Zeran's home phone number in Seattle, Washington. As a result of this anonymously perpetrated prank, Zeran received a high volume of calls, comprised primarily of angry and derogatory messages, but also including death threats. Zeran could not change his phone number because he relied on its availability to the public in running his business out of his home. Later that day, Zeran called AOL and informed a company representative of his predicament. The employee assured Zeran that the posting would be removed from AOL's bulletin board but explained that as a matter of policy AOL would not post a retraction. The parties dispute the date that AOL removed this original posting from its bulletin board.

On April 26, the next day, an unknown person posted another message advertising additional shirts with new tasteless slogans related to the Oklahoma City bombing. Again, interested buyers were told to call Zeran's phone number, to ask for "Ken," and to "please call back if busy" due to high demand. The angry, threatening phone calls intensified. Over the next four days, an unidentified party continued to post messages on AOL's bulletin board, advertising additional items including bumper stickers and key chains with still more offensive slogans. During this time period, Zeran called AOL repeatedly and was told by company representatives that the individual account from which the messages were posted would soon be closed. Zeran also reported his case to Seattle FBI agents. By April 30, Zeran was receiving an abusive phone call approximately every two minutes.

Meanwhile, an announcer for Oklahoma City radio station KRXO received a copy of the first AOL posting. On May 1, the announcer related the message's contents on the air, attributed them to "Ken" at Zeran's phone number, and urged the listening audience to call the number. After this radio broadcast, Zeran was inundated with death threats and other violent calls from Oklahoma City residents. Over the next few days, Zeran talked to both KRXO and AOL representatives. He also spoke to his local police, who subsequently surveilled his home to protect his safety. By May 14, after an Oklahoma City newspaper published a story exposing the shirt advertisements as a hoax and after KRXO made an on-air apology, the number of calls to Zeran's residence finally subsided to fifteen per day.

Zeran first filed suit on January 4, 1996, against radio station KRXO in the United States District Court for the Western District of Oklahoma. On April 23, 1996, he filed this separate suit against AOL in the same court. Zeran did not bring any action against the party who posted the offensive messages. After Zeran's suit against AOL was transferred to the Eastern District of Virginia pursuant to 28 U.S.C. § 1404(a), AOL answered Zeran's complaint and interposed 47 U.S.C. § 230 as an affirmative defense. AOL then moved for judgment on the pleadings pursuant to Fed.R.Civ.P. 12(c). The district court granted AOL's motion, and Zeran filed this appeal.

II.

A.

Because § 230 was successfully advanced by AOL in the district court as a defense to Zeran's claims, we shall briefly examine its operation here. Zeran seeks to hold AOL liable for defamatory speech initiated by a third party. He argued to the district court that once he notified AOL of the unidentified third party's hoax, AOL had a duty to remove the defamatory posting promptly, to notify its subscribers of the message's false nature, and to effectively screen future defamatory material. Section 230 entered this litigation as an affirmative defense pled by AOL. The company claimed that Congress immunized interactive computer service providers from claims based on information posted by a third party.

The relevant portion of § 230 states: "No provider or user of an interactive computer service shall be treated as the publisher or speaker of any information provided by another information content provider." 47 U.S.C. § 230(c)(1).[2] By its plain language, § 230 creates a federal immunity to any cause of action that would make service providers liable for information originating with a third-party user of the service. Specifically, § 230 precludes courts from entertaining claims that would place a computer service provider in a publisher's role. Thus, lawsuits seeking to hold a service provider liable for its exercise of a publisher's traditional editorial functions—such as deciding whether to publish, withdraw, postpone or alter content—are barred.

The purpose of this statutory immunity is not difficult to discern. Congress recognized the threat that tort-based lawsuits pose to freedom of speech in the new and burgeoning Internet medium. The imposition of tort liability on service providers for the communications of others represented, for Congress, simply another form of intrusive government regulation of speech. Section 230 was enacted, in part, to maintain the robust nature of Internet communication and, accordingly, to keep government interference in the medium to a minimum. In specific statutory findings, Congress recognized the Internet and interactive computer services as offering "a forum for a true diversity of political discourse, unique opportunities for cultural development, and myriad avenues for intellectual activity." *Id.* § 230(a)(3). It also found that the Internet and interactive computer services "have flourished, to the benefit of all Americans, *with a minimum of government regulation.*" *Id.*

---

2. Section 230 defines "interactive computer service" as "any information service, system, or access software provider that provides or enables computer access by multiple users to a computer server, including specifically a service or system that provides access to the Internet and such systems operated or services offered by libraries or educational institutions." 47 U.S.C. § 230(e)(2). The term"information content provider" is defined as "any person or entity that is responsible, in whole or in part, for the creation or development of information provided through the Internet or any other interactive computer service." *Id.* § 230(e)(3). The parties do not dispute that AOL falls within the CDA's "interactive computer service" definition and that the unidentified third party who posted the offensive messages here fits the definition of an "information content provider."

§ 230(a)(4) (emphasis added). Congress further stated that it is "the policy of the United States ... to preserve the vibrant and competitive free market that presently exists for the Internet and other interactive computer services, unfettered by Federal or State regulation." *Id.* § 230(b)(2) (emphasis added).

None of this means, of course, that the original culpable party who posts defamatory messages would escape accountability. While Congress acted to keep government regulation of the Internet to a minimum, it also found it to be the policy of the United States "to ensure vigorous enforcement of Federal criminal laws to deter and punish trafficking in obscenity, stalking, and harassment by means of computer." *Id.* § 230(b)(5). Congress made a policy choice, however, not to deter harmful online speech through the separate route of imposing tort liability on companies that serve as intermediaries for other parties' potentially injurious messages.

Congress' purpose in providing the § 230 immunity was thus evident. Interactive computer services have millions of users. See *Reno v. ACLU*, ___ U.S. at ___ , 117 S.Ct. at 2334 (noting that at time of district court trial, "commercial online services had almost 12 million individual subscribers"). The amount of information communicated via interactive computer services is therefore staggering. The specter of tort liability in an area of such prolific speech would have an obvious chilling effect. It would be impossible for service providers to screen each of their millions of postings for possible problems. Faced with potential liability for each message republished by their services, interactive computer service providers might choose to severely restrict the number and type of messages posted. Congress considered the weight of the speech interests implicated and chose to immunize service providers to avoid any such restrictive effect.

Another important purpose of § 230 was to encourage service providers to self-regulate the dissemination of offensive material over their services. In this respect, § 230 responded to a New York state court decision, *Stratton Oakmont, Inc. v. Prodigy Servs. Co.*, 1995 WL 323710 (N.Y.Sup.Ct. May 24, 1995). There, the plaintiffs sued Prodigy—an interactive computer service like AOL—for defamatory comments made by an unidentified party on one of Prodigy's bulletin boards. The court held Prodigy to the strict liability standard normally applied to original publishers of defamatory statements, rejecting Prodigy's claims that it should be held only to the lower "knowledge" standard usually reserved for distributors. The court reasoned that Prodigy acted more like an original publisher than a distributor both because it advertised its practice of controlling content on its service and because it actively screened and edited messages posted on its bulletin boards.

Congress enacted § 230 to remove the disincentives to self-regulation created by the *Stratton Oakmont* decision. Under that court's holding, computer service providers who regulated the dissemination of offensive material on their services risked subjecting themselves to liability, because such regulation cast the service provider in the role of a publisher. Fearing that the specter of liability would therefore deter service providers from blocking and screening offensive material, Congress enacted § 230's broad immunity "to remove disincentives for the development and utilization of blocking and filtering technologies that empower parents to restrict their children's access to objectionable or inappropriate online material." 47 U.S.C. § 230(b)(4). In line with this purpose, § 230 forbids the imposition of publisher liability on a service provider for the exercise of its editorial and self-regulatory functions.

B.

Zeran argues, however, that the § 230 immunity eliminates only publisher liability, leaving distributor liability intact. Publishers can be held liable for defamatory statements contained in their works even absent proof that they had specific knowledge of the statement's inclusion. W.Page Keeton et al., *Prosser and Keeton on the Law of Torts* § 113, at 810 (5th ed.1984). According to Zeran, interactive computer service providers like AOL are normally considered instead to be distributors, like traditional news vendors or book sellers. Distributors cannot be held liable for defamatory statements contained in the materials they distribute unless it is proven at a minimum that they have actual knowledge of the defamatory statements upon which liability is predicated. *Id.* at 811 (explaining that distributors are not liable "in the absence of proof that they knew or had reason to know of the existence of defamatory matter contained in matter published"). Zeran contends that he provided AOL with sufficient notice of the defamatory statements appearing on the company's bulletin board. This notice is significant, says Zeran, because AOL could be held liable as a distributor only if it acquired knowledge of the defamatory statements' existence.

Because of the difference between these two forms of liability, Zeran contends that the term "distributor" carries a legally distinct meaning from the term "publisher." Accordingly, he asserts that Congress' use of only the term "publisher" in § 230 indicates a purpose to immunize service providers only from publisher liability. He argues that distributors are left unprotected by § 230 and, therefore, his suit should be permitted to proceed against AOL. We disagree. Assuming *arguendo* that Zeran has satisfied the requirements for imposition of distributor liability, this theory of liability is merely a subset, or a species, of publisher liability, and is therefore also foreclosed by § 230.

The terms "publisher" and "distributor" derive their legal significance from the context of defamation law. Although Zeran attempts to artfully plead his claims as ones of negligence, they are indistinguishable from a garden variety defamation action. Because the publication of a statement is a necessary element in a defamation action, only one who publishes can be subject to this form of tort liability. Restatement (Second) of Torts § 558(b) (1977); Keeton et al., *supra*, § 113, at 802. Publication does not only describe the choice by an author to include certain information. In addition, both the negligent communication of a defamatory statement and the failure to remove such a statement when first communicated by another party—each alleged by Zeran here under a negligence label—constitute publication. In fact, every repetition of a defamatory statement is considered a publication. Restatement (Second) of Torts § 577.

In this case, AOL is legally considered to be a publisher. "[E]very one who takes part in the publication ... is charged with publication." *Id.* Even distributors are considered to be publishers for purposes of defamation law:

> Those who are in the business of making their facilities available to disseminate the writings composed, the speeches made, and the information gathered by others may also be regarded as participating to such an extent in making the books, newspapers, magazines, and information available to others as to be regarded as publishers. They are intentionally making the contents available to others, sometimes without knowing all of the contents—including the defamatory content—and sometimes without any opportunity to ascertain, in advance, that any defamatory matter was to be included in the matter published. They are intentionally making the contents available to others, sometimes without knowing all of the contents— including the defamatory content—and sometimes without any opportunity to ascertain, in advance, that any defamatory matter was to be included in the matter published.

Id. at 803. AOL falls squarely within this traditional definition of a publisher and, therefore, is clearly protected by § 230's immunity.

Zeran contends that decisions like *Stratton Oakmont* and *Cubby, Inc. v. CompuServe Inc.*, 776 F.Supp. 135 (S.D.N.Y.1991), recognize a legal distinction between publishers and distributors. He misapprehends, however, the significance of that distinction for the legal issue we consider here. It is undoubtedly true that mere conduits, or distributors, are subject to a different standard of liability. As explained above, distributors must at a minimum have knowledge of the existence of a defamatory statement as a prerequisite to liability. But this distinction signifies only that different standards of liability may be applied *within* the larger publisher category, depending on the specific type of publisher concerned. *See* Keeton et al., *supra*, § 113, at 799–800 (explaining that every party involved is charged with publication, although degrees of legal responsibility differ). To the extent that decisions like *Stratton* and *Cubby* utilize the terms "publisher" and "distributor" separately, the decisions correctly describe two different standards of liability. *Stratton* and *Cubby* do not, however, suggest that distributors are not also a type of publisher for purposes of defamation law.

Zeran simply attaches too much importance to the presence of the distinct notice element in distributor liability. The simple fact of notice surely cannot transform one from an original publisher to a distributor in the eyes of the law. To the contrary, once a computer service provider receives notice of a potentially defamatory posting, it is thrust into the role of a traditional publisher. The computer service provider must decide whether to publish, edit, or withdraw the posting. In this respect, Zeran seeks to impose liability on AOL for assuming the role for which § 230 specifically proscribes liability—the publisher role.

Our view that Zeran's complaint treats AOL as a publisher is reinforced because AOL is cast in the same position as the party who originally posted the offensive messages. According to Zeran's logic, AOL is legally at fault because it communicated to third parties an allegedly defamatory statement. This is precisely the theory under which the original poster of the offensive messages would be found liable. If the original party is considered a publisher of the offensive messages, Zeran certainly cannot attach liability to AOL under the same theory without conceding that AOL too must be treated as a publisher of the statements.

Zeran next contends that interpreting§ 230 to impose liability on service providers with knowledge of defamatory content on their services is consistent with the statutory purposes outlined in Part IIA. Zeran fails, however, to understand the practical implications of notice liability in the interactive computer service context. Liability upon notice would defeat the dual purposes advanced by § 230 of the CDA. Like the strict liability imposed by the *Stratton Oakmont* court, liability upon notice reinforces service providers' incentives to restrict speech and abstain from self-regulation.

If computer service providers were subject to distributor liability, they would face potential liability each time they receive notice of a potentially defamatory statement—from any party, concerning any message. Each notification would require a careful yet rapid investigation of the circumstances surrounding the posted information, a legal judgment concerning the information's defamatory character, and an on-the-spot editorial decision whether to risk liability by allowing the continued publication of that information. Although this might be feasible for the traditional print publisher, the sheer number of postings on interactive computer services would create an impossible burden in the Internet context. Because service providers would be subject to liability only for the publication of information, and not for its removal, they would have a natural incentive simply to remove messages upon notification, whether the contents were defamatory or not. Thus, like strict liability, liability upon notice has a chilling effect on the freedom of Internet speech.

Similarly, notice-based liability would deter service providers from regulating the dissemination of offensive material over their own services. Any efforts by a service provider to investigate and screen material posted on its service would only lead to notice of potentially defamatory material more frequently and thereby create a stronger basis for liability. Instead of subjecting themselves to further possible lawsuits, service providers would likely eschew any attempts at self-regulation.

More generally, notice-based liability for interactive computer service providers would provide third parties with a no-cost means to create the basis for future lawsuits. Whenever one was displeased with the speech of another party conducted over an interactive computer service, the offended party could simply "notify" the relevant service provider, claiming the information to be legally defamatory. In light of the vast amount of speech communicated through interactive computer services, these notices could produce an impossible burden for service providers, who would be faced with ceaseless choices of suppressing controversial speech or sustaining prohibitive liability. Because the probable effects of distributor liability on the vigor of Internet speech and on service provider self-regulation are directly contrary to § 230's statutory purposes, we will not assume that Congress intended to leave liability upon notice intact.

Zeran finally contends that the interpretive canon favoring retention of common law principles unless Congress speaks directly to the issue counsels a restrictive reading of the § 230 immunity here. See *United States v. Texas*, 507 U.S. 529, 534, 113 S.Ct. 1631, 1634–35, 123 L.Ed.2d 245 (1993). This interpretive canon does not persuade us to reach a different result. Here, Congress has indeed spoken directly to the issue by employing the legally significant term "publisher," which has traditionally encompassed distributors and original publishers alike.

The decision cited by Zeran, *United States v. Texas*, also recognized that abrogation of common law principles is appropriate when a contrary statutory purpose is evident. *Id.* This is consistent with the Court's earlier cautions against courts' application of the canon with excessive zeal: " 'The rule that statutes in derogation of the common law are to be strictly construed does not require such an adherence to the letter as would defeat an obvious legislative purpose or lessen the scope plainly intended to be given to the measure.' " *Isbrandtsen Co. v. Johnson*, 343 U.S. 779, 783, 72 S.Ct. 1011, 1014, 96 L.Ed. 1294 (1952) (quoting *Jamison v. Encarnacion*, 281 U.S. 635, 640, 50 S.Ct. 440, 442, 74 L.Ed. 1082 (1930)). Zeran's argument flies in the face of this warning. As explained above, interpreting § 230 to leave distributor liability in effect would defeat the two primary purposes of the statute and would certainly "lessen the scope plainly intended" by Congress' use of the term "publisher."

Section 230 represents the approach of Congress to a problem of national and international dimension. The Supreme Court underscored this point in *Reno v. ACLU*, finding that the Internet allows "tens of millions of people to communicate with one another and to access vast amounts of information from around the world.[It] is 'a unique and wholly new medium of worldwide human communication.' " ___ U.S. at ___ , 117 S.Ct. at 2334 (citation omitted). Application of the canon invoked by Zeran here would significantly lessen Congress' power, derived from the Commerce Clause, to act in a field whose international character is apparent. While Congress allowed for the enforcement of "any State law that is consistent with [§ 230]," 47 U.S.C. § 230(d)(3), it is equally plain that Congress' desire to promote unfettered speech on the Internet must supersede conflicting common law causes of action. Section 230(d)(3) continues: "No cause of action may be brought and no liability may be imposed under any State or local law that is inconsistent with this section." With respect to federal-state preemption, the Court has advised: "[W]hen Congress has 'unmistakably . . . ordained,' that its enactments alone are to regulate a part of commerce, state laws regulating that aspect of commerce must fall. The result is compelled whether Congress' command is explicitly stated in the statute's language or implicitly contained in its structure and purpose." *Jones v. Rath Packing Co.*, 430 U.S. 519, 525, 97 S.Ct. 1305, 1309, 51 L.Ed.2d 604 (1977) (citations omitted). Here, Congress' command is explicitly stated. Its exercise of its commerce power is clear and counteracts the caution counseled by the interpretive canon favoring retention of common law principles.

III.

The CDA was signed into law and became effective on February 8, 1996. Zeran did not file his complaint until April 23, 1996. Zeran contends that even if § 230 does bar the type of claim he brings here, it cannot be applied retroactively to bar an action arising from AOL's alleged misconduct prior to the CDA's enactment. We disagree. * * *

IV.

For the foregoing reasons, we affirm the judgment of the district court.

AFFIRMED.

Note

In 1997, Matt Drudge, author of the DRUDGE REPORT, published on the Internet accusations of spousal abuse against White House aide Sidney Blumenthal. Blumenthal sued both Drudge and America Online on the basis that the reports were false. Drudge had a written agreement with AOL which made his web site available to all AOL members. AOL filed for summary judgement in the case, and the court granted the motion on the basis of § 230 of the Communications Decency Act of 1996. The court noted that whether or not it was a wise decision, Congress decided not to treat providers of interactive computer services as publishers. Therefore such services are immune from liability for their failure to edit, withhold or restrict access to material disseminated through their systems. Since the plaintiffs could show no evidence that Drudge was an agent or employee of AOL, the service provider could not be found liable. The case proceeded against Drudge himself. *Blumenthal v. Drudge*, 992 F. Supp. 44 (D.D.C. 1998).

C. DUTY TO PROVIDE ACCURATE INFORMATION TO THOSE AFFECTED

HERMES v. PFIZER, INC.

United States Court of Appeals, Fifth Circuit, 1988.
848 F.2d 66.

PER CURIAM:

In this Mississippi diversity suit a jury returned a verdict of $800,000 against defendant Pfizer, Inc. as compensation for plaintiff Laura Hermes' personal injury resulting from the use of the prescription drug Sinequan, a Pfizer product. We reject Pfizer's arguments that the evidence of the drug's potential side effect was insufficient to trigger a duty to warn and that there was insufficient evidence that the drug was a cause of injury, and we affirm.

I

A gynecologist prescribed Sinequan, a tricyclic antidepressant, for Laura Hermes, a 50–year old post-hysterectomy patient. Several days after taking the medication, Hermes developed "extrapyramidal" symptoms or a "hunting jaw." Hermes sought treatment by an oral surgeon who referred her to a neurologist. The condition appears to be permanent.

Hermes filed this suit against Pfizer alleging strict liability and negligence. Hermes offered the testimony of Dr. Dewey Metts, the oral surgeon, Dr. Joe Jackson, the treating neurologist, Dr. Michael Bourgeois, the prescribing gynecologist, Dr. James O'Donnell, an expert in adverse drug reactions and licensed pharmacist, and, as an adverse witness, Salvatore Giorgiani a Pfizer employee responsible for maintaining adverse drug reactions reports. Pfizer presented the testimony of Dr. James Matheny, an expert in pharmacology. Dr. Armin Haerer, a neurologist who examined Hermes under court order, also testified at trial.

II

Pfizer argues that the court erred in denying its motions for directed verdict, judgment n.o.v., and new trial because the evidence on the issues of duty to warn and causation was insufficient to support a jury verdict. On review of a motion for directed verdict or judgment n.o.v., we apply the test announced in *Boeing Co. v. Shipman*,[3] whether, in a light most favorable to the party opposing the motion, reasonable people could not arrive at a contrary verdict. In reviewing a motion for new trial, we ask whether the verdict is against the great weight of the evidence.

A

A key issue in this appeal is whether Pfizer had a duty to warn Hermes of the possible side effect she experienced, whether it knew or

---

3.   411 F. 2d 365 (5th Cir.1969).

should have known that the taking of Sinequan could cause permanent hunting jaw. Whether there is a duty to warn turns on the manufacturer's actual knowledge and its "constructive knowledge as measured by scientific literature and other available means of communication." A manufacturer has a duty to keep abreast of research, adverse reaction reports, and other scientific literature pertaining to its product.

Pfizer argues that there was insufficient evidence of any knowledge of the possible side effect. It argues that not one expert testified that there had been any report of symptoms such as those experienced by Hermes. It cites to *Johnston v. Upjohn Co.*,[9] in which the court held that "if such a reaction had never occurred before, defendant could not know about it or in the exercise of the required degree of care could not have found out about it, and absent knowledge of such reaction, there could be no duty to warn."

Pfizer argues that in any event there is no evidence that it breached any duty to warn, pointing to its instructions insert and reference in *Physician's Desk Reference*, which noted the possibility of temporary extrapyramidal symptoms. Pfizer contends that it had no duty to warn of *permanent* symptoms because it "knew" of none.

Hermes argues, on the other hand, that Pfizer knew or should have known of the side effect. Her expert, O'Donnell, unequivocally stated that Sinequan could cause temporary and permanent hunting jaw. The jury also had before it an FDA computer printout of adverse drug reaction reports concerning Sinequan, evidence that reports of extrapyramidal symptoms were recorded as early as 1970.

We are persuaded that this evidence was enough for the jury to have concluded that Pfizer had sufficient knowledge to trigger a duty to warn. The court did not err in denying Pfizer's motion on this ground. * * *

We AFFIRM.

Questions

1. Assume that a hospital is contemplating acquiring a sophisticated computer system to assist in detection of illness. What factors, as an attorney, would you consider in the formulation of your advice to your client, the hospital, about whether or not to acquire the system?

2. Should a computer company which provides a service be required to do so in such a way as to maximize (or nearly maximize) the benefits of the system? Should it matter if health and/or safety are involved?

3. For example, should a computer company which provides computerized analysis of blood be required to (a) keep its programs current with the latest blood tests; (b) develop sophisticated blood tests on its own in order to provide maximum service?

9.   442 S.W.2d 93, 94 (Mo.App.1969)

D. DUTY OF GOVERNMENT AGENCIES TO OPERATE ON THE BASIS OF ACCURATE INFORMATION

MESIAR v. HECKMAN

Supreme Court of Alaska, 1998.
964 P.2d 445.

BRYNER, JUSTICE.

I. INTRODUCTION

Art Heckman, Fred Lamont, and Martin Kelley (collectively Heckman) engage in commercial or subsistence fishing on the Yukon River drainage; on behalf of themselves and similarly situated resource users, they sued David Mesiar and the Alaska Department of Fish and Game (collectively ADF & G) for negligent operation of a sonar fish counter that ADF & G relied on to make fisheries closure decisions for the Yukon River drainage during the 1994 fishing season. The main issues presented are whether ADF & G owes Heckman an actionable duty to use reasonable care in fisheries data collection and management, and, alternatively, whether ADF & G is immune from tort liability for negligent data collection. We conclude that ADF & G owes no actionable duty to Heckman and do not reach the immunity question.

II. FACTS AND PROCEEDINGS

The Commissioner of ADF & G has the responsibility to "manage, protect, maintain, improve, and extend the fish, game, and aquatic plant resources of the state in the interest of the economy and general well-being of the state." Title 16, Chapter 5 of the Alaska Statutes gives ADF & G broad powers to carry out its statutory responsibilities, including the power to summarily order emergency openings and closures of fishing periods; such orders have the force and effect of law.

In 1994 the Board of Fisheries promulgated 5 AAC 01.249 as a guideline for managing the fall chum-salmon run from July 16 through December 31 in the Yukon River drainage. The regulation included provisions governing mandatory closures and setting time limits for different fisheries—commercial, sport, personal use, and subsistence—depending on the projected run size.

In order to explain and supplement 5 AAC 01.249, ADF & G issued Regional Information Report No. 3A94–23, the "Yukon Area Commercial and Subsistence Salmon Fisheries 1994 Management Plan." In this plan, ADF & G stated that the sonar project near Pilot Station would be the primary method by which it would assess the fall chum salmon run. ADF & G set guidelines for operating the sonar and, in an internal memorandum entitled "Project Operational Plan for the Lower Yukon River Sonar," described these guidelines, as well as the sonar equipment itself and how it would be used in counting fish on the Yukon.

As a result of low salmon counts, ADF & G closed fisheries on the Yukon during parts of the 1994 fall chum season under 5 AAC 01.249. In response, Heckman filed a class action against ADF & G employee David Mesiar and ADF & G, alleging that Mesiar, who operated the sonar counter near Pilot Station, negligently miscounted the run, thereby precipitating unnecessary closures and restrictions on Yukon River drainage chum fisheries.

ADF & G moved to dismiss Heckman's complaint for failure to state a claim, arguing primarily that it owed no actionable duty to Heckman and that, even if it did owe a duty, it had immunity from tort suits arising out of fisheries management decisions under AS 09.50.250(1)'s discretionary function exception. Superior Court Judge pro tem Mark Wood denied ADF & G's motion, holding that ADF & G owed Heckman a duty to operate sonar counting equipment in a nonnegligent manner and that, though fisheries closure decisions themselves are immune discretionary functions, ministerial data collection functions supporting those decisions are not.

ADF & G petitioned this court to review Judge Wood's ruling. We granted the petition and now consider whether Heckman's cause of action for negligent fish counting can be sustained against ADF & G's assertions that it had no duty and is immune from liability. We begin by considering the issue of duty.

III.   ADF & G OWES HECKMAN NO ACTIONABLE DUTY.

A.   *The Relationship between ADF & G and Heckman Is the Same as the Relationship between ADF & G and Any Other Alaska Fisheries Resource User.*

The initial step in deciding whether an action for negligence can be maintained is to consider whether a duty exists. Whether an actionable duty exists is a question of law and public policy. " 'Duty' is not sacrosanct in itself, but is only an expression of the sum total of those considerations of policy which lead the law to say that the particular plaintiff is entitled to protection." *City of Kotzebue v. McLean*, 702 P.2d 1309 (Alaska 1985) (quoting William L. Prosser, *The Law of Torts* § 53, at 325 (4th ed. 1971)). In *McLean* we adopted an *ad hoc* approach to duty determinations, explaining that we "first define the class of cases to which our rulings will apply, then weigh the factors which support and oppose the imposition of liability in that class of cases."

In the first phase of duty analysis that *McLean* describes—defining the class of cases to which our ruling applies—we must bear in mind that duty is at heart a question of policy centering on the basic relationship between the parties rather than on the nature of their conduct on a given occasion. *See* W. Page Keeton et al., *Prosser and Keeton on the Law of Torts* § 53, at 356 (5th ed. 1984). Particular conduct becomes important only when a duty is imposed; the conduct then helps to determine the applicable standard of care: "It is better to reserve 'duty' for the problem of the *relation* between individuals which imposes upon one a legal obligation for the benefit of the other, and to deal with particular conduct in terms of a legal standard of what is required to meet [that] obligation." *Id.* (emphasis added). As we noted in *Kooly*, we must take "a generalized approach which asks whether a duty of care should be imposed in the general class of cases" exemplified by the case before the court. *Kooly*, 958 P.2d at 1109. This generalized approach is necessary because " 'fact-intensive inquiries pertain to the issues of breach, causation, and damages, not the threshold legal question of whether a duty exists.' " *Id.* (quoting *Bolieu v. Sisters of Providence in Washington*, 953 P.2d 1233, 1241 (Alaska 1998)).

The threshold issues, then, are what sort of relationship exists between the parties, and what class of cases does that relationship define. Heckman seems to argue that the parties' relationship is narrow and specific—that Mesiar was essentially counting salmon for the benefit of persons engaging in the Yukon River fall chum-salmon run. But ADF & G more broadly characterizes the relationship at issue here as the basic relationship between a resource manager and a resource user: "Fisheries management and population sampling are inexact processes and for every season and every fishery closure (or opening) there will be disappointed users." ADF & G contends that imposing "an actionable common law duty on a state to collect data for fisheries or public resource management in a non-negligent manner" would be virtually unprecedented. And it claims that recognizing such a broad duty "will encourage annual class-action suits to challenge unpopular ADF & G decisions."

In our view, ADF & G accurately characterizes the relationship at issue in this case and the class of cases it defines. Common-law principles and the common-use clause in article VIII, section 3, of the Alaska Constitution "impose upon the state a trust duty to manage the fish, wildlife and water resources of the state for *the benefit of all the people.*" *Owsichek v. State, Guide Licensing & Control Bd.*, 763 P.2d 488, 495 (Alaska 1988) (emphasis added). Alaska Statutes 16.05.020(2) reflects this constitutional mandate: "The [ADF & G] commissioner shall ... manage ... the fish ... resources of the state in the interest of the economy and *general* well-being of the state[.]" AS 116.05.020(2) (emphasis added). Alaska Statutes 16.05.092 also mirrors the constitutional mandate, requiring ADF & G to "develop and continually maintain a comprehensive, coordinated state plan for the orderly present and long-range rehabilitation, enhancement, and development of all aspects of the state's fisheries *for the perpetual use, benefit, and enjoyment of all citizens.*" AS 16.05.092(1) (emphasis added).

ADF & G undoubtedly designed its sonar chum-salmon counting project to benefit Heckman and other Yukon River resource users. But Heckman and other Yukon River users were not the exclusive beneficiaries of the program. As part of ADF & G's overall resource-management effort, the sonar project served all resource users and potential users in Alaska. Heckman did stand to gain or lose from ADF & G's efforts more immediately and directly than other Alaskans. But this gave him no special power to demand a higher level of performance from the agency, and it gave him no vested right to recover damages in the event of ADF & G's failure.

In short, Heckman's relationship to ADF & G was that of a resource user to a resource manager. In performing his job as operator of the sonar fish counters, Mesiar collected data for ADF & G, not for Heckman. And in making decisions based on Mesiar's data, ADF & G acted not for the particular and immediate benefit of Heckman and other users of the fall chum-salmon run then in progress, but for the broader benefit of short-term and long-term resource users statewide. If ADF & G owed Heckman an actionable duty of due care in counting fish during the fall chum run, logic would dictate that the agency owed the same duty to all resource users who might claim foreseeable injury as a result of ADF & G's failure to exercise due care in any ministerial aspect of any resource-management program.

The relationship between resource manager and resource user, then, is "the class of cases to which our ruling[ ] will apply." *McLean,* 702 P.2d at 1314. We must now turn to the second phase of our duty analysis, which requires us to "weigh the factors which support and oppose the imposition of liability in [this] class." *Id.*

B. The State Owes No Duty to Heckman under the D.S.W. Duty Analysis.

1. The D.S.W. factors

In *D.S.W. v. Fairbanks North Star Borough School District,* 628 P.2d 554, 555 (Alaska 1981), we listed the following public policy considerations as relevant in determining if an actionable duty of care exists:

> The foreseeability of harm to the plaintiff, the degree of certainty that the plaintiff suffered injury, the closeness of the connection between the defendant's conduct and the injury suffered, the moral blame attached to the defendant's conduct, the policy of preventing future harm, the extent of the burden to the defendant and consequences to the community of imposing a duty to exercise care with resulting liability for breach, and the availability, cost and prevalence of insurance for the risk involved.

Id. (quoting *Peter W. v. San Francisco Unified Sch. Dist.,* 60 Cal.App.3d 814, 131 Cal. Rptr. 854, 859–60). Applying these factors to the present case, we conclude that no actionable duty should be found to exist.

a. Foreseeability of harm, certainty of injury, and connection between conduct and injury

In *Mattingly v. Sheldon Jackson College,* 743 P.2d 356, 361 (Alaska 1987), we held that, for purely economic harm, the identifiable class of plaintiffs must be particularly foreseeable in number, type, and economic expectations. ADF & G argues that the harm to Heckman is not foreseeable or certain because the class of plaintiffs is not particularized. Heckman counters that ADF & G knew that its closure decisions would be based on the sonar numbers and that any inaccuracy could therefore result in harm to Heckman. In Heckman's view, the closures thus caused certain harm and were a direct result of the negligent sonar operation.

Both parties are correct. Heckman is correct in asserting that ADF & G's closure decisions predictably and specifically harmed users of the Yukon River drainage fall chum run. But ADF & G is also correct in observing that identifying plaintiffs and specific damages, as contemplated by *Mattingly*, is problematic. ADF & G's resource-management decisions foreseeably affect many resource users other than those fishing the fall run upstream from the counters; the benefits to one class of users often will harm others, creating a potential conflict between classes of resource users alleging differing harms.

In any fisheries-regulation scheme, the interests of some classes of resource users at times become adverse to those of others; a management decision that benefits some inevitably will harm others. For instance, premature closures on the lower river allow more fish to reach upper-river users and may result in a larger escapement, providing future benefits to the ocean-fishing industry. The argument that Heckman's damages are foreseeable and certain thus proves too much: almost all fisheries-management decisions have predictable adverse effects on one class of resource users or another; because virtually any management action may be characterized as negligent, recognizing an actionable duty of due care to Heckman would foreseeably expose ADF & G to litigation for almost any future management decision. Hence, the foreseeability of harm to Heckman is not a dispositive factor.

b. Moral blame attached to ADF & G's conduct

Virtually all negligence may be viewed as morally blameworthy. Yet in determining the existence of a duty, we have sometimes attached little moral blame to negligent conduct; at other times, we have emphasized this factor. ADF & G accurately observes that the differing treatment our case law accords to the blameworthiness of various negligent acts reflects distinctions in the types of risk they involve. Our cases have ascribed particular significance to the moral blameworthiness of negligence that creates a risk of death or serious personal injury; in contrast, we have ascribed little blameworthiness to ordinary negligence that merely causes economic or purely emotional harm.

We certainly do not mean to trivialize the serious and substantial harm that ADF & G's alleged negligence may have caused Heckman and similarly situated resource users; but this harm is nonetheless primarily economic. We conclude that, when ordinary negligence creates a risk of economic harm only, moral blameworthiness is not a prominent factor for purposes of determining the existence of an actionable duty.

c. Policy of preventing future harm

Heckman argues that future negligence in implementing sonar plans would be deterred by imposing a duty on ADF & G. We find the argument unpersuasive.

As we have already pointed out in our discussion of foreseeability, ADF & G's closure orders have different impacts on potentially conflicting groups of resource users. Recognizing an actionable duty to avoid negligent closures based on inaccurate sonar counts could impede ADF & G's ability to manage for all users by encouraging it to base closure decisions on the demands of a single user group. It is far from clear that an actionable duty of care would deter reliance on inaccurate data. To the contrary, the prospect of an action for damages might merely encourage ADF & G to succumb to the demands of the nearest and loudest group of resource users, regardless of the accuracy of ADF & G's data.

> d.   *The extent of the burden to the defendant and consequences to the community of imposing a duty*

We find it likely that burdensome consequences would ensue if we declared actionable a public duty like the one ADF & G owes to all fish and wildlife resource users in Alaska. Allowing a cause of action against a state agency for negligent management decisions would open the door to endless damage claims by unlimited groups of resource users. Almost any management action might support a claim for damages. And in contemplating any proposed action, ADF & G might face competing threats of suit by processors and fishing vessel owners, by upstream and downstream residents, or by groups of resource users representing subsistence, commercial, and sport fishing interests.

It makes no difference that Heckman does not allege negligence arising from a management decision involving policy and discretion, but instead alleges a series of objectively verifiable flaws in implementing and monitoring ADF & G's sonar fish-counting project. ADF & G routinely bases its management decisions on data and information gathered from a wide array of sources. Holding the agency accountable in damages for mistakes in the information underlying its decisions would likely discourage it from acting on any but the clearest information. Yet hesitation prompted by fear of premature action might easily lead to cries of harm, and accompanying suits, from resource users whose interests lay in prompt and vigorous agency initiatives. Caught in the middle by competing threats of litigation in the event of either action or inaction, the agency ultimately might be driven by fear of litigation to heed the loudest threats, rather than to rely on sound principles of resource management.

In sum, once we recognized an actionable duty of care in gathering data, an alleged breach of the duty might provide an inroad for challenging broader, policy-based decisions. And the very awareness of this possibility might prompt ADF & G to alter its approach to making management decisions. The foreseeable negative consequences to the community would be that the state's resources would not be conserved for the benefit of all Alaskans, as article VIII, section 3 of the Alaska

Constitution requires. Public policy dictates that ADF & G be free from such coercion in collecting data and making management decisions.

e. Availability of insurance

The record contains no meaningful information concerning the availability or potential cost of insurance to protect the State from damages claims arising from negligent resource-management decisions. But given the unprecedented nature of a cause of action for damages stemming from negligent resource management, and given further that almost any management decision will harm some resource users and generate a risk of suit, we think it unlikely that the State could find or afford insurance. As a practical matter, it seems likely that the State would absorb all costs of litigation, in effect becoming a guarantor of Alaska's ability to ensure fish and wildlife resources to its citizens. This result hardly seems desirable.

2. The D.S.W. factors do not warrant a finding of duty.

Heckman cites no cases, and we are aware of none, holding that mere negligence by an agency charged with a general public duty of resource management supports a claim for damages by an affected resource user. But there are significant similarities between the present case and D.S.W., which involved the State's alleged negligence in fulfilling an analogous, broad-based public responsibility: providing public education to children. In D.S.W., we declined to find an actionable right to a non-negligent education:

> Few of our institutions, if any, have aroused the controversies, or incurred the public dissatisfaction, which have attended the operation of the public schools. . . . To hold them to an actionable "duty of care," in the discharge of their academic functions, would expose them to the tort claims—real or imagined—of disaffected students and parents in countless numbers.

628 P.2d at 555–56 (quoting *Peter W. v. San Francisco Unified Sch. Dist.*, 60 Cal.App.3d 814, 131 Cal.Rptr. 854, 861 (1976)). As ADF & G correctly asserts, fisheries management, much like academic management, is an area fraught with controversy of the kind that invites litigation. We would greatly compound the volatility surrounding fisheries issues by allowing a cause of action for negligent resource-management decisions. Holding ADF & G "to an actionable 'duty of care,' . . . would expose [it] to the tort claims—real or imagined—of disaffected [resource users] in countless numbers." *Id.*

IV. CONCLUSION

We conclude that the relationship between Heckman and ADF & G does not support an actionable duty. Accordingly, we REVERSE the superior court's denial of ADF & G's motion to dismiss.

E. COMPUTERIZED BUSINESS RECORDS AS EVIDENCE

UNITED STATES v. WHITAKER

United States Court of Appeals, Seventh Circuit, 1997.
127 F.3d 595.

BAUR, CIRCUIT JUDGE.

Frank Whitaker was charged in Counts One and Four of a four-count superseding indictment. Count One charged Whitaker with conspiring to distribute marijuana in violation of 21 U.S.C. § 846 and Count Four alleged that the United States was entitled to forfeiture pursuant to 21 U.S.C. §§ 841(a)(1), 846, and 853. A jury found Whitaker guilty on Count One. He waived trial by jury as to the Count Four forfeiture charge and the district court found him guilty. On November 17, 1995, the district court sentenced Whitaker to 180 months on Count One, to be followed by five years of supervised release. The district court also ordered Whitaker to forfeit to the government $235,535.00 in assets, jointly and severally with certain co-defendants. Whitaker appeals, arguing that the district court abused its discretion by admitting computer records * * *

BACKGROUND

Frank Whitaker was involved in a large-scale narcotics conspiracy, headed by co-defendant Ralph Solis, which was responsible for distributing large quantities of marijuana from early 1991 until March 22, 1994. After an investigation and statements by cooperating codefendants, a superseding indictment was returned on November 22, 1994 against Whitaker, Ralph Solis, Peter Krell, Jeffrey Freund, John Follman, Anthony Gibbons, and Gary Frost, charging them with being members of this drug conspiracy. Testimony at trial established that the marijuana distribution organization operated in the Southern District of Illinois, the Eastern District of Missouri, Texas, Minnesota, and elsewhere. * * *

In addition to testimonial evidence as to Whitaker's position and role in Solis' organization, the government also introduced documents and physical evidence to prove Whitaker's involvement. This evidence included leases for the warehouse and the apartment, a tape-recorded conversation between Aulabaugh and Solis which implicated Whitaker, hotel receipts indicating that Whitaker had called Frost's residence, Solis' address book containing Whitaker's telephone number listed under his nickname, "Gator," as well as the telephone numbers for Aulabaugh and Frost, and paperwork found in the van which contained Whitaker's name. * * *

The government also introduced printouts of computer records into evidence. Frost used the computer records to keep track of drug transactions from approximately October 5, 1993 until February 24, 1994. Frost had shown the records and his computerized method for keeping track of drug transactions to Hartline, and other coconspirators knew that Frost kept computer records of the drug business. These computer records were seized from Frost's residence on February 25, 1994. FBI Special Agent Jay Keeven testified at trial as to the seizure of the records. FBI Special Agent Eric Daniel Clouse also testified as an expert witness about the computer records. He testified that, in his opinion, the records pertained to a marijuana-trafficking business. The records contained an account named "Me," which, as Agent Clouse testified, referred to the person running the business and doing the transactions, and an account named "Cruz," which was Solis' nickname. The "Cruz" account contained a notation that read "Cash Gator $38,000" on October 16, 1993, which corresponded with a $38,000 reduction in the "Me" account. A similar notation of "Cash Gator $49,000" with a corresponding reduction in the "Me" account also appeared on October 27, 1993. "Gator" was Whitaker's nickname.

Frost was one of Hartline's retail customers. Hartline testified that he recruited Frost into the conspiracy in early 1991 when he asked to use Frost's residence in Granite City, Illinois, as an unloading and storage site for marijuana. Frost was paid for the use of his residence and was also given first-pick of the marijuana for his own distribution purposes. Hartline was arrested for possession of marijuana on March 2, 1992, and began to ease himself out of the organization. Frost took over Hartline's business and role in the conspiracy. Couriers continued bringing marijuana to Frost's residence, and Frost continued distributing it to his own customers and to former customers of Hartline. * * *

Analysis

No. 95–3809—FRANK WHITAKER

1. *Admission of Computer Printouts*

Whitaker's first argument on appeal is that the district court erred in admitting the printouts of Frost's computer records against him because they were not properly authenticated and because the government did not lay a proper foundation. He also argues that these records were critical to the government's case because they established Whitaker's link to the conspiracy, and their admission into evidence violated his due process rights to a fair trial under the Fifth Amendment. The government responds that Whitaker did not properly object to the lack of authentication of the computer records, but merely objected to the lack of foundation. The government therefore contends that we can review this matter only for plain error, which, it believes, Whitaker cannot show.

First, while it is true that a specific objection made on the wrong grounds and overruled precludes a party from raising a specific objection on other, tenable grounds on appeal, we do not have to deal with that problem here. Although Whitaker's counsel may not have used the buzzword "authentication," he did timely and properly object to both the foundation and the authentication of the computer records during Agent Keeven's testimony. * * *

* * * We therefore review the district court's decision to admit the records for abuse of discretion and not, as the government suggests, for plain error. * * *

Federal Rule of Evidence 901(a) provides the requirement for authentication of evidence:

> The requirement of authentication or identification as a condition precedent to admissibility is satisfied by evidence sufficient to support a finding that the matter in question is what its proponent claims.

Fed.R.Evid. 901(a). Whitaker argues that the prosecution failed to comply with the requirements of Rule 901(a) with respect to the computer printouts because it never supplied witnesses who had personal knowledge of the computer system's operation or who could confirm the accuracy of the input to and output from the computer.

The government laid the foundation for the computer records and provided their authentication through the testimony of FBI Special Agent Jay Keeven. Agent Keeven testified that the records were retrieved from Frost's computer, which was seized during the execution of a federal search warrant of Frost's home in February 1994. The records were retrieved from the computer using the Microsoft Money program. Agent Keeven was present when that program was installed on the computer and when the records were retrieved. Agent Keeven testified concerning his personal knowledge and his personal participation in obtaining the printouts. On cross-examination, the defense did not ask Agent Keeven any questions about how the disks were formatted, what type of computer was used, or any other questions of a technical nature. In sum, his testimony was sufficient to establish the authenticity of the computer records of the drug business, and the district court was correct in admitting the records.

Later in the trial, after the testimony of Agent Keeven, the government called FBI Agent Clouse to the stand as an expert to interpret the computer records for the jury. Agent Clouse testified that he worked for the Racketeering Records Analysis Unit of the FBI, and as part of that work he had examined suspected drug and money laundering records in more than 400 cases to determine whether they were clandestine in nature and what notations on those records meant. The court accepted Agent Clouse as an expert in the field of analysis of suspected drug records.

Whitaker attempts to discredit Agent Clouse's testimony by pointing out that Agent Clouse effectively admitted on cross-examination that he was not an expert on computers. Agent Clouse did testify on cross-examination that did not know whether the documents were properly retrieved from the computer and that his totals could be affected if the documents were retrieved improperly. That is irrelevant, because that was not the purpose of Agent Clouse's testimony. He was called as a witness to interpret the records, not to testify as to the method by which they were retrieved—that was the purpose of Agent Keeven's testimony. Agent Keeven had already testified as to how and when the records were retrieved. Agent Clouse, rather, provided expert testimony as to the meaning of the records, and he certainly was qualified to interpret and explain the records to the jury. As he stated, "I can vouch for the results that I got from the documents that I have." Agent Clouse testified that the computer records he was asked to interpret did indeed represent "records of a marijuana distribution business." Agent Clouse then went on to interpret government enlargements of charts in order to help the jury understand the information he had garnered from the drug records. He testified that the records covered the time period from October 5, 1993 until February 24, 1994. He explained to the jury how the "Me" Account reflects "the person who is actually running the business." He also testified as to notations on the records referring to "Gator" and "Sly." He testified that those notations on October 10, 16, and 27, 1993, with references to "Gator" involved $20,000 on October 10, $38,000 on October 16, and $49,000 on October 27. These notations corresponded to ingoing and outgoing cash flows from the "Me" accounts into various other accounts. Agent Clouse testified that he knew the names on the accounts because they corresponded to the names of the computer files. It was not Agent Clouse's duty as a witness to authenticate or lay the foundation for the records; he was testifying as to the interpretation of the records once they were retrieved from the Microsoft Money personal finance program.

Whitaker is incensed by the fact that codefendant Gary Frost assisted Agent Keeven in retrieving the computer records from his computer and by the fact that the government did not establish a chain of custody for the computer or the contemporaneously-seized disks. Whitaker argues: "The fact that the prosecution allowed Frost access to his former computer while it was in government custody to assist in producing the key piece of physical evidence against Whitaker, undermines, rather than supports, the authenticity of the printouts." He believes that allowing Frost access to the computer could have affected the requirement that the computer and disks be in substantially the same condition as when the crime was committed. He believes that with a few rapid keystrokes, Frost could have easily added Whitaker's alias, "Gator" to the printouts in order to finger Whitaker and to appear more helpful to the government. This is almost wild-eyed speculation and without some evidence to support such a scenario, we will not disturb the trial judge's ruling.

* * *

For the foregoing reasons, the judgment and sentence of Frank Whitaker in No. 95–3809 are AFFIRMED. * * *

F. COMPUTER–GENERATED EVIDENCE

COMMERCIAL UNION INSURANCE
CO. v. BOSTON EDISON CO.

Supreme Judicial Court of Massachusetts, 1992.
412 Mass. 545, 591 N.E.2d 165.

ABRAMS, JUSTICE.

The plaintiffs, former coowners of the building at One Beacon Street in Boston (building), brought an action for breach of contract and restitution for money paid by mutual mistake against the Boston Edison Company (Edison), claiming that Edison had overcharged them for steam usage at the building between January, 1974, and January 10, 1979. * * * At trial, the judge directed a verdict for the plaintiffs on liability on their restitution claim, and the jury awarded damages of $650,000 on that claim. The jury found for Edison on the plaintiffs' contract claim. The judge entered final judgment on the plaintiffs' jury verdict in the amount of $1,590,371. We allowed Edison's application for direct review. On appeal, Edison claims errors based on the admission in evidence of a computer simulation and expert opinions based on the simulation. * * * We affirm.

Facts. Under the terms of an agreement between Edison and the plaintiffs, Edison supplied and the plaintiffs purchased steam for the air conditioning, cooking, and space and water heating systems in the building.

Due to a problem with the metering system of which the parties were unaware, the meter overregistered the amount of steam being used. The problem came to light when the building manager, having taken several unsuccessful steps to reduce the steam bills by conserving steam usage in the building, finally shut down the steam system entirely, only to discover that the low-range steam meter nevertheless continued to register steam flow at eighteen percent. The problem was traced to the meter having been defectively installed when the building was built. During the time that the faulty metering system was in place, Edison had charged the plaintiffs $3,756,531.30 for steam used.

Edison does not dispute that it overcharged the plaintiffs during the relevant time period; rather, it disputes the amount of the overcharge. Prior to the litigation, Edison reviewed numerous steam usage charts for the relevant period and, applying a "correction formula" recommended by the meter manufacturer, concluded that the meter was off by four percent, rather than the eighteen percent recorded by the building manager and asserted by the plaintiffs. Edison nevertheless decided to split the difference between its and the plaintiffs' estimated percentage of error. Basing its overcharge calculations on a system error of eleven percent, Edison offered $93,764.86 to the plaintiffs. * * * The plaintiffs rejected Edison's calculations as premised on the erroneous assumption that the percentage of error had remained constant throughout the five-year period.

The plaintiffs relied on a computer simulation to make their own calculations of actual steam usage. The computer program, called TRACE (Trane Air Conditioning Economics), consists of scientific formulae and algorithms concerning heat transfer, building materials, operating characteristics of various heating and air handling equipment, and weather history, among other things. To generate a simulation, the computer program uses data specifying a particular building's construction materials, operating patterns, architectural details, latitude, longitude, outside air flow, and heating, ventilating and air conditioning equipment, among other things.

Evidentiary issues regarding TRACE. Edison moved in limine to exclude the TRACE evidence on the grounds that the data and equations used in the simulation were neither accurate nor complete, and that the program had not achieved general acceptance by the community of scientists involved. The judge, defining the relevant scientific community as heating, ventilating and air conditioning (HVAC) and building design professionals, determined that this group had accepted TRACE as scientifically reliable. At trial, following a voir dire of the plaintiffs' expert, the judge further found that the program data and equations were accurate and complete, and ruled admissible the TRACE evidence and related expert testimony.

Edison claims error in the admission of the TRACE evidence. First, Edison argues that the results of the TRACE simulation are inadmissible hearsay, and the judge therefore erred in admitting them in evidence. We disagree.

The function of computer programs like TRACE "is to perform rapidly and accurately an extensive series of computations not readily accomplished without use of a computer." *Schaeffer v. General Motors Corp.*, 372 Mass. 171, 177, 360 N.E.2d 1062 (1977). We permit experts to base their testimony on calculations performed by hand, cf., e.g., *Anthony's Pier Four, Inc. v. HBC Assocs.*, 411 Mass. 451, 478, 583 N.E.2d 806 (1991); *Kroeger v. Stop & Shop Cos., Inc.*, 13 Mass.App.Ct. 310, 323, 432 N.E.2d 566 (1982). There is no reason to prevent them from performing the same calculations, with far greater rapidity and accuracy, on a computer. Therefore, as we indicated in *Schaeffer, supra*, 372 Mass. at 177–178, 360 N.E.2d 1062, we treat computer-generated models or simulations like other scientific tests, and condition admissibility on a sufficient showing that: (1) the computer is functioning properly; (2) the input and underlying equations are sufficiently complete and accurate (and disclosed to the opposing party, so that they may challenge them); and (3) the program is generally accepted by the appropriate community of scientists. See *Commonwealth v. Fatalo*, 346 Mass. 266, 269, 191 N.E.2d 479 (1963).

Edison urges us to reject the computer simulation evidence. We decline to do so. We note that we are not the first jurisdiction to recognize that computer models or simulations may be used to assist the fact finder. Generally courts have permitted computer models in cases not easily susceptible of other forms of proof. See, e.g., *Seattle Master Builders Ass'n v. Pacific Northwest Elec. Power & Conservation Planning Council*, 786 F.2d 1359, 1370 (9th Cir.1986), *cert. denied*, 479 U.S. 1059, 107 S.Ct. 939, 93 L.Ed.2d 989 (1987) (allowing use of computer simulations of value of energy conservation methods based on principles derived from American Society of Heating, Refrigerating and Air Conditioning Engineers "Handbook of Fundamentals" to determine energy conservation value); *Perma Research & Dev. v. Singer Co.*, 542 F.2d 111, 115 (2d Cir.), *cert. denied*, 429 U.S. 987, 97 S.Ct. 507, 50 L.Ed.2d 598 (1976) (results of computer simulation used to form basis of expert testimony regarding feasibility of perfection of automobile anti-skid device); *United States v. Dioguardi*, 428 F.2d 1033, 1037 (2d Cir.), *cert. denied*, 400 U.S. 825, 91 S.Ct. 50, 51, 27 L.Ed.2d 54 (1970) (computer analysis employed to determine when defendant would have exhausted his inventory, had he not concealed assets); *Pearl Brewing Co. v. Joseph Schlitz Brewing Co.*, 415 F.Supp. 1122, 1134 (S.D.Tex.1976) (computer simulation used to test varying market conditions in price-fixing case); *United States v. United Technologies Corp.*, 1977–2 Trade Cas. (CCH) par. 61,647, 1977 WL 1470 (1977) (econometric model used in antitrust case); *In re Sugar Indus. Antitrust Litig.*, 73 F.R.D. 322, 353 (E.D.Pa. 1976) (expert could rely on statistical model to formulate his opinion as to class damages in complex antitrust case); *Messex v. Louisiana Dep't of Highways*, 302 So.2d 40, 44 (La.App.1974) (computer simulation of automobile accident used to assist court in determining whether defendant had reasonable opportunity to avoid accident). There is no reason to exclude computer simulations provided the computer simulation meets the appropriate standards of admissibility.

Edison next argues that the judge erred in determining that the TRACE program, at least as employed to estimate past steam heat consumption rather than predict future consumption, has been generally accepted by the relevant community of scientists. There was no error.

In determining whether TRACE is generally accepted by the relevant community of scientists, we make our "own determination without regard to the conclusions of the trial or motion judge." *Commonwealth v. Curnin*, 409 Mass. 218, 223, 565 N.E.2d 440 (1991). In so doing, we "may properly consider not only the evidence in the record but also the reasoning and conclusions of other courts and the writings of experts." *Id.*

The plaintiffs offered evidence showing that TRACE has been used by engineers and HVAC design professionals to model energy consumption in over 40,000 buildings. The most common applications for TRACE include comparing the energy efficiency of alternative heating and cooling systems, and predicting a building's energy consumption. Where TRACE is used for the latter purpose, the predictions are quite accurate. California requires a computer analysis of building energy consumption before a new building permit is issued for a multi-story building. The

California Energy Commission has approved TRACE for this purpose, pursuant to Cal.Code Regs., Tit. 20, § 1409 (1990). TRACE also is used to recreate past energy consumption in buildings. There is no reason for disturbing the judge's conclusion simply because, in this case, TRACE was used to calculate past, rather than future or hypothetical, energy consumption—that is, because the TRACE input consisted of historical rather than hypothetical facts about the building's operations and weather conditions.

Edison further argues that HVAC engineers are not the relevant community of scientists for purposes of determining whether TRACE has been generally accepted. We have said that "the requirement of the *Frye* [v. *United States*, 293 F. 1013 (D.C.Cir.1923)] rule of general acceptability is satisfied, in our opinion, if the principle is generally accepted by those who would be expected to be familiar with its use." *Commonwealth v. Lykus*, 367 Mass. 191, 203, 327 N.E.2d 671 (1975). The evidence showed that approximately eighty percent of TRACE users are HVAC engineers. Edison proposes that the relevant community of scientists is "the community involved in the field of fluid flow measurement or custody transfer fluids." Edison's argument amounts to the following: those who use meters to measure energy consumption, rather than those who use computer simulations, should pass on the validity of the computer simulation. We reject this argument.

Edison also argues that the evidence was insufficient to support the judge's conclusion that the data and equations used in the TRACE program were accurate and complete, because the judge did not have access to the thousands of pages of coding of the TRACE program. This argument is without merit. As discussed supra at 168 the judge is required to determine (1) the completeness and accuracy of the data and underlying equations, and (2) whether the program is generally accepted by the appropriate community of scientists. Edison's argument confounds these two requirements. Because "[t]hose most qualified [to assess the general validity of a scientific method such as a computer simulation] are not judges, but rather are scientists with special knowledge who are most familiar with the method or theory in question," *Commonwealth v. Mendes*, 406 Mass. 201, 205, 547 N.E.2d 35 (1989), the judge is required to determine only whether TRACE is generally accepted by the appropriate community of scientists. The judge need not determine whether all the complex, underlying coding is complete and accurate.

In Schaeffer v. General Motors Corp., 372 Mass. 171, 178, 360 N.E.2d 1062 (1977), we held that the judge must "conduct a hearing in the absence of the jury on the question whether the tests conducted and results ascribed thereto meet the prescribed standards for the admissibility of such evidence." In ruling on the admissibility of the TRACE program, the judge received and reviewed, among other things, the depositions (and attached exhibits) of three people involved in performing the simulation; three affidavits submitted by the plaintiffs' experts; seven affidavits submitted by Edison's experts (including responsive affidavits); articles regarding TRACE and computer evidence generally; the section of the California state administrative code which approves the use of TRACE; and numerous memoranda of law. Furthermore, as noted above, the judge conducted a three-hour voir dire of the plaintiffs' chief TRACE experts. Edison maintains that the *Schaeffer* hearing requirement was not fulfilled in this case because not all the witnesses were called to testify in person. We decline to hold that in all cases only a voir dire hearing of all the relevant witnesses can satisfy the *Schaeffer* hearing requirement.

Another requirement set out in *Schaeffer* is that the judge must "put into the record, by dictation, for the transcript or otherwise, the findings of fact made by him as the basis for the admission or exclusion of the evidence in question." *Schaeffer, supra* at 178, 360 N.E.2d 1062. Edison argues that the judge did not comply with this second *Schaeffer* requirement. We reject this argument, too. In this case, the judge issued seven pages of findings regarding the general acceptance of TRACE, and read into the record her findings that the input used was accurate.

Edison argues that the opinion of one of the plaintiffs' experts as to the amount of steam used in the building during the relevant time period was inadmissible because it was based on facts or data not independently admissible. *Cf. Department of Youth Servs. v. A Juvenile*, 398 Mass. 516, 527–532, 499 N.E.2d 812 (1986). Given our conclusion that the TRACE results are admissible, this claim fails.

Edison further argues that it was denied a fair opportunity to prepare effective cross-examination of the plaintiffs' expert witnesses because it was not furnished with the actual coding of the TRACE program (i.e., how the algorithms described in the manuals were written and arranged into computer language). As a result, it claims, the TRACE results and expert opinions should not have been admitted. The judge found and ruled that the TRACE program itself is proprietary and confidential.[5] Edison suggests that it was entitled to the information, even if it were proprietary. Cf. *Perma Research & Dev. v. Singer Co.*, 542 F.2d 111, 115 (2d Cir.1976) (no abuse of discretion where judge refused to order disclosure of proprietary program). We need not reach this issue, however, because the judge was justified in rejecting Edison's request for the underlying coding on the basis that it was not made in a timely manner. Edison did not ask for the coding until it filed a third request for production of documents. At the time of the third request,

---

5. The equations and procedures on which the program is based, however, are set forth in the publicly available standard reference handbook of the American Society of Heating, Refrigerating and Air Conditioning Engineers, Inc. (ASHRAE). Edison had nine manuals on TRACE, setting forth in detail the input needed by the TRACE program and the mathematical equations and algorithms which form the basis of the program. The equations in the program are standard ASHRAE algorithms and physical laws of heat transfer. In addition, Edison had the opportunity to review all the input used in the TRACE simulation for this litigation, and one of Edison's own experts created energy simulation computer programs similar to TRACE, relying on the same type of algorithms.

one scheduled trial date already had come and gone. There was no error in the judge's ruling that disclosure was not required. * * *

Judgment affirmed.

Questions

The results of the above cases indicate that computerized evidence has gained acceptance both in criminal and civil cases. What are the implications for our increasingly mechanized society? What measures should be taken to ensure the accuracy and validity of computerized data? What would you consider as a factor disqualifying computerized data as evidence?

Chapter XI

ACCESS TO INFORMATION IN COMPUTERIZED FORM

A. ACCESS TO GOVERNMENT DATABANKS

DELORME PUBLISHING COMPANY, INC. v. NATIONAL OCEANIC AND ATMOSPHERIC ADMINISTRATION OF THE UNITED STATES DEPARTMENT OF COMMERCE

United States District Court, D. Maine, 1996.
917 F.Supp. 867.

HORNBY, DISTRICT JUDGE.

I have ruled that the National Oceanic and Atmospheric Administration's ("NOAA") electronic "raster" compilations of its nautical charts—compilations that can be read by computers—are "agency records" subject to disclosure under the Freedom of Information Act ("FOIA") unless a specific exemption applies. *DeLorme Pub. Co. v. NOAA*, 907 F.Supp. 10 (D.Me.1995). I now conclude that NOAA may withhold its raster compilations under FOIA Exemption 3 and the Federal Technology Transfer Act for five years from the date of their development.

I. BACKGROUND

The case is presented on cross-motions for summary judgment, but there are no material facts genuinely in dispute. In October 1993, NOAA, through its National Ocean Service, initiated the process of selecting a private partner to participate in a cooperative research and development agreement ("CRADA") to produce an electronic nautical charting system. Such public-private cooperation is authorized and encouraged by the Federal Technology Transfer Act ("FTTA"). 15 U.S.C. § 3710a. A number of firms, including the plaintiff DeLorme, expressed an interest in the project, but NOAA ultimately selected BSB Electronic Charts ("BSB") as its private partner. NOAA and BSB signed an initial CRADA in August of 1994. As part of its anticipated contribution to the CRADA, NOAA created 202 digitized raster compilations of nautical charts during 1993 and 1994 by scanning the color negatives used to create NOAA's paper charts. Another 21 raster files were created between August and November 1994, where BSB's role was to "work[ ] side-by-side with [Agency] personnel ... performing scanning, processing and related activities." Enabnit Decl. at ¶ 18. In November of 1994,

DeLorme sent NOAA two FOIA requests seeking disclosure of all the raster compilations and certain documents relating to the CRADA. NOAA refused to produce any of the raster compilations and some of the documents. As a result, DeLorme brought this FOIA lawsuit.

NOAA claims that three FOIA exemptions apply to the digitized versions of its nautical charts and permit it to refuse disclosure. Specifically, NOAA argues that the raster compilations are exempt from disclosure under Exemption 3, 5 U.S.C. § 552(b)(3), because the FTTA authorizes their protection; Exemption 2, § 552(b)(2), because they relate to "the internal personnel rules and practices" of NOAA; and Exemption 5, § 552(b)(5), because they are "intra-agency memorandums" that would not ordinarily be obtainable through discovery in a lawsuit against the Agency.

As to the *documents* requested, NOAA argues that the portions it has withheld are exempt from disclosure under both Exemption 5 and Exemption 6, § 552(b)(6), which protects against unwarranted invasions of privacy.

II. FOIA EXEMPTION 3

FOIA Exemption 3 allows an agency to withhold records that are "specifically exempted from disclosure by [a] statute" other than FOIA, as long as the statute: "(A) requires that the matters be withheld from the public in such a manner as to leave no discretion on the issue, or (B) establishes particular criteria for withholding or refers to particular types of matters to be withheld." 5 U.S.C. § 552(b)(3).

NOAA contends that the FTTA is an exempting statute. 15 U.S.C. § 3710 *et seq.* As amended in 1989, the FTTA contains a provision, similar to FOIA Exemption 4, limiting disclosure, in certain circumstances, of "commercial ... information that is privileged or confidential." 15 U.S.C. § 3710a(c)(7). Examining an agency's Exemption 3 claim ordinarily requires analysis of whether the statute in question is an "exempting statute" within the meaning of Exemption 3 and, if so, whether the requested information is "included within" that statute's protection, *Aronson v. IRS*, 973 F.2d 962, 964 (1st Cir.1992), but DeLorme has not contested NOAA's assertion that the FTTA qualifies and therefore has waived any arguments to the contrary.

Because the FTTA is an Exemption 3 statute, "FOIA de novo review normally ends," and review of the agency's interpretation of the statute's protection "must take place under more deferential, administrative law standards." *Id.* at 967; see also *Church of Scientology Int'l v. Dept. of Justice*, 30 F.3d 224, 235 (1st Cir.1994). Those standards are governed by the *Chevron* doctrine and typically require courts to give considerable deference to an agency's construction of an ambiguous statute. *Chevron U.S.A. Inc. v. Natural Resources Defense Council, Inc.*, 467 U.S. 837, 104 S.Ct. 2778, 81 L.Ed.2d 694 (1984); *Strickland v. Comm'r Dept. Human*

Services, 48 F.3d 12 (1st Cir.), *cert. denied*, 516 U.S. 850, 116 S.Ct. 145, 133 L.Ed.2d 91 (1995).

However, "the deference accorded to an administrative agency's interpretations depends on the extent to which the matters at issue depend peculiarly on the agency's field of expertise." *McCuin v. Sec'y of Health and Human Services*, 817 F.2d 161, 168 (1st Cir.1987). The Supreme Court has stated that, when Congress does not entrust a single agency with the task of administering a statute, "[t]here is ... not the same basis for deference predicated on expertise" that the Court found in *Chevron. Bowen v. American Hosp. Ass'n*, 476 U.S. 610, 643 n. 30, 106 S.Ct. 2101, 2120 n. 30, 90 L.Ed.2d 584 (1986). In *Bowen*, the Court did not defer to an agency's interpretation of a statute protecting the rights of handicapped persons because the statute affected all government agencies, and 27 agencies had promulgated regulations under the statute. *Id.* Similarly, the statute at issue in this case, the FTTA, has broad application and has been implemented by more than a dozen agencies. To defer to NOAA's interpretation of the statute would thus "lay the groundwork for a regulatory regime in which either the same statute is interpreted differently by [different] agencies or the one agency that happens to reach the courthouse first is allowed to fix the meaning of the text for all." *Rapaport v. Dep't of Treasury, Office of Thrift Supervision*, 59 F.3d 212, 216–17 (D.C.Cir.1995) . Therefore, I continue to proceed *de novo*.

Congress enacted the FTTA in 1986 "to improve the transfer of commercially useful technologies from the Federal laboratories and into the private sector" to strengthen the nation's military and economic competitiveness. S.Rep. No. 283, 99th Cong., 2d Sess. 1 (1986), *reprinted in* 1986 U.S.C.C.A.N. 3442. Toward that end, the Act "authorizes a broad range of cooperative research and development arrangements where there is a mutual interest between the laboratory mission and ... private sector organizations." *Id.* at 10, 1986 U.S.C.C.A.N. at 3451.

In 1989, Congress amended the FTTA to provide, with respect to cooperative research and development ventures, two types of protection from disclosure for "commercial ... information that is privileged or confidential." 15 U.S.C. § 3710a(c)(7). First, the Act *prohibits* an agency from disclosing such information if it "is obtained in the conduct of research or as a result of activities under this chapter [Title 15, Ch. 63, Technology Innovation] from a non-Federal party participating in a [CRADA]." § 3710a(c)(7)(A). Second, the act *allows* an agency to withhold information for up to five years if that information "results from research and development activities under this chapter and that would be ... commercial ... information that is privileged or confidential if the information had been obtained from a non-Federal party participating in a [CRADA]." § 3710a(c)(7)(B). In other words, if qualifying information is obtained from the CRADA's private partner—in this case BSB—it cannot be disclosed. However, if qualifying information is obtained from the agency and would have been protected if it had come from the private partner, the agency has the discretion to withhold it, but only for a five-year period. Congress concluded that such protection was necessary because "the threat of disclosure under [FOIA] of commercial information, developed under the CRADA or otherwise, has been the biggest reason to date for companies declining to enter CRADAs." H.R.Conf.Rep. No. 331, 101st Cong., 1st Sess. 761 (1989), *reprinted in* 1989 U.S.C.C.A.N. 977, 1150.

A. The 202 Raster Files Created in Anticipation of the CRADA

NOAA maintains that it may withhold for five years under § 3710a(c)(7)(B) the 202 raster compilations it created prior to signing the CRADA because: (1) the raster files are information resulting from "research and development activities"; (2) those activities were "conducted under" the Technology Innovation chapter of Title 15; and (3) the raster files would be "commercial" and "confidential" information if obtained from the private partner. DeLorme contests each assertion.

1. Research and Development Activities

The FTTA does not define "research and development." That term is defined elsewhere in Title 15, however, to include, "a systematic application of knowledge toward the production of useful materials, devices, and systems or methods, including design, development, and improvement of prototypes and new processes to meet specific requirements." 15 U.S.C. § 638(e)(5). Although DeLorme insists that NOAA's production of the raster files entailed nothing more than the mechanical process of feeding the chart films into an electronic scanner, and no research and development, that is too narrow a focus. FTTA protection is available for "information that results from research and development activities." § 3710a(c)(7)(B). The raster files have been created as one step in the larger process of developing NOAA's nautical data—previously limited to paper charts—into an end-product suitable for reliable and efficient computer usage by consumers in conjunction with global positioning technology. That process clearly entails "a systematic application of knowledge toward production of useful materials [or] devices." § 638(e)(5).

2. Conducted Under

The second issue is whether the 202 initial raster files were the result of research and development activities "conducted under" the Technology Innovation chapter of Title 15, 15 U.S.C. § 3701 *et seq.* NOAA asserts that it created them in anticipation of entering into a CRADA. DeLorme does not contest that assertion, but argues that only research and development occurring after a CRADA is finalized comes "under" the chapter. The FTTA does not define what it means by activities "conducted under" the statute. Standing alone, the phrase is obviously broad and not limited to what happens after a particular

CRADA is signed. The legislative history supports a broad reading. * * * I conclude that the 202 raster files NOAA created in anticipation of CRADA qualify as "activities conducted under" the Technology Innovation chapter.

3. Commercial and Confidential Information

The final issue is whether the 202 raster files qualify as "commercial" and "confidential" information. Although these terms are statutorily undefined, the circuit courts are nearly unanimous on their meanings. "Commercial" is given its ordinary meaning and applies broadly to information in which a private party would have a commercial interest if it had submitted the information to the government. *Public Citizen Health Research Group v. FDA*, 704 F.2d 1280, 1290 (D.C.Cir.1983). The raster files at issue here certainly are of commercial interest to BSB.

In determining whether commercial information is "confidential," courts do not focus upon "whether the information has customarily been regarded as confidential," but instead look to "the potential harm that will result from disclosure." *9 to 5 Org. v. Bd. of Governors of the Fed. Reserve Sys.*, 721 F.2d 1, 10 (1st Cir.1983). Therefore, commercial information:

> is "confidential" for purposes of the exemption if disclosure of the information is likely to have either of the following effects: (1) to impair the Government's ability to obtain necessary information in the future; or (2) to cause substantial harm to the competitive position of the person from whom the information was obtained.

Id. at 8, quoting *National Parks and Conservation Ass'n v. Morton*, 498 F.2d 765, 770 (D.C.Cir.1974). NOAA argues that both effects exist in this case. It asserts that, assuming that the information hypothetically had come from BSB—as § 3710a(c)(7)(B) requires for this analysis—disclosure of the raster files would (1) impair the government's efforts under the FTTA by discouraging private firms from participating in CRADAs in the future, and (2) harm BSB's competitive position by giving the information to competitors after BSB had invested considerable resources in developing the data for commercial application. NOAA "is in the best position to determine the effect of disclosure on its ability to obtain necessary technical information" in the future, and it has "plausibly supported" its conclusion "in some detail." *Orion Research Inc. v. EPA*, 615 F.2d 551, 554 (1st Cir.), *cert. denied*, 449 U.S. 833, 101 S.Ct. 103, 66 L.Ed.2d 38 (1980). I conclude that the raster compilations meet the test of confidential information.

In summary, because the 202 raster files created in anticipation of the CRADA are commercial and confidential information resulting from research and development activities conducted under the FTTA, NOAA is entitled to prevent their disclosure for up to five years from the date of their development under § 3710a(c)(7)(B).

B. The 21 Raster Files Created During the CRADA

NOAA also seeks protection for 21 raster compilations created after it entered into the joint research and development agreement with BSB. These 21 raster files could be withheld by NOAA for up to five years, if NOAA generated them, on the reasoning I have just given. NOAA, however, claims that the files were jointly created by the Agency and BSB and are therefore subject to mandatory and permanent protection from disclosure as information "obtained . . . from a non-Federal party participating in a [CRADA]." § 3710a(c)(7)(A). Taking the facts in a light most favorable to NOAA, BSB's only role was as follows: "BSB personnel worked side-by-side with [NOAA] . . . performing scanning, processing and related activities necessary to create the compilations." I agree with DeLorme that the presence of BSB personnel during the scanning process is insufficient to convert the rasters into information "obtained from" a private party. These raster files are entitled only to the five-year protection of § 3710a(c)(7)(B).

C. "Vector Conversions" of the Raster Files

DeLorme also seeks access to "vector conversions" of the raster files. A vector conversion is a database containing verbal descriptions of chart features and their attributes. NOAA claims, after a thorough search of its records, that it has never possessed any such vector conversions. To avert summary judgment on this point, DeLorme is required to show either "that [NOAA] might have discovered" the vector conversions had it undertaken a "reasonable search," or that the Agency acted in bad faith. *Maynard v. CIA*, 986 F.2d 547, 560 (1st Cir.1993). DeLorme has shown neither. I therefore conclude that NOAA has fulfilled its obligations under the FOIA with regard to the vector conversions; an agency cannot "withhold" records that are not in its possession.

III. FOIA Exemption 2

Although I find that NOAA may protect the raster files from disclosure for up to five years from the date of their development, I also address NOAA's Exemption 2 claim because it offers the potential for indefinite protection.

FOIA Exemption 2 allows an agency to withhold records "related solely to the internal personnel rules and practices of an agency." 5 U.S.C. § 552(b)(2). Urging a broad interpretation of the exemption, NOAA argues that the raster compilations sought by DeLorme qualify for protection because they shed light upon the Agency's internal charting practices.

NOAA bears the burden of proving that the raster files are exempted "under clearly delineated statutory language." *Tax Analysts v. Dept. of Justice*, 845 F.2d 1060, 1064 (D.C.Cir.1988), quoting S.Rep. No. 813, 89th Cong., 1st Sess. 3 (1965), *aff'd*, 492 U.S. 136, 109 S.Ct. 2841, 106 L.Ed.2d 112 (1989). "Congress intended that Exemption 2 be interpreted narrowly and specifically." *Dep't of Air Force v. Rose*, 425 U.S. 352, 365,

96 S.Ct. 1592, 1601, 48 L.Ed.2d 11 (1976), quoting *Vaughn v. Rosen*, 523 F.2d 1136, 1142 (D.C.Cir.1975). In *Rose*, the Court noted that "[t]he phrasing for Exemption 2 is traceable to congressional dissatisfaction with the exemption from disclosure under former § 3 of the Administrative Procedure Act [APA] of 'any matter related solely to the internal management of an agency.'" 425 U.S. at 362, 96 S.Ct. at 1600 (emphasis added). Thus, the Court concluded that Congress intended Exemption 2 to have a "narrower reach" than the APA exemption for the internal management category. *Id.* at 363, 96 S.Ct. at 1600.

The statutory language of Exemption 2 is pretty unambiguous. It is difficult to see how the raster compilations could, under any stretch of the imagination, be said to be "related solely to the internal personnel rules and practices" of NOAA. Nevertheless, I recognize that the D.C. Circuit, which has the most experience in dealing with FOIA, has spilled a lot of ink over the meaning of this phrase. Initially, judges within that court reached an apparent impasse over whether the term "personnel" modified "practices" as well as "rules." The D.C. Circuit ultimately came up with a new position that interpreted the whole phrase as meaning "rules and practices governing agency personnel," giving examples like job training rules. *Crooker v. BATF*, 670 F.2d 1051, 1056 (D.C.Cir.1981) (en banc). For policy reasons, that circuit also has replaced the statutory language "related solely to" with the judicial gloss "predominantly," *id.* at 1068, 1074, and now seems to view the test as whether the item in question "shed[s] significant light" on such a rule or practice. *Schwaner v. Dep't of Air Force*, 898 F.2d 793, 797 (D.C.Cir. 1990).

Whether I follow the plain language of FOIA Exemption 2 or the creative gloss the D.C. Circuit has added, NOAA's argument is still too broad. The raster compilations simply do not shed significant light upon anything having to do with personnel matters or rules or practices governing agency personnel, and they are neither solely nor predominantly related to such matters. These files are not at all like the law enforcement guidelines, *Dirksen v. Dep't of Health and Human Servs.*, 803 F.2d 1456, 1458–59 (9th Cir.1986), hiring criteria, *Nat'l Treasury Employees Union v. U.S. Customs Service*, 802 F.2d 525, 528–29 (D.C.Cir.1986), or investigative techniques, *Windels, Marx, Davies & Ives v. Dep't of Commerce*, 576 F.Supp. 405, 412 (D.D.C.1983), protected in the cases upon which NOAA relies. Instead, the raster files are electronic compilations of data assembled by NOAA to fulfill the agency's mission. Nothing in Exemption 2 supports the proposition that government "information may be withheld simply because it manifests an agency practice of collecting the information."

IV. FOIA Exemption 5

NOAA claims that the raster compilations may also be withheld under FOIA Exemption 5, which protects certain agency memoranda and letters. 5 U.S.C. § 552(b)(5). Consistent with the policies of the FTTA, 15 U.S.C. § 3710a(c)(7)(B), however, NOAA seeks protection under Exemption 5 only for a maximum period of five years. Because I have ruled that NOAA may withhold the raster compilations for up to five years under Exemption 3, the Agency's Exemption 5 arguments are moot.

V. THE CRADA DOCUMENTS

Although NOAA turned over most of the CRADA-related documents DeLorme sought, it withheld a portion of one page pursuant to FOIA Exemption 6, § 552(b)(6), and three other pages in their entirety pursuant to Exemption 5, § 552(b)(5). DeLorme has failed to respond to the arguments put forth by NOAA to justify its withholding of those documents, and I treat the issue as waived.

VI. CONCLUSION

For the foregoing reasons, I find that NOAA has properly invoked Exemption 3, § 552(b)(3), and the FTTA, § 3710a(c)(7)(B), to withhold the raster files for up to 5 years from the date of their development.

Summary judgment shall be entered for the defendant and against the plaintiff. There is no need to rule on DeLorme's motion to strike certain portions of NOAA's statement of material facts, as I have not relied upon any of the contested portions in reaching my conclusions. NOAA's motion to amend its statement of material facts is therefore MOOT. Oral argument as requested by NOAA is unnecessary. Because DeLorme has not "substantially prevailed" in this litigation, I DENY its request for an award of attorney fees. See 5 U.S.C. § 552(a)(4)(E).

SO ORDERED.

Notes

1. If the Freedom of Information Act applied to all information in the possession of the United States government, the government would not be able to get licenses to use existing trade secret information, without paying the huge price necessary to induce the seller to give up its trade secret to the world.

2. But suppose the government decides to create new information that did not exist before. There are three ways that it can cover the cost of creating the information. It can create the information internally using its own staff and equipment; it can pay a private party to create the information for the government with the understanding that the information will enter the public domain; or it can pay a smaller amount to a private party to create the information with the understanding that the private party can exploit the information as a trade secret. The Federal Technology Transfer Act and the Freedom of Information Act implement these options.

B. ACCESS TO COMPUTERIZED DATA IN LITIGATION

NATIONAL UNION ELECTRIC CORPORATION v. MATSUSHITA ELECTRIC INDUSTRIAL CO., LTD.

IN RE JAPANESE ELECTRICAL PRODUCTS ANTITRUST LITIGATION

United States District Court, Eastern District of Pennsylvania, 1980.
494 F.Supp. 1257.

MEMORANDUM OPINION AND ORDER

(Discovery Request for Computer Material)

EDWARD R. BECKER, DISTRICT JUDGE.

This Memorandum Opinion addresses a motion styled "Request of Certain Defendants for the Production by National Union Electric Corporation (NUE) of Certain Computer Materials." More specifically, defendants request NUE to cause its computer experts to perform the work necessary to create a computer readable tape containing certain data previously supplied by NUE to defendants in printed form in answers to interrogatories.

The relevant interrogatories requested:

— NUE's annual and monthly sales, in dollars and units, for monochrome and color television receivers, by model (Interrogatories 1 and 2)

— NUE's annual and monthly production, in dollars and units, for monochrome and color television receivers, by model (Interrogatories 3 and 4)

— Model numbers for television receivers produced or sold by NUE, including various characteristics of the sets (e. g. the number of square inches on the viewing screen of the picture tube) (Interrogatory No. 5).

In answer to the interrogatories, NUE furnished certain TV sales and production data, and certain model by model price data in the form of a computer generated paper printout. The printout can, of course, be read by defense counsel. However, it cannot be read by defense counsel's computer. Because defense counsel contend that they cannot effectively analyze the data until the data can be read by their computer, they have brought the present motion. Defendants' counsel concede that they could themselves replicate what they seek from NUE if they were to undertake the expensive and time consuming process of having clerical personnel manually create a data base identical to NUE's by reading each piece of data in NUE's computer paper printout and key-punching it into a computer readable device. They estimate that this process would take two months and cost many thousands of dollars. On the other hand, defendants submit that it would be a comparatively simple matter for NUE's computer people to rerun the program which caused the computer to assemble and to print this data in paper reports, substituting a new instruction to extract and print the same data onto a computer-readable form like magnetic tape. Defendants are willing to pay the cost of this operation.

There is a subtle play on words involved in this motion. Lawyers and judges often talk of "production" in terms of Rule 34 of the Federal Rules of Civil Procedure as involving the delivery to the opposing party of some existing document or tangible object. In connection with the present motion, however, the word "produce" is used in the sense of "manufacture"; i.e. NUE is being asked to manufacture or produce something which did not exist theretofore. NUE maintains that the discovery rules do not cognize such a request and that, in any event, what defendants request is protected by the work product privilege, F.R.Civ.P. 26(b)(3), because it reflects mental impressions, analysis, conclusions or thoughts of NUE's counsel or their representatives. NUE thus resists the motion.

NUE's work product objection stems ultimately from the fact that the data at issue was compiled under counsel's direction from raw data which has been available for defendants' inspection and copying in this litigation. NUE asserts that the process for establishing the computer base for the data at issue involved detailed "decision analysis", i.e. the sentient selection by counsel from voluminous raw material of a limited amount of data for inclusion in that base, and that the fruits of that process are therefore protected under the work product rubric. Acknowledging that the work product privilege is but a qualified evidentiary privilege, NUE adds that the defendants do not have substantial need for the computer tape, within the meaning of F.R.Civ.P. 26(b) (3), because they could create the tape themselves by the method described above. Given the colossal cost of this litigation, NUE suggests that the time and cost necessary to produce the tape is modest and that it does not constitute undue hardship within the meaning of the rule.

When this matter first came on for hearing, we denied the motion for discovery, in part because we misunderstood it, and in part because it was couched in different form than it now is. We were under the impression at that time that the defendants were seeking data stored by the plaintiffs somewhere within their computer software, which differed from the material on the paper printout, and further that the data was arrayed in a particular way so that disclosure might have revealed something about NUE's trial strategy. So viewed, the information sought would have been similar to plaintiff's trial support system which was protected from discovery under the work product notion in *In re: IBM Peripherals EDP Devices Antitrust Litigation*, 5 Computer Law Service Rep. 878 (N.D.Cal.1975). An affidavit filed by NUE's computer expert explains that NUE, through its counsel, did in fact create a litigation support system on the basis of selection by counsel of a number of documents out of many for inclusion in a computer data base. However, the defendants do not in fact seek a computer disc, or a computer tape extracted from that disc, which contains information selected for use in such a litigation support system. Rather, defendants' request is limited to exactly the same data (in the same arrangement) which NUE furnished defendants in paper computer printout reports. We are thus faced with a different question from that which we originally perceived.

It is true, as NUE complains, that no computer tape in the form requested by the defendants exists, and that the relief requested by defendants would require "the creation (e.g. manufacture) of a physical object not now in existence". The principal question before us, however, is whether that which defendants seek production (or manufacture) of is work product within the meaning of the Federal Rules. We conclude that it is not.

Ordinarily, in addressing the question whether given material is work product, we would turn to precedent, including the seminal case of *Hickman v. Taylor*, 329 U.S. 495, 67 S.Ct. 385, 91 L.Ed. 451 (1947). We have canvassed the cases, but find nothing helpful. We are, therefore, constrained to analyze the facts before us in terms of the language of Rule 26. We have done so, but have failed to discover any "mental impressions, conclusions, opinions, or legal theories" therein. Neither do we find any "trial strategy". Rather, we find that all the defendants seek is precisely the same data as is contained in the computer printouts which were furnished in discovery. To the extent that an issue exists as to selection and arrangement of that data, it appears that it is the defendants who decided what data NUE was to gather and how it should be arranged by virtue of the framing of their interrogatories. Moreover, to the extent that any "decision analysis" by NUE was involved, the paper computer printout has already revealed whatever data, activity, or other "decisional analysis" considerations were present.

As defendants note, the only difference between what defendants already have and what they request is that a computer cannot read what NUE has previously produced. That is a mechanical, not a qualitative, difference. It must be remembered that the actual data being sought is model-by-model production, sales, and price data, which is not claimed to have been the product of any attorney input. And, finally, it must be noted that it is clear from the affidavits which have been filed that NUE does not have to produce its entire data base or computerized trial support system in order to adequately respond to defendants' request Rather, as defendants' affidavits demonstrate, in order to produce the computer-printed information in a tape form, all that is necessary is for NUE's computer specialist to re-run the instructions used to extract and print the computer reports on paper with a new instruction to print the results on computer-readable form like magnetic tape rather than in paper copy form To repeat, what is sought is not work product within the meaning of Rule 26.

In view of the foregoing analysis we must confront the only remaining question, i.e. whether there is anything in the federal discovery rules which relieves NUE from the obligation to perform the labor necessary to produce the requested tape. Notwithstanding NUE's protestations, both common sense and a growing body of precedent support defendants' request. While we can find no case in which the court has ordered the programming of a computer to manufacture a computer tape not theretofore in physical existence, a number of cases have ordered the production, in the Rule 34 sense, of computer materials.

In *Quadrini v. Sikorsky Aircraft Division, United Aircraft Corporation*, 74 F.R.D. 594 (D.Conn.1977) Judge Newman granted defendant's motion to compel plaintiff to produce, inter alia, data processing cards, which are a type of computer-readable materials. In *Pearl Brewing Co. v. Jos. Schlitz Brewing Co.*, 415 F.Supp. 1122, 1134–41 (S.D.Tex.1976), Judge Bue allowed defendants under Rule 26(b)(4)(B) to inspect and copy "the entire system documentation" i.e., the underlying computer program which performed certain analysis prepared by certain experts for plaintiff's computer-generated model. In *Adams v. Dan River Mills, Inc.*, 54 F.R.D. 220, 222 (W.D.Va.1972), the court ordered production of computer-readable data material, saying:

> "Because of the accuracy and inexpensiveness of producing the requested documents in the case at bar, this court sees no reason why the defendant should not be required to produce the computer cards or tapes . . . to the plaintiff."

And, in *United States v. Davey*, 543 F.2d 996 (2d Cir.1976), an Internal Revenue summons proceeding, the Court of Appeals ordered the respondent to produce magnetic tapes in its possession, which contained financial data, even though the same information had already been proffered to the Internal Revenue Service in printout form. The district court in Davey had ordered production of the computer tapes, commenting that their production would make unnecessary "a great deal of manual examination of many thousands of printout pages." 404 F.Supp. 1283, 1284 (S.D.N.Y.1975), rev'd on other grounds, *Davey, supra*. The Second Circuit affirmed on this point. It noted that "inspection of the requested tapes . . . would . . . insure greater accuracy and a substantial saving in auditing time," and held that the taxpayer could not "give the IRS requested information in an inconvenient form with a view to immunizing itself from demands for other records containing the same relevant information in a more convenient form." 543 F.2d at 1000.

As some of the decisions have observed, the 1970 amendments to Rule 34 of the Federal Rules of Civil Procedure made it clear that computerized records are subject to requests for production. Those amendments added to the list in Rule 34(a)(1) of matters subject to production the language "and other data compilations from which information can be obtained, translated, if necessary, by the respondent through detection devices into reasonably usable form." The 1970 Advisory Committee Notes explained:

The inclusive description of "documents" is revised to accord with changing technology. It makes clear that Rule 34 applies to electronic data compilations from which information can be obtained only with the use of detection devices, and that when the data can as a practical matter be made usable by the discovering party only through respondent's devices, respondent may be required to use his devices to translate the data into usable form. In many instances, this means that respondent will have to supply a print-out of computer data.

48 F.R.D. 487, 527 (1970). The Rule thus provides that data be produced in a "reasonably usable form." The Advisory Committee contemplated that this usable form would often consist of a printout of the data stored electronically, but did not preclude production of the information in an electronic medium. The Manual for Complex Litigation, on the other hand, views the production of computer data records in machine-readable form as primary in complex cases, with the production of printouts as a secondary alternative:

In the computer context, the basic types of machine records commonly utilized include: (1) punched cards; (2) paper and magnetic tapes; and (3) a variety of other machine oriented components which record and store data. In the absence of special considerations such as privilege, work product immunity, or the presence of industrial or trade secrets in the machine, readable computerized data (including computerized analyses) in any of the above-mentioned forms should be freely discoverable. If the discovering party has data processing equipment that is compatible with that of the owners of the computer records, *delivery of the machine-readable version of the information, or a copy thereof*, will often be sufficient. When the discovering party's equipment is not compatible, or he has no computer equipment, delivery of a print-out of the machine-readable records may provide a reasonable alternative mode of discovery.

While a printout might be "reasonably usable" within the meaning of Rule 34, the production of a party's data in a form which is directly readable by the adverse party's computers is the preferred alternative, according to the editors of the Manual for Complex Litigation.

Although there may be some difference between requiring the production of existing tapes and requiring a party to so program the computer as to produce data in computer-readable as opposed to printout form, we find it to be a distinction without a difference, at least in the circumstances of this case. As we have noted, the defendants have expressed their willingness to pay the costs of whatever operations are necessary to manufacture a computer-readable tape. As a result, the problem of allocating the burden of discovery expense, which might be significant in otherwise similar situations, see Horning, supra, at 675–87, is nonexistent here. Apart from the possible expense, the manufacture of a machine-readable copy of a computer disc is in principle no different from the manufacture of a photocopy of a written document, a common enough method of responding to a request for document production.

It may well be that Judge Charles E. Clark and the framers of the Federal Rules of Civil Procedure could not foresee the computer age. However, we know we now live in an era when much of the data which our society desires to retain is stored in computer discs. This process will escalate in years to come; we suspect that by the year 2000 virtually all data will be stored in some form of computer memory. To interpret the Federal Rules which, after all, are to be construed to "secure the just, speedy, and inexpensive determination of every action," in a manner which would preclude the production of material such as is requested here, would eventually defeat their purpose.

Defendants' request will be granted.

An appropriate order follows.

DISCOVERY OF COMPUTERIZED DATA

Federal Judicial Center, Manual for Complex Litigation, Third, 1993.

Computerized data have become commonplace in litigation. Such data include not only conventional information but also such things as operating systems (programs that control a computer's basic functions), applications (programs used directly by the operator, such as word processing or spreadsheet programs), computer-generated models, and other sets of instructions residing in computer memory. Any discovery plan must address the relevant issues, such as the search for, location, retrieval, form of production and inspection, preservation, and use at trial of information stored in mainframe or personal computers or accessible "online." For the most part, such data will reflect information generated and maintained in the ordinary course of business. Some computerized data, however, may have been compiled in anticipation of or for use in the litigation (and may therefore be entitled to protection as trial preparation materials). Discovery requests may themselves be transmitted in computer-accessible form; interrogatories served on computer disks, for example, could then be answered using the same disk, avoiding the need to retype them. Finally, computerized data may form the contents for a common document depository.

Rule 34 provides for the production, inspection, and copying of computerized data (i.e., "data compilations from which information can be obtained, translated, if necessary, by the respondent through detection devices into reasonably usable form"); Rule 33(d) permits parties to answer interrogatories by making available for inspection and copying business records, including "compilations," where "the burden of deriving or ascertaining the answer is substantially the same for the party serving the interrogatory as for the party served." The court will need to consider, among other things, whether production and inspection should be in computer-readable form (such as by translation onto CD–ROM disks) or of printouts (hard copies); what information the producing party must be required to provide (such as manuals and similar materials) to facilitate the requesting party's access to and inspection of the producing party's data; whether to require the parties to agree on a standard format for production of computerized data; and how to minimize and allocate the costs of production (such as the cost of computer runs or of special programming to facilitate production) and equalize the burdens on the parties. The cost of production may be an issue, for example, where production is to be made of E-mail (electronic mail) or voice-mail messages erased from hard disks but capable of being retrieved.

Computer-stored data and other information responsive to a request will not necessarily be found in an appropriately labeled file. Broad database searches may be necessary, and this may expose confidential or irrelevant data to the opponent's scrutiny unless appropriate safeguards are installed. Similarly, some data may be maintained in the form of compilations that may themselves be entitled to trade secret protection or that reflect attorney work product, having been prepared by attorneys in contemplation of litigation. Data may have been compiled, for example, to produce studies and tabulations for use at trial or as a basis for expert opinions.

In general, the Federal Rules of Evidence apply to computerized data as they do to other types of evidence. Computerized data may, however, raise unique issues concerning the accuracy and authenticity of the database. Accuracy may be impaired as a result of incorrect or incomplete entry of data, mistakes in output instructions, programming errors, damage and contamination of storage media, power outages, and equipment malfunctions. The proponent of computerized evidence has the burden of laying a proper foundation by establishing its accuracy. Issues concerning accuracy and reliability of computerized evidence, including any necessary discovery, should be addressed during pretrial proceedings and not raised for the first time at trial.

When the data are voluminous, verification and correction of all items may not be feasible. In such cases, verification may be made of a sample of the data. Instead of correcting the errors detected in the sample—which might lead to the erroneous representation that the compilation is free from error—evidence may be offered (or stipulations made) by way of extrapolation from the sample of the effect of the observed errors on the entire compilation. Alternatively, it may be feasible to use statistical methods to determine the probability and range of error.

The complexity, general unfamiliarity, and rapidly changing character of the technology involved in the management of computerized materials may at times make it appropriate for the court to seek the assistance of a special master or neutral expert. Alternatively, the parties may be called on to provide the court with expert assistance, in the form of briefings on the relevant technological issues.

Notes And Questions

Would a computerized litigation system developed by one party in a complex litigation, be discoverable by the other party? *See In re IBM Peripheral EDP Devices Antitrust Litigation*, 5 Computer L.Serv. 878 (N.D.Calif. 1975).

ANTI–MONOPOLY, INC. v. HASBRO, INC.

United States District Court, Southern District of New York,1996.
1996 WL 22976.

PECK, UNITED STATES MAGISTRATE JUDGE:

This Court's November 3, 1995 Opinion and Order granted plaintiff's motion to compel defendants to produce certain data in computerized (electronic) form:

> The law is clear that data in computerized form is discoverable even if paper "hard copies" of the information have been produced, and that the producing party can be required to design a computer program to extract the data from its computerized business records, subject to the Court's discretion as to the allocation of the costs of designing such a computer program. The application of these principles to the facts of this case, however, require further negotiation by the parties.

By letter motion dated December 8, 1995, plaintiff Anti–Monopoly now moves to compel defendants Hasbro and Toys "R" Us ("TRU") to produce the computerized data "without requiring plaintiff to pay any of defendants' costs." For the reasons discussed below, the Court denies plaintiff's motion. If plaintiff wants the computerized information, it will have to pay defendants' reasonable costs of creating computer programs to extract the requested data from defendants' computers.

ANALYSIS

This Court's November 3, 1995 Opinion foretold today's result:

> The Court further notes that, as in *Matsushita* [*National Union Electric Corp. v. Matsushita Electric Industrial Co.*, 494 F. Supp. 1257, 1258–62 (E.D.Pa.1980)], further Court rulings may depend on plaintiff's willingness to pay defendants' costs in creating the required computer program.

Plaintiff Anti–Monopoly has presented two main arguments as to why it should not have to bear the costs.

"Plaintiff's first argument is that it has not asked defendants to do any programming or translating. Plaintiff has merely asked that defendants produce the requested data processing records for plaintiff to copy." The flaw in this argument is that plaintiff does not present any evidence that the requested data is available for production by defendants without the need for programming. Defendants have presented affidavits from Helen Averett and Nelson Chaffee, the respective heads of TRU's and Hasbro's Management Information Systems ("MIS") Departments. Both Ms. Averett and Mr. Chaffee swear that in order to extract this information from the computer (and in some cases from older stored computer tapes), "it is necessary to write a computer program and execute that program." The Court accepts these sworn representations.

Plaintiff appears to be arguing that if defendants merely "dumped" all of their computer data without writing a program to extract the data plaintiff seeks, there would be no programming costs involved. Plaintiff cites no case support for this proposition. If the data plaintiff requested existed in a computer report format so it could be copied without needing special programming (or more than de minimis programming), then plaintiff would not have to pay. But the requested data here does not exist as such in defendants' computer, and can be extracted only by special programming. Plaintiff cannot avoid that cost by telling defendants to "dump" their computer data, including data not requested or relevant in a Rule 26 discovery sense. Such a ruling would fly in the face of the cases cited above that require the requesting party to pay for computerized data to be extracted where a program has to be written. This is especially so here since plaintiff is a competitor of Hasbro and a supplier to TRU, and in spite of the confidentiality order, plaintiff should not be given irrelevant computerized business data of competitors.

"Plaintiff's second argument is that justice requires that the [cost] burden of production be borne by defendants because plaintiff has no assets with which to pay these costs." *In Oppenheimer Fund, Inc. v. Sanders*, 437 U.S. 340, 361–62, 98 S.Ct. 2380, 2395 (1978) the Supreme Court held that:

> Although in some circumstances the ability of a party to bear a burden may be a consideration, the test in this respect should be whether the cost is substantial; not whether it is "modest" in relation to ability to pay. In the context of a lawsuit in which the defendants [with assets over $500 million] deny all liability, the imposition on them of a threshold expense of $16,000 . . . can hardly be viewed as an insubstantial burden.

Here, the estimated cost of $1,680 as to Hasbro and $5–6000 as to TRU is not "insubstantial," and in addition, plaintiff has not shown that it could extract the needed data for less if defendants merely "dumped" the data as plaintiff requests.

Conclusion

The data plaintiff seeks cannot be retrieved from defendants' computers without special programming. Plaintiff should pay for that programming. Plaintiff cannot avoid that by asking defendants to "dump" their computer files including irrelevant data. Plaintiff's real argument is that defendants can afford this cost and plaintiff cannot. That does not provide a basis to impose these costs on defendants in this case. Accordingly, plaintiff's motion is denied. If plaintiff wants this computer data, it must pay defendants' reasonable programming expense to retrieve the requested data.

SO ORDERED.

IN RE POTASH ANTITRUST LITIGATION

United States District Court, D. Minnesota, 1996.
1996 WL 757185.

ERICKSON, UNITED STATES MAGISTRATE JUDGE.

I. INTRODUCTION

This matter came before the undersigned United States Magistrate Judge pursuant to a special assignment, made in accordance with the provisions of Title 28 U.S.C. § 636(b)(1)(A), upon the Plaintiffs' Motion for Sanctions.

For reasons which follow, we deny the Plaintiffs' Motion.

II. FACTUAL BACKGROUND

On April 11, 1994, the Plaintiffs served their First Request for Production of Documents. In this request, the Plaintiffs sought the comprehensive production of data which pertained to the potash transactions, that had been made by the Defendants, during the seven year period from 1987 through 1993. Document Request No. 53 illustrates the scope of the contemplated production:

> 53.   Documents which record, refer or relate to the total sales for each year in the relevant period or portion thereof the total dollar value of potash sold to the class of direct purchasers of potash alleged in the Amended Complaints in this action and any such documents which specify the dollar value of sales of each individual type, grade or particle size of potash sold to members of the class.

On May 31, 1994, the Defendants served their Responses and, on June 21, 1994, counsel for the parties met to discuss those Responses. At that conference, defense counsel advised that the Defendants, with two exceptions, had recently provided Economists, Inc. ("EI"), whom they had retained for consulting purposes, with electronic transaction data for the period from 1987 through 1993, and that they were prepared to provide the Plaintiffs with the same electronic data base. Thereafter, on July 1, 1994, the Defendants forwarded their computer tapes, and their diskettes which contained the same data, together with a description of the electronic file contents. However, on July 11, the Plaintiffs notified the Defendants that they had encountered difficulties in interpreting the information.

Thereafter, on July 29, 1994, the Plaintiffs informally requested that the Defendants produce an electronic database, which had been prepared by Dr. Joseph McAnneny, who was an economist with EI, and which had been referenced in a report that the Defendants had filed in opposition to the Plaintiffs' Class Certification Motion. Notwithstanding their objection, that the McAnneny Database was nondiscoverable work product, the Defendants offered to supply that Database, so long as the Plaintiffs were willing to share in the cost of its production. By letter dated August 8, 1996, the Plaintiffs responded by reiterating the difficulties that they had been experiencing in translating the Defendants' computerized data which had been produced on July 1.

In order to more fully address the Plaintiffs' concerns, the Defendants arranged for a telephone conference, on August 19, 1994, between the computer experts of both the Plaintiffs and the Defendants. After that conference, the Defendants directed EI to prepare responses to the additional questions that had been posed by the Plaintiffs' computer expert. These responses were provided to the Plaintiffs on September 23, 1994.

Earlier, however, on September 12, 1994, the Plaintiffs had moved to strike Dr. McAnneny's affidavit or, in the alternative, to effectively compel the Defendants to provide the McAnneny Database. In response to this Motion, the Defendants had argued that the Plaintiffs were not entitled to obtain the McAnneny Database free of charge, and had reported that they had "put in place a procedure that would permit plaintiffs' experts to obtain EI's assistance to create an intermediate database of their own, using the same transaction records and file layouts with which EI started its study of potash prices."

On March 30, 1995—in excess of six months after they had received EI's response to their computer expert's list of questions—the Plaintiffs' propounded a Third Request for Production of Documents. In this Request, the Plaintiffs sought three categories of information: 1) electronic transaction data for the period from 1984 through 1986, similar to that which had been provided, on July 1, 1994, for the period from 1987 to 1993; 2) printouts of the transaction data for the period from 1984 through 1993; and, 3) documents pertaining to the transaction data for the 1987–1993 period.

After conducting a "meet and confer," the Plaintiffs advised that, with respect to the transaction data produced on July 1, 1994, they "wanted documents 'that would shed light on what the transactional database produced to plaintiffs means,' in particular, 'manuals explaining how defendants kept records in the computer database, manuals on how the files are maintained and what the different fields mean.'" On May 24, 1995, the Plaintiffs were advised that the Defendants were prepared to provide the requested information. By June 23, 1995, the "manuals" were produced by each of the Defendants who maintained such documents in their possession. According to the uncontradicted Declaration of Kerry Lynn Edwards ("Edwards"), who serves as counsel for one of the Defendants, Plaintiffs' counsel never "raise[d] any specific problem or issue concerning the content or interpretation of the transaction data that had been produced to the plaintiffs on July 1, 1994," notwithstanding the fact that she and Plaintiffs' counsel had engaged in "meet and confer" discussions concerning the other two categories of information, that had been sought in the Plaintiffs' March 30, 1995 Request for Production of Documents—namely, the printouts, and the transaction data for 1984 through 1986.

On July 28, 1995, Dr. Gordon C. Rausser, who has served as the Plaintiffs' expert witness, submitted an Expert Report which included his calculation of the damages that the Plaintiffs are purported to have suffered as a result of the alleged conspiracy. Rather than predicate his damage calculation upon the Defendants' actual transaction data, Dr. Rausser used price information that was gathered, and published, by Green Markets, which is an industry newsletter. In explaining the source of the data, upon which he premised his damage calculations, Dr. Rausser advised:

> The use of aggregate Green Markets data is appropriate for this analysis. The defendants have yet to produce sufficient information on the structure and content of their specific transaction data to permit reliable analysis. The information that has been produced regarding these transaction data, however, indicate that the Green Markets data provides a good representation of defendants' specific price levels. For instance, the correlation between the Green Markets data used in my analysis, and the PCS transaction data is over 80%.

The Defendants take issue with Dr. Rausser's assertion that the Green Markets price information is an acceptable substitute for the Defendants' actual sales data. According to Dr. Robert S. Stillman ("Dr. Stillman"), who is the Defendants' damages expert, "on average, the Green Markets prices exceeded the PCS 'at the mine' prices" by approximately $9 per short ton.

In May of 1995, the Defendants provided Lexecon, Inc. ("Lexecon"), which is an economics consulting firm with whom Dr. Stillman is affiliated, the same electronic transaction data that had been produced to the Plaintiffs on July 1, 1994. According to the Defendants, by late August, or by early September of 1995, the Defendants had discovered complications in the electronic transaction data that had been generated by PCS, IMC, Kalium, and Noranda. As to PCS, Lexecon determined that PCS had, in the ordinary course of its business operations, incorrectly entered data into its computer base, which related to the $35 rebate. Deposition of Robert Stillman at 54–55, attached as Exhibit 31, Defs.'Jt.Sanc.Dec. In contrast, the error in IMC's data related to an omission of something less than 100 transactions, out of a total of several hundred thousand transactions, for the period from 1987 to 1993. With respect to Kalium's data, the problem pertained to a data field which listed original invoice numbers. Apparently, after Lexecon had uncovered a discrepancy among Kalium's invoices, Kalium determined that some, but not all, of the original invoice numbers were posted incorrectly. Lastly, as to Noranda, Lexecon determined that certain data spikes, which were observed in its data, were attributable to a malfunction in the procedure that Noranda had employed to deduct freight costs. Apparently, the problem only existed in five of the 84 months of data that Noranda had provided, and the problem caused the actual prices to appear larger than they were. Assertedly—and it has not been controverted—until these errors were discovered, the Defendants were not aware of their existence.

On September 18, 1995, the Defendants filed the Reports of their experts. By September 26, 1995, each of the four Defendants, who had discovered errors in its electronic transactional data, had provided the Plaintiffs with corrected diskettes and tapes. In addition, the Defendants agreed to have Lexecon review EI's responses to the questions of the Plaintiffs' computer experts, that had been discussed in September of 1994, and they directed Lexecon to promptly transmit any additions, deletions or clarifications. Less than one week later, the Defendants forwarded the results of Lexecon's review. Whereas EI's initial responses had encompassed nearly 33 pages, we are informed that Lexecon's corrections amounted to little more than 20 lines of material.

As noted, Dr. Rausser filed his Expert Report on July 27, 1995. In that Report, Dr. Rausser revealed that the Plaintiffs were intending to argue that "noncollusive" price levels could be derived by computing the minimum prices that the Canadian Defendants could have charged in order to comply with the Suspension Agreement. According to the Defendants, up until that time, the Plaintiffs had not provided any indication that they were interested in the Defendants' efforts to comply with the Suspension Agreement. Thereafter, in response to an inquiry from Lexecon, which, in turn, was triggered by Dr. Rausser's Report, counsel for PCS located a collection of computer printouts that documented PCS's attempt to monitor its compliance with the Agreement. After reviewing these documents, Andrew Rosenfield, who is the Defendants' liability expert, and who is also affiliated with Lexecon, informed PCS that he might refer to those documents in his Expert Report. According to Gerald Zingone ("Zingone"), who serves as counsel for PCS, a decision was reached, to send the monitoring documents to the Plaintiffs immediately, rather than to wait and provide the documents with Rosenfield's Expert Report. As a result, PCS produced these monitoring documents on August 23, 1995.

On August 28, 1995, the Plaintiffs informed PCS that they regarded the monitoring documents as being responsive to one or more of the categories of documents that they had sought in their April 12, 1994, Request for Production of Documents . Unfortunately, the Plaintiffs did not identify the document request or requests, that they felt to be applicable. Also on August 28, the Plaintiffs submitted a list of questions, which related to the monitoring documents, and which received PCS's responses on September 1, 1995. According to Zingone, the Plaintiffs followed, with a few additional questions, which he answered by telephone, and by a letter dated September 5, 1995. Notably, Zingone has averred that the Plaintiffs "never asked one additional question concerning the monitoring documents," and "did not ask PCS to voluntarily produce any of those individuals familiar with the monitoring documents for deposition."

Pursuant to Rule 26(e)(2), Federal Rules of Civil Procedure, the Plaintiffs request that we declare the Green Markets data, which Dr. Rausser utilized in his Expert Report, to be the best available information. Further, they urge that the Defendants should be precluded from using any of the corrected computer data, that they had not produced to the Plaintiffs prior to September of 1995. In addition, the Plaintiffs seek to exclude from the Trial, any of PCS's documentation which relates to its internal monitoring of the Suspension Agreement.

III. DISCUSSION

A. *Standard of Review.* Rule 26(e)(2), Federal Rules of Civil Procedure, governs the supplementation of responses to discovery:

> A party is under a duty seasonably to amend a prior response to an interrogatory, request for production, or request for admission if the party learns that the response is in some material respect incomplete or incorrect and if the additional or corrective information has not otherwise been made known to the other parties during the discovery process or in writing.

Although the Rule does not contain a specific sanction for failing to supplement discovery, "[f]ew would question a court's inherent power to discipline breaches of [the rule], even in the absence of a court order." *Campbell Indus. v. MN Gemini*, 619 F.2d 24, 27 (9th Cir. 1980).

As our Court of Appeals has observed, "[t]he purpose of our modern discovery procedure is to narrow the issues, to eliminate surprise, and to achieve substantial justice." *Mawby v. United States*, 999 F.2d 1252, 1254 (8th Cir. 1993). To that end, the Trial Court has wide discretion in fashioning a proper sanction for an improper failure to supplement. Among the sanctions available to the Court, for such a violation of the Rule, are an "exclusion of evidence, continuance, or other action, as the court may deem appropriate." B. *Legal Analysis.* With these principles as our guide, we separately address the Plaintiffs' Motion as it pertains to the transaction databases, and to PCS's monitoring documents. Given the Record before us, we conclude that an award of sanctions is unwarranted.

1. *The Transaction Databases.* The Plaintiffs maintain that, despite clear knowledge of the flaws in the databases, the Defendants silently waited to "ambush" them with those errors. According to the Plaintiffs, the Defendants awaited the filing of the parties' Expert Reports before revealing the irregularities in their databases. They further assert that, because they were denied the necessary information to comprehend the Defendants' sales data, the Defendants "should not be heard to criticize Dr. Rausser's use of the Green Markets data." We disagree.

As a threshold consideration, we note that the Record does not support the Plaintiffs' assertion that they repeatedly informed the Defendants that their databases were incomplete, or were not capable of interpretation. Instead, the Record verifies that, following the Plaintiffs' receipt of EI's explanatory answers, in September of 1994, which, in itself, followed the Defendants' provision of their own computer expert for telephonic consultation with the Plaintiffs' computer expert, the Plaintiffs did not voice—formally or informally—a substantive concern, over the transaction databases, until March 30, 1995. At that time, the Plaintiffs requested certain interpretive manuals, which the Defendants promptly furnished. While acknowledging their receipt of these manuals, the Plaintiffs now contend that those documents "did not assist plaintiffs' expert economist, Dr. Gordon Rausser, in understanding the database." We find it significant, however, that, with the sole exception of this Motion, the Plaintiffs did not previously challenge the adequacy of the Defendants' response to this aspect of their Request for Documents of March 30, 1995. Moreover, notwithstanding an ample opportunity to do so, the Plaintiffs did not serve a single deposition notice, pursuant to Rule 30(b)(6), Federal Rules of Civil Procedure, so as to ascertain the information that they were lacking, nor did they approach the Court with a request for further discovery, if they felt that one of their limited depositions should not be used for such a purpose.

Next, the Plaintiffs argue that the fact that the four Defendants produced corrected databases, within one week of each other, and not until their expert had filed his initial Report, supports their inference that the Defendants deferred disclosing the corrections until that disclosure suited their own needs. In response, the Defendants maintain that the near simultaneity of their responses was owing to Lexecon's contemporaneous inquiry into their transaction data. Given the uncontested averments before us, we find support for the Defendants' position, which outweighs the Plaintiffs' suspicions of wrongdoing. The four Defendants who supplied the amended diskettes—namely, Noranda, PCS, IMC, and Kalium—first learned of the errors, based upon the investigation by Lexecon, in late July, August, and September of 1995, respectively, all of which occurred after Dr. Rausser's Report was completed. Accordingly, we find no evidence to support the Plaintiffs' urging that we ascribe a bad faith motive to the Defendants, based upon the timing by which the information was provided.

Lastly, we are not persuaded by the Plaintiffs' claims of prejudice. First, the Plaintiffs have failed to demonstrate how the corrections, to the transaction databases of Noranda, PCS, IMC, and Kalium, were essential to the Plaintiffs' understanding of the sales transactions of those Defendants. This may best be illustrated by the deficiencies associated with IMC's computerized data. As noted, apparently, in the recording of this information into its computer system, IMC inadvertently omitted less than 100 documents, over a seven year period. How that omission could appreciably affect the Plaintiffs' capacity to understand that data is neither self-obvious, nor has it been made clear.

As to PCS, it should be sufficient to note that, at his deposition, Dr. Rausser conceded that PCS's data was accurate, verified, and interpretable. Furthermore, notwithstanding the Plaintiffs' claim that they were harmed, because Dr. Rausser could not use the actual sales data, the Plaintiffs have failed to adequately explain why Dr. Rausser did not either attempt to employ the numbers, that had been provided, in his supplemental report or, if time was a critical factor, why they did not request a continuance. In the absence of a showing that the Plaintiffs' predicament—if, indeed, that is what they confronted—was not a direct result of their own failure to fully discover on a timely basis and, in the further absence of any showing that the requested information was critical to an understanding of the Defendants' sales transactions, we deny the Plaintiffs' Motion for Sanctions as being without merit.

2. *The PCS Monitoring Documents.* The Plaintiffs contend that the documents, which disclose PCS's attempt to monitor its compliance with the Suspension Agreement, should be excluded from evidence at Trial. Although not argued in their written submissions, the Plaintiffs asserted, at the Hearing on this Motion, that these documents were responsive to two discovery requests that were included in their April 12, 1994, Request for Production of Documents. Specifically, the Plaintiffs draw our attention to Document Requests Nos. 18 and 38, which read as follows:

18. Each document referring or relating to the effect on sales volumes, market position or share of the market of any potash producer as a result of changes in published or list prices, discounts, bids, bases for bids, or actual transaction prices.

* * *

38. All documents or computer print outs reflecting summaries, compilations, or analyses of sales of potash by you (sic) company for each location, division, or other subdivision and on a company-wide basis.

Insofar as we are aware, the documents at issue have not been submitted for our review, although we have been informed that some 1700 pages of computations have been provided by PCS, which are directed toward its compliance with the Suspension Agreement. Whether these documents can truly be said to respond to either of these Requests is not a judgment that we can meaningfully make on the basis of the Record before us. Accordingly, we turn to an ascertainment of any prejudice to the Plaintiffs by the purported lateness in their discovery of this information.

In this respect, the Plaintiffs fare no better for they have neglected to demonstrate, other than by conclusory declaration, that an Order of preclusion is warranted. Notably, there is no evidence to support the Plaintiffs' assertion that PCS acted in bad faith, nor do we find any basis upon which to conclude that the information, as provided, could not be utilized by Dr. Rausser, or relied upon in the cross-examination of the Defendants' experts. Other logistical details, if any there be, can be addressed in a Motion in limine to the Trial Court. Finding no bad faith on PCS's part, and no showing of prejudice to the Plaintiffs, even if the disclosures are assumed to have been untimely, we deny the Motion for Sanctions as unwarranted.

NOW, THEREFORE, It is—

ORDERED:

That the Plaintiffs' Motion for Sanctions is denied.

Chapter XII

FIRST AMENDMENT RIGHTS

A. INTRODUCTION

The growth of computer technology over the past decade has led to numerous constitutional concerns. The Internet is a unique form of communication in that it allows users to access information and communicate via the World Wide Web, chat rooms, e-mail and by the creation of permanent online sites. This growth has led to questions in terms of the amount of protection the constitution will grant online users and how this protection will be granted.

There are two primary Internet-related constitutional issues being disputed within the courts, jurisdiction and the First Amendment. A previous chapter discussed jurisdiction. This chapter will address the First Amendment. The issue is the extent to which the First Amendment will protect the free exchange of ideas and the expression of diversified viewpoints on the Internet.

B. IS THERE A RIGHT TO HAVE E–MAIL DELIVERED?

CYBER PROMOTIONS, INC. v. AMERICA ONLINE, INC.

AMERICA ONLINE, INC. v. CYBER PROMOTIONS, INC.

United States District Court, E.D. Pennsylvania, 1996.
948 F.Supp. 436.

WEINER, DISTRICT JUDGE.

These cases present the novel issue of whether, under the First Amendment to the United States Constitution, one private company has the unfettered right to send unsolicited e-mail advertisements to subscribers of another private online company over the Internet and whether the private online company has the right to block the e-mail advertisements from reaching its members. The question is important because while the Internet provides the opportunity to disseminate vast amounts of information, the Internet does not, at least at the present time, have any means to police the dissemination of that information. We therefore find that, in the absence of State action, the private online service has the right to prevent unsolicited e-mail solicitations from reaching its subscribers over the Internet.

The cases have their genesis in a letter dated January 26, 1996, in which American Online, Inc. ("AOL") advised CyberPromotions, Inc. ("Cyber") that AOL was upset with Cyber's dissemination of unsolicited e-mail to AOL members over the Internet. * * *

On May 8, 1996, Cyber filed a First Amended Complaint in Civil Action No. 96–2486 in which it asserted the same four claims it asserted in its original Complaint and added a declaratory judgment claim (Count V). Cyber seeks, *inter alia*, a "declaration that [it] has the right to send to AOL members via the Internet unsolicited e-mail advertisements." Amended Complaint at p. 21. Cyber also asks the Court to "permanently enjoin [ ] AOL ... from ... directly or indirectly preventing AOL members from receiving [Cyber's] e-mail messages." *Id.* * * *

AOL has vehemently argued throughout the brief history of these suits that Cyber has no right to send literally millions of e-mail messages each day to AOL's Internet servers free of charge and resulting in the overload of the e-mail servers. Indeed, the court has received a plethora of letters from disgruntled AOL members who object to having to receive Cyber's unsolicited e-mail whenever they sign on to AOL despite repeated attempts to be removed from Cyber's lists. Cyber, on the other hand, has contended that without the right to send unsolicited e-mail to AOL members, it will go out of business.

Recognizing that Cyber's contention that it has the right to send unsolicited e-mail to AOL members over the Internet implicates the First Amendment and therefore is a threshold issue, the Court directed the parties to brief the following issue: Whether Cyber has a right under the First Amendment of the United States Constitution to send unsolicited e-mail to AOL members via the Internet and concomitantly whether AOL has the right under the First Amendment to block the e-mail sent by Cyber from reaching AOL members over the Internet. In response, AOL has filed a document entitled "Motion for Partial Summary Judgment of America Online, Inc. on First Amendment issues." Specifically, AOL seeks summary judgment on Cyber's declaratory judgment claim asserted in Count V of Cyber's First Amended Complaint. Cyber has filed a document entitled "Plaintiff's Memorandum in Support of its First Amendment Right to Send Internet E–Mail to Defendant's Members."

The Court also directed the parties to enter into a Stipulation of Facts solely for the purpose of resolving the First Amendment issue. Pursuant to the Court's directive, the parties have stipulated to the following facts:

1.   Cyber is a corporation organized and existing under the laws of the Commonwealth of Pennsylvania, having a place of business at 1255 Passmore Street, 1st Floor, Philadelphia, Pennsylvania 19111.

2.   AOL is a corporation organized and existing under the laws of the State of Delaware with its principal place of business at 22000 AOL Way, Dulles, Virginia 20166.

3.   AOL was and is a private online company that has invested substantial sums of its own money in equipment, name, software and reputation. AOL is not owned in whole or in part by the government.

4.   AOL is owned by shareholders, and its stock trades on the New York Stock Exchange.

5.   AOL is not a government entity or political subdivision.

6.   AOL's members or subscribers pay prescribed fees for use of AOL resources, access to AOL and access and use of AOL's e-mail system and its connection to the Internet.

7.   AOL's e-mail system operates through dedicated computers known as servers, which consist of computer hardware and software purchased, maintained and owned by AOL. AOL's computer servers have a finite, though expandable, capacity to handle e-mail. All Internet e-mail from non-AOL members to AOL customers or members and from AOL customers or members to non-AOL members requires the use of AOL's computer hardware and software in combination with the hardware and software of the Internet and the hardware and software of the non-AOL members.

8.   Private companies compete with AOL in the online business.

9.   There has been no government involvement in AOL's business decision to institute or reinstitute a block directed to Internet e-mail sent by Cyber to AOL members or subscribers.

10.   Although the Internet is accessible to all persons with just a computer, a modem and a service provider, the constituent parts of the Internet (namely the computer hardware and software, servers, service providers and related items) are owned and managed by private entities and persons, corporations, educational institutions and government entities, who cooperate to allow their constituent parts to be interconnected by a vast network of phone lines.

11.   In order for non-AOL members to send Internet e-mail to AOL members, non-AOL members must utilize a combination of their own hardware and software, the Internet and AOL's network.

12.   To obtain its initial access to the Internet, AOL obtained an Internet address and domain name from IANA, a clearinghouse that routinely and ministerially assigns Internet addresses and domain names.

13.   Cyber, an advertising agency incorporated in 1996, provides advertising services for companies and individuals wishing to advertise their products and services via e-mail.

14.   Cyber sends its e-mail via the Internet to members of AOL, members of other commercial online services and other individuals with an Internet e-mail address.

15. AOL provides its subscribing members with one or more e-mail addresses so that members can exchange e-mail with one another and exchange e-mail (both sending and receiving) over the Internet with non-AOL members.

16. AOL has attached to its Memorandum of Law in Support of its Motion for Partial Summary Judgment on First Amendment Issues three sets of examples of e-mail messages sent by Cyber to AOL members. The first set (Tab 1) consists of a multi-page set of advertisements; the second set (Tab 2) consists of an exclusive or single-advertiser e-mail; and the third set (Tab 3) consists of a document called by Cyber an "e-mag." Under each tab are two examples, the first selected by AOL and the second selected by Cyber. The Court has reviewed all of the examples and notes that many of the ads include get-rich-quick ads, weight loss ads, health aid promises and even phone sex services.

17. To attract membership, AOL offers a variety of services, options, resources and support, including content-based services, access to stock quotes, children's entertainment, news, and the ability to send and receive Internet e-mail to and from non-AOL members.

In addition to the parties's Stipulation of Facts, it is necessary for resolution of the issue before us to relate some of the factual findings about the Internet itself made earlier this year by our court in *American Civil Liberties Union v. Reno*, 929 F.Supp. 824 (E.D.Pa.1996). They are as follows:

18. "The Internet is ... a unique and wholly new medium of worldwide human communication." *Id.* at 844.

19. The Internet is "a giant network which interconnects innumerable smaller groups of linked computer networks." *Id.* at 830. In short, it is "a global Web of linked networks and computers ... " *Id.* at 831.

20. "The Internet is an international system." *Id.* It is "a decentralized, global medium of communications—or 'cyberspace'—that links people, institutions, corporations, and governments around the world. This communications medium allows any of the literally tens of millions of people with access to the Internet to exchange information." *Id.*

21. "No single entity—academic, corporate, governmental, or non-profit—administers the Internet. It exists and functions as a result of the fact that hundreds of thousands of separate operators of computers and computer networks independently decided to use common data transfer protocol to exchange communications and information with other computers (which in turn exchange communications and information with still other computers)." *Id.* at 832.

22. Computer users have a wide variety of avenues by which to access the Internet. *Id.* One such avenue is "through one of the major national commercial 'online services' such as [AOL] ... *Id.* at 833. These online services offer nationwide computer networks (so that subscribers can dial-in to a local telephone number), and the services provide extensive and well organized content within their own proprietary com-

puter networks. In addition to allowing access to the extensive content available *within* each online service, the services also allow subscribers to link to the much larger resources of the Internet." *Id.* (emphasis in original). "The major commercial online services have almost twelve million individual subscribers across the United States." *Id.* Approximately six million individuals are subscribers of AOL.

23.   There are a number of different ways to communicate over the Internet. One such way "is via electronic mail, or 'e-mail', comparable in principle to sending a first class letter. One can address and transmit a message to one or more other people." *Id.* at 834.

24.   "[T]he content on the Internet is as diverse as human thought." *Id.* at 842.

25.   "Communications over the Internet do not 'invade' an individuals's home or appear on one's computer screen unbidden. Users seldom encounter content 'by accident.' " *Id.* at 844.

26.   Unlike a radio or television, "the receipt of information on the Internet requires a series of affirmative steps more deliberate and directed than merely turning a dial." *Id.* at 845. * * *

In its Motion for Partial Summary Judgment, AOL contends that Cyber has no First Amendment right to send unsolicited e-mail to AOL members over the Internet because AOL is not a state actor, AOL's e-mail servers are not public fora in which Cyber has a right to speak, Cyber's right to use AOL's, service free of charge, does not substantially outweigh AOL's right to speak or not to speak, and that AOL's restrictions on mass e-mail solicitations are tailored to serve a substantial interest. Motion for Partial Summary Judgment at 6. Because we find AOL is not a state actor and none of its activities constitute state action, we need not consider AOL's remaining First Amendment contentions.

The First Amendment to the United States Constitution states that "Congress shall make no law respecting an establishment of religion, or prohibiting the free exercise thereof; or abridging the freedom of speech, or of the press." The United States Supreme Court has recognized that "the constitutional guarantee of free speech is a guarantee only against abridgement by government, federal or state." *Hudgens v. NLRB*, 424 U.S. 507, 513, 96 S.Ct. 1029, 1033, 47 L.Ed.2d 196 (1976). Only recently, the Supreme Court has stated that "the guarantees of free speech . . . guard only against encroachment by the government and 'erec[t] no shield against merely private conduct.' " *Hurley v. Irish–American Gay Group of Boston*, ___ U.S. ___ , ___ , 115 S.Ct. 2338, 2344, 132 L.Ed.2d 487 (1995) (citation omitted).

In the case sub judice, the parties have stipulated that AOL is a private online company that is not owned in whole or part by the government. Stipulation of Facts at ¶ 3. (emphasis added). The parties have further stipulated that "AOL is not a government entity or political subdivision." *Id.* at ¶ 5. They have also stipulated that there has been no government involvement in AOL's business decision to institute or reinstitute a block directed to Internet e-mail sent by Cyber to AOL members or subscribers. *Id.* at ¶ 9.

Despite these stipulations, Cyber argues that AOL's conduct has the character of state action. As a general matter, private action can only be considered state action when "there is a sufficiently close nexus between the State and the challenged action of [the private entity] so that the action of the latter may be fairly treated as that of the State itself." *Blum v. Yaretsky*, 457 U.S. 991, 1004, 102 S.Ct. 2777, 2786, 73 L.Ed.2d 534 (1982). Recently, our Court of Appeals observed that the Supreme Court appears to utilize three distinct tests in determining whether there has been state action. *Mark v. Borough of Hatboro*, 51 F.3d 1137, 1142 (3d Cir.1995). First, we must consider whether " 'the private entity has exercised powers that are traditionally the *exclusive* prerogative of the state.' " *Id.* (quoting *Blum v. Yaretsky*, 457 U.S. at 1004–05, 102 S.Ct. at 2785–86. (emphasis in *Mark*)). This test is known as the exclusive public function test. If the private entity does not exercise such powers, we must consider whether " 'the private entity has acted with the help of or in concert with state officials.' " *Mark*, 51 F.3d at 1142 (quoting *McKeesport Hospital v. Accreditation Council for Graduate Medical Ed.*, 24 F.3d 519, 524 (3d Cir.1994)). The final test is whether " '[t]he State has so far insinuated itself into a position of interdependence with … [the acting party] that it must be recognized as a joint participant in the challenged activity.' " *Mark*, 51 F.3d at 1142 (quoting *Krynicky v. University of Pittsburgh*, 742 F.2d 94, 98 (3d Cir.1984)).

With regard to the first test, AOL exercises absolutely no powers which are in any way the prerogative, let alone the *exclusive* prerogative, of the State. In *ACLU, supra*, this Court previously found that no single entity, including the State, administers the Internet. *ACLU*, 929 F.Supp. at 832. Rather, the Court found that the Internet is a "global Web of linked networks and computers" which exists and functions as the result of the desire of hundreds of thousands of computer operators and networks to use common data transfer data protocol to exchange communications and information. *Id.* In addition, "the constituent parts of the Internet … are owned and managed by private entities and persons, corporations, educational institutions and government entities, who co-operate to allow their constituent parts to be interconnected by a vast network of phone lines." Stipulation of Facts at ¶ 10. As a result, tens of millions of people with access to the Internet can exchange information. AOL is merely one of many private online companies which allow its members access to the Internet through its e-mail system where they can exchange information with the general public. The State has absolutely no interest in, and does not regulate, this exchange of information between people, institutions, corporations and governments around the world.

Cyber argues, however, that "by providing Internet e-mail and acting as the sole conduit to its members' Internet e-mail boxes, AOL has opened up that part of its network and as such, has sufficiently devoted this domain for public use. This dedication of AOL's Internet e-mail accessway performs a public function in that it is open to the public, free of charge to any user, where public discourse, conversations and commercial transactions can and do take place." Cyber's Memorandum in Support of its First Amendment Right to Send Internet E–Mail to Defendant's Members at 13. Cyber therefore contends that AOL's Internet e-mail accessway is similar to the company town in *Marsh v. Alabama*, 326 U.S. 501, 66 S.Ct. 276, 90 L.Ed. 265 (1946), which the Supreme Court found performed a public function and therefore was a state actor.

In *Marsh*, a Jehovah's Witness was convicted of criminal trespass for distributing literature without a license on a sidewalk in a town owned by a private company. The Supreme Court found that since the private company owned the streets, sidewalks, and business block, paid the sheriff, privately owned and managed the sewage system, and owned the building where the United States post office was located, the company, in effect, operated as the municipal government of the town. *Marsh*, 326 U.S. at 502–03, 66 S.Ct. at 276–77. "[T]he owner of the company town was performing the full spectrum of municipal powers and stood in the shoes of the State." *Lloyd Corp. v. Tanner*, 407 U.S. 551, 569, 92 S.Ct. 2219, 2229, 33 L.Ed.2d 131 (1972). The Court observed that "[t]he more an owner, for his advantage, opens up his property for use by the public in general, the more do his rights become circumscribed by the statutory and constitutional rights of those who use it." Marsh, 326 U.S. at 506, 66 S.Ct. at 278. As a result, the Court found state action in "the State['s] ... attempt[ ] to impose criminal punishment on appellant for undertaking to distribute religious literature in a company town ..." *Marsh*, 326 U.S. at 509, 66 S.Ct. at 280. Our Court of Appeals has noted that "*Marsh* has been construed narrowly." *Cable Investments, Inc. v. Woolley*, 867 F.2d 151, 162 (3d Cir.1989).

By providing its members with access to the Internet through its e-mail system so that its members can exchange information with those members of the public who are also connected to the Internet, AOL is not exercising *any* of the municipal powers or public services traditionally exercised by the State as did the private company in Marsh. Although AOL has technically opened its e-mail system to the public by connecting with the Internet, AOL has not opened its property to the public by performing any municipal power or essential public service and, therefore, does not stand in the shoes of the State. Marsh is simply inapposite to the facts of the case *sub judice*.

Cyber also argues that AOL's Internet e-mail connection constitutes an exclusive public function because there are no alternative avenues of communication for Cyber to send its e-mail to AOL members. As support for this proposition, Cyber directs our attention to the decisions of the Supreme Court in *United States Postal Service v. Greenburgh Civic Assn's*, 453 U.S. 114, 101 S.Ct. 2676, 69 L.Ed.2d 517 (1981); *Lloyd Corp. v. Tanner*, 407 U.S. 551, 92 S.Ct. 2219, 33 L.Ed.2d 131 (1972) and *Amalgamated Food Employees Union v. Logan Valley Plaza*, 391 U.S.

308, 88 S.Ct. 1601, 20 L.Ed.2d 603 (1968). Of these decisions, only the *Lloyd* decision is helpful to Cyber.

In *Greenburgh*, a civic association challenged a federal statute which prohibited the deposit of unstamped "mailable matter" in a letterbox approved by the United States Postal Service. The civic association contended that the First Amendment guaranteed them the right to deposit, without postage, their notices, circulars, flyers in such letterboxes. The Supreme Court upheld the constitutionality of the statute, finding that neither the enactment nor the enforcement of the statute was geared in any way to the content of the message sought to be placed in the letterbox. The Court also noted that the statute did not prevent individuals from going door-to-door to distribute their message or restrict the civic organization's right to use the mails. Greenburgh, however, did not involve the issue of whether there was state action. It therefore is inapplicable to the issue of whether AOL's conduct constitutes state action.

In *Logan Valley*, a case involving peaceful picketing directed solely at one establishment within a shopping center, the Court reviewed the Marsh decision in detail, emphasized the similarities between a shopping center and a company town and concluded that a shopping center is the "functional equivalent" of the business district in Marsh. As a result, the Court held that the picketers had a First Amendment right to picket within a shopping center. *Logan Valley*, however, was subsequently overruled by *Lloyd*, *supra*. Hudgens v. National Labor Relations Board, 424 U.S. 507, 96 S.Ct. 1029, 47 L.Ed.2d 196 (1976). ("[W]e make clear now, if it was not clear before, that the rationale of *Logan Valley* did not survive the Court's decision in the *Lloyd* case.")

In *Lloyd*, a group of individuals sought to distribute handbills in the interior of a privately owned shopping center. The content of the handbills was not directed at any one establishment in the shopping center but instead was directed at the Vietnam War. The Court noted that, unlike the situation in *Logan Valley* where the protestors had no other alternative to convey their message at the single establishment in the shopping center, the protesters in *Lloyd* could distribute their message about the Vietnam war on any public street, sidewalk or park outside the mall. The Court therefore found that "[i]t would be an unwarranted infringement of property rights to require [the protesters] to yield to the exercise of First Amendment under circumstances where adequate alternative avenues of communication exist." *Lloyd*, 407 U.S. at 567, 92 S.Ct. at 2228. The *Lloyd* Court went on to reject the individuals' functional equivalency argument, finding that the private shopping center neither assumed the full spectrum of municipal powers nor stood in the shoes of the state, as did the private company in Marsh. The Court held that, "[t]he First and Fourteenth Amendments safeguard the rights of free speech and assembly by limitations on state action, not on action by the owner of private property used nondiscriminatorily for private purposes only." *Lloyd*, 407 U.S. at 567, 92 S.Ct. at 2228 (emphasis in original).

Cyber has numerous alternative avenues of sending its advertising to AOL members. An example of another avenue Cyber has of sending its advertising to AOL members over the Internet is the World Wide Web which would allow access by Internet users, including AOL customers, who want to receive Cyber's e-mail. Examples of non-Internet avenues include the United States mail, telemarketing, television, cable, newspapers, magazines and even passing out leaflets. Of course, AOL's decision to block Cyber's e-mail from reaching AOL's members does not prevent Cyber from sending its e-mail advertisements to the members of competing commercial online services, including CompuServe, the Microsoft Network and Prodigy.

Having found that AOL is not a state actor under the exclusive public function test, we evaluate whether AOL is a state actor under the remaining two tests, i.e. whether AOL is acting with the help of or in concert with state officials and whether the State has put itself in a position of interdependence with AOL such that it must be considered a participant in AOL's conduct. These tests actually overlap one another.

In its Memorandum, Cyber does not specifically argue that AOL is acting in concert with state officials. Indeed, the two major cases from the Supreme Court which have found state action under this test are clearly distinguishable from the case *sub judice*. See, *Adickes v. S.H. Kress & Co.*, 398 U.S. 144, 90 S.Ct. 1598, 26 L.Ed.2d 142 (1970) (finding a conspiracy between a private actor and a state official to engage in unlawful discrimination constituted action under color of law for purposes of 42 U.S.C. § 1983); *Lugar v. Edmondson Oil Co.*, 457 U.S. 922, 102 S.Ct. 2744, 73 L.Ed.2d 482 (1982) (finding private creditor's prejudgment attachment petition upon which clerk of state court issued a writ of attachment and sheriff executed the writ on property of private debtor was state action under § 1983).

Rather, Cyber relies on the "joint participation" doctrine and contends that "AOL's use of the Court to obtain injunctive relief and/or damages [which it seeks in its prayer for relief in its counterclaim] and its assertions of federal and state statutory law, which if applicable to Cyber's activities, would violate Cyber's First Amendment rights." Cyber's Memorandum at 15.

In *Edmonson v. Leesville Concrete Co.*, 500 U.S. 614, 111 S.Ct. 2077, 114 L.Ed.2d 660 (1991) the Supreme Court refined the joint participation test by announcing that courts must ask "first whether the claimed constitutional deprivation resulted from the exercise of a right or privilege having its source in state authority; and second, whether the private party charged with the deprivation could be described in all fairness as a state actor." *Edmonson*, 500 U.S. at 620, 111 S.Ct. at 2082–83. Under the first prong, the inquiry is "under what authority did the private person engage in the allegedly unlawful acts." *Mark*, 51 F.3d at 1144.

In the case sub judice, the parties have stipulated that "[t]here has been no government involvement in AOL's business decisions with respect to e-mail sent by Cyber nor in any AOL decision to institute or reinstitute a block directed to Internet e-mail sent by Cyber to AOL members or subscribers." Stipulation of Facts at ¶ 9. As a result, Cyber is unable to satisfy even the first prong of the joint participation test.

In addition, our Court of Appeals has stated that "[m]erely instituting a routine civil suit does not transform a litigant's actions into those taken under color of state law." *Tunstall v. Office of Judicial Support*, 820 F.2d 631, 634 (3d Cir.1987). The *Tunstall* Court concluded that the filing of a quiet title action in state court by a purchaser of land to complete the seizure of plaintiff's property did not involve state action since the suit "did not attempt any seizure of property with the cooperation of state officials as in the Lugar line of cases." *Id.* In addition, the United States Court of Appeals for the Eleventh Circuit has found that a regulated utility did not act under color of state law when it obtained a temporary restraining order from a state court. *Cobb v. Georgia Power Co.*, 757 F.2d 1248 (11th Cir.1985). The United States Court of Appeals for the Second Circuit has held that the mere filing of a state law contempt proceeding does not constitute joint participation so as to satisfy the color of state law requirement under 42 U.S.C. § 1983. *Dahlberg v. Becker*, 748 F.2d 85 (2d Cir.1984).

Perhaps recognizing the futility of its argument, Cyber contends in its Reply Memorandum that "[i]t is not Cyber's position that the mere filing of an action provides a party with the requisite state action to assert a First Amendment violation. Rather it is the Court's participation with the litigant in issuing or enforcing an order which impinges on another's First Amendment rights. *Grandbouche v. Clancy*, 825 F.2d 1463, 1466 (10th Cir.1987)." Reply Memorandum at 7. In *Grandbouche*, the United States Court Appeals for the Tenth Circuit stated that the first Amendment "may be applicable in the context of discovery orders, even if all of the litigants are private entities." The Court found government action present as a result of a magistrate's order compelling discovery and the trial court's enforcement of that order.

We are troubled by the *Grandbouche* decision because it has the effect of creating government action every time a magistrate simply signs, and a trial judge enforces, a discovery order. Therefore, even if this Court had enforced a discovery order (which we have not), we would not follow the *Grandbouche* decision.

In sum, we find that since AOL is not a state actor and there has been no state action by AOL's activities under any of the three tests for state action enunciated by our Court of Appeals in *Mark*, Cyber has no right under the First Amendment to the United States Constitution to send unsolicited e-mail to AOL's members. It follows that AOL, as a private company, may block any attempts by Cyber to do so. * * *

Although we have found that Cyber has no right under the First Amendment of the United States Constitution or under the Constitutions of Pennsylvania or Virginia to send unsolicited e-mail to members of AOL, we will not, at this time, enter judgment on Count V of Cyber's First Amended Complaint for declaratory relief. This is because Cyber contends in its Reply brief that "many more issues ... have to be addressed since there are numerous reasons beyond the First Amendment which will permit Cyber to send e-mail to AOL members." Cyber's Reply Memorandum at 1. Therefore, we will simply declare that Cyber has no right under the First Amendment to the United States Constitution or under the Constitutions of Pennsylvania or Virginia to send unsolicited e-mail over the Internet to members of AOL. We will allow Cyber ten days from the date of this Memorandum Opinion and Order to submit a list of the theories other than the First Amendment it believes entitles it to send unsolicited e-mail to members of AOL.

An Order to that effect follows.

ORDER

The motion of American Online, Inc. for partial summary judgment on First Amendment issues is GRANTED in part and DENIED in part.

The Court declares that Cyber Promotions, Inc. does not have a right under the First Amendment to the United States Constitution or under the Constitutions of Pennsylvania and Virginia to send unsolicited e-mail advertisements over the Internet to members of American Online, Inc. and, as a result, American Online, Inc. may block any attempts by Cyber Promotions, Inc. to do so.

Cyber Promotions, Inc. shall, within ten days of the date of this Order, submit to the Court a list of the theories other than the First Amendment which it believes entitles it to send unsolicited e-mail to members of American Online, Inc.

Either party may request that we issue an Order certifying our decision for an immediate interlocutory appeal to the United States Court of Appeals for the Third Circuit.

IT IS SO ORDERED. * * *

Note And Question

Under 47 U.S.C. § 227(1)(C), it is unlawful, "to use any telephone facsimile machine, computer, or other device to send an unsolicited advertisement to a telephone facsimile machine". This provision was held to be Constitutional in *Destination Ventures, Ltd. v. F.C.C.*, 46 F.3d 54 (9th Cir.1995). Should similar legislation be adopted to forbid unsolicited e-mail advertisements? Would such legislation be Constitutional?

C. PORNOGRAPHY AND INDECENCY

RENO v. AMERICAN CIVIL LIBERTIES UNION

Supreme Court of the United States, 1997.
521 U.S. 844, 117 S.Ct. 2329, 138 L.Ed.2d 874.

JUSTICE STEVENS delivered the opinion of the Court.

At issue is the constitutionality of two statutory provisions enacted to protect minors from "indecent" and "patently offensive" communications on the Internet. Notwithstanding the legitimacy and importance of the congressional goal of protecting children from harmful materials, we agree with the three-judge District Court that the statute abridges "the freedom of speech" protected by the First Amendment.

I

The District Court made extensive findings of fact, most of which were based on a detailed stipulation prepared by the parties. See 929 F.Supp. 824, 830–849 (E.D.Pa.1996). The findings describe the character and the dimensions of the Internet, the availability of sexually explicit material in that medium, and the problems confronting age verification for recipients of Internet communications. Because those findings provide the underpinnings for the legal issues, we begin with a summary of the undisputed facts.

The Internet

The Internet is an international network of interconnected computers. It is the outgrowth of what began in 1969 as a military program called "ARPANET," which was designed to enable computers operated by the military, defense contractors, and universities conducting defense-related research to communicate with one another by redundant channels even if some portions of the network were damaged in a war. While the ARPANET no longer exists, it provided an example for the development of a number of civilian networks that, eventually linking with each other, now enable tens of millions of people to communicate with one another and to access vast amounts of information from around the world. The Internet is "a unique and wholly new medium of worldwide human communication."

The Internet has experienced "extraordinary growth." The number of "host" computers—those that store information and relay communications—increased from about 300 in 1981 to approximately 9,400,000 by the time of the trial in 1996. Roughly 60% of these hosts are located in the United States. About 40 million people used the Internet at the time of trial, a number that is expected to mushroom to 200 million by 1999.

Individuals can obtain access to the Internet from many different sources, generally hosts themselves or entities with a host affiliation. Most colleges and universities provide access for their students and faculty; many corporations provide their employees with access through an office network; many communities and local libraries provide free access; and an increasing number of storefront "computer coffee shops" provide access for a small hourly fee. Several major national "online services" such as America Online, CompuServe, the Microsoft Network, and Prodigy offer access to their own extensive proprietary networks as well as a link to the much larger resources of the Internet. These commercial online services had almost 12 million individual subscribers at the time of trial.

Anyone with access to the Internet may take advantage of a wide variety of communication and information retrieval methods. These methods are constantly evolving and difficult to categorize precisely. But, as presently constituted, those most relevant to this case are electronic mail ("e-mail"), automatic mailing list services ("mail exploders," sometimes referred to as "listservs"), "newsgroups," "chat rooms," and the "World Wide Web." All of these methods can be used to transmit text; most can transmit sound, pictures, and moving video images. Taken together, these tools constitute a unique medium—known to its users as "cyberspace"—located in no particular geographical location but available to anyone, anywhere in the world, with access to the Internet.

E-mail enables an individual to send an electronic message—generally akin to a note or letter—to another individual or to a group of addressees. The message is generally stored electronically, sometimes waiting for the recipient to check her "mailbox" and sometimes making its receipt known through some type of prompt. A mail exploder is a sort of e-mail group. Subscribers can send messages to a common e-mail address, which then forwards the message to the group's other subscribers. Newsgroups also serve groups of regular participants, but these postings may be read by others as well. There are thousands of such groups, each serving to foster an exchange of information or opinion on a particular topic running the gamut from, say, the music of Wagner to Balkan politics to AIDS prevention to the Chicago Bulls. About 100,000 new messages are posted every day. In most newsgroups, postings are automatically purged at regular intervals. In addition to posting a message that can be read later, two or more individuals wishing to communicate more immediately can enter a chat room to engage in real-time dialogue—in other words, by typing messages to one another that appear almost immediately on the others' computer screens. The District Court found that at any given time "tens of thousands of users are engaging in conversations on a huge range of subjects." It is "no exaggeration to conclude that the content on the Internet is as diverse as human thought."

The best known category of communication over the Internet is the World Wide Web, which allows users to search for and retrieve information stored in remote computers, as well as, in some cases, to communicate back to designated sites. In concrete terms, the Web consists of a vast number of documents stored in different computers all over the world. Some of these documents are simply files containing information.

However, more elaborate documents, commonly known as Web "pages," are also prevalent. Each has its own address—"rather like a telephone number." Web pages frequently contain information and sometimes allow the viewer to communicate with the page's (or "site's") author. They generally also contain "links" to other documents created by that site's author or to other (generally) related sites. Typically, the links are either blue or underlined text—sometimes images.

Navigating the Web is relatively straightforward. A user may either type the address of a known page or enter one or more keywords into a commercial "search engine" in an effort to locate sites on a subject of interest. A particular Web page may contain the information sought by the "surfer," or, through its links, it may be an avenue to other documents located anywhere on the Internet. Users generally explore a given Web page, or move to another, by clicking a computer "mouse" on one of the page's icons or links. Access to most Web pages is freely available, but some allow access only to those who have purchased the right from a commercial provider. The Web is thus comparable, from the readers' viewpoint, to both a vast library including millions of readily available and indexed publications and a sprawling mall offering goods and services.

From the publishers' point of view, it constitutes a vast platform from which to address and hear from a world-wide audience of millions of readers, viewers, researchers, and buyers. Any person or organization with a computer connected to the Internet can "publish" information. Publishers include government agencies, educational institutions, commercial entities, advocacy groups, and individuals. Publishers may either make their material available to the entire pool of Internet users, or confine access to a selected group, such as those willing to pay for the privilege. "No single organization controls any membership in the Web, nor is there any centralized point from which individual Web sites or services can be blocked from the Web."

Sexually Explicit Material

Sexually explicit material on the Internet includes text, pictures, and chat and "extends from the modestly titillating to the hardest-core." These files are created, named, and posted in the same manner as material that is not sexually explicit, and may be accessed either deliberately or unintentionally during the course of an imprecise search. "Once a provider posts its content on the Internet, it cannot prevent that content from entering any community." Thus, for example,

> "when the UCR/California Museum of Photography posts to its Web site nudes by Edward Weston and Robert Mapplethorpe to announce that its new exhibit will travel to Baltimore and New York City, those images are available not only in Los Angeles, Baltimore, and New York City, but also in Cincinnati, Mobile, or Beijing—wherever Internet users live. Similarly, the safer sex instructions that Critical Path posts to its Web site, written in street language so that the

teenage receiver can understand them, are available not just in Philadelphia, but also in Provo and Prague."

Some of the communications over the Internet that originate in foreign countries are also sexually explicit.

Though such material is widely available, users seldom encounter such content accidentally. "A document's title or a description of the document will usually appear before the document itself . . . and in many cases the user will receive detailed information about a site's content before he or she need take the step to access the document. Almost all sexually explicit images are preceded by warnings as to the content." For that reason, the "odds are slim" that a user would enter a sexually explicit site by accident. Unlike communications received by radio or television, "the receipt of information on the Internet requires a series of affirmative steps more deliberate and directed than merely turning a dial. A child requires some sophistication and some ability to read to retrieve material and thereby to use the Internet unattended."

Systems have been developed to help parents control the material that may be available on a home computer with Internet access. A system may either limit a computer's access to an approved list of sources that have been identified as containing no adult material, it may block designated inappropriate sites, or it may attempt to block messages containing identifiable objectionable features. "Although parental control software currently can screen for certain suggestive words or for known sexually explicit sites, it cannot now screen for sexually explicit images." [Nevertheless, the evidence indicates that "a reasonably effective method by which parents can prevent their children from accessing sexually explicit and other material which parents may believe is inappropriate for their children will soon be available]."

Age Verification

The problem of age verification differs for different uses of the Internet. The District Court categorically determined that there "is no effective way to determine the identity or the age of a user who is accessing material through e-mail, mail exploders, newsgroups or chat rooms." The Government offered no evidence that there was a reliable way to screen recipients and participants in such fora for age. Moreover, even if it were technologically feasible to block minors' access to newsgroups and chat rooms containing discussions of art, politics or other subjects that potentially elicit "indecent" or "patently offensive" contributions, it would not be possible to block their access to that material and "still allow them access to the remaining content, even if the overwhelming majority of that content was not indecent."

Technology exists by which an operator of a Web site may condition access on the verification of requested information such as a credit card number or an adult password. Credit card verification is only feasible, however, either in connection with a commercial transaction in which the card is used, or by payment to a verification agency. Using credit card possession as a surrogate for proof of age would impose costs on non-commercial Web sites that would require many of them to shut down. For that reason, at the time of the trial, credit card verification was "effectively unavailable to a substantial number of Internet content providers." Moreover, the imposition of such a requirement "would completely bar adults who do not have a credit card and lack the resources to obtain one from accessing any blocked material."

Commercial pornographic sites that charge their users for access have assigned them passwords as a method of age verification. The record does not contain any evidence concerning the reliability of these technologies. Even if passwords are effective for commercial purveyors of indecent material, the District Court found that an adult password requirement would impose significant burdens on noncommercial sites, both because they would discourage users from accessing their sites and because the cost of creating and maintaining such screening systems would be "beyond their reach." * * *

In sum, the District Court found:

"Even if credit card verification or adult password verification were implemented, the Government presented no testimony as to how such systems could ensure that the user of the password or credit card is in fact over 18. The burdens imposed by credit card verification and adult password verification systems make them effectively unavailable to a substantial number of Internet content providers." *Ibid.* (finding 107).

II

The Telecommunications Act of 1996, Pub.L. 104–104, 110 Stat. 56, was an unusually important legislative enactment. As stated on the first of its 103 pages, its primary purpose was to reduce regulation and encourage the rapid deployment of new telecommunications technologies. The major components of the statute have nothing to do with the Internet; they were designed to promote competition in the local telephone service market, the multichannel video market, and the market for over-the-air broadcasting. The Act includes seven Titles, six of which are the product of extensive committee hearings and the subject of discussion in Reports prepared by Committees of the Senate and the House of Representatives. By contrast, Title V—known as the "Communications Decency Act of 1996" (CDA)—contains provisions that were either added in executive committee after the hearings were concluded or as amendments offered during floor debate on the legislation. An amendment offered in the Senate was the source of the two statutory provisions challenged in this case. They are informally described as the "indecent transmission" provision and the "patently offensive display" provision

The first, 47 U.S.C.A. § 223(a) (Supp.1997), prohibits the knowing transmission of obscene or indecent messages to any recipient under 18 years of age. It provides in pertinent part:

"(a) Whoever—

"(1) in interstate or foreign communications—

. . . . .

"(B) by means of a telecommunications device knowingly—

"(i) makes, creates, or solicits, and

"(ii) initiates the transmission of,

"any comment, request, suggestion, proposal, image, or other communication which is obscene or indecent, knowing that the recipient of the communication is under 18 years of age, regardless of whether the maker of such communication placed the call or initiated the communication;

. . . . .

"(2) knowingly permits any telecommunications facility under his control to be used for any activity prohibited by paragraph (1) with the intent that it be used for such activity,

"shall be fined under Title 18, or imprisoned not more than two years, or both."

The second provision, § 223(d), prohibits the knowing sending or displaying of patently offensive messages in a manner that is available to a person under 18 years of age. It provides:

"(d) Whoever—

"(1) in interstate or foreign communications knowingly—

"(A) uses an interactive computer service to send to a specific person or persons under 18 years of age, or

"(B) uses any interactive computer service to display in a manner available to a person under 18 years of age,

"any comment, request, suggestion, proposal, image, or other communication that, in context, depicts or describes, in terms patently offensive as measured by contemporary community standards, sexual or excretory activities or organs, regardless of whether the user of such service placed the call or initiated the communication; or

"(2) knowingly permits any telecommunications facility under such person's control to be used for an activity prohibited by paragraph (1) with the intent that it be used for such activity,

"shall be fined under Title 18, or imprisoned not more than two years, or both."

The breadth of these prohibitions is qualified by two affirmative defenses. See § 223(e)(5). One covers those who take "good faith, reasonable, effective, and appropriate actions" to restrict access by minors to the prohibited communications. § 223(e)(5)(A). The other covers those who restrict access to covered material by requiring certain designated forms of age proof, such as a verified credit card or an adult identification number or code. § 223(e)(5)(B).

III

On February 8, 1996, immediately after the President signed the statute, 20 plaintiffs filed suit against the Attorney General of the United States and the Department of Justice challenging the constitutionality of §§ 223(a)(1) and 223(d). A week later, based on his conclusion that the term "indecent" was too vague to provide the basis for a criminal prosecution, District Judge Buckwalter entered a temporary restraining order against enforcement of § 223(a)(1)(B)(ii) insofar as it applies to indecent communications. A second suit was then filed by 27 additional plaintiffs, the two cases were consolidated, and a three-judge District Court was convened pursuant to § 561 of the Act. After an evidentiary hearing, that Court entered a preliminary injunction against enforcement of both of the challenged provisions. Each of the three judges wrote a separate opinion, but their judgment was unanimous. * * *

Judge Buckwalter concluded that the word "indecent" in § 223(a)(1)(B) and the terms "patently offensive" and "in context" in § 223(d)(1) were so vague that criminal enforcement of either section would violate the "fundamental constitutional principle" of "simple fairness," id., at 861, and the specific protections of the First and Fifth Amendments, id., at 858. He found no statutory basis for the Government's argument that the challenged provisions would be applied only to "pornographic" materials, noting that, unlike obscenity, "indecency has not been defined to exclude works of serious literary, artistic, political or scientific value." Id., at 863. Moreover, the Government's claim that the work must be considered patently offensive "in context" was itself vague because the relevant context might "refer to, among other things, the nature of the communication as a whole, the time of day it was conveyed, the medium used, the identity of the speaker, or whether or not it is accompanied by appropriate warnings." Id., at 864. He believed that the unique nature of the Internet aggravated the vagueness of the statute. Id., at 865, n. 9.

Judge Dalzell's review of "the special attributes of Internet communication" disclosed by the evidence convinced him that the First Amendment denies Congress the power to regulate the content of protected speech on the Internet. Id., at 867. His opinion explained at length why he believed the Act would abridge significant protected speech, particularly by noncommercial speakers, while "[p]erversely, commercial pornographers would remain relatively unaffected." Id., at 879. He construed our cases as requiring a "medium-specific" approach to the analysis of the regulation of mass communication, id., at 873, and concluded that the Internet—as "the most participatory form of mass speech yet developed," id., at 883—is entitled to "the highest protection from governmental intrusion," ibid.

The judgment of the District Court enjoins the Government from enforcing the prohibitions in § 223(a)(1)(B) insofar as they relate to "indecent" communications, but expressly preserves the Government's right to investigate and prosecute the obscenity or child pornography activities prohibited therein. The injunction against enforcement of §§ 223(d)(1) and (2) is unqualified because those provisions contain no separate reference to obscenity or child pornography.

The Government appealed under the Act's special review provisions, § 561, 110 Stat. 142–143, and we noted probable jurisdiction, see 519 U.S. ___ , 117 S.Ct. 554, 136 L.Ed.2d 436 (1996). In its appeal, the Government argues that the District Court erred in holding that the CDA violated both the First Amendment because it is overbroad and the Fifth Amendment because it is vague. While we discuss the vagueness of the CDA because of its relevance to the First Amendment overbreadth inquiry, we conclude that the judgment should be affirmed without reaching the Fifth Amendment issue. We begin our analysis by reviewing the principal authorities on which the Government relies. Then, after describing the overbreadth of the CDA, we consider the Government's specific contentions, including its submission that we save portions of the statute either by severance or by fashioning judicial limitations on the scope of its coverage.

IV

In arguing for reversal, the Government contends that the CDA is plainly constitutional under three of our prior decisions: (1) *Ginsberg v. New York*, 390 U.S. 629, 88 S.Ct. 1274, 20 L.Ed.2d 195 (1968); (2) *FCC v. Pacifica Foundation*, 438 U.S. 726, 98 S.Ct. 3026, 57 L.Ed.2d 1073 (1978); and (3) *Renton v. Playtime Theatres, Inc.*, 475 U.S. 41, 106 S.Ct. 925, 89 L.Ed.2d 29 (1986). A close look at these cases, however, raises— rather than relieves—doubts concerning the constitutionality of the CDA.

In *Ginsberg*, we upheld the constitutionality of a New York statute that prohibited selling to minors under 17 years of age material that was considered obscene as to them even if not obscene as to adults. We rejected the defendant's broad submission that "the scope of the constitutional freedom of expression secured to a citizen to read or see material concerned with sex cannot be made to depend on whether the citizen is an adult or a minor." 390 U.S., at 636, 88 S.Ct. at 1279. In rejecting that contention, we relied not only on the State's independent interest in the well-being of its youth, but also on our consistent recognition of the principle that "the parents' claim to authority in their own household to direct the rearing of their children is basic in the structure of our society."

In four important respects, the statute upheld in Ginsberg was narrower than the CDA. First, we noted in Ginsberg that "the prohibition against sales to minors does not bar parents who so desire from purchasing the magazines for their children." *Id.*, at 639, 88 S.Ct., at 1280. Under the CDA, by contrast, neither the parents' consent—nor even their participation—in the communication would avoid the application of the statute. Second, the New York statute applied only to commercial transactions, *id.*, at 647, 88 S.Ct., at 1284–1285, whereas the

CDA contains no such limitation. Third, the New York statute cabined its definition of material that is harmful to minors with the requirement that it be "utterly without redeeming social importance for minors." *Id.*, at 646, 88 S.Ct., at 1284. The CDA fails to provide us with any definition of the term "indecent" as used in § 223(a)(1) and, importantly, omits any requirement that the "patently offensive" material covered by § 223(d) lack serious literary, artistic, political, or scientific value. Fourth, the New York statute defined a minor as a person under the age of 17, whereas the CDA, in applying to all those under 18 years, includes an additional year of those nearest majority.

In *Pacifica*, we upheld a declaratory order of the Federal Communications Commission, holding that the broadcast of a recording of a 12–minute monologue entitled "Filthy Words" that had previously been delivered to a live audience "could have been the subject of administrative sanctions." 438 U.S., at 730, 98 S.Ct., at 3030 (internal quotations omitted). The Commission had found that the repetitive use of certain words referring to excretory or sexual activities or organs "in an afternoon broadcast when children are in the audience was patently offensive" and concluded that the monologue was indecent "as broadcast." *Id.*, at 735, 98 S.Ct., at 3033. The respondent did not quarrel with the finding that the afternoon broadcast was patently offensive, but contended that it was not "indecent" within the meaning of the relevant statutes because it contained no prurient appeal. After rejecting respondent's statutory arguments, we confronted its two constitutional arguments: (1) that the Commission's construction of its authority to ban indecent speech was so broad that its order had to be set aside even if the broadcast at issue was unprotected; and (2) that since the recording was not obscene, the First Amendment forbade any abridgement of the right to broadcast it on the radio.

In the portion of the lead opinion not joined by Justices Powell and Blackmun, the plurality stated that the First Amendment does not prohibit all governmental regulation that depends on the content of speech. *Id.*, at 742–743, 98 S.Ct., at 3036–3037. Accordingly, the availability of constitutional protection for a vulgar and offensive monologue that was not obscene depended on the context of the broadcast. *Id.*, at 744–748, 98 S.Ct., at 3037–3040. Relying on the premise that "of all forms of communication" broadcasting had received the most limited First Amendment protection, *id.*, at 748–749, 98 S.Ct., at 3039–3040, the Court concluded that the ease with which children may obtain access to broadcasts, "coupled with the concerns recognized in Ginsberg," justified special treatment of indecent broadcasting. *Id.*, at 749–750, 98 S.Ct., at 3040–3041.

As with the New York statute at issue in *Ginsberg*, there are significant differences between the order upheld in *Pacifica* and the CDA. First, the order in *Pacifica*, issued by an agency that had been regulating radio stations for decades, targeted a specific broadcast that represented a rather dramatic departure from traditional program content in order to designate when—rather than whether—it would be permissible to air such a program in that particular medium. The CDA's broad categorical prohibitions are not limited to particular times and are not dependent on any evaluation by an agency familiar with the unique characteristics of the Internet. Second, unlike the CDA, the Commission's declaratory order was not punitive; we expressly refused to decide whether the indecent broadcast "would justify a criminal prosecution." *Id.*, at 750, 98 S.Ct., at 3041. Finally, the Commission's order applied to a medium which as a matter of history had "received the most limited First Amendment protection," *id.*, at 748, 98 S.Ct., at 3040, in large part because warnings could not adequately protect the listener from unexpected program content. The Internet, however, has no comparable history. Moreover, the District Court found that the risk of encountering indecent material by accident is remote because a series of affirmative steps is required to access specific material.

In *Renton*, we upheld a zoning ordinance that kept adult movie theatres out of residential neighborhoods. The ordinance was aimed, not at the content of the films shown in the theaters, but rather at the "secondary effects"—such as crime and deteriorating property values— that these theaters fostered: " 'It is th[e] secondary effect which these zoning ordinances attempt to avoid, not the dissemination of "offensive" speech.' " 475 U.S., at 49, 106 S.Ct., at 930 (quoting *Young v. American Mini Theatres, Inc.*, 427 U.S. 50, 71, n. 34, 96 S.Ct. 2440, 2453, n. 34, 49 L.Ed.2d 310 (1976)). According to the Government, the CDA is constitutional because it constitutes a sort of "cyberzoning" on the Internet. But the CDA applies broadly to the entire universe of cyberspace. And the purpose of the CDA is to protect children from the primary effects of "indecent" and "patently offensive" speech, rather than any "secondary" effect of such speech. Thus, the CDA is a content-based blanket restriction on speech, and, as such, cannot be "properly analyzed as a form of time, place, and manner regulation." 475 U.S., at 46, 106 S.Ct., at 928. See also *Boos v. Barry*, 485 U.S. 312, 321, 108 S.Ct. 1157, 1163, 99 L.Ed.2d 333 (1988) ("Regulations that focus on the direct impact of speech on its audience" are not properly analyzed under *Renton*); *Forsyth County v. Nationalist Movement*, 505 U.S. 123, 134(1992) ("Listeners' reaction to speech is not a content-neutral basis for regulation").

These precedents, then, surely do not require us to uphold the CDA and are fully consistent with the application of the most stringent review of its provisions.

V

In *Southeastern Promotions, Ltd. v. Conrad*, 420 U.S. 546, 557, 95 S.Ct. 1239, 1245–1246, 43 L.Ed.2d 448 (1975), we observed that "[e]ach medium of expression ... may present its own problems." Thus, some of our cases have recognized special justifications for regulation of the broadcast media that are not applicable to other speakers, see *Red Lion Broadcasting Co. v. FCC*, 395 U.S. 367, 89 S.Ct. 1794, 23 L.Ed.2d 371 (1969); *FCC v. Pacifica Foundation*, 438 U.S. 726, 98 S.Ct. 3026, 57 L.Ed.2d 1073 (1978). In these cases, the Court relied on the history of extensive government regulation of the broadcast medium, see, *e.g., Red Lion*, 395 U.S., at 399–400, 89 S.Ct., at 1811–1812; the scarcity of available frequencies at its inception, see, *e.g., Turner Broadcasting System, Inc. v. FCC*, 512 U.S. 622, 637–638, 114 S.Ct. 2445, 2456–2457, 129 L.Ed.2d 497 (1994); and its "invasive" nature, see *Sable Communications of Cal., Inc. v. FCC*, 492 U.S. 115, 128 109 S.Ct. 2829, 2837–2838, 106 L.Ed. 2d 93 (1989).

Those factors are not present in cyberspace. Neither before nor after the enactment of the CDA have the vast democratic fora of the Internet been subject to the type of government supervision and regulation that has attended the broadcast industry. Moreover, the Internet is not as "invasive" as radio or television. The District Court specifically found that "[c]ommunications over the Internet do not 'invade' an individual's home or appear on one's computer screen unbidden. Users seldom encounter content 'by accident.' " 929 F.Supp., at 844 (finding 88). It also found that "[a]lmost all sexually explicit images are preceded by warnings as to the content," and cited testimony that " 'odds are slim' that a user would come across a sexually explicit sight by accident." *Ibid.*

We distinguished *Pacifica* in *Sable,* 492 U.S., at 128, 109 S.Ct. at 2837, on just this basis. In *Sable*, a company engaged in the business of offering sexually oriented prerecorded telephone messages (popularly known as "dial-a-porn") challenged the constitutionality of an amendment to the Communications Act that imposed a blanket prohibition on indecent as well as obscene interstate commercial telephone messages. We held that the statute was constitutional insofar as it applied to obscene messages but invalid as applied to indecent messages. In attempting to justify the complete ban and criminalization of indecent commercial telephone messages, the Government relied on Pacifica, arguing that the ban was necessary to prevent children from gaining access to such messages. We agreed that "there is a compelling interest in protecting the physical and psychological well-being of minors" which extended to shielding them from indecent messages that are not obscene by adult standards, 492 U.S., at 126, 109 S.Ct., at 2836–2837, but distinguished our "emphatically narrow holding" in *Pacifica* because it did not involve a complete ban and because it involved a different medium of communication, *id.*, at 127, 109 S.Ct., at 2837. We explained that "the dial-it medium requires the listener to take affirmative steps to receive the communication." *Id.*, at 127–128, 109 S.Ct., at 2837. "Placing a telephone call," we continued, "is not the same as turning on a radio and being taken by surprise by an indecent message." *Id.*, at 128, 109 S.Ct. at 2837.

Finally, unlike the conditions that prevailed when Congress first authorized regulation of the broadcast spectrum, the Internet can hardly be considered a "scarce" expressive commodity. It provides relatively unlimited, low-cost capacity for communication of all kinds. The Government estimates that "[a]s many as 40 million people use the Internet today, and that figure is expected to grow to 200 million by 1999." This dynamic, multifaceted category of communication includes not only traditional print and news services, but also audio, video, and still images, as well as interactive, real-time dialogue. Through the use of chat rooms, any person with a phone line can become a town crier with a voice that resonates farther than it could from any soapbox. Through the use of Web pages, mail exploders, and newsgroups, the same individual can become a pamphleteer. As the District Court found, "the content on the Internet is as diverse as human thought." 929 F.Supp., at 842 (finding 74). We agree with its conclusion that our cases provide no basis for qualifying the level of First Amendment scrutiny that should be applied to this medium.

VI

Regardless of whether the CDA is so vague that it violates the Fifth Amendment, the many ambiguities concerning the scope of its coverage render it problematic for purposes of the First Amendment. For instance, each of the two parts of the CDA uses a different linguistic form. The first uses the word "indecent," 47 U.S.C.A. § 223(a) (Supp.1997), while the second speaks of material that "in context, depicts or describes, in terms patently offensive as measured by contemporary community standards, sexual or excretory activities or organs," § 223(d). Given the absence of a definition of either term, this difference in language will provoke uncertainty among speakers about how the two standards relate to each other and just what they mean. Could a speaker confidently assume that a serious discussion about birth control practices, homosexuality, the First Amendment issues raised by the Appendix to our *Pacifica* opinion, or the consequences of prison rape would not violate the CDA? This uncertainty undermines the likelihood that the CDA has been carefully tailored to the congressional goal of protecting minors from potentially harmful materials.

The vagueness of the CDA is a matter of special concern for two reasons. First, the CDA is a content-based regulation of speech. The vagueness of such a regulation raises special First Amendment concerns because of its obvious chilling effect on free speech. See, *e.g., Gentile v. State Bar of Nev.*, 501 U.S. 1030, 1048–1051, 111 S.Ct. 2720, 2731–2733, 115 L.Ed.2d 888 (1991). Second, the CDA is a criminal statute. In addition to the opprobrium and stigma of a criminal conviction, the CDA threatens violators with penalties including up to two years in prison for each act of violation. The severity of criminal sanctions may well cause speakers to remain silent rather than communicate even arguably unlawful words, ideas, and images. See, *e.g., Dombrowski v. Pfister*, 380 U.S. 479, 494, 85 S.Ct. 1116, 1125, 14 L.Ed.2d 22 (1965). As a practical matter, this increased deterrent effect, coupled with the "risk of discriminatory enforcement" of vague regulations, poses greater First Amendment concerns than those implicated by the civil regulation reviewed in *Denver Area Ed. Telecommunications Consortium, Inc. v. FCC*, 518 U.S. 727, 116 S.Ct. 2374, 135 L.Ed.2d 888 (1996).

The Government argues that the statute is no more vague than the obscenity standard this Court established in *Miller v. California*, 413

U.S. 15, 93 S.Ct. 2607, 37 L.Ed.2d 419 (1973). But that is not so. In *Miller*, this Court reviewed a criminal conviction against a commercial vendor who mailed brochures containing pictures of sexually explicit activities to individuals who had not requested such materials. *Id.*, at 18, 93 s.Ct., at 2611–2612. Having struggled for some time to establish a definition of obscenity, we set forth in Miller the test for obscenity that controls to this day:

> "(a) whether the average person, applying contemporary community standards would find that the work, taken as a whole, appeals to the prurient interest; (b) whether the work depicts or describes, in a patently offensive way, sexual conduct specifically defined by the applicable state law; and (c) whether the work, taken as a whole, lacks serious literary, artistic, political, or scientific value." *Id.*, at 24, 93 S.Ct., at 2615 (internal quotation marks and citations omitted).

Because the CDA's "patently offensive" standard (and, we assume *arguendo*, its synonymous "indecent" standard) is one part of the three-prong *Miller* test, the Government reasons, it cannot be unconstitutionally vague.

The Government's assertion is incorrect as a matter of fact. The second prong of the *Miller* test—the purportedly analogous standard—contains a critical requirement that is omitted from the CDA: that the proscribed material be "specifically defined by the applicable state law." This requirement reduces the vagueness inherent in the open-ended term "patently offensive" as used in the CDA. Moreover, the *Miller* definition is limited to "sexual conduct," whereas the CDA extends also to include (1) "excretory activities" as well as (2) "organs" of both a sexual and excretory nature.

The Government's reasoning is also flawed. Just because a definition including three limitations is not vague, it does not follow that one of those limitations, standing by itself, is not vague. Each of *Miller*'s additional two prongs—(1) that, taken as a whole, the material appeal to the "prurient" interest, and (2) that it "lac[k] serious literary, artistic, political, or scientific value"—critically limits the uncertain sweep of the obscenity definition. The second requirement is particularly important because, unlike the "patently offensive" and "prurient interest" criteria, it is not judged by contemporary community standards. See *Pope v. Illinois*, 481 U.S. 497, 500, 107 S.Ct. 1918, 1920–1921, 95 L.Ed.2d 439 (1987). This "societal value" requirement, absent in the CDA, allows appellate courts to impose some limitations and regularity on the definition by setting, as a matter of law, a national floor for socially redeeming value. The Government's contention that courts will be able to give such legal limitations to the CDA's standards is belied by *Miller's* own rationale for having juries determine whether material is "patently offensive" according to community standards: that such questions are essentially ones of *fact*. * * *

VII

We are persuaded that the CDA lacks the precision that the First Amendment requires when a statute regulates the content of speech. In order to deny minors access to potentially harmful speech, the CDA effectively suppresses a large amount of speech that adults have a constitutional right to receive and to address to one another. That burden on adult speech is unacceptable if less restrictive alternatives would be at least as effective in achieving the legitimate purpose that the statute was enacted to serve.

In evaluating the free speech rights of adults, we have made it perfectly clear that "[s]exual expression which is indecent but not obscene is protected by the First Amendment." *Sable*, 492 U.S., at 126, 109 S.Ct., at 2836. See also *Carey v. Population Services Int'l*, 431 U.S. 678, 701, 97 S.Ct. 2010, 2024, 52 L.Ed.2d 675 (1977) ("[W]here obscenity is not involved, we have consistently held that the fact that protected speech may be offensive to some does not justify its suppression"). Indeed, *Pacifica* itself admonished that "the fact that society may find speech offensive is not a sufficient reason for suppressing it." 438 U.S., at 745, 98 S.Ct., at 3038.

It is true that we have repeatedly recognized the governmental interest in protecting children from harmful materials. See *Ginsberg*, 390 U.S., at 639, 88 S.Ct., at 1280; *Pacifica*, 438 U.S., at 749, 98 S.Ct., at 3040. But that interest does not justify an unnecessarily broad suppression of speech addressed to adults. As we have explained, the Government may not "reduc[e] the adult population . . . to . . . only what is fit for children." *Denver*, 518 U.S., at 759, 116 S.Ct., at 2393 (internal quotation marks omitted) (quoting *Sable*, 492 U.S., at 128). "[R]egardless of the strength of the government's interest" in protecting children, "[t]he level of discourse reaching a mailbox simply cannot be limited to that which would be suitable for a sandbox." *Bolger v. Youngs Drug Products Corp.*, 463 U.S. 60, 74–75, 103 S.Ct. 2875, 2884–2885, 77 L.Ed.2d 469 (1983).

The District Court was correct to conclude that the CDA effectively resembles the ban on "dial-a-porn" invalidated in *Sable*. 929 F.Supp., at 854. In *Sable*, 492 U.S., at 129, 109 S.Ct., at 2838, this Court rejected the argument that we should defer to the congressional judgment that nothing less than a total ban would be effective in preventing enterprising youngsters from gaining access to indecent communications. *Sable* thus made clear that the mere fact that a statutory regulation of speech was enacted for the important purpose of protecting children from exposure to sexually explicit material does not foreclose inquiry into its validity. As we pointed out last Term, that inquiry embodies an "overarching commitment" to make sure that Congress has designed its statute to accomplish its purpose "without imposing an unnecessarily great restriction on speech." *Denver*, 518 U.S., at 741, 116 S.Ct., at 2385.

In arguing that the CDA does not so diminish adult communication, the Government relies on the incorrect factual premise that prohibiting a transmission whenever it is known that one of its recipients is a minor would not interfere with adult-to-adult communication. The findings of the District Court make clear that this premise is untenable. Given the size of the potential audience for most messages, in the absence of a viable age verification process, the sender must be charged with knowing that one or more minors will likely view it. Knowledge that, for instance, one or more members of a 100–person chat group will be minor—and therefore that it would be a crime to send the group an indecent message—would surely burden communication among adults.

The District Court found that at the time of trial existing technology did not include any effective method for a sender to prevent minors from obtaining access to its communications on the Internet without also denying access to adults. The Court found no effective way to determine the age of a user who is accessing material through e-mail, mail exploders, newsgroups, or chat rooms. 929 F.Supp., at 845 (findings 90–94). As a practical matter, the Court also found that it would be prohibitively expensive for noncommercial—as well as some commercial—speakers who have Web sites to verify that their users are adults. *Id.*, at 845–848 (findings 95–116). These limitations must inevitably curtail a significant amount of adult communication on the Internet. By contrast, the District Court found that "[d]espite its limitations, currently available user-based software suggests that a reasonably effective method by which *parents* can prevent their children from accessing sexually explicit and other material which parents may believe is inappropriate for their children will soon be widely available." *Id.*, at 842 (finding 73) (emphases added).

The breadth of the CDA's coverage is wholly unprecedented. Unlike the regulations upheld in *Ginsberg* and *Pacifica*, the scope of the CDA is not limited to commercial speech or commercial entities. Its open-ended prohibitions embrace all nonprofit entities and individuals posting indecent messages or displaying them on their own computers in the presence of minors. The general, undefined terms "indecent" and "patently offensive" cover large amounts of nonpornographic material with serious educational or other value. Moreover, the "community standards" criterion as applied to the Internet means that any communication available to a nation-wide audience will be judged by the standards of the community most likely to be offended by the message. The regulated subject matter includes any of the seven "dirty words" used in the *Pacifica* monologue, the use of which the Government's expert acknowledged could constitute a felony. It may also extend to discussions about prison rape or safe sexual practices, artistic images that include nude subjects, and arguably the card catalogue of the Carnegie Library.

For the purposes of our decision, we need neither accept nor reject the Government's submission that the First Amendment does not forbid a blanket prohibition on all "indecent" and "patently offensive" messages communicated to a 17–year old—no matter how much value the message may contain and regardless of parental approval. It is at least clear that the strength of the Government's interest in protecting minors is not equally strong throughout the coverage of this broad statute. Under the CDA, a parent allowing her 17–year-old to use the family computer to obtain information on the Internet that she, in her parental judgment, deems appropriate could face a lengthy prison term. See 47 U.S.C.A. § 223(a)(2) (Supp.1997). Similarly, a parent who sent his 17–year-old college freshman information on birth control via e-mail could be incarcerated even though neither he, his child, nor anyone in their home community, found the material "indecent" or "patently offensive," if the college town's community thought otherwise.

The breadth of this content-based restriction of speech imposes an especially heavy burden on the Government to explain why a less restrictive provision would not be as effective as the CDA. It has not done so. The arguments in this Court have referred to possible alternatives such as requiring that indecent material be "tagged" in a way that facilitates parental control of material coming into their homes, making exceptions for messages with artistic or educational value, providing some tolerance for parental choice, and regulating some portions of the Internet—such as commercial web sites—differently than others, such as chat rooms. Particularly in the light of the absence of any detailed findings by the Congress, or even hearings addressing the special problems of the CDA, we are persuaded that the CDA is not narrowly tailored if that requirement has any meaning at all.

VIII

In an attempt to curtail the CDA's facial overbreadth, the Government advances three additional arguments for sustaining the Act's affirmative prohibitions: (1) that the CDA is constitutional because it leaves open ample "alternative channels" of communication; (2) that the plain meaning of the Act's "knowledge" and "specific person" requirement significantly restricts its permissible applications; and (3) that the Act's prohibitions are "almost always" limited to material lacking redeeming social value.

The Government first contends that, even though the CDA effectively censors discourse on many of the Internet's modalities—such as chat groups, newsgroups, and mail exploders—it is nonetheless constitutional because it provides a "reasonable opportunity" for speakers to engage in the restricted speech on the World Wide Web. Brief for Appellants 39. This argument is unpersuasive because the CDA regulates speech on the basis of its content. A "time, place, and manner" analysis is therefore inapplicable. See *Consolidated Edison Co. of N.Y. v. Public Serv. Comm'n of N.Y.*, 447 U.S. 530, 536, 100 S.Ct. 2326, 2332–2333, 65 L.Ed.2d 319 (1980). It is thus immaterial whether such speech would be feasible on the Web (which, as the Government's own expert acknowledged, would cost up to $10,000 if the speaker's interests were not accommodated by an existing Web site, not including costs for database management and age verification). The Government's position is equivalent to arguing that a statute could ban leaflets on certain subjects as long as individuals are free to publish books. In invalidating a number of laws that banned leafletting on the streets regardless of their content—we explained that "one is not to have the exercise of his liberty of expression in appropriate places abridged on the plea that it may be exercised in some other place." *Schneider v. State of N.J. (Town of Irvington)*, 308 U.S. 147, 163, 60 S.Ct. 146, 151–152, 84 L.Ed. 155 (1939).

The Government also asserts that the "knowledge" requirement of both §§ 223(a) and (d), especially when coupled with the "specific child" element found in § 223(d), saves the CDA from overbreadth. Because both sections prohibit the dissemination of indecent messages only to persons known to be under 18, the Government argues, it does not require transmitters to "refrain from communicating indecent material to adults; they need only refrain from disseminating such materials to persons they know to be under 18." Brief for Appellants 24. This argument ignores the fact that most Internet fora—including chat rooms, newsgroups, mail exploders, and the Web—are open to all comers. The Government's assertion that the knowledge requirement somehow protects the communications of adults is therefore untenable. Even the strongest reading of the "specific person" requirement of § 223(d) cannot save the statute. It would confer broad powers of censorship, in the form of a "heckler's veto," upon any opponent of indecent speech who might simply log on and inform the would-be discoursers that his 17–year-old child—a "specific person ... under 18 years of age," 47 U.S.C. § 223(d)(1)(A) (Supp.1997)—would be present.

Finally, we find no textual support for the Government's submission that material having scientific, educational, or other redeeming social value will necessarily fall outside the CDA's "patently offensive" and "indecent" prohibitions. See also n. 37, supra.

IX

The Government's three remaining arguments focus on the defenses provided in § 223(e)(5). First, relying on the "good faith, reasonable, effective, and appropriate actions" provision, the Government suggests that "tagging" provides a defense that saves the constitutionality of the Act. The suggestion assumes that transmitters may encode their indecent communications in a way that would indicate their contents, thus permitting recipients to block their reception with appropriate software. It is the requirement that the good faith action must be "effective" that makes this defense illusory. The Government recognizes that its proposed screening software does not currently exist. Even if it did, there is no way to know whether a potential recipient will actually block the encoded material. Without the impossible knowledge that every guardian in America is screening for the "tag," the transmitter could not reasonably rely on its action to be "effective."

For its second and third arguments concerning defenses—which we can consider together—the Government relies on the latter half of § 223(e)(5), which applies when the transmitter has restricted access by requiring use of a verified credit card or adult identification. Such verification is not only technologically available but actually is used by commercial providers of sexually explicit material. These providers, therefore, would be protected by the defense. Under the findings of the District Court, however, it is not economically feasible for most noncommercial speakers to employ such verification. Accordingly, this defense would not significantly narrow the statute's burden on noncommercial speech. Even with respect to the commercial pornographers that would be protected by the defense, the Government failed to adduce any evidence that these verification techniques actually preclude minors from posing as adults. Given that the risk of criminal sanctions "hovers over each content provider, like the proverbial sword of Damocles," the District Court correctly refused to rely on unproven future technology to save the statute. The Government thus failed to prove that the proffered defense would significantly reduce the heavy burden on adult speech produced by the prohibition on offensive displays.

We agree with the District Court's conclusion that the CDA places an unacceptably heavy burden on protected speech, and that the defenses do not constitute the sort of "narrow tailoring" that will save an otherwise patently invalid unconstitutional provision. In *Sable*, 492 U.S., at 127, 109 S.Ct., at 2837, we remarked that the speech restriction at issue there amounted to " 'burn[ing] the house to roast the pig.' " The CDA, casting a far darker shadow over free speech, threatens to torch a large segment of the Internet community.

X

At oral argument, the Government relied heavily on its ultimate fallback position: If this Court should conclude that the CDA is insufficiently tailored, it urged, we should save the statute's constitutionality by honoring the severability clause, see 47 U.S.C. § 608, and construing nonseverable terms narrowly. In only one respect is this argument acceptable.

A severability clause requires textual provisions that can be severed. We will follow § 608's guidance by leaving constitutional textual elements of the statute intact in the one place where they are, in fact, severable. The "indecency" provision, 47 U.S.C.A. § 223(a) (Supp.1997), applies to "any comment, request, suggestion, proposal, image, or other communication which is obscene or indecent." (Emphasis added.) Appellees do not challenge the application of the statute to obscene speech, which, they acknowledge, can be banned totally because it enjoys no First Amendment protection. See *Miller*, 413 U.S., at 18, 93 S.Ct., at 2611–2612. As set forth by the statute, the restriction of "obscene" material enjoys a textual manifestation separate from that for "indecent" material, which we have held unconstitutional. Therefore, we will sever the term "or indecent" from the statute, leaving the rest of § 223(a) standing. In no other respect, however, can § 223(a) or § 223(d) be saved by such a textual surgery.

The Government also draws on an additional, less traditional aspect of the CDA's severability clause, 47 U.S.C., § 608, which asks any reviewing court that holds the statute facially unconstitutional not to invalidate the CDA in application to "other persons or circumstances" that might be constitutionally permissible. It further invokes this Court's admonition that, absent "countervailing considerations," a statute should "be declared invalid to the extent it reaches too far, but otherwise left intact." *Brockett v. Spokane Arcades, Inc.*, 472 U.S. 491, 503–504, 105 S.Ct. 2794, 2801–2802, 86 L.Ed.2d 394 (1985). There are two flaws in this argument.

First, the statute that grants our jurisdiction for this expedited review, 47 U.S.C.A. § 561 (Supp.1997), limits that jurisdictional grant to actions challenging the CDA "on its face." Consistent with § 561, the plaintiffs who brought this suit and the three-judge panel that decided it treated it as a facial challenge. We have no authority, in this particular posture, to convert this litigation into an "as-applied" challenge. Nor, given the vast array of plaintiffs, the range of their expressive activities, and the vagueness of the statute, would it be practicable to limit our holding to a judicially defined set of specific applications.

Second, one of the "countervailing considerations" mentioned in Brockett is present here. In considering a facial challenge, this Court may impose a limiting construction on a statute only if it is "readily susceptible" to such a construction. *Virginia v. American Booksellers Assn., Inc.*, 484 U.S. 383, 397, 108 S.Ct. 636, 645, 98 L.Ed.2d 782 (1988). See also *Erznoznik v. Jacksonville*, 422 U.S. 205, 216, 95 S.Ct. 2268, 2276, 45 L.Ed.2d 125 (1975) ("readily subject" to narrowing construction). The open-ended character of the CDA provides no guidance what ever for limiting its coverage.

This case is therefore unlike those in which we have construed a statute narrowly because the text or other source of congressional intent identified a clear line that this Court could draw. *Cf., e.g., Brockett*, 472 U.S., at 504–505, 105 S.Ct., at 2802 (invalidating obscenity statute only to the extent that word "lust" was actually or effectively excised from statute); *United States v. Grace*, 461 U.S. 171, 180–183, 103 S.Ct. 1702, 1708–1710, 75 L.Ed.2d 736 (1983) (invalidating federal statute banning expressive displays only insofar as it extended to public sidewalks when clear line could be drawn between sidewalks and other grounds that comported with congressional purpose of protecting the building, grounds, and people therein). Rather, our decision in *United States v. National Treasury Employees Union*, 513 U.S. 454, 479 (1995), is applicable. In that case, we declined to "dra[w] one or more lines between categories of speech covered by an overly broad statute, when Congress has sent inconsistent signals as to where the new line or lines should be drawn" because doing so "involves a far more serious invasion of the legislative domain." This Court "will not rewrite a . . . law to conform it to constitutional requirements." *American Booksellers*, 484 U.S., at 397, 108 S.Ct., at 645.

XI

In this Court, though not in the District Court, the Government asserts that—in addition to its interest in protecting children—its "[e]qually significant" interest in fostering the growth of the Internet provides an independent basis for upholding the constitutionality of the CDA. Brief for Appellants 19. The Government apparently assumes that the unregulated availability of "indecent" and "patently offensive" material on the Internet is driving countless citizens away from the medium because of the risk of exposing themselves or their children to harmful material.

We find this argument singularly unpersuasive. The dramatic expansion of this new marketplace of ideas contradicts the factual basis of this contention. The record demonstrates that the growth of the Internet has been and continues to be phenomenal. As a matter of constitutional tradition, in the absence of evidence to the contrary, we presume that governmental regulation of the content of speech is more likely to interfere with the free exchange of ideas than to encourage it. The interest in encouraging freedom of expression in a democratic society outweighs any theoretical but unproven benefit of censorship.

For the foregoing reasons, the judgment of the district court is affirmed.

It is so ordered.

Notes and Comments

1. James Barrows was convicted under New York Penal Law § 235.22 for disseminating indecent material to minors over the Internet. An intermediate appellate court overturned the conviction on the grounds that the law was unconstitutionally vague and overbroad. *People v. Barrows*, 177 Misc.2d 712, 677 N.Y.S.2d 672 (1998). In making this determination, the appellate court relied upon the analysis in *Reno v. American Civil Liberties Union*. The appellate court found that upholding the statute would result in chilling the free speech of adults. In the absence of a clear moral standing as to what is and is not appropriate for children, the statute could not be upheld.

2. A year later in *People v. Foley*, 692 N.Y.S.2d 248 (1999), a different New York appellate court upheld the same statute that was struck down in *Barrows*. This court held that generally the statute would accomplish the Legislature's goal in protecting children from cybersex abuse. While the court recognized that there could possibly exist instances in which the statute could be applied in a manner which would "render it unconstitutionally overbroad," these situations would be few and could be cured by a case-by-case analysis. *Cyberspace, Communications, Inc. v. Engler*, 55 F. Supp.2d 737 (1999) held that for Michigan to regulate the dissemination of material it must establish that the statute has met the requirement for content-based restrictions on speech.

3. Legislation to protect children on the Internet is politically popular. No sooner is one law struck down than Congress enacts another law and civil libertarians bring suit against to stop enforcement. Therefore there is likely to be continued litigation over the Constitutionality of Internet censorship laws.

AMERICAN CIVIL LIBERTIES UNION v. RENO

United States Court of Appeals, Third Circuit, 2000.
217 F.3d 162.

GARTH, CIRCUIT JUDGE:

This appeal "presents a conflict between one of society's most cherished rights—freedom of expression—and one of the government's most profound obligations—the protection of minors." *American Booksellers v. Webb*, 919 F.2d 1493, 1495 (11th Cir.1990). The government challenges the District Court's issuance of a preliminary injunction which prevents the enforcement of the Child Online Protection Act, Pub.L. No. 105–277, 112 Stat. 2681 (1998) (codified at 47 U.S.C. § 231) ("COPA"), enacted in October of 1998. At issue is COPA's constitutionality, a statute designed to protect minors from "harmful material" measured by "contemporary community standards" knowingly posted on the World Wide Web ("Web") for commercial purposes.

We will affirm the District Court's grant of a preliminary injunction because we are confident that the ACLU's attack on COPA's constitutionality is likely to succeed on the merits. Because material posted on the Web is accessible by all Internet users worldwide, and because current technology does not permit a Web publisher to restrict access to its site based on the geographic locale of each particular Internet user, COPA essentially requires that every Web publisher subject to the statute abide by the most restrictive and conservative state's community standards in order to avoid criminal liability. Thus, because the standard by which COPA gauges whether material is "harmful to minors" is based on identifying "contemporary community standards" the inability of Web publishers to restrict access to their Web sites based on the geographic locale of the site visitor, in and of itself, imposes an impermissible burden on constitutionally protected First Amendment speech.

In affirming the District Court, we are forced to recognize that, at present, due to technological limitations, there may be no other means by which harmful material on the Web may be constitutionally restricted, although, in light of rapidly developing technological advances, what may now be impossible to regulate constitutionally may, in the not-too-distant future, become feasible.

I. BACKGROUND

COPA was enacted into law on October 21, 1998. Commercial Web publishers subject to the statute that distribute material that is harmful to minors are required under COPA to ensure that minors do not access the harmful material on their Web site. COPA is Congress's second attempt to regulate the dissemination to minors of indecent material on the Web/Internet. The Supreme Court had earlier, on First Amendment grounds, struck down Congress's first endeavor, the Communications Decency Act, ("CDA") which it passed as part of the Telecommunications Act of 1996.[1] See *Reno v. ACLU*, 521 U.S. 844, 117 S.Ct. 2329, 138 L.Ed.2d 874 (1997) ("Reno II"). To best understand the current challenge to COPA, it is necessary for us to briefly examine the CDA.

A. CDA

The CDA prohibited Internet users from using the Internet to communicate material that, under contemporary community standards, would be deemed patently offensive to minors under the age of eighteen. See *Reno II*, 521 U.S. at 859–60. In so restricting Internet users, the CDA provided two affirmative defenses to prosecution; (1) the use of a credit card or other age verification system, and (2) any good faith effort to restrict access by minors. *See id.* at 860. In holding that the CDA violated the First Amendment, the Supreme Court explained that without defining key terms the statute was unconstitutionally vague. Moreover, the Court noted that the breadth of the CDA was "wholly unprecedented" in that, for example, it was "not limited to commercial speech or commercial entities ... [but rather] [i]ts open-ended prohibitions embrace all nonprofit entities and individuals posting indecent messages or displaying them on their own computers." *Id.* at 877.

Further, the Court explained that, as applied to the Internet, a community standards criterion would effectively mean that because all Internet communication is made available to a worldwide audience, the content of the conveyed message will be judged by the standards of the community most likely to be offended by the content. See *id.* at 877–78. Finally, with respect to the affirmative defenses authorized by the CDA, the Court concluded that such defenses would not be economically feasible for most noncommercial Web publishers, and that even with respect to commercial publishers, the technology had yet to be proven effective in shielding minors from harmful material. See *id.* at 881. As a result, the Court held that the CDA was not tailored so narrowly as to achieve the government's compelling interest in protecting minors, and that it lacked the precision that the First Amendment requires when a statute regulates the content of speech. See *id.* at 874. See also *United States v. Playboy Entertainment Group, Inc.*, ___ U.S. ___ , 120 S.Ct. 1878, ___ L.Ed.2d ___ , 2000 WL 646196 (U.S. May 22, 2000).

B. COPA

COPA, the present statute, attempts to "address[ ] the specific concerns raised by the Supreme Court" in invalidating the CDA. H.R. Rep. No. 105–775 at 12 (1998); See S.R. Rep. No. 105–225, at 2 (1998). COPA prohibits an individual or entity from:

> knowingly and with knowledge of the character of the material, in interstate or foreign commerce by means of the World Wide Web,

---

1. For ease of reference the various applicable cases will be referred to as follows: *ACLU v. Reno*, 929 F.Supp. 824 (E.D.Pa. 1996), hereinafter "*Reno I*" (addressing CDA); *Reno v. ACLU*, 521 U.S. 844, 117 S.Ct. 2329, 138 L.Ed.2d 874 (1997), hereinafter "*Reno II*" (striking down the CDA as unconstitutional); *ACLU v. Reno*, 31 F.Supp.2d 473 (E.D.Pa.1999), hereinafter "*Reno III*" (case currently on appeal addressing constitutionality of COPA).

mak[ing] any communication for *commercial* purposes that is available to any minor and that includes any material that is harmful to minors.

47 U.S.C. § 231(a)(1) (emphasis added). As part of its attempt to cure the constitutional defects found in the CDA, Congress sought to define most of COPA's key terms. COPA attempts, for example, to restrict its scope to material on the Web rather than on the Internet as a whole; to target only those Web communications made for "commercial purposes"; and to limit its scope to only that material deemed "harmful to minors."

Under COPA, whether material published on the Web is "harmful to minors" is governed by a three-part test, *each* of which must be found before liability can attach:

> (A) the average person, applying *contemporary community standards*, would find, taking the material as a whole and with respect to minors, is designed to appeal to, or is designed to pander to, the prurient interest;

> (B) depicts, describes, or represents, in a manner patently offensive with respect to minors, an actual or simulated sexual act or sexual contact, an actual or simulated normal or perverted sexual act, or a lewd exhibition of the genitals or post-pubescent female breast; and

> (C) taken as a whole, lacks serious, literary, artistic, political, or scientific value for minors.

47 U.S.C. § 231(e)(6) (emphasis added). The parties conceded at oral argument that this "contemporary community standards" test applies to those communities within the United States, and not to foreign communities. Therefore, the more liberal community standards of Amsterdam or the more restrictive community standards of Tehran would not impact upon the analysis of whether material is "harmful to minors" under COPA.

COPA also provides Web publishers subject to the statute with affirmative defenses. If a Web publisher "has restricted access by minors to material that is harmful to minors" through the use of a "credit card, debit account, adult access code, or adult personal identification number . . . a digital certificate that verifies age . . . or by any other reasonable measures that are feasible under available technology," then no liability will attach to the Web publisher even if a minor should nevertheless gain access to restricted material under COPA. 47 U.S.C. § 231(c)(1). COPA violators face both criminal (maximum fines of $50,000 and a maximum prison term of six months, or both) and civil (fines of up to $50,000 for each day of violation) penalties.

C.   Overview of the Internet and the World Wide Web

* * *

It is essential to note that under current technology, Web publishers cannot "prevent [their site's] content from entering any geographic community." *Reno* III, 31 F.Supp.2d at 484. As such, Web publishers cannot prevent Internet users in certain geographic locales from accessing their site; and in fact the Web publisher will not even know the geographic location of visitors to its site. See *American Libraries*, 969 F.Supp. at 171. Similarly, a Web publisher cannot modify the content of its site so as to restrict different geographic communities to access of only certain portions of their site. Thus, once published on the Web, existing technology does not permit the published material to be restricted to particular states or jurisdictions. * * *

II. ANALYSIS

* * *

A. *Reasonable probability of success on the merits*

We begin our analysis by considering what, for this case, is the most significant prong of the preliminary injunction test—whether the ACLU met its burden of establishing a reasonable probability of succeeding on the merits in proving that COPA trenches upon the First Amendment to the United States Constitution. Initially, we note that the District Court correctly determined that as a content-based restriction on speech, COPA is "both presumptively invalid and subject to strict scrutiny analysis." See *Reno* III, 31 F.Supp.2d at 493. As in all areas of constitutional strict scrutiny jurisprudence, the government must establish that the challenged statute is narrowly tailored to meet a compelling state interest, and that it seeks to protect its interest in a manner that is the least restrictive of protected speech. See, *e.g.*, *Schaumburg v. Citizens for a Better Environment*, 444 U.S. 620, 637, 100 S.Ct. 826, 63 L.Ed.2d 73 (1980); *Sable Comm of Calif. v. FCC*, 492 U.S. 115, 126 (1989). These principles have been emphasized again in the Supreme Court's most recent opinion, *United States v. Playboy Entertainment Group, Inc.*, __ U.S. __ , 120 S.Ct. 1878, __ L.Ed.2d __ , 2000 WL 646196 (U.S. May 22, 2000), where the Court, concerned with the "bleeding" of cable transmissions, held § 505 of the Telecommunications Act of 1996 unconstitutional as violative of the First Amendment.

It is undisputed that the government has a compelling interest in protecting children from material that is harmful to them, even if not obscene by adult standards. See *Reno III*, 31 F.Supp.2d at 495 (citing *Sable*, 492 U.S. at 126 (1989); *Ginsberg v. New York*, 390 U.S. 629, 639–40, 88 S.Ct. 1274, 20 L.Ed.2d 195 (1968)). At issue is whether, in achieving this compelling objective, Congress has articulated a constitutionally permissible means to achieve its objective without curtailing the protected free speech rights of adults. See Reno III, 31 F.Supp.2d at 492 (citing Sable, 492 U.S. at 127; Butler v. Michigan, 352 U.S. 380, 383, 77 S.Ct. 524, 1 L.Ed.2d 412 (1957)). As we have observed, the District Court found that it had not—holding that COPA was not likely to succeed in surviving strict scrutiny analysis.

We base our particular determination of COPA's likely unconstitutionality, however, on COPA's reliance on "contemporary community standards" in the context of the electronic medium of the Web to identify material that is harmful to minors. The overbreadth of COPA's definition of "harmful to minors" applying a "contemporary community standards" clause—although virtually ignored by the parties and the amicus in their respective briefs but raised by us at oral argument—so concerns us that we are persuaded that this aspect of COPA, without reference to its other provisions, must lead inexorably to a holding of a likelihood of unconstitutionality of the entire COPA statute.

Hence we base our opinion entirely on the basis of the likely unconstitutionality of this clause, even though the District Court relied on numerous other grounds.

As previously noted, in passing COPA, Congress attempted to resolve all of the problems raised by the Supreme Court in striking down the CDA as unconstitutional. One concern noted by the Supreme Court was that, as a part of the wholly unprecedented broad coverage of the CDA, "the 'community standards' criterion as applied to the Internet means that any communication available to a nationwide audience will be judged by the standards of the community most likely to be offended by the message." *Reno II*, 521 U.S. at 877–78. We are not persuaded that the Supreme Court's concern with respect to the "community standards" criterion has been sufficiently remedied by Congress in COPA.

Previously, in addressing the mailing of unsolicited sexually explicit material in violation of a California obscenity statute, the Supreme Court held that the fact-finder must determine whether " 'the average person, applying contemporary community standards' would find the work taken as a whole, [to appeal] to the prurient interest." *Miller v. California*, 413 U.S. 15, 24, 93 S.Ct. 2607, 37 L.Ed.2d 419 (1973) (quoting *Kois v. Wisconsin*, 408 U.S. 229, 230, 92 S.Ct. 2245, 33 L.Ed.2d 312 (1972)). In response to the Supreme Court's criticism of the CDA, Congress incorporated into COPA this *Miller* test, explaining that in so doing COPA now "conforms to the standards identified in *Ginsberg*, as modified by the Supreme Court in *Miller v. California*, 413 U.S. 15, 93 S.Ct. 2607, 37 L.Ed.2d 419 (1973)." H.R. Rep. No. 105–775 at 13 (1998); 47 U.S.C. S 231(e)(6)(A). Even in so doing, Congress remained cognizant of the fact that "the application of community standards in the context of the Web is controversial." H.R. Rep. No. 107–775, at 28. Nevertheless, in defending the constitutionality of COPA's use of the *Miller* test, the government insists that "there is nothing dispositive about the fact that [in COPA] commercial distribution of such [harmful] materials occurs through an online, rather than a brick and mortar outlet." See Reply Brief at 18 n. 3.

Despite the government's assertion, "[e]ach medium of expression 'must be assessed for First Amendment purposes by standards suited to it, for each may present its own problems.' " *Reno III*, 31 F.Supp.2d at 495 (quoting *Southeastern Promotions, Ltd. v. Conrad*, 420 U.S. 546,

557, 95 S.Ct. 1239, 43 L.Ed.2d 448 (1975)). See also *United States v. Playboy Entertainment Group, Inc.*, ___ U.S. ___, at ___, 120 S.Ct. 1878, ___ L.Ed.2d ___ , at ___ , 2000 WL 646196, at *8 (U.S. May 22, 2000). In considering "the unique factors that affect communication in the new and technology-laden medium of the Web," we are convinced that there are crucial differences between a "brick and mortar outlet" and the online Web that dramatically affect a First Amendment analysis. *Id.*

Unlike a "brick and mortar outlet" with a specific geographic locale, and unlike the voluntary physical mailing of material from one geographic location to another, as in Miller, the uncontroverted facts indicate that the Web is not geographically constrained. See *Reno III*, 31 F.Supp.2d at 482–92; American Libraries, 969 F.Supp. at 169 ("geography, however, is a virtually meaningless construct on the Internet"). Indeed, and of extreme significance, is the fact, as found by the District Court, that Web publishers are without any means to limit access to their sites based on the geographic location of particular Internet users. As soon as information is published on a Web site, it is accessible to all other Web visitors. See *American Libraries*, 969 F.Supp. at 166; Reno III, 31 F.Supp.2d at 483. Current technology prevents Web publishers from circumventing particular jurisdictions or limiting their site's content "from entering any [specific] geographic community." *Reno* III, 31 F.Supp.2d at 484. This key difference necessarily affects our analysis in attempting to define what contemporary community standards should or could mean in a medium without geographic boundaries.

In expressing its concern over the wholly unprecedented broad coverage of the CDA's scope, the Supreme Court has already noted that because of the peculiar geography-free nature of cyberspace, a "community standards" test would essentially require every Web communication to abide by the most restrictive community's standards. See *Reno II*, 521 U.S. at 877–78. Similarly, to avoid liability under COPA, affected Web publishers would either need to severely censor their publications or implement an age or credit card verification system whereby any material that might be deemed harmful by the most puritan of communities in any state is shielded behind such a verification system. Shielding such vast amounts of material behind verification systems would prevent access to protected material by any adult seventeen or over without the necessary age verification credentials. Moreover, it would completely bar access to those materials to all minors under seventeen—even if the material would not otherwise have been deemed "harmful" to them in their respective geographic communities.

The government argues that subjecting Web publishers to varying community standards is not constitutionally problematic or, for that matter, unusual. The government notes that there are numerous cases in which the courts have already subjected the same conduct to varying community standards, depending on the community in which the conduct occurred. For example, the Supreme Court has stated that "distributors of allegedly obscene materials may be subjected to varying community standards in the various federal judicial districts into which they transmit the material [but that] does not render a federal statute unconstitutional because of the failure of the application of uniform national standards of obscenity." *Hamling v. United States*, 418 U.S. 87, 106, 94 S.Ct. 2887, 41 L.Ed.2d 590 (1974). Similarly, the government cites to the "dial-a-porn" cases in which the Supreme Court has held that even if the "audience is comprised of different communities with different local standards" the company providing the obscene material "ultimately bears the burden of complying with the prohibition on obscene messages" under each community's respective standard. *Sable Comm. of California v. F.C.C.*, 492 U.S. 115, 125–26, 109 S.Ct. 2829, 106 L.Ed.2d 93 (1989).

These cases, however, are easily distinguished from the present case. In each of those cases, the defendants had the ability to control the distribution of controversial material with respect to the geographic communities into which they released it. Therefore, the defendants could limit their exposure to liability by avoiding those communities with particularly restrictive standards, while continuing to provide the controversial material in more liberal-minded communities. For example, the pornographer in *Hamling* could have chosen not to mail unsolicited sexually explicit material to certain communities while continuing to mail them to others. Similarly, the telephone pornographers ("dial-a-porn") in Sable could have screened their incoming calls and then only accepted a call if its point of origination was from a community with standards of decency that were not offended by the content of their pornographic telephone messages.

By contrast, Web publishers have no such comparable control. Web publishers cannot restrict access to their site based on the geographic locale of the Internet user visiting their site. In fact, "an Internet user cannot foreclose access to . . . work from certain states or send differing versions of . . . communication[s] to different jurisdictions . . . The Internet user has no ability to bypass any particular state." *American Libraries Ass'n v. Pataki*, 969 F.Supp. 160 (S.D.N.Y.1997). As a result, unlike telephone or postal mail pornographers, Web publishers of material that may be harmful to minors must "comply with the regulation imposed by the State with the most stringent standard or [entirely] forego Internet communication of the message that might or might not subject [the publisher] to prosecution." *Id.* * * *

III. Conclusion

Due to current technological limitations, COPA—Congress' laudatory attempt to achieve its compelling objective of protecting minors from harmful material on the World Wide Web—is more likely than not to be found unconstitutional as overbroad on the merits. Because the ACLU has met its burden in establishing all four of the necessary elements to obtain a preliminary injunction, and the District Court properly exercised its discretion in issuing the preliminary injunction, we will affirm the District Court's order.

In so affirming, we approvingly reiterate the sentiments aptly noted by the District Court: "sometimes we must make decisions that we do not like. We make them because they are right, right in the sense that the law and the Constitution, as we see them, compel the result." *Reno III*, 31 F.Supp.2d at 498. We also express our confidence and firm conviction that developing technology will soon render the "community standards" challenge moot, thereby making congressional regulation to protect minors from harmful material on the Web constitutionally practicable. Indeed, in the context of dealing with technology to prevent the "bleeding" of cable transmissions, the Supreme Court in *United States v. Playboy Entertainment Group, Inc.*, __ U.S. __ at __ , 120 S.Ct. 1878, __ L.Ed.2d __ at __ , 2000 WL 646196 at *4 (U.S. May 22, 2000) recognized, as do we, that "technology may one day provide another solution."

Therefore, we will affirm the District Court's order dated February 1, 1999, issuing a preliminary injunction.

Note

1. This decision gives the World Wide Web stronger protection from censorship than that enjoyed by print media. Any censorship, of course, is likely to be futile, since purveyors of pornography can easily move offshore.

MAINSTREAM LOUDOUN v. BOARD OF TRUSTEES OF THE LOUDOUN COUNTY LIBRARY

United States District Court, E.D. Virginia, 1998.
2 F.Supp.2d 783.

BRINKEMA, DISTRICT JUDGE.

Before the Court are defendants' Motion to Dismiss the Individual Defendants and Motion to Dismiss for Failure to State a Claim or, in the Alternative, for Summary Judgment, in a case of first impression, involving the applicability of the First Amendment's free speech clause to public libraries' content-based restrictions on Internet access.

I. BACKGROUND

The plaintiffs in this case are an association, Mainstream Loudoun, and ten individual plaintiffs, all of whom are both members of Mainstream Loudoun and adult patrons of Loudoun County public libraries. Defendants are the Board of Trustees of the Loudoun County Public Library, five individual Board members, and Douglas Henderson, Loudoun County's Director of Library Services. The Loudoun County public library system has six branches and provides patrons with access to the Internet and the World Wide Web. Under state law, the "management and control" of this library system is vested in a Board of Trustees (the "Library Board"). *See* Va.Code Ann. § 42.1–35. Library Board members are appointed by County officials and are not elected. *See id.* In addition to their management and control duties, Virginia Code § 42.1–35 directs the Library Board to "adopt such bylaws, rules and regulations for their own guidance and for the government of the free public library system as may be expedient."

On October 20, 1997, the Library Board voted to adopt a "Policy on Internet Sexual Harassment" (the "Policy"), which requires that "[s]ite-blocking software . . . be installed on all [library] computers" so as to: "a. block child pornography and obscene material (hard core pornography)"; and "b. block material deemed Harmful to Juveniles under applicable Virginia statutes and legal precedents (soft core pornography)." To implement the Policy, the Library Board chose "X–Stop," a commercial software product intended to limit access to sites deemed to violate the Policy.

Plaintiffs allege that the Policy impermissibly blocks their access to protected speech such as the Quaker Home Page, the Zero Population Growth website, and the site for the American Association of University Women–Maryland. They also claim that there are no clear criteria for blocking decisions and that defendants maintain an unblocking policy that unconstitutionally chills plaintiffs' receipt of constitutionally protected materials.

Based on the above allegations, plaintiffs bring this action under 42 U.S.C. § 1983 against the Library Board and against five individual Library Board members in both their personal and official capacities, and Director of Library Services Douglas Henderson in his official capacity. Plaintiffs allege that the Policy imposes an unconstitutional restriction on their right to access protected speech on the Internet, and seek declaratory and injunctive relief, as well as costs and attorneys' fees pursuant to 42 U.S.C. § 1988.[1]

II. IMMUNITY ISSUES

A. *Legislative Immunity*

* * *

[W]e find that the Library Board and its members are not entitled to legislative immunity in their enforcement role. * * *

B. *Communications Decency Act Immunity*

Defendants also claim that they are immune from suit under section 509 of the Telecommunications Act of 1996, now codified at 47 U.S.C. § 230. Section 230 is entitled "Protection for private blocking and screening of offensive material," and provides at § 230(c)(2) that:

> No provider or user of an interactive computer service shall be held liable on account of . . . any action voluntarily taken in good faith to

---

1. In a February 24, 1998 Order, this Court granted a Motion to Intervene as Plaintiffs made by several individuals and organizations which publish speech on the Internet. Intervenors argue that defendants have unconstitutionally interfered with their First Amendment rights as speakers to communicate with Loudoun County library patrons. The intervenors' claim is not explicitly at issue in the motions now before the Court.

restrict access to or availability of material that the provider or user considers to be obscene, lewd, lascivious, filthy, excessively violent, harassing, or otherwise objectionable, whether or not such material is constitutionally protected.

The Act defines "interactive computer service" to include "a service or system that provides access to the Internet [that is] offered by libraries or educational institutions." 47 U.S.C. § 230(e)(2). Based on the above language, defendants argue that they are absolutely immune from suit for their decision to promulgate and enforce the Policy.

Although defendants' interpretation of § 230(a)(2) is facially attractive, it is not supported by that section's legislative history or relevant case law. At the beginning of § 230, Congress states that "[i]t is the policy of the United States ... to preserve the vibrant and competitive free market that presently exists for the Internet and other interactive computer services, unfettered by federal or state regulation." 47 U.S.C. § 230(b)(2). Interpreting § 230, the Fourth Circuit has explained that:

> The purpose of [§ 230] statutory immunity is not difficult to discern. Congress recognized the threat that tort-based lawsuits pose to freedom of speech in the new and burgeoning Internet medium. The imposition of tort liability on service providers for the communications of others represented, for Congress, simply another form of intrusive government regulation of speech. Section 230 was enacted, in part, to maintain the robust nature of Internet communication and, accordingly, to keep government interference in the medium to a minimum.

Zeran v. America Online Inc., 129 F.3d 327, 330 (4th Cir.1997). The Fourth Circuit went on to explain that "[a]nother important purpose of § 230 was to encourage service providers to self-regulate the dissemination of offensive materials over their services." *Id.* at 331. Thus, as its name implies, § 230 was enacted to minimize state regulation of Internet speech by encouraging *private* content providers to self-regulate against offensive material; § 230 was not enacted to insulate government regulation of Internet speech from judicial review. Even if § 230 were construed to apply to public libraries, defendants cite no authority to suggest that the "tort-based" immunity to "civil liability" described by § 230 would bar the instant action, which is for declaratory and injunctive relief. *See* 47 U.S.C. § 230(a)(2); *Zeran*, 129 F.3d at 330. We therefore hold that 47 U.S.C. § 230 does not bar this action.

* * *

III. STANDING

* * *

Defendants also allege that no individual plaintiff claims to have requested that a site be unblocked and had that request denied; however, we find that no such allegation is necessary to confer standing. *See Lamont v. Postmaster General*, 381 U.S. 301, 85 S.Ct. 1493, 14 L.Ed.2d

398 (1965). In *Lamont*, the plaintiff sued to invalidate a federal statute that directed the Postmaster General not to deliver a publication deemed "communist propaganda" without a written request from the plaintiff. *See id.* 381 U.S. at 302–04. Plaintiff refused to make such a written request, claiming that the requirement imposed an unconstitutional burden on his First Amendment right to receive protected speech. *See id.* at 304–05. Despite plaintiff's refusal to seek access to restricted materials, the Supreme Court allowed him to maintain his First Amendment claim. *See id.* In accordance with Lamont, the plaintiffs in this case need not allege that they actually requested that a particular site be unblocked. Instead, plaintiffs need only allege that they were unable to access otherwise protected materials as a result of the Policy. Because the Complaint contains such allegations, the first requirement of *Maryland Highways Contractors* is satisfied here. *See* 933 F.2d at 1250. * * *

IV. Plaintiffs' First Amendment Claim

In their Motion to Dismiss for Failure to State a Claim, or, in the Alternative, for Summary Judgment, defendants concede that the Policy prohibits access to speech on the basis of its content. However, defendants argue that the "First Amendment does not in any way limit the decisions of a public library on whether to provide access to information on the Internet." Indeed, at oral argument, defendants went so far as to claim that a public library could constitutionally prohibit access to speech simply because it was authored by African–Americans, or because it espoused a particular political viewpoint, for example pro-Republican. Thus, the central question before this Court is whether a public library may, without violating the First Amendment, enforce content-based restrictions on access to Internet speech.

No cases directly address this issue. However, the parties agree that the most analogous authority on this issue is *Board of Education v. Pico*, 457 U.S. 853, 102 S.Ct. 2799, 73 L.Ed.2d 435 (1982), in which the Supreme Court reviewed the decision of a local board of education to remove certain books from a high school library based on the board's belief that the books were "anti-American, anti-Christian, anti-Sem[i]tic, and just plain filthy." *Id.* 457 U.S. at 856. The Second Circuit had reversed the district court's grant of summary judgment to the school board on plaintiff's First Amendment claim. A sharply-divided Court voted to affirm the Court of Appeal's decision to remand the case for a determination of the school board's motives. However, the Court did not render a majority opinion. Justice Brennan, joined by three Justices, wrote what is commonly referred to as the "plurality" opinion. Justice Brennan held that the First Amendment necessarily limits the government's right to remove materials on the basis of their content from a high school library. *See id.* at 864–69 (plurality op.). Justice Brennan reasoned that the right to receive information is inherent in the right to speak and that "the State may not, consistently with the spirit of the First Amendment, contract the spectrum of available knowledge." *Id.* at 866 (quoting *Griswold v. Connecticut*, 381 U.S. 479, 482, 85 S.Ct. 1678,

14 L.Ed.2d 510 (1965)); *see also Stanley v. Georgia*, 394 U.S. 557, 564, 89 S.Ct. 1243, 22 L.Ed.2d 542 (1969) ("the Constitution protects the right to receive information and ideas"). Justice Brennan explained that this principle was particularly important given the special role of the school's library as a locus for free and independent inquiry. *See id.* 457 U.S. at 869. At the same time, Justice Brennan recognized that public high schools play a crucial inculcative role in "the preparation of individuals for participation as citizens" and are therefore entitled to great discretion "to establish and apply their curriculum in such a way as to transmit community values." *Id.* at 863–64 (quoting *Ambach v. Norwick*, 441 U.S. 68, 76–77, 99 S.Ct. 1589, 60 L.Ed.2d 49 (1979) (internal quotation marks omitted)). Accordingly, Justice Brennan held that the school board members could not remove books "simply because they dislike the ideas contained [in them]," thereby "prescrib[ing] what shall be orthodox in politics, nationalism, religion, or other matters of opinion," but that the board might remove books for reasons of educational suitability, for example pervasive vulgarity. *Id.* 457 U.S. at 872 (quoting *West Va. Bd. of Educ. v. Barnette*, 319 U.S. 624, 642, 63 S.Ct. 1178, 87 L.Ed. 1628 (1943)) (internal quotation marks omitted).

In a concurring opinion, Justice Blackmun focused not on the right to receive information recognized by the plurality, but on the school board's discrimination against disfavored ideas. Justice Blackmun explicitly recognized that *Pico's* facts invoked two significant, competing interests: the inculcative mission of public high schools and the First Amendment's core proscription against content-based regulation of speech. *See id.* 457 U.S. at 876–79 (Blackmun, J., concurring). Justice Blackmun noted that the State must normally demonstrate a compelling reason for content-based regulation, but that a more limited form of protection should apply in the context of public high schools. *See id.* at 877–78. Balancing the two principles above, Justice Blackmun agreed with the plurality that the school board could not remove books based on mere disapproval of their content but could limit its collection for reasons of educational suitability or budgetary constraint. *See id.* at 879.

Dissenting, Chief Justice Burger, joined by three Justices, concluded that any First Amendment right to receive speech did not affirmatively obligate the government to provide such speech in high school libraries. *See id.* at 888 (Burger, C.J., dissenting). Chief Justice Burger reasoned that although the State could not constitutionally prohibit a speaker from reaching an intended audience, nothing in the First Amendment requires public high schools to act as a conduit for particular speech. *See id.* at 885–89. Chief Justice Burger explained that such an obligation would be inconsistent with public high schools' inculcative mission, which necessarily requires schools to make content-based choices among competing ideas in order to establish a curriculum and educate students. *See id.* at 889.

Defendants contend that the *Pico* plurality opinion has no application to this case because it addressed only decisions to remove materials from libraries and specifically declined to address library decisions to acquire materials. *See id.* at 861–63, 871–72 (plurality op.). Defendants liken the Internet to a vast Interlibrary Loan system, and contend that restricting Internet access to selected materials is merely a decision not to acquire such materials rather than a decision to remove them from a library's collection. As such, defendants argue, the instant case is outside the scope of the Pico plurality.

In response, plaintiffs argue that, unlike a library's collection of individual books, the Internet is a "single, integrated system." Pl. Brief at 14 (quoting *ACLU v. Reno*, 929 F.Supp. 824, 838 (E.D.Pa.1996)), *aff'd*, ___ U.S. ___, 117 S.Ct. 2329, 138 L.Ed.2d 874 (1997). As plaintiffs explain, "[t]hough information on the Web is contained in individual computers, the fact that each of these computers is connected to the Internet through [World Wide Web] protocols allows all of the information to become part of a single body of knowledge." Pl. Brief at 15 (quoting *Reno*, 929 F.Supp. at 836). Accordingly, plaintiffs analogize the Internet to a set of encyclopedias, and the Library Board's enactment of the Policy to a decision to "black out" selected articles considered inappropriate for adult and juvenile patrons.

After considering both arguments, we conclude that defendants have misconstrued the nature of the Internet. By purchasing Internet access, each Loudoun library has made all Internet publications instantly accessible to its patrons. Unlike an Interlibrary loan or outright book purchase, no appreciable expenditure of library time or resources is required to make a particular Internet publication available to a library patron. In contrast, a library must actually expend resources to restrict Internet access to a publication that is otherwise immediately available. In effect, by purchasing one such publication, the library has purchased them all. The Internet therefore more closely resembles plaintiffs' analogy of a collection of encyclopedias from which defendants have laboriously redacted portions deemed unfit for library patrons. As such, the Library Board's action is more appropriately characterized as a removal decision. We therefore conclude that the principles discussed in the *Pico* plurality are relevant and apply to the Library Board's decision to promulgate and enforce the Policy.

Plaintiffs also contend that the plurality's decision in *Pico* establishes a blanket rule that removal decisions by libraries may not be resolved on summary judgment. We find plaintiffs' reading of *Pico* to be oversimplistic. It is true that a majority of the *Pico* Court voted to remand the case for a determination of the school board's motives, impliedly rejecting the unfettered discretion defendants claim. *See id.* at 875. At the same time, however, a majority of the Court could not agree on the degree of discretion available to school libraries. *See id.* at 856 (plurality op.); 875 (Blackmun, J., concurring); *cf. id.* at 883 (White, J., concurring). Nor did any of the Pico Justices directly address the special circumstances that obtain in public libraries. It would therefore be inappropriate for this Court to deny defendants' Motion without first determining the scope of discretion available to the Library Board to remove materials on the basis of their content.

Defendants argue that any limitation on their discretion to remove materials would force them to act as an unwilling conduit of information, and urge this Court to adopt the position of the Pico dissent. Defendants interpret the dissent to mean that they are entitled to unfettered discretion in deciding what materials to make available to library patrons.

Adopting defendants' position, however, would require this Court to ignore the *Pico* plurality's decision to remand the case, as discussed above. Moreover, all of the *Pico* Justices, including the dissenters, recognized that any discretion accorded to school libraries was uniquely tied to the public school's role as educator. *See id.* at 863–64, 869–71 (plurality op.); 875–76, 879 (Blackmun, J., concurring) ("Certainly, the unique environment of the school places substantial limits on the extent to which official decisions may be restrained by First Amendment values."); *cf. id.* at 889–92 (Burger, C.J., dissenting) ("Whatever role the government might play as a conduit of information, schools in particular ought not be made a slavish courier of the material of third parties.... How are 'fundamental values' to be inculcated except by having school boards make content-based decisions about the appropriateness of retaining materials in the school library and curriculum [?]"); 909–10 (Rehnquist, J., dissenting) ("When it acts as an educator ... the government is engaged in inculcating social values and knowledge in relatively impressionable young people.... In short, actions by the government as educator do not raise the same First Amendment concerns as actions by the government as sovereign."); 921 (O'Connor, J., dissenting) (stating that "in this case the government is acting in its special role as educator"). Of even more significance to our case is Justice Rehnquist's observation that high school libraries must be treated differently from public libraries. *See id.* at 915 (Rehnquist, J., dissenting) ("Unlike university or public libraries, elementary and secondary school libraries are not designed for freewheeling inquiry."). Indeed, Chief Justice Burger and Justice Rehnquist justified giving public schools broad discretion to remove books in part by noting that such materials remained available in public libraries. *See id.* at 892 (Burger, C.J., dissenting) ("Books may be acquired from ... public libraries, or other alternative sources unconnected with the unique environment of the local public schools."); 915 (Rehnquist, J., dissenting) ("[T]he most obvious reason that petitioners' removal of the books did not violate respondents' right to receive information is the ready availability of the books elsewhere.... The books may be borrowed from a public library."). Accordingly, neither the dissent nor the plurality of *Pico* can be said to support defendants' argument that public libraries enjoy unfettered discretion to remove materials from their collections.

To the extent that *Pico* applies to this case, we conclude that it stands for the proposition that the First Amendment applies to, and limits, the discretion of a public library to place content-based restrictions on access to constitutionally protected materials within its collection. Consistent with the mandate of the First Amendment, a public library, "like other enterprises operated by the State, may not be run in such a manner as to 'prescribe what shall be orthodox in politics, nationalism, religion, or other matters of opinion.'" *Id.* at 876 (Blackmun, J., concurring) (quoting *Barnette*, 319 U.S. at 642).

Furthermore, the factors which justified giving high school libraries broad discretion to remove materials in *Pico* are not present in this case. The plaintiffs in this case are adults rather than children. Children, whose minds and values are still developing, have traditionally been afforded less First Amendment protection, particularly within the context of public high schools. See *Tinker v. Des Moines Sch. Dist.*, 393 U.S. 503, 506, 89 S.Ct. 733, 21 L.Ed.2d 731 (1969). In contrast, adults are deemed to have acquired the maturity needed to participate fully in a democratic society, and their right to speak and receive speech is entitled to full First Amendment protection. Accordingly, adults are entitled to receive categories of speech, for example "pervasively vulgar" speech, which may be inappropriate for children. See *Reno v. ACLU*, ___ U.S. ___, ___, 117 S.Ct. 2329, 2346, 138 L.Ed.2d 874 (1997); *Sable Communications v. FCC*, 492 U.S. 115, 126, 109 S.Ct. 2829, 106 L.Ed.2d 93 (1989).

More importantly, the tension Justice Blackmun recognized between the inculcative role of high schools and the First Amendment's prohibition on content-based regulation of speech does not exist here. *See Pico*, 457 U.S. at 876–80 (Blackmun, J., concurring). Public libraries lack the inculcative mission that is the guiding purpose of public high schools. Instead, public libraries are places of freewheeling and independent inquiry. *See id.* at 914 (Rehnquist, J., dissenting). Adult library patrons are presumed to have acquired already the "fundamental values" needed to act as citizens, and have come to the library to pursue their personal intellectual interests rather than the curriculum of a high school classroom. As such, no curricular motive justifies a public library's decision to restrict access to Internet materials on the basis of their content.

Finally, the unique advantages of Internet speech eliminate any resource-related rationale libraries might otherwise have for engaging in content-based discrimination. The Supreme Court has analogized the Internet to a "vast library including millions of readily available and indexed publications," the content of which "is as diverse as human thought." *Reno*, 117 S.Ct. at 2335. Unlike more traditional libraries, however, there is no marginal cost associated with acquiring Internet publications. Instead, all, or nearly all, Internet publications are jointly available for a single price. Indeed, it costs a library more to restrict the content of its collection by means of blocking software than it does for the library to offer unrestricted access to all Internet publications. Nor do Internet publications, which exist only in "cyberspace," take up shelf space or require physical maintenance of any kind. Accordingly, considerations of cost or physical resources cannot justify a public library's decision to restrict access to Internet materials. *Cf. Pico*, 457 U.S. at 909 (Rehnquist, J., dissenting) (budgetary considerations force schools to choose some books over others); 879 n. 1 (Blackmun, J., concurring) (same).

In sum, there is "no basis for qualifying the level of First Amendment scrutiny" that must be applied to a public library's decision to restrict access to Internet publications. *Reno*, 117 S.Ct. at 2344. We are therefore left with the First Amendment's central tenet that content-based restrictions on speech must be justified by a compelling governmental interest and must be narrowly tailored to achieve that end. *See Simon & Schuster, Inc. v. Members of the N.Y. State Crime Victims Bd.*, 502 U.S. 105, 118, 112 S.Ct. 501, 116 L.Ed.2d 476 (1991). This principle was recently affirmed within the context of Internet speech. *See Reno*, 117 S.Ct. at 2343–48. Accordingly, we hold that the Library Board may not adopt and enforce content-based restrictions on access to protected Internet speech absent a compelling state interest and means narrowly drawn to achieve that end.

This holding does not obligate defendants to act as unwilling conduits of information, because the Library Board need not provide access to the Internet at all. Having chosen to provide access, however, the Library Board may not thereafter selectively restrict certain categories of Internet speech because it disfavors their content. In accord with this holding is Lamont, discussed supra, in which the Court held that the Post Office could not constitutionally restrict access to speech it considered "communist propaganda," stating that " '[t]he United States may give up the post-office when it sees fit, but while it carries it on the use of the mails is almost as much a part of free speech as the right to use our tongues.' " *Lamont*, 381 U.S. at 305 (quoting *Milwaukee Soc. Dem. Pub. Co. v. Burleson*, 255 U.S. 407, 437, 41 S.Ct. 352, 65 L.Ed. 704 (1921) (Holmes, J., dissenting)); *see id.* 381 U.S. at 310 ("If the Government wishes to withdraw a subsidy or a privilege, it must do so by means and on terms which do not endanger First Amendment rights.") (Brennan, J., concurring). Similarly, in this case, the Library Board need not offer Internet access, but, having chosen to provide it, must operate the service within the confines of the First Amendment.

A. *Obscenity, Child Pornography, and Speech "Harmful to Juveniles"*

Having determined that a public library must satisfy strict scrutiny before it may engage in content-based regulation of protected speech, we now consider the speech regulated by the Policy. The Policy prohibits access to three types of speech: obscenity, child pornography, and materials deemed "[h]armful to [j]uveniles." Complaint Ex. 1. Obscenity and child pornography are not entitled to the protections of the First Amendment, and the government may legitimately restrict access to such materials. *See New York v. Ferber*, 458 U.S. 747, 102 S.Ct. 3348, 73 L.Ed.2d 1113 (1982) (child pornography); *Miller v. California*, 413 U.S. 15, 93 S.Ct. 2607, 37 L.Ed.2d 419 (1973) (obscenity). Indeed, "[t]ransmitting obscenity and child pornography, whether via the Internet or other means, is already illegal under federal law for both adults and juveniles." *Reno*, 117 S.Ct. at 2348 n. 44. In the instant case, however, plaintiffs allege that the X–Stop filtering software chosen by defendants restricts many publications which are not obscene or pornographic, including materials unrelated to sex altogether, such as the Quaker's website. Moreover, plaintiffs allege that X–Stop fails to block access to pornographic materials arguably covered by the Policy. Most importantly, plaintiffs allege that the decision as to which materials to block is made by a California corporation based on secret criteria not disclosed even to defendants, criteria which may or may not bear any relation to legal definitions of obscenity or child pornography. As such, plaintiffs argue that the means called for by the Policy are not narrowly tailored to any legitimate interest defendants may have in regulating obscenity and child pornography.

The Policy also prohibits access to materials which are "deemed Harmful to Juveniles under applicable Virginia statutes and legal precedents." This appears to be a reference to Virginia Code § 18.2–390, which defines materials "Harmful to Juveniles" to include sexual content that:

> (a) predominately appeals to the prurient, shameful or morbid interest of juveniles, (b) is patently offensive to prevailing standards in the adult community as a whole with respect to what is suitable material for juveniles, and (c) is, when taken as a whole, lacking in serious literary, artistic, political or scientific value for juveniles.

Plaintiffs allege that the Policy improperly limits adult Internet speech to what is fit for children. In support, plaintiffs cite *Reno*, 117 S.Ct. at 2329. In *Reno*, the Supreme Court held that a content-based Internet regulation intended to prevent the transmission of material harmful to minors was unconstitutional because it suppressed speech adults were constitutionally entitled to send and receive. The Court stated:

> It is true that we have repeatedly recognized the governmental interest in protecting children from harmful materials. But that interest does not justify an unnecessarily broad suppression of speech addressed to adults. As we have explained, the Government may not "reduc[e] the adult population ... to ... only what is fit for children."

Id. 117 S.Ct. at 2346 (quoting *Denver Area Telecomm. Consortium v. FCC*, 518 U.S. 727, 116 S.Ct. 2374, 2393, 135 L.Ed.2d 888 (1996)) (citations omitted). The Court went on to cite *Bolger v. Youngs Drug Products Corp.*, 463 U.S. 60, 103 S.Ct. 2875, 77 L.Ed.2d 469 (1983), for the proposition that: " '[R]egardless of the strength of the government's interest' in protecting children, '[t]he level of discourse reaching a mailbox simply cannot be limited to that which would be suitable for a sandbox.' " *Reno*, 117 S.Ct. at 2346 (quoting *Bolger*, 463 U.S. at 74–75). Applying Reno to the instant case, it is clear that defendants may not, in the interest of protecting children, limit the speech available to adults to what is fit for "juveniles." As plaintiffs point out, even when government regulation of content is undertaken for a legitimate purpose, whether it be to prevent the communication of obscene speech or materials harmful to children, the means it uses must be a "reasonable response to the threat" which will alleviate the harm "in a direct and material way."

Turner Broadcasting v. FCC, 512 U.S. 622, 624, 114 S.Ct. 2445, 129 L.Ed.2d 497 (1994). Plaintiffs have adequately alleged a lack of such reasonable means here. As such, plaintiffs have stated a valid First Amendment claim which may go forward.

B. The Unblocking Policy

Defendants contend that, even if the First Amendment limits the Library Board's discretion to remove materials, the unblocking procedure ensures the constitutionality of the Policy because it allows library staff to make certain that only constitutionally unprotected materials are blocked. Under the unblocking policy, library patrons who have been denied access to a site may submit a written request which must include their name, telephone number, and a detailed explanation of why they desire access to the blocked site. The library staff then "decide[s] whether the request should be granted." Def. Brief at 3.

Plaintiffs argue that the unblocking procedure constitutes an unconstitutional burden on the right of library patrons to access protected speech, citing *Lamont*, 381 U.S. at 301. The statute at issue in *Lamont* directed the Postmaster General not to deliver "communist propaganda" to postal patrons unless they first returned to the Post Office a card bearing their names and addresses and specifically requesting that such materials be sent to them. *See id.* at 302–04. The Supreme Court held the statute to be "unconstitutional because it require[d] an official act (viz., returning the reply card) as a limitation on the unfettered exercise of the addressees' First Amendment rights." *Id.* at 305. In particular, the Court noted the severe chilling effect of forcing citizens to publicly petition the Government for access to speech it clearly disfavored. *See id.* at 307.

Here, as in *Lamont*, the unblocking policy forces adult patrons to petition the Government for access to otherwise protected speech, for example speech "Harmful to Juveniles." Indeed, the Loudoun County unblocking policy appears more chilling than the restriction at issue in *Lamont*, because it grants library staff standardless discretion to refuse access to protected speech, whereas the statute at issue in *Lamont* required postal employees to grant access requests automatically. As such, defendants' alleged unblocking procedure does not in any way undercut plaintiffs' First Amendment claim.

V. Conclusion

For the reasons set forth above, defendants' Motion to Dismiss the Individual Defendants will be GRANTED, and their Motion to Dismiss for Failure to State a Claim will be GRANTED IN PART as to certain plaintiffs and DENIED in all other respects. As to defendants' Motion in the Alternative for Summary Judgment, this Court holds that several material factual issues remain which mandate against summary judgment at this time. These include, but are not limited to, defendants' justification for the Policy, the Internet sites blocked by X–Stop, and the degree of defendants' knowledge of and control over the sites X–Stop blocks. Accordingly, defendants' Motion in the Alternative for Summary Judgment will also be DENIED. An appropriate order will issue. * * *

D. INTELLECTUAL PROPERTY RIGHTS VERSUS FREE SPEECH

CPC INTERNATIONAL, INC. v. SKIPPY INC.

United States Court of Appeals, Fourth Circuit, 2000.
214 F.3d 456.

Wilkinson, Chief Judge:

This case involves a protracted dispute over the use of the trademark SKIPPY. In 1986, CPC International, the maker of Skippy Peanut Butter, brought suit against Skippy, Incorporated, for trademark infringement and unfair competition. The district court enjoined Skippy from communicating that CPC has no rights in the trademark SKIPPY for food products. In 1998, Skippy created the web site Skippy.com. CPC alleged that the web site violated the 1986 order, and the district court ordered Skippy to remove about ten pages of material from its web site. Because the district court's injunction lacks the findings and specificity required by Fed.R.Civ.P. 65(d) and because its substantial breadth raises serious First Amendment concerns, we vacate the injunction and remand for further proceedings.

I.

In 1923, Percy L. Crosby created a cartoon featuring a school-aged child named Skippy. The cartoon was syndicated and the Skippy character was marketed in cartoon books, magazine articles, and novels. Crosby obtained a federal trademark SKIPPY for cartoons depicting the humorous juvenile character. This mark was transferred to appellant Skippy, Incorporated, sometime after 1932. Appellant Joan Crosby Tibbetts is Percy Crosby's daughter and the current president of Skippy. Skippy currently owns a trademark SKIPPY for the cartoon comic strip.

CPC International and its predecessors have sold peanut butter in the United States under the trademark SKIPPY since 1933. CPC owns a federal trademark SKIPPY for peanut butter.

In 1986, CPC brought suit alleging that Skippy had engaged in trademark infringement and unfair competition. Skippy had licensed the right to use "the word mark SKIPPY, the comic strip SKIPPY, [and] the fanciful character SKIPPY" on the packaging of caramel corn, popcorn, and nuts. CPC Int'l, Inc. v. Skippy, Inc., 651 F.Supp. 62, 65 (E.D.Va. 1986). The district court found that the use of the mark SKIPPY on caramel corn or any other food product constituted trademark infringement because it would create a likelihood of confusion with CPC's trademark in SKIPPY Peanut Butter. *See id.* at 67.

Accordingly, the district court issued an order (the 1986 order) that enjoined Skippy and Joan Tibbetts (1) "from continuing to offer to license, offer to sell, distribute, advertise or promote a caramel corn and peanut product or any other food product under the trademark SKIPPY or any mark confusingly similar thereto"; and (2) "from communicating in any manner with anyone that [Skippy's] rights in the trademark SKIPPY include the right to use SKIPPY on peanut butter and food products and, conversely, that CPC has no rights in the SKIPPY trademark in connection with these products."

In 1997, Skippy registered the domain name Skippy.com. The web site recounted the "Life and Times" of Percy Crosby, including his childhood, military career, and the popular success enjoyed by the Skippy cartoon character. It also included stories of an FBI investigation, "CPC's Malicious Prosecution," and "CPC's Fraud on the Courts." A "legal notice" on the web site stated "SKIPPY and the image of the character SKIPPY are trademarks and copyrights of SKIPPY, INC. Neither these marks nor the copyrighted works of Percy Crosby may be used without the permission of SKIPPY, INC."

The instant case arises out of CPC's motion to show cause why Skippy and Tibbetts should not be held in contempt of the 1986 order. On September 9, 1999, the district court ordered Skippy and Tibbetts to remove permanently significant portions of the web site. The passages to be deleted were highlighted and attached to the order. The court also enjoined appellants from "providing others with any of the deleted material on the Skippy.com website or any material that violates the Court's [1986 order]." On September 21, 1999, the district court entered a final order, which provided that upon showing of further violations of the 1986 order the court would impose a $500 per day damage award against appellants. Skippy and Tibbetts now appeal.

II.

It is important at the outset to define the precise focus of this lawsuit. This is not a defamation suit, and it is only an unfair competition suit insofar as it challenges Skippy's compliance with the 1986 order. The case involves solely CPC's motion to show cause why Skippy should not be held in contempt for violation of the 1986 order. Rather than addressing Skippy's conduct under the terms of that order, the district court simply issued a sweeping injunction requiring the wholesale removal of material from Skippy's web site.

We find that the district court's injunctive decree suffers from two related deficiencies. First, the injunction fails to comply with the terms of Fed.R.Civ.P. 65(d). Second, the injunction's substantial overbreadth raises serious First Amendment concerns. We shall address each of these problems in turn.

A.

Rule 65(d) provides, "Every order granting an injunction . . . shall set forth the reasons for its issuance; shall be specific in terms; shall describe in reasonable detail . . . the act or acts sought to be restrained." * * * What is to be removed is clear from the [District Court's] order;

however, the reason for redacting these materials is not. Such a terse and sweeping injunction does not comply with the requirements of Rule 65(d).

B.

The absence of proper findings serves to illuminate a further defect in the district court's order. The injunction against Skippy is not narrowly tailored to remedy specific violations of the 1986 order. As such it implicates serious First Amendment concerns.

The First Amendment prohibits not only statutory abridgment but also judicial action that restrains free speech. *See New Orleans Steamship Ass'n v. General Longshore Workers, ILA Local* 1418, 626 F.2d 455, 462 (5th Cir.1980). The Supreme Court has recognized the risks of overbroad injunctions, especially when First Amendment considerations are at stake. An injunction must "burden no more speech than necessary to serve a significant government interest." *Madsen v. Women's Health Center, Inc.*, 512 U.S. 753, 765, 114 S.Ct. 2516, 129 L.Ed.2d 593 (1994); *see also NAACP v. Claiborne Hardware Co.*, 458 U.S. 886, 924 n. 67, 102 S.Ct. 3409, 73 L.Ed.2d 1215 (1982) (injunction must be vacated or "modified to restrain only unlawful conduct"). Injunctions must be narrowly tailored and should prohibit only unlawful conduct. An "order must be tailored as precisely as possible to the exact needs of the case." *Carroll v. President and Comm'rs of Princess Anne*, 393 U.S. 175, 184, 89 S.Ct. 347, 21 L.Ed.2d 325 (1968).

The district court failed to articulate any correlation between the redactions and the government's interest in enforcing trademark law. The basic objectives of trademark law are to encourage product differentiation, promote the production of quality goods, and provide consumers with information about the quality of goods. *See Qualitex Co. v. Jacobson Prods. Co.*, 514 U.S. 159, 163–64, 115 S.Ct. 1300, 131 L.Ed.2d 248 (1995). It is hard to see what "significant government interest" is served here. CPC's trademark has not been used for any commercial gain, nor has the trademark been used in a way that confuses the public. *See Anheuser–Busch, Inc. v. L & L Wings, Inc.*, 962 F.2d 316, 321–22 (4th Cir.1992). In the 1986 case, the district court found that when Skippy licensed the SKIPPY trademark for use on food products this constituted unfair competition because of the possibility of confusion between the caramel corn products and CPC's Skippy Peanut Butter. *See CPC Int'l*, 651 F.Supp. at 67. The web site, however, does not create any such confusion between the Skippy cartoon character and Skippy Peanut Butter. While there certainly is a strong state interest in preventing trademark infringement and unfair competition, there has been no finding that suppressing significant portions of Skippy's web site serves such an interest.

First Amendment interests are at stake here because Ms. Tibbetts tells her side of the story on the Skippy web site—how a big corporation worked to steal her father's cartoon trademark and then used the trademark to make a fortune. This is an admittedly partisan account and one that vexes CPC. Yet just because speech is critical of a corporation and its business practices is not a sufficient reason to enjoin the speech. As the First Circuit stated, if a trademark owner could "enjoin the use of his mark in a noncommercial context found to be negative or offensive, then a corporation could shield itself from criticism by forbidding the use of its name in commentaries critical of its conduct." *L.L. Bean, Inc. v. Drake Publishers, Inc.*, 811 F.2d 26, 33 (1st Cir.1987).

It is important that trademarks not be "transformed from rights against unfair competition to rights to control language." Mark A. Lemley, The Modern Lanham Act and the Death of Common Sense, 108 Yale L.J. 1687, 1710–11 (1999). Such a transformation would diminish our ability to discuss the products or criticize the conduct of companies that may be of widespread public concern and importance. *See id.* "Much useful social and commercial discourse would be all but impossible if speakers were under threat of an infringement lawsuit every time they made reference to a person, company or product by using its trademark." *New Kids on the Block v. New Am. Publ'g, Inc.*, 971 F.2d 302, 307 (9th Cir.1992). The 1999 injunction broadly removes most of the speech on the web site. By redacting purely editorial and historical comments, the injunction is not narrowly tailored. The Constitution will not tolerate such a wholesale suppression of speech.

Contrary to CPC's assertions, there is no reason to deny full First Amendment protection to Skippy. The redacted portions of the web site are not commercial speech. Speech is commercial in nature if it does "no more than propose a commercial transaction." *Virginia State Bd. of Pharmacy v. Virginia Citizens Consumer Council, Inc.*, 425 U.S. 748, 762, 96 S.Ct. 1817, 48 L.Ed.2d 346 (1976) (internal quotation marks omitted). Here, the only place where a commercial transaction was even conceivably proposed was in Skippy's "legal notice," which states "for information about licensing these images and trademarks, please contact Joan Crosby Tibbetts." Indeed, this warning was not even among the redacted portions of the web site, and continues to be displayed.

Beyond the warning, the original web site did not offer any products for sale or represent that Skippy possessed the trademark for use on food products. The web site served a primarily informational purpose, not a commercial one. The instant case is thus distinguishable from *Board of Trustees of the State University v. Fox*, in which the Supreme Court held that "Tupperware parties" that offered products for sale constituted commercial speech notwithstanding the fact that they included discussions on home economics. 492 U.S. 469, 474–75, 109 S.Ct. 3028, 106 L.Ed.2d 388 (1989). This case is also distinct from *Bolger v. Youngs Drug Products Corporation*, which held that advertising pamphlets for contraceptives were commercial speech even though they contained factual information about public issues such as family planning. 463 U.S. 60, 67–68, 103 S.Ct. 2875, 77 L.Ed.2d 469 (1983). Both *Fox* and *Bolger* involved commercial speech supplemented by comments related to the marketed product.

By contrast, the speech on the Skippy web site did not propose a commercial transaction. The web site simply tells one woman's story about her family and recounts her view of CPC's actions and the legal events surrounding the trademark SKIPPY. Throughout most of the web site the trademark SKIPPY is used as part of editorial and historical commentary. As such it is a protected form of expression. "The freedom of speech and of the press guaranteed by the Constitution embraces at least the liberty to discuss publicly and truthfully all matters of public concern without previous restraint or fear of subsequent punishment." *Thornhill v. Alabama*, 310 U.S. 88, 101–02, 60 S.Ct. 736, 84 L.Ed. 1093 (1940). Before closing off such comments, the district court must articulate the state's interest and then narrowly draw an injunction to prohibit only illegal conduct and nothing more. *See Madsen*, 512 U.S. at 765.

III.

Because the injunction fails to comply with the requirements of Rule 65(d) and because it raises serious First Amendment concerns, we vacate the injunction and remand for further proceedings in accordance with this opinion.

VACATED AND REMANDED

Note

Faber used "ballysucks.com" as the name of a Internet domain devoted to criticism of the Bally health clubs. The holder of the "Bally" trademark sued for trademark infringement. The court held that Faber's use of the domain name was protected by First Amendment. *Bally Total Fitness Holding Corp. v. Faber,* 29 F.Supp.2d 1161, 1167 (C.D.Cal.1998). While the *Bally* case occurred before the adoption of the Anticybersquatting Consumer Protection Act, the holding obviously is still good law, because the First Amendment, of course, would trump any act of Congress.

E. ANONYMOUS AND PSEUDONYMOUS COMMUNICATIONS

AMERICAN CIVIL LIBERTIES UNION OF GEORGIA v. MILLER

United States District Court, N.D. Georgia, 1997.
977 F.Supp. 1228.

SHOOB, SENIOR DISTRICT JUDGE.

This action is before the Court on plaintiffs' motion for preliminary injunction and defendants' motion to dismiss. For the reasons stated below, the Court grants plaintiffs' motion and denies defendants' motion.

FACTUAL BACKGROUND

Plaintiffs bring this action for declaratory and injunctive relief challenging the constitutionality of Act No. 1029, Ga. Laws 1996, p.

1505, codified at O.C.G.A. § 16–9–93.1 ("act" or "statute"). The act makes it a crime for

> any person ... knowingly to transmit any data through a computer network ... for the purpose of setting up, maintaining, operating, or exchanging data with an electronic mailbox, home page, or any other electronic information storage bank or point of access to electronic information if such data uses any individual name ... to falsely identify the person ...

and for

> any person ... knowingly to transmit any data through a computer network ... if such data uses any ... trade name, registered trademark, logo, legal or official seal, or copyrighted symbol ... which would falsely state or imply that such person ... has permission or is legally authorized to use [it] for such purpose when such permission or authorization has not been obtained.

The parties vigorously dispute the scope of the act. Plaintiffs, a group of individuals and organization members who communicate over the internet, interpret it as imposing unconstitutional content-based restrictions on their right to communicate anonymously and pseudonymously over the internet, as well as on their right to use trade names, logos, and other graphics in a manner held to be constitutional in other contexts.

Plaintiffs argue that the act has tremendous implications for internet users, many of whom "falsely identify" themselves on a regular basis for the purpose of communicating about sensitive topics without subjecting themselves to ostracism or embarrassment. Plaintiffs further contend that the trade name and logo restriction frustrates one of the internet's unique features—the "links" that connect web pages on the World Wide Web and enable users to browse easily from topic to topic through the computer network system. Plaintiffs claim that the act's broad language is further damaging in that it allows for selective prosecution of persons communicating about controversial topics.

Defendants contend that the act prohibits a much narrower class of communications. They interpret it as forbidding only fraudulent transmissions or the appropriation of the identity of another person or entity for some improper purpose. Defendants ask the Court to abstain from exercising jurisdiction in this case in order to give the Georgia Supreme Court an opportunity to definitively interpret the act.

Motion for Preliminary Injunction

In order to prevail on a preliminary injunction motion, plaintiffs must establish 1) a substantial likelihood of success on the merits; 2) a substantial threat of irreparable injury if the injunction is not granted; 3) that the threatened injury to the plaintiffs outweighs the harm an injunction may cause defendants; and 4) that granting the injunction would not disserve the public interest. *Teper v. Miller*, 82 F.3d 989, 992–

93 n. 3 (11th Cir.1996). The Court concludes that plaintiffs have satisfied each of these requirements and are thus entitled to injunctive relief.

1. Likelihood of Success on the Merits

In their motion to dismiss, defendants assert two affirmative defenses which, if persuasive, would make plaintiffs' success on the merits unlikely. First, defendants argue that because plaintiffs have not been prosecuted or threatened with prosecution under the act, no live controversy exists and plaintiffs therefore lack standing to bring this action. The Court concludes, however, that plaintiffs do have standing because "a credible threat of prosecution" exists. *Graham v. Butterworth*, 5 F.3d 496, 499 (11th Cir.1993). When plaintiffs filed this action "they intended to engage in arguably protected conduct, which the statute seemed to proscribe." *Id.* at 499. Furthermore, the rules of standing are relaxed in the first amendment context where "the statute's alleged danger is, in large measure, one of self-censorship; a harm that can be realized even without an actual prosecution." *Virginia v. American Booksellers Ass'n*, 484 U.S. 383, 384, 108 S.Ct. 636, 638, 98 L.Ed.2d 782 (1988).

Defendants also ask the Court to abstain from exercising jurisdiction over this case on the grounds that the law is ambiguous and in need of state court interpretation. However, abstention should rarely be invoked in cases involving facial challenges to statutes allegedly violative of the first amendment. *Dombrowski v. Pfister*, 380 U.S. 479, 489–90, 85 S.Ct. 1116, 1122, 14 L.Ed.2d 22 (1965) (holding abstention "inappropriate for cases [where] ... statutes are justifiably attacked on their face as abridging free expression"). The reluctance to abstain in first amendment cases recognizes that the delay abstention imposes has a further chilling effect on speech. *Zwickler v. Koota*, 389 U.S. 241, 252, 88 S.Ct. 391, 397–98, 19 L.Ed.2d 444 (1967). * * *

Having addressed defendants' affirmative defenses, the Court concludes that plaintiffs are likely to prevail on the merits of their claim. It appears from the record that plaintiffs are likely to prove that the statute imposes content-based restrictions which are not narrowly tailored to achieve the state's purported compelling interest. Furthermore, plaintiffs are likely to show that the statute is overbroad and void for vagueness.

First, because "the identity of the speaker is no different from other components of [a] document's contents that the author is free to include or exclude," *McIntyre v. Ohio Elections Comm'n*, 514 U.S. 334, 340–42, 115 S.Ct. 1511, 1516, 131 L.Ed.2d 426 (1995), the statute's prohibition of internet transmissions which "falsely identify" the sender constitutes a presumptively invalid content-based restriction. *See R.A.V. v. St. Paul*, 505 U.S. 377, 382, 112 S.Ct. 2538, 2542–43, 120 L.Ed.2d 305 (1992). The state may impose content-based restrictions only to promote a "compelling state interest" and only through use of "the least restrictive means to further the articulated interest." *Sable Communications of California, Inc. v. FCC*, 492 U.S. 115, 126, 109 S.Ct. 2829, 2836, 106 L.Ed.2d 93 (1989). Thus, in order to overcome the presumption of invalidity, defendants must demonstrate that the statute furthers a compelling state interest and is narrowly tailored to achieve it.

Defendants allege that the statute's purpose is fraud prevention, which the Court agrees is a compelling state interest. However, the statute is not narrowly tailored to achieve that end and instead sweeps innocent, protected speech within its scope. Specifically, by its plain language the criminal prohibition applies regardless of whether a speaker has any intent to deceive or whether deception actually occurs. Therefore, it could apply to a wide range of transmissions which "falsely identify" the sender, but are not "fraudulent" within the specific meaning of the criminal code.

Defendants respond that the act does not mean what it says and that, instead, a variety of limiting concepts should be engrafted onto it. First, defendants propose to add an element of fraud, or a specific intent requirement of "intent to defraud" or "intent to deceive" to the act. None of these terms or phrases appears in the statute, however, although they are expressly included in other Georgia criminal statutes which require proof of specific intent. *See, e.g.,* O.C.G.A. §§ 10–1–453, 16–9–1(a), 16–9–2, and 16–8–3.

Second, defendants contend that the act applies only to persons who misappropriate the identity of another specific entity or person. Again, there is nothing in the language of the act from which a reasonable person would infer such a requirement, and the General Assembly has specifically included analogous elements when it meant to do so. *See* O.C.G.A. § 10–1–453.

Third, defendants seek to limit the restriction on use of trade names, marks, and seals by collapsing the act's two clauses—suggesting that "use" of a mark is prohibited only when it would "falsely identify" the user. Without explanation, this construction borrows the "false identification" portion of the first clause and applies it to the second. In addition to not making sense grammatically, the interpretation also imports into the second clause all of the previously discussed interpretive problems with the phrase "falsely identify."

In construing a statute, the Court must "follow the literal language of the statute 'unless it produces contradiction, absurdity or such an inconvenience as to insure that the legislature meant something else.' " *Telecom*USA, Inc. v. Collins,* 260 Ga. 362, 363, 393 S.E.2d 235 (1990) (citing *Department of Transp. v. City of Atlanta,* 255 Ga. 124, 137, 337 S.E.2d 327 (1985)). Only if a statute is "readily susceptible to a narrowing construction" may such an interpretation be applied to save a questionable law. *American Booksellers Ass'n,* 484 U.S. at 397. The words and phrases defendants seek to add to the act appear nowhere in it. Moreover, defendants' attempt to interpret the act is so confusing and contradictory that it could not possibly constitute grounds for rejecting the act's plain language. Even if the Court could impose a limiting construction on the act, defendants' brief provides no real guidance on what that construction should be, but instead offers a variety of very different possible interpretations in hopes that the Court will select one. The Court concludes, therefore, that the act is not readily susceptible to a limiting construction and that its plain language is not narrowly tailored to promote a compelling state interest.

For similar reasons, plaintiffs are likely to succeed on their overbreadth claim because the statute "sweeps protected activity within its proscription." *M.S. News Co. v. Casado*, 721 F.2d 1281, 1287 (10th Cir.1983) (citing *Erznoznik v. City of Jacksonville*, 422 U.S. 205, 212–13 (1975)). In the first amendment context, the overbreadth doctrine, which invalidates overbroad statutes even when some of their applications are valid, *United States v. Salerno*, 481 U.S. 739, 745, 107 S.Ct. 2095, 2100, 95 L.Ed.2d 697 (1987), is based on the recognition that "the very existence of some broadly written laws has the potential to chill the expressive activity of others not before the Court." *Forsyth County v. Nationalist Movement*, 505 U.S. 123, 129, 112 S.Ct. 2395, 2401, 120 L.Ed.2d 101 (1992).

The Court concludes that the statute was not drafted with the precision necessary for laws regulating speech. On its face, the act prohibits such protected speech as the use of false identification to avoid social ostracism, to prevent discrimination and harassment, and to protect privacy, as well as the use of trade names or logos in noncommercial educational speech, news, and commentary—a prohibition with well-recognized first amendment problems. Therefore, even if the statute could constitutionally be used to prosecute persons who intentionally "falsely identify" themselves in order to deceive or defraud the public, or to persons whose commercial use of trade names and logos creates a substantial likelihood of confusion or the dilution of a famous mark, the statute is nevertheless overbroad because it operates unconstitutionally for a substantial category of the speakers it covers. *Village of Schaumburg v. Citizens for a Better Environment*, 444 U.S. 620, 634, 100 S.Ct. 826, 834–35, 63 L.Ed.2d 73 (1980).

Finally, plaintiffs are likely to succeed on their claim that the statute is unconstitutionally vague. The void-for-vagueness doctrine requires a criminal statute to "define the criminal offense with sufficient definiteness that ordinary people can understand what conduct is prohibited and in a manner that does not encourage arbitrary and discriminatory enforcement." *Kolender v. Lawson*, 461 U.S. 352, 357, 103 S.Ct. 1855, 1858, 75 L.Ed.2d 903 (1983). Like the overbreadth doctrine, the policies underlying the vagueness rule apply with special force where the statute at issue restricts speech. *ACLU v. Reno*, 929 F.Supp. 824, 860 (E.D.Pa.1996). The Court concludes that plaintiffs are likely to prove that the statute is void for vagueness because it 1) does not give fair notice of the scope of conduct it proscribes; 2) is conducive to arbitrary enforcement; and 3) infringes upon plaintiffs' free expression. *See Grayned v. City of Rockford*, 408 U.S. 104, 108–09, 92 S.Ct. 2294, 2298–99, 33 L.Ed.2d 222 (1972).

First, the act fails to give fair notice of proscribed conduct to computer network users by failing to define the following terms and phrases: "falsely identify," "use," "falsely imply," and "point of access to electronic information." These undefined terms provide inadequate notice of the scope of proscribed conduct to persons of ordinary intelligence and thus void the act for vagueness.

The statute criminalizes computer transmissions which "falsely identify" the sender, yet fails to state whether or not proof of specific intent to deceive, or proof of actual deception, is required. Plaintiffs' affidavits demonstrate that, although they have no intent to deceive when sending transmissions which may "falsely identify" them and, indeed, have many legitimate and important reasons for concealing their identity, they cannot determine whether or not their conduct violates the act.

Similarly, the portion of the act relating to trade names and logos fails to define or adequately limit the word "use." Other statutes protecting intellectual property expressly limit the definition of "use" to use in a commercial context. *See, e.g.,* 15 U.S.C. § 1125 (federal trademark infringement law); O.C.G.A. § 10–1–440(b) (1994) (defining "use" within the meaning of Georgia trademark infringement laws); O.C.G.A. § 10–1–450 (1994) (Georgia trademark infringement law). In contrast, the only limiting concept of "use" in the act is that such use must "falsely imply" that permission to use the mark has been obtained. This restriction, which is also undefined and suffers from the same vagueness problems as the term "falsely identify," fails to provide sufficiently specific notice of proscribed conduct.

Finally, the act fails to explain the phrase "any data ... over the transmission facilities or through the network facilities of a local telephone network for the purpose of ... exchanging data with ... a point of access to electronic information." Plaintiffs contend that this phrase could mean that the act applies not only to computer transmissions per se, but also to transmissions by telephone, fax machine, answering machine, voice mail system, pager, or any other electronic device which might be connected to computer network facilities. The act provides no guidance about these potential applications.

Second, the act's vague provisions create a risk of arbitrary and discriminatory enforcement. As plaintiffs point out, not only does the act fail to notify potential defendants of proscribed conduct, but it also fails to notify law enforcement officials of what exactly is prohibited. The act's failure to specifically articulate proscribed conduct affords prosecutors and police officers substantial room for selective prosecution of persons who express minority viewpoints.

Third, the act's vagueness is particularly harmful because it chills protected expression. Plaintiffs' affidavits indicate that they have already altered what they believe to be innocent and legitimate behavior because of their inability to discern what exactly the act proscribes. Without court intervention, this self-censorship will continue until the act is amended, revoked, or definitively interpreted by the state supreme court.

For all of these reasons, the Court concludes that plaintiffs are likely to succeed on their claim that the act is void for vagueness, overbroad, and not narrowly tailored to promote a compelling state interest.

2. *Substantial threat of irreparable injury*

Plaintiffs have also demonstrated a substantial threat of irreparable injury in the absence of a preliminary injunction. The Supreme Court has held that "[t]he loss of First Amendment freedoms, for even minimal periods of time, unquestionably constitutes irreparable injury." *Elrod v. Burns*, 427 U.S. 347, 373, 96 S.Ct. 2673, 2690, 49 L.Ed.2d 547 (1976). As described above, the act has already induced self-censorship. The Court concludes, therefore, that failure to enjoin enforcement of the act will force plaintiffs either to continue self-censorship or to risk criminal prosecution. Thus, plaintiffs have demonstrated a substantial threat of irreparable injury unless a preliminary injunction is issued.

3. *Balance of hardships*

The balance of hardships weighs heavily in plaintiffs' favor. As stated above, plaintiffs will suffer irreparable injury if prosecution under the statute is not enjoined. In contrast, Georgia already has in place many less restrictive means to address fraud and misrepresentation—the interests defendants claim the act at issue promotes. *See, e.g.*, O.C.G.A. § 16–8–3 (1996) (theft by deception); O.C.G.A. § 16–9–93(a)(2) (1996) (computer theft by deception); O.C.G.A. § 10–1–453 (1994) (unauthorized and deceitful use of name or seal of another); O.C.G.A. § 10–1–393 (Supp.1996) (unfair and deceptive consumer trade practices). Defendants contend that these statutes do not fully reach problematic behavior over the internet, but they fail adequately to explain why. If the act prevents some ill-defined category of fraud or deception not covered by existing laws, defendants do not articulate why they have a compelling interest in preventing that conduct on the internet but have done nothing to prevent the same practices in the print media. Therefore, the Court concludes that plaintiffs face substantially greater harms if the act is allowed to stand than defendants face if its enforcement is enjoined.

4. *Promotion of the Public Interest*

Finally, for all the reasons set forth above, a preliminary injunction will advance the public interest. "No long string of citations is necessary to find that the public interest weighs in favor of having access to a free flow of constitutionally protected speech." *Reno*, 929 F.Supp. at 851.

5. *Conclusion*

For the foregoing reasons, the Court DENIES defendants' motion to dismiss [#11–1], GRANTS plaintiffs' motion for preliminary injunction [#3–1], and enjoins defendants from enforcing O.C.G.A. § 16–9–93.1

pending a final determination on the merits of plaintiffs' complaint.
* * *

Notes

1. In the early and mid–1990s, many of those who posted messages in the public bulletin boards and discussion groups on "Usenet" hid their identities by using an anonymous forwarding service run as a public service by Johan Helsingius in Finland. However, when forced in a copyright suit to reveal the identity of one of the anonymous users, Mr. Helsingius closed his service. Peter H. Lewis, "Behind an Internet Message Service's Close," New York Times, Sept. 6, 1996, Sec. D, p. 2, col. 4. Various substitutes have been proposed from time to time.

2. What would be the legal and practical implications of the creation of a system that allowed totally anonymous sending of e-mail and creating of untraceable websites?

F. ENCRYPTION SOFTWARE AND THE FIRST AMENDMENT

JUNGER v. DALEY

United States Court of Appeals, Sixth Circuit, 2000.
209 F.3d 481.

BOYCE F. MARTIN, JR., CHIEF JUDGE.

This is a constitutional challenge to the provisions of the Export Administration Regulations, 15 C.F.R. Parts 730–74, that regulate the export of encryption software. Peter D. Junger appeals the district court's grant of summary judgment in favor of Secretary Daley and the other defendants.

The district court found that encryption source code is not sufficiently expressive to be protected by the First Amendment, that the Export Administration Regulations are permissible content-neutral restrictions, and that the Regulations are not subject to a facial challenge as a prior restraint on speech. Subsequent to the district court's holding and the oral arguments before this Court, the Bureau of Export Administration issued an interim final rule amending the regulations at issue. *See* Revisions to Encryption Items, 65 Fed.Reg. 2492 (2000) (to be codified at 15 C.F.R. Parts 734, 740, 742, 770, 772, 774). Having concluded that the First Amendment protects computer source code, we reverse the district court and remand this case for further consideration of Junger's constitutional claims in light of the amended regulations.

ENCRYPTION AND SOFTWARE BACKGROUND

Encryption is the process of converting a message from its original form ("plaintext") into a scrambled form ("ciphertext"). Most encryption today uses an algorithm, a mathematical transformation from plaintext to ciphertext, and a key that acts as a password. Generally, the security of the message depends on the strength of both the algorithm and the key.

Encryption has long been a tool in the conduct of military and foreign affairs. Encryption has many civil applications, including protecting communication and data sent over the Internet. As technology has progressed, the methods of encryption have changed from purely mechanical processes, such as the Enigma machines of Nazi Germany, to modern electronic processes. Today, messages can be encrypted through dedicated electronic hardware and also through general-purpose computers with the aid of encryption software.

For a general-purpose computer to encrypt data, it must use encryption software that instructs the computer's circuitry to execute the encoding process. Encryption software, like all computer software, can be in one of two forms: object code or source code. Object code represents computer instructions as a sequence of binary digits (0s and 1s) that can be directly executed by a computer's microprocessor. Source code represents the same instructions in a specialized programming language, such as BASIC, C, or Java. Individuals familiar with a particular computer programming language can read and understand source code. Source code, however, must be converted into object code before a computer will execute the software's instructions. This conversion is conducted by compiler software. Although compiler software is typically readily available, some source code may have no compatible compiler.

REGULATORY BACKGROUND

The Export Administration Regulations create a comprehensive licensing scheme to control the export of nonmilitary technology, software, and commodities. In 1996, the President transferred export jurisdiction over nonmilitary encryption items from the State Department to the Commerce Department's Bureau of Export Administration.

The Regulations are structured around the Commodity Control List, which lists items subject to export control. *See* 15 C.F.R. Part 774. Each item on the List is given an Export Control Classification Number that designates the category of the controlled item and the reasons why the government controls the item's export. *See* 15 C.F.R. § 738.2. The reasons for control affect the nature and scope of the export controls.

Encryption software, including both source code and object code, is regulated under Export Control Classification Number 5D002 for national security reasons. *See id.* § 772 Supp. 1. In addition, encryption technology and encryption hardware are regulated for national security reasons under different Classification Numbers. Generally, the Regulations require a license for the export of all encryption items to all foreign destinations, except Canada. *See* 65 Fed.Reg. 2492, 2499 (to be codified at 15 C.F.R. § 742.15(a)). Although the regulations provide some exceptions, most encryption software in electronic form remains subject to the license requirements for export. Encryption software in printed form, however, is not subject to the Regulations. *See* 15 C.F.R. § 734.3(b)(2).

The Regulations define "export" as the "actual shipment or transmission of items subject to the EAR out of the United States." *Id.* § 734.2(b)(1). For encryption software, the definition of "export" also includes publication of the software on the Internet, unless steps are taken to restrict foreign access to the Internet site. *See* 65 Fed.Reg. 2492, 2496 (to be codified at 15 C.F.R. § 734.2(b)(9)(ii)).

Factual Background

Peter Junger is a professor at the Case Western University School of Law. Junger maintains sites on the World Wide Web that include information about courses that he teaches, including a computers and the law course. Junger wishes to post on his web site encryption source code that he has written to demonstrate how computers work. Such a posting is defined as an export under the Regulations.

On June 12, 1997, Junger submitted three applications to the Commerce Department, requesting determinations of commodity classifications for encryption software programs and other items. On July 4, the Export Administration told Junger that Classification Number 5D002 covered four of the five software programs he had submitted. Although it found that four programs were subject to the Regulations, the Export Administration found that the first chapter of Junger's textbook, *Computers and the Law*, was an allowable unlicensed export. Though deciding that the printed book chapter containing encryption code could be exported, the Export Administration stated that export of the book in electronic form would require a license if the text contained 5D002 software. Since receiving the classification determination, Junger has not applied for a license to export his classified encryption source code.

Junger filed this action to make a facial challenge to the Regulations on First Amendment grounds, seeking declaratory and injunctive relief that would permit him to engage in the unrestricted distribution of encryption software through his web site. Junger claims that encryption source code is protected speech. The district court granted summary judgment in favor of the defendants, holding that encryption source code is not protected under the First Amendment, that the Regulations are permissible content-neutral regulations, and that the Regulations are not subject to facial challenge on prior restraint grounds.

We review the grant of summary judgment *de novo. See Smith v. Wal–Mart Stores, Inc.,* 167 F.3d 286, 289 (6th Cir.1999).

The issue of whether or not the First Amendment protects encryption source code is a difficult one because source code has both an expressive feature and a functional feature. The United States does not dispute that it is possible to use encryption source code to represent and convey information and ideas about cryptography and that encryption source code can be used by programmers and scholars for such informational purposes. Much like a mathematical or scientific formula, one can describe the function and design of encryption software by a prose explanation; however, for individuals fluent in a computer programming language, source code is the most efficient and precise means by which to communicate ideas about cryptography.

The district court concluded that the functional characteristics of source code overshadow its simultaneously expressive nature. The fact that a medium of expression has a functional capacity should not preclude constitutional protection. Rather, the appropriate consideration of the medium's functional capacity is in the analysis of permitted government regulation.

The Supreme Court has explained that "all ideas having even the slightest redeeming social importance," including those concerning "the advancement of truth, science, morality, and arts" have the full protection of the First Amendment. *Roth v. United States*, 354 U.S. 476, 484, 77 S.Ct.1304, 1 L.Ed. 2d 1498 (1957) (quoting 1 JOURNALS OF THE CONTINENTAL CONGRESS 108 (1774)). This protection is not reserved for purely expressive communication. The Supreme Court has recognized First Amendment protection for symbolic conduct, such as draft-card burning, that has both functional and expressive features. *See United States v. O'Brien*, 391 U.S. 367, 88 S.Ct. 1673, 20 L.Ed.2d 672 (1968).

The Supreme Court has expressed the versatile scope of the First Amendment by labeling as "unquestionably shielded" the artwork of Jackson Pollack, the music of Arnold Schoenberg, or the Jabberwocky verse of Lewis Carroll. *Hurley v. Irish–American Gay, Lesbian and Bisexual Group*, 515 U.S. 557, 569, 115 S.Ct. 2338, 132 L.Ed.2d 487 (1995). Though unquestionably expressive, these things identified by the Court are not traditional speech. Particularly, a musical score cannot be read by the majority of the public but can be used as a means of communication among musicians. Likewise, computer source code, though unintelligible to many, is the preferred method of communication among computer programmers.

Because computer source code is an expressive means for the exchange of information and ideas about computer programming, we hold that it is protected by the First Amendment.

The functional capabilities of source code, and particularly those of encryption source code, should be considered when analyzing the governmental interest in regulating the exchange of this form of speech. Under intermediate scrutiny, the regulation of speech is valid, in part, if "it furthers an important or substantial governmental interest." *O'Brien*, 391 U.S. at 377, 88 S.Ct. 1673. In *Turner Broadcasting System v. FCC*, 512 U.S. 622, 664, 114 S.Ct. 2445, 129 L.Ed.2d 497 (1994), the Supreme Court noted that although an asserted governmental interest may be important, when the government defends restrictions on speech "it must do more than simply 'posit the existence of the disease sought to be cured.'" *Id.* (quoting *Quincy Cable TV, Inc. v. FCC*, 768 F.2d 1434, 1455 (D.C.Cir.1985)). The government "must demonstrate that the recited harms are real, not merely conjectural, and that the regulation will in fact alleviate these harms in a direct and material way." *Id.* We recognize that national security interests can outweigh the interests of protected speech and require the regulation of speech. In the present case, the record does not resolve whether the exercise of presidential power in furtherance of national security interests should overrule the interests in allowing the free exchange of encryption source code.

Before any level of judicial scrutiny can be applied to the Regulations, Junger must be in a position to bring a facial challenge to these regulations. In light of the recent amendments to the Export Administration Regulations, the district court should examine the new regulations to determine if Junger can bring a facial challenge.

For the foregoing reasons, we REVERSE the district court and REMAND the case to the district court for consideration of Junger's constitutional challenge to the amended regulations.

Note

Similar issues were raised in *Bernstein v. United States Department of Justice*, 176 F.3d 1132 (9th Cir.1999), opinion withdrawn pending hearing en banc, 192 F.3d 1308 (9th Cir.1999). The new regulations mentioned in *Junger* may make these cases moot unless export controls on cryptography are again strengthened.

Index

References are to Pages

ACCESS TO INFORMATION IN COMPU-TERIZED FORM
Freedom of Information Act, 734–741
Government databanks, access to, 734–741
Litigation, access to computerized data, 742–758

ACCURACY OF INFORMATION
See also Defamation
Duty of government agency to operate on basis of accurate information, 716–723
Duty to provide accurate information to those affected, 715–716
Evidence
Computer-generated evidence, 728–733
Computerized business records as evidence, 724–727

ANITCYBERSQUATING CONSUMER PROTECTION ACT
Domain names, 387 et seq.

ANONYMOUS COMMUNICATIONS
First Amendment rights, 812–819

ANTITRUST
Generally, 582–633
Agreements in violation of antitrust laws, 621–632
Horizontal restraints, 632–63
Tie-in sales, 583–620

ARBITRATION
Domain names, 399–405

BACKUP COPIES
Copyright, 120–126

BANKRUPTCY
Software users, protecting, 530–531

BUSINESS RECORDS
Evidence, computerized business records as, 724–727

CABLE TELEVISION FACILITIES
Internet access over cable television facilities, 572–581

CHILD ONLINE PROTECTION ACT
First Amendment rights, 790–797

CHILDREN'S ONLINE PRIVACY PROTECTION ACT
Generally, 649–652

COMMUNICATIONS DECENCY ACT OF 1996
First Amendment rights, 774–789

COMPETITION
See also Antitrust
Restricting e-competition, 542–569

COMPUTER PROGRAM
Copyright definition, 2

CONTRACTS
See also E–Commerce and Software Contracts
Antitrust, agreements in violation of antitrust laws, 621–632
Trade secrets, protecting against disclosure by negotiated contracts, 366–370

CONTRIBUTORY COPYRIGHT INFRINGEMENT
Generally, 182–197

COPYRIGHT
Generally, 1–216
Backup copies, 120–126
Computer program, definition, 2
Constitutional basis, 1–2
Contributory infringement, 182–197
Copies, 66–71, 120–126
Copyright Act of 1976, 2–4, 136–137
Copyrightability, 4–65
Copyright-like protection, 208–216
Creativity, 10–29
Data, copyrightability of computer-created compilations, 10–19
Derivative works, 71–75
Digital audio works, 75–85
Exclusive rights of copyright owner
Circumvention of technological measures, 85–93
Copies, 66–71

COPYRIGHT—Cont'd

Exclusive rights of copyright owner —Cont'd

Derivative works, 71–75

Digital audio works, 75–85

Limitations, 93–145

Performance and display, 75

Rental, 75

Factual data, computer-created compilation of, 10–19

Fair use, 93–120

First sale, 136–145

Fixation, 4–10

Idea and expression, merger of, 54–60

Infringement

Contributory infringement, 182–197

Direct infringement, 146–182

Vicarious infringement, 197–200

Internet service providers, privileges of, 126–136

Limitations on exclusive rights

Generally, 93–145

Backup copies, 120–126

Fair use, 93–120

First sale, 136–145

Internet service providers, privileges of, 126–136

Look and feel, 164 et seq.

Menu command hierarchy, 42 et seq.

Merger of idea and expression, 54–60

Methods of operation, 30–54

Microcode, 3, 55 et seq.

MP3, 107 et seq.

Napster, 110 et seq., 126 et seq.

Network effects, 30 et seq.

Operating system programs, 33 et seq.

Ownership of copyright, 65 et seq.

Performance and display, 75

Preemption of state law, 200–207

Rental, 75

ROMs, 4–9

Scenes a faire doctrine, 60–65

Semiconductor Chip Protection Act, 208–216

Software, copyrightability, 4–10

Star pagination, 20–30

Subject matter, 4–65

Switching costs, 30 et seq.

Vicarious infringement, 197–200

COPYRIGHT ACT OF 1976

Generally, 2–4, 136–137

DEFAMATION

Generally, 619–714

Immunity of internet service providers, 706–714

DERIVATIVE WORKS

Copyright, 71–75

DIGITAL AUDIO WORKS

Copyright, 75–85

DOCTRINE OF EQUIVALENTS

Patents, 338–339

DOMAIN NAMES

Anitcybersquating Consumer Protection Act, 387 et seq.

Arbitration, 399–405

In rem jurisdiction over domain names, 484–488

Internet Corporation for Assigned Names and Numbers, 399

Trademark rights in internet domain names, 387–399

E–COMMERCE AND SOFTWARE CONTRACTS

Generally, 495–569

Bankruptcy, protecting software users, 530–531

Consumer protection by Federal Trade Commission, 535–541

Electronic Signatures in Global and National Commerce Act, 501–502, 511–513

Federal Trade Commission, consumer protection by, 535–541

Gambling, 550 et seq.

Paperfree transactions, 498–510

Restricting e-competition, 542–569

Self-help, 531–535

Signatures, authentication of, 510–513

Taxation, 541–542

Tort as alternative to contract claims, 518–530

Unauthorized practice of law, 557–569

Uniform Computer Information Transactions Act, 502–510, 513–516, 534–535

Uniform Electronic Transactions Act, 499–501, 513

ECONOMIC ESPIONAGE ACT OF 1996

Generally, 345–346

ELECTRONIC COMMUNICATIONS PRIVACY ACT

Generally, 640–642, 657, 682–683

ELECTRONIC SIGNATURES IN GLOBAL AND NATIONAL COMMERCE ACT, 501–502, 511–513

E–MAIL

First Amendment rights to have e-mail delivered, 759–769

Junk e-mail filters, 469–471

ENABLEMENT

Patents, 304–319

ENCRYPTION SOFTWARE

First Amendment rights, 819–823

EUROPEAN UNION PRIVACY LAW

Generally, 684–691

EVIDENCE

Computer-generated evidence, 728–733

EVIDENCE—Cont'd
Computerized business records as evidence, 724–727

FAIR USE
Copyright, 93–120

FEDERAL TRADE COMMISSION
Consumer protection, 535–541

FILE WRAPPER ESTOPPEL
Patents, 338

FIRST AMENDMENT RIGHTS
Generally, 759–823
Anonymous and pseudonymous communications, 812–819
Child Online Protection Act, 790–797
Communications Decency Act of 1996, 774–789
E-mail, right to have delivered, 759–769
Encryption software, 819–823
Intellectual property rights versus free speech, 808–812
Library restrictions on internet access, 797–808
Pornography and indecency, 770–808

FIRST SALE
Copyright, 136–145

FIXATION
Copyright, 4–10

FREE SPEECH
See First Amendment Rights

FREEDOM OF INFORMATION ACT
Access to information in computerized form, 734–741

GAMBLING
E-commerce and software contracts, 550 et seq.

GOVERNMENT AGENCIES
See also Privacy
Accuracy of information, duty of government agency to operate on basis of accurate information, 716–723
Databanks, access to government databanks, 734–741
Federal Trade Commission, consumer protection by, 535–541
Trade secrets, protecting against disclosure by government agencies, 355–366

HORIZONTAL RESTRAINTS
Antitrust, 632–63

IDEA AND EXPRESSION
Copyright, merger of idea and expression, 54–60

INDECENCY
First Amendment rights, 770–808

INFORMATION
See Accuracy of Information; Access to Information in Computerized Form

INFRINGEMENT
See Copyright; Patents

INPUT MEANS
Patents, 328 et seq.

INTERNET COMMUNICATIONS
Interference with internet communications, 461–471

INTERNET CORPORATION FOR ASSIGNED NAMES AND NUMBERS
Domain names, 399

INTERNET JURISDICTION
Constitutional limits on reach of long-arm statutes, 476–484
Domain names, in rem jurisdiction over, 484–488
In rem jurisdiction over domain names, 484–488
Long-arm statutes, reach of, 472–484
Persons not doing business on internet, jurisdiction over, 489–494

INTERNET SERVICE PROVIDERS
Copyright privileges, 126–136
Defamation, immunity of internet service providers, 706–714

JUNK E-MAIL FILTERS
Interference with internet communications, 469–471

JURISDICTION
See Internet Jurisdiction

LIBEL
See Defamation

LIBRARIES
Internet access, First Amendment rights and library restrictions, 797–808

LINE SHARING
Telecommunications, 570–572

LITIGATION
Access to computerized data, 742–758

LOOK AND FEEL
Copyright, 164 et seq.

MEANS FOR
Patents, 319 et seq.

MENU COMMAND HIERARCHY
Copyright, 42 et seq.

METATAGS
Generally, 426 et seq.

METHODS OF OPERATION
Copyright, 30–54

MICROCODE
Copyright, 3, 55 et seq.

MISAPPROPRIATION
Product standards and trademarks, 408–461
Trade secrets, 342–355

MP3
Copyright, 107 et seq.

NAPSTER
Copyright, 110 et seq., 126 et seq.

NETWORK EFFECTS
Copyright, 30 et seq.

NETWORKED COMPUTER METHODS PATENT
Generally, 219–223

NON–OBVIOUSNESS
Patents, 287–304

NOVELTY AND ANTICIPATION
Patents, 283–287

OPERATING SYSTEM PROGRAMS
Copyright, 33 et seq.

PAPERFREE TRANSACTIONS
E-commerce and software contracts, 498–510

PATENTS
    Generally, 217–341
Claim interpretation, 319 et seq.
Doctrine of equivalents, 338–339
Eligibility for patent protection, 223–232
Enablement, 304–319
File wrapper estoppel, 338
Infringement, 319 et seq.
Input means, 328 et seq.
Means for, 319 et seq.
Networked computer methods patent, 219–223
Non-obviousness, 287–304
Novelty and anticipation, 283–287
Prosecution history estoppel, 338
Reverse doctrine of equivalents, 338
Subject matter patentable, 232–283
User stations, 324 et seq.

PERFORMANCE AND DISPLAY
Copyright, 75

PORNOGRAPHY
First Amendment rights, 770–808

PREEMPTION OF STATE LAW
Copyright, 200–207

PRIVACY
    Generally, 634–691
Children's Online Privacy Protection Act, 649–652

PRIVACY—Cont'd
Electronic Communications Privacy Act, 640–642, 657, 682–683
European Union privacy law, effect of, 684–691
Government records
    Disclosure of information by government, restricting, 671–676
    Use of information by government, restricting, 657–671
Government-compelled disclosures, restricting, 635–649
Non-government collection of information, restricting, 649–657
Private parties
    Collection of information, restricting non-government, 649–657
    Disclosure of information in private-party records, restricting, 676–683

PRODUCT STANDARDS
Misappropriation, 408–461

PROSECUTION HISTORY ESTOPPEL
Patents, 338

PSEUDONYMOUS COMMUNICATIONS
First Amendment rights, 812–819

RENTAL
Copyright, 75

REVERSE DOCTRINE OF EQUIVALENTS
Patents, 338

ROMS
Copyright, 4–9

SCENES A FAIRE DOCTRINE
Copyright, 60–65

SELF–HELP
E-commerce and software contracts, 531–535

SEMICONDUCTOR CHIP PROTECTION ACT
Generally, 208–216

SHRINKWRAP LICENSES
Protecting trade secrets, 370–386

SIGNATURES
Authentication, 510–513
Electronic Signatures in Global and National Commerce Act, 501–502, 511–513

SLANDER
See Defamation

SOFTWARE
    See also Copyright; E–Commerce and Software Contracts; Patents
Computer program, copyright definition, 2
Encryption software, First Amendment rights, 819–823

SPAM
Interference with internet communications, 461–471

STAR PAGINATION
Copyright, 20–30

SWITCHING COSTS
Copyright, 30 et seq.

TAXATION
E-commerce and software contracts, 541–542

TELECOMMUNICATIONS
Generally, 570–581
Cable television facilities, internet access over, 572–581
Line sharing, 570–572

TIE–IN SALES
Antitrust, 583–620

TRADE SECRETS
Generally, 342–386
Contracts, protecting against disclosure by negotiated contracts, 366–370
Economic Espionage Act of 1996, 345–346
Government agencies, protecting against disclosure by, 355–366
Improper means, taking by, 342–355
Misappropriation, 342–355

TRADE SECRETS—Cont'd
Shrinkwrap licenses, protecting trade secrets by, 370–386
Uniform Computer Information Transactions Act, 383–386
Uniform Trade Secrets Act, 343–345

TRADEMARKS
Domain names, trademark rights in, 387–399
Metatags, 426 et seq.
Misappropriation, 408–461

UNAUTHORIZED PRACTICE OF LAW
E-commerce and software contracts, 557–569

UNIFORM COMPUTER INFORMATION TRANSACTIONS ACT (UCITA)
Generally, 137, 207, 383–386, 504–510, 513–516, 534–535

UNIFORM ELECTRONIC TRANSACTIONS ACT
Generally, 499–501, 513

UNIFORM TRADE SECRETS ACT, 343–345

USER STATIONS
Patents, 324 et seq.

VICARIOUS COPYRIGHT INFRINGEMENT
Generally, 197–200